STRATEGY

Process, Content, Context

An International Perspective

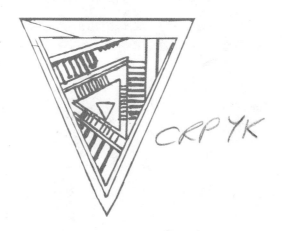

CRPYK

STRATEGY
Process, Content, Context

An International Perspective

BOB DE WIT

Rotterdam School of Management
Erasmus University
The Netherlands

RON MEYER

Rotterdam School of Management
Erasmus University
The Netherlands

with the assistance of
MARC HUYGENS

WEST PUBLISHING COMPANY

Minneapolis/St. Paul ▼ *New York* ▼ *Los Angeles* ▼ *San Francisco*

Text design: Roslyn M. Stendahl, Dapper Design
Copyediting Sections I-V: Giselle Weiss
Composition: Printing Arts, Inc.

WEST'S COMMITMENT TO THE ENVIRONMENT

In 1906, West Publishing Company began recycling materials left over from the production of books. This began a tradition of efficient and responsible use of resources. Today, up to 95 percent of our legal books and 70 percent of our college and school texts are printed on recycled, acid-free stock. West also recycles nearly 22 million pounds of scrap paper annually—the equivalent of 181,717 trees. Since the 1960s, West has devised ways to capture and recycle waste inks, solvents, oils, and vapors created in the printing process. We also recycle plastics of all kinds, wood, glass, corrugated cardboard, and batteries, and have eliminated the use of Styrofoam book packaging. We at West are proud of the longevity and the scope of our commitment to the environment.

Production, Prepress, Printing and Binding by West Publishing Company.

 TEXT IS PRINTED ON 10% POST CONSUMER RECYCLED PAPER   PRINTED WITH SOY INK™

COPYRIGHT ©1994 by   WEST PUBLISHING COMPANY
                      610 Opperman Drive
                      P.O. Box 64526
                      St. Paul, MN 55164-0526

Library of Congress Cataloging-in-Publication Data

de Wit, Bob
    Strategy—process, content, context: an international
    perspective / Bob de Wit, Ron Meyer.
    p.   cm.
    Includes index.

    ISBN 0-314-03213-4 (pbk.)

    1. Strategic planning.   2. Corporate planning.   3. International
    business enterprises.   I. Meyer, Ron.   II. Title.

HD30.28.W59 1994
658.4'012--dc20   94-5919
                                                          CIP

STRATEGY
Process, Content, Context

An International Perspective

BOB DE WIT

Rotterdam School of Management
Erasmus University
The Netherlands

RON MEYER

Rotterdam School of Management
Erasmus University
The Netherlands

with the assistance of
MARC HUYGENS

WEST PUBLISHING COMPANY

Minneapolis/St. Paul ▼ *New York* ▼ *Los Angeles* ▼ *San Francisco*

Text design: Roslyn M. Stendahl, Dapper Design
Copyediting Sections I-V: Giselle Weiss
Composition: Printing Arts, Inc.

WEST'S COMMITMENT TO THE ENVIRONMENT

In 1906, West Publishing Company began recycling materials left over from the production of books. This began a tradition of efficient and responsible use of resources. Today, up to 95 percent of our legal books and 70 percent of our college and school texts are printed on recycled, acid-free stock. West also recycles nearly 22 million pounds of scrap paper annually—the equivalent of 181,717 trees. Since the 1960s, West has devised ways to capture and recycle waste inks, solvents, oils, and vapors created in the printing process. We also recycle plastics of all kinds, wood, glass, corrugated cardboard, and batteries, and have eliminated the use of Styrofoam book packaging. We at West are proud of the longevity and the scope of our commitment to the environment.

Production, Prepress, Printing and Binding by West Publishing Company.

 TEXT IS PRINTED ON 10% POST CONSUMER RECYCLED PAPER   PRINTED WITH SOY INK

Library of Congress Cataloging-in-Publication Data

de Wit, Bob
    Strategy—process, content, context: an international
    perspective / Bob de Wit, Ron Meyer.
    p.   cm.
    Includes index.

    ISBN 0-314-03213-4 (pbk.)

    1. Strategic planning.   2. Corporate planning.   3. International
    business enterprises.   I. Meyer, Ron.   II. Title.

HD30.28.W59 1994
658.4'012--dc20   94-5919
                                                          CIP

Contents

Chapter 6
Multibusiness Level Strategies: On Cash and Competencies 263

Chapter 7
Multicompany Level Strategies: On Confrontation and Cooperation 318

SECTION IV
THE STRATEGY CONTEXT 362

Chapter 8
The Industry Context: On Compliance and Choice 364

Section VI
CASES

PREFACE

Most strategic management textbooks that are currently available look surprisingly similar. The most important characteristics shared by these books are:

–the use of a simplified *step-by-step strategic planning approach* as the books' structure;

–the presentation of a *limited number of theories* as accepted wisdom, from which prescriptions can easily be derived;

–the "translation" of original articles and papers into the textbook authors' own words to create *easily digestible pieces of text;*

–the focus of theories, examples, and cases on the *American* (or recently also British) context.

The uniformity of these books is less surprising if one considers the shared educational philosophy underlying these works. Their approach to teaching strategic management can be labelled as "instructional." Students are "told" how to tackle strategic management problems in a number of steps, with the objective of "training" the students to be able to repeat these steps in case discussions and in later business life.

Although we share the ideal of educating students in a manner that leads to the retention of applicable knowledge and skills, we do not believe that instruction and training are the best modes of teaching at the university level. Our educational philosophy is based on tossing students into the midst of the academic debate. We believe that students should be confronted with a large number of different perspectives. Students must learn to deal with conflicting and overlapping ideas, approaches, and paradigms without becoming paralysed and unable to solve concrete strategic management problems. In other words, it is our view that strategic management education at the university level must not program students but should help create flexible strategic thinkers, able to translate thought into action.

It is for this reason that our book differs on all four of the previously mentioned points. The key characteristics of this book are:

–a balanced coverage of all of the main themes of strategic management, namely, *the strategy process, the strategy content, and the strategy context;*

–a *broad representation of differing, and often conflicting, theories and approaches,* reflecting the richness of current debate among academics and practicioners in the field of strategic management;

–the *use of original articles and papers,* to offer the reader a firsthand account of thinkers' ideas and theories;

–an *international orientation,* reflected in the choice of topics, articles, examples, and cases.

In the following paragraphs the rationale behind the choices for these characteristics will be explained. Following this discussion, the structure of the book and the ways in which it can be employed will be further clarified.

Strategy: Process, Content, and Context

This textbook intends to give an overview of all essential aspects of strategic management. It is therefore important to recognize what the key dimensions of the field of strategic management actually are. To clarify the categorisation made, the opening sentence of Michael Porter's well-known book *Competitive Strategy* (1980) is a useful illustration: "The essence of formulating competitive strategy is relating a company to its environment." Whether one agrees with Porter or not, his statement is interesting in this context because it can be broken down into three parts that reflect the three dimensions of strategic management:

1. The first part of the statement, "the essence of formulating," indicates that there must be a process at play. Whether structured or unstructured, formal or informal, rational or irrational, the organisation must proceed through a number of steps before it can arrive at a strategy. This dimension of strategic management, which looks at the how of strategy, is referred to as the *strategy process.*

2. The middle part of the statement, "competitive strategy," indicates that the strategy process must result in a strategic "product." This output of the strategy process is a course of action to be followed by the company that will allow for the fulfilment of the company's objectives in the face of competitive pressures. This dimension of strategic management, which looks at the what, not the how, of strategy is referred to as *strategy content.*

3. The final part of the statement, "is relating a company to its environment," indicates that strategies are developed to suit varying organisational and environmental contexts. Of course, each company has its own unique characteristics and must operate in its own unique environment. However, many companies and environments share common characteristics, on the basis of which they can be grouped into categories. These categories of firms and environments are often faced with the same strategic problems and opportunities and require similar types of strategic responses. This dimension of strategic management is referred to as the *strategy context.*

This distinction between strategy process, strategy content and strategy context is also made by Pettigrew (1988) and Mintzberg (1990). In accordance with their views, it must be emphasized that process, content, and context are not the "elements" of strategic management, but its "dimensions." Elements can be taken apart and examined in isolation, but this is not the case with the strongly interrelated aspects process, content, and context. Strategic phenomena can be examined from a process, content, or context *perspective,* as you could look at a box's length, width, or height, depending on where you stand. The exclusive choice of any of the three angles gives only a limited view of the object under investigation. To obtain "depth" of understanding of strategy, it is therefore necessary to merge the process, content, and context vantages into a *three-dimensional view* of strategic management.

This book takes such a three-dimensional view of strategic management by paying equal attention to each dimension for all essential topics. The balanced coverage of process, content, and context topics is reflected in the book's structure. Of the nine main chapters, three chapters are spent on each of the three dimensions.

Theoretical Approaches: The State of the Current Debate

We do not believe that a university-level textbook on strategic management should provide an unnecessarily simplified view of the field. Strategic management cannot easily be represented by just one school of thought. Hence, for this book we have selected the theories, ideas, approaches, and perspectives that represent the most important contributions to the current discussions conducted within the field. This decision was made for the following reasons:

1. *Lack of a mainstream.* Some fields of science are dominated by a mainstream of thought, that can be recognized by a high measure of consensus among researchers with regard to basic premises and fundamental theories. This characteristic allows textbooks the luxury of merely transferring established knowledge to readers. The field of strategic management, however, has no significant body of shared views but is fragmented into competing schools of thought (for classifications see Bailey and Johnson, 1992; Mahoney and Pandian, 1992; Mintzberg, 1990; Schoemaker, 1993; Teece, Pisano, and Shuen, 1990; Whittington, 1993). It is interesting to speculate about the reasons for this lack of consensus, as for instance Whitley (1984) has done, but here we are primarily concerned with the consequences. The main conclusion, which we believe must be drawn, is that the reader is not benefited by a book limited to the views of only one school of thought. Quite the contrary; in the absence of a dominant mainstream, a book should seek to present a wider variety of perspectives and allow the reader to draw his or her own conclusions.

2. *Strategy cannot be taught.* Diverse perspectives also make didactical sense. Students can be instructed how to repair a car, how to solve a mathematical problem, and how to remove an infected appendix. Yet it is our opinion that it is impossible to tell anyone how to think strategically. Repairing a car requires following a fixed number of steps, so educating a mechanic focuses on "programming" this behaviour and fine-tuning the required manual skills. Strategy, however, falls into the same category as creativity—by its very essence it cannot be programmed. Strategic thinking is, as for instance Von Clausewitz points out, an art (this discussion about the nature of strategy is pursued at greater length in chapter 1). Strategy can therefore not be taught, though it can be learned. Learning how to think and act strategically involves understanding others' successful behaviour, testing new ideas in practice, and reflecting on results. As a consequence, the role of formal teaching is not to instruct but to facilitate the learning process by presenting the state of the art of current thought, challenging students' modes of thinking, and offering alternative ways of approaching strategic issues. In other words, we believe there is no better way to get students thinking strategically than to throw them into the arena of current academic debate, while simultaneously demanding that they apply their thinking to practical strategic problems.

3. *Diversity of target audience.* The primary target audience of this book is in Europe. It hardly needs to be argued that this audience is highly heterogeneous, especially when viewed from a cultural angle. In our opinion this cultural diversity demands a wide variety of perspectives, since many theories, ideas, and approaches are more applicable in one culture than in others. Most strategic management writers have not explicitly recognized the cultural assumptions underlying their work and have therefore failed to realize that their ideas "do not travel well." We believe that much of the debate going on among schools of thought is rooted in differing assumptions about national, industry, and corporate cultures. A book for the heterogeneous European market must offer a range of perspectives so that readers can themselves decide which approaches suit their context best. Moreover, the increasing number of managers that need to operate in two or more cultures can use the diversity of views presented in this book to reflect on the need to adapt their own perspective to other local situations.

The need to represent a variety of perspectives suggested a book structure in which the main schools of thought directly confront one another. While the division of the book into chapters has been on the basis of topic (using the distinction process, content, context), the buildup of each individual chapter reflects the various views held on the topic by key strategic management writers. In this way, each of the major strategic management topics is discussed from two or more different angles.

Use of the Original Articles

A third major distinguishing characteristic of this book is its use of the original works of the most important authors in the field of strategic management. Thousands of journal articles and books were scanned to select those writings of high quality and clarity that reflect the most important schools of thought in each topic area.

Given the importance of a diversity of perspectives, it should come as no surprise that we decided to let the writers speak for themselves, and not through an interpretative filter. Indeed, the strength of many of the ideas lies partially in the way they are put forward.

Rather than attempting to add value by rewriting others' ideas, we concentrated our efforts on selecting the right readings, editing them well, and organizing them so the key strategic management topics would be clearly debated from a variety of angles.

An International Orientation

The fourth and last major distinguishing characteristic of this book is its international orientation. In contrast to most English language textbooks currently available, which have primarily been written for the North American market, this book has been explicitly developed with an international audience in mind. The benefits of this choice to readers are the following:

1. *International perspectives.* While ideas recognize no borders, many schools of thought are more popular (and possibly more appropriate) in some countries than in others. In the diversity of views, ideas, and theories expressed in this book, most perspectives that are popular internationally are given fair representation. To us it is unimportant what the nationality of each author is, as long as the perspectives valued internationally receive ample attention.

2. *International context.* If strategy process and content are heavily influenced by the context in which they are situated, it follows that firms operating in international markets should pay explicit attention to the international context. This book therefore devotes an entire chapter to the international environment's impact on both strategy process and strategy content. Since the target audience for this book is in Europe, and this context has characteristics all its own, the final chapter has been set aside to focus on how the current issues unique to the European situation might have an influence on strategy process and content.

3. *International cases.* It almost speaks for itself that an internationally oriented textbook, focused on an audience in Europe, should offer cases representing a wide variety of countries. In this book, the cases cover most European countries, Japan and the United States.

Structure of the Book

The four distinctive characteristics outlined in the previous paragraphs have resulted in an unconventional book structure, which requires some short clarification:

Differentiation between chapters. As mentioned earlier, the chapters have been organized by *topic*. One section of three chapters is devoted to strategy process issues, the next section of three chapters focuses on strategy content, while in the last section of three chapters the discussion centres on topics in the area of strategy context. How the sections have been split into separate chapters will be explained in the introduction to each section. These three main sections are preceded by an introductory chapter, that explores the questions What is strategy? and Who is a strategist? Finally, there is also a closing chapter that delves deeper into the specific strategic management issues of the European environment.

Sequence of chapters. There is no significant reason for the process section to proceed the content section. Hence, they can be swapped if this is deemed convenient. The context section does assume previous knowledge of the process and content sections. Within each section the chapters have also been placed in a logical order, which will be explained in the introduction to each section.

Differentiation and sequencing within chapters. The sequence of the articles within each chapter gives a fair representation of the development of the debates within each topic area and also roughly follows publication dates. It should be emphasized that the final sequence of the articles has been determined on the basis of didactical arguments, not on the grounds of our preferences. To clarify the choice and sequence of articles, each chapter begins with a short introduction. These introductions present an overview of the most important schools of thought on the topic and indicate how each article contributes to the debate at hand. Each chapter is also accompanied by a short discussion of recommended readings and cases.

Editing of articles. To keep the size of the book within acceptable limits, most readings have had to be reduced in length, while extensive footnotes and references have had to be dropped. At all times this editing has been guided by the principle that the author's key ideas and arguments must be preserved intact. To compensate for the loss of references in each article, a combined list of the most important references has been added to the end of each chapter.

Organisation of the cases. The cases have not been sprinkled throughout the text, but have been placed together in the second half of the book. This division between text and cases has been made because most cases can be used together with more than one chapter. Which cases relate to which chapters is indicated in a table at the beginning of the case section of the book. Furthermore, tables identify the case companies' country of origin and the industry focus.

Target Audience

When it comes to clothing, it is well-known that one-size-fits-all garments usually fit no one. A good strategist realizes that this principle applies to more products than just clothing. This book therefore clearly focuses on one user segment, *European university-level management institutes.* This segment includes all university-level institutes throughout Europe, such as business schools, business administration faculties, business economics faculties, and management sciences institutes, whose objective is to educate individuals who are, or would like to become, managers. This book is suitable as:

An introductory strategic management text. This book allows students unfamiliar with strategic management to move quickly from introduction to state of the art. Test versions of this book have been used successfully at the senior bachelor's and master's levels, as well as for executive education.

An advanced strategic management text. Some schools might prefer to employ this book as an advanced strategic management text after a "classical" step-by-step book has been discussed. This book is well suited for such a two-staged approach, since most chapters start by recapitulating the classical approach and then go on to other approaches.

Although this book has been put together with a primary audience of European university-level management schools in mind, this does not mean that other audiences should not be interested in its contents. This book should also appeal to:

Non-European management schools. For the many non-European management schools that are also interested in an international perspective on strategic management, this book is a good introduction. An added benefit is that this book travels relatively well across cultures, owing to the variety of approaches presented.

Non-university-level management schools. Many non-university-level management schools do not shun academic developments, but follow them at a distance. Often they offer specialization courses toward the end of their programmes intended to give selected students an opportunity to close the gap between them and university-level programmes. Under these circumstances, this book might be the appropriate advanced strategic management text.

Nonmanagement schools. Increasingly, traditional university faculties in Europe have been forced to offer their students a better career perspective. This has resulted in an explosion of courses and specializations in the area of management within university departments as diverse as medicine ("health-care management"), engineering ("industrial management"), political science ("public sector management"), and anthropology ("cross-cultural management"). If management studies make up a significant proportion of the curriculum, the advanced level of this textbook might suit the requirements of the programme.

Nonstudents. Finally, there is no reason why practicioners should not pick up this book. While a classical textbook might not challenge views already held by managers, this book's variety of perspectives should stimulate managers to reconsider their opinions.

References

Bailey, A., and G. Johnson, How Strategies Develop in Organisations, in D. Faulkner and G. Johnson (Eds.), *The Challenge of Strategic Management*, Kogan Page, London, 1992.

Mahoney, J. T. and J. R. Pandian, The Resource-Based View within the Conversation of Strategic Management, *Strategic Management Journal,* June 1992.

Mintzberg, H., Strategy Formation: Schools of Thought, in J. W. Frederickson (Ed.), *Perspectives on Strategic Management*, Harper & Row, New York, 1990.

Pettigrew, A., *The Management of Strategic Change*, Basil Blackwell, Oxford, 1988.

Porter, M. E., *Competitive Strategy,* Free Press, Boston, 1980.

Schoemaker, P. J. H., Strategic Decisions in Organizations: Rational and Behavioural Views, *Journal of Management Studies*, January 1993.

Teece, D. J., Pisano, G., and A. Shuen, Firm Capabilities, Resources, and the Concept of Strategic Management, CCC Working Paper No. 90-8, December 1990.

Whitley, R., The Fragmented State of Management Studies: Reasons and Consequences, *Journal of Management Studies*, Autumn, 1984.

Whittington, R., *What Is Strategy and Does It Matter?* Routledge, London, 1993.

ACKNOWLEDGEMENTS

This book is not the product of our labours alone—we are merely its architects. As architects we have been responsible for the underlying philosophy and general design of this book. We have determined the necessary structure and the building materials needed. However, for the realisation of our ideas we have been dependent on the skills, support, and input of a very large number of other people.

Foremost, this book would not have been possible without the high quality building blocks supplied by external authors. We are much indebted to these writers, and to their publishers, and greatly appreciate their good will and cooperative spirit. Without their collaboration we would not have been able to create the structure of the book as we had envisioned.

Furthermore, we wish to thank all those people who have provided feedback on our "blueprints." Without the valuable responses from many colleagues, our learning, and the quality of this book, would never have progressed as far. The same is true with regard to the very useful comments and ideas brought forward by our students. During the last two years, concept versions of the manuscript were tested on these students, who proved to be very insightful commentators. Their feedback has resulted in many significant improvements in the text.

An architect is also dependent on time, money, and a stimulating work environment. We have been lucky that the Rotterdam School of Management in general, and our department in particular, have provided these essential circumstances. We are especially grateful for the support we have received from our department and the freedom we were granted to structure the writing process and determine the book content as we saw fit.

Once all the blueprints and building blocks are ready, someone must start building. In this case, our publisher, West, has played this important role of realising our intentions. Their enthusiasm, flexibility, professionalism, and lack of red tape have all expediated the process of transforming our ideas into the book in front of you. Special thanks are due to David Godden, who supported this project from the beginning and who was always there when needed.

Last, but not least, we would like to express our appreciation to two individuals who helped us intensively during the designing process. First, we would like to thank Wolfgang Tiegs, who spent months scanning the globe for interesting cases and came up with most of the material included in this book. Most of all, however, we would like to thank our assistant Marc Huygens, who for the past two years has worked on every aspect of our project. We realize that we have been lucky to find such a committed and multitalented person, willing to go far beyond the call of duty.

SECTION I
STRATEGY
AND MANAGEMENT

CHAPTER 1: INTRODUCTION
On Strategy and Strategists

CHAPTER 1
INTRODUCTION:
ON STRATEGY AND STRATEGISTS

Strategy. Power and knowledge.
Science when mere knowing; Art
when doing is the object.
 —Karl von Clausewitz
  1780–1831, German military theorist

Introduction

In a book entitled *Strategy*, it would seem reasonable to expect chapter 1 to begin with a clear-cut definition of the phenomenon called strategy, which would be employed with consistence in all subsequent chapters. An early and precise definition of the topic under study would help to avoid conflicting interpretations of what should be considered strategy and, by extension, what should be understood by the term *strategic management*. However, we believe that any such sharp definition of strategy here would actually be a disservice to the reader. It would suggest that there is widespread agreement among strategy practicioners, researchers, and theorists as to what strategy exactly is. Even a quick glance through current literature on the topic indicates otherwise (Mintzberg, 1990).

As stated in the preface, this book does not favour any one school of thought over another. On the contrary, it is the explicit intention to expose the reader to the most important perspectives on the strategy topic. Picking one definition would imply taking sides. Hence, chapter 1 cannot firmly define anything, but does offer some working definitions as focal points for further debate. In other words, this section can set the stage for the discussion on what strategy is, which must be carried through into the subsequent chapters. This is exactly the objective of what you are about to read. It is not the intention to define, but to interest, to stimulate, to invigorate—basically to tickle your brain. In the process, more questions will be raised than answers given.

The Articles

As the subtitle to this chapter indicates, the two main questions to be explored here are What is strategy? and Who is a strategist? The opening article, "The First Strategists" by Stephen Cummings, places both of these questions in a historical perspective. Cummings takes the reader back to the ancient Greeks, to whom we owe the term *strategy*, in a quest to uncover some fundamental characteristics of military strategy and strategists, which he believes are still important for business strategists today. The charm of this article lies not only in its clear and concise rendition of Hellenic thought, but also in its ability to place the current state of the art of strategic thinking in the humbling context of history. This reading convincingly points out that many seemingly modern strategy issues are actually millennia old. The development of the business strategy field may be a recent academic trend, stretching no further back than the 1960s, but outside commerce many of the great minds throughout history have occupied themselves with the topic of strategy, especially in the fields of war (see, for instance, the famous Chinese theorist Sun Tzu's *The Art of Strategy*) and politics (e.g., Niccolo Machiavelli's *The Prince*). The debate, which Cummings opens with this article, is to what extent the principles of military strategy can be applied to the business context. Can business strategists learn from military strategists, and vice versa? Stated even more broadly, to what measure are there parallels between strategy in such diverse fields as war, politics, sports, biology, and business? Are there universal principles of strategy? The extent to which the strategy principles of one area are valid in another is a recurrent theme in strategy literature.

The second article, "Defining the Concept of Strategy", does exactly what its title promises to do, not by giving a five-line dictionary definition, but by trying to identify a number of fundamental characteristics of strategy in the business context. The author, Arnoldo Hax, skillfully seeks the common ground between the major schools of thought within the field of strategy, attempting to put forward a number of key features of strategy on which most researchers would agree. Therefore, this article is well suited as a starting point for the discussion on what strategy actually is.

The debate is only really opened in the next article, by Henry Mintzberg and James Waters, entitled "Of Strategies: Deliberate and Emergent." They argue, quite simply, that strategy is not only what is *intended*, but also what is *realized*. While most theorists focus almost exclusively on intended strategy, the authors of this article stress that a shift of focus toward realized strategy offers an entirely different perspective on the strategy process. It allows the researcher to distinguish between realized strategies that were intended ("deliberate"), those which were unintended ("emergent"), and a variety of partially intended strategies between these two extremes. The question that the Mintzberg and Waters article raises is whether an emergent strategy is strategy at all, or just "muddling through" under a fancy name. This is a fundamental issue with far reaching consequences and is therefore only raised, but not pursued, in chapter 1. In their article, Mintzberg and Waters stick to the introductory nature of this chapter and only explore the definition of strategy. However, they light a match and the fireworks go off in chapter 2.

The fourth article, "Art or Science of Strategy," is actually a compilation of key passages from the military classic *On War*, which was originally published in 1832 after the death of its author, the Prussian military theorist Karl von Clausewitz. Although Von Clausewitz was a "practicioner"—he was a general who participated in many campaigns—his book is one of the first works to view war and strategy from a scientific perspective. The reason for including this short article in chapter 1 is to begin yet another debate on the nature of strategy—is it art or science? Does strategy more closely resemble painting or mathematics? If strategy can be reduced to a number of principles and laws, that can be logically combined and manipulated, then strategy is a rational activity, that can be approached with scientific means. If strategy is an art, however, which cannot be captured by logic or laws, then the state of mind of the strategist is far more important than his scientific training. Von Clausewitz argues that strategy is a combination of both, yet in his text he seems to favour art over science.

This two-hundred-year-old question is further pursued in the fifth article, "The Mind of the Strategist," by Kenichi Ohmae. This article is actually a part of the introduction to his book of the same title, in which he clearly takes a position in the debate, arguing that strategy is far more an art than a science. He is not against rational analysis but believes that it should not dominate over creativity and intuition. Ohmae's remarks raise some interesting questions. In the context of this introduction, an important question is: If a significant part of strategy is art, how can individuals prepare themselves to become strategists? There are many opinions with regard to the qualities a strategist needs and the methods for obtaining these qualities (see, for example, Cummings's article), yet few publications in the field of strategy have been devoted to this issue.

One of the most pleasurable articles to deal with the qualities of the strategist is the sixth and last article in this chapter, "Are You a Strategist or Just a Manager?" by Hans Hinterhuber and Wolfgang Popp. Written in a playful style, their article lists ten qualities they believe may indicate strategy potential. All ten qualities have been framed as questions, so individuals can test their own abilities and establish priorities to work on. Since Hinterhuber and Popp believe that strategy is difficult to learn, they also suggest that these ten points can be used by companies as criteria when selecting potential strategists. Of course, the question is whether it is really all this simple—are these the qualities of a strategist and can an acid test be developed to identify an individual's strategy potential? As with the issues raised by the previous articles, these questions are too fundamental to be answered in chapter 1. They will run as underground streams throughout the entire book, occasionally springing to the surface.

Recommended Cases

Two relatively short and accessible cases, "A.F.C. Ajax" and "Euro Disneyland S.C.A.," have been specially developed for this introductory chapter. The Ajax case is a playful rendition of the strategic issues faced by this famous Dutch football club. Their prime strategist, chairman Michael van Praag, must develop a strategy to deal with the club's loss of world class players to Italian and Spanish teams. This case offers the reader the opportunity to employ all of the ideas presented in this chapter's articles within an out-of-the-ordinary business context. Euro Disneyland is a more traditional business case about the problems encountered by the Disney amusement park situated outside of Paris. The chief strategist, Philippe Bourguignon, must find an answer to the lack of interest among Europeans for this exact duplicate of the American Disneyland. As with the Ajax case, the Euro Disneyland case gives the reader ample opportunity to apply all of the chapter's concepts to the situation at hand.

■ THE FIRST STRATEGISTS†

By Stephen Cummings

Origin of Strategy

The word *strategy* derives from the ancient Athenian position of *strategos*. The title was coined in conjunction with the democratic reforms of Kleisthenes (508–7 B.C.), who developed a new sociopolitical structure in Athens after leading a popular revolution against a Spartan-supported oligarchy. Kleisthenes instituted ten new tribal divisions, which acted as both military and political subunits of the district of Athens. At the head of each tribe was elected a strategos. Collectively, the ten incumbent *strategoi* formed the Athenian war council. This council and its individual members, by virtue of the kudos granted them, also largely controlled nonmilitary politics.

Strategos was a compound of *stratos*; which meant "army," or more properly an encamped army *spread out* over ground (in this way *stratos* is also allied to *stratum*) and *agein*, "to lead." The emergence of the term paralleled increasing military decision-making complexity. Warfare had evolved to a point where winning sides no longer relied on the deeds of heroic individuals, but on the co-ordination of many units of men each fighting in close formation. Also, the increasing significance of naval forces in this period multiplied the variables a commander must consider in planning action. Consequently, questions of co-ordination and synergy among the various emergent units of their organizations became imperative considerations for successful commanders.

Of what interest are the origins of strategy to those engaging in strategic activities and decision making in organizations today? In the words of Adlai Stevenson, we can see our future clearly and wisely only when we know the path that leads to the present. Most involved in corporate strategy have little knowledge of where that path began. A great deal of insight into strategy can be gained from examining those from whom we inherit the term. The first strategists, the Greek strategoi, perhaps practiced strategy in its purest sense.

Strategy and Strategist as Defined by Ancient Theorists

Aineias the Tactician, who wrote the earliest surviving Western volume on military strategy, How to Survive under Siege, in the mid–fourth century B.C., was primarily concerned with how to deploy available manpower and other resources to best advantage. The term strategy is defined in more detail by Frontinus in the first century A.D., as "everything achieved by a commander, be it characterized by foresight, advantage, enterprise, or resolution."

Ancient Athenian theorists also had clear ideas about the characteristics that were necessary in an effective strategos. According to Xenophon, a commander "must be ingenious, energetic, careful, full of stamina and presence of mind, loving and tough, straightforward and crafty, alert and deceptive, ready to gamble everything and

†**Source:** Reprinted with permission from *Long Range Planning*, "Brief Case: The First Strategists", June 1993, Pergamon Press Ltd. Oxford, England.

wishing to have everything, generous and greedy, trusting and suspicious." These criteria for identifying an excellent strategist still ring true.

Xenophon goes on to describe the most important attribute for an aspiring strategos/statement as "knowing the business which you propose to carry out." The Athenians in this period were very concerned that their leaders had an awareness of how things worked at the "coal-face." Strategoi were publicly elected by their fellow members of the Athenian organization; and to be considered a credible candidate, one had to have worked one's way into this position by demonstrating prowess at both individual combat and hands-on military leadership. Wisdom was considered to be a citizen's ability to combine political acumen and practical intelligence, and strategoi should be the wisest of citizens. The organization's future lay in the hands of these men and, ipso facto, the strategic leadership of the Athenian organization was not to consider itself immune from hardship when times were tough: "No man was fitted to give fair and honest advice in council if he has not, like his fellows, a family at stake in the hour of the city's danger."

To the ancient Athenians strategy was very much a line function. The formulation of strategy was a leadership task. The Athenian organization developed by Kleisthenes was extremely recursive. The new tribes, and the local communities that these tribes comprised, formed the units and subunits of the army, and were, in their sociopolitical structures, tantamount to the city-state in microcosm. Decision makers at all levels of the corporation were expected to think strategically, in accordance with the behaviour exhibited by those in leadership roles at higher levels of the Athenian system. Strategoi were expected both to direct and take part in the thick of battle, leading their troops into action. For a strategos not to play an active combat role would have resulted in a significant diminution in the morale of those fighting for his tribe.

Practical Lessons from the Strategoi

If military practice is identified as a metaphor for business competition, the strategic principles of the great strategoi still provide useful guides for those in the business of strategy formulation today. For Pericles, perhaps the greatest of the Athenian strategoi, the goal of military strategies was "to limit risk while holding fast to essential points and principles." His often quoted maxims of "Opportunity waits for no man" and "Do not make any new conquests during the war" are still applicable advice in a modern business environment.

Epaminondas of Thebes was said to have brought the two arms of his military corporation, infantry and cavalry, together in a "fruitful organizational blend." The Theban's strategic principles included economy of force coupled with overwhelming strength at the decisive point; close co-ordination between units and meticulous staff planning combined with speed of attack; and as the quickest and most economical way of winning a decision, defeat of the competition not at his weakest point but at his strongest. Epaminondas was Philip of Macedon's mentor, and it was largely due to the application of the Theban's innovations that the Macedonian army grew to an extent where it was able to realize Alexander the Great's (Philip's son) vast ambitions. The close integration of all its individual units became the major strength of the Macedonian army organization.

Alexander himself is perhaps the most famous ancient exponent of a contingency approach to strategy. It is often told that as a young man he was asked by his tutor Aristotle what he would do in a given situation. Alexander replied that his answer would depend on the circumstances. Aristotle described a hypothetical set of circumstances and asked his original question again. To this the student answered, "I cannot tell until the circumstances arise." In practice Alexander was not often caught without a "plan B." An example is related by Frontinus: "At Arbela, Alexander, fearing the numbers of the enemy, yet confident in the valour of his own troops, drew up a line of battle facing in all directions, in order that the men, if surrounded, might be able to fight from any side."

Ancient Approaches to the Learning of Strategy

The ancient Greeks took great interest in both the practical and theoretical aspects of strategic leadership. They favoured the case method as the best means of passing this knowledge from one generation of strategists to the next. Frontinus argued that "in this way commanders will be furnished with specimens of wisdom and foresight, which will serve to foster their own power of conceiving and executing like deeds." Aineias and Xenophon also used and championed such methods in ways that would please any Harvardophile. The best-crafted exposition of the case method, however, belongs to Plutarch, biographer to the ancient world's greatest leaders:

> It is true, of course, that our outward sense cannot avoid apprehending the various objects it encounters, merely by virtue of their impact and regardless of whether they are useful or not: but a man's conscious intellect is something which he may bring to bear or avert as he chooses, and can very easily transfer . . . to another object as he sees fit. For this reason, we ought to seek out virtue not merely to contemplate it, but to derive benefit from doing so. A colour, for example, is well suited to the eye if its bright and agreeable tones stimulate and refresh the vision, and in the same way we ought to apply our intellectual vision to those models which can inspire it to attain its own proper virtue through the sense of delight they arouse. . . . [Such a model is] no sooner seen than it rouses the spectator into action, and yet it does not form his character by mere imitation, but by promoting the understanding of virtuous deeds it provides him with a dominating purpose.

Now, as then, our strategic vision can be refreshed and stimulated through studying the character and deeds of the great strategic leaders of the past.

■ DEFINING THE CONCEPT OF STRATEGY†

By Arnoldo Hax

What is strategy? Once upon a time strategy could be defined as a rendition of the CEO's personal mission statement, rationalized by the corporate planner, and bought into by the executive committee and chief stockholders. But even this simplistic and somewhat cynical answer begs the question of how the strategy was really formed. Did it flash through a CEO's mind while at his or her morning ablutions or was it a logical model for growing the business, developed after years of studying the industry and the capabilities of the firm? Now that more and more line managers are becoming responsible for planning and strategies, and the sum of their increasingly fast-paced

†**Source:** This article is reprinted from "Redefining the Concept of Strategy", *Planning Review*, (May/June 1990), with permission from The Planning Forum, The International Society for Strategic Management and Planning.

decisions may affect a firm's strategy almost overnight or create a new implicit aspect of it, it's time for a fresh look at what strategy is and how it may come about.

But providing a simple definition is not easy. There are some elements of strategy that have universal validity and can be applied to any institution. However, other elements are heavily dependent on the nature of the firm, its constituencies, its structure, and its culture.

Six Dimensions of Strategy

To clarify the definition process, it is useful to consider the concept of strategy separately from the process of strategy formation. Let's start by assuming that strategy actually embraces all the critical activities of a firm. Let's also hypothesize that strategy provides a sense of unity, direction, and purpose, as well as facilitating the necessary changes induced by a firm's environment. The following six critical dimensions must therefore be included in any unified definition of the concept of strategy.

Strategy as a Coherent, Unifying, and Integrative Pattern of Decisions

Many business people would accept the definition that strategy is the major force that provides a comprehensive and integrative blueprint for an organization as a whole. As such, strategy gives rise to the plans that assure that the basic objectives of the total enterprise are fulfilled. This assumes that strategy is conscious, explicit, and proactive.

But skeptics can offer many examples of firms where strategy is implicit, murkily communicated, and practiced covertly. By expanding our definition we can include even firms that practice strategy as a black art. So, broadly defined, strategy is the pattern of decisions a firm makes.

This definition has historical validity. Strategy is a matter of record—it emerges from what the firm does. To examine strategy as an evolutionary process, we can study the nature of an organization's decision making and its resulting performance. Strategic patterns can be discerned by examining major changes or discontinuities in a firm's direction. These may be caused by changes in its top management or changes triggered by important external events that call for strategic repositioning.

Analyzing a firm in terms of these historical eras usually provides a more or less coherent strategic pattern. Significant strategies emerge. They are discovered by following the footprints of the major steps a firm has taken in the past. Often this path of strategic footprints—like a woodland trail that heads toward a mountain peak on the horizon—indicates the organization's future destination.

Strategy as a Means of Establishing an Organization's Purpose in Terms of its Long-Term Objectives

This classical view looks at strategy as a way of explicitly shaping the long-term goals and objectives of an organization; of defining the major action programs needed to achieve those objectives; and of deploying the necessary resources.

To make this concept useful, we first need to define a firm's long-term objectives. If these change constantly, the value of this approach decreases. There should be little change in this area unless external conditions or internal shifts call for a reexamination of the long-term commitments. Nothing could be more debilitating to a firm than an erratic reorientation of its objectives without substantive reasons. Continuous strategic redirections simply end up confusing all of a firm's stakeholders—but most importantly, its customers, employees, and stockholders.

The desirable stability of long-term objectives does not, however, preclude frequent refining of a firm's programs. This is accomplished by continually reexamining the short-term strategic action programs that are congruent with long-term objectives.

This approach makes it clear that resource allocation is a firm's most critical step in strategic implementation. The alignment between strategic objectives and programs on the one hand, and the allocation of a firm's overall resources—human, financial, technological, and physical—on the other, is required to achieve strategic effectiveness.

Strategy as a Definition of a Firm's Competitive Domain

It has long been recognized that one of the central concerns of strategy is defining the businesses a firm is in or intends to be in. The process of definition requires strategy makers to address issues of growth, diversification, and divestment.

A key step in defining a formal strategic planning process is effective business segmentation. Segmentation is a crucial step in business analysis, strategic positioning, resource allocation, and portfolio management. Segmentation explicitly identifies a firm's domain: Where is it going to be engaged in competitive actions, and how is it going to compete?

The basic questions to be addressed are, What businesses are we in? and What businesses should we be in? If a firm operating in a complex and dynamic business environment has never attempted to respond seriously to these questions, it may at first find them trivial. Yet, extracting a clear-cut answer from an experienced group of managers when these questions are addressed for the first time is often a surprisingly difficult procedure. Consensus is hard to come by.

The issues are further complicated because business segmentation ultimately has an enormous impact on defining the organizational structure of the firm. Consciously or unconsciously, issues of turf and executive responsibilities tend to have a major influence on the way these questions are addressed.

Strategy as a Response to External Opportunities and Threats and to Internal Strengths and Weaknesses as a Means of Achieving Competitive Advantage

According to this perspective, the central thrust of strategy is to achieve a long-term sustainable advantage over a firm's key competitors in every business in which it participates. This view of strategy is what underlies most of the modern analytical approaches used to support the search for a favorable competitive position. It recognizes that:

■ The ultimate objective is for a firm to achieve a long-term competitive advantage over its key competitors in all of its businesses.

■ This competitive advantage is the result of a thorough understanding of the external and internal forces that strongly affect an organization. Externally, a firm must recognize its relative industry attractiveness and trends, and the characteristics of the major competitors. This helps generate the discovery of the opportunities and threats that must be reckoned with. Internally, a firm must identify its competitive capabilities. This leads to the defining of its strengths and weaknesses.

■ Strategy allows organizations to achieve a viable match between their external environment and their internal capabilities. The role of strategy is not viewed simply as a passive response to the opportunities and threats presented by the external environment, but rather as a process of continuously and actively adapting the organization to meet the demands of a changing environment.

Given this perspective, it is now easy to see that the fundamental framework of business strategy encompasses three primary focal points:

- The business unit, which is the central subject of analysis.
- The industry structure, which determines the key environmental trends.
- The internal competencies, which define the ways to compete.

Thus, the long-term objectives, strategic action programs, and resource allocation priorities adapt to the role the business unit intends to play within the total portfolio of the firm's businesses. They also adapt to the favorable or unfavorable trends of the industry structure, as well as to the internal capabilities a firm needs to deploy in order to achieve the desired competitive position.

Strategy as a Logical System for Differentiating Managerial Tasks at Corporate, Business, and Functional Levels

The various hierarchical levels in the organization have quite different managerial responsibilities in terms of their contribution to defining the strategy of the firm. The corporate level is responsible for tasks that need the fullest scope in order to be addressed properly. Primarily, this means defining a firm's overall mission; validating proposals emerging from business and functional levels; identifying and exploiting linkages between distinct but related business units; and allocating resources with a sense of strategic priorities.

The business level is the proper place for all of the activities needed to enhance the competitive position of each individual business unit.

The key assignment of the functional level is to develop the necessary competencies—in finance, administrative infrastructure, human resources, technology, procurement, logistics, manufacturing, distribution, marketing, sales, and services— needed to sustain competitive advantage. Recognizing the differences in these managerial roles, and integrating them harmoniously, is another key dimension of strategy.

Regardless of the structure adopted by a firm, three highly differentiated strategic concerns still remain: The first addresses the organization as a whole (corporate strategy); the second is intrinsic to the business unit (business strategy); and the third involves the development of functional capabilities (functional strategy).

Strategy as a Definition of the Economic and Noneconomic Contribution the Firm Intends to Make to Its Stakeholders

The notion of stakeholders has gained importance as an element of strategic concern in the past few years. The term *stakeholders* refers to everyone who directly or indirectly receives the benefits or sustains the costs that result from a firm's actions. Stakeholders include shareholders, employees, managers, customers, suppliers, debt holders, communities, government, and others.

"Taking care of the stakeholders" is an extremely useful way of looking at a firm's concerns. In a profit-making organization, the proverbial bottom line becomes an important objective; but it can also become a dangerous trap. Managers must guard against looking at short-term profitability as the ultimate driving force. Sustained profitability is the legitimate and deserved reward of a job well done—one that emanates from being responsible to a firm's remaining stakeholders.

Toward a Unified Concept of Strategy

The concept of strategy embraces the overall purpose of an organization. It is not surprising, therefore, that defining it properly means examining the many facets that make up the whole. By combining them, we arrive at a more comprehensive definition of strategy.

From this unifying point of view, strategy becomes a fundamental framework through which an organization can assert its vital continuity, while at the same time purposefully managing its adaptation to the changing environment to gain competitive advantage. Strategy includes the formal recognition that the recipients of the results of a firm's actions are the wide constituency of its stakeholders. Therefore, the ultimate objective of strategy is to address stakeholders' benefits—to provide a base for establishing the host of transactions and social contracts that link a firm to its stakeholders.

■ OF STRATEGIES, DELIBERATE AND EMERGENT†

By Henry Mintzberg and James Waters

How do strategies form in organizations? Since strategy has almost inevitably been conceived in terms of what the leaders of an organization "plan" to do in the future, strategy formation has, not surprisingly, tended to be treated as an analytic process for establishing long-range goals and action plans for an organization, that is, as one of formulation followed by implementation. As important as this emphasis may be, we would argue that it is seriously limited, that the process needs to be viewed from a wider perspective so that the variety of ways in which strategies actually take shape can be considered.

For over ten years now, we have been researching the process of strategy formation based on the definition of strategy as a pattern in a stream of decisions. Streams of behaviour could be isolated and strategies identified as patterns or consistencies in such streams. The origins of these strategies could then be investigated, with particular attention paid to exploring the relationship between leadership plans and intentions and what the organizations actually did. Using the label "strategy" for both of these phenomena—one called *intended*, the other *realized*—encouraged that exploration.

Comparing intended strategy with realized strategy, as shown in figure 1-1, has allowed us to distinguish *deliberate* strategies—realized as intended—from *emergent* strategies—patterns or consistencies realized despite, or in the absence of, intentions.

†**Source:** This article was originally published in *Strategic Management Journal* (July/September 1985). Reproduced by permission of John Wiley and Sons Limited.

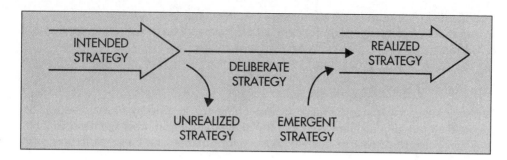

FIGURE 1-1
Types of Strategies

Pure Deliberate and Pure Emergent Strategies

For a strategy to be perfectly deliberate—that is, for the realized strategy (pattern in actions) to form exactly as intended—at least three conditions would seem to have to be satisfied. First, there must have existed precise intentions in the organization, articulated at a relatively concrete level of detail, so that there can be no doubt about what was desired before any actions were taken. Second, because organization means collective action, to dispel any possible doubt about whether or not the intentions were organizational, they must have been common to virtually all the actors: either shared as their own or else accepted from leaders, probably in response to some sort of controls. Third, these collective intentions must have been realized exactly as intended, which means that no external force (market, technological, political, etc.) could have interfered with them. The environment, in other words, must have been either perfectly predictable, totally benign, or else under the full control of the organization. These three conditions constitute a tall order, so that we are unlikely to find any perfectly deliberate strategies in organizations. Nevertheless, some strategies do come rather close, in some dimensions if not all.

For a strategy to be perfectly emergent, there must be order—consistency in action over time—in the absence of intention about it. (No consistency means no strategy or at least unrealized strategy—intentions not met.) It is difficult to imagine action in the total absence of intention—in some pocket of the organization if not from the leadership itself—such that we would expect the purely emergent strategy to be as rare as the purely deliberate one. But again, our research suggests that some patterns come rather close, as when an environment directly imposes a pattern of action on an organization.

Thus, we would expect to find tendencies in the directions of deliberate and emergent strategies rather than perfect forms of either. In effect, these two form the poles of a continuum along which we would expect real-world strategies to fall. Such strategies would combine various states of the dimensions we have discussed above: leadership intentions would be more or less precise, concrete and explicit, and more or less shared, as would intentions existing elsewhere in the organization; central control over organizational actions would be more or less firm and more or less pervasive; and the environment would be more or less benign, more or less controllable, and more or less predictable.

Below we introduce a variety of types of strategies that fall along this continuum, beginning with those closest to the deliberate pole and ending with those most reflective of the characteristics of emergent strategy. We present these types, not as any firm or exhaustive typology (although one may eventually emerge), but simply to explore this continuum of emergentness of strategy and to try to gain some insights into the notions of intention, choice, and pattern formation in the collective context we call organization.

The Planned Strategy

Planning suggests clear and articulated intentions, backed up by formal controls to ensure their pursuit, in an environment that is acquiescent. In other words, here (and only here) does the classic distinction between formulation and implementation hold up.

In this first type, called *planned* strategy, leaders at the center of authority formulate their intentions as precisely as possible and then strive for their implementation—their translation into collective action—with a minimum of distortion, "surprise free." To ensure this, leaders must first articulate their intentions in the form of a plan, to minimize confusion, and then elaborate this plan in as much detail as possible in the form of budgets, schedules, and so on to preempt discretion that might impede its realization. Those outside the planning process may act, but insofar as possible they are not allowed to decide. Programs that guide their behaviour are built into the plan, and formal controls are instituted to ensure pursuit of the plan and the programs.

But the plan is of no use if it cannot be applied as formulated in the environment surrounding the organization, so the planned strategy is found in an environment that is, if not benign or controllable, then at least rather predictable. Some organizations are powerful enough to impose their plans on their environments. Others are able to predict their environments with enough accuracy to pursue rather deliberate, planned strategies. We suspect, however, that many planned strategies are found in organizations that simply extrapolate established patterns in environments they assume will remain stable. In fact, strategies appear not to be conceived in planning processes so much as elaborated from existing visions or copied from standard industry recipes; planning thus becomes programming, and the planned strategy finds its origins in one of the other types of strategies described below.

Although few strategies can be planned to the degree described above, some do come rather close, particularly in organizations that must commit large quantities of resources to particular missions and so cannot tolerate unstable environments. They may spend years considering their actions, but once they decide to act, they commit themselves firmly. In effect, they deliberate so that their strategies can be rather deliberate. Our study of the United States government's escalation of military activity in Vietnam revealed a rather planned strategy. Once Lyndon Johnson announced his decision to escalate in 1965, the military planners took over and articulated the intentions in detail (or pulled out existing contingency plans), and pursued the strategy vigorously until 1968, when it became clear that the environment was less controllable than it had seemed.

The Entrepreneurial Strategy

In this second type of strategy, we relax the condition of precise, articulated intentions. Here, one individual in personal control of an organization is able to impose his or her vision of direction on it. Because such strategies are common in entrepreneurial firms tightly controlled by their owners, they are called *entrepreneurial* strategies.

In this case, the force for pattern or consistency in action is individual vision, the central actor's concept of his or her organization's place in its world. This is coupled with an ability to impose that vision on the organization through his or her personal control of its actions (e.g., through giving direct orders to its operating personnel). Of course, the environment must again be co-operative. But entrepreneurial strategies most commonly appear in young and/or small organizations (where personal control is feasible) that are able to find relatively safe niches in their environments. Indeed, the selection of such niches is an integral part of the vision. These strategies can, however, sometimes be found in larger organizations as well, particularly under conditions of crisis where all the actors are willing to follow the direction of a single leader who has vision and will.

Is the entrepreneurial strategy deliberate? Intentions do exist. But they derive from one individual who need not articulate or elaborate them. Indeed, for reasons discussed below, he or she is typically unlikely to want to do so. Thus, the intentions are both more difficult to identify and less specific than those of the planned strategy. Moreover, there is less overt acceptance of these intentions on the part of other actors in the organization. Nevertheless, so long as those actors respond to the personal will of the leader, the strategy would appear to be rather deliberate.

In two important respects, an entrepreneurial strategy can have emergent characteristics as well. First, vision provides only a general sense of direction. Within it, there is room for adaptation: the details of the vision can emerge en route. Second, because the leader's vision is personal, it can also be changed completely. To put this another way, since here the formulator is the implementor, step by step, that person can react quickly to feedback on past actions or to new opportunities or threats in the environment. He or she can thus reformulate vision.

It is this adaptability that distinguishes the entrepreneurial strategy from the planned one. Visions contained in single brains would appear to be more flexible, assuming the individual's willingness to learn, than plans articulated through hierarchies, which comprise many brains. Adaptation (and emergentness) of planned strategies is discouraged by the articulation of intentions and by the separation between formulation and implementation. Psychologists have shown that the articulation of a strategy locks it into place, impeding willingness to change it. The separation of implementation from formulation gives rise to a whole system of commitments and procedures, in the form of plans, programs, and controls elaborated down a hierarchy. Instead of one individual being able to change his or her mind, the whole system must be redesigned. Thus, despite the claims of flexible planning, the fact is that organizations plan not to be flexible but to realize specific intentions. It is the entrepreneurial strategy that provides flexibility, at the expense of the specificity and articulation of intentions.

The Ideological Strategy

Vision can be collective as well as individual. When the members of an organization share a vision and identify so strongly with it that they pursue it as an ideology, then they are bound to exhibit patterns in their behaviour, so that clear realized strategies can be identified. These may be called *ideological* strategies.

Can an ideological strategy be considered deliberate? Since the ideology is likely to be somewhat overt (e.g., in programs of indoctrination), and perhaps even articulated (in rough, inspirational form, such as a credo), intentions can usually be identified. The question thus revolves around whether these intentions can be considered organizational and whether they are likely to be realized as intended. In an important sense, these intentions would seem to be most clearly organizational. Whereas the intentions of the planned and entrepreneurial strategies emanate from one center and are accepted passively by everyone else, those of the ideological strategy are positively embraced by the members of the organization.

As for their realization, because the intentions exist as a rough vision, they can presumably be adapted or changed. But collective vision is far more immutable than individual vision. All who share it must agree to change their collective mind. Moreover, ideology is rooted in the past, in traditions and precedents (often the institutionalization of the vision of a departed, charismatic leader: one person's vision has become everyone's ideology). So people resist changing it. The object is to interpret "the word," not to defy it. Finally, the environment is unlikely to impose change: the purpose of ideology, after all, is to change the environment or else to insulate the organization from it. For all these reasons, ideological strategy would normally be highly deliberate, perhaps more so than any type of strategy except the planned one.

We have not as yet studied any organization dominated by an ideology. But such strategies do seem to occur in certain organizations described in the literature, notably in certain Israeli kibbutzim, "distinctive colleges," and some charitable institutions.

The Umbrella Strategy

Now we begin to relax the condition of tight control (whether bureaucratic, personal, or ideological) over the mass of actors in the organization and, in some cases, the condition of tight control over the environment as well. Leaders who have only partial control over other actors in an organization may design what can be called *umbrella* strategies. They set general guidelines for behaviour—define the boundaries—and then let other actors manoeuvre within them. In effect, these leaders establish kinds of umbrellas under which organizational actions are expected to fall—for example that all products should be designed for the high-priced end of the market (no matter what those products might be).

When an environment is complex, and perhaps somewhat uncontrollable and unpredictable as well, a variety of actors in the organization must be able to respond to it. In other words, the patterns in organizational actions cannot be set deliberately in one central place, although the boundaries may be established there to constrain them. From the perspective of the leadership (if not, perhaps, the individual actors), therefore, strategies are allowed to emerge, at least within these boundaries. In fact, we can label the umbrella strategy not only deliberate and emergent (intended at the center in its broad outlines but not in its specific details), but also "deliberately emergent" (in the sense that the central leadership intentionally creates the conditions under which strategies can emerge).

Like the entrepreneurial strategy, the umbrella strategy represents a certain vision emanating from the central leadership. But here those who have the vision do not control its realization; instead they must convince others to pursue it. The umbrella at least puts limits on the actions of others and ideally provides a sense of direction as well. Sometimes the umbrella takes the form of a more specific target. In the 1960s, for example, the U.S. Nationál Aeronautics and Space Administration (NASA) concentrated its efforts on putting a man on the moon. In the light of this specific target, all kinds of strategies emerged, as various technical problems were solved by thousands of different specialists.

We have so far described the umbrella strategy as one among a number of types that are possible. But in some sense, virtually all real-world strategies have umbrella characteristics. That is, in no organization can the central leadership totally preempt the discretion of others (as was assumed in the planned and entrepreneurial strategies), and by the same token, in none does a central leadership defer totally to others (unless it has ceased to lead). Almost all strategy-making behaviour involves, therefore, to some degree at least, a central leadership with some sort of intention trying to direct, guide, cajole, or nudge others with ideas of their own. When the leadership is able to direct, we move toward the realm of planned or entrepreneurial strategies; when it can hardly nudge, we move toward the realm of more emergent strategies. But in the broad range between these two can always be found strategies with umbrella characteristics.

In its pursuit of an umbrella strategy—which means, in essence, defining general direction subject to varied interpretation—the central leadership must monitor the behaviour of other actors to assess whether the boundaries are being respected. Like us, it searches for patterns in streams of actions. When actors are found to stray outside the boundaries (inadvertently or intentionally), the central leadership has three choices: to stop them, ignore them (perhaps for a time, to see what will happen), or adjust to them. In other words, when an arm pokes outside the umbrella, you either pull it in, leave it there (although it might get wet), or move the umbrella over to cover it.

In this last case, the leadership exercises the option of altering its own vision in response to the behaviour of others. Indeed, this would appear to be the place where much effective strategic learning takes place—through leadership response to the initiatives of others. Leadership that is never willing to alter its vision in such a way forgoes important opportunities and tends to lose touch with its environment (although, of course, one too willing to do so may be unable to sustain any central direction). The umbrella strategy thus requires a light touch, maintaining a subtle balance between proaction and reaction.

The Process Strategy

Similar to the umbrella strategy is what can be called the *process* strategy. Again, the leadership functions in an organization in which other actors must have considerable discretion to determine outcomes, owing to an environment that is complex and perhaps also unpredictable and uncontrollable. But instead of trying to control strategy content at a general level, through boundaries or targets, the leadership instead needs to exercise influence indirectly. Specifically, it controls the process of strategy making while leaving the content of strategy to other actors. Again, the resulting behaviour would be deliberate in one respect and emergent in others: the central leadership designs the system that allows others the flexibility to evolve patterns within it.

Leadership may, for example, control the staffing of the organization, thereby determining who gets to make strategy if not what that strategy will be (all the while knowing that control of the former constitutes considerable influence over the latter). Or it may design the structure of the organization to determine the working context of those who make strategy.

Divisionalized organizations of a conglomerate nature commonly use strategies: central headquarters creates the basic structure, establishes the systems, and appoints the division managers, who are then expected to d strategies for their own businesses. Note that techniques such as those introdu the Boston Consulting Group to manage the business portfolios of division companies, by involving headquarters in the business strategies to some e approximate umbrella strategies.

The Unconnected Strategy

The *unconnected* strategy is perhaps the most straightforward of all. One part of the organization with considerable discretion—a subunit, sometimes even a single individual—because it is only loosely coupled to the rest is able to realize its own pattern in its stream of actions.

How deliberate or emergent are these unconnected strategies? Since they come neither from a central leadership nor from intentions in the organization at large, they would seem to be relatively emergent from the perspective of the entire organization. But from the perspective of the unit or individual involved, clearly they can be deliberate or emergent, depending on the prior existence of intentions.

Some unconnected strategies directly contradict umbrella strategies (or even more centrally imposed planned or entrepreneurial ones), in effect developing on a clandestine basis. President Kennedy's directive to defuse the missile bases in Turkey during the Cuban Missile Crisis was deliberately ignored by the military leaders. Even though the strategy is likely to be deliberate from the point of view of its proponents, it cannot be articulated as such: they cannot reveal their intentions. To minimize their risk of exposure, they seek to realize intentions subtly, action by action, as if the strategy were emergent. Of course, that increases the chances that the intentions will get deflected along the way. If they do not, there is still the risk that the leadership will realize what is happening—will recognize the pattern in the stream of actions—and stop the strategy. Leadership can, however, play the game too, waiting to see what happens, knowing it, too, can learn from clandestine behaviour. If the strategy should prove successful, it can always be accepted and broadened—internalized in the system as a (henceforth) deliberate strategy. Our suspicion is that much strategic adaptation results from unconnected strategies (whether clandestine or not) that succeed and so pervade the organization.

The Consensus Strategy

In no strategy so far discussed have we totally dropped the condition of prior intention. The next type is rather more clearly emergent. Here many different actors naturally converge on the same theme, or pattern, so that it becomes pervasive in the organization, without the need for any central direction or control. We call it the *consensus* strategy. Unlike the ideological strategy, in which a consensus forms around a system of beliefs (thus reflecting intentions widely accepted in the organization), the consensus strategy grows out of the mutual adjustment among different actors as they learn from each other and from their various responses to the environment and thereby find a common, and probably unexpected, pattern that works for them.

In other words, the convergence is not driven by any intentions of a central management, nor even by prior intentions widely shared among the other actors. It just evolves as the result of a host of individual actions. Of course, certain actors may actively promote the consensus, perhaps even negotiate with their colleagues to attain it (as in the congressional form of government). But the point is that it derives more from collective action than from collective intention.

When convergence is on a general theme rather than a specific activity, it is likely to develop more gradually: individual actions would take time to be understood and to pervade the organization as precedents. An electronics manufacturer may find itself concentrating on high-quality products after it has achieved success with a number of such products, or a university may find itself over the years favoring the sciences over the humanities as its members come to realize where its real strengths lie.

The Imposed Strategy

All the strategies so far discussed have derived in part at least from the will (if not the intentions) of actors within the organization. The environment has been considered, if not benign, then at least acquiescent. But strategies can be *imposed* from outside as well; that is, the environment can directly force the organization into a pattern in its stream of actions, regardless of the presence of central controls. The clearest case of this occurs when an external individual or group with a great deal of influence over the organization imposes a strategy on it. We saw this in our study of state-owned Air Canada, when the minister who created and controlled the airline in its early years forced it to buy and fly a particular type of aircraft. Here the imposed strategy was clearly deliberate, but not by anyone in the organization. However, given its inability to resist, the organization had to resign itself to the pursuit of the strategy, so that it became, in effect, deliberate.

Sometimes the environment rather than people per se imposes strategies on organizations, simply by severely restricting the options open to them. Air Canada "chose" to fly jet aeroplanes and later wide-body aeroplanes. But did it? Could any world class airline have decided otherwise? Again, the organization has internalized the imperative so that the question of strategic choice becomes a moot point. To draw from another of our studies, did Lyndon Johnson choose to escalate the United States' involvement in Vietnam in 1965? Kennedy's earlier intended strategy of providing advisers for the South Vietnamese became an emergent strategy of engagement in a hot war, imposed by the environment (namely the actions of the Viet Cong; of course, to the extent that the military advisers intended to fight, the strategy might be more accurately described as clandestine). The result was that by the time Johnson faced the decision to escalate, the pressures were almost inescapable. So he "decided," and the strategy became a planned one.

Many planned strategies in fact seem to have this determined quality to them—that they are pursued by organizations resigned to co-operating with external forces. One is reminded here of the king in the story of *The Little Prince*, who only gave orders that could be executed. He claimed, for example, that he could order the sun to set, but only at a certain time of the day. The point is that when intentions are sufficiently malleable, everything can seem deliberate.

Reality, however, seems to bring organizations closer to a compromise position between determinism and free choice. Environments seldom preempt all choice, just as they seldom offer unlimited choice. That is why purely determined strategies are probably as rare as purely planned ones. Alternatively, if the umbrella strategy is the most realistic reflection of leadership intention, then the partially imposed strategy may be the most realistic reflection of environmental influence. Just as we argued earlier that virtually all real-world strategies have umbrella characteristics, so too we add here that virtually all have environmental boundaries.

Emerging Conclusions

In our view, the fundamental difference between deliberate and emergent strategy is that whereas the former focuses on direction and control—getting desired things done—the latter opens up the notion of strategic learning. Defining strategy as intended and conceiving it as deliberate, as has traditionally been done, effectively precludes the notion of strategic learning. Once intentions have been set, attention is

FIGURE 1-2
Strategic Learning

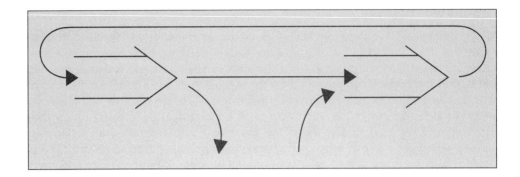

riveted on realizing them, not on adapting them. Messages from the environment tend to get blocked out. Adding the concept of emergent strategy, based on the definition of strategy as realized, opens up the process of strategy making to the notion of learning.

Emergent strategy itself implies learning what works—taking one action at a time in search for that viable pattern or consistency. It is important to remember that emergent strategy means not chaos but, in essence, unintended order. It is also frequently the means by which deliberate strategies change. As shown in figure 1-2, in the feedback loop added to our basic diagram, it is often through the identification of emergent strategies—patterns never intended—that managers and others in the organization come to change their intentions. This is another way of saying that not a few deliberate strategies are simply emergent ones that have been uncovered and subsequently formalized. Of course, unrealized strategies are also a source of learning, as managers find out which of their intentions do not work, rejected either by their organizations themselves or by environments that are less than acquiescent.

We wish to emphasize that emergent strategy does not have to mean that management is out of control, only—in some cases at least—that it is open, flexible, and responsive, in other words, willing to learn. Such behaviour is especially important when an environment is too unstable or complex to comprehend, or too imposing to defy. Openness to such emergent strategy enables management to act before everything is fully understood—to respond to an evolving reality rather than having to focus on a stable fantasy. Emergent strategy also enables a management that cannot be close enough to a situation, or know enough about the varied activities of its organization, to surrender control to those who have information current and detailed enough to shape realistic strategies. Whereas more deliberate strategies tend to emphasize central direction and hierarchy, the more emergent ones open the way for collective action and convergent behaviour.

By the same token, deliberate strategy is hardly dysfunctional. Managers need to manage too—sometimes even to impose intentions on their organizations—to provide a sense of direction. That can be partial, as in the cases of umbrella and process strategies, or it can be comprehensive, as in the cases of planned and entrepreneurial strategies. When the necessary information can be brought to a central place and environments can be largely understood and predicted (or at least controlled), then it may be appropriate to suspend strategic learning for a time to pursue intentions with as much determination as possible.

Our conclusion is that strategy formation walks on two feet, one deliberate, the other emergent. As noted earlier, managing requires a light, deft touch—to direct in order to realize intentions while at the same time responding to an unfolding pattern of action. The relative emphasis may shift from time to time, but not the requirement to attend to both sides of the phenomenon.

■ ART OR SCIENCE OF STRATEGY†

By Karl von Clausewitz

The choice between these terms seems to be still unsettled; no one seems to know rightly on what grounds it should be decided, and yet the thing is simple. *Knowing* is different from *doing*. The doing cannot properly stand in any book, and therefore also *art* should never be the title of a book. But because we have accustomed ourselves to combine under the name of *theory of art*, or simply *art*, the branches of knowledge necessary for the practice of an art, it is consistent to call everything art when the object is to carry out the doing (e.g., art of building) and science when merely knowledge is the object (e.g., science of mathematics). That in every art certain sciences may be included should not perplex us. But it is worth observing that there is also no science without a mixture of art. The reason is that however plain the difference between knowledge and power, it is difficult to trace out their line of separation in man himself. All thinking is indeed art. Where judgement begins, there art begins. Even the perception of the mind is judgement and consequently art. If it is impossible to imagine a human being possessing merely the faculty of cognition, devoid of judgement or the reverse, so also art and science can never be completely separated from each other.

Once more, where the object is creation and production, there is the province of art; where the object is investigation and knowledge, science holds sway. After all this it results of itself that it is more fitting to say art of strategy, than science of strategy. Strategy theory, therefore, will content itself to assist the commander to the insight into things which, blended with his whole thought, makes his course easier and surer, but never forces him into opposition with himself in order to obey an objective truth. All principles, rules and methods exist to offer themselves for use as required, and it must always be left for judgement to decide whether or not they are suitable. Theory must never be used as norms for a standard, but merely as aids to judgement.

Strategy forms the plan, and to this end it links together the series of acts which are to lead to the final decision; that is, it makes the plans for the separate campaigns and regulates the combats to be fought in each. As these are all things which to a great extent can only be determined on conjectures, some of which turn out incorrect, while a number of other arrangements pertaining to details cannot be made at all beforehand, it follows as a matter of course that strategy must go with the army to the field in order to arrange particulars on the spot and to make the modifications in the general plan which incessantly become necessary. Strategy can therefore never take its hand from the work for a moment. Theory will therefore attend on strategy in the determination of its plans, or, as we more properly say, it will throw a light on things and bring out prominently the little that there is of principle or rule.

It may sound strange that more strength of will is required to make an important decision in strategy than in tactics. In the latter we are hurried on with the moment. A commander feels himself borne along in a strong current, against which he durst not contend without the most destructive consequences; he suppresses the rising fears and boldly ventures farther. In strategy, where all goes at a slower rate, there is more

---

†**Source:** This article was adapted with permission from chapters 3 and 5 (book 2) and chapter 1 (book 3) of *On War*, Penguin Books, 1982.

room allowed for our own apprehensions and those of others, for objections and remonstrances, consequently also for unseasonable regrets; and as we do not see things in strategy as we do at least half of them in tactics, but everything must be conjectured and assumed, the convictions produced are less powerful. The consequence is that most generals, when they should act, remain stuck fast in bewildering doubts.

■ THE MIND OF THE STRATEGIST[†]

By Kenichi Ohmae

As a consultant I have had the opportunity to work with many large Japanese companies. Among them are many companies whose success you would say must be the result of superb strategies. But when you look more closely, you discover a paradox. They have no big planning staffs, no elaborate gold-plated strategic planning processes. Some of them are painfully handicapped by a lack of the resources—people, money, and technology—that seemingly would be needed to implement an ambitious strategy. Yet despite all these handicaps, they are outstanding performers in the marketplace. Year after year, they manage to build market share and create wealth.

How do they do it? The answer is easy. They may not have a strategic planning staff, but they do have a strategist of great natural talent, usually the founder or chief executive. Often—especially in Japan, where there are no business schools—these outstanding strategists have had little or no formal business education, at least at the college level. They may never have taken a course or read a book on strategy. But they have an intuitive grasp of the basic elements of strategy. They have an idiosyncratic mode of thinking in which company, customers, and competition merge in a dynamic interaction out of which a comprehensive set of objectives and plans for action eventually crystallizes.

Insight is the key to this process. Because it is creative, partly intuitive, and often disruptive of the status quo, the resulting plans might not even hold water from the analyst's point of view. It is the creative element in these plans and the drive and will of the mind that conceived them that give these strategies their extraordinary competitive impact.

Both in Japan and in the West, this breed of natural or instinctive strategist is dying out or is at least being pushed to the sidelines in favor of rational, by-the-numbers strategic and financial planners. Today's giant institutions, both public and private, are by and large not organized for innovation. Their systems and processes are all oriented toward incremental improvement—doing better what they are already doing. In the United States, the pressure of innumerable social and governmental constraints on corporate activities—most notably, perhaps, the proliferation of government regulations during the 1960s and 1970s—has put a premium on talent for adaptation and reduced still further the incentive to innovate. Advocates of bold and ambitious strategies too often find themselves on the sidelines, labeled as losers, while the rewards go to those more skilled at working within the system. This is especially true in mature industries, where actions and ideas often move in narrow grooves, forcing out innovators. Conversely, venture capital groups tend to attract flexible, adaptive minds.

[†]**Source:** This article was adapted with permission from the introduction to *The Mind of the Strategist*, McGraw-Hill, 1982.

In all times and places, large institutions develop cultures of their own, and success is often closely tied to the ability to conform. In our day, the culture of most business corporations exalts logic and rationality; hence, it is analysts rather than innovators who tend to get ahead. It is not unreasonable to say that many large U.S. corporations today are run like the Soviet economy. In order to survive, they must plan ahead comprehensively, controlling an array of critical functions in every detail. They specify policies and procedures in meticulous detail, spelling out for practically everyone what can and what cannot be done in particular circumstances. They establish hurdle rates, analyze risks, and anticipate contingencies. As strategic planning processes have burgeoned in these companies, strategic thinking has gradually withered away.

My message, as you will have guessed by now, is that successful business strategies result not from rigorous analysis but from a particular state of mind. In what I call the mind of the strategist, insight and a consequent drive for achievement, often amounting to a sense of mission, fuel a thought process that is basically creative and intuitive rather than rational. Strategists do not reject analysis. Indeed they can hardly do without it. But they use it only to stimulate the creative process, to test the ideas that emerge, to work out their strategic implications, or to ensure successful execution of high-potential "wild" ideas that might otherwise never be implemented properly. Great strategies, like great works of art or great scientific discoveries, call for technical mastery in the working out but originate in insights that are beyond the reach of conscious analysis.

■ ARE YOU A STRATEGIST OR JUST A MANAGER?†

By Hans Hinterhuber and Wolfgang Popp

Perhaps the greatest strategist of all time was not a business executive or an entrepreneur but a general. Helmuth von Moltke, chief of the Prussian and German general staffs from 1858 to 1888, engineered the strategy behind the military victories that allowed Otto von Bismarck to assemble a loose league of German states into a powerful empire. Moltke possessed two important characteristics that made him a superior strategist:

- The ability to understand the significance of events without being influenced by current opinion, changing attitudes, or his own prejudices.
- The ability to make decisions quickly and to take the indicated action without being deterred by a perceived danger.

The two characteristics support each other—and apply to managers and entrepreneurs as much as to generals and national leaders. But what makes a strategist out of a manager? There is no test that can precisely evaluate an individual's strategic management competence. But there are key questions whose answers can indicate the level of that competence. Managers who answer these questions in the form of a self-administered test can draw practical conclusions about their strategic abilities. Such a questionnaire makes the process of selecting good managers more objective, clear, and simple. At the same time, this method can provide individual managers with an instrument for developing their own management personalities.

Strategy Can't Be Taught

Helmuth von Moltke's superior strategies won the Austrio-Prussian War in 1866 and the Franco-Prussian War in 1871. Instead of giving specific orders, Moltke issued "directives," guidelines for autonomous decision making. In the past, Prussian officers were discouraged from acting on their own; military commanders controlled most actions from the top. But Moltke turned such tradition on its head by expecting his officers to show individual initiative.

According to Moltke, strategy is applied common sense and cannot be taught. Moltke's general conception of strategy—viewing all obvious factors in the right perspective—cannot be learned in any school.

So, what does it actually take to be a strategist? Our questionnaire summarizes the criteria we use to identify good strategists.

Do I Have an Entrepreneurial Vision?

Gottlieb Duttweiler started Migros Cooperative, now the largest Swiss supermarket chain, in 1925 with five Ford Model-T trucks loaded with sugar, coffee, rice, macaroni, shortening, and soap—and a vision of scrapping traditional distribution structures to help society's poorer classes. Enrico Mattei, founder of ENI (Ente Nazionale Idrocarburi), the Italian state-owned petroleum company, envisioned making Italy relatively self-sufficient in oil and natural gas. The president of a Swiss technological institute wanted to create conditions that would enable a member of his faculty to win the Nobel Prize.

As these and countless other examples demonstrate, there is always a vision at the beginning of any entrepreneurial activity, any major company restructuring program, any new phase in a person's life. Such visions are guides comparable to the North Star. The leader of a caravan in the desert, where sandstorms constantly change the landscape, looks to the patterns of the stars in the sky to stay on course. The stars are not the destination, but they do provide dependable guides for the journey to the next oasis, no matter which direction the caravan comes from, how well it is equipped for the trip, or how rough the terrain may be. Of course, the stars may point the way, but any Bedouin who hopes to reach the oasis safely knows to keep one eye on the ground to avoid quicksand—and to trust his caravan leader's sense of orientation.

Like the North Star, a manager's vision is not a goal. Rather, it is an orientation point that guides a company's movement in a specific direction. If the vision is realistic and appeals both to the emotions and the intelligence of employees, it can integrate and direct a company. Every entrepreneur who claims to possess strategic management competence should be able to state his or her vision clearly, in just a few sentences.

Of course, a vision may be more or less important to different companies and managers. A successful company intent on steering its present course may need the ability to focus more than the ability to create vision.

Do I Have a Corporate Philosophy?

When a vision is put into concrete terms, it becomes a corporate philosophy: the ideological creed of both entrepreneurs and their top managers. A good corporate philosophy is like a good battle cry and, as George Bernard Shaw pointed out, a good battle cry is half the battle.

A family-owned company in Austria follows a set of guiding principles, stating that the company should grow, but no faster than it can finance growth with internal resources. Decisions of the advisory board become binding only if they are unanimous. Family members are not allowed to engage in private business activity. The company enters into no co-operation agreements with other companies. But at Olivetti, CEO Carlo De Benedetti has taken a completely different tack: his corporate philosophy emphasizes co-operation agreements, joint ventures, alliances, and the incorporation of his companies in strategic networks.

The corporate philosophy of a company is like the worldview of an individual— that combination of the most essential elements in a person's character. Of course, it is important for a landlady sizing up a potential lodger to know something about his income; but it is also important for her to judge his character and basic ideology. Similarly, an entrepreneur locked in cutthroat competition with a competitor should learn something about the competitor's products and resources; however, it is even more important for the entrepreneur to know the opponent's corporate philosophy.

Entrepreneurs and top managers who lose battles or even wars to competitors have probably failed in assessing the long-term intentions of those competitors.

Do I Have Competitive Advantages?

Moltke noted that strategy is "the evolution of the original guiding idea according to continually changing circumstances." In business, the guiding idea is to assume a unique position in the market segment in which the company operates, based on permanently maintainable competitive advantages. In other words, one tries to become number one or number two—or at least to belong to the small group of leading competitors in any market segment.

But a company can capture a leading market position only if it offers customers a better product or a better solution to a problem at a favourable price. The central element of any strategy consists of creating permanent competitive advantages that in the ideal case establish a virtual monopoly in the market. The guiding idea of Franz Voelkl, a successful German ski manufacturer and former upstart, is "the one who builds his skis slowest builds the fastest skis." When racers wearing Voelkl's skis won gold medals during the Alpine World Championships at Lake Placid and Vail, sales boomed, confirming his guiding idea and competitive advantage. Customers who want success also want to use a successful product. Unlike his competitors, Voelkl's company produces all of the ski components in-house, including the wooden core, edges, and boot soles. This sort of manufacturing depth has produced a technically superior product—and a leap from fifteenth place to one of the top positions in the world ski market within ten years.

Artur Doppelmayr, an Austrian manufacturer of aerial transport systems, believes his main competitive advantage—in addition to innovative equipment design—is his service system. This allows Doppelmayr's company to come to the assistance of users within twenty-four hours anywhere in the world. Doppelmayr provides total quality management, standardization and reduction of components, a worldwide system of warehouses, and skilled personnel prepared to move immediately in emergency cases.

Both of these examples demonstrate strategies that have indirect effects. In the case of a direct strategy, such as taking the offensive in a price war, material and financial resources determine success rather than psychological factors or new-product development time. But when a company adopts an indirect strategy, such as a marketing plan that focuses on a product's overall benefits to customers—or excluding competitors via a clever policy of alliances—material and financial resources fade into the background.

Because of the acceleration of change and the increasing complexity of all human institutions, managers must learn to use indirect strategies. These are usually more effective and a better guarantee of lasting success than direct strategies, although even indirect strategies require financial and material resources.

Do My Employees Use Their Ability to Act Freely in the Interest of the Company?

In theory, the strategically managed company is a confederation of entrepreneurs, with management responsibility vested in strategic business units. These microenterprises are centers for integrated action, backed by the whole corporation's resources, and headed by entrepreneurial-minded managers. Following Helmuth von Moltke's example, corporate management should issue directives to the managers responsible for these strategic business units—but not detailed instructions. Directives are guidelines for decisions reached autonomously and usually have a stimulating effect. Effective directives combine the strategic intention of top management with the initiative and creativity of the individual manager.

The success of a company essentially depends on the extent to which managers use their ability to act freely in the company's interest. Bismarck once remarked that "courage on the battlefield is common among us. But you will frequently find very respectable people lacking in civil courage." He was talking about the courage to stand up for one's convictions; presumably, this also means the courage not to act on directives from top management—if this helps to implement strategic intentions better than passive obedience. Consequently, top management must allow directives to be modified and offer latitude for interpretation.

In everyday management practice, business unit managers must be familiar with the overall corporate vision, philosophy, and strategic intentions in order to act in accordance with them—even if the particular competitive situation forces managers to deviate from an agreement struck with corporate management. If managers are not, the blame lies less with them than with their superiors, who probably also lack strategic management competence. No business unit manager can be expected to act independently and take initiative in the interest of his or her company without knowing the corporate vision, philosophy, and directives.

Have I Built an Organization That Implements My Vision?

Entrepreneurs and top managers who feel they can improve matters by meddling at lower levels are usually mistaken. When they try, they assume functions normally carried out by other people, make the performance of those people superfluous, and add to their own management duties so much that they can no longer get everything done. These observations, which were made by Moltke, raise two useful questions in assessing strategic management competence: Are all management positions filled with people who think and act entrepreneurially? Are their duties, authority, and responsibilities such that they can formulate and implement strategies autonomously in the interest of the company? The answer to both questions will be no if managers unable to meet strategic demands remain in their positions—and if the organization does not permit employees to take entrepreneurial initiative along strategic lines.

Of course, there is always a discrepancy between how the actual organization operates and how it is formally described on paper. Within limits, in fact, such a discrepancy is desirable. Capable top managers rely on elasticity and uncertainty in the organizational system in order to offer outstanding employees the possibility of taking action autonomously. Therefore, the extent to which top management has erected an organization that promotes creative behaviour and permits effective implementation of strategies reflects the general level of strategic management competence.

Are Line Managers Involved in Strategic Planning?

Strategic planning is the job of line managers who are responsible for implementing a strategy. For that reason, the key to successful execution of strategy is the early involvement of line managers in the strategic planning process.

Successful companies familiarize line managers with strategic instruments in training courses and make sure they know the strategic intentions of their superiors; the function of the planning staff is no longer strategic planning. Rather, it is strategic analysis of critical sectors and business areas that are or may become important for the company. Both functions support line managers—and both line managers and planning staff monitor progress in the execution of strategies.

If line managers are not involved in the process of strategic planning, top management certainly cannot claim a high level of strategic management competence. The same is true if strategic control is not carried out effectively or is used as a means of political manoeuvring. For example, in an Italian textile company, line managers are supposed to be free to plan and execute strategies; however, top managers use a strategic controller to quash the views of those who disagree with their personal expectations or priorities.

Is the Corporate Culture in Harmony with the Strategies?

The more business strategies and corporate culture are in true harmony, the higher the level of strategic management competence. Companies can only create an atmosphere of maximum creativity, for example, if they reduce hierarchical elements to a minimum. Outstanding companies are usually products of excellent entrepreneurs and managers who have created a corporate culture in which their vision, company philosophy, and strategies can be implemented by employees who think independently and take initiative.

Do I Point Out Directions and Take New Approaches?

The value of great entrepreneurs or managers seems to come more from the fact that they lived than from what they accomplished. This is a counterintuitive conclusion; yet, sooner or later, all great business accomplishments are surpassed. What, therefore, is permanent about competent strategic management? Some possibilities include:

- The directions great entrepreneurs and managers take, not the limits they set.
- The projects, programs, and directions they initiate, not what they finish.
- The questions they raise, not the answers they find or already know.
- The paths they take, not the objectives they actually attain.
- The employees they select to carry on their vision, not the buildings they erect.

What is permanent about entrepreneurial capabilities and performance lies more in spontaneity than in education, more in originality and intuition than in learning, more in personal greatness than in specific, narrow capabilities.

Whatever an entrepreneur launches with a vision can have effects that last for decades—but what he or she has to offer in terms of solutions to individual problems often passes into oblivion quickly. Good strategists also have the ability to make employees and the outside world understand and embrace their visions.

Helmuth von Moltke is the best example of a man who knew the secret of always being armed with a "system of assistants" and transmitted the authority of his personality to his underlings. Hermann Keyserling—a German philosopher and founder of the School of Wisdom, popular in Europe in the 1920s—noted that having integrity means being totally honest with oneself and others, never pretending to be what one is not, and acting in accordance with one's essential personality. Ultimately, a manager who is a good strategist must have such integrity.

Have I Been Lucky in My Life So Far?

As Moltke observed, the good strategist also needs good luck. Put another way, strategic management competence includes the ability to place oneself in a position that favors being lucky. Many successful entrepreneurs and managers actually accomplished very little on their own. Their success required numerous other events to converge with their professional choices, which produced the "luck" they needed.

To tackle a tough challenge with good prospects for success, managers either need to feel deep down that they are up to the task or else to trust luck to help them get the job done. However, luck in this connection does not mean mere chance; rather, it means that the serendipitous difficulties inherent in such challenges tend to stimulate and strengthen precisely those character traits necessary to succeed.

Do I Make a Contribution to the Development of Society—and Myself?

Entrepreneurs and managers who possess a high level of strategic management competence may make individual mistakes, but they do not allow themselves to be deterred from the vision, corporate philosophy, or continued development of their guiding idea. They comprehend the big picture intuitively, remaining above mundane matters and deliberately avoiding identification with them. They experience relationships both inside and outside the company, as well as strategy formulation and implementation, within an overall context. They also are affected more consciously and directly by the big picture than by isolated events.

This highest level of strategic management competence is achieved only through a lifetime of work and training. It is absolutely unthinkable for entrepreneurs or managers worthy of the name to feel they have ever reached the final goal, have a perfect solution to a problem, or have spoken the last word on any subject.

This "something" at which managers should aim over and above professional fulfillment of their managerial duties is described beautifully by Robert Louis Stevenson: "You've had success in life if you have lived decently, laughed frequently, and loved a lot; won the respect of clever men and the love of children; filled out your place and accomplished your tasks; if you have left the world a better place than you found it, perhaps in the form of an improved strain of poppy, a perfect poem, or a saved soul; if you always appreciated the beauty of nature and also said so; if you saw the best in other people and always did your best."

How can we tell the difference between a visionary strategist and an unrealistic dreamer? The answer must be based on a reconstruction of the person's life: what he or she has accomplished or set in motion to date. In the end, strategists can be identified by measuring:

- The nature of the vision they had at the beginning of each phase of their career or life.
- The way in which they kept modifying their guiding ideas to suit changing conditions.
- The extent to which—and under what conditions—they put those ideas into action or led others to do so.

Our evaluation procedure can help top management distinguish between average managers and good strategists. When top managers look at the questions, they can learn something about the initiative and self-confidence of those who took the test. This can help them in improving the company's managerial effectiveness. In fact, if the self-evaluation of managers is carried out realistically, the company average indicates overall strategic management competence.

Napoleon often said that he had to be present personally if his armies were to win; but the battlefields on which his soldiers fought became so large he couldn't be everywhere at once. Consequently, the strategist in either military or business situations must be not only a student but also a teacher. He or she needs employees who are thoroughly schooled in the organization's values and strategies; only then will directives be understood and carried out even in difficult situations where the strategist cannot take personal action.

In this sense, top strategists are symbols rather than examples, because employees have the right to run their own lives. But when employees have been trained in strategic thought and action on the job—and management agrees about certain basic values such as the importance of individual initiative and creativity—a company legitimately becomes a federation of entrepreneurs.

■ CONCLUDING REMARKS TO CHAPTER 1

While the above readings touch on many aspects of strategy, it is important to dwell for a moment on two specific characteristics of strategy before moving on to the main body of the text, since they have a significant impact on the structure and focus of this book. The two aspects of strategy that require further investigation are the *levels* and *dimensions* of strategy.

strategy content.

Levels of Strategy

Strategies can be made for different groupings of individuals and tasks w
organisation. The lowest level of aggregation is one person (individual st
while the highest level of aggregation encompasses all people within the org
(companywide strategies). The most common analytical distinction
aggregation levels made in strategic management literature is between the f
business, and corporate levels, as Hax also does in his article. Strategy iss
1. *functional level* refer to questions regarding specific functional aspects of a
(operations strategy, marketing strategy, financial strategy, and so on). Stra
2. *business level* requires the integration of functional level strategies for a dis
products and/or services that are intended for a specific group of custon
companies only operate in one such business, so that this is the high
aggregation within the firm. Strategy at the *corporate level* (also called mu
level) requires the integration of two or more business-level strategies.

While analytically appealing, these three levels are difficult to isolate in reality. Although it would be so much simpler if all strategy issues could be separated into these three tidy categories, in practice there are no *discrete* borderlines between them. The levels are so strongly interdependent that the boundaries between them are *fuzzy*. For strategists this means they must resist the temptation to view functional, business, and corporate strategy issues in isolation, which is easier said than done. In the last ten years many "modern" companies have reorganised themselves into business units to increase focus and accountability. While this may have led to some substantial improvements, it has increased the risk of viewing business and corporate strategy as separate issues—Prahalad and Hamel (see chapter 6) even speak of the "tyranny of the strategic business unit." The reader should therefore be alert to "isolationist" thinking and should develop a tolerance for the fuzziness that the interrelationship of levels entails.

The focus of this book will be on the business and corporate levels, although of course this will often necessitate consideration of strategy issues at the functional level. The interdependence between business and corporate levels will be explicitly dealt with in chapter 6.

In addition to the functional, business, and corporate levels of strategy mentioned by Hax, this book will also devote attention to an even higher level of aggregation than the entire company. When strategies are made for groups of two or more companies, this is referred to as the *multicompany* or *network level* of strategy. Multicompany strategies are needed to give direction to, for example, joint ventures, strategic alliances, and networks of organisations. This level of strategy is still in an early phase of development, both in theory and in practice, and therefore most literature, including the articles in this book, pay scant attention to network strategy issues. Given the growing importance of this subject, however, this book will devote an entire chapter (chapter 7) to the topic of the multicompany level of strategy.

Dimensions of Strategy

In the preface to this book, the distinction between the strategy dimensions—process, content and context—was introduced. The strategy process was defined as the manner in which strategies come about ("how"), while the strategy content was defined as the output of the strategy process ("what"). The strategy context, finally, was defined as the set of circumstances under which both the process and content were determined ("where, when, who, and why").

As in the case of strategy levels, an elegant analytical distinction is made, which is a very useful tool for structuring both thoughts and chapters, but yet again, it is impossible to view each category in isolation. For instance, the manner in which the strategy process is organised will have a significant impact on the resulting strategy content, and likewise the content of the current strategy will strongly influence the way in which the strategy process will be conducted in future. Hence, process, content, and context are not separate elements of the strategy phenomenon that can be dealt with individually but are the strongly interrelated dimensions of every strategic issue. Every strategy question is by its nature three-dimensional, possessing process, content, and context characteristics; only the understanding of all three dimensions, and their interaction, will give the strategist real depth of understanding.

However, paying simultaneous and balanced attention to all three strategy dimensions is about as difficult as playing three-dimensional chess. Furthermore, most strategy research, by its very nature, is more analytic than synthetic—focusing on just a few variables at once. Consequently, most writings in the field of strategy, including most of the articles in this book, tend to favour just one, or at most two, dimensions, which is usually complex enough, given the need to remain comprehensible. Hence, it is almost inescapable that it is up to the reader to piece together these complementary unidimensional, or "flat," articles into a three-dimensional view of strategy.

Conclusion

The field of strategy is fraught with analytical distinctions that isolate phenomena that in reality are highly interdependent. Not only do the functional-business-corporate-network and process-content-context distinctions present us with serious difficulties when applied too rigourously, but as will be seen in the following chapters, such distinctions as strategy formulation versus implementation, organisation versus environment, and strategy versus structure can also wreak havoc if both categories are treated as absolute and/or unrelated. As stated earlier, the temptation to oversimplify must be resisted. The reader who wishes to understand the nature of strategy must develop a tolerance for fuzzy category boundaries and an eye for the interdependence of seemingly independent phenomena.

The temptation to overcomplicate must, however, also be resisted. Therefore, many of these distinctions have been used—with caution—to structure this text. Most importantly, the process-content-context distinction has been employed to organise the main sections of this book. Directly following this chapter, Section II will start with a look at the strategy process. Section III will subsequently deal with the strategy content, while Section IV is devoted to the strategy context. Finally, Section V focuses on the special topic of this book, the European context and its impact on strategy process and content.

References and Suggested Readings

Ackoff, R. L., *Creating the Corporate Future*, Wiley, New York, 1980.

Clausewitz, K. von, *On War*, Penguin, 1982.

Cummings, S., Brief Case: The First Strategists, *Long Range Planning*, June 1993, pp. 133–135.

Hax, A. C., Redefining the Concept of Strategy and the Strategy Formation Process, *Planning Review*, May/June 1990, pp. 34–40.

Henderson, B. D., The Origin of Strategy, *Harvard Business Review*, November/December 1989, pp. 139–143.

Hinterhuber, H. H., and W. Popp, Are You a Strategist or Just a Manager? *Harvard Business Review*, January/February 1992, pp. 105–113.

James, B. G., *Business Wargames*, Penguin, Harmondsworth, 1985.

Liddell-Hart, B. H., *Strategy*, Second Edition, Praeger, New York, 1967.

Machiavelli, N., *The Prince, and the Discources*, Modern Library, New York, 1950.

Mintzberg, H., The Manager's Job: Fact and Folklore, *Harvard Business Review*, July/August 1975, pp. 49–61.

Mintzberg, H., The Strategy Concept I: Five P's for Strategy, *California Management Review*, Fall 1987, pp. 11–24.

Mintzberg, H., The Strategy Concept II: Another Look at Why Organizations Need Strategies, *California Management Review*, Fall 1987, pp. 25–32.

Mintzberg, H., Strategy Formation: Schools of Thought, in Frederickson, J. W., (Ed.), *Perspectives on Strategic Management*, Harper & Row, New York, 1990.

Mintzberg, H., and J. A. Waters, The Mind of the Strategist(s), in Srivasta, S. (Ed.), *The Executive Mind*, Jossey-Bass, San Francisco, 1983.

Mintzberg, H., and J. A. Waters, Of Strategies: Deliberate and Emergent, *Strategic Management Journal*, July/September 1985, pp. 257–272.

Ohmae, K., *The Mind of the Strategist*, McGraw-Hill, 1982.

Rappaport, A., CFOs and Strategists: Forging a Common Framework, *Harvard Business Review*, May/June 1992, pp. 84–91.

Schon, D. A., *The Reflective Practitioner: How Professionals Think in Action*, Temple Smith, London, 1983.

Whittington, R., *What Is Strategy and Does It Matter?* Routledge, London, 1993.

Wing, R. L., *The Art of Strategy: A New Translation of Sun Tzu's Classic "The Art of War"*, Doubleday, New York, 1988.

Wrapp, H. E., Good Managers Don't Make Policy Decisions, *Harvard Business Review*, September/October 1967, pp. 91–99.

Zaleznik, A., Managers and Leaders: Are They Different? *Harvard Business Review*, May/June 1977, pp. 67–78.

SECTION II
THE STRATEGY PROCESS

*Plans are nothing. Planning
is everything.*
  —*Dwight D. Eisenhower
    1890–1969, American general and president*

In the previous section, when unravelling the three dimensions of strategy, the strategy process was defined as the way by which strategies come about. In this section, the focus will be on these dynamics of strategy formation—how do, and should, organisations develop, implement, evaluate, and adapt their strategies over time?

There are three important characteristics of this section the reader should take note of before being thrown as a rugby ball into the scrum of competing approaches to the strategy process:

1. *Integral process* The section does not merely focus on the manner by which strategies are initially formulated, but views the integral strategy process, by including decision making, implementation, evaluation, and adjustment as topics of discussion. In the terms of Mintzberg and Waters (chapter 1), it is not only the development of the intended strategy that is our concern, but the way by which the *intended* and *emergent* result in a *realized* strategy.

2. *Description and prescription* This section strives to strike a balance between the description of how most companies actually go about making strategy and the prescription of how they might improve their current process. This dual objective, of explanation and suggestion, actually follows the arguments put forward by Von Clausewitz in chapter 1. After all, we are interested in both the *knowing* and the *doing* of strategy, and therefore a balanced mix of decription and prescription is required.

3. *Abstraction levels* This section views the topic of strategy process at three abstraction levels. At the highest level of abstraction, fundamentally different ways of thinking about strategy formation can be recognized. We refer to these deep-rooted differences between the various schools of thought as conflicting *strategy process paradigms*. At a lower level of abstraction, differing paradigms translate into differing approaches to structuring strategy formation within the company. We refer to these varying procedures as questions at the level of *strategy process organisation*. Finally, different ways of organizing the strategy process will require different types of analytical techniques. This level of abstraction is referred to as that of *strategy process tools*.

The structure of this section closely follows these abstraction levels. Chapter 2 starts with the fundamental discussion between the main schools of thought—the planners and the incrementalists. Their differing strategy process paradigms are contrasted to make clear on which points they agree and on which principles they conflict. Authors from related schools of thought are also given the opportunity to state their case. Chapter 3 builds on chapter 2 by taking the debate between the planners and incrementalists to the "work floor." Obviously, their differing philosophies will lead to different ways of actually organizing the strategy process. Finally, chapter 4 will offer the reader some concrete analytical techniques that might be needed in the strategy process. These basic tools will also be of use in all subsequent case discussions.

Chapter 2
Strategy Process Paradigms:
On Plans and Patterns

To plan. To bother about the
best method of accomplishing an
accidental result.
  —Ambrose Bierce
    1842–1914, American novelist

Introduction

Picture, for a moment, an experiment whereby a large number of Western managers are asked to lie down on the couch of a psychoanalyst and are instructed to say the first word that comes to mind when hearing the term *strategy*. Probably the most common response would be "planning." This should not be surprising, since most textbooks on the subject of business and corporate strategy prescribe a planning approach, and many companies seem to be willing to follow this advice. So, for many practicing managers *strategic planning* and the *strategy process* seem to be more or less synonymous.

However, the popularity of strategic planning does not prove that it is the best way—or even a realistic way—of going about making and implementing strategy. Especially over the last ten years there has been mounting criticism of strategic planning. Some authors offer ideas for reforming the planning approach, while, at the other extreme, writers express sentiments that are more in line with Bierce's remark that planning is basically a waste of time. All critics would agree, however, that there is some degree of truth in Ackoff's (1980) comparison of most strategic planning to Indian rain dancing—both activities require "medicine men" and extensive rituals, yet have at best a minor impact on what they seek to influence.

This question of whether a planning perspective is the most fruitful way of approaching the strategy process is central to the discussion in this chapter. This is not a debate on details, but on principles. Various schools of thought on this subject employ such fundamentally differing assumptions in their argumentation that we speak of divergent *strategy process paradigms*. It is the intention of this chapter to provide the reader with insight into the main strategy process paradigms and to discover in what ways they differ. The consequences of each paradigm for the practical organisation of the strategy process is the central topic of chapter 3.

Which strategy process paradigms are there? Chaffee (1985) recognizes three main strategy process models, while Bailey and Johnson (1992) identify six approaches. Mintzberg (1990a) even outlines ten different schools of thought! Such quantitative differences would seem to suggest a lack of agreement on which major approaches exist, but this is not really the case—the different numbers are largely due to how broadly the authors have defined their categories. If the category boundaries are drawn quite broadly, the various schools of thought can be grouped into two fundamentally different approaches to the strategy process, namely the *planning* approach and the *incrementalist* approach.

These two paradigms correspond to the two terms in this chapter's subtitle. The planning approach views strategy as a *plan*—to be fully formulated, explicitly and rationally, and only then implemented. In the terms of Mintzberg and Waters (see chapter 1) the planning approach focuses on *deliberate* strategies. The incrementalist approach views strategy as a *pattern* in the stream of organisational activities—strategy is formulated, implemented, tested, and adapted, sometimes rationally, sometimes influenced by nonrational behaviour, but always in small steps and on a continuous basis, blurring the distinction between formulation and implementation. Thus the incrementalist approach focuses on *emergent* strategies. The planning approach can be caricatured as mechanistic ("think then do"), while the incrementalist approach can be caricatured as organic ("think-convince-try-argue-learn-think-etc.").

The structure of this chapter resembles the traditional manner of organising debates. First, both sides are allowed to make opening statements clarifying their points of view, which are then followed by a heated exchange of arguments. And as always, the public is the judge of who has won.

The Articles

The planning approach is "defended" by two articles. The first article, "The Concept of Corporate Strategy," by Kenneth Andrews, is an obvious representative for the planning approach, due to its historical impact. Together with Igor Ansoff, Andrews is seen as the godfather of strategic management, and the textbook from which this article has been drawn, *Business Policy: Text and Cases* (Christensen, Andrews, et al), has probably been one of the most influential textbooks in the field. In a nutshell, Andrews argues that strategy formulation should be viewed as a rational and explicit *design* issue and that strategy implementation is merely "a series of subactivities which are primarily administrative." Although he speaks of strategy as a *pattern*, he means only a pattern of decisions (consistency of intended strategy), not a pattern of organisational activities (consistency of realized strategy) as the incrementalists do.

One aspect that distinguishes Andrews from many others employing the planning paradigm is that he does not detail the formal organisation needed to arrive at plans and to ensure their implementation. His work focuses on the analytical steps needed to conceive a strategy, but his prescriptions are largely divorced from the organisational context. His perspective seems to resemble that of the chess grand master—a solitary, rational strategist engaged in a cerebral process. He therefore stresses the role of the

CEO as *the* architect of strategy, which has led Mintzberg (1990a) to dub this the *design* school, as opposed to the *planning* school, of thought.

Most literature employing the planning paradigm, however, does not focus on the cerebral processes of the CEO, but on the formal processes within the organisation. Therefore, a second article detailing these formal strategy steps within the company has been added as a complement to Andrews's work. This article—confusingly entitled "A Descriptive Model of Strategic Management," since it is clearly prescriptive—is the condensed introduction to a popular American strategic management textbook. The authors, Thomas Wheelen and David Hunger, have developed a very clear "cascade" model of the strategy process, where decisions of a higher order, such as mission and strategy, are first taken and then flow to lower levels where they are translated into programs, budgets, and finally actions. Despite their remark that feedback loops are possible, their model is basically *linear* (Chaffee, 1985), placing it firmly within the planning tradition.

In the third article, "Logical Incrementalism," the opposing approach states its case. It seems only fair that the very person who popularized the term *logical incrementalism*, James Quinn, should be selected as the spokesman. In this article, Quinn does not reject formal planning as a useful activity, but he argues that it is only one of the "building blocks" for achieving incremental strategic change. According to Quinn, writers who exalt the virtues of formal strategic planning make faulty assumptions about the "knowability" of the environment ("cognitive limits") and the rationality and controllability of organisations ("process limits"). No organisation can entirely "know" its environment, and therefore surprises are always possible. Thus Quinn argues that it is in the best interest of most organisations to remain flexible and uncommitted as long as possible, instead of locking the organisation into long-term strategies. Furthermore, since few environments are stable, most organisations must constantly adapt—they must monitor, experiment, learn and change on a continuous basis, which makes long-term planning virtually impossible, if not dangerous (in the same vein, Chaffee, 1985, speaks of the need for an *adaptive* mode of strategy development, while Mintzberg, 1990a, speaks of the *learning* school of thought). Finally, since organisations are not mechanical systems, but social systems, achieving strategic change involves changing attitudes and cultures, building commitment and political manoeuvring—essential informal aspects that are disregarded in formal planning models. All these arguments, Quinn believes, make grand plans foolhardy and suggest that a "one small step at a time" frame of mind is a far better strategy process paradigm.

While the planning and incrementalist approaches differ on many accounts, they both share the assumption that a rational proactive strategist can steer the organisation. Therefore, both are not only *descriptive* (incrementalism more so than planning) but also strongly *prescriptive*—advising the strategist how best to go forward. There is a different school of thought, however, that does not assume rational managers and that views strategy as "the product of the political, cognitive, and cultural fabric of the organisation." This school of thought, which Quinn refers to in his article as *power-behavioural*, but is also called *interpretative* (Chaffee, 1985), and *political* and *cultural* (Bailey and Johnson, 1992; Mintzberg, 1990), is named the *organisational action* view of the strategy process in the fourth article of this chapter. This article by Gerry Johnson, entitled "Rethinking Incrementalism," challenges many commonly held views and contains excellent examples of how the strategy process can form the strategist—not the other way around! Johnson agrees with Quinn that incrementalism makes more sense than planning, but points out that Quinn was too optimistic when using the term *logical*, since the "rationality" of every member of the organisation is limited by politics, perceptions, beliefs, myths, and rituals.

With these four articles, the stage has been set for the real debate to begin. This debate actually took place in the pages of the *Strategic Management Journal*, with Henry Mintzberg speaking on behalf of the incrementalist approach, and Igor Ansoff, representing the planning approach. Their contributions to the *Strategic Management Journal* have been condensed into the fifth and final article in this chapter, "A Discussion on Strategy Process Paradigms." Mintzberg confidently concludes that the final score is "Learning 1, Planning 0," but of course it is actually up to the reader to decide who made the most points.

Recommended Readings and Cases

Readers who wish to pursue the planning approach to strategy are recommended to begin with *Implanting Strategic Management* by Igor Ansoff. For those more interested in the incrementalist approach, James Quinn's *Strategies for Change* is still a good starting point. For a better understanding of the political processes involved in strategy formation the reader might want to turn to Andrew Pettigrew's *Management of Strategic Change*, while the cultural processes are vividly described in Gerry Johnson's *Strategic Change and the Management Process*. For a short overview of the various schools of thought, we would suggest "How Strategies Develop in Organisations" by Andy Bailey and Gerry Johnson; but if the reader has more time, Henry Mintzberg's much longer article "Strategy Formation: Schools of Thought" is also highly recommended.

The two cases that have been selected to accompany this chapter are "The Guns of August" and "Litton Industries and Texas Instruments." The first case, taken from a book by the historian Barbara Tuchman, gives a short rendition of the German and French military strategies during the first few weeks of World War I. The strategy process paradigms employed by the two belligerents closely resemble the radical extremes of planning and incrementalism. As such, this case provides a striking illustration of the advantages, but more particularly the pitfalls, inherent in the two strategy process paradigms. The second case, "The Swatch," by Arieh Ullmann, allows the reader to think through which strategy process paradigm best suits a particular business situation. Ullmann describes how Dr. Ernst Thomke, managing director of ETA, a major Swiss watch company, develops a plan to revolutionize the watch concept. By breaking with the industry recipe, the Swatch redefines the competitive game within the industry. The question is whether this method of strategy formation is the best way to proceed in the future. As with "The Guns of August," this case allows the reader to explore the pros and cons of the paradigms presented in this chapter.

■ THE CONCEPT OF CORPORATE STRATEGY†

By Kenneth Andrews

What Strategy Is

Corporate strategy is the pattern of decisions in a company that determines and reveals its objectives, purposes, or goals, produces the principal policies and plans for achieving those goals, and defines the range of business the company is to pursue, the kind of economic and human organization it is or intends to be, and the nature of the economic and noneconomic contribution it intends to make to its shareholders, employees, customers, and communities. In an organization of any size or diversity, *corporate strategy* usually applies to the whole enterprise, while *business strategy*, less comprehensive, defines the choice of product or service and market of individual businesses within the firm. Business strategy, that is, is the determination of how a company will compete in a given business and position itself among its competitors. Corporate strategy defines the businesses in which a company will compete, preferably in a way that focuses resources to convert distinctive competence into competitive advantage. Both are outcomes of a continuous process of strategic management that we will later analyze in detail.

The strategic decision contributing to this pattern is one that is effective over long periods of time, affects the company in many different ways, and focuses and commits a significant portion of its resources to the expected outcomes. The pattern resulting from a series of such decisions will probably define the central character and image of a company, the individuality it has for its members and various publics, and the position it will occupy in its industry and markets. It will permit the specification of particular objectives to be attained through a timed sequence of investment and implementation decisions and will govern directly the deployment or redeployment of resources to make these decisions effective.

Some aspects of such a pattern of decisions may be in an established corporation unchanging over long periods of time, like a commitment to quality, or high technology, or certain raw materials, or good labor relations. Other aspects of a strategy must change as or before the world changes, such as product line, manufacturing process,or merchandising and styling practices. The basic determinants of company character, if purposefully institutionalized, are likely to persist through and shape the nature of substantial changes in product-market choices and allocation of resources.

It would be possible to extend the definition of strategy for a given company to separate a central character and the core of its special accomplishment from the manifestations of such characteristics in changing product lines, markets, and policies designed to make activities profitable from year to year. *The New York Times*, for example, after many years of being shaped by the values of its owners and staff, is now so self-conscious and respected an institution that its nature is likely to remain unchanged, even if the services it offers are altered drastically in the direction of other outlets for its news-processing capacity.

It is important, however, not to take the idea apart in another way, that is, to separate goals from the policies designed to achieve those goals. The essence of the

---

†**Source:** This article was adapted with permission from chapter 2 of *The Concept of Corporate Strategy,* Irwin, Homewood, 1987.

definition of strategy I have just recorded is pattern. The interdependence of purposes, policies, and organized action is crucial to the particularity of an individual strategy and its opportunity to identify competitive advantage. It is the unity, coherence, and internal consistency of a company's strategic decisions that position the company in its environment and give the firm its identity, its power to mobilize its strengths, and its likelihood of success in the marketplace. It is the interrelationship of a set of goals and policies that crystallizes from the formless reality of a company's environment a set of problems an organization can seize upon and solve.

What you are doing, in short, is never meaningful unless you can say or imply what you are doing it for: the quality of administrative action and the motivation lending it power cannot be appraised without knowing its relationship to purpose. Breaking up the system of corporate goals and the character-determining major policies for attainment leads to narrow and mechanical conceptions of strategic management and endless logic chopping.

We should get on to understanding the need for strategic decisions and for determining the most satisfactory pattern of goals in concrete instances. Refinement of definition can wait, for you will wish to develop definition in practice in directions useful to you.

Summary Statements of Strategy

Before we proceed to clarification of this concept by application, we should specify the terms in which strategy is usually expressed. A summary statement of strategy will characterize the product line and services offered or planned by the company, the markets and market segments for which products and services are now or will be designed, and the channels through which these markets will be reached. The means by which the operation is to be financed will be specified, as will the profit objectives and the emphasis to be placed on the safety of capital versus level of return. Major policy in central functions such as marketing, manufacturing, procurement, research and development, labor relations, and personnel, will be stated where they distinguish the company from others, and usually the intended size, form, and climate of the organization will be included.

Each company, if it were to construct a summary strategy from what it understands itself to be aiming at, would have a different statement with different categories of decision emphasized to indicate what it wanted to be or do.

Reasons for Not Articulating Strategy

For a number of reasons companies seldom formulate and publish a complete strategy statement. Conscious planning of the long-term development of companies has been until recently less common than individual executive responses to environmental pressure, competitive threat, or entrepreneurial opportunity. In the latter mode of development, the unity or coherence of corporate effort is unplanned, natural, intuitive, or even nonexistent. Incrementalism in practice sometimes gives the appearance of consciously formulated strategy, but may be the natural result of compromise among coalitions backing contrary policy proposals or skillful improvisatory adaptation to external forces. Practicing managers who prefer muddling through to the strategic process would never commit themselves to an articulate strategy.

Other reasons for the scarcity of concrete statements of strategy include the desirability of keeping strategic plans confidential for security reasons and ambiguous to avoid internal conflict or even final decision. Skillful incrementalists may have plans in their heads that they do not reveal, to avoid resistance and other trouble in their own organization. A company with a large division in an obsolescent business that it intends to drain of cash until operations are discontinued could not expect high morale and cooperation to follow publication of this intent. In a dynamic company, moreover, where strategy is continually evolving, the official statement of strategy, unless couched in very general terms, would be as hard to keep up to date as an organization chart. Finally, a firm that has internalized its strategy does not feel the need to keep saying what it is, valuable as that information might be to new members.

Deducing Strategy from Behavior

In your own company you can do what most managements have not done. In the absence of explicit statements and on the basis of your experience, you may deduce from decisions observed what the pattern is and what the company's goals and policies are, on the assumption that some perhaps unspoken consensus lies behind them. Careful examination of the behavior of competitors will reveal what their strategy must be. At the same time none of us should mistake apparent strategy visible in a pattern of past incremental decisions for conscious planning for the future. What will pass as the current strategy of a company may almost always be deduced from its behavior, but a strategy for a future of changed circumstance may not always be distinguishable from performance in the present. Strategists who do not look beyond present behavior to the future are vulnerable to surprise.

Formulation of Strategy

Corporate strategy is an organization process, in many ways inseparable from the structure, behavior, and culture of the company in which it takes place. Nevertheless, we may abstract from the process two important aspects, interrelated in real life but separable for the purposes of analysis. The first of these we may call formulation, the second implementation. Deciding what strategy should be may be approached as a rational undertaking, even if, as in life, emotional attachments (to metal skis or investigative reporting) may complicate choice among future alternatives (for ski manufacturers or alternative newspapers). The principal subactivities of strategy formulation as a logical activity include identifying opportunities and threats in the company's environment and attaching some estimate or risk to the discernible alternatives. Before a choice can be made, the company's strengths and weaknesses should be appraised together with the resources on hand and available. Its actual or potential capacity to take advantage of perceived market needs or to cope with attendant risks should be estimated as objectively as possible. The strategic alternative that results from matching opportunity and corporate capability at an acceptable level of risk is what we may call an *economic strategy*.

The process described thus far assumes that strategists are analytically objective in estimating the relative capacity of their company and the opportunity they see or anticipate in developing markets. The extent to which they wish to undertake low or high risk presumably depends on their profit objectives. The higher they set the latter, the more willing they must be to assume a correspondingly high risk that the market opportunity they see will not develop or that the corporate competence required to excel competition will not be forthcoming.

So far we have described the intellectual processes of ascertaining what a company *might do* in terms of environmental opportunity, of deciding what it *can do* in terms of ability and power, and of bringing these two considerations together in optimal equilibrium. The determination of strategy also requires consideration of what alternatives are preferred by the chief executive and perhaps by his or her immediate associates as well, quite apart from economic considerations. Personal values, aspirations, and ideals do, and in our judgment quite properly should, influence the final choice of purposes. Thus what the executives of a company *want to do* must be brought into the strategic decision.

Finally strategic choice has an ethical aspect—a fact much more dramatically illustrated in some industries than in others. Just as alternatives may be ordered in terms of the degree of risk they entail, so may they be examined against the standards of responsiveness to the expectations of society the strategist elects. Some alternatives may seem to the executive considering them more attractive than others when the public good or service to society is considered. What a company *should do* thus appears as a fourth element of the strategic decision.

The ability to identify the four components of strategy—(1) market opportunity, (2) corporate competence and resources, (3) personal values and aspirations, and (4) acknowledged obligations to segments of society other than stockholders—is easier to exercise than the art of reconciling their implications in a final choice of purpose. Taken by itself each consideration might lead in a different direction.

If you put the various aspirations of individuals in your own organization against this statement you will see what I mean. Even in a single mind contradictory aspirations can survive a long time before the need to calculate trade-offs and integrate divergent inclinations becomes clear. Growth opportunity attracted many companies to the computer business after World War II. The decision to diversify out of typewriters and calculators was encouraged by growth opportunity and excitement that captivated the managements of RCA, General Electric, and Xerox, among others. But the financial, technical, and marketing requirements of this business exceeded the capacity of most of the competitors of IBM. The magnet of opportunity and the incentive of desire obscured the calculations of what resources and competence were required to succeed. Most crucially, where corporate capability leads, executives do not always want to go. Of all the components of strategic choice, the combination of resources and competence is most crucial to success.

The Implementation of Strategy

Since effective implementation can make a sound strategic decision ineffective or a debatable choice successful, it is as important to examine the processes of implementation as to weigh the advantages of available strategic alternatives. The

FIGURE 2-1
The Strategy Process

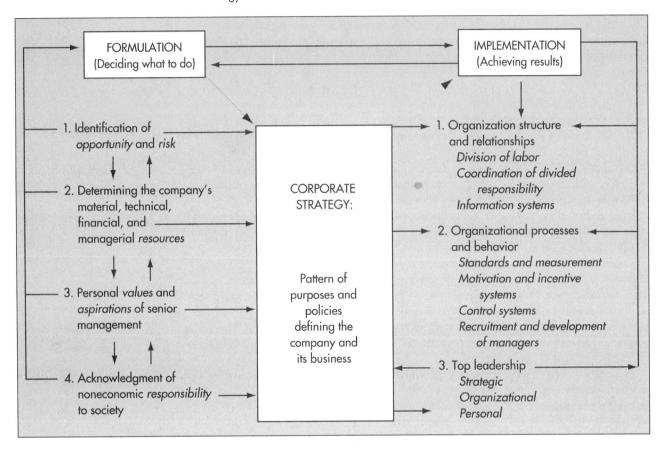

implementation of strategy comprises a series of subactivities that are primarily administrative. If purpose is determined, then the resources of a company can be mobilized to accomplish it. An organizational structure appropriate for the efficient performance of the required tasks must be made effective by information systems and relationships permitting coordination of subdivided activities. The organizational processes of performance measurement, compensation, management development—all of them enmeshed in systems of incentives and controls—must be directed toward the kind of behavior required by organizational purpose. The role of personal leadership is important and sometimes decisive in the accomplishment of strategy. Although we know that organizational structure and processes of compensation, incentives, control, and management development influence and constrain the formulation of strategy, we should look first at the logical proposition that structure should follow strategy in order to cope later with the organizational reality that strategy also follows structure. When we have examined both tendencies, we will understand and to some extent be prepared to deal with the interdependence of the formulation and implementation of corporate purpose. Figure 2-1 may be useful in understanding the analysis of strategy as a pattern of interrelated decisions.

Criteria for Evaluation

How is the actual or proposed strategy to be judged? How are we to know that one strategy is better than another? A number of important questions can regularly be asked. As is already evident, no infallible indicators are available. With practice they will lead to reliable intuitive discriminations.

- *Is the strategy identifiable and has it been made clear either in words or in practice?* The degree to which attention has been given to the strategic alternatives available to a company is likely to be basic to the soundness of its strategic decision. To cover in empty phrases ("Our policy is planned profitable growth in any market we can serve well") an absence of analysis of opportunity or actual determination of corporate strength is worse than to remain silent, for it conveys the illusion of a commitment when none has been made. The unstated strategy cannot be tested or contested and is likely therefore to be weak. If it is implicit in the intuition of a strong leader, the organization is likely to be weak and the demands the strategy makes upon it are likely to remain unmet. A strategy must be explicit to be effective and specific enough to require some actions and exclude others.

- *Does the strategy exploit fully domestic and international environmental opportunity?* The relation between market opportunity and organizational development is a critical one in the design of future plans. Unless growth is incompatible with the resources of an organization or the aspirations of its management, it is likely that a strategy that does not purport to make full use of market opportunity will be weak also in other aspects. Vulnerability to competition is increased by lack of interest in market share.

- *Is the strategy consistent with corporate competence and resources, both present and projected?* Although additional resources, both financial and managerial, are available to companies with genuine opportunity, the availability of each must be finally determined and programmed along a practicable time scale. This may be the most difficult question in this series.

- *Are the major provisions of the strategy and the program of major policies of which it is comprised internally consistent?* One advantage of making as specific a statement of strategy as is practicable is the resultant availability of a careful check on fit, unity, coherence, compatibility, and synergy—the state in which the whole of anything can be viewed as greater than the sum of its parts.

- *Is the chosen level of risk feasible in economic and personal terms?* The riskiness of any future plan should be compatible with the economic resources of the organization and the temperament of the managers concerned.

- *Is the strategy appropriate to the personal values and aspirations of the key managers?* Conflict between personal preferences, aspirations, and goals of the key members of an organization and the plan for its future is a sign of danger and a harbinger of mediocre performance or failure.

- *Is the strategy appropriate to the desired level of contribution to society?* To the extent that the chosen economic opportunity of the firm has social costs, such as air or water pollution, a statement of intention to deal with these is desirable and prudent.

- *Does the strategy constitute a clear stimulus to organizational effort and commitment?* Generally speaking, the bolder the choice of goals and the wider range of human needs they reflect, the more successfully they will appeal to the capable membership of a healthy and energetic organization.

- *Are there early indications of the responsiveness of markets and market segments to the strategy?* A strategy may pass with flying colors all the tests so far proposed, and may be in internal consistency and uniqueness an admirable work of art. But if within a time period made reasonable by the company's resources and the original plan the strategy does not work, then it must be weak in some way that has escaped attention.

A business enterprise guided by a clear sense of purpose rationally arrived at and emotionally ratified by commitment is more likely to have a successful outcome, in terms of profit and social good, than a company whose future is left to guesswork and chance. Conscious strategy does not preclude brilliance of improvisation or the welcome consequences of good fortune. Its cost is principally thought and work for which it is hard but not impossible to find time.

■ A DESCRIPTIVE MODEL OF STRATEGIC MANAGEMENT†

By Thomas Wheelen and David Hunger

The process of strategic management involves four basic elements: (1) *environmental scanning,* (2) *strategy formulation,* (3) *strategy implementation,* and (4) *evaluation and control.*

At the corporate level, the strategic management process includes activities that range from environmental scanning to the evaluation of performance. Top management scans both the external environment for opportunities and threats, and the internal environment for strengths and weaknesses. The factors that are most important to the corporation's future are referred to as strategic factors and are summarized with the acronym SWOT, standing for strengths, weaknesses,

†**Source:** This material is reprinted with permission from chapter 1 of *Strategic Management and Business Policy,* Fourth Edition, Addison-Wesley Publishing Company, Inc. Copyright © 1992.

FIGURE 2-2
Strategic Management Model

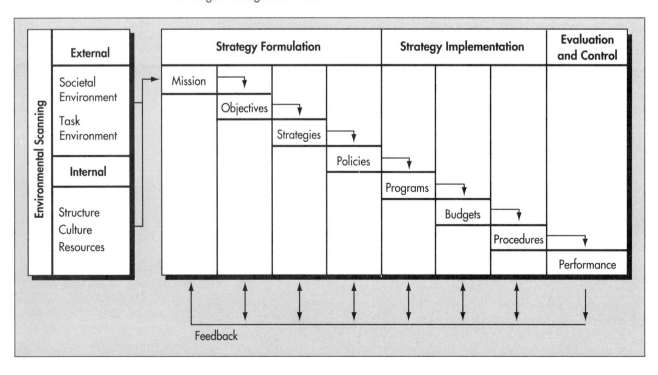

opportunities, and threats. Once these are identified, top management evaluates the strategic factors and determines the corporate mission. The first step in the formulation of strategy, a statement of mission, leads to a determination of corporate objectives, strategies, and policies. These strategies and policies are implemented through programs, budgets, and procedures. Finally, performance is evaluated, and information is fed back into the system so that adequate control of organizational activities is ensured. Figure 2-2 depicts this process as a continuous one.

Environmental Scanning: External

The *external environment* consists of variables (opportunities and threats) that are outside the organization and not typically within the short-run control of top management. These variables form the context within which the corporation exists. The external environment has two parts: task environment and societal environment. The task environment includes those elements or groups that directly affect and are affected by an organization's major operations. Some of these are stockholders, governments, suppliers, local communities, competitors, customers, creditors, labor unions, special interest groups, and trade associations. The task environment of a corporation is often referred to as its industry. The societal environment includes more

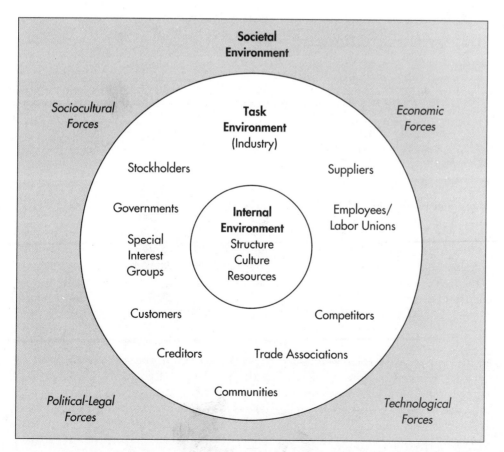

FIGURE 2-3
Environmental Variables

general forces—ones that do not directly touch the short-run activities of the organization but that can, and often do, influence its long-run decisions. Such economic, sociocultural, technological, and political-legal forces are depicted in figure 2-3 in relation to a firm's total environment.

Environmental Scanning: Internal

The *internal environment* of a corporation consists of variables (strengths and weaknesses) that are within the organization itself and not usually within the short-run control of top management. These variables form the context in which work is done. They include the corporation's structure, culture, and resources. The *corporate structure* is the way a corporation is organized in terms of communication, authority, and workflow. It is often referred to as the chain of command and is graphically described in an organization chart. The *corporation's culture* is that pattern of beliefs, expectations, and values shared by the corporation's members. In a firm norms typically emerge that define the acceptable behavior of people from top management down to the operative employees. *Corporate resources* are assets that form the raw material for the production of an organization's products or services. These assets include people and managerial talent as well as financial assets, plant facilities, and skills and abilities within functional areas.

Strategy Formulation

Strategy formulation is the development of long-range plans for the effective management of environmental opportunities and threats, in light of corporate strengths and weaknesses. It includes defining the corporate mission, specifying achievable objectives, developing strategies, and setting policy guidelines.

Mission

The corporate *mission* is the purpose or reason for the corporation's existence. For example, the mission of a savings and loan (S&L) association might be to provide mortgage money to people of the community. By fulfilling this mission, the S&L would hope to provide a reasonable rate of return to its depositors. A mission may be narrow or broad in scope. A *narrow mission* clearly limits the scope of the corporation's activities in terms of product or service offered, the technology used, and the market served. The above-mentioned S&L has the narrow mission of providing mortgage money to the people of the community. The problem with such a narrow statement of mission is that it might restrict the use of future opportunities for growth. A broad mission widens the scope of the corporation's activities to include many types of products or services, markets, and technologies. A *broad mission* of the same S&L might be to offer financial services to anyone, regardless of location. The problem with such a broad statement of mission is that it does not clearly identify which area the corporation wishes to emphasize and might confuse employees and customers.

A well-conceived mission statement defines the fundamental, unique purpose that sets a business apart from other firms of its type and identifies the scope of the business's operations in terms of products offered and markets served. Surveys of large North American corporations reveal that approximately 60 to 75 percent of them have formal, written statements of mission. A high percentage of the rest have an unwritten, informal mission.

The concept of a corporate mission implies that throughout a corporation's many activities there should be a common thread or unifying theme and that corporations with such a common thread are better able to direct and administer their many activities. In acquiring new firms or in developing new products, such a corporation looks for strategic fit, that is, the likelihood that new activities will mesh with present ones in such a way that the corporation's overall effectiveness and efficiency will be increased. A common thread may be common distribution channels or similar customers, warehousing economies or the mutual use of research and development, better use of managerial talent, or any of several possible synergistic effects.

Objectives

The corporate mission, as depicted in figure 2-2, determines the parameters of the specific objectives to be defined by top management. These objectives are listed as end results of planned activity. They state what is to be accomplished by when and should be quantified if possible. (The term *goal* is often confused with *objective*. In contrast to an objective, a goal is an open-ended statement of what one wishes to accomplish with no quantification of what is to be achieved and no time criteria for completion.) The achievement of corporate objectives, however, should result in a corporation's fulfilling its mission.

It is likely that some corporations have no formal objectives; rather, they have vague, verbal ones that are typically not ranked by priority. It is even more likely that such a corporation's specified, written objectives are not the "real" (personal and probably unpublishable) objectives of top management.

Strategies

A *strategy* of a corporation forms a comprehensive master plan stating how the corporation will achieve its mission and objectives. It maximizes competitive advantage and minimizes competitive disadvantage.

Just as many firms have no formal objectives, many chief executive officers (CEOs) have unstated, incremental, or intuitive strategies that have never been articulated or analyzed. If pressured, these executives might state that they are following a certain strategy. This stated or *explicit* strategy is one with which few could quarrel, such as the development and acquisition of new product lines. Further investigation, however, might reveal the existence of a very different *implicit* strategy. For example, the prestige of a banker in one community is strictly a function of the bank's asset size. Top management, therefore, tends to choose strategies that will increase total bank assets rather than profits. An extremely profitable small bank is in the eyes of the community still just another unimportant small bank. Often the only way to spot the implicit strategies of a corporation is to look not at what top management says, but at what it does. Implicit strategies can be derived from corporation policies, programs approved (and disapproved), and authorized budgets. Programs and divisions favored by budget increases and staffed by managers who are considered to be on the fast promotion track reveal where the corporation is putting its money and its energy.

Policies

Flowing from the strategy, *policies* provide broad guidance for decision making throughout the organization. Policies are thus broad guidelines that serve to link the formulation of strategy with its implementation.

Corporate policies are broad guidelines for divisions to follow in compliance with corporate strategy. These policies are interpreted and implemented through each division's own objectives and strategies. Divisions may then develop their own policies that will be guidelines for their functional areas to follow.

Strategy Implementation

Strategy implementation is the process by which strategies and policies are put into action through the development of programs, budgets, and procedures. This process might involve changes within the overall culture, structure, and/or management system of the organization. Except when such drastic corporate-wide changes are needed, however, the implementation of strategy is typically conducted by middle- and lower-level managers with review by top management. Sometimes referred to as operational planning, strategy implementation often involves day-to-day decisions in resource allocation.

Programs

A *program* is a statement of the activities or steps needed to accomplish a single-use plan. It makes the strategy action oriented. It may involve restructuring the corporation or changing the company's internal culture concerning how people get things done.

Budgets

A *budget* is a statement of a corporation's programs in dollar terms. Used in planning and control, it lists the detailed cost of each program. Many corporations demand a certain percentage return on investment, often called a hurdle rate, before top management will approve a new program. This is done to ensure that the new program will significantly add to the corporation's profit performance, and thus build shareholder value. The budget thus not only serves as a detailed plan of the new strategy in action, it also specifies through pro forma financial statements the expected impact on the firm's future financial situation.

Procedures

Sometimes termed standard operating procedures (SOP), *procedures* are a system of sequential steps or techniques that describe in detail how a particular task or job is to be done. They typically detail the various activities that must be carried out for completion of the corporation's program.

Evaluation and Control

Evaluation and control is the process in which corporate activities and performance results are monitored so that actual performance can be compared with desired performance. Managers at all levels use the resulting information to take corrective action and resolve problems. Although evaluation and control is the final major element of strategic management, it also can pinpoint weaknesses in previously implemented strategic plans and thus stimulate the entire process to begin again.

For evaluation and control to be effective, managers must obtain clear, prompt, and unbiased feedback from the people below them in the corporation's hierarchy. The model in figure 2-2 indicates how feedback in the form of performance data and activity reports runs through the entire management process. Using this feedback, managers compare what is actually happening with what was originally planned in the formulation stage.

■ LOGICAL INCREMENTALISM†

By James Quinn

"When I was younger I always conceived of a room where all these [strategic] concepts were worked out for the whole company. Later I didn't find any such room . . . . The strategy [of the company] may not even exist in the mind of one man. I certainly don't know where it is written down. It is simply transmitted in the series of decisions made." (Interview quote)

Introduction

When well-managed major organizations make significant changes in strategy, the approaches they use frequently bear little resemblance to the rational-analytical systems so often touted in the planning literature. The full strategy is rarely written down in any one place. The processes used to arrive at the total strategy are typically fragmented, evolutionary, and largely intuitive. Although one can usually find embedded in these fragments some very refined pieces of formal strategic analysis, the real strategy tends to evolve as internal decisions and external events flow together to create a new, widely shared consensus for action among key members of the top management team. Far from being an abrogation of good management practice, the rationale behind this kind of strategy formulation is so powerful that it perhaps provides the normative model for strategic decision making, rather than the step-by-step "formal systems planning" approach so often espoused.

The Formal Systems Planning Approach

A strong normative literature states what factors should be included in a systematically planned strategy and how to analyze and relate these factors step-by-step. The main elements of this "formal" planning approach include:

- analyzing one's own internal situation: strengths, weaknesses, competencies, problems;
- projecting current product lines, profits, sales, investment needs into the future;
- analyzing selected external environments and opponents' actions for opportunities and threats;

†**Source:** This article was orginally published as "Strategic Change: 'Logical Incrementalism,'" in *Sloan Management Review* (Fall 1978). Reproduced by permission of John Wiley and Sons Limited.

- establishing broad goals as targets for subordinate groups' plans;
- identifying the gap between expected and desired results;
- communicating planning assumptions to the divisions;
- requesting proposed plans from subordinate groups with more specific target goals, resource needs, and supporting action plans;
- occasionally asking for special studies of alternatives, contingencies, or longer-term opportunities;
- reviewing and approving divisional plans and summing these for corporate needs;
- developing long-term budgets presumably related to plans;
- implementing plans; and
- monitoring and evaluating performance (presumably against plans, but usually against budgets).

While this approach is excellent for some purposes, it tends to focus unduly on measurable quantitative factors and to underemphasize the vital qualitative, organizational, and power-behavioral factors that so often determine strategic success in one situation versus another. In practice, such planning is just one building block in a continuous stream of events that really determine corporate strategy.

The Power-Behavioral Approach

Other investigators have provided important insights on the crucial psychological, power, and behavioral relationships in strategy formulation. Among other things, these have enhanced understanding about: the multiple goal structures of organizations, the politics of strategic decisions, executive bargaining and negotiation processes, "satisficing" (as opposed to maximizing) in decision making, the role of coalitions in strategic management, and the practice of "muddling" in the public sphere. Unfortunately, however, many power-behavioral studies have been conducted in settings far removed from the realities of strategy formulation. Others have concentrated solely on human dynamics, power relationships, and organizational processes and ignored the ways in which systematic data analysis shapes and often dominates crucial aspects of strategic decisions. Finally, few have offered much normative guidance for the strategist.

The Study

Recognizing the contributions and limitations of both approaches, I attempted to document the dynamics of actual strategic change processes in some ten major companies as perceived by those most knowledgeably and intimately involved in them. Several important findings have begun to emerge from these investigations:

- Neither the power-behavioral nor the formal systems planning paradigm adequately characterizes the way successful strategic processes operate.
- Effective strategies tend to emerge from a series of "strategic subsystems," each of which attacks a specific class of strategic issue (e.g., acquisitions, divestitures, or major reorganizations) in a disciplined way, but which blends incrementally and opportunistically into a cohesive pattern that becomes the company's strategy.
- The logic behind each subsystem is so powerful that to some extent it may serve as a normative approach for formulating these key elements of strategy in large companies.

- Because of cognitive and process limits, almost all of these subsystems—and the formal planning activity itself—must be managed and linked together by an approach best described as logical incrementalism.

- Such incrementalism is not muddling. It is a purposeful, effective, proactive management technique for improving and integrating both the analytical and behavioral aspects of strategy formulation.

This article will document these findings, suggest the logic behind several important subsystems for strategy formulation, and outline some of the management and thought processes executives in large organizations use to synthesize them into effective corporate strategies. Such strategies embrace those patterns of high-leverage decisions (on major goals, policies, and action sequences) that affect the viability and direction of the entire enterprise or determine its competitive posture for an extended time period.

Critical Strategic Issues

Although certain "hard data" decisions (e.g., on product-market position or resource allocations) tend to dominate the analytical literature, executives identified other "soft" changes that have at least as much importance in shaping their concern's strategic posture. Most often cited were changes in the company's

- overall organizational structure or its basic management style;
- relationships with the government or other external interest groups;
- acquisition, divestiture, or divisional control practices;
- international posture and relationships;
- innovative capabilities or personnel motivations as affected by growth;
- worker and professional relationships reflecting changed social expectations and values;
- past or anticipated technological environments.

When executives were asked to "describe the processes through which their company arrived at its new posture" vis-á-vis each of these critical domains, several important points emerged. First, few of these issues lent themselves to quantitative modeling techniques or perhaps even formal financial analyses. Second, successful companies used a different subsystem to formulate strategy for each major class of strategic issues, yet these subsystems were quite similar among companies even in very different industries. Finally, no single formal analytical process could handle all strategic variables simultaneously on a planned basis. Why?

Precipitating Events

Often external or internal events over which managements had essentially no control would precipitate urgent, piecemeal, interim decisions that inexorably shaped the company's future strategic posture. One clearly observes this phenomenon in the decisions forced on General Motors by the 1973–74 oil crisis; the shift in posture pressed upon Exxon by sudden nationalizations; or the dramatic opportunities allowed for Haloid Corporation and Pilkington Brothers Ltd by the unexpected inventions of xerography and float glass.

In these cases, analyses from earlier formal planning cycles did contribute greatly, as long as the general nature of the contingency had been anticipated. They broadened the information base available (as in Exxon's case), extended the options considered (Haloid-Xerox), created shared values to guide decisions about precipitating events in consistent directions (Pilkington), or built up resource bases, management flexibilities, or active search routines for opportunities whose specific nature could not be defined in advance (General Mills, Pillsbury). But no organization—no matter how brilliant, rational, or imaginative—could possibly foresee the timing, severity, or even the nature of all such precipitating events. Further, when these events did occur there might be neither time, resources, nor information enough to undertake a full formal strategic analysis of all possible options and their consequences. Yet early decisions made under stress conditions often meant new thrusts, precedents, or lost opportunities that were difficult to reverse later.

An Incremental Logic

Recognizing this, top executives usually consciously tried to deal with precipitating events in an incremental fashion. Early commitments were kept broadly formative, tentative, and subject to later review. In some cases neither the company nor the external players could understand the full implications of alternative actions. All parties wanted to test assumptions and have an opportunity to learn from and adapt to the others' responses. For example: Neither the potential producer nor user of a completely new product or process (like xerography or float glass) could fully conceptualize its ramifications without interactive testing. All parties benefited from procedures that purposely delayed decisions and allowed mutual feedback. Some companies, like IBM or Xerox, have formalized this concept into "phase program planning" systems. They make concrete decisions only on individual phases (or stages) of new product developments, establish interactive testing procedures with customers, and postpone final configuration commitments until the latest possible moment.

Similarly, even under pressure, most top executives were extremely sensitive to organizational and power relationships and consciously managed decision processes to improve these dynamics. They often purposely delayed initial decisions, or kept such decisions vague, in order to encourage lower-level participation, to gain more information from specialists, or to build commitment to solutions. Even when a crisis atmosphere tended to shorten time horizons and make decisions more goal oriented than political, perceptive executives consciously tried to keep their options open until they understood how the crisis would affect the power bases and needs of their key constituents.

Incrementalism in Strategic Subsystems

One also finds that an incremental logic applies in attacking many of the critical subsystems of corporate strategy. Those subsystems for considering diversification moves, divestitures, major reorganizations, or government-external relations are typical and will be described here. In each case conscious incrementalism helps to (1) cope with both the cognitive and process limits on each major decision, (2) build the logical-analytical framework these decisions require, and (3) create the personal and organizational awareness, understanding, acceptance, and commitment needed to implement the strategies effectively.

The Diversification Subsystem

Strategies for diversification, either through research and development (R&D) or acquisitions, provide excellent examples. The formal analytical steps needed for successful diversification are well documented. However, the precise directions that R&D may project the company can only be understood step-by-step as scientists uncover new phenomena, make and amplify discoveries, build prototypes, reduce concepts to practice, and interact with users during product introductions. Similarly, only as each acquisition is sequentially identified, investigated, negotiated for, and integrated into the organization can one predict its ultimate impact on the total enterprise.

A step-by-step approach is clearly necessary to guide and assess the strategic fit of each internal or external diversification candidate. Incremental processes are also required to manage the crucial psychological and power shifts that ultimately determine the program's overall direction and consequences. These processes help unify both the analytical and behavioral aspects of diversification decisions. They create the broad conceptual consensus, the risk-taking attitudes, the organizational and resource flexibilities, and the adaptive dynamism that determine both the timing and direction of diversification strategies. Most important among these processes are:

- *Generating a genuine, top-level psychological commitment to diversification.* General Mills, Pillsbury, and Xerox all started their major diversification programs with broad analytical studies and goal-setting exercises designed both to build top-level consensus around the need to diversify and to establish the general directions for diversification. Without such action, top-level bargaining for resources would have continued to support only more familiar (and hence apparently less risky) old lines, and this could delay or undermine the entire diversification endeavor.

- *Consciously preparing to move opportunistically.* Organizational and fiscal resources must be built up in advance to exploit candidates as they randomly appear. And a "credible activist" for ventures must be developed and backed by someone with commitment power. All successful acquirers created the potential for profit centered divisions within their organizational structures, strengthened their financial-controllership capabilities, took action to create low-cost capital access, and maintained the shortest possible communication lines from the acquisitions activist to the resource-committing authority. All these actions integrally determined which diversifications actually could be made, the timing of their accession, and the pace at which they could be absorbed.

- *Building a "comfort factor" for risk taking.* Perceived risk is largely a function of one's knowledge about a field. Hence well-conceived diversification programs should anticipate a trial-and-error period during which top managers reject early proposed fields or opportunities until they have analyzed enough trial candidates to "become comfortable" with an initial selection. Early successes tend to be "sure things" close to the companies' past (real or supposed) expertise. After a few successful diversifications, managements tend to become more confident and accept other candidates—farther from traditional lines—at a faster rate. Again, the way this process is handled affects both the direction and pace of the actual program.

- *Developing a new ethos.* If new divisions are more successful than the old—as they should be—they attract relatively more resources and their political power grows. Their most effective line managers move into corporate positions, and slowly the company's special competency and ethos change. Finally, the concepts and products that once dominated the company's culture may decline in importance or even disappear. Acknowledging these ultimate consequences to the organization at the beginning of a diversification program would clearly be impolitic, even if the manager both desired and could predict the probable new ethos. These factors must be handled adaptively, as opportunities present themselves and as individual leaders and power centers develop.

Each of the above processes interacts with all others (and with the random appearance of diversification candidates) to affect action sequences, elapsed time, and ultimate results in unexpected ways. Complexities are so great that few diversification programs end up as initially envisioned. Consequently, wise managers recognize the limits to systematic analysis in diversification, and use formal planning to build the "comfort levels" executives need for risk taking and to guide the program's early directions and priorities. They then modify these flexibly, step-by-step, as new opportunities, power centers, and developed competencies merge to create new potentials.

The Divestiture Subsystem

Similar practices govern the handling of divestitures. Divisions often drag along in a less-than-desired condition for years before they can be strategically divested. In some cases, ailing divisions might have just enough yield or potential to offer hoped-for viability. In others, they might represent the company's vital core from earlier years, the creations of a powerful person nearing retirement, or the psychological touchstones of the company's past traditions.

Again, in designing divestiture strategies, top executives had to reinforce vaguely felt concerns with detailed data, build up managers' comfort levels about issues, achieve participation in and commitment to decisions, and move opportunistically to make actual changes. In many cases, the precise nature of the decision was not clear at the outset. Executives often made seemingly unrelated personnel shifts or appointments that changed the value set of critical groups, or started a series of staff studies that generated awareness or acceptance of a potential problem. They might then instigate goal assessment, business review, or "planning" programs to provide broader forums for discussion and a wider consensus for action. Even then they might wait for a crisis, a crucial retirement, or an attractive sale opportunity to determine the timing and conditions of divestiture. In some cases, decisions could be direct and analytical. But when divestitures involved the psychological centers of the organization, the process had to be much more oblique and carefully orchestrated.

The Major Reorganization Subsystem

It is well recognized that major organizational changes are an integral part of strategy. Sometimes they constitute a strategy themselves, sometimes they precede and/or precipitate a new strategy, and sometimes they help to implement a strategy. However, like many other important strategic decisions, macro-organizational moves are typically handled incrementally and outside of formal planning processes. Their effects on personal or power relationships preclude discussion in open forums and reports of such processes.

In addition, major organizational changes have timing imperatives (or "process limits") all their own. In making any significant shifts, the executive must think through the new roles, capabilities, and probable individual reactions of the many principals affected. He may have to wait for the promotion or retirement of a valued colleague before consummating any change. He then frequently has to bring in, train, or test new people for substantial periods before he can staff key posts with confidence. During this testing period he may substantially modify his original concept of the reorganization, as he evaluates individuals' potentials, their performance in specific roles, their personal drives, and their relationships with other team members.

Because this chain of decisions affects the career development, power, affluence, and self-image of so many, the executive tends to keep close counsel in his discussions, negotiates individually with key people, and makes final commitments as late as possible in order to obtain the best matches between people's capabilities, personalities, and aspirations and their new roles. Typically, all these events do not come together at one convenient time, particularly the moment annual plans are due. Instead the executive moves opportunistically, step-by-step, selectively moving people toward a broadly conceived organizational goal, which is constantly modified and rarely articulated in detail until the last pieces fit together.

The Government-External Relations Subsystem

Almost all companies cited government and other external activist groups as among the most important forces causing significant changes in their strategic postures during the periods examined. However, when asked "How did your company arrive at its own strategy vis-à-vis these forces?" it became clear that few companies had cohesive strategies (integrated sets of goals, policies, and programs) for government-external relations, other than lobbying for or against specific legislative actions. To the extent that other strategies did exist, they were piecemeal, ad hoc, and had been derived in a very evolutionary manner. Yet there seemed to be very good reasons for such incrementalism. The following are two of the best short explanations of the way these practices develop:

> We are a very large company, and we understand that any massive overt action on our part could easily create more public antagonism than support for our viewpoint. It is also hard to say in advance exactly what public response any particular action might create. So we tend to test a number of different approaches on a small scale with only limited or local company identification. If one approach works, we'll test it further and amplify its use. If another bombs, we try to keep it from being used again. Slowly we find a series of advertising, public relations, community relations actions that seem to help. Then along comes another issue and we start all over again. Gradually the successful approaches merge into a pattern of actions that becomes our strategy.

> I [the president] start conversations with a number of knowledgeable people . . . . I collect articles and talk to people about how things get done in Washington in this particular field. I collect data from any reasonable source. I begin wide-ranging discussions with people inside and outside the corporation. From these a pattern eventually emerges. It's like fitting together a jigsaw puzzle. At first the vague outline of an approach appears like the sail of a ship in a puzzle. Then suddenly the rest of the puzzle becomes quite clear. You wonder why you didn't see it all along. And once it's crystallized, it's not difficult to explain to others.

In this realm, uncontrollable forces dominate. Data are very soft, often can be only subjectively sensed, and may be costly to quantify. The possible responses of individuals and groups to different stimuli are difficult to determine in advance. The number of potential opponents with power is very high, and the diversity in their viewpoints and possible modes of attack is so substantial that it is physically impossible to lay out probabilistic decision diagrams that would have much meaning. Results are unpredictable and error costs extreme. Even the best intended and most rational-seeming strategies can be converted into disasters unless they are thoroughly and interactively tested.

Formal Planning in Corporate Strategy

What role do classical formal planning techniques play in strategy formulation? All companies in the sample do have formal planning procedures embedded in their management direction and control systems. These serve certain essential functions. In a process sense, they

- provide a discipline forcing managers to take a careful look ahead periodically;
- require rigorous communications about goals, strategic issues, and resource allocations;
- stimulate longer-term analyses than would otherwise be made;
- generate a basis for evaluating and integrating short-term plans;
- lengthen time horizons and protect long-term investments such as R&D;
- create a psychological backdrop and an information framework about the future against which managers can calibrate short-term or interim decisions.

In a decision-making sense, they

- fine-tune annual commitments;
- formalize cost-reduction programs;
- help implement strategic changes once decided on (for example, coordinating all elements of Exxon's decision to change its corporate name).

Formal Plans Also "Increment"

Although individual staff planners were often effective in identifying potential problems and bringing them to top management's attention, the annual planning process itself was rarely (if ever) the initiating source of really new key issues or radical departures into new product/market realms. These almost always came from precipitating events, special studies, or conceptions implanted through the kinds of "logical incremental" processes described above.

In fact, formal planning practices actually institutionalize incrementalism. There are two reasons for this. First, in order to utilize specialized expertise and to obtain executive involvement and commitment, most planning occurs from the bottom up in response to broadly defined assumptions or goals, many of which are longstanding or negotiated well in advance. Of necessity, lower-level groups have only a partial view of the corporation's total strategy, and command only a fragment of its resources. Their power bases, identity, expertise, and rewards also usually depend on their existing products or processes. Hence, these products or processes, rather than entirely new departures, should and do receive their primary attention. Second, most managements purposely design their plans to be "living" or "evergreen." They are intended only as frameworks to guide and provide consistency for future decisions made incrementally. To act otherwise would be to deny that further information could have a value. Thus, properly formulated formal plans are also a part of an incremental logic.

Special Studies

Formal planning was most successful in stimulating significant change when it was set up as a special study on some important aspect of corporate strategy. For example, when it became apparent that Pilkington's new float glass process would work, the company formed a Directors' Float Glass Committee consisting of all internal directors associated with float glass "to consider the broad issues of float glass [strategy] in both the present and the future." The committee did not attempt detailed plans. Instead, it tried to deal in broad concepts, identify alternate routes, and think through the potential consequences of each route some ten years ahead. Of some of the key strategic decisions it was later remarked, "It would be difficult to identify an exact moment when the decision was made . . . . Nevertheless, over a period of time a consensus crystallized with great clarity."

Such special strategic studies represent a subsystem of strategy formulation distinct from both annual planning activities and the other subsystems exemplified above. Each of these develops some important aspect of strategy, incrementally blending its conclusions with those of other subsystems, and it would be virtually impossible to force all these together to crystallize a completely articulated corporate strategy at any one instant.

Total Posture Planning

Occasionally, however, managements do attempt very broad assessments of their companies' total posture. Shortly after becoming CEO of General Mills, James McFarland decided that his job was "to take a very good company and move it to greatness," but that it was up to his management group, not himself alone, to decide what a great company was and how to get there. Consequently he took some thirty-five of the company's topmost managers away for a three-day management retreat. On the first day, after agreeing to broad financial goals, the group broke up into units of six to eight people. Each unit was to answer the question, What is a great company? from the viewpoints of stockholders, employees, suppliers, the public, and society. Each unit reported back at the end of the day, and the whole group tried to reach a consensus through discussion.

On the second day the groups, in the same format, assessed the company's strengths and weaknesses relative to the defined posture of "greatness." The third day focused on how to overcome the company's weaknesses and move it toward a great company. This broad consensus led, over the next several years, to the surveys of fields for acquisition, the building of management's initial comfort levels with certain fields, and the acquisition-divestiture strategy that characterized the McFarland era at General Mills.

Yet even such a major endeavor is only a portion of a total strategic process. Values that had been built up over decades stimulated or constrained alternatives. Precipitating events, acquisitions, divestitures, external relations, and organizational changes developed important segments of each strategy incrementally. Even the strategies articulated left key elements to be defined as new information became available, polities permitted, or particular opportunities appeared. Major product thrusts proved unsuccessful. Actual strategies therefore evolved as each company overextended, consolidated, made errors, and rebalanced various thrusts over time. And it was both logical and expected that this would be the case.

Logical Incrementalism

All of the above suggest that strategic decisions do not lend themselves to aggregation into a single massive decision matrix where all factors can be treated relatively simultaneously in order to arrive at a holistic optimum. Many have spoken of the cognitive limits that prevent this. Of equal importance are the process limits—that is, the timing and sequencing imperatives necessary to create awareness, build comfort levels, develop consensus, select and train people, and so forth—that constrain the system yet ultimately determine the decision itself. Unlike the preparation of a fine banquet, it is virtually impossible for the manager to orchestrate all internal decisions, external environmental events, behavioral and power relationships, technical and informational needs, and actions of intelligent opponents so that they come together at any precise moment.

Can the Process Be Managed?

Instead, the executive usually deals with the logic of each subsystem of strategy formulation largely on its own merits and usually with a different subset of people. He tries to develop or maintain in his own mind a consistent pattern among the decisions made in each subsystem. Knowing his own limitations and the unknowability of the events he faces, he consciously tries to tap the minds and psychic drives of others. He often purposely keeps questions broad and decisions vague in early stages to avoid creating undue rigidities and to stimulate others' creativity. Logic, of course, dictates that he make final commitments *as late as possible* consistent with the information he has.

Consequently, many a successful executive will initially set only broad goals and policies that can accommodate a variety of specific proposals from below, yet give a sense of guidance to the proposers. As they come forward the proposals automatically and beneficially attract the support and identity of their sponsors. Being only proposals, the executive can treat these at less politically charged levels, as specific projects rather than as larger goal or policy precedents. Therefore, he can encourage, discourage, or kill alternatives with considerably less political exposure. As events and opportunities emerge, he can incrementally guide the pattern of escalated or accepted proposals to suit his own purposes without getting prematurely committed to a rigid solution set that unpredictable events might prove wrong or that opponents find sufficiently threatening to coalesce against.

A Strategy Emerges

Successful executives link together and bring order to a series of strategic processes and decisions spanning years. At the beginning of the process it is literally impossible to predict all the events and forces that will shape the future of the company. The best executives can do is to forecast the forces most likely to impinge on the company's affairs and the ranges of their possible impact. They then attempt to build a resource base and a corporate posture so strong in selected areas that the enterprise can survive and prosper despite all but the most devastating events. They consciously select market/technological/product segments the concern can dominate given its resource limits, and place some side bets in order to decrease the risk of catastrophic failure or to increase the company's flexibility for future options.

They then proceed incrementally to handle urgent matters, start longer-term sequences whose specific future branches and consequences are perhaps murky, respond to unforeseen events as they occur, build on successes, and brace up or cut losses on failures. They constantly reassess the future, find new congruencies as events unfurl, and blend the organization's skills and resources into new balances of dominance and risk aversion as various forces intersect to suggest better—

but never perfect—alignments. The process is dynamic, with neither a real beginning nor end.

Strategy deals with the unknowable, not the uncertain. It involves forces of such great number, strength, and combinatory powers that one cannot predict events in a probabilistic sense. Hence logic dictates that one proceed flexibly and experimentally from broad concepts toward specific commitments, making the latter concrete as late as possible in order to narrow the bands of uncertainty and to benefit from the best available information. This is the process of logical incrementalism.

■ RETHINKING INCREMENTALISM†

By Gerry Johnson

There exist a number of models to account for the process of strategic management. One such framework is provided by Chaffee, who proposes three generic categories. Her first is the "linear" model corresponding to what others have called the planning (Mintzberg), rational (Peters and Waterman), rational comprehensive or synoptic (Fredrickson) approach. It is a model of strategy making that assumes a progressive series of steps of goal setting, analysis, evaluation, selection, and the planning of implementation to achieve an optimal long-term direction for the organization.

Chaffee's second category is the "adaptive" model of strategic management, a term also used by Mintzberg. This model corresponds to the idea of incremental strategic change discussed previously and, as we have seen, the explanations for this phenomenon vary considerably from those who see incrementalism as essentially logical or rational to those who account for the phenomenon in terms of satisficing behaviour in a political, or programmed, context or within the cognitive limits of management.

It is this cognitive view of strategy formulation that leads us to Chaffee's third category—the "interpretative" model. Weick argues that there is a "presumption of logic" in meeting a complex situation; this logic is rooted in the beliefs and assumptions that managers hold, a cognitive map that provides a view of the world, helps interpret the changes the organization faces, and provides appropriate responses. These organizational sets of beliefs and assumptions have been variously referred to in management literature as paradigms, interpretative schemes, and ideational culture. The result of the application of such cognitive maps is well documented: the danger is of "groupthink" as the application of "collective cognitive resources to develop rationalisations in line with shared illusions about the invulnerability of . . . organizations" (Janis, 1985). Other researchers have shown the extent to which symbolic aspects of the organization—stories and myths, rituals and ceremonies, and the language of the organization—act to legitimize and preserve such core beliefs and assumptions held within the organization.

Arguably these three models more generally embrace two broad thrusts about views on strategy formulation. The one is that strategy formulation can be accounted for by logical, rational processes either through the planning mode or through the adaptive, logical incremental mode. In either event the manager is a proactive strategy

†**Source:** This article was originally published in *Strategic Management Journal* (January/February 1988). Reproduced by permission of John Wiley and Sons Limited.

formulator consciously seeking to understand a complex environment, so as to establish causal patterns and formulate strategy by configuring organizational resources to meet environmental needs. The other view is an "organizational action" view of strategy formulation where strategy is seen as the product of political, programmatic, cognitive, or symbolic aspects of management. In what follows we will take a closer look at a case, the retail clothing company Coopers, in order to assess the extent to which these differing views explain the strategic development of the company.

Explaining Strategic Management Processes

A Rational View of Strategy Formulation

It might appear that the notion of strategy as a logical response to environmental change is supported at least insofar as over the period 1970–1985 the company did apparently try to make strategic changes in response to a changing business environment. However, the observation that strategies change with environmental changes tells us little about the processes of strategic decision making. If we were to account for such decisions in terms of linear, rational planning models, we would expect to find strong evidence and a significant impact of systematic environmental scanning, clear objective setting and evaluation of strategic options against such objectives, and probably a planning infrastructure through which this took place. In fact, in Coopers throughout the period studied there was little evidence of any of this, and as will be seen, when such activity did take place, it had relatively little impact. We have to account for the observed strategic changes in other ways.

However, the managers themselves expressed views about the management of strategy which square well with rational but incremental models of strategic management—views that mirror closely Quinn's notion of logical incrementalism. These views included the following:

- Small movements in strategy allow deliberate experimentation and sensing of the environment through action; if such small movements prove successful, then further development of strategy can take place.

- Shareholders expect short-term returns; therefore it is not sensible to commit large sums of money or other resources to major shifts in strategy.

- It is better to make continual adjustments to strategy so as to keep in line with market changes; if this is not done, then the company's strategy will become atrophied and over time will lead to the need for radical repositioning.

- Opportunistic managements are able to search for ways in which they can take advantage of the matching of a historic and developing strategy with a developing market.

- The nature of retailing is particularly suited to incremental adjustment, since there are few really fixed costs and assets. It is much less of a commitment and risk to try out a new strategy, because it can be done by opening a few new shops, or adjusting merchandise in shops; if this does not work, then the shops can be disposed of, or the merchandise sold off with relatively little loss.

- In a business in which there is high regard for people it is important not to "rock the boat" too much; people will go along with change much more readily if it is gradual and they can become used to it.

The danger is that of assuming that the logic of the processes described by the managers is necessarily a reasonable description of the processes that account for strategy formulation. This research was concerned with studying strategic change as a longitudinal, contextual process, rather than as the espoused theory of managers. It will be shown that a somewhat different picture of the process of strategic management emerges if patterns of development of strategy in the business are examined in terms of the events, dramas, and routines of organization life and the belief systems of managers.

An "Organizational Action" View of Strategy Formulation and Implementation

An "organizational action" view of strategy formulation argues that strategy can best be seen as the product of the political, cognitive and cultural fabric of the organization. The expectation would be that strategic decisions could be explained better in terms of political processes than analytical procedures; that cognitive maps of managers are better explanations of their perceptions of the environment and their strategic responses than are analysed position statements and evaluative techniques; and that the legitimacy of these cognitive maps is likely to be reinforced through the myths and rituals of the organization.

Discernible from the analysis of the interviews with managers was a common set of beliefs and assumptions taken for granted by those managers; it was tacit knowledge, primarily about the modes of operation in the organization, typically in terms of trading procedures, organization, and control, seen as bestowing beneficial competences and capabilities on the organization. For Coopers this set of beliefs and assumptions could be characterized and summarized thus: low cost, good value, merchandise bought in bulk by experienced buyers, yielding high margins, linked to the tight centralized control of stock and distribution provides a secure position in our particular market niche. Moreover, we can take decisions fast because of centralized "entrepreneurial" top management and rely on speedy implementation by loyal staff with years of experience in the business.

This set of beliefs amounts to what other writers have referred to as a paradigm: those sets of assumptions, usually implicit, about what sort of things make up the world, how they act, how they hang together, and how they may be known.

In Coopers over most of the years under study the buyers in particular exercised high degrees of power in the business. The link between the paradigm and the power bases in the company is an observation made by many researchers: "power accrued to those sub-units which could best deal with organisational uncertainty" (Pfeffer and Salancik). The merchandise strategy was perceived to have the effect of insulating the company from market threats; the price and margin advantages reduced the likelihood of competitive incursions and buffered them against downturns in demand. Changes in fashion were seen to be less important than for some other companies because they had elected to concentrate on "commodity" merchandise policies. It was the merchandise strategy that became the mechanism through which company profits were to be guaranteed, and this became central within the set of assumptions about the basis on which the business could compete in an uncertain world.

The dominance of buying and merchandise could be seen in the shop window displays of the 1970s, crowded with every item of merchandise the shop stocked with an emphasis given to what the buyers had procured. The assumption of the dominant importance of merchandise and buying was also symbolized in the greater freedom and discretion enjoyed by buyers in an otherwise tightly controlled business. The rituals of socialization ensured that everyone knew of the company way of retailing and acknowledged organizational features of loyalty, long service, and deference to senior executives not only as proper but beneficial. The nature of top management in the firm, its perceived entrepreneurial flair, the speed of decision making, and the centrality of the chief executive were enshrined in myths showing how this had been so throughout the history of the company. In short, the tenets of the paradigm were, indeed, legitimized symbolically.

Cases in the Formulation and Implementation of Strategy

The extent to which these characteristics of organizational action help explain the formulation of strategy in the company, and in so doing the observed phenomenon of incremental strategic change, can best be shown by using some brief examples from the company's history.

Younger Fashions: A Process of Lobbying and Incremental Adjustment   Prior to the mid-1970s the company had concentrated on what managers described as a "pile it high and sell it cheap" approach to clothes for the working man. However, there were managers in the business well aware of fashion changes in the market early in the 1970s; junior management, mainly from the relevatively lower power base of the retail side of the company, were lobbying for merchandise changes over a period of years, but their appeals for change were ignored or blocked by senior managers. It was these senior managers, and in particular senior merchandise executives, who were most wedded to, and arguably derived power from, the established and hitherto successful strategy. Moreover, those resisting change could draw on a whole raft of justifications for such resistance, usually embedded in organizational routines: lead times on high-volume purchasing were long; more fashionable items might jeopardize volume purchases and hence margins; it would be more difficult to control a widening merchandise range; in any case, profit growth was continuing, and there was no other serious competitor in their market sector. In short, they could draw upon well-established bases of the strategic success of the business to defend the legitimacy of the approach upon which their power had been built.

However, it has to be noted that those from within the business who were advocating change were also conceiving of problems and solutions within much the same paradigm constraints. To them the customer was much the same as he always had been: he just wanted access to some more fashionable goods. Moreover it was seen as a merchandise problem that could be resolved through a change in merchandise by buyers whose ability was highly regarded. It was not, for example, seen as a problem to do with shop ambience, or requiring a change in definition of target market.

The resolution of the problem was through the mechanism of what managers saw as logically incremental action. It can also be seen as a change in strategy defined in terms of the paradigm and implemented gradually so as not to interfere with what was "known to work." Fashion was defined as imitating what other fashionable retailers demonstrated they could sell in volume. There was to be no loss of control on stocks: distribution was retained at the centre and shops had to "qualify" for new stock on the evidence of past sales of the limited range of fashion merchandise available. The shops themselves were hardly changed.

The Response to Declining Performance: 1980–81   By the middle of 1981 the company was in a state of serious performance decline. The period provides some examples of a management team faced with a problem it found difficult to understand, making sense of it through, and exerting greater efforts within, its paradigm, whilst seeking to preserve the legitimacy of that paradigm from the threats of growing counterevidence.

Performance decline had to do with an economic downturn regarded as temporary. In the meantime, the paradigm offered a menu of responses to the problems the business faced. This included tightening controls and cutting controllable costs. It also meant that managers sought to do better what they had always done: to stack the merchandise higher, pack windows more fully, and make sure staff were selling more aggressively.

Whilst most managers may have accepted that the market would return, a newly arrived marketing director was convinced, through market research he had commissioned, of the dubious reliability of Coopers' traditional market. The research report not only questioned the validity of management's conception of the clothing market but attacked their way of operating within it. The response to such questioning was much as Pfeffer has indicated: "Attacks on the dominant beliefs or paradigm of the organization are likely to be met with counter argument and efforts to reinforce the paradigm." The resistance was concerned with more than the report itself: it was also addressed at the new director.

Formalizing Explanatory Models

Examination of the processes of strategic change in Coopers bears out many of the phenomena that characterize incremental strategic change explained in terms of an organizational action perspective. The patterns of change are indeed evolutionary; strategic decisions build upon history and what managers at least perceive to be the core strength of the business. Decisions came about after long periods of incubation following identification of problems or opportunities through highly qualitative assessment. High levels of solicitation and bargaining characterized both problem definition and the selection of solutions. The primacy of cognitive maps in the interpretation of environmental stimuli, the configuration of responses, and strategy implementation is also evident; and it becomes clear that these belief sets are relatively commonly held within the organization and persistent, forming an organizational paradigm. Moreover, the mediatory and legitimizing role of symbolic aspects of the organization is also borne out. Building on all this we can move toward more integrated explanatory models of strategic management that arguably help in understanding the complexity of strategic management.

The Nature of the Paradigm

We need to start by distinguishing between what is meant by the paradigm and what is meant by strategy. Following Mintzberg we can distinguish between intended and realized strategy. Realized strategy is taken to mean the observable output of an organization's activity in terms of its positioning over time. Intended strategy means the strategy that managers espouse, perhaps in some sort of formal plan, public statement or explanation. The paradigm, on the other hand, is a more generalized set of beliefs about the organization and the way it is or should be and, since it is taken for granted and not problematic, may be difficult to surface as a coherent statement. It is more likely to emerge in the explanations and stories of managers. The point is that both intended and realized strategies are likely to be configured within the parameters of the paradigm.

FIGURE 2-4
The Cultural Web of an
Organization

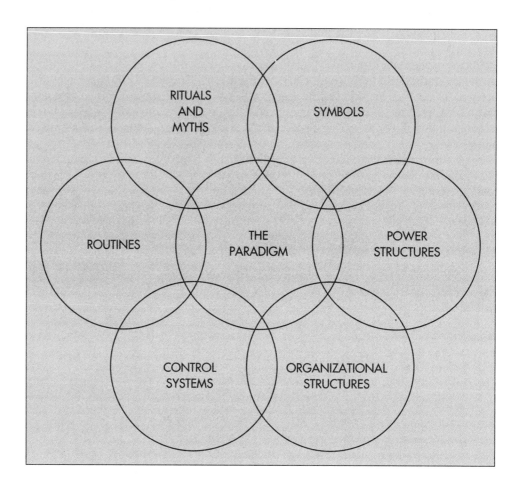

There were discernible reasons why the paradigm would be resistant to rapid change. First, the internal consistency of the paradigm as observed was self-preserving and self-legitimizing. It is not an easy matter to challenge or repudiate a construct of an internally supportive and consistent whole. Second, and particularly significant in terms of understanding management implications, we need to understand the paradigm not just as a system of beliefs and assumptions; it is preserved and legitimized in a "cultural web" of organizational action in terms of myths, rituals, symbols, control systems, and formal and informal power structures that support and provide relevance to core beliefs (see figure 2-4). At Coopers the assumptions about the approach to buying and merchandising, and the emphasis on centralized control of current costs and assets, were not only linked themselves, but institutionalized, indeed capitalized, in the stock control and distribution systems. This is the inertia of technical organizational commitment, and is not likely to be ignored or overturned.

Further, the constructs of the paradigm are closely linked to the power structures in the organization. In effect, the paradigm represents the internally constructed belief set about uncertainty reduction, so it is likely that those most associated with operationalizing these beliefs will be most powerful in the organization. This point is of some significance. Strategic change processes traditionally advocated in the literature are linked to rational analytical planning models. The notion that it is through analysis of the business environment and the competitive position of the firm that managers yield insights into strengths and weaknesses that help identify the need and opportunities for change overlooks the political implications of such analysis. Such analysis was undertaken in Coopers. In the period following the analysis the evidence it provided was either denied by management, discredited, or led to minimal change. The reason for this was not that the analysis lacked clarity or cogency; quite the reverse: it pointedly questioned tenets of beliefs fundamental to the strategies being followed by the organization; in other words it raised explicit challenges to the paradigm and, as such, constituted not an intellectual analytical questioning of strategy, but a political threat to those whose power was most associated with it. Clarity of analysis is not, in itself, a sufficient basis to break the powerful momentum of the fundamental assumptions embraced within the paradigm, and indeed can actually increase resistance to change.

An Integrated Model of Process

The proposition arising from the analysis of the events at Coopers is that environmental signals will be reordered in terms of the paradigm. Some environmental signals will simply not be seen as relevant in terms of the paradigm, and will be ignored. Signals from the environment might also be seen as "dissonant" with the paradigm; that is they might be actual or potential perceived threats to its basis, or not capable of being dealt with strictly within its bounds. Dissonance with the paradigm is potentially threatening to its integrity, and responses to such a threat follow a pattern:

- Dissonance will be mediated symbolically; that is, the symbolic mechanisms within which the paradigm is embedded will perform the role of maintaining the legitimacy of the paradigm in the face of the apparent threat.

- Since the threat may take the form of a political challenge to those most associated with core constructs of the paradigm, it may well be strongly resisted.

- Managers will seek to resolve the extent to which elements of the environment and the paradigm are in a state of dissonance. It is here that the most significant acts of strategic adaptation take place. The evidence throughout the period under study here is that such consonance might be achieved by (1) making sense of counterstimuli in the terms of paradigm rather than questioning or reconstructing the paradigm; or (2) where necessary marginally adjusting the paradigm, but from within its own bounds, and whilst maintaining its essential form.

The Notion of Strategic Drift

The paradigm effectively defines environmental "reality" and responses to environmental change. Quinn's logical notion is that strategic change, through environmental sensing by managers within subsystems and the interplay between subsystems, and continual testing out of new strategies, results in a learning and readjustment process in organization by which the organization keeps itself in line with environmental changes. This notion is summarized in figure 2-5a. The argument here is different: that managers may well see themselves as managing logically incrementally, but that such consciously managed incremental change does not necessarily succeed in keeping pace with environmental change. Indeed, it is argued that there is a high risk that it will not. The situation at Coopers as it evolved through the 1970s was not as shown in figure 2-5a, but rather as shown in figure 2-5b. Gradually the incrementally adjusted strategic changes and the environmental, particularly market, changes moved apart.

FIGURE 2-5
Incremental Change and
'Strategic Drift'

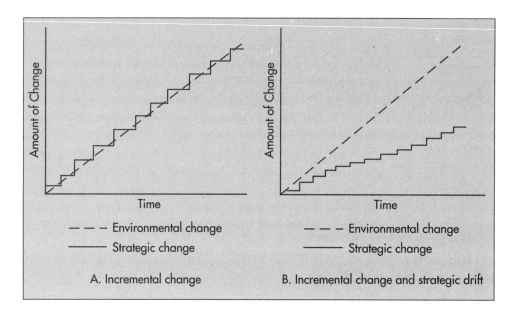

A. Incremental change

B. Incremental change and strategic drift

Conclusions and Normative Implications

The question remains how it might be possible to achieve more nearly effective adaptive incremental strategic management and avoid strategic drift.

If strategy is to be managed effectively, a "constructive tension" must exist between what is necessary to preserve and what must be changed—a tension, for example, between the need for managers to question and challenge and the preservation of core values and organizational mission; between the need for new ideas and directions and the need for continuity and preservation of the core business. This necessary tension is what Peters and Waterman call "simultaneous loose-tight properties" or "the coexistence of firm central direction and maximum individual autonomy." It is a view echoed elsewhere but more specifically at the cultural and cognitive levels. Meyer has argued that the reason one organization is more likely to adopt strategies divergent from its previous strategies than another is because it has a more heterogeneous organizational "ideology," as manifested, for example, in terms of organizational images and symbols. A number of writers have argued that such ideological heterogeneity can be built into management systems in a variety of ways, for example, through organic management styles with a removal or reduction of hierarchical lines of reporting and communication; through deliberate challenging and assumption-surfacing devices, either formally promulgated or as part of the organizational culture; through the active involvement of "outsiders" with less adherence to organizational culture or the organization's paradigm; and through the avoidance of "segmentalist" structures.

Findings here also bear out those who argue the power of symbolic mechanisms for strategic management and change. The point they argue is that strategic issues have traditionally been seen as linked to analytical and planning mechanisms of management, and as such run the risk of not being "owned" by those within the organization. They point out that successful organizations are good at managing change, not by talking about it at an analytical level but by demonstrating it at a symbolic and therefore more meaningful level in terms of the interpretative models suggested here and as illustrated in figure 2-4. Such organizations approach the management of change through the very artifacts (symbolic and political) that otherwise preserve the integrity of the paradigm and prevent change.

None of this is to say that the planning and analytical methods advocated in so much of the literature are of no relevance. It is rather to argue that planning and analysis are necessary but not sufficient, and need to be understood as mechanisms for problem and opportunity identification and strategy evaluation rather than as a mechanism for strategic change. Indeed, the argument can be advanced that planning and analytical mechanisms are likely to give rise to resistance to change unless they take place within a context where the mechanisms for managing strategic change through the social, cultural, political, cognitive and symbolic devices of the organization are already in place.

Overall, the results of the study emphasize the importance of understanding strategic management processes essentially in terms of organization action perspectives, and argue for the continued development of models that more precisely explain both strategy formulation and implementation in these terms.

■ A DISCUSSION ON STRATEGY PROCESS PARADIGMS†

Round 1: Reconsidering the Basic Premises of Strategic Management

By Henry Mintzberg

The literature that can be subsumed under *strategy formation* is vast, diverse, and since 1980 has been growing at an astonishing rate.

A good deal of this literature naturally divides itself into distinct schools of thought. In another publication (Mintzberg, 1990a), this author has identified ten of these. Three are prescriptive in orientation, treating strategy formation as a process of conceptual design, formal planning, and analytical positioning (the latter including much of the research on the content of competitive strategies). Six other schools deal with specific aspects of the process in a descriptive way, and are labeled the entrepreneurial school (concerned with strategy formation as a visionary process), the cognitive school (a mental process), the learning school (an emergent process), and the environmental school (a passive process). A final school, also descriptive, but integrative and labeled configurational, by seeking to delineate the stages and sequences of the process, helps to place the findings of these other schools in context.

This paper addresses itself to the first of these schools, in some ways the most entrenched of the ten. Its basic framework underlies almost all prescription in this field and, accordingly, has had enormous impact on how strategy and the strategy-making process are conceived in practice as well as in education and research. Hence

†**Source:** This article was adapted from a series of three articles, published in *Strategic Management Journal* and originally entitled: "The Design School: Reconsidering the Basic Premises of Strategic Management" (1990), "Critique of Henry Mintzberg's The Design School: Reconsidering the Basic Premises of Strategic Management" (1991), and "Learning 1, Planning 0: Reply to Igor Ansoff" (1991). Reproduced by permission of John Wiley and Sons Limited.

our discussion, and especially critique, of this school can in some ways be taken as a commentary on the currently popular beliefs in the field of strategic management in general. Our intention, however, is not to dismiss so important a school of thought, but rather to understand it better and so place it into its natural context, and thereby open up thinking in the field in general.

Origins of the Design School

Ostensibly the simplest and most fundamental view of strategy formation is as a process of informal conception—the use of a few essential concepts to design "grand strategy." Of these concepts the most essential is that of congruence or match. In the words of the design school's best-known proponents: "Economic strategy will be seen as the match between qualification and opportunity that positions a firm in its environment" (Christensen, Andrews, Bower, Hamermesh, and Porter, 1982). Capture Success seems to be the motto of the design school; find out what you are good at and match it with what the world wants and needs. These capabilities or qualifications have been variously referred to as distinctive competence, differential, competitive, or comparative advantage (the latter more commonly used in the context of public policy); or more simply (and broadly), an organization's strengths and weaknesses.

The Christensen et al. book quoted from above, entitled *Business Policy: Text and Cases*, first appeared in 1965 and quickly became the dominant textbook in the field, as well as the dominant voice for this school of thought. Certainly its text portion, attributed in the various editions to coauthor Kenneth Andrews, stands as the most outspoken and one of the clearest statements of this school. Given the impact that this rendition of the design school has had over the years—as well as its clarity and forcefulness of expression—we shall use it as a primary source in the discussion that follows, referring to it as the Andrews text.

Our depiction of the basic design school model (similar to Andrews's own figure of the development of economic strategy, but with other elements of his discussion added) is shown in figure 2-6.

Premises Underlying the Design School

Running through all of the literature that we identified with this school are a number of fundamental premises about the process of strategy formation.

Premise 1: Strategy Formation Should Be a Controlled, Conscious Process of Thought

It is not action that receives the greatest attention from the design school so much as reason—strategies formed through a tightly controlled process of conscious human thought. Action follows, once the strategies have been fully formulated. This theme runs through all of Andrews's writings, for example, in the comment that managers "know what they are really doing" only if they make strategy as "deliberate as possible" or, more simply, in reference to his "thesis" about "conscious strategy" that should be "consciously implemented." But this is perhaps made most clear in his

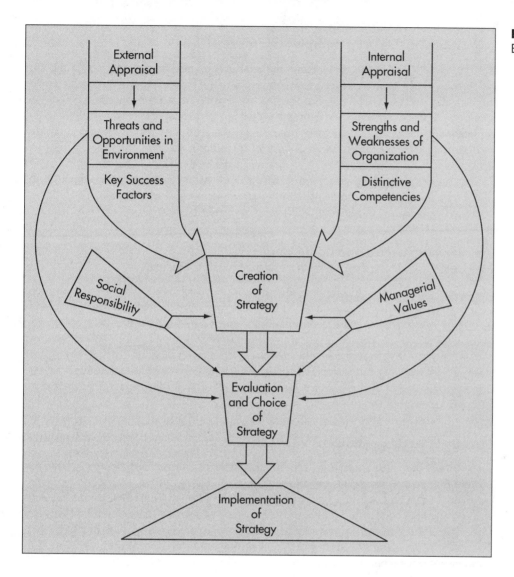

FIGURE 2-6
Basic Design School Model

comment that while the model may be simple, it is not necessarily natural—it must be learned, formally.

Premise 2: Responsibility for Control and Consciousness Must Rest with the Chief Executive Officer: That Person is *the* Strategist

To the design school, ultimately there is only one strategist, and that is the manager who sits at the apex of the organizational hierarchy. In Hayes's terms, "This 'command-and-control' mentality allocates all major decisions to top management, which imposes them on the organization and monitors them through elaborate planning, budgeting, and control systems" (1985).

It might be noted that this premise not only relegates other members of the organization to subordinate roles in strategy formation, but it also precludes external actors from the process altogether (except for the directors, who Andrews believes must review strategy).

Premise 3: The Model of Strategy Formation Must Be Kept Simple and Informal

Fundamental to the model is the belief that elaboration and formalization will sap it of its essence. This premise in fact goes with the last: one way to ensure that strategy can be controlled in one mind is to keep the process simple. As Andrews writes: "When the variety of what must be known cannot be reduced by a sharply focused strategy to the capacity of a single mind and when the range of a company's activities spans many industries and technologies, the problems of formulating a coherent strategy begin to get out of hand."

This premise, together with the first, forces Andrews to tread a fine line throughout his text, between nonconscious intuition on one side and formal analysis on the other, a position he seems to characterize as an act of judgment.

Premise 4: Strategies Should Be Unique: The Best Ones Result from a Process of Creative Design

The choice of objectives and the formulation of policy to guide action in the attainment of objectives depend on many variables unique to a given organization and situation. It is not possible to make useful generalizations about the nature of these variables or to classify their possible combinations in all situations.

As a result of this premise, the design school says little about the content of strategies themselves, but instead concentrates on the process by which they should be developed. And that process above all should be a "creative act," building on distinctive competence.

Premise 5: Strategies Emerge from This Design Process Fully Formulated

This school offers little room to incrementalist views or emergent strategies. It is the big picture that results from the process—the grand strategy, an overall concept of the business. This is no Darwinian view of strategy formation but the Biblical version, with strategy the final conception. There is, in other words, a strong implication that strategy as perspective appears at a point in time, fully formulated, ready to be implemented. The assumption is that the strategist is able to line up alternative strategies before him to be evaluated so that one can be definitively chosen.

Premise 6: Strategies Should Be Explicit and, If Possible, Articulated, Which Also Favors Their Being Kept Simple

Andrews believes that strategies should at least be explicit to those who make them and, if at all possible, articulated so that others in the organization can understand them: "The unstated strategy cannot be tested or contested and is likely therefore to be weak . . . . A strategy must be explicit to be effective and specific enough to require some action and exclude others."

If strategies are to be so articulated, it also follows that they have to be kept rather simple: to the point, easily stated to be easily understood. "Simplicity is the essence of good art," writes Andrews, "a conception of strategy brings simplicity to complex organizations."

Premise 7: Finally, Only After These Unique, Full-blown, Explicit, and Simple Strategies Are Fully Formulated Can They Then Be Implemented

We have already noted the sharp distinction this school makes between the formulation of strategies on one hand and their implementation on the other. Consistent with classical notions of rationality—diagnosis, prescription, then action—the design school clearly separates thinking from acting.

Central to this distinction is the associated premise that structure must follow strategy. As Andrews puts it: "Corporate strategy must dominate the design of organizational structure and processes."

Andrews's Qualifications

While these seven premises are clearly evident in Andrews's text, as noted earlier he does qualify virtually all of them. Most are presented as asides or afterthoughts, while his real commitment remains to the premises themselves, as of course is natural if he is not to undermine his own position.

By ultimately remaining true to its premises, Andrews positions the design school in its own niche, distinguishing it particularly from the planning and positioning schools on one side, which by elaborating the model shift it from the realm of judgment to that of analysis, and the entrepreneurial school on the other, which by mystifying the whole process locks it into the inaccessible (and unteachable) realm of intuition. The outstanding question is, How large is that niche; How much of the viable strategic behavior of organizations, whether for purposes of description *or* prescription, is it reasonably able to encompass?

Critique of the Design School

Assessment of Strengths and Weaknesses: Thinking versus Learning

Our critique of the design school revolves around one central theme: its promotion of thought independent of action, strategy formation above all as a process of *conception*, rather than as one of *learning*. We can see this most clearly in a fundamental step in the formulation process, the assessment of strengths and weaknesses.

How does an organization know its strengths and weaknesses? On this, the design school is quite clear—by consideration, assessment, judgment supported by analysis, in other words, by conscious thought. One gets the image of executives sitting around a table discussing the strengths, weaknesses, and distinctive competences of an organization, much as do students in a case study class. Having decided what these are, they are then ready to design strategies.

In his article on "strategic capability," Lenz (1980) critiques the use of an "organizational frame of reference"—usually based on some abstract ideal or a comparison with the situation of the past—with an external frame of reference. In other words, internal capability has to be assessed with respect to external context. But the problem of assessing strengths and weaknesses may go deeper still. Might competences not also be distinctive to time, even distinctive to application? And can any organization really be sure of its strengths before it tests them empirically?

Every strategic change involves some new experience, a step into the unknown, the taking of some kind of risk. Therefore, no organization can ever be sure in advance whether an established competence will prove to be a strength or a weakness. In its retail diversification efforts, a supermarket chain we studied was surprised to learn that discount stores, which seemed so compatible with its food store operations, did not work out well, while fastfood restaurants, ostensibly so different, did. The similarities of the discount store business—how products were displayed, moved about by customers, checked out—were apparently overwhelmed by the subtle but different characteristics of merchandising-styling, obsolescence, and so on. On the other hand, the restaurants may have looked very different, but they moved simple, basic, perishable, commodity-like products through an efficient chain of distribution much like the supermarket business did. The point we wish to emphasize is, How could the firm have known ahead of time? The discovery of what business it was to be in could not be undertaken on paper, but had to benefit from the results of testing and experience. (And the conclusion suggested from such experiences is that strengths generally turn out to be far narrower than expected and weaknesses, consequently, far broader.)

Structure Follows Strategy . . . as the Left Foot Follows the Right

While the design school tends to promote the dictum, first articulated by Chandler (1962), that structure should follow strategy and be determined by it, in fact its model also accepts the opposite. Since the assessment of organizational strengths and weaknesses is an intrinsic part of the model, a basic input to strategy formulation, and since structure is a key component of this input, housing the organization's capabilities, then structure must play a major role in determining strategy too, by constraining and conditioning it as well as guiding it.

While this may be an obvious point, hardly disputed even within the design school, it does have a broader implication, an important one in our critique of this school's model of strategy formation. No ongoing organization ever wipes the slate clean when it changes its strategy. The past counts, just as does the environment, and the structure is a significant part of that past. Claiming that strategy must take precedence over structure amounts to claiming that strategy must take precedence over the established capabilities of the organization, clearly an untenable proposition. By overemphasizing strategy, and the ability of the strategist to act rather freely, the design school slights, not just the environment, but also the organization itself. Structure may be malleable, but it cannot be altered at will just because a leader has conceived a new strategy. Many organizations have come to grief over just such a belief.

We conclude, therefore, that structure follows strategy as the left foot follows the right in walking. In effect, strategy and structure both support the organization. None takes precedence; each always precedes the other, and follows it, except when they move together, as the organization jumps to a new position. Strategy formation is an integrated system, not an arbitrary sequence.

Making Strategy Explicit: Promoting Inflexibility

Once strategies have been created, via the conscious assessment of strengths and weaknesses, among other things, the model calls for their articulation. While recognizing some reasons for not making strategy explicit, this school generally considers an unwillingness to articulate strategy as evidence of fuzzy thinking, or else of political motive. But there are other, often more important, reasons not to articulate strategy, which strike at the basic assumptions of the design school.

The reasons generally given for the need to articulate strategy are, first, that only an explicit strategy can be discussed, investigated, and debated; second, that only by making strategy explicit can it serve its prime function of knitting people together to "provide coherence to organizational action"; and third, that an articulated strategy can generate support—can rally the troops, so to speak, and reassure outside influencers. These all sound like excellent reasons for articulating strategy. And they are—so long as all the conditions are right. The most important of these is that the strategist is sure—knows where he or she wants to go, and has few serious doubts about the viability of that direction. In other words, the design school implicitly assumes conditions of stability or predictability. But organizations have to cope with conditions of uncertainty too.

Organizations must function not only *with* strategy, but also *during* periods of the formulation and reformulation of strategy, which cannot happen instantaneously. "It is virtually impossible for a manager to orchestrate all internal decisions, external environmental events, behavioral and power relationships, technical and informational needs, and actions of intelligent opponents so that they come together at a precise moment" [see Quinn's previous article]. Indeed, sometimes organizations also need to function during periods of unpredictability, when they cannot possibly hope to articulate any viable strategy. The danger during such periods is not the lack of explicit strategy but exactly the opposite—"premature closure," the reification of speculative tendencies into firm commitments. When strategists are not sure, they had better not articulate strategies, for all the reasons given above.

Moreover, even when it makes sense to articulate strategies because they appear to be viable well into the future, the dangers of doing so must still be recognized. Explicit strategies, as implied in the reasons for wanting them, are blinders designed to focus direction and so to block out peripheral vision. Thus, they can impede strategic change when it does become necessary: to put this another way, a danger in articulating strategy is that while strategists may be sure for now, they can never be sure forever. The more clearly articulated the strategy, the more deeply imbedded it becomes in the habits of the organization as well as the minds of its strategists. There is, in fact, evidence from the laboratories of cognitive psychology that the explication of a strategy—even having someone articulate what he or she is about to do anyway—locks it in, breeding a resistance to later change.

Another reason not to articulate strategy is that pronouncements of it, often necessarily superficial, can engender a false sense of understanding. Andrews argues that "a conception of strategy brings simplicity to complex organizations." True enough. But at what price?

To summarize, the problems of making strategy explicit essentially bring us back to the need to view strategy formation as a learning process, at least in some contexts. Sure strategies must often be made explicit, for purposes of investigation, coordination, and support. The questions are when? and how? and when not? There is undoubtedly a need for closure at certain points in an organization's history, moments when the process of strategy formation must be suspended temporarily to articulate clear strategies. But this need should not lead us to believe that it is natural for strategies to appear fully developed all of a sudden, nor should it allow us to ignore the periods during which strategies must evolve.

Separation of Formulation from Implementation: Detaching Thinking from Acting

How can anyone really question this distinction, or even the assumption that formulation must precede implementation? After all, this is just another version of the basic form of rationality that underlies Western thinking—in its simplest form, that to act you must first know what you want to accomplish. Think first, then do.

All that would be fine were the world only cooperative. Unfortunately, often it is not, in many cases for good reason, whether the resistance to the intended strategy comes from the environment in which it is to be implemented, the organization that is supposed to do the implementing, or even from the strategy itself.

Sometimes the "implementors" who make up the rest of the organization are perfectly willing to proceed as directed from the center, but the environment simply renders the strategy a failure. It may change unpredictably, so that the intended strategy becomes useless, or it may remain so unstable that no specific strategy can be useful. Despite implications to the contrary, the external environment is not some kind of pear to be plucked from the tree of external appraisal, but a major and sometimes unpredictable force to be reckoned with.

In other cases it is not the environment but the implementors within the organization who resist. They may, of course, be narrow-minded bureaucrats too wedded to their traditional ways to know a good new strategy when they see one, or small-minded ones who do not understand the new strategy, or bloody-minded ones who prefer to go their own way. But sometimes they are right-minded people who do what they do to serve the organization despite its leadership. They may resist implementation because they know the intended strategies to be unfeasible—that the organization will not be capable of realizing them or, once realized, they will fail in an unsuitable external environment.

Implementational failure can also occur without inhospitable environments and resistant organizations. The problem can lie in the strategy itself; indeed, in part at least, it almost always does. For one thing, no intended strategy can ever be so precisely defined that it covers every eventuality. Moreover, while the formulators may be few, the implementors are typically many, functioning at different levels and in different units and places, each with their own values and interpretations. They are not robots, nor are the systems that control them airtight. The inevitable result is some slipping between formulation and implementation.

"Slippage" is a term used in the public sector to mean that strategic intentions get distorted on their way to implementation; "drift" is another term used there for realized strategies that differ from intended ones. Here, however, we would like to take a position beyond both concepts.

Certainly much formulation is ill-conceived, just as much implementation is badly executed. But often the fundamental difficulty lies not on either side, but in conceiving a distinction between formulation and implementation in the first place.

Behind the premise of the formulation-implementation dichotomy lies a set of very ambitious assumptions: first, that the formulator can be fully, or at least sufficiently, informed to formulate viable strategies; and second, that the environment is sufficiently stable, or at least predictable, to ensure that the strategies formulated will remain viable after implementation. Under some conditions at least, one or the other of these assumptions proves false.

In an unstable environment, or one too complex to be comprehended in a single brain, the dichotomy has to be collapsed in one of two ways. If the necessary information can be comprehended in one brain, but the environment is unpredictable—or perhaps more commonly, takes time to figure out after an unexpected shift—then the "formulator" may have to "implement" him- or herself. In other words, thinking and action must proceed in tandem, closely associated: the thinker exercises close control over the actions. The leader (or a small group) develops some preliminary ideas, tries them out tentatively, modifies them, tries again, and continues until a viable strategy emerges, much as Quinn described the process, or continues to act even if one does not.

Such close control of a leader over both formulation and implementation is characteristic of the entrepreneurial mode of strategy making, where power is highly centralized in a flexible organization. It may sometimes be "opportunistic," as Andrews claims, but such opportunism can be necessary, in and of itself or more productively perhaps, as a means to experiment and learn.

Where there is too much information to be comprehended in one brain—for example, in organizations dependent on a great deal of sophisticated expertise, as in high-technology firms, hospitals, and universities—then the strategy may have to be worked out on a collective basis. Here, then, the dichotomy collapses in the other direction: the implementors become the formulators.

Both situations—formulators implementing and implementors formulating—amount to the same thing in one important respect: the organizations are *learning*. Andrews's great mistake was dismissing organizational learning by considering it opportunism. Even though he recognized the intertwining of formulation and implementation in practice, his making of the distinction *conceptually* led him to underestimate the important role of such learning, individually and especially collectively, over time, in strategy formation. More generally, the design school, by implicitly assuming that strategic learning somehow takes place in one head for a limited period of time and then stops, so that strategies can be articulated and implementation can begin, denied processes that have often proved critical to the creation of novel and effective strategies.

Out of all this discussion comes a whole range of possible relationships between thought and action. There are times when thought does, and should, precede action and guide it primarily, so that, despite some inevitable slippage, the dichotomy between formulation and implementation does hold up, more or less.

Other times, however, especially during or immediately after a major unexpected shift in the environment, thought must be so bound up with action in an interactive and continuous process that learning becomes a better label, and concept, for what happens then is "formulation-implementation."

And then, perhaps most common, are a whole range of possibilities in between—"implementation as evolution," as Majone and Wildavsky (1978) put it—where there is thought, then there is action, this produces learning that alters thought, followed by adjustments to action, and so on. Intended strategies exist, but realized strategies have emergent as well as deliberate characteristics. Here words like *formulation* and *implementation* should be used only with caution, as should the design school model of strategy formation.

The Design School: Context and Contribution

Our critique has not been intended to dismiss the design school model, but rather the assumption of its universality, that it somehow represents the one best way to make strategy.

Andrews thought it sufficient to delineate one model and then add qualifications to it. The impression left was that this was the way to make strategy, although with nuance, sometimes more, sometimes less. But that had the effect of associating strategy making with deliberate, centralized behavior and of slighting the equally important needs for emergent behavior and organizational learning. Another extreme—the "grassroots model"—makes no more sense, since it overstates equally. But by positioning these two at ends of a continuum, we can begin to consider real-world needs along it.

That is why the field of strategic management has need for these different schools of thought, so long as each is considered carefully in its own appropriate context.

Accordingly, we can begin to delineate the conditions that should encourage an organization to tilt toward the design school model end of the continuum. We see a set of four in particular.

- One brain can, in principle, handle all of the information relevant for strategy formation.
- That brain has full, detailed, intimate knowledge of the situation in question.
- The relevant knowledge is established and set before a new intended strategy has to be implemented—in other words, the situation is relatively stable or at least predictable.
- The organization in question is prepared to cope with a centrally articulated strategy.

These conditions suggest some clear contexts in which the design school model would seem to apply best—its own particular niche, so to speak, related to time as well as situation. In other words, this is a model to be applied only in certain kinds of organizations, and even there only in certain circumstances. Above all is the organization that needs a major reorientation, a new conception of its strategy. *The design school model would seem to apply best at the junction of major shift for an organization, coming out of a period of changing circumstances and into one of operating stability.*

The structural context Andrews seemed to favor for his model (although he would hardly use the label we are about to apply to it), and the one that appears to be most appropriate for the period of reconception of strategy in an existing organization, is what we call machine bureaucracy (see Mintzberg's article in chapter 9). This is structure characterized by a centralization of authority and a relatively stable context of operations, typically used in mass production and the mass delivery of services. Machine bureaucracies commonly pursue highly articulated and stable strategies. They therefore require in periods of reconception much of what the design school has to offer: a process whereby someone in central command somehow pulls the new conception together—defines it if not actually creates it—and then articulates it fully so that everyone else can implement it and then pursue it.

But there is an interesting anomaly here. The call from the design school for personalized and creative forms of strategic management (one strategist, strategies as novel conceptions) is not really compatible with machine bureaucracy, which tends to rely on standardized procedures and detached forms of control. In other words, machine bureaucracies are not mobiles to effect strategic change but stabiles for the continued pursuit of given strategies. For example, our own research on strategy formation suggests that chief executives of machine bureaucracies tend to be caretakers of existing strategies—fine-tuners of set directions rather than champions of radically new ones, in part because of the constraints imposed by their own standardized procedures. These organizations are, after all, machines dedicated to the pursuit of efficiency in very specific domains. Indeed, the whole array of mechanisms proposed in the design school's own model of implementation—performance measures, incentive systems, various other control procedures, not to mention the articulation of strategy itself, as noted earlier—once in place act not to promote change in strategy but to resist it. Formal implementation, ironically, impedes reformulation.

Major reformulation in machine bureaucracy typically occurs through a form of revolution; power is centralized around a single leader who acts personally and decisively to unfreeze existing practices and impose a new vision. In other words, in such "turnarounds," the organization tends to revert to the more flexible simple structure and to its more entrepreneurial mode of strategy making, at least until it has developed a new realized strategy, after which it tends to settle back down to its old machine bureaucratic way of functioning.

As for more complex types of organizations, which depend on expertise for their functioning, as we have argued elsewhere, "professional bureaucracies" and "adhocracies" cannot rely on the conventional prescriptive approaches to strategy making, whether design, planning, or positioning school-oriented, but must instead tilt toward the learning end of the continuum, developing strategies that are more emergent in nature through processes that have more of a grassroots orientation.

Round 2: Response to Henry Mintzberg

By Igor Ansoff

According to Mintzberg, for all intents and purposes, all of the prescriptive schools for strategy formulation should be committed to the garbage heap of history, leaving the field to the emerging strategy school he represents.

Many readers will recognize that the author of this paper is a forty-year-long card-carrying member of one of the schools that Henry confines to obscurity. These readers are also likely to know that my entire professional career has been focused on helping organizations manage their strategic behavior in unpredictable environments. Thus, if I am to accept his verdict, I have spent forty years contributing solutions that are not useful in the practice of strategic management.

Therefore, it should not be surprising that I rise in defense of at least one prescriptive school (the one to which I belong) in an effort to set the record straight and thus salvage a lifetime of work that has received a modicum of acceptance by practicing managers.

Mintzberg's Model of Strategy Formation

The critique is not confined to proving that the design school's and other prescriptive schools' principles are wrong. Interwoven with the critique are Mintzberg's own descriptive assertions about the real world, which he proceeds to convert into prescriptions for the manner in which strategy formation should take place in organizations. Sprinkled throughout the text, these prescriptions are neither summarized nor logically connected.

Therefore, the summary given below is this writer's attempt at a faithful summary of Henry's proposals.

- The central prescription is that with minor exceptions, all organizations should use what Mintzberg calls the emergent-strategy approach to strategy formation, using a trial-and-experience process.

- The output of this process is an observable strategy that is the logical pattern underlying the historical sequence of successful trials.
- Except for minor exceptions, this strategy should not be made explicit.
- It is not possible to formulate strategy in unpredictable environments.
- Nor is it possible to formulate a viable strategy in predictable environments.
- It is not possible to forecast the future with complete confidence.

Mintzberg's concern with managers' need "to be sure," and his assertion that they "cannot" act before they are sure, permeates the paper and is used as a basis for several descriptions and prescriptions, including the following:

- Managers should not make statements about the future if they are not totally sure of what they are saying.
- Managers should not evaluate their organization's strengths and weaknesses until they become evident from the trial-and-error experience.
- In complex organizations it is not possible to plan and coordinate an organization-wide process of strategy formulation.

Henry's prescription can be named as one of implicit strategy formation, under which strategy need not be a part of manager's concern, except under special circumstances. Managers should allow strategy and capabilities to evolve organically, through trial and experience, and focus their attention on the operating efficiency of the organization. Thus, Mintzberg prescribes a world free of explicit strategy formulation and free of strategic managers.

Critique of Mintzberg's Model

Self-Denial of a Chance to Study the Business Environment

It is strange how in his paper Mintzberg repeatedly commits sins of which he accuses the design and the other prescriptive schools. One of these is the accusation directed at the design school that it "slight[s] the environment in favor of a focus on the organization."

Henry's paper shows that he commits the same sin. This slight of the environment is unfortunate. If he had taken the minimum trouble to peruse the cover pages of *Business Week* for the past four to five years, he would have easily found the following information:

- In today's world, different types of organizations have different environments. Thus, since the 1940s the environment of many business firms has progressively become more and more turbulent, unpredictable, and surprising. On the other hand, the not-for-profit organization enjoyed a relatively placid environment until the 1970s.
- Within the two classes of organizations, the environments of different industries became differentiated. At one extreme, some organizations continue to enjoy a relatively placid existence; at the other extreme are organizations experiencing very high turbulence.
- The level of environmental turbulence has become a driving force that dictates strategic responses necessary for success.
- In high-turbulence environments success comes to firms which use strategies which are discontinuous from their historical strategies.
- In low-turbulence environments success comes to firms which use strategies of incremental development of their historically successful product development.

■ The final characteristic of the environment neglected by Mintzberg is the acceleration of the speed of change in the environment that has occurred during the past thirty years.

The latter aspect of the environment puts in doubt the major prescription Mintzberg offers in his paper. In turbulent environments, the speed at which changes develop is such that firms which use the emerging strategy formation advocated by Mintzberg endanger their own survival. When they arrive on a market with a new product or service, such firms find the market preempted by more foresightful competitors who plan their strategic moves in advance.

Failure to Meet Validity Tests for Prescriptive and Descriptive Observations

To be valid, a descriptive observation must meet a single test: it must be an accurate observation of reality. A prescription must pass a much more rigorous test: it must offer evidence that use of the prescription will enable an organization to meet the objective by which it judges its success.

Mintzberg seems oblivious to the need for evidence to support his descriptive statements, and he converts descriptions into prescriptions without offering any evidence that they will bring success to organizations using them. Without any prior evidence, Henry offers the following description: ."Sometimes organizations . . . need to function during periods of unpredictability, *when they cannot possibly hope to articulate any viable strategy* [emphasis added]." Having stated the description, Henry offers the following prescription, again without any supporting evidence: "When strategists are not sure, they had better not articulate strategies, *for all the reasons given above* [emphasis added]."

However, a careful and multiple rereading of the preceding text fails to reveal any "reason," only Mintzberg's unarticulated conviction, which permeates the paper, that strategy formulation is impossible unless the environment is "stable and predictable."

We must now deal with the origin of this conviction.

Descriptive Definition of Strategy

If Henry had taken the trouble to acquaint himself with the history and current practice of strategic management, he would have found widespread use of explicit a priori strategy formulation. Furthermore, he would have found that this formulation is typically used in environments in which managers are not sure about the future. Thus, once more, Henry's assertion is contradicted by facts. In this case the explanation is twofold.

The first is the black-and-white picture of the environment painted by Mintzberg: managers are either sure or totally unsure about the future. In the real world of management these two extremes are rarely observable. In practice, managers are typically partially unsure. And they formulate strategy precisely because being unsure makes it dangerous to assume that the firm's future will be an extrapolation of the past.

The second explanation is found in the difference between Henry's definition of the concept of strategy and the definition used in practice. His definition is *descriptive*, since in order to identify the strategy it is necessary to wait until a series of strategic moves has been completed. But the concept used in practice is *prescriptive* and stipulates that strategy should be formulated in advance of the events that make it necessary. Thus Henry's failure to differentiate between descriptive and prescriptive statements once again places him in the position of contradicting observable reality.

Use of the Existential Model of Learning

The model of organizational learning advocated by Mintzberg consists of a sequential trial-and-error process, neither preceded nor interrupted nor followed by cognitive strategy formulation. To be sure, under special circumstances he allows the possibility of postexperience strategy diagnosis. But nowhere in the paper does he suggest that the diagnosed strategy should in any way affect the choice of subsequent strategic moves. In fact, as cited before, Mintzberg considers explicit strategies to be "blinders designed to block out peripheral vision."

This model of learning is the oldest one in human history. It was the model of prehistoric man when he ventured from his cave in search for food. It was also the model of the master builders in the Middle Ages who created glorious cathedrals by repeating lessons learned from past successes, without understanding what made the cathedrals stand or fall. This was also the model used to train new apprentices by putting them to work under direct guidance of experienced master builders. We shall refer to it as the *existential* model of learning.

Henry's insistence on exclusive use of this most rudimentary model of learning in formation of strategy is ironic, because it is the model on which the Harvard Business School case method, which he criticizes at length, was originally built.

The Enlightenment ushered a new model that recognized the importance of cognition in human affairs. In this model decision making is the first stage, followed by implementation of the decision. It became the standard model of the natural sciences, and it was the model used in early prescriptions for strategic planning. We shall call this model the *rational* model of learning.

The rational model has several advantages over the existential:

- In cases in which decision making is less time-consuming than trial and error, the rational model saves time by selecting action alternatives that are most likely to produce success. This time saving is of great importance in organizations that find themselves in rapidly changing environments.
- It permits additional savings of time through starting strategic response in anticipation of need to act—a process called strategic planning.
- It reduces the number of strategic errors and reduces costs by eliminating the probable "nonstarters" from the list of possible strategic moves.

Thus, the rational model becomes particularly important when the cost of a failed trial is very high, as in the case of diversification by business firms.

Mintzberg makes no mention of the fact that the rational model is a legitimate alternative to the existential model. Henry neglects two facts that are readily available in the literature of the prescriptive schools.

The first is that the strategy concept used in practice does not specify alternatives. On the contrary, it sets guidelines for the *kinds* of opportunities the firm wants to develop through research and creativity. The second fact is that successful practitioners of strategy typically use a strategic control mechanism that periodically reviews and, if necessary, revises the strategy in light of experience. Thus, use of explicit strategy in successful practice is not rigid and does not preclude attention to new opportunities outside the scope of strategy. But use of explicit strategy does control erratic deviations from the strategy. Use of strategic control converts the rational learning mode into a more sophisticated one. The model becomes a chain of cognition-trial-cognition-trial, ad infinitum. We will refer to it as *strategic learning* model (Ansoff and McDonnell, 1990).

Failure to Identify Relevant Context

The most curious and damaging aspect of Mintzberg's model of strategy formation lies in his failure to identify the context in which his model is valid. It is curious because, as already discussed in this paper, Mintzberg does identify the context for the design school model. And in his other work he was one of the first researchers to call attention to the importance of a contextual view of organizational structures (see chapter 9).

And yet, it is the opinion of this writer that if streamlined and put into proper context, Mintzberg's model of strategy has demonstrable validity, both descriptively and prescriptively, and represents an insightful and important contribution to strategic management.

Empirical research (Ansoff and Sullivan, 1990) shows that Mintzberg's prescriptive model is a valid prescription for organizations that seek to optimize their performance in environments in which strategic changes are incremental and the speed of the changes is slower than the speed of the organizational response.

Finally, it is necessary to recognize that the context of the Mintzberg's descriptive validity is much larger than the prescriptive. This context includes firms that are successful in extrapolative business environments (in business jargon those are called market-driven firms); firms in discontinuous environments that are suffering from loss of competitiveness; and it includes a majority of the not-for-profit organizations in the United States.

Round 3: Learning 1, Planning 0; Reply to Igor Ansoff

By Henry Mintzberg

While debates abound about rationality versus incrementalism, or planning versus learning, and great gobs of wonderfully scientific statistics have been collected on the subject (not the best of which is that whole "does planning pay?" literature, which never proved anything), we do have one rather tangible data point. It is Richard Pascale's account by several Honda executives about how they developed on-site the strategy that captured two-thirds of the American motorcycle market. What is especially fascinating about this messy account is that it stands in sharp contrast to the brilliantly rational strategy imputed to these executives by BCG consultants, who apparently never bothered to ask.

Honda's success, if we are to believe those who did it and not those who figured it, was built precisely on what they initially believed to be one of Igor's "probable 'nonstarters'"—namely, the small motorcycle. Their own prior assumptions were that a market without small motorcycles would not buy small motorcycles. Had they a proper planning process in place, as Igor describes it in these pages, this nonstarter would have been eliminated at the outset—plan "rationally" and be done with it. But Honda was badly managed in this regard, and so a few Japanese managers, riding around on those little things in Los Angeles, were pleasantly surprised. They learned. (General Motors was apparently well managed in this regard, because a product development manager there once told me that they had a minivan on the drawing boards long before Chrysler ever did but that this "probable nonstarter" was scuttled in the planning process!)

We think we are so awfully smart. We can work it all out in advance, so cleverly, we "rational" human beings, products of the Enlightenment. We can predict the future, identify the nonstarters, impose our minds on all that matter. And why not. After all, aren't we the ones who live in turbulent times? That makes us important, doesn't it?

Come on, Igor. Of course we need to think. Of course we want to be rational. But it's a complicated world out there. We both know that we shall get nowhere without an emergent learning alongside deliberate planning. If we have discovered anything at all these many years, it is, first, that the conception of a novel strategy is a creative process (of synthesis), for which there are no formal techniques (analysis), and second, that to program these strategies throughout complex organizations, and out to assenting environments, we often require a good deal of formal analysis. So the two processes can intertwine. I'll use your words: "cognition-trial-cognition-trial, etc." We may differ on where to begin, but once it has gone on for a while, who cares? (Does it matter if the chicken or the egg came first?) You call it strategic learning. I have no problem with that so long as you don't pretend it can be formalized. And in return I'll promise never to claim that planning shouldn't be formalized. (Sounds like a good deal to me!)

Winston Churchill is reported to have defined planning as "deciding to put one foot in front of the other." I like to say that strategy and structure proceed like two feet walking: strategy always precedes structure, and always follows it too. And so it is with planning and learning.

Our problem, in practice and academia, has always been one of imbalance, the assumption that planning (or learning) could do it all. As I see things, long ago we may have been weak on rational analysis, but today we have an excess of it. What you call the age of enlightenment has become blinding. Contrary to your criticism, I *am* well aware of the "widespread use of explicit a priori strategy formulation" in our organizations—that is exactly the problem. For example, I have come to suspect that Harvard's great success may be business's great failure. In other words, the real danger of the design school may be in providing a seductive model whose superficial "rationality" in the classroom can so easily get promoted into the executive suite.

You claim, Igor, that rationality saves time. Maybe that is all too true: in formulating detached, easy strategies in case study discussions, later in executive meetings, that are not meant to be implemented, and later cannot be, and in giving all those whiz kids a head start down the fast track. They can certainly tell a probable nonstarter from a winner, at least a priori.

And let's not let ourselves be seduced by the "facts," or by "science." A score of 1 to 0 for informal learning over formal planning reflects not the wealth of management practice, but the poverty of the performance of all of us at the game of research.

References and Suggested Readings

Aaker, D. A., *Strategic Market Management*, Third Edition, Wiley, New York, 1992.

Ackoff, R. L., *Creating the Corporate Future*, Wiley, New York, 1980.

Andrews, K. R., *The Concept of Corporate Strategy*, Third Edition, Irwin, Homewood, IL, 1987.

Ansoff, H. I., *Corporate Strategy: An Analytical Approach to Business Policy for Growth and Expansion*, McGraw-Hill, New York, 1965.

Ansoff, H. I., Critique of Henry Mintzberg's The "Design School": Reconsidering the Basic Premises of Strategic Management, *Strategic Management Journal*, September 1991, pp. 449–461.

Ansoff, H. I., and E. McDonnell, *Implanting Strategic Management,* Second Edition, Prentice Hall, New York, 1990.

Ansoff, H. I., and P. Sullivan, Competitiveness through Strategic Response, in Gilman, R. (Ed.), *Making Organizations More Competitive: Constantly Improving Everything Inside and Outside the Organization,* Jossey-Bass, San Francisco, 1990.

Astley, W. G., Axelsson, R., Butler, R. J., Hickson, D. J., and D. C. Wilson, Complexity and Cleavage: Dual Explanations of Strategic Decision Making, *Journal of Management Studies,* October 1982, pp. 357–375.

Bailey, A., and G. Johnson, How Strategies Develop in Organizations, in Faulkner, D., and G. Johnson (Eds.), *The Challenge of Strategic Management,* Kogan Page, London, 1992.

Bowman, C., and G. Johnson, Surfacing Competitive Strategies, *European Management Journal,* June 1992, pp. 210–219.

Chaffee, E. E., Three Models of Strategy, *Academy of Management Review,* January 1985, pp. 89–98.

Chandler, A. D., *Strategy and Structure: Chapters in the History of the American Industrial Enterprise,* MIT Press, Cambridge, MA, 1962.

Channon, D. F., Strategy Formulation as an Analytical Process, *International Studies of Management and Organization,* Summer 1977, pp. 41–57.

Christensen, C. R., Andrews, K. R., Bower, J. L., Hamermesh, R. G., and M. E. Porter, *Business Policy: Text and Cases,* Fifth and Sixth Editions, Irwin, Homewood, IL, 1982 and 1987.

Cohen, M. D., March, J. G., and J. P. Olsen, A Garbage Can Model of Organization Choice, *Administrative Science Quarterly,* March 1972, pp. 1–25.

Cyert, R. M., and J. G. March, *A Behavioral Theory of the Firm,* Prentice Hall, Englewood Cliffs, NJ, 1963.

Edwards, J. P., Strategy Formulation as a Stylistic Process, *International Studies of Management and Organizations,* Summer 1977, pp. 13–27

Fahey, L., On Strategic Management Decision Processes, *Strategic Management Journal,* January/March 1981, pp. 43–60.

Faulkner, D., and G. Johnson, *The Challenge of Strategic Management,* Kogan Page, London, 1992.

Frederickson, J. W., Strategic Process: Questions and Recommendations, *Academy of Management Review,* October 1983, pp. 565–575.

Goold, M., Research Notes and Communications Design, Learning and Planning: A Further Observation on the Design School Debate, *Strategic Management Journal,* February 1992, pp. 169–170.

Hayes, R. H., Strategic Planning – Forward in Reverse?, *Harvard Business Review,* November/December 1985, pp. 111–119.

Hedberg, B., and S. A. Jonsson, Strategy Formation as a Discontinuous Process, *International Studies of Management and Organization,* Summer 1977, pp. 88–109.

Idenburg, P. J., Four Styles of Strategy Development, *Long Range Planning,* December 1993, pp. 132–137.

Janis, I. L., Sources of Error in Strategic Decision Making, in Pennings, J. M. (Ed.), *Organizational Strategy and Change,* Jossey-Bass, San Francisco, 1985.

Johnson, G., Rethinking Incrementalis.m, *Strategic Management Journal*, January/February 1988, pp. 75–91.

Johnson, G., *Strategic Change and the Management Process*, Basil Blackwell, Oxford, 1987.

Kagano, T., Nonaka, K., Sakakibara, K., and A. Okumura, *Strategic versus Evolutionary Management: A US-Japan Comparison of Strategy and Organization*, Advanced Series in Management, Elsevier, Amsterdam, 1985.

Lenz, R. T. Strategic Capability: A Concept and Framework for Analysis, *Academy of Management Review*, April 1980, pp. 225–234.

Lindblom, C. E., The Science of Muddling Through, *Public Administration Review*, Spring 1959, pp. 79–88.

Lindblom, C. E., Still Muddling, Not Yet Through, *Public Administration Review*, November/December 1979, pp. 517–526.

Lyles, M. A., Formulating Strategic Problems, Empirical Analysis and Model Development, *Strategic Management Journal*, January/March 1981, pp. 61–75.

MacMillan, I. C., *Strategy Formulation: Political Concepts*, West, St. Paul, MN, 1978.

Majone, G., and A. Wildavsky, Implementation as Evolution, *Policy Studies Review Annual*, 1978, pp. 103–117.

Miller, D., and P. H. Friesen, Structural Change and Performance: Quantum vs. Piecemeal-Incremental Approaches, *Academy of Management Journal*, December 1982, pp. 867–892.

Mintzberg, H., Patterns in Strategy Formation, *Management Science*, May 1978, pp. 934–948.

Mintzberg, H., Crafting Strategy, *Harvard Business Review*, July/August 1987, pp. 66–75.

Mintzberg, H., Strategy Formation: Schools of Thought, in Frederickson, J. (Ed.), *Perspectives on Strategic Management*, Harper & Row, New York, 1990.

Mintzberg, H., The Design School: Reconsidering the Basic Premises of Strategic Management, *Strategic Management Journal*, March 1990, pp. 171–195.

Mintzberg, H., Learning 1, Planning 0: Reply to Igor Ansoff, *Strategic Management Journal*, September 1991, pp. 463–466.

Mintzberg, H., Raisinghani, O., and A. Theoret, The Structure of Unstructured Decision Processes, *Administrative Science Quarterly*, June 1976, pp. 246–275.

Nelson, R. R., and S. G. Winter, *An Evolutionary Theory of Economic Change*, Harvard University Press, Cambridge, MA, 1982.

Noel, A., Strategic Cores and Magnificent Obsessions: Discovering Strategy Formulation through Daily Activities of CEOs, *Strategic Management Journal*, Summer 1989, pp. 33–49.

Pascale, R. T., Perspectives on Strategy: The Real Story Behind Honda's Success, *California Management Review*, Spring 1984, pp. 47–72.

Peters, T. J., and R. H. Waterman, *In Search of Excellence*, Harper & Row, New York, 1982.

Pettigrew, A. M., Strategy Formulation as a Political Process, *International Studies of Management and Organization*, Summer 1977, pp. 78–87.

Pettigrew, A. M., *The Management of Strategic Change*, Basil Blackwell, Oxford, 1988.

Pfeffer, J., and G. R. Salancik, *The External Control of Organizations, A Resource Dependency Perspective*, Harper & Row, New York, 1978.

Pondy, I. R., and A. S. Huff, Achieving Routine in Organizational Change, *Journal of Management,* Summer 1985, pp. 102–116.

Quinn, J. B., Strategic Goals: Process and Politics, *Sloan Management Review,* Fall 1977, pp. 21–37.

Quinn, J. B., Strategic Change: "Logical Incrementalism," *Sloan Management Review,* Fall 1978, pp. 7–21.

Quinn, J. B., *Strategies for Change,* Irwin, Homewood, IL, 1980.

Schwenk, C. R., Cognitive Simplification Processes in Strategic Decision Making, *Strategic Management Journal,* April/June 1984, pp. 111–128.

Shrader, C. B., Taylor, I., and D. R. Dalton, Strategic Planning and Organizational Performance: A Critical Appraisal, *Journal of Management,* Summer 1984, pp. 149–171.

Shrivastava, P., Is Strategic Management Ideological? *Journal of Management,* Fall 1986, pp. 363–377.

Shrivastava, P., and J. H. Grant, Empirically Derived Models of Strategic Decision-Making Processes, *Strategic Management Journal,* April/June 1985, pp. 97–113.

Stacey, R. D., *Strategic Management and Organisational Dynamics,* Pitman Publishing, London, 1993.

Weick, K. E., Substitutes for Corporate Strategy, in Teece, D. J. (Ed.), *The Competitive Challenge: Strategies for Industrial Innovation and Renewal,* Ballinger, Cambridge, MA, 1987.

Wheelen, T. L., and J. D. Hunger, *Strategic Management and Business Policy,* Fourth Edition, Addison-Wesley, 1992.

Wissema, J. G., Van der Pol, H. W., and H. M. Messer, Strategic Management Archetypes, *Strategic Management Journal,* January/March 1980, pp. 37–47.

Chapter 3
Strategy Process Organisation:
On Procedures and Perspectives

Prediction is very difficult,
especially about the future.
 —*Niels Bohr*
  1885–1962, Danish physicist

Introduction

The fundamental discussion on strategy process paradigms in chapter 2 was not solely intended to be intellectually stimulating. For the strategist, a debate on principles is not an end, but a means—a useful starting point when trying to organise the strategy process. After all, the use of different strategy process paradigms will "translate" into different ways of setting up, conducting, and participating in the strategy process.

In chapter 3 this step from strategy process principles to *strategy process organisation* will be the main focus. The articles in this chapter will explore how the planning and incrementalist approaches can actually be used to structure and influence the formulation and implementation of strategy.

The structure of this chapter closely resembles that of chapter 2—the opening articles are slanted toward the planning approach, while the later articles take a more strongly incrementalist point of view. However, while it was the intention of chapter 2 to polarise the debate on paradigms so that the ends of the planning-incrementalist continuum were clearly established, the discussion in chapter 3 is more evenly spread out between the two extremes.

It should be pointed out that as the articles move from a planning to an incrementalist approach, their attention slowly shifts from formal to informal aspects of the strategy process organisation. This difference in emphasis is reflected in the subtitle of this chapter. The first articles focus on *procedures*—the formal structure of the strategic planning system. In these articles issues such as planning steps, timetables, process participants, formal responsibilities, information systems, use of analytical techniques, budgeting procedures, and control systems are discussed. Gradually, however, there is a shift in the focus of the articles toward *perspectives*—the way of thinking and behaving in the organisation that will influence the effectiveness of the strategy process. These articles deal with issues such as management style, leadership roles, strategic vision, creating organisational awareness, political decision making, and mental models as important ingredients of the strategy process organisation. Again it is up to the readers to select—or, more likely, combine—approaches they believe will lead to the most effective way of going about making strategy.

The Articles

Two of the most well-known writers on the topic of formal planning systems are Balaji Chakravarthy and Peter Lorange. The first article in this chapter, "Managing the Strategy Process," is taken from their book of the same name. In this article, Chakravarthy and Lorange "translate" the general planning models as outlined in chapter 2 into organisational *procedures*. The framework they present is a general blueprint that details the strategic planning steps an organisation must go through sequentially to arrive at an effective strategy. Their focus on formalisation of the strategy process by means of organisational procedures, structural mechanisms, and fixed tasks places their approach firmly within the mainstream of the planning tradition. What distinguishes Chakravarthy and Lorange's framework from many other prescriptive planning models is that it places more emphasis on the fact that the strategic planning system cannot exist in an organisational vacuum. They explicitly argue that the strategic planning system must be linked to the monitoring, control, incentive, and staffing systems of the organisation to be effective, since plans must not only be made, but also implemented.

The following two articles in this chapter accept the necessity of a formalised strategic planning system as proposed by Chakravarthy and Lorange, but argue that in practice such systems have many shortcomings that need to be remedied. The first of these "reformist" articles is a rather mild critique entitled "Is Your Planning System Becoming Too Rational?" As the title indicates, the authors of this article, R. T. Lenz and Marjorie Lyles, believe that many strategic planning systems are too formalised, inflexible, and excessively quantitative—in short, too rational. They argue that while there is nothing wrong with formal planning itself, planning systems can easily degenerate into a bureaucratic state of overrationality if the wrong planning culture evolves. Factors such as the professionalisation of the planner's job, emphasis on planning routine, and the unquestioning use of analytical techniques all reinforce the downward spiral. The "antidote" that Lenz and Lyles propose is a change in the planning culture, mainly by creating awareness about the role that strategic planning should play within the organisation.

The criticisms of the second "reformer," Thomas Marx, go a step further. In his article, "Removing the Obstacles to Effective Strategic Planning," Marx unconditionally supports the need for strategic planning, but does not believe that the procedures currently employed to operationalise planning are particularly effective. In fact, he argues that many of the characteristics normally associated with planning, such as "formal presentations, large meetings, massive planning books, and regularly scheduled, annual reviews," are actually the obstacles to strategic planning that need to be removed. The crux of Marx's argument is that excessive formalisation is a developmental phase that most strategic planning systems go through. He therefore recommends that companies should not abandon planning but should progress beyond this formalisation phase and develop a more "lean and mean" strategic planning system.

The fourth article in this chapter, "Linking Planning and Implementation," is even further removed from the traditional planning approach. The authors of this article, L. J. Bourgeois and David Brodwin, argue that one of the most fundamental problems inherent in most strategic planning systems is the split between the formulation and implementation of strategy. Most planning systems, according to Bourgeois and Brodwin, separate the "thinkers," who formulate, from the "doers," who implement. Often the thinking is limited to the CEO, while the rest of the organisation must execute the plans handed to them. There are situations, the authors stress, where it makes sense to have this *top-down approach* to the strategy process ("the CEO as master planner"). However, Bourgeois and Brodwin believe there are many more circumstances in which a *bottom-up approach* would be more effective ("the CEO as guide and judge"). Such a bottom-up approach, which the authors call *crescive*, would make it possible to address formulation and implementation simultaneously, allowing strategies to *emerge* during the process. Adapting the traditional strategic planning system by incorporating the crescive approach would endow a formal planning system with many incremental characteristics—making it an interesting compromise between the planning and incrementalist perspectives.

The fifth article in this chapter, "Managing Strategic Change," by James Quinn, is the obvious choice to represent the incrementalist school of thought. This article, which was written as a follow-up to Quinn's article in chapter 2, "translates" the basic premises of logical incrementalism into an actual methodology for managing the strategy process and achieving strategic change. His approach stresses measures for building organisational awareness, understanding, and psychological commitment; overcoming personal and political resistance to change; and dealing with varying lead times and sequencing problems in critical decisions.

Since Quinn's article was published, researchers within the incrementalist tradition have had a particular interest in the related topics of strategic change, strategic flexibility and strategic learning. One of the most stimulating contributions in this newest crop of writings is "Building Learning Organizations." This article by Peter Senge is the sixth and final article of this chapter. While Quinn aspires to change our approach to the strategy process, Senge intends to change our approach to the entire organisation. He argues that the performance of organisations will increasingly depend on their ability to learn and change. In the context of this chapter, his message is that tinkering with the planning system is insufficient to ensure superior organisational performance over the long run. For an effective strategy process to evolve, the way the entire organisation is managed must be changed. The roles of management must be redefined and new management skills must be acquired to enable the organisation to learn.

Recommended Readings and Cases

Although formal planning systems are in widespread use, writings on this topic are largely of a how-to textbook nature. If the reader is interested in such a prescriptive guide, Balaji Chakravarthy and Peter Lorange's *Managing the Strategy Process: A Framework for a Multibusiness Firm* is a good place to start. Much more has been published on strategic learning, change, and flexibility. Arie de Geus has written an interesting article, "Planning as Learning," in which he describes Royal Dutch Shell's use of the planning system to encourage learning. An 'eminence grise' in the area of organisational learning is Chris Argyris, who's more recent book *Overcoming Organizational Defenses: Facilitating Organizational Learning* is also good reading. On the topic of strategic change, Rosabeth Moss Kanter's *The Change Masters* is an excellent starting point. Finally, in the area of strategic flexibility we would recommend J. Stuart Evans's *Strategic Flexibility for High Technology Manoeuvres* as a stimulating reading.

The two cases included in this book that fit this chapter best are the "Strategic Planning at Oldelft" and "Kao Corporation" cases. The Oldelft case, by Ron Meyer, focuses on the formal planning system, while the Kao case, by Sumantra Ghoshal and Charlotte Butler, deals with the organisation's strategic learning ability. Oldelft is a medium-sized high technology company with its home base in the Netherlands, that is struggling to develop an effective formal planning system. This case details the evolution of the planning system in the company and presents the reader with the opportunity to think of ways of improving the formal process. Kao is a very large Japanese fast-moving consumer goods producer that is quickly expanding abroad. This case explains how the company organises its learning and asks the reader to consider how its learning ability can be retained as the company moves beyond the borders of Japan.

■ MANAGING THE STRATEGY PROCESS†

By Balaji Chakravarthy and Peter Lorange

Steps in the Strategy Process

There are five distinct steps in the strategy process (see figure 3-1). The first three steps involve the strategic planning system; the final two steps cover the role of the monitoring, control, and learning system and the incentives and staffing systems, respectively.

The Strategic Planning System

The purpose of the first step in the planning system, *objectives setting*, is to determine a strategic direction for the firm and each of its divisions and business units. Objectives setting calls for an open-ended reassessment of the firm's business environments and

---

†**Source:** This article was adapted with permission from chapter 1 of *Managing the Strategy Process: A Framework for a Multibusiness Firm*, Prentice Hall, Englewood Cliffs, New Jersey, © 1991.

FIGURE 3-1
The Strategy Process

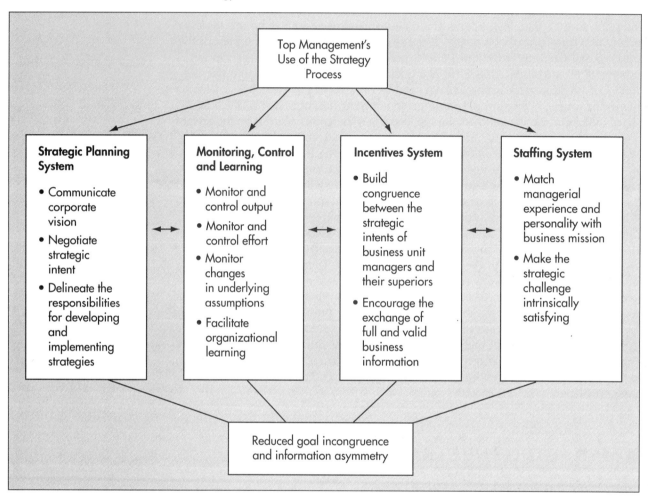

its strengths in dealing with these environments. At the conclusion of this step, there should be agreement at all levels of the organization on the goals that should be pursued and the strategies that will be needed to meet them. It is worth differentiating here between objectives and goals. Objectives refer to the strategic intent of the firm in the long run. Goals, on the other hand, are more specific statements of the achievements targeted for certain deadlines—goals can be accomplished, and when that happens the firm moves closer to meeting its objectives. Objectives represent a more enduring challenge.

The second step, *strategic programming*, develops the strategies identified in the first step and defines the cross-functional programs that will be needed to implement the chosen strategies. Cross-functional cooperation is essential to this step. At the end of the strategic programming step a long-term financial plan is drawn for the firm as a whole and each of its divisions, business units, and functions. On top of the financial projections from existing operations, the long-term financial plan overlays both the expenditures and revenues associated with the approved strategic programs of an organizational unit. The time horizon for these financial plans is chosen to cover the typical lead times that are required to implement the firm's strategic programs. A five-year financial plan is, however, very common. The purpose of the five-year financial plan is to ensure that the approved strategic programs can be funded through either the firm's internally generated resources or externally financed resources.

The third step, *budgeting*, defines both the strategic and operating budgets of the firm. The strategic budget helps identify the contributions that the firm's functional departments, business units, and divisions will be expected to make in a given fiscal year in support of the firm's approved strategic programs. It incorporates new product/market initiatives. The operating budget, on the other hand, provides resources to functional departments, business units, and divisions so that they can sustain their existing momentum. It is based on projected short-term activity levels, given past trends. Failure to meet the operating budget will hurt the firm's short-term performance, whereas failure to meet the strategic budget will compromise the firm's future.

The Monitoring, Control, and Learning System

The fourth step in the strategy process is *monitoring, control, and learning*. Here the emphasis is not on output but on meeting key milestones in the strategic budget and on adhering to planned spending schedules. Strategic programs, like strategic budgets, are monitored for the milestones reached and for adherence to spending schedules. In addition, the key assumptions underlying these programs are validated periodically. As a natural extension to this validation process, even the agreed-on goals at various levels are reassessed in the light of changes to the resources of the firm and its business environment.

The Incentives and Staffing Systems

The fifth and final step in the strategy process is *incentives and staffing*. One part of this is the award of incentives as contracted to the firm's managers. If the incentives system is perceived to have failed in inducing the desired performance, redesigning the incentives system and reassessing the staffing of key managerial positions are considered at this step.

Linking Organizational Levels and Steps in Strategic Planning

An effective strategy process must allow for interactions between the organizational levels and iterations between the process steps. Figure 3-2 describes some of the interactions and iterations in the strategic planning steps. The formal interactions in the process are shown in the figure by the solid line that weaves up and down through the organizational levels and across the three steps. The informal interactions that complement the formal interactions are shown by dotted loops.

Objectives Setting

The first formal step of the strategy process commences soon after top management reaffirms or modifies the firm's objectives at the beginning of each fiscal year. Embedded in these objectives should be the vision of the chief executive officer (CEO)

FIGURE 3-2

Steps in the Strategy Process

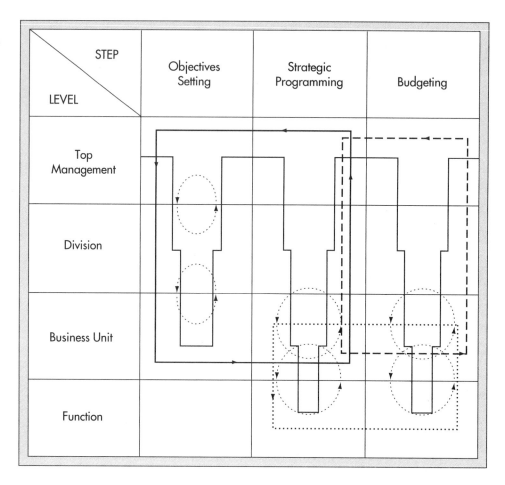

and his or her top management team. Top management's vision helps specify what will make the firm great. An elaboration of this vision can be done through a formal statement of objectives. However, it is not the formality of a firm's objectives but rather the excitement and challenge that top management's vision can bring to a firm's managers that is important to the strategy process.

Along with its communication of corporate objectives, top management must provide a forecast on key environmental factors. Assumptions on exchange rates, inflation, and other economic factors—as well as projections on the political risks associated with each country—are best compiled centrally so as to ensure objectivity and consistency. These objectives and forecasts are then discussed with a firm's divisional and business unit managers.

Once the corporate objectives are decided, top management negotiates, for each division and business unit in the firm, goals that are consistent with these objectives. The nature of these negotiations can vary. In some firms, top management may wish to set goals in a top-down fashion; in others, it may invite subordinate managers to participate in the goal-setting process. Managers are encouraged to examine new strategies and modify existing ones in order to accomplish their goals. The proposed strategies are approved at each higher level in the organizational hierarchy, then eventually by top management. Top management tries to make certain that the strategies as proposed are consistent with the firm's objectives and can be supported with the resources available to the firm. Modifications, where necessary, are made to the objectives, goals, and strategies in order to bring them in alignment. Another important outcome of the objectives-setting step is to build a common understanding across the firm's managerial hierarchy of the goals and strategies that are intended for each organizational unit.

The objectives-setting step in figure 3-2 does not include the functional departments. As we observed earlier, the primary role of these departments is a supporting one. They do not have a profit or growth responsibility, and their goals cannot be decided until the second step, when strategic programs in support of approved business unit goals begin to be formed. It is not uncommon, however, for key functional managers to be invited to participate in the objectives-setting step either as experts in a corporate task force or, more informally, as participants in the deliberations that are held at the business unit level.

It is important that divisional proposals be evaluated on an overall basis as elements of a corporate portfolio and not reviewed in a sequential mode. In the latter case, the resulting overall balance in the corporate portfolio would be more or less incidental, representing the accumulated sum of individual approvals. It makes little sense to attempt to judge in isolation whether a particular business family or business strategy is attractive to the corporate portfolio. That will depend on a strategy's fit with the rest of the portfolio and on the competing investment opportunities available to the firm in its business portfolio.

Strategic Programming

This second step in the process has two purposes: (1) to forge an agreement between divisional, business unit, and functional managers on the strategic programs that have to be implemented over the next few years and (2) to deepen the involvement of functional managers in developing the strategies that were tentatively selected in the first step.

The strategic programming step begins with a communication from top management about the goals and strategies that were finally approved for the firm's divisions and business units. The divisional manager then invites his or her business unit and functional managers to identify program alternatives in support of the approved goals and strategies. Examples of strategic programs include increasing market share for an existing product, introducing a new product, and launching a joint marketing campaign for a family of divisional products. As in these examples, a strategic program typically requires the cooperation of multiple functional departments.

However, the functional specialties within a firm often represent different professional cultures that do not necessarily blend easily. Further, day-to-day operating tasks can be so demanding that the functional managers may simply find it difficult to participate in the time-consuming cross-functional teamwork. A key challenge for both divisional and business managers is to bring about this interaction.

The proposed strategic programs travel up the hierarchy for approval at each level. At the division level, the programs are evaluated not only for how well they support the approved strategies but also for how they promote synergies within the firm. Synergies can come from two sources: through economies of scale and/or economies of scope. The creation of synergies based on economies of scale calls for a sharing of common functional activities—such as research and development (R&D), raw materials procurement, production, and distribution—so as to spread over a larger volume the overhead costs associated with these functions. The creation of economies of scope, on the other hand, requires a common approach to the market. Examples of such an approach include the development of a common trademark, the development of products/services that have a complementary appeal to a customer group, and the ability to offer a common regional service organization for the firm's diverse businesses.

At the corporate level, the proposed strategic programs provide an estimate of the resources that will be required to support the divisional and business unit goals. These goals, as well as their supporting strategies, are once again reassessed; and where needed, modifications are sought in the proposed strategic programs. As noted earlier, a long-term financial plan is drawn at this stage for the firm as a whole and each of its organizational units. The approved strategic programs are communicated to the divisions, business units, and functional departments at the beginning of the budgeting cycle.

Budgeting

When top management decides on the strategic programs that the firm should pursue, it has de facto allocated all of the firm's human, technological, and financial resources that are available for internal development. This allocation influences the strategic budgets that may be requested at each level in the organizational hierarchy.

The strategic budgets, together with the operating budgets of the various organizational units, are consolidated and sent up for top management approval. When top management finally approves the budgets of the various organizational units, before the start of a new budget year, it brings to a close what can be a year-long journey through the three steps of the strategy-making subprocess. The strategy implementation subprocess is then set into motion. Even though the two subprocesses are described sequentially here, it is important to mention that even as the budget for a given year is being formed, the one for the prior year will be under implementation. Midcourse corrections to the prior year's budget can have an impact on the formulation of the current budget.

If the actual accomplishments fall short of the strategic budget, in particular, the negative variance may suggest that the firm's managers failed to implement its chosen strategy efficiently. But it can also suggest that the strategic programs that drive this budget may have been ill conceived or even that the goals underlying these programs may have been specified incorrectly. The monitoring, control, and learning system provides continuous information on both the appropriateness of a strategic budget and the efficiency with which the budget is implemented. This information, based on the implementation of the prior year's strategic budget, can trigger another set of iterations between the three strategy-making steps, calling into question the goals and strategies on which the current year's budget are based. These iterations are shown by the dotted rectangles in figure 3-2.

■ IS YOUR PLANNING SYSTEM BECOMING TOO RATIONAL?[†]

By R.T. Lenz and Marjorie Lyles

Is Your Planning Becoming *too* Rational?

During the past three years, we have been involved in a study of strategic planning processes in several financial and commercial organizations. Our findings, when combined with insight gathered from consulting relationships, reveal a disconcerting trend. With increasing frequency we have observed a variety of bureaucratic processes within organizations and technical developments from without that are causing many planning processes to become too rational. By this we mean a condition in which the strategic planning process has become inflexible, formalized, and excessively quantitative. In this state, the planning system seems to develop an inertia all of its own that can stifle creative thought and frustrate the most able managers. It appears to be a major contributor to the disenchantment experienced by many line and staff members for whom planning has lost its glow.

Excessive Rationality: Its Basic Character and Origins

Nothing would be more comforting than to suggest that the tendency toward excessive rationality in a planning system stems from a single source. If it were so, the problem would be easily recognizable and, probably, rather straightforward to resolve. Unfortunately, it appears that this tendency has multiple origins—none of which is abnormal in organizational life and all of which occur over rather lengthy periods of time. The collective effect of independent decisions and commitments made in the midst of daily administrative affairs can result in an overly rationalized planning process. Its early symptoms are usually felt by managers who sense that the demands placed on them to plan are burdensome in terms of time requirements, and that creativity, innovation, and entrepreneurship are not rewarded. The resulting tension and frustration are mirrored in the remarks of one manager whose views are becoming increasingly widespread:

> "Thank God it's over; now let's get back to work. This is my third strategy review. Same damn outcome. Nothing resolved. Every year we get together, fill in the forms—some of which don't even fit my business (and the planning instruction manual gets thicker by the year), make a two-and-one-half-hour presentation. We never get to the strategic issues. The discussion gets bogged down in nitpicking and number crunching; then we simply run out of time. Nobody really cares what's in the strategic plans. We must put on a good show, appear to be innovative, and go through the ritual. What really counts is the one-year operating budget."

It would be misleading to suggest that either researchers, consultants, or practitioners fully understand the constellation of forces that cause a planning process to become bureaucraticized and ritualistic. Precise answers to such questions will,

†**Source:** Reprinted with permission from *Long Range Planning*, "Paralysis by Analysis: Is Your Planning System Becoming Too Rational?", August 1985, Vol. 18, Pergamon Press Ltd. Oxford, England.

FIGURE 3-3
Forces Contributing to Overrationalized Planning

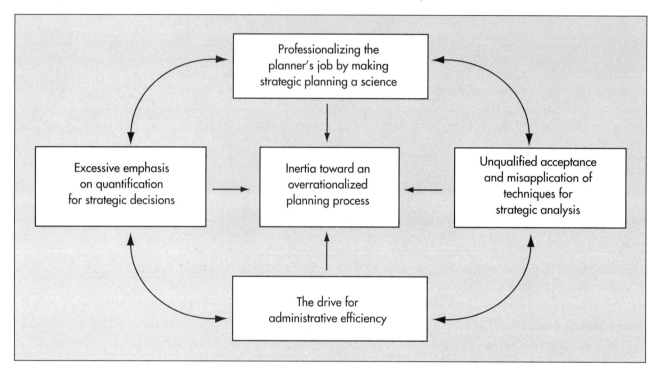

undoubtedly, be forthcoming as more field studies of organizations are undertaken. As it now stands, however, it is clear that both basic administrative processes within most firms and technological developments from outside contribute to excessive rationality. Figure 3-3 includes some of the more salient processes whose overall effect, if not guarded against, is to generate inertia within the planning system toward an overrationalized state.

Any classification of such diverse processes is at this point somewhat arbitrary. Nevertheless, the tendency toward too much rationality seems to be manifest in

- the growing professionalization of the planner's job;
- excessive emphasis on quantification in strategic decision making;
- a drive to make planning routine and administratively efficient;
- the unqualified acceptance and improper use of techniques for strategic analysis.

These processes influence each other in ways that can lead to a self-perpetuating cycle of organizational momentum. Gaining some appreciation for this requires more insight into each process.

Professionalizing the Planner's Job

One of the most important processes, particularly during the last decade, is the growth of planning as a profession. Both corporations and schools of business have done much to single out strategic planning as a high-potential career path. Fast-track programs in major business firms and university curricular developments have contributed to an aura and attractiveness that make careers in planning virtually irresistible. If popular business literature were to be taken at face value, one would come to believe that the corporate planner is a key influential who has the "king's ear" on every strategic decision.

A requirement for maintaining the professional mystique of planning is to cast it into the mold of an exact science. With the help of academicians and consultants this is precisely what has occurred. First came the necessary jargon. Terms such as strategic business unit, growth-share matrix, and GAP analysis became buzzwords of the planning professional. These provided outward and visible signs required to gain and sustain respectability in organizational life. Accompanying this special vocabulary are a variety of research findings and analytical techniques reputed to reveal "laws" of the marketplace. Armed with both an arcane language and a special knowledge of lawful (i.e., predictable) strategic relationships, corporate planning has come to be a "scientific" profession.

The hazards of permitting the planning function to gain professional and scientific status in organizational life are manifold, and more will be said of it later. What is worth noting at this point is that planners are first and foremost staff. Therefore, they feel vulnerable with respect to their organizational status—particularly when going one-on-one with strong line managers. It should come as no surprise, then, that a safe harbor for the corporate planner is specialized knowledge and complex analytical procedures. These are more than tools of the trade: they are independent bases of power for offsetting the prerogatives and stature of line executives and serve as a means for surviving the vagaries of corporate life.

Excessive Emphasis on Quantification

A second process that can make a planning system overly rational is excessive emphasis on quantification. This emphasis is directed at both information used as inputs to the planning process and the level of detail embodied in the corporate plan itself. In each instance there operates an implicit belief that the level of quantification and certainty are directly correlated.

A pervasive belief among many line and staff members is that only quantifiable data are sufficiently reliable bases for planning. Other data, though useful for explaining empirical relationships, lack the "hardness" or certainty required for planning. Beliefs of this sort are seldom expressed nor do they have to be. Nevertheless, they greatly bias the scope and character of information used to plan. Critically important qualitative information, especially that regarding emerging societal values, life-style changes, new directions in technology, and so on, is frequently lost in the shuffle. Partly, this is because models for strategy analysis and most management information systems can only accommodate numbers.

The desire of staff to establish solid planning assumptions is not the only factor contributing to the drive for quantification and certainty. Line managers also share part of the blame. One of the most often observed phenomena in organizational life is the direct correlation between the age of a planning system and the level of detail used for analysis and exhibited in the strategic plan. There are exceptions, of course, but the tendency is for line managers to demand and receive each year more detailed information for preparing plans. Corporate planners are then expected to incorporate such detail into the plan itself. In companies we have seen, the increasing emphasis on detail reflects a continuing quest for certainty. Unfortunately, in most firms this quest proves to be a mirage. What managers usually encounter with increasing levels of detail is not greater certainty, but more ambiguity. As strategic problems are sliced into smaller and smaller pieces, they become fragmented and disjointed. What is lost is coherence.

The Drive for Administrative Efficiency

A third force that can contribute to planning becoming too rational is a drive for administrative efficiency. This drive is not consciously coordinated and typically occurs simultaneously in many parts of an organization. It is usually undertaken to save time and make the planning process less of a chore to manage.

A central administrative problem in organizational life is that of sustaining commitment and enthusiasm to essential tasks. Planning is no exception. A distinct problem with planning processes, however, is that once they are implemented a raft of little decisions are made whose overall effect is to reduce the effectiveness of the process. In the early years of planning the process is usually "loose." That is, it is open to a wide spectrum of information and emphasis is placed on gaining fresh insight into emerging strategic issues. Typically there develops a dense, semistructured pattern of executive interaction. As time passes this looseness begins to be regarded as inefficient. Steps are then taken to improve planning effectiveness by making the process more routine and predictable. Initial changes usually center on standardizing data inputs and the format of planning documents. Unfortunately, this even occurs when strategically significant differences in businesses and markets are blurred by a standard format. Subsequently, attention centers on establishing a timetable for data preparation, meetings, and so on to facilitate more systematic coordination of effort. These decisions are taken throughout an organization in the name of improving the efficiency of the planning process.

Our experience suggests that the dual forces of administrative efficiency and planning effectiveness pull in opposite directions. To obtain more of one you must be ready to give up some of the other. This duality is not merely an academic abstraction. Rather, it is an operational characteristic. As planning systems are made more efficient, the time devoted to creative thought is inevitably reduced. The driving force in the planning process becomes the agreed-upon timetable. Demands for data in fixed formats and formalized executive interactions with a previously established agenda are not conducive to innovative thought and entrepreneurship.

In no sense are we suggesting that a planning process be left entirely unstructured. We are proposing that there is a delicate balance to be maintained between administrative efficiency and planning system effectiveness. And unless executives are alert to this issue, the scale can easily be tipped in a way that undermines the prospect of an organization for achieving strategic success.

Unqualified Acceptance and Misapplication of Analytical Techniques

Findings stemming from the PIMS Program, [see chapter 8, the Baden-Fuller and Stopford article] contributions from finance concerning capital budgeting, the Boston Consulting Group's concept of portfolio analysis, [see chapter 4] and recent outgrowths of industrial organization economics are milestones in strategic thought. These and similar techniques are powerful tools for competitive analysis. However, their function and limits are often ignored in the quest for certainty in strategic decision making. Planning becomes overrationalized when one or more of these techniques become the dominant framework for defining and evaluating strategic choices. The following problems are typical of this condition:

- The particular analytical model used becomes a "filter" that frames managerial thinking. In this mode the model's parameters and structure define strategic problems in such a way that the model can deal with them. Thus, emerging, ill-defined strategic issues that often prove decisive may not be detected because they either do not correspond to variables in the model or fall outside its analytical scope. In a sense, unqualified acceptance of a model for strategy analysis can seriously impair the capacity of an organization to spot problems sufficiently well in advance to formulate and implement a response.

- Many strategy analysis techniques place undue emphasis on a single criterion as the basis for strategic decision making. Both the present-value method and the Boston Consulting Group's portfolio model are primarily concerned with cash flows. Their implication is that the strategic significance of investment decisions and managing a portfolio of diverse businesses is summarized by streams of cash. For the executive, strategic choices are a complex, multidimensional problem. They involve matters that cannot be incorporated by a single measure. Misapplication of these or similar techniques can lead to strategic errors biased by short-term financial considerations that undermine the infrastructure of an organization necessary to sustain it over the long run.

- Proponents of particular analytical techniques usually make it a point to remind potential users of the scope, limits, and assumptions of each technique. Unfortunately, these are often ignored at great risk. The PIMS findings, for example, are based on product life cycle. Whether lawful relationships revealed in this program hold under other circumstances is not known. Thus, generalizing can be perilous. The portfolio model and experience curve (which underpins the BCG portfolio matrix) also have limits. Managers lulled into a false sense of security with these models can wake up to find that competitors placing greater emphasis on product innovation are expanding into new markets with higher rates of return.

- Deterministic thinking often supplants entrepreneurial creativity in strategy making. By this we mean when managers implicitly assume that relationships specified by an analytical model are inevitable and result from irresistible economic and technological trends. For example, some drawing on PIMS research argue that high profits are the outcome of a large market share. Therefore, one should pursue share. This is a case of overgeneralizing a deterministic relationship. It ignores other factors such as profit margins, cost structure, and barriers to industry competitors. The potency of these factors is clear in the world of commerce, which is replete with examples of firms with small market share that are extremely profitable.

The four processes presented in figure 3-3 are primary contributors to excessive rationality in the planning process. Certainly, not all firms experience these in the same proportion. Some never experience them at all. The point is that such processes operate among evolutionary developments that facilitate the normal adaptation of planning systems as organizations grow. When planning becomes too rational it is onerous, dysfunctional, and incapable of producing clear strategic thinking. Organizational consequences of this condition can be very serious.

Organizational Consequences of an Excessively Rational Planning Process

When a planning process becomes too rational, its effects are not localized. Instead, they affect persons in key roles throughout an organization. Of particular importance are the chief executive officer, the corporate planner, senior-level line managers, and board members. Such persons experience the effects somewhat differently. For this reason each deserves individual consideration.

Chief Executive Officer

There are two discernible effects on a chief executive when a planning system becomes too rational. First, the shifting pattern of people, values, aspirations, and commitments that comprise the milieu of executive action seems strangely irrelevant. The organization is discussed as if it were an abstraction to be referenced by carefully defined strategic variables and subject to immutable competitive laws. Intangible qualities of organization that constitute its social structure and sense of collective purpose seem unimportant in the wake of empirical data and statistically verified relationships. A second effect of excessive rationality concerns the role of the chief executive. If strategy formulation is developed within the parameters of a single model, the specification of strategy becomes merely a constrained choice problem. The executive's role is recast from that of institutional leader to one of clerk: in lieu of inventing a future for the organization is an annual endorsement of an inevitable course of action. Admittedly, these effects are exaggerated. But the central point remains that when planning becomes too rational it is devoid of meaning for many senior executives because of its incapacity to capture the complexity of strategic issues.

When confronted with this situation we have seen executives exhibit a variety of responses. Two of these are particularly detrimental to the success of the strategic planning process. One response is to withdraw support from an active participation in the process. It goes without saying that this seriously undermines the integrity of the planning effort by giving mixed signals to other executives. Without visible and enthusiastic support from the chief executive, strategic planning is doomed to failure.

A second and equally destructive consequence of overrationalized planning is for the chief executive officer (CEO) to form a coterie of senior managers for making strategic decisions. Such a group usually comprises certain key executives who share basic values with the chief executive and possess a similar view of the world. Matters of real strategic significance are confronted and dealt with by this group outside of the formal process of strategic planning. Relatively mundane aspects of planning occur within prescribed channels. In this situation the formal planning process can take on the role of an annual exercise that affords little in the way of innovative thought. Few other executive actions have a greater negative impact on the overall effectiveness of strategic planning than withdrawing visible support.

Corporate Planner

Although to some it may seem ironic, corporate planners are often victims of excessive rationality in planning. In their effort to attain organizational respectability as vital contributors to strategic decision making, the trappings of the "science of planning" sometimes create a snare. The snare is slowly fashioned out of the increasingly intricate network of models, data, analytical techniques, and formal procedures. If the process goes too far, these factors establish an intellectual cocoon of abstractions whose relationship to the administrative experiences of line managers is, at best, tenuous. Increasing sophistication can breed increasing irrelevance and the development of a ponderous planning apparatus.

An organizational consequence of such circumstances is to prevent the planner from acting as an otherwise creative agent in the planning process. In place of internal consultant, counselor, and confidant to managers struggling with tough strategic choices, the corporate planner becomes merely a gadfly insuring that deadlines are met and procedures adhered to. The planning process ceases to be an instrument and becomes an end in itself. Administrative success is equated with completing the plan on schedule and in the correct format. For the planner there is little time for creative analysis of strategic opportunities sensed by line managers, since such projects are often precluded by the formal demands of the planning system. Innovation suffers as the planner's role changes from one of catalyst to one of weary coordinator.

Senior Line Managers

By now it must be clear that line managers, too, are victims of too much rationality in planning. They suffer at the hands of executive leadership when an overrationality causes the CEO to withdraw from or bypass the strategic planning process. Such executive actions communicate contradictory signals to midlevel managers. In one breath these managers are reminded of the importance of strategic planning. It is made clear that planning will require much of them and that they will be rewarded if well done. If, simultaneously, the CEO personally disengages from the planning process, what are line managers to do?

Under such circumstances, managers expected to conduct the planning process experience role stress and feelings of ambiguity about planning. These experiences often surface in the form of dysfunctional behaviors that reduce the effectiveness of the planning process. Midlevel managers often send the same mixed signals to subordinates that they have received from their chief executive. Thus, the facade of planning is maintained while the substance of planning is lost. There develops a mere chain of compliance. Managers at all levels come to view the strategic planning process as the nearly unbearable annual ritual that in the end means little.

When the quality of participation in the planning process gravitates from enthusiastic support to reluctant compliance, the capacity of the system to facilitate adaptation is severely impaired. Missing are the priceless inputs from line managers that help an organization sense out shifting environmental contingencies. Early signals of strategic significance are ignored. Without antennae of this sort, the corporation is, at least with respect to subtle changes in competitive conditions, flying blind. If the planning process ceases to be a forum in which entrepreneurial thought and action are encouraged, ambitious, able managers are forced to find other outlets for their creativity. If these are not available, morale declines and a generation of future executives are compelled to conclude that strategic planning is simply another administrative burden they must bear while ascending the organizational hierarchy.

Board Members

Board members are, perhaps, the most unwitting victims of excessive rationality in planning. This stems from the fact that they are usually trying to reach an accommodation between two conflicting pressures that make board membership difficult. One source of pressure is rising public expectations of a board member's responsibility for a corporation's strategic behavior. A second source of pressure is the difficulty even able board members have in comprehending the complexity and scope of corporate actions. Many directors, despite good intentions, have an inadequate understanding of both current strategy and broad issues affecting strategic success.

To the besieged board member the appearance of certainty conveyed by a highly rational planning process is alluring indeed. Its pseudoscientific trappings provide a sense of stability in a world that often appears turbulent. Armed with sophisticated planning procedures, executives can bring to board members in simple black-and-white the immutable logic supporting their chosen course of action. If questions arise, staff can be summoned to deliver a litany of arcane terminology and statistical mumbo jumbo sufficient to blunt the most earnest inquiry. For the board member, an overrationalized planning process can become an opiate for coping with the stress of rising expectations and the increasing complexity of strategic choices.

Guidelines for Preventing an Overrationalized Planning Process

The occurrence of excessive rationality in strategic planning is a result of a myriad of complex administrative and technical processes. However, these processes are not inevitable in the sense that nothing can be done to arrest their momentum. At first blush, it may appear to be fruitful to engage the sources presented in figure 3-3 directly. This approach, however, will probably yield only modest results. Instead, our suggestion is to take action on three broad fronts with the intent of blunting the overall inertia toward excessive rationality.

Developing a Planning Culture

Simply stated, a culture is a group of individuals who have shared values. For planning to succeed, it is essential that a culture be developed in which the purpose and limits of planning are widely recognized and fully understood. This is a particularly important function of the president, but does not stop there. Organizations that we are familiar with that have experienced success in this area spend a great amount of energy to develop shared values. Typically, corporate planners work with line executives on a continuous basis and in a variety of roles. Stress is placed on consultation throughout the planning process. Efforts are made to counsel, coach when necessary, and reflect organization-wide opinion to line executives preparing plans.

Regardless of the specific approaches employed, persons must be made to understand that the strategic planning process is a means for the continual identification and response to strategic issues that may affect the long-term growth and development of an enterprise. In this capacity, it should facilitate problem formulation, sensing out of values and aspirations, consensus building, and settling on a strategy consistent with a firm's unique capabilities. In no sense, however, is strategy making an exact science. It is, instead, a combination of analytical techniques, administrative processes, and human judgment that bears elements of both art and science.

Probing Evaluation of Plans

In most companies where planning has become too rational, plans are usually presented rather than scrutinized. This occurs, in part, because of the heavy emphasis on quantification. Managers tend to use planning meetings as a forum for providing information in the form of graphs, charts, and tables. If evaluation does take place, it usually centers on the fine adjustments to particular numbers (e.g., sales, market share) rather than the strategy and tactics behind it.

In order to prevent this excessive concern with detail and producing the "right numbers," two steps can be taken. First, during the strategy formulation phase, stress should be placed on the assumptions underlying strategy alternatives. Every strategy alternative and final strategic plan are underpinned by a host of assumptions. Some assumptions may stem from data used during analysis (e.g., interest rates, GNP). Other assumptions are peculiar to specific analytical techniques (e.g., declining costs, cash flows, rates of technological innovation). If assumptions in either of these areas are unwarranted, conclusions that result are also likely to be unwarranted. In light of these circumstances, we suggest that staff and line executives be encouraged to examine in considerable detail assumptions supporting strategic alternatives facing a firm.

In addition to careful evaluation of assumptions, a second step is helpful in preventing excessive rationality in planning. During strategy review sessions, managers should be pressed to express in words the substance of their strategy and why they expect it to work. This compels managers to deal with qualitative factors likely to affect the proposed strategy (e.g., competitors' reactions, technological innovation). As one executive in our field study remarked: "If my managers cannot explain their strategy in simple language, then they don't have a strategy—all they have are a bunch of numbers." Lately, companies have been turning more and more toward a verbal synopsis of strategy in lieu of seemingly endless quantitative analyses. This changes the basic character and role of strategy review sessions. Instead of primarily serving as occasions for providing information, they become settings for careful thought and probing analysis. Thus, the prospect for creativity and innovation is enhanced.

Planning Process Audits

We recommend periodic audits of the strategic planning process. These may be conducted by a task force comprised of both participants in the planning process and those with no direct involvement. The latter could be a consultant, an outside board member, or an executive from another firm or division. The team should develop audit criteria before initiating their evaluation. The following are some criteria for getting started. This list is by no means all-inclusive.

- Do those engaged in the planning process understand its basic purpose and structure?
- Does the strategic planning process facilitate the identification and interpretation of strategic issues?
- Is there a balance between quantitative and qualitative information that sets the stage for innovative thought and action?
- Given the utility of information obtained, is the time required to gather and interpret it excessive?
- Does the planning process provide a means for fully discussing dissenting viewpoints?
- Are managers encouraged and rewarded for entrepreneurial initiatives?
- Are intangibles such as managerial values, aspirations, and acknowledged responsibilities to society explicitly incorporated into final strategic choices?
- Does the process provide adequate time for strategy implementation and evaluation?

■ REMOVING THE OBSTACLES TO EFFECTIVE STRATEGIC PLANNING†

By Thomas Marx

From its origins in the early 1960s through the late 1970s, strategic business planning held the business community spellbound with its promises of "sustainable competitive advantage" and the superior financial returns that would flow from it. No insignificant amount of this appeal was traceable to the veiled hint that these superior returns were the inevitable result of adhering strictly to the logical process being prescribed.

The strength of planning's appeal to the business community could be measured by the magnitude of the resources committed to the process by companies large and small. Huge amounts were expended for training managers in the methods of strategic planning, for compiling and analyzing the mountains of information that lie below the business plans sitting on desk tops like the tips of icebergs, and for writing, reviewing and monitoring the business plans. Entirely new organizations (strategic business units) were created to develop the plans and entirely new staffs (corporate strategic planning) were created to lead them through this process. The consumption of resources was enormous but so were the promised benefits.

Today, strategic business planning is in considerable disarray. The total resources devoted to planning at most companies steadily declined throughout the 1980s as the promised benefits often failed to materialize. Many companies at the forefront of strategic business planning only a few years ago have now substantially reduced the scope of their planning activity or abandoned it altogether. Those abandoning strategic business planning are comforted by the new conventional wisdom that "the Japanese don't plan."

Strategic business planning frequently has not delivered the promised benefits because it has failed to overcome the numerous bureaucratic obstacles that lie in its path. These obstacles are illustrated aptly by Jack Welch's description of the problems encountered with strategic business-planning at General Electric—the company that pioneered the strategic business planning process in the 1960s: "Our planning system was dynamite when we first put it in. The thinking was fresh, the form mattered little—the format got no points. It was idea-oriented. We then hired a head of planning and he hired two vice presidents and then he hired a planner, and the books got thicker and the printing got more sophisticated, and the covers got harder and the drawings got better. The meetings kept getting larger. Nobody can say anything with 16 or 18 people there."

The premise of this article is that while substantial reform of the planning process is urgently needed, it would be a major mistake to abandon strategic business planning in the face of the twin competitive and regulatory challenges facing most companies in the 1990s. Simultaneously meeting the increasing challenges of global competition, responding to the opportunities created by the tumultuous political, social, and economic changes throughout Europe and addressing the growing concerns for the protection of the environment from ozone depletion, greenhouse gases, and toxic wastes will require a strategic planning capability few firms currently possess, and even fewer will possess in the near future if the abandonment of strategic business planning continues. At the same time, it is imperative that the bureaucratic obstacles to effective strategic planning be eliminated. The trick is to avoid throwing out the baby with the bath water.

†**Source:** Reprinted with permission from *Long Range Planning*, "Removing the Obstacles to Effective Strategic Planning", August 1991, Vol. 24, Pergamon Press Ltd. Oxford, England.

FIGURE 3-4

Phases in the Development of Strategic Planning (Gluck, Kaufman, and Walleck, 1982)

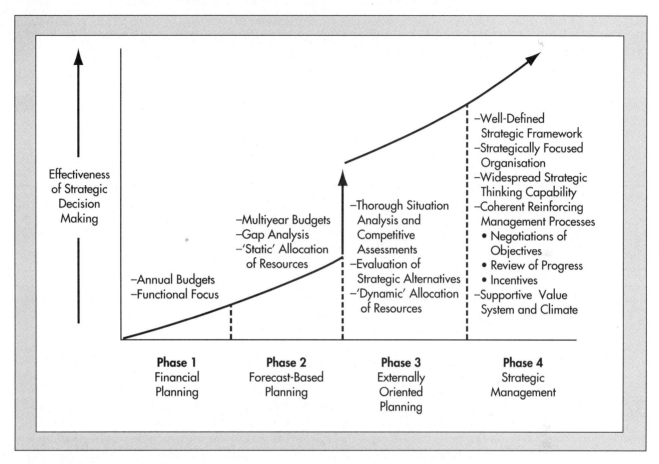

Obstacles to Effective Strategic Business Planning

The obstacles to an effective planning process can best be explained in the context of the four classical developmental phases of strategic business-planning systems, as shown in figure 3-4.

The promised benefits of strategic business planning are only realized in the latter stages of phase 3 and in the final phase in which planning is fully integrated with operating decision making and resource allocation throughout the company. Prior to this, management encounters the bulk of the cost of planning with only the promise of future benefits. Since management's tolerance for such a state of affairs is not without serious limits, the task is to move through the first three phases of planning as quickly as possible. Passage through the first two phases proceeds smoothly enough at most companies. The extension of annual financial planning to a three- to five-year horizon occurs naturally as the length of investment paybacks, contractual commitments, and product cycles grows with the success and maturity of the company. The introduction of forecasting techniques in phase 2 imposes no great burdens on the organization if one excludes the despair of those who expected to foretell the future with reasonable accuracy.

TABLE 3-1
Obstacles to Effective
Strategic Planning

Phase 3 Obstacles	Phase 4 Characteristics
Planning Processes	
Uniform procedures	Flexible procedures
Regularly scheduled reviews	Scheduled as needed
Strict time limits on reviews	As much time as needed
Formal presentations	Informal presentations
Numerous observers	Decision makers only
Massive paperwork	Ten-page plans
Restricted discussion	Open dialogue
No decisions	Decisions mandatory
Process emphasized	Results emphasized
Content of the Plans	
Data, numbers, facts	Business intelligence
Financial analysis	Strategic analysis
Short-term focus	Long-term focus
Generic strategies	Strategic action plans
Monitoring and Reward Processes	
Random progress reviews	Regular progress reviews
Limited accountability	Strict accountability

It is in phase 3 of the planning process that the difficult processes really begin. It is here that the company is organized, for planning purposes, into strategic business units (SBUs); extensive training is required; thorough analyses of competitors and the external environment and an inventory of internal strengths and weaknesses are undertaken; and formal business plans are written, reviewed, and monitored for the first time. It is also here that the organizational changes are most severe, and that the planning process becomes most vulnerable to its natural enemies—inertia, entrenched interests, and risk aversity. It is at this point that many companies, unable to steer the process safely through the many obstacles encountered in phase 3, abandon planning altogether.

The obstacles typically encountered in phase 3 of the planning process relate to the planning process itself, to the content of the business plans, and to the monitoring and reward processes essential to the successful implementation of the business plans. The basic obstacles encountered in phase 3 are shown in table 3-1 where they are contrasted with the characteristics of an effective phase 4 strategic business-planning process.

Planning Processes

The planning processes themselves often raise numerous obstacles to effective planning in phase 3. When these processes are seriously flawed, they are incapable of producing sound strategic business plans.

Uniform Procedures   Effective strategic business-planning procedures must be flexible and relatively unstructured. They must be tailored to the individual needs of the SBU in terms of process and content. This customizing ensures that the unique strategic issues affecting each SBU are effectively analyzed, presented and reviewed. This cannot occur if each plan is forced into a rigid, uniform mold. An effective strategic plan cannot be developed by requiring the SBUs to answer standardized questions and to complete mass-produced forms. Thus, a uniform planning process imposed upon the SBUs without regard for their individual industry circumstances and competitive positions is the first and, perhaps, most common obstacle to effective strategic business planning incurred at the entrance to phase 3.

Regularly Scheduled Reviews   The importance of flexibility to meet the unique needs of each SBU extends to the timing of the business plan reviews. Strategic business plan reviews should be scheduled as needed whether that is every three months or every three years. All SBU plans do not have to be reviewed every year or at the same time of year. Regularly scheduled, annual business plan reviews for every SBU elevate form over substance and serve as another obstacle to effective business planning.

Strict Time Limits on Reviews   The time allotted to the business plan reviews should be adequate to enable management to comprehend and to respond to the competitive issues facing the SBU, whether it be two hours or two days. Further, the initial time set aside for the business plan review should be determined by the SBU, which knows its situation and needs best. A failure by top management to make adequate time available for reviewing the plans results in hasty reviews and poor decisions (if any decisions are made), and signals a lack of commitment to the process by top management. The setting of strict (often two-hour) time limits for each business plan review thus becomes another obstacle to effective business planning.

Formal Presentations   The importance of informal presentations of the business plans cannot be overemphasized. Formal presentations, complete with slides and prepared text, are often crafted to limit discussion and to minimize the open probing needed to test the rigor of the business plans. Formal presentations are thus a major obstacle to effective planning.

Numerous Observers   Attendance at the business plan reviews should be strictly limited to key decision makers. The presence of numerous observers is another obstacle to effective planning because their presence discourages the candid discussion needed, and reduces the likelihood that any important decisions will be made. More often than not, these observers are not present to add value to the planning process, but rather are only there to protect the interests of other staffs and operating units.

Massive Paperwork   Planning by the pound (or kilo) is a common affliction that strikes companies entering phase 3 of the planning process. If the plan is much more than fifteen to twenty pages, the value of the paper probably exceeds the value of the plan. A good plan goes right to the key competitive issues and strategic action plans. To be sure, a great deal of analysis lies behind the plans, but the analysis is not the plan, and 100 pages of analysis does not substitute for 10 pages of strategic actions. A company that is planning by the pound is not planning. Thick notebooks are the work of analysts, not of strategists. Massive paperwork thus only serves as another obstacle to effective business planning by often delaying strategic reviews.

Restricted Discussion   The purpose of the business plan review is to elicit open discussion of the strategic opportunities and threats confronting the SBU, and to test the rigor of the SBU's strategic action plans. The SBU should be seeking top management's counsel, not trying to sell it a bill of goods. At the same time, top management should be trying to understand and assist the SBU in formulating the most effective strategic responses to its external opportunities and threats within the limits of the company's operating and capital budgets. A lack of such open dialogue and the shared understanding it creates thus becomes another obstacle to effective planning.

No Decisions   Perhaps the most critical element of all in the review process is whether top management makes decisions based on the business plans. This is the bottom line as far as the effectiveness of the business-planning process is concerned. The most important decisions, of course, are the allocations of resources. If the business plan is reviewed favorably but no resources are committed, it becomes perfectly clear to all that the real decisions are being made outside the business-planning system.

Process Counts   One of the most serious failings in the development of the planning process is the substitution of the process for the plans. This is perhaps more a symptom of a failing process than a cause of failure per se since the alleged value of the process serves as a ready justification for the continued expenditure of resources for planning when expected results are lacking. This perceived value of the process often results from a naive presumption that the process inexorably leads to superior financial performance. However, since the process provides employment and perhaps status and enhanced career opportunities for those charged with overseeing it, there is a built-in demand for the process regardless of actual results. Here, as with several instances above, the elevation of the process and thus of form over substance acts as a major obstacle to effective business planning. The process itself does not count. Only the quality of the plans count. If you hear "but we learned a lot from the process," strategic business planning at your company is starting to fail. If you hear this repeatedly, it has probably already failed.

Content of the Plans

Having established that it is the quality of the plans and not the process that counts, and that uniform, formal processes are major obstacles to effective planning, we must also be alert to several major obstacles that can result from the content of the plans themselves.

Data, Numbers, Facts   Strategic plans often lack the essential business intelligence needed to make major business decisions. Instead, one finds pages and pages of data, numbers, and facts that are often of very limited value to strategic decision making. Those responsible for developing the business plans are typically more secure presenting indisputable facts than they are in proposing strategic actions on the basis of specific assumptions and hypotheses, both of which arise because of the great uncertainty that necessitates strategic planning in the first place. Forecasts of the courses the economy and industry are likely to take, assumptions about the most important legislative issues likely to arise, and hypotheses about the strategic actions key competitors are likely to take and what the impacts of such possible actions might be on the SBU are essential to the formulation of strategic action plans. These forecasts, assumptions, and hypotheses, however, can easily be challenged, unlike the underlying raw data, numbers, and facts. They are therefore often avoided, especially in companies with strong risk-averse cultures. However, without the business intelligence that is created from these hypotheses, management is poorly equipped to make the critical strategic decisions necessary. Thus, the substitution of basic data, numbers, and facts for business intelligence is a major obstacle to effective business planning.

Financial Analysis   It is not uncommon for the strategic business plan to be little more than an elaborate budget. In this case, the plans consist largely of financial forecasts, often with the focus of management's attention on next year's budget. A preoccupation with the financial numbers, unfortunately, effectively precludes real strategic planning. If management is satisfied with the numbers, it pays no attention to the business plans or to the strategies for achieving the numbers. If it is not satisfied with the numbers, it again pays no attention to the business plan, but rather orders some recalculation of the numbers.

Since there is usually neither adequate time nor interest in re-doing the actual business plan, consistency between the planned strategic actions and the financial projections vanishes. Subsequent budget or head-count cutbacks may further increase the gulf between the plan and the numbers so that the plan may no longer be implementable or relevant. Management should, of course, be concerned with the financial implications of the business plan over the entire planning horizon. However, every number in the budget should be supported with a set of actions for achieving it. The substitution of a five-year budget for a five-year business plan is thus a major, though not uncommon, obstacle to effective planning.

Short-Term Focus   While most business plans cover a three- to five-year time horizon or longer, many companies focus on the coming year; especially if the emphasis is on the budget as discussed above, then managers defer concerns about the later years. Of course, this serves only to perpetuate an annual business planning or budgeting process that in turn precludes the discussion of most topics strategic in nature. This short-term focus stems largely from the emphasis on budgeting, on quarterly financial reporting, and on the greater predictability of the near term.

Generic Strategies   Business strategies range in level of detail from grand portfolios and generic strategies (compete on the basis of product differentiation, low cost, or niche marketing) to specific functional strategies (provide the fastest delivery in the industry) and detailed tactics (add three new delivery trucks at each zone office). While the appropriate level of strategic detail to include in the business plans varies with the size, diversity, and organizational structure of the company, a common obstacle to effective business planning is the substitution of generic strategies for a set of integrated strategic action plans.

Generic strategies, which could apply equally to any number of business units, seldom provide any clue about how the SBU will actually achieve competitive advantage, and thus offer no foundation for management's review of the business plan. For example, a generic strategy to compete on the basis of greater product differentiation provides no indication about how the SBU will achieve this differentiation, its ability to do so, or the impact on cost, quality, and other key success factors. What is needed for effective planning is a set of specific strategic actions integrated into a cohesive overall plan for gaining competitive supremacy.

Monitoring and Reward Processes

The monitoring and reward systems are critical elements in the business-planning process. The likelihood that the plan will be successfully implemented without effective monitoring and reward systems is remote. These two systems are also frequently the source of major obstacles to effective planning during phase 3 of the business-planning process.

Random Progress Reviews   While there is a need for substantial flexibility so that business plan reviews can be scheduled as needed, progress toward achieving the goals in the business plan should be reviewed on a regular basis—usually quarterly or semiannually, depending on business dynamics and management quality. If progress is not reviewed regularly, the plans are not likely to be effectively implemented because "what counts gets counted." With no systematic reviews to monitor progress and to discuss needed course corrections, the plans quickly become irrelevant to the operation of the business. Without effective monitoring, there is also no basis for accountability, which is essential to the successful implementation of the business plan.

Limited Accountability   A successful planning process requires that those responsible for carrying out the plans be held accountable for doing so, and be rewarded or penalized accordingly. If rewards are not tied directly to business plan performance, the plans will not be implemented and the objectives will not be achieved, unless fortuitously. The managers of the SBUs respond to the reward system, not the business-planning system. The successful implementation of the business plans thus requires that the two be inextricably linked. SBU managers will quickly deviate from or abandon the business plans altogether to pursue those objectives for which they believe they will be rewarded.

In order to avoid or eliminate these obstacles, it is helpful to recognize that in most organizations they seem to originate from a small set of underlying or root causes that are rather easy to identify.

Avoiding the Obstacles

The numerous obstacles to effective strategic business planning typically encountered in phase 3 of the planning process have one of four basic root causes: a lack of commitment to the process by top management; staff, rather than line-management control of the process; entrenched self-interests that are threatened by the business-planning process and which thus result in turf wars; and a corporate culture that discourages entrepreneurship and risk taking. The impact of these four factors on the success of business planning is often greatly magnified by the fact that these factors can be highly interdependent and mutually reinforcing. Thus, avoiding or controlling these four root causes is essential to eliminating the many obstacles to strategic business planning. These interrelationships are shown in table 3-2 where the obstacles discussed above are related to their root causes.

Lack of Management Commitment	Staff Control	Entrenched Interests	Corporate Culture
Strict time limits	Uniform process	Numerous observers	Data, numbers, facts
Restricted discussion	Regular schedule	No decisions	Generic strategies
Short-term focus	Formal presentation		Limited accountability
Financial emphases	Massive paperwork		
No decisions	Process emphasis		
Random progress reviews			
Limited accountability			

TABLE 3-2
The Root Causes of Failure in Strategic Planning

Management Commitment

The most fundamental cause of many of the obstacles to effective strategic business planning, and often the ultimate cause of its failure, is a lack of commitment to business planning by the top management of the company. This, not uncommon, lack of enthusiasm for strategic business planning by top management generates more problems than any other single factor. Further, it often results in staff control of the process by default, and the additional obstacles this creates. A lack of commitment by top management also permits entrenched interest groups, threatened by the planning process, to raise additional obstacles to the process. The lack of management commitment may also in part stem from a tradition of risk aversity, so there are likely to be major cultural obstacles to strategic business planning as well.

Given the significant consequences of inadequate executive support, the perplexing question arises why a company would commit substantial resources to strategic business planning without a solid commitment to the process from top management. There are several explanations for this apparent inconsistency. First, strategic business planning rapidly came to be considered a requirement of sound management by academics and management consultants. Many companies were therefore anxious to implement such a process even before they understood it fully. Managers were more prepared to spend money for a business-planning process than they were to change the way they managed the company, and often more interested in the visible trappings of business planning than in its substance. As it became clear that managers' roles in the company might have to change, often very substantially, their enthusiasm for strategic planning typically waned considerably.

In the strategic business planning process, top management is responsible for determining which businesses the company should be in, for allocating resources among those businesses, and for developing synergies among them to maximize overall stockholder wealth rather than the profits of individual SBUs. The top executives are not directly involved in the management of the SBUs. This separation of SBU and corporate management responsibilities gives the top executives the time, perspective, and motivation to allocate resources among SBUs to maximize the total value of the company. For many executives, this transition from a more traditional operating to a strategic role represents a fundamental change that was not fully anticipated, and for which they are often not prepared.

In other companies, the planning process may have been urged on management from lower levels within the company, especially from staffs intrigued with the new analytical techniques, and may have never received more than tacit endorsement from the top management. And, of course, top management's initial enthusiasm for planning has generally waned as the financial results have failed to materialize as quickly as they may have been promised by zealous staffers or outside consultants. For any or all of these reasons, top management's commitment to strategic business planning at many companies is far less than appears to casual observers.

A lack of commitment to the strategic business planning process by top management is clearly evidenced by strict time limits on the business plan reviews, restricted discussion at these reviews, and a primary focus on the short term and on short-term financial performance in particular. The most direct and deleterious result of a lack of management commitment to the planning process, however, is the failure to make decisions based on the business plans. The approval of the plans without commitment of the resources needed to implement them is the most common, obvious, and condemning statement of management's lack of commitment to the process, regardless of the visible trappings, amount of expenditures, and size of the planning books. The lack of management commitment to strategic planning is also clearly manifest in a failure to conduct systematic performance reviews and to hold people accountable for achieving business plan goals.

To remove these major obstacles to effective strategic business planning, top management's absolute commitment to the planning process must be secured. This commitment is not measured so much by a willingness to spend money for planning but by a willingness to accept the strategic, as opposed to operating, role that the planning process defines for the top management, and to make decisions on the basis of the strategic business plans. This commitment must clearly be understood to represent a fundamental change in the way key resource decisions are made. Management must also be willing to make a long-term commitment to the business-planning process. Results should not be promised prematurely in order to sell the process to the top management.

Staff Control

Many of the obstacles noted earlier occur when staff, rather than line management, control the business-planning process. Staff are prone to placing more emphasis on the process, on the uniformity and formality of the process, and on massive amounts of analysis rather than strategic action plans and bottom-line results. This should not be surprising since the process is the result from the staff's perspective. The development and implementation of the actual strategic plans are the responsibility of line management—not staff. When line management is in control of the process, the focus will be on the bottom-line results for which they are responsible and will be held accountable. When staffs control the process, business planning often takes on a life of its own quite unrelated to bottom-line results.

The most effective way to avoid staff control is to employ in the central planning group primarily people from operating units to which they will return shortly. Such personnel on temporary assignment to the planning staff will maintain their bottom-line focus. A few staff experts are needed to maintain the continuity of the planning process and to train managers and analysts in planning techniques, but their numbers should be kept to the minimum. Staff control can also be avoided by leaving much of the responsibility for the business-planning process—format, timing, instructions, and so on—with the operating units rather than with the central planning staff.

Entrenched Interests

The introduction of strategic business planning may be perceived as a serious threat to the power and status of numerous entrenched interest groups throughout the company. For example, business planning is often seen as a threat to the financial departments, which may control the budgeting process, because they foresee being replaced as an important decision-making unit as the company moves from phase 2 to phase 3 business planning. The creation of SBUs as planning organizations may also threaten the power of divisional managements or central office staffs that previously held more functional control over operations. Somewhat surprisingly, planning may also threaten the top management itself. Unfamiliarity with the new strategic roles, analytical techniques, and decision-making systems may threaten at least some members of top management. This is especially likely for top managers who are more accustomed to making operating as opposed to strategic decisions. The reduced scope of their direct involvement in the operations of the SBUs may be perceived as a serious loss of power and prestige by some top managers.

The presence of numerous observers at the business plan reviews is usually a reliable indicator of the amount of resistance to business planning from the entrenched interests that feel threatened by the new planning process. And the lack of decisions based on the business plans may be testimony to their ability to keep critical decisions outside the strategic business-planning process.

To avoid these obstacles, all of the major affected interests throughout the company should be invited to participate in the development of the strategic business-planning process, and each should be assigned an essential role in this new process. This should not prove difficult because, properly executed, strategic business planning is a process for effectively integrating all of the company's resources in the pursuit of common, corporate goals. Beyond this, an absolute commitment to the process by the top management is the most effective means of dispelling such resistance.

Corporate Culture

The company's attitude toward risk taking and entrepreneurship is a critical factor in the success of strategic business planning. Effective long-term business planning requires a culture that encourages entrepreneurial responses to risks and uncertainty. A highly risk-averse company will find it difficult to formulate explicit long-term plans, and to assign explicit accountability for carrying them out. Management, of course, cannot avoid risks by refusing to address them. Management can, however, avoid, or at least attempt to avoid, accountability for the mistakes and failures that are inevitable in an uncertain environment. If the culture will not tolerate such failures, entrepreneurialism and risk taking will be driven out of the business plans, and they will degenerate to nothing more than indisputable data, facts, and numbers, rather than valuable business intelligence. Implementation will be limited to generic strategies and ambiguous, qualitative, and easily achieved objectives rather than specific action strategies and measurable goals against which the SBU management can be held accountable.

To avoid such sterile and defensive (protecting the SBU from failure and accountability) business plans, the corporate culture must visibly promote and reward entrepreneurialism and risk taking. It must permit failure—otherwise the SBUs will not try aggressively to succeed. Most SBUs will emphasize avoiding failures that are readily identifiable and for which they will be held accountable. Changing a risk-averse culture to one that promotes entrepreneurialism and risk taking is equally essential and difficult. As De Geus has articulated well, an effective planning process can aid the organizational learning so essential to developing new perspectives and attitudes toward the future. The company must clearly announce the new behaviour that is desired, it must explain the business context that makes this new behaviour essential to the continued success of the firm, and most importantly, it must visibly reward the desired behaviour.

Summary and Conclusions

Strategic business planning has not consistently delivered the promised financial benefits because it has often fallen victim to a number of formidable, bureaucratic obstacles. As a result, many firms today are seriously rethinking their prior commitments to the business-planning process. This, however, is not the time to abandon strategic business planning, especially for those companies simultaneously facing growing worldwide competition and social demands. This is the time to begin removing the obstacles to effective strategic business planning so that these demands can be met.

There is a subtle but significant danger in the process of removing the obstacles to effective strategic business planning. The elimination of these obstacles by such leading companies as General Electric may well be mistakenly interpreted as an abandonment of business planning by other companies who will then dismantle their own strategic business-planning processes. This is a serious danger because the bureaucratic obstacles to planning, described in the second section of this article, have become so intricately embedded in the planning process that they are often seen as essential components of the process rather than obstacles to it. Nowhere is this better illustrated than in the mistaken notion that the Japanese do not plan. It is the lack of the most visible obstacles to effective strategic business planning in the Japanese systems that leads to this misperception. The elimination of formal presentations, large meetings, massive planning books, and regularly scheduled, annual reviews is not the abandonment of planning—it is the liberation of planning!

■ LINKING PLANNING AND IMPLEMENTATION†

By L. J. Bourgeois and David Brodwin

Most discussions of strategic planning focus on how to formulate strategy. There are several tools and techniques in widespread use. Management consulting firms offer strategic planning on a commodity basis, and business-school programs are adorned with methodologies for choosing the "best" strategy.

By contrast, scant attention has been given to how to implement those strategies. Yet many people have recognized that problems with implementation in many companies

†**Source:** This article was originally published as "Putting Your Strategy into Action," in *Strategic Management Planning* (March/May 1983). Reprinted by permission of the authors.

have resulted in failed strategies and abandoned planning efforts. This article will identify many of these implementation problems and then offer some remedies for them.

Five Ways Companies Implement Strategy

In studying the management practices of a variety of companies, we have found that their approaches to strategy implementation can be categorized into one of five basic descriptions. In each one, the chief executive officer plays a somewhat different role and uses distinctive methods for developing and implementing strategies. We have given each description a title to distinguish its main characteristics.

The first two descriptions represent traditional approaches to implementation. Here the CEO (chief executive officer) formulates strategy first, and thinks about implementation later.

- *The Commander Approach.* The CEO concentrates on formulating the strategy, giving little thought to how the plan will be carried out. He either develops the strategy himself or supervises a team of planners. Once he's satisfied that he has the best strategy, he passes it along to those who are instructed to "make it happen."

- *The Organizational Change Approach.* Once a plan has been developed, the executive puts it into effect by taking such steps as reorganizing the company structure, changing incentive compensation schemes, or hiring staff.

The next two approaches involve more recent attempts to enhance implementation by broadening the bases of participation in the planning process.

- *The Collaborative Approach.* Rather than develop the strategy in a vacuum, the CEO enlists the help of his senior managers during the planning process in order to ensure that all the key players will back the final plan.

- *The Cultural Approach.* This is an extension of the collaborative model to involve people at middle and sometimes lower levels of the organization. It seeks to implement strategy through the development of a corporate culture throughout the organization.

The final approach takes advantage of managers' natural inclination to develop opportunities as they are encountered.

- *The Crescive Approach.* In this approach, the CEO addresses strategy planning and implementation simultaneously. He is not interested in planning alone, or even in leading others through a protracted planning process. Rather, he tries, through his statements and actions, to guide his managers into coming forward as champions of sound strategies.

In studying these five approaches we noticed several trends. First, the two traditional methods are gradually being supplanted by the others. Second, companies are focusing increasingly on organizational issues involved in getting a company to adapt to its environment and to pursue new opportunities or respond to outside threats. Finally, we see a trend toward the CEO playing an increasingly indirect and more subtle role in strategy development.

Method 1: The Commander Approach

The typical scenario depicting the most traditional approach to strategy formulation and implementation is as follows: After the CEO approves the strategic plan, he calls his top managers into a conference room, presents the strategy and tells them to implement it.

The CEO is involved only with formulating the strategy. He assumes that an exhaustive analysis must be completed before any action can be taken, so the CEO typically authorizes an extensive study of the firm's competitive opportunities. In general, focusing on the planning succeeds in at least giving the CEO a sense of direction for his firm, which helps him make difficult day-to-day decisions and also reduces uncertainty within the organization.

However, this approach can be implemented successfully only if several conditions are met. First, the CEO must wield a great deal of power so he can simply command implementation. Otherwise, unless the proposed strategy poses little threat to organizational members, implementation cannot be achieved very easily.

Second, accurate information must be available to the strategist before it becomes obsolete. Since good strategy depends on high-quality information, it is important that critical information entering the firm at lower levels is being compiled, digested, and transmitted upward quickly.

Third, the strategist must be insulated from personal biases and political influences that can impinge on the plan. Managers are likely to propose strategies favorable to their own divisions but not necessarily to the corporation as a whole.

One problem with this approach is that it often splits the firm into "thinkers" and "doers," and those charged with the doing may not feel that they are part of the game. The general manager must dispel any impression that the only acceptable strategies are those developed by himself and his planning staff, or he may find himself faced with an extremely unmotivated, uninnovative group of employees.

Method 2: The Organizational Change Approach

With this approach, the CEO makes the strategy decisions and then paves the way for implementation by redesigning the organizational structure, personnel assignments, information systems, and compensation scheme.

This method goes beyond the first one by having the CEO consider how to put the plan into action. The CEO basically uses two sets of tools: (1) changing the structure and staffing to focus attention on the firm's new priorities and (2) revising systems for planning, performance measurement, and incentive compensation to help achieve the firm's strategic goals.

The first set of tools—changing the organizational structure and staffing—has been the traditional approach espoused in most business strategy texts.

The second set of tools involves adjusting administrative systems. Various planning, accounting, and control tools, such as those governing capital and operating budgets, can be used to help achieve desired goals. For example, if the firm's strategy calls for investing certain businesses and harvesting others, or for channeling profits from one national unit into funding others, these goals should be featured prominently in the capital budgeting procedures so that business-unit managers can effectively plan their resource requests and others can effectively evaluate them.

Performance measures should be designed so that they target meaningful short-term milestones in order to monitor progress toward strategic goals. The incentive compensation scheme should then be tied into the clear-cut numerical terms of the performance measures. At a minimum, the general manager must ensure that the current compensation plan isn't thwarting the achievement of the strategy in ways such as rewarding short-term profitability at the expense of longer-term growth.

Unlike the first approach, in this method the CEO doesn't merely command his subordinates to put the plan into action. He supervises the implementation and may only reveal the strategy gradually, rather than in one bold proclamation.

However, it usually is inadequate for the CEO simply to tack implementation onto strategy. This approach doesn't deal with problems of obtaining accurate information nor does it buffer the planner from political pressures. Also, as in the first approach, imposing the strategy downward from the top executives still causes motivational problems among the doers at lower levels.

In addition, another problem can develop when the CEO manipulates the systems and structures of the organization in support of a particular strategy. The general manager may be losing important strategic flexibility.

Some of these systems, particularly incentive compensation, take a long time to design, install, and become effective. If a dramatic change in the environment suddenly demands a major shift in the strategy, it may be very difficult to change the firm's course, since all the "levers" controlling the firm have been set firmly in support of the now-obsolete game plan.

Method 3: The Collaborative Approach

In contrast to the two earlier approaches in which the chief executive makes most of the strategic and organizational decisions, the collaborative approach extends strategic decision making to the organization's top management team. The purpose here is to get the top managers to help develop and support a good set of goals and strategies.

In this model, the CEO employs group dynamics and brainstorming, techniques to get managers with different points of view to contribute to the strategic process. Our research indicates that in effective top management teams the executives will have conflicting goals and perceptions of the external environment, so the CEO will want to extract whatever group wisdom is inherent in these different perspectives.

The typical scenario depicting this approach should be familiar to readers: With key executives and division managers, the CEO embarks on a weeklong planning retreat. At the retreat, each participant presents his or her own ideas of where the firm should head. Extensive discussions follow, until the group reaches a consensus around the firm's longer-range mission and near-term strategy. Upon returning to their respective offices, each participant charges ahead in the agreed-upon direction.

The collaborative approach overcomes two key limitations of the previous two methods. By incorporating information from executives who are closer to the line operations and by engaging several points of view, it helps provide better information than the CEO alone would have. Also, because participation breeds commitment, this method helps overcome any resistance from top managers—which improves the possibility of successful implementation.

However, what the collaborative approach gains in team commitment may come at the expense of "strategic perfection." That is, it results in a compromise that has been negotiated among players with different points of view. The strategy may not be as dynamic as one CEO's vision, but it will be more politically feasible.

A second criticism of the collaborative approach is that it is not "real" collective decision making from an organizational standpoint, because the managers—the organizational elite—cannot or will not give up centralized control. In effect, this approach still retains the wall separating thinkers from doers, and it fails to draw upon the resources of personnel throughout the organization. Our fourth approach to strategy implementation overcomes that shortcoming.

Method 4: The Cultural Approach

The cultural approach extends the benefits of collective participation into lower levels of the organization in order to get the entire organization committed to the firm's goals and strategies.

In this approach, the CEO sets the game plan and communicates the direction in which the firm should move, but he then gives individuals the responsibility of determining the details of how to execute the plan. To a large extent, the cultural approach represents the latest wave of management techniques promulgated to (and, in some cases, enthusiastically adopted by) American managers seeking the panacea to our current economic woes in the face of successful Japanese competition.

The implementation tools used in building a strong corporate culture range from such simple notions as publishing a company creed and singing a company song to much more complex techniques. The complex—and usually effective—tools involve implementing strategy by employing the concept of "third-order control."

Since implementation involves controlling the behavior of others, we can think of three levels of control. First-order control involves direct supervision. Second-order control involves using rules, procedures, and organizational structure to guide the behavior of others. Third-order control is a much more subtle—and potentially more powerful—means of influencing behavior through shaping the norms, values, symbols, and beliefs that managers and employees use in making day-to-day decisions.

The key distinction between managers using the cultural approach and those simply engaged in "participative management," is that these executives understand that corporate culture should serve as the handmaiden to corporate strategy, rather than proselytize "power equalization" and the like for its own sake.

Some of the tools used in the cultural approach involve some readily identifiable personnel practices, such as long-term employment, slow promotion of employees, less-specialized career paths, and consensus decision making. For many managers, the cultural approach will also lead to change in their management style; it will involve much more interaction where subordinates will be seen as planners.

Once an organizational culture is established that supports the firm's goals, the chief executive's implementation task is 90 percent done. With a cadre of committed managers and workers, the organization more or less carries itself through cycles of innovation in terms of new products and processes at the workbench, followed by assimilation and implementation at the lower levels.

The most visible cost of this system also yields its primary strength: consensus decision making and other culture-inculcating activities consume enormous amounts of time. But the payoff can be speedy execution and reduced gamesmanship among managers. At Westinghouse, as William Coates, executive vice president of the corporation construction group, described it, "We spend a lot of time trying to get a consensus, but once you get it, the implementation is instantaneous. We don't have to fight any negative feelings."

Based on our assessment of the nature of the companies generally held up as examples of this approach to strategic management, we have reached some tentative conclusions about the organizational characteristics for which it is best suited. The cultural approach works when power is decentralized, where there are shared goals between the organization and its participants, and where the organization is stable and growing.

But the cultural method has several limitations. For one, it works only with informed and intelligent people (note that most of the examples are firms in high-technology industries). Second, it consumes enormous amounts of time to implement.

Third, it can foster such a strong sense of organizational identity among employees that it becomes almost a handicap—that is, it can be difficult to have outsiders at top levels because the executives won't accept the infusion of alien blood.

In addition, companies with excessively strong cultures often will suppress deviance, impede attempts to change, and tend to foster homogeneity and inbreeding. The intolerance of deviance can be a problem when innovation is critical to strategic success. But a strong culture will reject inconsistency.

To handle this conformist tendency, companies such as IBM, Xerox, and General Motors have separated their ongoing research units and their new product-development efforts, sometimes placing them in physical locations far enough away to shield them from the corporation's culture.

Homogeneity can stifle creativity, encouraging nonconformists to leave for more accepting pastures and thereby robbing the firm of its innovative talent. The strongest criticism of the cultural approach is that it has such an overwhelming indoctrinal air about it. It smacks of faddism and may really be just another variant of the CEO-centered approaches (i.e., the previously discussed commander and organizational change approaches). As such, it runs the risk of maintaining the wall between thinkers and doers.

Although each of the approaches discussed can be effective in certain companies and business environments, none has proved adequate for complex companies in highly diversified or rapidly changing environments. The best way to implement strategy in this challenging situation is by what we have identified as the cescive approach. The name means "growing," indicating that under this method the CEO cultivates or allows strategies to grow from *within* the company instead of imposing the strategies of top management onto the firm.

Method 5: The Crescive Approach

The crescive approach differs from others in several respects. First, instead of strategy being delivered downward by top management or a planning department, it moves upward from the doers (salespeople, engineers, production workers) and lower middle-level managers. Second, strategy becomes the sum of all the individual proposals that surface throughout the year. Third, the top management team shapes the employees' premises, that is, their notions of what would constitute strategic projects. Fourth, the chief executive functions more as a judge, evaluating the proposals that reach his desk, than as a master planner.

Why Did the Crescive Approach Arise?

At first, the crescive approach may sound too risky. After all, it calls for the chief executive to relinquish a lot of control over the strategy-making process, seemingly leaving to chance the major decisions that determine the long-term competitive strength of the company.

To understand why the crescive approach is sometimes appropriate, you need to recognize five constraints that impinge on the chief executive as he sets out to develop and implement a strategy.

1. *The chief executive cannot monitor all significant opportunities and threats.* If the company is highly diversified, it is impossible for senior management to stay abreast of developments in all of the firm's different industries. Similarly, if an industry is shifting very quickly (e.g., personal computers), information collected at lower levels often becomes stale before it can be assimilated, summarized, and passed up the ranks. Even in more stable industries, the time required to process information upward through many

management levels can mean that decisions are being made based on outdated information.

As a result, in many cases the CEO must abandon the effort to plan centrally. Instead, an incentive scheme or "free-market" environment is established to encourage operating managers to make decisions that will further the long-range interests of the company.

2. *The power of the chief executive is limited.* The chief executive typically enjoys substantial power derived from the ability to bestow rewards, allocate resources, and reduce uncertainty for members of the organization. Thus, to an extent, the executive can impose his or her will on other members of the organization.

However, the chief executive is not omnipotent. Employees can always leave the firm, and key managers wield control over information and important client relationships. As a result, the CEO must often compromise on programs he wishes to implement.

Research indicates that new projects led by managers who were coerced into the leadership role fail, regardless of the intrinsic merit of the proposal. In contrast, a second-best strategy championed by a capable and determined advocate may be far more worthwhile than the optimum strategy with only lukewarm support.

3. *Few executives have the freedom to plan.* Although it is often said that one of the most important jobs of an executive is to engage in thoughtful planning, research shows that few executives actually set aside time to plan. Most spend the majority of their work days attending to short-range problems.

Thus, any realistic approach to strategic planning must recognize that executives simply don't plan much. They are bombarded constantly by requests from subordinates. So they shape the company's future more through their day-to-day decisions—encouraging some projects and discouraging others—than by sweeping policy statements or written plans. This process has been described as logical incrementalism because it is a rational process that proceeds in small steps rather than by long leaps.

4. *Tight control systems hinder the planning process.* In formulating strategies, top managers rely heavily on subordinates for up-to-date information, strategic recommendations, and approval of the operating goals.

The CEO's dependence on his subordinate managers creates a thorny control problem. In essence, if managers know they'll be accountable for plans they formulate or the information they provide, they have an incentive to bias their estimates of their division's performance.

A branch of decision science called agency theory, suggests how this situation should be handled. First, if the CEO wants his managers to deliver unbiased estimates, he cannot hold them tightly accountable for the successful implementation of each strategic proposal. Without such accountability, he places great emphasis on commitment as a force for getting things done.

Second, in order to assess the true ability and motivation of any subordinate, the CEO must observe him over a long period of time on a number of different projects. Occasional failures should be expected, tolerated, and not penalized.

One means to promote the ongoing flow of strategic information is to establish a special venture capital fund to take advantage of promising ideas that arise after the strategic and operating plans have been completed. Like the IBM Fellows or the Texas Instruments Idea programs, this approach allows opportunities to be seized and developed by their champions within the company.

5. *Strategies are produced by groups, not individuals.* Strategies are rarely created by single individuals. They are usually developed by groups of people, and they incorporate different perspectives on the business. The problem with group decisions is that groups tend to avoid uncertainty and to smooth over conflicts prematurely.

To reduce the distortions that can result from group decision making, the CEO can concentrate on three tools: first, encouraging an atmosphere that tolerates expression of different opinions; second, using organizational development techniques (such as group dynamics exercises) to reduce individual defensiveness and to increase the receptivity of

Approach	The CEO's Strategic Question	CEO's Role
I. Commander Approach	"How do I formulate the optimal strategy?"	Master Planner
II. Change Approach	"I have a strategy in mind—now how do I implement it?"	Architect of Implementation
III. Collaborative Approach	"How do I involve top management in planning so they will be committed to strategies from the start?"	Coordinator
IV. Cultural Approach	"How do I involve the whole organization in implementation?"	Coach
V. Crescive Approach	"How do I encourage managers to come forward as champions of sound strategies?"	Premise Setter and Judge

TABLE 3-3
The Five Approaches to Strategic Management

the group to discrepant data; and third, establish separate planning groups at the corporate level and in the line organization.

How the CEO Can Use the Crescive Approach

As the preceding discussion indicates, the CEO of a large corporation simply cannot be solely responsible for forming and implementing strategy. The crescive approach suggests that the CEO can solicit and guide the involvement of lower-level managers in the planning and implementation process in five ways:

- By keeping the organization open to new and potentially discrepant information
- By articulating a general strategy of superordinate goals to guide the firm's growth
- By carefully shaping the premises by which managers at all levels decide which strategic opportunities to pursue
- By manipulating systems and structures to encourage bottom-up strategy formulations
- By approaching day-to-day decisions as part of strategy formulation in the logical incrementalist manner described above

One of the most important and potentially elusive of these methods is the process of shaping managers' decision-making premises. The CEO can shape these premises in at least three ways. First, the CEO can emphasize a particular theme or strategic thrust ("We are in the information business") to direct strategic thinking. Second, the planning methodology endorsed by the CEO can be communicated to affect the way managers view the business. Third, the organizational structure can indicate the dimensions on which strategies should focus. A firm with a product-divisional structure will probably encourage managers to generate strategies for domination in certain product categories, whereas a firm organized around geographical territories will probably evoke strategies to secure maximum penetration of all products in particular regions.

To conclude, a summary of the five approaches, the strategic question each addresses, and the CEO's role in each is given in table 3-3. The choice of method should depend on the size of the company, the degree of diversification, the degree of geographical dispersion, the stability of the business environment, and finally, the managerial style currently embodied in the company's culture.

■ MANAGING STRATEGIC CHANGE[†]

By James Quinn

Executives managing strategic change in large organizations should not—and do not—follow highly formalized textbook approaches in long-range planning, goal generation, and strategy formulation. Instead, they artfully blend formal analysis, behavioral techniques, and power politics to bring about cohesive, step-by-step movement toward ends that initially are broadly conceived, but that are then constantly refined and reshaped as new information appears. Their integrating methodology can best be described as logical incrementalism. Managers *consciously* and *proactively* move forward *incrementally*:

- to improve the quality of information utilized in corporate strategic decisions;
- to cope with the varying lead times, pacing parameters, and sequencing needs of the "subsystems" through which such decisions tend to be made;
- to deal with the personal resistance and political pressures any important strategic change encounters;
- to build the organizational awareness, understanding, and psychological commitment needed for effective implementation;
- to decrease the uncertainty surrounding such decisions by allowing for interactive learning between the enterprise and its various impinging environments;
- to improve the quality of the strategic decisions themselves by (1) systematically involving those with most specific knowledge, (2) obtaining the participation of those who must carry out the decisions, and (3) avoiding premature momenta or closure that could lead the decision in improper directions.

How does one manage the complex incremental processes that can achieve these goals? The following is perhaps the most articulate short statement on how executives proactively manage incrementalism in the development of corporate strategies:

Typically you start with general concerns, vaguely felt. Next you roll an issue around in your mind till you think you have a conclusion that makes sense for the company. You then go out and sort of post the idea without being too wedded to its details. You then start hearing the arguments pro and con, and some very good refinements of the idea usually emerge. Then you pull the idea in and put some resources together to study it so it can be put forward as more of a formal presentation. You wait for "stimuli occurrences" or "crises," and launch pieces of the idea to help in these situations. But they lead toward your ultimate aim. You know where you want to get. You'd like to get there in six months. But it may take three years, or you may not get there.

Because of differences in organizational form, management style, or the content of individual decisions, no single paradigm can hold for all strategic decisions. However, very complex strategic decisions in my sample of large organizations tended to evoke certain kinds of broad process steps. These are briefly outlined below. While these process steps occur generally in the order presented, stages are by no means orderly or discrete. Executives do consciously manage individual steps proactively, but it is doubtful that any one person guides a major strategic change sequentially through all the steps. Developing most strategies requires numerous loops back to earlier stages as unexpected issues or new data dictate. Or decision times can become compressed and require short-circuiting leaps forward as crises occur. Nevertheless, certain patterns are clearly dominant in the successful management of strategic change in large organizations.

Creating Awareness and Commitment—Incrementally

Although many of the sample companies had elaborate formal environmental scanning procedures, most major strategic issues first emerged in vague or undefined terms, such as "organizational overlap," "product proliferation," "excessive exposure in one market," or "lack of focus and motivation." Some appeared as "inconsistencies" in internal action patterns or "anomalies" between the enterprise's current posture and some perception of its future environment. Early signals may come from anywhere and may be difficult to distinguish from the background noise of ordinary communications. Crises, of course, announce themselves with strident urgency in operations control systems. But if organizations wait until signals reach amplitudes high enough to be sensed by formal measurement systems, smooth, efficient transitions may be impossible.

Need Sensing: Leading the Formal Information System

Effective change managers actively develop informal networks to get objective information—from other staff and line executives, workers, customers, board members, suppliers, politicians, technologists, educators, outside professionals, government groups, and so on—to sense possible needs for change. They purposely use these networks to short-circuit all the careful screens their organizations build up to "tell the top only what it wants to hear."

To avoid undercutting intermediate managers, such bypassing has to be limited to information gathering, with no implication that orders or approvals are given to lower levels. Properly handled, this practice actually improves formal communications and motivational systems as well. Line managers are less tempted to screen information and lower levels are flattered to be able "to talk to the very top." Since people sift signals about threats and opportunities through perceptual screens defined by their own values, careful executives make sure their sensing networks include people who look at the world very differently than do those in the enterprise's dominating culture. Effective executives consciously seek options and threat signals beyond the status quo.

In some cases executives quickly perceive the broad dimensions of needed change. But they still may seek amplifying data, wider understanding of issues, or greater organizational support before initiating action. Far from accepting the first satisfactory (satisficing) solution—as some have suggested they do—successful managers seem to consciously generate and consider a broad array of alternatives. Why? They want to stimulate and choose from the most creative solutions offered by the best minds in their organizations. They wish to have colleagues knowledgeable enough about issues to help them think through all the ramifications. They seek data and arguments sufficiently strong to dislodge preconceived ideas or blindly followed past practices. They do not want to be the prime supporters of losing ideas or to have their organizations slavishly adopt "the boss's solution." Nor do they want—through announcing decisions too early—to prematurely threaten existing power centers, which could kill any changes aborning.

Even when executives do not have in mind specific solutions to emerging problems, they can still proactively guide actions in intuitively desired directions—by defining what issues staffs should investigate, by selecting principal investigators, and by controlling reporting processes. They can selectively "tap the collective wit" of their organizations, generating more awareness of critical issues and forcing initial thinking down to lower levels to achieve greater involvement. Yet they can also avoid irreconcilable opposition, emotional overcommitment, or organizational momenta beyond their control by regarding all proposals as "strictly advisory" at this early stage.

As issues are clarified and options are narrowed, executives may systematically alert ever-wider audiences. They may first shop key ideas among trusted colleagues to test responses. Then they may commission a few studies to illuminate emerging alternatives, contingencies, or opportunities. But key players might still not be ready to change their past action patterns or even be able to investigate options creatively. Only when persuasive data are in hand and enough people are alerted and on board to make a particular solution work might key executives finally commit themselves to it. Building awareness, concern, and interest to attention-getting levels is often a vital—and slowly achieved—step in the process of managing basic changes.

Changing Symbols: Building Credibility

As awareness of the need for change grows, managers often want to signal the organization that certain types of changes are coming, even if specific solutions are not in hand. Knowing they cannot communicate directly with the thousands who would carry out the strategy, some executives purposely undertake highly visible actions that wordlessly convey complex messages that could never be communicated as well—or as credibly—in verbal terms. Organizations often need such symbolic moves—or decisions they regard as symbolic—to build credibility behind a new strategy. Without such actions even forceful verbiage might be interpreted as mere rhetoric.

Legitimizing New Viewpoints

Often before reaching specific strategic decisions, it is necessary to legitimize new options that have been acknowledged as possibilities, but that still entail an undue aura of uncertainty or concern. Because of their familiarity, older options are usually perceived as having lower risks (or potential costs) than newer alternatives. Therefore, top managers seeking change often consciously create forums and allow slack time for their organizations to talk through threatening issues, work out the implications of new solutions, or gain an improved information base that will permit new options to be evaluated objectively in comparison with more familiar alternatives. In many cases, strategic concepts that are at first strongly resisted gain acceptance and support simply by the passage of time, if executives do not exacerbate hostility by pushing them too fast from the top.

Many top executives consciously plan for such gestation periods and often find that the strategic concept itself is made more effective by the resulting feedback.

Tactical Shifts and Partial Solutions

At this stage in the process, guiding executives might share a fairly clear vision of the general directions for movement. But rarely does a total new corporate posture emerge full grown—like Minerva from the brow of Jupiter—from any one source. Instead, early resolutions are likely to be partial, tentative, or experimental. Beginning moves often appear as mere tactical adjustments in the enterprise's existing posture. As such, they encounter little opposition, yet each partial solution adds momentum in new directions. Guiding executives try carefully to maintain the enterprise's ongoing strengths while shifting its total posture incrementally at the margin toward new needs. Such executives themselves might not yet perceive the full nature of the strategic shifts they have begun. They can still experiment with partial new approaches and learn without risking the viability of the total enterprise. Their broad early steps can still legitimately lead to a variety of different success scenarios. Yet logic might dictate that they wait before committing themselves to a total new strategy. As events unfurl, solutions to several interrelated problems might well flow together in a not-yet-perceived synthesis.

Broadening Political Support

Often these broad emerging strategic thrusts need expanded political support and understanding to achieve sufficient momentum to survive. Committees, task forces, and retreats tend to be favoured mechanisms for accomplishing this. If carefully managed, these do not become the "garbage cans" of emerging ideas, as some observers have noted. By selecting the committee's chair, membership, timing, and agenda, guiding executives can largely influence and predict a desired outcome, and can force other executives toward a consensus. Such groups can be balanced to educate, evaluate, neutralize, or overwhelm opponents. They can be used to legitimize new options or to generate broad cohesion among diverse thrusts, or they can be narrowly focused to build momentum. Guiding executives can constantly maintain complete control over these "advisory processes" through their various influences and veto potentials.

In addition to facilitating smooth implementation, many managers reported that interactive consensus-building processes also improve the quality of the strategic decisions themselves and help achieve positive and innovative assistance when things otherwise could go wrong.

Overcoming Opposition: "Zones of Indifference" and "No Lose" Situations

Executives of basically healthy companies in the sample realized that any attempt to introduce a new strategy would have to deal with the support its predecessor had. Barring a major crisis, a frontal attack on an old strategy could be regarded as an attack on those who espoused it perhaps properly—and brought the enterprise to its present levels of success. There often exists a variety of legitimate views on what could and should be done in the new circumstances a company faces. And wise executives do not want to alienate people who would otherwise be supporters. Consequently, they try to get key people behind their concepts whenever possible, to co-opt or neutralize serious opposition if necessary, or to find "zones of indifference" where the proposition would not be disastrously opposed. Most of all they seek "no lose" situations that will motivate all the important players toward a common goal.

But such tactics do not always work. Successful executives surveyed tended to honor legitimate differences in viewpoints and noted that initial opponents often shaped new strategies in more effective directions and became supporters as new information became available. But strong-minded executives sometimes disagreed to the point where they had to be moved or stimulated to leave; timing could dictate very firm top-level decisions at key junctions. Barring crises, however, disciplinary steps usually occurred incrementally as individual executives' attitudes and competencies emerged vis-à-vis a new strategy.

Structuring Flexibility: Buffers, Slacks, and Activists

Typically there are too many uncertainties in the total environment for managers to program or control all the events involved in effecting a major change in strategic direction. Logic dictates, therefore, that managers purposely design flexibility into their organizations and have resources ready to deploy incrementally as events demand. Planned flexibility requires (1) proactive horizon scanning to identify the general nature and potential impact of opportunities and threats the firm is most likely to encounter, (2) creating sufficient resource buffers—or slacks—to respond effectively as events actually unfurl, (3) developing and positioning "credible activists" with a psychological commitment to move quickly and flexibly to exploit specific opportunities as they occur, and (4) shortening decision lines from such people (and key operating managers) to the top for the most rapid system response. These—rather than precapsuled (and shelved) programmes to respond to stimuli that never quite occur as expected—are the keys to real contingency planning.

Systematic Waiting and Trial Concepts

The prepared strategist may have to wait for events, as Roosevelt awaited a trauma like Pearl Harbor. The availability of desired acquisitions or real estate might depend on a death, divorce, fiscal crisis, management change, or an erratic stock market break. Technological advances may have to await new knowledge, inventions, or lucky accidents. Despite otherwise complete preparations, a planned market entry might not be wise until new legislation, trade agreements, or competitive shakeouts occur. Organizational moves have to be timed to retirements, promotions, management failures, and so on. Very often the specific strategy adopted depends on the timing or sequence of such random events.

Solidifying Progress—Incrementally

As events move forward, executives can more clearly perceive the specific directions in which their organizations should—and realistically can—move. They can seek more aggressive movement and commitment to their new perceptions without undermining important ongoing activities or creating unnecessary reactions to their purposes. Until this point, new strategic goals might remain broad, relatively unrefined, or even unstated except as philosophic concepts. More specific dimensions might be incrementally announced as key pieces of information fall into place, specific unanswered issues approach resolution, or significant resources have to be formally committed.

Creating Pockets of Commitment

Early in this stage, guiding executives may need to actively implant support in the organization for new thrusts. They may encourage an array of exploratory projects for each of several possible options. Initial projects can be kept small, partial, or ad hoc, neither forming a comprehensive program nor seeming to be integrated into a cohesive strategy. Executives often provide stimulating goals, a proper climate for imaginative proposals, and flexible resource support, rather than being personally identified with specific projects. In this way they can achieve organizational involvement and early commitment without focusing attention on any one solution too soon or losing personal credibility if it fails.

In order to maintain their own objectivity and future flexibility, some executives choose to keep their own political profiles low as they build a new consensus. If they seem committed to a strategy too soon, they might discourage others from pursuing key issues that should be raised. By stimulating detailed investigations several levels down, top executives can seem detached yet still shape both progress and ultimate outcomes—by reviewing interim results and specifying the timing, format, and forums for the release of data. When reports come forward, these executives can stand above the battle and review proposals objectively, without being personally on the defensive for having committed themselves to a particular solution too soon. From this position they can more easily orchestrate a high-level consensus on a new strategic thrust. As an added benefit, negative decisions on proposals often come from a group consensus that top executives can simply confirm to lower levels, thereby preserving their personal veto for more crucial moments. In many well-made decisions people at all levels contribute to the generation, amplification, and interpretation of options and information to the extent that it is often difficult to say who really makes the decision.

Focusing the Organization

In spite of their apparent detachment, top executives do focus their organizations on developing strategies at critical points in the process. While adhering to the rhetoric of specific goal setting, most executives are careful *not* to state new goals in concrete terms before they have built a consensus among key players. They fear that they will prematurely centralize the organization, preempt interesting options, provide a common focus for otherwise fragmented opposition, or cause the organization to act prematurely to carry out a specified commitment. Guiding executives may quietly shape the many alternatives flowing upward by using what Wrapp refers to as "a hidden hand." Through their information networks they can encourage concepts they favor, let weakly supported options die through inaction, and establish hurdles or tests for strongly supported ideas with which they do not agree but which they do not wish to oppose openly.

Since opportunities for such focusing generally develop unexpectedly, the timing of key moves is often unpredictable. A crisis, a rash of reassignments, a reorganization, or a key appointment may allow an executive to focus attention on particular thrusts, add momentum to some, and perhaps quietly phase out others. Most managers surveyed seemed well aware of the notion that "if there are no other options, mine wins." Without being Machiavellian, they did not want misdirected options to gain strong political momentum and later have to be terminated in an open bloodbath. They also did not want to send false signals that stimulated other segments of their organizations to make proposals in undesirable directions. They sensed very clearly that the patterns in which proposals are approved or denied will inevitably be perceived by lower echelons as precedents for developing future goals or policies.

Managing Coalitions

Power interactions among key players are important at this stage of solidifying progress. Each player has a different level of power determined by his or her information base, organizational position, and personal credibility. Executives legitimately perceive problems or opportunities differently because of their particular values, experiences, and vantage points. They will promote the solutions they perceive as the best compromise for the total enterprise, for themselves, and for their particular units. In an organization with dispersed power, the key figure is the one who can manage coalitions. Since no one player has all the power, regardless of that individual's skill or position, the action that occurs over time might differ greatly from the intentions of any of the players. Top executives try to sense whether support exists among important parties for specific aspects of an issue and try to get partial decisions and momenta going for those aspects. As comfort levels or political pressures within the top group rise in favor of specific decisions, the guiding executive might, within his or her concept of a more complete solution, seek—among the various features of different proposals—a balance that the most influential and credible parties can actively support. The result tends to be a stream of partial decisions on limited strategic issues made by constantly changing coalitions of the critical power centers. These decisions steadily evolve toward a broader consensus, acceptable to both the top executive and some dominant coalition among these centers.

As a partial consensus emerges, top executives might crystallize issues by stating some broad goals in more specific terms for internal consumption. Finally, when sufficient general acceptance exists and the timing is right, the goals may begin to appear in more public announcements.

Formalizing Commitment by Empowering Champions

As each major strategic thrust comes into focus, top executives try to ensure that some individual or group feels responsible for its goals. If the thrust will project the enterprise in entirely new directions, executives often want more than mere accountability for its success—they want real commitment. A significantly new major thrust, concept, product, or problem solution frequently needs the nurturing hand of someone who genuinely identifies with it and whose future depends on its success.

In some cases, top executives have to wait for champions to appear before committing resources to risky new strategies. They may immediately assign accountability for less dramatic plans by converting them into new missions for ongoing groups.

From this point on, the strategy process is familiar. The organization's formal structure has to be adjusted to support the strategy. Commitment to the most important new thrusts has to be confirmed in formal plans. Detailed budgets, programs, controls, and reward systems have to reflect all planned strategic thrusts. Finally, the guiding executive has to see that recruiting and staffing plans are aligned with the new goals and that—when the situation permits—supporters and persistent opponents of intended new thrusts are assigned to appropriate positions.

Continuing the Dynamics by Eroding Consensus

The major strategic changes studied tended to take many years to accomplish. The process was continuous, often without any clear beginning or end. The decision process constantly moulded and modified management's concerns and concepts. Radical crusades became the new conventional wisdom, and over time totally new issues emerged. Participants or observers were often not aware of exactly when a particular decision had been made or when a subsequent consensus was created to supersede or modify it; the process of strategic change was continuous and dynamic.

Once the organization arrives at its new consensus, the guiding executive has to move immediately to insure that this new position does not become inflexible. In trying to build commitment to a new concept, individual executives often surround themselves with people who see the world in the same way. Such people can rapidly become systematic screens against other views. Effective executives therefore purposely continue the change process, constantly introducing new faces and stimuli at the top. They consciously begin to erode the very strategic thrusts they may have just created—a very difficult, but essential, psychological task.

Integration of Processes and of Interests

In the large enterprises observed, strategy formulation was a continuously evolving analytical-political consensus process with neither a finite beginning nor a definite end. It generally followed the sequence described above. Yet the total process was anything but linear. It was a groping, cyclical process that often circled back on itself, with frequent interruptions and delays. Pfiffner aptly describes the process of strategy formation as being "like fermentation in biochemistry, rather than an industrial assembly line."

Such incremental management processes are not abrogations of good management practice. Nor are they Machiavellian or consciously manipulative manoeuvres. Instead, they represent an adaptation to the practical psychological and informational problems of getting a constantly changing group of people with diverse talents and interests to move together effectively in a continually dynamic environment. Much of the impelling force behind logical incrementalism comes from a desire to tap the talents and psychological drives of the whole organization, to create cohesion, and to generate identity with the emerging strategy. The remainder of that force results from the interactive nature of the random factors and lead times affecting the independent subsystems that compose any total strategy.

The Role of Formal-Analytical Techniques

At each stage of strategy development, effective executives constantly try to visualize the new patterns that might exist among the emerging strategies of various subsystems. As each subsystem strategy becomes more apparent, both its executive team and top-level groups try to project its implications for the total enterprise and to stimulate queries, support, and feedback from those involved in related strategies. Perceptive top executives see that the various teams generating subsystem strategies have overlapping members. They require periodic updates and reviews before higher echelon groups that can bring a total corporate view to bear. They use formal planning processes to interrelate and evaluate the resources required, benefits sought, and risks undertaken vis-à-vis other elements of the enterprise's overall strategy. Some use scenario techniques to help visualize potential impacts and relationships. Others utilize complex forecasting models to better understand the basic interactions among subsystems, the total enterprise, and the environment. Still others use specialized staffs, "devil's advocates" or "contention teams," to make sure that all important aspects of their strategies receive a thorough evaluation.

All the formal methodologies help, but the real integration of all the components in an enterprise's total strategy eventually takes place only in the minds of high-level executives. Each executive may legitimately perceive the intended balance of goals and thrusts differently. Some of these differences may be openly expressed as issues to be resolved when new information becomes available. Some differences may remain unstated—hidden agendas to emerge at later dates. Others may be masked by accepting so broad a statement of intention that many different views are included in a seeming consensus, when a more specific statement might be divisive. Nevertheless, effective strategies do achieve a level of understanding and consensus sufficient to focus action.

Conclusions

In recent years, there has been an increasingly loud chorus of discontent about corporate strategic planning. Many managers are concerned that despite elaborate strategic planning systems, costly staffs for planning, and major commitments of their own time, their most elaborately analyzed strategies never get implemented. These executives and their companies generally have fallen into the trap of thinking about strategy formulation and implementation as separate, sequential processes. They rely on the awesome rationality of their formally derived strategies and the inherent power of their positions to cause their organizations to respond. When this does not occur, they become bewildered, if not frustrated and angry. Instead, successful managers in the companies observed acted logically and incrementally to improve the quality of information used in key decisions; to overcome the personal and political pressures resisting change; to deal with the varying lead times and sequencing problems in critical decisions; and to build the organizational awareness, understanding, and psychological commitment essential to effective strategies. By the time the strategies began to crystallize, pieces of them were already being implemented. Through the very processes they used to formulate their strategies, these executives had built sufficient organizational momentum and identity with the strategies to make them flow toward flexible and successful implementation.

■ BUILDING LEARNING ORGANIZATIONS†

By Peter Senge

The Nature of Learning

Human beings are designed for learning. No one has to teach an infant to walk, or talk, or master the spatial relationships needed to stack eight building blocks that don't topple. Children come fully equipped with an insatiable drive to explore and experiment. Unfortunately, the primary institutions of our society are oriented

†**Source:** Reprinted from "The Leader's New Work: Building Learning Organizations," *Sloan Management Review*, Fall, 1990, by permission of the publisher. Copyright © 1990 by the Sloan Management Review Assocation. All rights reserved.

predominantly toward controlling rather than learning, rewarding individuals for performing for others rather than for cultivating their natural curiosity and impulse to learn. The young child entering school discovers quickly that the name of the game is getting the right answer and avoiding mistakes—a mandate no less compelling to the aspiring manager.

"Our prevailing system of management has destroyed our people," writes W. Edwards Deming, leader in the quality movement."People are born with intrinsic motivation, self-esteem, dignity, curiosity to learn, joy in learning. The forces of destruction begin with toddlers—a prize for the best Halloween costume, grades in school, gold stars, and on up through the university. On the job, people, teams, divisions are ranked—reward for the one at the top, punishment at the bottom. Management by Objectives (MBO), quotas, incentive pay, business plans, put together separately, division by division, cause further loss, unknown and unknowable."

Ironically, by focusing on performing for someone else's approval, corporations create the very conditions that predestine them to mediocre performance. Over the long run, superior performance depends on superior learning.

If anything, the need for understanding how organizations learn and accelerating that learning is greater today than ever before. The old days when a Henry Ford, Alfred Sloan, or Tom Watson learned for the organization are gone. In an increasingly dynamic, interdependent, and unpredictable world, it is simply no longer possible for anyone to "figure it all out at the top." The old model, "the top thinks and the local acts," must now give way to integrating thinking and acting at all levels. While the challenge is great, so is the potential payoff.

Adaptive Learning and Generative Learning

The prevailing view of learning organizations emphasizes increased adaptability. Given the accelerating pace of change, or so the standard view goes, "the most successful corporation of the 1990s," according to Fortune magazine, "will be something called a learning organization, a consummately adaptive enterprise."

But increasing adaptiveness is only the first stage in moving toward learning organizations. The impulse to learn in children goes deeper than desires to respond and adapt more effectively to environmental change. The impulse to learn, at its heart, is an impulse to be generative, to expand our capability. This is why leading corporations are focusing on *generative* learning, which is about creating, as well as *adaptive* learning, which is about coping.

The total quality movement in Japan illustrates the evolution from adaptive to generative learning. With its emphasis on continuous experimentation and feedback, the total quality movement has been the first wave in building learning organizations. But Japanese firms' view of serving the customer has evolved. In the early years of total quality, the focus was on "fitness to standard," making a product reliably so that it would do what its designers intended it to do and what the firm told its customers it would do. Then came a focus on "fitness to need," understanding better what the customer wanted and then providing products that reliably met those needs. Today, leading-edge firms seek to understand and meet the "latent need" of the customer— what customers might truly value but have never experienced or would never think to ask for.

Generative learning, unlike adaptive learning, requires new ways of looking at the world, whether in understanding customers or in understanding how to better manage a business. For years, U.S. manufacturers sought competitive advantage in aggressive controls on inventories, incentives against overproduction, and rigid adherence to production forecasts. Despite these incentives, their performance was eventually eclipsed by Japanese firms who saw the challenges of manufacturing differently. They realized that eliminating delays in the production process was the key to reducing instability and improving cost, productivity, and service. They worked to build networks of relationships with trusted suppliers and to redesign physical production processes to reduce delays in materials procurement, production setup, and in-process inventory—much higher-leverage approach to improving both cost and customer loyalty.

As Boston Consulting Group's George Stalk has observed, the Japanese saw the significance of delays because they saw the process of order entry, production scheduling, materials procurement, production, and distribution as an integrated system (see chapter 5, for Stalk's original article). "What distorts the system so badly is time," observes Stalk—the multiple delays between events and responses. "These distortions reverberate throughout the system, producing disruptions, waste, and inefficiency." Generative learning requires seeing the systems that control events. When we fail to grasp the systemic source of problems, we are left to "push on" symptoms rather than eliminate underlying causes. The best we can ever do is adaptive learning.

The Leader's New Work

Our traditional view of leaders—as special people who set the direction, make the key decisions, and energize the troops—is deeply rooted in an individualistic and nonsystemic worldview. Especially in the West, leaders are heroes—great men (and occasionally women) who rise to the fore in times of crisis. So long as such myths prevail, they reinforce a focus on short-term events and charismatic heroes rather than on systemic forces and collective learning.

Leadership in learning organizations centers on subtler and ultimately more important work. In a learning organization, leaders' roles differ dramatically from that of the charismatic decision maker. Leaders are designers, teachers, and stewards. These roles require new skills: the ability to build shared vision, to bring to the surface and challenge prevailing mental models, and to foster more systemic patterns of thinking. In short, leaders in learning organizations are responsible for building organizations where people are continually expanding their capabilities to shape their future—that is, leaders are responsible for learning.

Creative Tension: The Integrating Principle

Leadership in a learning organization starts with the principle of creative tension. Creative tension comes from seeing clearly where we want to be, our "vision," and telling the truth about where we are, our "current reality." The gap between the two generates a natural tension.

Creative tension can be resolved in two basic ways: by raising current reality toward the vision, or by lowering the vision toward current reality. Individuals, groups, and organizations who learn how to work with creative tension learn how to use the energy it generates to move reality more reliably toward their visions.

Without vision there is no creative tension. Creative tension cannot be generated from current reality alone. All the analysis in the world will never generate a vision. Many who are otherwise qualified to lead fail to do so because they try to substitute analysis for vision. They believe that, if only people understood current reality, they would surely feel the motivation to change. They are then disappointed to discover that people resist the personal and organizational changes that must be made to alter reality. What they never grasp is that the natural energy for changing reality comes from holding a picture of what might be that is more important to people than what is.

But creative tension cannot be generated from vision alone; it demands an accurate picture of current reality as well. Vision without an understanding of current reality will more likely foster cynicism than creativity. The principle of creative tension teaches that *an accurate picture of current reality is just as important as a compelling picture of a desired future.*

Leading through creative tension is different from solving problems. In problem solving, the energy for change comes from attempting to get away from an aspect of current reality that is undesirable. With creative tension, the energy for change comes from the vision, from what we want to create, juxtaposed with current reality. While the distinction may seem small, the consequences are not. Many people and organizations find themselves motivated to change only when their problems are bad enough to cause them to change. This works for a while, but the change process runs out of steam as soon as the problems driving the change become less pressing. With problem solving, the motivation for change is extrinsic. With creative tension, the motivation is intrinsic. This distinction mirrors the distinction between adaptive and generative learning.

New Roles

The traditional authoritarian image of the leader as "the boss calling the shots" has been recognized as oversimplified and inadequate for some time. According to Edgar Schein, "Leadership is intertwined with culture formation." Building an organization's culture and shaping its evolution is the "unique and essential function" of leadership. In a learning organization, the critical roles of leadership—designer, teacher, and steward—have antecedents in the ways leaders have contributed to building organizations in the past. But each role takes on new meaning in the learning organization and, as will be seen in the following sections, demands new skills and tools.

Leader as Designer

The functions of design, or what some have called social architecture, are rarely visible; they take place behind the scenes. The consequences that appear today are the result of work done long in the past, and work today will show its benefits far in the future. Those who aspire to lead out of a desire to control, or gain fame, or simply to be at the center of the action will find little to attract them to the quiet design work of leadership.

But what, specifically, is involved in organizational design? "Organization design is widely misconstrued as moving around boxes and lines," says Hanover's O'Brien. "The first task of organization design concerns designing the governing ideas of purpose, vision, and core values by which people will live." Few acts of leadership have a more enduring impact on an organization than building a foundation of purpose and core values.

If governing ideas constitute the first design task of leadership, the second design task involves the policies, strategies, and structures that translate guiding ideas into business decisions. Leadership theorist Philip Selznick calls policy and structure the "institutional embodiment of purpose." "Policy making (the rules that guide decisions) ought to be separated from decision making," says Jay Forrester. "Otherwise, short-term pressures will usurp time from policy creation."

Traditionally, writers like Selznick and Forrester have tended to see policy making and implementation as the work of a small number of senior managers. But that view is changing. Both the dynamic business environment and the mandate of the learning organization to engage people at all levels now make it clear that this second design task is more subtle. Henry Mintzberg has argued that strategy is less a rational plan arrived at in the abstract and implemented throughout the organization than an "emergent phenomenon." Successful organizations "craft strategy" according to Mintzberg, as they continually learn about shifting business conditions and balance what is desired and what is possible. The key is not getting the right strategy but fostering strategic thinking.

Behind appropriate policies, strategies, and structures are effective learning processes; their creation is the third key design responsibility in learning organizations. This does not absolve senior managers of their strategic responsibilities. Actually, it deepens and extends those responsibilities. Now they are not only responsible for ensuring that an organization has well-developed strategies and policies but also for ensuring that processes exist whereby these are continually improved.

In the early 1970s, Shell was the weakest of the big seven oil companies. Today, Shell and Exxon are arguably the strongest, both in size and financial health. Shell's ascendance began with frustration. Around 1971 members of Shell's Group Planning in London began to foresee dramatic change and unpredictability in world oil markets. However, it proved impossible to persuade managers that the stable world of steady growth in oil demand and supply they had known for twenty years was about to change. Despite brilliant analysis and artful presentation, Shell's planners realized, in the words of Pierre Wack, that they "had failed to change behavior in much of the Shell organization." Progress would probably have ended there, had the frustration not given way to a radically new view of corporate planning.

As they pondered this failure, the planners' view of their basic task shifted: "We no longer saw our task as producing a documented view of the future business environment five or ten years ahead. Our real target was the microcosm (the 'mental model') of our decision makers." Only when the planners reconceptualized their basic task as fostering learning rather than devising plans did their insights begin to have an impact. The initial tool used was "scenario analysis," through which planners encouraged operating managers to think through how they would manage in the future under different possible scenarios. It mattered not that the managers believed the planners' scenarios absolutely, only that they became engaged in ferreting out the implications. In this way, Shell's planners conditioned managers to be mentally prepared for a shift from low prices to high prices and from stability to instability. The results were significant. When the Organisation of Petroleum Exporting Countries (OPEC) became a reality, Shell quickly responded by increasing local operating company control (to enhance maneuverability in the new political environment), building buffer stocks, and accelerating development of non-OPEC sources—actions that its competitors took much more slowly or not at all.

Somewhat inadvertently, Shell planners had discovered the leverage of designing institutional learning processes whereby, in the words of former planning director De Geus, "Management teams change their shared mental models of their company, their markets, and their competitors." Since then, "planning as learning" has become a byword at Shell, and Group Planning has continually sought out new learning tools that can be integrated into the planning process. Some of these are described below.

Leader as Teacher

Leader as teacher does *not* mean leader as authoritarian expert whose job it is to teach people the "correct" view of reality. Rather, it is about helping everyone in the organization, oneself included, to gain more insightful views of current reality. This is in line with a popular emerging view of leaders as coaches, guides, or facilitators. In learning organizations, this teaching role is developed further by virtue of explicit attention to people's mental models and by the influence of the systems perspective.

The role of leader as teacher starts with bringing to the surface people's mental models of important issues. No one carries an organization, a market, or a state of technology in his or her head. What we carry in our heads are assumptions. These mental pictures of how the world works have a significant influence on how we perceive problems and opportunities, identify courses of action, and make choices.

One reason that mental models are so deeply entrenched is that they are largely tacit. Ian Mitroff, in his study of General Motors, argues that an assumption that prevailed for years was that, in the United States, "Cars are status symbols. Styling is therefore more important than quality." The Detroit automakers didn't say, "We have a *mental model* that all people care about is styling." Few actual managers would even say publicly that all people care about is styling. So long as the view remained unexpressed, there was little possibility of challenging its validity or forming more accurate assumptions.

But working with mental models goes beyond revealing hidden assumptions. Reality, as perceived by most people in most organizations, means pressures that must be borne, crises that must be reacted to, and limitations that must be accepted. Leaders as teachers help people *restructure their views of reality* to see beyond the superficial conditions and events into the underlying causes of problems and therefore to see new possibilities for shaping the future.

Specifically, leaders can influence people to view reality at three distinct levels: events, patterns of behavior, and systemic structure.

Systemic Structure (Generative)
↓
Patterns of Behavior (Responsive)
↓
Events (Reactive)

The key question becomes, Where do leaders predominantly focus their own and their organization's attention?

Contemporary society focuses predominantly on events. The media reinforces this perspective, with almost exclusive attention to short-term, dramatic events. This focus leads naturally to explaining what happens in terms of those events: "The Dow Jones average went up sixteen points because high fourth-quarter profits were announced yesterday."

Pattern-of-behavior explanations are rarer, in contemporary culture, than event explanations, but they do occur. Trend analysis is an example of seeing patterns of behavior. A good editorial that interprets a set of current events in the context of long-term historical changes is another example. Systemic, structural explanations go even further by addressing the question, What causes the patterns of behavior?

In some sense, all three levels of explanation are equally true. But their usefulness is quite different. Event explanations—who did what to whom—doom their holders to a reactive stance toward change. Pattern-of-behavior explanations focus on identifying long-term trends and assessing their implications. They at least suggest how, over time, we can respond to shifting conditions. Structural explanations are the most powerful. Only they address the underlying causes of behavior at a level such that patterns of behavior can be changed.

By and large, leaders of our current institutions focus their attention on events and patterns of behavior, and under their influence, their organizations do likewise. That is why contemporary organizations are predominantly reactive, or at best responsive—rarely generative. On the other hand, leaders in learning organizations pay attention to all three levels, but focus especially on systemic structure; largely by example, they teach people throughout the organization to do likewise.

Leader as Steward

This is the subtlest role of leadership. Unlike the roles of designer and teacher, it is almost solely a matter of attitude. It is an attitude critical to learning organizations.

While stewardship has long been recognized as an aspect of leadership, its source is still not widely understood. I believe Robert Greenleaf came closest to explaining real stewardship, in his seminal book Servant Leadership. There, Greenleaf argues that "the servant leader *is* servant first. . . . It begins with the natural feeling that one wants to serve, to serve *first*. This conscious choice brings one to aspire to lead. That person is sharply different from one who is leader first, perhaps because of the need to assuage an unusual power drive or to acquire material possessions."

Leaders' sense of stewardship operates on two levels: stewardship for the people they lead and stewardship for the larger purpose or mission that underlies the enterprise. The first type arises from a keen appreciation of the impact one's leadership can have on others. People can suffer economically, emotionally, and spiritually under inept leadership. If anything, people in a learning organization are more vulnerable because of their commitment and sense of shared ownership. Appreciating this naturally instills a sense of responsibility in leaders. The second type of stewardship arises from a leader's sense of personal purpose and commitment to the organization's larger mission. People's natural impulse to learn is unleashed when they are engaged in an endeavor they consider worthy of their fullest commitment. Or, as Lawrence Miller puts it, "Achieving return on equity does not, as a goal, mobilize the most noble forces of our soul."

New Skills

New leadership roles require new leadership skills. These skills can only be developed, in my judgment, through a lifelong commitment. It is not enough for one or two individuals to develop these skills. They must be distributed widely throughout the organization. This is one reason that understanding the disciplines of a learning organization is so important. These disciplines embody the principles and practices that can widely foster leadership development.

Three critical areas of skills (disciplines) are building shared vision, surfacing and challenging mental models, and engaging in systems thinking.

Building Shared Vision

The skills involved in building shared vision include the following:

- *Encouraging personal vision.* Shared visions emerge from personal visions. It is not that people only care about their own self-interest—in fact, people's values usually include dimensions that concern family, organization, community, and even the world. Rather, it is that people's capacity for caring is personal.

- *Communicating and asking for support.* Leaders must be willing to continually share their own vision, rather than being the official representative of the corporate vision. They also must be prepared to ask, "Is this vision worthy of your commitment?" This can be difficult for a person used to setting goals and presuming compliance.

- *Visioning as an ongoing process.* Building shared vision is a never-ending process. At any one point there will be a particular image of the future that is predominant, but that image will evolve. Today, too many managers want to dispense with the "vision business" by going off and writing the Official Vision Statement. Such statements almost always lack the vitality, freshness, and excitement of a genuine vision that comes from people asking, "What do we really want to achieve?"

- *Blending extrinsic and intrinsic visions.* Many energizing visions are extrinsic—that is, they focus on achieving something relative to an outsider, such as a competitor. But a goal that is limited to defeating an opponent can, once the vision is achieved, easily become a defensive posture. In contrast, intrinsic goals like creating a new type of product, taking an established product to a new level, or setting a new standard for customer satisfaction can call forth a new level of creativity and innovation. Intrinsic and extrinsic visions need to coexist; a vision solely predicated on defeating an adversary will eventually weaken an organization.

- *Distinguishing positive from negative visions.* Many organizations only truly pull together when their survival is threatened. Similarly, most social movements aim at eliminating what people don't want: for example, antidrug, antismoking, or antinuclear arms movements. Negative visions carry a subtle message of powerlessness: people will only pull together when there is sufficient threat. Negative visions also tend to be short term. Two fundamental sources of energy can motivate organizations: fear and aspiration. Fear, the energy source behind negative visions, can produce extraordinary changes in short periods, but aspiration endures as a continuing source of learning and growth.

Surfacing and Testing Mental Models

Many of the best ideas in organizations never get put into practice. One reason is that new insights and initiatives often conflict with established mental models. The leadership task of challenging assumptions without invoking defensiveness requires reflection and inquiry skills possessed by few leaders in traditional controlling organizations.

- *Seeing leaps of abstraction.* Our minds literally move at lightning speed. Ironically, this often slows our learning, because we leap to generalizations so quickly that we never think to test them. We then confuse our generalizations with the observable data upon which they are based, treating the generalizations as if they were data.

- *Balancing inquiry and advocacy.* Most managers are skilled at articulating their views and presenting them persuasively. While important, advocacy skills can become counterproductive as managers rise in responsibility and confront increasingly complex issues that require collaborative learning among different, equally knowledgeable people. Leaders in learning organizations need to have both inquiry and advocacy skills.

- *Distinguishing espoused theory from theory in use.* We all like to think that we hold certain views, but often our actions reveal deeper views. For example, I may proclaim that people are trustworthy, but never lend friends money and jealously guard my possessions. Obviously, my deeper mental model (my theory in use), differs from my espoused theory. Recognizing gaps between espoused views and theories in use (which often requires the help of others) can be pivotal to deeper learning.

- *Recognizing and defusing defensive routines.* As one CEO (chief executive officer) in our research program puts it, "Nobody ever talks about an issue at the eight o'clock business meeting exactly the same way they talk about it at home that evening or over drinks at the end of the day." The reason is what Chris Argyris calls defensive routines, entrenched habits used to protect ourselves from the embarrassment and threat that come with exposing our thinking. For most of us, such defenses began to build early in life in response to pressures to have the right answers in school or at home. Organizations add new levels of performance anxiety and thereby amplify and exacerbate this defensiveness. Ironically, this makes it even more difficult to expose hidden mental models, and thereby lessens learning. The first challenge is to recognize defensive routines, then to inquire into their operation. Those who are best at revealing and defusing defensive routines operate with a high degree of self-disclosure regarding their own defensiveness.

Systems Thinking

We all know that leaders should help people see the big picture. But the actual skills whereby leaders are supposed to achieve this are not well understood. In my experience, successful leaders often are "systems thinkers" to a considerable extent. They focus less on day-to-day events and more on underlying trends and forces of change. But they do this almost completely intuitively. The consequence is that they are often unable to explain their intuitions to others and feel frustrated that others cannot see the world the way they do.

One of the most significant developments in management science today is the gradual coalescence of managerial systems thinking as a field of study and practice. This field suggests some key skills for future leaders:

- *Seeing interrelationships, not things, and processes, not snapshots.* Most of us have been conditioned throughout our lives to focus on things and to see the world in static images. This leads us to linear explanations of systemic phenomenon.

- *Moving beyond blame.* We tend to blame each other or outside circumstances for our problems. But it is poorly designed systems, not incompetent or unmotivated individuals, that cause most organizational problems. Systems thinking shows us that there is no outside—that you and the cause of your problems are part of a single system.

- *Distinguishing detail complexity from dynamic complexity.* Some types of complexity are more important strategically than others. Detail complexity arises when there are many variables. Dynamic complexity arises when cause and effect are distant in time and space, and when the consequences over time of interventions are subtle and not obvious to many participants in the system. The leverage in most management situations lies in understanding dynamic complexity, not detail complexity.

- *Focusing on areas of high leverage.* Some have called systems thinking the "new dismal science" because it teaches that most obvious solutions don't work—at best, they improve matters in the short run, only to make things worse in the long run. But there is another side to the story. Systems thinking also shows that small, well-focused actions can produce significant, enduring improvements, if they are in the right place. Systems thinkers refer to this idea as the principle of leverage. Tackling a difficult problem is often a matter of seeing where the high leverage lies, where a change—with a minimum of effort—would lead to lasting, significant improvement.

■ *Avoiding symptomatic solutions.* The pressures to intervene in management systems that are going awry can be overwhelming. Unfortunately, given the linear thinking that predominates in most organizations, interventions usually focus on symptomatic fixes, not underlying causes. This results in only temporary relief, and it tends to create still more pressures later on for further, low-leverage intervention. If leaders acquiesce to these pressures, they can be sucked into an endless spiral of increasing intervention. Sometimes the most difficult leadership acts are to refrain from intervening through popular quick fixes and to keep the pressure on everyone to identify more enduring solutions.

The consequences of leaders who lack systems-thinking skills can be devastating. Many charismatic leaders manage almost exclusively at the level of events. They deal in visions and in crises, and little in-between. Under their leadership, an organization hurtles from crisis to crisis. Eventually, the worldview of people in the organization becomes dominated by events and reactiveness. Many, especially those who are deeply committed, become burned out. Eventually, cynicism comes to pervade the organization. People have no control over their time, let alone their destiny.

Similar problems arise with the "visionary strategist," the leader with vision who sees both patterns of change and events. This leader is better prepared to manage change. He or she can explain strategies in terms of emerging trends, and thereby foster a climate that is less reactive. But such leaders still impart a responsive orientation rather than a generative one.

Many talented leaders have rich, highly systemic intuitions but cannot explain those intuitions to others. Ironically, they often end up being authoritarian leaders, even if they don't want to, because only they see the decisions that need to be made. They are unable to conceptualize their strategic insights so that these can become public knowledge, open to challenge and further improvement.

Developing Leaders and Learning Organizations

In a recently published retrospective on organization development in the 1980s, Marshall Sashkin and N. Warner Burke observe the return of an emphasis on developing leaders who can develop organizations. They also note Schein's critique that most top executives are not qualified for the task of developing culture. Learning organizations represent a potentially significant evolution of organizational culture. So it should come as no surprise that such organizations will remain a distant vision until the leadership capabilities they demand are developed. "The 1990s may be the period," suggest Sashkin and Burke, "during which organization development and (a new sort of) management development are reconnected."

I believe that this new sort of management development will focus on the roles, skills, and tools for leadership in learning organizations. Undoubtedly, the ideas offered above are only a rough approximation of this new territory. The sooner we begin seriously exploring the territory, the sooner the initial map can be improved—and the sooner we will realize an age-old vision of leadership:

The wicked leader is he who the people despise.
The good leader is he who the people revere.
The great leader is he who the people say, "We did it ourselves."
    —*Lao Tsu*

References and Suggested Readings

Argyris, C., Double Loop Learning in Organizations, *Harvard Business Review*, September/October 1977, pp. 115–125.

Argyris, C., *Overcoming Organizational Defenses: Facilitating Organizational Learning*, Prentice Hall, Boston, 1990.

Argyris, C., Teaching Smart People How to Learn, *Harvard Business Review*, May/June 1991, pp. 99–109.

Beck, P. W., Corporate Planning for an Uncertain Future, *Long Range Planning*, August 1982, pp. 12–21.

Bourgeois, L. J., and D. R. Brodwin, Putting Your Strategy into Action, *Strategic Management Planning*, March/May 1983.

Bourgeois, L. J., and D. R. Brodwin, Strategic Implementation: Five Approaches to an Elusive Phenomenon, *Strategic Management Journal*, July/September 1984, pp. 241–264.

Bresser, R. K., and R. C. Bishop, Dysfunctional Effects of Formal Planning: Two Theoretical Explanations, *Academy of Management Review*, October 1983, pp. 588–599.

Chakravarthy, B. S., and P. Lorange, *Managing the Strategy Process: A Framework for a Multibusiness Firm*, Prentice Hall, 1991.

De Geus, A. P., Planning as Learning, *Harvard Business Review*, March/April 1988, pp. 70–74.

Deming, W. E., *Quality, Productivity, and Competitive Position*, MIT Press, Cambridge, MA, 1982.

Evans, J. S., Strategic Flexibility for High Technology Manoeuvres: A Conceptual Framework, *Journal of Management Studies*, January 1991, pp. 69–89.

Fiol, C. M., and M. A. Lyles, Organizational Learning, *Academy of Management Review*, October 1985, pp. 803–813.

Forrester, J. W., A New Corporate Design, *Sloan Management Review*, Fall 1965, pp. 5–17.

Fowley, D., The New Breed of Strategic Planning, *Business Week*, September 17, 1984, pp. 52–57.

Frederickson, J. W., The Strategic Decision Process and Organizational Structure, *Academy of Management Review*, April 1986, pp. 280–297.

Gluck, F. W., Kaufman, S. P. and A. S. Walleck, The Four Phases of Strategic Management, *Journal of Business Strategy*, Winter 1982, pp. 9–21.

Gluck, F. W., Kaufman, S. P., and A. S. Walleck, Strategic Management for Competitive Advantage, *Harvard Business Review*, July/August 1980, pp. 154–161.

Gray, D. H., Uses and Misuses of Strategic Planning, *Harvard Business Review*, January/February 1986, pp. 89–97.

Greenleaf, R. K., *Servant Leadership: A Journey into the Nature of Legitimate Power and Greatness*, Paulist Press, New York, 1977.

Grinyer, P. H., and P. McKiernan, Generating Major Change in Stagnating Companies, *Strategic Managment Journal*, Summer 1990, pp. 131–146.

Hayes, R. H., Strategic Planning—Forward in Reverse? *Harvard Business Review*, November/December 1985, pp. 111–119.

Johnson, G., *Strategic Change and the Management Process*, Basil Blackwell, Oxford, 1987.

Johnson, G., Managing Strategic Change—Strategy, Culture, and Action, *Long Range Planning*, February 1992, pp. 28–36.

Kanter, R., *The Change Masters: Innovation for Productivity in the American Corporation*, Basic Books, New York, 1983.

Lenz, R. T., and M. A. Lyles, Paralysis by Analysis: Is Your Planning System Becoming Too Rational? *Long Range Planning*, August 1985, pp. 64–72.

Majone, G., and A. Wildavsky, Implementation as Evolution, *Policy Studies Review Annual*, II, 1978, pp. 103–117.

Marx, T. G., Removing the Obstacles to Effective Strategic Planning, *Long Range Planning*, August 1991, pp. 21–28.

Mason, R., and I. Mitroff, *Challenging Strategic Planning Assumptions*, Wiley, New York, 1981.

Melin, L., Strategies in Managing Turnaround, *Long Range Planning*, February 1985, pp. 80–86.

Mills, D. Q., and B. Friesen, The Learning Organization, *European Management Journal*, June 1992, pp. 146–156.

Mintzberg, H., Crafting Strategy, *Harvard Business Review*, July/August 1987, pp. 66–75.

Mitroff, I., *Break-Away Thinking*, Wiley, New York, 1988.

Pennings, J. H., Introduction: On the Nature and Theory of Strategic Decisions, in Pennings, J. M. (Ed.), *Organizational Strategy and Change*, Jossey-Bass, San Francisco, 1985.

Pettigrew, A. M., *The Management of Strategic Change*, Basil Blackwell, Oxford, 1988.

Pondy, I. R., and A. S. Huff, Achieving Routine in Organizational Change, *Journal of Management*, Summer 1985, pp. 102–116.

Quinn, J. B. Managing Strategic Change, *Sloan Management Review*, Summer 1980, pp. 3–20.

Quinn, J. B., *Strategies for Change*, Irwin, Homewood, IL, 1980.

Schein, E. H., *Organizational Culture and Leadership*, Jossey-Bass, San Francisco, 1985.

Schoeffler, S., Buzzell, R. D., and D. F. Heany, Impact of Strategic Planning on Profit Performance, *Harvard Business Review*, March/April 1974, pp. 137–145.

Selznick, P., *Leadership in Administration: A Sociological Interpretation*, Harper & Row, New York, 1957.

Senge, P. M., *The Fifth Discipline: The Art and Practice of the Learning Organization*, Doubleday, New York, 1990.

Senge, P. M., The Leader's New Work: Building Learning Organizations, *Sloan Management Review*, Fall 1990, pp. 7–23.

Shrivastava, P., A Typology of Organizational Learning Systems, *Journal of Management Studies*, January 1983, pp. 7–28.

Tichy, N., *Managing Strategic Change*, Wiley, New York, 1983.

Vasconcellos e Sá J., Does Your Strategy Pass the No Test? *European Management Journal*, June 1989, pp. 177–179.

CHAPTER 4
STRATEGY PROCESS TOOLS:
ON PLOTTING AND PORTFOLIOS

*He uses statistics as a drunken
man uses lamp-posts—for support
rather than illumination.*
  —Andrew Lang
    1844–1912, Scottish writer

Introduction

At the beginning of Section II a distinction was made between three abstraction levels: paradigms, organisation, and tools. Chapter 4 is devoted to the latter—the analytical instruments and techniques used to facilitate the strategy process.

Often this down-to-earth topic of *plotting and portfolios* does not appeal to the imagination in the same way other subjects do. In most cases, people would prefer to debate grand strategy rather than submerge themselves in the intricacies of an analytical grid or flow diagram. Yet, as is the case for most arts, mastery of certain basic techniques can enable the individual—brush techniques help the painter, musical notation assists the composer, and fingerprint analysis supports the work of the detective. Knowledge of these techniques doesn't make someone an artist, but makes becoming one, or being one, a bit easier. It is for this reason that this chapter offers the reader a toolbox filled with a number of the most well-known and often used strategy process techniques.

This objective has made the organisation of this chapter entirely different from all the others in this book. While the other chapters have one central topic, which is approached from competing perspectives, this chapter offers only one tool for each step in the strategy process. The reason for limiting the number of tools to just nine, while there are hundreds of rivalling techniques available, is purely pragmatic—you have to be able to carry this book around without feeling like a weight lifter!

Furthermore, in the following chapters more tools are gradually added to the basic set presented here.

There is a danger attached to presenting only one tool for each aspect of the strategy process. The danger lies in the fact that techniques are never objective—they are always based on theories belonging to a certain school of thought. Hence, tools are always partisan in the debates between opposing approaches to strategy. The reader must, therefore, be critical and employ each framework with care, realizing its assumptions and limits. Never may these tools be used as the drunk uses a lamppost.

To assist the reader, this introduction will point out which biases are wrapped up in each tool and which alternative tools are available in later chapters. However, in general, techniques have been selected that are in widespread use and not particular to only one school of thought.

For convenience, the articles have been arranged roughly to follow the steps of a strategic planning cycle. The first article deals with mission definition, while the second and third are about external analysis. The fourth, fifth, and sixth articles focus on different aspects of internal analysis, while the seventh article is about strategic option evaluation. Finally, the eight and ninth articles deal with strategy implementation and control.

The Articles

Although determining the organisation's mission is an essential part of the strategy process, this topic has been largely neglected by management writers. Therefore, for lack of a well-known tool, an excellent recent article by Andrew Campbell and Sally Yeung, "Creating a Sense of Mission," has been selected for this chapter. In this article, Campbell and Yeung present an integrative framework that can be used to determine and develop a company's mission. Furthermore, they indicate how the concept of mission ties in with related concepts such as vision and strategic intent (also see C. K. Prahalad and Yves Doz's article "The Dynamics of Global Competition" in chapter 10).

The next two articles in this chapter are concerned with different aspects of external analysis. The first of the two, "Macroenvironmental Analysis" by Peter Ginter and Jack Duncan, does exactly what the title suggests—it presents a methodology for scanning and analysing trends in the *macro* environment, focusing on social, economic, political, and technological developments. The second article, "The Structural Analysis of Industries" by Michael Porter, on the other hand, presents a methodology for analysing the *meso* environment. While Ginter and Duncan's approach is rather general, Porter's analytical technique is strongly rooted in economics (industrial organisation), which has led to some criticisms, especially from noneconomists. The main criticisms of Porter's framework concern its neglect of the role of government and its assumption of rationality—no attention is paid to industry cultures and politics, or to irrational behaviour of industry participants. Supplementary external analysis tools are presented later on in this text, particularly in chapter 8.

The next three articles deal with different aspects of internal analysis. The first of this trio is again an article by Michael Porter, "The Value Chain." This article, taken from his book *Competitive Advantage*, presents a framework for the systematic disaggregation of a firm into its strategically relevant activities. Splitting the organisation up into separate value-adding activities by means of the "value chain" tool allows the analyst to identify what the company does more cheaply or better than its competitors. In other words, this technique can be employed to single out the firm's specific competitive strengths and weaknesses. However, the value chain tool has the same type of limitations as Porter's industry analysis tool does. Due to the economic rationality with which Porter approaches his analysis, "soft" factors such as corporate culture, political processes, and organisational mission are not identified using this framework.

The second well-known framework included in this chapter that can be used as an internal analysis tool is "The 7S Model," by Robert Waterman, Tom Peters and Julien Phillips. This article was originally titled "Structure is Not Organisation," because the authors argue that many managers mistakenly equate the organisation to its more tangible aspects, structure and strategy. Less tangible elements of the organisation such as skills, staff, systems, style, and superordinate goals are often ignored. The model of organisations presented by Waterman, Peters, and Phillips encompasses all of these elements, making it a useful tool for thinking about, and analysing, organisations. Although the 7S model is not as detailed as the value chain, it is a complementary tool owing to its inclusion of the "soft" factors neglected by Porter.

"Portfolio Analysis" by Charles Hofer and Dan Schendel is the third and last article dealing with the topic of internal analysis. This article, taken from their book *Strategy Formulation: Analytical Concepts*, gives a short and clear summary of the most popular business portfolio matrices in use. These matrices can be used at the corporate level to plot the current strategic position of each of the company's various business units. The overview thus obtained can indicate strengths and weaknesses in the company's total portfolio of businesses. The widespread use of these portfolio techniques has led to the selection of this article for this chapter. However, the reader is warned that business portfolio grids are heavily criticised for a variety of reasons. The most important comments are directed at the oversimplification and overquantification of reality inherent in the matrices. These significant criticisms are discussed at length throughout chapter 6.

After mission definition, external analysis, and internal analysis, the next step in the strategic planning cycle followed by this chapter would normally be *strategic option formulation*. However, since all of the following chapters of this book are concerned with strategy options, and many basic tools are presented, this chapter will skip this topic. Therefore, the seventh article included here deals directly with the subject of *strategic option evaluation*. This article, "The Evaluation of Business Strategy" by Richard Rumelt, outlines four hurdles that a strategic option must be able to overcome before being considered a viable candidate for adoption.

The eighth article, "Implementing Strategy" by Lawrence Hrebiniak and William Joyce, presents one of the most well-known frameworks for executing a chosen strategic option. Their methodology is comprehensive, paying attention to both operational planning and organisational design issues—integrating concerns brought forward by both the planning and incrementalist schools of thought. It should be noted, however, that on the whole their approach is more skewed to the planning than to the incrementalist side of the spectrum.

As Hrebiniak and Joyce point out, once the implementation of strategy has been initiated, strategic controls must be put into place to ensure adherence to the objectives set. In the ninth and final article of this chapter, "Creating a Strategic Control System," Stephen Bungay and Michael Goold present a strategic control methodology. While their framework specifically focuses on how corporate management can use strategic controls to monitor and guide the strategy implementation of its business units, their methodology can be used to create a strategic control system at any level within the organisation. Here too, however, it must be noted that the approach taken is far more in line with the planning than the incrementalist perspective.

Recommended Readings and Cases

As was noted before, defining the company's mission is not an activity easily approached by the use of a framework. Therefore, for further reading we would recommend two publications that do not arrive at any fixed techniques. Derek Abell's *Defining the Business: The Starting Point of Strategic Planning* is a good early work, while Gary Hamel and C. K. Prahalad's "Strategic Intent" contains quite a few stimulating insights.

In the area of external analysis, this book does not touch on a number of very specific tools such as strategic group analysis, forecasting methods, and scenario techniques. Readers interested in strategic group analysis should start at the source, Michael Porter's *Competitive Strategy: Techniques for Analyzing Industries and Competitors,* while those curious about the uses of forecasting should turn to one of its proponents first, Spyros Makridakis, for instance, in his book *Forecasting, Planning and Strategy of the 21st Century.* Good initial readings on the topic of scenarios include Steven Schnaars's "How to Develop and Use Scenarios" and Pierre Wack's two sequential articles "Scenarios: Uncharted Waters Ahead" and "Scenarios: Shooting the Rapids."

For a useful compilation of both internal and external analysis tools, R. Dyson's textbook *Strategic Planning: Models and Analytical Techniques* is handy, while Alan Rowe, Richard Mason, Karl Dickel, and Neil Snyder's *Strategic Management: A Methodological Approach* includes a wide variety of tools for each aspect of the strategy process. For a good overview of strategic option evaluation methods we can also recommend Gerry Johnson and Kevan Scholes's textbook *Exploring Corporate Strategy.*

As stated at the outset, this chapter differs in character from all others in this book, because there is no "debate" on which it centres. The techniques presented here can, in principle, be employed in all of the cases included in this book. However, two cases have been selected that are particularly well suited to this chapter. The first case, "The Body Shop International" was written by Andrew Campbell to fit with the topic of mission. The Body Shop case is an excellent illustration of how "a sense of mission" can drive an organisation. The second case, "Sportis," on the other hand, describes how a Polish clothing company without a sense of direction is trying to survive the upheaval in Central Europe. The author, Max Boisot, explains how the firm is heavily dependent on the volatile Russian market, and he indicates that the company must reorient itself. This setting allows the reader to employ almost all tools discussed in this chapter. Furthermore, as a wrap-up of Section II, this case is also useful for a more general discussion on how the company should organise its strategy process.

■ CREATING A SENSE OF MISSION†

By Andrew Campbell and Sally Yeung

Many managers misunderstand the nature and importance of mission, while others fail to consider it at all. As far back as 1973, Peter Drucker observed: "That business purpose and business mission are so rarely given adequate thought is perhaps the most important cause of business frustration and failure." Unfortunately, his comment is as true today as it was then.

†**Source:** Reprinted with permission from *Long Range Planning,* August 1991, Pergamon Press Ltd. Oxford, England.

The reason for this neglect is due in part to the fact that mission is still a relatively uncharted area of management. Most management thinkers have given mission only a cursory glance, and there is little research into its nature and importance. What research there is has been devoted to analysing mission statements and attempting to develop checklists of items that should be addressed in the statement. Indeed, a major problem is that mission has become a meaningless term—no two academics or managers agree on the same definition. Some speak of mission as if it is commercial evangelism, others talk about strong corporate cultures, and still others talk about business definitions. Some view mission as an esoteric and somewhat irrelevant preoccupation that haunts senior managers, while others see it as the bedrock of a company's strength, identity and success—its personality and character.

Despite the diversity of opinion about mission, it is possible to distinguish two schools of thought. Broadly speaking, one approach describes mission in terms of business strategy, while the other expresses mission in terms of philosophy and ethics.

The strategy school of thought views mission primarily as a strategic tool, an intellectual discipline that defines the business's commercial rationale and target market. Mission is something that is linked to strategy but at a higher level. In this context, it is perceived as the first step in strategic management. It exists to answer two fundamental questions: What is our business? and What should it be?

The strategy school of mission owes its birth to an article, "Marketing Myopia," that appeared in the *Harvard Business Review* in 1960. The author, Ted Levitt, a Harvard marketing professor, argued that many companies have the wrong business definition. Most particularly, companies define their businesses too narrowly. Levitt reasoned that a railroad company should see its business as moving people rather than railroading, an oil company should define its business as energy, and a company making tin cans should see itself as a packaging business. Managers, Levitt argued, should spend time carefully defining their business so that they focus on customer need rather than on production technology.

More recently, it has become common for companies to include a statement of what their business is in the annual report. Corning Glass states: "We are dedicated to the total success of Corning Glass Works as a worldwide competitor. We choose to compete in four broad business sectors. One is Specialty Glass and Ceramics, our historical base, where our technical skills will continue to drive the development of an ever-broadening range of products for diverse applications. The other three are Consumer Housewares, Laboratory Sciences, and Telecommunications. Here we will build on existing strengths, and the needs of the markets we serve will dictate the technologies we use and the range of products and services we provide."

In contrast, the second school of thought argues that mission is the cultural "glue" that enables an organization to function as a collective unity. This cultural glue consists of strong norms and values that influence the way in which people behave, how they work together, and how they pursue the goals of the organization. This form of mission can amount to a business philosophy that helps employees to perceive and interpret events in the same way and to speak a common language. Compared to the strategic view of mission, this interpretation sees mission as capturing some of the emotional aspects of the organization. It is concerned with generating cooperation among employees through shared values and standards of behaviour.

IBM seems to subscribe to the cultural view of mission. The company describes its mission in terms of a distinct business philosophy, which in turn produces strong cultural norms and values. For IBM, "the basic philosophy, spirit and drive of the business" lies in three concepts: respect for the individual, dedication to service, and a quest for superiority in all things.

Is it possible to reconcile these two different interpretations? Are they conflicting theories or are they simply separate parts of the same picture? We believe these theories can be synthesized into a comprehensive single description of mission. We also believe that some of the confusion over mission exists because of a failure to appreciate that it is an issue that involves both the hearts (culture) and minds (strategy) of employees. It is something that straddles the world of business and the world of the individual.

Building a Definition of Mission

Our definition, which we have illustrated in figure 4-1, includes four elements— purpose, strategy, behaviour standards, and values. A strong mission, we believe, exists when the four elements of mission link tightly together, resonating and reinforcing each other.

Purpose

What is the company for? For whose benefit is all the effort being put in? Why should a manager or an employee do more than the minimum required? For a company these questions are the equivalent of a person asking, Why do I exist? The questions are deeply philosophical and can lead boards of directors into heated debate. Indeed, many companies do not even attempt to reach a conclusion about the nature of their overall purpose.

However, where there does appear to be an overall idea of purpose, companies fall into three categories. First there is the company that claims to exist for the benefit of the shareholders. For these companies the purpose is to maximize wealth for the shareholders. All decisions are assessed against a yardstick of shareholder value. Hanson, a conglomerate focused on Britain and the United States, is one example. Lord Hanson repeatedly states, "The shareholder is king." Unlike many companies whose

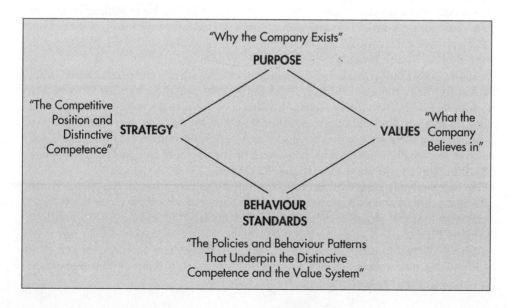

FIGURE 4-1
The Ashridge Mission Model

chairmen claim to be working primarily for the shareholders, Lord Hanson believes what he says and manages the business to that end. Hence Martin Taylor, a director, feels quite free to say: "All of our businesses are for sale all of the time. If anyone is prepared to pay us more than we think they are worth we will sell. We have no attachment to any individual business."

Most managers, however, are not as single-minded as Lord Hanson. They do not believe that the company's only purpose is to create wealth for shareholders. They acknowledge the claims of other stakeholders such as customers, employees, suppliers, and the community. Faced with the question: "Is your company in business to make money for shareholders, make products for customers, or provide rewarding jobs for employees?" they will answer yes to all three.

The second type of company, therefore, is one that exists to satisfy all its stakeholders. In order to articulate this broader idea of purpose these companies have written down their responsibilities to each stakeholder group. Ciba-Geigy is an example. It has published the company's business principles under four headings—the public and the environment, customers, employees, and shareholders. Under the heading of the public and the environment it has five paragraphs describing principles such as: "We will behave as a responsible corporate member of society and will do our best to cooperate in a responsible manner with the appropriate authorities, local and national."

In practice it can be argued that the multiple-stakeholder view of purpose is more a matter of pragmatism than arbitrary choice. In a competitive labour market, a company that totally ignored its employees' needs would soon find its labour costs soaring as it fought to stem the tide of rising employee turnover. But what is important is the psychology of statements of purpose. Lord Hanson is saying that he is expecting his managers to put the allegiance of employees after the interests of shareholders in their list of priorities. Other companies say they have equal priority. For employees this makes them very different companies.

Managers in the third type of company are dissatisfied by a purpose solely aimed at satisfying stakeholder needs. They have sought to identify a purpose that is greater than the combined needs of the stakeholders, something to which all the stakeholders can feel proud of contributing. In short, they aim toward a higher ideal. The planning director in one company, operating in a depressed region of Britain, explained: "I don't get excited about making money for shareholders. I like to help business succeed. That's something I can get excited about. I believe our future depends on it—I don't just mean this company, it's about the future of the nation, even the international community—it's about world peace and that sort of thing."

At The Body Shop, a retailer of cosmetics, managers talk about "products that don't hurt animals or the environment." At Egon Zehnder the purpose is to be the worldwide leader in executive search. Whether these companies have an almost moral crusade, like The Body Shop, or whether they just aspire to be the best, like Egon Zehnder, they have all reached beyond the stakeholder definition of purpose. Each stakeholder, whether shareholder, employee, or supplier, can feel that doing business with the company supports some higher-level goal.

We believe that leaders will find it easier to create employees with commitment and enthusiasm if they choose a purpose aimed at a higher ideal. We have met individuals committed to shareholders or to the broader definition of stakeholders, but we believe that it is harder for this commitment to grow. Purposes expressed in terms of stakeholders tend to emphasize their different selfish interests. Purposes aimed at higher ideals seek to deny these selfish interests or at least dampen their legitimacy. This makes it easier to bind the organization together.

Strategy

To achieve a purpose in competition with other organizations, there needs to be a strategy. Strategy provides the commercial logic for the company. If the purpose is to be the best, there must be a strategy explaining the principles around which the company will become the best. If the purpose is to create wealth, there must be a strategy explaining how the company will create wealth in competition with other companies.

Strategy will define the business that the company is going to compete in, the position that the company plans to hold in that business and the distinctive competence or competitive advantage that the company has or plans to create.

Behaviour Standards

Purpose and strategy are empty intellectual thoughts unless they can be converted into action, into the policy and behaviour guidelines that help people to decide what to do on a day-to-day basis.

Egon Zehnder's strategy is to be more professional than other executive search consultants. Connected with this it has a set of policies about how consultants should carry out assignments, called the systematic consulting approach. One of the policies is that consultants should not take on a search assignment unless they believe it will benefit the client. Another policy is that there should be a backup consultant for every assignment in order to ensure a quality service to the client. Supporting this systematic approach are behaviour standards about cooperation. These are ingrained into the culture rather than written on tablets of stone. An Egon Zehnder consultant willingly helps another consultant within his or her office or from other offices around the world.

The logic for the cooperation is a commercial logic. The firm wants to be the best. This means being better at cooperation than its competitors. As a result it needs a behaviour standard that makes sure consultants can help each other. This commercial logic is the left-brain logic of the firm.

Human beings are emotional, however, and are often driven more by right-brain motives than left-brain logic. To capture the emotional energy of an organization the mission needs to provide some philosophical or moral rationale for behaviour to run alongside the commercial rationale. This brings us to the next element of our definition of mission.

Values

Values are the beliefs and moral principles that lie behind the company's culture. Values give meaning to the norms and behaviour standards in the company and act as the "right brain" of the organization.

In many organizations corporate values are not explicit and can only be understood by perceiving the philosophical rationale that lies behind management behaviour. For example, consultants in Egon Zehnder believe in cooperative behaviour because they are committed to the firm's strategy. But they also believe in cooperative behaviour because they feel that it is "right."

Egon Zehnder people can also be moral about certain aspects of the systematic approach. The policy of not taking on an assignment unless the consultant believes it is good for the client highlights a moral as much as a commercial rationale. Other executive search companies will take on any assignment, they argue. But Egon

Zehnder puts the interests of the client first and will advise the client against an assignment even if it means lost revenues. It is a professional code of behaviour. As professionals they feel a moral duty to advise the client to do what is best for the client rather than what is best for Egon Zehnder. There is a commercial rationale for this behaviour, but the moral rationale is stronger.

Values can provide a rationale for behaviour that is just as strong as strategy. It is for this reason that the framework in figure 4-1 has a diamond shape. There are two rationales that link purpose with behaviour. The commercial rational or left-brain reasoning is about strategy and what sort of behaviour will help the company outperform competitors in its chosen arena. The emotional, moral, and ethical rationale or right-brain reasoning is about values and what sort of behaviour is ethical: the right way to treat people, the right way to behave in our society.

Our definition of mission includes both these rationales linked together by a common purpose.

A Sense of Mission: The Emotional Bond

A sense of mission is an emotional commitment felt by people toward the company's mission. But even in companies with very strong missions there are many people who do not feel an emotional commitment.

A sense of mission occurs, we believe, when there is a match between the values of an organization and those of an individual. Because organizational values are rarely explicit, the individual senses them through the company's behaviour standards. For example, if the behaviour standard is about cooperative working, the individual will be able to sense that helpfulness is valued above individual competition. If the individual has a personal value about the importance of being helpful and cooperative, then there is a values match between the individual and the organization. The greater the link between company policies and individual values, the greater the scope for the individual's sense of mission.

We see the values match as the most important part of a sense of mission because it is through values that individuals feel emotional about their organizations. Commitment to a company's strategy does not, on its own, constitute a sense of mission. It is not unusual for groups of managers to discuss their company's purpose and strategy and reach an intellectual agreement. However, this intellectual agreement does not necessarily translate into an emotional commitment, and hence the strategic plan does not get implemented. The emotional commitment comes when the individual personally identifies with the values and behaviours lying behind the plan, turning the strategy into a mission and the intellectual agreement into a sense of mission.

Recognizing the personal nature of a sense of mission is important because it has two implications. First, no organization can hope to have 100 per cent of its employees with a sense of mission, unless it is very small. People are too varied and have too many individual values for it to be possible for a large organization to achieve a values match for all its employees. Second, careful recruitment is essential. People's values do not change when they change companies. By recruiting people with compatible values, companies are much more likely to foster a sense of mission.

Mission and Sense of Mission

We have defined the terms *mission* and *sense of mission* at some length and been at pains to draw a distinction between these two concepts because we believe managers are frequently confused by them.

Mission is an intellectual concept that can be analysed and discussed unemotionally. Like strategy, mission is a set of propositions that can be used to guide the policies and behaviours of a company. However, mission is a larger concept than strategy. It covers strategy and culture. The strategy element of mission legislates what is important to the commercial future of the company. The values element of mission legislates what is important to the culture of the company. When the two are in tune, reinforcing each other and bound by a common purpose, the mission is strong. When there are contradictions and inconsistencies, the mission is weak.

Sense of mission is not an intellectual concept: it is an emotional and deeply personal feeling. The individual with a sense of mission has an emotional attachment and commitment to the company, what it stands for, and what it is trying to do.

A company with a clear mission does not necessarily have employees with a sense of mission. Some individuals may have a sense of mission with varying degrees of intensity. Many will not. Over time the number of employees with a sense of mission will increase as the policies of the mission become implemented and embedded in the company culture.

Mission and Vision

Warren Bennis and Burt Nanus identify vision as a central concept in their theory of leadership. "To choose a direction, a leader must first have developed a mental image of a possible and desirable future state of the organization. This image, which we call a vision, may be as vague as a dream or as precise as a goal or mission statement," they say. "The critical point is that a vision articulates a view of a realistic, credible, attractive future for the organization, a condition that is better in some important ways than what now exists." So far as the word *vision* has a meaning in business language, this quote captures its distinguishing features as well as its vagueness.

A vision and a mission *can* be one and the same. A possible and desirable future state of the organization can include all of the elements of mission—purpose, strategy, behaviour standards, and values. But vision and mission are not fully overlapping concepts. Vision refers to a future state, "a condition that is better . . . than what now exists," whereas mission more normally refers to the present. Marks and Spencer's mission, "to raise the standards of the working man," was being achieved throughout the 1950s and 1960s and is still being accomplished today. It is a timeless explanation of the organization's identity and ambition. When a vision is achieved, a new vision needs to be developed; but a mission can remain the same and members of the organization can still draw strength from their common and timeless cause.

A vision is, therefore, more associated with a goal, whereas a mission is more associated with a way of behaving. We believe that mission is the more powerful concept and we take issue with Bennis and Nanus for using the word *vision* without separating the two concepts. Vision is valuable because goals are valuable, but it is the clarity of mission rather than vision that we believe is the strength of a great leader.

In times of change, a new mission will be difficult to distinguish from a vision because the new mission will be a mental image of a desirable future state. Hence, our difference of opinion is not, in practice, a serious one. Nevertheless we have two concerns with vision as a concept. First, a vision begins to lose its power when it is achieved. It is no longer a driving force for action and the organization can begin to lose direction. This can happen to companies that strive for market leadership: once achieved, the ambition that drove the company drains away, leaving it directionless. Second, if a vision is so ambitious that it is unlikely to be achieved in the next five or ten years, it loses its power to motivate and stimulate. It becomes too ambitious and unrealistic.

Mission is a much more timeless concept. It is concerned with the way the organization is managed today (behaviour standards) and its purpose. Both of these are enduring ideas and can supply an unbounded source of fulfillment and energy.

Mission and Strategic Intent

Strategic intent is another concept that overlaps with vision and mission. Hamel and Prahalad comment: "On the one hand strategic intent envisions a desired leadership position and establishes the criterion the organization will use to chart its progress. Komatsu set out to 'encircle Caterpillar.' Canon sought to 'beat Xerox,' Honda strove to become a second Ford, an automotive pioneer. All are expressions of strategic intent. At the same time strategic intent is more than just unfettered ambition. (Many companies possess an ambitious strategic intent yet fall short of their goals.) The concept also encompasses an active management process that includes: focusing the organization's attention on the essence of winning; motivating people by communicating the value of the target; leaving room for individual and team contributions; sustaining enthusiasm by providing new operational definitions as circumstances change; and using intent consistently to guide resource allocations."

Strategic intent is a concept that draws from both vision and mission. It includes a desired future state, a goal defined in competitive terms that is more a part of vision than of purpose. It also encompasses a definition of strategy that is fundamentally the same as the use of strategy within mission. Strategic intent is, therefore, closest in concept to the traditional definition of mission: What business are we in and what strategic position do we seek?

However, we see strategic intent as suffering from the same problem as vision, in that once the intent has been achieved, the organization is liable to lose direction. The problem with goals is that they have to be reset as they are achieved. Purpose has the advantage of being everlasting.

We also see strategic intent as being a left-brain concept. Hamel and Prahalad argue that intent should motivate people "by communicating the value of the target." We have not found many managers who are motivated by a target, unless it is a short-term objective or milestone. Managers we have spoken to are motivated more by the organization's current values than by some distant ambition. Strategic intent is, in our view, a less powerful concept than mission because it fails to include values and behaviour standards, the keys to long-standing employee commitment and enthusiasm.

Mission Planning

Our research has shown us that mission can be analysed and discussed in as rigorous a way as strategy. In other words, managers can do mission planning in the same way that they do strategic planning. In fact, strategic planning is a subset of mission planning. Mission planning is more sophisticated than strategic planning; it helps managers formulate strategies that will fit their organization.

One of the reasons that so many strategies fail to get further than the pages of a beautifully bound planning document is that they are strategies, not missions: they fail to build on the values and behaviour standards that already exist in the organization and they do not inspire the emotions of the managers and employees who are expected to put them into practice.

Mission planning goes beyond strategic planning in three ways:

■ It involves an analysis of employee values and organization behaviour to assess the changes needed.

■ It focuses on identifying behaviour standards that are central to the implementation of strategy and symbolic of the new value system.

■ It encourages discussion of the organization's commitment to its stakeholders and to some higher-level purpose.

Mission planning forces managers to think through the behavioural implications of their plans; it prompts them to articulate an inspirational reason for any new plans; and it prevents them from sidestepping the issue of whether existing managers and employees are capable of responding to the challenge. Mission planning is where strategy, organization, and human resource issues come together. It asks managers to take a holistic view of their organization and its environment before developing a plan of action.

We believe that leaders of multibusiness companies should be promoting mission planning at the business unit level in the same way that most companies currently promote strategic planning. The first step is to extend mission thinking into the periodic strategic planning process:

■ Ask managers in charge of business units to include issues of purpose, values, and behaviour standards along with their presentation at the strategy review.

■ Ask them whether or not their organization is culturally aligned with their strategy.

■ Ask them what their three most important behaviour standards are.

Initially these questions will get little attention, superficial discussion, and insufficient analysis. But the process will have started. Managers at the centre will be able to identify issues of concern and ask for further clarification or follow-up with the business unit informally. The mission questions at the next strategy review can be more targeted, moving the thinking forward again.

In a highly developed process it may become necessary to separate the mission discussion from the strategy discussion in the same way that most companies have found it beneficial to separate the strategy discussion from the budget discussion.

Many managers at headquarters have argued to us that although they can see the relevance and importance of mission thinking at the business unit level, they can see no value in it at the headquarters level of a diversified company. A corporate-level mission would be considered an imposition, discouraging diverse businesses from developing their own diverse missions.

We do not disagree with this view, yet we still consider that it is possible to have a headquarters mission and a set of diverse business unit missions. Mission can be treated in the same way as strategy. Because it is possible, in fact necessary, to have a corporate strategy and a different strategy for each business unit, it is possible to have a corporate mission and a different mission for each business unit. With good strategic planning the strategies at different levels and between sister companies do not clash and can reinforce each other. In the same way, good mission planning ensures compatibility between the different missions.

■ MACROENVIRONMENTAL ANALYSIS†

By Peter Ginter and Jack Duncan

For many of today's organizations, success or failure, profit or loss, growth or decline depend on how well they respond to macrosocial, -economic, -technological, or -political/regulatory changes—the external macroenvironment.

Analysis of these areas involves the study of current and potential change and the assessment of the impact of changes on the organization.

Generally, the process of macroenvironmental analysis consists of four interrelated activities—scanning, monitoring, forecasting, and assessing. More specifically, macroenvironmental analysis involves:

- *scanning* macroenvironments for warning signs and possible environmental changes that will effect the business;
- *monitoring* environments for specific trends and patterns;
- *forecasting* future directions of environmental changes;
- *assessing* current and future trends in terms of the effects such changes would have on the firm.

Sport shoes provide a good example of the importance of environmental forces. Adidas, Converse, and Keds all missed or underestimated the size and strength of the upper-price running-shoe market and the extensive emphasis on health it signaled. A lack of response to such signals provided just the opportunity Nike needed to successfully enter the market.

While macroenvironmental analysis is a crucial part of systematic strategic planning, there may be many frustrations in its management and few guidelines to help managers understand and use the process:

- Inability to organize for effective environmental scanning
- Difficulty in matching individual beliefs and detectable trends
- Inability to obtain pertinent and timely information
- Delays between the occurrence of external events and management's ability to interpret them
- General inability to respond quickly enough to take advantage of the trends detected
- Motivation of the management team to discuss the issues

†**Source:** Reprinted with permission from *Long Range Planning*, December 1990, Pergamon Press Ltd. Oxford, England.

Engaging in Macroenvironmental Analysis

Before beginning macroenvironmental analysis, the following five questions should be considered. Answers to these questions will provide insight into the level of commitment that will be required by the organization.

Does My Organization Need Macroenvironmental Analysis?

Macroenvironmental analysis, like other aspects of managerial action, must be economical if it is to be successful. That is, the benefits must exceed the costs. Therefore, in answering the first question managers need to look at the potential benefits of systematic macroenvironmental analysis. A few of the more important are:

- Macroenvironmental analysis increases managerial awareness of environmental changes.
- A higher environmental awareness enhances strategic planning by enriching industry and market analysis, increasing our understanding of multinational settings, improving diversification and resource allocation decisions, and facilitating energy planning and risk management.
- Macroenvironmental analysis focuses the manager's attention on the primary influences of strategic change.
- Macroenvironmental analysis provides time to anticipate opportunities and carefully develop responses to change (i.e., an early warning system).

It can be argued that the need for macroenvironmental analysis increases when organizations are large, have diverse product lines, require large investments, face complex and turbulent markets, and experience high competitive threats.

More specifically, A. H. Mesch, based on his experiences in an operating division of Sun Exploration and Production Company, developed seven specific criteria for deciding if an organization needs macroenvironmental analysis:

- Does the external business environment influence capital allocations and the decision-making process?
- Have previous long-range plans been scrapped because of unexpected changes in the environment?
- Have there been unpleasant surprises in the external business environment?
- Is competition growing in the industry?
- Is the business more marketing oriented and more concerned about the ultimate customer?
- Do more and different kinds of external forces seem to be influencing decisions, and does there seem to be more interplay among them?
- Is management unhappy with past forecasting and planning efforts?

A "yes" to any of these questions suggests the need to consider adding or expounding the macroenvironmental analysis efforts in your organizations. The more "yes" answers, the more urgent the need.

Which Areas of the Environment Should I Analyse?

After establishing the need for macroenvironmental analysis, the next question is, Which areas of the macroenvironment should we scan, monitor, forecast, and assess? The theoretical and empirical literature suggest that there is a need to engage in scanning, monitoring, forecasting, and assessing in at least the macrosocial, -economic, -technological, and -political/regulatory environments. It is no longer sufficient to monitor only events and trends in your own industry.

For example, by the turn of the century it is estimated that 30 per cent of a new car's cost will be accounted for by aerospace-style computer electronics. Such technological improvements include computer gearshift, heads-up display, collision avoidance and navigation systems, and adaptive lights. Automobile industry management must scan, monitor, forecast, and assess these changes (changes in the technological environment) if their products are to be competitive in the year 2000.

Since external environments are vast and diverse, managers must carefully select promising trends and events to analyse. In fact, "It has become necessary to restrain executives from roaming the external environment with enthusiastic indiscipline."

At Royal Dutch/Shell, for example, attention was focused on variables such as oil demand by market class (economic), refining capacity construction worldwide (political and economic), likelihood of government intervention in different markets (political), alternative sources of fuels (technological), and so on.

How Much Information Do I Need and Where Do I Get It?

Managers are justifiably concerned about the amounts and sources of information for macroenvironmental analysis. Sometimes only a little information is needed to make strategic decisions and at other times it is necessary to gather large amounts of data. There are at least some conditions under which large amounts of information are required.

- The need for information increases as the scope or magnitude of the decision under consideration increases. Magnitude is measured in terms of the decision's potential impact on long-term return on investment and other goals and subgoals of the total organization or any of its component parts.
- The need for information increases as the urgency or timeliness of the decision increases.
- The need for information increases when the decision involves a problem as opposed to an activity that is going well. If the decision relates to something with which we have less experience, our need for information increases.
- The need for information increases as the relationship of the decision to some major long-range plan increases.

When these conditions are present, it is important that we have an ongoing macroenvironmental analysis effort and established sources of information.

Companies use a number of information sources inside and outside the organization. Inside sources should always be exploited, while outside sources should be used to a greater or lesser extent, depending on the nature of the decision under consideration.

For most companies, personal sources greatly exceed impersonal sources in terms of importance. Inside the company, subordinates and other managers are the greatest source of information. In fact, most companies have far more internal information than they expect. Vast amounts of relevant decision-making data frequently exist in research personnel, planners, economists, and executive specialists in geographical areas of the firm's operations or relevant functions. People inside the firm provide rich and valuable industrial, technological, and political information that may not be available elsewhere.

Outside sources are usually numerous and include customers, suppliers, bankers, and consultants. Also included in this category are business associates, and chance encounters with people outside the manager's organization who possess valuable strategic information. External impersonal sources are trade publications, conferences, and activities of trade associations. Outside agencies that supply forecasts and technical information about the environment can be useful as can consultants. Outside forecasts typically consider a broader range of issues and variables and often fill gaps left in the less objective analyses of inhouse specialists. Consultants can frequently provide in-depth studies on topics selected by the analysis staff and provide more objective assessments of the information uncovered in the process of analysis.

What Techniques Can I Use to Analyse Important Trends and Events?

This is the most neglected of the five questions addressed. It is the least examined because it is not quantitative and is the most subjective. As William Dill noted: "The complexity of what we find and the grossness of most of the data that we collect are not consistent with the standards of precision and parsimony that social scientists have come to respect."

There are few procedures for incorporating "fuzzy" issues into the planning process. The ones that are available are usually characterized as judgmental, speculative, or conjectural. In recent years a variety of techniques have been suggested for dealing more effectively with this confusing aspect of macroenvironmental analysis. Three methods most frequently mentioned as being effective are the delphi technique or the systematic solicitation of expert opinion, the diffusion process, and scenario development. These techniques can be used to study emerging trends in the macrosocial, -economic, -political, and -technological environments.

Traditional delphi techniques have undergone a great deal of change in the context of macroenvironmental analysis. The revised methodology involves:

■ identifying recognized experts in the area of interest;

■ seeking their cooperation and participation;

■ providing these experts with an initial position paper on the status of the issue;

■ personal interviews with each expert;

Sometimes more than a single interview is necessary, but in addition, some authors have suggested studying the "diffusion" of ideas that may eventually influence the environment. Based on the product adoption process, the Battelle approach traces the adoption of emerging values throughout society. This process traces ideas from their initial inception through various stages of adoption. Continuous observation and plotting of values and new ideas through this process allows key influences to be identified, monitored, and evaluated in terms of their effect on relevant environmental areas.

Few techniques of environmental analysis have been as extensively developed as the Royal Dutch/Shell scenario models. These scenarios served two main purposes important to any serious planner. First, the process had a protective goal whereby the company was able to anticipate and understand the risks involved in doing its business. Second, the process had an entrepreneurial goal. Its aim was not just to protect but to discover new strategic options of which Shell was previously unaware. Scenarios, at least as they are used at Royal Dutch/Shell, are fundamental aids to changing the mental models in ways that allow managers to generate options for the future while assuming acceptable levels of risk.

For any method adopted for macroenvironmental analysis, Terry proposed the use of a simple philosophy. The macroenvironmental analysis process becomes operational through the following principles:

- Macroenvironmental scanning should consider possible influences on the company. Only when the major issues are considered should the refining process, weighing, and priority-setting process be initiated.

- Recognize that the purpose of the scanning process is not to accurately predict the future but to identify those issues most likely to impact on the company and be prepared to cope with them when they arise.

- The results of macroenvironmental analysis should be used proactively rather than the company assuming a reactive stance toward the environment.

- It is not sufficient for managers to understand the plan that results from the macroenvironmental analysis; it is crucial that they understand the thinking that has led to the development of strategic and tactical key issues. It is advantageous for as many managers as possible to take part in macroenvironmental analysis.

- An important aspect of macroenvironmental analysis is that it focuses managers' attention on what lies outside the organization and allows them to create an organization that can adapt to and learn from that environment.

What Procedures and Organizational Structures Are Most Appropriate for Analysing the Macroenvironment?

Having answered all the preceding questions, the manager's attention should now turn to developing procedures for the process and an organizational structure to accomplish it. Unfortunately, most macroenvironmental analysis activity in the past was informal, unsophisticated, and largely an individual effort directed to person-specific interests. As a consequence, there are few useful frameworks for developing models and procedures.

Procedures   The literature reports three general types of macroenvironmental analysis procedural modes. These are regular, irregular, and continuous. The regular model is comprehensive and systematic. Its focus is retrospective in that it employs simple extrapolations of the recent past into the near future. The irregular model is a type of ad hoc macroenvironmental analysis generally activated by some unexpected environmental event. The continuous model emphasizes the monitoring of various environmental subsystems rather than specific events. The scenario approach we have used previously, while being activated by unexpected events, is continuous in character and intent.

Structuring the Process   Most companies use one of several variations to position their macroenvironmental analysis units. Some of the more common variations are corporate/strategic planning departments; product/market areas, divisions, or strategic business units; marketing research departments; legal departments; public relations or public affairs departments; think tanks; and concept groups. The corporate/strategic planning department, the product/market group, and strategic business unit are the most frequently used. However, companies in the most advanced stages of strategic planning prefer to place their macroenvironmental analysis units in separate departments.

One study of U.S. and foreign firms found that most macroenvironmental analysis units are located organizationally within formal planning departments. When found elsewhere, macroenvironmental analysis units are housed in public affairs and government relations departments. In a study of ten leading-edge corporations, there was considerable variety in the design of macroenvironmental analysis units—"a variety of positions within organizational hierarchies serve as the primary locus of environmental intelligence gathering and interpretation." Where structures existed, the variations could be classified according to the role the unit was designed to play in the organization. These roles logically fell under three headings—public-policy role, strategic planning integrated role, and function-oriented role.

Firms exhibiting a public-policy role placed primary attention on early detection of emerging issues that were suspected to be harbingers of large-scale shifts in societal attitudes, laws, social norms, and roles. Most units organized in this manner have direct access to top-level executives in the corporation, while linkage with the strategic planning process is tenuous at best and sometimes virtually nonexistent. Companies using the strategic planning integrated structure in macroenvironmental analysis focus on both general and industry levels of the environment and subsequently play an integrative role in the strategic planning process. In contrast to the public-policy role, companies with a function-oriented role for scanning centered activities on only those aspects of the environment that impinge directly on the activities of the function within the organization as whole. As a result these units may be housed in functional departments. The advantages and disadvantages of these administrative structures are presented in table 4-1.

A continuous or proactive approach is most appropriate for firms committed to strategic planning and concerned about the influence of the macroenvironment. Companies in advanced stages of strategic planning will benefit most by separating the macroenvironmental analysis operations from the unit primarily responsible for strategic planning. Companies with fewer environmental influences may benefit by incorporating macroenvironmental analysis within the strategic planning of other functional departments. Even with a separate macroenvironmental analysis unit, it may be useful to have certain line managers continually monitoring specific aspects of the external environment and periodically providing environmental information to the macroenvironmental analysis unit. At a minimum, periodic interviews with key line managers and executives should be conducted.

Structure	Advantages	Disadvantages
Public Policy	Direct access to power structure	Establishing legitimacy
	New perspective for top executive group	Survival depends on "sponsoring" manager
	Stimulates long-term strategic thinking	No direct planning linkage
	Access to the "corporate vision"	Must compete with strategic planners for top management attention
Integrated Planning	Direct access to strategic planning process	Pressure to become short range in analysis
	Can integrate corporate and business level environmental issues	Need to conform to planning procedures and formats
	Opportunity to directly influence corporate strategy	Tension between line and staff viewpoints
Function Oriented	Environment is more easily defined	Restricted environmental focus
	Direct input to key strategy decisions	Short-term orientation
	No competition with planning for management attention	Limited prospect for unconventional thinking
	Close line-staff interaction	Requires clear and stable concept of strategy

TABLE 4-1
Advantages and Disadvantages of Different Macroenvironmental Analysis Administrative Structures (Lenz and Engledow, 1986)

Regardless of its position in the organizational structure, the assessment of environmental information should (1) be systematic; (2) consider diverse opinions; and (3) divorce the findings from the personal beliefs of the managers. Judgmental techniques such as brainstorming, scenarios, and impact analysis can identify emerging issues, but management must still speculate about their impact. Macroenvironmental analysis, like general management, requires a good deal of judgment and experience.

■ THE STRUCTURAL ANALYSIS OF INDUSTRIES†

By Michael Porter

The essence of strategy formulation is coping with competition. Yet it is easy to view competition too narrowly and too pessimistically. While one sometimes hears executives complaining to the contrary, intense competition in an industry is neither coincidence nor bad luck.

Moreover, in the fight for market share, competition is not manifested only in the other players. Rather, competition in an industry is rooted in its underlying economics, and competitive forces exist that go well beyond the established combatants in a particular industry. Customers, suppliers, potential entrants, and substitute products are all competitors that may be more or less prominent or active depending on the industry.

The state of competition in an industry depends on five basic forces, which are diagrammed in figure 4-2. The collective strength of these forces determines the ultimate profit potential of an industry. It ranges from intense in industries where no company earns spectacular returns on investment, to mild in industries where there is room for quite high returns.

In the economists' "perfectly competitive" industry, jockeying for position is unbridled and entry to the industry very easy. This kind of industry structure, of course, offers the worst prospect for long-run profitability. The weaker the forces collectively, however, the greater the opportunity for superior performance.

Whatever their collective strength, the corporate strategist's goal is to find a position in the industry where his or her company can best defend itself against these forces or can influence them in its favor. The collective strength of the forces may be painfully apparent to all the antagonists; but to cope with them, the strategist must delve below the surface and analyze the sources of each. For example, what makes the industry vulnerable to entry? What determines the bargaining power of suppliers?

Knowledge of these underlying sources of competitive pressure provides the groundwork for a strategic agenda of action. They highlight the critical strengths and weaknesses of the company, animate the positioning of the company in its industry, clarify the areas where strategic changes may yield the greatest payoff, and highlight the places where industry trends promise to hold the greatest significance as either opportunities or threats. Understanding these sources also proves to be of help in considering areas for diversification.

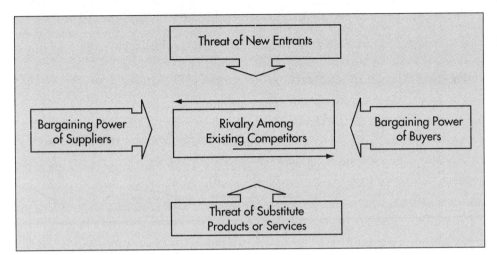

Contending Forces

The strongest competitive force or forces determine the profitability of an industry and so are of greatest importance in strategy formulation. For example, even a company with a strong position in an industry unthreatened by potential entrants will earn low returns if it faces a superior or a lower-cost substitute product. In such a situation, coping with the substitute product becomes the number one strategic priority.

Different forces take on prominence, of course, in shaping competition in each industry. In the oceangoing tanker industry the key force is probably the buyers (the major oil companies), while in tires it is powerful original equipment manufacturer (OEM) buyers coupled with tough competitors. In the steel industry the key forces are foreign competitors and substitute materials.

Every industry has an underlying structure, or a set of fundamental economic and technical characteristics, that gives rise to these competitive forces. The strategist, wanting to position his company to cope best with its industry environment or to influence that environment in the company's favor, must learn what makes the environment tick.

This view of competition pertains equally to industries dealing in services and to those selling products. To avoid monotony in this article, I refer to both products and services as "products." The same general principles apply to all types of business.

A few characteristics are critical to the strength of each competitive force. I shall discuss them in this section.

Threat of Entry

New entrants to an industry bring new capacity, the desire to gain market share, and often substantial resources. Companies diversifying through acquisition into the industry from other markets often leverage their resources to cause a shake-up.

The seriousness of the threat of entry depends on the barriers present and on the reaction from existing competitors that the entrant can expect. If barriers to entry are high and a newcomer can expect sharp retaliation from the entrenched competitors, obviously he will not pose a serious threat of entering.

There are six major sources of barriers to entry:

■ *Economies of scale.* These economies deter entry by forcing the aspirant either to come in on a large scale or to accept a cost disadvantage. Scale economies in production, research, marketing, and service are probably the key barriers to entry in the mainframe computer industry, as Xerox and General Electric sadly discovered. Economies of scale can also act as hurdles in distribution, utilization of the sales force, financing, and nearly any other part of a business.

■ *Product differentiation.* Brand identification creates a barrier by forcing entrants to spend heavily to overcome customer loyalty. Advertising, customer service, being first in the industry, and product differences are among the factors fostering brand identification.

■ *Capital requirements.* The need to invest large financial resources in order to compete creates a barrier to entry, particularly if the capital is required for unrecoverable expenditures in up-front advertising or research and development (R&D). Capital is necessary not only for fixed facilities but also for customer credit, inventories, and absorbing start-up losses. While major corporations have the financial resources to invade almost any industry, the huge capital requirements in certain fields, such as computer manufacturing and mineral extraction, limit the pool of likely entrants.

■ *Cost disadvantages independent of size.* Entrenched companies may have cost advantages not available to potential rivals, no matter what their size and attainable economies of scale. These advantages can stem from the effects of the learning curve (and of its first cousin, the experience curve), proprietary technology, access to the best raw materials sources, assets purchased at preinflation prices, government subsidies, or favorable locations. Sometimes cost advantages are legally enforceable, as they are through patents.

■ *Access to distribution channels.* The new boy on the block must, of course, secure distribution of his product or service. A new food product, for example, must displace others from the supermarket shelf via price breaks, promotions, intense selling efforts, or some other means. The more limited the wholesale or retail channels are and the more that existing competitors have these tied up, obviously the tougher that entry into the industry will be. Sometimes this barrier is so high that to surmount it, a new contestant must create its own distribution channels.

■ *Government policy.* The government can limit or even foreclose entry to industries with such controls as license requirements and limits on access to raw materials. The government also can play a major indirect role by effecting entry barriers through controls such as air and water pollution standards and safety regulations.

The potential rival's expectations about the reaction of existing competitors also will influence its decision on whether to enter. The company is likely to have second thoughts if incumbents have previously lashed out at new entrants or if

■ the incumbents possess substantial resources to fight back, including excess cash and unused borrowing power, productive capacity, or clout with distribution channels and customers;

■ the incumbents seem likely to cut prices because of a desire to keep market share or because of industrywide excess capacity;

■ industry growth is slow, affecting its ability to absorb the new arrival and probably causing the financial performance of all the parties involved to decline.

Changing Conditions

From a strategic standpoint there are two important additional points to note about the threat of entry. First, it changes, of course, as these conditions change. Second, strategic decisions involving a large segment of an industry can have a major impact on the conditions determining the threat of entry. For example, the actions of many U.S. wine producers in the 1960s to step up product introductions, raise advertising levels, and expand distribution nationally surely strengthened the entry roadblocks by raising economies of scale and making access to distribution channels more difficult.

Powerful Suppliers and Buyers

Suppliers can exert bargaining power on participants in an industry by raising prices or reducing the quality of purchased goods and services. Powerful suppliers can thereby squeeze profitability out of an industry unable to recover cost increases in its own prices. By raising their prices, soft drink concentrate producers have contributed to the erosion of profitability of bottling companies because the bottlers, facing intense competition from powdered mixes, fruit drinks, and other beverages, have limited freedom to raise *their* prices accordingly. Customers likewise can force down prices, demand higher quality or more service, and play competitors off against each other—all at the expense of industry profits.

The power of each important supplier or buyer group depends on a number of characteristics of its market situation and on the relative importance of its sales or purchases to the industry compared with its overall business.

A *supplier* group is powerful if:

- It is dominated by a few companies and is more concentrated than the industry it sells to.
- Its product is unique or at least differentiated, or if it has built up switching costs. Switching costs are fixed costs buyers face in changing suppliers. These arise because, among other things, a buyer's product specifications tie it to particular suppliers, it has invested heavily in specialized ancillary equipment or in learning how to operate a supplier's equipment (as in computer software), or its production lines are connected to the supplier's manufacturing facilities (as in some manufacture of beverage containers).
- It is not obliged to contend with other products for sale to the industry. For instance, the competition between the steel companies and the aluminum companies to sell to the can industry checks the power of each supplier.
- It poses a credible threat of integrating forward into the industry's business. This provides a check against the industry's ability to improve the terms on which it purchases.
- The industry is not an important customer of the supplier group. If the industry is an important customer, suppliers' fortunes will be closely tied to the industry, and they will want to protect the industry through reasonable pricing and assistance in activities like R&D and lobbying.

A *buyer* group is powerful if:

- It is concentrated or purchases in large volumes. Large-volume buyers are particularly potent forces if heavy fixed costs characterize the industry, which raises the stakes to keep capacity filled.
- The products it purchases from the industry are standard or undifferentiated. The buyers, sure that they can always find alternative suppliers, may play one company against another.

■ The products it purchases from the industry form a component of its product and represent a significant fraction of its cost. The buyers are likely to shop for a favorable price and purchase selectively. Where the product sold by the industry in question is a small fraction of buyers' costs, buyers are usually much less price sensitive.

■ It earns low profits, which creates great incentive to lower its purchasing costs. Highly profitable buyers, however, are generally less price sensitive (that is, of course, if the item does not represent a large fraction of their costs).

■ The industry's product is unimportant to the quality of the buyers' products or services. Where the quality of the buyers' products is very much affected by the industry's product, buyers are generally less price sensitive. Industries in which this situation obtains include oil field equipment, where a malfunction can lead to large losses, and enclosures for electronic medical and test instruments where the quality of the enclosure can influence the user's impression about the quality of the equipment inside.

■ The industry's product does not save the buyer money. Where the industry's product or service can pay for itself many times over, the buyer is rarely price sensitive; rather, he is interested in quality. This is true in services like investment banking and public accounting, where errors in judgment can be costly and embarrassing.

■ The buyers pose a credible threat of integrating backward to make the industry's product. The Big Three auto producers and major buyers of cars have often used the threat of self-manufacture as a bargaining lever. But sometimes an industry engenders a threat to buyers that its members may integrate forward.

Most of these sources of buyer power can be attributed to consumers as a group as well as to industrial and commercial buyers; only a modification of the frame of reference is necessary. Consumers tend to be more price sensitive if they are purchasing products that are undifferentiated, expensive relative to their incomes, and of a sort where quality is not particularly important.

The buying power of retailers is determined by the same rules, with one important addition. Retailers can gain significant bargaining power over manufacturers when they can influence consumers' purchasing decisions, as they do in audio components, jewelry, appliances, sporting goods, and other goods.

Strategic Action

A company's choice of suppliers to buy from or buyer groups to sell to should be viewed as a crucial strategic decision. A company can improve its strategic posture by finding suppliers or buyers who possess the least power to influence it adversely.

Most common is the situation of a company being able to choose whom it will sell to—in other words, buyer selection. Rarely do all the buyer groups a company sells to enjoy equal power. Even if a company sells to a single industry, segments usually exist within that industry that exercise less power (and that are therefore less price sensitive) than others. For example, the replacement market for most products is less price sensitive than the overall market.

As a rule, a company can sell to powerful buyers and still come away with above-average profitability only if it is a low-cost producer in its industry or if its product enjoys some unusual, if not unique, features.

If the company lacks a low-cost position or a unique product, selling to everyone is self-defeating because the more sales it achieves, the more vulnerable it becomes. The company may have to muster the courage to turn away business and sell only to less-potent customers. Of course, some industries do not enjoy the luxury of selecting "good" buyers.

Substitute Products

By placing a ceiling on prices it can charge, substitute products or services limit the potential of an industry. Unless it can upgrade the quality of the product or differentiate it somehow (as via marketing), the industry will suffer in earnings and possibly in growth.

Manifestly, the more attractive the price-performance trade-off offered by substitute products, the firmer the lid placed on the industry's profit potential.

Substitutes not only limit profits in normal times; they also reduce the bonanza an industry can reap in boom times. In 1978 the producers of fiberglass insulation enjoyed unprecedented demand as a result of high energy costs and severe winter weather. But the industry's ability to raise prices was tempered by the plethora of insulation substitutes, including cellulose, rock wool, and styrofoam. These substitutes are bound to become an even stronger force once the current round of plant additions by fiberglass insulation producers has boosted capacity enough to meet demand (and then some).

Substitute products that deserve the most attention strategically are those that (1) are subject to trends improving their price-performance trade-off with the industry's product, or (2) are produced by industries earning high profits. Substitutes often come rapidly into play if some development increases competition in their industries and causes price reduction or performance improvement.

Jockeying for Position

Rivalry among existing competitors takes the familiar form of jockeying for position—using tactics like price competition, product introduction, and advertising slugfests. Intense rivalry is related to the presence of a number of factors:

- Competitors are numerous or are roughly equal in size and power. In many U.S. industries in recent years foreign contenders, of course, have become part of the competitive picture.

- Industry growth is slow, precipitating fights for market share that involve expansion-minded members.

- The product or service lacks differentiation or switching costs, which locks in buyers and protects one combatant from raids on its customers by another.

- Fixed costs are high or the product is perishable, creating strong temptation to cut prices. Many basic materials businesses, like paper and aluminum, suffer from this problem when demand slackens.

- Capacity is normally augmented in large increments. Such additions, as in the chlorine and vinyl chloride businesses, disrupt the industry's supply-demand balance and often lead to periods of overcapacity and price cutting.

- Exit barriers are high. Exit barriers, like very specialized assets or management's loyalty to a particular business, keep companies competing even though they may be earning low or even negative returns on investment. Excess capacity remains functioning, and the profitability of the healthy competitors suffers as the sick ones hang on. If the entire industry suffers from overcapacity, it may seek government help—particularly if foreign competition is present.

■ The rivals are diverse in strategies, origins, and "personalities." They have different ideas about how to compete and continually run head-on into each other in the process.

As an industry matures, its growth rate changes, resulting in declining profits and (often) a shakeout. In the booming recreational vehicle industry of the early 1970s, nearly every producer did well; but slow growth since then has eliminated the high returns, except for the strongest members, not to mention many of the weaker companies.

While a company must live with many of these factors—because they are built into industry economics—it may have some latitude for improving matters through strategic shifts. For example, it may try to raise buyers' switching costs or increase product differentiation. A focus on selling efforts in the fastest-growing segments of the industry or on market areas with the lowest fixed costs can reduce the impact of industry rivalry. If it is feasible, a company can try to avoid confrontation with competitors having high exit barriers and can thus sidestep involvement in bitter price cutting.

Formulation of Strategy

Once the corporate strategist has assessed the forces affecting competition in his industry and their underlying causes, he can identify his company's strengths and weaknesses. The crucial strengths and weaknesses from a strategic standpoint are the company's posture vis-à-vis the underlying causes of each force. Where does it stand against substitutes? Against the sources of entry barriers?

Then the strategist can devise a plan of action that may include (1) positioning the company so that its capabilities provide the best defense against the competitive force; and/or (2) influencing the balance of the forces through strategic moves, thereby improving the company's position; and/or (3) anticipating shifts in the factors underlying the forces and responding to them, with the hope of exploiting change by choosing a strategy appropriate for the new competitive balance before opponents recognize it.

■ THE VALUE CHAIN†

By Michael Porter

Competitive advantage cannot be understood by looking at a firm as a whole. It stems from the many discrete activities a firm performs in designing, producing, marketing, delivering, and supporting its product. Each of these activities can contribute to a firm's relative cost position and create a basis for differentiation. A cost advantage, for example, may stem from such disparate sources as a low-cost physical distribution system, a highly efficient assembly process, or superior sales force utilization. Differentiation can stem from similarly diverse factors, including the procurement of high-quality raw materials, a responsive order entry system, or a superior product design.

FIGURE 4-3
The Value System

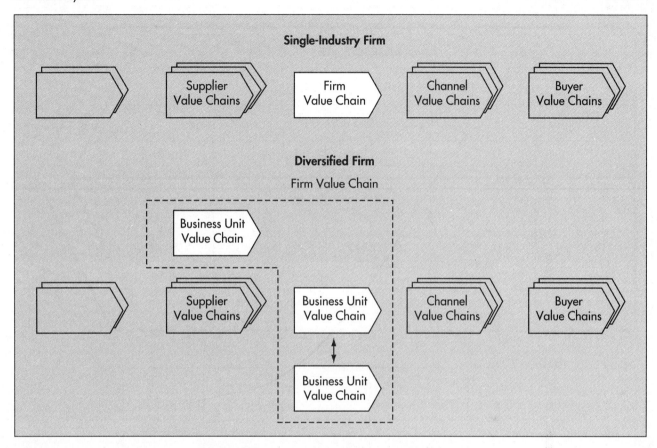

A systematic way of examining all the activities a firm performs and how they interact is necessary for analyzing the sources of competitive advantage. In this article, I introduce the *value chain* as the basic tool for doing so. The value chain disaggregates a firm into its strategically relevant activities in order to understand the behavior of costs and the existing and potential sources of differentiation. A firm gains competitive advantage by performing these strategically important activities more cheaply or better than its competitors.

A firm's value chain is embedded in a larger stream of activities that I term the *value system*, illustrated in figure 4-3. Suppliers have value chains (*upstream value*) that create and deliver the purchased inputs used in a firm's chain. Suppliers not only deliver a product but also can influence a firm's performance in many other ways. In addition, many products pass through the value chains of channels (*channel value*) on their way to the buyer. Channels perform additional activities that affect the buyer, as well as influence the firm's own activities. A firm's product eventually becomes part of its *buyer's value chain*. The ultimate basis for differentiation is a firm and its product's role in the buyer's value chain, which determines buyer needs. Gaining and sustaining competitive advantage depends on understanding not only a firm's value chain but how the firm fits in the overall value system.

FIGURE 4-4
The Generic Value Chain

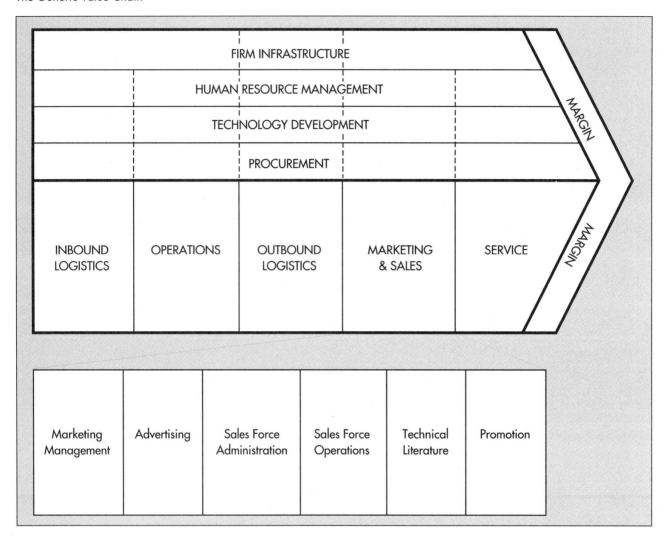

The Value Chain

Every firm is a collection of activities that are performed to design, produce, market, deliver, and support its product. All these activities can be represented using a value chain, shown in figure 4-4. A firm's value chain and the way it performs individual activities are a reflection of its history, its strategy, its approach to implementing its strategy, and the underlying economics of the activities themselves.

The relevant level for constructing a value chain is a firm's activities in a particular industry (the business unit). An industry- or sector-wide value chain is too broad because it may obscure important sources of competitive advantage. Though firms in the same industry may have similar chains, the value chains of competitors often differ.

In competitive terms, value is the amount buyers are willing to pay for what a firm provides them. Value is measured by total revenue, a reflection of the price a firm's product commands and the units it can sell. A firm is profitable if the value it commands exceeds the costs involved in creating the product. Creating value for buyers that exceeds the cost of doing so is the goal of any generic strategy. Value, instead of cost, must be used in analyzing competitive position since firms often deliberately raise their cost in order to command a premium price via differentiation.

The value chain displays total value, and consists of *value activities* and *margin*. Value activities are the physically and technologically distinct activities a firm performs. These are the building blocks by which a firm creates a product valuable to its buyers. Margin is the difference between total value and the collective cost of performing the value activities. Margin can be measured in a variety of ways. Supplier and channel value chains also include a margin that is important to isolate in understanding the sources of a firm's cost position, since supplier and channel margin are part of the total cost borne by the buyer.

Every value activity employs *purchased inputs, human resources* (labor and management), and some form of *technology* to perform its function. Each value activity also uses and creates *information*, such as buyer data (order entry), performance parameters (testing), and product failure statistics. Value activities may also create financial assets such as inventory and accounts receivable, or liabilities such as accounts payable.

Value activities can be divided into two broad types, *primary* activities and *support* activities. Primary activities, listed along the bottom of figure 4-4, are the activities involved in the physical creation of the product and its sale and transfer to the buyer, as well as after-sale assistance. In any firm, primary activities can be divided into the five generic categories shown in this figure. Support activities support the primary activities and each other by providing purchased inputs, technology, human resources, and various firmwide functions. The dotted lines reflect the fact that procurement, technology development, and human resource management can be associated with specific primary activities as well as support the entire chain. Firm infrastructure is not associated with particular primary activities but supports the entire chain.

Identifying Value Activities

Identifying value activities requires the isolation of activities that are technologically and strategically distinct. Value activities and accounting classifications are rarely the same. Accounting classifications (e.g., burden, overhead, direct labor) group together activities with disparate technologies, and separate costs that are all part of the same activity.

Primary Activities

There are five generic categories of primary activities involved in competing in any industry, as shown in figure 4-4. Each category is divisible into a number of distinct activities that depend on the particular industry and firm strategy:

- *Inbound logistics.* Activities associated with receiving, storing, and disseminating inputs to the product, such as material handling, warehousing, inventory control, vehicle scheduling, and returns to suppliers.

- *Operations.* Actitivies associated with transforming inputs into the final product form, such as machining, packaging, assembly, equipment maintenance, testing, printing, and facility operations.
- *Outbound logistics.* Activities associated with collecting, storing, and physically distributing the product to buyers, such as finished goods warehousing, material handling, delivery vehicle operation, order processing, and scheduling.
- *Marketing and sales.* Activities associated with providing a means by which buyers can purchase the product and inducing them to do so, such as advertising, promotion, sales force, quoting, channel selection, channel relations, and pricing.
- *Service.* Activities associated with providing service to enhance or maintain the value of the product, such as installation, repair, training parts supply, and product adjustment.

Support Activities

Procurement.   Procurement refers to the *function* of purchasing inputs used in the firm's value chain, not to the purchased inputs themselves. Purchased inputs include raw materials, supplies, and other consumable items as well as assets such as machinery, laboratory equipment, office equipment, and buildings. Though purchased inputs are commonly associated with primary activities, purchased inputs are present in every value activity including support activities. For example, laboratory supplies and independent testing services are common purchased inputs in technology development, while an accounting firm is a common purchased input in firm infrastructure. Like all value activities, procurement employs a "technology," such as procedures for dealing with vendors, qualification rules, and information systems.

Procurement tends to be spread throughout a firm. Some items such as raw materials are purchased by the traditional purchasing department, while other items are purchased by plant managers (e.g., machines), office managers (e.g., temporary help), salespersons (e.g., meals and lodging), and even the chief executive officer (e.g., strategic consulting). I use the term *procurement* rather than *purchasing* because the usual connotation of purchasing is too narrow among managers. The dispersion of the procurement function often obscures the magnitude of total purchases, and means that many purchases receive little scrutiny.

A given procurement activity can normally be associated with a specific value activity or activities it supports, though often a purchasing department serves many value activities and purchasing policies apply firmwide. The cost of procurement activities themselves usually represents a small if not insignificant portion of total costs, but often has a large impact on the firm's overall cost and differentiation. Improved purchasing practices can strongly affect the cost and quality of purchased inputs, as well as of other activities associated with receiving and using the inputs, and interacting with suppliers.

Technology Development.   Every value activity embodies technology, be it know-how, procedures, or technology embodied in process equipment. The array of technologies employed in most firms is very broad, ranging from those technologies used in preparing documents and transporting goods to those technologies embodied in the product itself. Moreover, most value activities use a technology that combines a number of different subtechnologies involving different scientific disciplines. Machining, for example, involves metallurgy, electronics, and mechanics.

Technology development consists of a range of activities that can be broadly grouped into efforts to improve the product and the process. I term this category of activities technology development instead of research and development because R&D has too narrow a connotation to most managers. Technology development tends to be associated with the engineering department or the development group. Typically, however, it occurs in many parts of a firm, although this is not explicitly recognized. Technology development may support any of the numerous technologies embodied in value activities, including such areas as telecommunications technology for the order entry system, or office automation for the accounting department. It does not solely apply to technologies directly linked to the end product. Technology development also takes many forms, from basic research and product design to media research, process equipment design, and servicing procedures. Technology development that is related to the product and its features supports the entire chain, while other technology development is associated with particular primary or support activities.

Human Resource Management. Human resource management consists of activities involved in the recruiting, hiring, training, development, and compensation of all types of personnel. Human resource management supports both individual primary and support activities (e.g., hiring of engineers) and the entire value chain (e.g., labor negotiations). Human resource management activities occur in different parts of a firm, as do other support activities, and the dispersion of these activities can lead to inconsistent policies. Moreover, the cumulative costs of human resource management are rarely well understood nor are the trade-offs in different human resource management costs, such as salary compared with the cost of recruiting and training due to turnover.

Firm Infrastructure. Firm infrastructure consists of a number of activities including general management, planning, finance, accounting, legal, government affairs, and quality management. Infrastructure, unlike other support activities, usually supports the entire chain and not individual activities. Depending on whether a firm is diversified or not, firm infrastructure may be self-contained or divided between a business unit and the parent corporation. In diversified firms, infrastructure activities are typically split between the business unit and corporate levels (e.g., financing is often done at the corporate level while quality management is done at the business unit level). Many infrastructure activities occur at both the business unit and corporate levels, however.

Firm infrastructure is sometimes viewed only as "overhead," but can be a powerful source of competitive advantage. In a telephone-operating company, for example, negotiating and maintaining ongoing relations with regulatory bodies can be among the most important activities for competitive advantage. Similarly, proper management information systems can contribute significantly to cost position, while in some industries top management plays a vital role in dealing with the buyer.

Activity Types

Within each category of primary and support activities, there are three activity types that play a different role in competitive advantage:

- *Direct.* Activities directly involved in creating value for the buyer, such as assembly, parts machining, sales force operation, advertising, product design, recruiting.
- *Indirect.* Activities that make it possible to perform direct activities on a continuing basis, such as maintenance, scheduling, operation of facilities, sales force administration, research administration, vendor record keeping.

■ *Quality assurance.* Activities that ensure the quality of other activities, such as monitoring, inspecting, testing, reviewing, checking, adjusting, and reworking. Quality assurance is *not* synonymous with quality management, because many value activities contribute to quality.

Every firm has direct, indirect, and quality assurance value activities. All three types are present not only among primary activities but also among support activities. In technology development, for example, actual laboratory teams are direct activities, while research administration is an indirect activity.

The role of indirect and quality assurance activities is often not well understood, making the distinction among the three activity types an important one for diagnosing competitive advantage. In many industries, indirect activities represent a large and rapidly growing proportion of cost and can play a significant role in differentiation through their effect on direct activities. Despite this, indirect activities are frequently lumped together with direct activities when managers think about their firms, though the two often have very different economics. There are often trade-offs between direct and indirect activities—more spending on maintenance lowers machine costs. Indirect activities are also frequently grouped together into "overhead" or "burden" accounts, obscuring their cost and contribution to differentiation.

Quality assurance activities are also prevalent in nearly every part of a firm, though they are seldom recognized as such. Testing and inspection are associated with many primary activities. Quality assurance activities outside of operations are often less apparent though equally prevalent. The cumulative cost of quality assurance activities can be very large, as recent attention to the cost of quality has demonstrated. Quality assurance activities often affect the cost or effectiveness of other activities, and the way other activities are performed in turn affects the need for and types of quality assurance activities. The possibility of simplifying or eliminating the need for quality assurance activities through performing other activities better is at the root of the notion that quality can be "free."

Defining the Value Chain

To diagnose competitive advantage, it is necessary to define a firm's value chain for competing in a particular industry. Starting with the generic chain, individual value activities are identified in the particular firm. Each generic category can be divided into discrete activities, as illustrated for one generic category in figure 4-4.

Defining relevant value activities requires that activities with discrete technologies and economics be isolated. Broad functions such as manufacturing or marketing must be subdivided into activities. The product flow, order flow, or paper flow can be useful in doing so. Subdividing activities can proceed to the level of increasingly narrow activities that are to some degree discrete. Every machine in a factory, for example, could be treated as a separate activity. Thus the number of potential activities is often quite large.

The appropriate degree of disaggregation depends on the economics of the activities and the purposes for which the value chain is being analyzed. Here, the basic principle is that activities should be isolated and separated that (1) have different economics, (2) have a high potential impact of differentiation, or (3) represent a significant or growing proportion of cost. In using the value chain, successively finer disaggregations of some activities are made as the analysis exposes differences important to competitive advantage; other activities are combined because they prove to be unimportant to competitive advantage or are governed by similar economics.

Selecting the appropriate category in which to put an activity may require judgment and can be illuminating in its own right. Order processing, for example, could be classified as part of outbound logistics or as part of marketing. In a distributor, the role of order processing is more a marketing function. Similarly, the sales force often performs service functions. Value activities should be assigned to categories that best represent their contribution to a firm's competitive advantage. If order processing is an important way in which a firm interacts with its buyers, for example, it should be classified under marketing.

Everything a firm does should be captured in a primary or support activity. Value activity labels are arbitrary and should be chosen to provide the best insight into the business. Labeling activities in service industries often causes confusion because operations, marketing, and after-sale support are often closely tied. Ordering of activities should broadly follow the process flow, but ordering is judgmental as well. Often firms perform parallel activities, whose order should be chosen to enhance the intuitive clarity of the value chain to managers.

Linkages within the Value Chain

Although value activities are the building blocks of competitive advantage, the value chain is not a collection of independent activities but a system of interdependent activities. Value activities are related by linkages within the value chain. Linkages are relationships between the way one value activity is performed and the cost or performance of another.

Linkages can lead to competitive advantage in two ways: optimization and coordination. Linkages often reflect trade-offs among activities to achieve the same overall result. For example, a more costly product design, more stringent materials specifications, or greater in-process inspection may reduce service costs. A firm must optimize such linkages reflecting its strategy in order to achieve competitive advantage.

Linkages may also reflect the need to coordinate activities. On-time delivery, for example, may require coordination of activities in operations, outbound logistics, and service (e.g., installation). The ability to coordinate linkages often reduces cost or enhances differentiation. Better coordination, for example, can reduce the need for inventory throughout the firm. Linkages imply that a firm's cost or differentiation is not merely the result of efforts to reduce cost or improve performance in each value activity individually. Much of the recent change in philosophy toward manufacturing and toward quality—strongly influenced by Japanese practice—is a recognition of the importance of linkages.

■ THE 7S FRAMEWORK†

By Robert Waterman, Thomas Peters, and Julien Phillips

The Belgian surrealist René Magritte painted a series of pipes and titled the series *Ceci n'est pas une pipe:* this is not a pipe. The picture of the thing is not the thing. In the same way, a structure is not an organization. We all know that, but like as not, when we reorganize what we do is to restructure. Intellectually, all managers and consultants know that much more goes on in the process of organizing than charts, boxes, dotted lines, position descriptions, and matrices can possibly depict. But all too often we behave as though we didn't know it; if we want change, we change the structure.

Our assertion is that productive organizational change is not simply a matter of structure, although structure is important. It is not so simple as the interaction between strategy and structure, although strategy is critical too. Our claim is that effective organizational change is really the relationship between structure, strategy, systems, style, skills, staff, and something we call superordinate goals. (The alliteration is intentional: it serves as an aid to memory.)

Our central idea is that organizational effectiveness stems from the interaction of several factors—some not especially obvious and some underanalyzed. Our framework for organizational change, graphically depicted in figure 4-5, suggests several important ideas:

- First is the idea of a multiplicity of factors that influence an organization's ability to change and its proper mode of change. Why pay attention to only one or two, ignoring the others? Beyond structure and strategy, there are at least five other identifiable elements. The division is to some extent arbitrary, but it has the merit of acknowledging the complexity identified in the research and segmenting it into manageable parts.

- Second, the diagram is intended to convey the notion of the interconnectedness of the variables—the idea is that it's difficult, perhaps impossible, to make significant progress in one area without making progress in the others as well. Notions of organizational change that ignore its many aspects or their interconnectedness are dangerous.

- In a recent article on strategy, *Fortune* commented that perhaps as many as 90 percent of carefully planned strategies don't work. If that is so, our guess would be that the failure is a failure in execution, resulting from inattention to the other *S*'s. Just as a logistics bottleneck can cripple a military strategy, inadequate systems or staff can make paper tigers of the best-laid plans for clobbering competitors.

- Finally, the shape of the diagram is significant. It has no starting point or implied hierarchy. A priori, it isn't obvious which of the seven factors will be the driving force in changing a particular organization at a particular point in time. In some cases, the critical variable might be strategy. In others, it could be systems or structure.

Structure

To understand this model of organizational change better, let us look at each of its elements, beginning—as most organizational discussions do—with structure. What will the new organization of the future be like? If decentralization was the trend of the

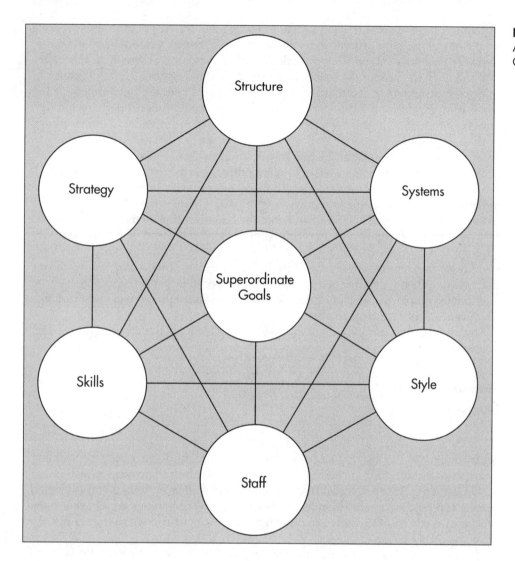

FIGURE 4-5
A New View of
Organization

past, what is next? Is it matrix organization? What will "Son of Matrix" look like? Our answer is that those questions miss the point.

The central problem in structuring today is not the one on which most organizational designers spend their time—that is, how to divide up tasks. It is one of emphasis and coordination—how to make the whole thing work. The challenge lies not so much in trying to comprehend all the possible dimensions of organizational structure as in developing the ability to focus on those dimensions currently important to the organization's evolution—and to be ready to refocus as the crucial dimensions shift.

Strategy

If structure is not enough, what is? Obviously, there is strategy. It was Alfred Chandler who first pointed out that structure follows strategy, or more precisely, that a strategy of diversity forces a decentralized structure. Throughout the past decade, the corporate world has given close attention to the interplay between strategy and structure. Certainly, clear ideas about strategy make the job of structural design more rational.

By strategy we mean those actions a company plans in response to or anticipation of changes in its external environment—its customers, its competitors. Strategy is the way a company aims to improve its position vis-à-vis competition—perhaps through low-cost production or delivery, perhaps by providing better value to the customer, perhaps by achieving sales and service dominance. It is, or ought to be, an organization's way of saying: "Here is how we will create unique value."

As the company's chosen route to competitive success, strategy is obviously a central concern in many business situations—especially in highly competitive industries where the game is won or lost on share points. But "structure follows strategy" is by no means the be-all and end-all of organizational wisdom. We find too many examples of large, prestigious companies around the world that are replete with strategy and cannot execute any of it. There is little if anything wrong with their structures; the causes of their inability to execute lie in other dimensions of our framework. When we turn to nonprofit and public-sector organizations, moreover, we find that the whole meaning of strategy is tenuous—but the problem of organizational effectiveness looms as large as ever.

Strategy, then, is clearly a critical variable in organizational design—but much more is at work.

Systems

By *systems* we mean all the procedures, formal and informal, that make the organization go, day by day and year by year: capital budgeting systems, training systems, cost-accounting procedures, budgeting systems. If there is a variable in our model that threatens to dominate the others, it could well be systems. Do you want to understand how an organization really does (or doesn't) get things done? Look at the systems. Do you want to change an organization without disruptive restructuring? Try changing the systems.

A large consumer goods manufacturer was recently trying to come up with an overall corporate strategy. Textbook portfolio theory seemed to apply: Find a good way to segment the business, decide which segments in the total business portfolio are most attractive, invest most heavily in those. The only catch: reliable cost data by segment were not to be had. The company's management information system was not adequate to support the segmentation.

Another intriguing aspect of systems is the way they mirror the state of an organization. Consider a certain company we'll call International Wickets. For years management has talked about the need to become more market oriented. Yet astonishingly little time is spent in their planning meetings on customers, marketing, market share, or other issues having to do with market orientation. One of their key systems, in other words, remains *very* internally oriented. Without a change in this key system, the market-orientation goal will remain unattainable no matter how much change takes place in structure and strategy.

To many business managers the word *systems* has a dull, plodding, middle-management sound. Yet it is astonishing how powerfully systems changes can enhance organizational effectiveness—without the disruptive side effects that so often ensue from tinkering with structure.

Style

It is remarkable how often writers, in characterizing a corporate management for the business press, fall back on the word *style*. Tony O'Reilly's style at Heinz is certainly not AT&T's, yet both are successful. The trouble we have with style is not in recognizing its importance, but in doing much about it. Personalities don't change, or so the conventional wisdom goes.

We think it important to distinguish between the basic personality of a top-management team and the way that team comes across to the organization. Organizations may listen to what managers say, but they believe what managers do. Not words, but patterns of actions are decisive. The power of style, then, is essentially manageable.

One element of a manager's style is how he or she chooses to spend time. As Henry Mintzberg has pointed out, managers don't spend their time in the neatly compartmentalized planning, organizing, motivating, and controlling modes of classical management theory. Their days are a mess or so it seems. There's a seeming infinity of things they might devote attention to. No top executive attends to all of the demands on his time; the median time spent on any one issue is nine minutes.

What can a top manager do in nine minutes? Actually, a good deal. He can signal what's on his mind; he can reinforce a message; he can nudge people's thinking in a desired direction. Skillful management of his inevitably fragmented time is, in fact, an immensely powerful change lever.

Another aspect of style is symbolic behavior. Companies most successful in finding mineral deposits typically have more people on the board who understand exploration or have headed exploration departments. Typically they fund exploration more consistently (that is, their year-to-year spending patterns are less volatile). They define fewer and more consistent exploration targets. Their exploration activities typically report at a higher organizational level. And they typically articulate better reasons for exploring in the first place.

This suggests a second attribute of style that is by no means confined to those at the top. Our proposition is that a corporation's style, as a reflection of its culture, has more to do with its ability to change organization or performance than is generally recognized.

Staff

Staff (in the sense of people, not line/staff) are often treated in one of two ways. At the hard end of the spectrum, we talk of appraisal systems, pay scales, formal training programs, and the like. At the soft end, we talk about morale, attitude, motivation, and behavior.

Top management is often, and justifiably, turned off by both these approaches. The first seems too trivial for their immediate concern ("Leave it to the personnel department"), the second too intractable ("We don't want a bunch of shrinks running around, stirring up the place with more attitude surveys").

Our predilection is to broaden and redefine the nature of the people issue. What do the top-performing companies do to foster the process of developing managers? How, for example, do they shape the basic values of their management cadre? Our reason for asking the question at all is simply that no serious discussion of organization can afford to ignore it (although many do). Our reason for framing the question around the development of managers is our observation that the superbly performing companies pay extraordinary attention to managing what might be called the socialization process in their companies. This applies especially to the way they introduce young recruits into the mainstream of their organizations and to the way they manage their careers as the recruits develop into tomorrow's managers.

Considering people as a pool of resources to be nurtured, developed, guarded, and allocated is one of the many ways to turn the "staff" dimension of our 7S framework into something not only amenable to, but worthy of, practical control by senior management.

We are often told, "Get the structure 'right' and the people will fit" or "Don't compromise the 'optimum' organization for people considerations." At the other end of the spectrum we are earnestly advised, "The right people can make any organization work." Neither view is correct. People do count, but staff is only one of our seven variables.

Skills

We added the notion of skills for a highly practical reason: It enables us to capture a company's crucial attributes as no other concept can do. A strategic description of a company, for example, might typically cover markets to be penetrated or types of products to be sold. But how do most of us characterize companies? Not by their strategies or their structures. We tend to characterize them by what they do best. We talk of IBM's orientation to the marketplace, its prodigious customer service capabilities, or its sheer market power. We talk of Du Pont's research prowess, Procter & Gamble's product management capability, ITT's financial controls, Hewlett-Packard's innovation and quality, and Texas Instruments' project management. These dominating attributes, or capabilities, are what we mean by skills.

Now why is this distinction important? Because we regularly observe that organizations facing big discontinuities in business conditions must do more than shift strategic focus. Frequently they need to add a new capability, that is to say, a new skill. The Bell System, for example, is currently striving to add a formidable new array of marketing skills. Small copier companies, upon growing larger, find that they must radically enhance their service capabilities to compete with Xerox. Meanwhile Xerox needs to enhance its response capability in order to fend off a host of new competition. These dominating capability needs, unless explicitly labeled as such, often get lost as the company "attacks a new market" (strategy shift) or "decentralizes to give managers autonomy" (structure shift).

Additionally, we frequently find it helpful to *label* current skills, for the addition of a new skill may come only when the old one is dismantled. Adopting a newly "flexible and adaptive marketing thrust," for example, may be possible only if increases are accepted in certain marketing or distribution costs. Dismantling some of the distracting attributes of an old "manufacturing mentality" (that is, a skill that was perhaps crucial in the past) may be the only way to insure the success of an important change program. Possibly the most difficult problem in trying to organize effectively is that of weeding out old skills—and their supporting systems, structures, and so on—to ensure that important new skills can take root and grow.

Superordinate Goals

The word *superordinate* literally means "of higher order." By superordinate goals we mean guiding concepts—a set of values and aspirations, often unwritten, that go beyond the conventional formal statement of corporate objectives.

Superordinate goals are the fundamental ideas around which a business is built. They are its main values. But they are more as well. They are the broad notions of future direction that the top management team wants to infuse throughout the organization. They are the way in which the team wants to express itself, to leave its own mark.

In a sense, superordinate goals are like the basic postulates in a mathematical system. They are the starting points on which the system is logically built, but in themselves are not logically derived. The ultimate test of their value is not their logic but the usefulness of the system that ensues. Everyone seems to know the importance of compelling superordinate goals. The drive for their accomplishment pulls an organization together. They provide stability in what would otherwise be a shifting set of organizational dynamics.

Unlike the other six S's, superordinate goals don't seem to be present in all, or even most, organizations. They are, however, evident in most of the superior performers.

To be readily communicated, superordinate goals need to be succinct. Typically, therefore, they are expressed at high levels of abstraction and may mean very little to outsiders who don 't know the organization well. But for those inside they are rich with significance. Within an organization, superordinate goals, if well articulated, make meanings for people. And making meanings is one of the main functions of leadership.

Conclusion

We have passed rapidly through the variables in our framework. What should the reader have gained from the exercise?

We started with the premise that solutions to today's thorny organizational problems that invoke only structure—or even strategy and structure—are seldom adequate. The inadequacy stems in part from the inability of the two-variable model to explain why organizations are so slow to adapt to change. The reasons often lie among our other variables: systems that embody outdated assumptions, a management style that is at odds with the stated strategy, the absence of a superordinate goal that binds the organization together in pursuit of a common purpose, the refusal to deal concretely with "people problems" and opportunities.

At its most trivial, when we merely use the framework as a checklist, we find that it leads into new terrain in our efforts to understand how organizations really operate or to design a truly comprehensive change program. At a minimum, it gives us a deeper bag in which to collect our experiences.

More important, it suggests the wisdom of taking seriously the variables in organizing that have been considered soft, informal, or beneath the purview of top management interest. We believe that style, systems, skills, superordinate goals can be observed directly, even measured—if only they are taken seriously. We think that these variables can be at least as important as strategy and structure in orchestrating major change; indeed, they are almost critical for achieving necessary, or desirable, change. A shift in systems, a major retraining program for staff, or the generation of top-to-bottom enthusiasm around a new superordinate goal could take years. Changes in strategy and structure, on the surface, may happen more quickly. But the pace of real change is geared to all seven S's.

At its most powerful and complex, the framework forces us to concentrate on interactions and fit. The real energy required to redirect an institution comes when all the variables in the model are aligned. One of our associates looks at our diagram as a set of compasses. "When all seven needles are all pointed the same way," he comments, "you're looking at an organized company."

■ PORTFOLIO ANALYSIS†

By Charles Hofer and Dan Schendel

For corporate level strategy, the principal visual constructs are business portfolio matrices that help to depict the firm's scope, the major component of corporate strategy. The simplest such matrix is a four-square grid developed by the Boston Consulting Group (BCG). A typical BCG matrix is depicted in figure 4-6. Here, each of the company's businesses is plotted according to the growth rates of the industry in which it competes and its relative competitive position (measured through market share) in that industry, with the size of each circle being proportional to the size of the business involved.

Businesses plotted in the upper left quadrant are called stars by BCG because they are growing rapidly while being roughly self-sustaining in terms of cash flow. As such, BCG feels they probably represent the best profit and growth opportunities available to a company.

Businesses in the lower left quadrant are called cash cows, because with their combination of low growth and high market share they could, and usually do, have entrenched, superior market positions with low costs, low growth rates, and the attendant low demands for investment funds that permit them to generate large cash surpluses. Cash cows thus pay the dividends and interest, provide debt capacity, pay the overhead, and provide the funds to reinvest elsewhere.

Businesses in the lower right quadrant of the matrix are called dogs by BCG because they usually are not very profitable owing to their relatively high-cost competitive position. Under periods of high inflation, dogs may not even generate enough cash to maintain their existing position, weak as it is. Thus BCG feels companies should try to liquidate any such businesses they have.

Businesses in the upper right quadrant are referred to as question marks or wildcats. They usually have the worst cash flow position of all since their cash needs are high because of growth and their cash generation is low because of low market share. Consequently, BCG feels there are only two viable strategies for a question mark business—grow it into a star or divest it.

Once the company's current position is plotted on such a grid, a projection can be made of its future position, assuming no change in its strategy. Viewed together, these two matrices—present and projected—not only help describe the scope and competitive advantage components of the firm's corporate strategy but also assist in the identification of some of the major strategic issues that face the firm. Such a grid also isolates some of the basic characteristics of each unit's business strategy.

†**Source:** This article was adapted from chapter 2 of *Strategy Formulation: Analytical Concepts*, West, 1978.

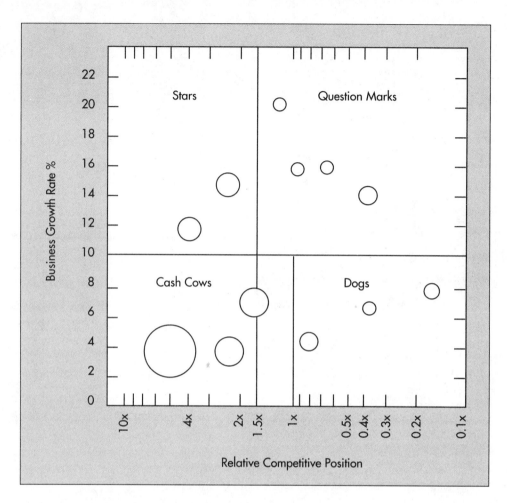

FIGURE 4-6
The BCG Business
Portfolio Matrix

Several criticisms have been raised about the use of BCG-type business portfolios. The most significant of these are:

- The use of a four-cell matrix is too simplistic since the world contains not only highs and lows, but middle positions as well.

- Growth rate is inadequate as a descriptor of overall industry attractiveness. There are, for example, some industries with high growth rates in demand that never have been very profitable because supply has grown even faster.

- Market share is inadequate as a description of overall competitive position because it depends so heavily on a definition of the market. Mercedes has a small share of the total auto market but a very high share of the luxury auto market, which may be a more relevant definition to use.

Figure 4-7 depicts a nine-cell "business screen," developed by General Electric, that overcomes most of these difficulties. On it, both industry attractiveness and competitive position are measures determined through an analysis and weighing of a variety of subfactors, including growth rate and market share. On this screen, the area of the circles is proportional to the size of the industries in which the various businesses compete. The pie slices within the circles reflect each business's market share.

FIGURE 4-7
The General Electric
Business Screen

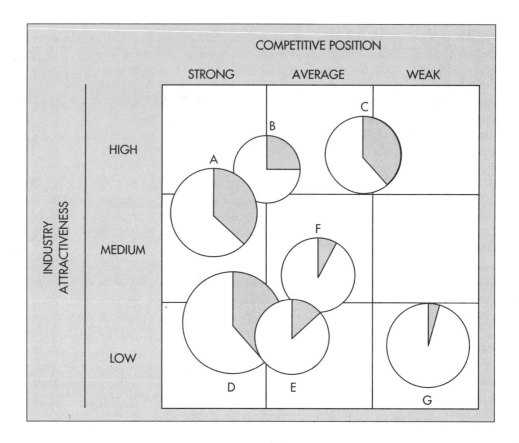

Consequently, their areas are also proportional to the sizes of the businesses they represent.

Here again, the firm's future position can be forecast, and the present and forecast matrices used both to help describe the firm's scope and competitive position and to identify some of the more important strategic issues facing the firm. In figure 4-7, for example, business C has a far larger market share than normal, given its competitive position ranking. Assuming both assessments are correct, one major strategic issue would be to identify the factors responsible for business C's poor competitive position and to assess whether these might be overcome at reasonable cost.

The principal difficulty with the GE business screen is that it does not depict as effectively as it might the positions of new businesses that are just starting to grow in new industries. In such instances, it may be preferable to use a fifteen-cell matrix in which businesses are plotted in terms of their competitive position and their stage of product/market evolution (see figure 4-8). As with the GE business screen, circles represent the sizes of the industries involved, and the pie wedges, the market shares of the businesses involved. Again, future positions can be plotted and used to identify major strategic issues. Thus in figure 4-8 one should ask why business B has not been able to secure a higher share of the market, given its strong competitive position.

Overall, each of the three business portfolio matrices described has strengths and weaknesses. In most situations, we recommend they be used in a two-stage process. First, a tentative plot of the corporate portfolio should be obtained using the BCG matrix because it is simplest and requires the least data. This tentative plot then can be

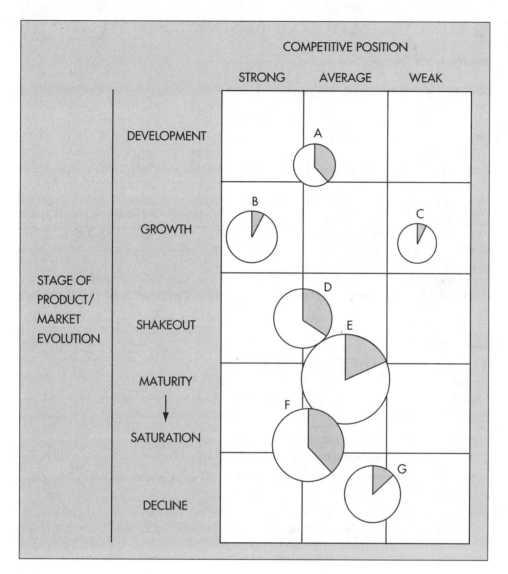

FIGURE 4-8
A Product/Market Evolution
Portfolio Matrix

used to highlight businesses that may require special attention during stage 2, either because of their importance or because they do not perform as they should based on the initial plot. During the second stage a choice should be made between the GE and the product/market evolution matrix according to the nature of the company's business. If most of the businesses represent aggregations of several product/market segments, the GE matrix is superior. However, if most consist of individual or small groups of related product/market segments, a product/market evolution matrix should be used.

■ THE EVALUATION OF BUSINESS STRATEGY†

By Richard Rumelt

Strategy can neither be formulated nor adjusted to changing circumstances without a process of strategy evaluation. Whether performed by an individual or as part of an organizational review procedure, strategy evaluation forms an essential step in the process of guiding an enterprise.

For many executives strategy evaluation is simply an appraisal of how well a business performs. Has it grown? Is the profit rate normal or better? If the answers to these questions are affirmative, it is argued that the firm's strategy must be sound. Despite its unassailable simplicity, this line of reasoning misses the whole point of strategy—that the critical factors determining the quality of current results are often not directly observable or simply measured, and that by the time strategic opportunities or threats do directly affect operating results, it may well be too late for an effective response. Thus, strategy evaluation is an attempt to look beyond the obvious facts regarding the short-term health of a business and appraise instead those more fundamental factors and trends that govern success in the chosen field of endeavor.

The Challenge of Evaluation

However it is accomplished, the products of a business strategy evaluation are answers to these three questions:

- Are the objectives of the business appropriate?
- Are the major policies and plans appropriate?
- Do the results obtained to date confirm or refute critical assumptions on which the strategy rests?

Devising adequate answers to these questions is neither simple nor straightforward. It requires a reasonable store of situation-based knowledge and more than the usual degree of insight. In particular, the major issues that make evaluation difficult and with which the analyst must come to grips are these:

- Each business strategy is unique. For example, one paper manufacturer might rely on its vast timber holdings to weather almost any storm while another might place primary reliance in modern machinery and an extensive distribution system. Neither strategy is wrong or right in any absolute sense; both may be right or wrong for the firms in question. Strategy evaluation must, then, rest on a type of situational logic that does not focus on one best way but that can be tailored to each problem as it is faced.

- Strategy is centrally concerned with the selection of goals and objectives. Many people, including seasoned executives, find it much easier to set or try to achieve goals than to evaluate them. In part this is a consequence of training in problem structuring. It also arises out of a tendency to confuse *values*, which are fundamental expressions of human personality, with objectives, which are *devices* for lending coherence to action.

- Formal systems of strategic review, while appealing in principle, can create explosive conflict situations. Not only are there serious questions as to who is qualified to give an

†**Source:** This article was originally published in *Business Policy and Strategic Management,* edited by W. F. Glueck (McGraw-Hill, 1980). Reproduced with permission.

objective evaluation, the whole idea of strategy evaluation implies management by "much more than results" and runs counter to much of currently popular management philosophy.

The Principles of Strategy Evaluation

For our purposes a strategy is a set of objectives, policies, and plans that taken together define the scope of the enterprise and its approach to survival and success. Alternatively, we could say that the particular policies, plans, and objectives of a business express its strategy for coping with a complex competitive environment.

One of the fundamental tenets of science is that a theory can never be proven to be absolutely true. A theory can, however, be declared absolutely false if it fails to stand up to testing. Similarly, it is impossible to demonstrate conclusively that a particular business strategy is optimal or even to guarantee that it will work. One can, nevertheless, test it for critical flaws. Of the many tests that could justifiably be applied to a business strategy, most will fit within one of these broad criteria:

- *Consistency.* The strategy must not present mutually inconsistent goals and policies.
- *Consonance.* The strategy must represent an adaptive response to the external environment and to the critical changes occurring within it.
- *Advantage.* The strategy must provide for the creation and/or maintenance of a competitive advantage in the selected area of activity.
- *Feasibility.* The strategy must neither overtax available resources nor create unsolvable subproblems.

A strategy that fails to meet one or more of these criteria is strongly suspect. It fails to perform at least one of the key functions that are necessary for the survival of the business. Experience within a particular industry or other setting will permit the analyst to sharpen these criteria and add others that are appropriate to the situation at hand.

Consistency

Gross inconsistency within a strategy seems unlikely until it is realized that many strategies have not been explicitly formulated but have evolved over time in an ad hoc fashion. Even strategies that are the result of formal procedures may easily contain compromise arrangements between opposing power groups.

Inconsistency in strategy is not simply a flaw in logic. A key function of strategy is to provide coherence to organizational action. A clear and explicit concept of strategy can foster a climate of tacit coordination that is more efficient than most administrative mechanisms. Many high-technology firms, for example, face a basic strategic choice between offering high-cost products with high custom-engineering content and lower-cost products that are more standardized and sold at higher volume. If senior management does not enunciate a clear, consistent sense of where the corporation stands on these issues, there will be continuing conflict between sales, design, engineering, and manufacturing people. A clear, consistent strategy, by contrast, allows a sales engineer to negotiate a contract with a minimum of coordination—the trade-offs are an explicit part of the firm's posture.

Organizational conflict and interdepartmental bickering are often symptoms of a managerial disorder but may also indicate problems of strategic inconsistency. Here are some indicators that can help sort out these two different problems:

- If problems in coordination and planning continue despite changes in personnel and tend to be issue rather than people based, they are probably due to inconsistencies in strategy.
- If success for one organizational department means, or is interpreted to mean, failure for another department, the basic objective structure is inconsistent.
- If, despite attempts to delegate authority, operating problems continue to be brought to the top for the resolution of *policy* issues, the basic strategy is probably inconsistent.

A final type of consistency that must be sought in strategy is between organizational objectives and the values of the management group. Inconsistency in this area is more of a problem in strategy formulation than in the evaluation of a strategy that has already been implemented. It can still arise, however, if the future direction of the business requires changes that conflict with managerial values. The most frequent source of such conflict is growth. As a business expands beyond the scale that allows an easy informal method of operation, many executives experience a sharp sense of loss. While growth can of course be curtailed, it often will require special attention to a firm's competitive position if survival without growth is desired. The same basic issues arise when other types of personal or social values come into conflict with existing or apparently necessary policies: the resolution of the conflict will normally require an adjustment in the competitive strategy.

Consonance

The way in which a business relates to its environment has two aspects: the business must both match and be adapted to its environment and it must at the same time compete with other firms that are also trying to adapt. This dual character of the relationship between the firm and its environment has its analog in two different aspects of strategic choice and two different methods of strategy evaluation.

The first aspect of fit deals with the basic mission or scope of the business and the second with its special competitive position or "edge." Analysis of the first is normally done by looking at changing economic and social conditions over time. Analysis of the second, by contrast, typically focuses on the differences across firms at a given time. We call the first the generic aspect of strategy and the second, competitive strategy. Table 4-2 summarizes the differences between these concepts.

TABLE 4-2
Generic Versus
Competitive Strategy

	Generic	**Competitive**
Measure of success	Sales growth	Market Share
Return to the firm	Value added	Return on investment
Function	Provision of value to the customer	Maintaining or obtaining a defensible position
Basic strategic tasks	Adapting to change and innovation	Creating barriers and deterring rivals
Method of expressing strategy	Product/market terms, functional terms	Policies leading to defensible position
Basic approach to analysis	Study of group of businesses over time	Comparison across rivals at a given time

The notion of consonance, or matching, therefore, invites a focus on generic strategy. The role of the evaluator in this case is to examine the basic pattern of economic relationships that characterize the business and determine whether or not sufficient value is being created to sustain the strategy. Most macroanalysis of changing economic conditions is oriented toward the formulation or evaluation of generic strategies. For example, a planning department forecasts that within ten years home appliances will no longer use mechanical timers or logic. Instead, microprocessors will do the job more reliably and less expensively. The basic message here for the makers of mechanical timers is that their generic strategies are becoming obsolete, especially if they specialize in major home appliances. Note that the threat in this case is not to a particular firm, competitive position, or individual approach to the marketplace but to the basic generic mission.

One major difficulty in evaluating consonance is that most of the critical threats to a business are those that come from without, threatening an entire group of firms. Management, however, is often so engrossed in competitive thinking that such threats are only recognized after the damage has reached considerable proportions.

The key to evaluating consonance is an understanding of why the business, as it currently stands, exists at all and how it assumed its current pattern. Once the analyst obtains a good grasp of the basic economic foundation that supports and defines the business, it is possible to study the consequences of key trends and changes. Without such an understanding, there is no good way of deciding what kinds of changes are most crucial, and the analyst can quickly be overwhelmed with data.

Advantage

It is no exaggeration to say that competitive strategy is the art of creating or exploiting those advantages that are most telling, enduring, and most difficult to duplicate.

Competitive strategy, in contrast to generic strategy, focuses on the differences among firms rather than their common missions. The problem it addresses is not so much, "How can this function be performed?" but "How can *we* perform it either better than, or at least instead of our rivals?" The chain supermarket, for example, represents a successful generic strategy. As a way of doing business, of organizing economic transactions, it has replaced almost all the smaller owner-managed food shops of an earlier era. Yet a potential or actual participant in the retail food business must go beyond this generic strategy and find a way of competing in the business. As another illustration, American Motors' early success in compact cars was generic— other firms soon copied the basic product concept. Once this happened, AMC had to try to either forge a strong competitive strategy in this area or seek a different type of competitive arena. Competitive advantages can normally be traced to one of three roots:

- superior resources
- superior skills
- superior position

The advantages produced by the first two are obvious. They represent the ability of a business to do more and/or do it better than its rivals. The critical analytical issue here is the question of which skills and resources represent advantages in which competitive arenas. The skills that make for success in the aerospace electronics industry, for instance, do not seem to have much to do with those needed in consumer electronics. Similarly, what makes for success in the early phases of an industry life cycle may be quite different from what ensures top performance in the later phases.

The idea that certain arrangements of one's resources can enhance their combined effectiveness, and perhaps even put rival forces in a state of disarray, is at the heart of the traditional notion of strategy. This kind of "positional" advantage is familiar to military theorists, chess players, and diplomats. Position plays a crucial role in business strategy as well.

Positional advantage can be gained by foresight, superior skill and/or resources, or just plain luck. Once gained, a good position is defensible. This means that it (1) returns enough value to warrant its continued maintenance and (2) would be so costly to capture that rivals are deterred from full-scale attacks on the core of the business. Position, it must be noted, tends to be self-sustaining as long as the basic environmental factors that underlie it remain stable. Thus entrenched firms can be almost impossible to unseat even if their raw skill levels are only average. And when a shifting environment allows position to be gained by a new entrant or innovator, the results can be spectacular.

The types of positional advantage that are most well known are those associated with size or scale. As the scale of operations increases, most firms are able to reduce both the marginal and the total cost of each additional unit produced. Marginal costs fall due to the effects of learning and more efficient processes, and total costs per unit fall even faster as fixed overheads are spread over a larger volume of activity. The larger firm can simply take these gains in terms of increased profitability or it can invest some of the extra returns in position-maintaining activities. By engaging in more research and development, being first to go abroad, having the largest advertising budget, and absorbing the costs involved with acting as an industry spokesman, the dominant business is rechanneling the gains obtained from its advantages into activities designed to maintain those advantages. This kind of positive feedback is the source of the power of position-based advantages—the policies that act to enhance position do not require unusual skills; they simply work most effectively for those who are already in the position in the first place.

While it is not true that larger businesses always have the advantages, it is true that larger businesses will tend to operate in markets and use procedures that turn their size to advantage. Large national consumer-products firms, for example, will normally have an advantage over smaller regional firms in the efficient use of mass advertising, especially network TV. The larger firm will, then, tend to deal in those products where the marginal effect of advertising is most potent, while the smaller firms will seek product-market positions that exploit other types of advantage.

Not all positional advantages are associated with size, although some type of uniqueness is a virtual prerequisite. The principal characteristic of good position is that it permits the firm to obtain advantage from policies that would not similarly benefit rivals without the position. For example, Volkswagen in 1966 had a strong, well-defined position as the preeminent maker of inexpensive, well-engineered, functional automobiles. This position allowed it to follow a policy of not changing its body styling. The policy both enhanced VW's position and reduced costs. Rivals could not similarly benefit from such a policy unless they could also duplicate the other aspects of VW's position. At the other end of the spectrum, Rolls-Royce employed a policy of deliberately limiting its output, a policy that enhanced its unique position and that could do so only because of its position in the first place. Mintzberg calls strongly defensible positions and the associated policies "gestalt strategies," recognizing that they are difficult either to analyze or attack in a piecemeal fashion.

Another type of positional advantage derives from successful trade names. These brands, especially when advertised, place retailers in the position of having to stock them, which in turn reinforces the position and raises the barrier to entry still further.

Such famous names as Sara Lee, Johnson & Johnson, and Kraft greatly reduce, for their holders, both the problems of gaining wide distribution for new products and obtaining trial use of new products by the buying public.

Other position-based advantages follow from such factors as:

- Owning special raw material sources or long-term supply contracts.

- Being geographically located near key customers in a business involving significant fixed investment and high transport costs.

- Being a leader in a service field that permits or requires the building of a unique experience base while serving clients.

- Being a full-line producer in a market with heavy trade-up phenomena.

- Having a wide reputation for providing a needed product or service reliably and dependably.

In each case, the position permits competitive policies to be adopted that can serve to reinforce the position. Whenever this type of positive-feedback phenomena is encountered, the particular policy mix that creates it will be found to be a defensible business position. The key factors that sparked industrial success stories such as IBM and Eastman Kodak were the early and rapid domination of strong positions opened up by new technologies.

Feasibility

The final broad test of strategy is its feasibility. Can the strategy be attempted within the physical, human, and financial resources available? The financial resources of a business are the easiest to quantify and are normally the first limitation against which strategy is tested. It is sometimes forgotten, however, that innovative approaches to financing expansion can both stretch the ultimate limitations and provide a competitive advantage, even if it is only temporary. Devices such as captive finance subsidiaries, sale-leaseback arrangements, and tying plant mortgages to long-term contracts have all been used effectively to help win key positions in suddenly expanding industries.

The less quantifiable but actually more rigid limitation on strategic choice is that imposed by the individual and organizational capabilities available.

In assessing the organization's ability to carry out a strategy, it is helpful to ask three separate questions.

- Has the organization demonstrated that it possesses the problem-solving abilities and/or special competences required by the strategy? A strategy, as such, does not and cannot specify in detail each action that must be carried out. Its purpose is to provide structure to the general issue of the business's goals and approaches to coping with its environment. It is up to the members and departments of the organization to carry out the tasks defined by strategy. A strategy that requires tasks to be accomplished that fall outside the realm of available or easily obtainable skill and knowledge cannot be accepted. It is either infeasible or incomplete.

- Has the organization demonstrated the degree of coordinative and integrative skill necessary to carry out the strategy? The key tasks required of a strategy not only require specialized skill, but often make considerable demands on the organization's ability to integrate disparate activities.

- Does the strategy challenge and motivate key personnel, and is it acceptable to those who must lend their support? The purpose of strategy is to effectively deploy the unique and distinctive resources of an enterprise. If key managers are unmoved by a strategy, not excited by its goals or methods, or strongly support an alternative, it fails in a major way.

Conclusions

In most medium—to large-size firms, strategy evaluation is not a purely intellectual task. The issues involved are too important and too closely associated with the distribution of power and authority for either strategy formulation or evaluation to take place in an ivory tower environment. In fact, most firms rarely engage in explicit formal strategy evaluation. Rather, the evaluation of current strategy is a continuing process and one that is difficult to separate from the normal planning, reporting, control, and reward systems of the firm. From this point of view, strategy evaluation is not so much an intellectual task as it is an organizational process.

As process, strategy evaluation is the outcome of activities and events that are strongly shaped by the firm's control and reward systems, its information and planning systems, its structure, and its history and particular culture. Thus its performance is, in practice, tied more directly to the quality of the firm's strategic management than to any particular analytical scheme. In particular, organizing major units around the primary strategic tasks and making the extra effort required to incorporate measures of strategic success in the control system may play vital roles in facilitating strategy evaluation within the firm.

Ultimately, a firm's ability to maintain its competitive position in a world of rivalry and change may be best served by managers who can maintain a dual view of strategy and strategy evaluation—they must be willing and able to perceive the strategy within the welter of daily activity *and* to build and maintain structures and systems that make strategic factors the object of current activity.

■ IMPLEMENTING STRATEGY†

By Lawrence Hrebiniak and William Joyce

The methods and problems of strategy implementation have received less attention than have those of strategy formulation. This is peculiar, because both practical and academic experience indicates that decisions made in implementing strategy have a substantial impact on organizational performance. There appears to be no unified, logical, normative approach for implementing strategy.

We believe, however, that much more has been written about strategy implementation than is apparent from a survey of titles of books and articles in academic and professional journals. The problem is not that we know too little about strategy implementation but that what we do know is fragmented among several "fields" of organization and management study. Each of these fields or approaches has focused on critical aspects of the strategy implementation process, providing key insights into how it should be managed. What remains, however, is a need for an integrated view of the implications of this knowledge for the theory and practice of strategy implementation.

Key Questions and Principles in Implementing Strategy

When answering the questions central to the implementation process, we believe that managers are guided by two critical principles. These are the principle of *intended rationality* and the principle of *minimum intervention*.

The Principle of Intended Rationality

In recent years there has been considerable interest in theories of limited rationality in decision making. March and Simon have argued that the classical economic theory of rational decision making does not adequately attend to the limited information-handling capacity of decision makers. The classical model assumes that decision makers have knowledge of all alternatives, the consequences of all alternatives, and a consistent preference-ordering and decision rule that allows choice from among them. Bounded rationality requires modification of this rational choice model, as discussed by March:

> "Because of such limits, the decision process that is used differs in some significant ways from the decision process anticipated by a more classical formulation. Decision making is seen as problem solving, search, and incremental trial and error. Described as 'muddling through' by Lindblom, as 'feedback-react' procedures by Cyert and March, and as 'cybernetic' by Steinbruner, incremental, limited rationality is usually contrasted with long-run planning, forecasts, and commitments. The intelligence of organizational action is seen as lying not in the capability to know everything in advance but in the ability to make marginal improvements by monitoring problems and searching for solutions. Thus theories of limited rationality are essentially theories of search or attention: What alternatives are considered? What information is used?"

We believe that recognition of bounded rationality and the limited actions of the classical economic decision model are essential to a theory of strategy implementation. The major consequence of limited rationality is to require that large strategic problems be "factored" into smaller, more manageable proportions for implementation. This process delimits the "candidates" for attention, allowing more rational decision given limited decision capacity.

We must be careful not to become so enamored of theories of limited rationality that we propose theories of nonrationality and rationality in their place. Our contention is that managers *intend* to be rational when formulating and implementing strategy, but that rationality is bounded by limited cognitive and information-processing capacities. Within limitations, the intention of managers is to (1) focus on utilitarian outcomes in strategic planning, (2) design organizations to minimize costs of coordination and optimize efficiency and effectiveness, and (3) develop incentives and controls that motivate and reinforce acceptable performance. Other factors (e.g., amount of slack resources) may determine the intensity with which rationality is pursued, but the basic pursuit, in our opinion, is central and pervasive in most organizations. Individual values and perceptions affect the process of formulating and implementing strategy, and individual behavior based on perceptions of rewards and costs may *not* always coincide or be consistent with organizational rationality and the attainment of superordinate organizational goals. The political or self-aggrandizing nature of individual behavior potentially can militate against and detract from desired organizational outcomes.

The point is that these facts actually support the existence of rationality in organizations. Individuals behave in such a way as to maximize personal rewards and minimize costs and negative feedback. Clearly, most behavior in utilitarian organizations is individually rational. The need, then, when implementing strategy is to try to ensure that desirable outcomes at the individual level are consistent with and support positive outcomes at the organizational level.

The principle of intended rationality implies that any approach to implementing strategy must confront two problems. First, the limited rationality of decision makers requires that large strategic problems be factored into more local and manageable proportions to reduce the *complexity* of implementation activities. Second, long-term strategic objectives must be factored into shorter-term operating objectives, and control mechanisms must be established to ensure *consistency* of individual and organizational rationality in pursuing these objectives.

A useful approach to strategy implementation also addresses a third issue: the efficient utilization of human, financial, and strategic resources. The next organizing concept, the principle of minimum intervention, addresses such issues directly.

The Principle of Minimum Intervention

This principle has its roots in many areas of organizational science and management practice and is implicit in the discussions of organizational design by Lawrence and Lorsch, Galbraith, and Thompson; of strategy formulation by Chandler and, more explicitly, of organizational development by Harrison. There is a general confluence in all this work that indicates that managers who are intendedly rational attempt to implement strategy within constraints of economic efficiency, choosing those courses of action that solve their problems with minimum costs to the organization.

This position is clear in Galbraith's approach to organizational design in which he argues implicitly that the traditional bureaucratic structural mechanisms be utilized as initial solutions to design problems. Only when these basic structures become overloaded by complex information-processing requirements should more complex and, thus, more costly techniques be used.

Similarly, in the strategy literature, Chandler argues that organizations do not change their structures when implementing strategy until they are forced to do so by operating inefficiencies. The resulting adjustment represents the minimum action needed to return to a state of efficient operation and increased economic performance.

Harrison has made these points quite explicitly in the organizational development literature noting that as the depth of intervention increases, not only do costs increase but so do the risks of unintended consequences for individuals. This concept can be expanded to argue that the principle of minimum intervention has a humanistic as well as a rational side; managers should implement strategy with minimum disruption of the individual's tasks, habits, and lives. In large systems in need of complex implementation efforts, however, such disruptions may be likely, placing human as well as logical constraints on the size and efficiency of implementation.

These considerations may be stated more generally in the following form: *In implementing strategy managers should change only what is necessary and sufficient to produce an enduring solution to the strategic problem being addressed.*

The point is that faced with a problem, the organization should respond in such a way as to solve it, but not at unnecessary financial or human cost. To confront a strategic problem by restructuring the entire organization when, in fact, it is possible to achieve acceptable results with a less far-reaching and pervasive approach (e.g., changes in incentives or controls) makes little sense. Violation of the principle of minimum intervention only results in unnecessary change and potentially negative impact on individuals responsible for the strategy implementation process.

Strategy Implementation: Planning and Design Problems

The two basic activities in implementing strategy are *planning* and *organizational design*. Although each of these has implications for the other, they have often been discussed separately, as if successful strategy implementation could be accomplished through either. This view has emphasized linkages and variables *within* each process or set of activities to the detriment of relationships between them. Some researchers, for example, have productively focused on such issues as the implications of corporate-level strategy for the development of business-level strategies specifying how the firm will compete in each of several, possibly related, businesses. Others have emphasized the implications of structural differentiation for achieving integration and coordination of effort toward some desired organizational end. Planners and organizational designers, that is, have tended to confine their thinking about strategy implementation to their own presumably separate fields. In contrast, we believe that both planning and organizational design are vital; both are interdependent and must be considered when implementing strategy.

Primary Structural Choices

Strategy formulation represents the starting point for the implementation actions in figure 4-9. Because a strategy applies to the entire organization, it must be broken

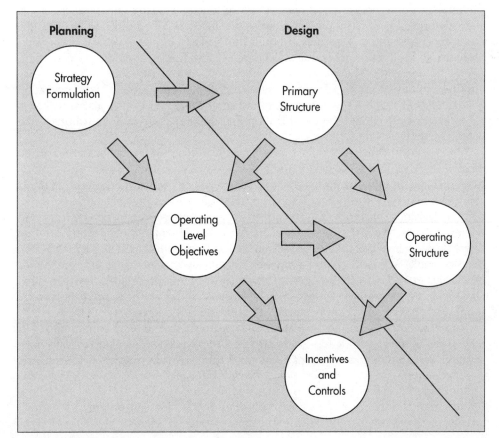

FIGURE 4-9
Strategy Implementation Model

down into smaller elements and ultimately short-range objectives. This causes a problem, because complex strategies imply complex and interdependent objectives, and planning processes alone are insufficient to ensure consistency and unity of direction. Also, decision makers have limited information-handling capabilities, as noted earlier. It is impossible for all managers to work simultaneously with a complex strategy and to comprehend adequately the interdependencies and diverse information involved.

Faced with such a situation, managers take action to reduce the scope of their plans to manageable proportions. In implementing strategy, this requires that managers first make choices about organizational design or the structural units within which efficiency and greater rationality are a reasonable expectation. Thompson argues that structure is the fundamental vehicle by which organizations achieve bounded rationality, and we refer to such decisions as primary structural choices in figure 4-9.

Primary structure denotes the *major operating units of the entire organization.* At this level of the implementation model, we argue that strategy formulation affects the creation or alteration of these primary units or elements. A strategy of diversification that results in the acquisition of another organization and its inclusion as a separate operating unit represents one example of the creation of primary structure. Primary structure, then, deals with the differentiation of the organization into its major components or parts. To facilitate the attainment of complex strategic objectives and plans, these objectives and plans must be reduced to smaller, more manageable proportions. Decisions about primary structure create the operating units that are most appropriate for this reduction process and, consequently, for the successful implementation of strategy.

We are arguing here that primary structure follows strategy, mainly because the strategic decisions of the type noted earlier are made at a point in time prior to the creation or alteration of the structural units that serve to implement the chosen plans. Structure also follows strategy, at least in part, because further attempts at establishing operating objectives and plans would be futile without the bounded rationality afforded within an appropriately chosen structural configuration. To set operating objectives that relate logically to longer-term strategic ends and plans, it first is necessary to differentiate the organization into smaller parts that contribute to the overall effort.

The choice of a primary structure clearly involves decisions about major organizing modes. Depending upon strategy and the costs involved, firms choose from among functional, geographic, or multidivisional structures, or even a hybrid representing a combination of basic forms. Similarly, strategic choices about product market position involve decisions concerning the customers or clients to serve, major competitors, and what regulation to expect. These decisions determine at what points the organization depends on or is vulnerable to changes in its environment. Rationality demands that managers take action to control elements of these environments to allow economic efficiency in the face of ambiguous or shifting competitive situations. In such circumstances, for example, managers may choose to acquire critical suppliers, thereby minimizing the threats to performance from uncertain relationships with them.

Numerous other examples abound in the organization and strategy literature, but they all make the same point: primary structure in part depends on and follows from strategy. The dominant direction of influence at this level is from strategy to structure.

Establishing Operating-Level Objectives

This is the third major component of the implementation model in figure 4-9. Operating-level objectives *are the strategic and short-term objectives of the major differentiated units of the organization.* Simply stated, objectives must now be set consistent with the choice or definition of structure. Integration of the operating objectives of major subunits with corporate strategic aims and plans is now possible because of the prior determination of primary structure. In a sense, then, planning at the operating level follows from and is delimited by structure. The formulation of operating unit or business strategy, given the existence of primary structure, reflects the constraints and opportunities in the prevailing situation.

This step represents the point in the planning process at which strategic objectives are developed for the operating units and are then translated into specific, short-term measures of performance. Focusing first on strategic objectives, it is helpful to picture the longtime existence of autonomous divisions or businesses that comprise the primary structure of the organization. Strategy formulation includes portfolio analysis and related issues of resource allocation at the corporate level. But strategy formulation also occurs at the divisional or business level. In the case of existing businesses or divisions, strategy formulation at the corporate and subunit levels may occur virtually simultaneously, but the former is clearly more global, whereas the latter reflects more limited local concerns. Strategy formulation at the corporate level includes assessment of, and resource allocations for, separate businesses or divisions; formulation at operating levels focuses more limitedly on a single business's or division's concerns, including its market strategy and intraunit allocation of resources.

The process of setting operating-level objectives also includes the translation of long-term strategic aims into specific short-term objectives for the operating units. Rather than trying to focus on the entire implementation process, managers at this stage are concerned with more local problems and objectives. Specific action plans are developed to implement portions of the strategy determined in the formulation process. Structure now constrains strategy implementation because managers focus on strategic issues relating only to their segments of the business, and these segments are determined by choices of the primary structure. Complex strategic issues cannot be easily elaborated into consistent, operational objectives and action plans without first establishing a zone of discretion within which managers can take action and commit resources. Primary structure establishes these boundaries and, once identified, reduces the information that must be processed during the establishment of operating objectives by reducing the number of inputs and outputs that must be considered.

It is clear, too, from the preceding discussion that operating-level objectives depend on previous choices of primary structure as well as on the basic strategy position of the entire organization. But the operating objectives obviously require local structure and processes for implementation as well. The next component of our model—operating structure—is created as a response to specific operating objectives originating from the first three strategy implementation activities. Thus, again, structure follows strategy and the planning process.

Operating Structure

Most of the theory and practice in the area of organizational design is devoted to operating structure, which refers to *the structure and, to some degree, related processes (e.g., coordination) within the major units that represent the primary structure of the organization.* Operating structure is the fourth component of the implementation process shown in figure 4-9. At this stage, managers must make decisions about the specific structure of the major components of the organization. In a sense, it is possible now to talk about organization designs rather than a single design; different divisions or businesses within the organization can face different situations and thus have different operating structures. The choice of operating structure depends in part on choices made at the three previous stages of implementation process, and the designer has many approaches to help at this point of implementation.

Decisions about operating structures fall into two broad categories: structural *differentiation*, or how to divide labor and departmentalize to achieve operating objectives; and *integration*, namely, the methods to be used to coordinate the various activities that have been segmented by differentiation decisions. Davis and Lawrence and others argue that organizations are created to solve problems and to carry out tasks that one person acting alone cannot accomplish. When more than one person come together to accomplish a task, criteria of efficiency dictate that work be divided to allow each person to become more expert at smaller portions of the task. This ultimately poses a problem, because once having divided the labor, it remains to coordinate the activities of workers toward the completion of the "whole" task.

Lawrence and Lorsch have provided extremely useful discussions and much needed research concerning these dual problems of differentiation and integration. We would add to their position by noting that while differentiation always precedes and often is antagonistic to integration, it is also clear that differentiation decisions, when defining operating structure, are usually made while simultaneously considering feasible integrating mechanisms. Thus concerns with differentiation and integration are not always sequential, although the actual techniques to achieve the latter follow the former.

The picture of implementing strategy, however, is not yet complete, because the creation of structure is not sufficient to ensure that individuals will adapt their own goals to those of the organization. Some strategy of obtaining individual and organizational goal congruence is required; great care in the formulation of strategy and development of operating structure and objectives can be negated by a lack of commitment or involvement among individuals charged with their implementation. Similarly, given individual rationality, it is unwise to allow individuals to benefit at the expense of or detriment to desired organizational outcomes. In essence what is required, then, is the careful development of an *incentive and control plan*, the fifth component of our model in figure 4-9 on page 195.

Incentive and Controls

Lorange (1980) and others propose that the planning process should contain a component dealing with the control of performance with respect to operating objectives. Individual and group rewards become an important aspect of strategy implementation because they control performance with respect to these desired ends. But incentive plans must be consistent with more than the operating objectives. The primary means of implementing operating-level objectives is the operating structure, whereas the primary means of controlling progress toward these objectives is the incentive plan. All three must be consistent with one another, with the dominant direction of influence from objectives to structure and then to incentives. Thus, the incentive plan must reinforce the structure and related management processes. Thorndike's "law of effect" definitely is most salient here: behavior that is reinforced tends to be repeated. This simple but powerful idea indicates the critical role of incentive planning for strategy formulation. The development of reward systems must support strategy implementation, thereby forming the fifth primary component of the implementation process. In this case, reward or incentive plans follow structure, and the cycle of planning decisions-design decisions continues within the implementation process.

To motivate behavior that is consistent with short-term and strategic objectives, it is vital to develop rewards and controls that take into account and integrate the short-run operation of the organization and its needs for long-run survival. People in utilitarian organizations are individually rational; successful implementation of strategy requires that individual motivations do not militate against the achievement of organizational rationality and the attainment of desired organizational outcomes. Similarly, control systems must guarantee the consistency and appropriateness of behavior or performance against objectives, but not at the expense of the innovation, creativity, and organizational learning that are so crucial for adaptability and long-term viability.

Change Management

The final component of the implementation process is change management, and it is a component whose importance should not be underestimated. All the previous components of the model deal with implementation, representing a logical chain of action choices that, as we describe them, are sequentially dependent upon one another. However, despite the fact that each of these addresses implementation, it is still necessary to confront more directly the critical problems inherent in changing strategic and operating objectives and primary and operating structures. Managers must make decisions about the "journalistic" questions of a strategy implementation: the who, what, where, and when of changing. The final portion of the model develops criteria for such changes as well as a specific approach to complex strategy implementation involving the simultaneous manipulation of several components of the model.

Strategy Implementation and Organizational Change

While it is true that everything depends on everything else in strategy implementation, it is also true that there is a dominant direction to this dependence deriving from the principle of intended rationality. *Not all elements of the basic model will be relevant in all situations;* we need ways of choosing or deciding the factors that are relevant in any given situation. Because the costs of strategy implementation increase with the size of the problem, this suggests the criterion of choosing, which we defined as the principle of minimum intervention.

The principle of minimum intervention provides a criterion for choosing where to begin an intervention. As the size of the strategic problem increases, we work backward in the basic model of figure 4-9 from the incentive and control component, through the various action steps, toward formulation itself. Small strategic problems may require only an adjustment in incentive plans, whereas larger problems may require changes in operating structures and consequently in all components of the model that follow this segment. In all cases the principle is the same: change only those portions of the system that must be changed to produce an enduring solution to the strategic problem.

After having decided which of the implementation components must be considered, we must decide how they will be implemented; that is, whether they will be implemented sequentially, in the order of the basic model, or whether they should all be considered jointly or concurrently. Generally managers prefer to implement strategy sequentially because the type of interdependence among components of the implementation process can be managed by plan. Concurrent or complex interventions or changes imply that "everything depends on everything else," that all components of the process are reciprocally interdependent. This type of dependence must be managed by mutual adjustment, a more costly form of coordination than plan, leading managers to prefer sequential implementation. However, other factors constrain this choice, the principle one of which we call the *implementation horizon*.

Implementation Horizon

Strategic problems have an additional important property beyond their size, and that is the time limit within which they must be solved. This is called the planning horizon: the time within which implementation must be accomplished.

The implementation horizon is determined by answering a number of questions, including, How long will the organization stay in business if it continues in its activities as it is today? If the answer to this question is several years, sequential strategy implementations are feasible. It is possible in this case for managers to approach the problem or threat in parts, methodically moving on only after each preceding part is handled or treated appropriately. If the answer to the implementation horizon question is that time is of the essence—for example, three to six months—it is clear that generally complex concurrent interventions must be undertaken to implement strategy.

The effect of shorter implementation horizons is to increase the number of components of the basic model that must be considered concurrently. Generally, the shorter the implementation horizon, the more complex the change, and consequently the more costly the adjustment in strategy. Under norms of rationality and the principle of minimum intervention, managers prefer to sequence implementation activities, beginning with the smallest component that will produce an enduring solution to the strategic problem.

The combination of these two primary characteristics of a strategic problem—size of problem and implementation horizon—determines the style chosen to implement strategy. Their combination implies that even small strategic problems can be difficult when coupled with short implementation horizons. The joint effect is a "velocity of change" that can produce costs approximating those of larger changes accomplished within longer implementation horizons.

A Typology of Strategy Implementations

The combination of these dimensions describes a rough taxonomy of types of strategy implementation efforts as shown in figure 4-10. There is a logical progression of costs among the four strategies—from simple evolutionary strategic change, through managerial and sequential implementation, and ending with complex implementations. This sequence implies that the most significant costs of implementation arise from the sheer magnitude of the problems being undertaken and that for any such problem the time available for implementation will have a secondary but important effect. Each of the types is now discussed briefly.

Evolutionary implementations are utilized when the strategic problem is small and the implementation horizon is long. Usually such changes are not recognized as changes at all but simply as "differences" in the way in which things are done over time. Under norms of intended rationality, managers take local actions to improve organizational performance, but without reference to any implementation plan. Because the size of the

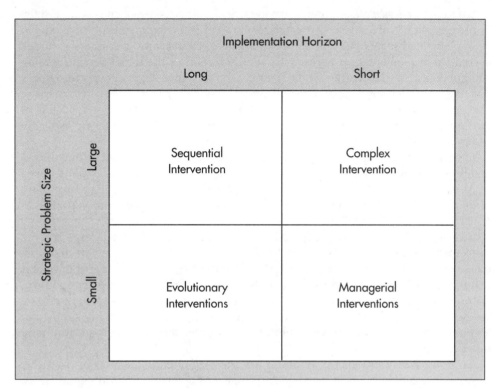

FIGURE 4-10
A Typology of Strategy
Implementation

problem is small, many implementations focus on latter stages of the implementation model and often are personnel related, as the emphasis is on incentives, controls, and motivations. Consequently, they are not sequential or complex interventions because only one component of the model is generally considered.

Connections between actions taken in evolutionary implementation are generally not recognized, and suboptimization occurs. Because such implementations are small, the costs of suboptimization are also small, and organizational slack is sufficient to absorb the minor inefficiencies. This type of implementation is effective as long as there are no major shifts in strategy and the organization has elaborated basic operating structures consistent with the strategic plan. Organizations implementing strategy in this mode are often "reactors" because of the few contingencies posed by their environment.

Managerial implementations occur when the size of the strategic problem is small, but the time available to implement the strategy is short. This can occur due to minor shifts in the business environment that require adjustment, but for which evolutionary implementations are undesirable due to the short time frame and cost of suboptimization. By definition, the planning horizon is short, and concerted action is imperative. Under criteria of intended rationality, organizations will develop implementation plans focusing on only one of the latter components: for example, structure or personnel-related decisions. Because the problem is not serious, usually only one component of the model is considered, and the effects of decisions on other components are ignored. Slack is usually sufficient to absorb these costs because the implementation is small and secondary effects are usually minor. Business environments are still relatively stable, posing no significant threats but requiring relatively frequent small adjustments.

Sequential implementations occur when the size of a strategic problem is large, but the implementation horizon is long enough to allow several components of the model to be implemented sequentially. Because this involves several components of the model, successful implementation necessitates consideration of the dependencies among components as well as within them. Planning for such interdependencies recognizes that any significant strategic change will involve change in several areas. In such cases, concerted action is required to avoid suboptimization, for now slack is unavailable or too costly an alternative. Connections among components of the model are explicitly recognized and accommodated, and are managed sequentially.

In this mode, an implementation begins with a specific component of the process and proceeds through all succeeding steps in turn, the key contingencies being posed by previous steps. Because such interdependencies can be managed by plan, sequenced interventions are preferred to the next type, complex interventions, in which planning is very difficult.

Complex implementations occur when the size of strategic problems is large and the implementation horizon is too short to allow sequencing of activities. In this case, managerial decisions about any one aspect of implementation both depend on and influence decisions in all other areas. Because of this reciprocal dependence, coordination by plan is impossible, and generally more costly face-to-face mechanisms are necessary. Organizations may establish task forces for implementing strategy to accommodate the higher needs for information processing arising from mutually interdependent activities.

Complex interventions occur under a variety of circumstances. For example, complex implementation is required in the face of a severe environmental shock requiring immediate adaptation. Generally, complex interventions are becoming more common as business environments become more complex and turbulent. In the face of rapid change, large adjustments in strategy are needed more frequently, implying more costly and complex implementations that pose new challenges for managers.

■ CREATING A STRATEGIC CONTROL SYSTEM†

By Stephen Bungay and Michael Goold

Why Have Strategic Controls?

Businesses need a balance between managing for short-term profits and for long-term strategic position (i.e., future profits). But on the principle that what you cannot measure, you cannot manage, it is very difficult to manage for long-term position without some measurement of it. Companies need some specific measures of the progress of their long-term strategies to build into their control systems, for what a company chooses to control explicitly is what its people will focus their attention on. A strategic control system ensures that the immense effort often put into preparing lengthy and detailed strategic plans is in fact translated into action, and the learning process is consolidated.

†**Source:** Reprinted with permission from *Long Range Planning*, "Creating a Strategic Control System", June 1991, Vol. 24, pp. 32–39, Pergamon Press Ltd. Oxford, England.

Strategic controls are of particular value to those at the centre of a diversified company with responsibility for controlling, monitoring, and guiding the development of operating units. For example:

- They are a means of clarifying what good performance is. Everybody wants to know three things: Where are we going? What do you want from me? and How am I doing? The control system can give answers to all of those questions, for it secures commitment to objectives that are tangible and complement financial ratios.

- They confer an ability to make explicit trade-offs between profit and investment/growth. Without them, when the going gets tough, budgetary pressures will tend to derail strategic goals, and in the same way, a strong short-term financial performance can make it hard to uncover underlying problems.

- They can be a way of introducing strategic "stretch" as well as financial stretch. Most people are motivated by targets that are difficult but just achievable, and it is often only by being set tough targets that they realize what they can achieve. Setting a competitive goal raises the sights of the business and gives it something worth striving for.

- They allow management in the business unit and at the centre to take action in a more timely way if the situation of a business is deteriorating. The alternative is to rely on gut feelings that something is wrong or wait until the bottom line proves the point. The right controls can not only give an early warning of impending problems but can suggest a diagnosis that enables management to take appropriate corrective action.

What Are Strategic Controls?

The measures actually adopted as strategic controls vary greatly, and are dependent on the nature of the business. In general, strategic controls can be considered to be nonfinancial performance measures or milestones. For example, for a company like Nestlé in a fast-moving consumer goods business, market share relative to other leading competitors is a vital measure, whereas for a research intensive business like ICI Pharmaceuticals, some measure of the quality of the R&D pipeline of new drugs is critical. Whatever measures are chosen should focus on objectives that are essential for achieving long-term competitive advantage in the business.

Strategic controls can be open to quantification, but sometimes their very nature mitigates against this. An interesting example of the use of both quantitative and qualitative strategic controls is offered by Honda. Honda places great emphasis on the measurement of nonfinancial controls at all levels. At the corporate level, although the centre believes in exercising as little direct control as possible over operations, it monitors customer satisfaction very closely. Honda supplements industry surveys with the company's own research that focuses on ascertaining the causes of problems. An overriding goal of Honda's senior management is to come top of these ratings.

In contrast to the formal way in which the customer satisfaction ratings are monitored, Honda pursues its second major goal in a more informal way, as it is not quantified. This goal, which it takes as seriously as the customer ratings, is to have high levels of "employee excitement" in all departments. Employee excitement is monitored by senior managers who are expected to visit their departments and report on it on a regular basis.

In addition to these two strategic controls, a host of operational factors (such as utilization, machine break-down rates, cycle times, waste levels, and so on) are measured at each Honda plant. They too are nonfinancial performance measures, but they have a different status from the two strategic controls, which are regarded as fundamental. Achieving top scores in customer satisfaction ratings is the company's overriding goal; employee excitement is a leading indicator of the company's ability to fulfil the goal, for doing so depends on continuous improvement, which Honda believes will only come about if employees remain highly motivated. Its controls complement each other and open the company up to enable it to learn rapidly: both learning what customers' needs are and encouraging employees to learn how to satisfy those needs better next time.

The choice of strategic objectives therefore needs to be based on a thorough assessment of what a company needs to do to achieve competitive advantage in its business. But once chosen, they are only effective when used in a control process through which monitoring and learning can take place. While the choice of objectives should be driven by the nature of the business, the development of an appropriate control process should be determined by the circumstances of the company and its management.

Developing a Strategic Control Process

Most major companies now have a strategic planning system that they use to help them manage their long-term position. It is in the context of the strategic planning process that strategic controls have their place.

A strategic planning process can only add value if the dialogue between the centre and the operating units is of high quality. In order to achieve high-quality dialogue, it is necessary for both the centre and the operating companies to invest in a period of building the requisite skills. Both must understand the sources of competitive advantage in the business, both must talk a common language, and most fundamentally, both must trust each other.

The effectiveness of the process is therefore as dependent on management skills, knowledge, and attitudes as it is on the focus of strategy. Controls can be particularly valuable in helping to develop these skills, which is an inherently slow process. Use of them can focus attention on the key success factors, keep discussion at the level of strategy, not operations, and facilitate the building of trust, by forcing both parties to be explicit about what they are collectively seeking to achieve. Instead of one party judging what the other is proposing, common ownership of the strategy is ensured. It follows that the planning process of which controls are an element should itself evolve with the skills of those engaged in it.

Stages in the Development of a Strategic Control Process

It is possible to think about the development of an effective strategic control process in terms of a number of broad phases that tend to merge into each other. First, the process presupposes the decentralization of responsibility for setting strategy into business units that are capable of operating with some degree of autonomy. Only when suitable organizational structure is in place can proper planning systems be developed. The second phase is the development of a formal planning process to create strategic-planning skills in the business units, and establish a common basis for dialogue with the centre. This should begin by focusing on competitive analysis and then move on to the definition of objectives and controls as part of the skill-building process. As the planning process evolves, it tends to grow in sophistication, and it carries within itself the danger of stultification into a formal routine. The third phase, therefore, which is as yet less common in practice, is to reduce the formality of the plans and shift the emphasis onto the controls. But the effectiveness of this stage will be greatly improved by the learning resulting from the previous ones, for it presupposes a high level of knowledge and understanding on the part of all those involved. Let us review each of these stages in more depth.

Aligning Appropriate Structures

The establishment of an organizational structure with business units capable of being treated as separate strategic entities is a move many companies made during the 1980s. The question in the 1990s, however, is much more often whether the delegation of authority and the lack of cross-links between operating units has gone too far. The problems that can arise are well expressed by this comment from Digital:

> "We had a structure based on product-market businesses and accountabilities. But there were lots of difficulties and problems. Because of separate accountability it was difficult to provide an integrated approach to large accounts. There were lots of boundary disputes. Instead of being strategists, the product people were being policemen, accountants and lawyers. Now we are trying to encourage people to work together in a more flexible fashion."

Being organized into autonomous units is good for the development of business-specific competences, but can prevent the transfer of intrabusiness capabilities across the whole organization. One of the roles the centre will increasingly have to adopt is therefore to act as guardian and developer of the company's capabilities. An important mechanism for doing this is the choice of controls. Strategic controls can be used to monitor the extent of cross-business interaction, to develop sensitivity to market changes that cut across business units, and to avoid a blinkered concentration by each business unit exclusively on its own bottom line.

Building Skills

Once the appropriate structure is in place, a formal (though not necessarily extensive) planning system can be introduced, in which line management has responsibility for the plans and the analysis that goes into them. The initial focus should be on the analysis of the businesses themselves and of competitors to isolate the key success factors and articulate what, if any, change in direction is needed. Established beliefs should be tested and thinking forced beyond the platitudinous.

Line managers can only be expected to accept planning responsibility and perform well if they are given adequate support. They will need training and explicit help in improving the clarity and cogency of their thinking, the focus of their plans, and their communication skills.

The centre's role is to ask questions that prompt reflection on what matters most and to draw out an articulate account of what makes each business tick. The operational leaders should be prompted by questioning to discover issues for themselves and to think through the options they have in addressing them. In this way, as the line learns to think strategically, the centre learns about the business. Both are necessary if the control process is to work effectively. Insight is more important than precision and rigorous thought more important than pages of numbers.

BCG has developed a simple tool, dubbed a strategy statement, for helping companies to create strategic plans that can double as control documents (see figure 4-11). In every business, each of the six topics is summarized on just one page,

FIGURE 4-11
The Strategy Statement as Control Document

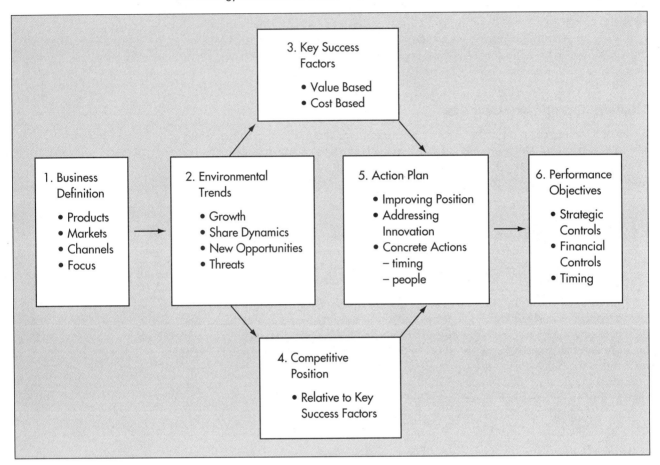

with the whole document containing the essentials of the strategy, its rationale, and the control mechanisms. The main role is played by line management, with central staff or consultants providing the necessary support (see figure 4-12). The conciseness of the document greatly facilitates its use as a control device, and producing it imposes valuable discipline: it really does make it necessary to concentrate on what matters most. Conciseness has even more point here—too many controls will be confusing and ineffective, and we generally find that only three or four at a maximum are what is required. The strategy statement has been used successfully to develop strategy in diversified businesses and to give the centre an economical means of ensuring that strategy implementation takes place, and monitoring the progress of the resulting changes in direction.

Once a strategic planning process of this sort has been introduced, it may well be some years before the necessary skills are developed for it to work well. As the first sets of plans will be relatively unsophisticated, they are unlikely to be pushed through to clear, specific targets or milestones, and control will probably be informal. The value of planning is as much in the learning effect of the process as the result, deepening the understanding of the business and competitors and creating a language understood by both the centre and the line.

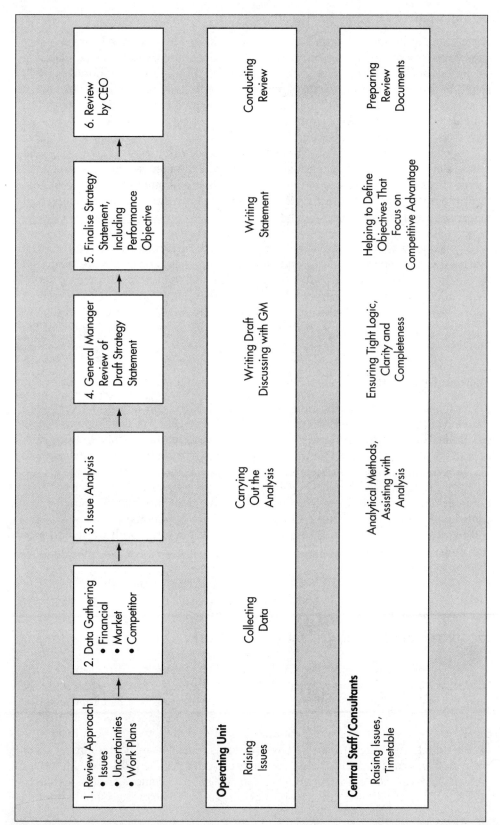

FIGURE 4-12
Stages in Writing a Control Document

Setting Control Targets

Targets should be set and agreed in formal discussions between the board member responsible for the operating company and the operating executive. The planning document should be ready in good time for the discussion and should contain suggestions for appropriate controls, the reasons why they are the key measures of success, and what means could be adopted to measure them. This discussion can be quite detailed, covering, for example, how market share should be defined and how the necessary data can be collected.

Proper preparation is essential to enable a sensible discussion to take place, and central staff can help to define questions and structure the agenda. Once the targets are agreed, tracking systems need to be put in place that will often involve information technology (IT) investments to produce the requisite data on the management information system (MIS). Without this investment, however, the exercise will often be futile.

To make strategic controls effective, it is vital to integrate the strategic control process into budgeting. If it is not, and particularly if the two processes are controlled by different corporate departments, strategic goals will tend to be hijacked by short-term budgetary pressures, no matter how explicit they are. In particular, management priorities may change, and attention may shift from the long-term goals established in the strategic planning process to short-term financial targets that emerge from the budget.

Dismantling the Bureaucracy

When the strategic planning process is well established and strategic controls are routinely agreed, the process can move into its final stage. Plans can begin to be less elaborate, formal requirements can be relaxed, and the discussions between the operating companies and the centre can focus much more on the controls themselves. The bureaucracy can be reduced now that everyone has mastered it, and as time goes on, the meetings can also become less formal. Plans themselves, as opposed to controls, can be reviewed on a three- or five-year cycle, rather than annually, or restricted to a consideration of major ventures (such as potential acquisitions) or changes in the competitive or market environment. The formal apparatus built up in order to introduce the process and build skills should be dismantled once this has been accomplished.

How to Make Strategic Controls Work

The main problems companies encounter in building a strategic control system are the cost of setting up the planning system in the first place, which is mainly management time; the cost of defining key success factors in some businesses, which may mean an intensive study; overcoming the initial hostility of line managers, who will tend to regard the process as a waste of time until they find that they learn from it; and the time required to educate all those involved, which is usually years not months. None of these problems can be totally avoided, but they can be anticipated. The most important factor in achieving success is therefore to create realistic expectations on all sides and to give due allowance for the time and resources necessary. The process should itself be carefully planned, or the problems will quickly seem to outweigh the benefits and morale will suffer.

There are a few important lessons about how to make strategic control work successfully. It is necessary to:

- Invest in the training necessary and adopt an appropriate style in reviewing plans, especially in the early stages.
- Invest in careful preparation before review sessions, as good questions are vital.
- Set stretching targets, but only a limited number.
- Follow through, take it seriously, and make actions and words consistent.
- Create an explicit link with financial targets and budgets, integrating the two processes (or none of it will be taken seriously at all).
- Show that the operating company benefits from the process (e.g., through the business becoming easier to manage) and give strong support for success (so that another real benefit becomes the approval of senior management or a better relationship with the centre).

Strategic control processes are still relatively rare, though a number of companies have made a start in parts of their operations. We believe that over the next decade their use will increase as more and more organizations discover the benefits of not just planning for the long term, but building long-term thinking into day-to-day operations.

References and Suggested Readings

Abell, D., *Defining the Business—The Starting Point of Strategic Planning*, Prentice Hall, Englewood Cliffs, NJ, 1980.

Bennis, W., and B. Nanus, *Leaders: The Strategies for Taking Charge*, Harper & Row, New York, 1985.

Bungay, S., and M. Goold, Creating a Strategic Control System, *Long Range Planning*, June 1991, pp. 32–39.

Campbell, A., Devine, M., and S. Yeung, *A Sense of Mission*, Hutchinson, London, 1990.

Campbell, A., and S. Yeung, Creating a Sense of Mission, *Long Range Planning*, August 1991, pp. 10–20.

Chandler, A. D., *Strategy and Structure: Chapters in the History of the American Industrial Enterprise*, MIT Press, Cambridge, MA, 1962.

Cyert, R. M. and J. G. March, *A Behavioral Theory of the Firm*, Prentice Hall, Englewood Cliffs, NJ, 1963.

Davis, S., and P. R. Lawrence, *Matrix*, Addison-Wesley, Reading, MA, 1978.

Dill, W. R., The Impact of Environment on Organizational Development, in Milick, S., and E. H . Van Ness (Eds.), *Concepts and Issues in Administrative Behavior*, Prentice Hall, Englewood Cliffs, NJ, 1962.

Drucker, P., *Management: Tasks, Responsibilities, Practices*, Harper & Row, New York, 1973.

Dyson, R., *Strategic Planning: Models and Analytical Techniques*, Wiley, New York, 1990.

Fahey, L., and V. K. Narayanan, *Macroenvironmental Analysis for Strategic Management*, West, St. Paul, MN, 1986.

Galbraith, J. R., *Designing Complex Organizations,* Addison-Wesley, Reading, MA, 1972.

Galbraith, J. R., Strategy and Organization Planning, *Human Resource Management,* Spring/Summer 1983, pp. 63–77.

Galbraith, J. R., and R. K. Kazanjian, *Strategy Implementation: Structure, Systems, and Process,* Second Edition, West, St. Paul, MN, 1986.

Ginter, P. M., and W. J. Duncan, Environmental Analysis for Strategic Management, *Long Range Planning,* December 1990, pp. 91–100.

Goold, M., and J. J. Quinn, *Strategic Control: Milestones for Long-Term Performance,* Hutchinson, London, 1990.

Hamel, G., and C. K. Prahalad, Strategic Intent, *Harvard Business Review,* May/June 1989, pp. 63–77.

Harrison, R., Choosing the Depth of Organizational Intervention, *Journal of Applied Behavioral Science,* 1970, pp. 181–201.

Hax, A. C., and N. S. Maljuf, *Strategic Management: An Integrated Perspective,* Prentice Hall, Englewood Cliffs, NJ, 1984.

Hofer, C. W., and D. E. Schendel, *Strategy Formulation: Analytical Concepts,* West, St. Paul, MN, 1978, pp. 30–34.

Hrebiniak, L. G., and W. F. Joyce, *Implementing Strategy,* Macmillan, New York, 1984.

Johnson, G. and K. Scholes, *Exploring Corporate Strategy,* Third Edition, Prentice Hall, Hamel Hempstead, 1993.

Lawrence, P. R., and J. W. Lorsch, *Organization and Environment,* Harvard University Press, Cambridge, MA, 1967.

Lenz, R. T. and J. L. Engledow, Environmental Analysis Units and Strategic Decision-Making: A Field Study of Selected "Leading-Edge" Corporations, *Strategic Management Journal,* January/February 1986, pp. 69–89.

Levitt, T., Marketing Myopia, *Harvard Business Review,* July/August 1960, pp. 45–56.

Lindblom, C. E., The Science of Muddling Through, *Public Administration Review,* Spring 1959, pp. 79–88.

Lorange, P., *Corporate Planning,* Prentice Hall, Englewood Cliffs, NJ, 1980.

Lorange, P., Scott, M. F., and S. Ghoshal, *Strategic Control,* West, St. Paul, MN, 1986.

Makridakis, S., *Forecasting, Planning, and Strategy for the 21st Century,* Free Press, New York, 1990.

March, J. G., Decisions in Organizations and Theories of Choice, in Van de Ven, A. H., and W. F. Joyce (Eds.), *Perspectives on Organizational Design and Behavior,* John Wiley & Sons, New York, 1981.

March, J. G. and H. A. Simon, *Organizations,* Wiley, New York, 1958.

Mesch, A. H., Developing an Effective Environmental Assessment Function, *Managerial Planning,* March/April 1984, pp. 17–22.

Millet, S. M., How Scenarios Trigger Strategic Thinking, *Long Range Planning,* October 1988, pp. 61–68.

Mintzberg, H., Strategy Making in Three Modes, *California Management Review,* Winter 1973, pp. 44–53.

Porter, M. E., How Competitive Forces Shape Strategy, *Harvard Business Review,* March/April 1979, pp. 137–145.

Porter, M. E., *Competitive Strategy: Techniques for Analyzing Industries and Competitors*, Free Press, New York, 1980.

Porter, M. E., *Competitive Advantage: Creating and Sustaining Superior Performance*, Free Press, New York, 1985.

Rowe, A. J., Mason, R. O., Dickel, K. E., and N. H. Snyder, *Strategic Management: A Methodological Approach*, Third Edition, Addison-Wesley, New York, 1989.

Rumelt, R. P., The Evaluation of Business Strategy, in Glueck, W. F., *Business Policy and Strategic Management*, Third Edition, McGraw-Hill, New York, 1980.

Schnaars, S. P., How to Develop and Use Scenarios, *Long Range Planning*, February 1987, pp. 105–114.

Stevenson, H. H., Defining Corporate Strengths and Weaknesses, *Sloan Management Review*, Spring 1976, pp. 51–68.

Terry, P. T., Mechanisms for Environmental Scanning, *Long Range Planning*, June 1977, pp. 2–9.

Thompson, J. D., *Organizations in Action*, McGraw-Hill, New York, 1967.

Thorndike, E. L., *The Elements of Psychology*, Seiler, New York, 1905.

Tilles, S., How to Evaluate Strategy, *Harvard Business Review*, July/August 1963, pp. 111–121.

Wack, P., Scenarios: Uncharted Waters Ahead, *Harvard Business Review*, September/October 1985, pp. 73–89.

Wack, P., Scenarios: Shooting the Rapids, *Harvard Business Review*, November/December 1985, pp. 139–150.

Waterman, R. H., Peters, T. J., and J. R. Phillips, Structure is Not Organization, *Business Horizons*, June 1980, pp. 14–26.

Section III
The Strategy Content

hapter 1 defined strategy content as the output of the strategy process—the intended or realized course of action selected to achieve the company's long-term objectives. In this section the focus will be on these "patterns in the stream of decisions or actions" called strategy content. Important issues in this section include questions such as What types of strategy are there? What can they be based on? In which directions do they lead? and What are their advantages and pitfalls?

Three introductory remarks should first be made before the reader is flung into the arena of conflicting perspectives on strategy content:

1. *Interaction process-content.* As discussed in chapter 1, strategy process and strategy content are two sides of the same coin, much in the same way light has wave and particle characteristics. Hence, the pragmatic split into a process and content section should not entice the reader into considering both aspects in isolation. In the three chapters of this section all articles focus on strategy content, but many have important implications for, or are significantly impacted by, the strategy process. Some authors identify this interaction, but more often than not it is left undiscussed. Hence, we encourage the reader to actively consider the relationship between content and process when going through this section.

2. *Description and prescription.* As in the previous chapters, it is the intention in this section to strike a balance between articles focused on prescription and those leaning more toward description—after all, we are interested both in the strategies that companies actually pursue and the strategic options that seem promising for the future. The reader should be forewarned, however, that many authors blur the line between analysis and recommendation. This places the burden on the reader to critically distinguish between facts, assumptions, interpretations, and suggestions.

3. *Aggregation levels.* In chapter 1 it was argued that strategy could be made at the *functional, business, corporate, and network levels*, and it was stated that this book would focus on the latter three. It was also pointed out that—while a useful analytical distinction—business-, corporate-, and network-level issues can no less be viewed as entirely separate than can strategy

formulation and implementation. Nevertheless, since it would be fruitless to lump all strategy content articles into one chapter, they have been split depending on whether business, corporate, or network issues are predominant.

This section has been structured using this distinction between these three levels of strategy. Chapter 5 starts with strategy content issues concerning the business level. The main focus is the question, What should be the primary *basis of strategy* when relating the company to its environment? Two important perspectives on this question can be distinguished—the positioning approach and the resource-based approach. Articles from both schools of thought are presented to clarify where agreement and difference of opinion exist. The discussion is concluded with an article that attempts to bridge the gap between the two approaches.

The "basis of strategy" discussion is not only important for the business level, but also for the corporate level, since many authors argue that in a multibusiness firm all businesses should share a common basis (common competitive advantages and/or competences). Chapter 6 focuses on this issue of *multibusiness synergy*. A distinction is made between three main schools of thought—the portfolio approach, the linkages approach, and the core competences approach. Here, too, articles representing all three perspectives are included to clarify the points of agreement and contention. And again the chapter is closed by a reading that attempts to incorporate all three approaches into one framework.

Finally, chapter 7 discusses the topic of network-level strategy. Each author in this chapter explores the possibilities and necessities of *multicompany cooperation*, both vertically (within the value system) and horizontally (with competitors). The debate centres on the question to what extent companies should embed themselves in networks. A distinction is made between the two main schools of thought—the discrete organisation perspective and the network perspective. Since the discrete organisation perspective views the environment as predominantly competitive, authors in this tradition do not see any necessity for, or legitimacy in, network-level strategies. They may find chapter 7 to be a waste of trees. Therefore, in this chapter the burden lies on the network school of thought to convince the reader that the multicompany level of strategy is both analytically useful and in practice essential to companies' survival.

CHAPTER 5
BUSINESS LEVEL STRATEGIES: *ON COMPETITION AND CAPABILITIES*

*Advantage is a better soldier
than rashness.*
　—*William Shakespeare*
　　1564–1616, English dramatist and poet

Introduction

The central question in this chapter is quite simple: What is a good strategy? The answers given by strategy theorists are, however, quite diverse. "Two strategy researchers, three opinions" is overstated, but the variety of perspectives on the topic is dauntingly large. When reduced to their bare essentials, however, the diversity of views can be categorized into two fundamentally different approaches to strategy content—the *positioning approach* and the *resource-based approach* (often also referred to as the *capabilities-based approach*). It is the intention of this chapter to structure the debate on the basic characteristics of a good strategy by presenting a limited number of articles representing these two major schools of thought.

In the previous chapter Rumelt outlined four basic characteristics of a good strategy on which most strategy theorists seem to agree. He argued that strategies must be *feasible* (implementable) and *consistent* (no mutually exclusive goals or policies). In line with Shakespeare, Rumelt also stated that strategies must provide a competitive *advantage*. Finally, he also noted the necessity of *consonance*—a fit between the organisation and its environment. It is the interpretation of this last principle that forms the dividing line between the positioning school and the resource-based approach.

While both schools of thought share the assumption that some sort of match between the firm and the outside world must be established, what divides them is their approach to achieving a fit. The positioning school (a name popularised by Mintzberg, 1990) places most emphasis on *adapting the company to its environment*. Its basic assumption is that the environment largely determines the firm's freedom to manoeuvre. Therefore, the structure of the environment is of primary importance—a good strategy is one that positions the firm within the environment. The challenge for the strategist is to find a position that is defensible against the attacks of existing and potential competitors and against the bargaining power of buyers and suppliers. This school of thought by no means denies the firm's ability to also shape its surroundings. However, its basic assumption is that the environment has far more influence on shaping firms' strategies than the other way around.

Since the underlying logic of the positioning approach is to first understand the environment and then position the firm, it is also referred to as the *outside-in* approach. The resource-based approach looks at the issue of relating the firm to its environment from the opposite direction and is therefore also labelled the *inside-out* perspective. The resource-based view places most emphasis on *adapting the environment to the company*. Its basic assumption is that a company can use superior organisational resources and capabilities to modify the industry structure and/or change the rules of the competitive game. Therefore, development of distinctive organisational qualities is of primary importance—a good strategy is one that uses unique abilities and resources to change industry standards to one's own advantage. The challenge to the strategist is to find and develop capabilities that are difficult to imitate and will distinguish the company from its competitors in the long run. It should be noted that the resource-based approach does not deny that firms must often adapt themselves to the environment. The argument put forward by authors taking a resource-based approach is that adaptation alone is basically short term and reactive, leading the company to lose its ability to create its own future.

Both approaches seek consonance between firm and environment, but differ in their emphasis on who should adapt most. Whether a business should adopt "competitiveness through positioning" or "advantage through capabilities" as its *basis of strategy* is a question readers must answer themselves at the end of this chapter.

The structure of this chapter largely follows the historical development of the debate in the strategy content literature. The kickoff is by the positioning school, followed by a number of articles representing the resource-based perspective. Finally, the last article explores the possibility of linking the two approaches.

The Articles

The opening article of this chapter, "Generic Competitive Strategies," has been taken from one of Michael Porter's more recent books, but its central concepts were originally introduced in his first book, *Competitive Strategy*. Since Porter is considered by all to be the most important theorist in the positioning tradition, it seems only logical to start with his basic framework. In his article, Porter states that positioning vis-à-vis the five forces (see chapter 4) "determines whether a firm's profitability is above or below the industry average." He argues that long run above-average performance results from selecting one of the three defensible positions available to the strategist: *cost leadership, differentiation,* or *focus*. According to Porter, these three options, or *generic strategies*, are the only feasible ways of achieving a sustainable competitive advantage. A firm that does not make a clear choice between one of the three generic strategies is "stuck in the middle" and will suffer below-average performance.

The second article in this chapter, "Time—The Next Source of Competitive Advantage" by George Stalk, does not explicitly contest Porter's view that the essence of strategy is choosing one of the three types of defensible industry positions. Stalk's point is only that in the past *speed* has not been sufficiently recognized as an important contributor to cost leadership or differentiation advantage. He argues that traditionally most attention has been paid to static sources of competitive advantage—for example, low wages and economies of scale as building blocks of a cost leadership strategy. In his opinion, the efficient use of time can lead to both lower cost and more differentiation. Although Stalk does not directly contradict Porter, his perspective is different. Stalk's emphasis on swiftness as an important organisational capability and his implicit suggestion that this skill might be used to rewrite the rules of competition indicate that he believes that strategy is more than a game of positioning.

In the next article, Stalk, writing together with Philip Evans and Lawrence Shulman, leaves no doubt that he favours the resource-based—they call it capabilities-based—approach to strategy content. In this article, "Competing on Capabilities," Stalk, Evans, and Shulman argue that the key to competitive success lies in identifying and developing "the hard-to-imitate organizational capabilities that distinguish a company from its competitors in the eyes of the customers." In their view, the positioning school's way of looking at the world is too static. Competition, they believe, is increasingly unlike chess, a "war of position," and more like an interactive video game, a "war of movement." Therefore, a company should not build static market share but should develop organisational capabilities that allow the firm to "move quickly in and out of products, markets, and even entire businesses." The flexibility gained by superior capabilities can be used to consistently change the rules of the competitive game in one's own industry, but can also be employed to rewrite the rules in entirely different industries. Stalk, Evans, and Shulman refer to companies seeking to transfer their most important business processes to different industries as *capabilities predators*. The capabilities-based perspective is, therefore, not only an important approach to business strategy but also to corporate strategy (in chapter 6, Prahalad and Hamel expand on the resource-based approach to corporate strategy).

In the fourth article of this chapter, "From Innovation to Outpacing," Xavier Gilbert and Paul Strebel expand on the idea of competition as a "war of movement" mentioned by Stalk, Evans, and Shulman. In the same vein, Gilbert and Strebel argue that the traditional positioning approach assumes that the product life cycle is a given to which the firm must adapt itself. They believe, on the other hand, that companies with the ability to continually innovate can shape the product life cycle themselves. The capability to create innovative products is, however, not enough. Companies must also be able to put together a complete "formula" and offer it at a competitive price. Here the authors explicitly contradict Porter. While Porter argues that companies striving for cost leadership and differentiation at the same time are "stuck in the middle," Gilbert and Strebel argue that the successful firms they have observed were capable of introducing new formulas that were simultaneously innovative and competitively priced—a combination that is difficult to beat. Developing the organisational capability to gain product leadership and cost leadership at the same time is what the authors refer to as an *outpacing strategy*.

In the fifth article, "Strategy as Stretch and Leverage," Gary Hamel and C. K. Prahalad go yet a step further, provocatively questioning the fundamental notion of consonance. They argue that most thinking on the topic of "strategic fit" is static, focusing on the match between existing resources and opportunities. However, they argue that existing *resources* are relatively unimportant compared with *resourcefulness*— the way an organisation uses, supplements, and upgrades its resources to build new competitive advantages. An organisation's capacity to *leverage* its resources—to get the biggest bang for its bucks—is the key to sustained competitiveness, according to the authors. They state that leveraging can be achieved by using capabilities across business units, improving them through cooperation with other firms, employing them where the returns are highest, and focusing them on company priorities. But to focus the entire organisation and to motivate it to continually learn and upgrade its capabilities is a difficult task. According to Hamel and Prahalad, what is needed is *stretch*—a purposely created misfit between the firm and its environment by means of "a chasm between ambition and resources." Companies must reach for a goal that is out of all proportion to their current resources and capabilities. This *strategic intent* can focus an organisation's attention and motivate individuals over a prolonged period of time. Hence, in Hamel and Prahalad's view, the essence of strategy is neither smart positioning nor the skilful allocation of existing resources, but the ambition to continually leverage existing resources, improve capabilities, and learn new skills (note how this point ties in with Peter Senge's article on the learning organisation in chapter 3).

After these readings, one question becomes inescapable: How far apart are the positioning and resource-based approaches? Are they contradictory or complementary perspectives? This introduction has focused on their differences, and therefore a sixth article has been included in this chapter as an example of how the two perspectives might be integrated. In this article, "How to Link Vision to Core Capabilities," Paul Schoemaker provides a methodology for combining the outside-in and inside-out approaches. The intention of his framework is to aid strategists in identifying "those core capabilities that will be effective for multiple strategic segments in several different possible futures."

Recommended Readings and Cases

Readers who wish to gain a better understanding of the positioning school's ideas should, of course, start with Michael Porter's *Competitive Strategy: Techniques for Analyzing Industries and Competitors*. An interesting follow-up reading would be Pankaj Ghemawat's *Commitment: The Dynamic of Strategy*. For a good overview of the resource-based approach, the reader is advised to turn to Robert Grant's article, "The Resource-Based Theory of Competitive Advantage: Implications for Strategy Formulation," or to a paper entitled "Firm Capabilities, Resources, and the Concept of Strategy: Four Paradigms of Strategic Management" by David Teece, G. Pisano, and A. Shuen. A stimulating follow-up reading would be James Quinn's *Intelligent Enterprise: A Knowledge and Service Based Paradigm for Industry*.

The two cases that have been selected for this section are the "Amstrad PLC" and "Canon" cases. The Amstrad case, written by John Hendry, describes the "technology of yesterday" strategy employed by this British consumer electronics firm. Amstrad has explicitly chosen to use old, proven technologies in its products, while creating an advantage by its quick response to consumer demand. This case is particularly well suited to the first three articles in this chapter, since the company's success can be explained from both a positioning and a capabilities perspective. Of course, the question is which of these two perspectives will be most beneficial when setting a course for the company's future. The Canon case, by Sumantra Ghoshal and Mary Ackenhusen, on the other hand, explains how this Japanese multinational is focused on "competing on capabilities." Many of the concepts discussed in this chapter, such as outpacing, leveraging resources, and learning are well illustrated by the Canon case. Here, too, the question is which actions—and perspective—the company should take to ensure future successes.

■ GENERIC COMPETITIVE STRATEGIES†

By Michael Porter

Positioning determines whether a firm's profitability is above or below the industry average. A firm that can position itself well may earn high rates of return even though industry structure is unfavorable and the average profitability of the industry is therefore modest.

The fundamental basis of above-average performance in the long run is *sustainable competitive advantage*. Though a firm can have a myriad of strengths and weaknesses vis-à-vis its competitors, there are two basic types of competitive advantage a firm can possess: low cost or differentiation. The significance of any strength or weakness a firm possesses is ultimately a function of its impact on relative cost or differentiation. Cost advantage and differentiation in turn stem from industry structure. They result from a firm's ability to cope with the five forces better than its rivals.

The two basic types of competitive advantage combined with the scope of activities for which a firm seeks to achieve them lead to three *generic strategies* for achieving above-average performance in an industry: cost leadership, differentiation, and focus. The focus strategy has two variants, cost focus and differentiation focus. The generic strategies are shown in figure 5-1.

Each of the generic strategies involves a fundamentally different route to competitive advantage, combining a choice about the type of competitive advantage sought with the scope of the strategic target in which competitive advantage is to be achieved. The cost leadership and differentiation strategies seek competitive advantage in a broad range of industry segments, while focus strategies aim at cost advantage (cost focus) or differentiation (differentiation focus) in a narrow segment. The specific actions required to implement each generic strategy vary widely from industry to industry, as do the feasible generic strategies in a particular industry. While selecting and implementing a generic strategy is far from simple, they are the logical routes to competitive advantage that must be probed in any industry.

The notion underlying the concept of generic strategies is that competitive advantage is at the heart of any strategy, and achieving competitive advantage requires a firm to make a choice—if a firm is to attain a competitive advantage, it must make a choice about the type of competitive advantage it seeks to attain and the scope within which it will attain it. Being all things to all people is a recipe for strategic mediocrity and below-average performance, because it often means that a firm has no competitive advantage at all.

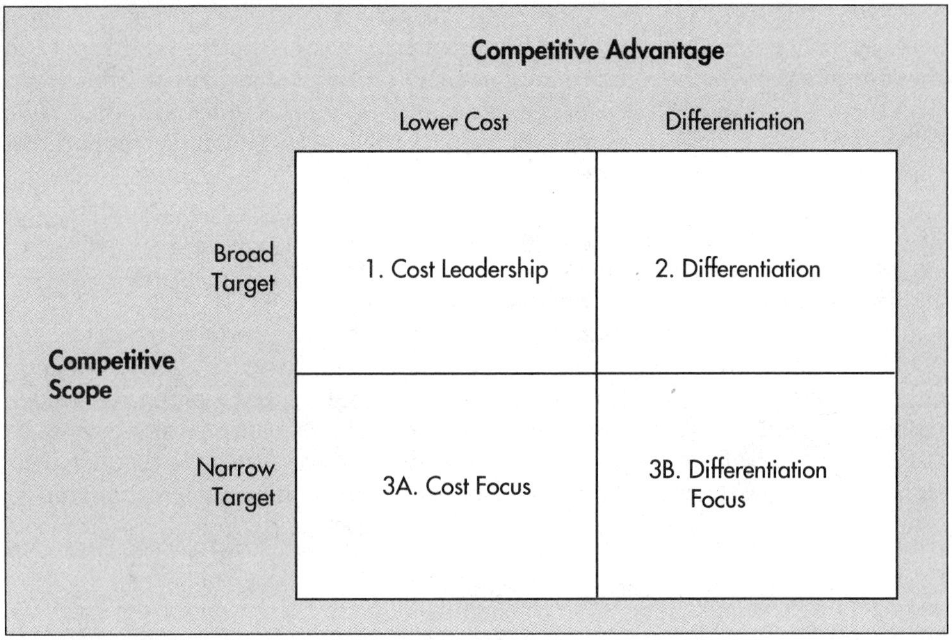

FIGURE 5-1
Three Generic Strategies

Competitive Advantage

	Lower Cost	Differentiation
Broad Target	1. Cost Leadership	2. Differentiation
Narrow Target	3A. Cost Focus	3B. Differentiation Focus

Competitive Scope

Cost Leadership

Cost leadership is perhaps the clearest of the three generic strategies. In it, a firm sets out to become *the* low-cost producer in its industry. The firm has a broad scope and serves many industry segments, and may even operate in related industries—the firm's breadth is often important to its cost advantage. The sources of cost advantage are varied and depend on the structure of the industry. They may include the pursuit of economies of scale, proprietary technology, preferential access to raw materials, and other factors. In TV sets, for example, cost leadership requires efficient-size picture tube facilities, a low-cost design, automated assembly, and global scale over which to amortize research and development (R&D). In security guard services, cost advantage requires extremely low overhead, a plentiful source of low-cost labor, and efficient training procedures because of high turnover. Low-cost producer status involves more than just going down the learning curve. A low-cost producer must find and exploit all sources of cost advantage. Low-cost producers typically sell a standard, or no-frills, product and place considerable emphasis on reaping scale or absolute cost advantages from all sources.

If a firm can achieve and sustain overall cost leadership, then it will be an above-average performer in its industry provided it can command prices at or near the industry average. At equivalent or lower prices than its rivals, a cost leader's low-cost position translates into higher returns. A cost leader, however, cannot ignore the bases of differentiation. If its product is not perceived as comparable or acceptable by buyers, a cost leader will be forced to discount prices well below competitors' to gain sales. This may nullify the benefits of its favorable cost position. Texas Instruments (in watches) and Northwest Airlines (in air transportation) are two low-cost firms that fell into this trap. Texas Instruments could not overcome its disadvantage in differentiation and exited the watch industry. Northwest Airlines recognized its problem in time, and has instituted efforts to improve marketing, passenger service, and service to travel agents to make its product more comparable to those of its competitors.

A cost leader must achieve *parity* or *proximity* in the bases of differentiation relative to its competitors to be an above-average performer, even though it relies on cost leadership for its competitive advantage. Parity in the bases of differentiation allows a cost leader to translate its cost advantage directly into higher profits than competitors'. Proximity in differentiation means that the price discount necessary to achieve an acceptable market share does not offset a cost leader's cost advantage and hence the cost leader earns above-average returns.

The strategic logic of cost leadership usually requires that a firm be *the* cost leader, not one of several firms vying for this position. Many firms have made serious strategic errors by failing to recognize this. When there is more than one aspiring cost leader, rivalry among them is usually fierce because every point of market share is viewed as crucial. Unless one firm can gain a cost lead and "persuade" others to abandon their strategies, the consequences for profitability (and long-run industry structure) can be disastrous, as has been the case in a number of petrochemical industries. Thus cost leadership is a strategy particularly dependent on preemption, unless major technological change allows a firm to radically change its cost position.

Differentiation

The second generic strategy is differentiation. In a differentiation strategy, a firm seeks to be unique in its industry along some dimensions that are widely valued by buyers. It selects one or more attributes that many buyers in an industry perceive as important, and uniquely positions itself to meet those needs. It is rewarded for its uniqueness with a premium price.

The means for differentiation are peculiar to each industry. Differentiation can be based on the product itself, the delivery system by which it is sold, the marketing approach, and a broad range of other factors. In construction equipment, for example, Caterpillar Tractor's differentiation is based on product durability, service, spare parts availability, and an excellent dealer network. In cosmetics, differentiation tends to be based more on product image and the positioning of counters in the stores.

A firm that can achieve and sustain differentiation will be an above-average performer in its industry if its price premium exceeds the extra costs incurred in being unique. A differentiator, therefore, must always seek ways of differentiating that lead to a price premium greater than the cost of differentiating. A differentiator cannot ignore its cost position, because its premium prices will be nullified by a markedly inferior cost position. A differentiator thus aims at cost parity or proximity relative to its competitors by reducing cost in all areas that do not affect differentiation.

The logic of the differentiation strategy requires that a firm choose attributes in which to differentiate itself that are *different* from its rivals'. A firm must truly be unique at something or be perceived as unique if it is to expect a premium price. In contrast to cost leadership, however, there can be more than one successful differentiation strategy in an industry if there are a number of attributes that are widely valued by buyers.

Focus

The third generic strategy is focus. This strategy is quite different from the others because it rests on the choice of a narrow competitive scope within an industry. The focuser selects a segment or group of segments in the industry and tailors its strategy to serving them to the exclusion of others. By optimizing its strategy for the target segments, the focuser seeks to achieve a competitive advantage in its target segments even though it does not possess a competitive advantage overall.

The focus strategy has two variants. In *cost focus* a firm seeks a cost advantage in its target segment, while in *differentiation focus* a firm seeks differentiation in its target segment. Both variants of the focus strategy rest on *differences* between a focuser's target segments and other segments in the industry. The target segments must either have buyers with unusual needs or else the production and delivery system that best serves the target segment must differ from that of other industry segments. Cost focus exploits differences in cost behavior in some segments, while differentiation focus exploits the special needs of buyers in certain segments. Such differences imply that the segments are poorly served by broadly targeted competitors who serve them at the same time as they serve others. The focuser can thus achieve competitive advantage by dedicating itself to the segments exclusively. Breadth of target is clearly a matter of degree, but the essence of focus is the exploitation of a narrow target's differences from the balance of the industry. Narrow focus in and of itself is not sufficient for above-average performance.

A good example of a focuser who has exploited differences in the production process that best serves different segments is Hammermill Paper. Hammermill has increasingly been moving toward relatively low-volume, high-quality specialty papers, where the larger paper companies with higher volume machines face a stiff cost penalty for short production runs. Hammermill's equipment is more suited to shorter runs with frequent setups.

A focuser takes advantage of suboptimization in either direction by broadly targeted competitors. Competitors may be *underperforming* in meeting the needs of a particular segment, which opens the possibility for differentiation focus. Broadly targeted competitors may also be *overperforming* in meeting the needs of a segment, which means that they are bearing higher than necessary cost in serving it. An opportunity for cost focus may be present in just meeting the needs of such a segment and no more.

If a focuser's target segment is not different from other segments, then the focus strategy will not succeed. In soft drinks, for example, Royal Crown has focused on cola drinks, while Coca-Cola and Pepsi have broad product lines with many flavored drinks. Royal Crown's segment, however, can be well served by Coke and Pepsi at the same time they are serving other segments. Hence Coke and Pepsi enjoy competitive advantages over Royal Crown in the cola segment due to the economies of having a broader line.

If a firm can achieve sustainable cost leadership (cost focus) or differentiation (differentiation focus) in its segment and the segment is structurally attractive, then the focuser will be an above-average performer in its industry. Segment structural attractiveness is a necessary condition because some segments in an industry are much less profitable than others. There is often room for several sustainable focus strategies in an industry, provided that focusers choose different target segments. Most industries have a variety of segments, and each one that involves a different buyer need or a different optimal production or delivery system is a candidate for a focus strategy.

Stuck in the Middle

A firm that engages in each generic strategy but fails to achieve any of them is "stuck in the middle." It possesses no competitive advantage. This strategic position is usually a recipe for below-average performance. A firm that is stuck in the middle will compete at a disadvantage because the cost leader, differentiators, or focusers will be better positioned to compete in any segment. If a firm that is stuck in the middle is lucky enough to discover a profitable product or buyer, competitors with a sustainable competitive advantage will quickly eliminate the spoils. In most industries, quite a few competitors are stuck in the middle.

A firm that is stuck in the middle will earn attractive profits only if the structure of its industry is highly favorable, or if the firm is fortunate enough to have competitors that are also stuck in the middle. Usually, however, such a firm will be much less profitable than rivals achieving one of the generic strategies. Industry maturity tends to widen the performance differences between firms with a generic strategy and those that are stuck in the middle, because it exposes ill-conceived strategies that have been carried along by rapid growth.

Becoming stuck in the middle is often a manifestation of a firm's unwillingness to make *choices* about how to compete. It tries for competitive advantage through every means and achieves none, because achieving different types of competitive advantage usually requires inconsistent actions. Becoming stuck in the middle also afflicts successful firms, who compromise their generic strategy for the sake of growth or prestige. A classic example is Laker Airways, which began with a clear cost-focus strategy based on no-frills operation in the North Atlantic market, aimed at a particular segment of the traveling public that was extremely price sensitive. Over time, however, Laker began adding frills, new services, and new routes. It blurred its image, and suboptimized its service and delivery system. The consequences were disastrous, and Laker eventually went bankrupt.

The temptation to blur a generic strategy, and therefore become stuck in the middle, is particularly great for a focuser once it has dominated its target segments. Focus involves deliberately limiting potential sales volume. Success can lead a focuser to lose sight of the reasons for its success and compromise its focus strategy for growth's sake. Rather than compromise its generic strategy, a firm is usually better off finding new industries in which to grow where it can use its generic strategy again or exploit interrelationships.

Pursuit of More Than One Generic Strategy

Each generic strategy is a fundamentally different approach to creating and sustaining a competitive advantage, combining the type of competitive advantage a firm seeks and the scope of its strategic target. Usually a firm must make a choice among them, or it will become stuck in the middle. The benefits of optimizing the firm's strategy for a particular target segment (focus) cannot be gained if a firm is simultaneously serving a broad range of segments (cost leadership or differentiation). Sometimes a firm may be able to create two largely separate business units within the same corporate entity, each with a different generic strategy. A good example is the British hotel firm Trusthouse Forte, which operates five separate hotel chains each targeted at a different segment. However, unless a firm strictly separates the units pursuing different generic strategies, it may compromise the ability of any of them to achieve its competitive advantage. A suboptimized approach to competing, made likely by the spillover among units of corporate policies and culture, will lead to becoming stuck in the middle.

Achieving cost leadership and differentiation is also usually inconsistent, because differentiation is usually costly. To be unique and command a price premium, a differentiator deliberately elevates costs, as Caterpillar has done in construction equipment. Conversely, cost leadership often requires a firm to forego some differentiation by standardizing its product, reducing marketing overhead, and the like.

Reducing cost does not always involve a sacrifice in differentiation. Many firms have discovered ways to reduce cost not only without hurting their differentiation but while actually raising it, by using practices that are both more efficient and effective or employing a different technology. Sometimes dramatic cost savings can be achieved with no impact on differentiation at all if a firm has not concentrated on cost reduction previously. However, cost reduction is not the same as achieving a cost advantage. When faced with capable competitors also striving for cost leadership, a firm will ultimately reach the point where further cost reduction requires a sacrifice in differentiation. It is at this point that the generic strategies become inconsistent and a firm must make a choice.

If a firm can achieve cost leadership and differentiation simultaneously, the rewards are great because the benefits are additive—differentiation leads to premium prices at the same time that cost leadership implies lower costs. An example of a firm that has achieved both a cost advantage and differentiation in its segments is Crown Cork and Seal in the metal container industry. Crown has targeted the so-called hard-to-hold uses of cans in the beer, soft drink, and aerosol industries. It manufactures only steel cans rather than both steel and aluminum. In its target segments, Crown has differentiated itself based on service, technological assistance, and offering a full line of steel cans, crowns, and canning machinery. Differentiation of this type would be much more difficult to achieve in other industry segments that have different needs. At the same time, Crown has dedicated its facilities to producing only the types of cans demanded by buyers in its chosen segments and has aggressively invested in modern two-piece steel-canning technology. As a result, Crown has probably also achieved low-cost producer status in its segments.

Sustainability

A generic strategy does not lead to above-average performance unless it is sustainable vis-à-vis competitors, though actions that improve industry structure may improve industrywide profitability even if they are imitated. The sustainability of the three generic strategies demands that a firm's competitive advantage resist erosion by competitor behavior or industry evolution. Each generic strategy involves different risks, which are shown in table 5-1.

The sustainability of a generic strategy requires that a firm possess some barriers that make imitation of the strategy difficult. Since barriers to imitation are never insurmountable, however, it is usually necessary for a firm to offer a moving target to

TABLE 5-1
Risks of the Generic
Strategies

Risks of Cost Leadership	Risks of Differentiation	Risks of Focus
Cost leadership is not sustained • competitors imitate • technology changes • other bases for cost leadership erode	Differentiation is not sustained • competitors imitate • bases for differentiation become less important to buyers	The focus strategy is imitated The target segment becomes structurally unattractive • structure erodes • demand disappears
Proximity in differentiation is lost	Cost proximity is lost	Broadly targeted competitors overwhelm the segment • the segment's differences from other segments narrow • the advantages of a broad line increase
Cost focusers achieve even lower cost in segments	Differentiation focusers achieve even greater differentiation in segments	New focusers subsegment the industry

its competitors by investing in order to continually improve its position. Each generic strategy is also a potential threat to the others—as table 5-1 shows, for example, focusers must worry about broadly targeted competitors and vice versa.

Table 5-1 can be used to analyze how to attack a competitor that employs any of the generic strategies. A firm pursuing overall differentiation, for example, can be attacked by firms that open up a large cost gap, narrow the extent of differentiation, shift the differentiation desired by buyers to other dimensions, or focus. Each generic strategy is vulnerable to different types of attacks.

In some industries, industry structure or the strategies of competitors eliminate the possibility of achieving one or more of the generic strategies. Occasionally no feasible way for one firm to gain a significant cost advantage exists, for example, because several firms are equally placed with respect to scale economies, access to raw materials, or other cost drivers. Similarly, an industry with few segments or only minor differences among segments, such as low-density polyethylene, may offer few opportunities for focus. Thus the mix of generic strategies will vary from industry to industry.

In many industries, however, the three generic strategies can profitably coexist as long as firms pursue different ones or select different bases for differentiation or focus. Industries in which several strong firms are pursuing differentiation strategies based on different sources of buyer value are often particulary profitable. This tends to improve industry structure and lead to stable industry competition. If two or more firms choose to pursue the same generic strategy on the same basis, however, the result can be a protracted and unprofitable battle. The worst situation is where several firms are vying for overall cost leadership. The past and present choice of generic strategies by competitors, then, has an impact on the choices available to a firm and the cost of changing its position.

The concept of generic strategies is based on the premise that there are a number of ways in which competitive advantage can be achieved, depending on industry structure. If all firms in an industry followed the principles of competitive strategy, each would pick different bases for competitive advantage. While not all would succeed, the generic strategies provide alternate routes to superior performance. Some strategic planning concepts have been narrowly based on only one route to competitive advantage, most notably cost. Such concepts not only fail to explain the success of many firms, but they can also lead all firms in an industry to pursue the same type of competitive advantage in the same way—with predictably disastrous results.

◼ TIME—THE NEXT SOURCE OF COMPETITIVE ADVANTAGE†

By George Stalk

Like competition itself, competitive advantage is a constantly moving target. For any company in any industry, the key is not to get stuck with a single simple notion of its source of advantage. The best competitors, the most successful ones, know how to keep moving and always stay on the cutting edge.

Today, time is on the cutting edge. The ways leading companies manage time—in production, in new product development and introduction, in sales and distribution—represent the most powerful new sources of competitive advantage. Though certain Western companies are pursuing these advantages, Japanese experience and practice provide the most instructive examples—not because they are necessarily unique but because they best illustrate the evolutionary stages through which leading companies have advanced.

Time-Based Competitive Advantage

While time is a basic business performance variable, management seldom monitors its consumption explicitly—almost never with the same precision accorded sales and costs. Yet time is a more critical competitive yardstick than traditional financial measurements.

Today's new-generation companies compete with flexible manufacturing and rapid-response systems, expanding variety and increasing innovation. A company that builds its strategy on this cycle is a more powerful competitor than one with a traditional strategy based on low wages, scale, or focus. These older, cost-based strategies require managers to do whatever is necessary to drive down costs: move production to or source from a low-wage country; build new facilities or consolidate old plants to gain economies of scale; or focus operations down to the most economic subset of activities. These tactics reduce costs but at the expense of responsiveness.

In contrast, strategies based on the cycle of flexible manufacturing, rapid response, expanding variety, and increasing innovation are time based. Factories are close to the customers they serve. Organizational structures enable fast responses rather than low costs and control. Companies concentrate on reducing if not eliminating delays and using their response advantages to attract the most profitable customers.

Many—but certainly not all—of today's time-based competitors are Japanese. Some of them are Sony, Matsushita, Sharp, Toyota, Hitachi, NEC, Toshiba, Honda, and Hino; time-based Western companies include Benetton, The Limited, Federal Express, Domino's Pizza, Wilson Art, and McDonald's. For these leading competitors, time has become the overarching measurement of performance. By reducing the consumption of time in every aspect of the business, these companies also reduce costs, improve quality, and stay close to their customers.

Breaking the Planning Loop

Companies are systems; time connects all the parts. The most powerful competitors understand this axiom and are breaking the debilitating loop that strangles much of traditional manufacturing planning.

Traditional manufacturing requires long lead times to resolve conflicts between various jobs or activities that require the same resources. The long lead times, in turn, require sales forecasts to guide planning. But sales forecasts are inevitably wrong; by definition they are guesses, however informed. Naturally, as lead times lengthen, the accuracy of sales forecasts declines. With more forecasting errors, inventories balloon and the need for safety stocks at all levels increases. Errors in forecasting also mean more unscheduled jobs that have to be expedited, thereby crowding out scheduled jobs. The need for longer lead times grows even greater and the planning loop expands even more, driving up costs, increasing delays, and creating system inefficiencies.

Managers who find themselves trapped in the planning loop often respond by asking for better forecasts and longer lead times. In other words, they treat the symptoms and worsen the problem. The only way to break the planning loop is to reduce the consumption of time throughout the system; that will, in turn, cut the need for lead time for estimates, for safety stocks, and all the rest. After all, if a company could ever drive its lead time all the way to zero, it would have to forecast only the next day's sales. While that idea of course is unrealistic, successful time-based competitors in Japan and in the West have kept their lead times from growing and some have even reduced them, thereby diminishing the planning loop's damaging effects.

Thirty years ago, Jay W. Forrester of MIT published a pioneering article in the Harvard Business Review, "Industrial Dynamics: A Major Breakthrough for Decision Makers" (July/August 1958), which established a model of time's impact on an organization's performance. Using "industrial dynamics"—a concept originally developed for shipboard fire control systems—Forrester tracked the effects of time delays and decision rates within a simple business system consisting of a factory, a factory warehouse, a distributor's inventory, and retailers' inventories. The numbers in figure 5-2 are the delays in the flow of information or product, measured in weeks. In this example, the orders accumulate at the retailer for three weeks, are in the mail for half a week, are delayed at the distributor for two weeks, go back into the mail for another half a week, and need eight weeks for processing at the factory and its warehouse. Then the finished product begins its journey back to the retailer. The cycle takes nineteen weeks.

FIGURE 5-2
Time in the Planning Loop (in weeks)

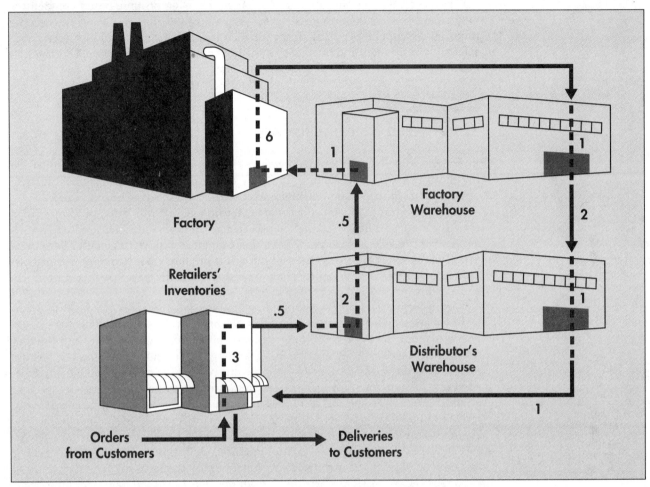

The system in this example is very stable—as long as retail demand is stable or as long as forecasts are accurate nineteen weeks into the future. But if unexpected changes occur, the system must respond. The chart, also taken from the Forrester article, shows what happens to this system when a simple change takes place: demand goes up 10 percent, then flattens. Acting on new forecasts and seeking to cut delivery delays, the factory first responds by ramping up production 40 percent. When management realizes—too late—that it has overshot the mark, it cuts production 30 percent. Too late again it learns that it has overcorrected. This ramping up and cutting back continue until finally the system stabilizes, more than a year after the initial 10 percent increase.

What distorts the system so badly is time: the lengthy delay between the event that creates the new demand and the time when the factory finally receives the information. The longer that delay, the more distorted is the view of the market. Those distortions reverberate throughout the system, producing disruption, waste, and inefficiency.

These distortions plague business today. To escape them, companies have a choice: they can produce to forecast or they can reduce the time delays in the flow of information and product through the system. The traditional solution is to produce to forecast. The new approach is to reduce time consumption.

Because time flows throughout the system, focusing on time-based competitive performance results in improvements across the board. Companies generally become time-based competitors by first correcting their manufacturing techniques, then fixing sales and distribution, and finally adjusting their approach to innovation. Ultimately, it becomes the basis for a company's overall strategy.

Time-Based Manufacturing

In general, time-based manufacturing policies and practices differ from those of traditional manufacturers along three key dimensions: length of production runs, organization of process components, and complexity of scheduling procedures.

When it comes to lot size, for instance, traditional factories attempt to maximize production runs while time-based manufacturers try to shorten their production runs as much as possible. In fact, many Japanese companies aim for run lengths of a single unit. The thinking behind this is as simple as it is fundamental to competitive success: reduced run lengths mean more frequent production of the complete mix of products and faster response to customers' demands.

Factory layout also contributes to time-based competitive advantage. Traditional factories are usually organized by process technology centers. For example, metal goods manufacturers organize their factories into shearing, punching, and braking departments; electronic assemblers have stuffing, wave soldering, assembly, testing, and packing departments. Parts move from one process technology center to the next. Each step consumes valuable time: parts sit, waiting to move; then move; then wait to be used in the next step. In a traditional manufacturing system, products usually receive value for only .05 percent to 2.5 percent of the time that they are in the factory. The rest of the time products sit waiting for something to happen.

Time-based factories, however, are organized by product. To minimize handling and moving of parts, the manufacturing functions for a component or a product are as close together as possible. Parts move from one activity to the next with little or no delay. Because the production process eliminates the need to pile and repile parts, they flow quickly and efficiently through the factory.

In traditional factories, scheduling is also a source of delay and waste. Most traditional factories use central scheduling that requires sophisticated materials resource planning and shop-floor control systems. Even though these systems are advanced, they still waste time: work orders usually flow to the factory floor on a monthly or weekly basis. In the meantime, parts can sit idle.

In time-based factories, local scheduling enables employees to make more production control decisions on the factory floor, without the time-consuming loop back to management for approval. Moreover, the combination of the product-oriented layout of the factory and local scheduling makes the total production process run more smoothly. Once a part starts through the production run, many of the requirements between manufacturing steps are purely automatic and require no intermediate scheduling.

These differences between traditional and time-based factories add up. Flexible factories enjoy big advantages in both productivity and time: labor productivity in time-based factories can be as much as 200 percent higher than in conventional plants; time-based factories can respond eight to ten times faster than traditional factories.

Flexible production means significant improvements in labor and net-asset productivity. These, in turn, yield reductions of up to 20 percent in overall costs and increases in growth for much less investment.

Toyota offers a dramatic example of the kinds of improvements that leading time-based competitors are making. Dissatisfied with the response time of a supplier, Toyota went to work. It took the supplier fifteen days to turn out a component after arrival of the raw materials at its factory. The first step was to cut lot sizes, reducing response time to six days. Next Toyota streamlined the factory layout, reducing the number of inventory holding points. The response time fell to three days. Finally Toyota eliminated all work-in-progress inventories at the supplier's plant. New response time: one day.

Toyota, of course, is not alone in improving manufacturing response times. Matsushita cut the time needed to make washing machines from 360 hours to just 2; Honda slashed its motorcycle fabricating time by 80 percent; in North America, companies making motor controllers and electrical components for unit air conditioners have improved their manufacturing response times by 90 percent.

Time-Based Sales and Distribution

A manufacturer's next challenge is to avoid dissipation of factory performance improvements in other parts of the organization. In Jay Forrester's example of the planning loop, the factory and its warehouse accounted for roughly one-half of the system's time. In actuality today, the factory accounts for one-third to one-half of the total time—often the most "visible" portion of time. But other parts of the system are just as important, if less apparent. For example, in the Forrester system, sales and distribution consume as much or more time than manufacturing.

What Forrester modeled, the Japanese experienced. By the late 1970s, leading Japanese companies were finding that inefficient sales and distribution operations undercut the benefits of their flexible manufacturing systems. Toyota, which at that time was divided into two separate companies, Toyota Motor Manufacturing and Toyota Motor Sales, again makes this point. Toyota Motor Manufacturing could manufacture a car in less than two days. But Toyota Motor Sales needed from fifteen to twenty-six days to close the sale, transmit the order to the factory, get the order scheduled, and deliver the car to the customer. By the late 1970s, the cost-conscious, competition-minded engineers at Toyota Manufacturing were angry at their counterparts at Toyota Motor Sales, who were frittering away the advantage gained in the production process. The sales and distribution function was generating 20 percent to 30 percent of a car's cost to the customer—more than it cost Toyota to manufacture the car!

Finally, in 1982 Toyota moved decisively to remedy the problem. The company merged Toyota Motor Manufacturing and Toyota Motor Sales. The company announced that it wanted to become "more marketing driven." While Toyota assured the public that the reorganization only returned it to its configuration in the 1950s, within eighteen months all the Toyota Motor Sales directors retired. Their jobs were left vacant or filled by executives from Toyota Motor Manufacturing.

The company wasted no time in implementing a plan to cut delays in sales and distribution, reduce costs, and improve customer service. The old system, Toyota found, had handled customer orders in batches. Orders and other crucial information would accumulate at one step of the sales and distribution process before dispatch to the next level, which wasted time and generated extra costs.

To speed the flow of information, Toyota had to reduce the size of the information batches. The solution came from a company-developed computer system that tied its salespeople directly to the factory scheduling operation. This link bypassed several levels of the sales and distribution function and enabled the modified system to operate with very small batches of orders.

Toyota expected this new approach to cut the sales and distribution cycle time in half—from four to six weeks to just two to three weeks across Japan. (For the Tokyo and Osaka regions, which account for roughly two-thirds of Japan's population, the goal was to reduce cycle time to just two days.) But by 1987 Toyota had reduced system responsiveness to eight days, including the time required to make the car. In the Forrester example, this achievement is equivalent to cutting the nineteen-week cycle to six weeks. The results were predictable: shorter sales forecasts, lower costs, happier customers.

Time-Based Innovation

A company that can bring out new products three times faster than its competitors enjoys a huge advantage. The effects of this time-based advantage are devastating; quite simply, American companies are losing leadership of technology and innovation—supposedly this country's source of long-term advantage.

Unless U.S. companies reduce their new product development and introduction cycles from 36–48 months to 12–18 months, Japanese manufacturers will easily out-innovate and outperform them. Taking the initiative in innovation will require even faster cycle times.

Residential air conditioners illustrate the Japanese ability to introduce more technological innovation in smaller increments—and how in just a few years these improvements add up to remarkably superior products. The Japanese introduce innovations in air conditioners four times faster than their American competitors; in technological sophistication the Japanese products are seven to ten years ahead of U.S. products.

Look at the changes in Mitsubishi Electric's three-horsepower heat pump between 1975 and 1985. From 1975 to 1979, the company did nothing to the product except change the sheet metal work, partly to improve efficiency but mostly to reduce materials costs. In 1979, the technological sophistication of the product was roughly equal to that of the U.S. competition. From this point on, the Japanese first established, and then widened the lead.

Using time-based innovation, Mitsubishi transformed its air conditioner. The changes came incrementally and steadily. Overall they gave Mitsubishi—and other Japanese companies on the same track—the position of technological leadership in the global residential air-conditioning industry.

In 1985, a U.S. air conditioner manufacturer was just debating whether to use integrated circuits in its residential heat pump. In view of its four- to five-year product development cycle, it could not have introduced the innovation until 1989 or 1990—putting the American company ten years behind the Japanese. Faced with this situation, the U.S. air conditioner company followed the example of many U.S. manufacturers that have lost the lead in technology and innovation: it decided to source its air conditioners and components from its Japanese competition.

Time-Based Strategy

The possibility of establishing a response-time advantage opens new avenues for constructing winning competitive strategies. At most companies, strategic choices are limited to three options:

- Seeking coexistence with competitors. This choice is seldom stable, since competitors refuse to cooperate and stay put.
- Retreating in the face of competitors. Many companies choose this course; the business press fills its pages with accounts of companies retreating by consolidating plants, focusing their operations, outsourcing, divesting businesses, pulling out of markets, or moving upscale.
- Attacking, either directly or indirectly. The direct attack involves the classic confrontation—cut price and add capacity, creating head-on competition. Indirect attack requires surprise. Competitors either do not understand the strategies being used against them or they do understand but cannot respond—sometimes because of the speed of the attack, sometimes because of their inability to mount a response.

Of the three options, only an attack creates the opportunity for real growth. Direct attack demands superior resources; it is always expensive and potentially disastrous. Indirect attack promises the most gain for the least cost. Time-based strategy offers a powerful new approach for successful indirect attacks against larger, established competitors.

■ COMPETING ON CAPABILITIES[†]

By George Stalk, Philip Evans, and Lawrence Shulman

In the 1980s, companies discovered time as a new source of competitive advantage. In the 1990s, they will learn that time is just one piece of a more far-reaching transformation in the logic of competition.

Companies that compete effectively on time—speeding new products to market, manufacturing just in time, or responding promptly to customer complaints—tend to be good at other things as well: for instance, the consistency of their product quality, the acuity of their insight into evolving customer needs, the ability to exploit emerging markets, enter new businesses, or generate new ideas and incorporate them in innovations. But all these qualities are mere reflections of a more fundamental characteristic: a new conception of corporate strategy that we call capabilities-based competition.

Four Principles of Capabilities-Based Competition

In industry after industry, established competitors are being outmaneuvered and overtaken by more dynamic rivals. In the years after World War II, Honda was a modest manufacturer of a 50-cc engine designed to be attached to a bicycle. Today it is challenging General Motors and Ford for dominance of the global automobile industry. Xerox invented xerography and the office copier market. But between 1976 and 1982, Canon introduced more than ninety new models, cutting Xerox's share of the midrange copier market in half. Today Canon is a key competitor not only in midrange copiers but also in high-end color copiers.

The greatest challenge to department store giants like Macy's comes neither from other large department stores nor from small boutiques but from The Limited, a $5.25 billion design, procurement, delivery, and retailing machine that exploits dozens of consumer segments with the agility of many small boutiques. Citicorp may still be the largest U.S. bank in terms of assets, but Banc One has consistently enjoyed the highest return on assets in the U.S. banking industry and now enjoys a market capitalization greater than Citicorp's.

These examples represent more than just the triumph of individual companies. They signal a fundamental shift in the logic of competition, a shift that is revolutionizing corporate strategy.

When the economy was relatively static, strategy could afford to be static. In a world characterized by durable products, stable customer needs, well-defined national and regional markets, and clearly identified competitors, competition was a "war of position" in which companies occupied competitive space like squares on a chessboard, building and defending market share in clearly defined product or market segments. The key to competitive advantage was *where* a company chose to compete. *How* it chose to compete was also important but secondary, a matter of execution.

Few managers need reminding of the changes that have made this traditional approach obsolete. As markets fragment and proliferate, "owning" any particular market segment becomes simultaneously more difficult and less valuable. As product life cycles accelerate, dominating existing product segments becomes less important than being able to create new products and exploit them quickly. Meanwhile, as globalization breaks down barriers between national and regional markets, competitors are multiplying and reducing the value of national market share.

In this more dynamic business environment, strategy has to become correspondingly more dynamic. Competition is now a "war of movement" in which success depends on anticipation of market trends and quick response to changing customer needs. Successful competitors move quickly in and out of products, markets, and sometimes even entire businesses—a process more akin to an interactive video game than to chess. In such an environment, the essence of strategy is not the structure of a company's products and markets but the dynamics of its behavior. And the goal is to identify and develop the hard-to-imitate organizational capabilities that distinguish a company from its competitors in the eyes of customers.

Companies like Wal-Mart, Honda, Canon, The Limited, or Banc One have learned this lesson. Their experience and that of other successful companies suggest four basic principles of capabilities-based competition:

- The building blocks of corporate strategy are not products and markets but business processes.
- Competitive success depends on transforming a company's key processes into strategic capabilities that consistently provide superior value to the customer.
- Companies create these capabilities by making strategic investments in a support infrastructure that links together and transcends traditional strategic business units (SBUs) and functions.

- Because capabilities necessarily cross functions, the champion of a capabilities-based strategy is the chief executive officer (CEO).

A capability is a set of business processes strategically understood. Every company has business processes that deliver value to the customer. But few think of them as the primary object of strategy. Capabilities-based competitors identify their key business processes, manage them centrally, and invest in them heavily, looking for a long-term payback.

What transforms a set of individual business processes into a strategic capability? The key is to connect them to real customer needs. A capability is strategic only when it begins and ends with the customer. Of course, just about every company these days claims to be "close to the customer." But there is a qualitative difference in the customer focus of capabilities-driven competitors. These companies conceive of the organization as a giant feedback loop that begins with identifying the needs of the customer and ends with satisfying them.

As managers have grasped the importance of time-based competition, for example, they have increasingly focused on the speed of new product *development*. But as a unit of analysis, new product development is too narrow. It is only part of what is necessary to satisfy a customer and, therefore, to build an organizational capability. Better to think in terms of new product *realization*, a capability that includes the way a product is not only developed but also marketed and serviced. The longer and more complex the string of business processes, the harder it is to transform them into a capability—but the greater the value of that capability once built because competitors have more difficulty imitating it.

Weaving business processes together into organizational capabilities in this way also mandates a new logic of vertical integration. At a time when cost pressures are pushing many companies to outsource more and more activities, capabilities-based competitors are integrating vertically to ensure that they, not a supplier or distributor, control the performance of key business processes. Even when a company doesn't actually own every link of the capability chain, the capabilities-based competitor works to tie these parts into its own business systems.

Another attribute of capabilities is that they are collective and cross-functional—a small part of many people's jobs, not a large part of a few. This helps explain why most companies underexploit capabilities-based competition. Because a capability is "everywhere and nowhere," no one executive controls it entirely. Moreover, leveraging capabilities requires a panoply of strategic investments across SBUs and functions far beyond what traditional cost-benefit metrics can justify. Traditional internal accounting and control systems often miss the strategic nature of such investments. For these reasons, building strategic capabilities cannot be treated as an operating matter and left to operating managers, to corporate staff, or still less to SBU heads. It is the primary agenda of the CEO. The prize will be companies that combine scale and flexibility to outperform the competition along five dimensions:

- *Speed.* The ability to respond quickly to customer or market demands and to incorporate new ideas and technologies quickly into products.
- *Consistency.* The ability to produce a product that unfailingly satisfies customers' expectations.
- *Acuity.* The ability to see the competitive environment clearly and thus to anticipate and respond to customers' evolving needs and wants.
- *Agility.* The ability to adapt simultaneously to many different business environments.
- *Innovativeness.* The ability to generate new ideas and to combine existing elements to create new sources of value.

Becoming a Capabilities-Based Competitor

Few companies are fortunate enough to begin as capabilities-based competitors. For most, the challenge is to become one.

The starting point is for senior managers to undergo the fundamental shift in perception that allows them to see their business in terms of strategic capabilities. Then they can begin to identify and link together essential business processes to serve customer needs. Finally, they can reshape the organization—including managerial roles and responsibilities—to encourage the new kind of behavior necessary to make capabilities-based competition work.

The experience of a medical-equipment company we'll call Medequip illustrates this change process. An established competitor, Medequip recently found itself struggling to regain market share it had lost to a new competitor. The rival had introduced a lower-priced, lower-performance version of the company's most popular product. Medequip had developed a similar product in response, but senior managers were hesitant to launch it. Their reasoning made perfect sense according to the traditional competitive logic. As managers saw it, the company faced a classic no-win situation. The new product was lower priced but also lower profit. If the company promoted it aggressively to regain market share, overall profitability would suffer.

But when Medequip managers began to investigate their competitive situation more carefully, they stopped defining the problem in terms of static products and markets. Increasingly, they saw it in terms of the organization's business processes. Traditionally, the company's functions had operated autonomously. Manufacturing was separate from sales, which was separate from field service. What's more, the company managed field service the way most companies do—as a classic profit center whose resources were deployed to reduce costs and maximize profitability. For instance, Medequip assigned full-time service personnel only to those customers who bought enough equipment to justify the additional cost.

However, a closer look at the company's experience with these steady customers led to a fresh insight: at accounts where Medequip had placed one or more full-time service representatives on-site, the company renewed its highly profitable service contracts at three times the rate of its other accounts. When these accounts needed new equipment, they chose Medequip twice as often as other accounts did and tended to buy the broadest mix of Medequip products as well. The reason was simple. Medequip's on-site service representatives had become expert in the operations of their customers. They knew what equipment mix best suited the customer and what additional equipment the customer needed. So they had teamed up informally with Medequip's salespeople to become part of the selling process. Because the service reps were on-site full-time, they were also able to respond quickly to equipment problems. And of course, whenever a competitor's equipment broke down, the Medequip reps were on hand to point out the product's shortcomings.

This new knowledge about the dynamics of service delivery inspired top managers to rethink how their company should compete. Specifically, they redefined field service from a stand-alone function to one part of an integrated sales and service capability. They crystallized this new approach in three key business decisions.

First, Medequip decided to use its service personnel not to keep costs low but to maximize the life-cycle profitability of a set of targeted accounts. This decision took the form of a dramatic commitment to place at least one service rep on-site with selected customers—no matter how little business each account currently represented.

The decision to guarantee on-site service was expensive, so choosing which customers to target was crucial; there had to be potential for considerable additional business. The company divided its accounts into three categories: those it dominated, those where a single competitor dominated, and those where several competitors were present. Medequip protected the accounts it dominated by maintaining the already high level of service and by offering attractive terms for renewing service contracts. The company ignored those customers dominated by a single competitor—unless the competitor was having serious problems. All the remaining resources were focused on those accounts where no single competitor had the upper hand.

Next Medequip combined its sales, service, and order entry organizations into cross-functional teams that concentrated almost exclusively on the needs of the targeted accounts. The company trained service reps in sales techniques so they could take full responsibility for generating new sales leads. This freed up the sales staff to focus on the more strategic role of understanding the long-term needs of the customer's business. Finally, to emphasize Medequip's new commitment to total service, the company even taught its service reps how to fix competitors' equipment.

Once this new organizational structure was in place, Medequip finally introduced its new low-price product. The result: the company has not only stopped its decline in market share but also *increased* share by almost 50 percent. The addition of the lower-priced product has reduced profit margins, but the overall mix still includes many higher-priced products. And absolute profits are much higher than before.

This story suggests four steps by which any company can transform itself into a capabilities-based competitor:

Shift the Strategic Framework to Achieve Aggressive Goals

At Medequip, managers transformed what looked like a no-win situation—either lose share or lose profits—into an opportunity for a major competitive victory. They did so by abandoning the company's traditional function, cost, and profit-center orientation and by identifying and managing the capabilities that link customer need to customer satisfaction. The chief expression of this new capabilities-based strategy was the decision to provide on-site service reps to targeted accounts and to create cross-functional sales and service teams.

Organize around the Chosen Capability and Make Sure Employees Have the Necessary Skills and Resources to Achieve It

Having set this ambitious competitive goal, Medequip managers next set about reshaping the company in terms of it. Rather than retaining the existing functional structure and trying to encourage coordination through some kind of matrix, they created a brand new organization—Customer Sales and Service—and divided it into "cells" with overall responsibility for specific customers. The company also provided the necessary training so that employees could understand how their new roles would help achieve new business goals. Finally, Medequip created systems to support employees in their new roles. For example, one information system uses CD-ROMs to give field-service personnel quick access to information about Medequip's product line as well as those of competitors.

Make Progress Visible and Bring Measurements and Reward into Alignment

Medequip also made sure that the company's measurement and reward systems reflected the new competitive strategy. Like most companies, the company had never known the profitability of individual customers. Traditionally, field-service employees were measured on overall service profitability. With the shift to the new approach, however, the company had to develop a whole new set of measures—for example, Medequip's "share-by-customer-by-product," the amount of money the company invested in servicing a particular customer, and the customer's current and estimated lifetime profitability. Team members' compensation was calculated according to these new measures.

Do Not Delegate the Leadership of the Transformation

Becoming a capabilities-based competitor requires an enormous amount of change. For that reason, it is a process extremely difficult to delegate. Because capabilities are cross-

EXHIBIT 5-1

How Capabilities Differ from Core Competencies: The Case of Honda

---

HOW CAPABILITIES DIFFER FROM CORE COMPETENCIES: THE CASE OF HONDA

In their influential 1990 HBR article, "The Core Competence of the Corporation," (see chapter 6) Gary Hamel and C. K. Prahalad mount an attack on traditional notions of strategy that is not so dissimilar from what we are arguing here. For Hamel and Prahalad, however, the central building block of corporate strategy is "core competence." How is a competence different from a capability, and how do the two concepts relate to each other?

Hamel and Prahalad define core competence as the combination of individual technologies and production skills that underly a company's myriad product lines. Sony's core competence in miniaturization, for example, allows the company to make everything from the Sony Walkman to videocameras to notebook computers. Canon's core competencies in optics, imaging, and microprocessor controls have enabled it to enter markets as seemingly diverse as copiers, laser printers, cameras, and image scanners.

As the above examples suggest, Hamel and Prahalad use core competence to explain the ease with which successful competitors are able to enter new and seemingly unrelated businesses. But a closer look reveals that competencies are not the whole story.

Consider Honda's move from motorcycles into other businesses, including lawn mowers, outboard motors, and automobiles. Hamel and Prahalad attribute Honda's success to its underlying competence in engines and power trains. While Honda's engine competence is certainly important, it alone cannot explain the speed with which the company has successfully moved into a wide range of businesses over the past 20 years. After all, General Motors (to take just one example) is also an accomplished designer and manufacturer of engines. What distinguishes Honda from its competitors is its focus on capabilities.

One important but largely invisible capability is Honda's expertise in "dealer management" — its ability to train and support its dealer network with operating procedures and policies for merchandising, selling floor planning, and service management. First developed for its motorcycle business, this set of business processes has since been replicated in each new business the company has entered.

Another capability central to Honda's success has been its skill at "product realization." Traditional product development separates planning, proving, and executing into three sequential activities: assessing the market's needs and whether existing products are meeting

Continued

functional, the change process can't be left to middle managers. It requires the hands-on guidance of the CEO and the active involvement of top line managers. At Medequip, the heads of sales, service, and order entry led the subteams that made the actual recommendations, but it was the CEO who oversaw the change process, evaluated their proposals, and made the final decision. His leading role ensured senior management's commitment to the recommended changes.

This top-down change process has the paradoxical result of driving business decision making down to those directly participating in key processes—for example, Medequip's sales and service staff. This leads to a high measure of operational flexibility and an almost reflexlike responsiveness to external change.

A New Logic of Growth: The Capabilities Predator

Once managers reshape the company in terms of its underlying capabilities, they can use these capabilities to define a growth path for the corporation. At the center of capabilities-based competition is a new logic of growth.

EXHIBIT 5-1 *(continued)*
How Capabilities Differ from Core Competencies: The Case of Honda

those needs; testing the proposed product; then building a prototype. The end result of this process is a new factory or organization to introduce the new product. This traditional approach takes a long time—and with time goes money.

Honda has arranged these activities differently. First, planning and proving go on continuously and in parallel. Second, these activities are clearly separated form execution. At Honda, the highly disciplined execution cycle schedules major product revisions every four years and minor revisions every two years. The 1990 Honda Accord, for example, which is the first major redesign of that model since 1986, incorporates a power train developed two years earlier and first used in the 1988 Accord. Finally, when a new product is ready, it is released to existing factories and organizations, which dramatically shortens the amount of time needed to launch it. As time is reduced, so are cost and risk.

Consider the following comparison between Honda and GM. In 1984, Honda launched its Acura division; one year later, GM created Saturn. Honda chose to integrate Acura into its existing organization and facilities. In Europe, for example, the Acura Legend is sold through the same sales force as the Honda Legend. The Acura division now makes three models – the Legend, Integra, and Vigor – and is turning out 300,000 cars a year. At the end of 1991, seven years after it was launched, the division had produced a total of 800,000 vehicles. More important, it had already introduced eight variations of its product line.

By contrast, GM created a separate organization and a separate facility for Saturn. Production began in late 1990, and 1991 will be its first full model year. If GM is lucky, it will be producing 240,000 vehicles in the next year or two and will have two models out.

As the Honda example suggests, competencies and capabilities represent two different but complementary dimensions of an emerging paradigm for corporate strategy. Both concepts emphasize "behavioral" aspects of strategy in contrast to the traditional structural model. But whereas core competence emphasizes technological and production expertise at specific points along the value chain, capabilities are more broadly based, encompassing the entire value chain. In this respect, capabilities are visible to the customer in a way that core competencies rarely are.

Like the "grand unified theory" that modern-day physicists are searching for to explain physical behavior at both the subatomic level and that of the entire cosmos, the combination of core competence and capabilities may define the universal model for corporate strategy in the 1990s and beyond.

In the 1960s, most managers assumed that when growth in a company's basic business slowed, the company should turn to diversification. This was the age of the multibusiness conglomerate. In the 1970s and 1980s, however, it became clear that growth through diversification was difficult. And so, the pendulum of management thinking swung once again. Companies were urged to "stick to their knitting"—that is, to focus on their core business, identify where the profit was, and get rid of everything else. The idea of the corporation became increasingly narrow.

Competing on capabilities provides a way for companies to gain the benefits of both focus and diversification. Put another way, a company that focuses on its strategic capabilities can compete in a remarkable diversity of regions, products, and businesses and do it far more coherently than the typical conglomerate can. Such a company is a "capabilities predator"—able to come out of nowhere and move rapidly from nonparticipant to major player and even to industry leader.

Capabilities-based companies grow by transferring their essential business processes—first to new geographic areas and then to new businesses. Wal-Mart CEO David Glass alludes to this method of growth when he characterizes Wal-Mart as "always pushing from the inside out; we never jump and backfill."

Strategic advantages built on capabilities are easier to transfer geographically than more traditional competitive advantages. Honda, for example, has become a manufacturer in Europe and the United States with relatively few problems. The quality of its cars made in the United States is so good that the company is exporting some of them back to Japan.

But the big payoff for capabilities-led growth comes not through geographical expansion but through rapid entry into whole new businesses. Capabilities-based companies do this in at least two ways. The first is by "cloning" their key business processes. Again, Honda is a typical example.

Most people attribute Honda's success to the innovative design of its products or the way the company manufactures them. These factors are certainly important. But the company's growth has been spearheaded by less visible capabilities. For example, a big part of Honda's original success in motorcycles was due to the company's distinctive capability in "dealer management," which departed from the traditional relationship between motorcycle manufacturers and dealers. Typically, local dealers were motorcycle enthusiasts who were more concerned with finding a way to support their hobby than with building a strong business. They were not particularly interested in marketing, parts-inventory management, or other business systems.

Honda, by contrast, managed its dealers to ensure that they would become successful businesspeople. The company provided operating procedures and policies for merchandising, selling, floor planning, and service management. It trained all its dealers and their entire staffs in these new management systems and supported them with a computerized dealer-management information system. The part-time dealers of competitors were no match for the better prepared and better financed Honda dealers.

Honda's move into new businesses, including lawn mowers, outboard motors, and automobiles, has depended on re-creating this same dealer-management capability in each new sector. Even in segments like luxury cars, where local dealers are generally more service oriented than those in the motorcycle business, Honda's skill at managing its dealers is transforming service standards. Honda dealers consistently receive the highest ratings for customer satisfaction among auto companies selling in the United States. One reason is that Honda gives its dealers far more autonomy to decide on the spot whether a needed repair is covered by warranty (see exhibit 5-1).

But the ultimate form of growth in the capabilities-based company may not be cloning business processes so much as creating processes so flexible and robust that the same set can serve many different businesses.

The Future of Capabilities-Based Competition

For the moment, capabilities-based companies have the advantage of competing against rivals still locked into the old way of seeing the competitive environment. But such a situation won't last forever. As more and more companies make the transition to capabilities-based competition, the simple fact of competing on capabilities will become less important than the specific capabilities a company has chosen to build. Given the necessary long-term investments, the strategic choices managers make will end up determining a company's fate.

■ FROM INNOVATION TO OUTPACING[†]

By Xavier Gilbert and Paul Strebel

Outpacing strategies rely on the explicit capability of a company to gain product leadership and cost leadership simultaneously. As the tennis player catches his opponent "on the wrong foot" by integrating his and the opponent's next few moves in one pattern, outpacing strategies also rely on the clustering of several complementary strategic moves. Their design and execution require new managerial and organizational approaches.

The Competitive Arena Has Changed

The competitive arena in most industry sectors has changed in many, widely publicized ways, such as globalization or deregulation. An important source of change that is less frequently discussed is the ability of some companies to modify the rules of the competitive game. They introduce a better offer, at a price that remains at least competitive with existing offers, in a way that makes it difficult for competitors to respond.

An example, is provided by Nintendo, the Japanese toy company. Initially a playing card manufacturer, Nintendo became famous in the early 1980s for its handheld electronic games. At that time, however, it was not even among the top ten toy companies in the world. By 1987, it had moved up to third rank and at the end of 1988, it had become the largest toy company in the world. Its return on sales was 15 percent, compared to less than 5 percent for most of the other industry players, worldwide.

In 1983, Nintendo had launched the Famicon, a family computer designed to provide computer-game images of unique quality, with fifty-two colors and TV-like sharpness. Such capabilities were traditionally associated with upper-end, professional

†**Source:** This article was originally published in *Business Quarterly*, Summer 1989, Vol. 54, #1, pp. 19–22. Reprinted with permission.

machines and had been out of reach for computer games. Nintendo did not think traditionally, however. Instead of following the standard approach of machines capable of doing everything plus high-quality image, it designed its product to provide high-quality images and very little else. For example, a keyboard was not thought to be important for computer games. As a result, the Famicon could be sold for a price unmatchable by other high-quality image machines. The result was a target selling price of ¥14,800 (about $60 at the time), as Nintendo had calculated that this was the average amount of money received by a Japanese teenager on New Year's Day.

But this was not all. Nintendo also devised a unique, complete competitive formula, from product design to retail. It selected subcontractors motivated by a desire to enter a new business. It committed to an initial order of three million integrated circuits to ensure that the supplier could reduce its manufacturing costs. It developed a low-cost distribution system for software, initially through vending machines that reloaded new software onto diskettes, and then through modems and public telephone lines. The result was unique perceived value for the computer-game players. The rug was pulled out literally from all other Japanese toy makers. In 1987, Bandai, the second largest Japanese toy maker, experienced a 16 percent decrease in sales, while its return on sales fell to 1.5 percent.

Why Traditional Strategies Do Not Work

The major weakness of the traditional strategic approaches is that they have been designed to identify and treat priorities sequentially. They have been product-life-cycle led, as if the product life cycle were a given to which the strategy should respond, rather than a process that the strategy should shape. Indeed, if the product life cycle were a given, there would be time for innovation, followed later with the development of a complete competitive formula for a broader market, again followed eventually with price competition. Within this frame of reference, innovative products may be expensive and rationalization may only come later, when all products become commodities.

In industry environments that are steered by companies capable of offering an innovative, competitively priced formula, however, such up-market or down-market repositioning remains not only ineffective, but dangerous. Companies that specialize in either product or cost leadership have difficulty shifting their emphasis. When such shifts have to be implemented in rapid sequence, not to mention simultaneously, the one-dimensional strategists have a hard time making ends meet.

A new strategic mind-set is required, one that relies less on dichotomies between moves and more on their complementarity. Rationalization can improve innovation and high value as perceived by the customer; innovation and high perceived value make cost-effective products more attractive for the customer. Successful companies have adopted this new strategic mind-set and are able to apply it repeatedly in a rapid sequence of complete moves.

The Profile of Winners

The strategies of some 100 companies in a wide range of industries, most evolving rapidly, have been examined by the authors and their colleagues over the last eight years. Some companies were initiating industry shifts; others were followers, redeploying their strategies to respond to industry changes; still others were caught by surprise, unable to respond to industry shifts. The successful companies, either in leading industry changes that caught their competitors on the wrong foot, or in responding effectively by capturing a share of the opportunity developed by the leaders, had four capabilities in common.

The Capability to Innovate

In leading or responding to an industry change, the successful companies had a capability to innovate. In some instances, they had initiated a "big bang" innovation; in most, they had produced incremental innovations. There were few examples of big bang innovations that had benefited the innovators. On the other hand, there were several examples of situations where a competitor other than the innovator had benefited from the opportunity created by the innovator's incomplete product idea, suggesting that innovation alone is not sufficient to create a durable competitive advantage.

The incremental innovations, which were far more numerous, consisted of providing a selected market segment with a better offer than the standard one, and of addressing new segments in this manner all the time. Examples were observed both in consumer products and in industrial goods of companies that had learned to innovate repeatedly by deploying a customized offer for each new market.

The capability to innovate often had to be applied in a "mature" environment, dominated by price competition and "commodity" products. The pressing need to rationalize and cut costs in these contexts generally kills any innovative capability. The successful companies, however, were able to compete on costs in a way that facilitated innovation. Nintendo's approach to rationalizing software distribution is an example.

The companies that used innovation to compete successfully had a couple of other characteristics in common. First, to avoid "buck-passing" exercises they had simpler organizational processes with fewer decision levels. Second, rapid information feedback from the market was seen as critical by the companies able to turn innovation into competitive advantage.

The Capability to Put Together a Complete Competitive Formula

The successful companies were also able to include, within their new competitive formula, a broad range of desirable benefits beyond the innovation itself, and thereby impose a new standard on the industry. The success of the IBM PC in a market that outsiders to the industry, such as Apple, Commodore, and Tandy, had just scratched, but with an incomplete formula, is an example.

The ability to recognize which features the market is really looking for distinguished the successful companies, which, in addition to their technological capabilities, were able to recognize the nontechnical market expectations that could serve as a basis for establishing a new standard. Several technology-oriented firms were observed that had difficulty in accepting that customer expectations do reflect needs and preferences other than technology. Not surprisingly, these companies had trouble in marketing their innovations. It took the founders of one computer company some eleven years to admit that "not even the best of systems will sell themselves."

A complete competitive formula encompasses not only an innovative product or service idea, but also the way it is promoted, distributed, supported, and used by the customer, all providing desirable benefits to the customer. Firms are not always aware of all the ingredients that make a product or service acceptable to a market segment. Putting together the complete formula requires that feedback from the market reach all the organization units that contribute to the competitive formula.

As a result, the ability to put together a complete competitive formula relies also on specific organizational characteristics. Highly compartmentalized organizations are not good at it. On the contrary, the capability of different functional areas to work together on the ingredients that will constitute the competitive formula, rather than in sequence, characterize the winners.

The Capability to Offer the New Formula at a Competitive Price

The capability to offer the new formula at a price competitive with that of previous offers clinches the competitive advantage and constitutes the outpacing strategy. The successful companies did not see innovation as a way to escape price competition; nor did they see innovation and rationalization as being mutually exclusive. On the contrary, they saw innovation and price competitiveness as inseparable. They could even use rationalization as a way to offer more value to the market by making all organization members closer to it and more responsible for it. As a result, they could design a new formula that while offering a higher perceived value, would help reduce costs at the same time. These companies were able to apply their resources to, and mobilize outside cooperation for, their new formula in ways that could be radically different from the prevailing industry habits. Their competitors could not respond without also making substantial changes to their approaches.

Several critical decisions are involved in the design of a formula that provides simultaneously higher perceived value and competitive prices. The offer must be unbundled and each of its elements reassessed with respect to its value for the selected market segment. Some elements of the previous offer, such as design features, positioning, distribution, or services, may turn out to be unnecessary or too expensive for the selected market segment, while others may be missing. They have to be assembled in the new formula in a coordinated manner.

The companies that were successful at designing a new, competitively priced formula were also able to use their organizations effectively. Their organizational processes allowed them to cut across functions to get an overview of the complete offer and to bring together all the needed resources in a coordinated manner. A sequential approach, where each function intervenes after the others have "done their job," will not provide this result.

The Capability to Perform These Moves Simultaneously

The last important characteristic of the successful companies was their capability to perform simultaneously, rather than sequentially, the development of the innovation, the assembly of a new complete formula and the rationalization of the formula. This capability is critical to catch competition on the wrong foot. It was perfectly illustrated by Nintendo's introduction of its Famicon. A complete formula, from design to distribution and service, was introduced all at once at a competitive price.

In some instances, however, successful companies are also able to "piggyback" on someone else's innovation. The source of their success, in this case, is the capability to put together a complete and competitively priced formula faster than the innovator. The frequent inability of the innovator to see the need for a complete formula, beyond the innovation, provides such opportunities. In particular, the early formulas often lack a suitable approach to distribution, which gives a chance to followers to address this aspect first. Indeed, with the progress of mass distribution, enormous rationalization opportunities exist, involving the development of partnerships with the channels.

These companies have been able to correct the inefficiencies of traditional organizational structures, particularly those of the matrix organizations, when there is a need to look at all the components of a competitive formula in a coordinated manner. Some successful companies, in different industries, have instituted, for example, a form of "roundtable" approach to allow the simultaneous consideration of the innovation of the complete formula needed to support it and of its competitive pricing.

In addition, successful companies are redesigning their organizational structures and processes to increase "throughput speed," from product development to meeting customer needs. With lower investment in goods in the pipeline and faster response to evolving customer needs, these companies are able, at the same time, to reduce costs, to provide more value to the customers, and to help their partners in the formula—suppliers, channels, and so on—to compete more effectively. A major European toy manufacturer has developed a partnership with retailers that allows it to capture sales information at the retailer level. As a result, it can reduce stock in the whole system, limit retailers' year-end carryover of unsold toys, and get quicker feedback on customer response; everyone wins.

The Need for Organizational Systems

The way the successful companies operated indicated that not only was a new strategic mind-set needed, but also new organizational concepts were implemented. Hierarchical organizations, relying on functional, geographic, or product specializations, with information systems that are equally specialized, cannot handle issues that are by definition multidimensional and multidisciplinary and that require constant adaptation by the organization. Their operating mode is sequential, while innovative, price-competitive formulas require coordinated, parallel work from a large number of vantage points.

The successful companies were able to use their organization as a pool of resources that could be networked in an evolving manner to be applied to changing competitive situations. People and information could be shared as a common resource with fewer hierarchical channels, which at the same time ensured a better use of these resources and a better outcome. In particular, information and feedback from the market, being more widely shared, affected all the steps of the development of a new competitive formula.

These "network" organizations could be observed at least on an ad hoc basis, and in some cases permanently, among the successful companies that were studied. It can be predicted that this form of organization will spread further in the future and that information technology will make a substantial contribution to its viability. Network organizations are the necessary complement to the new strategic mind-set that is needed to convert innovation into outpacing strategies.

■ STRATEGY AS STRETCH AND LEVERAGE[†]

By Gary Hamel and C. K. Prahalad

From Fit to Stretch

A good place to begin deconstructing our managerial frames is with the question, What is strategy? For a great many managers in large Western companies, the answer centers on three elements: the concept of fit or the relationship between the company and its competitive environment; the allocation of resources among competing investment opportunities; and a long-term perspective in which "patient money" figures prominently. From this perspective, "being strategic" implies a willingness to take the long view, and "strategic" investments are those that require a large and preemptive commitment of resources—betting bigger and betting earlier—as well as a distant return and substantial risk.

This dominant strategy frame is not wrong, only unbalanced. That every company must ultimately effect a fit between its resources and the opportunities it pursues, that resource allocation is a strategic task, and that managers must often countenance risk and uncertainty in the pursuit of strategic objectives all go without saying. But the predominance of these planks in corporate strategy platforms has obscured the merits of an alternative frame in which the concept of stretch supplements the idea of fit, leveraging resources is as important as allocating them, and the long term has as much to do with consistency of effort and purpose as it does with patient money and an appetite for risk.

To illustrate the effects of these opposing frames, imagine two companies competing in the same industry. Alpha, the industry leader, has accumulated a wealth of resources of every kind—human talent, technical skills, distribution access, well-known brands, manufacturing facilities, and cash flow—and it can fund just about any initiative it considers strategic. But its aspirations to remain atop its present perch, to grow as fast as its industry, and to achieve a 15 percent return on equity are modest. "Where do you go," Alpha's managers ask themselves, "when you're already number one?"

Beta, its rival, is a relative latecomer to the industry. It is much smaller than Alpha and has no choice but to make do with fewer people, a smaller capital budget, more modest facilities, and a fraction of Alpha's research and development (R&D) budget. Nevertheless, its ambitions belie its meager resource base. Beta's managers have every intention of knocking Alpha off its leadership perch. To reach this goal, they know that they must grow faster than Alpha, develop more and better products than Alpha, and build a worldwide brand franchise and a presence in every major market, all while expending fewer resources. The misfit between Beta's resources and its aspirations would lead most observers to challenge the feasibility of its goals, if not the sanity of its managers.

But consider the likely effects of Alpha's abundance and Beta's ambition on how the two companies frame their competitive strategies and marshal their resources.

Clearly, Alpha is much better placed to behave "strategically": to preempt Beta in building new plant capacity, to outspend Beta on R&D, to buy market share through aggressive pricing, and so on. Alpha's managers are likely to rest easily, confident that they can overpower their smaller rival in any confrontation. They are also likely to approach their battles with a mind-set reminiscent of World War I trench warfare—"Whoever runs out of ammunition first is the loser"—however resource-inefficient this approach may be.

Beta, on the other hand, is likely to adopt the tactics of guerrilla warfare in hopes of exploiting the orthodoxies of its more powerful enemy. It will search for undefended niches rather than confront its competitor in well-defended market segments. It will focus investments on a relatively small number of core competencies where management feels it has the potential to become a world leader. It might even find itself compelled to invent lean manufacturing with an emphasis on doing more with less.

The argument here is substantially more subtle than the oft-made point that small companies are more nimble. What distinguishes Beta from Alpha is not Beta's smaller resource base but the greater gap that exists between Beta's resources and its aspirations. In contrast, Alpha's problem is not that it is large—there's no inherent virtue in being small—but that it has insufficient stretch in its aspirations. Alpha's managers will not think and behave as if they were in a small, resource-restrained company. What bedevils Alpha is not a surfeit of resources but a scarcity of ambition.

The products of stretch—a view of competition as encirclement rather than confrontation, an accelerated product-development cycle, tightly knit cross-functional teams, a focus on a few core competencies, strategic alliances with suppliers, programs of employee involvement, consensus—are all elements of a managerial approach typically labeled "Japanese." But as the less than sterling performance of Japan's well-endowed banks and brokerage houses reminds us, there is no magic simply in being Japanese. Indeed, so-called Japanese management may have less to do with social harmony and personal discipline than it does with the strategic discipline of stretch. Companies like NEC, CNN, Sony, Glaxo, and Honda were united more by the unreasonableness of their ambitions and their creativity in getting the most from the least than by any cultural or institutional heritage. Material advantages are as poor a substitute for the creativity stretch engenders in Japan as they are in the United States or Europe. Creating stretch, a misfit between resources and aspirations, is the single most important task senior management faces.

From Allocation to Leverage

Allocating resources across businesses and geographies is an important part of top management's strategic role. But leveraging what a company already has rather than simply allocating it is a more creative response to scarcity. In the continual search for less resource-intensive ways to achieve ambitious objectives, leveraging resources provides a very different approach from the downsizing and delayering, the restructuring and retrenchment that have become common as managers contend with rivals around the world who have mastered the art of resource leverage.

There are two basic approaches to garnering greater resource productivity, whether those resources be capital or human. The first is downsizing, cutting investment and head count in hopes of becoming lean and mean—in essence, reducing the buck paid for the bang. The second approach, resource leveraging, seeks to get the most out of the resources one has—to get a much bigger bang for the buck. Resource leverage is essentially energizing, while downsizing is essentially demoralizing. Both approaches will yield gains in productivity, but a company that continually ratchets down its resource base without improving its capacity for resource leverage will soon find that downsizing and restructuring become a way of life—until investors locate a new owner or demand a management team with a better track record. Indeed, this is happening in the United States and in Europe as an increasing share of human and physical capital falls through acquisition, joint venture, and surrender of market share to competitors who are better at getting more from less.

The Arenas of Resource Leverage

Management can leverage its resources, financial and nonfinancial, in five basic ways: by *concentrating* them more effectively on key strategic goals; by *accumulating* them more efficiently; by *complementing* one kind of resource with another to create higher-order value; by *conserving* resources wherever possible; and by *recovering* them from the marketplace in the shortest possible time.

Let us look, one by one, at some of the components that make up these broad categories and ask the questions that managers must ask to assess the scope within their company for further resource leverage.

Concentrating Resources: Convergence and Focus

Leverage requires a strategic focal point, or what we have called a strategic intent, on which the efforts of individuals, functions, and businesses can converge over time. Komatsu's goal of "encircling Caterpillar," President Kennedy's challenge to "put a man on the moon by the end of the decade," British Airway's quest to become the "world's favorite airline," and Ted Turner's dream of global news all provided a strategic intent.

Yet in many, probably most, companies there is neither a strategic focal point nor any deep agreement on the company's growth trajectory. As a result, priorities shift constantly. Resources are squandered on competing projects. Potentially great ideas are abandoned prematurely. And the very definition of core business changes often enough to confuse both investors and employees. It is hardly surprising then that in many companies there is little cumulativeness to month-by-month and year-by-year strategic decisions.

Resource convergence is also unlikely if strategic goals fail to outlive the tenures of senior executives. Even with a high degree of resource leverage, the attainment of worldwide industry leadership may be a ten-year quest. Recasting the company's ambition every few years virtually guarantees that leadership will remain elusive. The target has to sit still long enough for all members of the organization to calibrate their sights, take a bead on the target, fire, adjust their aim, and fire again.

If convergence prevents the diversion of resources over time, focus prevents the dilution of resources at any given time. Just as a general with limited forces must pick his targets carefully, so a company must specify and prioritize the improvements it will pursue. Too many managers, finding their companies behind on cost, quality, cycle time, customer service, and other competitive metrics, have tried to put everything right at the same time and then wondered why progress was so painfully slow. No single business, functional team, or department can give adequate attention to all these goals at once. Without focused attention on a few key operating goals at any one time, improvement efforts are likely to be so diluted that the company ends up as a perpetual laggard in every critical performance area.

Dividing meager resources across a host of medium-term operational goals creates mediocrity on a broad scale. Middle managers are regularly blamed for failing to translate top-management initiatives into action. Yet middle management often finds itself attempting to compensate for top management's failure to sort out priorities, with the result that mixed messages and conflicting goals prevent a sufficient head of steam from developing behind any task.

Accumulating Resources: Extracting and Borrowing

Every company is a reservoir of experiences. Every day, employees come in contact with new customers, learn more about competitors, confront and solve technical problems, and discover better ways of doing things. But some companies are better than others at extracting knowledge from those experiences. Thus what differentiates companies over time may be less the relative quality or depth of their stockpile of experiences than their capacity to draw from that stockpile. Because experience comes at a cost, the ability to maximize the insights gained from every experience is a critical component of resource leverage. Being a "learning organization" is not enough; a company must also be capable of learning more efficiently than its competitors.

The capacity to learn from experience depends on many things: employees who are both reflective and well schooled in the art of problem solving; forums (such as quality circles) where employees can identify common problems and search for higher order solutions; an environment in which every employee feels responsible for the company's competitiveness; the willingness to fix things before they're broken; continuous benchmarking against the world's best practice. But learning takes more than the right tools and attitudes. It also requires a corporate climate in which the people who are closest to customers and competitors feel free to challenge long-standing practices. Unless top management declares open season on precedent and orthodoxy, learning and the unlearning that must precede it cannot begin to take place.

"Borrowing" the resources of other companies is another way to accumulate and leverage resources. The philosophy of borrowing is summed up in the remark of a Japanese manager that "you [in the West] chop down the trees, and we [in Japan] build the houses. " In other words, you do the hard work of discovery, and we exploit those discoveries to create new markets. It is instructive to remember that Sony was one of the first companies to commercialize the transistor and the charge-coupled device, technologies pioneered by AT&T's Bell Laboratories. Increasingly, technology is stateless. It crosses borders in the form of scientific papers, foreign sponsorship of university research, international licensing, cross-border equity stakes in high-tech start-ups, and international academic conferences. Tapping into the global market for technology is a potentially important source of resource leverage.

At the extreme, borrowing involves not only gaining access to the skills of a partner but also internalizing those skills. Internalization is often a more efficient way to acquire new skills than acquiring an entire company. In making an acquisition, the acquirer must pay both for the critical skills it wants and for skills it may already have. Likewise, the costs and problems of integrating cultures and harmonizing policy loom much larger in an acquisition than they do in an alliance.

NEC relied on hundreds of alliances, licensing deals, and joint ventures to bolster its product-development efforts and to gain access to foreign markets. Alliances with Intel, General Electric, Varian, and Honeywell, to name a few, multiplied NEC's internal resources. Indeed, NEC managers have been forthright in admitting that without the capacity to learn from their partners, their progress toward the goal of computers and communication would have been much slower.

Borrowing can multiply more than technical resources. Companies such as Canon, Matsushita, and Sharp sell components and finished products on an original equipment manufacturer (OEM) basis to Hewlett-Packard, Kodak, Thomson, Philips, and others to finance their leading-edge research in imaging, video technology, and flat-screen displays. Almost every Japanese company we have studied had a bigger share of world development spending in core competence areas and a bigger share of world manufacturing in core components than its brand share in end-product markets. The goal is to capture investment initiative from companies either unwilling or unable to invest in core competence leadership, in order to gain control of critical core competencies. Think of this as borrowing distribution channels and market share from downstream partners to leverage internal development efforts and reduce market risks.

In leveraging resources through borrowing, absorptive capacity is as important as inventive capacity. Some companies are systematically better at borrowing than others are, not least because they approach alliances and joint ventures as students, not teachers. Suffice it to say, arrogance and a full stomach are not as conducive to borrowing as humility and hunger. Captives of their own success, some companies are more likely to surrender their skills inadvertently than to internalize their partners' skills. We might call this negative leverage!

Borrowing can take a myriad of forms: welding tight links with suppliers to exploit their innovations: sharing development risks with critical customers; borrowing resources from more attractive factor markets (as, for example, when Texas Instruments employs relatively low-cost software programmers in India via a satellite hookup); participating in international research consortia to borrow foreign taxpayers' money. Whatever the form, the motive is the same, to supplement internal resources with resources that lie outside a company's boundaries.

Complementing Resources: Blending and Balancing

By blending different types of resources in ways that multiply the value of each, management transforms its resources while leveraging them. The ability to blend resources involves several skills: technological integration, functional integration, and new-product imagination.

It is possible that General Motors (GM) or Ford could outspend Honda in developing engine-related technologies like combustion engineering, electronic controls, and lean burn—and perhaps even attain scientific leadership in each area—but still lag Honda in terms of all-around engine performance because the U.S. companies were able to blend fewer technologies. Blending requires technology generalists, systems thinking, and the capacity to optimize complex technological trade-offs. Leadership in a range of technologies may count for little and the resources expended in such a quest may remain underleveraged if a company is not as good at the subtle art of blending as it is at brute-force pioneering.

Successfully integrating diverse functional skills like R&D, production, marketing, and sales is a second form of blending. Where narrow specialization and organizational chimneys exist, functional excellence is rarely translated into product excellence. In such cases, a company may outinvest its competitors in every functional area but reap much smaller rewards in the marketplace. Again, what is required is a class of generalists who understand the interplay of skills, technologies, and functions.

The third form of blending involves a company's ingenuity in dreaming up new-product permutations. Sony and 3M, for example, have demonstrated great imagination in combining core technologies in novel ways. Sony's "Walkman" brought together well-known functional components—headphones and an audiotape playback device—and created a huge market if not a new lifestyle. Yamaha combined a small keyboard, a microphone, and magnetically encoded cards to create a play-along karaoke piano for children. In these cases, the leverage comes not only from better amortizing past investments in core competencies but also from combining functional elements to create new markets.

Balancing is another approach to complementing resources. To be balanced, a company, like a stool, must have at least three legs: a strong product-development capability; the capacity to produce its products or deliver its services at world-class levels of cost and quality; and a sufficiently widespread distribution, marketing, and service infrastructure. If any leg is much shorter than the others, the company will be unable to exploit the investments it has made in its areas of strength. By gaining control over the missing resources, however, management can multiply the profits extracted from the company's unique assets.

Today many small, high-tech companies are unbalanced. While they can enter partnerships with companies that have complementary resources, the innovators are likely to find themselves in a poor bargaining position when it comes to divvying up profits. This imbalance explains why so many Japanese companies worked throughout the 1980s to set up their own worldwide distribution and manufacturing infrastructures rather than continue to borrow from their downstream partners. They realized they could fully capture the economic benefits of their innovations only if they owned all complementary resources. Today, in contrast, Japanese companies are acquiring innovators to complement their strong brand and manufacturing skills. Of the more than five hundred small, high-tech U.S. companies sold to foreign interests between 1988 and 1991, Japanese companies bought about two-thirds.

Whatever the nature of the imbalance, the logic is the same. A company cannot fully leverage its accumulated investment in any one dimension if it does not control the other two in some meaningful way. Rebalancing leads to leverage when profits captured by gaining control over critical complementary assets more than cover acquisition costs.

Conserving Resources: Recycling, Co-opting, and Shielding

The more often a given skill or competence is used, the greater the resource leverage. Sharp exploits its liquid-crystal-display competence in calculators, electronic pocket calendars, mini-TVs, large-screen-projection TVs, and laptop computers. Honda has recycled engine-related innovations across motorcycles, cars, outboard motors, generators, and garden tractors. It is little wonder that these companies have unmatched R&D efficiency. The common saying in Japan is, "No technology is ever abandoned, it's just reserved for future use." Honda and Sharp are proof of that maxim.

Recycling isn't limited to technology-based competencies. Brands can be recycled too. Familiarity with a high-quality "banner" brand can predispose customers at least to consider purchasing new products that bear the "maker's mark." Think of the leverage Sony gets when it launches a new product, thanks to the relatively modest incremental cost of building credibility with retailers and consumers and the implicit goodwill with which the product is imbued simply because it carries the Sony brand.

Banner branding cannot turn a loser into a winner. In fact, a lousy product will undermine the most respected brand. And in companies such as Unilever and Procter & Gamble, with a long history of product branding, it would be foolish to abandon well-loved brands for an unknown corporate banner. Yet even these companies are more and more apt to use their corporate monikers along with well-known product brands. For example, in working to build a strong presence in Japan, P&G recognized the added oomph its efforts would receive from a judicious use of its corporate name. Building brand leadership in a new market is always a slow and expensive process. But it becomes even more so when advertising budgets and customer awareness are fragmented across multiple brands.

Opportunities for recycling hard-won knowledge and resources are manifold. The ability to switch a production line quickly from making widgets to making gadgets, known as flexible manufacturing, is one. Others include sharing merchandising ideas across national sales subsidiaries, transferring operating improvements from one plant to another, using the same subsystem across a range of products, quickly disseminating ideas for better customer service, and lending experienced executives to key suppliers. But recycling will not occur without a strong organizational foundation. It requires a view of the corporation as a pool of widely accessible skills and resources rather than a series of fiefdoms.

Co-option provides another route to conserving resources. Enticing a potential competitor into a fight against a common enemy, working collectively to establish a new standard or develop a new technology, building a coalition around a particular legislative issue—in these and other cases, the goal is to co-opt the resources of other companies and thereby extend one's own influence. In borrowing resources, management seeks to absorb its partners' skills and make them its own; in co-opting resources, the goal is to enroll others in the pursuit of a common objective.

The process of co-option begins with a question: "How can I convince other companies that they have a stake in my success?" The logic is often, "My enemy's enemy is my friend." Philips has a knack for playing Sony and Matsushita against each other, enrolling one as a partner to block the other. Being slightly Machiavellian is no disadvantage when it comes to co-opting resources.

Sometimes co-option requires a stick as well as a carrot of common purpose. Typically, the stick is control over some critical resource, and the unstated logic here is, "Unless you play the game my way, I'll take my ball and go home." Fujitsu's relationship with its partners in the computer business is a good example. Each of these partners—ICL in Britain, Siemens in Germany, and Amdahl in the United States—shares a common objective to challenge the dominance of IBM. That is the carrot. The stick is the substantial, in some cases almost total, dependence of these companies on Fujitsu's semiconductors, central processors, disk drives, printers, terminals, and components.

To understand shielding, the third form of resource conservation, think about military tactics. Wise generals ensure that their troops are never exposed to unnecessary risks. They disguise their true intentions. They reconnoiter enemy territory before advancing. They don't attack heavily fortified positions. They feint to draw the enemy's forces away from the intended point of attack. The greater the enemy's numerical advantage, the greater the incentive to avoid a full frontal confrontation. The goal is to maximize enemy losses while minimizing the risk to one's own forces. This is the basis for "resource shielding."

Attacking a competitor in its home market, attempting to match a larger competitor strength-for-strength, accepting the industry leader's definition of market structure or "accepted industry practice" are strategies akin to John Wayne taking on all the bad guys single-handedly—and they work better in Hollywood than they do in global competition. In business, judo is more useful than a two-fisted brawl. The first principle in judo is to use your opponent's weight and strength to your own advantage: deflect the energy of your opponent's attack; get him off balance; then let momentum and gravity do the rest.

Searching for underdefended territory is another way to shield resources. Honda's success with small motorbikes, Komatsu's early forays into Eastern Europe, and Canon's entry into the "convenience" copier segment all failed to alert incumbents whose attention was focused elsewhere. Understanding a competitor's definition of its "served market" is the first step in the search for underdefended competitive space. The goal is to build up forces just out of sight of stronger competitors. This may be one reason why Toyota chose to launch the Lexus, its challenge to Mercedes-Benz, not in Germany but in California, where buyers are technologically sophisticated, value conscious, and not overly swayed by brand loyalty.

Recovering Resources: Expediting Success

The time between the expenditure of resources and their recovery through revenues is yet another source of leverage—the more rapid the recovery process, the higher the resource multiplier. A company that can do anything twice as fast as its competitors, with a similar resource commitment, enjoys a twofold leverage advantage. This rudimentary arithmetic explains, in part, why Japanese companies have been so intent on accelerating product-development times. Consider the effects of the two-to-one development-time advantage Japanese automakers traditionally held over their U.S. and European rivals. This lead not only allowed them to recoup investments more quickly but also gave them more up-to-date products and gave customers more excuses to abandon their brand loyalties.

But fast-paced product development is only one way of expediting recovery time. A company that has built a highly esteemed global brand will find customers eager to try out new products. This predisposition to buy can expedite recovery dramatically, since recovery time is measured not from product concept to product launch but from product concept to some significant level of world-market penetration.

Stretch without Risk

The essential element of the new strategy frame is an aspiration that creates by design a chasm between ambition and resources. For many managers, great ambition equals big risk. If managers at Ford, for instance, were simply to extrapolate past practices, they might believe that developing a car five times as good as the Escort (a potential Lexus beater, say) would require five times the resources. But stretch implies risk only when orthodox notions dictate how the ambition is to be achieved.

Stretch can beget risk when an arbitrarily short time horizon is set for long-term leadership goals. Impatience brings the risk of rushing into markets not fully understood, ramping up R&D spending faster than it can be managed, acquiring companies that cannot be digested easily, or rushing into alliances with partners whose motives and capabilities are poorly understood. Trouble inevitably ensues if resource commitments outpace the accumulation of customer and competitor insights. The job of top management is not so much to stake out the future as it is to help accelerate the acquisition of market and industry knowledge. Risk recedes as knowledge grows, and as knowledge grows, so does the company's capacity to advance.

The notion of strategy as stretch helps to bridge the gap between those who see strategy as a grand plan thought up by great minds and those who see strategy as no more than a pattern in a stream of incremental decisions. On the one hand, strategy as stretch is strategy by design, in that top management has a clear view of the goal line. On the other hand, strategy as stretch is strategy by incrementalism, in that top management must clear the path for leadership meter by meter. In short, strategy as stretch recognizes the essential paradox of competition: leadership cannot be planned for, but neither can it happen without a grand and well-considered aspiration.

■ HOW TO LINK VISION TO CORE CAPABILITIES[†]

By Paul Schoemaker

Senior executives commonly ponder such questions as "What might give us continued competitive advantage?" and "What new products should we make or markets should we enter and how?" These questions go to the heart of a firm's strategic vision—the shared understanding of what the firm should be and how it must change. I present a framework to help managers answer such questions critically and creatively. Knowing the answers constitutes the difference between muddling through and managing with confidence and foresight. The framework has four steps:

- Generate broad scenarios of possible futures that your firm may encounter
- Conduct a competitive analysis of the industry and its strategic segments
- Analyze your company's and your competition's core capabilities
- Develop a strategic vision and identify your strategic options

The information generated by the first three steps is plotted on a matrix that helps managers see the direction (step 4) they should take. The goal is to develop those core capabilities that will be effective for multiple strategic segments in several different possible futures. The methodology has been applied at corporate and divisional levels in U.S. and overseas firms and to functional strategy development as well (e.g., in marketing and R&D). It can prevent overconfidence and myopic framing of strategic issues from misleading the organization's planning effort. The methodology has successfully encouraged top management at several companies to break out of traditional frames of mind and challenge conventional wisdom.

Scenario Analysis

In an uncertain industry with intense competition, a company needs a method of analyzing its environment that is more fundamental than the typical methods of scanning and trend analysis. Companies confronted with major uncertainties, life-threatening competition, or sudden discontinuities may find the scenario method useful. The scenario method helps managers map out a wide range of possible futures,

---

†**Source:** This article is reprinted from *Sloan Management Review*, Fall 1992, by permission of the publisher. Copyright © 1992 by the Sloan Management Review Association. All rights reserved.

forcing them to "think outside the box." The method is well suited for addressing such external changes as deregulation, foreign competition, new technology, and increased environmental concerns. It exposes managers' assumptions (e.g., the government is the enemy) and knowledge gaps. Too often, corporate views about the future are myopic, short term, or concerned only with a few data points. Scenarios can challenge conventional wisdom and stretch people's thinking so they better appreciate long-term threats and opportunities.

The basic idea in scenario construction is to identify existing trends and key uncertainties and combine them into a few future worlds that are internally consistent and within the realm of the possible. The purpose of these scenarios is not to cover all eventualities but to discover the boundaries of future outcomes.

The first step is to determine the appropriate time frame and scope of the analysis. Next, we need to determine the scope and stakeholders (they can always be revised later if necessary). Regarding stakeholders, all parties should be considered, especially if they can flex their muscles.

The second step is to identify existing trends and conditions that will significantly affect the industry's future in known ways. Influence diagrams and causal maps are useful tools to reveal perceptions about trends and their interrelationships. The trends must be mutually compatible within the given time frame and widely agreed on.

Those trends that are not consensual should be treated as uncertainties, the third step in scenario construction. To identify key uncertainties, which is the heart of scenario thinking, it is useful to ask what three or four fundamental questions managers would like to pose to an oracle of Delphi, such as, "Will there be a fundamental technological breakthrough?" and "Will the United States-Japan trade conflict intensify or subside?" Other approaches to identifying key uncertainties are to examine issues of policy dispute or important upcoming decisions.

At this point, it is useful to discuss any interrelationships among the key uncertainties. For instance, a strong U.S. economy is likely to increase personal computer sales, spur research and development (R&D), and attract competitors. The latter, in turn, decreases industry concentration. Formal models can be used to capture such interconnections using cross-impact analysis or other conditional probabilities.

In step 4, the trends and uncertainties are combined into internally consistent, coherent, and wide-ranging scenarios. Do not limit yourself to internal viewpoints; vigorously pursue contrarian beliefs and outside perspectives.

To develop the scenarios, it is useful to start by putting all the negative elements in one scenario and all the positive elements in another. An important question is whether an "all-good" or "all-bad" scenario is internally consistent. It is often a matter of judgment whether certain elements go together. No simple recipe exists for creating consistent scenarios, nor would this be desirable. These extreme scenarios just offer wide starting points from which to develop different but consistent scenarios. Using common sense and strategic reflection, we might develop three scenarios as useful backdrops for strategic thinking.

Competitive Analysis

Whereas scenario analysis explores the general environment, competitive analysis focuses on each company's unique position, taking into account industry structure and the firm's own evolution. The industry analysis focuses on the forces and barriers (both entry and exit) to competition; the existing economies of scale, scope, and experience; and the stage of industry development, from emerging to mature and declining. It also includes softer analyses such as the attitudes, reputations, and past interactions among the players in terms of retaliation, coalitions, commitments, and so on. The nature of the industry partly determines the competing firms' size distribution (e.g., fragmented versus oligopolistic), scope (e.g., single versus multiproduct or domestic versus global), and strategies (low cost versus differentiation or innovation versus imitation). Also pertinent are the competing firms' unique histories and evolutions, as these determine what kind of resources and capabilities they have at their disposal.

Strategic Segmentation

The next step after competitive analysis is to identify all significant strategic segments the firm is or might be competing in. This is important because recent research suggests that on average, profitability varies far more across businesses within an industry than across industries. The focus of analysis, therefore, should be on each strategic business unit of the firm, within its industry context.

The concept of business segmentation has a long history, starting with product segmentation in the 1950s, market segmentation in the 1960s, and product/market segments in the 1970s and 1980s. In *product* segmentation, the focus is on the varying requirements and strategies from a manufacturing viewpoint. In *market* segmentation, the relevant aspects are the different needs and characteristics of each customer group. In *strategic* segmentation, the aim is to highlight and delineate the important but essentially different battlefields the firm is or might be competing in. Consequently, the focus is on such strategic factors as technologies used, customer needs satisfied, marketing channels, growth rates, innovation, forces of competition, entry and exit barriers, pricing practices, distribution channels, value chains, customer profiles, government regulation and protection, and so on.

The business segmentation task can be approached top down or bottom up. It can be performed intuitively or systematically. In the latter case, multidimensional scaling and cluster analyses may be useful tools to distill the relevant bases of segmentation and to identify the major segments. Whatever procedure is used, the analysis should yield a limited number—from two to eight—of business segments that differ fundamentally in their strategic nature. These strategic segments need not be pure, such as only product groupings or customer segments, but can be hybrids of product, market, technology, distribution, region, and pricing features.

Core Capabilities

Thus far our analysis has been externally focused—on the general future environment and competitors. The next step is to examine the firm internally, in terms of its core capabilities. The traditional approach is to score the firm on a large number of attributes, such as relative strength or weakness in R&D, engineering, manufacturing, marketing, sales, product quality, product line, employee morale, compensation, quality of personnel, reputation, and so on. Not all of these attributes, however, are of equal importance strategically. Moreover, many are symptoms of more fundamental characteristics that define the firm's essence. There are several ways to ascertain these more basic features.

The Firm as an Onion

Think of the firm as an onion made up of layers of functions, services, and production operations. Then ask which activities determine the firm's essence or core and which are at the periphery. For example, the outer layer may include product design, selling, or even marketing for one firm, whereas these skills and capabilities might constitute the core of another firm. Honda's core consists of the design and manufacturing of engines, which underlie its strengths in passenger cars, motorcycles, lawn mowers, and race cars. Other car manufacturers have different cores. Chrysler, for example, subcontracts major portions of its engine design and manufacturing. For biotech firms, a core capability would be R&D, including how to access academic know-how and commercialize it through strategic alliances. Selling and marketing, in contrast, fall in the outer layer for those biotech firms that license their products to established pharmaceutical firms.

The Firm as a Tree

An alternative way to explore core capabilities is to think of the firm as a tree. In this metaphor, the leaves and fruit represent the firm's end products and services. The branches constitute SBUs, which combine related products or services (e.g., midsize cars, heavy-duty lawn mowers, and 500-cc motorcycles). The trunk denotes core products, such as engines in Honda's case, which support each of the SBUs and end products. Lastly, the roots represent capabilities or core competencies that enable the firm to sustain its existing branches and grow new ones. Unlike a core product, a core capability (or competence) is not a stand-alone, sellable service or commodity. Examples of potential core capabilities include high-quality manufacturing, good supplier relations, service excellence, innovation, short product-development cycles, well-motivated employees, a marketing culture, and a strong service reputation. The challenge is to think of the firm not just in terms of its visible end products but also in terms of its invisible assets and core capabilities.

Strategic Assets

Above-average return can derive only from assets and skills that are hard to imitate. By definition, these assets and skills cannot be bought off the shelf but must be developed over time through investment and information exchange by the firm's human capital. By their nature, they involve time and evolution. For example, Apple could not have produced the Macintosh without learning first from the success of its Apple II and then from the failures of its Apple III and Lisa computers. This learning path entails micro-level interactions (among people, groups, and functions) that are hard to script, imitate, or even document. Indeed, the idiosyncrasy of this learning process is a desirable and necessary condition for competitive advantage. It makes a firm more immune to competition. For instance, 3M's well-known culture for innovation and Wal-Mart's distinctive approach to multiservice stores evolved in ways that are hard to duplicate and even harder to imitate swiftly.

In sum, firms differ fundamentally in the resources and capabilities they control. And since their capabilities developed slowly, firms are usually stuck with them in the short run. These "sticky assets" reflect the firm's unique history and limit the range of strategies realistically available to a firm. IBM could never become an Apple, nor Apple an IBM. Both have unique experiences and capabilities. It is crucial to understand what a firm's present core capabilities are and to what extent they need to be adjusted or replaced in view of the future scenarios. The following characteristics help define a core capability and can be used to score it relative to other core competencies:

- It evolved slowly through collective learning and information sharing
- Its development cannot be greatly speeded up by doubling investments
- It cannot be easily imitated by or transferred (sold) to other firms
- It confers competitive advantage in the eyes of customers
- It complements other capabilities in a "2+2=5" fashion
- Investment in it is largely irreversible; that is, the firm cannot cash it out

Key Success Factors

The identification of the core capabilities must occur in the context of an industry's key success factors (KSF). Think of KSFs as those strategic variables that a historian will pick to best discriminate winners from losers in your industry. For example, looking backward, raw material sourcing proved to be a KSF in the uranium and petroleum industries. Economies of scale were critical in steel and shipbuilding. Quality design was a core capability in the aircraft and stereo industries. For beer, films, and home appliances, distribution has been of overriding importance. The challenge in articulating a strategic vision is to identify the most important industry KSF, then to determine which core capabilities should be developed for one's own firm.

Core Capabilities Matrix

A strategic vision pulls together the insights obtained from examining the multiple scenarios, the industry's competitive structure, and the firm's (and competitors') distinct core capabilities. It helps to focus managerial attention and indicate which core capabilities the firm must develop further and how, so as to succeed in its chosen business segments.

Deciding which core capabilities should become the drivers for the future can be done systematically by juxtaposing the scenarios and the strategic segments. Figure 5-3 shows how a core capabilities matrix can be used to do this. This matrix, using Apple's core capabilities, lists the strategic segments on the vertical axis and the scenarios on the horizontal axis. For each cell, the core capabilities are listed that would help the firm do well in that segment under that scenario. Remember to use only those capabilities that are unique, important, controllable, durable, and that can generate excess profit.

One of the most important ways to look at the matrix is to identify the core capabilities that will be effective for multiple segments in a variety of future worlds. These are the capabilities a firm will want to leverage. They should be clearly identified and made an integral part of the company's overall strategic vision.

Let's look at some possible matrices. Figure 5-4 shows some prototypical matrix patterns. In matrix 1, a company operates in four strategic segments and has envisaged three possible future scenarios. The only place where core capabilities overlap is in

FIGURE 5-3
A Core Capabilities
Matrix for Apple

	Scenarios		
Strategic Segments	*Stagnation and Saturation*	*Computer Confusion*	*Computer Cornucopia*
Home	h, c, b, d	c, b, h, d	b, c, a, d
Education	c, h, d, e	c, d, h, a	d, c, e, b
Business	a, f, e, c	e, f, a, d	f, a, e, d
Workstations	g, d, e, a	d, g, h, e	d, f, g, b

Note: The top four capabilities are ranked within each cell in order of relative importance.

Legend for Core Capabilities:	*Frequency of Occurrence*
a. Highly knowledgeable salesforce	6
b. Access to distribution channels	5
c. User friendliness in product development	7
d. Availability of software and peripherals	11
e. Compatibility/integrative product line	7
f. Professional image — quality and reliability	4
g. Use of new and innovative technology	3
h. Low-cost position in manufacturing	5

segment B. An example might be a pharmaceutical firm's ability to get Food and Drug Administration approval (the core capability), which may be crucial for its patented drugs (segment B) in all possible futures. In other segments, each scenario requires a different set of core capabilities. Naturally, one's odds of success are greater if capabilities are developed that add value for multiple segments.

Matrix 2 depicts a company that will reap above-average returns, given its core capabilities, only if one scenario comes to pass. For example, superior brand management or service reputation could pay off in several product markets. This firm has a competitive advantage over firms operating in only one of these segments, but if one of the other scenarios comes true, its advantage may not mean much.

The more unique the capabilities and the more they overlap, the greater and more complex are their synergies. In matrix 3, there will always be some kind of synergy for segment C, no matter the future scenario, and this firm has greater odds of being competitive in the other segments, as they look strong for two of the three scenarios.

The ideal case would be matrix 4, with overlapping core competencies in every segment for every scenario. However, there is no guarantee that this state is achievable. A company may be able to achieve it by developing only those capabilities that are required in all cells, but if other important capabilities are thereby neglected, this approach will have its downside too.

Of course, it may be that few core capabilities appear more than once per cell. In that case, there may be no basis for a strategic vision in which multiple capabilities function in harmony at the corporate level. The firm may be little more than a collection of distinctly different companies operating in strategically different segments, whose core capabilities do not reinforce each other. Such lack of synergy is a serious issue. It

FIGURE 5-4
Prototypical Matrix Patterns

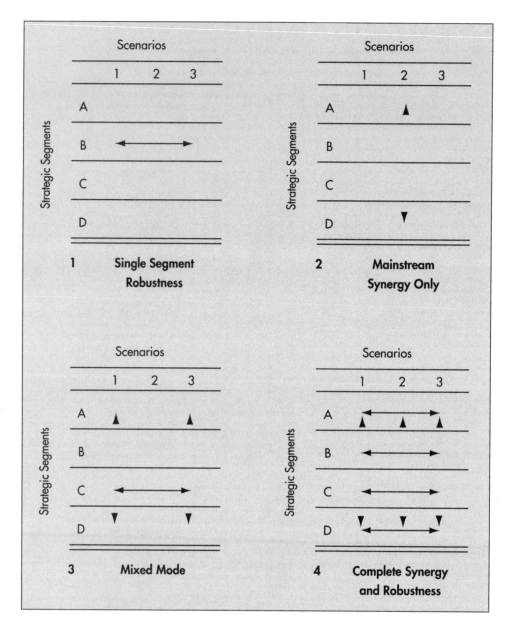

could cause conflicting signals and confusion, as multiple driving forces need to be managed and coordinated. Thus, strategic visions need to consider issues of organizational design, skill sharing, and culture. They must also address what practical options exist for moving the company in the desired direction.

It is instructive to rank the core capabilities within each cell because this naturally leads you to examine why rank-reversals occur across scenarios or segments. Also, it helps identify the robust and synergistic core competencies around which marketing, production, R&D, and personnel plans should develop.

No simple formula exists for identifying and ranking the core capabilities in each cell. This requires seasoned managerial judgment, creativity, and a keen sense of each segment's competitive structure. Scoring the various capabilities on the characteristics listed under Strategic Assets above will be helpful.

Strategic Vision

Although firms seldom publish their visions in detail, several examples have been described in the business press. Dow Chemical pursued a vision and framework developed by Herbert Dow over fifty years ago. It called for innovative manufacturing, forbidding copying or licensing; gaining control of raw material supplies; pursuing economies of scale and scope via vertical integration; and continually expanding capacity over business cycles. Essentially Dow's vision was to become a large-volume producer of commodity chemicals. This vision served it well for many decades, although Dow has lately focused more on specialty chemicals and higher-margin products.

Another venerable and successful vision guided Crown Cork & Seal. Until 1977 it pursued a strategy of being a differentiated low-cost producer of steel cans, crown bottle tops, and related container machinery for the beer, soft drink, food, and aerosol markets. Its competitive advantages derived from a low-cost position, flexibility in delivery, strong technical service, and a full line of packaging material and equipment. Crown's vision, however, also required major adjustment when some of its major markets were threatened, for example, by aluminum can makers. Thus, visions do not last forever and need periodic reassessment. For several decades, clear visions provided guidance and focus for these two organizations while generating high returns.

A sound vision that has been articulated and communicated by top management raises the firm's "strategic IQ" Lower-level echelons first internalize the vision and then pursue products and markets in line with it. Hence, a strategic vision helps managers decide which products and markets should and should not get resources. Even though a particular business may be profitable, unless it reinforces the core capabilities called for in the vision, it should not be high on the list for funding. In this sense, having a strategic vision redefines the rules for acting opportunistically or incrementally. The vision determines strategies, plans, and budgets. Similarly, the incentive system and performance reviews should be operationally linked to the vision and the strategies it calls for. This is the challenge of true strategic management.

Why should this method for generating a sound vision work? Strategic plans are essentially investments under uncertainty. Developing those core capabilities that will be effective in different futures positions the firm to do well in any future. And if those core capabilities are not easily imitated or destroyed, then when competitors realize the importance of those capabilities, they will not be able to easily acquire them.

Further, if the core capabilities overlap in multiple segments, the firm has more opportunities for success. A firm competing in four segments has six opportunities for synergies within pairs of segments, three possibilities for three-way synergies, and one chance at a four-way synergy. Juxtaposing these synergy opportunities with those of competitors should reveal if and where sustainable competitive advantages might be garnered.

The purpose of the matrix analysis, however, is not to instill risk aversion or excessive hedging. It is primarily an aid in deciding which capabilities to emphasize in view of their synergies over segments and resilience under different scenarios. This is done by first examining each cell in isolation and thereafter comparing the required capabilities across cells. Once the degrees of synergy and robustness have been ascertained, it can then be decided whether to play it safe (by developing primarily the common capabilities) or go all out and bet the company on one particular scenario or segment. As an empirical conjecture, I expect that firms that earn persistently high returns do so to a large extent by capitalizing on overlaps in their core capabilities matrix. Whether column or row overlap is more valuable will depend on time frames, risk levels, growth prospects, competitors, and other factors that are beyond my scope.

Conclusion

This article has examined how management teams might develop and test strategic visions to enhance future survival. Resilience is the key to prospering in a variety of futures, so it should be an important test of strategic vision and direction. Resilience or robustness does not just encourage optimization within the expected scenario but offers increased survival chances under less probable but potentially devastating scenarios.

Since multiple perspectives are needed, explicit vision building or testing is best conducted in small groups. In my experience, management teams need no more than two or three days to apply the above process at a qualitative, broad-brush level to their own situation. Especially if managers have done prior work on competitive analysis and understand past key success factors, the process can happen quickly once sound scenarios have been developed. Flexible facilitation, including techniques that encourage creative, nonlinear thinking, is essential to the successful application of this process in management teams. Usually, follow-up staff work is indicated for the scenarios or competitive portions, and external consultants may be useful if limited in-house resources or expertise exist.

This overall approach emphasizes a resource-based view of the firm. It is aimed at identifying and evolving those core capabilities that are important in multiple segments under alternate scenarios. By focusing the strategic vision on core capabilities needed in various possible futures and multiple strategic segments, synergies can be developed that give rise to surplus returns. Of course, these capabilities must not be easily transferable, for example, by a competitor merely hiring away a key employee. The less imitable the core capabilities are, and the more they indeed turn out to be the discriminating factors for business success, the greater their economic return. A firm's strategic vision essentially boils down to a bet on some perceived future or futures. The present methodology hedges this bet against a broad range of scenarios while extracting as much as possible from existing synergies. It strives for synergistic resilience in the development of a firm's core capabilities.

References and Suggested Readings

Aaker, D. A., Managing Assets and Skills: The Key to a Sustainable Competitive Advantage, *California Management Review*, Winter 1989, pp. 91–106.

Aaker, D. A., and B. Mascarenhas, The Need for Strategic Flexibility, *Journal of Business Strategy*, Fall 1984, pp. 74–82.

Amit, R., and P. J. Schoemaker, Strategic Assets and Organizational Rent, *Strategic Management Journal*, January 1993, pp. 33–46.

Barney, J. B., Asset Stocks and Sustained Competitive Advantage: A Comment, *Management Science*, December 1989, pp. 1511–1513.

Barney, J. B., Firm Resources and Sustained Competitive Advantage, *Journal of Management*, March 1991, pp. 99–120.

Blackburn, J. D., *Time-Based Competition*, Business One, Irwin, Homewood, IL, 1991.

Buzzell, R. D., Gale, B. T., and R. G. M. Sultan, Market Share—A Key to Profitability, *Harvard Business Review*, January/February 1975, pp. 97–106.

Collis, D. J., A Resource-Based Analysis of Global Competition: The Case of the Bearings Industry, *Strategic Management Journal*, Summer 1991, pp. 49–68.

De Meyer, A., Nakane, J., Miller, J. G., and K. Ferdows, Flexibility: The Next Competitive Battle—The Manufacturing Futures Survey, *Strategic Management Journal*, March/April 1989, pp. 135–144.

Dierickx, I., and K. Cool, Asset Stock Accumulation and Sustainability of Competitive Advantage, *Management Science*, December 1989, pp. 1504–1511.

Forrester, J. W., Industrial Dynamics: A Major Breakthrough for Decision Makers, *Harvard Business Review*, July/August 1958.

Ghemawat, P., Sustainable Advantage, *Harvard Business Review*, September/October 1986, pp. 53–58.

Ghemawat, P., *Commitment: The Dynamic of Strategy*, Free Press, New York, 1991.

Gilbert, X., and P. Strebel, From Innovation to Outpacing, *Business Quarterly*, Summer 1989, pp. 19–22.

Grant, R. M., The Resource-Based Theory of Competitive Advantage: Implications for Strategy Formulation, *California Management Review*, Spring 1991, pp. 114–135.

Gronhaug, K., and O. Nordhaug, Strategy and Competence in Firms, *European Management Journal*, December 1992, pp. 438–443.

Hall, R. A., A Framework Linking Intangible Resources and Capabilities to Sustainable Competitive Advantage, *Strategic Management Journal*, November 1993, pp. 607–618.

Hambrick, D. C., Operationalizing the Concept of Business-Level Strategy in Research, *Academy of Management Review*, October 1980, pp. 567–575.

Hamel, G., and C. K. Prahalad, Strategic Intent, *Harvard Business Review*, May/June 1989, pp. 63–76.

Hamel, G., and C. K. Prahalad, Strategy as Stretch and Leverage, *Harvard Business Review*, March/April 1993, pp. 75–84.

Harrigan, K. R., *Strategic Flexibility*, Lexington Books, Lexington, MA, 1985.

Henderson, B. D., The Application and Misapplication of the Experience Curve, *Journal of Business Strategy*, 1984, pp. 3–9.

Hendry, J., The Problem with Porter's Generic Strategies, *European Management Journal*, December 1990, pp. 443–450.

Itami, H., *Mobilizing Invisible Assets*, Harvard University Press, Cambridge, MA, 1987.

Mahoney, J. T., and J. R. Pandian, The Resource-Based View within the Conversation of Strategic Management, *Strategic Management Journal*, June 1992, pp. 363–380.

Meyer, C., *Fast Cycle Time: How to Align Purpose, Strategy, and Structure for Speed*, Free Press, New York, 1993.

Miller, D., The Generic Strategy Trap, *Journal of Business Strategy*, January/February 1992, pp. 37–42.

Nonaka, I., The Knowledge-Creating Company, *Harvard Business Review*, November/December 1991, pp. 96-104.

Penrose, E. T., *The Theory of the Growth of the Firm*, Basil Blackwell, London, 1959.

Peteraf, M. A., The Cornerstones of Competitive Advantage: A Resource-Based View, *Strategic Management Journal*, March 1993, pp. 179–191.

Peters, T. J., Time-Obsessed Competition, *Management Review*, September 1990, pp. 16–20.

Porter, M. E., *Competitive Strategy: Techniques for Analyzing Industries and Competitors*, Free Press, New York, 1980.

Porter, M. E., The Contributions of Industrial Organizations to Strategic Management, *Academy of Management Review*, October 1981, pp. 609–620.

Porter, M. E., *Competitive Advantage: Creating and Sustaining Superior Performance*, Free Press, New York, 1985.

Porter, M. E., Towards a Dynamic Theory of Strategy, *Strategic Management Journal*, Winter 1991, pp. 95–117.

Quinn, J. B., *Intelligent Enterprise: A Knowledge and Service Based Paradigm for Industry*, Free Press, New York, 1992.

Roos, J., and G. Von Krogh, Figuring Out Your Competence Configuration, *European Management Journal*, December 1992, pp. 422–427.

Rumelt, R. P., Schendel, D. E. and D. J. Teece, Strategic Management and Economics, *Strategic Management Journal*, Winter 1991, pp. 5–29.

Schoemaker, P. J. H., How to Link Vision to Core Capabilities, *Sloan Management Review*, Fall 1992, pp. 67–81.

Stalk, G., Time—The Next Source of Competitive Advantage, *Harvard Business Review*, July/August 1988, pp. 41–51.

Stalk, G., Evans, P., and L. E. Shulman, Competing on Capabilities: The New Rules of Corporate Strategy, *Harvard Business Review*, March/April 1992, pp. 57–69.

Stalk, G., and T. M. Hout, Redesign Your Organization for Time-Based Management, *Planning Review*, January/February 1990, pp. 4–9.

Teece, D. J., Pisano, G., and A. Shuen, *Firm Capabilities, Resources, and the Concept of Strategy: Four Paradigms of Strategic Management*, CCC Working Paper, December 1990.

Vandermerwe, S., and J. Rada, Servitization of Business: Adding Value by Adding Services, *European Management Journal*, Autumn 1988, pp. 314–324.

Wernerfelt, B., A Resource-Based View of the Firm, *Strategic Management Journal*, April/June 1984, pp. 171–180.

Wernerfelt, B., From Critical Resources to Corporate Strategy, *Journal of General Management*, Spring 1989, pp. 4–12.

CHAPTER 6
MULTIBUSINESS LEVEL STRATEGIES:
ON CASH AND COMPETENCIES

*Consider the little mouse, how sagacious
an animal it is which never entrusts its
life to one hole only.*
   —Plautus
     254–184 B.C., Roman playwright

Introduction

Just as mice see the benefit of more than one hole, so many companies believe in the
virtue of being active in more than one business. These firms have based their strategy
of diversification on the assumption that multibusiness involvement will lead to
synergies that outweigh the extra costs of managing a more complex organisation.
Corporate, or *multibusiness*, strategy deals with the identification and realisation of these
synergies. Or as Michael Porter puts it in his contribution to this chapter, "Corporate
strategy is what makes the corporate whole add up to more than the sum of its
business unit parts."

This is a definition of multibusiness strategy that most practicioners and theorists
can live with. Most also agree with the two key questions of corporate strategy
articulated by Porter: What businesses should the corporation be in and how should
the corporate centre manage its array of businesses? These two central questions are
referred to as the issues of *composition* and *control*.

This is, however, where widespread agreement ends. Opinions differ considerably
on how to determine the right corporate composition and the most effective type of
central control. Although it is always difficult to classify perspectives, it seems possible
to identify three distinct approaches to corporate strategy prevalent in strategic
management literature. These three approaches differ primarily with regard to the
type of synergies they emphasize. The perspective with the longest history, the *portfolio*

263

approach, focuses on business units sharing *financial resources (cash)* and the corporate centre exerting mainly financial control. The second perspective, which for lack of a commonly used name we shall refer to as the *linkages approach*, focuses on business units sharing *skills* and *activities*, while the corporate centre's role is to encourage these linkages between the business units' value chains. The third perspective, the *core competence approach,* focuses on building the corporation around fundamental *competencies* shared by all business units. In this view, the centre's responsibility for developing the corporation's core competencies gives it a dominant role in strategy development within the organisation.

It is the objective of this chapter to probe the question, What are the essential characteristics of a good corporate strategy? by presenting articles that are representative for these three approaches. The chapter's structure matches the chronological order in which the three approaches have been introduced into the field of strategy. The chapter is concluded by an article that borrows from all three perspectives, arguing that the validity of their premises depends on the particular circumstances. The authors of this last article set out to prove that there are "many best ways to make corporate strategy." It is up to the reader, however, to determine whether this is truly the case.

The Articles

The first article, "Portfolio Planning: Uses and Limits" by Philippe Haspeslagh, is a critical account of how a portfolio approach can be used to formulate corporate strategy. *Portfolio* entered the business vocabulary via the financial sector, where it refers to an investor's collection of shareholdings in different companies, purchased to spread investment risks. Transferred to corporate strategy, the portfolio approach views the corporate centre as an investor with financial stakes in a number of stand-alone business units. The "glue" keeping the company together is "cash," and the role of the centre is one of selecting a promising portfolio and keeping tight financial control—redirecting flows of cash from business units where prospects are dim ("cash cows" or "dogs"), to other business units where higher returns can be expected ("stars" or "question marks"). The strategic mission of each business unit is therefore also financial in orientation—grow, hold, milk, or divest, depending on the business unit's *position* on the portfolio grid (see the portfolio analysis tools discussed in chapter 4). A good corporate strategy strives for a balanced portfolio of mature cash generators and high potential return on investment (ROI) cash users. If the portfolio approach is strictly applied and only financial linkages exist between the business units, each can be run in isolation from the others. In other words, corporate diversity is managed by *disaggregation*—each business unit is run independently, with corporate headquarters focusing on resource allocation and financial control. However, as Haspeslagh admits, multiple interdependencies between business units often do exist, yet the portfolio approach provides little guidance on how to manage these.

In the second article of this chapter, "From Competitive Advantage to Corporate Strategy," Michael Porter stages a head-on attack against the popular portfolio approach, since he believes that the interdependencies between the business units are the very raison d'être of the multibusiness firm. He argues that shareholders are better at spreading investment risks than companies are, while capital markets are far better at providing financing. In his opinion, the value added by the corporate centre of a portfolio conglomerate usually does not outweigh the extra costs and constraints, making the corporate whole less than the sum of its business unit parts. Synergy between the parts can only be achieved, Porter argues, if the corporate centre strives to create and manage *value-adding linkages* between the various business units. In this article he focuses on the transfer of skills and the sharing of activities as the two ways of linking the value chains of different business units.

In the third article, "From Corporate Strategy to Parenting Advantage," Michael Goold and Andrew Campbell add two important considerations to Michael Porter's analysis. First, they point out that it is often difficult to determine in advance which linkages will actually add value. Especially in the case of a potential acquisition, Goold and Campbell argue that estimating the possible synergies is not as easy as Porter seems to suggest. Second, they believe that a parent company should not only add value to a new business unit, but should add *more* value than any other potential parent. Goold and Campbell argue that parent companies should ask themselves whether they offer the best potential synergies to a subsidiary. The corporation should only retain or acquire a business if they have such a *parenting advantage*.

In the fourth article, "The Core Competence of the Corporation," C. K. Prahalad and Gary Hamel make a case for even more linkages between the various business units of the company than Porter does. Porter believes that competition takes place at the business level, not the corporate level, and he is therefore inclined to view the business units as the primary drivers of competitiveness. Prahalad and Hamel disagree, explaining that competition actually does take place at the corporate level and hence that the roots of competitiveness lie not within the business units, but within the corporate whole. Employing the same resource-based approach as they did in chapter 5, Prahalad and Hamel argue that a company's diversification efforts should all spring from—and in turn reinforce—the corporation's core competencies. Their metaphor for the corporation is not an investor (portfolio approach) or linked chains (linkages approach), but a large tree—"the trunk and major limbs are core products, the smaller branches are business units, the leaves, flowers, and fruit are end products; the root system that provides nourishment, sustenance, and stability is the core competence." Because the individual business units both use and contribute to the corporation's core competencies, Prahalad and Hamel believe that too much decentralisation can be damaging. In their opinion, the corporate centre must play a dominant role in building the company's overarching abilities and should ensure that the firm's critical resources and competence carriers can easily be redeployed across business units.

So, what is the best way to run a multibusiness firm? In the fifth and final article, "Adding Value from Corporate Headquarters," Andrew Campbell and Michael Goold argue that there are "many best ways to make corporate strategy." In their study of sixteen large, diversified British companies, the authors witnessed the successful application of a variety of corporate management styles, largely spanning the spectrum of possible approaches discussed in the previous readings. In this article, Goold and Campbell take a contingency perspective, arguing that there are circumstances where a portfolio approach (which they call the *financial control* style) can be successful, but that other situations require more interdependencies between the business units and hence heavier involvement of the corporate centre in managing coordination (the *strategic control* and *strategic planning* styles). Goold and Campbell stress that each style of managing corporate strategy has benefits and drawbacks that the strategist must be aware of when deciding which style to adopt.

Recommended Readings and Cases

Whether one agrees with Goold and Campbell's synthesis or not, their book *Strategies and Styles: The Role of the Centre in Managing Diverse Corporations* is an excellent starting point for further reading on the different approaches to corporate strategy. For the same reason we would recommend "Why Diversify? Four Decades of Management Thinking" by Michael Goold and Kathleen Luchs. However, if the reader is more interested in other corporate strategy topics, such as mergers and acquisitions, vertical integration, and the role of the corporate supervisory board, that are too specific to be included in this chapter, other readings can be suggested. C. K. Prahalad and Richard Bettis's "The Dominant Logic: A New Linkage between Diversity and Performance," to which Goold and Campbell allude in their first article, gives a stimulating view on the potential fit of acquisition candidates. Philippe Haspeslagh and David Jemison's *Managing Acquisitions: Creating Value through Corporate Renewal* is a good initial reading on the topic of postacquisition integration. For a useful overview of vertical integration issues, the reader is advised to begin with Kathryn Rudie Harrigan's book *Strategies for Vertical Integration*. Finally, the role of the corporate supervisory (or nonexecutive) board is also an important topic, for which Ada Demb and Friedrich Neubauer's "How Can the Board Add Value?" can be recommended.

The two cases selected for this chapter are "Société Générale de Belgique" by D. Hover and J. Pringle, and "Corporate Strategy at Grand Metropolitan" by David Stadler and Andrew Campbell. Société Générale de Belgique (SGB) is a corporation with a large stake in many important Belgian industrial companies. Entirely in line with the main questions of the chapter, this case describes SGB's dilemmas with regard to the corporation's composition and the role that should be played by corporate headquarters. Readers are challenged to reflect on all of the perspectives presented in this chapter and to apply their own preferences to the SGB situation. The second case, on the British Grand Metropolitan company, describes a similar strategy problem, but in an entirely different industry and societal context, which gives rise to different considerations. The Grand Metropolitan case is also interesting because of the corporate strategy "fashions" that can be so nicely identified in the company's history.

■ PORTFOLIO PLANNING: USES AND LIMITS†

By Philippe Haspeslagh

The diversity of large industrial—and mostly multinational—corporations can be at once their greatest source of competitive advantage and the wellspring of their most fundamental difficulties. Diversity provides an opportunity for these companies to use cash flow generated by their mature basic businesses to gain new leadership positions. Internally, however, this same diversity also creates a managerial gap between the corporate level, which has the power to commit resources but often only a superficial knowledge of each business, and the business level, where managers have the substantive knowledge required to make resource allocation decisions but lack the "big

---

corporate picture." Corporate managers may often feel they are too far away to see the trees yet standing too close by to take in the forest.

In the late 1970s, a new generation of strategic planning approaches called portfolio planning spread across a wide range of companies in response to the problems and prospects of managing diversity.

Advocated by consulting firms like the Boston Consulting Group, McKinsey, and Arthur D. Little and touted by organizations like General Electric, Mead, and Olin, portfolio planning has struck the minds of many corporate executives. They speak a new strategic language and set up scores of bubble charts to explain their enthusiasm in corporate boardrooms. Most important, however, portfolio planning seems to have profoundly affected the way executives think about the management of their companies.

The Challenge: How Best to Manage Diversity

The basic challenge for the modern corporation lies in the sheer number of businesses over which it holds sway. Managers of large companies in the 1980s cannot possibly be familiar with all the relevant strategic aspects of each unit of their organizational structure.

Faced with this challenge, companies react in two ways. They may seek a substantive solution and simplify the problem by limiting their activities to businesses that are easy to comprehend or that share a common strategic logic. Or, to avoid the complexity of managing interrelatedness, they may treat their businesses as stand-alone units.

Usually, however, companies tackle the problem by developing a supra-administrative capability. The typical organization creates intermediate organizational levels (groups or sectors) and uses intermediate managers and administrative systems to measure, evaluate, and reward performance. Yet for all their sophistication, modern companies still experience difficulty in managing diversity.

Often top management is aware only of the short-term financial performance of its businesses (and even that is buried in the fragmentation of profit centers and the aggregation of reporting structures). Senior executives often end up delegating major decisions, which then become based on individual track records and managerial influence and heavily weighted by short-term career risks. Corporate top management becomes actively involved when dramatic across-the-board moves are called for. The uniformity of administrative systems indeed makes it very difficult to escape uniform pressures across all businesses.

As a result, a range of conflicts buffets almost any company. Even supposedly well-run organizations oscillate between periods of uniform emphasis on profits and emphasis on growth—often coinciding with the tenure of a particular chief executive officer (CEO). What is needed to counter these problems is a management system that provides (1) corporate-level visibility of performance on both strategic and financial terms, (2) selectivity in resource allocation, and (3) differentiation in administrative attention among businesses.

The Essence of Portfolio Planning: How It Helps

Portfolio planning recognizes that diversified companies are a collection of businesses, each of which makes a distinct contribution to the overall corporate performance and which should be managed accordingly. Putting the portfolio planning philosophy into place takes three steps as the typical company

- redefines businesses for strategic planning purposes as strategic business units (SBUs), which may or may not differ from operating units;
- classifies these SBUs on a portfolio grid according to the competitive position and attractiveness of the particular product market;
- uses this framework to assign each a "strategic mission" with respect to its growth and financial objectives and allocates resources accordingly.

The approach, then, allows management to see business performance as largely determined by the company's position within the industry. Companies can theoretically assess the strategic position of each of their enterprises and compare these positions using cash flow as the common variable. A verbal and graphic language facilitates communication across organizational levels. Finally, the approach helps build a framework for allocating resources directly and selectively and for differentiating strategic influence.

Focusing Debate on the Real Issues

Given the attractiveness of portfolio planning theory and its rapid acceptance by major companies, it is not surprising that the approach has stirred up much debate. Most of it has been ill focused, however, for proponents and critics alike are more interested in a dialogue about analytic techniques than in solving the practical problems inherent in implementation.

So they argue about which "portfolio grid" technology a company should choose between—the Boston Consulting Group growth/share matrix or the General Electric-McKinsey industry attractiveness/business position grid, the Arthur D. Little industry maturity-competitive position grid or the Shell directional policy matrix.

That discussion is sterile; the question of which grid to use and where to place a business on it is least important. The real issue is how a company can best define an SBU and assign a strategic mission to it. In short, what is a company to do with each of its businesses?

The decision on a strategic mission always requires a broad analysis of industry characteristics, competitive positions, expected competitive responses, financial resources, and the opportunities of other businesses in the portfolio. Whatever grid it chooses, a corporation's assessment comes down to a judgment heavily influenced by administrative considerations.

In selling a company on the what, the consultants sometimes forget the how. They make it appear that portfolio planning will emerge like a deus ex machina out on the corporate landscape—that its administration will pose no difficulties as long as top management has the will to implement it. A senior partner in a consulting firm explained his position as follows: "The challenge of portfolio planning really is analytical, not administrative. The way I see implementation is what I call the rule of the prince: once the analysis is done, a strong CEO should see to it that the portfolio strategy gets implemented."

The Use of Portfolio Planning

Diversified companies, particularly the large ones, widely practice the art of portfolio planning; for most of them, it is indeed much more than an analytic tool.

Since they face the greatest challenges, the bigger and more diverse among *Fortune* 1000 companies have introduced the technique. But among diversified industries, conglomerates rarely use portfolio planning, while diversified industrials often do.

Two-thirds of portfolio-planning companies oversee businesses that are related in some way. Moreover, companies usually attempt to integrate the management of these related businesses through the use of shared resources and staff at the corporate and group levels.

It is because of the difficulty they have in assessing the strategic performance of each of their businesses and allocating resources selectively that diversified industrials need a formal tool like portfolio planning. Conglomerates, on the other hand, speak portfolio-planning prose like Monsieur Jourdain in Molière's *Le Bourgeois gentilhomme*—"sans savoir." How well companies can incorporate these interdependencies in applying portfolio planning will be crucial to the success of the approach.

Portfolio planning companies tend to be international and likely to manage through complex organizational structures. Again, the ease with which the planning approach incorporates both a product and a market dimension will prove crucial to the company's success.

Structuring the Strategic Business Units

Before the introduction of portfolio planning, most companies divide up the corporate whole into organizational units (like divisions) on the basis of operating control considerations. Often these units lack the necessary autonomy appropriate for strategic planning and resource allocation.

Defining what constitutes a business unit is the first step in all strategic—not just portfolio—planning. In the case of portfolio planning, two theoretical principles underlie the definition:

- An organization must identify its various business units so that they can be regarded as independent for strategic purposes.
- Companies then should allocate resources directly to these SBUs to support whatever strategies are chosen.

The first principle is an attempt to solve the problem of inappropriate planning units by arriving at a good business definition on the basis of industry economics. Based on the experience curve, this definition sees a business as strategically independent if its value-added structure is such that market leadership in that business alone permits successful performance. To put it another way, a company looks at each market segment to see whether it can survive if it competes only in that segment.

The second principle, tying resource allocation directly to each SBU's strategic mission, attempts to solve the problems companies face with typical administrative systems. It hypothesizes that the practice of allocating resources on a project-by-project basis and the step-by-step aggregation of corporate operating results tend to shorten the focus of corporate management and create uniform rather than selective policies. To forge a dynamic strategy throughout the company, the theory states, a company must allocate its resources selectively and directly to strategically independent businesses.

SBUs without the Theoretical Mask

But that is the theory. It is the application of the theory of portfolio planning to the realities of corporate activities that is most difficult. Anyone simply reading the description of companies employing portfolio planning could list a multitude of obstacles and administrative hurdles; the ordinary manager is dumbfounded by all the possibilities for failure.

In practice, of course, SBUs are not—and cannot be—strategically autonomous units rooted in an industry's structure. A company can only determine the size, shape, and number of SBUs in the light of prior organizational constraints and history, the limits of its managers' intelligence and imagination, and the multiple interdependencies among businesses.

The Administrative Reality

Lest the theoreticians judge too harshly, the degree of diversification of most large companies obviates the possibility of simultaneous consideration of each relevant product/market segment at the corporate level. If the theory were strictly applied, a resulting grid would in most portfolio planning companies have over one hundred bubbles and in some over five hundred. It is no mere coincidence that portfolio planning companies—small and large alike—have ended up with, on the average, only thirty strategic business units (SBUs).

The end result is that, instead of single, homogenous units, most companies consider each SBU as a portfolio itself—not of different businesses but rather of product/market segments that often may have quite diverse grid positions and strategic missions. In fact, the more experienced companies are with portfolio planning, the more likely they are to treat the exercise as a multilevel operation.

The impact of this redefinition comes alive when you realize the degree to which related businesses of each company share resources along different dimensions. Companies create SBUs at the organizational level, where shared resources can be managed. Top management should therefore see nothing inherently wrong with business units that cut across different market segments and that have widely different positions on the grid or a variety of strategic missions. To the contrary, forcing uniform strategic missions onto the managers of business units leads to either rejection of the mission or buildup of inappropriate strategies.

Those companies most advanced in the art of portfolio planning structure it on two levels. When analyzing the whole corporate portfolio and making trade-offs among businesses, they look at the company in the aggregate. In this larger picture, the companies look at SBUs that are in most cases organizational units and assign them strategic missions that reflect the expected cash flow contribution to the whole company.

During the corporate plan review process, however, companies take a disaggregate view and look within those SBUs at the relevant strategic segments. These strategic segments are more likely to result from an analysis of the industry than from an accommodation to existing organizational structure. Their missions reflect the particular strategy the company wants a business unit manager to follow in each of his competitive arenas.

The definition of SBUs and strategic segments evolves throughout the introduction of the process. As the companies go through more planning cycles, the SBUs become more an organizational reality and the segment definition becomes finer. Often the segments are revised but the original SBU definition stays the same.

The definition of SBUs in each company raises two critical issues: how the company should define SBUs so as to accommodate the interdependencies and how a company can achieve the strategic aggregation and disaggregation that portfolio planning requires.

The question of interdependence, for example, creates nasty problems of the chicken-egg variety. One product/market segment may share manufacturing facilities with a few others, basic technology with an even broader group, and a sales organization with a different set of product/market segments. With all these differing dimensions, trade-offs must always be made. The guiding principle is that a company must define the SBU to incorporate control over those resources that will be the key strategic variables in the future. But how can the company do that before it knows the SBU's strategic mission?

Looking closer at the way in which the surveyed companies make these trade-offs in practice, you detect a bias toward cost efficiency in relation to responsiveness. Indeed, the business economics orientation of portfolio planning pushes cost structure as the only basis for business definition. In most industrial products and consumer durables companies, the market-based part of costs is small. Moreover, things like an SBU's responsiveness to local market conditions or governments are not quantifiable. As a result, these companies define SBUs along technological and manufacturing rather than market lines. Particularly in the international arena, many companies find that their worldwide SBUs are less responsive to local issues and cooler toward international activities than they were under the former international division structure and country plans.

Few Formal Administrative Changes

I found that in practice (except for considerations of capital investment and, of course, the strategic planning system itself) companies do not alter formal administrative systems in accordance with the strategic missions of SBUs. (If they did, theorists would see a high level of formal differentiation across businesses.) On one level, this attitude simply reflects the time needed to implement the planning system. For example, one company (acknowledged as a leader in portfolio planning) finally brought its management compensation system into line seven years after it had introduced the portfolio-planning process.

In addition, the reluctance to modify administrative systems across businesses is a good indication of the perceived benefits of administrative simplicity. Controllers have excellent arguments for keeping administrative procedures uniform.

More profoundly, however, the basis for this reluctance may lie within the nature of the SBUs themselves. As I've said, diversified industrials look at SBUs as portfolios of various segments; tying the formal systems to portfolio planning would mean going beyond the business units and would require the company to gear itself to the specific strategic mission of each segment.

The Importance of Informal Systems

Though successful companies did not change administrative systems to accommodate portfolio planning, their managers did informally adapt systems to fit the various businesses. Time and time again in the survey, this informal differentiation seemed to make the difference between portfolio planning as an isolated exercise and as an integral part of the management process. In fact, implementation depends on how well the CEO and other top managers can tailor their attention to each SBU, especially how they monitor strategic plans, how they weight the financial numbers *in light of the planning process,* and how and where they promote managers.

Not all companies are sophisticated about the process. For example, in one company, the CEO had enthusiastically endorsed portfolio planning as the wave of the future. But two years' worth of effort virtually went down the drain when every business manager found a telegram on his desk one morning from that same CEO requesting a 5 percent across-the-board cut in manpower.

The impact of portfolio planning is most profound on the corporate review process and the capital investment appraisal process. Corporate review of business plans becomes more intense and focuses on different variables than in other companies. Generally, portfolio-planning companies separate their strategic plan review from their financial review, so the planning process remains as meaningful as possible. As companies gain experience, the review goes into more and more of the detail of each segment within an SBU. My evidence indicates that the review process does shift from emphasis on short-term profits and sales objectives to long-term profits and sales targets and competitive analysis.

Tying Resource Allocation to Strategy

In a diversified company, strategy is essentially about resource allocation across businesses. In most companies, however, formal strategic planning is one thing and the capital investment appraisal process quite another.

My investigations show that companies engaging in process portfolio planning try to correct this inherent contradiction by tying the capital investment process closely to strategic planning. Not that many allocate resources primarily on the basis of strategies, but at least the business plan becomes an explicit element in the evaluation process for investment projects. Unfortunately, very few organizations tackle the allocation of strategic expenses (that is, investments that are expensed rather than capitalized, such as research and development (R&D), marketing, applications engineering) in the same way.

If resource allocation is what strategy is all about, then a fundamental question is whether portfolio planning actually affects the allocation of resources in the companies that adopt it. In general, the introduction of portfolio planning coincides with a perceived improvement in the allocation process. Both process and analytic portfolio planning help the company face the problem of marginal businesses. Changing the investment behavior of basic businesses or their attitudes toward risk that lead to inadequate funding of existing growth opportunities, however, requires a process approach to portfolio planning.

The one problem the approach does not address is the difficulty of generating new internal growth opportunities. I would add that on the basis of interviews I have conducted, the impact—if there is one at all—is rather negative. In theory, portfolio planning is about the allocation of all resources. In practice, however, companies focus on capital investment. The generation of new business requires explicit emphasis on human resource decisions and strategic expenses such as R&D and market research, only later to be followed by capital allocations.

On the most fundamental level, however, it appears that the impact of portfolio planning on resource allocation is a function of the degree and quality of its introduction. We can draw a road map of the potential benefits according to the stages of introduction. First, companies face up to those businesses with untenably weak market positions, make divestments, and inaugurate programs to increase market share. Next, businesses with growth opportunities feel liberated from short-term performance pressure and propose major growth programs from which the corporate level may not yet be ready to select.

In most cases, the investment inclination of base businesses changes slowly and requires the full commitment of top management behind certain power shifts. If a company has been overinvesting, all these resource demands may result in a resource crunch. The way that crunch is handled, in fact, gives a good indication of the degree to which portfolio planning has taken hold. If the company takes into account the various strategic missions of SBUs and counters the resource crunch selectively, then it has firmly established portfolio priorities. If, however, it institutes an across-the-board cut, you have a good sign that nothing has changed from the old days.

Current Fad or Basic Breakthrough?

Does portfolio planning constitute a step forward in the management of diversity, or is it simply a passing phenomenon? Often an administrative change, such as the introduction of a new planning system, is the way a CEO can address an organizational imbalance that might be at the root of a performance problem. Successful introduction may be self-defeating. The new system removes the problem and its own raison d'être.

It is true that in most companies the introduction of portfolio planning is triggered by a performance crisis and the need to allocate resources selectively in a capital-constrained environment.

Also, portfolio planning is not the discovery of the wheel. As I have defined it—the explicit recognition that a diversified company is a portfolio of businesses, each of which should make a distinct contribution to the overall corporate performance and should be managed accordingly—portfolio planning was practiced de facto by many companies before the development of formal "technology."

Yet along with most managers, I feel that in contrast to previous generations of planning approaches, portfolio planning is here to stay and represents an important improvement in management practice. After the initial portfolio imbalance is redressed, the approach can give companies a permanent added capacity for strategic control because it provides a framework within which the management process can be adapted to the evolving needs of the business. It also helps companies out of the dilemma between stifling centralization and dangerous decentralization. It allows them to reassert the primacy of the center in creating profit potential yet leave their strategic business units maximum operational autonomy in realizing that potential.

Portfolio planning can deliver on three fronts. The first is in the generation of good strategies, by promoting competitive analysis at the business level, more substantive discussion across levels, and strategy that capitalizes on the benefits of diversity at the corporate level. The second contribution is the promotion of more selective resource allocation trade-offs, not by solving the problems or eradicating the power game but by providing a focus for the issues and a vehicle for negotiation.

The most important contribution that portfolio planning can add is to the management process. The essence of managing diversity is the creation in each business of a pattern of influence that corresponds to the nature of the business, its competitive position, and its strategic mission. The benefit a company gets out of portfolio planning depends on its ability to create such a differentiated management process. Putting the approach into practice presents the company with some of its greatest challenges.

Success is based more on coping with administrative issues than on developing sophisticated analytic techniques. It requires a real commitment to good management and demands that an elegant theory be stretched to fit a complex reality.

■ FROM COMPETITIVE ADVANTAGE TO CORPORATE STRATEGY†

By Michael Porter

Corporate strategy, the overall plan for a diversified company, is both the darling and the stepchild of contemporary management practice—the darling because chief executive officers (CEOs) have been obsessed with diversification since the early 1960s, the stepchild because almost no consensus exists about what corporate strategy is, much less about how a company should formulate it.

A diversified company has two levels of strategy: business unit (or competitive) strategy and corporate (or companywide) strategy. Competitive strategy concerns how to create competitive advantage in each of the businesses in which a company competes. Corporate strategy concerns two different questions: what businesses the corporation should be in and how the corporate office should manage the array of business units.

Corporate strategy is what makes the corporate whole add up to more than the sum of its business unit parts.

The track record of corporate strategies has been dismal. I studied the diversification records of thirty-three large, prestigious U.S. companies over the 1950–1986 period and found that most of them had divested many more acquisitions than they had kept. The corporate strategies of most companies have dissipated instead of created shareholder value.

The need to rethink corporate strategy could hardly be more urgent. By taking over companies and breaking them up, corporate raiders thrive on failed corporate strategy. Fueled by junk bond financing and growing acceptability, raiders can expose any company to takeover, no matter how large or blue chip.

Recognizing past diversification mistakes, some companies have initiated large-scale restructuring programs. Others have done nothing at all. Whatever the response, the strategic questions persist. Those who have restructured must decide what to do next to avoid repeating the past; those who have done nothing must awake to their vulnerability. To survive, companies must understand what good corporate strategy is.

Premises of Corporate Strategy

Any successful corporate strategy builds on a number of premises. These are facts of life about diversification. They cannot be altered, and when ignored, they explain in part why so many corporate strategies fail.

Competition occurs at the business unit level. Diversified companies do not compete; only their business units do. Unless a corporate strategy places primary attention on nurturing the success of each unit, the strategy will fail, no matter how elegantly constructed. Successful corporate strategy must grow out of and reinforce competitive strategy.

Diversification inevitably adds costs and constraints to business units. Obvious costs such as the corporate overhead allocated to a unit may not be as important or subtle as the hidden costs and constraints. A business unit must explain its decisions to top management, spend time complying with planning and other corporate systems, live with parent company guidelines and personnel policies, and forgo the opportunity to motivate employees with direct equity ownership. These costs and constraints can be reduced but not entirely eliminated.

Shareholders can readily diversify themselves. Shareholders can diversify their own portfolios of stocks by selecting those that best match their preferences and risk profiles. Shareholders can often diversify more cheaply than a corporation because they can buy shares at the market price and avoid hefty acquisition premiums.

These premises mean that corporate strategy cannot succeed unless it truly adds value—to business units by providing tangible benefits that offset the inherent costs of lost independence and to shareholders by diversifying in a way they could not replicate.

Passing the Essential Tests

To understand how to formulate corporate strategy, it is necessary to specify the conditions under which diversification will truly create shareholder value. These conditions can be summarized in three essential tests:

- *The attractiveness test.* The industries chosen for diversification must be structurally attractive or capable of being made attractive.

- *The cost-of-entry test.* The cost of entry must not capitalize all the future profits.

- *The better-off test.* Either the new unit must gain competitive advantage from its link with the corporation or vice versa.

Of course, most companies will make certain that their proposed strategies pass some of these tests. But my study clearly shows that when companies ignored one or two of them, the strategic results were disastrous.

How Attractive Is the Industry?

In the long run, the rate of return available from competing in an industry is a function of its underlying structure. An attractive industry with a high average return on investment will be difficult to enter because entry barriers are high, suppliers and buyers have only modest bargaining power, substitute products or services are few, and the rivalry among competitors is stable. An unattractive industry like steel will have structural flaws, including a plethora of substitute materials, powerful and price-sensitive buyers, and excessive rivalry caused by high fixed costs and a large group of competitors, many of whom are state supported.

Diversification cannot create shareholder value unless new industries have favorable structures that support returns exceeding the cost of capital. If the industry doesn't have such returns, the company must be able to restructure the industry or gain a sustainable competitive advantage that leads to returns well above the industry average. An industry need not be attractive before diversification. In fact, a company might benefit from entering before the industry shows its full potential. The diversification can then transform the industry's structure.

In my research, I often found companies had suspended the attractiveness test because they had a vague belief that the industry "fit" very closely with their own businesses. In the hope that the corporate "comfort" they felt would lead to a happy outcome, the companies ignored fundamentally poor industry structures. Unless the close fit allows substantial competitive advantage, however, such comfort will turn into pain when diversification results in poor returns. Royal Dutch/Shell and other leading oil companies have had this unhappy experience in a number of chemicals businesses, where poor industry structures overcame the benefits of vertical integration and skills in process technology.

Another common reason for ignoring the attractiveness test is a low entry cost. Sometimes the buyer has an inside track or the owner is anxious to sell. Even if the price is actually low, however, a one-shot gain will not offset a perpetually poor business. Almost always, the company finds it must reinvest in the newly acquired unit, if only to replace fixed assets and fund working capital.

Diversifying companies are also prone to use rapid growth or other simple indicators as a proxy for a target industry's attractiveness. Many that rushed into fast-growing industries (personal computers, video games, and robotics, for example) were burned because they mistook early growth for long-term profit potential. Industries are profitable not because they are sexy or high tech; they are profitable only if their structures are attractive.

What Is the Cost of Entry?

Diversification cannot build shareholder value if the cost of entry into a new business eats up its expected returns. Strong market forces, however, are working to do just that. A company can enter new industries by acquisition or start-up. Acquisitions expose it to an increasingly efficient merger market. An acquirer beats the market if it pays a price not fully reflecting the prospects of the new unit. Yet multiple bidders are commonplace, information flows rapidly, and investment bankers and other intermediaries work aggressively to make the market as efficient as possible. In recent years, new financial instruments such as junk bonds have brought new buyers into the market and made even large companies vulnerable to takeover. Acquisition premiums are high and reflect the acquired company's future prospects—sometimes too well. Philip Morris paid more than four times book value for Seven-Up Company, for example. Simple arithmetic meant that profits had to more than quadruple to sustain the preacquisition return on investment (ROI). Since there proved to be little Philip Morris could add in marketing prowess to the sophisticated marketing wars in the soft-drink industry, the result was the unsatisfactory financial performance of Seven-Up and ultimately the decision to divest.

In a start-up, the company must overcome entry barriers. It's a real catch-22 situation, however, since attractive industries are attractive because their entry barriers are high. Bearing the full cost of the entry barriers might well dissipate any potential profits. Otherwise, other entrants to the industry would have already eroded its profitability.

In the excitement of finding an appealing new business, companies sometimes forget to apply the cost-of-entry test. The more attractive a new industry, the more expensive it is to get into.

Will the Business Be Better Off?

A corporation must bring some significant competitive advantage to the new unit, or the new unit must offer potential for significant advantage to the corporation. Sometimes, the benefits to the new unit accrue only once, near the time of entry, when the parent instigates a major overhaul of its strategy or installs a first-rate management team. Other diversification yields ongoing competitive advantage if the new unit can market its product, through the well-developed distribution system of its sister units, for instance. This is one of the important underpinnings of the merger of Baxter Travenol and American Hospital Supply.

When the benefit to the new unit comes only once, the parent company has no rationale for holding the new unit in its portfolio over the long term. Once the results of the one-time improvement are clear, the diversified company no longer adds value to offset the inevitable costs imposed on the unit. It is best to sell the unit and free up corporate resources.

The better-off test does not imply that diversifying corporate risk creates shareholder value in and of itself. Doing something for shareholders that they can do themselves is not a basis for corporate strategy. (Only in the case of a privately held company, in which the company's and the shareholder's risk are the same, is diversification to reduce risk valuable for its own sake.) Diversification of risk should only be a by-product of corporate strategy, not a prime motivator.

Executives ignore the better-off test most of all or deal with it through arm waving or trumped-up logic rather than hard strategic analysis. One reason is that they confuse company size with shareholder value. In the drive to run a bigger company, they lose sight of their real job. They may justify the suspension of the better-off test by pointing to the way they manage diversity. By cutting corporate staff to the bone and giving business units nearly complete autonomy, they believe they avoid the pitfalls. Such thinking misses the whole point of diversification, which is to create shareholder value rather than to avoid destroying it.

Concepts of Corporate Strategy

The three tests for successful diversification set the standards that any corporate strategy must meet; meeting them is so difficult that most diversification fails. Many companies lack a clear concept of corporate strategy to guide their diversification or pursue a concept that does not address the tests. Others fail because they implement a strategy poorly.

My study has helped me identify four concepts of corporate strategy that have been put into practice—portfolio management, restructuring, transferring skills, and sharing activities. While the concepts are not always mutually exclusive, each rests on a different mechanism by which the corporation creates shareholder value and each requires the diversified company to manage and organize itself in a different way.

TABLE 6-1
Concepts of Corporate Strategy

	Portfolio Management	Restructuring
Strategic Prerequisites	Superior insight into identifying and acquiring undervalued companies	Superior insight into identifying restructuring opportunities
	Willingness to sell off losers quickly or to opportunistically divest good performers when buyers are willing to pay large premiums	Willingness and capability to intervene to transform acquired units
	Broad guidelines for and constraints on the types of units in the portfolio so that senior management can play the review role effectively	Broad similarities among the units in the portfolio
	A private company or undeveloped capital markets	Willingness to cut losses by selling off units where restructuring proves unfeasible
	Ability to shift away from portfolio management as the capital markets get more efficient or the company gets unwieldy	Willingness to sell units when restructuring is complete, the results are clear, and market conditions are favorable
Organizational Prerequisites	Autonomous business units	Autonomous business units
	A very small, low-cost corporate staff	A corporate organization with the talent and resources to oversee the turnarounds and strategic repositionings of acquired units
	Incentives based largely on business unit results	Incentives based largely on acquired units' results
Common Pitfalls	Pursuing portfolio management in countries with efficient capital marketing and a developed pool of professional management talent	Mistaking rapid growth or a 'hot' industry as sufficient evidence of a restructuring opportunity
	Ignoring the fact that industry structure is not attractive	Lacking the resolve or resources to take on troubled situations and to intervene in management
		Ignoring the fact that industry structure is not attractive
		Paying lip service to restructuring but actually practicing passive portfolio management

TABLE 6-1 *(continued)*
Concepts of Corporate Strategy

	Transferring Skills	**Sharing Activities**
Strategic Prerequisites (continued)	Proprietary skills in activities important to competitive advantage in target industries Ability to accomplish the transfer of skills among units on an ongoing basis Acquisitions of beachhead positions in new industries as a base	Activities in existing units that can be shared with new business units to gain competitive advantage Benefits of sharing that outweigh the costs Both start-ups and acquisitions as entry vehicles Ability to overcome organizational resistance to business unit collaboration
Organizational Prerequisites (continued)	Largely autonomous but collaborative business units High-level corporate staff members who see their role primarily as integrators Cross-business-unit committees, task forces, and other forums to serve as focal points for capturing and transferring skills Objectives of line managers that include skills transfer Incentives based in part on corporate results	Strategic business units that are encouraged to share activities An active strategic planning role at group, sector, and corporate levels High-level corporate staff members who see their roles primarily as integrators Incentives based heavily on group and corporate results
Common Pitfalls (continued)	Mistaking similarity or comfort with new businesses as sufficient basis for diversification Providing no practical ways for skills transfer to occur Ignoring the fact that industry structure is not attractive	Sharing for its own sake rather than because it leads to competitive advantage Assuming sharing will occur naturally without senior management playing an active role Ignoring the fact that industry structure is not attractive

The first two require no connections among business units; the second two depend on them (see table 6-1). While all four concepts of strategy have succeeded under the right circumstances, today some make more sense than others. Ignoring any of the concepts is perhaps the quickest road to failure.

Portfolio Management

The concept of corporate strategy most in use is portfolio management, which is based primarily on diversification through acquisition. The corporation acquires sound, attractive companies with competent managers who agree to stay on. While acquired units do not have to be in the same industries as existing units, the best portfolio managers generally limit their range of businesses in some way, in part to limit the specific expertise needed by top management.

The acquired units are autonomous, and the teams that run them are compensated according to unit results. The corporation supplies capital and works with each to infuse it with professional management techniques. At the same time, top management provides objective and dispassionate review of business unit results. Portfolio managers categorize units by potential and regularly transfer resources from units that generate cash to those with high potential and cash needs.

In a portfolio strategy, the corporation seeks to create shareholder value in a number of ways. It uses its expertise and analytical resources to spot attractive acquisition candidates that the individual shareholder could not. The company provides capital on favorable terms that reflect corporatewide fund-raising ability. It introduces professional management skills and discipline. Finally, it provides high-quality review and coaching, unencumbered by conventional wisdom or emotional attachments to the business.

The logic of the portfolio management concept rests on a number of vital assumptions. If a company's diversification plan is to meet the attractiveness and cost-of-entry tests, it must find good but undervalued companies. Acquired companies must be truly undervalued because the parent does little for the new unit once it is acquired. To meet the better-off test, the benefits the corporation provides must yield a significant competitive advantage to acquired units. The style of operating through highly autonomous business units must both develop sound business strategies and motivate managers.

In most countries, the days when portfolio management was a valid concept of corporate strategy are past. In the face of increasingly well-developed capital markets, attractive companies with good managements show up on everyone's computer screen and attract top dollar in terms of acquisition premium. Simply contributing capital isn't contributing much. A sound strategy can easily be funded; small- to medium-size companies don't need a munificent parent.

Other benefits have also eroded. Large companies no longer corner the market for professional management skills; in fact, more and more observers believe managers cannot necessarily run anything in the absence of industry-specific knowledge and experience. Another supposed advantage of the portfolio management concept—dispassionate review—rests on similarly shaky ground since the added value of review alone is questionable in a portfolio of sound companies.

The benefit of giving business units complete autonomy is also questionable. Increasingly, a company's business units are interrelated, drawn together by new technology, broadening distribution channels, and changing regulations. Setting strategies of units independently may well undermine unit performance. The companies in my sample that have succeeded in diversification have recognized the value of interrelationships and understood that a strong sense of corporate identity is as important as slavish adherence to parochial business unit financial results.

But it is the sheer complexity of the management task that has ultimately defeated even the best portfolio managers. As the size of the company grows, portfolio managers need to find more and more deals just to maintain growth. Supervising dozens or even hundreds of disparate units and under chain-letter pressures to add more, management begins to make mistakes. At the same time, the inevitable costs of being part of a diversified company take their toll and unit performance slides while the whole company's ROI turns downward. Eventually, a new management team is installed that initiates wholesale divestments and pares down the company to its core businesses. The experiences of Gulf & Western, Consolidated Foods (now Sara Lee), and ITT are just a few comparatively recent examples. Reflecting these realities, the U.S. capital markets today reward companies that follow the portfolio management model with a "conglomerate discount"; they value the whole less than the sum of the parts.

In developing countries, where large companies are few, capital markets are undeveloped, and professional management is scarce, portfolio management still works. But it is no longer a valid model for corporate strategy in advanced economies. Nevertheless, the technique is in the limelight today in the United Kingdom, where it is supported so far by a newly energized stock market eager for excitement. But this enthusiasm will wane—as well it should. Portfolio management is no way to conduct corporate strategy.

Restructuring

Unlike its passive role as a portfolio manager, when it serves as banker and reviewer, a company that bases its strategy on restructuring becomes an active restructurer of business units. The new businesses are not necessarily related to existing units. All that is necessary is unrealized potential.

The restructuring strategy seeks out undeveloped, sick, or threatened organizations or industries on the threshold of significant change. The parent intervenes, frequently changing the unit management team, shifting strategy, or infusing the company with new technology. Then it may make follow-up acquisitions to build a critical mass and sell off unneeded or unconnected parts and thereby reduce the effective acquisition cost. The result is a strengthened company or a transformed industry. As a coda, the parent sells off the stronger unit once results are clear because the parent is no longer adding value and top management decides that its attention should be directed elsewhere.

When well implemented, the restructuring concept is sound, for it passes the three tests of successful diversification. The restructurer meets the cost-of-entry test through the types of companies it acquires. It limits acquisition premiums by buying companies with problems and lackluster images or by buying into industries with as yet unforeseen potential. Intervention by the corporation clearly meets the better-off test. Provided that the target industries are structurally attractive, the restructuring model can create enormous shareholder value. Some restructuring companies are Loew's, BTR, and General Cinema. Ironically, many of today's restructurers are profiting from yesterday's portfolio management strategies.

To work, the restructuring strategy requires a corporate management team with the insight to spot undervalued companies or positions in industries ripe for transformation. The same insight is necessary to actually turn the units around even though they are in new and unfamiliar businesses.

These requirements expose the restructurer to considerable risk and usually limit the time in which the company can succeed at the strategy. The most skillful proponents understand this problem, recognize their mistakes, and move decisively to dispose of them. The best companies realize they are not just acquiring companies but restructuring an industry. Unless they can integrate the acquisitions to create a whole new strategic position, they are just portfolio managers in disguise. Another important difficulty surfaces if so many other companies join the action that they deplete the pool of suitable candidates and bid their prices up.

Perhaps the greatest pitfall, however, is that companies find it very hard to dispose of business units once they are restructured and performing well. Human nature fights economic rationale. Size supplants shareholder value as the corporate goal. The company does not sell a unit even though the company no longer adds value to the unit. While the transformed units would be better off in another company that had related businesses, the restructuring company instead retains them. Gradually, it becomes a portfolio manager. The parent company's ROI declines as the need for reinvestment in the units and normal business risks eventually offset restructuring's one-shot gain. The perceived need to keep growing intensifies the pace of acquisition; errors result and standards fall. The restructuring company turns into a conglomerate with returns that only equal the average of all industries at best.

Transferring Skills

The purpose of the first two concepts of corporate strategy is to create value through a company's relationship with each autonomous unit. The corporation's role is to be a selector, a banker, and an intervenor.

The last two concepts exploit the interrelationships between businesses. In articulating them, however, one comes face-to-face with the often ill-defined concept of synergy. If you believe the text of the countless corporate annual reports, just about anything is related to just about anything else! But imagined synergy is much more common than real synergy. General Motors' purchase of Hughes Aircraft simply because cars were going electronic and Hughes was an electronics concern demonstrates the folly of paper synergy. Such corporate relatedness is an ex post facto rationalization of a diversification undertaken for other reasons.

Even synergy that is clearly defined often fails to materialize. Instead of cooperating, business units often compete. A company that can define the synergies it is pursuing still faces significant organizational impediments in achieving them.

But the need to capture the benefits of relationships between businesses has never been more important. Technological and competitive developments already link many businesses and are creating new possibilities for competitive advantage. In such sectors as financial services, computing, office equipment, entertainment, and health care, interrelationships among previously distinct businesses are perhaps the central concern of strategy.

To understand the role of relatedness in corporate strategy, we must give new meaning to this often ill-defined idea. I have identified a good way to start—the value chain. Every business unit is a collection of discrete activities ranging from sales to accounting that allow it to compete. I call them value activities. It is at this level, not in the company as a whole, that the unit achieves competitive advantage.

I group these activities in nine categories. Primary activities create the product or service, deliver and market it, and provide after-sale support. The categories of primary activities are inbound logistics, operations, outbound logistics, marketing and sales, and service. Support activities provide the input and infrastructure that allow the primary activities to take place. The categories are company infrastructure, human resource management, technology development, and procurement.

The value chain defines the two types of interrelationships that may create synergy. The first is a company's ability to transfer skills or expertise among similar value chains. The second is the ability to share activities. Two business units, for example, can share the same sales force or logistics network.

The value chain helps expose the last two (and most important) concepts of corporate strategy. The transfer of skills among business units in the diversified company is the basis for one concept. While each business unit has a separate value chain, knowledge about how to perform activities is transferred among the units. For example, a toiletries business unit, expert in the marketing of convenience products, transmits ideas on new positioning concepts, promotional techniques, and packaging possibilities to a newly acquired unit that sells cough syrup. Newly entered industries can benefit from the expertise of existing units and vice versa.

These opportunities arise when business units have similar buyers or channels, similar value activities like government relations or procurement, similarities in the broad configuration of the value chain (for example, managing a multisite service organization), or the same strategic concept (for example, low cost). Even though the units operate separately, such similarities allow the sharing of knowledge.

Of course, some similarities are common; one can imagine them at some level between almost any pair of businesses. Countless companies have fallen into the trap of diversifying too readily because of similarities; mere similarity is not enough.

Transferring skills leads to competitive advantage only if the similarities among businesses meet three conditions:

- The activities involved in the businesses are similar enough that sharing expertise is meaningful. Broad similarities (marketing intensiveness, for example, or a common core process technology such as bending metal) are not a sufficient basis for diversification. The resulting ability to transfer skills is likely to have little impact on competitive advantage.

- The transfer of skills involves activities important to competitive advantage. Transferring skills in peripheral activities such as government relations or real estate in consumer goods units may be beneficial but is not a basis for diversification.

- The skills transferred represent a significant source of competitive advantage for the receiving unit. The expertise or skills to be transferred are both advanced and proprietary enough to be beyond the capabilities of competitors.

The transfer of skills is an active process that significantly changes the strategy or operations of the receiving unit. The prospect for change must be specific and identifiable. Almost guaranteeing that no shareholder value will be created, too many companies are satisfied with vague prospects or faint hopes that skills will transfer. The transfer of skills does not happen by accident or by osmosis. The company will have to reassign critical personnel, even on a permanent basis, and the participation and support of high-level management in skills transfer is essential. Many companies have been defeated at skills transfer because they have not provided their business units with any incentives to participate.

Transferring skills meets the tests of diversification if the company truly mobilizes proprietary expertise across units. This makes certain the company can offset the acquisition premium or lower the cost of overcoming entry barriers.

The industries the company chooses for diversification must pass the attractiveness test. Even a close fit that reflects opportunities to transfer skills may not overcome poor industry structure. Opportunities to transfer skills, however, may help the company transform the structures of newly entered industries and send them in favorable directions.

The transfer of skills can be one-time or ongoing. If the company exhausts opportunities to infuse new expertise into a unit after the initial postacquisition period, the unit should ultimately be sold. The corporation is no longer creating shareholder value. Few companies have grasped this point, however, and many gradually suffer mediocre returns. Yet a company diversified into well-chosen businesses can transfer skills eventually in many directions. If corporate management conceives of its role in this way and creates appropriate organizational mechanisms to facilitate cross-unit interchange, the opportunities to share expertise will be meaningful.

By using both acquisitions and internal development, companies can build a transfer-of-skills strategy. The presence of a strong base of skills sometimes creates the possibility for internal entry instead of the acquisition of a going concern. Successful diversifiers that employ the concept of skills transfer may, however, often acquire a company in the target industry as a beachhead and then build on it with their internal expertise. By doing so, they can reduce some of the risks of internal entry and speed up the process. Two companies that have diversified using the transfer-of-skills concept are 3M and Pepsico.

Sharing Activities

The fourth concept of corporate strategy is based on sharing activities in the value chains among business units. Procter & Gamble, for example, employs a common physical distribution system and sales force in both paper towels and disposable diapers. McKesson, a leading distribution company, will handle such diverse lines as pharmaceuticals and liquor through superwarehouses.

The ability to share activities is a potent basis for corporate strategy because sharing often enhances competitive advantage by lowering cost or raising differentiation. But not all sharing leads to competitive advantage, and companies can encounter deep organizational resistance to even beneficial sharing possibilities. These hard truths have led many companies to reject synergy prematurely and retreat to the false simplicity of portfolio management.

A cost-benefit analysis of prospective sharing opportunities can determine whether synergy is possible. Sharing can lower costs if it achieves economies of scale, boosts the efficiency of utilization, or helps a company move more rapidly down the learning curve. The costs of General Electric's advertising, sales, and after-sales service activities in major appliances are low because they are spread over a wide range of appliance products. Sharing can also enhance the potential for differentiation. A shared order-processing system, for instance, may allow new features and services that a buyer will value. Sharing can also reduce the cost of differentiation. A shared service network, for example, may make more advanced, remote servicing technology economically feasible. Often, sharing will allow an activity to be wholly reconfigured in ways that can dramatically raise competitive advantage.

Sharing must involve activities that are significant to competitive advantage, not just any activity. P&G's distribution system is such an instance in the diaper and paper towel business, where products are bulky and costly to ship. Conversely, diversification based on the opportunities to share only corporate overhead is rarely, if ever, appropriate.

Sharing activities inevitably involves costs that the benefits must outweigh. One cost is the greater coordination required to manage a shared activity. More important is the need to compromise the design or performance of an activity so that it can be shared. A salesperson handling the products of two business units, for example, must operate in a way that is usually not what either unit would choose were it independent. And if compromise greatly erodes the unit's effectiveness, then sharing may reduce rather than enhance competitive advantage.

Many companies have only superficially identified their potential for sharing. Companies also merge activities without consideration of whether they are sensitive to economies of scale. When they are not, the coordination costs kill the benefits. Companies compound such errors by not identifying costs of sharing in advance, when steps can be taken to minimize them. Costs of compromise can frequently be mitigated by redesigning the activity for sharing. The shared salesperson, for example, can be provided with a remote computer terminal to boost productivity and provide more customer information. Jamming business units together without such thinking exacerbates the costs of sharing.

Despite such pitfalls, opportunities to gain advantage from sharing activities have proliferated because of momentous developments in technology, deregulation, and competition. The infusion of electronics and information systems into many industries creates new opportunities to link businesses. The corporate strategy of sharing can involve both acquisition and internal development. Internal development is often possible because the corporation can bring to bear clear resources in launching a new unit. Start-ups are less difficult to integrate than acquisitions. Companies using the shared-activities concept can also make acquisitions as beachhead landings into a new industry and then integrate the units through sharing with other units. Prime examples of companies that have diversified via using shared activities include P&G, Du Pont, and IBM. The fields into which each has diversified are a cluster of tightly related units. Marriott illustrates both successes and failures in sharing activities over time.

Following the shared-activities model requires an organizational context in which business unit collaboration is encouraged and reinforced. Highly autonomous business units are inimical to such collaboration. The company must put into place a variety of what I call horizontal mechanisms—a strong sense of corporate identity, a clear corporate mission statement that emphasizes the importance of integrating business unit strategies, an incentive system that rewards more than just business unit results, cross-business-unit task forces, and other methods of integrating.

A corporate strategy based on shared activities clearly meets the better-off test because business units gain ongoing tangible advantages from others within the corporation. It also meets the cost-of-entry test by reducing the expense of surmounting the barriers to internal entry. Other bids for acquisitions that do not share opportunities will have lower reservation prices. Even widespread opportunities for sharing activities do not allow a company to suspend the attractiveness test, however. Many diversifiers have made the critical mistake of equating the close fit of a target industry with attractive diversification. Target industries must pass the strict requirement test of having an attractive structure as well as a close fit in opportunities if diversification is to ultimately succeed.

Choosing a Corporate Strategy

Each concept of corporate strategy allows the diversified company to create shareholder value in a different way. Companies can succeed with any of the concepts if they clearly define the corporation's role and objectives, have the skills necessary for meeting the concept's prerequisites, organize themselves to manage diversity in a way that fits the strategy, and find themselves in an appropriate capital market environment. The caveat is that portfolio management is only sensible in limited circumstances.

A company's choice of corporate strategy is partly a legacy of its past. If its business units are in unattractive industries, the company must start from scratch. If the company has few truly proprietary skills or activities it can share in related diversification, then its initial diversification must rely on other concepts. Yet corporate strategy should not be a once-and-for-all choice but a vision that can evolve. A company should choose its long-term preferred concept and then proceed pragmatically toward it from its initial starting point.

Both the strategic logic and the experience of the companies I studied over the last decade suggest that a company will create shareholder value through diversification to a greater and greater extent as its strategy moves from portfolio management toward sharing activities. Because they do not rely on superior insight or other questionable assumptions about the company's capabilities, sharing activities and transferring skills offer the best avenues for value creation.

Each concept of corporate strategy is not mutually exclusive of those that come before, a potent advantage of the third and fourth concepts. A company can employ a restructuring strategy at the same time it transfers skills or shares activities. A strategy based on shared activities becomes more powerful if business units can also exchange skills. As the Marriott case illustrates, a company can often pursue the two strategies together and even incorporate some of the principles of restructuring with them. When it chooses industries in which to transfer skills or share activities, the company can also investigate the possibility of transforming the industry structure. When a company bases its strategy on interrelationships, it has a broader basis on which to create shareholder value than if it rests its entire strategy on transforming companies in unfamiliar industries.

My study supports the soundness of basing a corporate strategy on the transfer of skills or shared activities. The data on the sample companies' diversification programs illustrate some important characteristics of successful diversifiers. They have made a disproportionately low percentage of unrelated acquisitions, unrelated being defined as having no clear opportunity to transfer skills or share important activities. Even successful diversifiers such as 3M, IBM, and TRW have terrible records when they have strayed into unrelated acquisitions. Successful acquirers diversify into fields, each of which is related to many others. Procter & Gamble and IBM, for example, operate in eighteen and nineteen interrelated fields respectively and so enjoy numerous opportunities to transfer skills and share activities.

Companies with the best acquisition records tend to make heavier-than-average use of start-ups and joint ventures. Most companies shy away from modes of entry besides acquisition. My results cast doubt on the conventional wisdom regarding start-ups. These results demonstrate that while joint ventures are about as risky as acquisitions, start-ups are not. Moreover, successful companies often have very good records with start-up units, as 3M, P&G, Johnson & Johnson, IBM, and United Technologies illustrate. When a company has the internal strength to start up a unit, it can be safer and less costly to launch a company than to rely solely on an acquisition and then have to deal with the problem of integration. Japanese diversification histories support the soundness of start-up as an entry alternative.

My data also illustrate that none of the concepts of corporate strategy works when industry structure is poor or implementation is bad, no matter how related the industries are. Xerox acquired companies in related industries, but the businesses had poor structures and its skills were insufficient to provide enough competitive advantage to offset implementation problems.

Creating a Corporate Theme

Defining a corporate theme is a good way to ensure that the corporation will create shareholder value. Having the right theme helps unite the efforts of business units and reinforces the ways they interrelate as well as guides the choice of new businesses to enter. NEC Corporation, with its "C&C" (computers and communication) theme, provides a good example. NEC integrates its computer, semiconductor, telecommunications, and consumer electronics businesses by merging computers and communication.

It is all too easy to create a shallow corporate theme. CBS wanted to be an "entertainment company," for example, and built a group of businesses related to leisure time. It entered such industries as toys, crafts, musical instruments, sports teams, and hi-fi retailing. While this corporate theme sounded good, close listening revealed its hollow ring. None of these businesses had any significant opportunity to share activities or transfer skills among themselves or with CBS's traditional broadcasting and record businesses. They were all sold, often at significant losses, except for a few of CBS's publishing-related units. Saddled with the worst acquisition record in my study, CBS has eroded the shareholder value created through its strong performance in broadcasting and records.

Moving from competitive strategy to corporate strategy is the business equivalent of passing through the Bermuda Triangle. The failure of corporate strategy reflects the fact that most diversified companies have failed to think in terms of how they really add value. A corporate strategy that truly enhances the competitive advantage of each business unit is the best defense against the corporate raider. With a sharper focus on the tests of diversification and the explicit choice of a clear concept of corporate strategy, companies' diversification track records from now on can look a lot different.

■ FROM CORPORATE STRATEGY TO PARENTING ADVANTAGE†

By Michael Goold and Andrew Campbell

During the 1980s there has been a sea change in attitudes to corporate strategy. The fashion for diversification and "portfolio management" that prevailed in the 1960s and 1970s, has been replaced by a philosophy of "sticking to the knitting." Mindful of the dangers of too much diversity, many companies have been refocusing their portfolios on core business areas. For the same reasons, acquisitions that take a company into new businesses are now viewed with considerable suspicion. Unfortunately, a clear view on how much diversity is manageable and on what sorts of acquisitions are justifiable has not yet emerged to guide managers who are responsible for corporate strategy. Here, we would like to comment on Michael Porter's contribution to the continuing debate on corporate strategy, and point the way toward some new research directions we believe will be fruitful.

†**Source:** This article was originally published as "Brief Case: From Corporate Strategy to Parenting Advantage," in *Long Range Planning*, February 1991, Vol. 24, pp. 115–117. Reprinted with permission.

From Competitive Advantage to Corporate Strategy

In his frequently cited article "From Competitive Advantage to Corporate Strategy," Michael Porter claims that corporate strategy for diversified, multibusiness companies is intimately linked to competitive advantage at the business unit level. "Competition occurs at the business unit level. Diversified companies do not compete; only their business units do . . . . Successful corporate strategy must grow out of and reinforce competitive strategy." This leads him on to the "better-off test" as the crucial criterion for assessing diversification moves. "Either the new unit must gain competitive advantage from its link with the corporation or vice versa." Porter believes that the major reason for the failure of so many diversifications is that corporate managers ignore the better-off test or "deal with it through arm waving or trumped-up logic rather than hard strategic analysis."

We believe that the criticisms of corporate strategy that Porter makes, and the evidence of diversification failures that he has shown, are powerful. There are far too many examples of companies that lack a clear corporate strategy and where the contribution of the corporate level is to make the individual businesses in the portfolio worse off, not better off. Furthermore, a poor track record in acquisitions is frequently a result of lacking a sound corporate strategy based on the better-off test.

But Porter's account of corporate strategy leaves two vital questions open:

■ How can a company tell whether it will be able to make a given subsidiary better off? What "hard strategic analysis" can be done, or what experience can be drawn on, to give a reliable prediction of a company's ability to add value to a potential new business?

■ How much better off must the business be to justify a diversification move? Is any improvement enough, or can the better-off test be made more precise?

Deciding Whether a Given Subsidiary Will Be Better Off

How can we distinguish between real opportunities to make new units better off and apparently attractive moves that in the event fail? Many of the oil companies would no doubt wish that they had been more cautious in their acquisitions of minerals and other natural resources businesses. British Petroleum (BP), for example, found that they were not able to add much to Selection Trust, which they acquired in 1980, and have now divested to RTZ. This is very much the sort of diversification failure that Porter criticises, yet it was by no means obvious at the time of the acquisition that BP would not make Selection Trust better off. How could BP have determined before the event that they were not likely to make the minerals business better off?

Porter's suggested approach for applying the better-off test is to undertake a value chain analysis of the company's existing and new businesses as a basis for deciding where opportunities for improved performance lie. But this approach is by no means always sufficient. At the time of BP's acquisition of Selection Trust it seemed possible to claim that BP's skills in extractive industries would allow it to add value to Selection Trust. A value chain analysis, of the sort suggested by Porter, would probably have identified common activities or skills between, for example, oil exploration and minerals exploration, that could provide the basis for shared activities or skill transfer, and would therefore make Selection Trust better off.

In the event, less value was created through these relationships than had been expected. The differences between the oil and minerals businesses proved greater than anticipated. Further, and more importantly, the nature of competition and the key sources of competitive advantage (the "dominant logic") proved to be substantially different between oil and minerals. This meant that senior management reactions and decision-making processes were not appropriate for the new minerals business, thus offsetting the limited benefits that were available from the acquisition.

A value chain analysis is liable to miss the crucial differences in specific skills between businesses, and is a poor tool for quantifying benefits that may be available. More importantly, it is not suitable for unearthing essential differences in dominant logic between businesses. We need new concepts and new approaches for identifying and quantifying the specialist skills of parent organizations, and for determining how far differences in dominant logic may offset benefits that would otherwise be available.

The better-off test is conceptually useful, but as yet, it is not easy to apply in practice. Further research is needed to give it a much sharper and more usable cutting edge.

Parenting Advantage

Plainly, where a new business is not better off as part of the portfolio, the company's corporate strategy has destroyed rather than created value. But we believe that corporate strategy must ultimately pass a stiffer test than Porter proposes. The real goal for the corporation is that it adds *more* value to its business than any other potential parent.

As an example, consider the acquisition by a U.K. foods group of a particular U.K. snack business. Provided the new parent can bring a benefit such as improved marketing skills or better joint distribution, the acquisition will pass the better-off test. However, other potential parents might be able to bring much greater benefits. An international snacks company, such as Pepsico, might bring the potential for shared costs in research, product development, and marketing. A global food company, such as Unilever, might open up a wider range of new markets. The U.K. foods company is not the best parent for the acquisition in question, unless it adds *more* value than other possible parents.

Moreover, we take issue with Porter's claim that "diversified companies do not compete; only their business units do." An increasingly active market for corporate control means that there is constant explicit competition between diversified companies for the right to own and manage businesses, which from time to time break out openly in disputed acquisitions, mergers, breakups and management buyouts.

To justify their continuing stewardship of the businesses in their portfolios, corporate parents must be able to show that their businesses perform better under their ownership than they would under different ownership. In stock market terms, they must prevent "value gaps" from opening up between the price investors will pay for the businesses under the existing ownership, and the price other owners would be willing to pay for them. In corporate strategy terms, the parenting team must possess specialist skills or assets that allow them to add more value to their businesses than any other parent company could (i.e., to make them better off to a greater extent than any other parent company). We call their skills and assets parenting advantage, and we believe that parenting advantage is the basis of sound corporate strategy in the same way that competitive advantage is the basis of sound business unit strategy.

Porter has done us a service in drawing out the link from competitive advantage to corporate strategy. We propose that it is now time to move on from corporate strategy to parenting advantage.

■ THE CORE COMPETENCE OF THE CORPORATION†

By C. K. Prahalad and Gary Hamel

The most powerful way to prevail in global competition is still invisible to many companies. During the 1980s, top executives were judged on their ability to restructure, declutter, and delayer their corporations. In the 1990s, they'll be judged on their ability to identify, cultivate, and exploit the core competencies that make growth possible— indeed, they'll have to rethink the concept of the corporation itself.

Rethinking the Corporation

Once, the diversified corporation could simply point its business units at particular end-product markets and admonish them to become world leaders. But with market boundaries changing ever more quickly, targets are elusive and capture is at best temporary. A few companies have proven themselves adept at inventing new markets, quickly entering emerging markets, and dramatically shifting patterns of customer choice in established markets. These are the ones to emulate. The critical task for management is to create an organization capable of infusing products with irresistible functionality or, better yet, creating products that customers need but have not yet even imagined.

This is a deceptively difficult task. Ultimately, it requires radical change in the management of major companies. It means, first of all, that top managements of Western companies must assume responsibility for competitive decline. Everyone knows about high interest rates, Japanese protectionism, outdated antitrust laws, obstreperous unions, and impatient investors. What is harder to see, or harder to acknowledge, is how little added momentum companies actually get from political or macroeconomic "relief." Both the theory and practice of Western management have created a drag on our forward motion. It is the principles of management that are in need of reform.

The Roots of Competitive Advantage

In the short run, a company's competitiveness derives from the price/performance attributes of current products. But the survivors of the first wave of global competition, Western and Japanese alike, are all converging on similar and formidable standards for product cost and quality—minimum hurdles for continued competition, but less and less important as sources of differential advantage. In the long run, competitiveness derives from an ability to build, at lower cost and more speedily than competitors, the core competencies that spawn unanticipated products. The real sources of advantage are to be found in management's ability to consolidate corporatewide technologies and production skills into competencies that empower individual businesses to adapt quickly to changing opportunities.

Senior executives who claim that they cannot build core competencies either because they feel the autonomy of business units is sacrosanct or because their feet are held to the quarterly budget fire should think again. The problem in many Western companies is not that their senior executives are any less capable than those in Japan or that Japanese companies possess greater technical capabilities. Instead, it is their adherence to a concept of the corporation that unnecessarily limits the ability of individual businesses to fully exploit the deep reservoir of technological capability that many American and European companies possess.

The diversified corporation is a large tree. The trunk and major limbs are core products, the smaller branches are business units; the leaves, flowers, and fruit are end products. The root system that provides nourishment, sustenance, and stability is the core competence. You can miss the strength of competitors by looking only at their end products, in the same way you miss the strength of a tree if you look only at its leaves (see figure 6-1).

Core competencies are the collective learning in the organization, especially how to coordinate diverse production skills and integrate multiple streams of technologies.

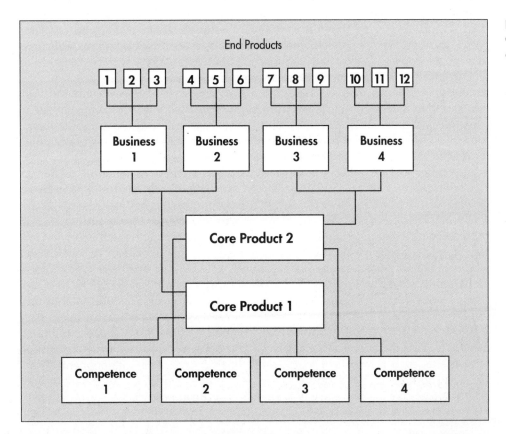

FIGURE 6-1
Competencies as the Roots of Competitiveness

Consider Sony's capacity to miniaturize or Philips's optical-media expertise. The theoretical knowledge to put a radio on a chip does not in itself assure a company the skill to produce a miniature radio no bigger than a business card. To bring off this feat, Casio must harmonize know-how in miniaturization, microprocessor design, materials science, and ultrathin precision casing—the same skills it applies in its miniature card calculators, pocket TVs, and digital watches.

If core competence is about harmonizing streams of technology, it is also about the organization of work and the delivery of value. Among Sony's competencies is miniaturization. To bring miniaturization to its products, Sony must ensure that technologists, engineers, and marketers have a shared understanding of customer needs and of technological possibilities. The force of core competence is felt as decisively in services as in manufacturing. Citicorp was ahead of others investing in an operating system that allowed it to participate in world markets twenty-four hours a day. Its competence in systems has provided the company the means to differentiate itself from many financial service institutions.

Core competence is communication, involvement, and a deep commitment to working across organizational boundaries. It involves many levels of people and all functions. World-class research in, for example, lasers or ceramics can take place in corporate laboratories without having an impact on any of the businesses of the company. The skills that together constitute core competence must coalesce around individuals whose efforts are not so narrowly focused that they cannot recognize the opportunities for blending their functional expertise with those of others in new and interesting ways.

Core competence does not diminish with use. Unlike physical assets, which do deteriorate over time, competencies are enhanced as they are applied and shared. But competencies still need to be nurtured and protected; knowledge fades if it is not used. Competencies are the glue that binds existing businesses. They are also the engine for new business development. Patterns of diversification and market entry may be guided by them, not just by the attractiveness of markets.

Consider 3M's competence with sticky tape. In dreaming up businesses as diverse as "Post-it" note pads, magnetic tape, photographic film, pressure-sensitive tapes, and coated abrasives, the company has brought to bear widely shared competencies in substrates, coatings, and adhesives and devised various ways to combine them. Indeed, 3M has invested consistently in them. What seems to be an extremely diversified portfolio of businesses belies a few shared core competencies.

In contrast, there are major companies that have had the potential to build core competencies but failed to do so because top management was unable to conceive of the company as anything other than a collection of discrete businesses. General Electric sold much of its consumer electronics business to Thomson of France, arguing that it was becoming increasingly difficult to maintain its competitiveness in this sector. That was undoubtedly so, but it is ironic that it sold several key businesses to competitors who were already competence leaders—Black & Decker in small electrical motors, and Thomson, which was eager to build its competence in microelectronics and had learned from the Japanese that a position in consumer electronics was vital to this challenge.

Management trapped in the strategic business unit (SBU) mind-set almost inevitably finds its individual businesses dependent on external sources for critical components, such as motors or compressors. But these are not just components. They are core products that contribute to the competitiveness of a wide range of end products. They are the physical embodiments of core competencies.

How Not to Think of Competence

Since companies are in a race to build the competencies that determine global leadership, successful companies have stopped imagining themselves as bundles of businesses making products. Canon, Honda, Casio, or NEC may seem to preside over portfolios of businesses unrelated in terms of customers, distribution channels, and merchandising strategy. Indeed, they have portfolios that may seem idiosyncratic at times: NEC is the only global company to be among leaders in computing, telecommunications, and semiconductors *and* to have a thriving consumer electronics business.

But looks are deceiving. In NEC, digital technology, especially VLSI and systems integration skills, is fundamental. In the core competencies underlying them, disparate businesses become coherent. It is Honda's core competence in engines and power trains that gives it a distinctive advantage in car, motorcycle, lawn mower, and generator businesses. Canon's core competencies in optics, imaging, and microprocessor controls have enabled it to enter, even dominate, markets as seemingly diverse as copiers, laser printers, cameras, and image scanners. Philips worked for more than fifteen years to perfect its optical-media (laser disc) competence, as did JVC in building a leading position in video recording. Other examples of core competencies might include mechantronics (the ability to marry mechanical and electronic engineering), video displays, bioengineering, and microelectronics. In the early stages of its competence building, Philips could not have imagined all the products that would be spawned by its optical-media competence, nor could JVC have anticipated miniature camcorders when it first began exploring videotape technologies.

Unlike the battle for global brand dominance, which is visible in the world's broadcast and print media and is aimed at building global "share of mind," the battle to build world-class competencies is invisible to people who aren't deliberately looking for it. Top management often tracks the cost and quality of competitors' products, yet how many managers untangle the web of alliances their Japanese competitors have constructed to acquire competencies at low cost? In how many Western boardrooms is there an explicit, shared understanding of the competencies the company must build for world leadership? Indeed, how many senior executives discuss the crucial distinction between competitive strategy at the level of a business and competitive strategy at the level of an entire company?

Let us be clear. Cultivating core competence does not mean outspending rivals on research and development. In 1983, when Canon surpassed Xerox in worldwide unit market share in the copier business, its R&D budget in reprographics was but a small fraction of Xerox's. Over the past twenty years, NEC has spent less on R&D as a percentage of sales than almost all of its American and European competitors.

Nor does core competence mean shared costs, as when two or more SBUs use a common facility—a plant, service facility, or sales force—or share a common component. The gains of sharing may be substantial, but the search for shared costs is typically a post hoc effort to rationalize production across existing businesses, not a premeditated effort to build the competencies out of which the businesses themselves grow.

Building core competencies is more ambitious and different than integrating vertically, moreover. Managers deciding whether to make or buy will start with end products and look upstream to the efficiencies of the supply chain and downstream toward distribution and customers. They do not take inventory of skills and look forward to applying them in nontraditional ways. (Of course, decisions about competencies *do* provide a logic for vertical integration. Canon is not particularly integrated in its copier business, except in those aspects of the vertical chain that support the competencies it regards as critical.)

Identifying Core Competencies—And Losing Them

At least three tests can be applied to identify core competencies in a company. First, a core competence provides potential access to a wide variety of markets. Competence in display systems, for example, enables a company to participate in such diverse businesses as calculators, miniature TV sets, monitors for laptop computers, and automotive dashboards—which is why Casio's entry into the handheld TV market was predictable. Second, a core competence should make a significant contribution to the perceived customer benefits of the end product. Clearly, Honda's engine expertise fills this bill.

Finally, a core competence should be difficult for competitors to imitate. And it will be difficult if it is a complex harmonization of individual technologies and production skills. A rival might acquire some of the technologies that comprise the core competence, but it will find it more difficult to duplicate the more-or-less comprehensive pattern of internal coordination and learning. JVC's decision in the early 1960s to pursue the development of a videotape competence passed the three tests outlined here. RCA's decision in the late 1970s to develop a stylus-based video turntable system did not.

Few companies are likely to build world leadership in more than five or six fundamental competencies. A company that compiles a list of twenty to thirty capabilities has probably not produced a list of core competencies. Still, it is probably a good discipline to generate a list of this sort and to see aggregate capabilities as building blocks. This tends to prompt the search for licensing deals and alliances through which the company may acquire, at low cost, the missing pieces.

Most Western companies hardly think about competitiveness in these terms at all. It is time to take a tough-minded look at the risks they are running. Companies that judge competitiveness, their own and their competitors', primarily in terms of the price/performance of end products are courting the erosion of core competencies—or making too little effort to enhance them. The embedded skills that give rise to the next generation of competitive products cannot be "rented in" by outsourcing and original equipment manufacturer (OEM) supply relationships. In our view, too many companies have unwittingly surrendered core competencies when they cut internal investment in what they mistakenly thought were just "cost centers" in favor of outside suppliers.

Of course, it is perfectly possible for a company to have a competitive product line up but be a laggard in developing core competencies—at least for a while. If a company wanted to enter the copier business today, it would find a dozen Japanese companies more than willing to supply copiers on the basis of an OEM private label. But when fundamental technologies changed or if its supplier decided to enter the market directly and become a competitor, that company's product line, along with all of its investments in marketing and distribution, could be vulnerable. Outsourcing can provide a shortcut to a more competitive product, but it typically contributes little to building the people-embodied skills that are needed to sustain product leadership.

Nor is it possible for a company to have an intelligent alliance or sourcing strategy if it has not made a choice about where it will build competence leadership. Clearly, Japanese companies have benefited from alliances. They've used them to learn from Western partners who were not fully committed to preserving core competencies of their own. Learning within an alliance takes a positive commitment of resources— travel, a pool of dedicated people, test-bed facilities, time to internalize and test what has been learned. A company may not make this effort if it doesn't have clear goals for competence building.

Another way of losing is forgoing opportunities to establish competencies that are evolving in existing businesses. In the 1970s and 1980s, many American and European companies—like General Electric, Motorola, GTE, Thorn, and General Electric Company (GEC)—chose to exit the color television business, which they regarded as mature. If by "mature" they meant that they had run out of new product ideas at precisely the moment global rivals had targeted the TV business for entry, then yes, the industry was mature. But it certainly wasn't mature in the sense that all opportunities to enhance and apply video-based competencies had been exhausted.

In ridding themselves of their television businesses, these companies failed to distinguish between divesting the business and destroying their video media-based competencies. They not only got out of the TV business but they also closed the door on a whole stream of future opportunities reliant on video-based competencies.

There are two clear lessons here. First, the costs of losing a core competence can be only partly calculated in advance. The baby may be thrown out with the bath water in divestment decisions. Second, since core competencies are built through a process of continuous improvement and enhancement that may span a decade or longer, a company that has failed to invest in core competence building will find it very difficult to enter an emerging market, unless, of course, it will be content simply to serve as a distribution channel.

American semiconductor companies like Motorola learned this painful lesson when they elected to forgo direct participation in the 256k generation of DRAM chips. Having skipped this round, Motorola, like most of its American competitors, needed a large infusion of technical help from Japanese partners to rejoin the battle in the 1-megabyte generation. When it comes to core competencies, it is difficult to get off the train, walk to the next station, and then reboard.

From Core Competencies to Core Products

The tangible link between identified core competencies and end products is what we call the core products—the physical embodiments of one or more core competencies. Honda's engines, for example, are core products, linchpins between design and development skills that ultimately lead to a proliferation of end products. Core products are the components or subassemblies that actually contribute to the value of the end products. Thinking in terms of core products forces a company to distinguish between the brand share it achieves in end product markets (for example, 40 percent of the U.S. refrigerator market) and the manufacturing share it achieves in any particular core product (for example, 5 percent of the world share of compressor output).

It is essential to make this distinction between core competencies, core products, and end products because global competition is played out by different rules and for different stakes at each level. To build or defend leadership over the long term, a corporation will probably be a winner at each level. At the level of core competence, the goal is to build world leadership in the design and development of a particular class of product functionality—be it compact data storage and retrieval, as with Philips's optical-media competence, or compactness and ease of use, as with Sony's micromotors and microprocessor controls.

To sustain leadership in their chosen core competence areas, these companies *seek to maximize their world manufacturing share in core products.* The manufacture of core products for a wide variety of external (and internal) customers yields the revenue and market feedback that, at least partly, determines the pace at which core competencies can be enhanced and extended. This thinking was behind JVC's decision in the mid-1970s to establish VCR supply relationships with leading national consumer electronics companies in Europe and the United States. In supplying Thomson, Thorn, and Telefunken (all independent companies at that time) as well as U.S. partners, JVC was able to gain the cash and the diversity of market experience that ultimately enabled it to outpace Philips and Sony. (Philips developed videotape competencies in parallel with JVC, but it failed to build a worldwide network of OEM relationships that would have allowed it to accelerate the refinement of its videotape competence through the sale of core products.)

JVC's success has not been lost on Korean companies like Goldstar, Samsung, Kia, and Daewoo, who are building core product leadership in areas as diverse as displays, semiconductors, and automotive engines through their OEM-supply contracts with Western companies. Their avowed goal is to capture investment initiative away from potential competitors, often U.S. companies. In doing so, they accelerate their competence-building efforts while "hollowing out" their competitors. By focusing on competence and embedding it in core products, Asian competitors have built up advantages in component markets first and have then leveraged off their superior products to move downstream to build brand share. And they are not likely to remain the low-cost suppliers forever. As their reputation for brand leadership is consolidated, they may well gain price leadership. Honda has proven this with its Acura line, and other Japanese carmakers are following suit.

Control over core products is critical for other reasons. A dominant position in core products allows a company to shape the evolution of applications and end markets. Such compact audio disc-related core products as data drives and lasers have enabled Sony and Philips to influence the evolution of the computer-peripheral business in optical-media storage. As a company multiplies the number of application arenas for its core products, it can consistently reduce the cost, time, and risk in new product development. In short, well-targeted core products can lead to economies of scale and scope.

The Tyranny of the SBU

The new terms of competitive engagement cannot be understood using analytical tools devised to manage the diversified corporation of twenty years ago, when competition was primarily domestic (GE versus Westinghouse, General Motors versus Ford) and all the key players were speaking the language of the same business schools and consultancies. Old prescriptions have potentially toxic side effects. The need for new principles is most obvious in companies organized exclusively according to the logic of SBUs. The implications of the two alternate concepts of the corporation are summarized in figure 6-2.

	SBU	Core Competence
Basis for competition	Competitiveness of today's products	Interfirm competition to build competencies
Corporate structure	Portfolio of businesses related in product-market terms	Portfolio of competencies, core products, and businesses
Status of the business unit	Autonomy is sacrosanct; the SBU "owns" all resources other than cash	SBU is a potential reservoir of core competencies
Resource allocation	Discrete businesses are the unit of analysis; capital is allocated business by business	Businesses and competencies are the unit of analysis: top management allocates capital and talent
Value added of top management	Optimizing corporate returns through capital allocation trade-offs among businesses	Enunciating strategic architecture and building competencies to secure the future

FIGURE 6-2
Two Concepts of the Corporation

Obviously, diversified corporations have a portfolio of products and a portfolio of businesses. But we believe in a view of the company as a portfolio of competencies as well. United States companies do not lack the technical resources to build competencies, but their top management often lacks the vision to build them and the administrative means for assembling resources spread across multiple businesses. A shift in commitment will inevitably influence patterns of diversification, skill deployment, resource allocation priorities, and approaches to alliances and outsourcing.

We have described the three different planes on which battles for global leadership are waged: core competence, core products, and end products. A corporation has to know whether it is winning or losing on each plane. By sheer weight of investment, a company might be able to beat its rivals to blue-sky technologies yet still lose the race to build core competence leadership. If a company is winning the race to build core competencies (as opposed to building leadership in a few technologies), it will almost certainly outpace rivals in new business development. If a company is winning the race to capture world manufacturing share in core products, it will probably outpace rivals in improving product features and the price/performance ratio.

Determining whether one is winning or losing end-product battles is more difficult because measures of product market share do not necessarily reflect various companies' underlying competitiveness. Indeed, companies that attempt to build market share by relying on the competitiveness of others, rather than investing in core competencies and world core-product leadership, may be treading on quicksand. In the race for global brand dominance, companies like 3M, Black & Decker, Canon, Honda, NEC, and Citicorp have built global brand umbrellas by proliferating products out of their core competencies. This has allowed their individual businesses to build image, customer loyalty, and access to distribution channels.

When you think about this reconceptualization of the corporation, the primacy of the SBU—an organizational dogma for a generation—is now clearly an anachronism.

Where the SBU is an article of faith, resistance to the seductions of decentralization can seem heretical. In many companies, the SBU prism means that only one plane of the global competitive battle, the battle to put competitive products on the shelf *today*, is visible to top management. What are the costs of this distortion?

Underinvestment in Developing Core Competencies and Core Products

When the organization is conceived of as a multiplicity of SBUs, no single business may feel responsible for maintaining a viable position in core products or be able to justify the investment required to build world leadership in some core competence. In the absence of a more comprehensive view imposed by corporate management, SBU managers will tend to underinvest. Recently, companies such as Kodak and Philips have recognized this as a potential problem and have begun searching for new organizational forms that will allow them to develop and manufacture core products for both internal and external customers.

SBU managers have traditionally conceived of competitors in the same way they've seen themselves. On the whole, they've failed to note the emphasis Asian competitors were placing on building leadership in core products or to understand the critical linkage between world manufacturing leadership and the ability to sustain development pace in core competence. They've failed to pursue OEM-supply opportunities or to look across their various product divisions in an attempt to identify opportunities for coordinated initiatives.

Imprisoned Resources

As an SBU evolves, it often develops unique competencies. Typically, the people who embody this competence are seen as the sole property of the business in which they grew up. The manager of another SBU who asks to borrow talented people is likely to get a cold rebuff. SBU managers are not only unwilling to lend their competence carriers but they may actually hide talent to prevent its redeployment in the pursuit of new opportunities. This may be compared to residents of an underdeveloped country hiding most of their cash under their mattresses. The benefits of competencies, like the benefits of the money supply, depend on the velocity of their circulation as well as on the size of the stock the company holds.

Western companies have traditionally had an advantage in the stock of skills they possess. But have they been able to reconfigure them quickly to respond to new opportunities? Canon, NEC, and Honda have had a lesser stock of the people and technologies that compose core competencies but could move them much quicker from one business unit to another. Corporate R&D spending at Canon is not fully indicative of the size of Canon's core competence stock and tells the casual observer nothing about the velocity with which Canon is able to move core competencies to exploit opportunities.

When competencies become imprisoned, the people who carry the competencies do not get assigned to the most exciting opportunities, and their skills begin to atrophy. Only by fully leveraging core competencies can small companies like Canon afford to compete with industry giants like Xerox. How strange that SBU managers, who are perfectly willing to compete for cash in the capital budgeting process, are unwilling to compete for people—the company's most precious asset. We find it ironic that top management devotes so much attention to the capital budgeting process yet typically has no comparable mechanism for allocating the human skills that embody core competencies. Top managers are seldom able to look four or five levels down into the organization, identify the people who embody critical competencies, and move them across organizational boundaries.

Bounded Innovation

If core competencies are not recognized, individual SBUs will pursue only those innovation opportunities that are close at hand—marginal product-line extensions or geographic expansions. Hybrid opportunities like fax machines, laptop computers, handheld televisions, or portable music keyboards will emerge only when managers take off their SBU blinkers. Remember, Canon appeared to be in the camera business at the time it was preparing to become a world leader in copiers. Conceiving of the corporation in terms of core competencies widens the domain of innovation.

Developing Strategic Architecture

The fragmentation of core competencies becomes inevitable when a diversified company's information systems, patterns of communication, career paths, managerial rewards, and processes of strategy development do not transcend SBU lines. We believe that senior management should spend a significant amount of its time developing a corporatewide strategic architecture that establishes objectives for competence building. A strategic architecture is a road map of the future that identifies which core competencies to build and their constituent technologies.

By providing an impetus for learning from alliances and a focus for internal development efforts, a strategic architecture like NEC's C&C (computers and communication) can dramatically reduce the investment needed to secure future market leadership. How can a company make partnerships intelligently without a clear understanding of the core competencies it is trying to build and those it is attempting to prevent from being unintentionally transferred?

Of course, all of this begs the question of what a strategic architecture should look like. The answer will be different for every company. But it is helpful to think again of that tree, of the corporation organized around core products and, ultimately, core competencies. To sink sufficiently strong roots, a company must answer some fundamental questions: How long could we preserve our competitiveness in this business if we did not control this particular core competence? How central is this core competence to perceived customer benefits? What future opportunities would be foreclosed if we were to lose this particular competence?

The architecture provides a logic for product and market diversification, moreover. An SBU manager would be asked: Does the new market opportunity add to the overall goal of becoming the best player in the world? Does it exploit or add to the core competence? At Vickers, for example, diversification options have been judged in the context of becoming the best power and motion control company in the world.

The strategic architecture should make resource allocation priorities transparent to the entire organization. It provides a template for allocation decisions by top management. It helps lower-level managers understand the logic of allocation priorities and disciplines senior management to maintain consistency. In short, it yields a definition of the company and the markets it serves. 3M, Vickers, NEC, Canon, and Honda all qualify on this score. Honda knew it was exploiting what it had learned from motorcycles—how to make high-revving, smooth-running, lightweight engines—when it entered the car business. The task of creating a strategic architecture forces the organization to identify and commit to the technical and production linkages across SBUs that will provide a distinct competitive advantage.

It is consistency of resource allocation and the development of an administrative infrastructure appropriate to it that breathes life into a strategic architecture and creates a managerial culture, teamwork, a capacity to change, and a willingness to share resources, to protect proprietary skills, and to think long term. That is also the reason the specific architecture cannot be copied easily or overnight by competitors. Strategic architecture is a tool for communicating with customers and other external constituents. It reveals the broad direction without giving away every step.

Redeploying to Exploit Competencies

If the company's core competencies, are its critical resource and if top management must ensure that competence carriers are not held hostage by some particular business, then it follows that SBUs should bid for core competencies in the same way they bid for capital. We've made this point glancingly. It is important enough to consider more deeply.

Once top management (with the help of divisional and SBU managers) has identified overarching competencies, it must ask businesses to identify the projects and people closely connected with them. Corporate officers should direct an audit of the location, number, and quality of the people who embody competence.

This sends an important signal to middle managers: core competencies are corporate resources and may be reallocated by *corporate* management. An individual business doesn't own anybody. SBUs are entitled to the services of individual employees so long as SBU management can demonstrate that the opportunity it is pursuing yields the highest possible payoff on the investment in their skills. This message is further underlined if each year in the strategic planning or budgeting process, unit managers must justify their hold on the people who carry the company's core competencies.

Also, reward systems that focus only on product-line results and career paths that seldom cross SBU boundaries engender patterns of behavior among unit managers that are destructively competitive. At NEC, divisional managers come together to identify next-generation competencies. Together they decide how much investment needs to be made to build up each future competency and the contribution in capital and staff support that each division will need to make. There is also a sense of equitable exchange. One division may make a disproportionate contribution or may benefit less from the progress made, but such short-term inequalities will balance out over the long term.

Incidentally, the positive contribution of the SBU manager should be made visible across the company. An SBU manager is unlikely to surrender key people if only the other business (or the general manager of that business who may be a competitor for promotion) is going to benefit from the redeployment. Cooperative SBU managers should be celebrated as team players. Where priorities are clear, transfers are less likely to be seen as idiosyncratic and politically motivated.

Transfers for the sake of building core competence must be recorded and appreciated in the corporate memory. It is reasonable to expect a business that has surrendered core skills on behalf of corporate opportunities in other areas to lose, for a time, some of its competitiveness. If these losses in performance bring immediate censure, SBUs will be unlikely to assent to skills transfers next time.

Finally, there are ways to wean key employees off the idea that they belong in perpetuity to any particular business. Early in their careers, people may be exposed to a variety of businesses through a carefully planned rotation program.

Competence carriers should be regularly brought together from across the corporation to trade notes and ideas. The goal is to build a strong feeling of community among these people. To a great extent, their loyalty should be to the integrity of the core competence area they represent and not just to particular businesses. In traveling regularly, talking frequently to customers, and meeting with peers, competence carriers may be encouraged to discover new market opportunities.

Core competencies are the wellspring of new business development. They should constitute the focus for strategy at the corporate level. Managers have to win manufacturing leadership in core products and capture global share through brand-building programs aimed at exploiting economies of scope. Only if the company is conceived of as a hierarchy of core competencies, core products, and market-focused business units will it be fit to fight.

Nor can top management be just another layer of accounting consolidation, which it often is in a regime of radical decentralization. Top management must add value by enunciating the strategic architecture that guides the competence acquisition process. We believe an obsession with competence building will characterize the global winners of the 1990s. With the decade underway, the time for rethinking the concept of the corporation is already overdue.

■ ADDING VALUE FROM CORPORATE HEADQUARTERS[†]

By Andrew Campbell and Michael Goold

Introduction

The key issue for the chief executive of a diversified company is: Do the separate businesses gain from membership of the whole? Is the whole greater than the sum of the parts? The test is whether business units perform better as part of the corporate portfolio than they would as independent companies. This is the harsh criterion that all central management groups should apply in rating their own effectiveness.

The same question also arises in comparing different companies. Often the issue is not only whether a business would be better off as part of a group than as an independent company, but also whether the business would prosper more in one group than another. In acquisition battles, such as the fight between Hanson Trust and United Biscuit for control of Imperial, the option of continued independence was ruled out early, and the outcome turned on judgements about which contender would make the better parent organisation.

For the last four years we have been studying the way that the corporate centre adds value to the business units. By looking at sixteen major British companies we have defined three broad categories of management style used by the centre—Strategic

[†]**Source:** This article was originally published in the *London Business School Journal* (Summer 1988). Reprinted by permission of the authors.

Planning (such as BP and UB), Strategic Control (such as Courtaulds and ICI), and Financial Control (such as Hanson and BTR).

We have found that the different styles cause value to be added in different ways. None of them proved to be inherently best. Each has strengths and weaknesses. Each adds value in a specific way and each can subtract value (i.e., make the business unit perform less well than it would as an independent company). Corporate managers faced with the problem of maximising their effectiveness need to understand the strengths and weaknesses of the different styles and how to get the best from the style they have chosen.

This article summarises the results of our research, explaining the differences between the styles and the different ways in which they add value to the portfolio of business units.

Why Different Styles Exist

We identified important tensions or trade-offs confronting corporate level managers. For example, the chief executive would like to help the business units by giving strong leadership from the centre, providing clear direction about which products and markets are suitable and how the units should compete. On the other hand, the chief executive would like to release the energies and entrepreneurial commitment of managers lower down by giving them wide autonomy to run their businesses as they please and to feel a sense of ownership. These two objectives are in conflict. The centre cannot simultaneously provide strong leadership and give autonomy to the business units. Hence we labeled it a tension facing corporate-level managers. The chief executive needs to decide where, on the scale of leadership versus autonomy, he wants to be positioned.

We identified four other similar tensions—coordination and cooperation versus clear responsibilities and accountability; thorough analysis and planning versus entrepreneurial speed of response; long-term strategic targets versus short-term financial targets; and flexible strategies (i.e., strategies that can be changed quickly to meet competitor moves) versus tight controls.

The three different styles (strategic planning, strategic control, and financial control) exist because it is possible to develop three different positionings against these tensions (see exhibit 6-1, "The Styles Matrix"). Hence, managers in the headquarters of Hanson Trust believe in autonomy for business units, clear accountability, entrepreneurial decision making, short-term financial targets, and tight controls. Alternatively, managers at the centre of BP believe in leadership from the centre, coordination and cooperation between different business units, thorough analysis and review of major decisions, long-term strategic targets, and flexible strategies. Exhibit 6-2 summarises the choices underlying each of the styles and compares these to the style used by the capital markets in relation to an independent company.

We also defined eight mechanisms through which the centre can add value to its business units. We recognised that the centre can only add value if it successfully influences (for the better) the strategies and actions of managers in the business units. The eight mechanisms are tools that the centre uses to influence strategy and actions. They are the organisation structure; the planning process; the use of themes, thrusts, or suggestions to guide managers; the degree to which the centre managers overlap between units; the resource allocation decisions taken by the centre; the objectives set

EXHIBIT 6-1
The Styles Matrix

The strategic planning, strategic control, and financial control styles form part of a continuum of ways headquarters can influence business units. The continuum has two dimensions: (1) planning influence, which expresses the degree to which strategy is centralised, and (2) control influence, which shows the importance companies attach to short-term financial targets.

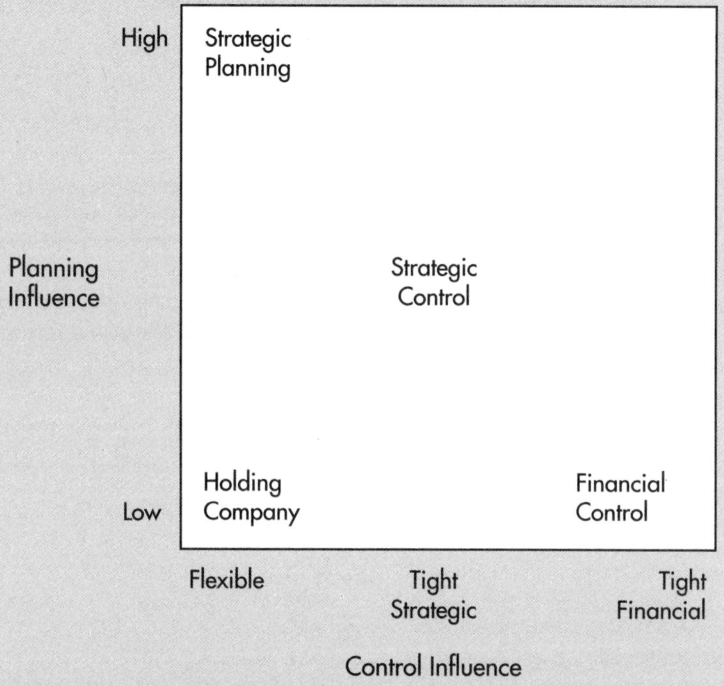

High	Strategic Planning	
Planning Influence	Strategic Control	
Low	Holding Company	Financial Control
	Flexible	Tight Strategic / Tight Financial

Control Influence

Companies that fall in the bottom left-hand corner can be labeled holding companies. In such organisations the centre has little influence over the subsidiaries. Our research found that successful companies moved away from the holding company style to one of the three alternatives.

The top right-hand corner of the matrix is blank because this style appears to be infeasible. Some companies in our research tried to combine a high degree of planning influence with tight short-term controls, but they have moved away from it. Either business unit managers became demotivated by a seemingly oppressive corporate centre, or headquarters failed to maintain sufficient objectivity to keep the controls tight.

for each unit; the closeness of monitoring against objectives; and the types of incentives and sanctions applied to managers who meet or fail to meet targets.

Each style uses these mechanisms in different ways and to different degrees, depending on the choices that have been made on the tensions. For example, a company that prizes coordination and cooperation, such as BP, has a matrix organization structure in its oil business that forces managers to coordinate over the big decisions. A company that believes in strong leadership, such as the Lex Service Group, guides business unit managers by often repeated themes, by defining the main thrusts of the organisation, and by making frequent suggestions or instructions. The choices managers make about the tensions affect the way the company uses these mechanisms.

EXHIBIT 6-2
Tensions in Corporate Level
Management

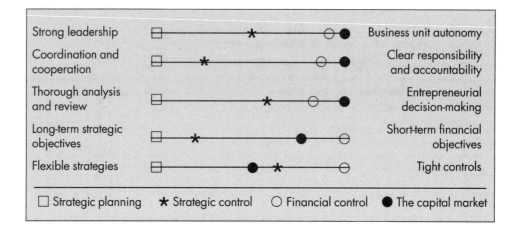

In this reading, we summarise the key features of each style against the eight mechanisms and we show how the features can both add value to the subsidiaries as well as subtract value. Some of the negative consequences of a style are intrinsic and unavoidable; others are pitfalls that can be avoided. While we recognise that no style is superior for all situations, we believe that managers who understand the style they are using will be able to avoid the pitfalls and make sure that the net contribution of the centre is positive rather than negative.

Strategic Planning

The strategic planning style is characterised by an emphasis on strategy, on long-term objectives, and on a cooperative, flexible management approach. Exhibit 6-3 summarises the key features.

The complex and overlapping organisational structures of these companies ensure that a variety of views on strategy will be expressed. They also allow the centre to inject its ideas into the formulation of strategy. So they bring the judgement and experience of a cross-section of senior managers into play to help define the best ways forward. This allows a wider discussion of issues and a more comprehensive search for new strategy options than would occur in an independent company. Coordinating committees and devices also allow strategies to be drawn together across a variety of businesses (or countries), to achieve benefits of synergy and integration that would not be available to separate companies. And strong staff groups at the centre allow economies of scope in the provision of central services.

EXHIBIT 6-3
Strategic Planning:
Key Features

Organisational structure and overlap management	— Multiple perspectives, matrix structures, strong staffs, coordination mechanisms
Planning process	— Extensive, strategic
Themes, thrusts, and suggestions	— Strong central leadership
Resource allocation	— Part of long-term strategy
Objectives	— Longer-term, strategic
Monitoring and controls	— Flexible

The drawback of this structure is that business managers have less clear-cut individual responsibilities, less control over their own destinies. The emphasis on cooperation between businesses and across levels, and the need to coordinate strategies, means that they have less unilateral authority to take decisions for their businesses that they personally feel are right. The inevitable price of multiple viewpoints and synergy is some loss of autonomy. This, in turn, can reduce motivation, unless a sense of shared purpose compensates for the loss of individual responsibility.

The *extensive planning processes* of the Strategic Planning companies are an important means for getting different views aired. They are a test of business unit thinking, and can help to prevent businesses from falling into outdated or inappropriate strategy patterns. By challenging business managers' "habits of mind," they perform a useful function that the independent company lacks. The questions posed by the central management in a Strategic Planning company should be much more informed, much more "strategic" than is possible for the outside investors and bankers to whom the independent company reports. This is a prime value of the planning processes of the Strategic Planning company. They also constitute a vehicle for the exercise of central leadership in strategic decision making, and a means by which the centre can learn more about the businesses. But extensive planning processes cannot avoid constraining business managers. As one line manager explained: "The decision-making and planning process in our company is very professional. We are very open about discussing things. We chew over important decisions at great length. My boss will get involved and his boss will join in the thinking. It's all very constructive and I am sure we make a better decision as a result. But somehow after all the discussion, I don't feel it's my decision anymore."

The need to communicate and justify plans to the centre inhibits freedom of action, slows down the decision process, and takes some ownership from lower levels of management. The independent company can be swifter and more entrepreneurial.

Furthermore, Strategic Planning processes are often cumbersome and confusing rather than probing and insightful. At their worst, they degenerate into rigid, bureaucratic exercises. The drawbacks of bureaucracy in planning may not be intrinsic to the Strategic Planning style, but it is an occupational hazard—a potential pitfall.

By providing *strong central leadership* through themes, thrusts, and suggestions, the Strategic Planning companies are able to embark on bolder, more aggressive strategies than would otherwise emerge. Central sponsorship can enlarge the ambitions of business management, ensure that resources are available to support investments, and help to overcome risk aversion. We have given examples in each Strategic Planning company of the sorts of business-building strategies that result, often looking toward the building of long-term advantage in major international businesses. It is doubtful whether these strategies would have been adopted by independent companies without a supportive and well-resourced parent in the background to underwrite the effort. It is in this context that mission statements and broad policies can be valuable, by defining what will receive priority from the centre.

The downside of strong leadership is equally clear. Close involvement by the centre in strategy development inevitably reduces both the objectivity of the centre in reviewing strategy, and the sense of personal "ownership" at the business level. This is the strong leadership-business autonomy tension .

Moreover, strong leadership can lead to a number of pitfalls. It can be seen as autocratic or ill-informed interference that overrules business-level ideas; bold strategies can become risky and overoptimistic; sound opportunities in noncore businesses may be turned down because they do not fit with the grand design. These pitfalls are frequently associated with the Strategic Planning style, although the best exponents of the style are able to avoid them. In companies such as BP, strong leadership blends into a cooperative attempt to work together for a common aim, thereby generating a sense of shared purpose and commitment that goes far to offset the disadvantages we have listed.

Resource allocation and objective setting in the Strategic Planning companies are aimed at the long-term development of the business. The centre acts as a sort of buffer to the capital market, protecting the business units from the need to satisfy the shorter-term performance criteria applied by the outside investor. This allows business managers to concentrate on building the core businesses, rather than trimming their sails with a view to meeting half-yearly earnings targets. It also means that they can make major acquisitions to support existing activities, or to build new ones, without an expectation that the payoff to such moves will come immediately. Clear priority can be given to long-term objectives.

There are a number of businesses in the Strategic Planning companies that have benefited from this strategic, long-term resource allocation process. Without it, BOC would be a weaker force in the worldwide gases business; Lex would not have built up its electronic component distribution business, BP would not have achieved its successes in oil and gas exploration. But there are others that, it can be argued, might have reacted more quickly to adversity, or avoided risky and unpromising investments, if they *had* been exposed to the disciplines of the external capital market.

Several managers in Strategic Planning companies made us aware of the dangers of too much emphasis on strategy and the long term. "The pressure on the long term took our eye off the short-term issues. They [corporate] and we undervalued the short-term profit impact of what we were doing," said one manager. "Too much strategy and not enough graft," was the conclusion of another.

We have also pointed out the difficulty in defining clear, objective, and measurable goals for monitoring long-term performance. This means that long-term performance measures open up the possibility of excuses. As Dick Giordano of BOC put it: "This is probably one of the most difficult challenges. How do you have milestones that measure strategic progress without allowing excuse making from business management?" But to point to these shortcomings is only to underline the tension that exists between giving priority to profits now or profits later, to short-term controls or long-term objectives. All Strategic Planning companies must accept some sacrifice in the clarity and enforceability of short-term objectives in order to allow for the allocation of resources to long-term aims.

Linked to this tension we noted that Strategic Planning companies are also prone to undue optimism about the future or to personal incentives that are not linked to strategies. Lacking both market disciplines and clear internal targets, the atmosphere can become too cosy. As one divisional manager put it: "As part of the corporate entity, we have this shield and blanket around us to protect us." This can mean that flexibility becomes tolerance, and tolerance becomes looseness. Motivation to perform is then at risk. The fact that the Strategic Planning companies have been relatively inactive in divestments, closures, and portfolio rationalisations, and that some have overextended themselves through rapid growth, is all evidence of this.

Furthermore, replacing the verdict of the stock market with subjective corporate assessments of strategic progress may not be an unmitigated gain. If second guessing what will impress the centre becomes the major goal, this can be even less conducive to strategic thinking than the short-term financial pressures of the City. It is in these circumstances that corporate "politics" flourish, with decisions taken to reinforce personal positions in the hierarchy, rather than to improve the strategies of the business.

TABLE 6-2
The Strategic Planning Style

Key Features	Added Value	Intrinsic Subtracted Value	Common But Avoidable Pitfalls
Complex, coordinated structure	Wider discussion of issues Synergy Central services	Less individual responsibility and authority	Can reduce motivation
Extensive, strategic planning process	More thorough search for best strategies	Less freedom of action Slower decisions	Can be cumbersome, confusing, bureaucratic
Strong central leadership	Bolder strategies Shared purpose and commitment	Less "ownership" by business Less objectivity by centre	Can become interference Can lead to risky and overambitious strategies
Long-term criteria	Building core businesses "Buffer" to capital market	Slower reactions to adversity Less clear targets	Can lead to overoptimism, "lip service"
Flexible controls	More tenacious pursuit of long-term goals More innovative, responsive strategies	Subjective assessments Less accountability	Can lead to politics

Finally, the *flexible control system* in the Strategic Planning companies adds value. By accepting that precise, short-term targets may have to be compromised in order to stay on track to build a business, it encourages a more tenacious pursuit of long-term goals. Furthermore, it is more tolerant of innovative strategies that carry with them the risk of failure, and of strategies that evolve continuously to meet the needs of rapidly changing markets. The centre in the Strategic Planning company is more sympathetic than the capital market to the manager who is struggling to create a major new business in a highly competitive and uncertain world.

Flexible controls, however, can never provide clear and objective standards of performance. Hence it is harder for both the centre and the business manager to know whether results are "on target." An element of judgement enters into the assessment of performance, and increases the scope for discretion. The price of flexibility is ambiguous performance measures and a reduced sense of personal accountability.

Table 6-2 summarises the key features and the added and subtracted value of the Strategic Planning style. We have divided the negative features of the style between those that are intrinsic and those that represent pitfalls that can be avoided. With skilful management the negative features of the style can be minimised or avoided by:

- sensitive, flexible, and selective planning processes;
- leadership;
- well-informed central management;
- shared purpose and commitment;
- avoiding overoptimism;
- incentives aligned with strategy;
- strenuous efforts to identify, measure, and act on strategic milestones.

But the style will always give less priority to individual accountability, responsibility, and incentives, and to short-term measures of performance.

Financial Control

At the opposite extreme to Strategic Planning lies Financial Control. Exhibit 6-4 summarises the key features of this style.

The *organisational structures* of the Financial Control companies stress *multiple, separate profit centres*, each with independent responsibilities. As far as possible, these structures replicate, for the profit centres, the circumstances of independent companies. The profit centres are set up to overlap as little as possible, and no attempt is made by the centre to coordinate between them. The profit centre manager is largely free to run his own show without interference from other parts of the company. "We believe in the importance of the individual line manager in achieving success for his business and for the group as a whole. The management system has been devised to give maximum responsibility to the line management," said Martin Taylor of Hanson Trust. There are advantages in the simplicity and clarity of this structure. In particular it gives early general management responsibility, thereby developing the skills needed for the long-term success of the company.

But the structure is less ambitious than that of the Strategic Planning companies. It adds no value in comparison to the independent company situation; but at least it avoids the negatives that are also associated with the more complex structures of Strategic Planning companies.

The *planning process* in the Financial Control companies *concentrates on budgets.* The emphasis is on the short term, and on agreeing targets rather than on the means by which they are going to be achieved. As with Strategic Planning companies, the centre probes the plans of business managers, but the nature of the questioning is very different. For Financial Control companies the primary value arises from the pressure it creates for "high-wire" standards of profitability and growth in profits, not from probing underlying strategic logic. As Lionel Stammers of BTR put it: "Many managers do not know what they can achieve until you ask them." The Financial Control companies add value by asking for performance that is more demanding than that insisted on by stockholders or bankers, and they exert pressure for performance much more continuously. An independent company can produce unexciting results for long periods, in some cases for many years, before market pressure will cause a change in management. But in Financial Control companies controls are tight.

As a by-product of the budgeting process, managers may also have to think again about the validity of the strategies they are following. If they are unable to satisfy corporate requirements, they may be forced to consider changes of direction. But the centre will not typically question strategies directly, or expect to make much contribution to the definition of new and preferable strategy options. And the emphasis is on next year's results, "the road ahead," not the long term. The focus on

EXHIBIT 6-4
Financial Control:
Key Features

Organisational structure and overlap management	— Clearly separate, profit centre responsibilities
Planning process	— Budgets
Themes, thrusts, and suggestions	— Business autonomy stressed
Resource allocation	— Project-based; short payback criteria
Objectives	— Shorter-term, financial
Monitoring and controls	— Very tight

results not strategies leaves managers more free to make their own decisions, provided they turn in the required performance. Furthermore, the planning process can be simpler and therefore less prone to "bureaucracy" than in Strategic Planning companies.

The major drawback of the planning process is that it cannot claim to add much value to the business manager in probing and thinking through his strategy options. Indeed, the short-term results orientation may distract him from tackling long-term issues. If the stock market is felt to create an unduly short-term orientation, the Financial Control style serves to reinforce this bias. We noted, for example, that a number of the subsidiaries of Financial Control companies are losing market share. Their managers explained that they are retreating from less profitable sections of the market, and that market share is not a useful objective. As one BTR manager put it: "We don't pride ourselves on market share. In fact, we don't like to refer to market share at all." It is this focus on the short term that causes critics of Financial Control companies to claim that they are gradually harvesting their competitive positions. Taken to extremes the style can encourage managers to milk their businesses by cutting back too far on investment.

Although the centre may make occasional suggestions, *business autonomy* is preserved. In the Financial Control companies by insisting that the final decision rests with business management and by avoiding any broad, top-down corporate themes, missions, or thrusts. This philosophy attempts to replicate the freedom of the independent company, and hence can obviously add little value when compared to it. If, however, constructive suggestions are made, but not imposed, the business manager may gain something that is denied to his fully independent counterpart. Nevertheless, it is clear that Financial Control does not attempt to add as much value in this respect as Strategic Planning; equally, however, it runs fewer risks of subtracting value.

The resource allocation process in the Financial Control companies adopts *objectives and criteria similar to the capital market.* There is no attempt to buffer the businesses from requirements for short-term profit. Rather, the Financial Control style sees itself as applying capital market criteria but in a much more thoroughgoing and efficient manner. With detailed information on each business and the ability to discriminate between them in resource allocation, the centre can ensure that funds flow only to those businesses whose proposals meet corporate criteria, and whose track records give confidence in their ability to deliver. The system reviews each investment on its merits, rather than as part of a long-term business strategy. It adds value by insisting that proposals will only be funded if they project high returns and fast paybacks, and if business managers appear committed to achieving their forecasts and have a track record of doing so in the past. By exposing all individual investments to this test, it goes much further than the capital markets in applying tough standards. The centre, however, does not pretend to have a detailed knowledge of each business's products and markets, or to be able to criticise, shape, and add value to the strategies behind the investment proposals .

The centre is more directly active in acquisitions and divestments. The search is for acquisition candidates whose assets are underperforming. Value is added to these acquisitions by increasing their profitability through the application of Financial Control disciplines. Conversely, divestments are made of businesses that do not respond to these criteria.

The clear emphasis on *short-term* profit *objectives* in resource allocation and acquisitions simplifies the management task. But it can also result in missed opportunities. We were told of a number of opportunities that had been considered and rejected because of the risk or the length of payback of the investment. Although it is not clear that the opportunities rejected would have resulted in substantial profit growth, it is probable that many more of these opportunities would have been taken up by Strategic Planning (or even Strategic Control) companies. One example is the market for standard gate arrays. Both GEC and Ferranti had the opportunity to enter the fast-growing MOS-technology segment at the early stages. Both rejected the opportunity. Ferranti chose to stay with its proven bipolar technology and GEC, after examining options, passed up the opportunity altogether. The bold strategies they rejected were pursued by LSI Logic, which now has a leading position worldwide. The short-term focus does preclude longer-term, more speculative investments. The tension remains and means that the Financial Control style will always create problems in businesses where long timescales are needed.

The main strength of the Financial Control style, however, is in the *tight controls* it imposes. Not only are budgets stretching; not only do investments demand short paybacks; but also the monitoring of results achieved and the feedback and follow through from the centre create strong incentives to deliver. The knowledge that there will be a speedy reaction to under- (or over-) achievement of monthly targets does create more motivation, more pressure for performance than is brought to bear on the managing director of an independent company. The simplicity of the criteria for judging performance also makes it easier for line managers to know where to focus their attention, and makes it perfectly clear who is doing a good job and succeeding, and who is not. Indeed, the knowledge that demanding standards have been set and can be seen to have been met is one of the prime motivating factors for successful managers in the Financial Control companies. A BTR division head commented that he would be willing to forgo £10,000 in salary in exchange for the psychological satisfaction of knowing he was going to be able to deliver on his budgeted objectives.

Those who do meet their objectives can be confident that they have earned the respect of the centre, and grow in self-confidence themselves. This has two benefits. It makes for a more open discussion of business issues with the centre, since the line manager can rely on his results rather than his words to impress the centre; and it creates a "winner's" psychology among business managers which makes them feel more capable of overcoming obstacles and pushing on to further peaks of performance.

But the tight control process also has its downside. It can stifle creativity, snuff out experimentation, and eliminate the entrepreneurial skunk works activities. There is less flexibility to respond to opportunities. The point was made by a Hanson Trust group chairman in this way: "Our business chief executives tend to be quite conservative in assessing the payback of potential investments. In order to preserve credibility with Hanson Trust, they will typically only promise what they are certain they can deliver. The chief executive knows he will be hung on it, and is therefore cautious rather than overambitious." At its worst, tight control can mean that everything is sacrificed to meeting specified control objectives at whatever cost to the underlying health of the business. The system can become a straitjacket, not a source of added value.

Table 6-3 summarises the key features and the added and subtracted value of the Financial Control style, again distinguishing between intrinsic problems and avoidable pitfalls. The negative features of this style can be minimised by:

- targets that require year-on-year *growth* in profits;
- leaving business managers in post long enough that they have to live with the consequences of the strategies they adopt;
- informed central managers who will offer constructive advice and suggestions but without imposing their views;

TABLE 6-3
The Financial Control Style

Key Features	Added Value	Intrinsic Subtracted Value	Common But Avoidable Pitfalls
Separate profit centres	Simplifies task Early general management responsibility	No coordination synergy	
Budgetary planning	Higher standards Challenges strategies that won't deliver Avoids "potholes"	Distracts from strategic issues	Can encourage milking the business
Business autonomy	Advice, not instructions	No cooperation, no "help" for businesses	
Short-term criteria	Clearer criteria "Efficient" internal capital market	Missed opportunities "Control games"	
Tight controls	Faster reaction More motivation "Winner's" psychology	Less flexibility and creativity	Can become a straitjacket

- willingness to question and override control objectives if it is clear that they will damage the health of the business;
- a winner's psychology to provide energy to maintain growth momentum; and
- acceptance that, in some businesses, the Financial Control style may be inappropriate.

But the style cannot avoid problems in businesses where long-term, coordinated strategies are needed, and cannot claim to provide much constructive help to business managers in the search for optimum strategies.

Strategic Control

Exhibit 6-5 shows the key features of the Strategic Control style, again expressed in terms that relate to our discussion of tensions. Strategic Control is a blend of the features found in Strategic Planning and Financial Control.

By *structuring themselves around individual profit centre businesses that are grouped into divisions*, Strategic Control companies claim to achieve the motivational benefits of decentralisation, while allowing important business overlaps to be managed at the business level. There is some added value from divisional coordination, but a minimum of interference with business managers.

This view may justify the divisional structure. But even if the divisional level is able to achieve synergies between businesses that would not be achieved independently, it is less clear how the corporate level adds value, structurally, to the divisions. Put simply, what would the divisions lose if they were set up as independent companies? As in Financial Control companies, the decentralised structure leaves little room for the centre to orchestrate the several businesses in the portfolio.

EXHIBIT 6-5
Strategic Control:
Key Features

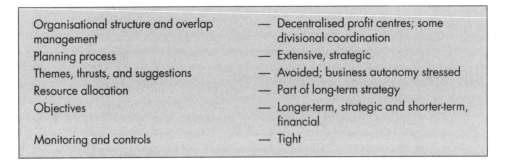

Organisational structure and overlap management	— Decentralised profit centres; some divisional coordination
Planning process	— Extensive, strategic
Themes, thrusts, and suggestions	— Avoided; business autonomy stressed
Resource allocation	— Part of long-term strategy
Objectives	— Longer-term, strategic and shorter-term, financial
Monitoring and controls	— Tight

Strategic Control companies argue that they make a prime contribution to divisional thinking via the quality controls in the *strategic review process.* The disciplines provide a continuing challenge that sharpens the thinking in the divisions and businesses. By its probing, the centre raises minimum standards of thinking and analysis, and prevents "habits of mind" from forming. The intention is similar to that of the Strategic Planning companies, although Strategic Control companies limit themselves to a questioning role, and do not propose their own views from the centre.

Although we have found some evidence to support these contentions, our research suggests that in reality the challenge to divisional thinking is not always helpful. Extensive planning processes run into the same problem of acting as a constraint that we described for the Strategic Planning companies. Moreover, bureaucracy grows quickly in Strategic Control companies because the centre is that much more distant from the businesses. One manager explained that the planning reviews in his company were a "whole series of rakings over, all of them too shallow." This means either that the centre may fail to be well-enough informed to ask useful questions, or that any benefits may be more than offset by the time-consuming and costly processes that they involve. "Net" added value is not always delivered by corporate planning processes. Only if these processes are sensitively designed and administered, and if the businesses in the portfolio are likely to respond to a second view can value be added by the centre.

Strategic Control companies generally *avoid major suggestions and initiatives* and are not active in coordinating between divisions or businesses. The emphasis on *business autonomy* is well caught by the chairman of a Vickers division, who said: "In giving freedom, it's a bit nerve-racking at times because you feel you're not in control, not in charge. But the result is that they take more initiative and they perform better. And they feel responsible for their actions whereas if you at the centre always ask questions, always try and monitor things very, very carefully, you get a reaction that they're not really responsible for the decisions, that you're really controlling things, and so if it goes wrong, it's as much your fault as it is theirs."

Strategic Control companies recognise that direction from the centre can subtract value. They stress the responsibility and independence of the business manager. However, this means that they are unlikely to add value by steering the development of strategy. Where ad hoc interventions do take place, our research would indicate that value was subtracted at least as often as it was added.

It is in *a resource allocation process that balances long- and short-term goals* that many Strategic Control companies add the most value. The centre provides access to a pool of resources, which can be made available for investment in long-term, large or risky projects. These projects might be turned down by outside investors, who have little knowledge of the business and who are often short-term or fashion driven in their attitudes, focusing more on past results than future prospects, and failing to assess technically complex or strategically innovative ideas. As Sir John Clark of Plessey argued: "City pressures make life difficult if you're trying to balance short-term profit pressure and the requirements of the business in terms of competitive advantage." Many of the business and divisional managements also see real value in this access to funding. "Probably the greatest benefit of being part of ICI is that they were willing to fund us through seventeen years of losses in getting the business going" (chairman, ICI Pharmaceuticals). "We were able to take a major step forwards in investment in new production capacity that would have been beyond us as an independent company" (chief executive, Howson Algraphy division, Vickers).

The downside of the long-term investment attitude is, of course, the same as in the Strategic Planning companies: a danger of undervaluing the importance of next year's profits. But the Strategic Control companies attempt to defend against this problem by balancing long-term objectives with short-term profit pressures. The ability of companies such as Courtaulds, ICI and Vickers to cut back drastically in some areas of their portfolios, while preserving growth momentum elsewhere, is evidence of their ability to make trade-offs of this sort. Indeed major corporate resource allocation decisions in the Strategic Control companies have concentrated at least as much on portfolio rationalisation and profitability improvement as on long-term investment.

In practice, however, there are numerous difficulties in achieving the right balance of objectives. Assessing more speculative, longer-term investments is hard. If the centre lacks close familiarity with the business, it may be forced to rely on the credibility of the sponsoring management team together with formal financial evaluations—much the same criteria as used by the outside investor. Where long-term projects *are* backed by the centre, the reason may be personal commitments to a business rather than clear-sighted strategic thinking. We encountered several examples of long-term and continued support for a business by the centre that cost the company far more than a hard-nosed and early closure would have done.

Reliance on corporate funds for investment can also be a source of problems since capital scarcity can cut out investments that might have been funded by the outside market. During the years of financial crisis, Vickers was unable to finance good proposals that were coming forward and Courtaulds was short of funds for investments even in growth areas. During this period Courtaulds applied across-the-board cash targets to all its businesses regardless of previous success or failure. Now the company has set up its major business groups with capital structures to resemble as closely as possible the conditions of the publicly quoted parent company. It believes that the groups should be better placed to identify the consequences of their investment plans to their own balance sheets and take proper action in a more differentiated fashion to control the financing consequences of their business performance. This is a long way from viewing the value of corporate management mainly in terms of its ability to allocate resources.

Lastly, although portfolio rationalisation has improved profitability ratios for the Strategic Control companies, it is less clear that divisions of these companies would have moved any less speedily to take corrective measures had they been independently set up. Strategic Control companies may move more decisively on rationalisation and exit decisions than Strategic Planning or Holding companies, but the discipline of the outside capital markets would in some cases have been more pressing than that provided by corporate management.

The resource allocation process in the Strategic Control companies therefore attempts to combine the "buffer" function of the Strategic Planning companies and the "efficiency" function of the Financial Control companies. In some respects this achieves the best of both worlds; but in others it encounters the disadvantages that come from the lack of a clear commitment to either. This follows from the basic tension between short- and long-term goals. Furthermore, uninformed long-term investments, naive portfolio pruning, and partisan preference for particular businesses are all potential—if avoidable—pitfalls for Strategic Control.

It is therefore only if the centre is genuinely better informed, closer to the businesses, and as objective as the outside investor that value is likely to be added.

Detailed monitoring and reporting allow the centre to pinpoint shortcomings more precisely; and incentives and *tight strategic and financial controls* create personal motivation in a much less blunt fashion than the outside capital market, where takeovers or palace revolutions are effectively the only sanctions against nonperforming management. Provided, therefore, that the control objectives are conducive to the prosperity of the business, Strategic Control adds value.

Our research suggests, however, that the definition of strategic control objectives is fraught with difficulty. First, the objectives that Strategic Control companies establish do not always embody the strategies they have agreed. Financial controls can crowd out strategic objectives, thereby damaging the long-term interests of the business. Or vague strategic goals can become an excuse for nonperformance. This means that the control process becomes bogged down in arguments over trade-offs, and the intention to create tight control languishes. Second, as in Financial Control, tight controls can subtract values through causing inflexibility and risk aversion in strategies.

There is an intrinsic conflict between encouraging long-term, creative, strategic thinking, and imposing tight, short-term controls. Two quotes from divisional managing directors in Strategic Control companies are relevant. The first illustrates the tension between strategy and control: "The centre is pressing us to grow. But it is unwilling to accept the negative impact on profitability this may entail." The second illustrates the uneasy balance between strategic and financial control, and the difficulty of being poised between them: "I asked the chief executive when I was appointed whether the company was a financial conglomerate or an industrial company. After four years the question still seems relevant, and the answer is always: 'Ask me again in six months' time.'" This remark found echoes in almost all the Strategic Control companies.

Making the controls supportive of flexible and innovative strategies is not easy. It can even be that the stock market, whose control process is less precise and rigorous, allows more latitude for business building than strategic controls that are poorly defined and insensitively applied.

Table 6-4 summarises the key features and the added and subtracted value of the Strategic Control style. The negative features of the style can be minimised by:

- flexible planning processes;
- willingness by the centre to spend the time necessary to get close to business unit strategies, to be knowledgeable about their competitive environments, and to discuss issues thoroughly;
- avoiding overoptimism;
- personal incentives aligned with strategy; and
- strenuous efforts to identify, measure, and act on strategic milestones.

But the style will always encounter difficulties in setting priorities between different sorts of objectives, and in encouraging business initiatives, while at the same time providing a check on strategic thinking from the centre.

TABLE 6-4
The Strategic Control Style

Key Features	Added Value	Intrinsic Subtracted Value	Common But Avoidable Pitfalls
Decentralised profit centres; divisional coordination	Little by centre	No central coordination	
Extensive, strategic planning process	Raises minimum standards of thinking and analysis Challenges habits of mind	Constraining	Can be bureaucratic; add cost, but little value
Business autonomy			Gratuitous suggestions
Long- and short-term criteria	Acceptance of longer-term investments Balanced objectives	Ambiguous objectives	Tolerance for low performers Capital rationing Uninformed investments and divestments
Tight controls	More motivation to perform	Risk aversion Subjective balancing of objectives	"Politics" "Lip service"

Summary

The best corporate parents have an understanding of the issues, trade-offs, and tension we have raised in this article. Companies like Tarmac and ICI have clearly chosen the style they want to use at the centre. They recognise the strengths and weaknesses of the style and work hard to get the most added value from the strengths and to minimise the negative consequences of the style's weak points. They are also articulate on the subject, explaining the management processes they use in terms of the benefits given to units in the portfolio.

It is common for managers in subsidiaries to complain about the interference and overhead burden of headquarters. Most corporate level managers think that this is to be expected. "Well of course they complain about the paperwork and fight the overhead allocations," said one planning manager, "I would do the same if I was in their shoes."

Yet we have found companies where the units praise the centre; where managers value the review meetings and budget planning meetings and where there is an atmosphere of trust and cooperation between layers in the hierarchy. This should be an objective of all companies. By understanding the differences between styles and the strengths and weaknesses of each style, we believe managers will be better able to create the trust and cooperation that some companies have achieved.

References and Suggested Readings

Andrews, K. R., Director's Responsibility for Corporate Strategy, *Harvard Business Review*, November/December 1980, pp. 30–42.

Bower, J. L., *Managing the Resource Allocation Process: A Study of Corporate Planning and Investment*, Irwin, Homewood, IL, 1972.

Buzzell, R. D., Is Vertical Integration Profitable? *Harvard Business Review*, January/February 1983, pp. 92–102.

Campbell, A., and M. Goold, Adding Value from Corporate Headquarters, *London Business School Journal*, Summer 1988, pp. 219–240.

Campbell, A., and K. Luchs, *Strategic Synergy*, Butterworth Heinemann, London, 1992.

Chakravarthy, B., and P. Lorange, *Managing the Strategy Process: A Framework for a Multibusiness Firm*, Prentice Hall, Englewood Cliffs, NJ, 1991.

Chatterjee, S., and B. Wernerfelt, The Link between Resources and Type of Diversification: Theory and Evidence, *Strategic Management Journal*, January 1991, pp. 33–48.

Demb, A., and F. Neubauer, How Can the Board Add Value? *European Management Journal*, June 1990, pp. 156–160.

Goold, M., and A. Campbell, *Strategies and Styles: The Role of the Centre in Managing Diverse Corporations*, Basil Blackwell, Oxford, 1987.

Goold, M., and A. Campbell, Many Best Ways to Make Strategy, *Harvard Business Review*, November/December 1987, pp. 70–76.

Goold, M., and A. Campbell, Brief Case: From Corporate Strategy to Parenting Advantage, *Long Range Planning*, February 1991, pp. 115–117.

Goold, M., Campbell, A., and K. Luchs, Strategies and Styles Revisited: Strategic Planning and Financial Control, *Long Range Planning*, October 1993, pp. 49–60.

Goold, M., and K. Luchs, Why Diversify? Four Decades of Management Thinking, *Academy of Management Executive*, August 1993, pp. 7–25.

Harrigan, K. R., *Strategies for Vertical Integration*, D. C. Heath, Lexington, MA, 1983.

Harrigan, K. R., Vertical Integration and Corporate Strategy, *Academy of Management Journal*, June 1985, pp. 397–425.

Haspeslagh, P., Portfolio Planning: Uses and Limits, *Harvard Business Review*, January/February 1982, pp. 58–73.

Haspeslagh, P., and D. Jemison, *Managing Acquisitions: Creating Value through Corporate Renewal*, Free Press, New York, 1991.

Hedley, B., Strategy and the Business Portfolio, *Long Range Planning*, February 1977, pp. 9–15.

Henderson, B. D., *On Corporate Strategy*, Abt Books, Cambridge, MA, 1979.

Mahoney, J. T., and J. R. Pandian, The Resource-Based View within the Conversation of Strategic Management, *Strategic Management Journal*, June 1992, pp. 363–380.

Montgomery, C. A., and B. Wernerfelt, Diversification, Ricardian Rents, and Tobin's Q, *Rand Journal of Economics*, Winter 1988, pp. 623–632.

Porter, M. E., From Competitive Advantage to Corporate Strategy, *Harvard Business Review,* May/June 1987, pp. 43–59.

Prahalad, C. K., and R. A. Bettis, The Dominant Logic: A New Linkage between Diversity and Performance, *Strategic Management Journal,* November/December 1986, pp. 485–601.

Prahalad, C. K., and G. Hamel, The Core Competence of the Corporation, *Harvard Business Review,* May/June 1990, pp. 79–91.

Ramanujam, V., and P. Varadarajan, Research on Corporate Diversification: A Synthesis, *Strategic Management Journal,* November/December 1989, pp. 523–551.

Rumelt, R. P., Diversification Strategy and Profitability, *Strategic Management Journal,* October/December 1982, pp. 359–369.

Young, D., Brief Case: Headquarters Staff—Products of History or Sources of Distinctive Skills, *Long Range Planning,* October 1993, pp. 139–141.

CHAPTER 7
MULTICOMPANY
LEVEL STRATEGIES:
ON CONFRONTATION
AND COOPERATION

*We have no eternal allies and we have
no perpetual enemies. Our interests
are eternal and perpetual, and the
interests it is our duty to follow.*
 —Henry John Temple
  1784–1865, English Prime Minister

Introduction

In chapter 1 it was indicated that many authors recognize a third strategy level in addition to the business and multibusiness levels. This level, the *multicompany* or *network* level, encompasses all strategy content issues with regard to cooperation between two or more organisations, for instance between the company and its suppliers, buyers, financiers, competitors, and public organisations. It is argued that at this level strategy has ceased to be the sole domain of one business unit or corporation and therefore must be developed jointly with other organisations.

 The importance of network level strategies is not necessarily widely accepted. On the contrary, Axelsson (1992) observes that "in the dominant perspective in literature, the environment is often treated as faceless (. . .) with the firm relating itself to this whole. In addition the firm is regarded as a distinct, clearly defined unit. Its boundaries are seldom questioned or considered problematical. It is a firm and it exists in a total environment. This environment is competitive." This quote reveals two important assumptions underlying the traditional strategy literature. First, there are *clear boundaries* between the organisation and the environment, and second, the environment is predominantly *competitive*.

Authors stressing the importance of network strategy usually disagree on both accounts. First, they point out that it is often unclear where the company ends and the environment begins. They argue that the classic distinction between *markets* and *hierarchies* (Williamson, 1975)—independent firms interacting under market conditions versus dependent, wholly owned subsidiaries interacting under the guidance of the corporate centre—is too black and white. In their view, a wide variety of relationships can exist between organisations, whereby both parties are neither dependent nor independent, but interdependent. Examples range from loosely coupled contracts through strategic alliances to more permanent long-term joint ventures. They point out that these hybrid forms are neither entirely internal nor external to the company, thereby blurring the boundaries between the firm and its environment.

The second assumption of the traditional view, that the environment is predominantly competitive, is also challenged. Most authors who emphasize the importance of multicompany strategy readily admit that organisations' goals and interests often conflict, which places their relationship within a competitive context. However, it is argued that organisations seldom have only conflicting interests. Usually organisations, even "competitors," have a large number of parallel interests, that can be best served by cooperation. Therefore, the complexity of multicompany strategy lies in finding the right balance between competing against, and working together with, other organisations, such as buyers, suppliers, competitors, financiers, and government bodies.

The structure of this chapter deviates from the "debate model" used in the other chapters because there are no well-known articles that explicitly argue the traditional, what we shall call *discrete organisation*, point of view. Most authors *assume* clear boundaries and predominantly competitive relationships but do not make a point of *defending* this perspective as the most useful approach to strategy content. This chapter therefore does not feature any articles taking the discrete organisation point of view, but contains five readings exploring the *fuzziness of organisational boundaries* and the *complexity of interrelationships* between the firm and its environment, referred to as the *network perspective*. It will be up to the reader to compare the network approach to the discrete organisation perspective and to judge what its merits are.

The Articles

The opening article of this chapter, "Why Should Firms Cooperate?" has been taken from the well-known book *Cooperative Strategies in International Business* by Farok Contractor and Peter Lorange. In this article the authors argue that cooperation and confrontation are complementary paths to business success, and they indicate under which circumstances collaborating with other organisations makes strategic sense. Beside these *cooperative rationales*, they also give an overview of the various types of *cooperative arrangements* that are possible, making a distinction between vertical cooperation (with buyers and suppliers) and horizontal cooperation (with similar organisations). As such, this article functions as a useful overview and introduction to the following readings.

The second article, "The Intellectual Holding Company," by James Quinn, Thomas Doorley, and Penny Paquette, expands on the topic of *vertical cooperation*. When writers employing the discrete organisation perspective view the value-creation system (or value chain), they focus on the optimal extent of vertical integration by means of ownership, given the bargaining power of buyers and suppliers. The authors of this article question the wisdom of building up powerful negotiation positions within the value-creation system by means of the absolute control of assets (ownership). They argue that the firm only needs to fully control a few strategically significant activities, while it can outsource or jointly control other less important activities. They stress that the company must be selective in what it wishes to control and should move beyond "hierarchies and markets" as the only ways to structure relationships with other organisations in the value-creation system. They believe that companies will increasingly become part of *loosely structured networks*, uniting temporarily for one purpose, yet remaining suppliers, competitors, or customers in other cases. Hence, companies must develop the capability to manage network relationships, which means that managers must become accustomed to fuzzy organisational boundaries and relationships that are simultaneously competitive and cooperative.

While Quinn, Doorley, and Paquette are primarily focused on vertical cooperation, the third article, "Collaborate with Your Competitors—and Win," expands on the topic of *horizontal cooperation*. In the discrete organisation perspective competitors should only compete—collaboration is frowned upon as collusion, or at best it is seen as a sign of weakness (if you can't beat them, join them). In the first article, however, Contractor and Lorange already mention a number of reasons why cooperation between competitors might be beneficial. In the third article, Gary Hamel, Yves Doz, and C. K. Prahalad focus on one cooperation rationale they believe should be paramount when engaging in *competitive collaboration*, namely, learning. In accordance with the resource-based approach discussed in chapters 5 and 6, the authors argue that cooperative ventures between competitors provide a window on each other's capabilities and offer the opportunity to acquire the other's skills and technologies. Hamel, Doz, and Prahalad urge companies only to enter strategic alliances if they have a well-developed capability to learn from their allies, clear objectives of what they wish to learn, and defenses against their allies' probing of their skills and technologies.

The fourth article, "The Firm as a Nexus of Treaties" by Torger Reve, integrates much of what is said in the preceding three articles. Reve proposes a framework that brings together all of the firm's horizontal and vertical relationships into one model. As the title of the article suggests, Reve does not view the firm as a legal entity within a perfect market system, but as a *strategic core* of capabilities engaging in a wide variety of vertical and horizontal *strategic alliances* to achieve competitive advantage. The value of this article is that it elegantly summarizes the *network view of the firm* in terms and concepts familiar to the writers using the traditional discrete organisation perspective.

The fifth and last article of this chapter, "Network Positions and Strategic Action" by Jan Johanson and Lars-Gunnar Mattson, takes the network concept one step further than the preceding articles do. The authors of the four other readings take a *microlevel* perspective, looking only at one-on-one relationships between the focal organisation and firms in the environment. Johanson and Mattson move beyond these *dyadic* relationships and take a *mesolevel* perspective, looking at the entire set of interrelationships within an industrial system. They argue that all strategic actions by firms are actually efforts to influence their position within a network. The authors therefore stress that a proper understanding of network dynamics is necessary for a firm to achieve strategic success.

Recommended Readings and Cases

Everyone who wishes to delve more deeply into the topic of organisational boundaries and interorganisational relationships would probably be much aided by going back to *the* classic in this area, Oliver Williamson's *Markets and Hierarchies*, to which so many others refer. For further reading on the subject of vertical relationships, Michael Best's *The New Competition* is an excellent choice. For horizontal relationships a good starting point would be *Strategic Alliances: Formation, Implementation, and Evolution*, by Peter Lorange and Johan Roos. If the reader is interested in moving beyond dyadic relationships, B. Axelsson and G. Easton's *Industrial Networks: A New View of Reality* is recommended. Finally, on the topic of managing relationships within networks, Jeffrey Pfeffer and Gerald Salancik's *The External Control of Organizations: A Resource Dependency Perspective* is a very interesting book to begin with.

The two cases selected to accompany this chapter are "Taurus Hungarian Rubber Works" by Joseph Wolfe, Gyula Bosnyak, and Janos Vecsenyi, and "CLG, EEIG" by Lluis Renart and Francesco Parés. The Taurus case describes the uncertain situation faced by this state-owned conglomerate. Within the centrally planned Hungarian economy, Taurus had grown into a very large company producing almost every rubber product needed within the country. With the shift toward a more market-driven economy, the company must build up relationships with other firms that can complement its technologies and provide it with access to the richer Western markets. Readers are confronted with the question of which relationships should be sought, what form they should take, and how they should be managed. The CLG, EEIG case is less open ended, as it explains how four medium-sized paint manufacturers from Britain, France, Germany, and Spain have entered into a strategic alliance. The main questions in this challenging case are how such a multicultural alliance must be managed and whether it will result in the competitive advantage hoped for by the participants.

■ WHY SHOULD FIRMS COOPERATE?[†]

By Farok Contractor and Peter Lorange

Nature is not always red in fang and claw. Cooperation and competition provide alternative or simultaneous paths to success. In business, as in nature, managers must learn the arts of competing and cooperating as equally valid aspects of corporate strategy. Cooperative aspects of international strategy have been relatively neglected until recently. In the past few years, however, there appears to have been a proliferation of international joint ventures, licensing, coproduction agreements, joint research programs, exploration consortia, and other cooperative relationships between two or more potentially competitive firms. The role of these relationships in international strategy is the focus of this article.

The traditional preference of international executives has largely been to enter a market or line of business alone. This seems to have been particularly true for the

---

†**Source:** Reprinted with the permission of Lexington Books, an imprint of Macmillan, Inc., from *Cooperative Strategies in International Business* by Farok J. Contractor and Peter Lorange, editors. Copyright © 1988 by Lexington Books.

larger multinationals, especially those based in the United States. Among smaller international companies and those based in Japan, Europe, and developing nations, there seems to have been a higher propensity to form cooperative relationships. Traditionally, cooperative arrangements were often seen as second-best to the strategic option of going it alone in the larger firms. Licensing, joint ventures, coproduction, and management service agreements have been viewed as options reluctantly undertaken, often under external mandates such as government investment laws or to cross protectionist entry barriers in developing and regulated economies. In several socialist and developing nations, this consideration remains important; association with local partners is more frequently necessary for market access and government permissions of various kinds.

What makes the recent spate of cooperative associations different is that they are typically being formed between firms in industrial free-market economies where there are few external regulatory pressures mandating a linkup. Instead of the traditional pattern of a large "foreign" firm trying to access a market by associating itself with a "local" partner, many of the recent partnerships involve joint activities in many stages of the value-added chain, such as production, sourcing, and research and development (R&D). These associations often involve firms of comparable rather than unequal size, both may be international in scope, and each may make similar rather than complementary contributions. Further, the territorial scope of some of these new cooperative ventures is global, rather than restricted to a single-country market as in the traditional pattern of joint ventures and contractual agreements. These new forms of cooperative ventures will be the focus of our discussion in this article.

An Alternative Paradigm for Multinational Operations

Cooperative arrangements are numerous enough to suggest that our stereotype of the multinational corporation may need to be changed. Traditionally, it has been seen as a monolithic entity, controlling or owning its inputs and outputs, and expanding alone into foreign markets, based on its technological, managerial, and marketing dominance. It could be seen as a transnational chain of control, "internalized" within the firm. In this view, the corporation reserves for itself the gains from global vertical and/or horizontal integration.

Today, we are in a more negotiated, circumscribed, competitive world, at least as far as several industries are concerned. In many situations, the international firm is better seen as a coalition of interlocked, quasi-arms-length relationships. Its strategic degrees of freedom are at once increased by the globalization of markets and decreased by the need to negotiate cooperative arrangements with other firms and governments. In linking up with another firm, one or both partners may enjoy options otherwise unavailable to them, such as better access to markets, pooling or swapping of technologies, enjoying larger economies of scale, and benefiting from economies of scope. These benefits are detailed later. As a corollary, each partner is less free to make its own optimizing decisions on issues such as product development, transfer prices, territorial scope, and retention of earnings versus dividend payout.

Types of Cooperative Arrangements

Between the two extremes of spot transactions undertaken by two firms, on the one hand, and their complete merger, on the other hand, lie several types of cooperative arrangements. These arrangements differ in the formula used to compensate each partner (the legal form of the agreement) as well as in the strategic impact on the global operations of each partner. Table 7-1 ranks these arrangements in order of increasing interorganizational dependence, which is generally, but not necessarily, correlated with strategic impact. This ranking is at present only in the form of a hypothesis, since no empirical work exists comparing the various types of cooperative agreements on the extent of interorganizational dependence they create.

For instance, technical training and start-up assistance agreements are usually of short duration. The company supplying the technology and training is typically compensated with a lump-sum amount and will thereafter have minimal links with the start-up company, unless, of course, there is an additional licensing agreement. Similarly, patent licensing involves a one-time transfer of the patent right. Compensation, however, is often in the form of a running royalty, expressed as a fraction of sales value. In component supply, contract assembly, buyback, and franchising agreements, the principal form of compensation for both partners is the markup on the goods supplied, although there could be a royalty arrangement as well, as typically is the case in franchising. The interdependence between the partners is thus somewhat greater because of delivery, quality control, and transfer-pricing issues associated with the supply of materials, as well as due to the global brand recognition in franchising.

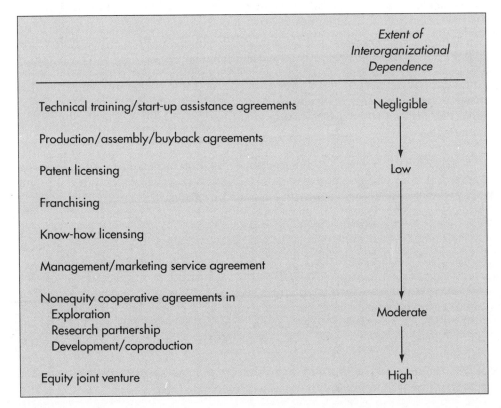

TABLE 7-1
Types of Cooperative Arrangements

Know-how licensing and management service agreements assume a closer degree of continuing assistance and organizational links. Studies show that most licensing involves the transfer of know-how, which is unpatented but proprietary information. It is not simply a matter of transferring a patent right or providing start-up training. It involves extended links between the two firms and ongoing interaction on technical or administrative issues. Payment in these cases will typically be in the form of a lump-sum fee plus running royalties.

The term *joint venture* often implies the creation of a separate corporation whose stock is shared by two or more partners, each expecting a proportional share of dividends as compensation. But many cooperative programs between firms involve joint activities without the creation of a new corporate entity. Instead, carefully defined rules and formulas govern the allocation of tasks, costs, and revenues.

Rationales for Cooperation

In addressing the conditions necessary for entering into a cooperative relationship, we shall take the viewpoint of any one partner and examine the contribution it makes to a given venture's strategy. It is critical to keep the strategy of one partner in mind. How central is the particular business domain of a joint venture for the partner? What opportunity losses must the partner reckon with as offsetting the benefits from a joint venture, such as limitations on future strategic flexibility and alternative use of management's capacity? Let us primarily discuss the benefits—the reasons for *forming* cooperative ventures.

In the broadest terms, joint ventures, licensing, and other types of cooperative arrangements can achieve at least seven more or less overlapping objectives. These are: (1) risk reduction, (2) economies of scale and/or rationalization, (3) technology exchanges, (4) co-opting or blocking competition, (5) overcoming government-mandated trade or investment barriers, (6) facilitating initial international expansion of inexperienced firms, and (7) vertical quasi-integration advantages of linking the complementary contributions of the partners in a "value chain." We have listed the major potential benefits that might be associated with each of these rationales in table 7-2. Each of these issues will be discussed in more detail in the following paragraphs.

When considering benefits from cooperative ventures in the broadest sense, they typically create value through either a *vertical* or *horizontal* arrangement. In considering the vertical value-addition process that takes place through a joint venture, it is useful to draw on the value chain approach suggested by Porter. The *combined* efforts of all partners must add up to a value chain that can produce a more competitive end result. It is important that the partners have complementary strengths, that they together cover all relevant know-how dimension needed, and that the strategies of the partners are compatible and not in conflict.

Instead of the partners making *complementary* contributions, an alternative model of cooperation is one in which the partners provide similar inputs to the venture. The rationales for the latter can be to limit excess capacity, to achieve risk reduction through joint efforts, and to save on costs, as we shall see shortly. Both models exist in international cooperative ventures, but their relative incidence and stability are not definitely known.

Let us now consider in more detail the seven areas for potentially generating benefits outlined in table 7-2.

TABLE 7-2
Strategic Contributions of
Joint Ventures (Adapted from
Contractor, 1986)

- *Risk Reduction*
  Product portfolio diversification
  Dispersion and/or reduction of fixed cost
  Lower total capital investment
  Faster entry and payback
- *Economies of Scale and/or Rationalization*
  Lower average cost from larger volume
  Lower cost by using comparative advantage of each partner
- *Complementary Technologies and Patents*
  Technological synergy
  Exchange of patents and territories
- *Co-opting or Blocking Competition*
  Defensive joint ventures to reduce competition
  Offensive joint ventures to increase costs and/or lower market share for a third company
- *Overcoming Government-Mandated Investment or Trade Barrier*
  Receiving permit to operate as a "local" entity because of local partner
  Satisfying local content requirements
- *Initial International Expansion*
  Benefit from local partner's know-how
- *Vertical Quasi Integration*
  Access to materials
  Access to technology
  Access to labor
  Access to capital
  Regulatory permits
  Access to distribution channels
  Benefits from brand recognition
  Establishing links with major buyers
  Drawing on existing fixed marketing establishment

Risk Reduction

Cooperative ventures can reduce a partner's risk by (1) spreading the risk of a large project over more than one firm, (2) enabling diversification in a product portfolio sense, (3) enabling faster entry and payback, and (4) cost subadditivity (the cost to the partnership is less than the cost of investment undertaken by each firm alone).

Developing, for instance, a new car or airplane is a multibillion-dollar undertaking. First, to state the obvious, a joint new undertaking such as the Boeing 767 project spreads the risk of failure (and the potential gains) over more than one party. This applies also to exploration consortia. But there are other subtler considerations, as can be illustrated by the General Motors-Toyota venture. To the extent that GM did not have to sink $2.5 billion into developing a new small car in the United States, it could invest the capital over a range of larger models. Given the public's fluctuating taste for smaller versus larger automobiles—something Detroit has been largely unsuccessful in predicting over the past two business cycles and oil shocks—a diversification of the product portfolio might insulate auto producers from such variability in demand, at least up to a point. Further, a joint venture can lower the total investment cost of a particular project, or the assets at risk, by combining expertise and slack facilities in the parent firms—the cost subadditivity factor. A good example is utility power pools that enable each regional electric company to make a lower investment than it would operating alone. Finally, the experience of all the partners—their mutual sharing or abdication of markets in favor of the joint venture corporation—make for faster entry with a better design and a quicker payback. Faster entry and certification are also strong factors in pharmaceutical-industry licensing. The industry's complaint is that because certification takes a long time, the monopoly advantage of a patent is eroded and there is not enough time to recoup R&D costs. Clinical testing performed by a licensee often speeds up the certification process.

Another dimension of risk reduction has to do with containing some of the political risk by linking up with a local partner. Such a partner may have sufficient political clout to steer the joint venture clear of local government action or interference. It may also be that the joint venture has come about as a result of the host government's industrial policy. In such a case, added political-risk reduction can be achieved; the government endorses the joint venture as being beneficial to its economic policy agenda. Government policies favoring joint ventures over fully owned investments are by no means peculiar to less-developed countries (LDCs). Japan has, in fact, been a role model for many developing nations.

Economies of Scale and Production Rationalization

"I think world trade in built-up vehicles will be largely replaced by trade in vehicle components . . . . The distinction between imports and domestics could very well become meaningless" (Donald Peterson, president of Ford). Underlying this remark are two distinct but related concepts. Production rationalization means that certain components or subassemblies are no longer made in two locations with unequal costs. Production of this item is transferred to the lower-cost location that enjoys the highest comparative advantage, thus lowering sourcing cost. But there is an added advantage. Because volume in the more advantageous location is now higher, *further* reduction in average unit cost is possible due to economies of larger scale. General Motors, for instance, has an extensive global interchange between its affiliates and joint venture partners such as Isuzu and Suzuki (in which it has had an admittedly passive equity stake, so far). Japan serves as a source for transaxles—transmission plus axle subassemblies—for assembly in markets such as Canada, Europe, South Africa, and Australia. Brazil serves as a source of small engines for Ford's U.S. and European markets. Other examples are abundant.

In many situations, too, particularly in more mature businesses, there may be excess capacity and need for industrial restructuring. A joint venture approach may be a practical vehicle for achieving this. Thus, production can be rationalized and output levels reduced within the joint venture context, thereby avoiding a "winner-loser" situation and a protracted stalemate. High exit barriers can thereby be overcome.

Exchanges of Complementary Technologies and Patents

Joint ventures, production partnerships, and licensing agreements may be formed in order to pool the complementary technologies of the partners. Several alliances in the pharmaceutical and biotechnology fields, for instance, are built on this rationale. Each partner contributes a missing piece. By pooling know-how and patents, a superior product is expected. In general, it is important to consider joint ventures as vehicles to bring together complementary skills and talents that cover different aspects of state-of-the-art know-how needed in high-technology industries. Such creations of "electric atmospheres" can bring out significant innovations not likely to be achieved in any one parent organization's "monoculture" context.

Moreover, *faster entry* into a market may be possible if the testing and certification done by one partner are accepted by the authorities in the other partner's territories. Or, one partner may cede the rights to a partially developed process to another firm, which refines it further, with the fruits of the development to be shared in a joint venture. This is a typical pattern among smaller and larger firms. In this regard, it is useful to remember that a patent is not merely a right to a process or design; it is also a right to a *territory*. Often, the marketing or territorial right is the dominant strategic issue. By pooling or swapping patents, companies also pool or swap territories. Research partnerships can have a similar intent.

A closely related issue has to do with the pressures faced by a company that has invested heavily in developing a new technological breakthrough. But on its own, it may not have sufficient production or global marketing resources to secure a rapid, global dissemination of the new technology, making it hard to achieve an acceptable payback for its investment. A joint venture approach can be an important vehicle in achieving such dissemination and realistically securing the necessary payback. This may be especially true for smaller firms lacking the internal financial and managerial resources to make their own investments or expand rapidly.

Paradoxically, this may also be true in giant diversified firms. Let us take General Electric (GE) as an example: it has scores of foreign affiliates, as well as several hundred licensing or production contracts plus minority joint ventures. For a company with the number of products GE has, the potential country/product combination of activities must add up to over ten thousand. Not even a giant firm can invest in all of these. Direct investment in fully owned subsidiaries is reserved for the most interesting combinations, while many of the rest are handled by cooperative ventures. Stopford and Wells confirm in their study that the propensity to form joint ventures is higher when the entry entails product diversification. Berg, Duncan, and Friedman indicate that large average firm size and rapid growth in an industry correlate positively with joint venture formation.

Co-opting or Blocking Competition

Potential (or existing) competition can be co-opted by forming a joint venture with the competitor or by entering into a network of cross-licensing agreements. The majority of these are defensive strategic moves. Besides other considerations mentioned earlier, blunting the Japanese auto penetration into the U.S. market is likely to have been one rationale for the GM-Toyota venture.

On the other hand, a joint venture may also be made in a more offensive vein. Caterpillar Tractor is said to have linked up with Mitsubishi in Japan in order to put pressure on the profits and market share that their common competitor Komatsu enjoyed in its important home market, Japan. Japan is said to generate 80 percent of Komatsu's global cash flow. Thus, even though the joint venture may not have great importance in itself for Caterpillar, it may act as a thorn in Komatsu's side and, thus, reduce its competitiveness outside Japan. Vickers suggests that many R&D partnerships are intended to quickly file patents to stake out the ground against competitors.

Of course, joint ventures are, quite properly, scrutinized by governments for their potential anticompetitive and welfare-limiting effects—but less stringently today, it seems, than a decade ago.

Overcoming Government-Mandated Investment and/or Trade Barriers

Here we come to one of the oldest and still common rationales for joint ventures—in many instances, host government policy makes the joint venture form the most convenient way to enter a market. An abundance of examples can be found, particularly in developing countries. Over the past few years, for instance, joint ventures with China have received much attention. We also have frequent examples of joint venture agreements being complemented by barter or countertrade arrangements. General Motors' venture with LZTK in Yugoslavia is an example of this. The joint venture, in fact, produces castings that GM buys for its German assembly lines; in return, GM is able to sell more cars in Yugoslavia by way of countertrade. These more-or-less protectionist policies are not exclusive to LDCs or planned economies. Mariti and Smiley describe how NATO prefers weapons systems developed by multinational consortia, whereby the purchasing countries can participate in parts manufacturing through a cooperative network. Japan is known for its more-or-less exclusionary policies, and this has been a major contributing factor to the hundreds of U.S. firms using the joint venture route as the most practical way to sell products in the Japanese market.

Facilitating Initial International Expansion

For medium—or small-sized companies lacking international experience, initial overseas expansion is often likely to be a joint venture. This may be especially true when the firm is from a socialist or developing country. In a typical scenario, such a firm has production capability, but lacks knowledge of foreign markets for which it depends on its partner. Embraer of Brazil, a highly successful aircraft manufacturer, was helped initially by its joint venture with Piper. It makes small commercial jets as well as fighters. Initially aiming for the Brazilian market, Embraer is now a strong exporter, landing orders even in the demanding U.S. market. It gives a good example of a joint venture partner that over time has been turning into a global competitor on its own.

In general, it is an expensive, difficult, and time-consuming business to build up a global organization and a significant international competitive presence. Joint ventures offer significant *time savings* in this respect. Even though one might consider building up one's market position independently, this may simply take too long to be viable. Even though acquisitions abroad might be another alternative for international expansion, it can often be hard to find good acquisition candidates at realistic price levels—many of the "good deals" may be gone. All of these considerations add to the attractiveness of the joint venture approach.

Vertical Quasi Integration

Several cooperative ventures involve each partner making essentially *similar* contributions, as described already. However, joint ventures, coproduction, research partnerships, and management or marketing service agreements can also be a form of vertical quasi integration, with each partner contributing one or more *different* elements in the production and distribution chains. The inputs of the partners are, in this case, *complementary*, not similar.

There is usually a strategic optimum, lying in *between* the extremes of complete vertical integration within one organization on the one hand and completely contractual relationships or outsourcing on the other hand. Sometimes, a cooperative relationship with another firm is the best way to reach this optimal middle ground.

Such ventures can be described as a mode of interfirm cooperation lying between the extremes of complete vertical integration (in one company) of the chain from raw materials to the consumer, to the opposite case where stages of production and distribution are owned by separate companies that contract with each other in conventional market mechanisms. Empirically, the latter case is observed only rarely. Examples may be found in pockets of the music and publishing industries. One even encounters firms with no assets other than an office that undertake production and sales by contracting out each stage to separate organizations, while they simply "manage" the entire chain. But such one-time contracts mean that none of the parties accept any obligation for future behavior. Strategic direction setting in any long-term sense may become next to impossible.

A firm may therefore integrate vertically (own more than one stage of the chain), because it may more easily permit longer-run strategic decisions. There is a large literature on vertical integration. Briefly stated, its advantages are these: (1) avoidance of interfirm contracting, transactions, and negotiations costs, (2) reduction in cost or achieving economies of scale from combining common administrative, production, transport, or information-processing activities in two or more stages of production or distribution, (3) internalizing technological or administrative abilities and secrets within a single firm, (4) gaining a better understanding of strategy within the industry as a whole (enabling the integrated firm to outperform its more fragmented competitors), and (5) the ability to implement technological changes more quickly and over more stages of the value chain.

On the other hand, there are drawbacks to integration as well. These drawbacks can be overcome to a certain extent by linking up with another firm, where integrating entirely within one firm may be difficult. First, there is the matter of capital investment cost, which may become too high for just one company to bear, especially when operating in a risky environment. We see that many joint ventures in uncertain investment fields such as semiconductor R&D or oil exploration are predicated simply on spreading the investment cost and risk.

Second, the vertically integrated firm tends to increase its fixed costs and, thus, its break-even point, thereby potentially increasing its vulnerability to cyclical fluctuation. In the aerospace industry, for instance, the cost of developing new airplanes is very high for even the largest participants, such as Boeing. The Boeing 767 is being built in a contracted coproduction cooperative venture with Japan Commercial Aircraft and Aeritalia. Not only are the development risks shared, but fixed costs of Boeing are lowered by contracting major portions of the aircraft to the other partners. There are other strategic advantages as well, such as helping the sales of the aircraft in Japan and Italy.

Third, forward integrating to internalize more elements of marketing channels requires market access, links with major buyers, and brand recognition, which can be a critical impediment in international expansion. The history of Japanese firms expanding into the U.S. market shows that in the early stages, they would link up with established U.S. companies. This typically gave them a "beachhead" and a longer learning period before developing channels of their own. Lastly, Porter indicates some other strategic disadvantages of full integration, such as reduced flexibility to environmental or technological change, dulled incentives for an individual operating unit to remain competitive if internal transfer prices do not reflect their external values, and being deprived of the marketing or technical insights available from outsiders.

A middle position between the two extremes of full integration and purely contractual relationships is often optimal for many companies. Joint ventures, coproduction, management service agreements, and so on provide a means whereby each partner can contribute its distinctive competencies. Many of the specific obligations of each partner may be defined in auxiliary agreements. Because they share in the equity of the venture or share the profits by a formula, the firms typically perceive that they have an overlapping if not identical strategy. The relationship is neither purely contractual nor entirely integrative. We may describe it as a mode of quasi integration.

Two Basic Patterns for Joint Venture Formation

We have discussed seven strategic rationales for forming cooperative relationships. In the broadest terms, they involve risk reduction, cost reduction, and an ability to enter markets or enhance revenues in a manner not possible for each firm alone.

A distinction was drawn between ventures in which the partners make similar inputs ("horizontal" ventures) versus ventures in which the contributions of the partners are complementary, with quasi-vertical integration providing *synergy*. Examples of partners making roughly similar contributions are found in the natural resources sector, oil and mineral exploration, real estate development, R&D ventures, and perhaps in large aerospace projects as well, where the dominant considerations appear to be an *accretion* of resources for the large investment involved and a spreading of risk over more participants.

Conclusion: Cooperative Ventures as an Alternative Form of International Business Operation

In this article, we have examined the strategic-management and industrial-organization rationales for forming cooperative ventures. We have not explored the cultural or behavioral problems of running them, nor have we examined in much detail the causes of their failure or success. There is a large literature on those topics; the thrust of that literature, perhaps unwittingly, seems to overemphasize the problems of running international joint ventures. There is, however, no hard evidence that their failure rate exceeds the normal corporate failure rate for comparable single-owner ventures. We have, however, claimed in this article that careful analysis prior to the decision of whether to go for a cooperative venture may be a most critical factor impacting future success of the cooperative venture (if such a venture is the decision outcome). The very fact that the partners have spent sufficient time to become truly clear about what they are entering into should be a major positive factor in this context.

The fact remains, nevertheless, that the strategic rationales prevailing when a cooperative venture was formed may shift over time. As a hypothesis for testing, let us propose that even though subsequent problems may develop (such as cultural difficulties, slower decision making, arguments over the rate and division of profits, disputes over sourcing, tensions in connection with the assignment of personnel, and disagreements on future expansion), these are still all less onerous problems when compared with an erosion of the fundamental strategic rationales proposed in this article. This erosion may come from external or environmental sources, such as when the technology contributed by one partner is obsolescent because of changes in the industry. Or the erosion may be internal, such as when one partner *learns* from the other, and the other partner then has nothing new to contribute. Ongoing viability of the venture depends on the *continuing* mutual dependence of the partners.

This article has specifically focused on the strategic and economic rationales for forming cooperative ventures. We have, by choice, not discussed "softer" issues, which also should be assessed before reaching a decision on whether to form a cooperative venture. Such issues might include the anticipated ease of working with the other partner; possible language difficulties, cultural differences, style incompatibilities, and differences in values and norms; the anticipated "political" climate within the context of the partners' organization; and the presence of a sufficiently strong "mentor" who will push the cooperative venture. We acknowledge the importance of incorporating these types of assessments into the decision on whether to go for a cooperative venture. However, we feel that the relative importance of these softer issues might be relatively lessened if a careful planning process has been undertaken, so that both partners understand the fundamental strategic and economic rationales involved.

It is possible that cooperative ventures will grow in importance as a mode of international business operations. However, we cannot be sure; in terms of strategic management of multinational operations, we have a trend and a countertrend. On the one hand, through regional economic integration plus convergence of standards and buyer preferences, in some industries there is the possibility of producing for a world market, with relatively minor variations in each nation. Centralized control and full ownership of affiliates is important for the implementation of an efficient and strategic direction in such corporations. On the other hand, we have pointed to examples in several industries where efficiency, risk reduction, and other strategic rationales make the cooperative mode of organization superior to an internalization or go-it-alone strategy. Moreover, the traditional impetus for joint ventures, licensing, and other contractual forms remains in many countries. Economic nationalism, protectionism, transport costs, differing local cultures and standards, as well as the presence of entrenched domestic firms encourage a linkup with a local company as a means of serving the particular needs of a geographic market and/or for getting political permission to produce and tap natural resources. These traditional types of cooperative ventures remains ubiquitous.

Negotiated arrangements between international firms such as joint ventures and technology-licensing agreements already vastly exceed controlled foreign affiliates by number, if not value. One model of the multinational corporation sees it as a closed, internalized administrative system that straddles national boundaries. An alternative paradigm proposed here is to view the international firm as a member of various open and shifting coalitions, each with a specific strategic purpose.

■ THE INTELLECTUAL HOLDING COMPANY†

By James Quinn, Thomas Doorley, and Penny Paquette

Service technologies are not just revolutionizing internal organizational configurations. They are restructuring whole industries'—and nations'—entire competitive postures. Service technologies now provide sufficient scale economies, flexibility, efficiency, and specialization potentials that outside vendors can supply many important corporate functions at greatly enhanced value and lower cost. Thus many of these functions should often be outsourced. Strategically approached, this does not "hollow out" the

†**Source:** Reprinted from "Technology in Services: Rethinking Strategic Focus," by James Quinn, Thomas Dooley, and Penny Paquette, *Sloan Management Review* (Winter 1990), by permission of the publisher. Copyright © 1990 by the Sloan Management Review Association. All rights reserved.

corporation. Instead, it decreases internal bureaucracies, flattens the organization, gives it a heightened strategic focus, and improves its competitive responsiveness. Taking advantage of this opportunity requires a whole new approach to strategy.

The "Intellectual Holding Company": Learning to Love the "Hollow Corporation"

Considering the enterprise as an intellectual holding company restructures the entire way one attacks strategy. One needs to ask, activity by activity, Are we really competitive with the world's best here? If not, can intelligent outsourcing improve our long-term position? Competitive analyses of service activities should not consider just the company's own industry, but should benchmark each service against "best-in-class" performance among all potential service providers and industries that might cross-compete within the analyzed category—both in the United States and abroad. This can completely change the focus of competitive analyses, creating a much more external, market-value orientation for the process.

As companies begin to outsource nonstrategic activities—particularly overheads—they often discover important secondary benefits. Managements concentrate more on their businesses' core strategic activities. Other internal costs and time delays frequently drop as long-standing bureaucracies disappear and political pressures decrease for annual increments to each department's budget. Managements begin to consider more carefully which departments really are critical to success, which activities can be cut to minimal levels and purchased as commodities, which must be maintained internally for strategic reasons, and which must be managed as the company's true source of competitive advantage. All this leads to a more compact organization, with fewer hierarchical levels. It also leads to a much sharper focus on recruiting, developing, and motivating the people who create most value in those areas where the company has special competencies.

Perhaps most important, management in the new environment shifts *away from* functional skills and the capacity to manage bureaucracies and *toward* more coordinative, strategic, and conceptual skills and the capacity to manage contract relationships. These are quite different from the skills that have dominated most companies—including start-up and emerging companies—in the past. One venture capitalist summarized the issue clearly:

"I keep trying to convince my partners and our client companies that we don't want to invest in hard assets. They are too short-lived and risky. We certainly don't want to invest in bureaucracies. We want to invest in people who have a clear viable concept, who can manage outside contracts with the best sources in the world, and who can concentrate their internal energies on that small core of activities that creates the real uniqueness and value-added for the company. That's where the action is today, but it's a tough sell against traditional thinking."

Dominating Those Services Crucial to Strategy

Many have expressed concerns about the hollowing out and loss of strategic capability outsourcing could cause. However, if the process is approached properly, careful outsourcing should increase both productivity and strategic focus. By limiting or getting rid of those activities (both production and service) where it can develop no strategic advantage—and where it is generally much weaker than the best outside sources—a company can increase the value it delivers to both customers and shareholders.

But a company must maintain command of those activities crucial to its strategic position. If it does not, it has essentially redefined the business it is in. For all other activities, if the company cannot see its way to strategic superiority, or if the activity is not essential to areas where it can attain such superiority, the company should consider outsourcing and actively managing any resulting relationships. But it is essential that the company plan and manage its outsourcing coalitions so that it does not become overly dependent on—and hence dominated by—its partner. In some cases this means consciously developing and maintaining alternate competitive sources or even strategically controlling critical stages in an overall process that might otherwise be totally outsourced.

In other cases, by creating a "strategic partnership" the company can even outsource a critical activity that another *noncompeting* company can perform more effectively— provided it can still control the crucial relationships with its customers.

Carefully developing the company's strategic focus around selected service activities—and partnering or outsourcing those where the company cannot excel—not only creates a stronger strategic focus, it can also prevent a takeover by those who might identify missed potentials as opportunities to substantially lower costs or raise post-takeover yields.

Highest Activity Share, Not Market Share, for Profits

Once a company develops great depth in certain selected service activities as its strategic focus, many individual products can spring off these "core" activities to give the firm a consistent corporate strategy for decades. Unfortunately, the true nature of these core capabilities is usually obscured by the tendency of organizations to think of their strengths in product—not activity or service—terms and by each functional group's need to see itself as the source of strategic strength. The key point is that a few *selected activities should drive strategy.* Knowledge bases, skill sets, and service activities are the things that generally can create continuing added value and competitive advantage.

Too much strategic attention has been paid to having a high share of the market. High share can be bought by inappropriate pricing or other short-term strategies. High market share and high profitability together come from having the highest relevant *activity* share in the marketplace—in other words, having the most effective presence in a service activity the market desires and thus gaining the experience curve and other benefits accruing to that high activity share. In service-dominated marketplaces—and most are—competitive analyses must focus on the relative potency of the activities or service power that undergird product positions. Too few strategists and companies realize this.

To be most effective, this service-activity dominance needs truly global development. As noted, the major value-added in most products today comes not from direct production or conversion processes, but from the technological improvements, styling, quality, marketing, timing, and financing contributions of service activities. Since these are knowledge-based intangibles that can be shipped cost-free anywhere, producers who expand their scope worldwide to tap the best knowledge and service sources available anywhere can obtain significant competitive advantage. Their capacity to command and coordinate service activities, supplier networks, and contract relations across broad geographical ranges has become perhaps the most important strategic weapon and scale economy for many of today's most competitive enterprises.

Avoiding Vertical Integration

Since most firms cannot afford to own or internally dominate all needed service activities, they tend to form coalitions, linking their own and their partners' capabilities through information, communication, and contract arrangements—rather than through ownership (i.e., vertical or horizontal integration). Because of their high value-added potentials, service companies and service activities within companies are central to many of these coalitions. An entirely new form of enterprise seems to be emerging, with a carefully conceived and limited set of "core strategic activities" (usually services) at its center, that allows a company to command and coordinate a constantly changing network of the world's best production and service suppliers on a global basis. This is a logical and most powerful extension of the *keiretsu* concept (linked networks of banks, producers, suppliers, and support-distribution companies) that has long been at the heart of Japan's trading success.

Given today's rapid technological advances, many enterprises find they can lower their risks and leverage their assets substantially by *avoiding* investments in vertical integration and managing "intellectual systems" instead of workers and machines. There are several reasons for this. First, well-managed outsourcing can put the world's very best talent at the disposal of the enterprise. Second, it decreases the firm's risk; if one unit in the system underperforms, the firm can quickly substitute competitors' components or services. Third, if new technologies suddenly appear, it is easier to switch sources. Fourth, if there is a cyclical or temporary drop in demand, the coordinating firm is not stuck with all the idle capacity and inventory swings of the entire production chain. Fifth, the system enjoys all of the motivation, flexibility, and lowered bureaucracy and overhead costs of a much more decentralized activity. With their high value and easy portability, the service inputs to these systems, especially, can be sourced anywhere in the world. The core strategy of a coordinating or systems company then becomes: Do only those things in-house that contribute to your competitive advantage, and try to source the rest from the world's best suppliers.

Manufacturing Industries Become "Service Networks"

Many industries are becoming loosely structured networks of service enterprises that join together temporarily for one purpose—yet are each other's suppliers, competitors, or customers elsewhere. Biotechnology provides an interesting example of this phenomenon; highly specialized companies are developing at each level of biotechnology. Many research groups or companies only identify and patent active biological entities (or proteins) at the laboratory level. Others only develop and license cell lines, which reproduce these entities. Still others create pilot-scale processes that can use the cell lines to produce proteins in sufficient quantities for clinical tests and commercialization. Other enterprises run clinical trials, and still others have the large-scale marketing expertise and distribution channels to reach wide markets.

Because of the relatively small scales, high risks, and expensive expertise needed at each level, it is often difficult for a single company to support the full chain of activities in-house. As a result, the industry is becoming structured as a number of multiple-level consortia; each enterprise has its own network of contract and information relationships involving a variety of research, clinical, production, and marketing groups around the world. Although biotechnology is commonly thought of as a manufacturing industry, all these are essentially service units, providing specialized activities for one another.

The semiconductor and electronics industries are moving toward a similar structure. Independent design, foundry, packaging, assembly, industrial distribution, kitting, configuration, systems analysis, networking, and value-added distributor groups do more than $15 billion worth of customized development, generating almost $140,000 of revenue per employee. Even large original equipment manufacturers (OEMs) are finding that these groups' specialization, fast turnarounds, advanced designs, and independent perspectives can lower costs, decrease investments, and increase value at all levels.

Strategically Redefining the "Focused Company"

Given the vast changes being wrought by new technologies, and the resulting potential for worldwide strategic outsourcing, the whole notion of what constitutes an "industry" or a "focused company" needs to be reexamined. True focus in strategy means the capacity to bring more power to bear on a selected sector than anyone else can. While this once meant owning the largest production facilities, research laboratories, or distribution channels supporting a single product line, this is no longer desirable or sufficient for most companies. Today, physical positions like a raw material source, a plant facility, or a product line rarely constitute a maintainable competitive advantage. They can be too easily bypassed, back-engineered, cloned, or slightly surpassed. A truly maintainable advantage usually derives from developing skill sets, experience factors, know-how, market understanding, databases, or distribution capabilities that others cannot reproduce and that lead to demonstrable value for the customer.

Two considerations are important. First, virtually all these sources of competitive advantage derive from *service activities*. Second, to the extent that these can be marshalled and integrated internally, they can successfully support extraordinarily wide product lines (à la Proctor & Gamble, 3M, IBM, Honda, Siemens, Mitsubishi, or Matsushita). For example: Honda's current multiple product strategy developed naturally out of its dominant skills in three key areas the design of small, efficient engines, the management of the technologies and logistics for small-scale assembly with extensive outsourcing of fabricated parts, and the creative management of offbeat distribution channels. Any product line using these became a natural extension for Honda, leading to today's ads that say you can fit "six Hondas in a two-car garage." The "six" doesn't refer to cars, but to a snow blower, a lawn mower, outdoor power tools, and so on. Similarly, 3M built on its research skills in three critical related technologies (abrasives, adhesives, and coating-bonding), a highly entrepreneurial development function, and broad-based distribution skills to create its diverse product line. Despite the seeming maturity of its basic technologies, as long as 3M stayed with these core skill areas it grew at a 10 percent annual rate and earned high margins. Although the firm stumbled when it tried to move into core activities beyond its origins, it quickly recovered when it refocused in the late 1980s.

Properly developed, a broad product or service line does not necessarily signify loss of focus if a firm can deploy especially potent service skills against selected marketplaces in a coordinated fashion. (In fact, a broad line may represent the leveraging of a less obvious strategic focus.) The key question is whether a company dominates a set of service skills that has importance to its customers—in other words, can bring more power to bear on this activity than anyone in the world. If so, the company can be a strategic success, provided it focuses its attention on that activity, obtains at least strategic parity through outsourcing elsewhere, and then blocks others from entering its markets by leveraging its skills across as broad a product line or customer base as it can dominate. Competitors must be defined as those with substitutable skill bases, not those with similar product lines. Product lines can be remarkably broad when the service skill base is deep enough to be dominating.

Conclusions

Most companies create a major portion of their incremental value and gain their real competitive advantage from a relatively few—generally service—activities. Much of the remaining enterprise exists primarily to permit these activities to take place. Yet managements typically spend an inordinate amount of their time, energy, and company resources dealing with these latter support functions—all of which decrease their attention to the company's truly crucial areas of strategic focus. Virtually all managers can benefit from a more carefully structured approach to managing their service activities strategically. Doing so involves defining each activity in the value-creation system as a service; carefully analyzing each such service activity to determine whether the company can become the best in the world at it; and eliminating, outsourcing, or joint venturing the activity to achieve "best-in-world" status when this is impossible internally. Perhaps most important, managers must recognize the cold reality that *not* achieving a strong enough competitive performance in each critical service activity will relegate the company to an inevitable loss of strategic advantage, provide lower profitability, and create a higher risk of takeover by those who do see the missed potentials.

■ COLLABORATE WITH YOUR COMPETITORS—AND WIN[†]

By Gary Hamel, Yves Doz, and C. K. Prahalad

Collaboration between competitors is in fashion. General Motors and Toyota assemble automobiles, Siemens and Philips develop semiconductors, Canon supplies photocopiers to Kodak, France's Thomson and Japan's JVC manufacture videocassette recorders. But the spread of what we call "competitive collaboration"—joint ventures, outsourcing agreements, product licensings, cooperative research—has triggered unease about the long-term consequences. A strategic alliance can strengthen both companies against outsiders even as it weakens one partner vis-à-vis the other. In particular, alliances between Asian companies and Western rivals seem to work against the Western partner. Cooperation becomes a low-cost route for new competitors to gain technology and market access.

Yet the case for collaboration is stronger than ever. It takes so much money to develop new products and to penetrate new markets that few companies can go it alone in every situation. ICL, the British computer company, could not have developed its current generation of mainframes without Fujitsu. Motorola needs Toshiba's distribution capacity to break into the Japanese semiconductor market. Time is another critical factor. Alliances can provide shortcuts for Western companies racing to improve their production efficiency and quality control.

We have spent more than five years studying the inner workings of fifteen strategic alliances and monitoring scores of others. Our research involves cooperative ventures between competitors from the United States and Japan, Europe and Japan, and the United States and Europe. We did not judge the success or failure of each partnership by its longevity—a common mistake when evaluating strategic alliances—but by the shifts in competitive strength on each side. We focused on how companies use competitive collaboration to enhance their internal skills and technologies while they guard against transferring competitive advantages to ambitious partners.

There is no immutable law that strategic alliances *must* be a windfall for Japanese or Korean partners. Many Western companies do give away more than they gain—but that's because they enter partnerships without knowing what it takes to win. Companies that benefit most from competitive collaboration adhere to a set of simple but powerful principles.

Collaboration is competition in a different form. Successful companies never forget that their new partners may be out to disarm them. They enter alliances with clear strategic objectives, and they also understand how their partners' objectives will affect their success.

Harmony is not the most important measure of success. Indeed, occasional conflict may be the best evidence of mutually beneficial collaboration. Few alliances remain win-win undertakings forever. A partner may be content even as it unknowingly surrenders core skills.

Cooperation has limits. Companies must defend against competitive compromise. A strategic alliance is a constantly evolving bargain whose real terms go beyond the legal agreement or the aims of top management. What information gets traded is determined day to day, often by engineers and operating managers. Successful companies inform employees at all levels about what skills and technologies are off-limits to the partner and monitor what the partner requests and receives.

Learning from partners is paramount. Successful companies view each alliance as a window on their partners' broad capabilities. They use the alliance to build skills in areas outside the formal agreement and systematically diffuse new knowledge throughout their organizations.

Why Collaborate?

Using an alliance with a competitor to acquire new technologies or skills is not devious. It reflects the commitment and capacity of each partner to absorb the skills of the other. We found that in every case in which a Japanese company emerged from an alliance stronger than its Western partner, the Japanese company had made a greater effort to learn.

Strategic intent is an essential ingredient in the commitment to learning. The willingness of Asian companies to enter alliances represents a change in competitive tactics, not competitive goals. NEC, for example, has used a series of collaborative ventures to enhance its technology and product competences. NEC is the only company in the world with a leading position in telecommunications, computers, and semiconductors—despite its investing less in research and development (R&D) (as a percentage of revenues) than competitors like Texas Instruments, Northern Telecom, and L.M. Ericsson. Its string of partnerships, most notably with Honeywell, allowed NEC to leverage its in-house R&D over the last two decades.

Western companies, on the other hand, often enter alliances to avoid investments. They are more interested in reducing the costs and risks of entering new businesses or markets than in acquiring new skills. A senior U.S. manager offered this analysis of his company's venture with a Japanese rival: "We complement each other well—our distribution capability and their manufacturing skill. I see no reason to invest upstream if we can find a secure source of product. This is a comfortable relationship for us."

An executive from this company's Japanese partner offered a different perspective: "When it is necessary to collaborate, I go to my employees and say, 'This is bad, I wish we had these skills ourselves. Collaboration is second best. But I will feel worse if after four years we do not know how to do what our partner knows how to do.' We must digest their skills."

The problem here is not that the U.S. company wants to share investment risk (its Japanese partner does too) but that the U.S. company has no ambition beyond avoidance. When the commitment to learning is so one-sided, collaboration invariably leads to competitive compromise.

Many so-called alliances between Western companies and their Asian rivals are little more than sophisticated outsourcing arrangements. General Motors buys cars and components from Korea's Daewoo. Siemens buys computers from Fujitsu. Apple buys laser printer engines from Canon. The traffic is almost entirely one way. These original equipment manufacturer (OEM) deals offer Asian partners a way to capture investment initiative from Western competitors and displace customer-competitors from value-creating activities. In many cases this goal meshes with that of the Western partner: to regain competitiveness quickly and with minimum effort.

Consider the joint venture between Rover, the British automaker, and Honda. Some twenty-five years ago, Rover's forerunners were world leaders in small car design. Honda had not even entered the automobile business. But in the mid-1970s, after failing to penetrate foreign markets, Rover turned to Honda for technology and product development support. Rover has used the alliance to avoid investments to design and build new cars. Honda has cultivated skills in European styling and marketing as well as multinational manufacturing. There is little doubt which company will emerge stronger over the long term.

Troubled laggards like Rover often strike alliances with surging latecomers like Honda. Having fallen behind in a key skills area (in this case, manufacturing small cars), the laggard attempts to compensate for past failures. The latecomer uses the alliance to close a specific skills gap (in this case, learning to build cars for a regional market). But a laggard that forges a partnership for short-term gain may find itself in a dependency spiral: as it contributes fewer and fewer distinctive skills, it must reveal more and more of its internal operations to keep the partner interested. For the weaker company, the issue shifts from, Should we collaborate? to With whom should we collaborate? to How do we keep our partner interested as we lose the advantages that made us attractive to them in the first place?

There's a certain paradox here. When both partners are equally intent on internalizing the other's skills, distrust and conflict may spoil the alliance and threaten its very survival. That's one reason joint ventures between Korean and Japanese companies have been few and tempestuous. Neither side wants to "open the kimono." Alliances seem to run most smoothly when one partner is intent on learning and the other is intent on avoidance—in essence, when one partner is willing to grow dependent on the other. But running smoothly is not the point; the point is for a company to emerge from an alliance more competitive than when it entered it.

One partner does not always have to give up more than it gains to ensure the survival of an alliance. There are certain conditions under which mutual gain is possible, at least for a time:

The partners' strategic goals converge while their competitive goals diverge. That is, each partner allows for the other's continued prosperity in the shared business. Philips and Du Pont collaborate to develop and manufacture compact discs, but neither side invades the other's market. There is a clear upstream/downstream division of effort.

The size and market power of both partners is modest compared with industry leaders. This forces each side to accept that mutual dependence may have to continue for many years. Long-term collaboration may be so critical to both partners that neither will risk antagonizing the other by an overtly competitive bid to appropriate skills or competences. Fujitsu's 1 to 5 size disadvantage with IBM means it will be a long time, if ever, before Fujitsu can break away from its foreign partners and go it alone.

Each partner believes it can learn from the other and at the same time limit access to proprietary skills. JVC and Thomson, both of whom make VCRs, know that they are trading skills. But the two companies are looking for very different things. Thomson needs product technology and manufacturing prowess; JVC needs to learn how to succeed in the fragmented European market. Both sides believe there is an equitable chance for gain.

How to Build Secure Defenses

For collaboration to succeed, each partner must contribute something distinctive: basic research, product development skills, manufacturing capacity, access to distribution. The challenge is to share enough skills to create advantage vis-à-vis companies outside the alliance while preventing a wholesale transfer of core skills to the partner. This is a very thin line to walk. Companies must carefully select what skills and technologies they pass to their partners. They must develop safeguards against unintended, informal transfers of information. The goal is to limit the transparency of their operations.

The type of skill a company contributes is an important factor in how easily its partner can internalize the skills. The potential for transfer is greatest when a partner's contribution is easily transported (in engineering drawings, on computer tapes, or in the heads of a few technical experts); easily interpreted (it can be reduced to commonly understood equations or symbols); and easily absorbed (the skill or competence is independent of any particular cultural context).

Western companies face an inherent disadvantage because their skills are generally more vulnerable to transfer. The magnet that attracts so many companies to alliances with Asian competitors is their manufacturing excellence—a competence that is less transferable than most. Just-in-time inventory systems and quality circles can be imitated, but this is like pulling a few threads out of an oriental carpet. Manufacturing excellence is a complex web of employee training, integration with suppliers, statistical process controls, employee involvement, value engineering, and design for manufacture. It is difficult to extract such a subtle competence in any way but a piecemeal fashion.

So companies must take steps to limit transparency. One approach is to limit the scope of the formal agreement. It might cover a single technology rather than an entire range of technologies; part of a product line rather than the entire line; distribution in a limited number of markets or for a limited period of time. The objective is to circumscribe a partner's opportunities to learn.

Moreover, agreements should establish specific performance requirements. Motorola, for example, takes an incremental, incentive-based approach to technology transfer in its venture with Toshiba. The agreement calls for Motorola to release its microprocessor technology incrementally as Toshiba delivers on its promise to increase Motorola's penetration in the Japanese semiconductor market. The greater Motorola's market share, the greater Toshiba's access to Motorola's technology.

Many of the skills that migrate between companies are not covered in the formal terms of collaboration. Top management puts together strategic alliances and sets the legal parameters for exchange. But what actually gets traded is determined by day-to-day interactions of engineers, marketers, and product developers: who says what to whom, who gets access to what facilities, who sits on what joint committees. The most important deals ("I'll share this with you if you share that with me") may be struck four or five organizational levels below where the deal was signed. Here lurks the greatest risk of unintended transfers of important skills.

Consider one technology-sharing alliance between European and Japanese competitors. The European company valued the partnership as a way to acquire a specific technology. The Japanese company considered it a window on its partner's entire range of competences and interacted with a broad spectrum of its partner's marketing and product development staff. The company mined each contact for as much information as possible.

For example, every time the European company requested a new feature on a product being sourced from its partner, the Japanese company asked for detailed customer and competitor analyses to justify the request. Over time, it developed a sophisticated picture of the European market that would assist its own entry strategy. The technology acquired by the European partner through the formal agreement had a useful life of three to five years. The competitive insights acquired informally by the Japanese company will probably endure longer.

Limiting unintended transfers at the operating level requires careful attention to the role of gatekeepers, the people who control what information flows to a partner. A gatekeeper can be effective only if there are a limited number of gateways through which a partner can access people and facilities. Fujitsu's many partners all go through a single office, the "collaboration section," to request information and assistance from different divisions. This way the company can monitor and control access to critical skills and technologies.

We studied one partnership between European and U.S. competitors that involved several divisions of each company. While the U.S. company could only access its partner through a single gateway, its partner had unfettered access to all participating divisions. The European company took advantage of its free rein. If one division refused to provide certain information, the European partner made the same request of another division. No single manager in the U.S. company could tell how much information had been transferred or was in a position to piece together patterns in the requests.

Collegiality is a prerequisite for collaborative success. But *too much* collegiality should set off warning bells to senior managers. CEOs or division presidents should expect occasional complaints from their counterparts about the reluctance of lower level employees to share information. That's a sign that the gatekeepers are doing their jobs. And senior management should regularly debrief operating personnel to find out what information the partner is requesting and what requests are being granted.

Limiting unintended transfers ultimately depends on employee loyalty and self-discipline. This was a real issue for many of the Western companies we studied. In their excitement and pride over technical achievements, engineering staffs sometimes shared information that top management considered sensitive. Japanese engineers were less likely to share proprietary information.

There are a host of cultural and professional reasons for the relative openness of Western technicians. Japanese engineers and scientists are more loyal to their company than to their profession. They are less steeped in the open give-and-take of university research since they receive much of their training from employers. They consider themselves team members more than individual scientific contributors. As one Japanese manager noted, "We don't feel any need to reveal what we know. It is not an issue of pride for us. We're glad to sit and listen. If we're patient we usually learn what we want to know."

Controlling unintended transfers may require restricting access to facilities as well as to people. Companies should declare sensitive laboratories and factories off-limits to their partners. Better yet, they might house the collaborative venture in an entirely new facility. IBM is building a special site in Japan where Fujitsu can review its forthcoming mainframe software before deciding whether to license it. IBM will be able to control exactly what Fujitsu sees and what information leaves the facility.

Finally, which country serves as "home" to the alliance affects transparency. If the collaborative team is located near one partner's major facilities, the other partner will have more opportunities to learn—but less control over what information gets traded. When the partner houses, feeds, and looks after engineers and operating managers, there is a danger they will "go native." Expatriate personnel need frequent visits from headquarters as well as regular furloughs home.

Enhance the Capacity to Learn

Whether collaboration leads to competitive surrender or revitalization depends foremost on what employees believe the purpose of the alliance to be. It is self-evident: to learn, one must want to learn. Western companies won't realize the full benefits of competitive collaboration until they overcome an arrogance borne of decades of leadership. In short, Western companies must be more receptive.

We asked a senior executive in a Japanese electronics company about the perception that Japanese companies learn more from their foreign partners than vice versa. "Our Western partners approach us with the attitude of teachers," he told us. "We are quite happy with this, because we have the attitude of students."

Learning begins at the top. Senior management must be committed to enhancing their companies' skills as well as to avoiding financial risk. But most learning takes place at the lower levels of an alliance. Operating employees not only represent the front lines in an effective defense but also play a vital role in acquiring knowledge. They must be well briefed on the partner's strengths and weaknesses and understand how acquiring particular skills will bolster their company's competitive position.

This is already standard practice among Asian companies. We accompanied a Japanese development engineer on a tour through a partner's factory. This engineer dutifully took notes on plant layout, the number of production stages, the rate at which the line was running, and the number of employees. He recorded all this despite the fact that he had no manufacturing responsibility in his own company, and that the alliance didn't encompass joint manufacturing. Such dedication greatly enhances learning.

Collaboration doesn't always provide an opportunity to fully internalize a partner's skills. Yet just acquiring new and more precise benchmarks of a partner's performance can be of great value. A new benchmark can provoke a thorough review of internal performance levels and may spur a round of competitive innovation. Asking questions like, Why do their semiconductor logic designs have fewer errors than ours? and Why are they investing in this technology and we're not? may provide the incentive for a vigorous catch-up program.

Competitive benchmarking is a tradition in most of the Japanese companies we studied. It requires many of the same skills associated with competitor analysis: systematically calibrating performance against external targets; learning to use rough estimates to determine where a competitor (or partner) is better, faster, or cheaper; translating those estimates into new internal targets; and recalibrating to establish the rate of improvement in a competitor's performance. The great advantage of competitive collaboration is that proximity makes benchmarking easier.

Indeed, some analysts argue that one of Toyota's motivations in collaborating with GM in the much-publicized NUMMI venture is to gauge the quality of GM's manufacturing technology. GM's top manufacturing people get a close look at Toyota, but the reverse is true as well. Toyota may be learning whether its giant U.S. competitor is capable of closing the productivity gap with Japan.

Competitive collaboration also provides a way of getting close enough to rivals to predict how they will behave when the alliance unravels or runs its course. How does the partner respond to price changes? How does it measure and reward executives? How does it prepare to launch a new product? By revealing a competitor's management orthodoxies, collaboration can increase the chances of success in future head-to-head battles.

Knowledge acquired from a competitor-partner is only valuable after it is diffused through the organization. Several companies we studied had established internal clearinghouses to collect and disseminate information. The collaborations manager at one Japanese company regularly made the rounds of all employees involved in alliances. He identified what information had been collected by whom and then passed it on to appropriate departments. Another company held regular meetings where employees shared new knowledge and determined who was best positioned to acquire additional information.

Proceed with Care—But Proceed

After World War II, Japanese and Korean companies entered alliances with Western rivals from weak positions. But they worked steadfastly toward independence. In the early 1960s, NEC's computer business was one-quarter the size of Honeywell's, its primary foreign partner. It took only two decades for NEC to grow larger than Honeywell, which eventually sold its computer operations to an alliance between NEC and Group Bull of France. The NEC experience demonstrates that dependence on a foreign partner doesn't automatically condemn a company to also-ran status. Collaboration may sometimes be unavoidable; surrender is not.

Managers are too often obsessed with the ownership structure of an alliance. Whether a company controls 51 percent or 49 percent of a joint venture may be much less important than the rate at which each partner learns from the other. Companies that are confident of their ability to learn may even prefer some ambiguity in the alliance's legal structure. Ambiguity creates more potential to acquire skills and technologies. The challenge for Western companies is not to write tighter legal agreements but to become better learners.

Running away from collaboration is no answer. Even the largest Western companies can no longer outspend their global rivals. With leadership in many industries shifting toward the East, companies in the United States and Europe must become good borrowers—much like Asian companies did in the 1960s and 1970s. Competitive renewal depends on building new process capabilities and winning new product and technology battles. Collaboration can be a low-cost strategy for doing both.

■ THE FIRM AS A NEXUS OF TREATIES[†]

By Torger Reve

Strategic Alliances

The strategic core consisting of assets of high specificity should always be governed within the boundaries of the firm. With no strategic core there is no economic rationale for the existence of the firm. Having defined and delimited the strategic core, the next step in strategic analysis is to analyse which economies can be obtained from the strategic core basis. Sometimes such an analysis would lead to an expansion of firm boundaries, for example, by vertical integration or horizontal acquisitions, but often the same economies can be obtained through strategic alliances with other firms relying on bilateral governance. Here an analysis of economies that can be obtained based in the strategic core is first presented, then realization of these economies through strategic alliances is discussed.

Basically four types of economy can be obtained starting from a given strategic core. For each type of economy there is a strategic expansion path. Thus the firm has four strategic expansion paths: downstream vertical integration, upstream vertical integration, horizontal integration, and diversification (see figure 7-1). Let us discuss these paths one by one.

The first two strategies both have to do with vertical integration. Vertical integration may result from technological factors producing externalities when successive stages of production and distribution are under separate ownership and control, or it may arise

†**Source:** This article was originally published as "The Firm as a Nexus of Internal and External Contracts," in *The Firm as a Nexus of Treaties,* edited by M. Aoki, M. Gustafsson, and O. E. Williamson, Sage Publications, Ltd. Copyright © 1990. Reprinted with permission.

FIGURE 7-1
Economies Based in the
Strategic Core

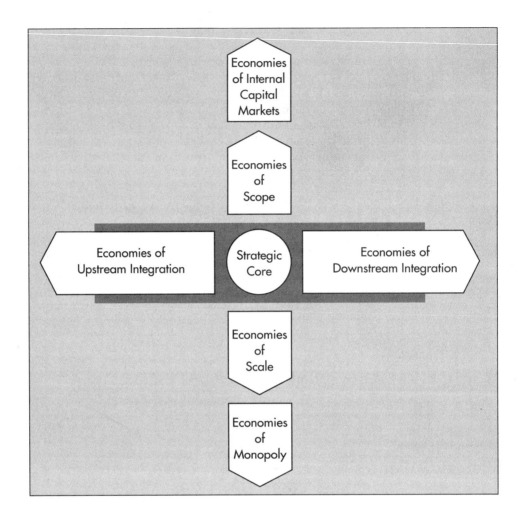

from informational and behavioural factors producing contracting difficulties when the parties are separate and independent. Economies of integration, I argue, can often be more efficiently obtained through vertical corporate agreements than through vertical integration by ownership. The question of ownership is actually of little importance here: it is the vertical control that matters from a strategy point of view. Vertical control can be obtained through ownership, but full vertical integration ties up capital resources and creates considerable management problems as the firm gets involved in successive stages of production or distribution where it has very little experience. Only in the few cases of very high asset specificity should full vertical integration be undertaken. When asset specificity is medium, external contracts can secure the necessary amount of vertical control. These phenomena have been extensively discussed elsewhere and lend themselves to the contractual analysis suggested by this article. Vertical marketing systems based on various types of bilateral governance are prevalent throughout most industries, as are subcontracting, licensing, and other co-operative agreements.

Two types of vertical integration or control should be distinguished: downstream integration means developing ties of co-ordination with customers, while upstream integration means developing ties of co-ordination with suppliers. When input resources are in short supply or require specific adjustments to the firm's production process, upstream integration should be considered. When customers represent the critical factor in the firm's success (which is naturally often the case), downstream integration should be considered. The study of long-lasting supplier and customer networks in industrial markets studied by Swedish researchers illustrates the importance of vertical relations through implicit contracting and trust, a phenomenon that has also been observed in the organization of Japanese industry. Both use the term *network* to denote the phenomenon. In Japan, production contracts and technological contracts are the most common vertical interfirm tie-ups, followed by marketing contracts, which are probably more common in Europe. A particular type of marketing contract that warrants mentioning is the franchising contract pioneered by American distributors. Franchising is a hierarchy-like exchange contract with strict central co-ordination, but ownership and operations are left to the local entrepreneur.

A traditional route for strategic expansion is through the exploitation of scale economies. Economies of scale can be obtained through investments in internal production capacity and growth, but a quicker route is through horizontal integration by mergers and acquisitions. Horizontal integration is often considered anticompetitive and is regulated through antitrust legislation, especially in the United States. In many other countries horizontal mergers and acquisitions are allowed on the grounds that international competitiveness needs to be strengthened, or simply from pure cost-scale arguments. Merger moves among some firms often lead to mergers among many of the remaining firms until some type of balance oligopoly results. One example is the international mergers which have taken place in the electrotechnical industry where three multinational companies—Asea Brown Boveri, Siemens, and General Electric—have formed to meet the Japanese giants in the same industry.

With the advent of new technology, for example, numerical control machines and other applications of information technology, technological scale requirements have been decreased in many industries. Thus scale arguments are more related to bargaining power in factor markets and leverage in capital markets than to traditional technological scale factors. Again there is a concern by legislators that horizontal strategies based on economies-of-scale arguments can develop into a potential domination strategy exploiting economies of monopoly with the loss of consumer welfare.

Scale economies can of course also be obtained through joint ventures rather than through mergers and acquisitions. Many managers avoid joint ventures because of the management problems involved when crossing organizational boundaries. Others see joint ventures as a means of horizontal expansion when capital resources are limited or the firm is facing other constraints on expansion.

A creative use of horizontal strategic alliances is to form such alliances in order to obtain advantages in vertical relations. Retailers form voluntary chains to be able to obtain better terms of trade with their suppliers and industrial vendors form joint venture companies to obtain large contracts with demanding customers.

The fourth path of strategic expansion is by exploiting economies of scope through related diversification. Economies of scope arise when some common skills are shared or utilized jointly. Such skills are found within the strategic core of the firm. Economies of scope give more precise meaning to the broader notion of synergy, which has been discussed in the strategy literature for decades. In principle, synergy can be traded between firms on the open market, but substantial contracting difficulties are likely to arise, as discussed at the start of the chapter. Economies of scope can therefore best be obtained through more specialized governance mechanisms, that is, by internal or bilateral governance.

Related diversification by ownership creates many of the problems mentioned under vertical integration, for example, large capital and managerial requirements. Again the alternative to consider is strategic alliances. In economies-of-scope situations the transacting parties have complementary assets that make them mutually interdependent. Such situations motivate firms to form co-operative agreements, and such agreements are also more likely to succeed. There are, however, problems involved in sharing strategic resources in joint ventures. Both parties have to go into the exchange with well-defined strategic cores that need to be protected in future exchange. Otherwise there is the risk that one party absorbs the core skills of the other party and abandons the joint venture. At the same time there has to be transfer of assets and skills to realize the alliance potential. The role of trust is essential here, as we will see in the section on incentives.

The discussion of the four types of economies—economies of downstream integration, upstream integration, scale, and scope—is significant in order to understand what is meant by complementary skills in external contracts. The strategic core contained core skills governed internally. Strategic alliances are contracts over complementary skills governed bilaterally. Skills are complementary when one of the four types of economy can be obtained when combining these skills with the strategic core. Evaluating such economies requires both organizational and economic analysis in order to achieve compatibility and profitability.

In this section the four types of strategic alliance corresponding to the four different strategic paths have been discussed as pure types. It was mentioned though that one type of alliance is sometimes formed to increase bargaining power in other alliances, for example, using horizontal alliances to influence vertical relationships. More complex sets of strategic alliances are found in Japanese *keiretsu* relationships of the major corporate groups. Here all four types of alliance constitute one big network organization. Similar patterns can be found for some of the major European corporations, for example Swedish Volvo, although the amount of capital control is typically higher.

While *keiretsu* relationships are built around a strong corporate core, such as Mitsui or Mitsubishi, network organizations are also found among smaller firms. In fact, the core skills that keep some of these network organizations together are simply the networking management capacity. An example has been given by Imai in the case of Dainichi's research and development (R&D) efforts in robotics. Dainichi is neither a robot manufacturer nor a robot user, but an integrator of manufacturers and users. Here interface skills become the strategic core of the network organization, and the full range of strategic alliances are activated to attain strategic goals.

These two types of network organizations—those that centre on a dominant corporate group and those that are built on interface skills—represent, in this author's view, business organizations of the future.

The Role of Incentives

There are basically two approaches to the agency problems of alliances. One is the economic approach in which self-interested actors choose a co-operative solution to increase joint profits. Transactions have to be protected by safeguards, and relations remain impersonal and unstable. Typically a game formulation is used for analysing such bilateral contracting.

The other approach is more behavioural in nature and attaches a value to the relationship between the parties. Under this approach the identity of the exchange party is critical, and relations tend to be long lasting. Contracts do not only apply to a particular transaction, thus both prior and future exchange matters. Social ties are built, and trust and solidarity develop between the parties. The exchange situation can best be described in terms of relations contracts. Relations contracts are characterized by relational norms such as role integrity, trust, preservation of relation, conflict resolution and supracontract norms.

In the economic approach bilateral exchange is formulated as a bargaining problem. In bargaining the pattern of dependence between the parties is often the determining factor, and the various bases of power available are activated by both parties. This does not mean that the parties cannot reach co-operative agreements, but they will search for the best solution to the game, exploiting fully their game position.

In the behavioural approach bilateral exchange can also be seen as a bargaining situation, but a more long-range view is taken. As is the case in repeated, co-operative games, transactions can be undertaken using trust, and long-lasting, transaction cost-efficient contracts.

In the first case, the pattern of dependencies may define imbalanced power, which allows for the use of authority and organizationlike incentives. In the second case, shared values and exchange norms tend to develop as interorganizational incentives. In both cases, skills in negotiations and relationship management may have an impact on the terms obtained.

Comparing governance in internal and external contracts shows organizational governance to be hard and authority based, while interorganizational governance tends to be soft and negotiation based. In reality, the two modes of governance penetrate each other. Thus negotiation supplements authority in organizations, and power supplements negotiations in bilateral governance.

In terms of strategic management the role of organizational and interorganizational incentives in maintaining core and complementary skills should be emphasized. Incentives need to be tailor-made to the assets in question depending on the asset specificity involved. Negotiations and relational skills tend to be more and more common in strategic management, given the importance of strategic alliances and mixed modes of organizational governance.

An Integrated Model of Strategy

The simple model of strategy developed here has two major elements: strategic core and strategic alliances. The strategic core is governed by internal contracts relying on organizational incentives, while the strategic alliances are governed by external contracts relying on interorganizational incentives. Core skills are high in asset specificity and are governed internally, while the complementary skills are of medium-asset specificity and governed through alliances. All other assets of low specificity are obtained in the market.

Strategic management according to this model is the alignment of strategic core and strategic alliances to obtain sustainable competitive advantage. The model is a normative model, arguing that efficiency gains can be obtained by drawing the efficient boundaries of the firm. Thus there is an optimal set of internal and external contracts that define the ideal strategic position of the firm under given external conditions. The model does not argue that this strategy optimum can easily be found,

FIGURE 7-2
Contracting Model of
Strategic Management

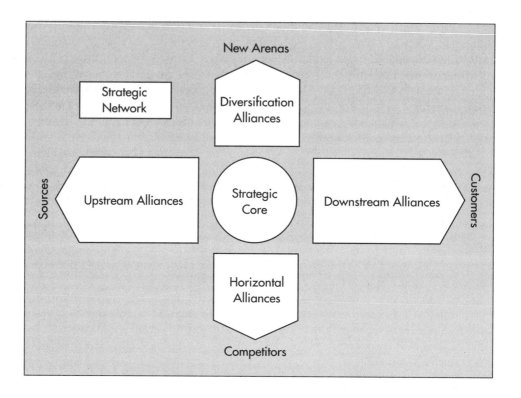

but at least it gives some guidance in distinguishing between efficient and nonefficient strategies. In addition to providing a theoretical underpinning of important aspects of strategic management, the concepts involved can easily be translated into managerial language. Strategy consists of critical skills and relationships held together by appropriate incentives. Skills and relationships need to be created, maintained, and developed, and efficient boundaries have to be established to economize on transaction costs.

Using the notion presented that strategic core can be identified within the value chain, there are four types of economies to be obtained—downstream and upstream integration, scale, and scope. When asset specificity is medium, such economies can most efficiently be obtained through strategic alliances, also of four types— downstream, upstream, horizontal, and diversification alliances (see figure 7-2).

Diversification alliances are limited to an exploitation of economies of scope, and thus only include related diversification. Unrelated diversification to exploit internal capital market economies is not considered further, given the economic rationale against this type of diversification.

Horizontal alliances are limited to an exploitation of economies of scale, and thus do not include the formation of cartels or monopolies, given that such alternatives are typically banned by antitrust legislation. In principle, all types of market imperfections can be exploited strategically, as strongly argued by Porter.

The contracting model of strategy developed in this article primarily deals with governance issues of efficient boundaries, arguing that governance advantages produce an advantageous strategic position. Such a model, I argue strongly, can fill in the organizational void of Porter's competitive-positioning model. Pedagogically, the positioning model and the contracting model can be integrated into one figure (see figure 7-3).

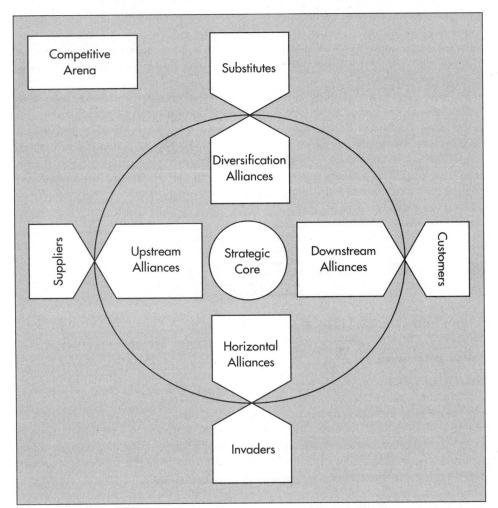

FIGURE 7-3
Integrated Model of
Strategic Management

Putting the two strategy models into one figure does not necessarily produce an integrated model of strategy. Some would even prefer to keep the two models separate and not make things even more complex. If positioning and contracting are the two major elements of strategy, positioning being the external component, and contracting the internal and bridging component, it should be possible to suggest linkages between the two.

Going back to the figure of the integrated model, we see how downstream and upstream alliances are ways of positioning the firm relative to its customers and suppliers. In fact, vertical alliances may be ways in which entry barriers are erected and market imperfections are exploited. At the same time, there are integration economies to be obtained from vertical alliances, for example, by superior logistics and marketing.

Horizontal alliances clearly have a role to play when it comes to potential invaders. Horizontal alliances may be formed with firms that are likely to be future invaders in order to preempt invasion. Furthermore, they may be formed to create entry barriers that make it more difficult for potential invaders to succeed.

Diversification alliances basically have the objective of taking the firm into another competitive arena, thus going beyond Porter's industry-type analysis. If diversification means forming technology contracts with other firms, it may also be a way of meeting substitutes in the existing competitive arena. Thus diversification alliances may be one way of technology transfer that makes the firm ready to meet challenges from substitutes in an existing competitive arena, or such alliances may be a way of moving the firm out of a mature competitive industry and into new arenas when new technology takes over.

Fully developed, an integrated model of strategy should capture the full repertoire of strategies a firm can activate. The model should point out the strategic expansion paths available, and it should demonstrate how the various alternatives interact. Furthermore, the model should allow for external changes to guide the firm in its adaptation to changing markets. This final factor shows the importance of joining the positioning model of strategy with the contracting model of strategy to stay with the original notion of strategy as the adaptation between organization and environment to attain strategic and economic goals.

■ NETWORK POSITIONS AND STRATEGIC ACTION†

By Jan Johanson and Lars-Gunnar Mattsson

Introduction

The basic idea in the industrial network model is that firms are engaged in networks of business relationships. The network structure, that is, the ways in which the firms are linked to each other, develops as a consequence of the firms transacting business with each other. At the same time, the network structure constitutes the framework within which business is carried out. This article develops and discusses a notion of strategic action in industrial networks. Strategic action is interesting not only in its consequences for firms, but also because of its implications for the dynamics of industrial systems.

There are three specific attributes of the network model that are central to the argument developed here. First, it views networks as sets of connected relationships between actors. Further, a distinction is made between two levels in the industrial system: the network of exchange relationships between industrial actors and the production system where resources are employed and developed in production. Resources and activities form the production system. The network of exchange relationships is viewed as a structure governing the production system. Second, the concept of network position is used to describe how the individual actors in the network are related to each other in a network structure. Third, both the means and ends of strategic action are closely linked to the position concept.

The choice of these three characteristics may be justified on the following grounds:

■ The separation of the actors in the network from the resources and activities in the production system is analytically helpful, first of all because the concept of strategic action presupposes actors. Actors have intentions, they make interpretations of conditions in the industrial system, and they act. It is also useful because there is not necessarily a one-to-one correspondence between a production system and a network of relationships. For

†**Source:** This article was originally published in *Industrial Networks: A New View of Reality*, edited by B. Axelsson and G. Easton (Routledge, 1992). Reprinted with permission.

example, an actor in a network may be engaged in exchange relationships covering several production systems or control different, widely separated clusters of resources in one production system. Correspondingly a production system may involve several actors who have no business relationships with each other.

■ The use of the position concept is not only a way to move from a dyadic to a network analysis, but it also provides a conceptual understanding of how the individual actor is related to, or rather embedded in, the environment.

■ The use of the position concept as both means and ends of strategic action makes it possible to give such action meaning in relation to the conditions for structural change in industrial networks. This is another way of saying that the individual actor's opportunities and constraints depend on the network and on the results of earlier strategic action. Thus, the notions of embeddedness and of investments in networks are given strategic meaning.

The Industrial System

In production systems, resources are employed, combined, and transformed in industrial production. Coordination and direction of activities in the production systems takes place through governance structures. The production system together with the governance structure constitutes the industrial system. The term *production* is taken in a wide sense to include all the different kinds of activities needed to create and use products and services (research and development, manufacturing, marketing, distribution, purchasing, and so on). The resources are dependent on each other in the sense that the outcome of the use of one resource is dependent on how another is used. The resources are more or less heterogeneous and specialised. The more they are specialised the stronger are the dependencies between actors. In the extreme case when two resources are completely specialised in a use where they are combined, they are completely complementary and there is a very high positive dependence between them. At the opposite extreme two specialised resources may be complete substitutes, in which case there is a high negative interdependence. On the whole, an operating production system can be characterised in terms of dependence between resources according to an industrial logic where resources are more or less complementary and/or substitutable inputs into, and outputs from, production.

Resource specialisation and interdependencies are, however, not solely determined by some technical imperative. In any specific situation they are a consequence of earlier use of the resources and of the structure of the production system. Resources are more or less heterogeneous, implying that they have properties in a number of different dimensions, so that, over time, they can be used in different ways, combined in different ways, and transformed in different ways. Thus, two heterogeneous resources that are combined can usually, through experience in use, become more specialised in their combined use leading to higher joint productivity, higher degrees of complementarity, and increased interdependence between them.

In such production systems, where there are innumerable, different, and changing resource interdependencies, there is a strong need for some kind of coordination between resources not only to economise their use, but also to create changes of an innovative nature. Traditionally two different governance modes are assumed to bring about this coordination: the hierarchy and the market. In the hierarchy, one supreme actor controls all the resources and brings about coordination. In the market model coordination takes place through price signals that inform the autonomous actors

FIGURE 7-4
Network Governance
in the Industrial System

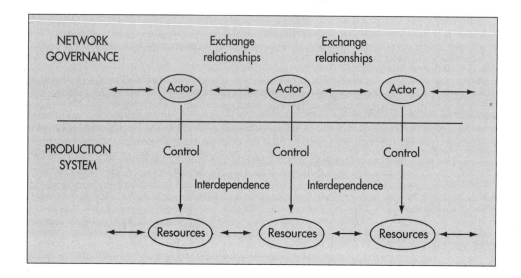

about the availability of, and need for, resources. In the present model it is assumed that the production system is governed through a network of exchange relationships between semiautonomous actors. The actors are engaged in and develop exchange relationships with each other and can in this way handle the interdependencies between the resources they control (see figure 7-4).

We assume a circular causal relation between the network level and the production level. Through the exchange relationships the actors learn about each other and develop some trust in each other. On that basis they adapt and develop their resource use to increase productivity, which also leads to increased resource interdependence between them. At the same time, as a result of interdependence, the actors develop their relationships, thus linking them closer to each other. Consequently, unless no other factors intervene, through current activities the specific dependencies and relationships will become gradually stronger and closer. However, as the specific relationship is embedded in a network of such relationships and since this focal dependence is only one in an intricate fabric of such dependencies, there are always intervening factors affecting the causal circle. Sometimes such forces are channelled via the network, sometimes they operate through the dependencies in the production system (see figure 7-5).

The exchange relationship is a mutual orientation of two actors toward each other. They are prepared to interact with each other in order to coordinate and develop

FIGURE 7-5
Interlinked Causal
Relationship/
Interdependence Circles

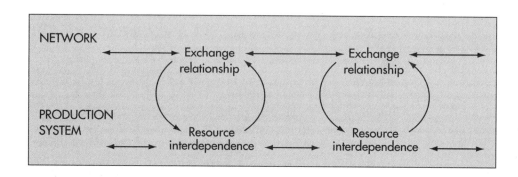

interdependent resources that each actor controls. They interact to get access to some of the resources controlled by the other actor. These exchange relationships develop over time and resources are used to establish, maintain, and develop them. Exchange relationships in networks may become lasting, especially if the heterogeneous resources controlled by the actors become adapted to each other and become highly specialised.

Exchange relationships also link actors indirectly to other actors with whom they do not have any such relationships. Actors in the industrial system also use resources that are interdependent without the actors having exchange relationships with each other. This is typically the case with competing actors. Similarly there may be interdependencies between actors with complementary resources, for example, complementary suppliers who have no exchange relationship with each other. If actors consider such interdependencies important, they may start interaction with each othcr, thus developing an exchange relationship. Correspondingly, actors may have more or less dormant relationships with each other, for historical or other reasons, without any resource dependencies between the resources they control. Such relationships may be used to combine resources, thus creating new productive resource interdependence.

Connected Relationships

A basic characteristic of networks is that relationships are connected; that is, exchange in one relationship is conditioned by exchange in others. The connections may be positive or negative. A positive connection between two relationships implies that exchange in one relationship has a positive effect on exchange in the other. This is, for instance, the case with relationships handling a sequence of interdependencies along a production chain. Correspondingly, two competing suppliers to a customer are usually negatively connected via that customer. The two cases are examples of simple connections via the resource interdependencies in the production system. It is apparent that connections in a network may be much more indirect and complex, so that two distant relationships in a network are connected with each other in multiple ways, some of which are positive and some negative.

However, the connections between relationships may also take place exclusively via the actors at the network level. In this case they are of a subjective nature and are a matter of intentions, strategies, views, and the "network theories" of the actors. Thus, an actor may, taking a long-term view of a market, consider two relationships as complementary in some sense, for instance, in terms of technical development. Similarly the actor may see two relationships as substitutes for each other in a foreign market entry. Thus, although there are no interdependencies on the production level, the two relationships may be negatively connected. Obviously, actor-mediated connections are much more ambiguous, fluid, and invisible than those that are resource interdependence-mediated. Nevertheless, they exist and have important implications for network development.

Since there are no objective criteria to decide which exchange relationships to include in networks and which to exclude, the boundaries of a specific network are necessarily fuzzy. However, certain interdependence criteria may be used. A production system can be delimited on the basis of resource interdependencies in relation to some focal product, technology, country, or region. The inclusion of relationships is then a matter of determining who the actors are who control relevant resources. The excluded relationships can then be regarded as belonging to other networks and as a means of providing links between networks. If, for example, the focal production system exists in a certain geographic area, relationships with actors outside that area should reasonably be considered as links to other networks. On the other hand, if there are strong interdependencies between resources in that area and resources in other areas, the focal production system should not be delimited on an area basis. One test of such delimitations is whether there are important exchange relationships with actors in other networks. Thus, if the exchange relationships included coordinated resources that according to a specific industrial logic belong to a specified focal production system, a test of the suitability of such a definition is if any excluded exchange relationships coordinate resources that have important influences on the included relationships.

Since we are interested in industrial development and structural change, influences from actors outside the focal network, that is, the network governing the focal production system, could be important. As an example, it is sufficient to mention internationalisation of competition. Even if it is apparent that the whole world is connected, we need, for analytical reasons, to consider production system boundaries. Thus, analytically there exist many networks and a specific actor may be engaged in several networks. To take another example, if we define a focal production system to exclude some of the resource interdependencies that one actor coordinates through exchange relationships, then this actor is defined as being involved in more than one network. This actor's resource interdependencies among several production systems might suggest that the delimitation of the production system as well as network should be "multi-industrial."

Network Perceptions

The actors in a network may view the network, its extensivity, and the nature of its exchange relationships in quite different ways and also differently from the description that might be provided by an outside analyst who is not an actor. First, the network is extensive and includes exchange relationships in which the actor is not directly involved. Second, even in those relationships where the actor is involved, the counterparts may view the relationships in different ways. Third, network analysis deals not only with the present but also with the past and the future, which means that the interpretations are influenced by different memories and different beliefs about the future. Since the actors form cognitive structures through experience and interpretations linked to theories about "reality," perceptions will be influenced by which conceptual framework the actors use. Whether the actor's "theory" is that the industrial system is governed by a network or by a market mechanism will obviously be of importance. This means that there is a potential normative value in the idea that a network has less clear boundaries than a "market structure," based on a traditional industrial organisation model. The actor with a network perspective will focus some attention on influences from "outside" actors and might therefore extend the network boundaries and thereby perhaps increase the possibilities for effective strategic action.

Positions in Networks

Each actor is engaged in a number of exchange relationships with other actors. These relationships define the position of the actor in the network. Since positions can be defined for all the actors in the network, the concept can be used to characterise network structure and network distance between actors. A basic attribute of exchange relationships is that they are established and developed over time and so this process can be viewed as an investment process. Thus, network positions are the result of investments in exchange relationships. Positions are a consequence of the cumulative nature of the use of resources to establish, maintain, and develop exchange relationships. The position of an actor also connects the separate, individual relationships with each other. The position characterises the actor's links to the environment and is therefore of strategic significance. The positions of all the actors in the network are also a major characteristic of the environment in which the actor is embedded. Furthermore, the position strongly influences the basis for an actor's development of exchange relationships in the future; that is, it forms the base for the actor's strategic actions.

Definitions of Positions

A distinction can be made between a limited and an extended definition of positions. The limited definition refers purely to the network level. According to the limited definition, the position of an actor is a matter of the exchange relationships of the actor and the identities of the counterparts in those relationships. The identities of the counterparts are, in consequence, a matter of their relationships to others. This corresponds to the way in which positions are used in sociometric network analyses and makes it possible for us to use all the usual measures for characterising network positions: interconnectedness, distance, and so on. When operationalising the limited definition it is possible to view relationships as integer variables that only take the values 0 and 1. It is, however, also possible to view relationships as continuous metric variables, defined on the same scale, with values between 0 and 1 depending on the strength of the relationship. Further, relationships may be conceived of as vectors with values depending on the strength of a number of bond dimensions—legal, social, and so forth.

The extended definition, however, refers in addition to the role the actors have in the production system. Thus, according to the extended definition, the position of an actor includes also the productive processes—in a broad sense—in which it is involved and its direct and indirect network interdependencies. The production role has two dimensions, one qualitative and one quantitative. The qualitative dimension describes which function the actor has in the production system. In a sequential chain linking the separate resources, the individual actor has one or more specific functions, for which the resources it controls are specialised. The quantitative dimension characterises the relative importance that the resources of the actor have in relation to the resources of other actors, that is, how much of the total quantity of substitutable resource is controlled by the actor. A network position gives an actor some power over resources controlled by other actors. This power is in no way absolute since exchange relationships by definition depend on voluntary mutual orientation and not on coercion.

Positions are Interrelated

Clearly, the positions of different actors in a network are more or less interrelated. This is the direct result of the basic assumption that networks are sets of connected exchange relationships. Connectedness means that exchange in one relationship is conditioned—facilitated or hindered—by exchange in another. Connectedness can occur on the production level. Through direct and indirect resource interdependencies, the positions of two actors are interrelated. This type of position interrelation may be described as objective. It is a matter of the industrial logic. The stronger the resource interdependencies, the stronger are the position interrelations. This means that the closer two actors are in a production chain, the stronger are their position interrelations. This means also that the more specialised the production of the actors is in relation to each other in a network, the stronger are their position interrelations. It means also that the more closed the production system is in relation to other production systems, the stronger are position interrelations in the system. Furthermore, positions of different actors may be positively or negatively connected to each other in the sense that when the position of one is strengthened the position of the other is strengthened or weakened. This can also be seen as a matter of the industrial logic.

However, interrelations between positions can also occur at the network level, which means that they are a matter of intentions and interpretations of the actors. They are of a subjective nature. It seems reasonable to assume that the longer the time perspective, the less important are the objective interdependencies driven by an industrial logic and the more important are the intentions and interpretations of the actors. Thus, in a long-term perspective, position interrelations become more of a subjective matter. The knowledge and the values of the actors are therefore important factors. Likewise it seems reasonable to assume that the smaller the investments in the production systems, the more important are the subjective views of the actors of the interrelations between positions. This does not mean that there are fewer position interrelations in soft industrial systems such as R&D or service industry systems than in manufacturing industry systems or that there are fewer position interrelations in the long term, only that they are more ambiguous. Generally, however, it can be assumed that the position interrelations are stronger the closer the actors are connected at the network level, as they will tend to have more analogous "network theories."

To sum up, the position of an actor is described by the characteristics of its exchange relationships. A limited, basic definition is that the position is a matter of with which actors the focal actor has exchange relationships. An extended definition of a position also involves the role of the actors in the production system. The role comprises the functions accorded by the industrial logic and the relative importance of the actors.

The position of an actor changes all the time, not only because new exchange relationships are developed, old ones interrupted, and others change in character, but also because the counterparts' positions are changing, and furthermore, the positions of third parties, with whom the focal actor has no direct relationships, are also changing. This follows from the definition of positions as being a matter of the identities of counterparts. But the ways in which positions change may differ depending on whether the changes take place on the actor (network) or on the resource (production system) level.

Strategic Action

In the general strategy literature, strategic actions are usually characterised as efforts by actors to influence their relationship with their environment. In the network approach this general notion is translated to mean that strategic actions are efforts by actors to influence (change or preserve) their position(s) in network(s). The following discussion is about such strategic action by one focal actor. Strategic objectives are defined in terms of network positions. Obviously, almost all actions in networks have some effect on network positions. This is, for instance, the case with action in an exchange relationship concerning current production. When two actors carry out exchange they develop their exchange relationships thus modifying their positions as well as those of other actors in the network. In this article, however, only action that aims primarily at the positions is considered strategic. Plainly, it is difficult to make a distinction between such position-directed action and more production-directed action.

This view of strategic action means that strategic action by a focal actor aims not only at increasing the post-action network effectiveness. It is also a matter of developing the base from which future action can proceed. Within the framework of the limited definition of network positions, strategic action aims at influencing actors, relationships, and network structures. It can be directed at the relationships of the focal actor, it can be directed at relationships between other actors in the network, or it can be directed at relationships with other networks. These goals may be achieved by breaking old relationships, establishing new ones, changing the character of existing ones, or preserving relationships endangered by adverse actions by other actors. The strategic action may also aim to influence actor-perceived mediated connections between relationships, such as whether and to what extent actors view relationships as complementary or competing. This is a matter of influencing their network theories. Such action may aim at influencing the network theories of a specific actor or a specific set of actors in a network. It may also aim at influencing or creating a dominant network theory in a network. This may imply attempts to make the network theories of different actors in the network more consistent. It may, however, also represent efforts to disconnect the network into two or more separate nets, where, for instance, the focal actor is the only link between the nets or where the focal actor has a strong position in one of the nets. Alternatively it may aim at connecting different sections more closely or at connecting different networks with each other.

Working within the framework of the extended definition of network positions, strategic action may also aim at restructuring the web of dependencies in the production system. An overall objective of such restructuring may be to develop the focal actor's role in the production system in a particular direction. Such action may, for instance, include weakening the dependence of the focal actor or reducing the dependence of a focal net on resources in certain other networks. This may include transforming specific dependencies between actors into more general dependencies that are not related to specific actors. The strategic action can also be designed to strengthen interdependencies in a production system in order, for instance, to create a specific dominant sequential chain of interdependencies. Correspondingly, it may aim at creating a set of dependencies around a certain resource controlled by the focal actor. Such actions may mean that general market dependencies are transformed into specific actor dependencies.

Using the limited definition of positions, the base for strategic action by a focal actor are its (1) network position, (2) resources, and (3) network theory. The three bases of strategic action are not unrelated. Thus the quantity and quality of the resources influence the resource interdependencies, which are closely related to the exchange relationships and consequently the network positions. The network position influences the network theory since that theory is to a large extent based on information channelled through the exchange relationships. Of the three types of strategic base the network position has a special status, since the strategic objectives are also defined in terms of network positions.

Internationalisation of the Firm

Let us finally illustrate the framework by discussing briefly strategic action in relation to the internationalisation of a focal firm. Such a strategic development involves, to an increasing degree, relationships cutting across national network boundaries. The focal firm begins internationalisation by establishing relationships with firms in other national networks. The first step may or may not involve control of production resources inside the new national network. Further internationalisation moves may include development of exchange relationships and positions in still more national networks and increased interdependency between the firm's positions in the different networks. The internationalisation of the firm can be seen as a consequence of strategic action by the firm to the extent that the moves are not the result of continuous development of current production activities or of actions taken by other actors.

The bases for internationalisation are, first, the firm's position, which can be used in various ways. Some of the exchange relationships in the old domestic network may be connected to existing or potential exchange relationships in the new network, depending to what extent these other firms have positions in those networks. Alternatively, the position of the actor in the old network can be communicated to actors in the new network thereby influencing their network theories so as to make them interested in becoming positively connected to the focal firm. A special case is that of actors who mutually exchange access to each other's positions in their respective networks. Observe, however, that the position in the old network can be a constraint on movement into new networks to the extent that commitments made in the old exchange relationships cannot be kept if new exchange relationships are added.

A second way that a firm may internationalise is that the firm's own resources can be made interdependent with resources controlled by actors in the other network. Quantitative and qualitative adjustments may or may not have to be made in order to establish and develop exchange relationships. Adjustments involve investments in new resources by the firm and purchase of already existing resources controlled by other actors. Another way to achieve the changes in resource structure is through explicit coordination with another firm.

Third, the firm's network theory not only directs the strategic action toward specific efforts to influence resources and positions, but can also be communicated to other actors in the network and thereby influence their action. For example, if the firm's network theory assumes expectations of network structure changes implying increasing interdependence between positions in different networks, that is, internationalisation, this view can influence other actors with whom joint strategic action is desired or it can be used to affect dominant network theories in the new networks.

So far the discussion concerns the situation when a focal firm starts moving into new networks. Let us now look at a situation when both the focal firm and many other actors have positions in many national networks. The interrelated nature of network positions in different networks makes it even more important to consider the network theories of actors in the further internationalisation moves. Strategic actions, involving explicit linkages between a focal firm's and one or more other actors' network positions, are to a large extent based on communication of network theories and may result in changes from negative to positive or from positive to negative connections between positions. So-called strategic alliances are a good example of this process in operation. They may create or handle interdependencies between production resources, but they also limit the number of potential alliances in the networks since some actors become appropriated. The survival of strategic alliances depends less on the extent to which resource coordination in the production system succeeds than on how network theories of both the involved and third actors develop.

Buying another firm is frequently referred to as a strategic action. An important issue in such a purchase is whether the buying firm can get control of the other firm's exchange relationships. In other words, can the focal firm take over the position as well as the resources. Depending on the network theory in the focal firm, the major aim of the acquisition may be to get control of the exchange relationships, to change their character, or to change the connections between exchange relationships. Control of exchange relationships through acquisitions is, however, never certain, since there are always two actors involved.

As national networks become increasingly interdependent, an obvious change in the actors' network theories is to regard the network boundaries as obsolete and to consider other boundaries as more relevant. Such changes in network theories might, for example, imply that the actors regard their positions as even more interdependent since they belong to the same network. Measures of network positions such as quantitative and qualitative aspects of resource interdependencies will become different when network boundaries change.

References and Suggested Readings

Aoki, M., Gustafsson, B., and O. E. Williamson, *The Firm as a Nexus of Treaties*, Sage, London, 1990.

Axelsson, B., and G. Easton, *Industrial Networks: A New View of Reality*, Wiley, New York, 1992.

Berg, S., Duncan, J., and P. Friedman, *Joint Venture Strategies and Corporate Innovation*, Oelgeschlager, Gunn and Hain, Cambridge, MA, 1982.

Best, M. H., *The New Competition: Institutions of Industrial Restructuring*, Polity, Cambridge, 1990.

Bleeke, J., and D. Ernst, The Way to Win in Cross-Border Alliances, *Harvard Business Review*, November/December 1991, pp. 127–135.

Borys, B., and D. B. Jemison, Hybrid Arrangements as Strategic Alliances: Theoretical Issues in Organizational Combinations, *Academy of Management Review*, April 1989, pp. 234–249.

Bronder, C., and R. Pritzl, Developing Strategic Alliances: A Conceptual Framework, for Successful Co-operation, *European Management Journal*, December 1992, pp. 412–421.

Charan, R., How Networks Reshape Organizations—For Results, *Harvard Business Review*, September/October 1991, pp. 104–115.

Contractor, F. J., International Business: An Alternative View, *International Marketing Review*, Spring 1986, pp. 74–85.

Contractor, F. J., and P. Lorange, Why Should Firms Cooperate? The Strategy and Economics Basis for Cooperative Ventures, in Contractor, F. J., and P. Lorange, *Cooperative Strategies in International Business*, Lexington Books, Lexington, MA, 1988.

Grabher, G., Rediscovering the Social in the Economics of Interfirm Relations, in Grabher, G. (Ed.), *The Embedded Firm: On the Socioeconomics of Industrial Networks*, Routledge, London, 1993.

Hamel, G., Competition for Competence and Interpartner Learning within International Strategic Alliances, *Strategic Management Journal,* Summer 1991, pp. 83–103.

Hamel, G., Doz, Y. L., and C. K. Prahalad, Collaborate with Your Competitors—and Win, *Harvard Business Review,* January/February 1989, pp. 133–139.

Harrigan, K. R., *Strategies for Joint Ventures,* D. C. Heath, Lexington, MA, 1985.

Harrigan, K. R., Strategic Alliances: Their New Role in Global Competition, *Columbia Journal of World Business,* Summer 1987, pp. 67–69.

Jarillo, J. C., and H. H. Stevenson, Cooperative Strategies—The Payoffs and the Pitfalls, *Long Range Planning,* February 1991, pp. 64–70.

Johanson, J., and L. G. Mattsson, Network Positions and Strategic Action—An Analytical Framework, in Axelsson, B. and G. Easton, *Industrial Networks: A New View of Reality,* Routledge, London, 1992.

Johnston, R., and P. R. Lawrence, Beyond Vertical Integration—The Rise of the Value-Adding Partnership, *Harvard Business Review,* July/August 1988, pp. 94–101.

Ketelhöhn, W., What Do We Mean by Cooperative Advantage? *European Management Journal,* March 1993, pp. 30–37.

Lewis, J. D., *Partnerships for Profit: Structuring and Managing Strategic Alliances,* Free Press, New York, 1990.

Lorange, P., and J. Roos, Why Some Strategic Alliances Succeed and Others Fail, *Journal of Business Strategy,* January/February 1991, pp. 25–30.

Lorange, P., and J. Roos, *Strategic Alliances: Formation, Implementation, and Evolution,* Blackwell, Cambridge, MA, 1992.

Mariti, P., and R. H. Smiley, Cooperative Agreements and the Organization of Industry, *Journal of Industrial Economics,* June 1983, pp. 437–451.

Miles, R. E., and C. C. Snow, Network Organizations: New Concepts for New Forms, *California Management Review,* Spring 1986, pp. 62–73.

Miles, R. E., and C. C. Snow, Causes of Failures in Network Organizations, *California Management Review,* Summer 1992, pp. 53–72.

Niederkofler, M., The Evolution of Strategic Alliances: Opportunities for Managerial Influence, *Journal of Business Venturing,* July 1991, pp. 237–257.

Pfeffer, J., and P. Nowak, Joint Ventures and Interorganizational Interdependence, *Administrative Science Quarterly,* September 1976, pp. 398–418.

Pfeffer, J., and G. R. Salancik, *The External Control of Organizations: A Resource Dependency Perspective,* Harper & Row, New York, 1978.

Porter, M. E., *Competitive Strategy: Techniques for Analyzing Industries and Competitors,* Free Press, New York, 1980.

Power, W. W., Neither Market Nor Hierarchy: Network Forms of Organization, *Research in Organizational Behavior,* 1990, pp. 295–336.

Quinn, J. B., Doorley, T. L., and P. C. Paquette, Technology in Services: Rethinking Strategic Focus, *Sloan Management Review,* Winter 1990, pp. 79–87.

Reve, T., The Firm as a Nexus of Internal and External Contracts, in Aoki, M., Gustafsson, B., and O. E. Williamson, *The Firm as a Nexus of Treaties,* Sage, London, 1990.

Robert, M., The Do's and Dont's of Strategic Alliances, *Journal of Business Strategy,* March/April 1992, pp. 50–53.

Ruigrok, W., and R. van Tulder, *The Ideology of Interdependence: The Link between Restructuring, Internationalisation and International Trade*, PhD Dissertation, University of Amsterdam, 1993.

Schaan, J. L., How to Control a Joint Venture Even as a Minority Partner, *Journal of General Management*, Autumn 1988, pp. 4–16.

Stopford, J. M. and L. Wells, *Managing the Multinational Enterprise*, Basic Books, New York, 1972.

Thorelli, H. B., Networks: Between Markets and Hierarchies, *Strategic Management Journal*, January/February 1986, pp. 37–51.

Williamson, O. E., *Markets and Hierarchies*, Free Press, New York, 1975.

Williamson, O. E., *The Economic Institutions of Capitalism: Firms, Markets, and Relational Contracting*, Free Press, New York, 1985.

SECTION IV
THE STRATEGY CONTEXT

*There never were, since the creation of
the world, two cases exactly parallel.*
—Philip Dormer Stanhope
1694–1773, English Secretary of State

While Stanhope was referring to the world of politics rather than to the world of business, his point that every situation is unique holds true in both. Every company's circumstances, every industry structure, and every competitive rivalry has unique characteristics distinguishing it from other business settings. In other words, the *strategy context* is different in each case.

One central question in this section is whether the uniqueness of each strategy context matters at all. At one extreme there are authors who implicitly assume, or explicitly argue, that the strategy process and/or the strategy content can be determined without regard to the specific business circumstances. To them the entire strategy context is irrelevant or at most of minor importance. Many of these "context-free" writers are in search of universal principles of strategy, applicable to every business situation. At the other extreme there are authors who argue that the best strategy process and the best strategy content depend on the specific business circumstances and that no general principles exist at all.

Most of the authors in this book have positioned themselves somewhere between these two radical extremes of *universality* and *specificity*. Leaning more to one side, there are many authors in this section who stress the preeminence of only one, or a limited set of, contextual variables—focusing for instance only on the importance of the industry structure or the company culture. Leaning more to the other side are writers who emphasize the importance of a wide variety of situational variables. These differing opinions confront the reader with the fundamental question: Which aspects of the strategy context truly have, or should have, an impact on the strategy process and the strategy content and how should the strategist deal with this influence?

Closely connected to this debate is the second theme of this section, the issue of *free choice* versus *determinism*. If one or more parts of the strategy context do have an impact on the strategy process and strategy content, how strong is this impact—does it nudge or push, influence or determine? Does the influence of the business's situation still allow for a high degree of liberty in choosing the strategy process and strategy content the strategist prefers, or are the process and content largely determined by the circumstances, leaving the strategist at most with the illusion of free choice?

As with the question of universalism versus specificity, here, too, few authors in this book can be found at the radical extremes, arguing or assuming complete free choice or absolute determinism. However, there are a wide variety of opinions with regard to the extent to which the strategy context constrains the liberty of the strategist. To one side there are a large number of authors emphasizing companys' ability to create their own future, while to the other side many authors emphasize strategists' inability to control the environment and even their own organisation.

These two themes, universalism versus specificity and free choice versus determinism, have been important criteria in the choice and arrangement of articles in this section. All three chapters in this section contain a variety of perspectives along each continuum, giving quite a few different answers to the question, How important is the strategy context? The division of articles between the three chapters has been done by identifying different parts of the strategy context. Although chapter 7 has just indicated how fuzzy the line between organisation and environment can be, we have nevertheless used these two general categories to make a first split between the articles. Chapter 9 contains the articles whose main focus is to evaluate the importance of the organisational context. The environmental context articles have been further divided into writings emphasizing the importance of industry-related characteristics (chapter 8) and articles concentrating on the influence of the international environment (chapter 10).

Chapter 8
The Industry Context:
On Compliance and Choice

*The reasonable man adapts himself to
the world; the unreasonable one
persists in trying to adapt the world
to himself. Therefore, all progress
depends on the unreasonable man.*
  —George Bernard Shaw
     1856–1950, Irish playwright and critic

Introduction

For a strategist it is important to know whether a company's survival and profitability can be significantly influenced by the strategist's cunning, or whether it is largely predetermined by the industry that the company happens to be in. If the company is comparable to an *acorn*, the height to which it will grow will largely depend on the earth into which it falls. In this case, the strategist can at best only seek the fertile soil of a promising industry. If, on the other hand, the company is comparable to an *artist*, its development will largely depend on its own creativity, intelligence, and drive. Environmental influences will have only a minor impact. In this case, the strategist has full command over the future of the company. This chapter seeks an answer to the question whether the company is more acorn or artist. Or, stated differently, the central issue is, To what extent does the industry context matter?

It is interesting to note that strategy researchers are not the only scientists trying to determine the impact of the environment on their object of study. In psychology the nature versus nurture debate has been going on for decades, while sociologists are also heavily divided on the topic of environmental determinism. Similar debates can also be witnessed in other fields, such as biology and medicine. What this indicates is that the question of environmental influence is neither unique nor easy to solve.

As put forward in the introduction to this section, there are two extreme answers possible to the question To what extent does the industry context matter? At the one extreme, it could be argued that the industry context fully determines the future of the company. In this view, strategy is merely doing things that are consistent with the "rules" or "laws" of the outside world. The company has no influence on the industry rules and has very little room to manoeuvre. In the subtitle to this chapter, this deterministic view is referred to as the *compliance* perspective. At the other extreme, it could be argued that a company has a multitude of ways to mould the industry structure, changing the rules of the game, as well as the possibility of switching over to other industries. Proponents of this perspective would fully agree with the remark by the Dutch poet Jules Deelder that "even within the limits of the possible, the possibilities are limitless." In this view, the firm has a broad range of strategic choices, the most important limit being the strategist's mindset. The industry structure is more the result of the firm's strategy than its starting point. Hence, in the subtitle to this chapter, this view is referred to as the *choice* perspective.

In this chapter, the first and the last article presented come very close to the compliance and choice extremes, while the other three readings can be found along the continuum between the two poles. After reading these five contributions it will be up to the reader to decide to what extent the industry context matters.

The Articles

The chapter starts off with a famous article by Michael Hannan and John Freeman, entitled "The Population Ecology of Organizations." In this article, Hannan and Freeman argue that to understand the pattern of survival and demise of *organisations*, it would be useful to borrow concepts developed to understand the survival and demise of *organisms*. In biology, the authors stress, scientists have long been researching why certain members of a population of organisms survive environmental changes while others do not. Two mechanisms seem to be at play simultaneously—*adaptation* and *selection*. Viewed at the level of the individual organisms, some are flexible enough to adapt themselves to new environmental circumstances while other individuals do not have this ability. Viewed at the level of the entire population, however, among the variety of individuals there will usually be some that by chance fit the new circumstances while others will never be suited to the changed environment. In other words, survivors are "selected" from the population by environmental influences. Transferring these ideas to organisational studies, Hannan and Freeman argue that most management literature takes an adaptation perspective, while there are many reasons to doubt organisations' ability to learn and adapt. They believe that the environment's power to select is very strong and therefore that a population ecology perspective can be very useful in understanding the relationship between an organisation and its environment. It is clear that in their perspective the company is an "acorn"—the industry determines the company's chances for survival and prosperity.

The author of the second article of this chapter also implicitly borrows some concepts from biology. In this article, entitled "Industry Evolution," Michael Porter explains how evolutionary processes within the industry context have a very strong impact on the survival and profitability of companies. In the terms of Hannan and Freeman, Porter recognizes both selection and adaptation processes. For instance,

Porter argues that the selection of fit companies is particularly strong as industries move into a mature phase of development: "When growth levels off in an industry . . . there is a period of turmoil as intensified rivalry weeds out the weaker firms." Porter does assume that companies can also adapt to changes in the industry's structure, but he argues that they first must understand the drivers of change. Beside "compliance" to the industry context, Porter emphasizes the possibility of "choice" as well. Or, in his own terms, he believes that firms can influence the evolution of the industry's structure. Hence, in Porter's opinion, the company has a certain degree of strategic freedom to determine its own fate, but ultimately the development of the industry structure is crucially important to the survival and profitability of the company. He presents the same view very succinctly in his article in chapter 4, where he states that "competition in an industry depends on five basic forces, which . . . determine the ultimate profit potential of an industry."

The author of the third article, "Selecting Strategies That Exploit Leverage," Milind Lele, takes largely the same perspective as Michael Porter does. In the positioning school tradition, Lele accords a large measure of importance to the industry context while recognizing the possibility that firms can also "change the terms of competition or the structure of the industry." What Lele adds to Porter's analysis is the consideration of the company's *competitive position* within the industry as an important environmental determinant of the company's freedom to manoeuvre. While Porter's article argues that industry evolution is an important external limitation, Lele argues that the company's competitive position in each evolutionary phase also curtails the strategist's free choice. Whether the company is the industry leader, second or third player, follower or new entrant will have a significant impact on the strategic options open to the company and on its profit potential.

In the fourth article of this chapter, entitled "Industry Breakpoints," Paul Strebel also adds an extra dimension to Porter's discussion on the impact of the industry context. Strebel specifies the different types of industry developments, ranging from *gradual* (evolutionary) changes to *radical* (revolutionary) changes. Gradual change can unfold as a trend, a cycle, or a turning point, while more radical change manifests itself as a breakpoint—a sharp and sudden *discontinuity* in the environment. Strebel argues that companies must understand the different types, and different drivers, of environmental change to be able to develop viable strategies. Since Strebel believes that the changing industry context can seriously inhibit a firm's chances of survival, but also leaves the firm with ample opportunity for creating new competitive advantages, this places his article somewhere between the "acorn" and "artist" views of the firm.

In the fifth and final article, Charles Baden-Fuller and John Stopford radically disagree with the compliance perspective as the title of the article indicates, "The Firm Matters, Not the Industry". As they say themselves, their view "contrasts sharply with the school of thought which believes that the fortune of a business is closely tied to its industry." They point out that only a fraction of the differences in profitability between business units can be attributed to industry characteristics, while more than half of the profit variations are due to the choice of strategy. In their opinion, profitability is largely determined by firms' creativity and imagination. Successful firms change the rules of the competitive game, introducing new *recipes* to the industry—a point of view that coincides with ideas expressed by the *resource-based* school of thought (see chapter 5). In the same vein, they challenge the widely held belief, also ventilated by Lele earlier in this chapter, that high market share is a cause of success in industries (Buzzell, Gale, and Sultan, 1975). Baden-Fuller and Stopford argue that high market share is the consequence of success, not the other way around. Hence, they do not believe that they can prescribe well-defined (or generic) approaches to the market ("in mature industries do this, in declining industries do that"), since the essence of competition is to divert from traditional solutions. The advice they can give is that companies must remain imaginative, constantly *rejuvenating* themselves. In their perspective, Shaw's "unreasonable man" will be better off in the end.

Recommended Readings and Cases

Readers wishing to extend their knowledge about the possible impact of the industry context on strategy content should probably start with Michael Porter's *Competitive Strategy: Techniques for Analyzing Industries and Competitors*. In this book he explores a variety of generic industry contexts (emerging, early maturity, declining, fragmented, and global) and discusses the threats and opportunities inherent in each. Robert Buzzell and Bradley Gale are also well known for their emphasis on the industry context. Their book, *The PIMS Principles: Linking Strategy to Performance*, which argues that there is a strong relationship between market share and profitability, makes for interesting reading.

Paul Strebel's article in this chapter has been taken from his book, *Breakpoints*, which is also highly recommended. The same is true for Charles Baden-Fuller and John Stopford's article, which has been adapted from their book *Rejuvenating the Mature Business*.

Finally, it should be noted that all readings in this chapter focus on the relationship between industry *context* and strategy *content*. Relatively little has been published that explicitly explores the relationship between industry context and strategy *process*, therefore no article on this topic was included in this chapter. We would recommend that the interested reader turn to *Managing the Strategy Process* by Balaji Chakravarthy and Peter Lorange, which gives a stimulating overview of the possible links between process and external context.

The two cases that have been specially selected for this chapter are "Royal Boskalis Westminster" by Ron Meyer, and "Cineplex Odeon Corporation" by Joseph Wolfe. Royal Boskalis Westminster is the world's largest dredging company, situated just outside of Rotterdam, in The Netherlands. The case describes the horrible state of the *cyclical* dredging industry, and the reader is confronted with the question how the company can survive in such an inhospitable industry context. This case offers the reader ample opportunity to reflect on the extent to which the company's options are open to free choice or dictated by the environment. In the second case, Cineplex, a large American cinema operator, is being faced with a different type of industry challenge. Cineplex's industry seems to be entering the *decline* phase of evolution due to the advent of competing technologies. The reader is asked to think about ways of dealing with the receding demand. Here again the question is whether Cineplex is in a declining business or whether decline is "merely a state of mind."

■ THE POPULATION ECOLOGY OF ORGANIZATIONS†

By Michael Hannan and John Freeman

Introduction

Analysis of the effects of the environment on organizational structure has moved to a central place in organizations theory and research in recent years. This shift has opened a number of exciting possibilities. As yet nothing like the full promise of the shift has been realized. We believe that the lack of development is due in part to/a failure to bring ecological models to bear on questions that are preeminently ecological. We argue for a reformulation of the problem in population ecology terms.

Although there is a wide variety of ecological perspectives, they all focus on selection. That is, they attribute patterns in nature to the action of selection processes. The bulk of the literature on organizations subscribes to a different view, which we call the adaptation perspective. According to the adaptation perspective, subunits of the organization, usually managers or dominant coalitions, scan the environment for opportunities and threats, formulate strategic responses, and adjust organizational structure appropriately.

The adaptation perspective is seen most clearly in the literature on management. Contributors to it usually assume a hierarchy of authority and control that locates decisions concerning the organization as a whole at the top. It follows then, that organizations are affected by their environments according to the ways in which managers or leaders formulate strategies, make decisions, and implement them. Particularly successful managers are able either to buffer their organizations from environmental disturbances or to arrange smooth adjustments that require minimal disruption of organizational structure.

Clearly, leaders of organizations do formulate strategies and organizations do adapt to environmental contingencies. As a result at least some of the relationship between structure and environment must reflect adaptive behavior or learning. But there is no reason to presume that the great structural variability among organizations reflects only or even primarily adaptation.

There are a number of obvious limitations on the ability of organizations to adapt. That is, there are a number of processes that generate structural inertia. The stronger the pressures, the lower the organizations' adaptive flexibility and the more likely that the logic of environmental selection is appropriate. As a consequence, the issue of structural inertia is central to the choice between adaptation and selection models.

Inertial pressures arise from both internal structure arrangements and environmental constraints. A minimal list of the constraints arising from internal considerations follows.

■ An organization's investment in plant, equipment, and specialized personnel constitutes assets that are not easily transferable to other tasks or functions. The ways in which such sunk costs constrain adaptation options are so obvious that they need not be discussed further.

†**Source:** Reprinted from *American Journal of Sociology*, March 1977, Vol. 82, pp. 929–964. Used with permission from the University of Chicago Press.

- Organizational decision makers also face constraints on the information they receive. Much of what we know about the flow of information through organizational structures tells us that leaders do not obtain anything close to full information on activities within the organization and environmental contingencies facing the subunits.

- Internal political constraints are even more important. When organizations alter structure, political equilibria are disturbed. As long as the pool of resources is fixed, structural change almost always involves redistribution of resources across subunits. Such redistribution upsets the prevailing system of exchange among subunits (or subunit leaders). So at least some subunits are likely to resist any proposed reorganization. Moreover, the benefits of structural reorganization are likely to be both generalized (designed to benefit the organization as a whole) and long run. Any negative political response will tend to generate short-run costs that are high enough that organizational leaders will forgo the planned reorganization.

- Finally, organizations face restraints generated by their own history. Once standards of procedure and the allocation of tasks and authority have become the subject of normative agreement, the costs of change are greatly increased. Normative agreements constrain adaptation in at least two ways. First, they provide a justification and an organizing principle for those elements that wish to resist reorganization (i.e., they can resist in terms of a shared principle). Second, normative agreements preclude the serious consideration of many alternative responses. For example, few research-oriented universities seriously consider adapting to declining enrollments by eliminating the teaching function. To entertain this option would be to challenge central organizational norms.

The external pressures toward inertia seem to be at least as strong. They include at least the following factors.

- Legal and fiscal barriers to entry and exit from markets (broadly defined) are numerous. Discussions of organizational behavior typically emphasize barriers to entry (state-licensed monopoly positions, and so on). Barriers to exit are equally interesting. There are an increasing number of instances in which political decisions prevent firms from abandoning certain activities. All such constraints on entry and exit limit the breadth of adaptation possibilities.

- Internal constraints upon the availability of information are paralleled by external constraints. The acquisition of information about relevant environments is costly, particularly in turbulent situations where the information is most essential. In addition, the type of specialists employed by the organization constrains both the nature of the information it is likely to obtain and the kind of specialized information it can process and utilize.

- Legitimacy constraints also emanate from the environment. Any legitimacy an organization has been able to generate constitutes an asset in manipulating the environment. To the extent that adaptation (e.g., eliminating undergraduate instruction in public universities) violates the legitimacy claims, it incurs considerable costs. So external legitimacy considerations also tend to limit adaptation.

- Finally, there is the collective rationality problem. One of the most difficult issues in contemporary economics concerns general equilibria. If one can find an optimal strategy for some individual buyer or seller in a competitive market, it does not necessarily follow that there is a general equilibrium once all players start trading. More generally, it is difficult to establish that a strategy that is rational for a single decision maker will be rational if adopted by a large number of decision makers.

A number of these inertial pressures can be accommodated within the adaptation framework. That is, one can modify and limit the perspective in order to consider choices within the constrained set of alternatives. But to do so greatly limits the scope of one's investigation. We argue that in order to deal with the various inertial pressures the adaptation perspective must be supplemented with a selection orientation.

Population Thinking in the Study of Organization-Environment Relations

The comparison of unit choice facing the organizational analyst with that facing the bioecologist is instructive. To oversimplify somewhat, ecological analysis is conducted at three levels: individual, population, and community. Events at one level almost always have consequences at other levels. Despite this interdependence, population events cannot be reduced to individual events (since individuals do not reflect the full genetic variability of the population) and community events cannot be simply reduced to population events. Both the latter employ a population perspective that is not appropriate at the individual level.

The situation faced by the organizations analyst is more complex. Instead of three levels of analysis, he faces at least five: (1) members, (2) subunits, (3) individual organizations, (4) populations of organizations, and (5) communities of (populations of) organizations. Levels 3–5 can be seen as corresponding to the three levels discussed for general ecology, with the individual organization taking the place of the individual organism. The added complexity arises because organizations are more nearly decomposable into constituent parts than are organisms. Individual members and subunits may move from organization to organization in a manner that has no parallel in nonhuman organization.

Instances of theory and research dealing with the effects of environments on organizations are found at all five levels. But, the common focus is on *the* organization and *its* environment. In fact, this choice is so widespread that there appears to be a tacit understanding that individual organizations are the appropriate units for the study of organization-environment relations.

We use the term *population* to refer to aggregates of organizations rather than members. Populations of organizations must be alike in some respect; that is, they must have some unit character. Unfortunately, identifying a population of organizations is no simple matter. The ecological approach suggests that one focus on common fate with respect to environmental variations. Since all organizations are distinctive, no two are affected identically by any given exogenous shock. Nevertheless, we can identify classes of organizations that are relatively homogeneous in terms of environmental vulnerability. Notice that the populations of interest may change somewhat from investigation to investigation depending on the analyst's concern. Populations of organizations referred to are not immutable objects in nature but are abstractions useful for theoretical purposes.

Taking our lead from distinguished ecologists, we suggest that a population ecology of organizations must seek to understand the distributions of organizations across environmental conditions and the limitations on organizational structures in different environments, and more generally seek to answer the question, Why are there so many kinds of organizations? Phrasing the question in this way opens the possibility of applying a rich variety of formal models to the analysis of the effects of environmental variations on organizational structure.

Hawley's Formulation of Human Ecology

We begin with Hawley's classic formulation of human ecology. However, we recognize that ecological theory has progressed enormously since sociologists last systematically applied ideas from bioecology to social organization. Nonetheless, Hawley's theoretical perspective remains a very useful point of departure. In particular we concentrate on the principle of isomorphism. This principle asserts that there is a one-to-one correspondence between structural elements of social organization and those units that mediate flows of essential resources into the system. It explains the variations in organizational forms in equilibrium. But any observed isomorphism can arise from purposeful adaptation of organizations to the common constraints they face or because nonisomorphic organizations are selected against. Surely both processes are at work in most social systems. We believe that the organizations literature has emphasized the former to the exclusion of the latter.

We suspect that careful empirical research will reveal that for wide classes of organizations there are very strong inertial pressures on structure arising both from internal arrangements (e.g., internal politics) and the environment (e.g., public legitimation of organizational activity). To claim otherwise is to ignore the most obvious feature of organizational life. Failing churches do not become retail stores; nor do firms transform themselves into churches. Even within broad areas of organizational action, such as higher education and labor union activity, there appear to be substantial obstacles to fundamental structural change. Research is needed on this issue. But until we see evidence to the contrary, we will continue to doubt that the major features of the world of organizations arise through learning or adaptation. Given these doubts, it is important to explore an evolutionary explanation of the principle of isomorphism. That is, we wish to embed the principle of isomorphism within an explicit selection framework.

Lotka-Volterra Models

In order to add selection processes we propose a competition theory using Lotka-Volterra models. This theory relies on growth models that appear suitable for representing both organizational development and the growth of populations of organizations. Recent work by bioecologists on Lotka-Volterra systems yields propositions that have immediate relevance for the study of organization-environment relations. These results concern the effects of changes in the number and mixture of constraints upon systems with regard to the upper bound of the diversity of forms of organization. We propose that such propositions can be tested by examining the impact of varieties of state regulation both on size distributions and on the diversity of organizational forms within broadly defined areas of activity (e.g., medical care, higher education, and newspaper publishing).

A more important extension of Hawley's work introduces dynamic considerations. The fundamental issue here concerns the meaning of isomorphism in situations in which the environment to which units are adapted is changing and uncertain. Should "rational" organizations attempt to develop specialized isomorphic structural relations with one of the possible environmental states? Or should they adopt a more plastic strategy and institute more generalized structural features? The isomorphic principle does not speak to these issues.

We suggest that the concrete implication of generalism for organizations is the accumulation and retention of varieties of excess capacity. To retain the flexibility of structure required for adaptation to different environmental outcomes requires that some capabilities be held in reserve and not committed to action. Generalists will always be outperformed by specialists who, with the same levels of resources, happen to have hit upon their optimal environment. Consequently, in any cross section the generalists will appear inefficient because excess capacity will often be judged waste. Nonetheless, organizational slack is a pervasive feature of many types of organizations. The question then arises, What types of environments favor generalists? Answering this question comprehensively takes one a long way toward understanding the dynamic of organization-environment relations.

Levins's Fitness-Set Theory

We begin addressing this question in the suggestive framework of Levins's fitness-set theory. This is one of a class of recent theories that relate the nature of environmental uncertainty to optimal levels of structural specialism. Levins argues that along with uncertainty one must consider the grain of the environment or the lumpiness of environmental outcomes. The theory indicates that specialism is always favored in stable or certain environments. When the environment shifts uncertainly among states that place very different demands on the organization, and the duration of environmental states is short relative to the life of the organization (variation is fine grained), populations of organizations that specialize will be favored over those that generalize. This is because organizations that attempt to adapt to each environmental outcome will spend most of their time adjusting structure and very little time in organizational action directed at other ends.

We doubt that many readers will dispute the contention that failure rates are high for new and/or small organizations. However, much of the sociological literature and virtually all of the critical literature on large organizations tacitly accepts the view that such organizations are not subject to strong selection pressures. While we do not yet have the empirical data to judge this hypothesis, we can make several comments. First, we do not dispute that the largest organizations individually and collectively exercise strong dominance over most of the organizations that constitute their environments. But it does not follow from the observation that such organizations are strong in any one period that they will be strong in every period. Thus, it is interesting to know how firmly embedded are the largest and most powerful organizations. Consider the so-called Fortune 500, the largest publicly owned industrial firms in the United States. We contrasted the lists for 1955 and 1975 (adjusting for pure name changes). Of those on the list in 1955, only 268 (53.6 percent) were still listed in 1975. One hundred twenty-two had disappeared through merger, 109 had slipped off the "500," and one (a firm specializing in Cuban sugar!) had been liquidated. The number whose relative sales growth caused them to be dropped from the list is quite impressive in that the large number of mergers had opened many slots on the list. So we see that whereas actual liquidation was rare for the largest industrial firms in the United States over a twenty-year period, there was a good deal of volatility with regard to position in this pseudodominance structure because of both mergers and slipping sales.

Second, the choice of time perspective is important. Even the largest and most powerful organizations fail to survive over long periods. For example, of the thousands of firms in business in the United States during the Revolution, only thirteen survive as autonomous firms and seven as recognizable divisions of firms. Presumably one needs a longer time perspective to study the population ecology of the largest and most dominant organizations.

Third, studying small organizations is not such a bad idea. The sociological literature has concentrated on the largest organizations for obvious design reasons. But if inertial pressures on certain aspects of structure are strong enough, intense selection among small organizations may greatly constrain the variety observable among large organizations. At least some elements of structure change with size, and the pressure toward inertia should not be overemphasized. Nonetheless we see much value in studies of the organizational life cycle that would inform us as to which aspects of structure get locked in during which phases of the cycle. For example, we conjecture that a critical period is that during which the organization grows beyond the control of a single owner/manager. At this time the manner in which authority is delegated, if at all, seems likely to have a lasting impact on organizational structure. This is the period during which an organization becomes less an extension of one or few dominant individuals and more an organization per se with a life on its own. If the selection pressures at this point are as intense as anecdotal evidence suggests they are, selection models will prove very useful in accounting for the varieties of forms among the whole range of organizations.

The optimism of the previous paragraph should be tempered by the realization that when one examines the largest and most dominant organizations, one is usually considering only a small number of organizations. The smaller the number, the less useful are models that depend on the type of random mechanisms that underlie population ecology models.

Fourth, we must consider what one anonymous reader, caught up in the spirit of our paper, called the antieugenic actions of the state in saving firms such as Lockheed from failure. This is a dramatic instance of the way in which large dominant organizations can create linkages with other large and powerful ones so as to reduce selection pressures. If such moves are effective, they alter the pattern of selection. In our view the selection pressure is bumped up to a higher level. So instead of individual organizations failing, entire networks fail. The general consequence of a large number of linkages of this sort is an increase in the instability of the entire system, and therefore we should see boom and bust cycles of organizational outcomes. Selection models retain relevance, then, when the systems of organizations are tightly coupled.

■ INDUSTRY EVOLUTION†

By Michael Porter

Structural analysis gives us a framework for understanding the competitive forces operating in an industry that are crucial to developing competitive strategy. It is clear, however, that industries' structures change, often in fundamental ways. Entry barriers and concentration have gone up significantly in the U.S. brewing industry, for example, and the threat of substitutes has risen to put a severe squeeze on acetylene producers.

Industry evolution takes on critical importance for formulation of strategy. It can increase or decrease the basic attractiveness of an industry as an investment opportunity, and it often requires the firm to make strategic adjustments. Understanding the process of industry evolution and being able to predict change are important because the cost of reacting strategically usually increases as the need for change becomes more obvious and the benefit from the best strategy is the highest for the first firm to select it. For example, in the early postwar farm equipment business, structural change elevated the importance of a strong exclusive dealer network backed by company support and credit. The firms that recognized this change first had their pick of dealers to choose from.

This article will present analytical tools for predicting the evolutionary process in an industry and understanding its significance for the formulation of competitive strategy.

Basic Concepts in Industry Evolution

The starting point for analyzing industry evolution is the framework of structural analysis (as described in Porter's second article in chapter 4). Industry changes will carry strategic significance if they promise to affect the underlying sources of the five competitive forces; otherwise changes are important only in a tactical sense. The simplest approach to analyzing evolution is to ask the following question: Are there any changes occurring in the industry that will affect each element of structure? For example, do any of the industry trends imply an increase or decrease in mobility barriers? An increase or decrease in the relative power of buyers or suppliers? If this question is asked in a disciplined way for each competitive force and the economic causes underlying it, a profile of the significant issues in the evolution of an industry will result.

Although this industry-specific approach is the place to start, it may not be sufficient, because it is not always clear what industry changes are occurring currently, much less which changes might occur in the future. Given the importance of being able to predict evolution, it is desirable to have some analytical techniques that will aid in anticipating the pattern of industry changes we might expect to occur.

The Product Life Cycle

The grandfather of concepts for predicting the probable course of industry evolution is the familiar product life cycle. The hypothesis is that an industry passes through a number of phases or stages—introduction, growth, maturity, and decline—illustrated in figure 8-1. These stages are defined by inflection points in the rate of growth of industry sales. Industry growth follows an S-shaped curve because of the process of innovation and diffusion of a new product. The flat introductory phase of industry growth reflects the difficulty of overcoming buyer inertia and stimulating trials of the new product. Rapid growth occurs as many buyers rush into the market once the product has proven itself successful. Penetration of the product's potential buyers is eventually reached, causing the rapid growth to stop and to level off to the underlying rate of growth of the relevant buyer group. Finally, growth will eventually taper off as new substitute products appear.

As the industry goes through its life cycle, the nature of competition will shift. I have summarized in table 8-1 the most common predictions about how an industry will change over the life cycle and how this should affect strategy.

The product life cycle has attracted some legitimate criticism:

■ The duration of the stages varies widely from industry to industry, and it is often not clear what stage of the life cycle an industry is in. This problem diminishes the usefulness of the concept as a planning tool.

■ Industry growth does not always go through the S-shaped pattern at all. Sometimes industries skip maturity, passing straight from growth to decline. Sometimes industry

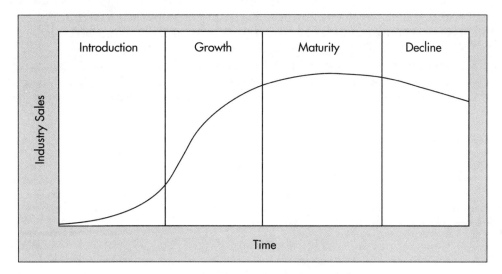

FIGURE 8-1
Stages of the Life Cycle

growth revitalizes after a period of decline, as has occurred in the motorcycle and bicycle industries and recently in the radio broadcasting industry. Some industries seem to skip the slow takeoff of the introductory phase altogether.

■ Companies can *affect* the shape of the growth curve through product innovation and repositioning, extending it in a variety of ways. If a company takes the life cycle as given, it becomes an undesirable self-fulfilling prophesy.

■ The nature of competition associated with each stage of the life cycle is *different* for different industries. For example, some industries start out highly concentrated and stay that way. Others, like bank cash dispensers, are concentrated for a significant period and then become less so. Still others begin highly fragmented; of these some consolidate (automobiles) and some do not (electronic component distribution). The same divergent patterns apply to advertising, research and development (R&D) expenditures, degree of price competition, and most other industry characteristics. Divergent patterns such as these call into serious question the strategic implications ascribed to the life cycle.

The real problem with the product life cycle as a predictor of industry evolution is that it attempts to describe *one* pattern of evolution that will invariably occur. And except for the industry growth rate, there is little or no underlying rationale for why the competitive changes associated with the life cycle will happen. Since actual industry evolution takes so many different paths, the life cycle pattern does not always hold, even if it is a common or even the most common pattern of evolution. Nothing in the concept allows us to predict when it will hold and when it will not.

A Framework for Forecasting Evolution

Instead of attempting to describe industry evolution, it will prove more fruitful to look underneath the process to see what really drives it. Like any evolution, industries evolve because some forces are in motion that create incentives or pressures for change. These can be called *evolutionary processes*.

Every industry begins with an *initial structure*—the entry barriers, buyer and supplier power, and so on that exist when the industry comes into existence. This structure is usually (though not always) a far cry from the configuration the industry will take later in its development. The initial structure results from a combination of underlying economic and technical characteristics of the industry, the initial constraints of small industry size, and the skills and resources of the companies that are early entrants. For example, even an industry like automobiles with enormous possibilities for economies of scale started out with labor-intensive, job-shop production operations because of the small volumes of cars produced during the early years.

TABLE 8-1
Predictions of Product Life-Cycle Theories about Strategy, Competition, and Performance

	Introduction	Growth	Maturity	Decline
Buyers and Buyer Behavior	High-income purchaser Buyer inertia Buyers must be convinced to try the product	Widening buyer group Consumer will accept uneven quality	Mass market Saturation Repeat buying Choosing among brands is the rule	Customers are sophisticated buyers of the product
Products and Product Change	Poor quality Product design and development key Many different product variations; no standards Frequent design changes Basic product designs	Products have technical and performance differentiation Reliability key for complex products Competitive product improvements Good quality	Superior quality Less product differentiation Standardization Less rapid product changes—more minor annual model changes Trade-ins become significant	Little product differentiation Spotty product quality
Marketing	Very high advertising/ sales (a/s) Creaming price strategy High marketing costs	High advertising, but lower percent of sales than introductory Most promotion of ethical drugs Advertising and distribution key for nontechnical products	Market segmentation Efforts to extend life cycle Broaden line Service and deals more prevalent Packaging important Advertising competition Lower a/s	Low a/s and other marketing
Manufacturing and Distribution	Overcapacity Short production runs High skilled-labor content High production costs Specialized channels	Undercapacity Shift toward mass production Scramble for distribution Mass channels	Some overcapacity Optimum capacity Increasing stability of manufacturing process Lower labor skills Long production runs with stable techniques Distribution channels pare down their lines to improve their margins High physical distribution costs due to broad lines Mass channels	Substantial over-capacity Mass production Specialty channels
R&D	Changing production techniques			

The evolutionary processes work to push the industry toward its *potential structure*, which is rarely known completely as an industry evolves. Embedded in the underlying technology, product characteristics, and nature of present and potential buyers, however, there is a range of structures the industry might possibly achieve, depending on the direction and success of research and development, marketing innovations, and the like.

	Introduction	Growth	Maturity	Decline
Foreign Trade	Some exports	Significant exports Few imports	Falling exports Significant imports	No exports Significant imports
Overall Strategy	Best period to increase market share R&D, engineering are key functions	Practical to change price or quality image Marketing the key function	Bad time to increase market share, particularly if low-share company Having competitive costs becomes key Bad time to change price image or quality image "Marketing effectiveness" key	Cost control key
Competition	Few companies	Entry Many competitors Lots of mergers and casualties	Price competition Shakeout Increase in private brands	Exits Fewer competitors
Risk	High risk	Risks can be taken here because growth covers them up	Cyclicality sets in	
Margins and Profits	High prices and margins Low profits Price elasticity to individual seller not as great as in maturity	High profits Highest profits Fairly high prices Lower prices than introductory phase Recession resistant High P/Es Good acquisition climate	Falling prices Lower profits Lower margins Lower dealer margins Increased stability of market shares and price structure Poor acquisition climate—tough to sell companies Lowest prices and margins	Low prices and margins Falling prices Prices might rise in late decline

It is important to realize that instrumental in much industry evolution are the investment decisions by both existing firms in the industry and new entrants. In response to pressures or incentives created by the evolutionary process, firms invest to take advantage of possibilities for new marketing approaches, new manufacturing facilities, and the like, which shift entry barriers, alter relative power against suppliers and buyers, and so on. The luck, skills, resources, and orientation of firms in the industry can shape the evolutionary path the industry will actually take. Despite potential for structural change, an industry may not actually change because no firm happens to discover a feasible new marketing approach; or potential scale economies may go unrealized because no firm possesses the financial resources to construct a fully integrated facility or simply because no firm is inclined to think about costs. Because innovation, technological developments, and the identities (and resources) of the particular firms either in the industry or considering entry into it are so important to evolution, industry evolution will not only be hard to forecast with certainty but also an industry can potentially evolve in a variety of ways at a variety of different speeds, depending on the luck of the draw.

Evolutionary Processes

Although initial structure, structural potential, and particular firms' investment decisions will be industry-specific, we can generalize about what the important evolutionary processes are. There are some predictable (and interacting) dynamic processes that occur in industry in one form or another, though their speed and direction will differ from industry to industry:

- long-run changes in growth
- changes in buyer segments served
- buyer's learning
- reduction of uncertainty
- diffusion of proprietary knowledge
- accumulation of experience
- expansion (or contradiction) in scale
- changes in input and currency costs
- product innovation
- marketing innovation
- process innovation
- structural change in adjacent industries
- government policy change
- entries and exits

Key Relationships in Industry Evolution

In the context of this analysis, *how* do industries change? They do not change in a piecemeal fashion, because an industry is an *interrelated system*. Change in one element of an industry's structure tends to trigger changes in other areas. For example, an innovation in marketing might develop a new buyer segment, but serving this new segment may trigger changes in manufacturing methods, thereby increasing economies of scale. The firm reaping these economies first will also be in a position to start backward integration, which will affect power with suppliers—and so on. One industry change, therefore, often sets off a chain reaction leading to many other changes.

It should be clear from the discussion here that whereas industry evolution is always occurring in nearly every business and requires a strategic response, there is no one way in which industries evolve. Any single model for evolution such as the product life cycle should therefore be rejected. However, there are some particularly important relationships in the evolutionary process that I will examine here.

Will the Industry Consolidate?

It seems to be an accepted fact that industries tend to consolidate over time, but as a general statement, it simply is not true. In a broad sample of 151 four-digit U.S. manufacturing industries in the 1963–72 time period, for example, 69 increased in four-firm concentration more than two percentage points, whereas 52 decreased more than two percentage points in the same period. The question of whether consolidation will occur in an industry exposes perhaps the most important interrelationships among elements of industry structure—those involving competitive rivalry, mobility barriers, and exit barriers.

Industry Concentration and Mobility Barriers Move Together

If mobility barriers are high or especially if they increase, concentration almost always increases. For example, concentration has increased in the U.S. wine industry. In the standard-quality segment of the market, which represents much of the volume, the strategic changes (high advertising, national distribution, rapid brand innovation, and so on) have greatly increased barriers to mobility. As a result, the larger firms have gotten further ahead of smaller ones, and few new firms have entered to challenge them.

No Concentration Takes Place If Mobility Barriers Are Low or Falling

Where barriers are low, unsuccessful firms that exit will be replaced be new firms. If a wave of exit has occurred because of an economic downturn or some other general adversity, there may be a temporary increase in industry concentration. But at the first signs that profits and sales in the industry are picking up, new entrants will appear. Thus a shakeout when an industry reaches maturity does not necessarily imply long-run consolidation.

Exit Barriers Deter Consolidation

Exit barriers keep companies operating in an industry even though they are earning subnormal returns on investment. Even in an industry with relatively high mobility barriers, the leading firms cannot count on reaping the benefits of consolidation if high exit barriers hold unsuccessful firms in the market.

Long-Run Profit Potential Depends on Future Structure

In the period of very rapid growth early in the life of an industry (especially after initial product acceptance has been achieved), profit levels are usually high. For example, growth in sales of skiing equipment was in excess of 20 percent per year in the late 1960s, and nearly all firms in the industry enjoyed strong financial results. When growth levels off in an industry, however, there is a period of turmoil as intensified rivalry weeds out the weaker firms. All firms in the industry may suffer financially during this adjustment period. Whether or not the remaining firms will enjoy above-average profitability will depend on the level of mobility barriers, as well as the other structural features of the industry. If mobility barriers are high or have increased as the industry has matured, the remaining firms in the industry may enjoy healthy financial results even in the new era of slower growth. If mobility barriers are low, however, slower growth probably means the end of above-average profits for the industry. Thus mature industries may or may not be as profitable as they were in their developmental period.

Changes in Industry Boundaries

Structural change in an industry is often accompanied by changes in industry boundaries. Industry evolution has a strong tendency to shift these boundaries. Innovations in the industry or those involving substitutes may effectively enlarge the industry by placing more firms into direct competition. Reduction in transportation cost relative to timber cost, for example, has made timber supply a world market rather than one restricted to continents. Innovations increasing the reliability and lowering the cost of electronic surveillance devices have put them into effective competition with security guard services. Structural changes making it easier for suppliers to integrate forward into the industry may well mean that suppliers effectively become competitors. Or buyers purchasing private label goods in large quantities and dictating product design criteria may become effective competitors in the manufacturing industry. Part of the analysis of the strategic significance of industry evolution is clearly an analysis of how industry boundaries may be affected.

Firms Can Influence Industry Structure

Industry structural change can be influenced by firms' strategic behavior. If it understands the significance of structural change for its position, the firm can seek to influence industry change in ways favorable to it, either through the way it reacts to strategic changes of competitors or in the strategic changes it initiates.

Another way a company can influence structural change is to be very sensitive to external forces that can cause the industry to evolve. With a head start, it is often possible to direct such forces in ways appropriate to the firm's position. For example, the specific form of regulatory changes can be influenced; the diffusion of innovations coming from outside the industry can be altered by the form that licensing or other agreements with innovating firms take; positive action can be initiated to improve the cost or supply of complementary products through providing direct assistance and help in forming trade associations or in stating their case to the government; and so on for the other important forces causing structural change. Industry evolution should not be greeted as a fait accompli to be reacted to, but as an opportunity.

■ SELECTING STRATEGIES
THAT EXPLOIT LEVERAGE†

By Milind Lele

Strategic leverage is a new concept that can help top management make better choices among various strategic options. By providing a framework to analyze a company's competitive position and the evolutionary state of its industry, strategic leverage is intended to support managers searching for effective answers to the basic question of the 1990s—Where should a company focus its long-term attention and scarce resources? Not only is this technique meant to help avoid wasting resources, it may also show management where to concentrate allocations in ways that will change the terms of the competition or even alter the basic structure of the industry or market.

Strategic leverage is defined as a company's ability to maneuver in an industry multiplied by the return for such a maneuver. In other words, it is the freedom to change position relative to competitors. *Return* describes the growth in revenue or market share that results from the change of position. If a company can change its channels of distribution, for example, and the market provides a significant return for such a maneuver, then it has successfully employed strategic leverage.

Managers can translate their understanding of their company's strategic leverage into specific objectives, strategies, and tactics by using a framework called the structure-position map (see figure 8-2). The methodology subdivides company's competitive position into four categories:

- The *leader* of the segment or industry
- The *second or third players*, that is, the companies closest to the leader in size, capabilities, and market share
- *Followers*, being all other players including niche players or specialty firms, but excluding entrants
- *Entrants*, firms entering the market for the first time, either by creating new capacity or through acquisition

Leaders. During the growth stage, the leading firm must try to define the game and set the overall pattern of competition. As the industry settles down into a period of slower growth, the leader's objective should be to limit price warfare. When that's not feasible, the leaders should move aggressively to consolidate the industry as an endgame strategy. During decline, the leader must try and change the game and, hopefully, reignite growth.

Second or third players. During the initial growth period, these firms must make every effort to define and modify the game and the overall terms of competition in their favor. As industry growth slows, they have two choices: play within the rules, or try to change the rules. If they elect to play within the rules, they can use them to nibble away at an unsuspecting (or lazy) leader's market share. Or they can exploit the rules by sawing the floor around the leader, possibly even moving into first place. As the industry starts to decline, they have to decide their endgame strategies: whether and when to exit, how to position themselves if they choose to stay, and whether to change the game itself.

Followers. Early on during the emerging or growth phases of the industry followers or would-be niche players must understand how the industry is likely to evolve (learn

---

†**Source:** This article was originally published in *Planning Review,* January/February 1992, Vol. 20, pp. 15–21. Reprinted with permission.

FIGURE 8-2

The Structure-Position Map: Company Competitive Position

Nature of Conflict	Leader	#2 or #3	Follower	Entrant	Industry Evolution
Win/Win	Define the game	Define/ modify the game	Learn the game Anticipate the rules	Exploit the game Become 1, 2, or 3	Emerging/ growth
Limited Warfare	Set, enforce the rules	Exploit the rules: *Nibble*	Raise barricades higher	Change the rules Change the game	Early Maturity
Win/Lose	Force consolidation	Change the rules: *Saw the floor*			Late Maturity
Lose/Lose	Change the game				Decline

the game), and how to exploit industry structure to create a niche (anticipate the rules). As industry growth slows, followers must create strong defenses (raise the barricades) to deter the major players from entering their market segment. During decline, these players are well entrenched and can survive for a long time, as shown by Rolls Royce in automobiles and Leica in 35-mm cameras. Alternatively, they may prefer to sell out, timing their exit for maximum gain.

Entrants. The objective of opportunistic entrants should be to skim the cream rapidly (exploit the game) and then to exit when industry growth slows to a crawl. Their goal is quick profits; consequently, they should avoid making any investments that raise their exit costs. Strategic entrants—companies who believe the emerging industry threatens their existing market or who possess core competencies that are central to the new industry—should aim at becoming key players (capturing first, second, or third place in the market). Otherwise, they're well advised to stay out.

How Leaders Can Exploit Leverage

A leader's choices may change definitively as a result of the interplay between structure, position, and industry evolution. Industry structure is not a major driver except indirectly, through the ease or difficulty of entry into the market. Strategic choices are governed more by industry evolution—the rate at which the industry is growing and how and when it is likely to mature—and a firm's competitive position. As the industry matures, structure and position move to the fore, overshadowing evolution. Structure determines whether limiting price competition is even feasible, while relative position dictates the degree to which a leader can set and enforce limits on price warfare. Later on, structural constraints, such as high exit barriers, may prevent a leader from forcing out other participants. This, in turn, can create highly destructive and debilitating price competition.

Growth or Win/Win

During the growth stage of industry evolution, the nature of the conflict is win/win; industry sales and profits are exploding, and there is little or no rivalry. Industry leaders are difficult to identify as market shares are changing rapidly, and different firms are trying to establish control over technology or market evolution. Therefore, in this context, the term *leader* refers to the half-dozen or so firms that are at the forefront of industry evolution in terms of technological changes, sales, and market development.

At this point, a company can choose among four basic objectives:

- It can try to maintain its leadership position as the industry evolves.
- It can opt to be a strong number two.
- It can use the profits from its temporary leadership position to find or create lucrative, defensible product or market niches.
- It can decide to sell out to a would-be entrant at an attractive price.

These objectives, in turn, decide a firm's strategies and tactics (see figure 8-3). If a firm wants to remain the leader or to be a strong second, its overall strategy must be differentiation. The firm's tactics must focus on controlling or influencing technological or market evolution and the number, types, and presence of its products in the channels of distribution. If the firm wants to find or create lucrative, secure niches, its strategy should be focused toward the differentiated end.

The central issue here is long-term positioning. As the industry matures, only two, or at most three, players are likely to be successful in establishing a unique, differentiated identity across the board, and only one firm can become the cost leader. Thus, unless they can find or create a niche, other front-runners risk being neither industry nor segment leaders, which means they earn substantially lower profits.

Consequently, a firm that is at the forefront during the growth stage must realistically assess its chances of being either first or second in the long run. If, as is likely, its prospects of remaining first or second are remote, then it should concentrate its energies on finding a secure niche that it is able to dominate. Alternatively, its interests may be better served by selling out to a potential entrant. Prices are likely to be very attractive, and the new owner may have the necessary financial and managerial resources.

The speed of industry evolution—whether anticipated or actual—determines the importance and the urgency of making these choices. In an industry that is growing relatively slowly, as was the case with the U.S. black-and-white television industry in the 1950s and early 1960s, leaders feel little pressure to select a particular positioning early on. However, in rapidly growing high-tech industries, he who hesitates is lost. Consequently, managers should concentrate the bulk of their efforts on capturing the most suitable positioning early, and on balancing the importance of technological leadership and market control.

FIGURE 8-3
Objectives, Strategies,
and Tactics—Leaders

	Objectives	Strategies	Tactical Issues
Win/Win	Maintain 1 Capture 2 Find/create niche	Differentiation (rarely cost) leadership Differentiated focus	Control of product/ market evolution Control of shelf space
Limited Warfare	Minimize price warfare	Entrenchment Consolidation	Flankers Price leadership Signaling
Win/Lose	End price wars Dominate	Consolidation Differentiation and cost leadership	Signaling Aggressive price and promotion tactics
Lose/Lose	Divest Dominate	—	—

Strategic decisions made during the growth stage have long-lasting effects. There are three typical mistakes:

■ Believing that a firm will maintain its initial technological or innovative leadership despite the near-certain entry of larger players with sizable vested interests;

■ Failing to recognize how industry forces—especially buyer (channel) power—change and adapt their strategies to these new realities;

■ Lacking clear, realistic long-term objectives.

Maturity: Limited Warfare or Win/Lose

As growth slows and the industry starts to mature, a leader must determine whether limited price competition is feasible, given the structure of the industry and the company's position and resources. If price warfare is containable, the leader's objective must be to establish and maintain the terms of competition, that is, the price differentials it will permit, price leadership, the types and intensity of promotion, and intermediaries' margins and pricing patterns.

Its strategy should be entrenchment—tightening its hold on major customers and intermediaries. The leader should not hesitate to use acquisitions, either to capture and control key market segments, or to further consolidate the industry and limit price competition. Tactical areas of primary concern are:

■ introducing or countering with appropriate flankers to ensure that competitors do not increase their shares;

■ maintaining price leadership, while ensuring that other players don't nibble away at its share.

If limited price warfare is unlikely because of industry structure or the leader's position, weak management must decide whether:

- to impose price discipline through consolidations if necessary;
- to dominate the industry by driving out weaker players through relentless price and product competition;
- to exit the industry.

The first two choices pose substantial risks. Reimposing price discipline may not be feasible without extensive (and expensive) consolidation. And high exit barriers, or the understandable reluctance of competitors to leave quietly, may make domination difficult, time-consuming, and expensive. Finally, at this stage of industry evolution, it may be difficult to find buyers offering attractive prices.

Decline or Lose/Lose

During decline there are essentially two choices—divest, or dominate and harvest. Divesting businesses may be difficult, in which case a firm may divest selectively, milking the existing investment. If a firm chooses to remain in the industry, it should move aggressively to consolidate the industry if at all possible—that is, if exit barriers are not too high. It should purchase smaller players or simply force them out by aggressively lowering its costs and prices, adding capacity, or taking other actions.

How Second or Third Players Can Exploit Leverage

During the growth phase, the second or third players' choices are the same as those faced by the eventual leader, particularly if, as is often the case, there are several potential contenders for leadership. However, the second or third players' choices become particularly interesting as the industry matures. At this point, a firm can make significant gains. If the nominal industry leader is weak, complacent, or preoccupied by other activities such as diversification efforts, a determined number two or a clever number three can substantially narrow the gap. Occasionally, it may even succeed in overtaking the leader.

The second or third players' options during industry maturity demonstrate the importance of strategic leverage (see figure 8-4). Only by thoroughly understanding where a company has any leverage and what industry forces shape its leverage, can a manager determine

- whether it is feasible to improve or change the firm's competitive position;
- which specific tactics—low-profile attacks on neglected segments, changes to product quality/price ratios, bypassing existing channels—are most likely to succeed;
- the potential risks of different approaches;
- the timing of such tactics.

Maturity: Limited Warfare

The main issue is whether a firm should work to maintain the status quo or increase its share without resorting to all-out price warfare, which is rarely successful. A firm can gain share on the leader either gradually, or more aggressively by consolidating its

FIGURE 8-4
Objectives, Strategies, and Tactics—Second or Third Players

	Objectives	Strategies	Tactical Issues

Win/Win	Capture 1
	Maintain 2/3
	Find/create niche
		Differentiation
		Differentiation
		  or cost leadership
		Focus
			How to accelerate
			  speed of product/
			  market evolution
			Shelf space

Limited Warfare	Maintain
	  status quo
	Increase share
	Capture 1
	Divest
		Follow/support
		  leader
		Nibble
		Saw the floor
			Signaling
			Flanking
			Attacking niches
			  or changing
			  performance/
			  price ratios

Win/Lose	Increase share/
	  strengthen
	  position
	Divest
		Selective attacks
		Acquisitions
		Changing terms
		  of game
			Target niches
			Acquisition of
			  niche players
			Channel changes

Lose/Lose	Minimize losses Divest	—	—

hold on the market a segment at a time. Which tactical variables will be important depend on the structure of the industry and the long-term objectives of the firm. However, signaling will be necessary either to demonstrate adherence to implicit terms of competition or to lull the leader into continued complacency.

Maturity: Win/Lose

Here, second or third players must decide whether to exit the industry, or to use industry warfare to increase share or otherwise strengthen position. If a firm chooses to stay in the industry and fight it out, then its strategy should be to increase its leverage by changing the rules of the game.

A tenacious competitor can use a variety of tactics to change the rules, for example, consolidation by acquiring players in important niches, price attacks in selective segments, or changes to the channels of distribution. The last tactic can be particularly effective, for channel roles change as industries evolve. However, market leaders are often reluctant to change existing channel strategies, with the result that they are often inefficient and, consequently, vulnerable to price attacks by competitors using more efficient alternatives.

Decline: Lose/Lose

Here, second or third players have only one choice: exit. The real issue is timing. Can a firm exit early enough to avoid distress-sale prices when the industry contracts violently?

What Followers Can and Cannot Do

Followers typically have very little leverage and must use it judiciously if they want to survive, let alone prosper. A follower's strategic choices are summarized in figure 8-5. When the industry is growing, the primary consideration for a follower is, Can we find or create a profitable, defensible niche where we can be first, or at worst second, in market position? If a firm cannot, it should sell out, preferably while industry growth is still high and potential entrants are numerous, thereby maximizing the returns to its shareholders. Exiting at this point is infinitely preferable to continuing until the industry matures and major players start to invade niche markets in search of continued growth.

While specific tactics vary from industry to industry, product or market specialization is crucial to delay the entry of major players into niche markets. Particularly in the absence of natural entry barriers, a firm can use such specialized knowledge to create switching costs, thus making it expensive or unattractive for customers to change over to less specialized or customized products or services offered by larger competitors. Specialized channels can also make it more difficult for major players to enter a niche by raising their selling costs or requiring them to change their price structure.

As an industry nears maturity, a firm must decide whether it wishes to continue as an active participant or exit by selling out. There is a strong case for exiting: As industry growth slows and competition intensifies, the niche player often finds it difficult to protect its position without significant investments.

Conversely, buyers may be plentiful—current major players wanting to consolidate their hold on the market; firms looking for a secure niche; and late entrants wishing to enter the market. Under the right circumstances, bidding wars can raise prices to such a level that the alternative, staying in for the long term, is no longer attractive.

FIGURE 8-5
Objectives, Strategies, and Tactics—Followers

	Objectives	Strategies	Tactical Issues
Win/Win	Find/create defensible niche Be acquired	Focus	Product/market specialization Channel selection
Limited Warfare	Maintain status quo Entrench in niche Displace 2 or 3 Be acquired	Strengthen defenses	Price control Service intensity
Win/Lose	Minimize share loss Be acquired	Increase value Create nuisance value	—
Lose/Lose	—	—	—

If a firm chooses to continue in the market, its strategy must be to strengthen its defenses against the inevitable attempts by the larger players to increase their revenues and profits by entering lucrative niches. Two tactics play a particularly important role in achieving this objective. The first is close control over pricing, to ensure that unduly high prices do not tempt firms into entering the market. This is especially important in segments where exit barriers are high. In such situations, it is essential to prevent entry. Once a firm enters, it is usually too expensive to drive it out.

The other key tactic is service intensity. By increasing the levels of service offered, the niche player can make customers reluctant to switch except for really steep price differentials. When coupled with aggressive pricing, service intensity creates a major hurdle for potential entrants. They must lower prices in order to capture any revenues at all, while their costs are higher due to the special needs of the segment and the higher service levels provided by established niche players.

After price warfare becomes widespread, early exit may be the niche player's only realistic choice, especially if the alternative is survival as a minor actor in a declining if not dying industry.

What Entrants Should Do

The objectives, strategies, and tactics for the two types of entrants—opportunistic and competitive—are summarized in figure 8-6. Two situations should be considered for entry—growing industries, and mature industries with limited price competition. There is no reason to enter declining industries or industries where price warfare is widespread.

Entrants in mature markets with limited price competition have two alternatives: Should the firm join in the status quo? Or should it try to conquer the market by changing the terms of competition or even the nature of the conflict itself? If a firm chooses to join the status quo, its strategy should be to maintain limited price conflict. Through carefully chosen market signals, it should reassure existing players that it does not intend to violate or significantly change the terms of competition within the industry.

More often, a firm enters a market with the intention of dominating or at least becoming a significant player. In this case, its strategy should be to saw the floor around the leader(s)—to change the terms of competition or, long term, the structure of the industry itself. Typical tactics will be to attack fringe or secondary market segments, change the overall price/performance ratio, or use different channels of distribution.

How to Change Strategic Leverage

Companies do not have to accept the limitations on strategic leverage imposed by structure or position. They can change the situation to their advantage in a number of ways. They can acquire other firms, thereby changing their competitive position. Or they can alter the competitive balance of the industry by creating strategic alliances. They can introduce new technology, which radically alters the structure of the industry. Alternatively, they can substantially increase industry capacity thereby intensifying price competition within the industry and, possibly, forcing smaller players to exit.

	Objectives	Strategies	Tactical Issues
Win/Win	Make shortterm gains and cash out *Opportunistic entrant* Capture 1, 2, or 3 *Competitive entrant*	Find, attack targets of opportunity Differentiation or cost leadership	Rapid product roll-out Minimal investment in facilities Participate/control/ product evolution
Limited Warfare	Join Conquer	Maintain status quo Change the rules Change the game Consolidate/ force exit	Signaling Changes in product/ price relationships Attacking key/ fringe segments
Win/Lose	—	—	—
Lose/Lose	—	—	—

FIGURE 8-6
Objectives, Strategies, and Tactics—Entrants

We can group these different possibilities into two main categories according to whether they change the terms of competition or the structure of the industry.

Changing the Rules

Managers can change the terms of competition in their industry in a number of ways:

- *They can attack pricing gaps.* Mazda changed the upscale sports car market with its RX-7, which looked "just like a Porsche, at half the price!" Essentially, Mazda was attacking an opening created by Porsche's continually increasing prices, which had stranded many buyers who wanted a Porsche but could not afford one.

- *They can change channels or channel roles.* In the late 1980s, Blockbuster Video consolidated the home video rental industry in a short four years by creating large, well-capitalized, and well-managed outlets.

- *They can raise the intensity of competition.* Firms can alter the tempo of competition by providing higher levels of service (Singapore Airlines); increasing advertising severalfold (Miller Brewing, Lotus); accelerating the rate of new product introductions (Sony in consumer electronics); or other tactical moves. When this occurs, rivals who lack financing or who are not as nimble are left behind.

- *They can change the value/price ratio.* This is precisely what the Japanese did in so many markets, and what Becton Dickinson did in disposable hypodermic syringes.

Changing the Game Itself

Sometimes companies find it desirable to change the basic structure of the industry itself. For example, when an industry is in late maturity, the leader may find it necessary to forcibly consolidate the industry. In other cases, a second or third player may find that changing the structure is the only way to overtake the leader.

- *Introduce new technology.* A major discontinuous shift in the basic technology usually changes the makeup of an industry. But this maneuver doesn't always take a major technological innovation. An industry can also be changed through marketing, logistical, or operational innovations. The Canon copier cartridge was an extension of the basic copier technology. But because it changed the underlying economics of sales, distribution, and service support, it made a major change in the copier industry.

- *Consolidate channels.* This approach has been used by countless firms. Consolidation is particularly effective when an industry is fragmented and both buyers and suppliers are weak.

- *Consolidate the industry.* American Airlines' aggressive pricing and promotional tactics (1989–90) appear to have had one aim: Consolidate the airline industry in order to keep price wars under control.

Framing the Right Issues

Managers can use the structure-position map, together with the knowledge of their company's leverage, to select their objectives and strategies and tactics. However, this framework is not intended to be applied mechanically or to eliminate a manager's freedom of choice.

The chief value of our approach is that it helps managers identify and frame the right issues by focusing on the areas of greatest concern and impact. Managerial skill and willingness to take calculated risks are still essential. And informed judgment is vital in determining which stage an industry is currently in and how rapidly it is evolving; in evaluating the firm's position relative to its competitors; and in assessing the likely risks and returns in altering the rules of the game—or even the game itself.

■ BREAKPOINTS[†]

By Paul Strebel

The small Swiss town of Wohlen in the canton of Aargau is home to an impressive turn-of-the-century building that once was the headquarters of Georges Meyer & Company, one of the world's leading straw hat manufacturers. The company originated in the straw-plaiting industry that emerged from the European countryside in the late sixteenth century. A major breakthrough occurred in 1860 when Georges Meyer and his partner introduced plaiting machines. By the 1950s, their company employed more than one thousand people, occupied a sprawling site that included manufacturing and dyeing facilities, and had agencies and representatives around the world. Georges Meyer's success attracted other competitors, primarily three Swiss companies, Dreyfuss, about half its size, and Breitschmid and Jacques Meier, each about a quarter of its size.

In the 1960s the industry was confronted unexpectedly with a major breakpoint: hats were out of fashion. The confined spaces inside automobiles and airplanes had been making hats more and more cumbersome for some time. Ever accelerating

†**Source:** This article has been adapted from chapters 1 and 2 of *Breakpoints*, Harvard Business School Press, 1992, pp. 9–47. Used with permission.

lifestyles left less and less time for the careful dressing and stately occasions so appropriate for hats. When these forces finally culminated in a shift in fashion, the impact on the straw braid industry was disastrous. Demand hit bottom.

Georges Meyer's competitors began moving into different but related activities. Dreyfuss exploited its agency network to distribute other products, especially those of 3M Corporation, with whom it developed a link. Breitschmid used its braiding know-how to manufacture cable sleeves, and in the process came up with the curl to the telephone handset cable. Jacques Meier moved into cellophane bags, capitalizing on the plastic film technology that had been used to encase the straw before braiding.

At Georges Meyer itself, rivalry between the three managing directors prevented the company from focusing on a single response to the discontinuity. Strong financial reserves allowed for several diversification attempts, including, for example, the manufacture of stuffed straw animals, all of which failed. By the early 1970s, business was so bad the company had to be liquidated. Georges Meyer converted to a property holding and investment company designed to manage the remaining assets, including the stately head office, and distribute the proceeds to the shareholders.

The demise of Georges Meyer illustrates how a breakpoint in the business environment, in this case a radical shift in fashion, triggered a breakpoint in demand, which turned into a strong force for change in the industry. The result was a sharp shift in the competitive rules of the game and a major breakpoint in the performance of the leading company.

Business discontinuities can be best recognized relative to recent trends and behavior in the industry, company, or business unit. The quantitative signs of a breakpoint take the form of shifts in performance trends. These are sharp changes in direction, up or down, in the quantitative performance of the industry, company, or business unit. When plotted on a graph, a performance shift generates a jump, a sudden rise or fall in the growth rate of the trend. The qualitative signs take the form of shifts in the competitive or organizational behavior of the industry, company, or business unit. These shifts involve qualitative changes in the rules of the industry or company game, which are reflected in the set of viable strategies.

Shifts in Industry Performance

The sales and profit data of industries and competitors, if broken down sufficiently, usually can be used to visualize the impact of a breakpoint. A Princeton statistician is said to have remarked often that a simple graph is worth the output from a thousand equations. To identify quantitative shifts in performance, one does not need to engage in complex statistical analysis. Rather one should decide on the key quantitative measure of performance for the business and find a way of graphing it that most simply reflects what is happening.

Consider the example in figure 8-7 of the Dutch audio-video market, radio and hi-fi equipment, tape recorders, TV, video recorders and cameras, compact discs, and so forth. Industry sales in millions of guilders are shown on the vertical axis. The overall shape of the curve reflects the early growth, followed by gradual maturing, of the Dutch audio-video market. (The slope of the line gives a direct indication of the industry's growth rate, because a log scale has been used on the vertical axis.)

Over forty years, distinct periods of rapid and low growth can be distinguished. During the 1950s, the audio technology developed during World War II was adapted

FIGURE 8-7
Sales Growth Rate Shifts in
the Dutch Audio-Video
Industry

Source: Data provided by
Philips N. V., Nederland,
Consumer Electronics Division.

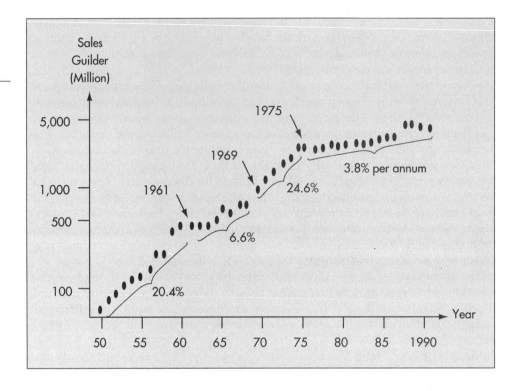

to civilian use. Rapid growth rates, averaging 20 percent per annum, persisted until 1960. The saturation of the market, combined with an economic slowdown, triggered a breakpoint in the growth of demand, followed by sharply lower growth rates during the early 1960s. Although interrupted by the introduction of the compact cassette and hi-fi stereo in 1964 and 1965, the slow growth continued until 1968, at an average annual rate of 6.6 percent.

In 1969, the surging sales of color TVs triggered another sharp breakpoint, this time in the direction of higher growth rates averaging almost 25 percent annually for six years. The oil price crisis hit in 1974, producing the next breakpoint in the direction of lower growth rates. Despite the success of video recorders and compact discs, the average growth rate was less than 4 percent during the 1980s. Without these new products the growth rate probably would have been negative.

The point is that industry performance trends do not necessarily change smoothly, or randomly. Rather an industry's performance may exhibit a sudden upturn or downturn that persists for some time. These shifts in industry performance are typically jumps in the growth rate of the performance measure.

Performance curves are often too aggregated to reflect key breakpoints that are important to managers. When industries or companies are complex and more mature, new-product breakpoints, for example, may be obscured by overlapping product life cycles. The video recorder and compact disc were of the same order of importance to competitors in the Dutch audio-video market as color TV. Yet the aggregate performance displayed merely a blip in its growth rate. To reflect these breakpoints, more detailed market segment data are necessary.

Shifts in Competitive Behavior

Industry growth-rate breakpoints are often accompanied by sharp shifts in competitive behavior. These breakpoints may be stimulated by external factors, such as the shift in fashion that affected the straw braid industry, or by internal life-cycle developments.

No matter where they originate, competitive shifts involve transitions between two well-known ways of competing. The two ways are illustrated by a value-cost diagram of the evolution of the personal computer industry (see figure 8-8). One possibility, shown with the vertical arrows, is to make the product better by increasing the value of a personal computer as perceived by the market; the other alternative, shown with the horizontal arrows, is to make the product cheaper by reducing the delivered cost of a given set of PC functions. Since the introduction of the PC, a progressive evolution has taken place toward increasing perceived value at declining delivered cost. Although competition takes place continually on both dimensions, in terms of growth, greater or lesser emphasis may be on perceived value or on delivered cost at different times.

During the development phase, competitive behavior revolved around attempts to develop the value of the product. Hundreds of small firms were competing with Apple to define the form and content of a personal computer. This value-based competition continued until IBM introduced what eventually became the market standard. The sudden entry of IBM triggered a breakpoint, toward an emphasis on matching the IBM standard and then reducing the delivered cost. Those firms unable to manage the shift in competitive emphasis, and unprotected by niche segments, went out of business in

FIGURE 8-8

Competitive Shifts in the Personal Computer Industry (Simplified View)

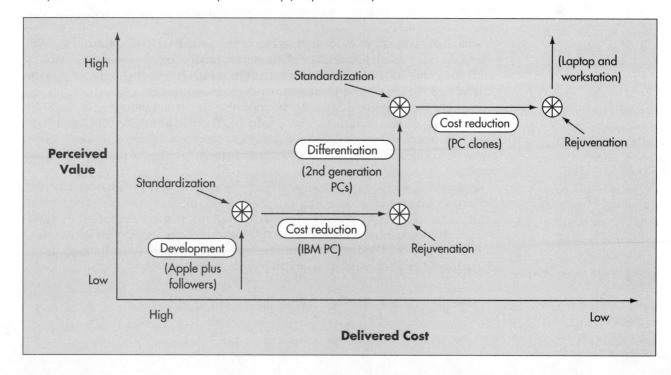

the shakeout that followed. To manage this breakpoint, Apple was forced to oust its founders and bring in a consumer-marketing expert.

Competition on lower delivered costs was dominant, especially with the entry of competitors from the Far East, until the leading competitors came out with a second-generation product. The emphasis on hard discs, better graphics, and greater speed triggered a second shift in market behavior back to competition around the value of the PC. To survive this shift, even the clone manufacturers in the Far East were forced to follow suit. Competitive behavior continued to revolve around value enhancement until the clone manufacturers caught up and switched the emphasis back to process cost reduction.

In the late 1980s, the PC industry went through yet another important shift back to value competition. In the growth segments, the product's function shifted toward the laptop and integrated workstations. As a workstation, the PC has become part of more complex information system networks with specialized applications for different end users.

Competitive shifts change the rules of the competitive game. They add a fundamentally new dimension to the competitive mix. Standardization shifts involve a move toward increasing competition around rationalization and delivered costs. Rejuvenation shifts involve a move toward competition around product development, differentiation, or customization, designed to increase perceived value. In effect, competitive shifts add a new layer of value, or lower cost, which significantly improves the product offering. As a result, over time, the industry progresses up along the diagonal in figure 8-8 toward product offerings with more perceived value per unit of real delivered cost.

Actual market cycles do not necessarily manifest a neat sequence of shifts. Several rejuvenations may succeed one another before a standardization occurs. Some market segments, such as designer clothing, which mostly depends on art or fashion, may rarely undergo standardization. Conversely, markets for commodities may experience successive price declines, based on process standardizations incorporating new technology, with few if any rejuvenations of the product or the service's perceived value.

With the shortening of product life cycles in today's markets, standardization shifts often follow closely on rejuvenation shifts. In fact, product innovation is not complete until the competitive formula has been standardized and the delivery system streamlined. This is needed to ensure that the fully augmented product reaches the market in a cost-effective manner. In the consumer electronics industry, for example, and in many service industries, new product introductions involve the immediate launching of a complete, standardized competitive formula. Therefore, it often makes no sense to talk about separate innovation and standardization shifts at the product level.

Competitive shifts only make sense at the industry sector level, when examining the behavior of competitors as a group. At this level, one can identify competitive breakpoints followed by periods of innovative activity, with a continuous stream of new products that have more or less fully standardized competitive formulas. Alternatively, breakpoints are followed by an emphasis on rationalization, characterized by a continual spate of cost reduction moves.

Breakpoints versus Turning Points

How sharp must the shifts be to qualify as discontinuous? To qualify as a breakpoint, the change should be sudden and radical, that is, rapid and fundamental in nature: it should create a noticeable break in the performance trend and break the rules of the competitive game, making recent experience useless.

However, radical change in a company's position may occur gradually over time. Change that is gradual and radical constitutes a turning point. Turning points are gradual and incremental, whereas breakpoints are sudden and sharp. Both are forms of radical change.

To first movers, a change that they create in the competitive game seems gradual. It appears to be a turning point. To followers, those companies that only wake up later on in response to the cumulative effect, the same change looks sharp and discontinuous, more like a breakpoint. When one or more of the change characteristics described in this article occur within a period of one year, or possibly two, casual observation suggests that most followers regard these transitions as breakpoints.

In lower-tech industries like beer and cosmetics, breakpoints may be relatively few and far between. In these industries, product and brand life cycles may be quite long, supporting long periods of continuity. Shiseido's first cosmetic product, Eudermine, a skin lotion with a distinctive wine red color and bottle design, is still on sale ninety years after its introduction. In high-tech industries like consumer electronics and computers, technological change is more rapid, product life cycles are much shorter, and breakpoints are correspondingly more frequent.

Performance shifts and behavioral shifts usually do not occur at the same time. Breakpoints caused by outside factors affect the performance of an industry or a company before its behavior changes. Thus, the plunging sales in the straw braid industry preceded the shifts in competitive strategy and behavior. Conversely, breakpoints that are initiated by players within the system will show up in behavioral shifts first, before performance shifts.

The important point is to identify potentially discontinuous change as early as possible. But because the features of a breakpoint, shifts in performance, for example, are only apparent after the breakpoint has occurred, one must be sensitive to the underlying forces, forces that have been gathering momentum, often, as we shall see, over a long period.

Forces of Change

The strength of a change force shows up in the rate of change it creates in the environment. Even though history never repeats itself exactly, forces of change are associated with recurring patterns that reflect different rates of change. The features of the more common patterns are:

- trends and trajectories;
- turning points, stimuli, and limits;
- cycles and recurring turning points.

These are listed according to the strength of the related force of change. Trends represent forces of change to the extent that they change the business environment. Emerging or declining trends are typically weak, whereas growing or mature trends are strong. A turning point (or breakpoint) shows up as a shift in the direction of a trend, up or down, which corresponds to a strong force of change. Cycles comprise major turning points, at irregular intervals, that involve reversals in the direction of trends, which makes the force of change even greater. Fortunately, as we shall see, there is a basic pattern in cyclical phenomena that can be used to anticipate cyclical turning points.

Trends and Trajectories

Existing trends are important, because playing out their implications is one of the best guides to the future. Peter Drucker, for one, says that he does not try to forecast the future, but he does take the consequences of existing trends very seriously. The increasing strain on the natural environment is a trend that cannot be reversed overnight, so its implications will be with us for many years to come. Similarly, ever wider diffusion of microprocessor technology has implications for innovation in many industries. Or, on a shorter timescale within one industry, a declining cost curve has pricing implications for all competitors.

Unfortunately, executives, caught up in the maelstrom of daily events, often have difficulty responding to the potential impact of otherwise obvious trends. In the construction machinery industry, the falling heavy-construction and housing markets were a fact well before the Saudi market collapsed. Even if the latter hadn't occurred, existing trends indicated that business could not continue as usual.

To internalize the potential impact of trends, it is vital that top management in particular become actively involved in continually scanning the environment. In most cases, it is not enough to read reports from the planning department. Rarely do critical reports get the attention they deserve, and even if they do, important reports are difficult to recognize as such if one hasn't been monitoring continually the development of critical factors in the environment. As Fred Gluck, a McKinsey director, put it: "Decision making based on somebody else's analysis of the situation is simply too risky and can't lead to bold initiative." The place to start scanning is with the drivers of demand in the main segments of the business, and with the factors affecting behavior on the supply side among the competitors, in the resource supply chain and distribution channels, and among the company's stakeholders.

Turning Points, Stimuli, and Limits

Changes in the direction of a trend can be either up, corresponding to increasing intensity or growth of the trend, or down, corresponding to less intensity or growth. The leading indicators of a potential upturn typically include new stimuli that replace or augment the basic drivers behind the trend. The indicators of a potential downturn include limits that inhibit or dampen the trend drivers.

Stimuli

The stimuli of an upturn take many different forms:

- Innovation in all its guises, but especially in new technology or products, is the most frequent and powerful stimulator of output trends.
- Emergence of a dominant design or standard product offering makes it possible to shift to much larger output.
- Specialization/customization opens up new and different market segments.
- Deregulation unleashes the stimulus of free competition.
- New management or a new approach may usher in a more dynamic organization.

Often more than one stimulus is involved at a time. New technology, or products, provide the stimulus for many upturns in tandem with evolving market needs. In the computer industry, new products have been introduced repeatedly against a background of increasing customer dissatisfaction with the real benefits provided by existing systems and an inclination to experiment rather than accept the industry's party line. It is worth recalling the number of discontinuities that IBM stimulated with successive generations of mainframe computers, reflecting the transitions from the vacuum tube to the transistor, and improvements in integrated circuits, each of which responded to growing client needs. DEC's minicomputer stimulated a breakpoint by allowing users to do most of their data processing in their own departments. Apple created the personal computer breakpoint by tapping independent software development to fill the latent need for customized data processing on the end user's desk. In the 1980s, DEC and others tried to capitalize on their experience in distributed data processing to introduce networking that met the desire to link disparate systems together. And, in an otherwise depressed computer industry during the early 1990s, Toshiba and Compaq kept the trend toward individual computing afloat with their laptops and portables.

Limits

The limits that presage a downturn also come in a variety of forms:

- natural laws of the sciences that put a physical limit on a trend
- carrying capacity/resource exhaustion
- saturation of markets
- negative feedback effects that undermine growth
- underinvestment that cuts off growth
- fragmentation and chaos in markets

Combined Limits and Stimuli

The presence of stimuli and limits pointing in the same direction sometimes makes it easier to identify a potential turning point or breakpoint, especially when new stimuli replace old limits. The most common example is the transition from one technology development curve to another.

The limits to a technology flatten its growth curve out at the top. The resulting slower growth and lower returns make investment in alternative technologies attractive. The higher potential return on alternative technologies increases the chances of a jump to a new generation of technology. Gerhard Mensch studied the times when 112 major technological innovations were commercialized. He found that many were bunched in the middle of major world depressions. The findings confirm the notion that major technology shifts often have their origin in the years of weak returns, years that reflect both the end of the existing generation of technology and the higher potential returns associated with new technology.

Competitive behavior during an industry life cycle also provides examples of how limits and stimuli may combine to create a turning point. The limits become increasingly apparent, for example, before competitive behavior shifts away from value competition. The return to product enhancement and customization declines. The offerings of competitors in the marketplace begin to look alike. Customers are less and less willing to pay for purely perceived value. At the same time, the stimuli for a shift toward more cost-based competition begin to make themselves felt. The convergence of the products favors the development of a dominant design which can be used to standardize the production delivery and service process. A broad potential market emerges sharing an implicit consensus about the basic features of a standard product offering.

The development of the generic drugs business in the pharmaceutical industry of the 1980s illustrates this interplay between limits and stimuli. For some time fewer and fewer new products were being launched, despite higher research and development spending. The cost of bringing a new product to the market increased, up to $100 million, while the process itself slowed to an average of ten years. Average volume growth for pharmaceuticals decreased from 15 percent in the 1970s to about 5 percent in the 1980s. In terms of stimuli for generics, there was growing worldwide political pressure for lower drug prices: in the United Kingdom, for example, profit ceilings had been set; in Japan, prices had already been submitted to an average 50 percent decrease. Moreover, the upcoming expiration of many major patents was opening the door for generics. In the United States, FDA approval had been greatly facilitated by the Waxman bill, while the increasing older population created more demand for cheaper medicine. The limits on the existing business and the stimuli in the direction of generics provided a strong signal about a possible major turning point in the pharmaceutical industry.

Cycles and Recurring Turning Points

A cyclical perspective on human affairs can be very useful for identifying the patterns that link turning points together. Yet, a cyclical view comes more naturally to executives in the East. Sony, for example, talks about a twenty-five-year cycle in audio technology, beginning with the phonograph in 1875, followed by the gramophone in 1900, the electrophone in 1924, the LP stereo in the early 1950s, and the CD player in the late 1970s. As Heitaro Nakajima, a former managing director of Sony, put it: "This leads us to suspect that the next major revolution will take place in the beginning of the 21st century. And what will that be? My personal guess is that it will probably be an all solid state recorder using semiconductor memories. It might be called a 'Silicon Recorder.'"

Managers in the East often interpret cycles as part of Tao, a process of continual flow and change. Its principal characteristic is ceaseless cyclical motion, the ultimate essence of reality in Chinese philosophy. The yin and the yang are two phases or states that set the limits for the cycles of change in the Tao: "The yang having reached its climax retreats in favor of the yin; the yin having reached its climax retreats in favor of the yang." Although there are many interpretations, the yin can be seen as cooperative, supportive, partial to collective effort. The yang is competitive, aggressive, more individualistic. According to the ancient *Book of Changes*, all of reality including business is in a constant state of tension, reflecting a dynamic interplay between these polar opposites.

In the language we have been using, cyclical change involves repeated turning points between opposing poles of behavior. The limits inherent in too much of one behavior create the opening for stimuli supporting the opposite type of behavior. Cycles incorporating the tension between opposing behaviors crop up everywhere, on the sociopolitical level, and the economic, industry corporate, and business unit levels. Sensitivity to the characteristics of typical cycles, like the sensitivity to stimuli and limits, is key to identifying the forces of change as early as possible.

Militating against the notion of cycles, however, is a deeply ingrained Western belief in some form of continuing progress. This belief has a long pedigree going back to Jacob's dream of a ladder that reaches up to the heavens. The theme was picked up by the Christian philosophers such as Augustine who used examples from the Old Testament. And in the Greek and Roman empires good was shown to triumph over evil. The philosophers of the eighteenth-century Enlightenment went further and fashioned the concept of freedom, a belief in progress, and above all a commitment to the scientific method. Indeed, the accomplishments of science, and especially its technological and economic spin-offs, are visible signs of continuing progress. Western economists, moreover, emphasize the notion of market equilibrium, the idea that deviations will be cut short by competitive forces that drive everything back to equilibrium. Nothing could be more foreign to the ideology of progressive equilibrium than the notion of repetitive turning points and cycles.

The importance of cycles for identifying the evolution of change forces over time, in the face of the widespread belief in continuing progress, makes it worthwhile to consider the features that are common to some typical cycles so that they can be recognized more quickly. Analogs to Darwin's evolutionary cycle of random mutation and natural selection are especially interesting.

In human organizations (markets and hierarchies) the evolutionary cycle corresponds to variety creation on the one hand, and efficient use of scarce resources on the other. This cycle provides a simple framework for identifying patterns of change in several arenas.

Sociopolitical Cycles

The first step is to identify the opposing poles of behavior that make up the cycle. Applying the cyclical view to the sociopolitical sphere, numerous pairs of opposing behaviors come to mind:

- individualism versus group orientation
- progressive versus conservative
- democratic versus dictatorial
- left wing versus right wing

To illustrate the evolutionary tension between variety creation and efficient use of scarce resources, we shall use the tension between individualism and group orientation. On one side is the individualist approach to sociopolitical affairs. On the other is the group—or community-oriented approach. Both reflect the pursuit of freedom, albeit in different, yet complementary, ways. Individualism reflects the yang tendency, an emphasis on freedom of choice, competition, a decentralized governance structure. It generates the variety that is the basis of evolutionary mutation. The group orientation embodies the yin view, an emphasis on freedom from want, by minimizing threats to survival through group effort and the protective authority of the state. This behavior provides the cohesion needed to prevail in the face of societal problems. Many variants of the two exist in dynamic tension with one another, often masked by an ideology of the "right" or the "left." An extreme version of one often encourages an extreme version of the other.

The deregulation of the U.S. airline industry is an example of how a sociopolitical turning point can trigger several industry discontinuities. The free-market ideology of Reagan led directly to the deregulation of the airline industry, which in turn spawned numerous new competitors and a growing variety of different flight offerings to the consumer. People's Express was one of the more flamboyant incarnations of the new competitive behavior. But the trend toward differentiation foundered on the limits imposed by a saturating market and rising costs. The demise of People's Express and then Pan American symbolized the turning point back toward competition based on disciplined efficiency and streamlined operations. This trend was stimulated in the early 1990s by a worldwide recession that forced airlines to search for economies of scale in alliances and mergers, for example, Swissair's links with Delta, SAS, and Singapore Airlines.

In the sociopolitical examples, two complementary turning points stand out that represent the extremes of the political cycle; each signals a shift from one of the two basic sociopolitical tendencies to the other. They are:

- Divergence and loosening of authority, marking a turning point away from a group orientation toward more individualism; and
- Convergence and tightening of authority, marking a turning point away from individualism toward more of a group orientation.

These shifts embrace a whole range from relatively smooth transitions that characterize turning points to the discontinuous change that epitomizes breakpoints. The lesson here is that the forces of political change are much easier to identify if they are stripped of their ideological content and interpreted in terms of an imperfect search for balance over time between the two opposing poles of a cyclical process.

Economic Cycles

Cyclical economic change is manifest all the time in the analysis of the business cycle. Alternating periods of expansion and contraction, higher and lower real-growth rates, can be clearly demarcated by business economists, albeit after the fact. Whatever the particular cause, cyclical fluctuations between expansion and contraction are an accepted fact of economic life. They can be characterized in terms of two related turning points:

- divergence away from existing economic activity toward greater expenditure, expansion, and new growth opportunities; and
- convergence around existing economic activity, toward less expenditure, contraction, and lower growth.

Divergence occurs in the trough of the business cycle, where the contraction has run its course. Managers, seeing the strengthening in demand relative to supply, begin to find opportunities for branching out. Convergence takes place at the peak of the cycle, when a perceived shortage of some input, for example, causes key economic actors to cut back their plans for expansion and, instead, consolidate existing activities.

In addition to shorter-term economic cycles, some economists see much longer cycles of fifty to sixty years, associated with major depressions like that of the 1930s. Looking at commodity prices, bond prices, wages, and bank liabilities, the controversial Russian economist Nikolai Kondratiev identified three great depressions, in the 1820s, 1870s, and 1930s. Apart from prices, Kondratiev associated "other empirical patterns" with his long waves: an increase in the number of technical inventions during the two decades before a long upswing; accentuated short-term cycles with longer upswings when the long cycle is rising; more social change during the "rising wave of a long cycle"; longer downswings when the long cycle is declining; and a long agricultural depression during the downswing. Although some of this theory may be no more than the output of a creative mind, it is remarkable how closely these patterns fit recent history.

The automobile industry, for example, was founded at the beginning of the Kondratiev cycle that began in the 1880s. The emergence of the industry saw the appearance of hundreds of small companies making automobiles—Switzerland alone had several of them. But few survived the major turning point toward efficiency that marked the top of the cycle, a turning point that gave birth to Ford's assembly line production of the Model T. The end of the Kondratiev cycle was marked by the Great Depression of the 1930s. It almost saw the end of Ford Motor Company as well. Henry Ford I refused to believe the shift in competitive behavior that accompanied the emergence of a new Kondratiev cycle, the differentiation of styles and colors that led to the founding of General Motors. Ford had to be removed from the board before his company could belatedly adapt to the new conditions. The top of the Kondratiev cycle in the 1960s again saw a shift toward the streamlining of production with the emergence of Toyota, Nissan, and Honda, a shift that put the American and European industries into a defensive position that has continued to this day.

Mainstream economic theory has little to say about long waves. Systematic long-run fluctuations don't exist, and there is a deathly silence about the possibility of breakpoints in the market environment. In terms of classical economic theory, the sustained growth over the past sixty years is indeed miraculous. Only half of it can be explained by an increased supply of the traditional economic variables: capital, labor, and land, including the impact of education. The other half is attributed to technological innovation, about which classical economics has little, if anything, to say. Technology is a so-called exogenous factor, a "deus ex machina."

Technology Cycles

Those who believe in long economic waves attribute them to bursts of technological innovation. Long-run economic growth seems to follow periods of intense innovation. A group of new technologies gives rise to a cluster of new industries that provide the engine of long-term growth, until they run out of steam. Joseph Schumpeter, the Austrian economist who was eclipsed by John Maynard Keynes in the 1930s, regarded innovation, the commercialization of inventions, as the basic force behind capitalist market economies: "The fundamental impulse that sets and keeps the capitalist engine in motion comes from the new consumers' goods, the new methods of production or transportation, the new markets, the new forms of industrial organization that capitalist enterprise creates."

Innovation, according to Schumpeter, is discontinuous. "Innovations appear, if at all, discontinuously in groups or swarms." He claimed that this periodic bunching of innovations is caused by the scarcity of entrepreneurial talent and the need for innovations to feed off one another. Long waves, according to Schumpeter, are characterized by a whole set of industries that use the same basic technological innovations on the supply side and possibly complement one another on the demand side. Thus, the microprocessor couples computers and telecommunications with a host of industries like banking, consumer electronics, transportation, machine tools, and robotics. To take advantage of the new technologies, existing industries have to regroup. While this diffusion and absorption process continues, a long upswing underpins the shorter economic cycles.

As we have noted already, the pace of innovation is stimulated by economic depression. Good and easy times reduce innovative activity: the relative return on new ventures is too low and the risk of loss too high. The economic success of the microprocessor takes attention away from other basic innovations that may be waiting in the wings; their time will come only when the microprocessor wave runs out of growth possibilities. When times are bad, the pressure of economic survival forces people to break out of old ways. The risk is low and there is little to lose.

The agricultural depression before the first industrial revolution stimulated the commercialization of textiles, iron, and steam power in England and Scotland. The depression of 1815–25, in turn, saw the emergence of steel and the railroads that opened up continental Europe and North America. During the depression from 1870 to 1885, electricity, the automobile, and chemicals got their start with the birth of such famous names as Daimler and Benz, Hoechst, and Philips Gloeilampenfabrieken. During the Great Depression of the 1930s, aircraft, electronics, and petrochemicals began to take off. The stagflation of the 1970s spawned the prolific microprocessor, the beginning of a genetic engineering revolution, the commercialization of the laser, and new materials like ceramics.

Although the exact timing of these innovations is controversial, the important point is that depression-driven innovation provides the beginning of long-run, technology-driven industry cycles. The entrepreneurial phase is followed by the diffusion of the innovations throughout related industries. This stimulates growth in many other existing industries. Eventually, the diffusion process runs out of steam and the long-run industry growth rate peaks. Competition increases in the decades ahead and the growth rate slows. Ultimately, the leading industries slide into a long stagflation, or depression, during which a new wave of innovations is born.

The turning points that make up a technology cycle can be characterized in the following way:

■ divergence of competitive behavior stimulated by the emergence of a new technology, based on widespread commercialization of an invention, or cluster of inventions, often accompanied by a swarm of entrepreneurs; and

■ convergence around the existing technology that reflects the exhaustion and drying up of potential improvements to the technology, accompanied by the saturation of possible end uses, marking the high point in the development of the technology.

From an executive point of view, these technology-related turning points are critical. Well-managed companies can deal with most short-term economic cycles by adjusting their growth and output. Turning points in the basic use of technology, however, mark the need for sharp changes in competitive behavior.

Competitive Cycles

It is in individual markets that the attributes of the product offerings supplied by competitors meet customer demands. Supply and demand evolve together in symbiosis, first one and then the other driving the process. The interplay between supply and demand creates competitive turning points and breakpoints. Although the government, the economy, or technology may play a role, competitive turning points are driven primarily by the behavior of competitors. This shows up most clearly in the service sector, where technology is less intrusive.

The two basic types of turning points that make up competitive cycles are:

- divergence away from an existing product or business system standard, corresponding to a shift in competitive emphasis from delivered cost to perceived value competition; and

- convergence around a product, or business system standard, corresponding to a shift in the opposite direction from perceived value to delivered cost competition.

Sensitivity to these turning points can go a long way toward facilitating the early identification of the forces for change implicit in the competitive cycle.

Basic Pattern in Cyclical Phenomena

The key to isolating strong forces of change is clearly the ability to anticipate cyclical turning points. Anticipating a turning point requires seeing the limits and stimuli that provoke it. Here the recognition of cyclical patterns is central, because cycles suggest the kinds of limits and stimuli to watch out for. The basic pattern involved in all of these cycles is summarized in figure 8-9.

The key to identifying the turning points is to realize that if the industry is presently in a period of divergence, the next turn of the cycle will bring convergence and vice versa. Thus, if you are in a divergent mode, focus on the indicators of emerging convergent forces and vice versa, since the next turn of the cycle will bring on the other type of change, supplanting the one prevailing now.

Experienced players normally have little difficulty describing the behavior that precedes common turning points: the behavior reflects an improved ability to manage scarce resources on the one hand (efficiency, price competition, technology diffusion, economic consolidation, sociopolitical cooperation), and on the other hand, the creation of greater variety (innovation, value competition, technology development, economic expansion, sociopolitical individualism). As an illustration, the typical behavior of industry change agents prior to competitive convergence (that often results in a price

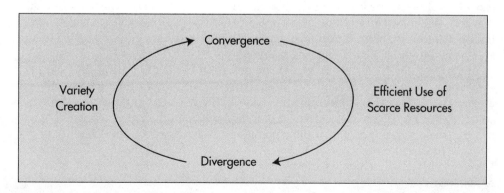

FIGURE 8-9
Basic Pattern in Cyclical Phenomena

war) and competitive divergence (that often leads to a new product breakthrough) is outlined below.

Leading indicators of convergence:

- Customers: the segmentation between customer groups looks increasingly artificial and starts to break down.
- Competitors: convergence is visible in increasingly similar products, service, and image.
- Potential competitors: very few, if any, new entrants on the horizon.
- Supply chain: suppliers and resources cannot easily be used as a source of competitive advantage.
- Channels: the bargaining power in the industry typically shifts downstream to the distribution channels.

Leading indicators of divergence:

- Customers: an increasingly saturated market for the standardized commodity product reflects itself in declining growth rates.
- Competitors: declining returns because of cost reduction and rationalization force competitors to look elsewhere.
- Potential competitors: restless customers attract new entrants.
- Supply chain: new sources of supply and new resources, especially new technology, are frequently the source of new product development.
- Channels: change in the distribution channels is mostly a lagging, rather than leading indicator of competitive product divergence.

A new product or service rarely takes over a market immediately. The concept and creation of a new product is often spontaneous, unstructured, and unpredictable. But the commercialization of the product and penetration of the market require very deliberate and visible action. Observing competitors that are experimenting is one of the important leading indicators.

Timing of Turning Points

Turning points vary in the timing of their potential impact. Because of longer-term trends and trajectories, turning points and cycles never repeat themselves in detail. Their timing may be irregular and their sequence cannot be taken for granted.

To pin down the timing of turning points, it is useful to look for a coincidence of forces. In the U.S. construction equipment industry, excess capacity, the decline in construction, rising interest rates, and the gradual saturation of the Middle Eastern market all pointed to a downturn in sales. The timing of the impact of these limits to growth, and hence the timing of the downturn, depended on how much additional demand was still left in the Middle East and in the overall U.S. economy. In general, the timing of a turning point depends on the strength of the existing trend relative to its limits and the stimuli promoting a new trend.

Identifying the forces of change in the environment is the critical first step in anticipating breakpoints. Sensitivity to the change forces and their timing is essential if they are not to be a threat, but rather an opportunity to be exploited. And yet many companies are not even aware of the established trends in their environment, not to mention the timing of potential turning points and cycles. The 1981 and 1991 history of the U.S. construction-machinery industry shows that those companies that do not learn how to identify change patterns and deal with their timing are condemned to repeat them.

■ THE FIRM MATTERS, NOT THE INDUSTRY†

By Charles Baden-Fuller and John Stopford

It is the firm that matters, not the industry. Successful businesses ride the waves of industry misfortunes; less successful business are sunk by them. This view contrasts sharply with the popular, but misguided, school of thought that believes that the fortune of a business is closely tied to its industry. Those who adhere to this view believe that some industries are intrinsically more attractive for investment than others. They (wrongly) believe that if a business is in a profitable industry, then its profits will be greater than if the business is in an unprofitable industry.

The Role of the Industry in Determining Profitability

Old views:

- Some industries are intrinsically more profitable than others.
- In mature environments it is difficult to sustain high profits.
- It is environmental factors that determine whether an industry is successful, not the firms in the industry.

New views:

- There is little difference in the profitability of one industry versus another.
- There is no such thing as a mature industry, only mature firms; industries inhabited by mature firms often present great opportunities for the innovative.
- Profitable industries are those populated by imaginative and profitable firms; unprofitable industries have unusually large numbers of uncreative firms.

This notion that there are "good" and "bad" industries is a theme that has permeated many strategy books. As one famous strategy writer put it:

"The state of competition in an industry depends on five basic competitive forces. . . . The collective strength of these forces determines the ultimate profit potential in the industry, where profit potential is measured in terms of long-run return on invested capital. . . . The forces range from intense in industries like tires, paper and steel—where no firm earns spectacular returns—to relatively mild like oil-field equipment and services, cosmetics and toiletries—where high returns are quite common" (Porter, 1980).

Unfortunately, the writer overstates his case, for the evidence does not easily support his claim. Choosing good industries may be a foolish strategy; choosing good firms is far more sensible. As noted in table 8-2, recent statistical evidence does not support the view that the choice of industry is important. At best only 10 per cent of the differences in profitability between one business unit and another can be related to their choice of industry. By implication, nearly 90 per cent of profitability variations are not explained by the choice of industry, and *at least half appear to be attributable to the choice of strategy*. Put simply, the correct choice of strategy appears to be at least five times more important than the correct choice of industry.

---

†**Source:** This article has been adapted from chapter 2 of *Rejuvenating the Mature Business,* Routledge, 1992, pp. 13–34. Used with permission.

TABLE 8-2
The Role of Industry Factors
Determining Firm
Performance

Percentage of Business Units' Profitability Explained by	
Choice of industry	8.3 percent
Choice of strategy	46.4 percent
Parent company	0.8 percent
Not explained—random	44.5 percent
Abstracted from Rumelt (1991).	

Mature Industries Offer Good Prospects for Success

It is often stated that market opportunities are created rather than found. Thus market research would never have predicted the large potential of xerography, laptop computers, or the pocket cassette recorder. Leaps of faith may be required. By analogy, low-growth mature markets or troubled industries are arguably ones that may offer greater chances of rewards than ones that appear to be glamorous and profitable. Our reasoning is simple. In general, profitable industries are more profitable because they are populated by more imaginative and more creative businesses. These businesses create an environment that attracts customers, grows the industry revenues, and makes the industry attractive. But creative and innovative businesses are also more fiercely competitive. To win in such environments may be difficult, as the pace of change may be rapid and the minimum standards high. In contrast, many less-profitable industries are populated by sleepy, uncreative businesses that fail to innovate. In such environments, the potential for success by a creative newcomer is greater. The demands of competition may be less exacting and the potential for attracting customers is better.

We do not wish to overstate our case, but rather to force the reader to focus attention away from the mentality of labelling and prejudging opportunities based only on industry profitability. For example, outsiders often point to low-growth industries and suggest that the opportunities are less than those in high-growth industries. Yet the difference in growth rates may be dependent on the ability of businesses in these industries to be creative and innovative. Until Honda came, the motorcycle market was in steady decline. By their innovations—of new bicycles with attractive features sold at reasonable prices—the market was once again revived. Thus we suggest that the growth rate of the industry is a reflection of the kinds of businesses in the industry, not the intrinsic nature of the environment.

Large Market Share Is the Reward, Not the Cause of Success

We believe that many managers are mistaken in the value they ascribe to market share. A large share of the market is often the symptom of success, but it is not always its cause. Banc One and Cook achieved significant positions in their industries because they were successful. For these organisations the sequence of events was success followed by growth, which was then cemented into greater success. Banc One has been doing things differently from many of its competitors for many years. It emphasised

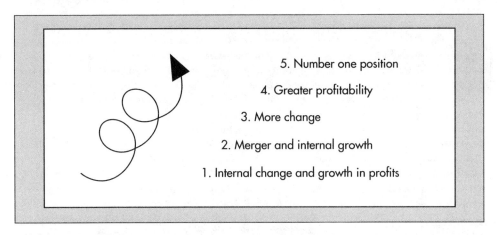

FIGURE 8-10
Upward Spiral of Creative
Business

operational efficiency and it quickly captured a significant position as a low cost, high quality data processor for other banks and financial service companies. It also emphasised service, in particular service to retail and commercial customers, which contrasted with the approach of many other banks that sought to compete solely on price or failed to appreciate what the customer really wanted. Mergers and growth have been an important part of Banc One's strategy, but in every case, the merged organisations have been changed to fit the philosophy of Banc One.

Market Share and Profitability

Old views:

- Large market share brings lower costs and higher prices and so yields greater profits.
- Small-share firms cannot challenge leaders.

New views:

- Large market share is the reward for efficiency and effectiveness.
- If they do things better, small-share firms can challenge the leaders.

For creative organisations we see an upward spiral (figure 8-10), and for organisations that are not creative, we see the cycles shown in figure 8-11.

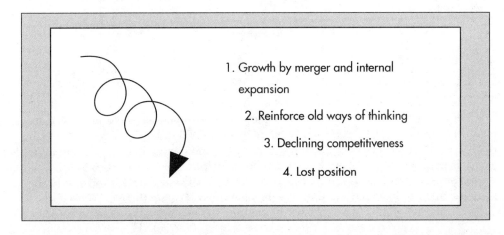

FIGURE 8-11
Downward Spiral of
Unchanging Business

EXHIBIT 8-1
Market Share and
Profitability

MARKET SHARE AND PROFITABILITY

There is a lively debate on the importance of market share in *explaining* business unit profitability. By *explaining* we do not mean *causing*. High market share could be the consequence of profitability, or the cause of both.

Those who advocate that large market share *leads* to greater profits point to the importance of several causal factors. First, large market share gives rise to the need to deliver large volumes of the service or good. These increased volumes in turn give rise to opportunities for costs savings by exploiting scale economies in production, service delivery, logistics, and marketing. Second, large market share permits the firm to benefit from experience or learning effects that also lower costs. Third, larger market share may allow the firm to charge higher prices. A product or service with a large share may seem intrinsically less risky to consumers. Finally, with a large market share, new entrants may be discouraged because they perceive the incumbent to have a substantial commitment to the industry through perceived or actual sunk costs.

In contrast, there are several who argue that these supposed benefits of large share are overrated. It is innovation that matters, innovators that realize new ways of competing can achieve their advantages by new approaches that do not necessarily need large market shares. However, those with new approaches may win market share, in which case large share is a reward for success. This Darwinian view of the market suggests that the competitive process is one where success goes to the firm that successfully innovates.

The strongest proponents of the importance of market share as a cause of success are Buzzell and Gale. Using the PIMS database drawn from a very large sample of business units across a range of industries, they asserted the existence of a strong relationship between relative market share and profitability. The figures below (Buzzell and Gale, 1987) suggest that a firm that has first rank in an industry will be more than twice as profitable as one of fourth rank.

Industry rank (by market share)	1	2	3	4	≤5
Pretax profits/sales (per cent)	12.7	9.1	7.1	5.5	4.5

However, these figures are misleading, for in a very large proportion of the industries studied, the firm with largest rank was *not* the most profitable. Often the picture is quite different; indeed according to the statistics published in Buzzell and Gale (1987) only 4 percent of the differences in profitability of one business unit versus another could be explained by differences in market share. Schmalensee (1985) in his extensive study of more than four hundred firms in U.S. manufacturing, found that less than 2 per cent of the variations in profitability between one business and another could be explained by differences in market share. Market share effects appear to be relatively unimportant across a wide sample of industries. Of course, market share may be important in specific instances, but this only goes to reinforce our basic point that the critical success is dependent on getting the right strategy.

Our assertions run counter to much of what has been written in conventional books on strategy, and what is believed in many corporate boardrooms (see exhibit 8-1). There is a common but incorrect belief among managers that being number one or number two in an industry gives the business unique advantages and that these are greatest in industries characterised by slow growth. With a large market share, it is often argued, the business can achieve lower costs and charge higher prices than its rivals. In slow-growth markets, it is argued, this may prove to be a decisive factor. This thinking ignores the importance of innovation, and believes that it is the size of the business that confers the advantage, not the new ways of doing things.

These false beliefs are widespread. They appear in many guises. At one extreme there are chief executives who say, "We are only interested in industries where we hold a number one or number two position." Such statements, if unaccompanied by an emphasis on innovation, will give out the wrong signal that high share will lead to success. At a more mundane level, managers are encouraged to write in their plans, "We should dominate the industry and seek success by capturing a number one position." Again, such statements are dangerous where the writer and reader believe that share by itself will bring success.

Growing market share is not the panacea for an organisation's ills, not even in mature slow-growing markets. The belief that gaining market share will lead to greater profitability comes from confusing cause and effect. Many successful businesses do have a large market share, but the causality is usually from success to share, not the other way. Successful businesses often (but not always) grow because they have discovered an overwhelming source of competitive advantage, such as quality at low cost. Such advantages can be used to displace the market share of even the most entrenched incumbents.

Competing Recipes

The crucial battles amongst firms in an industry are often centered around differing approaches to the market. Even in the so-called mature industries, where incumbent strategies have evolved and been honed over long time periods, it is new ideas that displace the existing leaders. Traditional wisdom has overstated the power of the generic approach (see exhibit 8-2) and underplayed the role of innovation. Banc One established its premier position by rejecting conventional orthodoxy and emphasising aspects hitherto neglected by industry leaders. Cook won in the steel castings industry

---

THE FALLACY OF THE GENERIC STRATEGY

It has been fashionable to suggest that there are a few *stable generic strategies* that offer fundamental choices to the organization. Typically these are described as a choice between a *low cost strategy or a differentiated strategy*. The low cost strategy involves the sacrifice of something—speed, variety, fashion, or even quality—in order to keep costs low, the lowest in the industry. In contrast, the high cost, differentiated strategy involves the focus on the very factors ignored by the others. The advocates of generic strategy make an (implicit or explicit) assertion: that the opposites cannot be reconciled. According to the generic strategists, it is not possible to be both low cost and high quality, or low cost and fashionable, or low cost and speedy. Trying to reconcile the opposites means being *stuck in the middle*. This, it is suggested, is the worst of both worlds.

Generic strategies are a fallacy. The best firms are striving all the time to reconcile the opposites. Cook did find a way to be both high quality and low cost, so, too, many of the other creative firms we studied. At any point in time, there are some combinations that have not yet been resolved, but firms strive to resolve them. Until McDonald's, the idea of consistency and low price for fast food had not been achieved on a large scale. McDonald's solved that problem. Benetton was but one of many firms that resolved the dilemma of fashion at low cost. Given the enormous rewards that accrue to those who can resolve the dilemmas of the opposites, it is not surprising that there are *no lasting or enduring generic strategies*.

EXHIBIT 8-2
The Fallacy of the Generic Strategy

by emphasising quality and service to the customer. Hotpoint emphasised variety and quality in its approach to both the retailers and the final consumers. No single approach works well in all industries, but rather a multiple set of approaches. Here we emphasise the more fundamental point: the real competitive battles are fought out between firms with a diversity of approaches to the market.

The Dynamics of Competition in Traditional Industries

Old view:

- Competition is based on firms following well-defined traditional (or generic) approaches to the market.

New view:

- The real battles are fought among firms taking different approaches, especially those that counter yesterday's ideas.

Conclusions

Organisations that have become mature and suffer from poor performance typically view themselves as prisoners of their environment. Often their managers blame everyone but themselves for their poor performance. Labelling their environment as mature or hostile, they identify excess capacity, unfair competition, adverse exchange rates, absence of demand, and a host of other factors to explain why they are doing badly. Alas, too often these external factors are not really the causes of their demise but rather the symptoms of their failure. This conclusion is not so new; others have made the point before, yet their words appear to have been forgotten. Hall (1980) in an article in the *Harvard Business Review* noted: "Even a cursory analysis of the leading companies in the eight basic industries leads to an important observation: survival and prosperity are possible even when the business environment turns hostile and industry trends change from favourable to unfavourable. In this regard, the casual advice frequently offered to competitors in basic industries—that is diversify, dissolve or be prepared for below average returns—seems oversimplified and even erroneous."

Of course all industries experience the roller coaster of economic upswings and downswings, but there are organisations that appear to ride the waves and others that appear to be submerged by them.

Those who are submerged all too often clutch at the wrong things in trying to escape their drowning. Seeking simple solutions such as industry recipes, the value of market share, or the need to amass large resources, they fail to appreciate the extent to which the rules of the game in an industry are always changing.

References and Suggested Readings

Aldrich, H. E., *Organizations and Environments*, Prentice Hall, Englewood Cliffs, NJ, 1979.

Astley, W. G., and C. J. Fombrun, Collective Strategy: Social Ecology of Organizational Environments, *Academy of Management Review*, October 1983, pp. 576–587.

Baden-Fuller, C. W. F., and J. M. Stopford, *Rejuvenating the Mature Business*, Routledge, London, 1992, pp. 13–34.

Buzzell, R. D., and B. T. Gale, *The PIMS Principles: Linking Strategy to Performance*, Free Press, New York, 1987.

Buzzell, R. D., Gale, B. T., and R. G. M. Sultan, Market Share—A Key to Profitability, *Harvard Business Review*, January/February 1975, pp. 97–106.

Chakravarthy, B., and P. Lorange, *Managing the Strategy Process: A Framework for a Multibusiness Firm*, Prentice Hall, Englewood Cliffs, 1991.

Dankbaan, B., Groenewegen, J., and H. Schenk (Eds.), *Perspectives in Industrial Organization*, Kluwer, Dordvecht, 1990.

Duncan, R., Characteristics of Organisational Environments and Perceived Environmental Uncertainty, *Administrative Science Quarterly*, September 1972, pp. 313–327.

Freeman, J., and W. Boeker, The Ecological Analysis of Business Strategy, *California Management Review*, Spring 1984, pp. 73–86.

Ghemawat, P., The Risk of Not Investing in a Recession, *Sloan Management Review*, Winter 1993, pp. 51–58.

Gilbert, X., and P. Strebel, Taking Advantage of Industry Shifts, *European Management Journal*, December 1989, pp. 398–402.

Hall, W. K., Survival Strategies in a Hostile Environment, *Harvard Business Review*, September/October 1980, pp. 75–85.

Hannan, M. T., and J. Freeman, The Population Ecology of Organizations, *American Journal of Sociology*, March 1977, pp. 929–964.

Harrigan, K. R., *Strategies for Declining Businesses*, D. C. Heath, Lexington, MA, 1980.

Harrigan, K. R., and M. E. Porter, End-Game Strategies for Declining Industries, *Harvard Business Review*, July/August 1983, pp. 111–120.

Hawley, A., *Human Ecology: A Theory of Community Structure*, Ronald, New York, 1950.

Hrebiniak, L. G., and W. F. Joyce, Organizational Adaptation: Strategic Choice and Environmental Determinism, *Administrative Science Quarterly*, September 1985, pp. 336–349.

Lawrence, P. R., and J. W. Lorsch, *Organization and Environment*, Harvard University Press, Cambridge, MA, 1967.

Lele, M. L., Selecting Strategies That Exploit Leverage, *Planning Review*, January/February 1992, pp. 15–21.

Lele, M. L., *Creating Strategic Leverage*, Wiley, New York, 1992.

Levin, S. A., Community Equilibrium and Stability: An Extension of the Competitive Exclusion Principle, *American Naturalist*, September/October 1970, pp. 413–423.

McKiernan, P., *Strategies of Growth*, Routledge, London, 1992.

Moore, J. F., Predators and Prey: A New Ecology of Competition, *Harvard Business Review*, May/June 1993, pp. 75–86.

Nelson, R. R., and S. G. Winter, *An Evolutionary Theory of Economic Change*, Harvard University Press, 1982.

Porter, M. E., *Competitive Strategy: Techniques for Analyzing Industries and Competitors*, Free Press, New York, 1980.

Rumelt, R., How Much Does Industry Matter?, *Strategic Management Journal*, March 1991, pp. 167–186.

Scherer, F. M., *Industrial Market Structure and Market Performance*, Second Edition, Houghton Mifflin, Boston, 1980.

Schmalensee, R., Do Markets Differ Much?, *American Economic Review*, June 1985, pp. 341–351.

Schnaars, S. P., When Entering Growth Markets, Are Pioneers Better Than Poachers? *Business Horizons*, March/April 1986, pp. 27–36.

Schofield, M., and D. Arnold, Strategies for Mature Businesses, *Long Range Planning*, October 1988, pp. 69–76.

Schumpeter, J. A., *Capitalism, Socialism and Democracy*, Third Edition, Harper & Row, New York, 1950.

Starbuck, W. H., and B. L. T. Hedberg, Saving an Organization from a Stagnating Environment, in Thorelli, H. B. (Ed.), *Strategy + Structure = Performance: The Strategic Planning Imperative*, Indiana University Press, Bloomington, 1977.

Strebel, P., Organizing for Innovation over an Industry Cycle, *Strategic Management Journal*, March/April 1987, pp. 117–124.

Strebel, P., Competitive Turning Points: How to Recognize Them, *European Management Journal*, June 1989, pp. 141–147.

Strebel, P., Dealing with Discontinuities, *European Management Journal*, December 1990, pp. 434–442.

Strebel, P. J., *Breakpoints*, Harvard Business School Press, Boston, 1992.

Woo, C. Y. Y., and A. C. Cooper, Strategies of Effective Low Share Businesses, *Strategic Management Journal*, July/September 1981, pp. 301–318.

CHAPTER 9
THE ORGANISATIONAL CONTEXT:
ON CONTROL AND CHAOS

We shape our environments, then
our environments shape us.
  —Winston Churchill
     1874–1965, British statesman and writer

Introduction

This chapter is the mirror image of chapter 8. While the central question in the previous chapter was, Does the company's *external* environment dictate strategy? this chapter focuses on the question, Does the company's *internal* environment dictate strategy? In other words, to what extent is the strategist restricted by the organisational context when developing new strategies? Are the firm's strategist and strategy, as Churchill suggests, merely the product of the company's way of doing things? If the organisation resembles a machine, such as a *vehicle*, then its direction can be determined by the person operating the steering controls. In this case, the leader has full command of the organisation's strategy, within the limits of what is technically feasible. If, however, the organisation resembles a complex uncontrollable system, such as the *weather*, then it can only develop gradually out of the current state of affairs, depending on the interactions of a large number of influencing factors. In this case, the strategy of the organisation is the result of "atmospheric" processes, which the "leader" is unable to control. This chapter seeks an answer to the question whether the company is more like a vehicle or like the weather. Or, stated differently, the central issue is, To what extent does the organisational context matter?

The alert reader will have recognized that the two extremes sketched above coincide with the poles of *deliberate* and *emergent* strategy described by Mintzberg and Waters in chapter 1. In the extreme mechanistic view of the organisation, the leader can design a strategy more or less from scratch, which the organisation attempts to implement as planned. The organisational structure is adapted to fit the proposed strategy— *structure follows strategy* (Chandler, 1962). Whether the intended strategy is also realized will depend on the difficulties encountered in the external environment, not on any internal factors. In short, when developing strategy, the leader matters, not the organisation. In the subtitle to this chapter, this view of the organisation is referred to as the *control* perspective.

If the other extreme position, that the organisation is a complex uncontrollable system, is adopted, then the conclusion must be drawn that strategy is not rationally designed but emerges as the result of political, social, cultural, and cognitive processes. In this perspective, it is not only true that *strategy follows structure* but also that strategy follows the other five *S*'s mentioned by Waterman, Peters, and Phillips in chapter 4. Strategy even follows strategy—the new strategy is the "captive" of the old strategy and can only differ from it slightly. In short, with regard to realized strategy, the organisation matters, not the leader. In the subtitle to this chapter, this view of the organisation is referred to as the *chaos* perspective. While in everyday usage the term *chaos* simply refers to a mess, in scientific usage the term refers to the nonlinear behaviour exhibited by complex systems. In other words, phenomena are "chaotic" if it is not easy to trace back how an interplay of factors has brought them about.

In this chapter, one article will be presented from the "control" end of the spectrum, arguing the importance of leadership. The next four articles are all somewhere in the middle of the continuum and explore how different aspects of the organisational context can limit the strategist's freedom to manoeuvre. The last article will be from the chaos end of the spectrum. At the end of the chapter, it will again be up to the reader to decide which perspective holds the most promise.

The Articles

The first article in this chapter, "The CEO: Leadership in Organizations" by Roland Christensen, Kenneth Andrews, Joseph Bower, Richard Hamermesh, and Michael Porter, is a part of the same well-known textbook, *Business Policy*, as is Kenneth Andrew's article in chapter 2. This reading is intended to represent a large body of literature that emphasizes the role of the organisation's leader as main strategic planner and chief strategy implementor. In line with most leadership literature, this article accords a large measure of importance to the CEO. If the organisation is led by an individual of "great human skill, sensitivity, administrative capability [. . .and] analytic intelligence of a higher order," the organisation will have a better chance of being successful. In other words, the organisation is a vehicle in need of a driver who knows where to go, how to get there, and is capable of roadside repairs if anything breaks down on the way. It is recognized that the organisational context is sometimes not entirely pliable and can limit the freedom of the CEO to make and implement strategy. However, this is not viewed as a disqualification of the control perspective, but as a failure of the CEO to lead. In short, the leader matters, not the organisational context. It is interesting to note that most strategy writers taking this point of view also exhibit a preference for the planning approach to the strategy process, as does Andrews in chapter 2.

The second article is the classic "Evolution and Revolution as Organizations Grow" by Larry Greiner. In this reading, Greiner argues that organisations are not stable state entities, but dynamic systems. He believes that as organisations grow they tend to go through continuous cycles of gradual development (evolution) and substantial turmoil (revolution). In his opinion, each stage of evolutionary growth creates its own problems, which eventually lead to a period of revolution. The type of solution found to the upheaval will in turn determine the nature of the next phase of gradual development. Greiner emphasizes that these dynamics are only partially controllable by top management—the organisation's history can create a momentum all its own. He recommends that management should analyse where they are in the developmental sequence and should adapt the organisational structure and management systems to fit these circumstances. Although Greiner is not a strategy researcher and does not draw explicit conclusions about what his ideas mean for making strategy, the reader can quite easily see what the consequences are. Greiner's analysis would seem to suggest that the organisation's approach to the strategy process and content might also need to be adapted to fit the phase of development. Making strategy in an entrepreneurial context might need to be done differently than in a diversified multinational. In other words, the organisational context matters—development might follow strategy, but the reverse is also the case.

The next article in this chapter, "A Strategic Typology of Organizations" by Raymond Miles, Charles Snow, Alan Meyer, and Henry Coleman, adds a second way in which the organisational context might be important in influencing the strategy process and content. The authors of this article focus not on the developmental phase of the organisation, but on its *strategy style* (although they never employ this term). They argue that organisations can approach strategic issues employing one of four different styles. They distinguish defenders, prospectors, analysers, and reactors, and argue that each type makes strategy in a significantly different way. They also believe that these styles are so strongly ingrained in organisations' culture that the flexibility to change from one type to another is very low. Hence, the freedom of strategists to mould the strategy process and content as they please is severely limited. In other words, strategy might form style but subsequently becomes style's captive.

In the fourth article, "The Effective Organization: Forces and Forms," Henry Mintzberg suggests yet another typology of organisations, based not on their development phase or strategy style but on the *forces* that dominate the organisation and on the *form* the organisation adopts. According to Mintzberg, much of what happens in organisations can be explained by the interplay of seven basic forces: direction, efficiency, proficiency, concentration, innovation, cooperation, and competition. When one of these forces dominates, the organisation draws toward the corresponding form: entrepreneurial, machine, professional, diversified, adhocracy, ideological, and political. Mintzberg argues that these seven forms are the most common *configurations*—organisations whose various characteristics of structure, strategy, and context are in natural coalignment. However, Mintzberg believes there are few circumstances where these configurations constitute effective organisations. More often, the conflicting demands placed on the organisation require managers to build their own unique solutions instead of slotting themselves into one of the seven configurations. Each unique solution includes a specific strategy process and content that fit with the organisation's situation. This is the *contingency approach*—adapting the strategy process and content to the organisational context. Hence, the organisation matters—strategy may influence the organisational forces and forms, but the opposite is also the case. As Mintzberg puts it himself, "structure follows strategy as the left foot follows the right!"

The fifth article, "The Icarus Paradox" by Danny Miller, expands on one of the points that Mintzberg also touches on, namely, the *failure of success*. In this reading, Miller argues that excellent companies can become blinded by success, thereby setting their own downfall into motion. Miller uses the metaphor of Icarus, who flew so high and close to the sun that his artificial wax wings melted and he plunged to his death. According to Miller, the very nature of success creates a self-destructive momentum within the organisation, which, if unchecked, will lead from riches to rags. The perils of success can only be combated, Miller believes, by continual learning and renewal. In the context of this chapter, Miller's point is that organisational dynamics are not easily controllable by the leader and therefore that the strategy process and content must be adjusted accordingly. The organisational context matters—a strategy might lead to success, but success will in turn breed its own strategies.

The sixth and last article is mysteriously entitled "Strategy as Order Emerging from Chaos." In this reading, Ralph Stacey takes the argument of uncontrollable organisational dynamics yet a step further than Miller does. In Stacey's perspective, leaders shouldn't even try to control the organisation and its strategy, as this is counterproductive. He states that "sometimes the best thing a manager can do is to let go and allow things to happen." His reasoning is that chaotic systems, like companies, have a self-organising ability, which "can produce controlled behaviour, even though no one is in control." Adding an arrow to the incrementalists' bow, he argues that real strategic change requires the chaos of contention and conflict to destroy old recipes (see Johnson, chapter 2) and to seek for new solutions. The "self-organizing processes of political interaction and complex learning" ensure that chaos does not result in disintegration. Hence, in Stacey's opinion, it is management's task to help create an atmosphere of bounded instability in which strategy can emerge. Leaders should manage the organisational context and let strategy develop spontaneously.

Recommended Readings and Cases

Readers interested in exploring the history of the strategy-organisation link can actually go quite far back, but we would suggest starting with Alfred Chandler's classic *Strategy and Structure: Chapters in the History of the American Industrial Enterprise*. For a better insight into the current thinking on the topic of leadership, the reader might want to begin with *Leaders: The Strategies for Taking Charge* by Warren Bennis and Burt Nanus, or Joseph Bower's *The Craft of General Management*. However, the reader is forewarned that much of this literature is not readily applicable in non-Anglo-Saxon cultures, as is made clear by Geert Hofstede in his article "Motivation, Leadership, and Organization: Do American Theories Apply Abroad?"

As for authors taking a less control-oriented perspective, we would recommend beginning with Edward Schein's *Organizational Culture and Leadership*. Richard Pascale's *Managing on the Edge: How Successful Companies Use Conflict to Stay Ahead* is also stimulating reading. Further yet toward the chaos side of the spectrum, Gerry Johnson's *Strategic Change and the Management Process* and Ralph Stacey's *Strategic Management and Organisational Dynamics* provide provocative ideas about the relationship between strategy and the organisational context. Finally, we would also recommend Graham Allison's classic *Essence of Decision: Explaining the Cuban Missile Crisis*, which gives an early account of the breadth of approaches described in this chapter.

The two cases selected to accompany this chapter are the "Scandinavian Airlines System in 1988" and "Cartier" cases. The SAS case is intended for a discussion focusing on the importance of leadership, while the Cartier case can be used to explore the issue of creative chaos. The SAS case, written by Sumantra Ghoshal, describes how this partially Danish, Norwegian, and Swedish company transformed itself from a bureaucratic airline into a market-driven, diversified travel corporation. A key role in this turnaround process seems to have been played by the CEO, Jan Carlzon. The reader is asked to think about the future direction of SAS and to reflect on the importance of the leader in setting, and holding, course. Naturally, the reader must also determine whether the leader actually has freedom to manoeuvre or whether he is locked in by uncontrollable organisational dynamics. The Cartier case, written by Sumantra Ghoshal, François-Xavier Huard, and Charlotte Butler, explains how this French producer of luxury jewellery and fragrances seeks to balance top-down control and bottom-up creative chaos. The CEO is a very strong individual, but the type of product requires a large measure of freedom within the organisation to ensure creativity and market responsiveness. The reader is thus challenged to think about the extent to which Cartier's future strategy can be controlled by the CEO.

■ THE CEO: LEADERSHIP IN ORGANIZATIONS†

By Roland Christensen, Kenneth Andrews, Joseph Bower, Richard Hamermesh, and Michael Porter

Management we regard as leadership in the informed, planned, purposeful conduct of complex organized activity. *General management* is, in its simplest form, the management of a total enterprise or of an autonomous subunit. The senior general manager in any organization is its chief executive officer, who for the purposes of simplicity we will often call the *president*.

We will begin by considering the *roles* that presidents must play. We will examine the *functions* or characteristic and natural actions that they perform in the roles they assume. We will try to identify *skills* or abilities that put one's perceptions, judgment, and knowledge to effective use in executive performance. As we look at executive roles, functions and skills, we may be able to define more clearly aspects of the *point of view* that provide the most suitable perspective for high-level executive judgment.

Many attempts to characterize executive roles and functions come to very little. Henri Fayol, originator of the classical school of management theory, identified the roles of planner, organizer, coordinator, and controller, initiating the construction by others of a later vocabulary of remarkable variety. Present-day students reject these categories as vague or abstract and indicative only of the objectives of some executive activity. Henry Mintzberg, who among other researchers has observed managers at work, identifies three sets of behavior—interpersonal, informational, and decisional. The interpersonal roles he designates as *figurehead* (for ceremonial duties), *leader* (of the work of his organization or unit), and *liaison agent* (for contacts outside his unit). Information roles can be designated as *monitor* (of information), *disseminator* (internally), and *spokesman* (externally). Decisional roles are called *entrepreneur, disturbance handler, resource allocator,* and *negotiator.*

Empirical studies of what managers do are corrective of theory but not necessarily instructive in educating good managers. That most unprepared managers act intuitively rather than systematically in response to unanticipated pressures does not mean that the most effective do so to the same extent. If in fact the harried, improvisatory, overworked performers of ten roles do not really know *what* they are

†**Source:** This article has been adapted from "The CEO: Leadership in Organizations," in *Business Policy: Text and Cases,* Sixth Edition, Irwin, Homewood, IL, 1987. Used with permission.

doing or have any priorities besides degree of urgency, then we are not likely to find out what more effective management is from categorizing their activities. On the other hand it is futile to offer unrealistic exhortations about long-range planning and organizing to real-life victims of forced expediency.

The simplification that will serve our approach to policy best will leave aside important but easily understood activities. The executive may make speeches, pick the silver pattern for the executive lunchroom, negotiate personally with important customers, and do many things human beings have to do for many reasons. Roles we may study in order to do a better job of general management can be viewed as those of *organization leader, personal leader*, and *chief architect of organization purpose*. As leader of persons grouped in a hierarchy of suborganizations, the president must be taskmaster, mediator, motivator, and organization designer. Since these roles do not have useful job descriptions saying what to do, one might better estimate the nature of the overlapping responsibility of the head of an organization than to draw theoretical distinctions between categories. The personal influence of leaders becomes evident as they play the role of communicator or exemplar and attract respect or affection. When we examine finally the president's role as architect of organization purpose, we may see entrepreneurial or improvisatory behavior if the organization is just being born. If the company is long since established, the part played may be more accurately designated as manager of the purpose-determining process or chief strategist.

The CEO as Organization Leader

Chief executives are first and probably least pleasantly persons who are responsible for results attained in the present as designated by plans made previously. Nothing that we will say shortly about their concern for the people in their organizations or later about their responsibility to society can gainsay this immediate truth. Achieving acceptable results against expectations of increased earnings per share and return on the stockholder's investment requires the CEO or president to be continually informed and ready to intervene when results fall below what had been expected. Changing circumstances and competition produce emergencies upsetting well-laid plans. Resourcefulness in responding to crisis is a skill that most successful executives develop early.

But the organizational consequences of the critical taskmaster role require presidents to go beyond insistence upon achievement of planned results. They must see as their second principal function the creative maintenance and development of the organized capability that makes achievement possible. This activity leads to a third principle—the integration of the specialist functions that enable their organizations to perform the technical tasks in marketing, research and development, manufacturing, finance, control, and personnel that proliferate as technology develops and tend to lead the company in all directions. If this coordination is successful in harmonizing special staff activities, presidents will probably have performed the task of getting organizations to accept and order priorities in accordance with the companies' objectives. Securing commitment to purpose is a central function of the president as organization leader.

The skills required by these functions reveal presidents not solely as taskmasters but as mediators and motivators as well. They need ability in the education and motivation of people and the evaluation of their performance, two functions that tend to work against one another. The former requires understanding of individual needs, which persist no matter what the economic purpose of the organization may be. The latter requires objective assessment of the technical requirements of the task assigned. The capability required here is also that required in the integration of functions and the mediation of the conflict bound to arise out of technical specialism. The integrating capacity of the chief executive extends to meshing the economic, technical, human, and moral dimensions of corporate activity and to relating the company to its immediate and more distant communities. It will show itself in the formal organizational designs that are put into effect as the blueprint of the required structured cooperation.

The perspective demanded of successful organization leaders embraces both the primacy of organizational goals and the validity of individual goals. Besides this dual appreciation, they exhibit an impartiality toward the specialized functions and have criteria enabling them to allocate organizational resources against documented needs. The point of view of the leader of an organization almost by definition requires an overview of its relations not only to its internal constituencies but to the relevant institutions and forces of its external environment. We will come soon to a conceptual solution of the problems encountered in the role of organization leader.

The CEO as Personal Leader

The functions, skills, and appropriate point of view of chief executives hold true no matter who they are or who makes up their organizations. The functions that accompany presidential performance of their role as communicator of purpose and policy, as exemplar, and as the focal point for the respect or affection of subordinates vary much more according to personal energy, style, character, and integrity. Presidents contribute as persons to the quality of life and performance in their organizations. This is true whether they are dynamic or colorless. By example they educate junior executives to seek to emulate them or simply to learn from their behavior what they really expect. They have the opportunity to infuse organized effort with flair or distinction if they have the skill to dramatize the relationship between their own activities and the goals of corporate effort.

All persons in leadership positions have or attain power that in sophisticated organizations they invoke as humanely and reasonably as possible in order to avoid the stultifying effects of dictatorship, dominance, or even markedly superior capacity. Formally announced policy, backed by the authority of the chief executive, can be made effective to some degree by clarity of direction, intensity of supervision, and the exercise of sanctions in enforcement. But in areas of judgment where policy cannot be specified without becoming absurdly overdetailed, chief executives establish in their own demeanor even more than in policy statements the moral and ethical level of performance expected.

The skills of the effective personal leader are those of persuasion and articulation made possible by saying something worth saying and by understanding the sentiments and points of view being addressed. Leaders cultivate and embody relationships between themselves and their subordinates appropriate to the style of leadership they have chosen or fallen into. Some of the qualities lending distinction to this leadership cannot be deliberately contrived, even by an artful schemer. The maintenance of personal poise in adversity or emergency and the capacity for development as an emotionally mature person are essentially innate and developed capabilities. It is probably true that some personal preeminence in technical or social functions is either helpful or essential in demonstrating leadership related to the president's personal contribution. Credibility and cooperation depend upon demonstrated capacity of a kind more tangible and attractive than, for example, the noiseless coordination of staff activity.

The CEO as Architect of Organization Purpose

To go beyond the organizational and personal roles of leadership, we enter the sphere of organization purpose, where we may find the atmosphere somewhat rare and the going less easy. We think students will note, as they see president after president cope or fail to cope with problems of various economic, political, social, or technical elements, that the contribution presidents make to their companies goes far beyond the apparently superficial activities that clutter their days.

The attention of presidents to organization needs must extend beyond answering letters of complaint from spouses of aggrieved employees to appraisal (for example) of the impact of their companies' information, incentive, and control systems upon individual behavior. Their personal contribution to their company goes far beyond easily understood attention to key customers and speeches to the Economic Club to the more subtle influence their own probity and character have on subordinates. We must turn now to activities even further out—away from immediate everyday decisions and emergencies. Some part of what a president does is oriented toward maintaining the development of a company over time and preparing for a future more distant than the time horizon appropriate to the roles and functions identified thus far.

The most difficult role—and the one we will concentrate on henceforth—of the chief executive of any organization is the one in which he serves as custodian of corporate objectives. The entrepreneurs who create a company know at the outset what they are up to. Their objectives are intensely personal, if not exclusively economic, and their passions may be patent protection and finance. If they succeed in passing successfully through the phase of personal entrepreneurship, where they or their bankers or families are likely to be the only members of the organization concerned with purpose, they find themselves in the role of planner, managing the process by which ideas for the future course of the company are conceived, evaluated, fought over, and accepted or rejected.

The presidential functions involved include establishing or presiding over the goal-setting and resource-allocation processes of the company, making or ratifying choice among strategic alternatives, and clarifying and defending the goals of the company against external attack or internal erosion. The installation of purpose in place of improvisation and the substitution of planned progress in place of drifting are probably the most demanding functions of the chief executive. Successful organization leadership requires great human skill, sensitivity, and administrative ability. Personal leadership is built upon personality and character. The capacity for determining and monitoring the adequacy of the organization's continuing purposes implies as well analytic intelligence of a high order. The president we are talking about is not a two-dimensional poster or television portrait.

The crucial skill of the president concerned with corporate purpose includes the creative generation or recognition of strategic alternatives made valid by developments in the marketplace and the capability and resources of the company. Along with this, in a combination not easily come by, runs the critical capacity to analyze the strengths and weaknesses of documented proposals. The ability to perceive with some objectivity corporate strengths and weaknesses is essential to sensible choice of goals, for the most attractive goal is not attainable without the strength to open the way to it through inertia and intense opposition, with all else that lies between.

Probably the skill most nearly unique to general management, as opposed to the management of functional or technical specialties, is the intellectual capacity to conceptualize corporate purpose and the dramatic skill to invest it with some degree of magnetism. As we will see, the skill can be exercised in industries less romantic than space, electronics, or environmental reclamation. No sooner is a distinctive set of corporate objectives vividly delineated than the temptation to go beyond it sets in. Under some circumstances it is the president's function to defend properly focused purpose against superficially attractive diversification or corporate growth that glitters like fool's gold. Because defense of proper strategy can be interpreted as mindless conservatism, wholly appropriate defense of a still valid strategy requires courage, supported by detailed documentation.

Continuous monitoring, in any event, of the quality and continued suitability of corporate purpose is over time the most sophisticated and essential of all the functions of general management alluded to here. The perspective that sustains this function is the kind of creative discontent that prevents complacency even in good times and seeks continuous advancement of corporate and individual capacity and performance. It requires also constant attention to the future, as if the present did not offer problems and opportunities enough.

■ EVOLUTION AND REVOLUTION AS ORGANIZATIONS GROW†

By Larry Greiner

Introduction

A small research company chooses too complicated and formalized an organizational structure for its young age and limited size. It flounders in rigidity and bureaucracy for several years and is finally acquired by a larger company.

Key executives of a retail store chain hold on to an organizational structure long after it has served its purpose because their power is derived from this structure. The company eventually goes into bankruptcy.

A large bank disciplines a "rebellious" manager who is blamed for current control problems, when the underlying cause is centralized procedures that are holding back expansion into new markets. Many younger managers subsequently leave the bank, competition moves in, and profits are still declining.

The problems of these companies, like those of many others, are rooted more in past decisions than in present events or outside market dynamics. Historical forces do indeed shape the future growth of organizations. Yet management, in its haste to grow, often overlooks such critical developmental questions as: Where has our organization been? Where is it now? And what do the answers to these questions mean for where we are going? Instead, its gaze is fixed outward toward the environment and the

---

†**Source:** Reprinted by permission of *Harvard Business Review.* "Evolution and Revolution as Organizations Grow," by Larry Greiner, (July/August 1972). Copyright © 1972 by the President and Fellows of Harvard College. All rights reserved.

future—as if more precise market projections will provide a new organizational identity.

Companies fail to see that many clues to their future success lie within their own organizations and their evolving states of development. Moreover, the inability of management to understand its organizational development problems can result in a company becoming "frozen" in its present stage of evolution or, ultimately, in failure, regardless of market opportunities.

My position in this article is that the future of an organization may be less determined by outside forces than it is by the organization's history. In stressing the force of history on an organization, I have drawn from the legacies of European psychologists (their thesis being that individual behavior is determined primarily by previous events and experiences, not by what lies ahead). Extending this analogy of individual development to the problems of organizational development, I shall discuss a series of developmental phases through which growing companies tend to pass. But, first, let me provide two definitions:

- The term *evolution* is used to describe prolonged periods of growth where no major upheaval occurs in organization practices.

- The term *revolution* is used to describe those periods of substantial turmoil in organization life.

As a company progresses through developmental phases, each evolutionary period creates its own revolution. For instance, centralized practices eventually lead to demands for decentralization. Moreover, the nature of management's solution to each revolutionary period determines whether a company will move forward into its next stage of evolutionary growth. As I shall show later, there are at least five phases of organizational development, each characterized by both an evolution and a revolution.

Key Forces in Development

During the past few years a small amount of research knowledge about the phases of organization development has been building. Some of this research is very quantitative, such as time-series analyses that reveal patterns of economic performance over time. The majority of studies, however, are case oriented and use company records and interviews to reconstruct a rich picture of corporate development. Yet both types of research tend to be heavily empirical without attempting more generalized statements about the overall process of development.

A notable exception is the historical work of Alfred D. Chandler, Jr., in his book *Strategy and Structure.* This study depicts four very broad and general phases in the lives of four large U.S. companies. It proposes that outside market opportunities determine a company's strategy, which in turn determines the company's organizational structure. This thesis has a valid ring for the four companies examined by Chandler, largely because they developed in a time of explosive markets and technological advances. But more recent evidence suggests that organizational structure may be less malleable than Chandler assumed; in fact, structure can play a critical role in influencing corporate strategy. It is this reverse emphasis on how organizational structure affects future growth that is highlighted in the model presented in this article.

From an analysis of recent studies, five key dimensions emerge as essential for building a model of organizational development:

- age of the organization
- size of the organization
- stages of evolution
- stages of revolution
- growth rate of the industry

I shall describe each of these elements separately, but first note their combined effect as illustrated in figure 9-1. Note especially how each dimension influences the other over time; when all five elements begin to interact, a more complete and dynamic picture of organizational growth emerges.

FIGURE 9-1
Model of Organizational Development

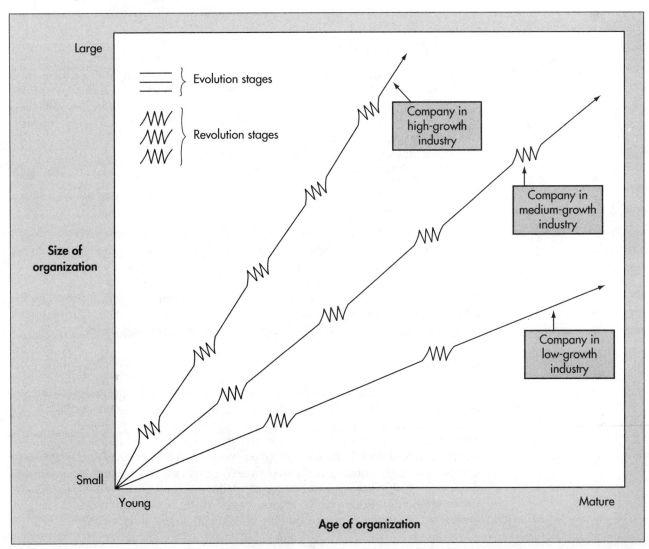

After describing these dimensions and their interconnections, I shall discuss each evolutionary/revolutionary phase of development and show (1) how each stage of evolution breeds its own revolution, and (2) how management solutions to each revolution determine the next stage of evolution.

Age of the Organization

The most obvious and essential dimension for any model of development is the life span of an organization (represented as the horizontal axis in figure 9-1). All historical studies gather data from various points in time and then make comparisons. From these observations, it is evident that the same organization practices are not maintained throughout a long time span. This makes a most basic point: management problems and principles are rooted in time. The concept of decentralization, for example, can have meaning for describing corporate practices at one time period but loses its descriptive power at another.

The passage of time also contributes to the institutionalization of managerial attitudes. As a result, employee behavior becomes not only more predictable but also more difficult to change when attitudes are outdated.

Size of the Organization

This dimension is depicted as the vertical axis in figure 9-1. A company's problems and solutions tend to change markedly as the number of employees and sales volume increase. Thus, time is not the only determinant of structure; in fact, organizations that do not grow in size can retain many of the same management issues and practices over lengthy periods. In addition to increased size, however, problems of coordination and communication magnify, new functions emerge, levels in the management hierarchy multiply, and jobs become more interrelated.

Stages of Evolution

As both age and size increase, another phenomenon becomes evident: the prolonged growth that I have termed the evolutionary period. Most growing organizations do not expand for two years and then retreat for one year; rather, those that survive a crisis usually enjoy four to eight years of continuous growth without a major economic setback or severe internal disruption. The term evolution seems appropriate for describing these quieter periods because only modest adjustments appear necessary for maintaining growth under the same overall pattern of management.

Stages of Revolution

Smooth evolution is not inevitable; it cannot be assumed that organization growth is linear. *Fortune*'s "500" list, for example, has had significant turnover during the last fifty years. Thus we find evidence from numerous case histories that reveals periods of substantial turbulence spaced between smoother periods of evolution.

I have termed these turbulent times the periods of revolution because they typically exhibit a serious upheaval of management practices. Traditional management practices, which were appropriate for a smaller size and earlier time, are brought under scrutiny by frustrated top managers and disillusioned lower-level managers. During such periods of crisis, a number of companies fail—those unable to abandon past practices and effect major organizational changes are likely either to fold or to level off in their growth rates.

The critical task for management in each revolutionary period is to find a new set of organization practices that will become the basis for managing the next period of evolutionary growth. Interestingly enough, these new practices eventually sow their seeds of decay and lead to another period of revolution. Companies therefore experience the irony of seeing a major solution in one time period become a major problem at a later date.

Growth Rate of the Industry

The speed at which an organization experiences phases of evolution and revolution is closely related to the market environment of its industry. For example, a company in a rapidly expanding market will have to add employees rapidly; hence, the need for new organizational structures to accommodate large staff increases is accelerated. While evolutionary periods tend to be relatively short in fast-growing industries, much longer evolutionary periods occur in mature or slowly growing industries.

Evolution can also be prolonged, and revolutions delayed, when profits come easily. For instance, companies that make grievous errors in a rewarding industry can still look good on their profit and loss statements; thus they can avoid a change in management practices for a longer period. The aerospace industry in its infancy is an example. Yet revolutionary periods still occur, as one did in aerospace when profit opportunities began to dry up. Revolutions seem to be much more severe and difficult to resolve when the market environment is poor.

Phases of Growth

With the foregoing framework in mind, let us now examine in depth the five specific phases of evolution and revolution. As shown in figure 9-2, each evolutionary period is characterized by the dominant *management style* used to achieve growth, while each revolutionary period is characterized by the dominant *management problem* that must be solved before growth can continue. The patterns presented in figure 9-2 seem to be typical for companies in industries with moderate growth over a long time period; companies in faster growing industries tend to experience all five phases more rapidly, while those in slower growing industries encounter only two or three phases over many years.

It is important to note that *each phase is both an effect of the previous phase and a cause for the next phase.* For example, the evolutionary management style in phase 3 of figure 9-2 is "delegation," which grows out of, and becomes the solution to, demands for greater "autonomy" in the preceding phase 2 revolution. The style of delegation used in phase 3, however, eventually provokes a major revolutionary crisis that is characterized by attempts to regain control over the diversity created through increased delegation.

The principal implication of each phase is that management actions are narrowly prescribed if growth is to occur. For example, a company experiencing an autonomy crisis in phase 2 cannot return to directive management for a solution—it must adopt a new style of delegation in order to move ahead.

FIGURE 9-2
The Five Phases of Growth

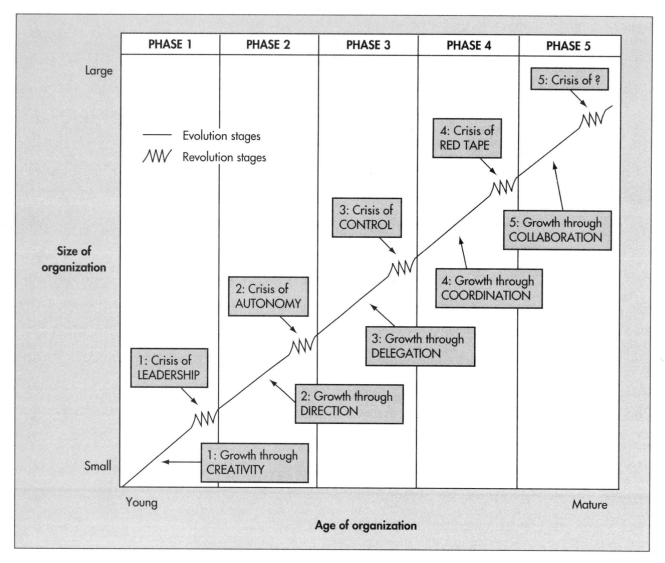

Phase 1: Creativity . . .

In the birth stage of an organization, the emphasis is on creating both a product and a market. Here are the characteristics of the period of creative evolution:

- The company's founders are usually technically or entrepreneurially oriented, and they disdain management activities; their physical and mental energies are absorbed entirely in making and selling a new product.

- Communication among employees is frequent and informal.

- Long hours of work are rewarded by modest salaries and the promise of ownership benefits.

- Control of activities comes from immediate marketplace feedback; the management acts as the customers react.

And the Leadership Crisis. All of the foregoing individualistic and creative activities are essential for the company to get off the ground. But therein lies the problem. As the company grows, larger production runs require knowledge about the efficiencies of manufacturing. Increased numbers of employees cannot be managed exclusively through informal communication; new employees are not motivated by an intense dedication to the product or organization. Additional capital must be secured, and new accounting procedures are needed for financial control.

Thus the founders find themselves burdened with unwanted management responsibilities. So they long for the "good old days," still trying to act as they did in the past. And conflicts between the harried leaders grow more intense.

At this point a crisis of leadership occurs, which is the onset of the first revolution. Who is to lead the company out of confusion and solve the managerial problems confronting it? Quite obviously, a strong manager is needed who has the necessary knowledge and skill to introduce new business techniques. But this is easier said than done. The founders often hate to step aside even though they are probably temperamentally unsuited to be managers. So here is the first critical developmental choice—to locate and install a strong business manager who is acceptable to the founders and who can pull the organization together.

Phase 2: Direction . . .

Those companies that survive the first phase by installing a capable business manager usually embark on a period of sustained growth under able and directive leadership. Here are the characteristics of this evolutionary period:

- A functional organizational structure is introduced to separate manufacturing from marketing activities, and job assignments become more specialized.
- Accounting systems for inventory and purchasing are introduced.
- Incentives, budgets, and work standards are adopted.
- Communication becomes more formal and impersonal as a hierarchy of titles and positions builds.
- The new manager and his key supervisors take most of the responsibility for instituting direction, while lower-level supervisors are treated more as functional specialists than as autonomous decision-making managers.

And the Autonomy Crisis. Although the new directive techniques channel employee energy more efficiently into growth, they eventually become inappropriate for controlling a larger, more diverse and complex organization. Lower-level employees find themselves restricted by a cumbersome and centralized hierarchy. They have come to possess more direct knowledge about markets and machinery than do the leaders at the top; consequently, they feel torn between following procedures and taking initiative on their own.

Thus the second revolution is imminent as a crisis develops from demands for greater autonomy on the part of lower-level managers. The solution adopted by most companies is to move toward greater delegation. Yet it is difficult for top managers who were previously successful at being directive to give up responsibility. Moreover, lower-level managers are not accustomed to making decisions for themselves. As a result, numerous companies flounder during this revolutionary period, adhering to centralized methods while lower-level employees grow more disenchanted and leave the organization.

Phase 3: Delegation . . .

The next era of growth evolves from the successful application of a decentralized organizational structure. It exhibits these characteristics:

- Much greater responsibility is given to the managers of plants and market territories.
- Profit centers and bonuses are used to stimulate motivation.
- The top executives at headquarters restrain themselves to managing by exception, based on periodic reports from the field.
- Management often concentrates on making new acquisitions that can be lined up beside other decentralized units.
- Communication from the top is infrequent, usually by correspondence, telephone, or brief visits to field locations.

The delegation stage proves useful for gaining expansion through heightened motivation at lower levels. Decentralized managers with greater authority and incentive are able to penetrate larger markets, respond faster to customers, and develop new products.

And the Control Crisis.   A serious problem eventually evolves, however, as top executives sense that they are losing control over a highly diversified field operation. Autonomous field managers prefer to run their own shows without coordinating plans, money, technology, and manpower with the rest of the organization. Freedom breeds a parochial attitude.

Hence, the phase 3 revolution is under way when top management seeks to regain control over the total company. Some top managements attempt a return to centralized management, which usually fails because of the vast scope of operations. Those companies that move ahead find a new solution in the use of special coordination techniques.

Phase 4: Coordination . . .

During this phase, the evolutionary period is characterized by the use of formal systems for achieving greater coordination and by top executives taking responsibility for the initiation and administration of these new systems. For example:

- Decentralized units are merged into product groups.
- Formal planning procedures are established and intensively reviewed.
- Numerous staff personnel are hired and located at headquarters to initiate company-wide programs of control and review for line managers.
- Capital expenditures are carefully weighed and parceled out across the organization.
- Each product group is treated as an investment center where return or invested capital is an important criterion used in allocating funds.
- Certain technical functions, such as data processing, are centralized at headquarters, while daily operating decisions remain decentralized.
- Stock options and companywide profit sharing are used to encourage identity with the firm as a whole.

All of these new co-ordination systems prove useful for achieving growth through more efficient allocation of a company's limited resources. They prompt field managers to look beyond the needs of their local units. While these managers still have much decision-making responsibility, they learn to justify their actions more carefully to a "watchdog" audience at headquarters.

And the Red-Tape Crisis.   But a lack of confidence gradually builds between line, and staff, and between headquarters and the field. The proliferation of systems and programs begins to exceed its utility; a red-tape crisis is created. Line managers, for example, increasingly resent heavy staff direction from those who are not familiar with local conditions. Staff people, on the other hand, complain about uncooperative and uninformed line managers. Together both groups criticize the bureaucratic paper system that has evolved. Procedures take precedence over problem solving, and innovation is dampened. In short, the organization has become too large and complex to be managed through formal programs and rigid systems. The phase 4 revolution is under way.

Phase 5: Collaboration . . .

The last observable phase in previous studies emphasizes strong interpersonal collaboration in an attempt to overcome the red-tape crisis. Where phase 4 was managed more through formal systems and procedures, phase 5 emphasizes greater spontaneity in management action through teams and the skillful confrontation of interpersonal differences. Social control and self-discipline take over from formal control. This transition is especially difficult for those experts who created the old systems as well as for those line managers who relied on formal methods for answers.

The phase 5 evolution, then, builds around a more flexible and behavioral approach to management. Here are its characteristics:

- The focus is on solving problems quickly through team action.
- Teams are combined across functions for task-group activity.
- Headquarters staff experts are reduced in number, reassigned, and combined in interdisciplinary teams to consult with, not to direct, field units.
- A matrix-type structure is frequently used to assemble the right teams for the appropriate problems.
- Previous formal systems are simplified and combined into single multipurpose systems.
- Conferences of key managers are held frequently to focus on major problem issues.
- Educational programs are utilized to train managers in behavioral skills for achieving better teamwork and conflict resolution.
- Real-time information systems are integrated into daily decision making.
- Economic rewards are geared more to team performance than to individual achievement.
- Experiments in new practices are encouraged throughout the organization.

And the ? Crisis.   What will be the revolution in response to this stage of evolution? Many large U.S. companies are now in the phase 5 evolutionary stage, so the answers are critical. While there is little clear evidence, I imagine the revolution will center on the "psychological saturation" of employees who grow emotionally and physically exhausted by the intensity of teamwork and the heavy pressure for innovative solutions.

My hunch is that the phase 5 revolution will be solved through new structures and programs that allow employees to periodically rest, reflect, and revitalize themselves. We may even see companies with dual organizational structures: a "habit" structure for getting the daily work done, and a "reflective" structure for stimulating perspective and personal enrichment. Employees could then move back and forth between the two structures as their energies are dissipated and refueled.

Implications of History

Let me now summarize some important implications for practicing managers. First, the main features of this discussion are depicted in table 9-1, which shows the specific management actions that characterize each growth phase. These actions are also the solutions that ended each preceding revolutionary period.

In one sense, I hope that many readers will react to my model by calling it obvious and natural for depicting the growth of an organization. To me this type of reaction is a useful test of the model's validity.

But at a more reflective level I imagine some of these reactions are more hindsight than foresight. Those experienced managers who have been through a developmental sequence can empathize with it now, but how did they react when in the middle of a stage of evolution or revolution? They can probably recall the limits of their own developmental understanding at that time. Perhaps they resisted desirable changes or were even swept emotionally into a revolution without being able to propose constructive solutions. So let me offer some explicit guidelines for managers of growing organizations to keep in mind.

Know Where You Are in the Developmental Sequence

Every organization and its component parts are at different stages of development. The task of top management is to be aware of these stages; otherwise, it may not recognize when the time for change has come, or it may act to impose the wrong solution.

Top leaders should be ready to work with the flow of the tide rather than against it; yet they should be cautious, since it is tempting to skip phases out of impatience. Each phase results in certain strengths and learning experiences in the organization that will be essential for success in subsequent phases. A child prodigy, for example, may be able to read like a teenager, but he cannot behave like one until he ages through a sequence of experiences.

I also doubt that managers can or should act to avoid revolutions. Rather, these periods of tension provide the pressure, ideas, and awareness that afford a platform for change and the introduction of new practices.

Recognize the Limited Range of Solutions

In each revolutionary stage it becomes evident that this stage can be ended only by certain specific solutions; moreover, these solutions are different from those that were applied to the problems of the preceding revolution. Too often it is tempting to choose solutions that were tried before, which makes it impossible for a new phase of growth to evolve.

Management must be prepared to dismantle current structures before the revolutionary stage becomes too turbulent. Top managers, realizing that their own managerial styles are no longer appropriate, may even have to take themselves out of leadership positions. A good phase 2 manager facing phase 3 might be wise to find

TABLE 9-1

Organization Practices during Evolution in the Five Phases of Growth

Category	PHASE 1	PHASE 2	PHASE 3	PHASE 4	PHASE 5
MANAGEMENT FOCUS	Make & sell	Efficiency of operations	Expansion of market	Consolidation of organization	Problem solving & innovation
ORGANIZATION STRUCTURE	Informal	Centralized & functional	Decentralized & geographical	Line-staff & product groups	Matrix of teams
TOP MANAGEMENT STYLE	Individualistic & entrepreneurial	Directive	Delegative	Watchdog	Participative
CONTROL SYSTEM	Market results	Standards & cost centers	Reports & profit centers	Plans & investment centers	Mutual goal setting
MANAGEMENT REWARD EMPHASIS	Ownership	Salary & merit increases	Individual bonus	Profit sharing & stock options	Team bonus

another phase 2 organization that better fits his talents, either outside the company or with one of its newer subsidiaries.

Finally, evolution is not an automatic affair; it is a contest for survival. To move ahead, companies must consciously introduce planned structures that not only are solutions to a current crisis but also are fitted to the *next* phase of growth. This requires considerable self-awareness on the part of top management, as well as great interpersonal skill in persuading other managers that change is needed.

Realize That Solutions Breed New Problems

Managers often fail to realize that organizational solutions create problems for the future (i.e., a decision to delegate eventually causes a problem of control). Historical actions are very much determinants of what happens to the company at a much later date. An awareness of this effect should help managers to evaluate company problems with greater historical understanding instead of "pinning the blame" on a current development. Better yet, managers should be in a position to *predict* future problems, and thereby to prepare solutions and coping strategies before a revolution gets out of hand.

A management that is aware of the problems ahead could well decide *not* to grow. Top managers may, for instance, prefer to retain the informal practices of a small company, knowing that this way of life is inherent in the organization's limited size, not in their congenial personalities. If they choose to grow, they may do themselves out of a job and a way of life they enjoy.

And what about the managements of very large organizations? Can they find new solutions for continued phases of evolution? Or are they reaching a stage where the government will act to break them up because they are too large?

Concluding Note

Clearly, there is still much to learn about processes of development in organizations. The phases outlined here are only five in number and are still only approximations. Researchers are just beginning to study the specific developmental problems of structure, control, rewards, and management style in different industries and in a variety of cultures.

One should not, however, wait for conclusive evidence before educating managers to think and act from a developmental perspective. The critical dimension of time has been missing for too long from our management theories and practices. The intriguing paradox is that by learning more about history we may do a better job in the future.

■ A STRATEGIC TYPOLOGY OF ORGANIZATIONS†

By Raymond Miles, Charles Snow, Alan Meyer, and Henry Coleman

An organization is both an articulated purpose and an established mechanism for achieving it. Most organizations engage in an ongoing process of evaluating their purposes—questioning, verifying, and redefining the manner of interaction with their environments. Effective organizations carve out and maintain a viable market for their goods or services. Ineffective organizations fail this market-alignment task. Organizations also constantly modify and refine the mechanism by which they achieve their purposes—rearranging their structure of roles and relationships and their managerial processes. Efficient organizations establish mechanisms that complement their market strategy, but inefficient organizations struggle with these structural and process mechanisms.

For most organizations, the dynamic process of adjusting to environmental change and uncertainty—*of maintaining an effective alignment with the environment while managing internal interdependencies*—is enormously complex, encompassing myriad decisions and behaviors at several organization levels. But the complexity of the adjustment process can be penetrated: by searching for patterns in the behavior of organizations, one can describe and even predict the process of organizational adaptation. This article presents a theoretical framework that managers and students of management can use to analyze an organization as an integrated and dynamic whole—a model that takes into account the interrelationships among strategy, structure, and process. Specifically, the framework has two major elements: (1) a general model of the process of adaptation that specifies the major decisions needed by the organization to maintain an effective alignment with its environment, and (2) an organizational typology that portrays different patterns of adaptive behavior used by organizations within a given industry or other grouping.

†**Source:** This article was originally published as "Organizational Strategy, Structure, and Process," in *Academy of Management Review* (July 1978). Reprinted with permission.

The Adaptive Cycle

We have developed a general model of the adaptive process that we call the *adaptive cycle*. Consistent with the strategic-choice approach to the study of organizations, the model parallels and expands ideas formulated by theorists such as Chandler, Child, Cyert and March, Drucker, Thompson, and Weick. Essentially, proponents of the strategic-choice perspective argue that organizational behavior is only partially preordained by environmental conditions and that the choices top managers make are the critical determinants of organizational structure and process. Although these choices are numerous and complex, they can be viewed as three broad "problems" of organizational adaptation: the *entrepreneurial problem*, the *engineering problem*, and the *administrative problem*. In mature organizations, management must solve each of these problems simultaneously, but for explanatory purposes, these adaptive problems can be discussed as if they occurred sequentially.

The Entrepreneurial Problem

The adaptive cycle, though evident in all organizations, is perhaps most visible in new or rapidly growing organizations (and in organizations that recently have survived a major crisis). In a new organization, an entrepreneurial insight, perhaps only vaguely defined at first, must be developed into a concrete *definition of an organizational domain: a specific good or service and a target market or market segment*. In an ongoing organization, the entrepreneurial problem has an added dimension. Because the organization has already obtained a set of "solutions" to its engineering and administrative problems, its next attempt at an entrepreneurial "thrust" may be difficult.

The Engineering Problem

The engineering problem involves the creation of a system that *operationalizes management's solution to the entrepreneurial problem*. Such a system requires management to select an appropriate technology (input-transformation-output process) for producing and distributing chosen products or services and to form new information, communication, and control linkages (or modify existing linkages) to ensure proper operation of the technology.

As solutions to these problems are reached, initial implementation of the administrative system takes place. There is no assurance that the configuration of the organization, as it begins to emerge during this phase, will remain the same when the engineering problem finally has been solved. The actual form of the organization's structure will be determined during the administrative phase as management solidifies relations with the environment and establishes processes for coordinating and controlling internal operations.

The Administrative Problem

The administrative problem, as described by most theories of management, is primarily that of reducing uncertainty within the organizational system, or, in terms of the present model, of rationalizing and stabilizing those activities that successfully solved problems faced by the organization during the entrepreneurial and engineering phases. Solving the administrative problem involves more than simply rationalizing the system already developed (uncertainty reduction); it also involves formulating and implementing those processes that will enable the organization to continue to evolve (innovation).

In the ideal organization, management would be equally adept at performing two somewhat conflicting functions: it would be able to create an administrative system (structure and processes) that could smoothly direct and monitor the organization's current activities without, at the same time, allowing the system to become so ingrained that future innovation activities are jeopardized. Such a perspective requires the administrative system to be viewed as both a *lagging* and *leading* variable in the process of adaptation. As a lagging variable, it must rationalize, through the development of appropriate structures and processes, strategic decisions made at previous points in the adjustment process. As a leading variable, the administrative system must facilitate the organization's future capacity to adapt by articulating and reinforcing the paths along which innovative activity can proceed.

The Strategic Typology

If one accepts the adaptive cycle as valid, the question becomes: How do organizations move through the cycle? That is, using the language of our model, what strategies do organizations employ in solving their entrepreneurial, engineering, and administrative problems? Our research and interpretation of the literature show that there are essentially three *strategic types* of organizations: Defenders, Analyzers, and Prospectors. Each type has its own unique strategy for relating to its chosen market(s), and each has a particular configuration of technology, structure, and process that is consistent with its market strategy. A fourth type of organization encountered in our studies is called the Reactor. The Reactor is a form of strategic "failure" in that inconsistencies exist among its strategy, technology, structure, and process.

Defenders

The Defender (i.e., top management) deliberately enacts and maintains an environment for which a stable form of organization is appropriate. Stability is chiefly achieved by the Defender's definition of, and solution to, its *entrepreneurial* problem. Defenders define their *entrepreneurial* problem as *how to seal off a portion of the total market in order to create a stable domain*, and they do so by producing only a limited set of products directed at a narrow segment of the total potential market. Within this limited domain, the Defender strives aggressively to prevent competitors from entering its "turf." Such behaviors include standard economic actions like competitive pricing or high-quality products, but Defenders also tend to ignore developments and trends outside of their domains, choosing instead to grow through market penetration and perhaps some limited product development. Over time, a true Defender is able to carve out and maintain a small niche within the industry that is difficult for competitors to penetrate.

Having chosen a narrow product-market domain, the Defender invests a great deal of resources in solving its *engineering* problem: *how to produce and distribute goods or services as efficiently as possible*. Typically, the Defender does so by developing a single core technology that is highly cost-efficient. Technology efficiency is central to the Defender's success since its domain has been deliberately created to absorb outputs on a predictable, continuous basis. Some Defenders extend technological efficiency to its limits through a process of vertical integration—incorporating each stage of production from raw materials supply to distribution of final outputs into the same organizational system.

Finally, the Defender's solution to its administrative problem is closely aligned with its solutions to the entrepreneurial and engineering problems. The Defender's *administrative* problem—*how to achieve strict control of the organization in order to ensure efficiency*—is solved through a combination of structural and process mechanisms that can be generally described as "mechanistic." These mechanisms include a top-management group heavily dominated by production and cost-control specialists, little or no scanning of the environment for new areas of opportunity, intensive planning oriented toward cost and other efficiency issues, functional structures characterized by extensive division of labor, centralized control, communications through formal hierarchical channels, and so on. Such an administrative system is ideally suited for generating and maintaining efficiency, and the key characteristic of stability is as apparent here as in the solution to the other two adaptive problems.

Pursued vigorously, the Defender strategy can be viable in most industries, although stable industries lend themselves to this type of organization more than turbulent industries (e.g., the relative lack of technological change in the food-processing industry generally favors the Defender strategy compared with the situation in the electronics industry). This particular form of organization is not without its potential risks. The Defender's *primary risk* is that of *ineffectiveness*—being unable to respond to a major shift in its market environment. The Defender relies on the continued viability of its single, narrow domain, and it receives a return on its large technological investment only if the major problems facing the organization continue to be of an engineering nature. If the Defender's market shifts dramatically, this type of organization has little capacity for locating and exploiting new areas of opportunity. In short, the Defender is perfectly capable of responding to today's world. To the extent that tomorrow's world is similar to today's, the Defender is ideally suited for its environment.

Prospectors

In many ways, Prospectors respond to their chosen environments in a manner that is almost the opposite of the Defender. In one sense, the Prospector is exactly like the Defender: there is a high degree of consistency among its solutions to the three problems of adaptation.

Generally speaking, the Prospector enacts an environment that is more dynamic than those of other types of organizations within the same industry. Unlike the Defender, whose success comes primarily from efficiently serving a stable domain, the Prospector's prime capability is that of finding and exploiting new product and market opportunities. For a Prospector, maintaining a reputation as an innovator in product and market development may be as important as, perhaps even more important than, high profitability. In fact, because of the inevitable "failure rate" associated with sustained product and market innovation, Prospectors may find it difficult consistently to attain the profit levels of the more efficient Defender.

Defining its *entrepreneurial* problem as *how to locate and develop product and market opportunities*, the Prospector's domain is usually broad and in a continuous state of development. The systematic addition of new products or markets, frequently combined with retrenchment in other parts of the domain, gives the Prospector's products and markets an aura of fluidity uncharacteristic of the Defender. To locate new areas of opportunity, the Prospector must develop and maintain the capacity to survey a wide range of environmental conditions, trends, and events. This type of organization invests heavily in individuals and groups who scan the environment for potential opportunities. Because these scanning activities are not limited to the organization's current domain, Prospectors are frequently the creators of change in their respective industries. Change is one of the major tools used by the Prospector to gain an edge over competitors, so Prospector managers typically perceive more environmental change and uncertainty than managers of the Defender (or the other two organization types).

To serve its changing domain properly, the Prospector requires a good deal of flexibility in its technology and administrative system. Unlike the Defender, the Prospector's choice of products and markets is not limited to those that fall within the range of the organization's present technological capability. The Prospector's technology is contingent upon both the organization's current *and* future product mix: entrepreneurial activities always have primacy, and appropriate technologies are not selected or developed until late in the process of product development. Therefore, the Prospector's overall *engineering* problem is *how to avoid long-term commitments to a single type of technological process*, and the organization usually does so by creating multiple, prototypical technologies that have a low degree of routinization and mechanization.

Finally, the Prospector's *administrative* problem flows from its changing domain and flexible technologies: *how to facilitate rather than control organizational operations.* That is, the Prospector's administrative system must be able to deploy and coordinate resources among numerous decentralized units and projects rather than to plan and control the operations of the entire organization centrally. To accomplish overall facilitation and coordination, the Prospector's structure-process mechanisms must be "organic." These mechanisms include a top-management group dominated by marketing and research and development experts, planning that is broad rather than intensive and oriented toward results not methods, product or project structures characterized by a low degree of formalization, decentralized control, lateral as well as vertical communications, and so on. In contrast to the Defender, the Prospector's descriptive catchword throughout its administrative as well as entrepreneurial and engineering solutions is flexibility.

Of course, the Prospector strategy also has it costs. Although the Prospector's continuous exploration of change helps to protect it from a changing environment, this type of organization runs the *primary risk* of *low profitability and overextension of resources.* While the Prospector's technological flexibility permits a rapid response to a changing domain, complete efficiency cannot be obtained because of the presence of multiple technologies. Finally, the Prospector's administrative system is well suited to maintain flexibility, but it may, at least temporarily, underutilize or even misutilize physical, financial, and human resources. In short, the Prospector is effective—it can respond to the demands of tomorrow's world. To the extent that the world of tomorrow is similar to that of today, the Prospector cannot maximize profitability because of its inherent inefficiency.

Analyzers

Based on our research, the Defender and the Prospector seem to reside at opposite ends of a continuum of adjustment strategies. Between these two extremes, a third type of organization is called the Analyzer. The Analyzer is a unique combination of the Prospector and Defender types and represents a viable alternative to these other strategies. A true Analyzer is an organization that attempts to minimize risk while maximizing the opportunity for profit—that is, an experienced Analyzer combines the strengths of both the Prospector and the Defender into a single system. This strategy is difficult to pursue, particularly in industries characterized by rapid market and technological change, and thus the word that best describes the Analyzer's adaptive approach is balance.

The Analyzer defines its *entrepreneurial* problem in terms similar to both the Prospector and the Defender: *how to locate and exploit new product and market opportunities while simultaneously maintaining a firm core of traditional products and customers*. The Analyzer's solution to the entrepreneurial problem is also a blend of the solutions preferred by the Prospector and the Defender: the Analyzer moves toward new products or new markets but only after their viability has been demonstrated. This periodic transformation of the Analyzer's domain is accomplished through imitation—only the most successful product or market innovations developed by prominent Prospectors are adopted. At the same time, the majority of the Analyzer's revenue is generated by a fairly stable set of products and customer or client groups— a Defender characteristic. Thus, the successful Analyzer must be able to respond quickly when following the lead of key Prospectors while at the same time maintaining operating efficiency in its stable product and market areas. To the extent that it is successful, the Analyzer can grow through market penetration as well as product and market development.

The duality evident in the Analyzer's domain is reflected in its *engineering* problem and solution. This type of organization must learn *how to achieve and protect an equilibrium between conflicting demands for technological flexibility and for technological stability*. This equilibrium is accomplished by partitioning production activities to form a dual technological core. The stable component of the Analyzer's technology bears a strong resemblance to the Defender's technology. It is functionally organized and exhibits high levels of standardization, routinization, and mechanization in an attempt to approach cost efficiency. The Analyzer's flexible technological component resembles the Prospector's technological orientation. In manufacturing organizations, it frequently includes a large group of applications engineers (or their equivalent) who are rotated among teams charged with the task of rapidly adapting new product designs to fit the Analyzer's existing stable technology.

The Analyzer's dual technological core thus reflects the engineering solutions of both the Prospector and the Defender, with the stable and flexible components integrated primarily by an influential applied research group. To the extent that this group is able to develop solutions that match the organization's existing technological capabilities with the new products desired by product managers, the Analyzer can enlarge its product line without incurring the Prospector's extensive research and development expenses.

The Analyzer's administrative problem, as well as its entrepreneurial and engineering problems, contains both Defender and Prospector characteristics. Generally speaking, the *administrative* problem of the Analyzer is *how to differentiate the organization's structure and processes to accommodate both stable and dynamic areas of operation*. The Analyzer typically solves this problem with some version of a matrix organization structure. Heads of key functional units, most notably engineering and production, unite with product managers (usually housed in the marketing department) to form a balanced dominant coalition similar to both the Defender and the Prospector. The product manager's influence is usually greater than the functional manager's since his or her task is to identify promising product-market innovations and to supervise their movement through applied engineering and into production in a smooth and timely manner. The presence of engineering and production in the dominant coalition is to represent the more stable domain and technology that are the foundations of the Analyzer's overall operations. The Analyzer's matrix structure is supported by intensive planning between the functional divisions of marketing and production, broad-gauge planning between the applied research group and the product managers for the development of new products, centralized control mechanisms in the functional divisions and decentralized control techniques in the product groups, and so on. In sum, the key characteristic of the Analyzer's administrative system is the proper differentiation of the organization's structure and processes to achieve a balance between the stable and dynamic areas of operation.

As is true for both the Defender and Prospector, the Analyzer strategy is not without its costs. The duality in the Analyzer's domain forces the organization to establish a dual technological core, and it requires management to operate fundamentally different planning, control, and reward systems simultaneously. Thus, the Analyzer's twin characteristics of stability and flexibility limit the organization's ability to move fully in either direction were the domain to shift dramatically. Consequently, the Analyzer's *primary risks* are both *inefficiency and ineffectiveness* if it does not maintain the necessary balance throughout its strategy-structure relationship.

Reactors

The Defender, the Prospector, and the Analyzer can all be proactive with respect to their environments, though each is proactive in a different way. At the extremes, Defenders continually attempt to develop greater efficiency in existing operations while Prospectors explore environmental change in search of new opportunities. Over time, these action modes stabilize to form a pattern of response to environmental conditions that is both *consistent* and *stable*.

A fourth type of organization, the Reactor, exhibits a pattern of adjustment to its environment that is both *inconsistent* and *unstable*; this type lacks a set of response mechanisms that it can consistently put into effect when faced with a changing environment. As a consequence, Reactors exist in a state of almost perpetual instability. The Reactor's "adaptive" cycle usually consists of responding inappropriately to environmental change and uncertainty, performing poorly as a result, and then being reluctant to act aggressively in the future. Thus, the Reactor is a "residual" strategy, arising when one of the other three strategies is improperly pursued.

Although there are undoubtedly many reasons why organizations become Reactors, we have identified three. First, *top management may not have clearly articulated the organization's strategy*. For example, one company was headed by a "one-man" Prospector of immense personal skills. A first-rate architect, he led his firm through a rapid and successful growth period during which the company moved from the design and construction of suburban shopping centers, through the construction and management of apartment complexes, and into consulting with municipal agencies concerning urban planning problems. Within ten years of its inception, the company was a loose but effective collection of semiautonomous units held together by this particular individual. When this individual was suddenly killed in a plane crash, the company was thrown into a strategic void. Because each separate unit of the company was successful, each was able to argue strongly for more emphasis on its particular domain and operations. Consequently, the new chief executive officer, caught between a number of conflicting but legitimate demands for resources, was unable to develop a unified, cohesive statement of the organization's strategy; thus, consistent and aggressive behavior was precluded.

A second and perhaps more common cause of organizational instability is that *management does not fully shape the organization's structure and processes to fit a chosen strategy.* Unless all of the domain, technological, and administrative decisions required to have an operational strategy are properly aligned, strategy is a mere statement, not an effective guide to behavior. One publishing company wished, in effect, to become an Analyzer—management had articulated a direction for the organization that involved operating in both stable and changing domains within the college textbook publishing industry. Although the organization comprised several key Defender and Prospector characteristics such as functional structures and decentralized control mechanisms, these structure-process features were not appropriately linked to the company's different domains. In one area where the firm wished to "prospect," for example, the designated unit had a functional structure and shared a large, almost mass-production technology with several other units, thereby making it difficult for the organization to respond to market opportunities quickly. Thus, this particular organization exhibited a weak link between its strategy and its structure-process characteristics.

The third cause of instability—and perhaps ultimate failure—*is a tendency for management to maintain the organization's current strategy-structure relationship despite overwhelming changes in environmental conditions.* Another organization in our studies, a food-processing company, had initially been an industry pioneer in both the processing and marketing of dried fruits and nuts. Gradually, the company settled into a Defender strategy and took vigorous steps to bolster this strategy, including limiting the domain to a narrow line of products, integrating backward into growing and harvesting, and assigning a controller to each of the company's major functional divisions as a means of keeping costs down. Within recent years, the company's market has become saturated, and profit margins have shrunk on most of the firm's products. In spite of its declining market, the organization has consistently clung to a Defender strategy and structure, even to the point of creating ad hoc cross-divisional committees whose sole purpose was to find ways of increasing efficiency further. At the moment, management recognizes that the organization is in trouble, but it is reluctant to make the drastic modifications required to attain a strategy and structure better suited to the changing market conditions.

Unless an organization exists in a "protected" environment such as a monopolistic or highly regulated industry, it cannot continue to behave as a Reactor indefinitely. Sooner or later, it must move toward one of the consistent and stable strategies of Defender, Analyzer, or Prospector.

■ THE EFFECTIVE ORGANIZATION: FORCES AND FORMS[†]

By Henry Mintzberg

What makes an organization effective? For a long time we thought we had the answer. Frederick Taylor told us about the "one best way" at the turn of the century, and organizations long pursued this Holy Grail. First it was Taylor's time and motion studies, later the participative management of the human relations people, in more

[†]**Source:** Reprinted from "The Effective Organization: Forces and Forms" by Henry Mintzberg, *Sloan Management Review*, Winter 1991, by permission of the publisher. Copyright 1991 by the Sloan Management Review Association. All rights reserved.

recent years the wonders of strategic planning. It was as if every manager had to see the world through the same pair of glasses, although the fashion for lenses changed from time to time.

Then along came the so-called contingency theorists, who argued that "it all depends." Effective organizations designed themselves to match their conditions. They used those time and motion studies for mass production, they used strategic planning under conditions of relative stability, and so forth. Trouble was, all this advice never came together: managers were made to feel like diners at a buffet table, urged to take a little bit of this and a little bit of that.

In a way, these two approaches to organizational effectiveness are reflected in the most popular management writings of today. I like to call them Peterian and Porterian. Tom Peters and Robert Waterman implore managers to "stick to their knitting" and to design their structures with "simultaneous loose-tight properties," among other best ways, while Michael Porter insists that they use competitive analysis to choose strategic positions that best match the characteristics of their industries. To Porter, effectiveness resides in strategy, while to Peters it is the operations that count—executing any strategy with excellence.

While I agree that being effective depends on doing the right thing as well as doing things right, as Peter Drucker put it years ago, I believe we have to probe more deeply to find out what really makes an organization effective. We need to understand what gets it to a viable strategy in the first place, what makes it excellent once it's there, and how some organizations are able to sustain viability and excellence in the face of change.

Some years ago I thought I had another answer. I argued that effective organizations "got it all together." By choosing "configuration," they brought their various characteristics of structure, strategy, and context into natural coalignment. For example, some achieved integration as efficient machines, while others coalesced around product innovation. In a sense, these organizations played jigsaw puzzle, fitting all the pieces of their operations into one neat image.

Recently, however, I have begun to wonder about configuration. There are certainly many effective organizations that seem to fit one image or another—IBM as that "big blue" machine, 3M as the product innovator. But some rather effective organizations do not, and even those that do sometimes confound things. How does that big blue machine come up with critical adaptations when it has to, and why does 3M have those tight financial controls? Thus I have begun to consider another view of organizational effectiveness, in which organizations do not slot themselves into established images so much as build their own unique solutions to problems. Do Your Own Thing is its motto, LEGO its metaphor.

This article builds a framework around these two approaches. It proposes that the effective organization plays LEGO as well as jigsaw puzzle. The pieces of the game are the forces that organizations experience; the integrating images are the forms that organizations take. Together, they constitute a powerful framework by which to diagnose and deal with the problems organizations face. Below I introduce the forces, as the basic building blocks of all organizations. Then I shall outline the framework that is to follow.

A System of Forces

Much of what happens in organizations can, in my experience, be captured by the interplay of seven basic forces. I array five of these around the outside of a pentagon and put two in the middle, as shown in figure 9-3. They are described below.

- First is the force for *direction*; this gives a sense of where the organization must go as an integrated entity. Without such direction—which today is apt to be called strategic vision, years ago grand strategy—the various activities of an organization cannot easily mesh to achieve common purpose.

- Next is the force for *efficiency*, which attempts to ensure a viable ratio of benefits gained to costs incurred. Without some concern for efficiency, all but the most protected of organizations must eventually falter. Efficiency generally means standardization and formalization; often it reduces to economy. In current practice, it focuses on rationalization and restructuring, among other things.

- Across from the force for efficiency is that for *proficiency*—for carrying out certain tasks with high levels of knowledge and skill. Without proficiency, the difficult work of organizations—whether surgery in the hospital or engineering in the corporation—just could not get done.

- Below efficiency is the force for *concentration*—for particular units to concentrate their efforts on serving particular markets. Without such concentration, it becomes difficult to manage an organization that is diversified.

- At the bottom right is the force for *innovation*. Organizations need central direction and focused concentration, and they need efficiency and proficiency. But they also need to discover new things for their customers and themselves—to adapt and to learn.

- Finally, inside the pentagon are two forces I call catalytic: *cooperation* and *competition*. One describes the pulling together of ideology, the other the pulling apart of politics. By ideology, I mean more than just the culture of an organization, I mean the rich culture of norms, beliefs, and values that knit a disparate set of people into a harmonious, cooperative entity. By politics I mean behavior that is technically not sanctioned or legitimate. It acts outside the bounds of legal authority and acknowledged expertise and therefore tends to be conflictive in nature. No serious organization is ever entirely free of politics, few perhaps of at least some vestiges of ideology.

This article's view of organizational effectiveness will be developed as follows. Taking these forces as fundamental and their interplay as key to understanding what goes on in organizations, I shall argue first that when one force dominates an organization, it is drawn toward a coherent, established form, described as *configuration*. That facilitates its management, but also raises the problem of *contamination*. When no single force dominates, the organization must instead function as a balanced *combination* of different forces, including periods of *conversion* from one form to another. But combination raises the problem of *cleavage*. Both contamination and cleavage require the management of *contradiction*, and here the catalytic forces, cooperation and competition, come into play. But these two forces are themselves contradictory, and so the effective organization must balance them as well. Put this all together and you get a fascinating game of jigsaw puzzle-cum-LEGO. This may seem complicated, but bear with me; reading about it here will prove a lot easier than managing it in practice. It may even help!

FIGURE 9-3
A System of Forces in
Organizations

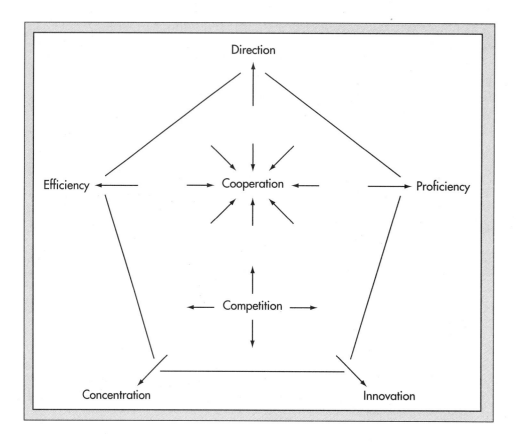

Configuration

Charles Darwin once wrote about "lumpers" as opposed to "splitters"—synthesizers who think in broad categories and prefer to slot things into well-established pigeonholes, as opposed to analyzers who tend to split things up finely. In a way, of course, we are all lumpers—we all like neat envelopes into which we can put our confusing experiences.

It is ironic, therefore, that in the field of management we do not have established categories by which to distinguish different organizations. Imagine biology without some system of species to consider living things. Biologists might well end up, for example, debating the "one best dwelling" for all mammals—bears as well as beavers. Silly as this example may seem, that is what we do in management all the time.

Configuration refers to any form of organization that is consistent and highly integrated. In the spirit of the jigsaw puzzle, a configuration is an image whose pieces all fit neatly together.

A Portfolio of Forms

In principle, all kinds of configurations are possible. In practice, however, only a few seem to occur commonly.

Our pentagon contains seven forces. I believe that configuration occurs when any one of these forces dominates an organization, driving it to a corresponding form. That gives us seven basic forms, described below, five of which are shown at the nodes of the pentagon, in figure 9-4.

- The *entrepreneurial* form tends to occur when the force for direction dominates an organization, so that the chief executive takes personal control of much of what goes on. This happens especially in startup and turnaround situations, both of which require the imposition of strong vision from the top; it also happens in small, owner-managed companies. As a result, there are few middle-management and staff positions, or else they are relatively weak. As a turnaround example, when Jan Carlzon took over the airline SAS in the early 1980s, he established direct links with the operating employees, bypassing much of the established administration and dispensing with many of the standard control systems in order to impose his new vision.

- The *machine* form tends to appear when the force for efficiency becomes paramount; this typically occurs in mass production and mass service organizations (automobile companies, retail banks, and so on) and in ones with an overriding need for control (as in nuclear power plants and many government departments). Here, especially in the larger, more mature organization, middle-management and staff functions are fully developed; they focus on regulating the work of the operating employees by imposing rules, regulations, and standards of various kinds.

- The *professional* form tends to arise when proficiency is the dominant force, as in hospitals, accounting practices, and engineering offices. What matters here is the drive to perfect existing skills and knowledge, rather than to invent new ones. This makes the professional organization a consummate pigeonholer: the hospital, for example, prefers to diagnose entering patients as quickly as possible so that it can get on with administering the most appropriate standardized treatment. This characteristic allows for the considerable autonomy found in these organizations: each professional works remarkably free of his or her colleagues, let alone of the managers ostensibly in charge.

- The *adhocracy* form develops in response to an overriding need for innovation. Again we have an organization of skilled experts. But here, because the organization exists to create novelty—such as the unique film or the new engineering prototype—the experts must combine their efforts in multidisciplinary project teams. Doing so requires a good deal of informal communication, with the result that the structure becomes fluid, sometimes called "intrapreneurial." Some adhocracy organizations, such as advertising agencies and think tank consulting firms, innovate directly on behalf of their clients. Others use project work to innovate for themselves, bringing their own new products or facilities on line— for example, some high-technology and chemical firms.

- The *diversified* form tends to arise when the force for concentration, particularly on distinct products and markets, overrides the others. Such organizations first diversify and then divisionalize. Each division is given relative autonomy, subject to the performance controls imposed by a small, central headquarters. The diversified form is, of course, best known in the world of large, conglomerate corporations. But when governments speak of accountability, they have much the same structure in mind.

- The forces for cooperation and for competition can sometimes dominate, too, giving rise to forms I call the *ideological* and the *political*. Examples of both are readily available: the spirited Israeli kibbutz is ideological, and the conflictive regulatory agency in which infighting takes over is political. But I believe these forms are not all that common, at least compared with the others discussed above, and so our discussion will proceed from here mainly on the basis of five forms and seven forces, shown in figure 9-4.

Do these forms really exist in practice? In one sense, they do not. After all, they are just words on pieces of paper, caricatures that simplify a complex reality. No serious

FIGURE 9-4
A System of Forces and
Forms in Organizations

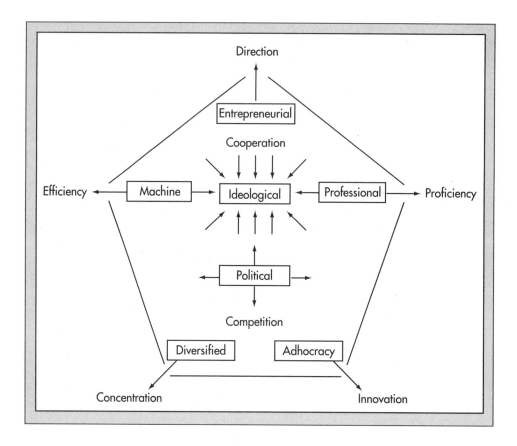

organization can be labeled a pure machine or a pure adhocracy. On the other hand, we can't carry reality around in our heads; we think in terms of simplifications, called theories or models, of which these forms are examples. We must, therefore, turn to a second question whether the forms are *useful*. And again I shall answer, yes and no.

While no configuration ever matches a real organization perfectly, some do come remarkably close; examples include the highly regulated Swiss hotel and the freewheeling Silicon Valley innovator. Just as species exist in nature in response to distinct ecological niches, so too do configurations evolve in human society. The hotel guest does not want surprises—no jack-in-the-box popping up when the pillow is lifted, thank you—just the predictability of that wake-up call at 8:00, not 8:07. But in that niche called advertising, the client that gets no surprises may well take its business elsewhere.

My basic point about configuration is simple: when the form fits, the organization may be well advised to wear it, at least for a time. With configuration, an organization achieves a sense of order, of integration. There is internal consistency, synergy among processes, fit with the external context. It is the organization without configuration, much like the individual without personality, that tends to suffer the identity crises.

Outsiders also appreciate configuration; it helps them to understand an organization. We walk into a McDonald's and know immediately what drives it, likewise a 3M. But more important is what configuration does for the managers: it makes the organization more manageable. With the course set, it is easier to steer, and also to deflect pressures that are peripheral. No configuration is perfect—the professional one, for example, tends to belittle its clients, while the machine one often alienates its workers—but there is something to be said for consistency. Closely controlled workers may not be happier than the autonomous ones of the professional organization, but they are certainly better off than ones confused by quality circles in the morning and time studies in the afternoon. Better to have the definition and discipline of configuration than to dissipate one's energies trying to be all things to all people.

Moreover, much of what we know about organizations in practice applies to specific configurations. There may not be any one best way, but there are certainly preferred ways in particular contexts—for example, time studies in machine organizations and matrix structures in adhocracies.

Thus, configuration seems to be effective for classification, for comprehension, for diagnosis, and for design. But only so long as everything holds still. Introduce the dynamics of evolutionary change and, sooner or later, configuration becomes ineffective.

Contamination by Configuration

In harmony, consistency, and fit lies configuration's great strength—and also its debilitating weakness. Experience shows that the dominant force sometimes dominates to the point of undermining all the others. For example, the quest for efficiency in a machine organization can almost totally suppress the capacity for innovation, while in an adhocracy the need for some modicum of efficiency often gets suppressed. I call this phenomenon *contamination*, although we might just as easily rephrase Lord Acton's dictum: among the forces of organizations, too, power tends to corrupt and absolute power corrupts absolutely. For example, the story of medical care in the United States could well be described as the contamination of efficiency by proficiency. No one can deny the primacy of proficiency—who would go to a hospital that favors efficiency?—but few people would defend the extent to which it has been allowed to dominate.

Machine organizations recognize this problem when they locate their research and development facilities far from the head office so that their capacity for innovation will not be contaminated by the technocratic staff. Unfortunately, while lead may block X rays, there is no known medium to shield the effects of a dominant culture. (The controller drops by, just to have a look: "What, no shoes? Can't they be creative dressed properly?") Of course, the opposite case is also well known. Just ask its members, "Who's the most miserable person in an adhocracy?" as I do in workshops with them. The inevitable reply is a brief silence followed by a few smiles, then growing laughter as everyone turns to some poor person cowering in the comer. Of course, it's the controller. Controllers may wear shoes, but that hardly helps them keep the lid on all the madness.

Contamination is another way of saying that a configuration is not merely a structure, not even merely a power system: each is a culture in its own right. Of course, contamination may seem like a small price to pay for being coherently organized. True enough. Until things go out of control.

Configuration out of Control

A configuration is geared not only to a general context but also to specific conditions—for example, a particular leader in an entrepreneurial organization, or a particular product and market in a machine one. Thus, when the need arises for change, the dominating force may act to hold the organization in place. Then other forces must come into play. But because of contamination, the other forces may well be too weak. And so the organization goes out of control. For example, a machine organization in need of a new strategy may find neither the direction of an entrepreneurial leader nor the innovation of intrapreneurial subordinates. And so its internal consistency is perpetuated while it falls increasingly out of touch with its context.

In addition, each configuration is capable of driving itself out of control. That is to say, each contains the seeds of its own destruction. These reside in its dominating force and come into play through the effects of contamination. With too much proficiency in a professional organization, unconstrained by efficiency and direction, the professionals become overindulged (as in many of today's universities, not to mention medicine); with too much technocratic regulation in a machine organization, free of the force for innovation, an obsession with control arises (as in far too much contemporary industry and government).

My colleagues, Danny Miller and Manfred Kets de Vries, have published an interesting book about The Neurotic Organization. They discuss organizations that become dramatic, paranoid, schizoid, compulsive, and depressive. In each case, a system that may once have been healthy has run out of control. Very roughly, I believe these five organizational neuroses correspond to what tends to happen to each of the five forms. The entrepreneurial organization tends to go out of control by becoming dramatic, as its leader, free of the other forces, takes the system off on a personal ego trip. The machine organization seems predisposed to compulsion once its analysts and their technocratic controls take over. Those who have worked in universities and hospitals understand the collective paranoid tendencies of professionals, especially when free of the constraining forces of administration and innovation. I need not dwell on the depressive effects of obsession with the "bottom line" in the diversified organization; the impact on morale and innovation are now widely appreciated. As for the adhocracy organization, its problem is that while it must continually innovate, it must also exploit the benefits of that innovation. One requires divergent thinking, the other convergent. Other forces help balance that tension; without them, the organization can easily become schizoid.

In effect, each form goes over the edge in its own particular way, so that behaviors that were once functional become dysfunctional when pursued to excess. Alongside excellence go the "perils of excellence." This is easily seen on our pentagon. Remove all the arrows but one at any node, and the organization, no longer anchored, flies off in that direction.

Containment of Configuration

Thus I conclude that truly effective organizations do not exist in pure form. What keeps a configuration effective is not only the dominance of a single force but also the constraining effects of other forces. I call this *containment*. For example, people inclined to break the rules may feel hard pressed in the machine organization. But without some of them, the organization may be unable to deal with unexpected problems. Similarly, administration may not be powerful in the professional organization, but if it is allowed to atrophy, anarchy inevitably results. Thus, to manage configuration effectively is to exploit one form but also to reconcile different forces. But how does the effective organization deal with this contradiction?

Combination

Configuration is a good thing when you can have it. Unfortunately, some organizations all of the time, and all organizations some of the time, *cannot*. They must instead balance competing forces.

Consider the symphony orchestra. Proficiency is clearly a critical force, but so, too, is direction: such an organization is not conceivable without highly skilled players as well as leadership from a strong conductor. The Russians apparently tried a leaderless orchestra shortly after the revolution, but soon gave it up.

I shall use the word *combination* for the organization that balances different forces. In effect, it does not make it near any one node of the pentagon but instead finds its place somewhere inside.

How common are combinations as compared with configurations? To some extent the answer lies in the eyes of the beholder: what looks like a relatively pure form to one person (a lumper) may look like a combination of forces to another (a splitter).

Kinds of Combinations

Combinations themselves may take a variety of forms. They may balance just two forces or several; these forces may meet directly or indirectly; and the balance may be steady over time or oscillate back and forth.

When only two of the five forces meet in rough balance, the organization might be described as a *hybrid*. This is the case with the symphony orchestra, which can be found somewhere along the line between the entrepreneurial and professional forms. Organizations can, of course, combine several forces in rough balance as well. Organizations that experience such multiple combinations are, of course, the ones that must really play LEGO.

Then there is the question of how the different forces interact with each other. In some cases, they confront each other directly; in others, they can be separated over time or place. The combination in the symphony orchestra must be close and pervasive— leadership and professional skill meet regularly, face-to-face. However, in organizations where different units favor different forces, they can act somewhat independently. And some organizations are lucky enough to buffer the effects of the different forces; in newspapers, the more professional editorial function simply hands over its camera-ready copy to the machinelike plant for production, and there is little need for interaction.

Finally, contrasting with the combinations maintained continuously are those that achieve balance in a dynamic equilibrium over time. In other words, power oscillates between the competing forces. Richard Cyert and James March wrote some years ago about the "sequential attention to goals" in organizations, where conflicting needs are attended to each in their own turn. For example, a period of innovation to emphasize new product development might be followed by one of consolidation to rationalize product lines.

Cleavage in Combinations

Necessary as it may sometimes be, all is not rosy in the world of combination. If configuration encourages contamination, which can drive the organization out of control, then combination encourages *cleavage*, which can have much the same effect. Instead of one force dominating, two or more forces confront each other and eventually paralyze the organization.

In effect, a natural fault line exists between any two opposing forces. Pushed to the limit, fissures begin to open up. In fact, Fellini made a film with exactly this theme. Called *Orchestra Rehearsal*, it is about musicians who revolt against their conductor, and so bring on complete anarchy, followed by paralysis. Only then are they prepared to cooperate with their leader, because only then do they realize he is necessary to perform effectively. But one need not turn to allegories to find examples of cleavage. It occurs in most combinations—for example, in the classic battles between the research and development (R&D) people, who promote new product innovation, and the production people, who want to stabilize manufacturing for operating efficiency. Cleavage can, of course, be avoided when the different forces are naturally buffered, as in the newspaper example. But few combination organizations are so fortunate.

I have discussed combination as if it is unavoidable in certain organizations, but implied that configuration is advantageous where possible, because it is more easily managed. But in reality, combination of one kind or another is necessary in every organization. The nodes of the pentagon, where the pure configurations lie, are only imaginary ideals. Indeed, any organization that reaches one is probably on its way out of control. It is the inside of the pentagon that has the space; that is where the effective organization must find its place. Some may fall close to one of the nodes, as configuration, *more or less*, while others may sit between nodes as combinations. But ultimately, configuration and combination are not so very different: one represents a tilt in favor of one force over others, the other more of a balance between forces. The question thus becomes again, How does the effective organization deal with the contradiction?

Conversion

So far our discussion has suggested that an organization finds its place in the pentagon and then stays there, more or less. But, in fact, few organizations get the chance to spend their entire lives in one place: their needs change, and they must undergo *conversion* from one configuration or combination to another.

Any number of external changes can cause such a conversion. An adhocracy organization may chance upon a great invention and settle down in machine form to exploit it. Or the stable market of a machine organization may suddenly become subject to so much change that it has to become innovative. Some conversions are, of course, temporary; the machine organization in trouble, for example, becomes entrepreneurial for a time to allow a forceful leader to impose new direction (so-called turnaround). This seems to describe Chrysler's experience when Iacocca arrived, as well as SAS's when Carlzon took over.

Cycles of Conversion

Of particular interest here is another type of conversion, which is somewhat predictable in nature because it is driven by forces intrinsic to the organization. Earlier

I discussed the seeds of destruction contained in each configuration. Sometimes they destroy the organization, but sometimes they destroy only the configuration and drive the organization toward a more viable form. For example, the entrepreneurial form is inherently vulnerable, dependent as it is on a single leader. It may work well for the young organization, but with aging and growth the need for direction may be displaced by the need for efficiency. Then conversion to the machine form becomes necessary—the power of one leader must be replaced by that of numerous administrators.

The implication is that organizations often go through stages as they develop—if they develop—possibly sequenced into life cycles. In fact, I have placed the forces and forms on the pentagon to reflect the most common of these, with the simple, earlier stages near the top and the more complex ones lower down.

What appears to be the most common life cycle, especially in business, occurs around the left side of the figure. Organizations generally begin in the entrepreneurial form, because startup requires clear direction and attracts strong leaders. As these organizations grow, many settle into the machine form to exploit increasingly established markets. But with greater growth, established markets can become saturated, which often drives the successful organization to diversify its markets and then divisionalize its structure, taking it finally to the bottom left of the pentagon.

Those organizations highly dependent on expertise, however, will instead go down the right side of the pentagon, using the professional form if their services are more standardized and the adhocracy form if they are more innovative. (Some adhocracies eventually settle down by converting to the professional form, where they can exploit certain of the skills they have developed; this happens often in the consulting business, for example.)

Ideology is shown above politics on the pentagon because it tends to be associated with the earlier stages of an organization's life, politics with the later ones. Any organization can, of course, have a strong culture, just as any can become politicized. But ideologies develop rather more easily in young organizations, especially with charismatic leadership in the entrepreneurial stage, whereas it is extremely difficult to build a strong and lasting culture in a mature organization. Politics, in contrast, typically spreads as the energy of a youthful organization dissipates and its activities become more diffuse. Moreover, ideologies tend to dissipate over time, as norms rigidify into procedures and beliefs become rules; then political activity tends to rise in its place. Typically, the old and spent organizations are the most politicized; indeed, it is often their political conflict that finally kills them.

Cleavage in Conversion

Conversions may be necessary, but that does not make them easy. Some do occur quickly, because a change is long overdue, much as a supersaturated liquid, below the freezing point, solidifies the moment it is disturbed. But most conversions require periods of prolonged and agonizing transition. Two sides battle, usually an old guard committed to the status quo and young "upstarts" in favor of the change.

The organization in transition becomes, of course, a form of combination, and it has the same problem of cleavage. Given that the challenge is to the very base of its power, however, there can be no recourse to higher authority to reconcile the conflict. Once again, then, the question arises: How does the effective organization deal with the contradiction?

Contradiction

The question of how to manage contradiction has concluded each section of this article. I believe the answer lies in the two forces in the middle of the pentagon. Organizations that have to reconcile contradictory forces, especially in dealing with change, often turn to the cooperative force of ideology or the competitive force of politics. Indeed, I believe that these two forces themselves represent a contradiction that must be managed if an organization is not to run out of control.

I have placed these two forces in the middle of the pentagon for a particular reason. While it is true that each can dominate an organization, and so draw it toward a distinct form (referred to earlier as ideological and political), I believe that these forces more commonly act differently from the other five. While the other forces tend to infiltrate parts of the organization, and so isolate them, these tend instead to *infuse* the entire organization. Thus I refer to them as *catalytic*, noting that one tends to be centripetal, drawing behavior inward toward a common core, and the other centrifugal, driving behavior away from any central tendency. I shall argue that both can promote change and also prevent it, and that either way the organization is sometimes rendered more effective, sometimes less.

Cooperation through Ideology

Ideology represents the force for cooperation in an organization, for collegiality and consensus. People pull together for the common good—"we" are in this together.

I use the word *ideology* here to describe a rich culture in an organization, the uniqueness and attractiveness of which binds the members tightly to it. They commit themselves personally to the organization and identify with its needs.

Such an ideology can infuse any form of organization. It is often found in the entrepreneurial form, because, as already noted, organizational ideologies are usually created by charismatic leaders. But after such leaders move on, these ideologies can sustain themselves in other forms too. Ideology encourages the members of an organization to look inward—to take their lead from the organization's own vision, instead of looking outward to what comparable organizations are doing. (Of course, when ideology is strong, there are no comparable organizations!)

This looking inward is represented on the pentagon by the direction of the arrows of cooperation. They form a circle facing inward, as if to shield the organization from outside influences. Ideology above all draws people to work together to take the organization where all of them believe it must go. In this sense, ideology should be thought of as the spirit of an organization, the life force that infuses the skeleton of its formal structure.

Thus the existence of an ideology would seem to render any particular configuration more effective. People get fired up to pursue efficiency, or proficiency, or whatever else drives the organization. When this happens to a machine organization—as in a McDonald's, which is very responsive to its customers and very sensitive to its employees—I like to call it a "snappy machine." Bureaucratic machines are not supposed to be snappy, but ideology changes the nature of their quest for efficiency. This, of course, is the central message of the Peters and Waterman book, In Search of Excellence: effectiveness is achieved, not by opportunism, not even by clever strategic positioning, but by a management that knows exactly what it must do ("sticks to its knitting") and then does it with the fervor of religious missionaries ("hands on, value driven").

There seems to be another important implication: ideology helps an organization to manage contradiction and so to deal with change. The different forces no longer need conflict in quite the same way. Infused with the common ideology, units used to opposing each other can instead pull together, reducing contamination and cleavage and so facilitating adaptation.

Such organizations can more easily reconcile opposing forces because what matters to their people is the organization itself, not any of its particular parts. If you believe in IBM more than marketing finesse or technical virtuosity per se, then when things really matter you will suspend your departmental rivalries to enable IBM to adapt.

In Competitive Strategy, Michael Porter warns about getting "stuck in the middle" between a strategy of "cost leadership" and one of "differentiation" (one representing the force for efficiency, the other representing quality and innovation). How, then, has Toyota been able to produce such high-quality automobiles at such reasonable cost? Why didn't Toyota get stuck in the middle?

I believe that Porter's admonition stems from the view, prevalent in U.S. management circles throughout this century and reflected equally in my discussion of configuration, that if an organization favors one particular force, then others must suffer. If the efficiency experts have the upper hand, then quality gets slighted; if the designers get their way, productive efficiency must lag; and so on. This may be true so long as an organization is managed as a collection of different parts—a portfolio of products and functions. But when the spirit of ideology infuses the structure, an organization takes on an integrated life of its own, and contradictions get reconciled.

So far I have discussed the reconciliation of contradictions between different people and units. But even more powerful can be the effect of reconciling these forces within individuals themselves. Where ideology is strong, not just the researchers are responsible for innovation, nor the accountants for efficiency; everyone internalizes the different forces in carrying out his or her own job. In metaphorical terms, it is easy to change hats if they are all emblazoned with the same insignia.

Limits to Cooperation

Overall, then, ideology sounds like a wonderful thing. But all is not rosy in the world of culture, either. For one thing, ideologies are difficult to build, especially in established organizations, and difficult to sustain once built. For another thing established ideologies can sometimes get in the way of organizational effectiveness.

The impression left by a good deal of current writing and consulting notwithstanding, ideology is not there for the taking, to be plucked off the tree of management technology like any other piece of fashionable fruit. As Karl Weick has argued, "A corporation doesn't *have* a culture. A corporation is a culture. That's why they're so horribly difficult to change." The fact is that there are no five easy steps to a better culture. At best, those steps lay down a thin veneer of impressions that wash off in the first political storm; at worst, they destroy whatever good remains in the prevailing culture. Effective ideologies are built slowly and patiently by committed leaders who establish compelling missions for their organizations, nurture them carefully, and care deeply about the people who make them work.

But even after an ideology is established, the time can come—and usually does eventually—when its effect is to render the organization ineffective, sometimes to the point of destroying it. This is suggested by Weick's comment that ideologies are "so horribly difficult to change."

I argued above that ideology promotes change by allowing an organization to reconcile contradictory forces. Now I should like to argue exactly the opposite case.

Ideology discourages change by forcing everyone to work within the same set of beliefs. In other words, strong cultures are immutable: they may promote change within their own boundaries, but they themselves are not to be changed. Receiving "the word" enables people to ask every question but one: the word itself must never be questioned.

I can explain this by introducing two views of strategy, one as position, the other as perspective. In one case, the organization looks down to specific product-market positions (as depicted in Michael Porter's work), in the other it looks up to a general philosophy of functioning (as in Peter Drucker's earlier writings about the "concept of a business"). I like to ask people in my management seminars whether Egg McMuffin was a strategic change for McDonald's. Some argue yes, of course, because it brought the firm into the breakfast market. Others dismiss this as a variation in product line— pure McDonald's, just different ingredients in a new package. Their disagreement concerns not the change at McDonald's so much as their implicit definition of strategy. To the former, strategy is position (the breakfast market), to the latter it is perspective (the McDonald's way). The important point here is that change of position *within* perspective is easy to accomplish (the McDonald's way, but now for breakfast), whereas change of perspective (a new way, that is, a new ideology) is extremely difficult. (Anyone for McDuckling à l'Orange?) The very ideology that makes an organization so adaptive within its own niche undermines efforts to move it to a different niche.

Thus, when change of a fundamental nature must be made—in strategy, structure, form, whatever—the ideology that may for so long have been the key to the organization's effectiveness suddenly becomes its central problem. Ideology becomes a force for the status quo; indeed, because those who perceive the need for change are forced to challenge it, the ideology begins to breed politics!

To understand this negative effect of ideology, take another look at figure 9-4. All those arrows face inward. The halo they form may protect the organization, but at the possible expense of isolating it from the outside world. In other words, ideology can cause the other forces to atrophy: direction comes to be interpreted in terms of an outmoded system of beliefs, forcing efficiency, proficiency, and innovation into ever-narrower corners. As the other arrows of the figure disappear, those of ideology close in on the organization, causing it to *implode*. That is how the organization dominated by the force of ideology goes out of control. It isolates itself and eventually dies. We have no need for the extreme example of a Jonestown to appreciate this negative consequence of ideology. We all know organizations with strong cultures that like that proverbial bird, flew in ever-diminishing circles until they disappeared up their own rear ends.

Competition through Politics

If the centripetal force of ideology, ostensibly so constructive, turns out to have a negative consequence, then perhaps the centrifugal force of politics, ostensibly so destructive, has a positive one.

Politics represents the force for competition within an organization—for conflict and confrontation. People pull apart for their own needs. "They" get in "our" way.

Politics can infuse any of the configurations or combinations, exacerbating contamination and cleavage. Indeed, both problems were characterized as intrinsically conflictive in the first place; the presence of politics for other reasons simply enhances them. The people behind the dominant force in a configuration—say, the accountants in a machine organization, or the experts in a professional one—lord their power over everyone else, while those behind each of the opposing forces in a hybrid relish any opportunity to do battle with each other to gain advantage. Thus, in contrast to a machinelike Toyota pulling together is the Chrysler Iaccoca first encountered, pulling apart; the ideology of an innovative Hewlett-Packard stands in contrast to the politics of a NASA during the Challenger tragedy. For every college that is distinctive, there are others that are destructive.

Politics is generally a parochial force in organizations, encouraging people to pursue their own ends. Infusing the parts of an organization with the competitive force of politics thus reinforces their tendency to fly off in different directions. At the limit, the organization dominated by politics goes out of control by *exploding*. Nothing remains at the core—no central direction, no integrating ideology, and, therefore, no directed effort at efficiency or proficiency or innovation.

In this respect, politics may be a more natural force than ideology. That is to say, organizations left alone seem to pull apart rather more easily than they pull together. Getting human beings to cooperate seems to require continual effort on the part of a dedicated management.

Benefits of Competition

But we cannot dismiss politics as merely divisive. Politics' constructive role in organizations is suggested by the very problems of ideology. If pulling together discourages people from addressing fundamental change, then pulling apart may be the only way to ensure that they do.

Most organizations have a deeply rooted status quo, reinforced especially by the forces of efficiency, proficiency, and ideology, all designed to promote development *within an established perspective*. Thus, to achieve fundamental change in an organization, especially one that has achieved configuration and, moreover, is infused with ideology, the established forces must be challenged, and that means politics. In the absence of entrepreneurial or intrapreneurial capabilities, and sometimes despite them, politics may be the only force capable of stimulating the change. The organization must, in other words, pull apart before it can pull together again. It appears to be inevitable that a great deal of the most significant change is driven not by managerial insight or specialized expertise or ideological commitment, let alone the procedures of planning, but by political challenge. I conclude that both politics and ideology can promote organizational effectiveness as well as undermine it. Ideology infused into an organization can be a force for revitalization, energizing the system and making its people more responsive. But that same ideology can also hinder fundamental change. Likewise, politics often impedes necessary change and wastes valuable resources. But political challenge may also be the only means to promote really fundamental change. Thus there remains one last contradiction to reconcile, that between ideology and politics themselves.

Combining Cooperation and Competition

The two catalytic forces of ideology and politics are themselves contradictory forces that have to be reconciled if an organization is to remain truly effective in the long run. Pulling together ideologically infuses life into an organization; pulling apart politically challenges the status quo; only by encouraging both can an organization sustain its viability. The centripetal force of ideology must contain and in turn be contained by the centrifugal force of politics. That is how an organization can keep itself from imploding or exploding—from isolating itself, on the one hand, and going off in all directions, on the other. Moreover, maintaining a balance between these two forces—in their own form of combination—can discourage the other forces from going out of control. Ideology helps secondary forces to contain a dominant one; politics encourages them to challenge it. All of this is somewhat reminiscent of that old children's game (with extended rules!): paper (ideology) covers scissors (politics) and can also help cover rocks (the force for efficiency), while scissors cut paper and can even wedge rocks out of their resting places.

Let me turn one last time to the arrows of the pentagon. Imagine first the diverging arrows of competition contained within the converging circle of cooperation. Issues are debated and people are challenged, but only within the existing culture. The two achieve an equilibrium, as in the case of the Talmudic scholars who fight furiously with each other over the interpretation of every word in their ancient books, yet close ranks to present a united front to the outside world. Is that not the very behavior we find in some of our most effective business corporations, IBM among others? Or reverse the relationship and put the arrows pulling apart outside those of the halo pulling together. Outside challenges keep a culture from closing in on itself.

Thus, I believe that only through achieving some kind of balance of these two catalytic forces can an organization maintain its effectiveness. That balance need not, however, be steady state. Quite the contrary. It should constitute a dynamic equilibrium over time, to avoid constant tension between ideology and politics. Most of the time, the cooperative pulling together of ideology, contained by a healthy internal competition, is to be preferred, so that the organization can vigorously pursue its established strategic perspective. But occasionally, when fundamental change becomes necessary, the organization has to be able to pull apart through the competitive force of politics. That seems to be the best combination of these two forces.

■ THE ICARUS PARADOX[†]

By Danny Miller

The fabled Icarus of Greek mythology is said to have flown so high, so close to the sun, that his artificial wax wings melted and he plunged to his death in the Aegean Sea. The power of Icarus's wings gave rise to the abandon that so doomed him. The paradox, of course, is that his greatest asset led to his demise. And that same paradox applies to many outstanding companies: their victories and their strengths so often seduce them into the excesses that cause their downfall. Success leads to specialization and exaggeration, to confidence and complacency, to dogma and ritual. This general tendency, its causes, and how to manage it are what this article is all about.

It is ironic that many of the most dramatically successful organizations are so prone to failure. The histories of outstanding companies demonstrate this time and again. In fact, it appears that when taken to excess the same things that drive success—focused, tried-and-true strategies; confident leadership; galvanized corporate cultures; and especially the interplay of all these elements—also cause decline. Robust, superior organizations evolve into flawed purebreds; they move from rich character to exaggerated caricature as all subtlety, all nuance, is gradually lost.

Many outstanding organizations follow such paths of deadly momentum—time-bomb trajectories of attitudes, policies, and events that lead to falling sales,

†**Source:** Reprinted from *Business Horizons*, January/February 1992. Copyright 1992 by the Foundation for the School of Business at Indiana University. Used with permission.

plummeting profits, even bankruptcy. These companies extend and amplify the strategies to which they credit their success. Productive attention to detail, for instance, turns into an obsession with minutiae; rewarding innovation escalates into gratuitous invention; and measured growth becomes unbridled expansion. In contrast, activities that were merely de-emphasized—not viewed as integral to the recipe for success—are virtually extinguished. Modest marketing deteriorates into lackluster promotion and inadequate distribution; tolerable engineering becomes shoddy design. The result: strategies become less balanced. They center more and more on a single core strength that is amplified unduly while other aspects are forgotten almost entirely.

Such changes are not limited to strategy. The heroes who shaped the winning formula gain adulation and absolute authority, while others drop to third-class citizenship. An increasingly monolithic culture impels firms to focus on an ever smaller set of considerations and to rally around a narrowing path to victory. Reporting relationships, roles, programs, decision-making processes—even target markets—come to reflect and serve the central strategy and nothing else. And policies are converted into rigid laws and rituals by avidly embraced credos and ideologies. By then, organizational learning has ceased, tunnel vision rules, and flexibility is lost.

This riches-to-rags scenario seduces some of our most acclaimed corporations; and in our research on outstanding companies we have found four principal examples of it, four very common "trajectories" of decline (see figure 9-5):

- The *focusing* trajectory takes punctilious, quality-driven *craftsmen* organizations with their masterful engineers and airtight operations, and turns them into rigidly controlled, detail-obsessed *tinkerers*—firms whose insular, technocratic monocultures alienate customers with perfect, but irrelevant, offerings.

- The *venturing* trajectory converts growth-driven, entrepreneurial *builders*—companies managed by imaginative leaders and creative planning and financial staffs—into impulsive, greedy *imperialists* who severely overtax their resources by expanding helter-skelter into businesses they know nothing about.

- The *inventing* trajectory takes *pioneers* with unexcelled R&D departments, flexible think tank operations, and state-of-the-art products, and transforms them into utopian *escapists* run by a cult of chaos-loving scientists who squander resources in the pursuit of hopelessly grand and futuristic inventions.

- Finally, the *decoupling* trajectory transforms *salesmen*—organizations with unparalleled marketing skills, prominent brand names, and broad markets into aimless, bureaucratic *drifters* whose sales fetish obscures design issues, and who produce a stale and disjointed line of "me too" offerings.

These four illustrative trajectories have trapped many of the firms we studied, including IBM, Polaroid, Procter & Gamble, Texas Instruments, ITT, Chrysler, Dome Petroleum, Apple Computer, A&P, General Motors, Sears, Digital Equipment, Caterpillar Tractor, Montgomery Ward, Eastern Airlines, Litton Industries, and Disney.

A Case History

The glorious but ultimately tragic history of ITT demonstrates well the course of the *venturing* trajectory. Harold Geneen was a manager's manager, a universally acclaimed financial wizard of unsurpassed energy, and the chief executive officer (CEO) and grand inquisitor of the diversified megaconglomerate ITT. It was Geneen, the entrepreneurial accountant, who took a ragtag set of stale, mostly European telecommunications operations and forged them into a cohesive corporate entity. With

FIGURE 9-5
The Four Trajectories

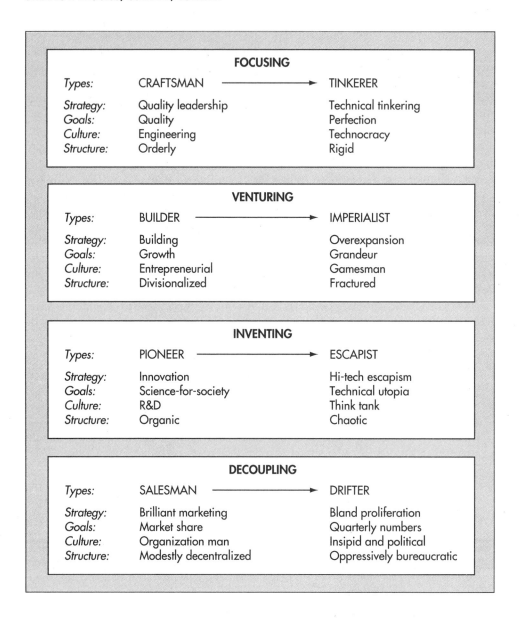

his accountant's scalpel, he weeded out weak operations; and with his entrepreneur's wand he revived the most promising ones. He installed state-of-the-art management information systems to monitor the burgeoning businesses on an ongoing basis. And he built a head office corps of young managers to help him control his growing empire and identify opportunities for creative diversification.

At first, this diversification paid off handsomely as it so aptly exploited the financial, organizational, and turnaround talents of Geneen and his crack staff. Many acquisitions were purchased at bargain prices and most beautifully complemented ITT's existing operations. Moreover, a divisional structure in which managers were responsible for the profitability of their units provided incentive for local initiative. Geneen's legendary control and information systems—with frequent appraisal meetings and divisional accountants reporting directly to the head office—ensured that most problems would be detected early and corrected.

Unfortunately, ITT's success at diversification and controlled decentralization led to too much more of the same. Their skills at acquisition and control made Geneen and his staff ever more confident that they could master complexity. So diversification went from a selective tactic to an ingrained strategy to a fanatical religion; decentralization and head office control were transformed from managerial tools into an all-consuming, lockstep way of life. The corporate *culture* worshipped growth, and it celebrated, lavishly paid, and quickly promoted only those who could attain it. The venturing trajectory had gotten under way, and the momentum behind it was awesome.

Loads of debt had to be issued to fund the acquisitions. In less than ten years, Geneen the imperialist bought a staggering 100 companies, a proliferation so vast it exceeded the complexity and scope of many nation-states—250 profit centers in all were set up. Geneen, quite simply, had created the biggest conglomerate on earth, encompassing 375,000 employees in eighty countries by 1977.

Even Geneen and his sophisticated staff troops, with all their mastery of detail and their status as information system gurus, could not manage, control, or even understand so vast an empire. But they tried, meddling in the details of their divisions, and pressing home the need to meet abstract and often irrelevant financial standards. Political games took place in which head office controllers would try to impress Geneen by making the divisions look bad. Divisional executives, in turn, would try to fool the controllers. It got to where more than 75 percent of divisional managers' schedules were taken up preparing budgets and going to meetings at the head office, leaving them little time to direct their own units.

This obsession with acquisitions and financial control detracted from the substance of divisional strategies. The product lines of many units were neglected and became stale. Return on capital fell, and by the late 1970s many of the divisions were experiencing major operating problems. A subsequent CEO, Rand Araskog, had to sell off more than 100 units in an attempt to revive the company, which shrunk the workforce by more than 60 percent. The great ITT had become a flabby agglomeration of gangrenous parts.

The general pattern is clear. Over time, ITT's success—or more specifically, its manager's reactions to success—caused it to amplify its winning strategy and to forget about everything else. It moved from sensible and measured expansion to prolific and groundless diversification; from sound accounting and financial control to oppressive dominance by head office hit men; and from invigorating divisionalization to destructive factionalism. The substance of basic businesses—their product lines and markets—was lost in a sea of financial abstractions. By concentrating exclusively on what it did best, ITT pushed strategies, cultures, and structures to dangerous extremes, and failed to develop in other areas. Greatness had paved the way to excess and decline as ITT the builder became ITT the imperialist.

Configuration and Momentum

The example of ITT reveals two notions that surfaced again and again when we looked at outstanding companies. We call these notions *configuration* and *momentum*.

Outstanding corporations are a bit like beautiful poems or sonatas—their parts or elements fit together harmoniously to express a theme. They are perhaps even more akin to living systems whose organs are intimately linked and tightly coordinated. Although organizations are less unified than organisms, they too constitute *configurations*: complex, evolving systems of mutually supportive elements organized around stable central themes. We found that once a theme emerges—a core mission or a central strategy, for example—a whole slew of routines, policies, tasks, and structures develop to implement and reinforce it. It is like seeding a crystal in a supersaturated solution: once a thematic particle is dropped into solution, the crystal begins to form naturally around it. Themes may derive from leaders' visions, the values and concerns of powerful departments, even common industry practices.

ITT's configuration, like all others, had a central theme and a "cast of players"—human, ideological, strategic, and structural—that completed the scenario. The theme was "rapid growth through expansion"; the cast of players included an entrepreneurial, ambitious CEO with a strategy of diversification and acquisition, a powerful financial staff who dominated because they could best implement this strategy, elaborate information systems and sophisticated controls, and even decentralized profit centers that infused expertise into the far-flung divisions amassed by diversification. All these "players" complemented each other and were essential to the enactment of the play. And as with all configurations, the parts only make sense with reference to the whole builder constellation.

Our research uncovered a number of exceptionally common but quite different configurations associated with stellar performance: builders, craftsmen, pioneers, and salesmen, each subject to its own evolutionary trajectory.

Our second finding showed that organizations keep extending their themes and configurations until something earthshaking stops them: a process we call *momentum*. Firms perpetuate and amplify one particular motif above all others as they suppress its variants. They choose one set of goals, values, and champions and focus more and more tightly around them. The powerful get more powerful; others become disenfranchised as firms move first toward consistency, and then toward obsession and excess. Organizations turn into their "evil twins"—extreme versions or caricatures of their former selves.

Once ITT began to diversify, for example, it accelerated its policy because it seemed successful; because it was very much in line with the dreams and visions of what leaders and their powerful financial staffs wanted; and because it was undergirded by a vast set of policies and programs. Similarly, having implemented their financial control systems, ITT continued to hone and develop them. After all, these systems were demanded by the expanding and diverse operations; they were favored by the growing staff of accountants; and they were the only way top managers could exert control over existing operations and still have time to scout out new acquisitions.

Momentum is also contagious and leads to a vicious cycle of escalation. As diversification increased at ITT, so did the size of the head office staff and the time spent on divisional meetings. The staff's role was to generate still more attractive candidates for diversification, and that's what they did. Diversification increased still further, requiring even larger legions of accountants and financial staff. And so the spiral continued. In short, momentum, by extending the builder configuration, led to the dangerous excesses of imperialism.

Outstanding organizations, it seems, extend their orientations until they reach dangerous extremes; their momentum issues in common trajectories of decline. And because successful types differ so much from one another, so will their trajectories.

The Trajectories

Our four trajectories emerged in a study we conducted of outstanding companies. Craftsmen, builders, pioneers, and salesmen were all susceptible to their own

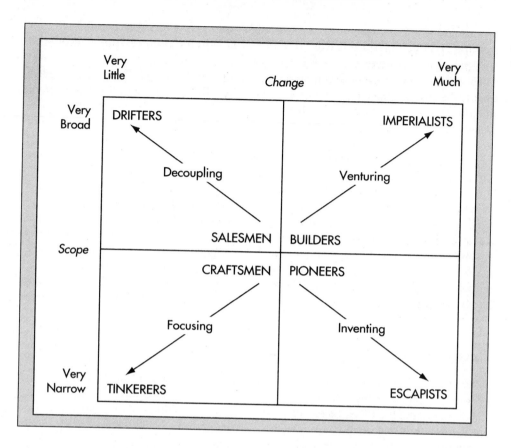

FIGURE 9-6
The Configurations and Trajectories Arrayed

trajectories, and firms of a given type followed remarkably parallel paths, albeit at differing speeds. For purposes of simple comparison, our four strategies are classified in figure 9-6 along two dimensions: *scope* is the range of products and target markets; *change* is the variability of methods and offerings. Excellent businesses are driven toward extremes along both of these dimensions (among others). Take scope. Firms that excel by focusing on one product or on a precisely targeted market ultimately come to rely on too narrow a set of customers, products, and issues. Conversely, firms that thrive by aggressively diversifying often become too complex, fragmented, and thinly spread to be effective. The same tendencies apply to strategic change as dynamic firms move toward hyperactivity, and conservative ones inch toward stagnation.

Craftsmen to Tinkerers: The Focusing Trajectory

Digital Equipment Corporation made the highest quality computers in the world. Founder Ken Olsen and his brilliant team of design engineers invented the minicomputer, a cheaper, more flexible alternative to its mainframe cousins. Olsen and his staff honed their minis until they absolutely could not be beat for quality and durability. Their VAX series gave birth to an industry legend in reliability, and the profits poured in.

But DEC turned into an engineering monoculture. Its engineers became idols, while its marketers and accountants were barely tolerated. Component specs and design standards were all managers understood. In fact, technological fine-tuning became such an all-consuming obsession that customers' needs for smaller machines, more economical products, and more user-friendly systems were ignored. The DEC PC, for example, bombed because it was so out of sync with the budgets, preferences, and shopping habits of potential users. Performance began to slip.

Craftsmen are passionate about doing one thing incredibly well: Their leaders insist on producing the best products for the market, their engineers lose sleep over micrometers, and their quality control staff rules with an iron and unforgiving hand. Details count. Quality is the primary source of corporate pride; it gets rewarded and recognized and is by far the paramount competitive advantage. Indeed, it is what the whole corporate culture is based on. Shoddiness is a capital offense. (There is also a cost leader variant of the craftsman).

But in becoming *tinkerers*, many craftsmen become parodies of themselves. They get so wrapped up in tiny technical details that they forget the purpose of quality is to attract and satisfy buyers. Products become overengineered but also overpriced; durable, but stale. Yesterday's excellent designs become today's sacrosanct anachronisms. And an ascendent engineering monoculture so engrosses itself in the minutiae of design and manufacture that it loses sight of the customer. Before long, marketing and R&D become the dull stepchildren, departments to be seen but not heard. Unfortunately, the bureaucratic strictures that grew up to enforce quality end up perpetuating the past and suppressing initiative.

Builders to Imperialists: The Venturing Trajectory

Charles "Tex" Thornton was a young Texas entrepreneur when he expanded a tiny microwave company into Litton Industries, one of the most successful high-technology conglomerates of the 1960s. Sales mushroomed from $3 million to $1.8 billion in twelve years. By making selective and related acquisitions, Litton achieved an explosive rate of growth. Its excellent track record helped the company amass the resources needed to accelerate expansion still further.

But Litton began to stray too far from familiar areas, buying larger and more troubled firms in industries it barely understood. Administrative officers and control systems became overtaxed, debt became unwieldy, and a wide range of problems sprang up in the proliferating divisions. The downward spiral at Litton was no less dramatic than its ascent.

Builders are growth driven, entrepreneurial companies with a zeal for expansion, merger, and acquisition. They are dominated by aggressive managers with ambitious goals, immense energy, and an uncanny knack for spotting lucrative niches of the market. These leaders have the promotional skills to raise capital, the imagination and initiative to exploit magnificent growth opportunities, and the courage to take substantial risks. They are also master controllers who craft acute, sensitive information and incentive systems to rein in their burgeoning operations.

But many builders become *imperialists*, addicted to careless expansion and greedy acquisition. In the headlong rush for growth they assume hair-raising risks, decimate resources, and incur scads of debt. They bite off more than they can chew, buying sick companies in businesses they do not understand. Structures and control systems become hopelessly overburdened. And a dominant culture of financial, legal, and accounting specialists further rivets managerial attention on expansion and diversification, while stealing time away from the production, marketing, and R&D matters that so desperately need to be addressed.

Pioneers to Escapists: The Inventing Trajectory

By the mid-1960s, Control Data Corporation of Minneapolis had become the paramount designer of supercomputers. Chief engineer Seymour Cray, the preeminent genius in a field of masters, had several times fulfilled his ambition to build the world's most powerful computer. He secluded himself in his lab in Chippewa Falls, working closely with a small and trusted band of brilliant designers. Cray's state-of-the-art 6600 supercomputer was so advanced it caused wholesale firing at IBM, whose engineers had been taken completely off guard by their diminutive competitor.

CDC's early successes emboldened it to undertake new computer development projects that were increasingly futuristic, complex, and expensive. Substantial lead times, major investments, and high risks were entailed, and many bugs had to be purged from the systems. Long delays in delivery occurred and costs mushroomed. Science and invention had triumphed over an understanding of competition, customers, and production and capital requirements.

Pioneers are R&D stars. Their chief goal is to be the first out with new products and new technology. Consistently at the vanguard of their industry, pioneers are, above all, inventors. Their major strengths are the scientific and technological capacities that reside within their brilliant R&D departments. Typically, pioneers are run by missionary leaders-in-lab-coats: PhDs with a desire to change the world. These executives assemble and empower superb research and design teams, and create a fertile, flexible structure for them to work in that promotes intensive collaboration and the free play of ideas.

Unfortunately, many pioneers get carried away by their coups of invention and become *escapists*—firms in hot pursuit of technological nirvana. They introduce impractical, futuristic products that are too far ahead of their time, too expensive to develop, and too costly to buy. They also become their own toughest competitors, antiquating prematurely many of their offerings. Worse, marketing and production come to be viewed as necessary evils, and clients as unsophisticated nuisances. Escapists, it seems, become victims of a utopian culture forged by their domineering R&D *wunderkinder*. Their goals, which soar to hopelessly lofty heights, are expressed in technological terms, rather than market or economic terms. And their loose "adhocracy" structures might suffice to organize a few engineers working in a basement, but only serve to breed chaos in complex organizations.

Salesmen to Drifters: The Decoupling Trajectory

Lynn Townsend ascended to the presidency of Chrysler at the youthful age of 42. He was known to be a financial wizard and a master marketer. "Sales aren't just made; sales are pushed," Townsend would say. In his first five years as president, he doubled Chrysler's U.S. market share and tripled its international one. He also conceived the five-year, fifty thousand-mile warranty. But Townsend made very few radical changes in Chrysler's products. Mostly he just marketed aggressively with forceful selling and promotion, and sporty styling.

Chrysler's success with its image-over-substance strategy resulted in increasing neglect of engineering and production. It prompted a proliferation of new models that could capitalize on the marketing program. But this made operations very complex and uneconomical. It also contributed to remote management-by-numbers, bureaucracy, and turf battles. Soon strategies lost focus and direction, and profits began to plummet.

Salesmen are marketers par excellence. That is their core strength. Using intensive advertising, attractive styling and packaging, attentive service, and penetrating distribution channels, they create and nurture high-profile brand names that make them major players within their industries. To place managers in especially close contact with their broad markets, salesmen are partitioned into manageable profit centers, each one of which is responsible for a major product line.

Unfortunately, salesmen tend to become unresponsive *drifters*. They begin to substitute packaging, advertising, and aggressive distribution for good design and competent manufacturing. Managers begin to believe they can sell anything as they concoct a mushrooming proliferation of bland, copycat offerings. This growing diversity of product lines and divisions makes it tough for top managers to master the substance of all their businesses. So they rely increasingly on elaborate bureaucracy to replace the hands-on management of products and manufacturing. Gradually drifters become unwieldy, sluggish behemoths whose turf battles and factionalism impede adaptation. In scenarios that come straight from Kafka, the simplest problems take months, even years to address. Ultimately, the leader is decoupled from his company, the company from its market, and product lines and divisions from each other.

Forces to Watch

In considering these four trajectories, you might want to keep in mind some of the "subtexts": the hidden causes at work behind the scenes that drive every one of them.

Sources of Momentum

Leadership Traps.   Failure teaches leaders valuable lessons, but good results only reinforce their preconceptions and tether them more firmly to their tried-and-true recipes. Success also makes managers overconfident, more prone to excess and neglect, and more given to shaping strategies to reflect their own preferences rather than those of the customers. Some leaders may even be *spoiled* by success—taking too much to heart their litany of conquests and the praise of their idolizing subordinates. They become conceited and obstinate, resenting challenges and ultimately isolating themselves from reality.

Monolithic Cultures and Skills.   The culture of the exceptional organization often becomes dominated by a few star departments and their ideologies. For example, because craftsmen see quality as the source of success, the engineering departments who create it and are its guarantors acquire ever more influence. This erodes the prominence of other departments and concerns, making the corporate culture more monolithic, more intolerant, and more avid in its pursuit of one single goal.

To make matters worse, attractive rewards pull talented managers toward rich, dominant departments, and bleed them away from less august units. The organization's skill set soon becomes spotty and unbalanced, compromising versatility and the capacity for reorientation.

Power and Politics.   Dominant managers and departments resist redirecting the strategies and policies that have given them so much power. Change, they reason, would erode their status, their resources, and their influence over rival executives and departments. The powerful, then, are more likely to reinforce and amplify prevailing strategies than to change them.

Structural Memories. Organizations, like people, have memories. They implement successful strategies using systems, routines, and programs. The more established and successful the strategy, the more deeply embedded it will be in such programs, and the more it will be implemented routinely, automatically, and unquestioningly. Indeed, even the premises for decision making—the cues that elicit attention and the standards used to evaluate events and actions—will be controlled by routines. Yesterday's programs will shape today's perceptions and give rise to tomorrow's actions. Again, continuity triumphs.

Configuration and Momentum

The qualities of leadership, culture, skills, power, and structure are by no means independent. They configure and interact to play out a central theme. Over time, organizations gradually adhere more consistently to that theme—so much so that an adaptable, intelligent company can turn into a specialized, monolithic machine.

Take the pioneer. Successful innovations reward and empower their creators, who will recruit and promote in their own images. The resulting horde of "R&D types" then set up the flexible structures and design projects they find so invigorating. This further encourages innovation and the search for clients who value it. Meanwhile, other departments begin to lose influence and resources, and their skills diminish. So cultures become monolithic, strategies more focused, skills more uneven and specialized, and blind spots more common. The firm has embarked on the inventory trajectory.

"Chain reactions" such as this make an organization more focused and cohesive. At first, this greatly benefits the firm. But ultimately, concentration becomes obsession. All prominent features become exaggerated, while everything else—auxiliary skills, supplementary values, essential substrategies, and constructive debate—vanishes.

The Paradox of Icarus

This brings us to the Icarus paradox that traps so many outstanding firms: Overconfident, complacent executives extend the very factors that contributed to success to the point where they cause decline. There are really two aspects to the paradox. The first is that *success can lead to failure*. It may engender overconfidence, carelessness, and other bad habits that produce excesses in strategies, leadership, culture, and structures. Icarus flew so well that he got cocky and overambitious.

The second aspect of the paradox is that many of the preceding causes of decline—galvanized cultures, efficient routines and programs, and orchestrated configurations—were also initially the causes of success. Or conversely, *the very causes of success, when extended, may become the causes of failure*. It is simply a case of "too much of a good thing." Unfortunately, it is very hard sometimes to distinguish between the focus, harmony, and passionate dedication necessary for outstanding performance, and the excesses and extremes that lead to decline.

Combating the Perils of Success

It is time now to turn from problems to cures—to suggest ways of avoiding the trajectories, of fending off the myopia induced by cohesive configurations. We will describe the "mirrors" managers can develop: the capacities for self-reflection and intelligence gathering that may help guard against excess and irrelevance.

Managers must confront a poignant paradox: Excellence demands focus, dedication, and cohesive configuration. But these are precisely the things that give rise to momentum, narrowness, complacency, and excess. So what to do?

Some successful organizations have adopted a few potentially powerful methods for avoiding problems. They

- build thematic, cohesive configurations;
- encourage their managers to reflect broadly and deeply about the direction of the company—in other words, they act telescopically, but reflect using mirrors;
- scan widely and monitor performance assiduously;
- where possible, temporarily decouple renewal activities from established operations, at least for a while.

Thematic Configurations

It is tempting to use the sources of momentum discussed above to derive the prescriptions for avoidance. Are worldviews too confining? Then dismantle them. Are cultures too monolithic? Then open them up. Are configurations too cohesive to allow meaningful adaptation? Then throw them into question, inject noise into the system, and make disruptive changes. Unfortunately, employing these remedies too freely might destroy the concentration and synergy so necessary for success.

In humans, greatness demands dedication and focus—a "living on the edge" quality. Prodigies in the arts are not known for their well-rounded lives. Brilliant scientists and entrepreneurs give up much of their family life. And superb college athletes are too preoccupied with training to excel at their studies. To do anything really well requires giving some things up. Because there is within us all only so much talent and energy, it must be focused for maximum effect.

The same logic holds for organizations. Concentration and synergy—not middle-of-the-road flexibility—are the hallmarks of greatness. Successful organizations zealously align their strategies, structures, and cultures around a central theme to create powerful, cohesive, brilliantly orchestrated configurations.

Conversely, middle-of-the-road strategies may be anathema to competitive advantage—the jack-of-all-trades is too often master of none. The same is true of culture and structure. Equality among marketing, production, and R&D departments might slow down decision making and prevent a coherent strategic theme from emerging. Similarly, organizational cultures that nurture too many dissidents might be stymied by conflict.

Managers, therefore, should reap the benefits of a well-tuned configuration without regret. They should take care not to kill their competitive edge by prematurely watering things down, introducing too much noise into the system, or permitting too many discordant practices.

I wish to amend Peters and Waterman's thesis: It is not just the pieces of a configuration—closeness to customers, innovation, high quality, differentiated products, loose-tight structures, or skunk works—that create excellence. Stardom is attained also *through* configuration, the way the pieces fit together—their complementarity, their organization. To achieve success—*form* or configuration must animate and orchestrate the *substance* of individual elements.

Liberating Self-Reflection

Unfortunately, configuration and synergy are usually attained at the cost of myopia. Stellar performers view the world through narrowing telescopes. One point of view takes over; one set of assumptions comes to dominate. The result is complacency and overconfidence.

The only way to avoid myopia and the resulting excesses of the trajectories is for managers to reflect on their own basic assumptions about customers, competitors, and what they deem good or bad about strategy, structure, and culture. They must search for the underlying values, presumptions, and attributions that drive their organization. Only after they become conscious of the various inbred premises for action can they begin to question them.

Gathering Information

Self-knowledge cannot be attained in a vacuum. Many of the best sources of such knowledge can be found outside the organization. To discover whether momentum is driving organizations toward dangerous excesses, managers must test their assumptions against reality—against evolving customer needs, new technologies, and competitive threats.

The whole point of gathering information is to create uneasiness, to combat complacency. Information must serve as the clarion call that awakens a somnolent system, the brakes that slow down a runaway trajectory. Combined with self-knowledge, it can prevent many of the excesses that have plagued our firms. What follows are some general maxims for corporate information gathering, written in the more lively prescriptive tone.

Dedication and Commitment. Information gathering should not be viewed as a routine accounting function; it is the sentinel that guards the fort. Gather and analyze information as if your company's life depends on it. It often does.

Counterintuitive Scanning. Look for trends in soft data you *do not* normally think are of central importance, then try to interpret them in a manner least favorable to the company. For example, salesmen should supplement the sales and market reports to which they are so addicted with indicators of product quality and manufacturing efficiency.

Getting Through to the Top. Make sure information goes to the powerful and is gathered by the bold. Don't ever shoot a messenger. Get people at high levels involved in the collection and analysis of information. Keep the game honest and reliable by using multiple sources of information.

Sources of Good Information: Operations. If you are a senior manager in particular, make sure you tour your operations. You could pretend to be a customer or try to buy your own products or services incognito. Talk to lots of employees at all levels. Get your teenage nephew hired and listen to his reports. Find out what people in plants, warehouses, and branches are saying. Peters and Austin call this "management by wandering around" (MBWA). It keeps managers in touch with "the first vibrations of the new."

Sources of Good Information: Customers.   Visit customers and have them visit you. Work on some projects together, and benefit from their free advice.

Sources of Good Information: Competitors.   Find out how the firm stacks up against its competitors in the minds of industry financial analysts. Buy and benchmark rivals' products. Determine what customers think of the competition's offerings and what new products your rivals are introducing.

Sources of Good Information: Performance Trends.   A static statistic tells us much less than a trend, so monitor everything over time. Plot graphs of information so that trends become apparent.

Going Beyond the Formal Information System.   Things change, but formal information systems reflect only the kind of news—mostly quantitative—that was important yesterday. Many acute challenges will not be captured. So use these systems creatively and go beyond them.

Pattern Recognition.   Use your ability to recognize patterns to discover what the mountain of data is saying. Are ominous trends developing that have a common and dangerous cause? Are symptoms intensifying? Is there a vicious cycle that explains this? Ask which configuration is emerging, which trajectory applies. Generate questions that would complete the picture and gather new data accordingly.

Enlist managers from the different functions in these tasks of probing and interpretation. Meet with them regularly, not to plug numbers into a pro forma budget, but solely to spot important threats and opportunities. This is the only way of finding out when it is time to change. No bells will ring when that happens. There are no hard-and-fast rules. It is all a matter of judgment. The only imperative is that all leaders must operate with the firm assumption that one day they will have to go to war with the past.

Learning and Innovating at the Boundaries

Concentrated, orchestrated configurations produce wonderful results but can slow learning and renewal. One way for a large organization to have its cake and eat it too is to establish small independent units to experiment and do new things outside of—that is, without disturbing—the configuration of existing operations. Firms might, for example, set up small-scale development teams that have the flexibility to get things done quickly and economically. Companies such as 3M give such teams much independence but limited resources, killing projects that remain unsuccessful after five years or so. Hewlett-Packard's small, agile teams collectively introduced products at the rate of eight per week in the mid-1980s. Some items went from conception to debugged prototype in just seventeen weeks.

Many Japanese companies also use such small development teams to increase the number of new product experiments. These teams always work outside the normal structure. They are populated by Young Turks with tremendous energy (the average age at Honda was twenty-seven), and are fast tracks for advancement. Most teams fail, but the ones that succeed go on to become very significant business units.

Conclusions

In his monumental *A Study of History*, Arnold Toynbee has painstakingly traced the rise and fall of twenty-one civilizations. All of these once great cultures, except perhaps our own, have collapsed or stagnated. Toynbee argued that their declines came not from natural disasters or barbarian invasions, but from internal rigidity, complacency, and oppression. He saw that some of the very institutions and practices responsible for ascendence ultimately evolved into the perverse idolatries that caused decline: "When the road to destruction has perforce to be trodden on the quest of life, it is perhaps no wonder that the quest should often end in disaster."

Organizations, too, are built into greatness and then launched toward decline by similar factors: focused strategies, galvanized cultures, specialized skills, efficient programs, and the harmonious configuration of all these things. When used with intelligence and sensitivity, these factors can make for tremendous success. But when taken to extremes, they spawn disaster. Ironically, success itself often induces the myopia and carelessness that lead to such excesses. Managers of thriving organizations must forever remain alert to such "perils of excellence."

◼ STRATEGY AS ORDER EMERGING FROM CHAOS†

By Ralph Stacey

Chaos and Self-Organization in Business

There are four important points to make on the recent discoveries about the complex behaviour of dynamic systems, all of which have direct application to human organizations.

Chaos Is a Form of Instability Where the Specific Long-Term Future Is Unknowable

Chaos in its scientific sense is an irregular pattern of behaviour generated by well-defined nonlinear feedback rules commonly found in nature and human society. When systems driven by such rules operate away from equilibrium, they are highly sensitive to selected tiny changes in their environments, amplifying them into self-reinforcing virtuous and vicious circles that completely alter the behaviour of the system. In other words, the system's future unfolds in a manner dependent upon the precise detail of what it does, what the systems constituting its environments do, and upon chance. As a result of this fundamental property of the system itself, specific links between cause and effect are lost in the history of its development, and the specific path of its long-term future development is completely unpredictable. Over the short term, however, it is possible to predict behaviour because it takes time for the consequences of small changes to build up.

†**Source:** Reprinted with permission from *Long Range Planning*, Vol. 26, No. 1, "Strategy as Order Emerging from Chaos," pp. 10–17. © 1993, Pergamon Press Ltd. Oxford, England.

Is there evidence of chaos in business systems? We would conclude that there was if we could point to small changes escalating into large consequences; if we could point to self-reinforcing vicious and virtuous circles; if we could point to feedback that alternates between the amplifying and the damping. It is not difficult to find such evidence.

Creative managers seize on small differences in customer requirements and perceptions to build significant differentiators for their products. Customers may respond to this by switching from other product offerings, leading to a virtuous circle; or they may switch away, causing the kind of vicious circle that Coca-Cola found itself caught up in when it made that famous soft drink slightly sweeter.

Managers create, or at the very least shape, the requirements of their customers through the product offerings they make. Sony created a requirement for personal hi-fi systems through its Walkman offering, and manufacturers and operators have created requirements for portable telephones. Sony and Matsushita created the requirement for video recorders, and when companies supply information systems to their clients, they rarely do so according to a complete specification—instead, the supplier shapes the requirement. When managers intentionally shape customer demands through the offerings they make, this feeds back into customer responses, and managers may increase the impact by intentionally using the copying and spreading effects through which responses to product offerings feed back into other customers' responses. When managers do this, they are deliberately using positive feedback—along with negative feedback controls to meet cost and quality targets, for example—to create business success.

A successful business is also affected by many amplifying feedback processes that are outside the control of its managers and produce effects that they did not intend. Successful businesses are quite clearly characterized by feedback processes that flip between the negative and the positive, the damping and the amplifying; that is, they are characterized by feedback patterns that produce chaos. The long-term future of a creative organization is absolutely unknowable, and no one can intend its future direction over the long term or be in control of it. In such a system long-term plans and visions of future states can be only illusions.

But in Chaos There Are Boundaries Around the Instability

While chaos means disorder and randomness in the behaviour of a system at the specific level, it also means that there is a qualitative pattern at a general, overall level. The future unfolds unpredictably, but it always does so according to recognizable familylike resemblances. This is what we mean when we say that history repeats itself, but never in the same way. We see this combination of unpredictable specific behaviour within an overall pattern in snowflakes. As two nearby snowflakes fall to the earth, they experience tiny differences in temperature and air impurities. Each snowflake amplifies those differences as they form, and by the time they reach the earth they have different shapes—but they are still clearly snowflakes. We cannot predict the shape of each snowflake, but we can predict that they will be snowflakes. In business, we recognize patterns of boom and recession, but each time they are different in specific terms, defying all attempts to predict them.

Chaos is unpredictable variety within recognizable categories defined by irregular features, that is, an inseparable intertwining of order and disorder. It is this property of being bounded by recognizable qualitative patterns that makes it possible for humans to cope with chaos. Numerous tests have shown that our memories do not normally store information in units representing the precise characteristics of the individual shapes or events we perceive. Instead, we store information about the strength of connection between individual units perceived. We combine information together into categories or concepts using family resemblance-type features. Memory emphasizes general structure, irregular category features, rather than specific content. We remember the irregular patterns rather than the specific features and we design our next actions on the basis of these memorized patterns. And since we design our actions in this manner, chaotic behaviour presents us with no real problem. Furthermore, we are adept at using analogical reasoning and intuition to reflect upon experience and adapt it to new situations, all of which is ideally suited to handling chaos.

Unpredictable New Order Can Emerge from Chaos through a Process of Spontaneous Self-Organization

When nonlinear feedback systems in nature are pushed far from equilibrium into chaos, they are capable of creating a complex new order. For example, at some low temperature the atoms of a particular gas are arranged in a particular pattern and the gas emits no light. Then, as heat is applied, it agitates the atoms causing them to move, and as this movement is amplified through the gas it emits a dull glow. Small changes in heat are thus amplified, causing instability, or chaos, that breaks the symmetry of the atoms' original behaviour. Then at a critical point, the atoms in the gas suddenly all point in the same direction to produce a laser beam. Thus, the system uses chaos to shatter old patterns of behaviour, creating the opportunity for the new. And as the system proceeds through chaos, it is confronted with critical points where it, so to speak, makes a choice between different options for further development. Some options represent yet further chaos and others lead to more complex forms of orderly behaviour, but which will occur is inherently unpredictable. The choice itself is made by spontaneous self-organization amongst the components of the system in which they, in effect, communicate with each other, reach a consensus, and commit to a new form of behaviour. If a more complex form of orderly behaviour is reached, it has what scientists call a dissipative structure, because continual attention and energy must be applied if it is to be sustained—for example, heat has to be continually pumped into the gas if the laser beam is to continue. If the system is to develop further, then the dissipative structure must be short-lived; to reach an even more complex state, the system will have to pass through chaos once more.

It is striking how similar the process of dealing with strategic issues in an organization is to the self-organizing phenomenon just outlined. The key to the effectiveness with which organizations change and develop new strategic directions lies in the manner in which managers handle what might be called their strategic issue agenda. That agenda is a dynamic, unwritten list of issues, aspirations, and challenges that key groups of managers are attending to. Consider the steps managers can be observed to follow as they handle their strategic issue agenda:

■ *Detecting and selecting small disturbances.* In open-ended strategic situations, change is typically the result of many small events and actions that are unclear, ambiguous, and confusing, with consequences that are unknowable. The key difficulty is to identify what the real issues, problems, or opportunities are, and the challenge is to find an appropriate and creative aspiration or objective. In these circumstances the organization has no alternative but to rely on the initiative of individuals to notice and pursue some issue, aspiration, or challenge. In order to do this, those individuals have to rely on their experience-based intuition and ability to detect analogies between one set of ambiguous circumstances and another.

■ *Amplifying the issues and building political support.* Once some individual detects some potential issue, that individual begins to push for organizational attention to it. A complex political process of building special interest groups to support an issue is required before it gains organizational attention and can thus be said to be on the strategic issue agenda.

■ *Breaking symmetries.* As they build and progress strategic issue agendas, managers are in effect altering old mental models, existing company and industry recipes, to come up with new ways of doing things. They are destroying existing perceptions and structures.

■ *Critical points and unpredictable outcomes.* Some issues on the agenda may be dealt with quickly, while others may attract attention, continuous or periodic, for a very long time. How quickly an issue is dealt with depends upon the time required to reach enough consensus and commitment to proceed to action. At some critical point, an external or internal pressure in effect forces a choice. The outcome on whether and how to proceed to action over the issue is unpredictable because it depends upon the context of power, personality, and group dynamic within which it is being handled. The result may or may not be action, and action will usually be experimental at first.

■ *Changing the frame of reference.* Managers in a business come to share memories of what worked and what did not work in the past—the organizational memory. In this way they build up a business philosophy, or culture, establishing a company recipe and in common with their rivals an industry recipe too. These recipes have a powerful effect on what issues will subsequently be detected and attended to; that is, they constitute a frame of reference within which managers interpret what to do next. The frame of reference has to be continually challenged and changed because it can easily become inappropriate to new circumstances. The dissipative structure of consensus and commitment is therefore necessarily short-lived if an organization is to be innovative.

These phases constitute a political and learning process through which managers deal with strategic issues, and the key point about these processes is that they are spontaneous and self-organizing: no central authority can direct anyone to detect and select an open-ended issue for attention, simply because no one knows what it is until someone has detected it; no one can centrally organize the factions that form around specific issues; nor can anyone intend the destruction of old recipes and the substitution of new ones since it is impossible to know what the appropriate new ones are until they are discovered. The development of new strategic direction requires the chaos of contention and conflict, and the self-organizing processes of political interaction and complex learning.

Chaos Is a Fundamental Property of Nonlinear Feedback Systems, a Category That Includes Human Organizations

Feedback simply means that one action or event feeds into another; that is, one action or event determines the next according to some relationship. For example, one firm repackages its product and its rival responds in some way, leading to a further action on the part of the first, provoking in turn yet another response from the second, and so on. The feedback relationship may be linear, or proportional, and when this is the case, the first firm will repackage its product and the second will respond by doing much the same. The feedback relationship could be nonlinear, or nonproportional, however, so that when the first firm repackages its product, the second introduces a new product at a lower price; this could lead the first to cut prices even further, so touching off a price war. In other words, nonlinear systems are those that use amplifying (positive) feedback in some way. To see the significance of positive feedback, compare it with negative feedback.

All effective businesses use negative or damping feedback systems to control and regulate their day-to-day activities. Managers fix short-term targets for profits and then prepare annual plans or budgets, setting out the time path to reach the target. As the business moves through time, outcomes are measured and compared with annual plan projections to yield variances. Frequent monitoring of those variances prompts corrective action to bring performance indicators back onto their planned paths; that is, variances feed back into corrective action and the feedback takes a negative form, so that when profit is below target, for example, offsetting action is taken to restore it. Scheduling, budgetary, and planning systems utilize negative feedback to keep an organization close to a predictable, stable equilibrium path in which it is adapted to its environment. While negative feedback controls a system according to prior intention, positive feedback produces explosively unstable equilibrium where changes are amplified, eventually putting intolerable pressure on the system until it runs out of control.

The key discovery about the operation of nonlinear feedback systems, however, is that there is a third choice. When a nonlinear feedback system is driven away from stable equilibrium toward explosive unstable equilibrium, it passes through a phase of bounded instability—there is a border between stability and instability where feedback flips autonomously between the amplifying and the damping to produce chaotic behaviour; a paradoxical state that combines both stability and instability.

All human interactions take the form of feedback loops simply because the consequences of one action always feed back to affect a subsequent one. Furthermore, all human interactions constitute nonlinear feedback loops because people under- and overreact. Since organizations are simply a vast web of feedback loops between people, they must be capable of chaotic, as well as stable and explosively unstable, behaviour. The key question is which of these kinds of behaviours leads an organization to success. We can see the answer to this question if we reflect upon the fundamental forces operating on an organization.

All organizations are powerfully pulled in two fundamentally different directions:

- *Disintegration.* Organizations can become more efficient and effective if they divide tasks, segment markets, appeal to individual motivators, empower people, promote informal communication, and separate production processes in geographic and other terms . These steps lead to fragmenting cultures and dispersed power that pull an organization toward disintegration, a phenomenon that can be seen in practice as companies split into more and more business units and find it harder and harder to maintain control.

- *Ossification.* To avoid this pull to disintegration, and to reap the advantages of synergy and coordination, all organizations are also pulled to a state in which tasks are integrated, overlaps in market segments and production processes managed, group goals stressed above individual ones, power concentrated, communication and procedures formalized, and strongly shared cultures established. As an organization moves in this direction it develops more and more rigid structures, rules, procedures, and systems until it eventually ossifies, consequences that are easy to observe as organizations centralize.

Thus, one powerful set of forces pulls every organization toward a stable equilibrium (ossification) and another powerful set of forces pulls it toward an explosively unstable equilibrium (disintegration). Success lies at the border between these states, where managers continually alter systems and structures to avoid attraction either to disintegration or to ossification. For example, organizations typically swing to centralization in one period, to decentralization in another, and back again later on. Success clearly lies in a nonequilibrium state between stable and unstable equilibria; and for a nonlinear feedback system, that is chaos.

Eight Steps to Create Order Out of Chaos

When managers believe that they must pull together harmoniously in pursuit of a shared organizational intention established before they act, they are inevitably confined to the predictable—existing strategic directions will simply be continued or innovations made by others will simply be imitated. When, instead of this, managers create the chaos that flows from challenging existing perceptions and promote the conditions in which spontaneous self-organization can occur, they make it possible for innovation and new strategic direction to emerge. Managers create such conditions when they undertake actions of the following kind.

Develop New Perspectives on the Meaning of Control

The activity of learning in a group is a form of control that managers do not normally recognize as such. It is a self-organizing, self-policing form of control in which the group itself discovers intention and exercises control. Furthermore, we are all perfectly accustomed to the idea that the strategic direction of local communities, nation-states, and international communities is developed and controlled through the operation of political systems, but we rarely apply this notion to organizations. When we do, we see that a sequence of choices and actions will continue in a particular direction only while those espousing that direction continue to enjoy sufficient support. This constitutes a form of control that is as applicable to an organization when it faces the conflicts around open-ended change, as it is to a nation. The lesson is that self-organizing processes can produce controlled behaviour even though no one is in control—sometimes the best thing a manager can do is to let go and allow things to happen.

Design the Use of Power

The distribution of power and the way in which it is used provide very important boundaries around the group learning process from which new strategic directions emerge. The application of power in particular forms has fairly predictable consequences for group dynamics. Where power is applied as force and consented to out of fear, the group dynamic will be one of submission, or where such power is not consented to, the group dynamic will be one of rebellion, either covert or overt. Power may be applied as authority, and the predictable group dynamic here is one in which members of the group suspend their critical faculties and accept instructions from those above them. Groups in states of submission, rebellion, or conformity are incapable of complex learning, that is, the development of new perspectives and new mental models.

The kind of group dynamics that are conducive to complex learning occur when highly competitive win/lose polarization is removed, and open questioning and public testing of assertions encouraged. When this happens, people use argument and conflict to move toward periodic consensus and commitment to a particular issue. That consensus and commitment cannot, however, be the norm when people are searching for new perspectives—rather, they must alternate between conflict and consensus, between confusion and clarity. This kind of dynamic is likely to occur when they most powerfully alternate the form in which they use their power: sometimes withdrawing and allowing conflict; sometimes intervening with suggestions; sometimes exerting authority.

Encourage Self-Organizing Groups

A group will be self-organizing only if it discovers its own challenges, goals, and objectives. Mostly, such groups need to form spontaneously—the role of top managers is simply to create the atmosphere in which this can happen. When top managers do set up a group to deal with strategic issues, however, they must avoid the temptation to write terms of reference, set objectives, or prod the group to reach some predetermined view. Instead top managers must present ambiguous challenges and take the chance that the group may produce proposals they do not approve of. For a group of managers to be self-organizing, it has to be free to operate as its members jointly choose, within the boundaries provided by their work together. This means that when they work together in this way, the normal hierarchy must be suspended for most of the time. Members are there because of the contributions they are able to make and the influence they can exert through those contributions and their own personalities. This suspension of the normal hierarchy can take place only if those on higher levels behave in a manner that indicates that they attach little importance to their position for the duration of the work of the group.

Provoke Multiple Cultures

One way of developing the conflicting countercultures required to provoke new perspectives is to rotate people between functions and business units. The motive here is to create cultural diversity as opposed to the current practice of using rotation to build a cadre of managers with the same management philosophy. Another effective way of promoting countercultures is that practised by Canon and Honda, where significant numbers of managers are hired at the same time, midway through their careers in other organizations, to create sizeable pockets of different cultures that conflict with the predominant one.

Present Ambiguous Challenges Instead of Clear Long-Term Objectives or Visions

Agendas of strategic issues evolve out of the clash between different cultures in self-organizing groups. Top managers can provoke this activity by setting ambiguous challenges and presenting half-formed issues for others to develop, instead of trying to set clear long-term objectives. Problems without objectives should be intentionally posed to provoke the emotion and conflict that lead to active search for new ways of doing things. This activity of presenting challenges should also be a two-way one, where top executives hold themselves open to challenge from subordinates.

Expose the Business to Challenging Situations

Managers who avoid taking chances face the certainty of stagnation and therefore the high probability of collapse in the long term, simply because innovation depends significantly on chance. Running for cover because the future is unknowable is in the long run the riskiest response of all. Instead, managers must intentionally expose themselves to the most challenging of situations. In his study of international companies, Michael Porter concludes that those who position themselves to serve the world's most sophisticated and demanding customers, who seek the challenge of competing with the most imaginative and competent competitors, are the ones who build sustainable competitive advantage on a global scale (see Michael Porter's article in chapter 10).

Devote Explicit Attention to Improving Group Learning Skills

New strategic directions emerge when groups of managers learn together in the sense of questioning deeply held beliefs and altering existing mental models rather than simply absorbing existing bodies of knowledge and sets of techniques. Such a learning process may well be personally threatening and so arouse anxiety that leads to bizarre group dynamics—this is perhaps the major obstacle to effective organizational learning. To overcome it, managers must spend time explicitly exploring how they interact and learn together—the route to superior learning is self-reflection in groups.

Create Resource Slack

New strategic directions emerge when the attitudes and behaviour of managers create an atmosphere favourable to individual initiative and intuition, to political interaction, and to learning in groups. Learning and political interaction are hard work, and they cannot occur without investment in spare management resources. A vital precondition for emergent strategy is thus investment in management resources to allow it to happen.

Conclusion

Practising managers and academics have been debating the merits of organizational learning as opposed to the planning conceptualization of strategic management (see chapter 2). That debate has not, however, focused clearly on the critical unquestioned assumptions upon which the planning approach is based, namely, the nature of causality. Recent discoveries about the nature of dynamic feedback systems make it clear that cause and effect links disappear in innovative human organizations, making it impossible to envision or plan their long-term futures. Because of this lack of causal connection between specific actions and specific outcomes, new strategic directions can only emerge through a spontaneous, self-organizing political and learning process. The planning approach can be seen as a specific approach applicable to the short-term management of an organization's existing activities, a task as vital as the development of a new strategic direction.

References and Suggested Readings

Ackoff, R. L., *Creating the Corporate Future*, Wiley, New York, 1980.

Allison, G. T., *Essence of Decision: Explaining the Cuban Missile Crisis*, Little, Brown, Boston, 1971.

Baden-Fuller, C. W. F., and J. M. Stopford, *Rejuvenating the Mature Business*, Routledge, London, 1992.

Barney, J. B., Organizational Culture: Can It Be a Source of Sustainable Competitive Advantage? *Academy of Management Review*, July 1986, pp. 656–665.

Bennis, W., and B. Nanus, *Leaders: The Strategies for Taking Charge*, Harper & Row, New York, 1985.

Bower, J. L. (Ed.), *The Craft of General Management*, Harvard Business School Publications, Boston, 1991.

Chandler, A. D., *Strategy and Structure: Chapters in the History of the American Industrial Enterprise*, MIT Press, Cambridge, MA, 1962.

Chandler, A. D., *The Visible Hand*, Harvard University Press, Cambridge, MA, 1977.

Channon, D., *The Strategy and Structure of British Enterprise*, Harvard University Press, Cambridge, MA, 1973.

Child, J., Organizational Structure, Environment, and Performance: The Role of Strategic Choice, *Sociology*, January 1972, pp. 2–22.

Christensen, C. R., Andrews, K. R., Bower, J. L., Hamermesh, R. G., and M. E. Porter, *Business Policy: Text and Cases*, Sixth Edition, Irwin, Homewood, IL, 1987.

Donaldson, G., and J. W. Lorsch, *Decision Making at the Top: The Shaping of Strategic Direction*, Basic Books, New York, 1983.

Drucker, P., *Management: Tasks, Responsibilities, Practices*, Harper & Row, New York, 1973.

Frederickson, J. W., The Strategic Decision Process and Organizational Structure, *Academy of Management Review*, April 1986, pp. 280–297.

Galbraith, J. R., Strategy and Organization Planning, *Human Resource Management*, Spring/Summer 1983, pp. 63–77.

Greiner, L. E., Evolution and Revolution as Organizations Grow, *Harvard Business Review*, July/August 1972, pp. 37–46.

Hampden-Turner, C., *Charting the Corporate Mind*, Free Press, New York, 1990.

Hoffman, R. C., Strategies for Corporate Turnarounds: What Do We Know about Them? *Journal of General Management*, Spring 1989, pp. 46–66.

Hofstede, G., Motivation, Leadership, and Organization: Do American Theories Apply Abroad? *Organizational Dynamics*, Summer 1980, pp. 42–63.

Hofstede, G., *Cultures and Organizations: Software of the Mind*, McGraw-Hill, London, 1991.

Johnson, G., *Strategic Change and the Management Process*, Blackwell, Oxford, 1987.

Kets de Vries, M. F. R., and D. Miller, *The Neurotic Organization*, Jossey-Bass, San Francisco, 1984.

Khandwalla, P. N., *The Design of Organizations*, Harcourt, Brace, Jovanovich, New York, 1977.

Lawrence, P. R., and J. W. Lorsch, Differentiation and Integration in Complex Organizations, *Administrative Science Quarterly*, March 1967, pp. 1–47.

March, J. G., and H. A. Simon, *Organizations*, Wiley, New York, 1958.

Miles, R. E., and C. C. Snow, *Organizational Strategy: Structure and Process*, McGraw-Hill, New York, 1978.

Miles, R. E., Snow, C. C., Meyer, A. D., and H. J. Coleman, Organizational Strategy, Structure, and Process, *Academy of Management Review*, July 1978, pp. 546–562.

Miller, D., *The Icarus Paradox: How Excellent Companies Can Bring About Their Own Downfall*, Harper Business, New York, 1990.

Miller, D., The Icarus Paradox: How Exceptional Companies Bring About Their Own Downfall, *Business Horizons*, January/February 1992, pp. 24–35.

Miller, D., The Architecture of Simplicity, *Academy of Management Review,* January 1993, pp. 116–138.

Miller, D., and M. Kets de Vries, *Unstable at the Top,* New American Library, New York, 1987.

Miller, D., and P. Friesen, Momentum and Revolution in Organizational Adaptation, *Academy of Management Journal,* December 1980, pp. 591–614.

Miller, D., and P. Friesen, *Organizations: A Quantum View,* Prentice Hall, Englewood Cliffs, N J, 1984.

Mintzberg, H., *The Structuring of Organizations,* Prentice Hall, Englewood-Cliffs, NJ, 1975.

Mintzberg, H., The Effective Organization: Forces and Forms, *Sloan Management Review,* Winter 1991, pp. 54–67.

Mitroff, I. I., *Stakeholders of the Organizational Mind: Toward a New View of Organizational Policy Making,* Jossey-Bass, San Francisco, 1983.

Nonaka, I., Creating Order out of Chaos: Self Renewal in Japanese Firms, *California Management Review,* Spring 1988, pp. 57–73.

Pascale, R. T., *Managing on the Edge: How Successful Companies Use Conflict to Stay Ahead,* Viking Penguin, London, 1990.

Pearson, A. E., Muscle-Build the Organization, in Bower, J. L. (Ed.), *The Craft of General Management,* Harvard Business School Publications, Boston, MA, 1991.

Peters, T., and N. Austin, A Passion for Excellence, *Fortune,* 13 May 1985, pp. 16, 20.

Peters, T. J., and R. H. Waterman, *In Search of Excellence,* Harper & Row, New York, 1982.

Pfeffer, J., and G. R. Salancik, Organizational Decision Making as a Political Process: The Case of a University Budget, *Administrative Science Quarterly,* June 1974, pp. 135–151.

Porter, M. E., *Competitive Strategy: Techniques for Analyzing Industries and Competitors,* Free Press, New York, 1980.

Schein, E. H., *Organizational Culture and Leadership,* Jossey-Bass, San Francisco, 1985.

Schwartz, H., and S. M. Davis, Matching Corporate Culture and Business Strategy, *Organizational Dynamics,* Summer 1981, pp. 30–48.

Selznick, P., *Leadership in Administration: A Sociological Interpretation,* Harper & Row, New York, 1957.

Simon, H. A., *The Sciences of the Artificial,* MIT Press, 1969.

Stacey, R. D., *Managing Chaos: Dynamic Business Strategies in an Unpredictable World,* Kogan Page, London, 1992.

Stacey, R. D., *Strategic Management and Organizational Dynamics,* Pitman, London, 1993.

Stopford, J. M., and C. Baden-Fuller, Corporate Rejuvenation, *Journal of Management Studies,* July 1990, pp. 399–415.

Taylor, B., Gilinsky, A., Hilmi, A., Hahn, D., and U. Grab, Strategy and Leadership in Growth Companies, *Long Range Planning,* June 1990, pp. 66–75.

Toynbee, A., *A Study of History,* Oxford University Press, London, 1947.

Tushman, M. L., Newman, W., and E. Romanelli, Convergence and Upheaval: Managing the Unsteady Pace of Organizational Evolution, in Tushman, M. L., O'Reilly, C. A., and D. Nadler (Eds.), *The Management of Organization: Strategy, Tactics, Analysis,* Harper and Row, New York, 1989.

Volberda, H. W., *Organizational Flexibility: Change and Preservation,* Wolters-Noordhoff, Groningen, 1992.

Weick, K. E., *The Social Psychology of Organizing,* Addison-Wesley, Reading, MA, 1979.

Whittington, R., *What Is Strategy and Does It Matter?* Routledge, London, 1993.

CHAPTER 10
THE INTERNATIONAL CONTEXT: *ON CONVERGENCE AND COUNTRIES*

*Every man takes the limits of
his own field of vision for
the limits of the world.*
—Arthur Schopenhauer
1788–1860, German philosopher

Introduction

This book features some authors whose world ends at the borders of their country, but fortunately most authors have a broader field of vision, even though the international dimension is often not explicitly mentioned in their work. In most articles, it is an implicit assumption that companies operate in an international arena, either because the firms have ventured abroad themselves or by virtue of their competitors, suppliers, buyers, or other stakeholders becoming more international. In this chapter, the international arena will no longer merely be assumed but will be the *explicit* focus of attention. In the following readings, the consequences of this international context for the strategy process and the strategy content will be explored.

While the international strategist is faced with a variety of challenges, one fundamental question lies at the heart of the issues that must be dealt with— *globalisation*. The process of globalisation refers to the growth of interdependencies between national markets on a worldwide scale. When speaking of these interdependencies, most researchers agree that the two extremes—entire *in*dependence and entire *inter*dependence—are rare at best. The entire independence of national markets for a certain type of product or service would mean that the buying behaviour, technologies, product features, prices, companies, and competitive dynamics in one country would have absolutely no effect on these factors in other countries. In such a case of *international fragmentation*, the world would be no more than an aggregation of unrelated national markets. At the other extreme, entire interdependence of the national markets for a certain type of product or service, the buying behaviour, technologies, product features, prices, companies, and competitive dynamics in countries around the world would be fully interrelated. In such a case of complete *international integration*, the world would be one *global* market.

While most strategy writers agree that few industries are at the extremes of the fragmentation-integration continuum, there is considerable debate on the extent to which the global integration of markets has progressed and will progress in future. More toward the integration pole, there are those who argue that a unified global market is imminent for almost all types of products and services. In their opinion, nationality and geography are becoming increasingly unimportant. In the subtitle, this view is referred to as the *convergence* perspective. More toward the fragmentation pole, there are those who emphasize the resilience of national cultures, regulations, politics, technologies, systems, and market structures. These authors argue that international markets will remain imperfect owing to the peculiarities of nations. In the subtitle to this chapter, this view is referred to as the perspective stressing the importance of *countries*.

It is the intention of this chapter to debate the extent, speed, inevitability, and consequences of globalisation by contrasting these two perspectives. The first two articles are by a radical and a moderate proponent of the convergence perspective, while the third article is by two authors who argue that country-specific factors are more important than the convergence thinkers are willing to accept. These first three articles of the chapter constitute the *standardisation-adaptation debate*; the question is which part of the company's strategy can be standardised worldwide and which part must be locally adapted. The fourth and fifth articles attempt to integrate the convergence and country-oriented perspectives, while simultaneously adding new issues to the standardisation-adaptation debate. The fourth article adds the considerations of global competition, while the fifth article adds the issue of transnational management. The last article leans most toward the "country" side of the spectrum, provocatively arguing that worldwide competitiveness is ultimately rooted in a strong home base. At the end of the chapter, however, readers will have to weigh the arguments and evidence themselves to decide what the impact of globalisation really is on strategy process and strategy content.

The Articles

The topic of international integration has long been an issue receiving significant academic attention. It was not until the early 1980s, however, that the subject developed into a full-fledged debate at the centre of strategic management. The article that has probably been the most influential in focusing this debate has been "The Globalization of Markets" by Theodore Levitt. In this article, Levitt boldly predicts that the world is quickly moving toward a converging commonality. According to Levitt, "the world's needs and desires have been irrevocably homogenized." He believes that the force driving this process is *technology*, which has facilitated communication, transport, and travel, while allowing for the development of superior products at low prices. His conclusion is that "the commonality of preference leads inescapably to the standardization of products, manufacturing, and the institutions of trade and commerce." The old-fashioned multinational corporation, which adapted itself to local circumstances, is "obsolete and the global corporation absolute."

In the second article of this chapter, "Managing in a Borderless World," Kenichi Ohmae takes a less radical view of global convergence. Like Levitt, Ohmae believes that customer needs around the world have become similar, while the fixed costs of meeting these needs have soared, making global products a necessity. However, while Levitt unabashedly argues for complete global standardisation of products, Ohmae believes that in most circumstances "the lure of a universal product is a false allure." In Ohmae's opinion, the challenge is to localise products while retaining global economies of scale. This means that global companies cannot be run in an entirely standard way by headquarters—local subsidiaries must be left with some freedom to become *insiders* in their own markets. Ohmae also argues that the headquarters of a global company cannot afford to be dominated by home-country thinking. Headquarters must see and think globally first, taking an *equidistant* perspective to the three major markets in the world, Japan, the United States, and Europe—the *triad powers* (see also Ohmae, 1985).

The next reading, "The Myth of Globalization" by Susan Douglas and Yoram Wind, goes much further than Ohmae in stressing the need for local adaptation. In this article, the authors react directly to "the sweeping and somewhat polemic character" of Levitt's argumentation. Douglas and Wind believe that many of the assumptions underlying Levitt's global standardisation philosophy are contradicted by the facts. They argue that the convergence of customer needs is not a one-way street; *divergence* trends are also noticeable. Furthermore, they argue that Levitt's emphasis on economies of scale in production and marketing as an irreversibly driving force of globalisation is misguided. According to Douglas and Wind, many new technologies have actually lowered the minimum efficient scale of operation, while there are also plenty of industries where economies of scale are not an important issue. The authors conclude by outlining the specific circumstances under which a strategy of global standardisation might be effective. Under all other circumstances, Douglas and Wind reiterate, the international strategist will have to search for the right balance between standardisation and adaptation.

In the fourth article, "The Dynamics of Global Competition," C. K. Prahalad and Yves Doz move beyond the standardisation-adaptation debate, which they see as only one of the questions posed by globalisation. They largely agree with Douglas and Wind that the international strategist should determine the extent of globalisation in a business and should adapt the organisation's response accordingly. But while Douglas and Wind hardly mention the influence of global competition on the company's international strategy choices, Prahalad and Doz place these considerations at the centre of attention. Prahalad and Doz argue that even in international markets that require extensive local adaptation and where economies of scale are low, the competition can be global. An aggressive competitor can use cross-border cash flows to finance market share battles and pay for the attack of other companies' profit-producing markets. According to Prahalad and Doz, companies that do not realize that "the essence of global competition . . . is the management of international cash flows and strategic coordination," but view the world on a country-by-country basis, might be in for an unpleasant surprise.

The next article, "Managing across Borders" by Christopher Bartlett and Sumantra Ghoshal, deals with the organisational implications of globalisation. In this reading, Bartlett and Ghoshal argue that interdependent national markets force the international company to coordinate across borders, as opposed to the old multinational corporation, which was organised on a country-by-country basis. *Global functional management* is needed to *learn* and transfer core competencies worldwide, while *global business management* with global product responsibilities is needed to achieve worldwide *efficiency* and integration. At the same time, however, most international companies must also have strong *geographic management* to be *responsive* to the local circumstances. Bartlett and Ghoshal argue that optimizing learning, efficiency, and responsiveness simultaneously is the challenge facing the new *transnational* organisation. They believe that every organisation must find its own dynamic balance between these forces; there is not one best organisational response to globalisation, because the extent of globalisation is never the same.

In the sixth and last article, "The Competitive Advantage of Nations," Michael Porter is concerned with the question whether international integration has made a company's nationality and home base irrelevant. In a perfect global market, geography should be unimportant—in a truly borderless world, customers, technologies, products, competitors, and infrastructures would be similar around the globe, and the nationality and location of the company would be insignificant. Even more, it would be to the advantage of companies to become nationless global citizens, as Ohmae seems to suggest. However, the more imperfect the international market, the more important could be the home country characteristics in determining the market behaviour and competitive advantage of the company. This is exactly the point made by Porter: the home country does matter to the firm's international competitiveness. Important differences between countries with regard to buyers, suppliers, competitors, related industries, and supporting infrastructure exist that make the company's home base important. Hence, the international strategist must realise, Porter argues, that "a global strategy supplements and solidifies the competitive advantage created at the home base; it is the icing, not the cake."

Recommended Readings and Cases

There have been few writers as radical as Levitt, but quite a large number of stimulating works from the convergence perspective. A good place for the interested reader to start would be Kenichi Ohmae's *Triad Power: The Coming of Global Competition* and George Yip's *Total Global Strategy*. For a stronger balancing of convergence and country-oriented views, the reader should turn to *The Multinational Mission* by C. K. Prahalad and Yves Doz, and *Competition in Global Industries* by Michael Porter.

Most of this literature emphasizes strategy content issues while largely neglecting strategy process aspects. A well-known exception is the article "Strategic Planning for a Global Business" by Balaji Chakravarthy and Howard Perlmutter. With regard to the management of large international companies, *Managing across Borders: The Transnational Solution* by Christopher Bartlett and Sumantra Ghoshal is highly recommended.

The two cases selected to accompany this chapter are "Saatchi & Saatchi" by Ron Meyer and "Nokia Data" by Kamran Kashani and Robert Howard. The Saatchi & Saatchi case is an example of a company following a global strategy, while the Nokia Data case describes how this Finnish company does the opposite by following a multidomestic strategy. The Saatchi & Saatchi case is particularly interesting because this British advertising agency has been a vocal adherent of the convergence perspective and has made Theodore Levitt a nonexecutive director of the firm. The case gives readers the opportunity to think about the number of industries that have "gone global," as they constitute the market segment Saatchi is focusing on. The Nokia

Data case is interesting because the company is in an industry many believe is highly globally integrated, while Nokia explicitly follows a multidomestic strategy. Readers are confronted with this paradox and must decide whether they think Nokia is on a suicide mission or whether the global context leaves the company far more loopholes than one might expect.

■ THE GLOBALIZATION OF MARKETS†

By Theodore Levitt

A powerful force drives the world toward a converging commonality, and that force is technology. It has proletarianized communication, transport, and travel. It has made isolated places and impoverished peoples eager for modernity's allurements. Almost everyone everywhere wants all the things they have heard about, seen, or experienced via the new technologies.

The result is a new commercial reality—the emergence of global markets for standardized consumer products on a previously unimagined scale of magnitude. Corporations geared to this new reality benefit from enormous economies of scale in production, distribution, marketing, and management. By translating these benefits into reduced world prices, they can decimate competitors that still live in the disabling grip of old assumptions about how the world works.

Gone are accustomed differences in national or regional preference. Gone are the days when a company could sell last year's models—or lesser versions of advanced products—in the less-developed world. And gone are the days when prices, margins, and profits abroad were generally higher than at home.

The globalization of markets is at hand. With that, the multinational commercial world nears its end, and so does the multinational corporation.

The multinational and the global corporation are not the same thing. The multinational corporation operates in a number of countries, and adjusts its products and practices in each—at high relative costs. The global corporation operates with resolute constancy—at low relative cost—as if the entire world (or major regions of it) were a single entity; it sells the same things in the same way everywhere.

Which strategy is better is not a matter of opinion but of necessity. Worldwide communications carry everywhere the constant drumbeat of modern possibilities to lighten and enhance work, raise living standards, divert, and entertain. The same countries that ask the world to recognize and respect the individuality of their cultures insist on the wholesale transfer to them of modern goods, services, and technologies. Modernity is not just a wish but also a widespread practice among those who cling, with unyielding passion or religious fervor, to ancient attitudes and heritages.

Who can forget the televised scenes during the 1979 Iranian uprisings of young men in fashionable French-cut trousers and silky body shirts thirsting with raised modern weapons for blood in the name of Islamic fundamentalism?

In Brazil, thousands swarm daily from preindustrial Bahian darkness into exploding coastal cities, there quickly to install television sets in crowded corrugated huts and, next to battered Volkswagens, make sacrificial offerings of fruit and fresh-killed chickens to Macumban spirits by candlelight.

A thousand suggestive ways attest to the ubiquity of the desire for the most advanced things that the world makes and sells—goods of the best quality and reliability at the lowest price. The world's needs and desires have been irrevocably homogenized. This makes the multinational corporation obsolete and the global corporation absolute.

Living in the Republic of Technology

Daniel J. Boorstin, author of the monumental trilogy *The Americans*, characterized our age as driven by "the Republic of Technology (whose) supreme law . . . is convergence, the tendency for everything to become more like everything else."

In business, this trend has pushed markets toward global commonality. Corporations sell standardized products in the same way everywhere—autos, steel, chemicals, petroleum, cement, agricultural commodities and equipment, industrial and commercial construction, banking and insurance services, computers, semiconductors, transport, electronic instruments, pharmaceuticals, and telecommunications, to mention some of the obvious.

Nor is the sweeping gale of globalization confined to these raw material or high-tech products, where the universal language of customers and users facilitates standardization. The transforming winds whipped up by the proletarianization of communication and travel enter every crevice of life.

Commercially, nothing confirms this as much as the success of McDonald's from the Champs Elysées to the Ginza, of Coca-Cola in Bahrain and Pepsi-Cola in Moscow, and of rock music, Greek salad, Hollywood movies, Revlon cosmetics, Sony televisions, and Levi jeans everywhere. "High-touch" products are as ubiquitous as high-tech.

Starting from opposing sides, the high-tech and the high-touch ends of the commercial spectrum gradually consume the undistributed middle in their cosmopolitan orbit. No one is exempt and nothing can stop the process. Everywhere everything gets more and more like everything else as the world's preference structure is relentlessly homogenized.

Consider the cases of Coca-Cola and Pepsi-Cola, which are globally standardized products sold everywhere and welcomed by everyone. Both successfully cross multitudes of national, regional, and ethnic taste buds trained to a variety of deeply ingrained local preferences of taste, flavor, consistency, effervescence, and aftertaste. Everywhere both sell well. Cigarettes, too, especially American-made, make year-to-year global inroads in territories previously held in the firm grip of other, mostly local, blends.

These are not exceptional examples. (Indeed their global reach would be even greater were it not for artificial trade barriers.) They exemplify a general drift toward the homogenization of the world and how companies distribute, finance, and price products. Nothing is exempt. The products and methods of the industrialized world play a single tune for all the world, and all the world eagerly dances to it.

Ancient differences in national tastes or modes of doing business disappear. The commonality of preference leads inescapably to the standardization of products, manufacturing, and the institutions of trade and commerce. Small nation-based markets transmogrify and expand. Success in world competition turns on efficiency in production, distribution, marketing, and management, and inevitably becomes focused on price.

The most effective world competitors incorporate superior quality and reliability into their cost structures. They sell in all national markets the same kind of products sold at home or in their largest export market. They compete on the basis of appropriate value—the best combinations of price, quality, reliability, and delivery for products that are globally identical with respect to design, function, and even fashion.

That, and little else, explains the surging success of Japanese companies dealing worldwide in a vast variety of products—both tangible products like steel, cars, motorcyles, hi-fi equipment, farm machinery, robots, microprocessors, carbon fibers, and now even textiles, and intangibles like banking, shipping, general contracting, and soon computer software. Nor are high-quality and low-cost operations incompatible, as a host of consulting organizations and data engineers argue with vigorous vacuity. The reported data are incomplete, wrongly analyzed, and contradictory. The truth is that low-cost operations are the hallmark of corporate cultures that require and produce quality in all that they do. High quality and low costs are not opposing postures. They are compatible, twin identities of superior practice.

To say that Japan's companies are not global because they export cars with left-side drives to the United States and the European continent, while those in Japan have right-side drives, or because they sell office machines through distributors in the United States but directly at home, or speak Portuguese in Brazil is to mistake a difference for a distinction. The same is true of Safeway and Southland retail chains operating effectively in the Middle East, and to not only native but also imported populations from Korea, the Philippines, Pakistan, India, Thailand, Britain, and the United States. National rules of the road differ, and so do distribution channels and languages. Japan's distinction is its unrelenting push for economy and value enhancement. That translates into a drive for standardization at high quality levels.

Vindication of the Model T

If a company forces costs and prices down and pushes quality and reliability up— while maintaining reasonable concern for suitability—customers will prefer its world-standardized products. The theory holds, at this stage in the evolution of globalization, no matter what conventional market research and even common sense may suggest about different national and regional tastes, preferences, needs, and institutions. The Japanese have repeatedly vindicated this theory, as did Henry Ford with the Model T. Most important, so have their imitators, including companies from South Korea (television sets and heavy construction), Malaysia (personal calculators and microcomputers), Brazil (auto parts and tools), Colombia (apparel), Singapore (optical equipment), and yes, even from the United States (office copiers, computers, bicycles, castings), Western Europe (automatic washing machines), Rumania (housewares), Hungary (apparel), Yugoslavia (furniture), and Israel (pagination equipment).

Of course, large companies operating in a single nation or even a single city don't standardize everything they make, sell, or do. They have product lines instead of a single product version, and multiple distribution channels. There are neighborhood, local, regional, ethnic, and institutional differences, even within metropolitan areas. But although companies customize products for particular market segments, they know that success in a world with homogenized demand requires a search for sales opportunities in similar segments across the globe in order to achieve the economies of scale necessary to compete.

Such a search works because a market segment in one country is seldom unique; it has close cousins everywhere precisely because technology has homogenized the globe. Even small local segments have their global equivalents everywhere and become subject to global competition, especially on price.

The global competitor will seek constantly to standardize his offering everywhere. He will digress from this standardization only after exhausting all possibilities to retain it, and he will push for reinstatement of standardization whenever digression and divergence have occurred. He will never assume that the customer is a king who knows his own wishes.

Trouble increasingly stalks companies that lack clarified global focus and remain inattentive to the economics of simplicity and standardization. The most endangered companies in the rapidly evolving world tend to be those that dominate rather small domestic markets with high value-added products for which there are smaller markets elsewhere. With transportation costs proportionately low, distant competitors will enter the now-sheltered markets of those companies with goods produced more cheaply under scale-efficient conditions. Global competition spells the end of domestic territoriality, no matter how diminutive the territory may be.

When the global producer offers his lower costs internationally, his patronage expands exponentially. He not only reaches into distant markets, but also attracts customers who previously held to local preferences and now capitulate to the attractions of lesser prices. The strategy of standardization not only responds to worldwide homogenized markets but also expands those markets with aggressive low pricing. The new technological juggernaut taps an ancient motivation—to make one's money go as far as possible. This is universal—not simply a motivation but actually a need.

The Hedgehog Knows

The difference between the hedgehog and the fox, wrote Sir Isaiah Berlin in distinguishing between Dostoevski and Tolstoy, is that the fox knows a lot about a great many things, but the hedgehog knows everything about one great thing. The multinational corporation knows a lot about a great many countries and congenially adapts to supposed differences. It willingly accepts vestigial national differences, not questioning the possibility of their transformation, not recognizing how the world is ready and eager for the benefit of modernity, especially when the price is right. The multinational corporation's accommodating mode to visible national differences is medieval.

By contrast, the global corporation knows everything about one great thing. It knows about the absolute need to be competitive on a worldwide basis as well as nationally and seeks constantly to drive down prices by standardizing what it sells and how it operates. It treats the world as composed of few standardized markets rather than many customized markets. It actively seeks and vigorously works toward global convergence. Its mission is modernity and its mode, price competition, even when it sells top-of-the-line, high-end products. It knows about the one great thing all nations and people have in common: scarcity.

Nobody takes scarcity lying down; everyone wants more. This in part explains division of labor and specialization of production. They enable people and nations to optimize their conditions through trade. The median is usually money.

Experience teaches that money has three special qualities: scarcity, difficulty of acquisition, and transience. People understandably treat it with respect. Everyone in the increasingly homogenized world market wants products and features that everybody else wants. If the price is low enough, they will take highly standardized world products, even if these aren't exactly what mother said was suitable, what immemorial custom decreed was right, or what market-research fabulists asserted was preferred.

The implacable truth of all modern production—whether of tangible or intangible goods—is that large-scale production of standardized items is generally cheaper within a wide range of volume than small-scale production. Some argue that CAD/CAM (computer aided design/computer aided manufacturing) will allow companies to manufacture customized products on a small scale—but cheaply. But the argument misses the point. If a company treats the world as one or two distinctive product markets, it can serve the world more economically than if it treats it as three, four, or five product markets.

Different cultural preferences, national tastes and standards, and business institutions are vestiges of the past. Some inheritances die gradually; others prosper and expand into mainstream global preferences. So-called ethnic markets are a good example. Chinese food, pita bread, country and western music, pizza, and jazz are everywhere. They are market segments that exist in worldwide proportions. They don't deny or contradict global homogenization but confirm it.

Many of today's differences among nations as to products and their features actually reflect the respectful accommodation of multinational corporations to what they believe are fixed local preferences. They believe preferences are fixed, not because they are but because of rigid habits of thinking about what actually is. Most executives in multinational corporations are thoughtlessly accommodating. They falsely presume that marketing means giving the customer what he says he wants rather than trying to understand exactly what he'd like. So they persist with high-cost, customized multinational products and practices instead of pressing hard and pressing properly for global standardization.

I do not advocate the systematic disregard of local or national differences. But a company's sensitivity to such differences does not require that it ignore the possibilities of doing things differently or better.

With persistence and appropriate means, barriers against superior technologies and economics have always fallen. There is no recorded exception where reasonable effort has been made to overcome them. It is very much a matter of time and effort.

A Failure in Global Imagination

Many companies have tried to standardize world practice by exporting domestic products and processes without accommodation or change—and have failed miserably. Their deficiencies have been seized on as evidence of bovine stupidity in the face of abject impossibility. Advocates of global standardization see them as examples of failures in execution.

In fact, poor execution is often an important cause. More important, however, is failure of nerve—failure of imagination.

Consider the case for the introduction of fully automatic home laundry equipment in Western Europe at a time when few homes had even semiautomatic machines.

The growing success of small, low-powered, low-speed, low-capacity, low-priced Italian machines, even against the preferred but highly priced and highly promoted brand in West Germany, was significant. It contained a powerful message that was lost on managers confidently wedded to a distorted version of the marketing concept according to which you give the customer what he says he wants. In fact the customers said they wanted certain features, but their behavior demonstrated they'd take other features provided the price and the promotion were right.

In this case it was obvious that under prevailing conditions, people preferred a low-priced automatic over any kind of manual or semiautomatic machine and certainly over higher priced automatics, even though the low-priced automatics failed to fulfil all their expressed preferences. The supposedly meticulous and demanding German consumers violated all expectations by buying the simple, low-priced Italian machines.

This case illustrates how the perverse practice of the marketing concept and the absence of any kind of marketing imagination let multinational attitudes survive when customers actually want the benefits of global standardization. People were asked what features they wanted in a washing machine rather than what they wanted out of life. Selling a line of products individually tailored to each nation is thoughtless. Managers who took pride in practising the marketing concept to the fullest did not, in fact, practice it at all. Data do not yield information except with the intervention of the mind. Information does not yield meaning except with the intervention of imagination.

Cracking the Code of Western Markets

Since the theory of the marketing concept emerged a quarter of a century ago, the more managerially advanced corporations have been eager to offer what customers clearly want rather than what is merely convenient. They have created marketing departments supported by professional market researchers of awesome and often costly proportions. And they have proliferated extraordinary numbers of operations and product lines—highly tailored products and delivery systems for many different markets, market segments, and nations.

Significantly, Japanese companies operate almost entirely without marketing departments or market research of the kind so prevalent in the West. Yet, in the colorful words of General Electric's chairman John F. Welch, Jr., the Japanese, coming from a small cluster of resource-poor islands, with an entirely alien culture and an almost impenetrably complex language, have cracked the code of Western markets. They have done it not by looking with mechanistic thoroughness at the way markets are different but rather by searching for meaning with a deeper wisdom. They have discovered the one great thing all markets have in common—an overwhelming desire for dependable, world-standard modernity in all things, at aggressively low prices. In response, they deliver irresistible value everywhere, attracting people with products that market-research technocrats described with superficial certainty as being unsuitable and uncompetitive.

The wider a company's global reach, the greater the number of regional and national preferences it will encounter for certain product features, distribution systems, or promotional media. There will always need to be some accommodation to differences.

In its highly successful introduction of Contac 600 (the timed-release decongestant) into Japan, SmithKline Corporation used thirty-five wholesalers instead of the one thousand-plus that established practice required. Daily contacts with the wholesalers and key retailers, also in violation of established practice, supplemented the plan, and it worked.

Denied access to established distribution institutions in the United States, Komatsu, the Japanese manufacturer of lightweight farm machinery, entered the market through over-the-road construction equipment dealers in rural areas of the Sunbelt, where farms are smaller, the soil sandier and easier to work. Here inexperienced distributors were able to attract customers on the basis of Komatsu's product and price appropriateness.

In cases of successful challenge to prevailing institutions and practices, a combination of product reliability and quality, strong and sustained support systems, aggressively low prices, and sales-compensation packages, as well as audacity and implacability, circumvented, shattered, and transformed very different distribution systems. Instead of resentment, there was admiration.

The differences that persist throughout the world despite its globalization affirm an ancient dictum of economics—that things are driven by what happens at the margin, not at the core. Thus, in ordinary competitive analysis, what's important is not the average price but the marginal price, what happens not in the usual case but at the interface of newly erupting conditions. What counts in commercial affairs is what happens at the cutting edge. What is most striking today is the underlying similarities of what is happening now to national preferences at the margin. These similarities at the cutting edge cumulatively form an overwhelming, predominant commonality everywhere.

To refer to the persistence of economic nationalism (protective and subsidized trade practices, special tax aids, or restrictions for home market producers) as a barrier to the globalization of markets is to make a valid point. Economic nationalism does have a powerful persistence. But, as with the present almost totally smooth internationalization of investment capital, the past alone does not shape or predict the future.

Reality is not a fixed paradigm, dominated by immemorial customs and derived attitudes, heedless of powerful and abundant new forces. The world is becoming increasingly informed about the liberating and enhancing possibilities of modernity. The persistence of the inherited varieties of national preferences rests uneasily on increasing evidence of, and restlessness regarding, their inefficiency, costliness, and confinement. The historic past, and the national differences respecting commerce and industry it spawned and fostered everywhere, is now subject to relatively easy transformation.

Cosmopolitanism is no longer the monopoly of the intellectual and leisure classes; it is becoming the established property and defining characteristic of all sectors everywhere in the world. Gradually and irresistibly it breaks down the walls of economic insularity, nationalism, and chauvinism. What we see today as escalating commercial nationalism is simply the last violent death rattle of an obsolete institution.

The successful global corporation does not abjure customization or differentiation for the requirements of markets that differ in product preferences, spending patterns, shopping preferences, and institutional or legal arrangements. But the global corporation accepts and adjusts to these differences only reluctantly, only after relentlessly testing their immutability, after trying in various ways to circumvent and reshape them.

■ MANAGING IN A BORDERLESS WORLD†

By Kenichi Ohmae

Most managers are nearsighted. Even though today's competitive landscape often stretches to a global horizon, they see best what they know best: the customers geographically closest to home. These managers may have factories or laboratories in a dozen countries. They may have joint ventures in a dozen more. They may source materials and sell in markets all over the world. But when push comes to shove, their field of vision is dominated by home-country customers and the organizational units that serve them. Everyone—and everything—else is simply part of "the rest of the world."

This nearsightedness is not intentional. No responsible manager purposefully devises or implements an astigmatic strategy. But by the same token, too few managers consciously try to set plans and build organizations as if they see all key customers equidistant from the corporate center. Whatever the trade figures show, home markets are usually in focus; overseas markets are not.

Effective global operations require a genuine equidistance of perspective. But even with the best will in the world, managers find that kind of vision hard to develop—and harder to maintain. Not long ago, the chief executive officer (CEO) of a major Japanese capital-goods producer cancelled several important meetings to attend the funeral of one of his company's local dealers. When I asked him if he would have done the same for a Belgian dealer, one who did a larger volume of business each year than his late counterpart in Japan, the unequivocal answer was no. Perhaps headquarters would have had the relevant European manager send a letter of condolence. No more than that. In Japan, however, tradition dictated the CEO's presence. But Japanese tradition isn't everything, I reminded him. After all, he was the head of a global, not just a Japanese organization. By violating the principle of equidistance, his attendance underscored distinctions among dealers. He was sending the wrong signals and reinforcing the wrong values. Poor vision has consequences.

It may be unfamiliar and awkward, but the primary rule of equidistance is to see—and to think—global first. Honda, for example, has manufacturing divisions in Japan, North America, and Europe—all three legs of the Triad—but its managers do not think or act as if the company were divided between Japanese and overseas operations. Indeed, the very word *overseas* has no place in Honda's vocabulary because the corporation sees itself as equidistant from all its key customers. At Casio, the top managers gather information directly from each of their primary markets and then sit down together once a month to lay out revised plans for global product development.

There is no single best way to avoid or overcome nearsightedness. An equidistant perspective can take many forms. However managers do it, however they get there,

†**Source:** Reprinted by permission of *Harvard Business Review*. "Managing in a Borderless World" by Kenichi Ohmae, May/June 1989. Copyright © 1989 by the President and Fellows of Harvard College. All rights reserved.

building a value system that emphasizes seeing and thinking globally is the bottom-line price of admission to today's borderless economy.

A Geography without Borders

On a political map, the boundaries between countries are as clear as ever. But on a competitive map, a map showing the real flows of financial and industrial activity, those boundaries have largely disappeared. What has eaten them away is the persistent, ever speedier flow of information—information that governments previously monopolized, cooking it up as they saw fit and redistributing in forms of their own devising. Today, of course, people everywhere are more and more able to get the information they want directly from all corners of the world.

Through this flow of information, we've become global citizens, and so must the companies that want to sell us things. Black-and-white television sets extensively penetrated households in the United States nearly a dozen years before they reached comparable numbers of viewers in Europe and Japan. With color television, the time lag fell to about five or six years for Japan and a few more for Europe. With videocassette recorders, the difference was only three or four years—but this time, Europe and Japan led the way; the United States, with its focus on cable TV, followed. With the compact disc, household penetration rates evened up after only one year. Now, with MTV available by satellite across Europe, there is no lag at all. New music, styles, and fashion reach all European youngsters almost at the same time they are reaching their counterparts in America. We all share the same information.

More than that, we are all coming to share it in a common language. Ten years ago when I would speak in English to students at Bocconi, an Italian university, most of them would listen to me through a translator. Last year, they listened to me directly in English and asked me questions in English. This is a momentous change. The preparation for 1992 has taken place in language much sooner than it has in politics. We can all talk to each other now, understand each other, and governments cannot stop us. "Global citizenship" is no longer just a nice phrase in the lexicon of rosy futurologists. It is every bit as real and concrete as measurable changes in GNP or trade flows. It is actually coming to pass.

The same is true for corporations. In the pharmaceutical industry, for example, the critical activities of drug discovery, screening, and testing are now virtually the same among the best companies everywhere in the world. Scientists can move from one laboratory to another and start working the next day with few hesitations or problems. They will find equipment with which they are familiar, equipment they have used before, equipment that comes from the same manufacturers.

When information flows with relative freedom, the old geographic barriers become irrelevant. Global needs lead to global products. For managers, this universal flow of information puts a high premium on learning how to build the strategies and the organizations capable of meeting the requirements of a borderless world.

What Is a Universal Product?

Imagine that you are the CEO of a major automobile company reviewing your product plans for the years ahead. Your market data tell you that you will have to develop four dozen different models if you want to design separate cars for each distinct segment of the Triad market. But you don't have enough world-class engineers to design so many models. You don't have enough managerial talent or enough money. No one does. Worse, there is no single "global" car that will solve your problems for you. America, Europe, and Japan are quite different markets with quite different mixes of needs and preferences. Worse still, as head of a worldwide company, you cannot write off any of these Triad markets. You simply have to be in each of them—and with first-rate successful products. What do you do?

If you are the CEO of Nissan, you first look at the Triad region by region and identify each market's dominant requirements. In the United Kingdom, for example, tax policies make it essential that you develop a car suitable for corporate fleet sales. In the United States, you need a sporty "Z" model as well as a four-wheel drive family vehicle. Each of these categories is what Nissan's president, Yutaka Kume, calls a "lead-country" model—a product carefully tailored to the dominant and distinct needs of individual national markets. Once you have your short list of lead-country models in hand, you can ask your top managers in other parts of the Triad whether minor changes can make any of them suitable for local sales. But you start with the lead-country models. "With this kind of thinking," says Mr. Kume, "we have been able to halve the number of basic models needed to cover the global markets and, at the same time, to cover 80 percent of our sales with cars designed for specific national markets."

Imagine, instead, if Nissan had taken its core team of engineers and designers in Japan and asked them to design only global cars, cars that would sell all over the world. Their only possible response would have been to add up all the various national preferences and divide by the number of countries. They would have had to optimize across markets by a kind of rough averaging. But when it comes to questions of taste and, especially, aesthetic preference, consumers do not like averages. They like what they like, not some mathematical compromise.

When it comes to product strategy, managing in a borderless world doesn't mean managing by averages. It doesn't mean that all tastes run together into one amorphous mass of universal appeal. And it doesn't mean that the appeal of operating globally removes the obligation to localize products. The lure of a universal product is a false allure. The truth is a bit more subtle.

For some kinds of products, however, the kind of globalization that Ted Levitt talks about makes excellent sense. One of the most obvious is, oddly enough, battery-powered products like cameras, watches, and pocket calculators. What makes these products successful across the Triad? Popular prices, for one thing, based on aggressive cost reduction and global economies of scale. Also important, however, is the fact that many general design choices reflect an in-depth understanding of the preferences of leading consumer segments in key markets throughout the Triad.

Another important cluster of these global products is made up of fashion-oriented, premium-priced branded goods. Gucci bags are sold around the world, unchanged from one place to another. They are marketed in virtually the same way. They appeal to an upper-bracket market segment that shares a consistent set of tastes and preferences. By definition, not everyone in the United States or Europe or Japan belongs to that segment. But for those who do, the growing commonality of their tastes qualifies them as members of a genuinely cross-Triad, global segment. There is even such a segment for top-of-the-line automobiles like the Rolls-Royce and the Mercedes-Benz. You can— in fact, should—design such cars for select buyers around the globe. But you cannot do that with Nissans or Toyotas or Hondas. Truly universal products are few and far between.

Insiderization

Some may argue that my definition of universal products is unnecessarily narrow, that many such products exist that do not fit neatly into top-bracket segments: Coca-Cola, Levi's jeans, things like that. On closer examination, however, these turn out to be very different sorts of things. Think about Coca-Cola for a moment. Before it got established in each of its markets, the company had to build up a fairly complete local infrastructure and do the groundwork to establish local demand. Today, because the company has done its homework and done it well, Coke is a universally desired brand. But it got there by a different route: local replication of an entire business system in every important market over a long period of time. When you walk into the 7-Eleven stores of the world and look for a bottle of cola, the one you pick depends on its location on the shelf, its price, or perhaps the special in-store promotion going on at the moment. In other words, your preference is shaped by the effects of the cola company's complete business system in that country.

Now, to be sure, the quality of that business system will depend to some extent on the company's ability to leverage skills developed elsewhere or to exploit synergies with other parts of its operations—marketing competence, for example, or economies of scale in the production of concentrates. Even so, your choice as a consumer rests on the power with which all such functional strengths have been brought to bear in your particular local market—that is, on the company's ability to become a full-fledged insider in that local market.

With fashion-based items, where the price is relatively high and the purchase frequency low, insiderization does not matter all that much. With commodity items, however, where the price is low and the frequency of purchase high, the insiderization of functional skills is all-important. There is simply no way to be successful around the world with this latter category of products without replicating your business system in each key market.

For industrial products companies, becoming an insider often poses a different set of challenges. Because these products are chosen largely on the basis of their performance characteristics, if they cut costs or boost productivity, they stand a fair chance of being accepted anywhere in the world. Even so, however, these machines do not operate in a vacuum. Their success may have to wait until the companies that make them have developed a full range of insider functions—engineering, sales, installation, finance, service, and so on. So, as these factors become more critical, it often makes sense for the companies to link up with local operations that already have these functions in place.

Financial services have their own special characteristics. Product globalization already takes place at the institutional investor level but much less so at the retail level. Still, many retail products now originate overseas, and the money collected from them is often invested across national borders. Indeed, foreign exchange, stock markets, and other trading facilities have already made money a legitimately global product.

In all these categories, then, as distinct from premium fashion-driven products like Gucci bags, insiderization in key markets is the route to global success. Yes, some top-of-the-line tastes and preferences have become common across the Triad. In many other cases, however, creating a global product means building the capability to understand and respond to customer needs and business system requirements in each critical market.

The Headquarters Mentality

By all reasonable measures, Coca-Cola's experience in Japan has been a happy one. More often than not, however, the path it took to insiderization—replicating a home-country business system in a new national market—creates many more problems than it solves. Managers back at headquarters, who have had experience with only one way to succeed, are commonly inclined to force that model on each new opportunity that arises. Of course, sometimes it will work. Sometimes it will be exactly the right answer. But chances are that the home-country reflex, the impulse to generalize globally from a sample of one, will lead efforts astray.

In the pharmaceutical industry, for example, Coca-Cola's approach would not work. Foreign entrants simply have to find ways to adapt to the Japanese distribution system. Local doctors will not accept or respond favorably to an American-style sales force.

One common problem with insiderization, then, is a misplaced home-country reflex. Another, perhaps more subtle, problem is what happens back at headquarters after initial operations in another market really start paying off. When this happens, in most companies everyone at home starts to pay close attention. Without really understanding why things have turned out as well as they have, managers at headquarters take an increasing interest in what is going on in Japan or wherever it happens to be.

Functionaries of all stripes itch to intervene. Corporate heavyweights decide they had better get into the act, monitor key decisions, ask for timely reports, take extensive tours of local activities. Every power-that-be wants a say in what has become a critical portion of the overall company's operations. When minor difficulties arise, no one is willing to let local managers continue to handle things themselves. Corporate jets fill the skies with impatient satraps eager to set things right.

We know perfectly well where all this is likely to lead. A cosmetics company, with a once enviable position in Japan, went through a series of management shake-ups at home. As a result, the Japanese operation, which had grown progressively more important, was no longer able to enjoy the rough autonomy that made its success possible. Several times, eager U.S. hands reached in to change the head of activities in Japan, and crisp memos and phone calls kept up a steady barrage of challenges to the unlucky soul who happened to be in the hot seat at the moment. Relations became antagonistic, profits fell, the intervention grew worse, and the whole thing just fell apart. Overeager and overanxious managers back at headquarters did not have the patience to learn what really worked in the Japanese market. By trying to supervise things in the regular "corporate" fashion, they destroyed a very profitable business.

This is an all-too-familiar pattern. With dizzying regularity, the local top manager changes from a Japanese national to a foreigner, to a Japanese, to a foreigner. Impatient, headquarters keeps fitfully searching for a never-never ideal "person on the spot." Persistence and perseverance are the keys to long-term survival and success. Everyone knows it. But headquarters is just not able to wait for a few years until local managers—of whatever nationality—build up the needed rapport with vendors, employees, distributors, and customers. And if, by a miracle, they do, then headquarters is likely to see them as having become too "Japanized" to represent their interests abroad. They are no longer "one of us." If they do not, then obviously they have failed to win local acceptance.

This headquarters mentality is not just a problem of bad attitude or misguided enthusiasm. Too bad, because these would be relatively easy to fix. Instead, it rests on—and is reinforced by—a company's entrenched systems, structures, and behaviors. Dividend payout ratios, for example, vary from country to country. But most global companies find it hard to accept low or no payout from investment in Japan, medium returns from Germany, and larger returns from the United States. The usual wish is to get comparable levels of return from all activities, and internal benchmarks of performance reflect that wish. This is trouble waiting to happen. Looking for 15 percent return on investment (ROI) a year from new commitments in Japan is going to sour a company on Japan very quickly. The companies that have done the best there—the Coca-Colas and the IBMs—were willing to adjust their conventional expectations and settle in for the long term.

It is no surprise that many of the most globally successful Japanese companies— Honda, Sony, Matsushita, Canon, and the like—have been led by a strong owner-founder for at least a decade. They can override bureaucratic inertia; they can tear down institutional barriers. In practice, the managerial decision to tackle wrenching organizational and systems changes is made even more difficult by the way in which problems become visible. Usually, a global systems problem first comes into view in the form of explicitly local symptoms. Rarely do global problems show up where the real underlying causes are.

Troubled CEOs may say that their Japanese operations are not doing well, that the money being spent on advertising is just not paying off as expected. They will not say that their problems are really back at headquarters with its superficial understanding of what it takes to market effectively in Japan. They will not say that it lies in the design of their financial reporting systems. They will not say that it is part and parcel of their own reluctance to make long-term, front-end capital investments in new markets. They will not say that it lies in their failure to do well the central job of any headquarters operation: the development of good people at the local level. Or at least they are not likely to. They will diagnose the problems as local problems and try to fix them.

Thinking Global

Top managers are always slow to point the finger of responsibility at headquarters or at themselves. When global faults have local symptoms, they will be slower still. When taking corrective action means a full, zero-based review of all systems, skills, and structures, their speed will decrease even further. And when their commitment to acting globally is itself far from complete, it is a wonder there is any motion at all. Headquarters mentality is the prime expression of managerial nearsightedness, the sworn enemy of a genuinely equidistant perspective on global markets.

In the early days of global business, experts like Raymond Vernon of the Harvard Business School proposed, in effect, a United Nations model of globalization. Companies with aspirations to diversify and expand throughout the Triad were to do so by cloning the parent company in each new country of operation. If successful, they would create a mini-UN of clonelike subsidiaries repatriating profits to the parent company, which remained the dominant force at the center. We know that successful companies enter fewer countries but penetrate each of them more deeply. That is why this model gave way by the early 1980s to a competitor-focused approach to globalization. By this logic, if we were a European producer of medical electronics equipment, we had to take on General Electric in the United States so that it would not come over here and attack us on our home ground. Today, however, the pressure for globalization is driven not so much by diversification or competition as by the needs and preferences of customers. Their needs have globalized, and the fixed costs of meeting them have soared. That is why we must globalize.

Managing effectively in this new borderless environment does not mean building pyramids of cash flow by focusing on the discovery of new places to invest. Nor does it mean tracking your competitors to their lair and preemptively undercutting them in their own home market. Nor does it mean blindly trying to replicate home-country business systems in new colonial territories. Instead, it means paying central attention to delivering value to customers—and to developing an equidistant view of who they are and what they want. Before everything else comes the need to see your customers clearly. They—and only they—can provide legitimate reasons for thinking global.

■ THE MYTH OF GLOBALIZATION[†]

By Susan Douglas and Yoram Wind

In recent years, globalization has become a key theme in every discussion of international strategy. Proponents of the philosophy of "global" products and brands, such as professor Theodore Levitt of Harvard, and the highly successful advertising agency, Saatchi and Saatchi, argue that in a world of growing internationalization, the key to success is the development of global products and brands, in other words, a focus on standardized products and brands worldwide. Others, however, point to the numerous barriers to standardization, and suggest that greater returns are to be obtained from adapting products and marketing strategies to the specific characteristics of individual markets.

The growing integration of international markets as well as the growth of competition on a worldwide scale implies that adoption of a global perspective has become increasingly imperative in planning strategy. However, to conclude that this mandates the adoption of a strategy of universal standardization appears naive and oversimplistic. In particular, it ignores the inherent complexity of operations in international markets, and the formulation of an effective strategy to penetrate these markets. While global products and brands may be appropriate for certain markets and in targeting certain segments, adopting such an approach as an universal strategy in relation to all markets may not be desirable, and may lead to major strategic blunders. Furthermore, it implies a product orientation, and a product-driven strategy, rather than a strategy grounded in a systematic analysis of customer behavior and response patterns and market characteristics.

The purpose of this article is thus to examine critically the notion that success in international markets necessitates adoption of a strategy of global products and brands. Given the restrictive characteristic of this philosophy, a somewhat broader perspective in developing global strategy is proposed which views standardization as merely one option in the range of possible strategies which may be effective in global markets.

The Traditional Perspective on International Strategy

Traditionally, discussion of international business strategy has been polarized around the debate concerning the pursuit of a uniform strategy worldwide versus adaptation to specific local market conditions. On the one hand, it has been argued that adoption of a uniform strategy worldwide enables a company to take advantage of the potential synergies arising from multicountry operations, and constitutes the multinational company's key competitive advantage in international markets. Others however, have argued that adaptation of strategy to idiosyncratic national market characteristics is crucial to success in these markets.

Fayerweather in his seminal work in international business strategy described the central issue as one of conflict between forces toward unification and those resulting in fragmentation. He pointed out that within a multinational firm, internal forces created pressures toward the integration of strategy across national boundaries. On the other hand, differences in the sociocultural, political, and economic characteristics of countries as well as the need for effective relations with the host society, constitute fragmenting influences that favor adaptation to the local environment.

Recent discussion of global competitive strategy echoes the same theme of the dichotomy between the forces that have triggered the globalization of markets and those that constitute barriers to global competition. Factors such as economies of scale in production, purchasing, faster accumulation of learning from operating worldwide, decrease in transportation and distribution costs, reduced costs of product adaptation, and the emergence of global market segments have encouraged competition on a global scale. However, barriers such as governmental and institutional constraints, tariff barriers and duties, preferential treatment of local firms, transportation costs, differences in customer demand, and so on, call for nationalistic or "protected niche" strategies.

Compromise solutions such as "pattern standardization" have also been proposed. In this case, a global promotional theme or positioning is developed, but execution is adapted to the local market. Similarly, it has been pointed out that even where a standardized product is marketed in a number of countries, its positioning may be adapted in each market. Conversely, the positioning may be uniform across countries, but the product itself adapted or modified.

Although this debate first emerged in the 1960s, it has recently taken on a new vigor with the widely publicized pronouncements of proponents of "global standardization" such as Professor Levitt and Saatchi & Saatchi.

The sweeping and somewhat polemic character of their argument has sparked a number of counterarguments as well as discussion of conditions under which such a strategy may be most appropriate. It has, for example, been pointed out that the potential for standardization may be greater for certain types of products such as industrial goods or luxury personal items targeted to upscale consumers, or products with similar penetration rates. Opportunities for standardization are also likely to occur more frequently among industrialized nations, and especially the Triad countries where customer interests as well as market conditions are likely to be more similar than among developing countries.

The role of corporate philosophy and organizational structure in influencing the practicality of implementing a strategy of global standardization has also been recognized. Here, it has been noted that few companies pursue the extreme position of complete standardization with regard to all elements of the marketing mix, and business functions such as R&D, manufacturing, and procurement in all countries throughout the world. Rather, some degree of adaptation is likely to occur relative to certain aspects of the firm's operations or in certain geographic areas. In addition, the feasibility of implementing a standardized strategy will depend on the autonomy accorded to local management. If local management has been accustomed to substantial autonomy, considerable opposition may be encountered in attempting to introduce globally standardized strategies.

An examination of such counterarguments suggests that there are a number of dangers in espousing a philosophy of global standardization for all products and services, and in relation to all markets worldwide. Furthermore, there are numerous difficulties and constraints to implementing such a strategy in many markets, stemming from external market conditions (such as government and trade regulation, competition, the marketing infrastructure, and so on), as well as from the current structure and organization of the firm's operations.

The Global Standardization Philosophy: The Underlying Assumptions

An examination of the arguments in favor of a strategy of global products and brands reveals three key underlying assumptions:

- Customer needs and interests are becoming increasingly homogeneous worldwide.
- People around the world are willing to sacrifice preferences in product features, functions, design, and the like for lower prices at high quality.
- Substantial economies of scale in production and marketing can be achieved through supplying global markets.

There are, however, a number of pitfalls associated with each of these assumptions. These are discussed here in more detail.

Homogenization of the World's Wants

A key premise of the philosophy of global products is that customers' needs and interests are becoming increasingly homogeneous worldwide. But while global segments with similar interests and response patterns may be identified in some product markets, it is by no means clear that this is a universal trend. Furthermore, there is substantial evidence to suggest an increasing diversity of behavior within countries, and the emergence of idiosyncratic country-specific segments.

Lack of Evidence of Homogenization. In a number of product markets ranging from watches, perfume, and handbags to soft drinks and fast foods, companies have successfully identified global customer segments, and developed global products and brands targeted to these segments. These include such stars as Rolex, Omega and Le Baume & Mercier watches, Dior, Patou or Yves St. Laurent perfume. But while these brands are highly visible and widely publicized, they are often, with a few notable exceptions such as Classic Coke or McDonald's, targeted to a relatively restricted upscale international customer segment.

Numerous other companies, however, adapt lines to idiosyncratic country preferences, and develop local brands or product variants targeted to local market segments. The Findus frozen food division of Nestlé, for example, markets fish cakes and fish fingers in the United Kingdom, but beef bourguignon and coq au vin in

France, and vitello con funghi and braviola in Italy. Similarly, Coca-Cola in Japan markets Georgia, cold coffee in a can, and Aquarius, a tonic drink, as well as Classic Coke and Hi-C.

Growth of Intracountry Segmentation Price Sensitivity.   Furthermore, there is a growing body of evidence that suggests substantial heterogeneity within countries. In the United States, for example, the VALS (Value of American Lifestyles) study has identified nine value segments, while other studies have identified major differences in behavior between regions and subcultural segments. Many other countries are also characterized by substantial regional differences as well as different lifestyle and value segments.

Similarly, in industrial markets, while some global segments, often consisting of firms with international operations, can be identified, there also is considerable diversity within and between countries. Often local businesses constitute an important market segment and, especially in developing countries, may differ significantly in technological sophistication, business philosophy and strategy, emphasis on product quality, and service and price, from large multinationals.

The evidence thus suggests that the similarities in customer behavior are restricted to a relatively limited number of target segments, or product markets, while for the most part, there are substantial differences between countries. Proponents of standardization counter that the international strategist should focus on similarities among countries rather than differences. This may, however, imply ignoring a major part of a local market, and the potential profits that may be obtained from tapping other market segments.

Universal Preference for Low Price at Acceptable Quality

Another critical component of the argument for global standardization is that people around the world are willing to sacrifice preferences in product features, functions, design, and the like for lower prices, assuming equivalent quality. Aggressive low pricing for quality products that meet the common needs of customers in markets around the world is believed to further expand the global markets facing the firm. Although an appealing argument, this has three major problems.

Lack of Evidence of Increased Price Sensitivity.   Evidence to suggest that customers are universally willing to trade off specific product features for a lower price is largely lacking. While in many product markets there is invariably a price-sensitive segment, there is no indication that this is on the increase. On the contrary, in many product and service markets, ranging from watches, personal computers, and household appliances to banking and insurance, an interest in multiple product features, product quality, and service appears to be growing.

Low Price Positioning Is a Highly Vulnerable Strategy.   Also, from a strategic point of view, emphasis on price positioning may be undesirable, especially in international markets, since it offers no long-term competitive advantage. A price-positioning strategy is always vulnerable to new technological developments that may lower costs, as well as to attack from competitors with lower overhead, and lower operating or labor costs. Government subsidies to local competitors may also undermine the effectiveness of a price-positioning strategy. In addition, price-sensitive customers typically are not brand or source loyal.

Standardized Low Price Can Be Overpriced in Some Countries and Underpriced in Others. Finally, a strategy based on a combination of a standardized product at a low price, when implemented in countries that vary in their competitive structure as well as the level of economic development, is likely to result in products that are overdesigned and overpriced for some markets and underdesigned and underpriced for others. Cost advantages may also be negated by transportation and distribution costs as well as tariff barriers and/or price regulation.

Economies of Scale of Production and Marketing

The third assumption underlying the philosophy of global standardization is that a key force driving strategy is product technology, and that substantial economies of scale can be achieved by supplying global markets. This does, however, neglect three critical and interrelated points: (1) technological developments in flexible factory automation enable economies of scale to be achieved at lower levels of output and do not require production of a single standardized product, (2) cost of production is only one and often not the critical component in determining the total cost of the product, and (3) strategy should not be solely product driven but should take into account the other components of a marketing strategy, such as positioning, packaging, brand name, advertising, PR, consumer and trade promotion and distribution.

Developments in Flexible Factory Automation. Recent developments in flexible factory automation methods have lowered the minimum efficient scale of operation and have thus enabled companies to supply smaller local markets efficiently, without requiring operations on a global scale. However, diseconomies may result from such operations due to increased transportation and distribution costs, as well as higher administrative overhead, and additional communication and coordination costs.

Furthermore, decentralization of production and establishment of local manufacturing operations enables diversification of risk arising from political events, fluctuations in foreign exchange rates, or economic instability. Recent swings in foreign exchange rates, coupled with the growth of offshore sourcing have underscored the vulnerability of centralizing production in a single location. Government regulations relating to local component and/or offset requirements create additional pressures for local manufacturing. Flexible automation not only implies that decentralization of manufacturing and production may be cost efficient but also makes minor modifications in products of models in the latter stages of production feasible, so that a variety of model versions can be produced without major retooling. Adaptations to product design can thus be made to meet differences in preferences from one country to another without loss of economies of scale.

Production Costs Are Often a Minor Component of Total Cost. In many consumer and service industries, such as cosmetics, detergents, pharmaceuticals, or financial institutions, production costs are a small fraction of total cost. The key to success in these markets is an understanding of the tastes and purchase behavior of target customers' distribution channels, and tailoring products and strategies to these rather than production efficiency. In the detergent industry, for example, mastery of mass-merchandising techniques and an effective brand management system are typically considered the key elements in the success of the giants in this field, such as Procter & Gamble (P&G) or Colgate-Palmolive.

The Standardization Philosophy Is Primarily Product Driven.   The focus on product- and brand-related aspects of strategy in discussions of global standardization is misleading since it ignores the other key strategy variables. Strategy in international markets should also take into consideration other aspects of the marketing mix, and the extent to which these are standardized across country markets rather than adapted to local idiosyncratic characteristics.

Requisite Conditions for Global Standardization

The numerous pitfalls in the rationale underlying the global standardization philosophy suggest that such a strategy is far from universally appropriate for all products, brands, or companies. Only under certain conditions is it likely to prove a "winning" strategy in international markets. These include: (1) the existence of a global market segment, (2) potential synergies from standardization, and (3) the availability of a communication and distribution infrastructure to deliver the firm's offering to target customers worldwide.

Existence of Global Market Segments

As noted previously, global segments may be identified in a number of industrial and consumer markets. In consumer markets these segments are typically luxury- or premium-type products. Global segments are, however, not limited to such product markets, but also exist in other types of markets, such as motorcycle, record, stereo equipment, and computer, where a segment with similar needs and wants can be identified in many countries.

In industrial markets, companies with multinational operations are particularly likely to have similar needs and requirements worldwide. Where the operations are integrated or coordinated across national boundaries, as in the case of banks or other financial institutions, compatibility of operational systems and equipment may be essential. Consequently, they may seek vendors who can supply and service their operations worldwide, in some cases developing global contrasts for such purchases. Similarly, manufacturing companies with worldwide operations may source globally in order to ensure uniformity in quality, service and price of components, and other raw materials throughout their operations.

Marketing of global products and brands to such target segments and global customers enables development of a uniform global image throughout the world. In some markets such as perfume or fashions, association with a specific country of origin or a foreign image in general may carry a prestige connotation. In other cases, for example, Sony electronic equipment, McDonald's hamburgers, Hertz or Avis car rental, IBM computers, or Xerox office equipment, it may help to develop a worldwide reputation for quality and service. Just as multinational corporations may seek uniformity in supply worldwide, some consumers who travel extensively may be interested in finding the same brand of cigarettes and soft drinks, or hotels, in foreign countries. This may be particularly relevant in product markets used extensively by international travelers.

While the existence of a potential global segment is a key motivating factor for developing a global product and brand strategy, it is important to note that the desirability of such a strategy depends on the size and economic viability of the segment in question, the strength of the segment's preference for the global brand, as well as the ability to reach the segment effectively and profitably.

Synergies Associated with Global Standardization

Global standardization may also have a number of synergistic effects. In addition to those associated with a global image noted above, opportunities may exist for the transfer of good ideas for products or promotional strategies from one country to another.

The standardization of strategy and operations across a number of countries may also enable the acquisition or exploitation of specific types of expertise that would not be feasible otherwise. Expertise in assessing country risk or foreign exchange risk, or in identifying and interpreting information relating to multiple country markets, for example, may be developed.

Such synergies are not, however, unique to a strategy of global standardization, but may also occur wherever operations and strategy are coordinated or integrated across country markets. In fact, only certain scale economies associated with product and advertising copy standardization, and the development of a global image as discussed earlier, are unique to global standardization.

Availability of an International Communication and Distribution Infrastructure

The effectiveness of global standardization also depends to a large extent on the availability of an international infrastructure of communications and distribution. As many corporations have expanded overseas, service organizations have followed their customers abroad to supply their needs worldwide.

Advertising agencies such as Saatchi & Saatchi, McCann Erickson, and Young & Rubicam now have an international network of operations throughout the world, while many research agencies can also supply services in major markets worldwide. With the growing integration of financial markets, banks, investment firms, insurance and other financial institutions are also becoming increasingly international in orientation and are expanding the scope of their operations in world markets. The physical distribution network of shippers, freight forwarding, export and import agents, customs clearing, invoicing and insurance agents is also becoming increasingly integrated to meet demand for international shipment of goods and services.

Improvements in telecommunications and in logistical systems have considerably increased capacity to manage operations on a global scale and hence facilitate adoption of global standardization strategies. The spread of telex and fax systems, as well as satellite linkages and international computer linkages, all contribute to the shrinking of distances and facilitate globalization of operations. Similarly, improvements in transportation systems and physical logistics such as containerization and computerized inventory and handling systems have enabled significant cost savings as well as reducing time required to move goods across major distances.

Operational Constraints to Effective Implementation of a Standardization Strategy

While adoption of a standardized strategy may be desirable under certain conditions, there are a number of constraints that severely restrict the firm's ability to develop and implement a standardized strategy.

External Constraints to Effective Standardization

The numerous external constraints that impede global standardization are well recognized. Here, three major categories are highlighted, namely, (1) government and trade restrictions; (2) differences in the marketing infrastructure, such as the availability and effectiveness of promotional media; (3) the character of resource markets, and differences in the availability and costs of resources; and (4) differences in competition from one country to another.

Government and Trade Restrictions.   Government and trade restrictions, such as tariff and other trade barriers, product, pricing or promotional regulation, frequently hamper standardization of the product line, pricing, or promotional strategy. Tariffs or quotas on the import of key materials, components, or other resources may, for example, affect production costs and thus hamper uniform pricing or alternatively result in the substitution of other components and modifications in product design. Local content requirements or compensatory export requirements, which specify that products contain a certain proportion of components manufactured locally or that a certain volume of production is exported to offset imports of components or other services, may have a similar impact.

The existence of cartels such as the European steel cartel, or the Swiss chocolate cartel, may also impede or exclude standardized strategies in countries covered by these agreements. In particular, they may affect adoption of a uniform pricing strategy as the cartel sets prices for the industry. Cartel members may also control established distribution channels, thus preventing use of a standardized distribution strategy. Extensive grey markets in countries such as India, Hong Kong, and South America may also affect administered pricing systems, and require adjustment of pricing strategies.

The Nature of the Marketing Infrastructure.   Differences in the marketing infrastructure from one country to another may hamper use of a standardized strategy. These may, for example, include differences in the availability and reach of various promotional media, in the availability of certain distribution channels or retail institutions, or in the existence and efficiency of the communication and transportation network. Such factors may, therefore, require considerable adaptation of strategy of local market conditions.

Interdependencies with Resource Markets.   Yet another constraint to the development of standardized strategies is the nature of resource markets, and their operation in different countries throughout the world as well as the interdependency of these markets with marketing decisions. Availability and cost of raw materials, as well as labor and other resources in different locations, will affect not only decisions regarding sourcing of and hence the location of manufacturing activities but also marketing strategy decisions such as product design. For example, in the paper industry, availability of cheap local materials such as jute and sugar cane may result in their substitution for wood fiber.

Cost differentials relative to raw materials, labor, management, and other inputs may also influence the trade-off relative to alternative strategies. For example, high packaging cost relative to physical distribution may result in use of cheaper packaging with a shorter shelf life and more frequent shipments. Similarly, low labor costs relative to media may encourage a shift from mass media advertising to labor-intensive promotion such as personal selling and product demonstration.

Availability of capital, technology, and manufacturing capabilities in different locations will also affect decisions about licensing, contract manufacturing, joint ventures, and other "make-buy" types of decisions for different markets, as well as decisions about countertrade, reciprocity, and other long-term relations.

The Nature of the Competitive Structure.   Differences in the nature of the competitive situation from one country to another may also suggest the desirability of adaptation strategy. Even in markets characterized by global competition, such as agricultural equipment and motorcycles, the existence of low-cost competition in certain countries may suggest the desirability of marketing stripped-down models or lowering prices to meet such competition. Even where competitors are predominantly other multinationals, preemption of established distribution networks may encourage adoption of innovative distribution methods or direct distribution to short-circuit an entrenched position. Thus, the existence of global competition does not necessarily imply a need for global standardization.

All such aspects thus impose major constraints on the feasibility and effectiveness of a standardized strategy, and suggest the desirability or need to adapt to specific market conditions.

Internal Constraints to Effective Standardization

In addition to such external constraints on the feasibility of a global standardization strategy, there are also a number of internal constraints that may need to be considered. These include compatibility with the existing network of operations overseas, as well as opposition or lack of enthusiasm among local management toward a standardized strategy.

Existing International Operations.   Proponents of global standardization typically take the position of a novice company with no operations in international markets, and hence fail to take into consideration the fit of the proposed strategy with current international activities. In practice, however, many companies have a number of existing operations in various countries. In some cases, these are joint ventures, or licensing operations or involve some collaboration in purchasing, manufacturing or distribution with other companies. Even where foreign manufacturing and distribution operations are wholly owned, the establishment of a distribution network will typically entail relationships with other organizations, for example, exclusive distributor agreements.

Such commitments may be difficult if not impossible to change in the short run, and may constitute a major impediment to adoption of a standardized strategy. If, for example, a joint venture with a local company has been established to manufacture and market a product line in a specific country or region, resistance from the local partner (or government authorities) may be encountered if the parent company wishes to shift production or import components from another location. Similarly, a licensing contract will impede a firm from supplying the products covered by the agreement from an alternative location for the duration of the contract, even if it becomes more cost efficient to do so.

Conversely, the establishment of an effective dealer or distribution network in a country or region may constitute an important resource to a company. The addition of new products to the product line currently sold or distributed by this network may therefore provide a more efficient utilization of company resources than expanding to new countries or geographic regions with the existing product line, as this would require substantial investment in the establishment of a new distribution network.

In addition, overseas subsidiaries may currently be marketing not only core products and brands from the company's domestic business, but may also have added or acquired local or regional products and brands in response to local market demand. In some cases, therefore, introduction of a global product or brand may be likely to cannibalize sales of local or regional brands.

Advocates of standardization thus need to take into consideration the evolutionary character of international involvement, which may render a universal strategy of global products and brands suboptimal. Somewhat ironically, the longer the history of a multinational corporation's involvement in foreign or international markets, and the more diversified and far-flung its operations, the more likely it is that standardization will not lead to optimal results.

Local Management Motivation and Attitudes.   Another internal constraint concerns the motivation and attitudes of local management with regard to standardization. Standardized strategies tend to facilitate or result in centralization in the planning and organization of international activities. Especially if input from local management is limited, this may result in a feeling that strategy is "imposed" by corporate headquarters, and/or not adequately adapted or appropriate in view of specific local market characteristics and conditions. Local management is likely to take the view "it won't work here—things are different," which will reduce their motivation to implement a standardized strategy effectively.

A Framework for Classifying Global Strategy Options

The adoption of a global perspective should not be viewed as synonymous with a strategy of global products and brands. Rather, for most companies such a perspective implies consideration of a broad range of strategic options of which standardization is merely one.

In essence, a global perspective implies planning strategy relative to markets worldwide rather than on a country-by-country basis. This may result in the identification of opportunities for global products and brands and/or integrating and coordinating strategy across national boundaries to exploit potential synergies of operating on an international scale. Such opportunities should, however, be weighed against the benefits of adaptation to idiosyncratic customer characteristics.

The development of an effective global strategy thus requires a careful examination of all international options in terms of standardization versus adaptation open to the firm.

A firm's international operations are likely to be characterized by a mix of strategies, including not only global products and brands, but also some regional products and brands and some national products and brands. Similarly, some target segments may be global, others regional, and others national. Hybrid strategies of this nature thus enable a company to take advantage of the benefits of standardization and potential synergies from operating on an international scale, while at the same time not losing those afforded by adaptation to specific country characteristics and customer preferences.

■ THE DYNAMICS OF GLOBAL COMPETITION†

By C. K. Prahalad and Yves Doz

As the emerging patterns of competition in a wide variety of businesses become of increasing concern, especially the intense competition brought about by overseas competitors, the words *global business* and *global competition* have entered the lexicon of most managers. However, the distinction between the intrinsic characteristics of a business—its cost structure, technology, and customers, for example, at a given point in time—and the characteristics of competition in that business is not always well understood. Further, labeling businesses as "global" or "multidomestic" may hide broad variations in the underlying managerial tasks. We shall develop a methodology for capturing the characteristics of a wide range of businesses or for understanding the "existing rules of the game" in a business. Then we shall go beyond the analysis of existing rules and examine how determined competitors often change those rules.

The Building Blocks

The building blocks of the methodology for mapping the characteristics of a business start with the managerial demands that it imposes on senior management.

Global Integration of Activities

Integration refers to the centralized management of geographically dispersed activities on an ongoing basis. Managing shipments of parts and subassemblies across a network of manufacturing facilities in various countries is an example of integration of activities.

The need for integration arises in response to pressures to reduce costs and optimize investment. Pressures to reduce cost may force location of plants in countries with low labor costs, such as South Korea, Taiwan, and Malaysia. Products are then shipped from those plants to the established markets of the United States and Europe. The same pressures may also lead to building large-scale, highly specialized plants to realize economies of scale. Ford's European operations and IBM's worldwide manufacturing operations are examples of the phenomenon. In either case, the goal is leveraging the advantages of low manufacturing cost. Managerially, that translates into a need for ongoing management of logistics that cut across multiple national boundaries.

Global Strategic Coordination

Strategic coordination refers to the central management of resource commitments across national boundaries in the pursuit of a strategy. It is distinct from the integration of ongoing activities across national borders. Typical examples would involve coordinating research and development (R&D) priorities across several laboratories, coordinating pricing to global customers, and facilitating transfers of technology from headquarters to subsidiaries and across subsidiaries. Unlike activity integration, strategic coordination can be selective and nonroutine.

†**Source:** Reprinted with the permission of The Free Press, a Division of Macmillan, Inc. from *The Multinational Mission: Balancing Local Demands and Global Vision*, by C. K. Prahalad and Yves L. Doz. Copyright © 1986 by The Free Press.

Strategic coordination is often essential to provide competitive and strategic coherence to resource commitments made over time by headquarters and various subsidiaries in multiple countries. The goal of strategic coordination is to recognize, build, and defend long-term competitive advantages. For example, headquarters may assign highly differentiated goals to various subsidiaries in the same business in order to develop a coherent response to competition.

Strategic coordination, like integration of activities, often involves headquarters and one or several subsidiaries. Coordination decisions transcend a single subsidiary.

Local Responsiveness

Local responsiveness refers to resource commitment decisions taken autonomously by a subsidiary in response to primarily local competitive or customer demands. In a wide variety of businesses, there may be no competitive advantage to be gained by coordinating actions across subsidiaries; in fact, that may prove to be detrimental.

Typically, businesses where there are no meaningful economies of scale or proprietary technology (e.g., processed foods) fall into this category. The need for significant local adaptation of products or differences in distribution across national markets may also indicate a need for local responsiveness.

Mapping the Characteristics of a Business

Let us take the case of Corning Glass. As of 1975 it operated internationally in six business categories with more than sixty thousand line items. The businesses were:

- Television products, which included supplying TV bulbs to original equipment manufacturers (OEM) like RCA, Philips, and Sylvania
- Electronic products, which consisted of components like resistors and capacitors used by computer, communication, and military equipment manufacturers
- Consumer products, chiefly Corning Ware, the leading cookware product in the United States
- Medical products, consisting of scientific instruments such as blood gas analyzers and diagnostic reagents
- Science products, specifically laboratory glassware
- Technical products, mostly ophthalmic products, which consisted of photochromatic eyeglass blanks, produced in a variety of thicknesses, curvatures, and so forth

Corning's overseas activities comprised fourteen major foreign manufacturing operations and a host of licensees. Its products were produced abroad, and the overseas sales volume was significant.

With such a spread of overseas activities in both manufacturing and marketing, should Corning treat all its businesses as global? Are there differences among those businesses that transcend the location of plants and the distribution of markets around the world?

It is a great temptation to categorize businesses as diverse as Corning Ware and electronic products as either global (meaning their activities can and should be integrated across borders) or multidomestic (meaning that they are local businesses in multiple countries). However, each business is subject to varying degrees of economic, competitive, and technological pressures that push it toward becoming global or toward remaining locally responsive. Some of the Corning businesses have to accommodate both pressures simultaneously.

The Integration-Responsiveness Grid

The Integration-Responsiveness (IR) grid provides us with a way of capturing the pressures on a given business—pressures that make *strategic coordination* and *global integration of activities* critical, as well as the pressures that make being sensitive to the diverse demands of various national markets and achieving *local responsiveness* critical.

We can use the following criteria for evaluating the pressures for global coordination and integration, as well as local responsiveness.

Pressures for Global Strategic Coordination

Importance of multinational customers. The dependence of a business on multinational original equipment manufacturer (OEM) customers imposes a need for global strategic coordination. For example, in the TV bulbs business, a significant portion of the total sales went to multinational original equipment manufacturer (OEM) customers like Philips and Sylvania. Multinational customers can, and often do, compare prices charged them by their suppliers around the world, demand the same level of service and product support, and have centralized vendor certification. The product is often sold at the center, say, to the OEM's product division, and delivered around the world—wherever the multinational customer may need it. The percentage of sales to multinational OEM customers and their importance to the business can thus dictate the need for global coordination. In the case of Corning Ware, the opposite was true. Its customers were mostly local, and it was primarily a mass-marketed item.

Presence of multinational competitors. The presence of competitors who operate in multiple markets indicates the potential for global competition. Consequently, it is crucial to gather intelligence on competitors across national markets, to understand their strategic intent, and to be ready to respond to their actions wherever most appropriate. The presence of multinational competitors calls for global strategic coordination. Competitors for Corning's various businesses ranged from global competitors in electronic products, to regional competitors in TV products, to local competitors in lab ware and Corning cookware.

Investment intensity. If an aspect of the business is investment intensive (e.g., R&D, manufacturing), the need to leverage that investment increases the need for global coordination. Worldwide product strategies have to be developed and implemented quickly to make the large initial investments profitable.

At Corning, the intensity of the R&D effort in the medical products business and the intensity of investment in manufacturing and product development in the electronics business indicated that a high level of global coordination and integration was required in those two businesses. In the lab ware business, the pressure for international strategic coordination was not felt.

Technology intensity. Technology intensity and the extent of proprietary technology often encourage firms to manufacture in only a few selected locations. Having fewer manufacturing sites allows easier control over quality, cost, and new product introduction. Centralized product development and manufacturing operations in a few locations result in global integration, particularly when the markets are widely dispersed.

Again, at Corning the technological intensity differed from business to business. For example, the lab ware required a very low technology as compared to the medical products business. Medical products had short life cycles, with constantly renewed markets, whereas lab ware had stable products and applications.

Pressure for cost reduction. Global integration is often a response to pressure for cost reduction. Cost reduction requires sourcing the product from low-factor-cost locations (global sourcing), or exploiting economies of scale and experience by building large plants that serve multiple national markets. Either approach to lowering costs imposes a need for global integration.

Some of Corning's businesses, such as electronic products, were subject to severe cost pressures, while others, like Corning Ware, were less so.

Universal needs. If the product meets a universal need and requires little adaptation across national markets, global integration is obviously facilitated.

Electronic products—capacitors, resistors—are good examples of universal products. They do not vary by country. On the other hand, Corning Ware is not universal. It must be adapted to suit various market needs. For example, the "oven-to-freezer" feature may be a big hit in the United States but may not be appropriate in France; a soufflé dish popular in France may not have a big market in the Midwest.

Access to raw materials and energy. Access to raw materials and a cheap and plentiful supply of energy can force manufacturing to be located in a specific area. Aluminum smelters, paper mills, and, increasingly, petrochemicals tend to be located where the raw materials are available. That tendency in some businesses suggests global coordination and integration. None of Corning's businesses had to contend with this issue.

Pressures for Local Responsiveness

Differences in customer needs. Businesses that thrive on satisfying a diverse set of customer needs, most of which is nation or region specific, require a locally responsive strategy.

Several businesses within Corning have satisfied country-specific needs. Corning Ware, technical materials, and to some extent chemical systems were designed with specific customers of individual countries in mind. On the other hand, electronic products met a universal need.

Differences in distribution channels. Differences in distribution channels in various countries and the differences in pricing, product positioning, promotion, and advertising that those differences entail indicate the need for local responsiveness.

In the lab ware business at Corning, the distribution system used to access the school systems in various countries varied; comparable differences in distribution channels characterized Corning Ware. On the other hand, in the electronic and TV products businesses, which were primarily serving OEM customers, the differences among national markets were only marginal.

Availability of substitutes and the need to adapt. If a product function is being met by local substitutes, with differing price-performance relationships in a given national market, or if the product must be significantly adapted to be locally competitive, then a locally responsive strategy is indicated.

Corning Ware had a significant number of substitutes—cooking ware made from other materials, as well as cooking ware promoted differently. It also needed to be adapted to suit local conditions. In the case of electronic products, neither condition was important: products were universal and faced no differentiated local substitutes.

Market structure. Market structure includes the importance of local competitors as compared to multinational ones, as well as the extent of their concentration. If local competitors tend to control a significant portion of the market and/or if the industry is not concentrated, then a locally responsive posture is most usually indicated (unless there are merits to competing globally to make the industry structure evolve in your favor). A fragmented industry with local competitors indicates that there may be no inherent advantages to size and scale, unless product and process technology can be changed.

Again, among Corning's businesses, lab ware had to compete in each national market with a large number of local competitors in a fragmented industry, while TV products had to cope with only a handful of large competitors in a globally concentrated industry.

Host government demands. Demands imposed by host governments for local self-sufficiency for a variety of reasons—from concerns of national development to concerns of national security—can force a business to become locally responsive.

Mapping Corning's Businesses in the Integration-Responsiveness Grid

It is obvious that Corning does not operate in any one type of business—either global or multidomestic. Each of its businesses is subject to a different combination of pressures toward global coordination and integration and toward local responsiveness—pressures that elude a simple either/or classification. We can identify the differences using the criteria we have developed, as shown in table 10-1.

The characteristics of the three businesses can now be captured in an Integration-Responsiveness Grid, as shown in figure 10-1. From the foregoing analysis, the following generalizations can be drawn:

1. The mapping of the characteristics of the various businesses illustrates the differences among them, even though all six businesses share the same corporate logo and all evolved out of the same broad glass technology. Because of those differences, managers must examine each business individually to develop strategies rather than treat them all alike.

2. Classifying businesses broadly as either global or local can be misleading. There are few businesses that are totally local. If there were no advantages to be gained in that business by a multinational corporation (MNC), then it is likely to be very fragmented with no scope for leveraging knowledge, products, financial muscle, or brands across markets. On the other hand, few businesses are totally global. A variety of factors, including the need for a responsive and differentiated local presence in various countries, make it difficult to ignore totally the demands of various national markets.

3. The purpose of the IR framework is to assess the *relative importance* of the two sets of conflicting demands on a business and to determine which of the two provides strategic leverage at a given point in time.

4. In the case of Corning, some businesses tend toward global integration (e.g., electronics, medical products). In those businesses, strategic advantage will accrue to the competitor who is organized to exploit the benefits of strategic coordination in investments, product policy, product development, pricing, monitoring competitors, and so forth. In businesses that tend toward local responsiveness (e.g., Corning Ware, lab ware), strategic advantage accrues to the firm that is sensitive to the need for decentralized pricing, promotion, and product policy. There may be little benefit in strategic coordination.

5. In Corning's case the real challenge to management is not in managing the extremes; it is in managing multifocal businesses, which demand sensitivity to both dimensions *at the same time,* as is the case with the TV products business. This implies that in such busi-

TABLE 10-1
Comparison of Three
Businesses within Corning

Criteria	Electronics	TV Products	Corning Ware
Pressures for Global Strategic Coordination			
Importance of multinational customers	high	high	low
Importance of multinational competitors	high	medium/high	low
Investment intensity	high	high	low/medium
Pressures for Global Operational Integration			
Technology intensity	medium	medium	low
Pressure for cost reduction	high	high	low
Universal needs	high	medium	low
Access to raw materials and energy	n/a	n/a	n/a
Need for Global Integration	*high*	*medium*	*low*
Pressures for Local Responsiveness			
Differences in customer needs	low	medium?	high
Differences in distribution	low	low	high
Need for substitutes and product adaptation	low	low	high
Market structure	concentrated	concentrated	fragmented
Host government demands	n/a	n/a	n/a
Need for Local Responsiveness	*low*	*medium*	*high*

nesses it is unwise to make a one-time trade-off in favor of either global integration or local responsiveness. Both demands have to be managed simultaneously.

Some Implications

Several managerial conclusions can be derived from mapping the characteristics of a business on the IR grid.

1. Corning's electronic components, which is high on the need for global integration and low on the need for local responsiveness, suggests that managers developing strategies for that business must pay considerably more attention to leveraging aspects like economies of scale, product development, global customers, and global competitors than to issues of local responsiveness. This also implies that resource allocation decisions with respect to key elements of strategy for that business (such as plant location and investment, pricing, product development, and key account management) may have to be centralized. In other words, for the electronic components business, the locus of strategic management is the central worldwide business management group. On the other hand, for Corning Ware or lab ware, the key strategic choices (pricing, promotion, choice of channels) have to be managed in a decentralized mode. The center for strategy making is the regional or the national subsidiary managers, as contrasted with the center for the electronic components business, as shown in figure 10-2.

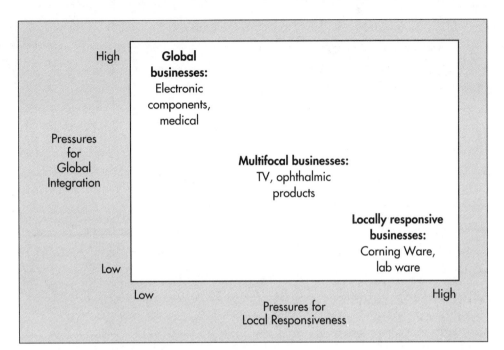

FIGURE 10-1
Integration – Responsiveness Grid: Characteristics of Corning's Business

2. In both those businesses representing the extremes—electronic components and Corning Ware—managers can make "clear one-time choices" of what aspects of the business to leverage. Therefore, a clear and simple organizational form—worldwide business management in the case of electronic components and area management in the case of Corning Ware—is possible. In other words, the relative simplicity of the strategic priorities enables a clear-cut choice of simple organization.

3. In the case of the TV business the strategic choice is not all that clear-cut. Some elements of strategy, like plant size and technology, may have to be managed centrally. On the other hand, deliveries, competitors, and some key customers may have to be managed both regionally and locally. That implies that managers cannot make a "one-time choice" on which of the two dimensions to leverage. They must *simultaneously focus their attention* on aspects of the business that require global integration and aspects that demand local responsiveness, and on varying degrees of strategic coordination. This need for *multiple focal points for managing* suggests that managers must reflect the need for multiple points of view—the need to integrate and be responsive at the same time—in the way that business is organized. That requires the organization to be multifocal or matrix.

In general, many businesses that have the characteristics of Corning's TV business will need a *multifocal* or matrix organization, despite all the problems of managing such an organization.

The IR grid is not just a tool for discovering the essential orientation of a business for strategy making. It also enables managers to decide on the appropriate form of organization to manage the strategic orientation desired.

Mapping the Dynamics of a Business on the IR Grid

While taking Corning to illustrate the basic approach to mapping the characteristics on the IR grid, we have assumed our data and have assessed the characteristics of a business at a given point in time, rather than the way it might change over time. For

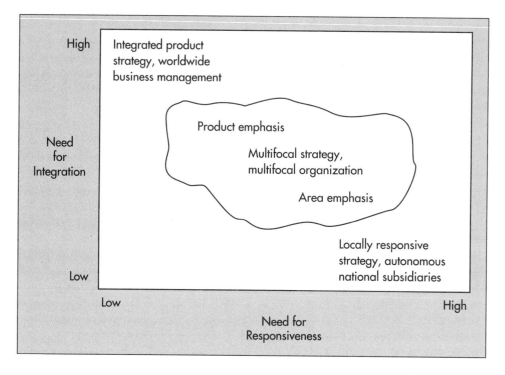

the strategist, the direction of possible change in the characteristics of a business is even more interesting than the situation at a given point in time. Now we shall identify the factors that can change the location of a business in the IR grid over time as well as suggest the type of data that might be useful in understanding such trends early.

Changes in Underlying Industry Economics

Shifts in the location of a business on the IR grid are often a result of shifts in the underlying economics of the industry. Let us take the example of ethylene oxide. During the early 1970s, most chemical firms operated plants of an annual capacity of 50 million to 75 million pounds. In most markets of the world, especially in the United States and Europe, that meant firms could dedicate a plant (or more) to each important national market. As each market could afford its own manufacturing and marketing facilities, and as ethylene oxide was a commodity product, managers could be very sensitive to local needs. In the early 1970s most firms operated with considerable local responsiveness and a low level of global integration. However, over the period 1972–75, several chemical firms, especially ICI in the United Kingdom, started building plants with a capacity as large as 250 million to 400 million pounds. The cost advantage arising from the economies of scale was around 12 to 15 percent over traditional, smaller plants. Because a single national market could not absorb the output of the large-scale plants, the firm had to coordinate prices, product specifications, logistics, and, most importantly, investments across several, so far autonomous, national markets. In a very short time, the center of gravity for strategy making in the ethylene oxide business for several chemical firms had shifted toward high need for integration and low need for responsiveness. Given a 12 to 15 percent cost advantage in a commodity chemical, few competitors could resist the pressure to build large plants in order to remain competitive. On the IR grid, the ethylene oxide business would be depicted as locally responsive until 1972.

Impact of Governments

During the same period drug companies also faced a shift in their business. The proprietary drug business, involving significant investment in R&D and requiring strict quality controls in manufacturing, is best managed centrally, from a few locations. However, the politics of health care in many countries around the world force drug firms to manufacture in multiple locations. They are also subject to local clinical testing, registration procedures, and pricing restrictions. As governments and quasi-government agencies control a significant portion of the health care budget in most countries, they are in a position to demand a high level of local responsiveness. That has forced most drug firms into simultaneously facing a high need for global integration and a high need for local responsiveness.

Shifts in the Competitive Focus of Customers

Supplier industries tend to follow the shifts in the industries they serve. For example, the automobile industry has become global in terms of its sourcing and design, as well as manufacturing. That trend has had impact on suppliers to the auto industry. For example, paint manufacturers, who manufacture paints for household use as well as car finishes, have typically operated on a locally responsive basis. The trend in the auto industry has forced one segment of their operations, car finishes, to become globally integrated. Product planners and purchasing agents in the auto industry would like to contract with a set of suppliers who can supply the same quality of car finish around the world. Yet the home paint segment is still locally responsive. Paint manufacturers who saw their business as essentially locally responsive had to contend with the realization that the auto industry internationalization was changing the nature of customer relations in a segment of their business; they had to recognize that they could no longer treat both segments of their business—car finishes and home paints—alike.

Firms Learn

The way a business is perceived in the IR grid may shift as firms learn about their businesses and see new opportunities and problems. For example, when a processed food firm, Nabisco, went overseas, its management assumed the businesses could be managed centrally and that the benefits of coordinating in advertising and product development outweighed the benefits of local responsiveness. It soon became apparent that the habits of consumers were harder to change in some of the businesses than originally thought; a locally responsive strategy made more sense.

Changing the "Rules of the Game"

Other firms saw opportunities to do exactly the opposite. Otis Elevator saw an opportunity in the late 1960s to integrate its operations in the elevator market in Europe. At that time the market was dominated by local firms; most MNCs also operated on a locally responsive mode. Through a process of acquisitions and consolidations, by standardizing elevator design, and by cutting costs, Otis changed the rules of the game. It changed the economics of the industry to a point where regional integration, if not global integration, became the dominant mode. The first company to initiate and exploit that change can gain a considerable advantage over its competitors, who are slower to move toward international integration.

The success of Japanese competitors in a variety of industries can be attributed to their ability to pick primarily locally responsive industries, even those populated by MNCs, and change them to globally integrated businesses. Examples abound. Traditional competitors who were multinational prior to the Japanese competitive thrust in the auto industry (e.g., General Motors), ball bearings (e.g., SKF), and television sets (e.g., Philips) operated on a locally responsive basis. They were caught off guard. Once a determined competitor changes the rules of the game, the degrees of freedom available to others may be limited, as in the case of ethylene oxide or in the auto and elevator industries.

The movement of a business within the IR grid is very much influenced by the perceptions, judgments, and ambitions of managers on how it can be resegmented or changed. Significant shifts in the location of a business in the IR grid imply that the key success factors in that business have changed dramatically, leading to shifts in strategy. Strategy development is therefore not just an exercise in assessing the "rules of the game" in a given business, at a given point in time (i.e., the location of a business in the IR grid); it is as much developing viable new rules of the game (i.e., identifying opportunities for mobility within the IR grid). That calls for marrying analysis of objective data and current industry patterns and managerial perceptions together with judgments on how the business can be changed.

IR Pressures May Affect Functions within a Business Differently

We have assumed, so far, in identifying the pressures for global integration and local responsiveness that the unit of analysis is a discrete business. In some cases, however, functions within a business may respond differently to those pressures. For example, in the computer industry, integrated R&D is common. Manufacturing may be somewhat decentralized, and marketing fairly locally responsive.

Functions such as R&D, manufacturing, marketing, and service may be used to identify pressures for global integration and local responsiveness, when each function represents a significant commitment of distinct types of resources and different underlying cost structures (significant economies of scale in R&D and the need for differentiated marketing tasks by country), and when internal mechanisms exist or can be developed to coordinate the functions that are managed differently.

Global Business versus Global Competition

We have so far examined the characteristics of a business using the IR grid and have identified factors that cause mobility of a business within that framework. However, the location of a business in the IR framework does not always identify the pattern of competition in a business. It is likely that if a business is high on global integration and low on local responsiveness, (e.g., semiconductors), it will be run, by most firms participating in that business, on a worldwide basis. On the other hand, a business high on local responsiveness and low on global integration (e.g., processed foods), is likely to be run with significant local autonomy. Businesses that are high on both dimensions (e.g., telecommunications, ethical drugs), may require a complex structure that accommodates the pressures of both integration and responsiveness. But those patterns do not identify the nature of competition that may exist in a given business. For example, the detergents business would be seen as locally responsive in the IR grid. There are no overwhelming economies of scale in the manufacture of detergents.

The technology is well known. Managing differences in distribution, promotion, and pricing across national markets are crucial. Based on that analysis, can we conclude that Unilever and Procter & Gamble are not involved in global competition? The computer industry will be regarded as a global business in the IR grid. Does that mean that all computer firms have to be global in their scope of operations or compete across the world? Computer firms like Nixdorf, ICL, Bull, and until recently Hitachi and Fujitsu competed primarily in their national markets, protected by privileged access to the public sector or to nationally defined customers. If we believe that the structural characteristics of a business—such as cost, technology, scale, customer profiles—*determine rather than influence* the pattern of a global competition, then the analysis developed before is adequate. However, if we believe that competitors influence the patterns of competition as much as the underlying characteristics of a business and that often they change those characteristics through competitive innovation, then we need to pay special attention to the role of *key competitors' strategic intentions in determining the patterns of global competition.*

Cost Structure versus Cash Flow

Most managers believe that cost reduction (or gaining cost parity with Japanese and Korean competitors) is the essence of the competitive problem faced by Western MNCs. We would like to suggest that global competition is not about cost reduction per se but about managing *global cash flows*. Consider, for example, the following scenario:

Let us assume that CPC, the consumer products MNC, has a dominant market share in the cooking oil business in Brazil. The product and the brand name are well established. Because of CPC's dominant share and the absence of large and viable competitors in that business in Brazil, CPC typically enjoys very high levels of profitability. Let us further assume that Unilever, sensing the profit potential in Brazil for packaged and branded cooking oil, introduces a similar product. To gain market entry, Unilever prices its product about 5 to 8 percent lower and promotes it heavily with the trade. What should the manager of CPC Brazil do? Obviously there are no great economies of scale in manufacturing in the packaged cooking oil business, and CPC does not enjoy a competitive advantage based purely on size in Brazil. Switching costs to customers are almost negligible. By the criteria we developed, packaged cooking oil is a "locally responsive" business.

We have posed this question to a large number of executives. In our experience, the response to the question is almost always "I will also lower prices and defend my market share" or "I will give better discounts to the trade and advertise more heavily" or "I am willing to sacrifice some profit margin in Brazil to defend my market share." When pushed to recognize the reality that any actions in Brazil—be it more advertising, more discounts, or price reductions—will all lead to deterioration of profits, managers typically would concede market share to the aggressor, in this case to Unilever. What are the lessons of this example?

1. Even though packaged cooking oil is a locally responsive business, it cannot be defended locally (in Brazil) against a determined global competitor like Unilever without a significant profit penalty. Unilever, in reducing prices and increasing discounts to the trade in Brazil, exposed only a very small percentage of its worldwide cash flow in that business. On the other hand, CPC exposed a significant percentage of its worldwide cash flow. Any price reduction by CPC in Brazil to counter Unilever's actions would hurt CPC more than it is likely to hurt Unilever. The only viable strategy for CPC is to search for Unilever's cash sanctuaries—whether in Germany or in the United Kingdom—and take

price action there. That is likely to put a "monkey wrench in Unilever's money machine" and reduce its ability to continue to fund market share battles in Brazil. Even though the characteristics of that business suggest that the business ought to be locally responsive, the ability of multimarket firms like Unilever and CPC to coordinate strategies and cash flows across markets creates a competitive arena that is global.

2. The essence of global competition, as illustrated by the CPC-Unilever example, is the *management of international cash flows and strategic coordination,* even when global integration across subsidiaries in terms of product flows does not take place. If CPC is to become an effective competitor against Unilever, it has to have viable operations in markets like Germany and the United Kingdom—Unilever's profit sanctuaries. The ability to retaliate against Unilever is conditional on CPC's having operations in Unilever's profit sanctuaries as well as the ability to coordinate actions strategically between the two subsidiaries— say Brazil and Germany. It assumes that the CPC manager in Germany is willing or can be persuaded to take a short-term profit penalty in order to support the Brazilian operations. As every MNC manager knows, few organizations have the ability to coordinate subsidiaries' actions—as, for example, in Brazil and Germany. Moreover, the internal systems (planning, performance measurement, and compensation) in most MNCs act as impediments to such strategic behavior.

3. MNCs that are preoccupied with costs may find themselves strategically vulnerable. In the example above, even if CPC had lower costs than Unilever in Brazil, Unilever's actions would erode CPC's profit margin. Unilever could take a profit penalty in Brazil as long as its profit sanctuaries remained uncontested in Germany and the United Kingdom. CPC's lower costs in Brazil allow it to sustain a competitive battle and to outlast Unilever only if Unilever also competes on a market-by-market basis and does not coordinate its strategies across markets.

Managing Cash Flows

The game of global competition revolves around cash flows. Recognition of that fact allows managers to emphasize not just the cost side of the equation but also the price side.

Managing the Cost Side

The goal of the strategist in managing the cost side is simply this: How do I get the lowest possible systemwide cost in this business? The factors to consider in determining the lowest possible net cost are the following:

Factor costs. Factor costs refer to the location-specific advantages that accrue to a manufacturer. Included in factor costs are labor cost differentials between alternative manufacturing locations, availability of cheap sources of raw materials or semifinished materials, and availability and access to low-cost capital, as well as preferential tax treatment in specific locations.

Exchange rate advantages. The volatility of exchange rates during the last decade has brought an additional dimension to the problem of a competitor's cost advantage.

Scale advantages. Cost advantages can accrue to manufacturers from the average age of plants and the level of their technological sophistication. Further, productivity advantages accruing from better utilization of equipment, materials, and labor can add an additional layer of cost advantage.

The Manufacturing System

The manufacturing system has to balance the three dimensions of the cost equation—labor costs, manufacturing scale and technology, and exchange rate fluctuations.

The strategist's task is not to reduce the impact of any one of those dimensions to the exclusion of others but to strike a balance among the three factors, as well as to manage the system flexibly. That entails the following:

1. The business must have a portfolio of manufacturing locations that allows the firm to exploit both factor cost advantages and the exchange rate differentials.

2. While the logic of a portfolio of manufacturing locations and flexible loading of those locations is appealing, there are several impediments to accomplishing that goal. The first impediment is the difficulty of integrating the activities of various national subsidiaries and varying the load assigned to them in the short term. Issues of performance evaluation, incentive compensation, national pride, and the stability of the work force interfere seriously with the ability to be flexible. National policies in various countries also restrict flexibility in the short term.

Managing the Price Side

The concern of the strategist in managing the price side is simply this: How do I get the highest net price in this business? Because there are significant price differentials for the same product and "functionality" in different markets, by developing a portfolio of markets the strategist can maximize the bet prices for the system as a whole. The factors to consider are as follows.

Structure of markets. The market of each country is unique in terms of its competitive structure. The intensity of competition, which determines price levels in various markets, is dependent on the number and the type of competitors, and the demand structure in a market. The relative market share of competitors in the market of a given country may also give us clues as to competitors who are motivated to take price action and thus drive margins down. It is important to realize that prices are constrained by market structure, competitive rivalry, and competitors' strategic intentions in a given market and not by cost to the firm. Although that is obvious, firms continue to think of prices in cost-plus terms and miss opportunities to exploit the market asymmetries around the world. In order to exploit the market asymmetries, the firm should have a market presence in a portfolio of markets.

The value of distribution and brand presence. Well-established brands with a quality image, like Sony in consumer electronics, command a premium. Further, control over the distribution channels brought about by a product line also allows for a premium.

The value of a product family. While the analysis so far has assumed a single business as the basic unit of analysis for competitive profiling, the value of a product family cannot be underestimated. For example, just as a firm can use its multinational market presence to cross-subsidize competitive battles (e.g., Unilever versus CPC in the example outlined before), a firm with a large product family can subsidize a given business within a market.

The Marketing System

Managing net prices is critical to managing a business's overall cash flow. That means firms should manage the marketing system. The strategist's role is to balance the three sources of price advantages available to the firm.

Strategic Intent: The Motor behind Global Competition

The discussion so far has concentrated on the nature of the armory that one needs to compete globally. It is important to recognize that the outcomes in global competition are determined not just by the size of the armory that the various players possess but also by how effectively and imaginatively they use their weapons. The strategic intent of various competitors, or their long-term vision, may be as important as the size and quality of their armories. We should distinguish the strategic intent from the strategies: *intent* is used here to describe long-term goals and aims, rather than detailed plans.

Building Layers of Competitive Advantage

In our research we can discern three types of firms—firms whose strategic intent is *global dominance*, even if, initially, they do not possess the strategic infrastructure to accomplish that goal; firms whose strategic intent is *defending domestic dominance*, even if they have operations in multiple markets; and those whose primary orientation is *local responsiveness*. The different strategic intents lead to very distinct approaches to competition and the use of competitive advantages, even if the strategic infrastructures appear not to be markedly dissimilar.

Loose Bricks: Building Layers of Competitive Advantage. Japanese firms in the consumer electronics business started with the strategic intent of global dominance, even though their strategic infrastructure during the 1960s did not extend beyond a well-protected home market. During the 1960s they were major exporters of black-and-white TV sets. By 1967 they had become the largest producers of black-and-white TVs; by the 1970s they had closed the gap in color sets. Japanese producers used their cost advantage, derived primarily from their low labor costs, to gain volume in the United States. Once they had secured that initial volume, they moved quickly to invest heavily in process and product technology, from which they gained scale and quality advantages. By the early 1970s the Japanese advantage was not only low labor costs but also greater reliability and quality based on superior manufacturing technology.

Japanese manufacturers recognized the transience of low labor cost as well as technology-based advantages. Volatile exchange rates and increases in labor costs as well as newer manufacturing technologies were rendering the sources of competitive advantages they had quite vulnerable. Throughout the 1970s Japanese TV makers invested heavily in order to create a strong brand presence in global markets and a distribution presence, thus adding another layer of competitive advantage.

Making global distribution and brand presence pay for themselves meant a high level of channel utilization. The Japanese force-fed the distribution channels by speeding up product development cycles and expanding across contiguous product families. Thus by the early 1980s, the Japanese competitive advantage had evolved from low-cost sourcing, to a technological advantage resulting in lower costs and higher quality, then to a global distribution and brand presence across a spectrum of consumer electronic products. The strategic intent of global dominance provided a basis for building on tactical and short-term advantages, deploying resources in such a way as to build "layers of competitive advantage." The Japanese position today in consumer electronics is formidable.

Defending Domestic Dominance.   RCA was prototypical of firms with a defend-domestic-dominance orientation. RCA owned most CTV patents and should rightly be regarded as the "father of color TV." However, RCA did not invest in overseas markets and was quite happy to concede the private label and the small CTV market to the Japanese. It saw itself as not only defending the U.S. market—its domestic base—but also defending only segments of the market, primarily the market for higher-priced sets. As a result, RCA allowed a market position for the Japanese, was unaware of their long-term goals in the United States, and was blindsided.

The Japanese threat was obvious by 1975-76, and American producers who were primarily concerned about domestic dominance were unable to respond. Convinced that the sources of Japanese competitive advantage lay in low labor costs, they transferred most of their manufacturing overseas. They also sought protection. Yet even with costs under control, these companies (RCA, GE, and Zenith) were still vulnerable because they had failed to understand the changing nature of the Japanese competitive advantage. Even as American producers closed the cost gap, the Japanese were cementing future profit foundations by investing in global brand positions. While Zenith and RCA dominated the color TV business in the United States, neither had a strong presence elsewhere. With no choice of competitive venue, U.S. companies were forced to fight every market share battle in their home profit sanctuary.

When American TV makers reduced prices at home, they subjected 100 percent of their sales volume to margin pressure. Matsushita could force such price action while exposing only a fraction of its own worldwide profitability. TVs were no more than one loose brick in the American consumer electronic market. The Japanese goal appears to be to knock down the entire wall. For example, with margins under pressure in the TV business, no American manufacturer had the stomach to develop its own video recorder. Today video tape recorders are the mainstay of profitability for many Japanese consumer electronics companies.

Companies defending domestic positions are often shortsighted about their competitor's strategic intentions. A company can understand its own vulnerability to global competition only by first understanding its rivals' intentions, and then carefully reasoning back to potential tactics. With no appreciation of strategic intent, defense-minded competitors are doomed to a perpetual game of catch-up.

Local Responsiveness.   Philips of The Netherlands is well-known virtually everywhere in the world. Like other long-standing MNCs, Philips has always benefited from the kind of international distribution system that U.S. companies often lack. Yet our evidence suggests that this advantage alone was not enough. Philips had its own set of problems in responding to the Japanese challenge.

Because laws prohibited Japanese producers from supplying finished sets for private-label sale, they supplied picture tubes instead. By concentrating on such volume-sensitive manufacturing, Japanese manufacturers skirted protectionist sentiment while exploiting the economies of scale gained from U.S. and Japanese experience.

Yet, just as they had not been content to remain private-label suppliers in the United States, Japanese companies were not content to remain component suppliers in Europe. They wanted to establish their own brand positions. Sony, Matsushita, and Mitsubishi set up local manufacturing operations in the United Kingdom. When the British began to fear a Japanese takeover of the local industry, Toshiba and Hitachi simply found U.K. partners. In moving the assembly line from the Far East to Europe, Japanese manufacturers incurred cost and quality penalties. Yet they regarded such penalties as acceptable costs for establishing strong European distribution and brand positions.

If we contrast Japanese entry strategies in the United States and Europe, it is clear that the tactics and timetables differed. Yet the long-term strategic intentions were the same, and the competitive advantage of Japanese producers evolved similarly in both markets. In both Europe and the United States, Japanese companies found an opening in the bottom half of the market—small-screen portables, along with other openings in the private label business in the United States and the picture tube business in Europe.

Philips was the only European manufacturer whose volume could fund the automation of manufacturing and the rationalization of product lines and components. Even though its volume was sufficient, Philips's manufacturing was spread across seven European countries. So it had to demonstrate (country by country, minister by minister, union by union) that the only alternative to protectionism was to support the development of Pan-European competitors. Philips also had to wrestle with independent subsidiaries not eager to surrender their autonomy in manufacturing and capital investment. By 1982 it was the world's largest color TV maker and had almost closed the cost gap with the Japanese producers. Even so, after ten years, rationalization plans are still incomplete.

Philips remains vulnerable to global competition because of the difficulties inherent in weaving disparate national subsidiaries into a coherent global competitive team. Low-cost manufacturing and international distribution give Philips two of the critical elements needed for global competition. Still needed is coordination of national business strategies.

Philips's national managers are jealous of their autonomy in marketing and strategy. With their horizon of competition often limited to a single market, national managers are poorly placed to assess their global vulnerability. They can neither fully understand nor adequately analyze the strategic intentions and market entry tactics of global competitors. Nor can they estimate the total resources available to foreign competitors for local market share battles.

Under such management pressure, companies like Philips risk responding to global competition on a purely local basis. Its Japanese competitors can "cherry pick" attractive national markets with little fear that their multinational rival will focus total company resources on retaliation in key markets.

The Concept of Critical Markets

Central to the arguments presented here is the notion of critical markets. In other words, to defend itself against determined global competitors who can cross-subsidize market share battles, a firm should be a multimarket competitor. That does not mean the firm should be present in all markets. Critical markets may be determined by seeking, at a minimum:

- markets that are the profit sanctuaries of the key competitors in that business;
- markets that provide volume and include the state-of-the-art customers;
- markets where the competitive intensity allows reasonable margins.

■ MANAGING ACROSS BORDERS†

By Christopher Bartlett and Sumantra Ghoshal

Recent changes in the international operating environment have forced companies to optimize *efficiency, responsiveness*, and *learning* simultaneously in their worldwide operations. To companies that previously concentrated on developing and managing one of these capabilities, this new challenge implies not only a total strategic reorientation but a major change in organizational capability, as well.

Implementing such a complex, three-pronged strategic objective would be difficult under any circumstances, but in a worldwide company the task is complicated even further. The very act of "going international" multiplies a company's organizational complexity. Typically, doing so requires adding a third dimension to the existing business—and function-oriented management structure. It is difficult enough balancing product divisions that bring efficiency and focus to domestic product-market strategies with corporate staffs whose functional expertise allows them to play an important counterbalance and control role. The thought of adding capable, geographically oriented management—and maintaining a three-way balance of organizational perspectives and capabilities among product, function, and area—is intimidating to most managers. The difficulty is increased because the resolution of tensions among product, function, and area managers must be accomplished in an organization whose operating units are often divided by distance and time and whose key members are separated by culture and language.

From Unidimensional to Multidimensional Capabilities

Faced with the task of building multiple strategic capabilities in highly complex organizations, managers in almost every company we studied made the simplifying assumption that they were faced with a series of dichotomous choices. They discussed the relative merits of pursuing a strategy of national responsiveness as opposed to one based on global integration; they considered whether key assets and resources should be centralized or decentralized; and they debated the need for strong central control versus greater subsidiary autonomy. How a company resolved these dilemmas typically reflected influences exerted and choices made during its historical development. In telecommunications, ITT's need to develop an organization responsive to national political demands and local specification differences was as important to its survival in the pre– and post–World War II era as was NEC's need to build its highly centralized technological manufacturing and marketing skills and resources in order to expand abroad in the same industry in the 1960s and 1970s.

When new competitive challenges emerged, however, such unidimensional biases became strategically limiting. As ITT demonstrated by its outstanding historic success and NEC showed by its more delayed international expansion, strong *geographic management* is essential for development of dispersed responsiveness. Geographic management allows worldwide companies to sense, analyze, and respond to the needs of different national markets.

Effective competitors also need to build strong *business management* with global product responsibilities if they are to achieve global efficiency and integration. These managers act as champions of manufacturing rationalization, product standardization, and low-cost global sourcing. (As the telecommunications switching industry globalized, NEC's organizational capability in this area gave it a major competitive advantage.) Unencumbered by either territorial or functional loyalties, central product groups remain sensitive to overall competitive issues and become agents to facilitate changes that, though painful, are necessary for competitive viability.

Finally, a strong, worldwide *functional management* allows an organization to build and transfer its core competencies—a capability vital to worldwide learning. Links between functional managers allow the company to accumulate specialized knowledge and skills and to apply them wherever they are required in the worldwide operations. Functional management acts as the repository of organizational learning and as the prime mover for its consolidation and circulation within the company. It was for want of a strongly linked research and technical function across subsidiaries that ITT failed in its attempt to coordinate the development and diffusion of its System 12 digital switch.

Thus, to respond to the needs for efficiency, responsiveness, and learning simultaneously, the company must develop a multidimensional organization in which the effectiveness of each management group is maintained and in which each group is prevented from dominating the others. As we saw in company after company, the most difficult challenge for managers trying to respond to broad, emerging strategic demands was to develop the new elements of multidimensional organization without eroding the effectiveness of their current unidimensional capability.

Overcoming Simplifying Assumptions

For all nine companies at the core of our study, the challenge of breaking down biases and building a truly multidimensional organization proved difficult. Behind the pervasive either/or mentality that led to the development of unidimensional capabilities, we identified three simplifying assumptions that blocked the necessary organizational development. The need to reduce organizational and strategic complexity has made these assumptions almost universal in worldwide companies, regardless of industry, national origin, or management culture.

- There is a widespread, often implicit assumption that roles of different organizational units are uniform and symmetrical; different businesses should be managed in the same way, as should different functions and national operations.

- Most companies, some consciously, most unconsciously, create internal interunit relationships on clear patterns of dependence or independence, on the assumption that such relationships *should* be clear and unambiguous.

- Finally, there is the assumption that one of corporate management's principal tasks is to institutionalize clearly understood mechanisms for decision making and to implement simple means of exercising control.

Those companies most successful in developing truly multidimensional organizations were the ones that challenged these assumptions and replaced them with some very different attitudes and norms. Instead of treating different businesses, functions, and subsidiaries similarly, they systematically *differentiated* tasks and responsibilities. Instead of seeking organizational clarity by basing relationships on dependence or independence, they built and managed *interdependence* among the different units of the companies. And instead of considering control their key task, corporate managers searched for complex mechanisms to *coordinate and co-opt* the differentiated and interdependent organizational units into sharing a vision of the company's strategic tasks. These are the central organizational characteristics of what we described as transnational corporations—those most effective in managing across borders in today's environment of intense competition and rapid, often discontinuous change.

From Symmetry to Differentiation

Like many other companies we studied, Unilever built its international operations under an implicit assumption of organizational symmetry. Managers of diverse local operating companies in products ranging from packaged foods to chemicals and detergents all reported to strongly independent national managers, who in turn reported through regional directors to the board.

By the mid-1970s, however, the entrenched organizational symmetry was being threatened. Global economic disruption caused by the oil crisis dramatically highlighted the very substantial differences in the company's businesses and markets and forced management to recognize the need to differentiate its organizational structures and administrative processes. While standardization, coordination, and integration paid high dividends in the chemical and detergent businesses, for example, important differences in local tastes and national cultures impeded the same degree of coordination in foods. As a result, the roles, responsibilities, and powers of the central product-coordination groups eventually began to diverge as the company tried to shake off the constraint of the symmetry assumption.

But as Unilever tackled the challenge of managing some businesses in a more globally coordinated manner, it was confronted with the question of what to coordinate. Historically, the company's philosophy of decentralized capabilities and delegated responsibilities resulted in most national subsidiaries becoming fully integrated, self-sufficient operations.

Over time, decentralization of all functional responsibilities became increasingly difficult to support. In the 1970s, for example, when arch-competitor Procter & Gamble's subsidiaries were launching a new generation of laundry detergents based on the rapeseed formula created by the parent company, most of Unilever's national detergent companies responded with their own products. The cost of developing thirteen different formulations was extremely high, and management soon recognized that not one was as good as P&G's centrally developed product. For the sake of cost control and competitive effectiveness, Unilever had to break with tradition and begin centralizing European product development. The company has since created a system in which central coordination is more normal, although very different for different functions such as basic research, product development, manufacturing, marketing, and sales.

Just as they saw the need to change symmetrical structures and homogeneous processes imposed on different businesses and functions, most companies we observed eventually recognized the importance of differentiating the management of diverse geographic operations. Despite the fact that various national subsidiaries operated with very different external environments and internal constraints, they all traditionally reported through the same channels, operated under similar planning and control systems, and worked under a set of common and generalized mandates.

Increasingly, however, managers recognized that such symmetrical treatment can constrain strategic capabilities. At Unilever, for example, it became clear that Europe's highly competitive markets and closely linked economies meant that its operating companies in that region required more coordination and control than those in, say, Latin America. Little by little, management increased the product-coordination groups' role in Europe until they had direct line responsibility for all operating companies in their businesses. Elsewhere, however, national management maintained its historic line management role, and product coordinators acted only as advisers. Unilever has thus moved in sequence from a symmetrical organization to a much more differentiated one differentiating by product, then by function, and finally by geography.

Recently, within Europe, differentiation by national units has proceeded even further. Operations in "key countries" such as France, Germany, and the United Kingdom are allowed to retain considerably more autonomy than those in "receiver countries" such as Switzerland, Sweden, Holland, and Denmark. While the company's overall commitment to decentralization is maintained, receiver countries have gradually become more dependent on the center for direction and support, particularly in the areas of product development and competitive strategy.

Unilever is far from unique. In all of the companies we studied, senior management was working to differentiate its organizational structure and processes in increasingly sophisticated ways. For example, Philips's consumer electronics division began experimenting with an organization differentiated by product life-cycle stage—high-tech products like CD players being managed with very different strategies and organization processes from those for stable high-volume products like color TVs, which, in turn, were managed differently from mature and declining products like portable radios. Procter & Gamble is differentiating the roles of its subsidiaries by giving some of them responsibilities as lead countries in product strategy development, then rotating that leadership role from product to product. Matsushita differentiates the way it manages its worldwide operations not on the basis of geography, but on the unit's strategic role. L. M. Ericsson, which had centralized most of the basic research on its digital switch, is now decentralizing development and applications responsibilities to a few key country subsidiaries that have the capability to contribute.

Thus, instead of deciding the overall roles of product, functional, and geographic management on the basis of simplistic dichotomies such as global versus domestic businesses or centralized versus decentralized organizations, many companies are creating different levels of influence for different groups as they perform different activities. Doing this allows the relatively underdeveloped management perspectives to be built in a gradual, complementary manner rather than in the sudden, adversarial environment often associated with either/or choices.

From Dependence or Independence to Interdependence

New strategic demands make organizational models of simple interunit dependence or independence inappropriate. The reality of today's worldwide competitive environment demands collaborative information sharing and problem solving, cooperative support and resource sharing, and collective action and implementation. Independent units risk being picked off one by one by competitors whose coordinated global approach gives them two important strategic advantages—the ability to integrate research, manufacturing, and other scale-efficient operations, and the opportunity to cross-subsidize the losses from battles in one market with funds generated by profitable operations in home markets or protected environments.

On the other hand, foreign operations totally dependent on a central unit must deal with problems reaching beyond the loss of local market responsiveness. They also risk being unable to respond effectively to strong national competitors or to sense potentially important local market or technical intelligence.

But it is not easy to change relationships of dependence or independence that have been built up over a long history. In most cases efforts to obtain cooperation by fiat or by administrative mechanisms have been disappointing. The independent units have feigned compliance while fiercely protecting their independence. The dependent units have found that the new cooperative spirit implies little more than the right to agree with those on whom they depend.

Yet some companies have gradually developed the capability to achieve such cooperation and to build what Rosabeth Kanter calls an "integrative organization." Of the companies we studied, the most successful did so not by creating new units, but by changing the basis of the relationships among product, functional, and geographic management groups. From relations based on dependence or independence, they moved to relations based on formidable levels of explicit, genuine interdependence. In essence, they made integration and collaboration self-enforcing by making it necessary for each group to cooperate in order to achieve its own interests. Companies were able to create such interdependencies in many ways.

NEC has developed reciprocal relationships among different parts of its organizations by creating a series of internal quasi markets. It builds cooperation between the R&D function and the different product groups by allocating only a part of the R&D budget directly to the company's several central laboratories. This portion is used to support basic and applied research in core technologies of potential value to the corporation as a whole. The remaining funds are allocated to the product groups to support research programs that reflect their priorities. In response to the product divisions' proposed projects, each research group puts forward proposals that it feels will lead to the desired product or process improvements. What follows is a negotiation process that results in the product divisions "buying" some of the proposals put up by the laboratories, while different R&D groups adopt some of the projects demanded by the product managers. In other words, NEC has created an internal market for ensuring that research is relevant to market needs.

Procter & Gamble employs an entirely different approach to creating and managing interdependencies. In Europe, for example, it formed a number of Eurobrand teams for developing product-market strategies for different product lines. Each team is headed by the general manager of a subsidiary that has a particularly well-developed competence in that business. It also includes the appropriate product and advertising managers from the other subsidiaries and relevant functional managers from the company's European headquarters. Each team's effectiveness clearly depends on the involvement and support provided by its members and, more important, by the organizational units they represent. Historically, the company's various subsidiaries had little incentive to cooperate. Now, however, the success of each team—and the reputation of the general manager heading it—depends on the support of other subsidiaries; this has made cooperation self-enforcing. Each general manager is aware that the level of support and commitment he can expect from the other members of the Eurobrand team depends on the support and contribution the product managers from his subsidiaries provide to the other teams. The interdependencies of these Eurobrand teams were able to foster teamwork driven by individual interests.

It is important to emphasize that the relationships we are highlighting are different from the interdependencies commonly observed in multiunit organizations. Traditionally, multinational corporation (MNC) managers have attempted to highlight what has been called "pooled interdependence" to make subunit managers responsive to global rather than local interests. (Before the Eurobrand team approach, for instance, P&G's European vice president often tried to convince independent-minded subsidiary managers to transfer surplus-generated funds to other more needy subsidiaries, in the overall corporate interest, arguing that, "Someday when you're in need they might be able to fund a major product launch for you.")

As the example illustrates, pooled interdependence is often too broad and amorphous to affect day-to-day management behavior. The interdependencies we described earlier are more clearly reciprocal, and each unit's ability to achieve its goals is made conditional upon its willingness to help other units achieve their own goals.

From Control to Coordination and Co-option

The simplifying assumptions of organizational symmetry and dependence (or independence) had allowed the management processes in many companies to be dominated by simple controls—tight operational controls in subsidiaries dependent on the center, and a looser system of administrative or financial controls in decentralized units. When companies began to challenge the assumptions underlying organizational relationships, however, they found they also had to adapt their management processes.

As organizations became, at the same time, more diverse and more interdependent, there was an explosion in the number of issues that had to be linked, reconciled, or integrated. The rapidly increasing flows of goods, resources, and information among organizational units increased the need for *coordination* as a central management function. But the costs of coordination are high, both in financial and human terms, and coordinating capabilities are always limited. Most companies, though, tended to concentrate on a primary means of coordination and control—"the company's way of doing things." Clearly, there was a need to develop multiple means of coordination, to rank the demands for coordination, and to allocate the scarce coordinating resources. The way in which one of our sample companies developed its portfolio of coordinative processes illustrates the point well.

During the late 1970s and early 1980s, Philips had gradually developed some sophisticated means of coordination. This greatly helped the company shape its historically evolved, nationally centered organization into the kind of multidimensional organization it needed to be in the 1980s. Coordinating the flow of goods in a global sourcing network is a highly complex logistical task, but one that can often be formalized and delegated to middle and lower-level management. By standardizing product specifications and rationalizing sourcing patterns through designating certain plants as international production centers (IPCs), Philips facilitated goods-flow coordination. By making these flows reasonably constant and forecastable, the company could manage them almost entirely through formal systems and processes. These became the main coordination mechanisms in the company's attempt to increase the integration of worldwide sourcing of products and components.

Coordinating the flow of financial, technical, and human resources, however, was not so easily routinized. Philips saw the allocation of these scarce resources as a reflection of key strategic choices and therefore managed the coordination process by centralizing many decisions. The board became heavily involved in major capital budgeting decisions; the product divisions reasserted control over product development, a process once jealously guarded by the national organizations; and the influential corporate staff bureau played a major role in personnel assignments and transfers.

But while goods flows could be coordinated through formalization, and resource flows through centralization, critical information flows were much more difficult to manage. The rapid globalization of the consumer electronics industry in the 1970s forced Philips to recognize the need to move strategic information and proprietary knowledge around the company much more quickly. While some routine data could be transferred through normal information systems, much of the information was so diverse and changeable that establishing formal processes was impossible. While some core knowledge had to be stored and transferred through corporate management, the sheer volume and complexity of information—and the need for its rapid diffusion—limited the ability to coordinate through centralization. Philips found that the most effective way to manage complex flows of information and knowledge was through various socialization processes: the transfer of people, the encouragement of informal communication channels that fostered information exchange, or the creation of forums that facilitated interunit learning.

Perhaps most well known is the company's constant worldwide transfer and rotation of a group of senior managers (once referred to internally as the Dutch Mafia, but today a more international group) as a means of transferring critical knowledge and experience throughout the organization. Philips also made more extensive use of committees and task forces than any other company we studied. Although the frequent meetings and constant travel were expensive, the company benefited not only from information exchange but also from the development of personal contacts that grew into vital information channels.

Even though they recognize the growing diversity of tasks facing them, a surprising number of companies have had great difficulty in differentiating the way they manage products, functions, or geographic units. The simplicity of applying a single planning and control system across businesses and the political acceptability of defining uniform job descriptions for all subsidiary heads were often allowed to outweigh the clear evidence that the relevant business characteristics and subsidiary roles were vastly different.

We have described briefly how companies began to remedy this situation by differentiating roles and responsibilities within the organization. Depending on their internal capabilities and on the strategic importance of their external environments, organizational units might be asked to take on roles ranging from that of strategic leader with primary corporatewide responsibility for a particular business or function, to simple implementer responsible only for executing strategies and decisions developed elsewhere.

Clearly, these roles must be managed in quite different ways. The unit with strategic leadership responsibility must be given freedom to develop responsibility in an entrepreneurial fashion, yet must also be strongly supported by headquarters. For this unit, operating controls may be light and quite routine, but coordination of information and resource flows to and from the unit will probably require intensive involvement from senior management. In contrast, units with implementation responsibility might be managed through tight operating controls, with standardized systems used to handle much of the coordination—primarily of goods flows. Because the tasks are more routine, the use of scarce coordinating resources could be minimized.

Differentiating organizational roles and management processes can have a fragmenting and sometimes demotivating effect, however. Nowhere was this more clearly illustrated than in the many companies that unquestioningly assigned units the "dog" and "cash cow" roles defined by the Boston Consulting Group's growth-share matrix in the 1970s. Their experience showed that there is another equally important corporate management task that complements and facilitates coordination effectiveness. We call this task *co-option*: the process of uniting the organization with a common understanding of, identification with, and commitment to the corporation's objectives, priorities, and values.

A clear example of the importance of co-option was provided by the contrast between ITT and NEC managers. At ITT, corporate objectives were communicated more in financial than in strategic terms, and the company's national entities identified almost exclusively with their local environment. When corporate management tried to superimpose a more unified and integrated global strategy, its local subsidiaries neither understood nor accepted the need to do so.

In contrast, NEC developed an explicitly defined and clearly communicated global strategy enshrined in the company's "C&C" motto—a corporatewide dedication to building business and basing competitive strategy on the strong link between computers and communications. Top management recognized that one of its major tasks was to inculcate the worldwide organization with an understanding of the C&C strategy and philosophy and to raise managers' consciousness about the global implications of competing in these converging businesses. By the mid-1980s, the company was confident that every NEC employee in every operating unit had a clear understanding of NEC's global strategy as well as of his or her role in it. Indeed, it was this homogeneity that allowed the company to begin the successful decentralization of its strategic tasks and the differentiation of its management processes.

Thus the management process that distinguished transnational organizations from simpler unidimensional forms was one in which control was made less dominant by the increased importance of interunit integration and collaboration. These new processes required corporate management to supplement its control role with the more subtle tasks of coordination and co-option, giving rise to a much more complex and sophisticated management process.

Sustaining a Dynamic Balance: Role of the "Mind Matrix"

Developing multidimensional perspectives and capabilities does not mean that product, functional, and geographic management must have the same level of influence on all key decisions. Quite the contrary. It means that the organization must possess a differentiated influence structure—one in which different groups have different roles for different activities. These roles cannot be fixed but must change continually to respond to new environmental demands and evolving industry characteristics. Not only is it necessary to prevent any one perspective from dominating the others, it is equally important not to be locked into a mode of operation that prevents reassignment of responsibilities, realignment of relationships, and rebalancing of power distribution. This ability to manage the multidimensional organizational capability in a flexible manner is the hallmark of a transnational company.

What is critical, is not just the structure, but also the mentality of those who constitute the structure. The common thread that holds together the diverse tasks we have described is a managerial mind-set that understands the need for multiple strategic capabilities, that is able to view problems from both local and global perspectives, and that accepts the importance of a flexible approach. This pattern suggests that managers should resist the temptation to view their task in the traditional terms of building a formal global matrix structure—an organizational form that in practice has proven extraordinarily difficult to manage in the international environment. They might be better guided by the perspective of one top manager who described the challenge as "creating a matrix in the minds of managers."

Our study has led us to conclude that a company's ability to develop transnational organizational capability and management mentality will be the key factor that separates the winners from the mere survivors in the emerging international environment.

■ THE COMPETITIVE ADVANTAGE OF NATIONS†

By Michael Porter

Companies, not nations, are on the front line of international competition. Yet, the characteristics of the home nation play a central role in a firm's international success. The home base shapes a company's capacity to innovate rapidly in technology and methods and to do so in the proper directions. It is the place from which competitive advantage ultimately emanates and from which it must be sustained. A global strategy supplements and solidifies the competitive advantage created at the home base; it is the icing, not the cake. However, on the one hand, while having a home base in the right nation helps a great deal, it does not ensure success. On the other hand, having a home base in the wrong nation raises fundamental strategic concerns.

The most important sources of national advantage must be actively sought and exploited, unlike low factor costs obtainable simply by operating in the nation. Internationally successful firms are not passive bystanders in the process of creating competitive advantage. Those we studied were caught up in a never-ending process of seeking out new advantages and struggling with rivals to protect them. They were positioned to benefit the most from their national environment. They took steps to make their home nation (and location within the nation) an even more favorable environment for competitive advantage. Finally, they amplified their home-based advantages and offset home-based disadvantages through global strategies that tapped selectively into advantages available in other nations.

Competitive advantage ultimately results from an effective combination of national circumstances and company strategy. Conditions in a nation may create an environment in which firms can attain international competitive advantage, but it is up to a company to seize the opportunity.

The Context for Competitive Advantage

These imperatives of competitive advantage constitute a mind-set that is not present in many companies. Indeed, the actions required to create and sustain advantage are

FIGURE 10-3
The Diamond

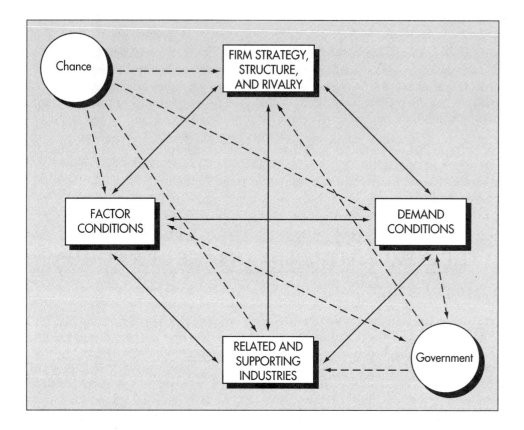

unnatural acts. Stability is valued in most companies, not change. Protecting old ideas and techniques becomes the preoccupation, not creating new ones.

The long-term challenge for any firm is to put itself in a position where it is most likely to perceive, and best able to address, the imperatives of competitive advantage. One challenge is to expose a company to new market and technological opportunities that may be hard to perceive. Another is preparing for change by upgrading and expanding the skills of employees and improving the firm's scientific and knowledge base. Ultimately, the most important challenge is overcoming complacency and inertia to act on the new opportunities and circumstances.

The challenge of action ultimately falls on the firm's leader. Much attention has rightly been placed on the importance of visionary leaders in achieving unusual organizational success. But where does a leader get the vision, and how is it transmitted in a way that produces organizational accomplishment? Great leaders are influenced by the environment in which they work. Innovation takes place because the home environment stimulates it. Innovation succeeds because the home environment supports and even forces it. The right environment not only shapes a leader's own perceptions and priorities but provides the catalyst that allows the leader to overcome inertia and produce organizational change.

Great leaders emerge in different industries in different nations, in part because national circumstances attract and encourage them. Visionaries in consumer electronics are concentrated in Japan, chemicals and pharmaceuticals in Germany and Switzerland, and computers in America. Leadership is important to any success story, but is not in and of itself sufficient to explain such successes. In many industries, the national environment provides one or two nations with a distinct advantage over

EXHIBIT 10-1
Elements of the Diamond

Competitive Advantages and Disadvantages

The "diamond" provides a framework for assessing import areas of competitive strength and weakness.

Factor Conditions. International rivals will differ in the mix and cost of available factors and the rate of factor creation. Swedish automobile firms, for example, benefit from the solidarity wage system that makes the wages of Swedish auto workers closer to those of other Swedish industries, but relatively lower than the wages of auto workers in other advanced nations.

Demand Conditions. Competitors from other nations will face differing segment structures of home demand, differing home buyer needs, and home buyers with various levels of sophistication. Demand conditions at their home base will help predict foreign competitors' directions of product change as well as their likely success in product development, among other things.

Related and Supporting Industries. Competitors based in other nations will differ in the availability of domestic suppliers, the quality of interaction with supplier industries, and the presence of related industries. Italian footwear firms and leather goods producers, for example, have early access to new tanned leather styles because of the world-leading Italian leather tanning industry.

Firm Strategy, Structure, and Rivalry. The environment in their home nation will strongly influence the strategic choices of foreign rivals. Italian packaging equipment firms, for example, reflect their Italian context. They are mostly small and managed by strong, paternal leaders. Owners of firms have personal relationships with significant buyers. This makes them unusually responsive to market trends and provides the ability to custom-tailor machinery to buyer circumstances.

---

their foreign competitors. Leadership often determines which particular firm or firms exploit this advantage.

More broadly, the ability of any firm to innovate has much to do with the environment to which it is exposed, the information sources it has available—and consults—and the types of challenges it chooses to face. Seeking safe havens and comfortable customer relationships only reinforces past behavior. Maintaining suppliers who are captive degrades a source of stimulus, assistance, and insight. Lobbying against stringent product standards sends the wrong signal to an organization about norms and aspirations.

Innovation grows out of pressure and challenge. It also comes from finding the right challenges to meet. The main role of the firm's leader is to create the environment that meets these conditions. One essential part of the task is to take advantage of the national "diamond" (see figure 10-3 and exhibit 10-1) that currently describes competition in the industry.

The New Rules for Innovation

A company should actively seek out pressure and challenge, not try to avoid them. Part of the task is to take advantage of the home nation in order to create the impetus for innovation. Some of the ways of doing so are:

- *Sell to the most sophisticated and demanding buyers and channels.* Some buyers (and channels) will stimulate the fastest improvement because they are knowledgeable and expect the best performance. They will set a standard for the organization and provide the most valuable feedback. However, sophisticated and demanding buyers and channels need not be the firm's only customers. Focusing on them exclusively may unnecessarily diminish long-term profitability. Nevertheless, serving a group of such buyers, chosen because their needs will challenge the firm's particular approach to competing, must be an explicit part of any strategy.

■ *Seek out the buyers with the most difficult needs.* Buyers who face especially difficult operating requirements (such as climate, maintenance requirements, or hours of use), who confront factor cost disadvantages in their own businesses that create unusual pressures for performance, who have particularly tough competition, or who compete with strategies that place especially heavy demands on the firm's product or service, are buyers that will provide the laboratory (and the pressure) to upgrade performance and extend features and services. Such buyers should be identified and cultivated. They become part of a firm's R&D program.

■ *Establish norms of exceeding the toughest regulatory hurdles or product standards.* Some localities (or user industries) will lead in terms of the stringency of product standards, pollution limits, noise guidelines, and the like. Tough regulating standards are not a hindrance but an opportunity to move early to upgrade products and processes. Older or simplified models can be sold elsewhere.

■ *Source from the most advanced and international home-based suppliers.* Suppliers who themselves possess competitive advantage, as well as the insight that comes from international activities, will challenge the firm to improve and upgrade as well as provide insights and assistance in doing so.

■ *Treat employees as permanent.* When employees are viewed as permanent instead of as workers who can be hired and fired at will, pressures are created that work to upgrade and sustain competitive advantage. New employees are hired with care, and continuous efforts are made to improve productivity instead of adding workers. Employees are trained on an ongoing basis to support more sophisticated competitive advantages.

■ *Establish outstanding competitors as motivators.* Those competitors who most closely match a company's competitive advantages, or exceed them, must become the standard of comparison. Such competitors can be a source of learning as well as a powerful focal point to overcome parochial concerns and motivate change for the entire organization.

The True Costs of Stability

These prescriptions may seem counterintuitive. The ideal would seem to be the stability growing out of obedient customers, captive and dependent suppliers, and sleepy competitors. Such a search for a quiet life, an understandable instinct, has led many companies to buy direct competitors or form alliances with them. In a closed, static world, monopoly would indeed be the most comfortable and profitable solution.

In reality, however, competition is dynamic. Complacent firms will lose to other firms who come from a more dynamic environment. Good managers always run a little scared. They respect and study competitors. Seeking out and meeting challenges is part of their organizational norm. By contrast, an organization that values stability and lacks self-perceived competition breeds inertia and creates vulnerabilities.

In global competition, the pressures of demanding local buyers, capable suppliers, and aggressive domestic rivalry are even more valuable and necessary for long-term profitability. These drive the firm to a faster rate of progress and upgrading than international rivals, and lead to sustained competitive advantage and superior long-term profitability. A tough domestic industry structure creates advantage in the international industry. A comfortable, easy home base, in contrast, leaves a firm vulnerable to rivals who enjoy greater dynamism at home.

Perceiving Industry Change

Beyond pressure to innovate, one of the most important advantages an industry can have is early insight into important needs, environmental forces, and trends that others have not noticed. Japanese firms had an early and clear warning about the importance of energy efficiency. American firms have often gotten a jump in seeing demand for new services, giving them a head start in many service industries. Better insight and early warning signals lead to competitive advantages. Firms gain competitive position before rivals perceive an opportunity (or a threat) and are able to respond.

Perceiving possibilities for new strategies more clearly or earlier comes in part from simply being in the right nation at the right time. Yet it is possible for a firm to more actively position itself to see the signals of change and act on them. It must find the right focus or location within the nation, and work to overcome the filters that distort or limit the flow of information.

Identify and serve buyers (and channels) with the most anticipatory needs. Some buyers will confront new problems or have new needs before others because of their demographics, location, industry, or strategy.

Discover and highlight trends in factor costs. Increases in the costs of particular factors or other inputs may signal future opportunities to leapfrog competitors by innovating to deploy inputs more effectively or to avoid the need for them altogether. A firm should know which markets or regions are likely to reflect such trends first.

Maintain ongoing relationships with centers of research and sources of the most talented people. A firm must identify the places in the nation where the best new knowledge is being created that is now or might become relevant to its industry. Equally important is to identify the schools, institutions, and other companies where the best specialized human resources needed in the industry are being trained.

Study all competitors, especially the new and unconventional ones. Rivals sometimes discover new ideas first. Innovators are often smaller, more focused competitors that are new to the industry. Alternatively, they may be firms led by managers with backgrounds in other industries not bound by conventional wisdom. Such "outsiders," with fewer blinders to cloud their perception of new opportunities and fewer perceived constraints in abandoning past practices, frequently become industry innovators.

Bring some outsiders into the management team. The incorporation of new thinking in the management process is often speeded by the presence of one or more "outsiders"—managers from other companies or industries or from the company's foreign subsidiaries.

Interchange within the National Cluster

A firm gains important competitive advantages from the presence in its home nation of world-class buyers, suppliers, and related industries. They provide insight into future market needs and technological developments. They contribute to a climate for change and improvement, and become partners and allies in the innovation process. Having a strong cluster at home unblocks the flows of information and allows deeper and more open contact than is possible when dealing with foreign firms. Being part of a cluster localized in a small geographic area is even more valuable.

Buyers, Channels, and Suppliers.   The first hurdle to be cleared in taking advantage of the domestic cluster is attitudinal It means recognizing that home-based buyers and suppliers are allies in international competition and not just the other side of transactions. A firm must also pursue:

- Regular senior management contact
- Formal and ongoing interchange between research organizations
- Reciprocity in serving as test sites for new products or services
- Cooperation in penetrating and serving international markets

Working with buyers, suppliers, and channels involves helping them upgrade and extend their own competitive advantages. Their health and strength will only enhance their capacity to speed the firm's own rate of innovation. Open communications with local buyers or suppliers, and early access to new equipment, services, and ideas, are important for sustaining competitive advantage. Such communication will be freer, more timely, and more meaningful than is usually possible with foreign firms.

Encouraging and assisting domestic buyers and suppliers to compete globally is one part of the task of upgrading them. A company's local buyers and suppliers cannot ultimately sustain competitive advantage in many cases unless they compete globally. Buyers and suppliers need exposure to the pressures of worldwide competition in order to advance themselves. Trying to keep them "captive" and prevent them from selling their products abroad is ultimately self-defeating.

An orientation toward closer vertical relationships is only just starting to take hold in many American companies, though it is quite typical in Japanese and Swedish companies. Interchange with buyers, channels, and suppliers always involves some tension, because there is inevitably the need to bargain with them over prices and service. In global industries, however, the competitive advantage to be gained from interchange more than compensates for some sacrifice in bargaining leverage. Interchange should not create dependence but interdependence. A firm should work with a group of suppliers and customers, not just one.

Related Industries.   Industries that are related or potentially related in terms of technology, channels, buyers, or the way buyers obtain or use products are potentially important to creating and sustaining competitive advantage. The presence in a nation of such industries deserves special attention. These industries are often essential sources of innovation. They can also become new suppliers, buyers, or even new competitors.

At a minimum, senior management should be visiting leading companies in related industries on a regular basis. The purpose is to exchange ideas about industry developments. Formal joint research projects, or other more structured ways to explore new ideas, are advisable where the related industry holds more immediate potential to affect competitive advantage.

Locating within the Nation.   A firm should locate activities and its headquarters at those locations in the nation where there are concentrations of sophisticated buyers, important suppliers, groups of competitors, or especially significant factor-creating mechanisms for its industry (such as universities with specialized programs or laboratories with expertise in important technologies). Geographic proximity makes the relationships within a cluster closer and more fluid. It also makes domestic rivalry more valuable for competitive advantage.

Serving Home Base Buyers Who Are International and Multinational

To transform domestic competitive advantage into a global strategy, a firm should identify and serve buyers at home that can also serve abroad. Such buyers are domestic companies that have international operations, individuals who travel frequently to other nations, and local subsidiaries of foreign firms. Targeting such buyers has two benefits. First, they can provide a base of demand in foreign markets to help offset the costs of entry. More important, they will often be sophisticated buyers who can provide a window into international market needs.

Improving the National Competitive Environment

Sustaining competitive advantage is not only a function of making the most of the national environment. Firms must work actively to improve their home base by upgrading the national diamond (see figure 10-3 and exhibit 10-1). A company draws on its home nation to extend and upgrade its own competitive advantages. The firm has a stake in making its home base a better platform for international success.

Playing this role demands that a company understand how each part of the "diamond" best contributes to competitive advantage. It also requires a long-term perspective, because the investments required to improve the home base often take years or even decades to bear fruit. What is more, short-term profits are elevated by foregoing such investments, and by shifting important activities abroad instead of upgrading the ability to perform them at home. Both actions will diminish the sustainability of a firm's competitive advantages in the long run.

Firms have a tendency to see the task of ensuring high-quality human resources, infrastructure, and scientific knowledge as someone else's responsibility. Another common misconception is that, because competition is global, the home base is unimportant. Too often, U.S. and British companies in particular leave investments in the national diamond to others or to the government. The result is that companies are well managed but lack the human resources, technology, and access to capable suppliers and customers needed to succeed against foreign rivals.

Where and How to Compete

A firm's home nation shapes where and how it is likely to succeed in global competition. Germany is a superb environment for competing in printing equipment, but does not offer one conducive to international success in heavily advertised consumer packaged goods. Italy represents a remarkable setting for innovation in fashion and furnishing, but a poor environment for success in industries that sell to government agencies or infrastructure providers.

Within an industry, a nation's circumstances also favor competing in particular industry segments and with certain competitive strategies. Given local housing conditions, for example, Japan is a good home base for competing globally in compact models of appliances and in appliances that are inherently compact (such as microwave ovens) but a poor home base for competing in full-sized refrigerators. Within compact appliances, the Japanese environment is particularly conducive to differentiation strategies based on rapid new model introduction and high product quality.

The national diamond becomes central to choosing the industries to compete in as well as the appropriate strategy. The home base is an important determinant of a firm's strengths and weaknesses relative to foreign rivals.

Understanding the home base of foreign competitors is essential in analyzing them. Their home nation yields them advantages and disadvantages. It also shapes their likely future strategies. The diamond serves as an important tool for competitor analysis in international industries.

Choosing Industries and Strategies

The likelihood that a firm can achieve breakthroughs or innovations of strategic importance in an industry is also influenced by its home nation. Innovation and entrepreneurial behavior is partly a function of chance. But it also depends to a considerable degree on the environment in which the innovator or entrepreneur works. The diamond has a strong influence on which nation (and even on which region within that nation) will be the source of an innovation.

Important innovations in Denmark, for example, have occurred in enzymes for food processing, in natural vitamins, in measuring instruments related to food processing, and in drugs isolated from animal organs (insulin and the anticoagulant heparin). These are hardly random in a nation whose exports are dominated by a large cluster of food-and-beverage-related industries. A firm or individual has the best odds of succeeding in innovation, or in creating a new business, where the national diamond provides the best environment.

The national circumstances most significant for competitive advantage depend on a firm's industry and strategy. In a resource—or basic factor-driven industry, the most important national attribute is a supply of superior or low-cost factors. In a fashion-sensitive industry, the presence of advanced and cutting-edge customers is paramount. In an industry heavily based on scientific research, the quality of factor-creating mechanisms in human resources and technology, coupled with access to sophisticated buyers and suppliers, is decisive.

Cost-oriented strategies are more sensitive to factor costs, the size of home demand, and conditions that favor large-scale plant investments. Differentiation strategies tend to depend more on specialized human resources, sophisticated local buyers, and world-class local supplier industries. Focus strategies rest on the presence of unusual demand in particular segments or on factor conditions or supplier access that benefits competing in a particular product range.

As competition globalizes, and as developments such as European trade liberalization and free trade between the United States and Canada promise to eliminate artificial distortions that have insulated domestic firms from market forces, firms must increasingly compete in industries and segments where they have real strengths. This must increasingly be guided by the national diamond.

A firm can raise the odds of success if it is competing in industries, and with strategies, where the nation provides an unusually fertile environment for competitive advantage. The questions in exhibit 10-2 are designed to expose such areas. Of major importance is a forward-looking view in answering these questions. The focus must be on the nature of evolving competition, not the past requirements for success.

Diversification

While diversification is part of company strategy in virtually every nation, its track record has been mixed at best. Widespread diversification into unrelated industries

EXHIBIT 10-2
The Home Base Diamond

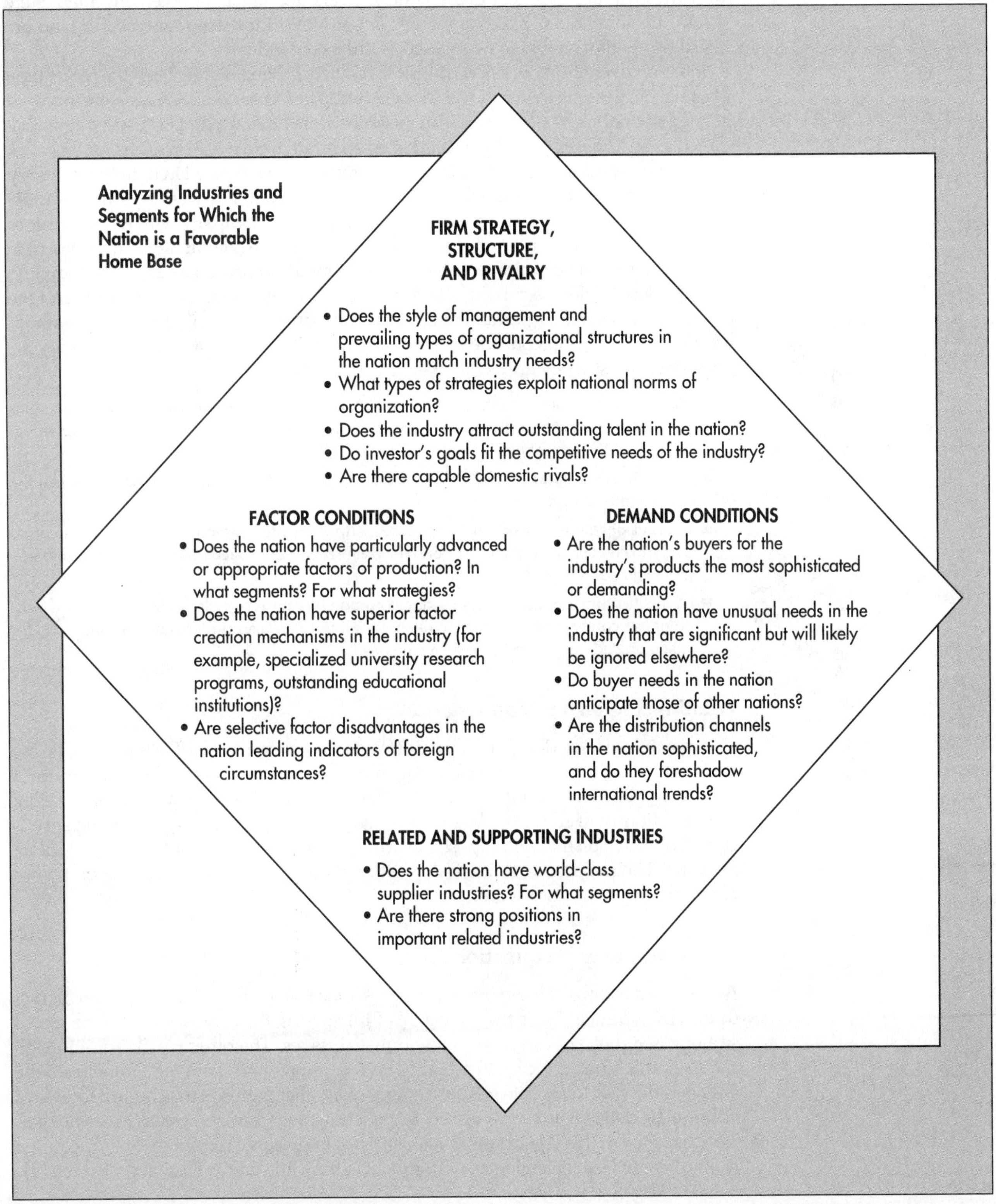

Analyzing Industries and Segments for Which the Nation is a Favorable Home Base

FIRM STRATEGY, STRUCTURE, AND RIVALRY

- Does the style of management and prevailing types of organizational structures in the nation match industry needs?
- What types of strategies exploit national norms of organization?
- Does the industry attract outstanding talent in the nation?
- Do investor's goals fit the competitive needs of the industry?
- Are there capable domestic rivals?

FACTOR CONDITIONS

- Does the nation have particularly advanced or appropriate factors of production? In what segments? For what strategies?
- Does the nation have superior factor creation mechanisms in the industry (for example, specialized university research programs, outstanding educational institutions)?
- Are selective factor disadvantages in the nation leading indicators of foreign circumstances?

DEMAND CONDITIONS

- Are the nation's buyers for the industry's products the most sophisticated or demanding?
- Does the nation have unusual needs in the industry that are significant but will likely be ignored elsewhere?
- Do buyer needs in the nation anticipate those of other nations?
- Are the distribution channels in the nation sophisticated, and do they foreshadow international trends?

RELATED AND SUPPORTING INDUSTRIES

- Does the nation have world-class supplier industries? For what segments?
- Are there strong positions in important related industries?

was rare among the international leaders we studied. They tended instead to compete in one or two core industries or industry sectors, and their commitment to these industries was absolute. For every widely diversified Hitachi or Siemens, there were several Boeings, Koenig & Bauers, FANUCs, Novo Industries, and SKFs, who are global competitors but heavily focused on their core industry.

Internal diversification, not acquisition, has to a striking degree been the motivation for achieving leading international market positions. Where acquisitions were involved in international success stories, the acquisitions were often modest or focused ones that served as an initial entry point or reinforced an internal entry. The reasons for this track record in diversification are not hard to understand when viewed in light of my theory.

Internal diversification facilitates a transfer of skills and resources that is quite difficult to accomplish when acquiring an independent company with its own history and way of operating. Internal entry tends to increase the overall rate of investment in factor creation. There is also an intense commitment to succeed in diversification into closely related fields because of the benefits that accrue to the base business and the effect on the overall corporate image. Unrelated diversification, particularly through acquisition, makes no contribution to innovation. The implications of my theory for diversification strategy are as follows:

- New industries for diversification should be selected where a favorable national diamond is present or can be created. Diversification proposals should be screened for the attractiveness of the home base.

- Diversification is most likely to succeed when it follows or extends clusters in which the firm already competes.

- Internal development of new businesses, supplemented by small acquisitions, is more likely to create and sustain competitive advantage than the acquisition of large, establishment companies.

- Diversification into businesses lacking common buyers, channels, suppliers, or close technological connections is not only likely to fail but will also undermine the prospects for sustaining advantage in the core businesses.

Locating Regional Headquarters

The principles I have described carry implications for the choice of where to locate the regional headquarters responsible for managing a firm's activities in a group of nations. Regional headquarters are best placed not for administrative convenience but in the nation with the most favorable national diamond. Of special importance is choosing a location that will expose the firm to significant needs and pressures lacking at home. The purpose is to learn as well as raise the odds that information passes credibly back to the home base.

Selective Foreign Acquisitions

Foreign acquisitions can serve two purposes. One is to gain access to a foreign market or to selective skills. Here the challenge of integrating the acquisition into the global strategy is significant but raises a few unusual issues. The other reason for a foreign acquisition is to gain access to a highly favorable national diamond. Sometimes the only feasible way to tap into the advantages of another nation is to acquire a local firm because an outsider is hard-pressed to penetrate such broad, systemic advantages. The challenge in this latter type of acquisition is to preserve the ability of the acquired firm to benefit from its national environment at the same time as it is integrated into the company's global strategy.

The Role of Alliances

Alliances, or coalitions, are final mechanisms by which a firm can seek to tap national advantages in other nations. Alliances are a tempting solution to the dilemma of a firm seeking the home-base advantages of another nation without giving up its own. Unfortunately, alliances are rarely a solution. They can achieve selective benefits, but they always involve significant costs in terms of coordination, reconciling goals with an independent entity, creating a competitor, and giving up profits. These costs make many alliances temporary and destined to fail. They are often transitional devices rather than stable arrangements.

No firm can depend on another independent firm for skills and assets that are central to its competitive advantage. If it does, the firm runs a grave risk of losing its competitive advantage in the long run. Alliances tend to ensure mediocrity, not create world leadership. The most serious risk of alliances is that they deter the firm's own efforts at upgrading. This may occur because management is content to rely on the partner. It may also occur because the alliance has eliminated a threatening competitor.

References and Suggested Readings

Bartlett, C. A., and S. Ghoshal, Managing across Borders: New Organizational Responses, *Sloan Management Review,* Fall 1987, pp. 43–53.

Bartlett, C. A., and S. Ghoshal, Organizating for Worldwide Effectiveness: The Transnational Solution, *California Management Review,* Fall 1988, pp. 54–74.

Bartlett, C. A., and S. Ghoshal, *Managing across Borders: The Transnational Solution,* Harvard Business School Press, New York, 1989.

Bartlett, C. A., and S. Ghoshal, What Is a Global Manager? *Harvard Business Review,* September/October 1992, pp. 124–132.

Chakravarthy, B. S., and H. W. Perlmutter, Strategic Planning for a Global Business, *Columbia Journal of World Business,* Summer 1985, pp. 3–10.

Douglas, S. P., Evolution of Global Marketing Strategy: Scale, Scope, and Synergy, *Columbia Journal of World Business,* Fall 1989, pp. 47–59.

Douglas, S. P., and Y. Wind, The Myth of Globalization, *Columbia Journal of World Business,* Winter 1987, pp. 19–29.

Fayerweather, J., *International Business Strategy and Administration,* Second Edition, Ballinger, Cambridge, MA, 1982.

Ghoshal, S., Global Strategy: An Organizing Framework, *Strategic Management Journal,* September/October 1987, pp. 425–440.

Ghoshal, S., and N. Nohria, Horses for Courses: Organizational Forms for Multinational Companies, *Sloan Management Review,* Winter 1993, pp. 23–35.

Gomes-Casseres, B., Joint Ventures in the Face of Global Competition, *Sloan Management Review,* Spring 1989, pp. 17–26.

Gugler, P., Building Transnational Alliances to Create Competitive Advantage, *Long Range Planning,* February 1992, pp. 90–99.

Hamel, G., and C. K. Prahalad, Do You Really Have a Global Strategy? *Harvard Business Review,* July/August 1985, pp. 139–148.

Hout, T. M., Porter, M. E., and E. Rudden, How Global Companies Win Out, *Harvard Business Review,* September/October 1982, pp. 98–108.

Kanter, R. M., *The Change Masters,* Simon and Schuster, New York, 1983.

Kogut, B., Designing Global Strategies: Comparative and Competitive Value-Added Chains, *Sloan Management Review,* Summer 1985, pp. 15–28.

Levitt, T., The Globalization of Markets, *Harvard Business Review,* May/June 1983, pp. 92–102.

Maljers, F. A., Inside Unilever: The Evolving Transnational Company, *Harvard Business Review,* September/October 1992, pp. 46–51.

Morrison, A. J., Ricks, D. A., and K. Roth, Globalization versus Regionalization: Which Way for the Multinational? *Organizational Dynamics,* Winter 1991, pp. 17–29.

Ohmae, K., *Triad Power: The Coming of Global Competition,* Macmillan, London, 1985.

Ohmae, K., The Global Logic of Strategic Alliances, *Harvard Business Review,* March/April 1989, pp. 143–154.

Ohmae, K., Managing in a Borderless World, *Harvard Business Review,* May/June 1989, pp. 152–161.

Ohmae, K., Planting for a Global Harvest, *Harvard Business Review,* July/August 1989, pp. 136–145.

Porter, M. E., *Competition in Global Industries,* Free Press, New York, 1986.

Porter, M. E., *The Competitive Advantage of Nations,* Macmillan, London, 1990.

Porter, M. E., New Global Strategies for Competitive Advantage, *Planning Review,* May/June 1990, pp. 4–14.

Prahalad, C. K., and Y. Doz, *The Multinational Mission,* Free Press, New York, 1987.

Quelch, J. A., and E. J. Hoff, Customizing Global Marketing, *Harvard Business Review,* May/June 1986, pp. 59–68.

Raffee, H., and R. T. Kreutzer, Organizational Dimensions of Global Marketing, *European Journal of Marketing,* 1989, pp. 43–57.

Teece, D. J., The Multinational Enterprise: Market Failure and Market Power Considerations, *Sloan Management Review,* Spring 1981, pp. 4–17.

Vernon, R., and L. T. Wells, *The Economic Environment of International Business,* Fourth Edition, Prentice Hall, Englewood Cliffs, NJ, 1986.

Welch, L. S., and R. Luostarinen, Internationalization: Evolution of a Concept, *Journal of General Management,* Winter 1988, pp. 34–55.

Wortzel, L. H., Global Strategies: Standardization versus Flexibility, in Vernon-Wortzel, H., and L. H. Wortzel (Eds.), *Global Strategic Management,* Wiley, New York, 1990.

Yip, G. S., Loewe, P. M. and M. Y. Yoshino, How to Take Your Company to the Global Market, *Columbia Journal of World Business,* Winter 1988, pp. 37–48.

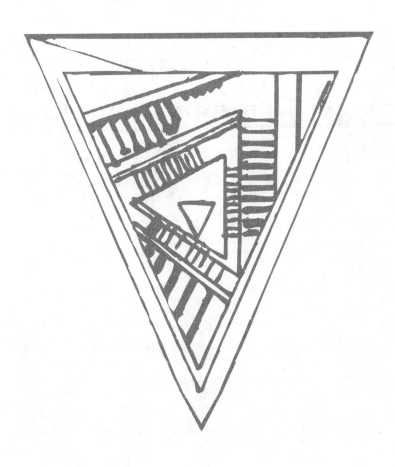

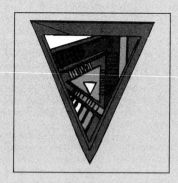

Section V
Strategy in Europe

Chapter 11: The European Context
On Subsidiarity and Synergy

CHAPTER 11
THE EUROPEAN CONTEXT:
ON SUBSIDIARITY AND SYNERGY

A great wind is blowing, and that gives
you either imagination or a headache.
—*Catherine II (The Great)*
1729–1796, Empress of Russia

Introduction

European integration was initiated with great enthusiasm, and for a while the battle cry "Europe 1992!" could make hearts beat faster. Since then, however, the integration process has progressed more slowly than anticipated, meeting stiff resistance from a variety of angles. It is a very legitimate question to wonder if, and how, European unification will proceed and what the strategic consequences of this will be. Will the European Community (EC) move beyond "the twelve," and what balance will be struck between the centrifugal forces of *subsidiarity* and the centripetal forces of *synergy?*

However, before pondering the broader Europe of the future, it is necessary to understand the Europe of the present and ask the fundamental question, Does the European context matter? In other words, does the unique European environment in general—including both EC and non-EC countries—and the process of European unification in particular, have a significant impact on both the strategy content and the strategy process of companies operating in the European arena? This question is equally significant for EC companies, non-EC European firms, and non-European corporations.

It is the intention of this chapter to seek an answer to this question by presenting three sets of two articles each. The objective of the first set of articles is to further clarify the European *context*, by closer examination of the economic integration policies of the European Community. The second set of articles deals with the strategy *content* repercussions of European integration, while the third set focuses on the strategy *process* consequences of unification. The reader will note that the debate in this chapter is, unfortunately, less advanced than the discussions in the previous chapters. Beside serving as a signal to European researchers, this implies that more responsibility rests with the reader to determine what the true importance of the European context is.

The Articles

This chapter appropriately starts off with the full text of the official EC report, which documents the expected economic gains of European integration. From this article, "The Economics of 1992" by Michael Emerson, Michel Aujean, Michel Catinat, Philippe Goybet, and Alexis Jacquemin, it becomes clear what the objectives of the "1992 programme" were and which specific internal market barriers the European Community intended to eliminate.

In the second article, "European Integration: Myths and Realities," John Kay reacts to the previous document and the "hype" surrounding it. The aim of his article is to distinguish the incorrect and often misleading clichés—the myths—from the real benefits—the realities. Kay discusses the three main realities of the 1992 programme: trade facilitation, the removal of nontariff barriers, and the liberalisation of public procurement. In each case, he gives a more detailed account of the probable economic consequences of integration than in the first article of this chapter.

The next two articles focus largely on the strategy content issues raised by the European context described above. The first of the pair, "The Strategic Implications of European Integration" by Herman Daems, takes a positioning approach to analyse how 1992 will shape competition. Using Porter's "five forces" analysis (see chapter 4), Daems reviews many of the consequences of the 1992 programme already identified by Kay and subsequently explores a number of strategic options available to companies to deal with these consequences.

The second of the pair of "content" articles, "Partnerships in Europe" by Yves Doz, presents a strategic reaction to 1992 not dwelled on by Kay or Daems. Doz argues that the commonly considered strategic options of competitive repositioning, national consolidations, and transnational mergers and acquisitions are all valuable "hard" restructuring methods. However, he believes that there are many situations, particularly in the European context, where the "softer" restructuring method of partnerships would be more suitable. In his opinion, joint ventures and alliances are "more likely to bring the same rationalisation and restructuration benefits as mergers are expected to provide."

The third set of articles deals primarily with the strategy process consequences of the European context. In the first article of this set, "Will Management Become European?" Keith Thurley and Hans Wirdenius introduce the term *European management*. By the term they mean "recognizable patterns of managerial behaviour and an approach to problem solving and decision making at all levels in organizations that establishes the identity of the management strategy as distinctly European, and particularly focuses on approaches to planning, implementing, and evaluating change." They argue that such a distinctly European flavour of making and implementing, strategy is necessary given the joint pressures of economic and legal integration in the face of continued cultural diversity. However, what European management will be like and how it will differ from non-European management styles is an issue Thurley and Wirdenius believe is still wide open.

In the last article, "Management Learning for Europe," Sybren Tijmstra and Kenneth Casler accept the challenge presented by Thurley and Wirdenius. In this reading, Tijmstra and Casler attempt to define how European management will differ from both American and Japanese management. Their argumentation focuses on the individual qualities that must be embodied in the European manager: (S)he must "have a solid core of technical and managerial competence, . . . display a genuine enthusiasm and empathy for different peoples and cultures, . . . be self-aware, conscious of his/her own personal values and cultural orientation, . . . and keen to accept changes." Tijmstra and Casler also indicate how such European managers must be educated and developed. However, because they focus on the individual manager, it remains a question how the strategy process within a European organisation might be different than elsewhere in the world. Moreover, it remains a question whether European-based companies should focus on "European management" if global markets are the battleground of the future.

Recommended Readings and Cases

Although there is not much literature on the impact of the European context on strategy process and strategy content, there are still a few stimulating articles and books to be found. We would first strongly recommend readers look at "European Myopia" by Orjan Sölvell and Ivo Zander as an antidote to excessive Eurocentrism. An interesting book exploring "Europeanness" is Transnational Business in Europe: Economic and Social Perspectives, by Jules van Dijck and A. Wentink. For a good industry-level perspective, the interested reader might want to start with *Competition in Europe* by Peter de Wolf.

The two cases selected to accompany this chapter are "Pharma Swede" and "Cap Gemini Sogeti." The Pharma Swede case, written by Kamran Kashani and Robert Howard, deals with the consequences of changing European pharmaceutical regulation for this Swedish company. Readers are asked to think about the impact of government regulation in general and the implications of European integration in particular. As such, Pharma Swede is a very specific case of how changing European rules could have a significant influence on the company's room to manoeuvre. The Cap Gemini Sogeti case, by Tom Elfring, does not look at the changing European regulatory environment, but at the consequences of the practical integration of the European economy. Cap Gemini Sogeti (CGS) is a French firm specializing in computer facilities management, customized computer system development, and management consultancy. CGS has chosen a pan-European strategy but must develop a transnational organisation to fit this ambition. This case gives readers the opportunity to consider what a "European" organisation should look like.

■ THE ECONOMICS OF EUROPEAN INTEGRATION†

By Michael Emerson, Michel Aujean, Michel Catinat,
Philippe Goybet, and Alexis Jacquemin

Purpose

The objective of the study "The Economics of 1992: The EC Commission's Assessment of the Economic Effect of Completing the Internal Market," is to contribute a deeper understanding of the channels through which the removal of the European Community's internal market barriers may result in economic gains. An attempt is made also to quantify the potential size of these gains. While quantification of such a complex process is indeed hazardous, the essential point is to ascertain not the exact but the broad orders of magnitude. The political effort required to complete the internal market will be very considerable. Will it be worth the trouble? The findings of this study are affirmative. A significant improvement in the Community's macroenvironment performance could indeed be made possible as a result of the numerous microeconomic measures proposed in the internal market programme. But a certain number of supporting conditions, beyond simply legislating the three hundred items in the White Paper, are also required to secure the potential economic gains.

The Nature of the Community's Internal Market Barriers

Tariffs and quantitative restrictions on trade have been largely eliminated in the Community. The remaining barriers essentially consist of

- differences in technical regulations between countries, which impose extra costs on intra-EC trade;
- delays at frontiers for customs purposes, and related administrative burdens for companies and public administrations, which impose further costs on trade;
- restrictions on competition for public purchases through excluding bids from other Community suppliers, which often result in excessively high costs of purchase;
- restrictions on freedom to engage in certain service transactions, or to become established in certain service activities in other Community countries, particularly financial and transport services, where the costs of market-entry barriers also appear to be substantial.

While quite a number of these individual barriers can be overcome at a moderate cost, when taken together with the oligopolistic structure of many markets, they add up to a considerable degree of noncompetitive segmentation of the market. This is suggested by the substantial consumer price differences between countries. This discrepancy between the gains from eliminating the direct costs of barriers and those from achieving a full, competitive integration of the market is of capital importance for

---

†**Source:** Reprinted from *The Economics of 1992* by Michael Emerson, et al (1988) by permission of Oxford University Press. Copyright © 1988 Commission of the European Communities.

the conclusions of this study. It has clear implications for how competition policy is to be conducted, alongside the removal of the technical, physical, and fiscal frontiers proposed in the White Paper.

The Nature of the Economic Gains to Be Measured

Since the economic concepts involved in this study are several and complex, it is important to be clear about the essentials at the outset.

The creation of a true European internal market will on the one hand suppress a series of constraints that today prevent enterprises from being as efficient as they could be and from employing their resources to the full, and on the other hand establish a more competitive environment that will incite them to exploit new opportunities. The removal of the constraints and the emergence of the new competitive incentives will lead to four principal types of effect:

- A significant reduction in costs due to a better exploitation of several kinds of economies of scale associated with the size of production units and enterprises

- An improved efficiency in enterprises, a rationalization of industrial structures, and a setting of prices closer to costs or production, all resulting from more competitive markets

- Adjustments between industries on the basis of a fuller play of comparative advantages in an integrated market

- A flow of innovations, new processes, and new products, stimulated by the dynamics of the internal market

These processes liberate resources for alternative productive uses, and when they are so used the total, sustainable level of consumption and investment in the economy will be increased. This is the fundamental criterion of economic gain.

These gains in economic welfare will also be reflected in macroeconomic indicators. It is implicit, in order to attain the highest sustainable level of consumption and investment, that productivity and employment be also of a high order. In particular, where rationalization efforts cause labour to be made redundant, this resource has to be successfully reemployed. Also implicit is a high rate of growth in the economy. The sustainability condition, moreover, requires that the major macroeconomic equilibrium constraints be respected, notably as regards price stability, balance of payments, and budget balances. It further implies a positive performance in terms of worldwide competitivity. These different objectives can, however, be achieved in different mixes; it is for macroeconomic policy to determine how to dispose of the potential economic gains made available by the microeconomic measures taken in order to complete the internal market.

Costs and prices are the key elements in the attempt to quantify the economic gains mentioned. The percentage reduction in costs or prices resulting from the removal of the market barriers, or change in competitive conditions, is the essential starting point in the quantification process. A first approximation of the economic gain in money terms may be arrived at by multiplying these percentage costs or price changes by the initial value of the goods or services in question. While this measure has the great merit of simplicity, it ignores some important secondary effects. The most important of these are seen in continuing and cumulative impacts on the economy that may follow from a change in the competitive environment. These and other effects, including those that distinguish the position of consumers and producers, are built into the quantification methods used in this study.

Empirical Estimates

Any estimates of the effects of a complex action like completing the internal market can only be regarded as very approximate. Apart from being subject to a number of policy conditions, such estimates are extremely difficult to make especially as regards some of the more speculative and long-term effects. With these strong reservations to be kept in mind, some rough orders of magnitude may be suggested. For perspective, the Community's total gross domestic product in 1985 (the base year for most estimates in this study) was 3300 billion ECU for the twelve member states (or 2900 billion ECU for the seven countries essentially covered by the empirical estimates that follow).

- The direct costs of frontier formalities, and associated administrative costs for the private and public sector, may be of the order of 1.8 percent of the value of goods traded within the Community or around 9 billion ECU.

- The total costs for industry of identifiable barriers in the internal market, including not only frontier formalities as above but also technical regulations and other barriers, have been estimated in opinion surveys of industrialists to average a little under 2 percent of those companies' total costs. This represents about 40 billion ECU or 3 percent of industrial value-added.

- Several industry studies corroborate these findings, with cost reductions of the order of 1 to 2 percent estimated to result for the food and beverage industry, construction materials, pharmaceuticals, and textiles and clothing, and 5 percent for automobiles. It is to be stressed that these relatively moderate figures typically reflect the cost of identifiable market barriers, and not the total gains that could be expected from a full, competitive integration of these product markets (see further below).

- In particular, industries and service sector branches subject to market entry restrictions could experience considerably bigger potential cost and price reductions. Examples include branches of industry for which government procurement is important (energy generating, transport, office and defence equipment), financial services (banking insurance and securities), and road and air transport. In these cases cost and price reductions often on the order of 10 to 20 percent, and even more in some cases, could be expected. For public procurement alone the gains could amount to around 20 billion ECU. For financial services also a range around 20 billion ECU in potential savings has been proposed, although the margin of uncertainty here is particularly large.

- The relatively large percentage reductions for some categories of public procurement reflect the fact that these estimates include the broader effects of open competition in these sectors, including the realization of previously unexploited economies of scale (which are not reflected in the figures reported in the first three points). A study of potential economies of scale in European industry shows that in more than half of all branches of industry, twenty firms of efficient size can coexist in the Community market, whereas the largest national markets could only have four each. It is evident, therefore, that only the European internal market could combine the advantages of technical and economic efficiency, twenty firms being more likely to assure effective competition than four firms. Comparing the present industrial Structure with a more rationalized but still less than optimal one, it is estimated that about one-third of European industry could profit from varying cost reductions of between 1 to 7 percent, yielding an aggregate cost saving on the order of 60 billion ECU.

- It becomes progressively more hazardous to suggest magnitudes for other types of gain resulting from enhanced competition, including the reduction of what has been termed "X-inefficiency." This covers a poor internal allocation of resources—human, physical, and financial. Conditions of weak competition cause X-inefficiency, and also permit excess profit margins (monopoly profits, or economic rent). There are, in this area, some sources of information ranging from industry case studies to theoretical models of corporate behaviour in different market environments. The costs of X-inefficiency may often be as great as those resulting from unexploited economies of scale. The total effect of moving to a competitive, integrated market, with fuller achievement of potential economies of scale and reduction of X-inefficiency, may be twice to three times the direct cost of identified barriers in an environment where competition is less effective.

■ The totality of the foregoing effects could be reflected, in the new equilibrium situation in the economy after several years, in a downward convergence of presently disparate price levels. Detailed information exists on these price differences at the consumer level, with and without indirect taxes. This permits a number of purely illustrative hypotheses to be examined, as regards the magnitude of savings that would be obtained in the event of different degrees of downward price convergence depending upon the extent of existing internal market barriers and the degree of natural protection represented by the transport costs and differences in tastes. Under one set of hypotheses, implying strong market integration but far from complete price convergence and with incomplete sectoral coverage, the gains amounted to about 140 billion ECU.

■ Overall these estimates offer a range, starting with around 70 billion ECU (2.5 percent of GDP) for a rather narrow conception of the benefits of removing the remaining internal market barriers, to around 125 to 190 billion ECU (4.25 to 6.5 percent of GDP) in the hypothesis of a much more competitive integrated market (as already indicated, the above amounts in ECU are scaled in relation to the 1985 GDP of seven member states, accounting for 88 percent of the EUR 12 total. The same percentages of GDP, for the 1988 GDP of EUR 12, give a range of around 175 to 255 billion ECU). Overall, it would seem possible to enhance the Community's annual potential growth rate, for both output and consumption by around 1 percentage point for the period up to 1992. In addition, there would be good prospects that longer-run dynamic effects could sustain a buoyant growth rate further into the 1990s.

■ The common assumptions underlying the foregoing estimates (notably the cumulative totals) are that (1) it might take five or possibly more years for the larger part of the effects to be reached, and (2) in any event it is assumed that micro- and macroeconomic policies would ensure that the resources released as costs are reduced are effectively reemployed productively. This concerns labour in particular. These were simplifying assumptions since it is not possible to project the evolution of complex economic structures in many dimensions at the same time (for example, by industry branch over time and for many economic variables). In order to make good some of these limitations, a number of macroeconomic simulation exercises have been conducted, injecting some of the foregoing estimates into macrodynamic models. For this purpose, the effects of the internal market programme have been grouped under four major headings, each having a different type of macroeconomic impact: (1) the removal of customs delays and costs, (2) the opening of public markets to competition, (3) the liberalization and integration of financial markets, and (4) more general supply-side effects, reflecting changes in the strategic behaviour of enterprises in a new competitive environment. The simulated macroeconomic results are presented, first, under the assumption of a passive macroeconomic policy, and second, under the assumption that improved room for manoeuvre is actively exploited.

● *With a passive macroeconomic policy.* The overall impact of the measures is manifest most strongly in the initial years in the downward pressure on prices and costs, but this is followed with only a modest time lag by increases in output. The major impacts, however, appear in the medium run after about five to six years, by which time a cumulative impact of +4.5 percent in terms of GDP and minus -6 percent in terms of the price level might be expected from a full implementation of the internal market programme.These macroeconomic simulations thus tend to converge with the results of the aggregated microeconomic calculations. The total impact on employment is initially slightly negative, but in the medium term it increases by about 2 million jobs (nearly 2 percent of the initial employment level). The budget balance is improved markedly, and the current account of the balance of payments is improved significantly. Each of the simulated measures or changes in economic behaviour contributes to the positive results, cutting costs and prices, stimulating gains in productivity and investment increasing real incomes and expenditure.

- *With a more active macroeconomic policy.* Since all the main indicators of monetary and financial equilibrium would be thus improved, it would be legitimate to consider adjusting medium term macroeconomic strategy onto a somewhat more expansionary trajectory. The extent of this adjustment would depend upon which constraint (inflation, budget, or balance of payments deficits) was considered binding. A number of variants are illustrated in the text. In the middle of the range, for example, lies a case in which the GDP level after a medium-term period might be 2.5 percent higher, in addition to the 4.5 percent gain suggested under the passive macroeconomic policy, thus totalling 7 percent. In this case, inflation would still have been held well below the course initially projected in the absence of the internal market programme, the budget balance would also be improved, while the balance of payments might be worsened by a moderate but sustainable amount.

- *The microeconomic and macroeconomic synthesis.* The foregoing paragraphs have set out quantitative estimates on matters that are extremely difficult to evaluate at all precisely. There should be no misunderstanding about the nature of such figures. They are the product of many sources of very approximate information, combined with economic assumptions and judgments that are defendable but also only approximate. The important conclusions are basically the following. The estimates have been assembled in an eclectic manner, using various techniques of microeconomic and macroeconomic analysis. These different approaches suggest consistent results. The potential gains from a full, competitive integration of the internal market are not trivial in macroeconomic terms. They could be about large enough to make the difference between a disappointing and very satisfactory economic performance for the Community economy as a whole.

■ Notwithstanding these qualifications, the largest benefits suggested above are unlikely to be overestimates of the potential benefit of fully integrating the Community's market. This is because the figures exclude some important categories of dynamic impact on economic performance. Three examples may be mentioned. First, there is increasing evidence that the trend rate of technological innovation in the economy depends on the presence of competition; only an integrated market can offer the benefits both of scale of operation and competition. Second, there is evidence in fast-growing high technology industries of dynamic or learning economies of scale, whereby costs decline as the total accumulated production of certain goods and services increases; market segmentation gravely limits the scope for these benefits and damages performance in key high-growth industries of the future. Third, the business strategies of European enterprises are likely to be greatly affected in the event of a rapid and extensive implementation of the internal market programme; a full integration of the internal market will foster the emergence of truly European companies, with structures and strategies that are better suited to securing a strong place in world market competition.

From the Removal of Technical Barriers to Full Market Integration

The range of quantitative estimates just presented draws attention to the major difference between

■ a narrow, technical, and short-term view of the costs of "tangibly" identifiable frontier barriers, such as customs delays and various regulations; and

■ a broader, strategic, and long-term view of the benefits from having a fully integrated, competitive, and rationalized internal market.

Since the magnitudes involved under the second concept are at least twice as big as under the first one, it is important to be clear about the conditions required to achieve the larger results.

- The most fundamental condition is the credibility of the operation: that within a medium-term period the European market environment is to be transformed in a way that will oblige all enterprises producing or marketing tradeable goods and services to adopt European business strategies. Businesses have in effect to make up their minds over two questions: (1) whether the market is going to be much more competitive or not, and (2) in the affirmative case, whether this will be combined with a more dynamic macroeconomic environment. This implies, in turn, being clear about the microeconomic and macroeconomic policies associated with the internal market policy.

- As regards microeconomic policies, the first condition for the credibility of the programme is that economic agents should easily be able to engage in arbitrage between national markets to profit from price differences, and so impose more nearly common and competitive price levels. This means that the frontiers must be truly open: drive-through at the geographic frontiers, open also for individuals to engage in cross-frontier shopping to add to competition for producers and distributors, and free of administrative complications within member states. Thus all the essential barriers have to be removed, otherwise the last remaining barriers may on their own be sufficient to restrain competition. The second condition, which concerns competition policy as regards public subsidies, is that enterprises contemplating European market strategies must be assured that if they advance in their penetration of other countries' markets, they will not find themselves confronted by defensive subsidies in those countries. For the medium-term planning of enterprises, what is most important is the degree of certainty surrounding their planning assumptions. Thus the barrier of uncertainty must be removed. Does the enterprise have to compete just with known commercial rivals or will it have also to compete with governments standing behind these rivals? Only the public authorities can assure this condition. In the first place the European Commission itself already has powers to restrain state subsidies, indeed forbid them where appropriate. But this needs to be reinforced by the demonstrable willingness of member states to accept these "rules of the game" rather than conduct long political and procedural struggles over illegal subsidy regimes. The third condition concerns competition policy addressed to private enterprises. Here it is necessary for the business world to understand clearly that commercial practices that tend to segment markets or lead to the abuse of dominant positions will be vigorously countered. At the present time, price discrimination between national markets is widespread and substantial to the considerable cost of consumers. Competition policy must, for the market to be fully integrated, make it clearly understood, for example, that parallel imports are to be welcomed wherever undue price differences are seen to exist.

- As regards macroeconomic policies, the issue is essentially whether demand policy will accommodate the increased potential for noninflationary growth and indeed be perceived as determined to do so over a medium-term period. This point has been illustrated by the simulations reported above. It is certain that implementation of the internal market programme will put downward pressure on costs and prices, and create the potential for greater noninflationary growth. It is not certain, however, how far this potential will materialize. From the standpoint of macroeconomic analysis there are a range of possibilities: the benefits from the more competitive market pressures may be taken mainly in the form of less price inflation, or mainly in the form of more output with unchanged inflation (i.e., activity is expanded to the point that the initial disinflationary impulse is completely offset by higher demand pressure), or by a more even mix of disinflation and output gains. Business opinion was relatively optimistic that increased sales and output would result, when surveyed for the present study in the late summer of 1987. On average, industrialists expect the internal market programme to lead to a lifting of total sales by about 5 percent over a period of years. This is entirely consistent with the other calculations reported above on the potential gains from market integration. It is necessary, however, that the credibility of these favourable expectations be supported by a well-coordinated, growth-oriented macroeconomic policy. If this is not done, the market liberalization process risks generating defensive and negative reactions in which case the viability of the programme could be threatened. While the approach adopted in this study is a structural one, and therefore does not discuss current issues of the world and European business cycles, the implementation of the internal market programme cannot, to be successful in practice, ignore current macroeconomic realities. Early 1988 sees a weakening of the world and European business cycles, and a much higher level of European exchange rates against the U.S. dollar and other currencies linked to it. Some international competitors are going to be well placed to make strategic gains in their share of a weakening European market. These trends hold out obvious dangers. While Europe must, of course, make its contribution to the rebalancing of the world economy, it must also take steps to safeguard the successful implementation of the internal market programme. These safeguards can be summarized under two headings: (1) support for the European business cycle, sufficient to counter its weakening in the short run, and favour the acceleration of growth thereafter, (2) endeavours to assure that international exchange rate adjustments are adequate but not excessive.

Adjustment Costs and the Distribution of Gains

Accelerated market integration certainly means that more people will have to change their jobs more frequently. However, the counterpart to this should be rising employment and rising real incomes in the aggregate, as the foregoing estimates and simulations have suggested. Experience suggests that the costs of market adjustments become very serious above all where necessary sectoral adjustments are delayed (for example agriculture and steel).

Difficult as it is to estimate the aggregate gains from market integration, this task is relatively manageable compared with that of forecasting its distribution by country or region. While the latter task has not been attempted, it is worth noting that neither economic theory nor relevant economic history can point to any clear-cut pattern of likely distributional advantage or disadvantage. Theories or vicious circles or divergence or regional fortunes resulting from market integration exist, but so do alternative theses that point to more balanced or indeterminate outcomes; the latter theses including important recent developments in the analysis of trade between industrialized countries. Smaller countries, in particular those having recently joined the Community with relatively protected economic structures, have proportionately the biggest opportunities for gain from market integration. In any case, policy instruments exist to provide an insurance policy to help initial losers recover (e.g., the Community's structural funds, whose substantial expansion has recently been agreed).

Final Remarks

The study supports the following essential conclusions:

- In the present condition of the European economy the segmentation and weak competitiveness of many markets means that there is a large potential for the rationalization of production and distribution structures, leading to improvements in productivity, and reductions in many costs and prices.

- The completion of the internal market could, if strongly reinforced by the competition policies of both the Community and member states, have a deep and extensive impact on economic structures and performance. The size of this impact, in terms of the potential for increased noninflationary growth, could be sufficient to transform the Community's macroeconomic performance from a mediocre to a very satisfactory one.

■ In order to achieve a prize of this magnitude, all the main features of the internal market programme would need to be implemented with sufficient speed and conviction, such that the credibility of the total operation is not just safeguarded, but reinforced. Implementation of half of the actions proposed in the White Paper will deliver much less than half of the total potential benefits.

■ In fact, more than full implementation of the White Paper is required in order to achieve the full potential benefits of an integrated European market. There must be a strong competition policy, which was discussed only in very summary terms in the White Paper. Macroeconomic policy has to be set on a coherent, growth-oriented strategy. The White Paper represents a policy aimed at making the supply potential of the Community economy more flexible and competitive. The counterpart in terms of the demand side needs to be clearly agreed among policymakers and credibly communicated to business and public opinion. In normal cyclical conditions it would be appropriate, as soon as sufficient market actions are beginning to be implemented, for macroeconomic policy to ratify these measures by ensuring that the economy climbs onto the higher growth trajectory.

■ EUROPEAN INTEGRATION: MYTHS AND REALITIES[†]

By John Kay

Introduction

This article looks beyond the—often absurd—hype that has surrounded the discussion of 1992 in the last years, and assesses the realities of what the programme means for business opportunities and business behaviour. We do so with some qualms.

There is a sense in which the real significance of 1992 lies in the hype, rather than in the programme itself. The marketing campaign has enjoyed a success far beyond its promoters' dreams in alerting business to the potential of the European markets and the opportunities for European ventures, and in restoring self-confidence in the European ideal. Objective reality may not have changed, but the manner in which it has been perceived has.

In this way, the spirit of 1992 may have taken on a significance greater than the detail of the programme. And the spirit is at once wider and narrower than the programme itself. Wider because it is already apparent that opportunities will be seized that were not taken before, not because there were official obstacles to them, but because business horizons were too national in outlook. Narrower, because in specific areas—such as public procurement or financial market liberalization—it is sincerity with which governments pursue the ideals of 1992 that matters, rather than the content of European Commission directives themselves.

But this emphasis on the spirit of 1992 is not in any way a justification of the woolly generalization that surrounds much discussion of the impact of 1992 on both public

[†]**Source:** This article was adapted from chapter 1 of *1992, Myths and Realities*, Center for Business Strategy, 1989. Used with permission.

and business policy. It is important to understand both what the spirit of 1992 does involve and what it does not. While phrases like "the creation of a single market of 320 million people" are effective ways of firing the public imagination, they are profoundly misleading as a guide to the real significance of economic integration. The cliché is dangerous because it invites business to believe that the European market will be more homogeneous after 1992 than it is now, in the same way that the British market is today more homogeneous than the European market (and, indeed, more homogeneous than the market in a large federal state, such as the United States). But there is not, and cannot be, anything in the 1992 programme that will bring about such an outcome. Trade liberalization has its primary effects on supply, not on demand. The reason why demand for many products varies across the European community is mainly because of differences in preferences, habits, language, culture, climate, and incomes that will be wholly unaffected by 1992. In this context, economic integration is about the creation of greater product diversity within national markets, not about the elimination of product diversity in international markets.

It follows that the view that the likely consequence of 1992 will be the standardization of European production in a smaller number of plants, offering consumers a reduced choice of products but also the benefit of lower prices from greater scale economies, is in most cases mistaken. It also follows that the idea that an appropriate immediate response to the approach of 1992 is to promote transnational mergers with a view to benefitting from such rationalization is also erroneous. If there were advantages in concentrating production on a small number of varieties of eurobeer, eurocars, eurobiscuits, and eurochocolate, there are few obstacles now to such concentration. The reason these developments do not occur is that the variety of consumer tastes—within countries as well as between them—demands a wider range of products. At the same time there are few scale economies that would become available by extending production beyond the levels of output that are already attained in a fragmented Europe. This will be as true after 1992 as before it.

This is not to say that 1992 will have no effects on the structure of markets or production, or that it will not benefit the European economy. The gains derive from the availability of wider product ranges within domestic markets, and this has been the principal consequence of economic integration so far; as a result of the promotion of greater competition through the liberalization of ossified national regulatory structures; and through the breakdown of comfortable domestic cartels. The potentially important effects come, in short, from new market entry, and they come in those industries where entry has in the past been inhibited—by domestic regulation or public procurement policies. It follows the merger that meets both the business and public policy requirement of 1992 is the merger that provides a springboard for such entry. With a few exceptions, merger between established market leaders in different member states is unlikely to be sensible business strategy, and where there are business advantages to it, there are public benefits in blocking it.

Completing the Internal Market

The measures that form most of the 1992 programme were first put forward in a Commission White Paper—Completing the Internal Market—in 1985. Some of the proposals aim to reduce obstacles to the rapid and economical distribution of goods within the Community. The most dramatic of these is the plan to abolish fiscal frontiers, thus reducing or eliminating border controls or intra-Community movements of goods and people. Many of the provisions are concerned with the elimination of nontariff barriers to trade—the ways in which differences in national standards and regulations have the intended or inadvertent effect of limiting market access to other Community producers. Many of the Commission's proposals are intended to promote the liberalization of public procurement policies—the use of public sector purchasing to promote national champions or to give preferences to local suppliers. The White Paper contains a now famous list of three hundred measures designed to promote these several objectives.

The Single European Act, which became effective in 1987, takes these measures further. It requires the Commission to bring forward proposals that would achieve the completion of the internal market by 31 December 1992. The relevant economic market is not determined simply by the presence or absence of trade barriers. In this sense there will not be a single European market in 1992, any more than there is a single British market now. For some commodities—such as aircraft—the relevant geographical market is already the world. For other goods and services—such as haircuts or concrete—the market is, and always will be, a local one.

There is a unified European market for some commodities now. There are also many for which it is not. Since the days of Alfred Marshall, economists have measured the extent of market unification by reference to the *law of one price*: in a single economic market, there can only be one price at which any particular commodity is sold. It is apparent that there is no single European market for any of the four commodities illustrated in table 11-1, even though three of them—cars, domestic appliances, and pharmaceuticals—are subject to extensive and growing international trade. We should not confuse the development of trade with the unification of markets, and the strategies appropriate to a single market are by no means the same as those appropriate to a group of interrelated markets. The issue of whether or not a unified market exists can be resolved only by references to the particular conditions under which particular commodities are sold. The nature of a market is defined by the nature of competition between buyers and sellers, not by governments, commissions, laws, or regulations. What governments, commissions, laws, and regulations can do—and all they can do—is to influence the nature of that competition.

Stages of Market Unification

In the first stage, national markets are distinct and entry by foreign manufacturers or their products is seriously restricted, by regulation, tariffs, or custom and practice. This is true at the moment, for example, of electricity and of most areas of insurance, where although commodities are potentially tradeable, in fact virtually no trade occurs. In a market as fragmented as this, there may be large and persistent differences in the

	German Cars	Pharmaceuticals	Life Insurance	Domestic Appliances
Belgium	100	100	100	100
France	115	78	75	130
West Germany	127	174	59	117
Italy	129	80	102	110
Netherlands	NA	164	51	105
United Kingdom	142	114	39	93

TABLE 11-1
Prices in European Markets (Belgium = 100)

Source: *European Economy,* March 1988; Nicolaides & Baden Fuller, 1987.

efficiencies of national industries and producers—as indeed there are in electricity and services.

The second stage of market unification is the linkage of distinct national markets. Here trade occurs, but the movement of goods is substantially controlled by the manufacturer and his agents. Much of the inefficiency that is likely to characterize autarky (i.e., economic self-sufficiency) will have been eliminated. It is unlikely that there will be large continuing differences in the efficiency of different companies, and most scale economies will have been realized. Prices, marketing strategies, and distribution systems will be variable. Nevertheless, distribution may still be inefficient, consumer choice in segmented markets limited, and competitive pressures less strong than they might be. The European markets for most manufactured goods are at this stage of development—cars and pharmaceuticals, for example.

The third stage of market unification is one in which trade is free at wholesale and retail level. Marketing and distribution systems converge, and prices tend to equality. Aircraft and oil markets are like this, for example, and for these (and for most commodity products) it is sensible to talk about a unified world market.

There are many reasons why markets are not yet unified, and the reasons vary substantially across different countries and commodities. The fragmentation that remains within the European Community is only to a very limited extent the result of trade barriers of a kind that is within the powers of the European Commission to remove. This is not to suggest that the implications of membership of the European Community are unimportant. It is a measure not of the Community's failure, but of its success, that the remaining inhibitions on trade within Europe are mostly not the result of artificial trade barriers.

Consequences of Programme Measures

If there are three main themes to the 1992 programme—trade facilitation, removal of nontariff barriers, and liberalization of procurement—there are, in turn, three main ways in which the plan may affect the structure of European markets:

- cost positions of competitors
- market segmentation
- entry of new competitors

The effect on relative cost positions of different competitors within existing markets means that companies exporting to other Community states will find their costs reduced, relative to their domestic competitors or companies outside the Community. Non-Community producers may also gain some cost advantage from lower costs of distribution within the Community.

Next, the completion of the internal market may undermine market segmentation. Manufacturers of branded commodities typically impose different pricing policies, supported by different mechanisms of promotion and distribution, in the various markets in which they compete. Some examples of this are to be found in the industries listed in table 11-1. Market unification may undermine the feasibility and desirability of such strategies. Finally, the 1992 programme may facilitate the entry of new competitors into markets that were previously closed, or unattractive.

The Commission hopes to reduce the costs associated with trade within the Community—this is the essence of the "internal market." The most important element of this—and certainly the most visible and tangible manifestation of the 1992 programme—is the plan to dismantle fiscal frontiers between states. In the

Commission's view, this requires the approximation of VAT rates and the harmonization of excise duties throughout Europe.

Reductions in distribution costs within the Community give competitive benefits to businesses in other Community states relative to both domestic and non-Community producers. The magnitude of these effects depends on the cost reductions generated by the internal market programme. It is quickly apparent, however, that these are unlikely to be large. A realistic assessment of the costs savings obtainable from reductions in distribution costs from a programme of administrative simplification and transport liberalization might, perhaps, be half that level—say between 1 and 1.5 per cent of the value of trade affected. A cost advantage of this magnitude will not have a material effect on the structure of production in most industries.

All this is not to say that the goal of greater freedom of movement for goods within the European Community should not be pursued, or that it will not give rise to benefits. But two general points emerge. The first is that to the extent that the market within the Community does continue to be fragmented, it does not appear that the costs associated with border formalities and inefficiencies in distribution systems are primarily responsible. The second is that it seems unlikely that the economic consequences of 1992 will be macroeconomic, or that we should look for major results from generalized trade liberalization. If there are major effects on industrial structure from 1992, we should look to industry-specific measures.

The Costs and Pattern of Distribution

One such industry-specific effect should be noted immediately. Although the cost savings identified above are not large relative to product prices, they are large relative to the costs of distribution. Thus the 1992 programme is likely to have much more substantial general effects on the structure of distribution than on the structure of production. Patterns of wholesale distribution will look significantly different if they can be organized with minimal regard for national boundaries. In addition, distribution costs will also be reduced by liberalization of regulations governing transport within the Community.

The readiness to use Benelux as a warehousing centre for the Community—which is already evident in many commodities—may be expected to increase. This will, in turn, carry a number of activities with it, such as blending, where the value added in processing is low. It may have consequential implications for shipping, where it may become attractive to import in bulk to a Benelux port rather than in smaller quantities to locations closer to the ultimate destination.

Will these effects extend to retail distribution? The pattern of retail distribution may be affected by cross-border shopping by consumers. While cross-border shopping would be part of an internal market, there is concern that it may be generated artificially by differences in tax rates. This is currently a problem in Ireland, around Luxembourg, and across some other Community borders. There is a possibility that such trade would increase, perhaps through the development of international mail order, unless the 1992 programme is effective in eliminating the opportunity or preventing the outcome.

Because cross-border shopping is very conspicuous, its significance is often exaggerated. Of all products, cars are most susceptible to cross-border transactions—the unit value of the purchase is (apart from houses) the highest of any item in consumer budgets, price differentials within the Community are large, the product is internationally branded and uniquely mobile. Yet personal imports into the United Kingdom, the highest priced of Community markets, have been only about 2 per cent of U.K. new car registrations.

Public Procurement

The potential significance of 1992 for the structure of European industry is greatest in the field of public procurement. In principle, public bodies may not discriminate between Community suppliers in their procurement policies and are required to advertise major contracts throughout the Community. In practice, cross-border purchasing by European governments is negligible.

One reason is that several areas of major significance are excluded. Defence is obviously a special case, and it is neither realistic nor wholly desirable to expect that markets will be opened completely in view of the special relationship between supplier and customer that defence procurement will often entail. The Community's requirement for open tendering does not at present cover telecommunications, water, energy, or transport. Thus the scope of the existing directive exempts purchases by all the major public utilities. These are important exclusions, and it is not too cynical to say that these industries are excluded precisely because they are important. The Commission's proposals include the elimination of these exemptions, although this has not yet been agreed by the Council of Ministers.

This draws attention to the underlying issue, however, that confronts any attempt to outlaw discrimination through legislation. The French government prefers to buy from French producers, but French consumers, faced with a wide range of potential suppliers, appear to do exactly the same. You can lead a horse to water, but you cannot make it drink or look into its mind and establish the reasons why it has refused to drink. The Commission is, however, anxious to do its best, particularly by extending the rights of complainants who feel they have been refused contracts on improper grounds. Such a complaint is, however, rarely a route to commercial success. It is rarely comfortable to be a member of an exclusive club if you have won your membership by court order, as campaigners against other kinds of discrimination are well aware.

In this area, above all, the spirit of 1992 is considerably more important than the letter. There is little the Commission can do to force protectionist national purchasing agencies to shop more widely if the protectionist instinct remains. But the internal market programme itself may erode that instinct. And differing attitudes to public expenditure and public intervention may lead agencies increasingly to rank value-for-money as a more important objective than the support of their national government's industrial policy.

The Removal of Nontariff Barriers to Trade

Of all existing distortions to trade within the Community, technical and administrative barriers to trade are the most significant and the most wide ranging. A study for the Commission based on a questionnaire distributed to twenty thousand European businesses rated technical standards and regulations, and administrative barriers, as the two most important obstacles to trade.

During most of the life of the Community, the Commission has attempted to overcome the problem of different national standards by securing agreement on a common European norm. These attempts were the subject of much derision—hence the jokes about eurosausages and eurobeer—and peculiarly vulnerable to political manoeuvering as different governments and companies attempted to use the Community as a formula for imposing norms disadvantageous to their competitors, or found it necessary to resist the strategic games of others who had got there first.

In 1985, the Commission adopted a "new approach" to these problems. The essence of the new approach is that the definition of European standards need not go beyond the basic objectives of consumer protection. The task of ensuring that products meet these requirements can then be delegated (to the British Standards Institution and its analogues in other sectors and other countries). The principle of mutual recognition then implies that member states must allow products that satisfy these requirements free access to their markets. They can impose different or more burdensome regulations on their own producers if they wish, but cannot use these as a basis for excluding other products.

The ability of manufacturers to engage in such price discrimination depends on their capacity to restrict parallel trade in the products concerned. National differences in standards or regulations are an important means of limiting such parallel trade. The figures in table 11-1 show the potential significance of 1992 for these industries if the ability to segment markets is undermined. There is little exaggeration in stating that the profitability of the European car and pharmaceutical markets have depended for the last decade on the high margins obtainable in the United Kingdom and West Germany respectively.

To what extent does the 1992 programme demand different strategies for market segmentation? In the car industry, for example, the ability to restrict parallel trade is maintained by three principal factors: the type approval system, the British habit of driving on the left-hand side of the road, and the relationship between motor manufacturers and distributors. These are archetypes of the main generic categories of device by which market segmentation can be sustained.

The first of these—*national approval requirements*—exemplifies the type of barrier to trade the 1992 programme aims to remove. A car may be imported into the principal European markets only if it has type approval—a certificate that demonstrates that it is in a class or model that satisfies local construction and use regulations. These regulations serve, in the main, genuine safety objectives. But a car that is purchased in one European country will not normally satisfy this criterion in another even if it is a model that is legally on sale in that other country. It will probably fail to satisfy these regulations in minor respects unless it has been adapted to the local specification, requiring considerable expense and the cooperation of the manufacturer. The result is an effective block on importation of the vehicle by anyone other than the agent of the manufacturer (note that personal, although not commercial, import into the United Kingdom is exempt from type approval requirements).

A second trade barrier arises because the British drive on the left-hand side of the road. This is an *internal standard*, the product of the historical evolution of the market in the United Kingdom. The British do not drive on the left in order to discourage the import of foreign cars, but this is the practical effect. Foreign cars are less convenient to use unless they are substantially modified, and these modifications can only be undertaken economically by the original manufacturer. There are many examples of domestic standards of this kind, some legally imposed, some privately adopted, some technically determined, some the result of local habit and usage. At one end of the spectrum, for example, there are differences in electricity plugs and sockets in member states (a situation that, contrary to widespread popular belief, will persist after 1992). At the other end of the spectrum, there are language differences that are critical to the packaging and labelling of many products.

All of these are obstacles to the free movement of goods and particularly to parallel trade between markets. Most of them are likely to be permanent, because the advantages of a common standard, although real, are insufficiently large to outweigh the costs of adoption.

The third obstacle to free trade in cars comes from the *relationship between manufacturers and their distributors*. A distributor will be reluctant to enter into parallel trade if this may jeopardize an important relationship with the supplying manufacturer. This is obviously important in the car market, and is facilitated by the block exemption of the manufacturers' selective distribution agreement under Article 85 of the Treaty of Rome. Although this exemption is due to expire in 1995, its elimination is not part of the 1992 programme.

Barriers of this kind are often significant. Substantial differences persist across European markets in the price of domestic appliances, although there do not appear to be any substantial technical obstacles to trade. Nor are there domestic standards that parallel imports would fail to meet in important respects, although there are minor issues associated with the validity and enforceability of guarantees and the language of packaging and instructions. The inevitable conclusion is that distributors of these products are reluctant to send models to any market other than that to which the manufacturer intended them to be consigned.

The 1992 programme will make the segmentation of the market by manufacturers somewhat more difficult, but the effects are unlikely to be large enough to undermine the existing pattern or price discrimination in any fundamental way.

Nontariff Barriers and Market Entry

The second principal effect of nontariff barriers to trade is to limit market entry. Trade restrictions may be aimed either at producers or at products. Since the inception of the European Community, both the treaty and the policy of the Commission have been aimed at the first kind of restrictions—which exclude foreign producers—and as far as trade in goods is concerned, this policy has now been almost completely successful. But in service industries, regulations that limit entry by foreign producers remain widespread, and an attack on these is a key element in the next phase of economic integration—before and after 1992.

In the pharmaceutical industry, entry restrictions are severe, mainly as a result of national registration requirements. In engineering, differences in standards generally represent a mixture of statutory rules and user preference. The automobile industry's mixture of differences in technical regulation and consumer habits is representative of the sector. Exclusion of foreign producers is common in financial and professional services, where authorization requirements are involved, but most nontariff barriers are directed at products rather than producers.

It should be clear that there are almost no useful generalizations about the probable effects of the attack on nontariff trade barriers contained in the 1992 programme. Industry-specific analysis is required.

Mergers Before, and After, 1992

It may come as a surprise to many people that it has been possible to write at length on the strategic implications of 1992 without so far discussing mergers and corporate restructuring. For many, this is the essence of what 1992 is about.

But it is clearly appropriate to look at the product market first. The implications of 1992 for corporate structure follow directly from its implications for the organization of production. If 1992 leads to increased competition and new entry, then that should be the basis for corporate reorganization. If, on the other hand, the impact of the 1992 programme on the product market is likely to be comparatively small, then mergers in anticipation of changes in the structure of production and distribution are inappropriate. In the discussion surrounding the recent acquisition of Rowntree by Nestlé, much was made of the relevance of 1992. But since it is difficult to see any important effects of the 1992 programme on the European chocolate market, it is very hard to see why the private profitability or public desirability of any proposed merger should be influenced by the programme.

Much discussion of the need for European mergers rests on a belief that economies of scale are pervasive throughout industry, that national markets within Europe are too small to allow these scale economies to be realized, and that major cost savings are to be obtained from the rationalization of European production into a smaller number of plants and companies.

There are, indeed, some industries for which this account is true. They are principally industries where fragmentation has been sustained by national purchasing policies. Promotion of national champions in airframe manufacture by the British and French governments failed to produce effective competitors to Boeing, and success in international markets has come only as a result of a European collaborative project. The absurd proliferation of public switching equipment systems in the European telecommunications industry, each designed for the specific requirements of a national post and telecommunications office, has raised costs to European consumers and reduced export markets for all the companies involved.

These industries, however, are very much the exception rather than the rule. Economies of scale are substantial but nonetheless unrealized because governments and their agencies are ready to accept substantial cost penalties in pursuing industrial policy objectives. Private sector customers, in the main, are not. Cars are more typical. This is an industry in which there are substantial economies of scale. As a result, there are indeed cost savings to be derived from the rationalization of production into a smaller number of producers and models.

So why does this not occur? The reason is not the fragmentation of the European market which has been described above. Car sales are effectively segmented into individual national markets, but production is already completely international. There are potential cost savings from rationalization, but it might be observed that precisely analogous "savings" could be derived from rationalization of the number of producers and models within the unified markets of the United States or Japan. This reduction in the number of models does not occur because the preference of consumers—as revealed in the marketplace—is for a wider range of products at somewhat higher prices. It is fortunate that this is so, since otherwise European car producers would already have disappeared from the market in the face of lower-cost Japanese competition. It is not apparent why the willingness, or otherwise, of consumers to pay more for commodities suited to their particular needs and preferences should be affected in any way by the 1992 programme. Indeed all the evidence we have suggests that the diversity of consumer tastes increases as markets widen and incomes rise.

Thus there are no reasons to anticipate that the completion of the internal market will have the consequence that fewer European car producers will produce larger numbers of cars. If type approval requirements are harmonized, there will be some savings to all producers (including smaller savings to non-Community producers) and some losses to manufacturers (particularly Ford and Rover) if market segmentation is undermined. Otherwise, it is difficult to see major changes in the relative positions of established Community producers. Similar observations can be made in most other markets, and the idea that the 1992 programme is likely to induce substantial structural change in manufactured foodstuffs or alcoholic drinks—where scale economies are exhausted at low levels of production, compared with the demands of 320 million people, and where consumer preferences for product diversity are clearly strong—seems fanciful in the extreme.

There are very few industries in which mergers between large established producers in different Community states are an appropriate response to 1992. It cannot, it seems, be repeated frequently enough that the larger relative size of American and Japanese companies in many sectors, particularly electricals and engineering, is the *result* of their greater success, not the *cause* of it; that such success has almost never been founded on the suppression of competition in their domestic markets; and that the evidence does not exist that there are important unexploited scale economies in many sectors of European industry.

The kind of merger that does make sense is that which provides a springboard for new entry, especially into markets where such entry has previously been restricted by domestic regulation, local cartels, or nationalism in procurement policies. It will rarely pay to buy large companies for these purposes, because their prices will reflect the rents that the protection they have received has enabled them to earn.

Another kind of merger that elements of the 1992 programme will facilitate is the growth of a European market in corporate control—the prospect that weakly managed companies, especially in the smaller European economies, may become vulnerable to hostile takeover from predators anxious to make more effective use of the assets involved. The stalking of Belgium's Société Générale by De Benedetti is the most striking example of what might become a different trend in European mergers. The British experience of the operations of the market for corporate control suggests that this development offers some advantages, but not unmixed or unambiguous ones.

■ THE STRATEGIC IMPLICATIONS OF EUROPEAN INTEGRATION†

By Herman Daems

The twelve members of the European Community have embarked on an ambitious programme. By 1 January 1993 they plan to eradicate most of the national borders and to lower some of the internal barriers that continue to restrict the free flow of people, products, services, and capital within the European Community. In this way the twelve European countries hope to create a large single market of some 322 million consumers

†**Source:** Reprinted with permission from "The Strategic Implications of Europe 1992," *Long Range Planning*, June 1990, Vol. 23, pp. 41–48, Pergamon Press Ltd. Oxford, England.

that they expect will make it profitable for companies, both European and non-European, to invest in new plants, new products, and new technologies. Companies located within the European Community and doing business there will no longer be handicapped by the wasteful market fragmentation that for decades has cut sharply into European competitiveness vis-à-vis Japan and the U.S.

There have at least been three different types of responses to the bold initiative of the European Community. First, there is the response of the Eurosceptics, who argue that Europe is a fiction. The endless squabbles in which Europeans engaged among themselves are for the Eurosceptics sufficient evidence that European integration has not worked in the past and will never work in the future. But there are also the Eurobashers. For the Eurobashers, 1992 is a smokescreen behind which Europe is building a fortress of trade barriers that will make it much more difficult for non-Europeans to do business with and in Europe. Many of the Eurobashers do not intend to make strategic adjustments; for them, Washington or Tokyo must take up the challenge that Europe will be mounting in the 1990s and they lobby the politicians for new trade policies against Europe. Then there are the Europhorics—they are euphoric about what they think is going to happen in the Old World. They envisage a United States of Europe, with one language, one culture, one currency, and even one president. The Europhorics are redesigning their European strategies from scratch. They will soon be disappointed as they discover that they have been planning for a Eurotopia.

It is obvious that the responses that I am describing here are stereotypes. But in one form or another I have encountered them in the discussions I have had with companies on both side of the Atlantic about the strategic implications of a border-free Europe. None of the above stereotypes is of course the correct response.

How 1992 Will Shape Competition

The immediate effect of the 1992 project will be a decline in the costs of doing business in a European market. The decline comes from a lowering of the costs of crossing borders. Several factors will be responsible for lower border crossing costs. First, the costs of shipment will go down as there will be fewer administrative hurdles at border crossings, less time will be lost in waiting for customs clearance, and shipment rates will go down as deregulation forces road haulage companies and airlines to compete more aggressively on price. Second, as goods and services cross borders, fewer product adjustments will be necessary in order to satisfy local legislation and standards. As a consequence of the lowering of the costs of crossing borders, companies will be able to expand their geographical markets in Europe. A company located in Belgium that before could only serve the Belgian market will after 1992 be able to compete in such neighbouring markets as Germany, Holland, and France. But this applies also to its competitors located in those countries. As companies will increasingly be able to penetrate each other's markets, traditional market boundaries will disappear and competitive arenas will be redrawn.

Rivalry

The disappearance of traditional market boundaries increases rivalry and leads to competitive battles. In some markets the battle will be fought on the basis of costs, as companies that have opportunities for lower costs because of a more cost-efficient location of their production facilities or because of unexploited economies of scale and unused productive capacity will try to use their cost advantage to improve their competitive position. But in other markets the battle will be over product specifications, as products that currently are not available in some markets can be supplied to such markets after Europe has become a border—and barrier-free economy.

Rivalry will particularly intensify in the short run. Indeed, companies will be eager to take advantage of the enlarging markets. Production facilities where opportunities for economies of scale exist will be expanded. When competitors simultaneously move to grab the cost advantages associated with expansion, a fierce battle can be expected, because in many industries demand growth will not be sufficient to absorb the expansion of capacity. Another reason why rivalry will become more intense is that collusive market-sharing arrangements will break down as traditional market positions come under pressure. In many industries companies are aware that the race to use capacity to fully exploit economies of scale and the breakdown in collusive market practices may be detrimental for industry profits. Therefore, companies in such industries as electronics and power generators have actively been pursuing mergers and strategic alliances. Through such mergers companies can rationalize capacity building and capacity utilization. Intraindustry mergers are already reducing the fragmentation of market structures and are increasing market concentration. Over the long haul this process of concentration will make rivalry less intense. The Commission is very concerned about this development and as a consequence has stepped up its efforts to monitor and police mergers and acquisitions that strengthen the market dominance of the key players in an industry.

Buyer Power

Competition in European markets will intensify as a consequence of increased rivalry, but increases in buyer power will also play a role. After the directives of the 1992 project have been implemented, buyers will have more options than ever before of obtaining goods and services from suppliers all over the European community. Buyers or arbitrageurs will compare prices in different European markets and will purchase products where prices are lowest. It will consequently be much more difficult to sustain the currently high levels of price discrimination in European markets. For multinational companies with nationally organized sales organizations in various European countries that have decentralized pricing, the increased buyer power can create many problems. German customers who have always bought from the German sales organization will now have the option of buying directly from the Italian sales organization of the company. As a consequence of 1992 it will be necessary to restructure national sales organizations in order to better coordinate their pricing and promotional activities.

Companies may also find that their local customers disappear. This is specifically the case for companies that serve markets of intermediate products. The 1992 project forces industrial buyers to rationalize their production facilities. This will lead to the closure of production facilities. A company that has served a specific production facility of an industrial buyer may find that by 1992 the facility is being closed down.

Power of Suppliers

Suppliers will also gain power, because with the expected decline in the cost of border-crossing costs they not only have the option to supply local users but they can also deliver goods and services to users in other European markets. In this way suppliers will no longer be at the mercy of their traditional local users. It is also possible that some of the traditional suppliers will relocate to a production site in another European country. This will affect the organization of purchasing and the logistics of supply.

Entry of New Competitors

The Europe 1992 project will also have an impact on the entry of new competitors. As suggested above, for companies already located within the European Community the lowering of the border-crossing costs will make it easier to penetrate new geographical markets. For companies like the Japanese car manufacturers, who so far have tended to serve Community markets with imports, it is not entirely clear what will happen after 1992. Some fear that they will be locked out and therefore are trying to invest in new production or assembly facilities in the Community or to buy up existing companies. The direct investments bring new and efficient capacity to the European market and therefore are likely to heat up competition in European markets. Some attempts are being made in Europe to impose restrictions on the plants that are being built by non-Community firms. The restrictions typically are local content requirements.

Substitutes

The threat to a local industry's profitability from the development of substitute products and services is probably in the short run not very great. But over the long haul the larger internal market will make it possible to increase the efficiency of the product development process and will speed up product innovation.

The Strategic Implications of Europe 1992

Here are some of the fundamental questions that a company should consider as it reviews its European business strategies:

- Will the company's competitive position be sustainable as competition heats up?
- What can the company do to shore up its position?
- In what European markets should the company compete and how should the company serve those markets?
- How should the company use its existing production facilities?
- Where should the company locate its various value activities?

Competitive Position

Companies that have built their competitive position on a low-cost strategy must evaluate to what extent their costs position will be eroded by the 1992 project. Two factors can be responsible for the erosion of the cost position.

Economies of scale. As markets enlarge because borders disappear and barriers diminish, opportunities arise for exploiting unrealized economies of scale. Some companies are in a better position than others to take advantage of these opportunities. The larger competitors in the industry will find it easier than the smaller ones in the industry to build a cost position on the basis of economies of scale, because they can most credibly make the investments to expand their production facilities. Very often the larger competitors are located in the larger countries. Competitors in large European countries will also benefit as national product standards become more homogeneous. Such competitors already have large volumes in their home country to achieve economies of scale and will be able to ship products to other European countries without having to incur costs for adjusting products to other standards. The cost position of the large competitors will also improve relative to the cost position of the smaller ones because the large competitors will be able to drastically cut the number of different product varieties they need to produce to serve all European markets. If the shift from national to Community standards imposes a one-time adjustment cost on the companies to achieve compliance, the larger companies again are in a better position than the smaller ones because the larger competitors will be able to spread the adjustment costs over a larger volume. For all these reasons it can be expected that competitors from the larger countries will have an advantage in defending cost-based competitive positions.

Cost-efficient locations. Companies with cost-efficient locations for their production facilities are in a better position to defend a cost-based competitive position as Europe 1992 becomes a reality than the companies that have not yet been able to invest in cost-efficient locations. The cost efficiency of a location can come from lower labour costs, fiscal advantages offered by the country where the facility is located, or from the transport savings that can be gained from the central position of the production sites. These factors usually work in opposite directions. Countries like Greece, Spain, and Portugal with the lowest labour costs are less centrally located than countries with relatively high labour costs like Belgium and the Netherlands. Consequently, labour-intensive plants will be moved to South European countries, while plants that manufacture products that are subject to high transportation costs will be concentrated in the centre of Europe.

For companies that rely on a strategy of product differentiation, the threat to the sustainability of their competitive position comes from the following three factors.

New products. As a consequence of freer markets, products that thus far have not been offered in a specific European market may by 1992 be introduced in that market. If such products offer different characteristics to consumers, they may well start eroding the position of the established products.

Price/value ratio. A substantial threat to differentiation strategies comes from sudden declines in price/value ratios. Market integration will enable some producers of differentiated products to realize economies of scale that in turn will give them the opportunity to price competing differentiated products out of the market.

Economies of scale in marketing. Differentiation strategies are often highly dependent on marketing efforts. As 1992 approaches, increased competition among media will make it cheaper to develop brand images for differentiated products on a European scale. The logistics of distribution can also be improved because of the 1992 project. It will no longer be necessary to build distribution organizations along national boundaries, and consequently cost savings will be available.

Defending a Competitive Position

What can companies do to avoid losing their competitive advantage in the new Europe? Basically the company can try to reverse the various threats that I described above. Instead of waiting for its competitors, the company should try to move first. This suggests that one of the critical elements in shoring up the company's competitive advantage in a business will be timing. Companies that wait until all the directives are implemented will find that their most dangerous competitors have already moved upon them. But moving early may not be enough. As I argued above, small players are bound to have a substantial handicap in exploiting the opportunities for economies of scale. Such players should evaluate if they can move from a cost-based advantage to a differentiation-based advantage. Despite the homogenizing of product standards, differentiation-based strategies are going to be easier in the post-1992 markets because companies will be able to reach small market niches in a variety of European countries and in this way will be able to build sufficient volume for an efficient production of the differentiated products. Smaller companies that have decided to defend a differentiation-based advantage may want to look for partners based in other Community states but with skills complementary to their own in order to facilitate the introduction of their products in markets that they have not entered so far. The complementarity of skills is necessary because it makes it easier to create a more stable alliance between the partners. If differentiation is not feasible, the smaller players may want to consider selling out to a larger player in the industry.

Mergers are also an alternative when the major players want to impose some order as the industry prepares itself for the transition to a post-1992 era.

Market Coverage Strategies

In what markets should a company compete and how should it be present in such markets? I will look at the question from the point of view of a Dutch company as it considers the Italian market. The first element (the vertical axis in figure 11-1) that the Dutch company needs to consider is the competitive strength of the local competitors in the Italian market. The second element (the horizontal axis) is the cost of crossing the Italian border with goods for delivery to the Italian market. These costs not only include the customs clearance costs and the costs of transportation but also the costs of adjusting products to Italian specifications. In the past when border-crossing costs were high, the Dutch company opted to create its own production facility in Italy to serve the market there because the Italians were weak competitors in their own market. The Dutch company preferred to invest in an Italian subsidiary because local production was cheaper than importing the goods from Holland. The fact that the

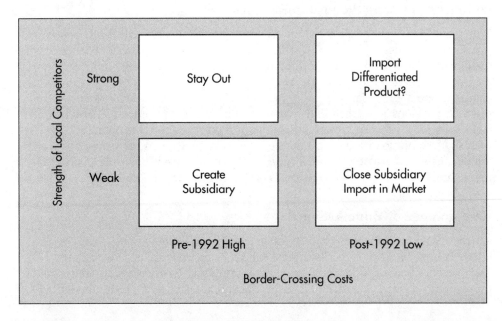

FIGURE 11-1
Analysis of 1992 Effect on Market Coverage Strategy

FIGURE 11-2

Analysis of 1992 Effect on
Production Plants

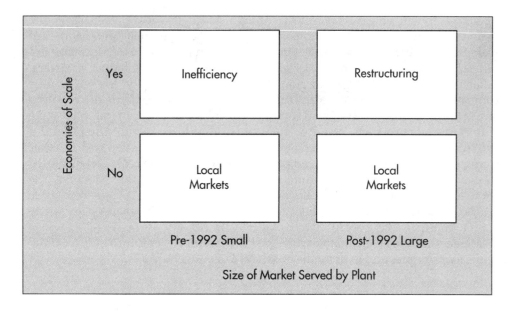

Italians were weak was crucial for the decision of the Dutch company, because if the Italians had been strong, the Dutch company would probably have stayed out of the Italian market. In the post-1992 era the situation will change because the border-crossing costs will decline. As long as its Italian competitors remain weak, it makes sense for the Dutch company to close its Italian subsidiary, as the Dutch company has spare capacity in its other European subsidiaries and can exploit economies of scale in those subsidiaries. The story would of course be different if in the past the Dutch company had decided to stay out of Italy. As a consequence of the 1992 project the Dutch company would probably want to reconsider the import opportunities in the Italian market, the more so because the position of its Italian competitors may have weakened for reasons that I described before.

Optimizing Existing Production Facilities

With the help of figure 11-2 a company can analyse what it needs to do with its existing production facilities. The two critical elements are the opportunities for economies of scale (vertical axis) and the size of the market it can reach and serve from its plants. Again a distinction can be made between the pre- and post-1992 period. If the company operates its plants at full capacity and no cost savings can be obtained from drastic expansions in the scale of its plants, the plants will typically serve local markets in an efficient way. For such a company not much will change in the post-1992 era. The plants will continue to serve local markets. However, if the company operates plants with inefficient sizes at less than full capacity, the company will be forced to drastically restructure its plants in order to become competitive in the post-1992 era.

Configuration of Value Activities

Where should the company locate its value activities in the new Europe? Again this is a complex question but a good analysis of it can be made with the help of figure 11-3. The relevant dimensions to consider are the Community-wide competitive strength of the company in such value activities as production, research and development (R&D),

and distribution and the locational advantages of a specific European country for these value activities. I will consider the case of a German company that wants to evaluate the configuration of its value activities. If the German company expects that it can hold on to its competitive position in the post-1992 era, and if Germany offers the best European location for doing product development and manufacturing, then there are no reasons for the company to relocate its activities. However, if because of high labour costs and transportation costs Germany no longer is the best European location for that value activity, then the company should move its operations to other European locations that have lower labour costs or are more centrally situated in Europe. The story changes when the German company expects to irreversibly lose its competitive strength in the post-1992 era. In that case, its strategic options depend on the locational advantages of Germany for the value activities of the company. If Germany has no locational advantages, then the threatened company should prepare for closure. However, if Germany is an ideal location, then the company may want to sell out to a stronger foreign competitor or look for a foreign partner to shore up its competitive position.

Organizational Consequences

There will also be organizational implications of the 1992 project. Companies that thus far have relied on national organizations to manage their European operations will need to take a hard look at that organization. Many companies, Philips is a prominent example, are doing this already, but many have found that there is a lot of resistance to the reorganization from the previous national powerhouses that feel threatened by the restructuring. The reorganization should help middle-sized companies that thus far have developed competitive strategies at national levels to integrate those strategies into a Community-wide competitive strategy, if not into a global strategy.

Several functions and activities will need to be reorganized to take full advantage of the single European market. The product development activity can now be organized

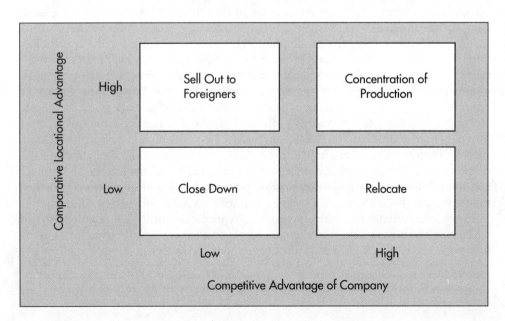

FIGURE 11-3
Analysis of 1992 Effect on Location of Production Centres

at a Community-wide level because adjustments to the new homogeneous product standards should be coordinated. In this way it will also be possible to speed up product development and to make the process more efficient. Purchasing should be organized in such a way that the company can take advantage from increased competition among suppliers. The logistical organization of supply must also be reviewed. Major changes could occur in the coordination of production operations. Some plants will be expanded while others will close down or take on new assignments. The physical distribution will no longer be organized along national lines and a rationalization of distribution centres will become possible. Sales organizations should continue to have a national prospective because they will have to respond to the typical national characteristics of the markets that will still be there after 1992. But the sales organizations will need to be coordinated at a Community level, because otherwise customers will take advantage of price and promotional differences between countries. The free movement of capital—if it is realized as planned—will make it possible to further centralize the finance function. Finally, the human resource function will have to prepare managers and workers for more cross-cultural cooperation.

■ PARTNERSHIPS IN EUROPE[†]

By Yves Doz

Background

The European economy is currently going through a fundamental transition, one characterized by a dramatic increase in international competitive demands. "1992," the Japanese challenge, increasing economies of scale and scope (particularly in R&D, marketing, and distribution), faster technological and market changes, swifter competitors' moves, and more demanding customers are all contributing to greater competitive pressures.

This increase in competitive demands is most challenging for the traditional national companies, those that had often diversified across a wide range of loosely related businesses in their home country rather than internationalized. Such companies lack both business focus and global competitive strength. Beyond the shelter of national protection and government procurement preferences, much of the European electronics industry followed this pattern of national diversification and limited internationalization. Up to the 1980s, companies such as AEG and Siemens, GEC and Plessey, Thomson and Matra or Thorn-Emi concentrated primarily on their domestic markets. Despite significant exceptions, such as ICI and BASF, the European chemical industry followed a somewhat similar pattern. Electrical engineering, heavy machinery, and metallurgy, too, were primarily national industries. Only the oil industry internationalized early, its product requiring a worldwide orientation. The 1970s and 1980s have also seen the emergence of a strong belief in market share in Europe as elsewhere. Neoclassical microeconomics, the strategy concepts put forward

†**Source:** This article was originally published as "Partnerships in Europe: The 'Soft Restructuring' Option?" in *Corporate and Industry Strategies for Europe*, edited by L. G. Mattsson and B. Stymne, Elsevier Science Publisher, 1991.

by consulting companies (the Boston Consulting Group in particular), and various empirical studies (for example the PIMS project) all propagated a concern for market share. These models and analyses posited relative scale and experience as the major determinants of long-term profits in individual businesses. The increase in efficiency brought by higher scale in production in numerous industries from the 1950s to the 1970s also contributed to the belief that higher market share brings success. Although some of the more recent academic research sheds some doubt on the empirical reality of market share and scale as determinants of profitability, belief in their relationship remains the cornerstone of many business strategies.

Unsurprisingly, growing exposure to global competition and the spreading belief in market share and scale drove a number of traditional European companies toward mergers, consolidation, and restructuring. In some cases, overextended, overdiversified groups such as AEG in Germany or Empain Schneider in France had to restructure under bankruptcy pressure. In other cases, takeover threats or successful takeovers forced restructuring (e.g., Société Générale de Belgique, Montedison, and Plessey). Some other companies initiated and carried out their own restructuring (e.g., Thorn-Emi in the United Kingdom, BSN in France).

One can identify three steps in many of the European restructuring efforts. The first of them often involves gaining clarity and transparency vis-à-vis the financial performance and strategic position of individual businesses. Decentralization, the setting up of "business units," portfolio analysis, and portfolio planning processes usually characterize this first step. An assessment of the competitive position of each business is usually a result. Value-based planning processes often follow, as the liberalization of capital markets and the emergence of a more open market for corporate control create greater concern for measurable value creation on the part of top management.

A second step has often been national consolidations, where national banks and frequently the state encourage the merger of weaker companies into stronger ones and the creation of national groups in the hope that they will become large enough to stand a chance in international competition. In France, Germany, Italy, and the United Kingdom, such a policy of consolidation into national "champions" has been at work for a long time in a wide range of industries, including heavy industrial equipment, computers, aircraft and space systems, chemicals, electrical machinery, robotics, and others. However, the success of these policies has often been marred by the usual post-merger integration issues preventing the potential value offered by the consolidations from actually being realized. Tensions between public and private sector corporate policies, financial performance expectations, and management styles have also been a barrier to such mergers, particularly in France and Italy, both of which have a vast, politically entrenched public sector.

A third step is transnational mergers and acquisitions, which have greatly increased of late. This solution is hardly new. Although much-publicized "megamergers" such as the Dunlop-Pirelli "alliance" or the VFW-Fokker merger have usually failed, they at least testify to the early strength of the phenomenon. It is far too early as yet to assess the success or failure of the current wave of mergers and acquisitions in Europe; however, the difficulty in successfully integrating merged operations and therefore in turning potential value into actual value creation raises some doubt as to their overall success.

This article argues that in many cases in which mergers and acquisitions may not take place or may fail, partnerships, joint ventures, and alliances represent a "softer" approach more likely to bring the same rationalisation and restructuration benefits as mergers are expected to provide. The first section reviews problems and sources of failures in mergers and acquisitions. The second section analyzes why and how partnerships and alliances may help overcome the difficulties faced by mergers and acquisitions, both at the business strategy level and the national policy level, when moving toward European industrial restructuring. To ignore the fact that partnerships and alliances also involve complex problems and often fail would be naive; thus, a third section presents our research on partnerships and alliances and alerts the reader to their pitfalls.

The Difficulties of "Hard" Restructuring

The Limits to Internal Growth

In an increasingly liberal European economy, it can be argued that natural selection processes among firms will play a growing role, and restructuring can be achieved by the autonomous growth of better-performing companies and the gradual disappearance of worse-performing companies. Over the long run this assertion may be true, although Europe has seen few of the very fast rises of new companies observed in the United States or even in Japan. Major corporate successes in Europe have been achieved more through acquisitions and realignments in business portfolios than through organic growth. In a conservative, relatively stable environment characterized by comparatively little overall economic growth, organic development is simply too slow. The opportunities for fast corporate growth are too few, the resources take too much time to mobilize, and the learning processes required to develop new competencies are too slow.

When technological and market conditions in an industry change rapidly, a patiently built success may be undone in a few years or even less, as exemplified by the demise of Nixdorf, a victim of standardization, in the computer industry. Companies cannot change their perspectives, their resource base, and their accumulated skills fast enough to be able to adjust to new conditions. The more successful the company has been with organic growth over a longer period of time, the more difficult it becomes to engage successfully in a major strategic transformation. Few companies manage to develop a rich and diverse enough portfolio of "core competencies" and deploy them in new configurations fast enough to meet changing market conditions on the basis of organic growth. Historically, European companies have seldom taken this approach to developing core competencies around activities common to several businesses, and therefore they tend to favor acquisitions over organic growth for restructuring. However, acquisitions come with their problems too.

The Limits of Mergers and Acquisitions

Mergers and acquisitions may fail to take place or to succeed: mergers that would make sense do not take place, while the success rate of those that do occur is not very high. By their own admission, managers polled in large-scale surveys on mergers and acquisitions reckon that only about one in four mergers meets the expectations they had for it.

Missed acquisition opportunities.   Some possible mergers do not take place. Public policy restrictions obviously play an important role, in particular as governments protect certain sectors. Europe, for example, has a dozen boilermakers and heavy electrical equipment suppliers where only a few can prosper in competitive market conditions. The protection of national champions, often themselves state-owned enterprises, has played a key role in maintaining fragmented supply structures in industries supplying technology-intensive and infrastructure goods to the governments, state-owned enterprises, or politically sensitive sectors of the economy such as farming.

In other cases, genuine antitrust, antimonopoly concerns have blocked mergers. The fear on the part of potential acquirers or merger candidates that their takeovers or mergers might bog down over lengthy public enquiries and government debates, such as in the case of GEC and Plessey in the United Kingdom, has led some companies to eschew potentially successful mergers.

The absolute size and patterns of ownership of companies may also rule out acquisitions or mergers. General Motors and Toyota could not acquire each other! Companies may also be privately owned or protected by elaborate ownership schemes that exclude takeovers and mergers. In Europe, a number of companies such as Philips are simply not to be taken over given the structure of their stock's voting rights; for others, key creditors such as Deutsche Bank in Germany or shareholders such as the Wallenberg group in Sweden usually have to support any major acquisition and need to play a pivotal role in it.

More interestingly, acquisitions may not take place because it is very difficult to put a price on the acquisition candidate. The value of a technology-intensive start-up is highly variable depending on one's assumptions about future research results, market growth, and continued commitment of key technical staff and managers. Valuation uncertainties may also prevent acquisitions from taking place. This is particularly true inasmuch as potential acquirers are increasingly aware of the risk of overpaying acquisitions that result from the dynamics of the acquisition decision process itself.

Lastly, attractive acquisition candidates may become scarcer. As companies refocus, the risk of overvaluation increases. A hedge against overvaluation was to acquire operations only from decentralized conglomerates that added little value, with the expectation that the acquirer could generate more synergies with the newly acquired business than its former owner. The acquired business thus had more value to its new owner than to its former one. As many companies now refocus their investments on their core business(es), the divestment of their "noncore" businesses creates opportunities for such acquisitions at first. Later such opportunities obviously become scarcer, as the firms have only kept businesses to which interdependencies with other businesses in their portfolios add value. The wave of mergers and acquisitions in the second half of the 1980s in the United States was in part a result of the refocusing strategies of major companies.

Failed acquisitions.   Research on postmerger integration suggests that the integration process often fails, in particular in acquisitions for which learning from the acquired company is important. In acquisitions that are not purely absorption of similar operations, the establishment and subsequent management of the interface between the acquired and acquiring companies are difficult. The key capabilities that this interface needs to provide are:

- *Bidirectionality*, that is, the willingness of both sides to reach out to the other in an effort to share competencies, in particular the willingness of the acquired firm to draw upon the skill and capabilities of the acquiring firm rather than having the latter impose its way.

- *A balance between continued learning and efficiency*, that is, between keeping the acquired operations relatively separate with their own identities and at the same time achieving "symbiosis" between the acquired and acquiring companies. When an acquisition is made with the objective of exploring a possible new industry or market domain, not overwhelming the acquired company with absorption pressures becomes critical, in particular for learning about this new domain.

- Enough *mutuality and adaptability* to make the acquiring company's management understand that its own approaches may have to change. It is not possible, particularly in an acquisition meant to combine skills, to put the whole burden of learning and adjustment on the acquired company. To create the most value, both the acquired and the acquiring companies must usually learn to work together, that is, both must adapt.

Yet, many acquiring companies do not seem to differentiate clearly between various acquisition integration approaches that depend on the nature of the benefits sought from the acquisition. It is also difficult for the acquiring company not to impose too many of its ways on the acquired company. While such imposition may make sense in absorption acquisitions, where the objective is full rationalization and integration and the disappearance of the acquired company as a separate entity, such an approach may prevent the creation of value when the objective requires the combination of resources and skills from both companies. In these cases acquisitions have to be managed more as partnerships than as absorptions.

Such problems are magnified when a large, well-established company acquires a smaller, entrepreneurial one from which it hopes to gain new skills and capabilities. In these circumstances, it is often difficult for the acquiring company to reach the appropriate balance between integrating its new acquisition fully (and destroying its innovativeness and even its existing skill base) and maintaining it at arm's length (and not allowing the transfer of skills). Such difficulties are sometimes made even worse in partial acquisitions by the ambiguity created, some managers seeing a partial acquisition as a partnership and others seeing it as equivalent to a full acquisition. Further, conflicts between the initial shareholders and the new ones are likely to be significant in the case of a partial acquisition.

Acquisitions are thus fraught with problems, particularly when the acquisition of skills and the transfer of competencies is one of the major goals. Potentially productive acquisitions may not take place, either because of public policy constraints, shareholding structure, or valuation uncertainties. Acquisitions are thus not always the shortcut to building capabilities that they are often said to constitute.

Yet, despite the limits of organic growth, and the shortcomings of acquisitions just discussed, the wave of industry restructuring started in Europe in the 1980s is likely to continue, representing a major challenge in the 1990s. The second section of this article explores how partnerships may, in some circumstances, overcome the difficulties faced by acquisitions and at the same time provide a shortcut to restructuring that organic growth and redirection would not allow.

Partnerships as an Alternative to "Hard" Restructuring

Partnerships and alliances may help overcome the problems that make acquisitions fail. Valuation uncertainties and thus the risk of acquisition overvaluation are decreased by partnerships. Partnerships provide a relatively low-cost opportunity to learn about the value of the partner's skills and resources before having to make a major resource commitment. The process of collaboration itself allows this assessment of skills and resources. Mergers obviously call for resource outlays before sufficient mutual experience is gained to decrease valuation uncertainties. In that sense partnerships may be more akin to leasing, possibly with an option to buy, than to buying.

Moreover, real opportunities to create value together may not be easily visible early on; the very process of collaboration, with the joint learning process it implies, may lead to discovery of further opportunities to create value. Thus the potential for value creation is not only better assessed in a partnership than in a merger, it is also increased in particular because postmerger "determinism," that is, the commitment to implement what was planned and used to justify the merger, often prevails over discovering new learning and value-creating opportunities.

Keeping options open, in terms of both what technologies and customers to pursue and what partners to develop deeper relations with, is likely to be of increasing importance in post-1992 Europe. Partnerships provide opportunities to speed up the adaptation of the firm to its environment, particularly when that adaptation requires shifts in the resource base of the firm. Internal resource base shifts in mature firms are often very slow. For instance, it was difficult for established pharmaceutical companies to respond quickly to the emergence of biotechnology as a new core technology without resorting to partnerships. The existing terms of employment, the resilience of R&D resource allocation processes, the unfamiliarity with new skills, and the difficulties in identifying, assessing, and recruiting key potential hirees in a new scientific field all conspired to stifle the internal development of biotechnology skills by major pharmaceutical companies. Similarly, the shift in value added in the information technology industry from hardware to services and "value-adding" solutions triggered many partnerships between traditional computer suppliers and software houses, specialized value-added resellers, and value-added service providers, all of which contribute specific complementary skills. Even companies that traditionally shunned partnerships, such as IBM and DEC, are now heavily involved in these relationships. Developing new in-house skills would be too slow for them to follow fast market and technology shifts successfully. Further, the dearth of specialized personnel would make the development of such in-house skills very uncertain.

Once the nature and extent of desired commitments are clear, partnerships may still allow a flexible learning process prior to an eventual merger. For example, the Thomson Semiconductors SGS-Ates merger evolved out of several partnerships between the two companies (mostly in the context of the ESPRIT program), which led managers from both sides to identify and assess more accurately their complementary capabilities and joint potential value. Some of the more subtle complementary capabilities could not have been identified without collaboration prior to the merger.

Since partnerships are less costly than mergers, multiple options may also be explored, not just in terms of technologies or applications, but also in terms of potential merger candidates. Partnerships with multiple partners may allow participants to identify potential merger opportunities better. To some extent, the history of collaborative projects in the defense systems field in Europe has cumulatively contributed to establishing or tarnishing the reputations of individual firms in various subfields and thus facilitates the choice of potential merger partners. After a series of collaborative agreements on individual projects, it becomes known in the industry who the "good" partners are and who are the "difficult" ones.

Partnerships may also solve the problem of unnecessary assets accompanying mergers and provide opportunities to leverage the partners' competencies better. Contrary to many acquisitions, where an entire corporate entity usually has to be taken over, partnerships may be quite focused. Nestlé and General Mills, for example, set up a joint venture solely for their breakfast cereals in Europe, remaining independent in all other areas. While acquisitions may also be targeted, in addition to the fact that the sale of unnecessary, unwanted parts of the acquired company is sometimes quite profitable (e.g., RJR's sale of Nabisco's European biscuit operations to

BSN following RJR's acquisition of Nabisco), partnerships usually involve less risk of tying up resources in unnecessary assets than do acquisitions. They allow the partners to lease or borrow assets, or rent the right to their use without major resource commitments and risks.

The more invisible and intangible the assets of a given company, the more a partnership will open a "window" to observe and copractice the skills of the partner, those very skills that build the partner's intangible assets. Partnerships may permit technology and skill transfers between companies when other mechanisms for such transfers usually fail. Obviously, though, the more the observed skills are system embedded, collective, culturally bound, and deeply rooted in a social fabric evolved over long periods of time, the less easily they transfer. Yet, an outright acquisition might quickly dissipate these skills. First, key employees who are the repository of the skills might leave. Second, the continuous honing of skills over time requires a high commitment on the part of employees; although they may not leave, being acquired by a large firm would probably lower their commitment. Third, in entrepreneurial firms where employees are often significant stock owners, an acquisition drastically changes the interests of the key employees. Fourth, intangible, tacit skills may take some time to be appreciated by the acquiring company, and quick reorganizing or refocusing action, seemingly useful in the short run, might rapidly destroy or at least inadvertently erode such tacit skills. The rather dismal track record of acquisitions of smaller "technology-based" entrepreneurial firms by larger ones testifies to the difficulty of internalizing tacit skills via acquisitions. Finally, not all companies can be acquired, even for a high price: Could General Motors acquire Toyota, with whom it collaborated to learn manufacturing skills?

Practicing skills together, using the partnership as a learning ground, may give vastly superior results. Such learning from partnerships may be further maximized in multiple partnerships. By having a network of focused partnerships with a series of different partners, each contributing specific skills, it becomes possible to assemble and combine a range of skills unmatched by other companies in the partner who occupies the nodal position in the network. While each of the other partners sees only the individual partnership he is involved in, the nodal company builds strength by drawing skills from all partners and combining them.

When strength in one business is dependent on core technologies and know-how common to several businesses, an acquisition disconnects the acquired business from the remainder of the related businesses in its previous company, and thus cuts off the supply of technologies and skills common to the several businesses. Insofar as the continued availability and updating of these skills is essential to success, a joint venture, which guarantees longer-term access to partners' independently developed skills, is preferable to an acquisition. For instance, Philips and DuPont have several joint ventures in the recording media field (tapes, compact discs). Their success is dependent on DuPont providing ongoing expertise in film and coating, which is developed at least partly in other businesses of DuPont in which Philips is not involved. Philips provides strength and expertise in consumer marketing and distribution, which are developed and leveraged across a whole range of businesses. In such circumstances partnerships are clearly preferable to acquisitions. The joint ventures allow Philips to borrow skills from Du Pont—and vice versa—on an ongoing basis. Companies with the greatest dissimilarity and complementarity of skills between them and with the greatest internal capability to renew and update their skill bases are most likely to be able to create value provided they pursue opportunities that call for the combination of their complementary skills. This may explain why partnerships between seemingly unrelated partners may offer the greatest returns.

The more each partner company focuses on a few core businesses and cultivates core skills common to these businesses, the greater the likelihood that a partnership will provide better longer-term access to critical skills than an acquisition. The current refocusing of corporate portfolios into core businesses is likely not only to ultimately reduce the number of acquisition candidates, but also to increase the advantage of partnerships over acquisitions because the businesses remaining in the portfolio are more closely related and more likely to share core competencies. It is only when the partnered operations themselves become the main source of the core skills to be used in other businesses of each partner that tensions may erupt, as the two partners may have quite different priorities for the joint business according to its interdependencies with each one's other businesses.

Conversely, the more the partnership is used to leverage each partner's skills jointly in order to exploit a totally new opportunity that neither could have exploited alone, the more new value is created and the more easily both partners' strategic priorities for the joint activity can converge.

In fact, the continued dependence of a partnership on the strategic priorities of two partners, as compared with one owner in the case of an acquisition, is probably the main weakness of partnerships relative to acquisitions. The continued compatibility of these priorities, as well as their relative intensity, are often put to question as the broader strategy of the partners evolves. This is a source of vulnerability and instability in partnerships. However, partnerships may then evolve toward acquisitions in which the most interested partner assumes complete ownership and control. Tentative empirical evidence suggests that partnerships indeed often end with one partner taking full control of a hitherto joint operation. In such a case the partnership may have fulfilled precisely the function suggested above: a transitional step toward acquisition that lowers the risks of acquisition to an acceptable level and increases the value-creating potential of the acquisition through a period of learning.

Obviously, though, this is not true for all partnerships. While the maintenance of two separate parent organizations lowers the initial stakes, it is no guarantee that the quality of the collaboration process will be high. On the contrary, the existence of two strong but different parents may prevent wholehearted cooperation and may ultimately foster conditions that prevent value creation. A partnership is superior to a merger only insofar as the collaboration process is managed in such a way as to provide for a convergence over time between the partners, and the development of enough sharing and trust to allow for value discovery and value creation.

Conditions for Alliance Success

While partnerships may overcome the difficulties of restructuring via organic growth or mergers and acquisitions, their success hinges on the putting in place and effective management of a series of interface processes. This section outlines the most important of them. They are:

- Convergence process
- Expectation adjustment process
- Consistency of position process
- Governance process
- Capability transfer process
- Top management monitoring process

Convergence Process

As discussed in the previous section, partnerships may allow a process of value discovery to take place between partners whose level of mutual trust and knowledge is low. One of the first tasks in a partnership is thus to increase mutual trust and knowledge, which can only occur through an interaction process. In the partnerships we have analyzed, this usually required a distinction between the negotiating and operating teams in order to avoid having concerns, fears, and stereotypes triggered by an often adversarial negotiation process transferred into the collaboration process. This can be achieved, for example, by including the future managers of the partnership in the negotiations in a "nice guy" position while corporate staffs and attorneys usually take a tougher stance. The convergence process also requires a "translation" capability between the partners, that is, understanding and redefining the partnership in the strategic context and organizational language of each partner.

Such translation improves mutual understanding and ability to communicate. It requires partners to invest in understanding each other's organization and way of doing things and each other's language (not only the obvious national tongue, but also the corporate languages, acronyms, symbolic expressions, styles of behavior, and so forth). Special task forces, off-site workshops, and joint projects can be used to promote such mutual comprehension.

The process of involvement of individuals in the alliance (buy-in) also needs to be carefully orchestrated. If redundancies are to take place in the partnership, they either need to be carried out very early and clearly justified or to be delayed until the relationship is cemented, and they must also be balanced between the partners. This is particularly important in partnerships that have the ambition to permanently restructure selected activities, and the independence of the partners in these activities is not to be maintained. The involvement of managers needs to be staged; premature pressures to create a "common" management team when the individuals involved do not understand or trust each other easily may result in the activation of defensive routines and a withdrawal into formal interactions that are unlikely to be effective.

The convergence process also requires that partners be ready to address common issues in the same time frame and with compatible speed. Yet the speed at which companies identify and analyze issues and their relative capacities to deal with them and reach a resolution vary greatly. This speed difference needs to be taken into account in designing a convergent collaboration process.

Expectation Adjustment Process

Partnerships frequently run into trouble. First, they usually start with overly optimistic expectations, the result of escalation in the negotiation process. Once started, partnerships are likely to incur costs and encounter tensions between the partners before payoffs are in sight. Focusing on operational day-to-day problems may also create a "halo" effect, that is, convey the impression in both partners' organizations that the partnership does not work well. Further, unless the convergence process is quite effective, this sense of crisis may lead to scapegoating between the partners, either toward "cultural incompatibilities" or toward each other's managers. Many partnerships with the potential to create value ultimately falter because managerial expectations about them collapse in an uncontrolled fashion.

Pressures for quick success, particularly when partnerships result from precarious strategic positions (a usual condition for partnerships aimed at restructuring), often add to the crisis. Partnerships are expected to deliver results rapidly and predictably.

While crises of expectation cannot be fully avoided, they can at least be anticipated or presumed and personnel in the partnership can be prepared for them. Keeping in sight the strategic benefits of the alliance, building a common framework to pursue these results, and communicating a joint ambition to the managers and specialized personnel involved in the relationship are important. A clearly defined joint ambition transcends the capabilities of each partner separately before the partnership.

Expectation crises can also be solved much more easily when the strategic context of both partners is clear and when the convergence process allows joint resolution of issues and problems.

Consistency of Position Process

Partnerships may suffer over time from a lack of consistency of position between the partners and within each partner. Between the partners the issue of strategic divergence is most obvious. Not much can be done about strategic divergence beyond the usual recommendation that the true mutual interests of the partners and the stability of their strategic contexts be assessed thoroughly at the beginning of the partnership. Hidden agendas, competitive issues, and lack of mutual understanding obviously make that difficult.

Treating the partnership as an evolutionary relationship, susceptible to adjustment and revision as the strategic interests of the partners evolve and as their willingness to contribute to the alliance shifts is the only workable approach over time. This obviously implies, however, that there is a certain fragility to partnerships as compared with acquisitions. Shared control creates an inescapable uncertainty.

Some joint venture managers try to shelter their operations from such uncertainty by distancing themselves from their corporate parents over time and creating an increasingly self-sufficient joint venture. While this may help them per se, it minimizes the value of the partnership to the parents and may create further tensions between the parents and the venture.

Consistency of position within each partner is often an even more tricky issue. Multiple units are involved in partnerships (functions, product lines, country units, and so on) and have different stakes in their success. They may also have different interpretations of what success means and of what is important. Their level of commitment also varies. "Smart" partner companies may exploit such internal discrepancies in their partner's organization in order to achieve their own goals and "cherry pick" their partners. Partnerships are thus a key test on organizational unity and strategic consistency. Weaknesses in either, or both, are likely to be magnified by partnerships. Off-line overlay structures created specifically to interface with partnerships may help, but only insofar as they are sufficiently connected with their own organization and have enough clout not just to present a unified facade, but also to mobilize resources and competencies from units with somewhat different perspectives and objectives.

Governance Process

The success of a partnership is also a function of the match between the characteristics of the task at hand and the nature of the governance structure adopted to run the partnership. While this is an obvious point, we observe that companies sometimes develop general rules and heuristics for choosing the form and the process of governance of their partnerships that do not make these contingent on the nature of the joint tasks.

Capability Transfer Process

The success of partnerships, particularly when the restructuring involves skill transfers and not merely scale pooling, also hinges on transferring enough skills to perform the joint task effectively, and yet to maintain enough exclusivity to key skills so that one's bargaining strength in the collaboration process is not eroded in an uncontrollable fashion.

Top Management Monitoring Process

The implication from the five key processes outlined above is that partnerships are obviously not a cost-free option to acquisitions. They may represent a different trade-off in the mix of costs, risks, and benefits to the participating companies. Partnerships may decrease the risk of being wrong under extensive valuation uncertainty vis-à-vis acquisitions; but this decrease in risk is achieved only with great managerial costs. Partnerships require constant management attention and constant efforts to create and extract value. While they decrease shorter-term risks, partnerships may increase longer-term risk, by keeping two partners actively involved, and then by carrying the risk of strategic divergence.

Conclusion

Despite the management difficulties outlined above, and the need for building and actively maintaining a series of processes between the partners and within the partners, partnerships represent a viable effective option to acquisitions, organic growth, and disjointed capability acquisitions (e.g., through licensing). They limit the financial risks and circumvent the public policy issues faced by many acquisitions, they are more narrowly focused on key capability acquisitions, and they allow the sharing of skills between partners on an ongoing basis. As European companies refocus their activities on core businesses, and learn to cultivate and leverage common core competencies across these various businesses, the advantage of partnerships over acquisitions or other firms of technology transfer is likely to further increase.

■ WILL MANAGEMENT BECOME EUROPEAN?[†]

By Keith Thurley and Hans Wirdenius

The European Management Model

The growing debate on the usefulness of the term *European management* has, in fact, only developed over the last few years, once the implications of the Single European Market (SEM) began to be apparent.

In spite of a flood of books on management topics and a rapid growth of management education and consulting services, there is still a gap between the

†**Source:** This article was originally published in *European Management Journal* (June 1991). Used by permission of the authors.

"knowledge in use," valued by practicing managers at all levels of organizational action, and the more abstract models and hypotheses argued to be important by management theorists. The currently highly appraised study of Michael Porter on his "national diamond," for example, could also therefore be seen to ignore the implications of the obvious fact that the local cultural and institutional practices of managers are clearly different in different societies, in that such differences may prevent managers from being able to follow strategies that are locally demanded from applying the Porter framework. Cultural assumptions, derived from previous education and the experience of managing in a particular society, not only mean that management practice is profoundly different in different societies, but that management theories, models, and prescriptions are also considerably affected by the language and concepts used and the type of goals that are seen as important. In sum, the European experience and formulation of management being different from American and Japanese experience, and the frameworks used by Americans and Japanese being different from those used by Europeans make it necessary now to distinguish "European" management as a possible alternative approach.

This "cultural" approach, of course, is obvious when applied to a nation like Japan with distinct history and practices that are seen as unique (for example, lifetime employment, seniority practices, and enterprise unionism). It is less obvious when applied to a continent that has many different national styles that contrast sharply with each other. Nevertheless, it is possible to distinguish overall values and assumptions which could be seen to be "European."

The politics of European integration are beginning to produce policies and directions by the European Commission that will actually alter the nature of European managers' roles and the relative importance of their priorities and goals. The proposal for a Regulation on the Statute for a European Company, published by the Commission in May 1989, for example, lays down a possible legal form of company that would stand apart from companies recognized by the laws of the twelve nations. Such a recognized international company would enable businesses to carry out cross-frontier restructuring by means of an international assets merger, rather than by use of a takeover bid. It would form the basis of joint subsidiaries and holding companies of international groups and it would also provide for choice in the forms of employee involvement and controls over the policies for disclosure of information and for auditing accounts across the Community. The creation of "European companies," along with the implication of the proposals for the Social Charter and the Action Programme for implementing the Social Charter, would clearly have an impact on managerial roles, goals, and relationships. Politically, it begins to look as though management in enterprises within the European Community will be quite different from management in organizations based outside the Community. European management, in a word, would have a different European legal basis and a distinctive form of organization.

The presence of competition and the need for policies for survival would drive managers in European enterprises to plan radical change policies at different levels of their organizations. Policies for enterprise renewal, programmes for developing and changing the nature and focus of middle management, and policies for improving the efficiency of production systems and the quality of the product would all lead to the need for a European management approach, grounded in the fact that it had to be seen as legitimate by employees and other stakeholders. The faster and the more radical changes are demanded, the more the need for a consciously moulded European approach, to be sustained by all the Social Partners. In this way, motivation could be released.

The argument for European management, therefore, was not simply based on recognition of cultural differences. It anticipated political pressures for a common approach, given the need for radical changes in organizational structures and performance.

A Definition

By the term *European management*, therefore, we mean recognizable patterns of managerial behaviour and an approach to problem solving and decision making at all levels in organizations that establishes the identity of the management strategy as distinctly European, and particularly focuses on approaches to planning, implementing and evaluating change. It is assumed that European management

- is emerging and cannot be said to exist except in limited circumstances;
- is broadly linked to the idea of European integration, which is continuously expanding further into different countries (i.e., the 12 countries);
- reflects key values such as pluralism, tolerance, and so on, but is not consciously developed from such values;
- is associated with a balanced stakeholder philosophy and the concept of Social Partners.

Objections

The first major objection to this argument rests with the judgement that there is a long-term trend of internationalization taking place in all societies and that we are at the beginning of constructing a global economy, far beyond the European sphere of influence. The need for global strategy, as argued by such writers as Ohmae, is hostile to any concept of a world built on political blocs or alliances. It is an argument that world companies cannot afford to be nationalistic. There is, of course, a recognition that the conditions for operations in different societies are important and require different policies and approaches. Basically, transnational corporations have to deal with this by joint ventures with local partners and by the hiring of local staff. Such companies, within the setting of European economies, can adapt by setting up local companies and tailoring their global strategies so that local political and cultural sensibilities are not offended. In essence, however, it means that it is wrong to perceive European ideas and values as the basis for strategies; all that is necessary is prudent modification of overall global policies and strategies.

The international construction industry is a good example of such an approach. By definition, construction is a temporary project-based activity, with a finite life. This means that international technical staff can be employed, temporarily, on project management in foreign countries. Of course, the acquisition of contracts requires a more permanent national branch structure for international construction firms. Public works tendering and construction work for local property developers and industrial companies mean that staff have to be employed in order to discover, through their local networks, what business is available. (Project management staff can also be used for such purposes.) Such national branch offices and companies, however, do not yet have to be created at the "European" level (at least until the European Commission has a large public works budget). It is, in fact, more efficient to concentrate in such offices local national staff who know the local scene and can advise the company on where the best business possibilities are likely to be found. There is no argument for European management here, therefore.

A second objective to the European management thesis lies with the idea of competitive advantage. According to this prescription, companies should seek out the definition of where their expertise is seen to lie. For American companies, for example, who are selling products that are identified with the American way of life (Levi's jeans, Coca-Cola, Apple, and so on) it would be positively harmful to be seen as European. Japanese companies selling cars or other consumer goods, even construction buildings, may well believe that their competitive advantage lies with their products and management being seen as Japanese, as this is identified with high quality. Even companies within Europe might find that their national character is important in marketing their products. This is particularly true of products that have a strong national image or that are identified with a special national advantage, such as a tradition of craftsmanship (Swiss watches).

Of course, there are examples of non-European companies that have succeeded in localizing their identity, so that they are no longer seen as foreign. Kellogg, Woolworth, Ford, Electrolux, and Shell are all examples of companies that have achieved a type of local United Kingdom identity. This has been achieved by a very strong localization of employees and managers and acquisition of a "local" company culture, usually after years of experience.

There are, in fact, no real examples of European companies in terms of their identity. SAS has a Scandinavian identity that is much disputed by the Scandinavian countries. Philips is genuinely European in its employment of managers and engineers from many countries but its identity is clearly Dutch. This is true of most European multinational companies (Fiat, Siemens, Thomson, and so on). This fact has been argued to mean that European management is simply a myth.

It can also be argued that even international service organizations, such as consultancies, may have international staff but are strongly oriented to selling products with a clear national origin and significance. There is every reason, for example, for McKinsey's to continue to appear both international and American in orientation. The "Americanness" of McKinsey prescriptions is, in fact, one of its main attractions.

The objections to the European management theories, therefore, are mainly related to the belief that internationalization is more important than building a European identity and to the evidence that national origin is often of considerable importance to company competitive advantage. Table 11-2 demonstrates this argument.

The Reasons for the Europeanization of Management

It is perfectly true that such objections effectively destroy any argument assuming a general trend toward European management or, alternatively, recommending European management as a style to be adopted in all circumstances. There is no reason to defend such arguments, which are clearly unlikely to be valid. What can be argued, however, is that there are several major factors that will, in the medium or long term, serve to produce the need for international companies operating in European countries to make a strategic choice whether to adopt a "European" managerial framework or a clear alternative. Such a choice is likely to be produced, first, by political pressures from the European Commission, the European Court, and in future, the European Parliament.

TABLE 11-2
Competitive Advantage
and National Identity:
Types of Situations

Type of Situation	Examples
Local national companies (selling mainly to local markets)	British Gas, Abbey National Building Society
Local national companies exporting to other European countries (or operating within them)	Rover, Volvo, BMW
Local national companies importing and distributing products from other countries	Amstrad
European multinationals with single national identity	Siemens, Olivetti, Renault, Porsche
European cross-national firms with double identity	Shell, Unilever, SAS
European national companies collaborating on a European product	British Aerospace, Sud Aviation (Airbus)
Non-European firms with local national identity	Kellogg, Ford
Non-European firms with foreign identity	NEC, Sony, Levi, IBM, Rank
National holding company and local company with national identity	Hansar Trust

It is important to underline that the EC is a new type of political entity. It is not likely to become a formal federation, exactly on the lines of the United States for two reasons. First, the world is also developing a global interdependence at the same time as European integration, and this means that the EC can never possess the type of national sovereignty and autonomy assumed by European states and the United States in the nineteenth and early twentieth centuries. It is probable, for example, that parts of the European economy, such as financial and capital markets, will be internationalized at a global level before full European integration can be achieved. So managers in some organizations will be mainly under controls and regulations of a proper international character, even inside the new Europe. Secondly, the EC exists as a constantly growing concept. It is best conceptualized as a set of concentric circles growing outward and it is obvious that Eastern Europe and Scandinavia are gradually going to have to be integrated into the European system. This means that it is an open system in which controls will be much stricter in some core geographical (and functional) areas than in peripheral areas. This is actually the strength of the European ideal.

A second major factor is related to the needs of transnational organizations to build a European planning and coordination centre. This need is already demonstrated by the existence of such European local organizations in the case of European and foreign multinational companies manufacturing, selling, and operating in several different countries. The creation of many joint ventures and agreements and the growth of international subcontractors and suppliers for manufacturing operations necessitate the creation of such planning and controlling organizations.

An example concerns the car industry. Japanese firms are now building plants in several European countries, particularly in the United Kingdom. The scale of production required to make such operations profitable—several million cars per year are planned—means that distribution sales and ordering systems will have to be created in Europe. The tendency of firms such as Toyota is to centralize all planning and ordering systems as well as research and development (R&D) in Japan. Factories are built in overseas countries as part of an integrated manufacturing logic, but at present there are no plans for an autonomous and comprehensive European organization dealing with all the functions of R&D, marketing, design, distribution and sales, and so on. It is easy to see how the pressures for creating such an organization will develop. Already an R&D centre is planned for Germany and a limited European organization has been started in Belgium, besides the main factories that will open in 1993 in the United Kingdom. Step by step, it is likely that there will be pressure within the company to decentralize decisions to the European level. Competition with European and U.S. carmakers in Europe will make such an organizational change much more necessary. A European local organization will need to integrate nationals of many countries to be effective. This provides the basis of need for European management, even within a Japanese organization as successful, dominant, and expanding as Toyota.

The third reason for predicting that transnational organizations will have to consider a strategic choice for European management rests with the personnel needs of such companies to develop a "European cadre" of senior employees. The concept of cadre in France covers both the senior, technical, and specialist, scientific personnel and the managerial and administrative personnel in an organization. It is, of course, an entirely French concept related to the output of the *grandes écoles*, which are responsible for producing most of the elite in France. Technologically sophisticated organizations need increasing numbers of such specialists in all functions. It is now generally recognized that competitive advantage rests with the level of "knowledge formation" developed in the firm, that is, the extent to which knowledge is built up continuously by study and experience. This clearly requires that managers and specialists will stay for considerable periods in the firm. European transborder organizations will increasingly find that such personnel will demand international careers within the European context. This could be found by interfirm mobility, but then the knowledge of the individual will be lost to the firm. This fact puts pressure on firms to provide such inter-organizational careers. The demand for creating a European level organization will then come from such pressures and this also presents the choice for and against a European management option.

Testing the Argument

In the case of European transnational organizations such as Siemens or Philips it is fairly obvious that ideas of European management are extremely useful as a framework for guiding the development and share of their European local product divisional organization. Such a framework provides a basis for legitimacy for their cross-national cooperation. This would also be true for joint ventures such as the Airbus organization linked to French, German, British, Italian and other manufacturing firms. There is little need to show the relevance of the argument to the human resource policies of such organizations.

As stated above, there are also non-European transnational organizations operating in Europe that depend on their foreign identity for their competitive advantage This may be true not only for their products, but also for their management organization. IBM never tries to appear European, even if it has a strong European organization. The appeal of the company rests on its strong and unique corporate culture, which is clearly North American in origin and style. This does not mean that IBM European managers cannot behave as Europeans in their personal daily work, but that the organization still preserves its distinct character.

The real test of the argument that European management will become an issue for strategic choice for many new transnational corporations operating in the Single European Market after 1992, however, lies with such foreign organizations, which personify "non-European values." In spite of the growth of European integration, it is fairly clear that there will remain many critical industries that have been penetrated by foreign multinational companies. Where this has happened or is about to happen, there is a critical test of whether the ideas of European management will be used as a basis for organization and strategies of change. If they are not used, then the Europe of the future will not only be extremely varied in its styles and approach to management, but will likely be very much more conflictual in relationships between employees, managers, and other stakeholders. It is also predictable that turnover will be higher, and this could handicap and limit effective knowledge formation.

We can therefore take the case, again, of Japanese transnational organizations operating in the electronics industry. Here, the product cycle is rapid and development costs are more and more crucial. Many Japanese electronics manufacturers and telecommunication firms are already starting to build European-level marketing organizations. The problems are complex for such firms. The product development process is at present based on close relationships in Japan between R&D laboratories, development factories, full-production factories, and sales branches. In spite of ever-growing numbers of European factories, the main European level activities are found in marketing. The problem for the Japanese is that short-cycle product development depends on close relationships between functional staff in the firm and with customers and suppliers. This cannot take place if marketing and production are in Europe, but all other functions are in Japan. Sooner or later, there has to be a European-level organization in which Europeans interact directly and not through Japan. Cross-national training, which has just started in such firms, will be necessary to allow effective networking. The fusion of the technical design, manufacturing, and marketing functions will have to be made within Europe. This again presents major problems for Japanese firms, but it is difficult to avoid.

The test of the argument, therefore, on Japanese firms reveals that although it is possible in early stages of development to persist with a traditional expatriate-run organization with local staff providing advice on local variations, there is increasingly a problem for Japanese firms that are ambitious enough to want to run large-scale cross-border European operations. In this case, the problem of how to structure and run the European-level organization becomes critical.

Conclusions

Our discussion has revealed that we have now reached a new stage in the debate on European management. It is still in embryo form in its shape and structure, that is, the values can be defined as well as many of the policy objectives, but structures are still a matter of debate.

We have seen that European management has a very different relevance in different types of business situations. We cannot predict that European management will become a dominant framework for managerial thinking and action, except in certain key situations. Local national identity and styles are likely to remain important for all local firms and it is only when transnational organization becomes necessary that the issue becomes a matter for strategic choice. The crucial factor determining the relevance of European management to firms, apart from the existence of transborder organization, is the basis for knowledge in the firm. If knowledge is primarily a local national creation (as in the case of the Swiss watch industry), then it is obvious that there is no real need for Europeanization. The European management framework is therefore relevant when the firm depends on building a really integrated team of cross-national members over a long period.

This means that basically there are four situations to consider. For European transnational organizations, where the basis of competitive advantage still lies in the national firm, then the European-level organization is only important as a coordinating function. European management is probably irrelevant to such firms.

In cases where European transnational organizations are dependent on European-level strategic decisions and where the Euroidentity is crucial to motivation, then European management is extremely important.

In the third situation of foreign transnational organizations with a strong and necessary national identity, there may be a severe conflict and problem of knowledge formation for the firm.

In the fourth case, as we discussed above, a foreign transnational organization may find it has to change its structure and management style in order to build a strong European-level coordinating, planning, and controlling organization. This case may also be highly conflictual.

■ MANAGEMENT LEARNING FOR EUROPE[†]

By Sybren Tijmstra and Kenneth Casler

Today, business managers and their organisations around the world operate in a challenging, complex environment, one in which flexibility, adaptability, and responsiveness are key factors of survival. As Europe changes economically, socially, and politically, as it grows more interdependent, a new business organisation is emerging, bringing with it a new management philosophy and business practices. "European" management—as opposed to North American and Japanese management—is now becoming recognizable. Its innovative approaches to business strategy, organisational structure, and operational issues arise from the specific nature of the European context.

European businesses are by no means out of the race for a world position, nor are they straggling far behind the frontrunners. The novelty is that they are attempting to run under a new banner—a European one—in order to unlock new potential and generate competitive advantage that should benefit European industry as a whole. This cannot happen in a state of national competition and economic fragmentation. Economic convergence is imposing new ways of thinking about products and services, innovative approaches to markets, changes in business organisation and operations: put simply, a European model of business and management.

†**Source:** This article was originally published in *European Management Journal*, March 1992, Vol. 10, pp. 30–38. Reprinted by permission.

The Need for European Managers

Like the United States and Japan, Europe wants to be seen as a supplier of high-value-added, high-intellectual-content products and services. Such products require large capital investments and sophisticated know-how to develop and market. The expertise of well-educated professionals, with backgrounds in high technology and advanced science, is especially vital. Also, critical mass in terms of financial leverage, production volumes, and market size is essential in sustaining viable positions both in the home market and in the world market.

For Europe, this means that fragmented, national markets must be transcended to achieve the necessary critical mass. Accepting a process of transnationalisation in nearly every business function (from research and development, procurement and logistics to human resource management) is simply a necessity at all levels of responsibility. Business managers and their organisations must develop the flexibility, adaptability, and responsiveness to face and benefit from the transnational market conditions in Europe today.

European Diversity, Concentration, and Integration

Social and cultural diversity is, and will remain, a dominant feature of European society. In every respect, this diversity is a resource that we must learn to tap. In business, the variety of existing organisational forms and management styles, different entrepreneurial attitudes, and human relations in the workplace pose definite challenges but also offer many opportunities to learn and to create new wealth. This diversity will also stretch our imaginations. To quote one recent article: "The creation of effective trans-European business organizations requires new managerial approaches and systems."

European integration is a key accelerator in this process of transnationalisation, which affects all levels of management today. The political pressure from European institutions to reduce economic fragmentation is intense and is reflected in efforts to complete the Single Market and Monetary Union. Likewise, Community programmes to establish a European Social Charter and Statutes for a European Company will change the way in which business operates. Gradually, these pressures to build a new socioeconomic and political framework will transform the business environment and lead to fundamental changes in the management mentality in Europe.

People and Organisations Need to Internationalise Profoundly

This transformation is a dynamic, open-ended process, affecting countries all across Europe, and not just the European Community. In this context managers need a greater international awareness and cross-cultural competence than before. International companies have always depended on a mobile corps of professionals and managers for their operations. A small team of expatriate managers have traditionally gained access to the top management and boardroom positions of such firms. Now the difference between international companies and European companies is that the latter need competent, international managers at all levels of the organisation. They must be armed with the skills and attitudes to operate in different cultural contexts, with people speaking different languages and holding different assumptions about life and work.

European managers can no longer work in geographical or functional isolation. They need to share their expertise throughout the organisation, frequently crossing national borders and language barriers. As more task forces and project groups include international team members, and as the transnational dimension of product development, production, and marketing intensifies, internationalism—i.e., international awareness, sensitivity, and competence—becomes the critical factor of success in the corporate culture in Europe. Management development for European and international responsibility becomes a particularly strategic issue.

European Management and Managers

The Europeanisation of organisations, management teams, and management approaches is affecting the larger companies adopting pan-European business strategies, but also a growing number of small and medium-sized companies are concerned by M&A activity, strategic alliances, subcontracting arrangements, and comakership relationships. Many of the critical issues that management will be grappling with in Europe in the 1990s have been discussed in recent publications. Among them are:

- Achieving improved productivity, product/service quality, and organisational flexibility
- Introducing new/more science and technology into products and services
- Managing integrated R&D, production, and marketing through "organic" work systems (task forces, project teams)
- Stimulating and organising "intrapreneurship" in international business networks
- Developing and managing the firm's international human resources

European companies will need to tackle these issues, paying special attention to the impact of the transnational/European dimension on business strategy, organisational structure, operating processes and procedures, and human resource and management development policies. These companies will need to:

- Focus more on international processes than structures
- Facilitate international networking
- Allow for "subtle and informal mechanisms" of control and coordination to encourage cross-cultural collaboration
- Build corporate identity and commitment across borders in order to achieve a common vision, shared values, and a coherent style within the organisation

Companies, regardless of size, that take a strategic commitment to the European marketplace will need to bring their management approach in line with these new realities.

Different Strategies Lead to Different Management Approaches

Since it can easily find itself in a variety of geographic and sociopolitical contexts, a European company's decision to serve specific markets has obvious implications for its business practices. A decision to position business operations for Europe, especially when this involves managing product development, manufacturing operations, and customer relations in different countries, will have critical consequences for the company's organisational structure, operational processes, management approach and style, and human resource requirements.

European Management Is Different
from American and Japanese Management

European management will differ considerably from both American and Japanese management. Thurley and Wirdenius argue that there are three reasons for this. First, European management involves mediating and capitalising on the diversity of European cultures. Second, the European Community is a novel political entity very unlike the United States of America or other existing federations. Finally, companies operating in Europe are facing serious competitive challenges resulting from political, social, and economic developments in the European "Community" and from economic globalisation trends that are shaking the foundations of industrialised society worldwide. European companies must necessarily undergo a transformation in all areas to achieve competitiveness.

The emergence of a European management approach has obvious implications for the profile, education, development, and management of European managers. It has been suggested that the European manager will have five characteristics that derive from operating in a transnational context:

- An ability to comprehend the European business environment, and specifically its cultural, social, political, and economic complexity
- An ability to imagine, create, and lead new forms of business (networks, task forces, coordinating units) that span borders and bridge cultures
- An ability to build commitment to a corporate identity and mission shared by all members of the organisation whatever their original cultural values
- An ability to win the support of "national" stakeholders in the company's different countries of operation
- An ability to accept and pursue transnational mobility to achieve a European career path

Underlying these characteristics are several important assumptions about the European manager. This person will probably:

- have a solid core of *technical and managerial competence* providing him/her with fundamental confidence in his/her ability to take up challenges. This expertise will reduce personal stress levels and also make him/her acceptable to colleagues.
- display a genuine *enthusiasm and empathy for different peoples and cultures* and a willingness to discover and accommodate divergent approaches to situations and problems. This means that s/he will have the language and cultural skills to overcome communication barriers and the personal skills to achieve goals and results in all European countries.
- be self-aware, conscious of *his/her own personal values and cultural orientation*. S/he will be mindful of the impact of his/her own bias on personal relations and performance in different cultural settings and will remain open to the values and preferences of these other cultures.
- be *willing and keen to accept changes* in the professional environment throughout his/her career. This flexibility and adaptability are hallmarks of a genuinely international personality.

National cultures and identities will remain a characteristic feature of European management throughout the 1990s and beyond. It is essential, therefore, that managers recognise and accommodate through their personal and professional thought and action the multiconformity—i.e., the many enlightening differences and complementarities—of Europe.

Management Learning for Europe:
The Education and Development of European Managers

The current process of Europeanisation is creating individual and organisational learning opportunities that must be structured and supported in order for European management to emerge successfully. Precareer education and postexperience development of European managers is an imperative and a challenge. The imperative is to transform national managers at senior and middle levels into European business leaders. The challenge is how.

There are three specific learning areas in which business leaders need to be developed for European management responsibilities (see figure 11-4). They are

- the European business environment,
- European management dynamics, and
- Europeanisation processes.

Each of these areas has several dimensions that the European manager needs to integrate and learn to be effective transnationally.

European Business Environment

First, the European business environment is structured by a number of elements, which are knowledge based (see figure 11-5). An awareness and understanding of these determinants is a sine qua non if the manager is to operate successfully across Europe.

Sociopolitical elements include the national heritage (history, culture, language) of each country of operation. They also include supranational efforts made within the European Community to integrate member states (e.g., institutions, legislation, regulation). These factors are, in fact, both hard and soft and include legal obligations (e.g., employee involvement) as well as attitudes to work, leisure, and the environment in each country. All must be considered in business decisions. In comparison with Japanese and American management issues, it may be said that there is a specific and necessary "learnable" European response to these issues.

Economic factors include national and Europe-wide industry dynamics as well as efforts to construct a single integrated economic community by 1993. Price controls, investment incentives, social charges, and so on will differ from country to country until harmonisation is achieved. Europe is far more fragmented than either the United States or Japan in this respect; European managers will require a specific knowledge base on European economic issues and must be open to new developments and change. Europe's economic fragmentation is likely to persist beyond 1993 and the ultimate framework will concern far more than the twelve member states of the European Community.

In regard to technological development, current internationalisation trends are introducing greater harmonisation across industrialised societies and rapidly reducing the technological gap. Masaru Ibuka, cofounder of Sony, has claimed that the age of technological leadership for the competitive edge is over. On the contrary, the competitive edge now lies in the marketing of the technology. In Europe as a whole technological sophistication may vary from country to country and business sector to business sector, but there are strong and definite harmonisation trends. More important

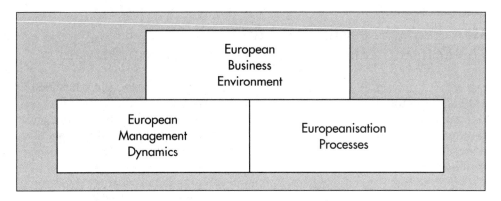

is the gradual convergence of lifestyles in Europe and indeed around the globe, which will have considerable impact on business sector and market dynamics throughout Europe, particularly in the area of marketing.

Although there still persist substantial differences between sectors in European countries, the effect of concentration trends and European integration will be to smooth out a number of the local differences over the long run. In respect of technology and business sectors, therefore, globalisation trends may be moving American, Japanese, and European managers in fairly similar directions, particularly in terms of the complexity and diversity that they need to manage. However, Europeans are likely to gain a competitive advantage for world markets with their knowledge of and sensitivity to culturally diverse markets acquired in the home market, where they learn to respond creatively, accurately, and rapidly to customers in many countries.

European Management Dynamics

A second area of learning of crucial importance to national managers, is the dynamics of national approaches to management in European countries (see figure 11-6). This covers the spectrum of soft management issues from business practices to leadership styles and personal values at work. There are two major determinants that illustrate the diversity of European management. They are

- the diversity of business cultures in Europe, where culture is understood to consist of the traditions, practices and values of both individuals and organisations, and

FIGURE 11-5
European Business
Environment

Sociopolitical Determinants	Economic Determinants
Business Sector Determinants	Technological Determinants

- the spectrum of management values, by which is meant the patterns of management behaviour that result from different educational systems, organisational models, and business practices.

The tapestry of business cultures in Europe is rich. Managers who operate transnationally need to understand and work within a mosaic of values and practices. They need to be creative, to recognise and adjust to diverse patterns of thought, judgement, perception, and behaviour and to be able to work with many different people, members of different "national" and organisational cultures.

An ability to read and understand cultural orientation across a broad spectrum of people and businesses in Europe is the hallmark of a European manager. It is best developed through exposure to different leadership styles, work styles, communication, and collaboration styles. This ability forms not only part of the individual's managerial know-how but also part of the organisation's knowledge base. A transnational business needs to build a management team whose members are both culturally sensitive and sufficiently international in origin to ensure that the "corporate culture" reflects the complex cultural environment in which it operates.

Management values are the sum of many factors: from individual preferences and attitudes about work and people at work, to specific organisational cultures and business practices, but also including an individual's technical knowledge and skills. The European environment is rich in terms of its different conceptions of what a manager is and does. The diverse national systems of management education and training, the different personnel recruitment and career management practices, corporate organisation, and management development policies all play a role in shaping the profile of the European manager. The European manager needs an understanding of this diversity in order to achieve both personal and professional goals. Organisations need a sophisticated knowledge of management recruitment, motivation, and development practices around Europe in order to attract management potential and retain valuable members of its international management team, offering challenging, attractive careers.

Europeanisation Processes

There is a third area of learning about European management that concerns companies whose competitive advantage no longer lies exclusively at the national level but at the level where corporate vision and strategic decisions are international, and more specifically, European. Such transnational firms are developing innovative organisational structures, flexible management processes, effective cross-cultural communication systems, and supranational corporate identities to fulfill their missions (see figure 11-7). They are able to synergise the contributions made by the different organisational units and people wherever they are located. To lead such an organisation, the management team needs an awareness of European differences and

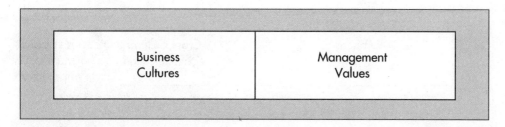

FIGURE 11-6
European Management Dynamics

| Business Cultures | Management Values |

similarities, on the one hand, and creative leadership and cross-border know-how, on the other. The ability and willingness to learn all the time is critical.

Firms across Europe will be experimenting with flatter organisational structures and decentralised units that enjoy autonomy and entrepreneurial responsibility in an integrated network. Increasingly such structures will rely on sophisticated but subtle planning and control coordination centres at the European level. It is of utmost importance in such organisational structures to achieve commitment to the corporate mission through shared values and a strong corporate identity. Competent, sensitive leadership is of the essence.

When the transnational dimension imprints the organisation, the complexity of its operations is magnified and effective communications become critical to operational success. The transnational organisation and the members of its management team will need cross-cultural communication skills to achieve its mission. These will necessarily include a knowledge of the languages and cultures in which the organisation operates, and an attitude of cooperation and learning to effectively bond the employees of the organisation wherever they work. People in different countries with differing personal and organisational values will have special need of bonding.

Delivering the European Manager

How will European business firms achieve these goals of greater international awareness and transnational competence in their organisations? How can they effectively form a European knowledge base to underpin operations in a marketplace of such diversity and complexity? How will they unite employees across a spectrum of countries into a shared vision and common identity? Current practice in several pioneering firms points towards at least three avenues of approach:

- European recruitment of managers
- European career paths and management assignments
- European management development

European Recruitment of Managers

Business organisations with a European strategy will need to recruit members of their management teams across borders. Since they will need access to both well-educated

FIGURE 11-7
Europeanisation Process

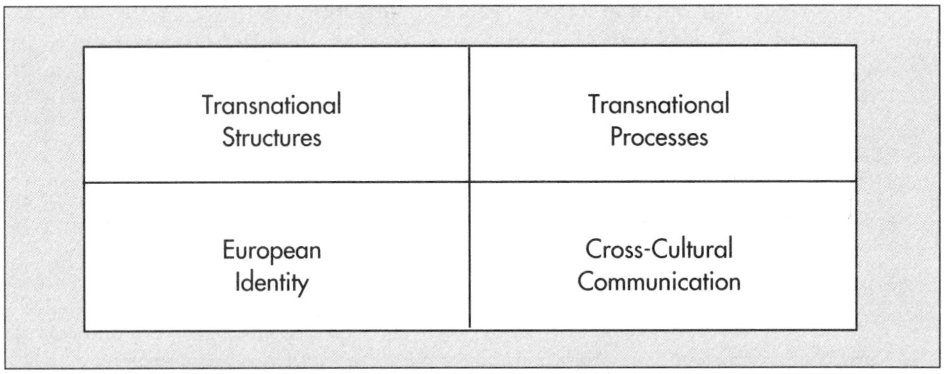

Transnational Structures	Transnational Processes
European Identity	Cross-Cultural Communication

young graduates and experienced business professionals, these companies will need to develop cross-border recruitment strategies, increasing their awareness and understanding of local national education systems and employment practices. This recruitment expertise will be a valuable asset to the European company and give it a competitive advantage over firms locked into national recruitment systems.

To succeed and be attractive to the pool of graduates and professionals in the employment market, European companies will also need a Europe-wide image and reputation. A number of leading companies in various countries in Europe have understood the importance of a strong corporate image at a European level, not only for the marketing of their products and services but for the recruitment of skilled employees as well. These companies usually have strong links with excellent educational institutions in several countries and pursue an active campus recruitment policy. Medium-sized companies, however, are just beginning to realise the importance of corporate image for recruitment purposes. They will recognise that special links with educational institutions can be a valuable asset, especially with European schools or national schools linked in an international network (e.g., Community of European Management Schools, which includes members in Belgium, Denmark, France, Germany, Italy, The Netherlands and Spain).

It is equally important that graduates and professionals have the requisite European education, expertise, exposure, and experience to be able to integrate the transnational organisational structures and promote the cross-border development strategies critical to business success in Europe. At present there are few management education centres that provide a genuinely European response to corporate management requirements. Many national business schools claim to offer international programmes and graduates. These claims, however, cannot be substantiated in many cases.

More business schools and management development centres need to develop the potential to assist European companies in useful ways with educational services and well-trained graduates. They too will need to restructure their educational resources to meet the demands and challenges of the emerging business environment in Europe.

There are at least six characteristics that an educational institution will need to develop in order to offer a genuinely European service to industry:

- The course and programme offerings must have a European/international orientation; European topics and issues form an integral part of all teaching and learning modules.

- The educational approach must be based on European/international materials and be supported by readings, case studies, project work, and international assignments to ensure awareness and understanding of cross-border business.

- The faculty must be European/international in composition to a very significant degree; a truly European business school will have as many as ten nationalities on the faculty with no single country representing more than 25 to 30 percent of the total.

- The course/programme participants must be international in origin; again one would expect at least ten nationalities to be represented in the student body with the largest national group weighing no more than 25 to 30 percent of the total.

- The institution will have multiple locations and operate as a transnational organisation; this structure must make sense in educational terms, otherwise it is a recipe for resource dispersion; the aim is to lever one's educational expertise in different markets and learn from these local contexts to offer an educational perspective on European management. The institution's own management team will be international in composition.

- The institution will have a European/international advisory board to guide and support its development. Such boards will include recognised academic members and corporate representatives whose organisations have achieved European management excellence.

In short, for an educational institution to offer the products and services that will be of value to European organisations managing cross-border development and business operations, it must itself be transnational. With expertise in the design, development, and delivery of international educational programmes for international audiences, the institution demonstrates that it fully understands the needs of European business.

European Career Paths and Management Assignments

Knowledge is a firm's most valuable asset. Successful human resource management aims to secure that the company's expertise and human capital is not lost or squandered. To members of the European management team it is essential to offer cross-border management assignments and career paths. Through multinational project teams and task forces, managers at all levels gain valuable exposure and experience, enhancing their ability to operate across borders. European projects bring together managers from different cultures, increase the exchange of expertise, and expand the knowledge base of the corporation. Companies must also be able to offer an international career path involving long-term management assignments in different countries and job rotations across borders and functions. This will ensure that the members of the management team develop Europe-wide experience, exposure, and expertise.

European Management Development

On-the-job experience and challenging assignments will sensitise management to the issues affecting individual and corporate performance in the context of day-to-day operations. In addition, management development programmes are necessary to reinforce and upgrade the core knowledge, technical skills, and individual attitudes that guarantee a firm's competitiveness. These programmes need to provide high-potential employees with both the hard and soft tools of management, from advanced functional knowledge and techniques to strategic awareness and leadership qualities. In the case of European organisations it is necessary to provide this training with an international perspective and to do so against the backdrop of transnational business operations. Therefore, European companies will offer on-the-job management training in a number of formats: in-company programmes, consortium programmes, and open courses. As frequently as possible this training will take place in a foreign country setting and with international participants. In general, companies will need to encourage and support individual efforts to upgrade and update their "human capital" in order to "meet the new demands of the working environment." Management learning for Europe will challenge individuals to the extreme and they will need to know that the entire organisation supports their efforts to learn.

References and Suggested Readings

Boisot, M., Territorial Strategies in a Competitive World: The Emerging Challenge to Regional Authorities, *European Management Journal*, September 1990, pp. 394–401.

Bournois, F., and J. Chauchat, Managing Managers in Europe, *European Management Journal*, March 1990, pp. 3–18.

Daems, H., The Strategic Implications of Europe 1992, *Long Range Planning,* June 1990, pp. 41–48.

De Wolf, P. (Ed.), *Competition in Europe,* Kluwer, Dordrecht, 1991.

Dijck, J. J. J. van, Transnational Management in an Evolving European Context, *European Management Journal,* December 1990, pp. 474–479.

Doz, Y., Partnerships in Europe: The "Soft Restructuring" Option? in Mattsson, L.-G., and B. Stymne, *Corporate and Industry Strategies for Europe,* Elsevier, Amsterdam, 1991.

Elfring, T., Structure and Growth of Business Services in Europe, in De Jong, H. W., (Ed.), *The Structure of European Industry,* Third Edition, Kluwer, Dordrecht, 1993.

Emerson, M., Aujean, M., Catinat, M., Goybet, P., and A. Jacquemin, *The Economics of 1992,* Oxford University Press, 1988.

Friberg, E. G., 1992: Moves Europeans Are Making, *Harvard Business Review,* May/June 1989, pp. 85–89.

Kay, J., Myths and Realities, in Davis, E. et al.: *1992, Myths and Realities,* Centre for Business Strategy, London, 1989.

Landreth, O. L., *European Corporate Strategy: Heading for 2000,* Macmillan, Basingstoke, 1992.

Mayes, D. G., *The European Challenge—Industry's Response to the 1992 Programme,* Harvester Wheatsheaf, London, 1991.

Nicolaides, P., and C. W. F. Baden-Fuller, *Price Discrimination and Product Differentiation in the European Domestic Appliance Market,* Centre for Business Strategy, London Business School, 1987.

Ohmae, K., *Triad Power: The Coming of Global Competition,* MacMillan, London, 1985.

Porter, M. E., *The Competitive Advantage of Nations,* MacMillan, London, 1990.

Rugman, A. M., and A. Verbeke, Europe 1992 and Competitive Strategies for North American Firms, *Business Horizons,* November/December 1991, pp. 76–81.

Sölvell, Ö., and I. Zander, European Myopia, in Mattsson, L.-G. and B. Stymne (Eds.), *Corporate and Industry Strategies for Europe,* Elsevier, Amsterdam, 1991.

Thurley, K., and H. Wirdenius, Will Management Become European? *European Management Journal,* June 1991, pp. 127–134.

Tijmstra, S., and K. Casler, Management Learning for Europe, *European Management Journal,* March 1992, pp. 30–38.

Van den Bosch, F. A. J., and A. A. van Prooijen, The Competitive Advantage of European Nations: The Impact of National Culture—A Missing Element in Porter's Analysis? *European Management Journal,* June 1992, pp. 173–177.

Van Tulder, R., and G. Junne, *European Multinationals in Core Technologies,* John Wiley, Chichester, 1988.

Wassenberg, A. F. P., Corporate Strategies, Industrial Policies, and Entrepreneurial Hybrids: A European Ménage à Trois, in Van Dijck, J. J. J., and A. A. L. G. Wentink (Eds.), *Transnational Business in Europe: Economic and Social Perspectives,* Tilburg University Press, 1992.

SECTION VI
CASES

As Locke correctly observed, true understanding requires more than just reading. Ideas, perspectives, and theories must be "chewed over" before they can be absorbed into our minds. One of the most common and beneficial ways of achieving this is by means of case discussions. Therefore, twenty-two cases have been included in this book, giving the reader ample opportunity to apply the theoretical concepts of the previous eleven chapters to practical situations.

To increase the accessibility of the cases, three tables have been included on the next pages, clarifying the content and potential usage of the cases. These tables deal with the following topics:

1. *Chapter coverage.* Table 1 indicates which cases are most suited to which chapters. The extent to which cases and chapters *fit* has been expressed by means of stars. Three stars means that there is an *excellent* fit between the case and the theoretical issues being discussed in the chapter. Two stars indicates that the fit is *good* and that the theoretical issues can be well illustrated by the case material. One star means that there is only a partial *(reasonable)* fit; the chapter's theory is of secondary importance to understanding the case issues. Table 1 shows that at least two cases have an excellent fit with each chapter.

2. *Country coverage.* Table 2 indicates which countries are dealt with in which cases. Two stars are used to signify that the country is a *primary* focus of the case. One star means that the country is discussed in the case, but that it is only of *secondary* importance to the case topic. Stars have only been placed in the Europe column if the broader European context is at issue. Table 2 illustrates the broad coverage of European and major non-European countries.

3. *Industry coverage.* Table 3 indicates which industries are dealt with in which cases. This table reflects the balanced coverage of service and product companies.

As the link between the theoretical chapters and the cases is the most important, the sequence of the cases in this section will be according to the chapters with which they have the best fit.

TABLE 1
Chapter Coverage

Section	I	II			III			IV			V
Chapter	**1**	**2**	**3**	**4**	**5**	**6**	**7**	**8**	**9**	**10**	**11**
Euro Disney	***	**							*		**
Ajax	***				*						**
Guns of August	*	***									
The Swatch	*	***	**	**	**			**	**	*	
Oldelft		**	***	**					*		
Kao		**	***		**		*			**	
The Body Shop				***	**	*	*	*	*		
Sportis		**	**	***	*			*			
Amstrad				*	***	**					
Canon			*		***	**	*	*			
SGB					*	***			*		
GrandMet			*		*	***			*		
CLG, EEIG			*		*		***	*	*		**
Taurus		*	*		**	*	***				
Royal Boskalis				*	*		**	***			
Cineplex		*		*	*	*		***			
SAS		*		**	**	**	*	*	***	*	*
Cartier		*	*		**	**			***	**	
Saatchi & Saatchi					*	**		*	*	***	*
Nokia Data					*			*		***	*
Pharma Swede					**		*	*		*	***
Cap Gemini		*	**		**	*	**	*	*	*	***

*** = Excellent fit
** = Good fit
* = Reasonable fit

TABLE 2
Country Coverage

Country	B	CAN	CH	CIS	D	DK	E	F	H	I	J	N	NL	PL	S	SF	UK	USA	EUR
Euro Disney								**											*
Ajax							*			*			**						*
Guns of August					**			**											
The Swatch			**															*	
Oldelft													**						
Kao											**								
The Body Shop																	**		
Sportis				*										**					
Amstrad																	**		
Canon											**								*
SGB	**																		
GrandMet																	**		
CLG, EEIG					**		**	**									**		**
Taurus									**										
Royal Boskalis	*										**								
Cineplex		*																**	*
SAS						**						**			**				*
Cartier								**											
Saatchi & Saatchi																	**		*
Nokia Data																**			*
Pharma Swede															**				**
Cap Gemini					*			**											**

** = Primary focus
 * = Secondary focus

B = Belgium	I = Italy
CAN = Canada	J = Japan
CH = Switzerland	N = Norway
CIS = Commonwealth of Independent States	NL = The Netherlands
	PL = Poland
D = Germany	S = Sweden
DK = Denmark	SF = Finland
E = Spain	UK = United Kingdom
F = France	USA = United States
H = Hungary	EUR = Europe

TABLE 3
Industry Coverage

Industry Type	Services	Industrial Goods	Consumer Goods	Nonbusiness	Specified
Euro Disney	*				Amusement
Ajax	*				Soccer
Guns of August				*	Military
The Swatch			*		Watches
Oldelft		*			Optical Electronics
Kao			*		Household Products, Personal Care Products
The Body Shop			*		Personal Care Products
Sportis			*		Protective Clothing
Amstrad			*		Consumer Electronics
Canon		*	*		Photocopiers, Computers, Cameras
SGB	*	*			Industrial Banking
GrandMet	*		*		Diversified
CLG, EEIG		*			Paint
Taurus		*			Rubber Products
Royal Boskalis	*				Dredging
Cineplex	*				Cinemas
SAS	*				Airlines
Cartier			*		Jewellery, Fragrances
Saatchi & Saatchi	*				Advertising, Consulting
Nokia Data		*	*		Computers
Pharma Swede			*		Pharmaceuticals
Cap Gemini	*				Consulting, Computer Software

■ EURO DISNEY S.C.A. A FAIRY TALE?[†]

By Marc Huygens and Ron Meyer

Standing with a glass of France's finest cognac in his hand, Philippe Bourguignon's eyes were fixed on the contours of the Eiffel Tower. From this luxurious apartment he had a superb view over all of the aesthetic splendour Paris offers at night. However, not all had been equally pleasant today, October 18, 1993. Quite the contrary, this morning had been one of the worst of his career. As chairman of Euro Disney, Bourguignon had been forced to announce the firing of 950 employees, almost 10 percent of the company's entire workforce, bringing the total number of employees down to approximately 11,000, from a high of 19,000. Since the opening of the amusement park on April 12, 1992, Euro Disney's continuing heavy losses had exceeded 1.5 billion French francs, making dramatic action inescapable.

Two years ago, the prospects had been so much more promising. Disney had been successful at transplanting its profitable American theme park concept to Japan, and Disney's corporate management expected to conquer Europe in the same manner. Disney's confidence was reflected in their attendance and profit projections, which showed that the Paris amusement park would pass the break-even point within a year of opening its gates.

Disney's management had much to be proud of. They had skilfully balanced the arguments of increased tourism and job creation, with the threat of Barcelona as an interesting alternative location, to negotiate a sweet deal with the French government: 4800 acres, 30 kilometres from Paris were sold in 1987 at 1971 agricultural prices. Moreover, the French government extended highways, subways, and railroad lines to the site of Marne la Vallée. Phase 1 of the detailed plan, including the theme park, six hotels with a total of 5,200 rooms, a convention centre, a golf course, and thirty-two nightclubs, bars, and restaurants, was completed on the day before opening. Furthermore, Euro Disney had entered into partnerships with companies such as American Express, Coca-Cola, Esso, IBM, Kodak, Mattel, Nestlé, Philips, and Renault. These companies had committed themselves to building or financing many of the attractions and state-of-the-art systems in return for favourable sales and/or promotion opportunities within the resort[1]. Phase 2, consisting of a film studio and a second theme park, was planned to start construction by the end of 1993.

However, Euro Disney also had its critics. On the investment side, many commentators questioned the financial arrangements made by the Walt Disney Corporation. Euro Disney had been created as a subsidiary, in which Walt Disney Corporation held only a 49 percent stake. The other stocks—sold for 72 French francs per share, while Walt Disney Corporation had purchased their stocks for only 10 French francs per share—would be tradeable on the Paris exchange. Euro Disney would be managed by the parent company, for which hefty management fees would be paid. Together with the considerable royalties, it was estimated that if sales progressed as planned, by 1997, 57 percent of Euro Disney's operating profit would go to the parent company.[2] Even if Euro Disney would lose money, Walt Disney Corporation would receive these fixed sources of income.

The most vocal critics, however, were those who feared a "cultural Chernobyl." These commentators saw in Disney's plans a form of "cultural imperialism," which the French government should prevent, not encourage. Some of these critics even predicted imminent failure, arguing that Europeans in general, and the French in particular, are too different from Americans for such a standardized product to survive being exported.

[†]**Source:** This case was written by Marc Huygens and Ron Meyer as a basis for class discussion, not to illustrate the correct or incorrect handling of a management situation. All information in this case was obtained from published sources. The authors would like to thank Bob de Wit for his useful comments.

[1]*Management Today*, September 1992, pp. 90–96.
[2]*Economist*, September 26, 1992, pp. 87–88.

As the park opened on April 12, 1992, and attendance rates remained far below expectations, management's response was to point at the economic downturn facing Europe. However, within a few months the American chairman of Euro Disney, Robert Fitzpatrick, was replaced by a Disney insider of French origin, Philippe Bourguignon. Placing the Frenchman at the head of the company was seen by many as a transition from an American to a European management style. According to Bourguignon, it was his task to "make every effort to blend into the local community by forging a unique blend of Disney tradition reflecting European expectations. One of our highest priorities will be to continue our effort to adapt to our European environment."[3]

---

[3] *Amusement Business*, April 12, 1993, pp. 1–2.

But ticket sales have remained low. Officially, the reasons for the disappointing attendance rates are the economic downturn in Europe, the devaluations of the U.K., Spanish, and Italian currencies, and the high entrance and hotel prices. Furthermore, those Europeans who do come fail to spend as liberally as American and Japanese visitors do. These factors, together with a lack of capital and the collapse of the French property market, have lead phase 2 to be postponed for at least one year.

It seemed clear to Bourguignon that the original strategy of Euro Disney had to be reconsidered. Adapting to the European context would definitely require more than breaking Disney's no-alcohol rule by serving wine in the restaurants. A more radical change would be necessary to turn Euro Disney into a profitable company. But what, he thought to himself, would the best strategy be?

A.F.C. AJAX: A WINNING CONCEPT?†

By Marc Huygens and Ron Meyer

As Ajax chairman, Michael van Praag, stood in front of his club's awards cabinet containing several of football's most sought after trophies, his mind was preoccupied with the recent loss of yet five more of his best players to southern European teams. At the end of the 1992–1993 season, Dennis Bergkamp and Wim Jonk had left for Inter Milan, Aron Winter had signed up with Lazio Roma, Brian Roy had gone to Foggia, and Marciano Vink had been lured to Genoa. Just a year before he had already lost three of his key players. As a football enthusiast, he was sad to see these world-class players leave Amsterdam and The Netherlands; but more important, as chairman of Ajax he was worried that his club might not be able to continue its successes after so many departures. He wondered what type of strategy could be devised to triumph once again in both national and international leagues, and he asked himself what he as chairman could do to bring such a strategy about.

Van Praag could feel the pressure of the fans' high expectations. They had grown accustomed to attractive football and to winning. Since the club's founding in 1900, Ajax had been national champion dozens of times, while winning five European Cups and one World Cup since 1970. Many of these accomplishments were realized during the period in which Michael van Praag's father was the chairman of Ajax, placing an even heavier burden on Van Praag to succeed.

Most football analysts were in agreement that the team's success had to a large extent been due to the unique system employed by Ajax. This system placed much more emphasis on offense than on defense and stressed technical over physical ability. Its key characteristic was that positions on the field were considered to be of the utmost importance, which meant that players had to be highly disciplined and team minded. The Ajax concept of football left little room for individualists and mavericks. "The system is holy…all actions must fit with the system."[1]

While the Ajax system had resulted in attractive offensive football and had differentiated Ajax from other clubs,[2] the system also had its drawbacks. First, the concept of offense was so deeply embedded in the club's culture that defensive football would not be tolerated—neither by the fans or by the club itself, even when a low-risk draw would be preferential. Second, the strict system made it very difficult to buy external players who would fit in. Yet buying external players was often a necessity, as Ajax's best people were lured away by the promise of fortune and fame in football-mad Italy and Spain.

Van Praag realized that it was almost impossible to offer his players the same salaries as in southern Europe, while the atmosphere surrounding football in these countries could also never be paralleled. In Italy and Spain, football is not an interesting pastime drawing a few thousand fans, as it is in The Netherlands; football is a way of life, drawing tens of thousands of fans. As a consequence of the higher attendance (bigger stadiums), more lucrative TV deals, better sponsoring contracts, and more generous benefactors, Italian and Spanish football clubs can work with budgets many times the multiple of Ajax's Dfl 17.5 million. Due to these countries' favourable tax climate, the players can also pocket more of their gross earnings. Add to this the celebrity status and hero worship of footballers in southern Europe, and it becomes obvious why the region is a magnet for talented players.

---

[1]Guus van Holland, "Uniek Ajax-model blijft illusie voor alle sportbonden" (Unique Ajax model remains an illusion for all sport federations), *NRC Handelsblad*, November 25, 1993.

[2]As Ajax players have moved abroad, so has the Ajax system. The former Ajax player Johan Cruyff, regarded by many as one of the best footballers of all time, employs the Ajax philosophy as trainer of F. C. Barcelona. A. C. Milan has also adopted many of the Ajax premises, after their purchase of the Ajax players Marco van Basten and Frank Rijkaard.

---

†**Source:** This case was written by Marc Huygens and Ron Meyer for class discussion, not to illustrate the effective or ineffective handling of a management situation. All information was obtained from public sources.

Luckily for Ajax the transfer of footballers to other teams has been a very lucrative business, bringing in vast amounts of money that could be reinvested in higher salaries and the purchase of external players. It worried Van Praag, however, that the European Commission had indicated that the buying and selling of players conflicted with Article 85 of European law. If this article, detailing an employee's freedom to seek alternative employment, would be applied strictly, the current transfer system would need to be abolished. This would mean that the barrier for Ajax players to switch to a southern European team would be lower still, and that their departure would leave Ajax empty-handed.

Van Praag was not the type of man to devise the necessary strategy all by himself. While he was very creative and accustomed to making important decisions, due to the fact that he also ran his own medium-sized electronics trading company, he still preferred to work in a team.[3] He was sure that developing a strategy together with the other voluntary members of the board and with Ajax's professional staff was best. In his opinion, he needed the input of such people as General Manager Arie van Eyden, Coach Louis van Gaal, Youth Development Manager Co Adriaanse, and Financial Manager Uri Coronel.

As Michael van Praag left Ajax's Amsterdam office, he decided to talk through some of his recent ideas and concerns at the next board meeting. He was very curious to hear whether his colleagues shared his concerns and whether they could jointly generate some new initiatives. He didn't expect the board to come up with an entirely new plan to fend off Ajax's problems, but he did hope to nudge Ajax more in the right direction.

---

[3]Lia Thorborg, "Het eerste kwartier willen ze met je over voetbal praten" (The first fifteen minutes they want to talk to you about football), *Elan*, January 1993, pp. 53–56.

THE GUNS OF AUGUST: GERMAN AND FRENCH STRATEGY IN 1914[†]

By Barbara W. Tuchman

The German View

Count Alfred von Schlieffen, Chief of the German General Staff from 1891 to 1906 was, like all German officers, schooled in Clausewitz's precept, "The heart of France lies between Brussels and Paris." It was a frustrating axiom because the path it pointed to was forbidden by Belgian neutrality, which Germany, along with the other four major European powers, had guaranteed in perpetuity. Believing that war was a certainty and that Germany must enter it under conditions that gave her the most promise of success, Schlieffen determined not to allow the Belgian difficulty to stand in Germany's way. Of the two classes of Prussian officer, the bullnecked and the wasp-waisted, he belonged to the second. Monocled and effete in appearance, cold and distant in manner, he concentrated with such single-mindedness on his profession that when an aide, at the end of an all-night staff ride in East Prussia, pointed out to him the beauty of the river Pregel sparkling in the rising sun the General gave a brief, hard look and replied, "An unimportant obstacle." So too, he decided, was Belgian neutrality.

The Belgian Question

A neutral and independent Belgium was the creation of England, or rather of England's ablest foreign minister, Lord Palmerston. Belgium's coast was England's frontier; on the plains of Belgium, Wellington had defeated the greatest threat to England since the Armada. Thereafter England was determined to make that patch of open, easily traversable territory a neutral zone and, under the post-Napoleon settlement of the Congress of Vienna, agreed with the other powers to attach it to the Kingdom of the Netherlands. Resenting union with a Protestant power, burning with the fever of the nineteenth-century nationalism, the Belgians revolted in 1830, setting off an international scramble. The Dutch fought to retain their province; the French, eager to reabsorb what they had once ruled, moved in; the autocratic states—Russia, Prussia, and Austria—bent on keeping Europe clamped under the vise of Vienna, were ready to shoot at the first sign of revolt anywhere.

Lord Palmerston outmaneuvered them all. He knew that a subject province would be an eternal temptation to one neighbor or another and that only an independent nation, resolved to maintain its own integrity, could survive as a safety zone. Through nine years of nerve, of suppleness, of never swerving from his aim, of calling out the British fleet when necessary, he played off all contenders and secured an international treaty guaranteeing Belgium as an "independent and perpetually neutral state." The treaty was signed in 1839 by England, France, Russia, Prussia, and Austria.

Ever since 1892, when France and Russia had joined in military alliance, it was clear that four of the five signatories of the Belgian treaty would be automatically engaged—two against two—in the war for which Schlieffen had to plan. Europe was a heap of swords piled as delicately as jackstraws; one could not be pulled out without moving the others. Under the terms of the Austro-German alliance, Germany was obliged to support Austria in any conflict with Russia. Under the terms of the alliance between France and Russia, both parties were obliged to move against Germany if either became involved in a "defensive war" with Germany. These arrangements made it inevitable that in any war in which she engaged, Germany would have to fight on two fronts against both Russia and France.

[†]**Source:** Reprinted with permission of Macmillan Publishing Company and Russell & Volkening, as agents for the author, from *The Guns of August* by Barbara W. Tuchman. Copyright ©1962 by Barbara W. Tuchman. Copyright renewed in 1990 by Barbara W. Tuchman. Subheadings inserted by James Brian Quinn to aid students.

What part England would play was uncertain; she might remain neutral; she might, if given cause, come in against Germany. That Belgium could be the cause was no secret. In Franco-Prussian War of 1870, when Germany was still a climbing power, Bismarck had been happy enough, upon a hint from England, to reaffirm the inviolability of Belgium. Gladstone had secured a treaty from both belligerents providing that if either violated Belgian neutrality, England would cooperate with the other to the extent of defending Belgium, though without engaging in the general operations of the war. Although there was something a little impractical about the tail of this Gladstonian formula, the Germans had no reason to suppose its underlying motive any less operative in 1914 than in 1870. Nevertheless, Schlieffen decided, in the event of war, to attack France by way of Belgium.

France First

His reason was "military necessity." In a two-front war, he wrote, "the whole of Germany must throw itself upon *one* enemy, the strongest, most powerful, most dangerous enemy, and that can only be France." Schlieffen's completed plan for 1906, the year he retired, allocated six weeks and seven-eighths of Germany's forces to smash France while one-eighth was to hold her eastern frontier against Russia until the bulk of her army could be brought back to face the second enemy. He chose France first because Russia could frustrate a quick victory by simply withdrawing within her infinite room, leaving Germany to be sucked into an endless campaign as Napoleon had been. France was both closer at hand and quicker to mobilize. The German and French armies each required two weeks to complete mobilization before a major attack could begin on the fifteenth day. Russia, according to German arithmetic, because of her vast distances, huge numbers, and meager railroads, would take six weeks before she could launch a major offensive, by which time France would be beaten.

The risk of leaving East Prussia, hearth of Junkerdom and the Hohenzollerns, to be held by only nine divisions was hard to accept, but Frederick the Great had said, "It is better to lose a province than split the forces with which one seeks victory," and nothing so comforts the military mind as the maxim of a great but dead general. Only by throwing the utmost numbers against the West could France be finished off quickly. Only by a strategy of envelopment, using Belgium as a pathway, could the German armies, in Schlieffen's opinion, attack France

successfully. His reasoning, from the purely military point of view, appeared faultless.

The German Army of a million and a half that was to be used against France was now six times the size it had been in 1870, and needed room to maneuver. French fortresses constructed along the frontiers of Alsace and Lorraine after 1870 precluded the Germans from making a frontal attack across the common border. A protracted siege would provide no opportunity, as long as French lines to the rear remained open, of netting the enemy quickly in a battle of annihilation. Only by envelopment could the French be taken from behind and destroyed. But at either end of the French lines lay neutral territory—Switzerland and Belgium. There was not enough room for the huge German Army to get around the French armies and still stay inside France. The Germans had done it in 1870 when both armies were small, but now it was a matter of moving an army of millions to outflank an army of millions. Space, roads, and railroads were essential. The flat plains of Flanders had them. In Belgium there was both room for the outflanking maneuver which was Schlieffen's formula for success as well as a way to avoid the frontal attack which was his formula for disaster.

Clausewitz, oracle of German military thought, had ordained a quick victory by "decisive battle" as the first object in offensive war. Occupation of the enemy's territory and gaining control of his resources was secondary. To speed an early decision was essential. Time counted above all else. Anything that protracted a campaign Clausewitz condemned. "Gradual reduction" of the enemy, or a war of attrition, he feared like the pit of hell. He wrote in the decade of Waterloo, and his works had been accepted as the Bible of strategy ever since.

The New Cannae

To achieve decisive victory, Schlieffen fixed upon a strategy derived from Hannibal and the Battle of Cannae. The dead general who mesmerized Schlieffen had been dead a very long time. Two thousand years had passed since Hannibal's classic double envelopment of the Romans at Cannae. Field gun and machine gun had replaced bow and arrow and slingshot, Schlieffen wrote, "but the principles of strategy remain unchanged. The enemy's front is not the objective. The essential thing is to crush the enemy's flanks . . . and complete the extermination by attack upon his rear." Under Schlieffen, envelopment became the fetish and frontal attack the anathema of the German General Staff.

Schlieffen's first plan to include the violation of Belgium was formulated in 1899. It called for cutting across the corner of Belgium east of the Meuse. Enlarged with each successive year, by 1905 it had expanded into a huge enveloping right wing sweep in which the German armies would cross Belgium from Liège to Brussel before turning southward, where they could take advantage of the open country of Flanders, to march against France. Everything depended upon a quick decision against France, and even the long way around through Flanders would be quicker than laying siege to the fortress line across the common border.

Schlieffen did not have enough divisions for a double envelopment of France à la Cannae. For this he substituted a heavily one-sided right wing that would spread across the whole of Belgium on both sides of the Meuse, sweep down through the country like a monstrous hayrake, cross the Franco-Belgian frontier along its entire width, and descend upon Paris along the Valley of the Oise. The German mass would come between the capital and the French armies which, drawn back to meet the menace, would be caught, away from their fortified areas, in the decisive battle of annihilation. Essential to the plan was a deliberately weak German left wing on the Alsace-Lorraine front which would tempt the French in that area forward into a "sack" between Metz and the Vosges. It was expected that the French, intent upon liberating their lost provinces, would attack here, and it was considered so much the better for the success of the German plan if they did, for they could be held in the sack by the German left wing while the main victory was obtained from behind. In the back of Schlieffen's mind always glimmered the hope that, as battle unfolded, a counterattack by his left wing could be mounted in order to bring about a true double envelopment—the "colossal Cannae" of his dreams. Sternly saving his greatest strength for the right wing, he did not yield to that vaulting ambition in his plan. But the lure of the left wing remained to tempt his successors.

Thus the Germans came to Belgium. Decisive battle dictated envelopment, and envelopment dictated the use of Belgian territory. The German General Staff pronounced it a military necessity; Kaiser and Chancellor accepted it with more or less equanimity. Whether it was advisable, whether it was even expedient in view of the probable effect on world opinion, especially on neutral opinion, was irrelevant. That it seemed necessary to the triumph of German arms was the only criterion. Germans had imbibed from 1870 the lesson that arms and war were the sole source of German greatness. They had been taught by Field Marshal von der Goltz, in his book *The Nation in Arms*, that "We have won our position through the sharpness of our sword, not through the sharpness of our mind." The decision to violate Belgian neutrality followed easily.

National Character

Character is fate, the Greeks believed. A hundred years of German philosophy went into the making of this decision in which the seed of self-destruction lay embedded, waiting for its hour. The voice was Schlieffen's, but the hand was the hand of Fichte who saw the German people chosen by Providence to occupy the supreme place in the history of the universe, of Hegel who saw them leading the world to a glorious destiny of compulsory *Kultur*, of Nietzsche who told them that Supermen were above ordinary controls, of Treitschke who set the increase of power as the highest moral duty of the state, of the whole German people, who called their temporal ruler the "All-Highest." What made the Schlieffen plan was not Clausewitz and the Battle of Cannae, but the body of accumulated egoism which suckled the German people and created a nation fed on "the desperate delusion of the will that deems itself absolute."

The goal, decisive battle, was a product of the victories over Austria and France in 1866 and 1870. Dead battles, like dead generals, hold the military mind in their dead grip, and Germans, no less than other peoples, prepare for the last war. They staked everything on decisive battle in the image of Hannibal, but even the ghost of Hannibal might have reminded Schlieffen that though Carthage won at Cannae, Rome won the war.

Old Field Marshal Moltke in 1890 foretold that the next war might last seven years—or thirty—because the resources of a modern state were so great it would not know itself to be beaten after a single military defeat and would not give up. His nephew and namesake who succeeded Schlieffen as Chief of Staff also had moments when he saw the truth as clearly. In a moment of heresy to Clausewitz, he said to the Kaiser in 1906, "It will be a national war which will not be settled by a decisive battle but by a long wearisome struggle with a country that will not be overcome until its whole national force is broken, and a war which will utterly exhaust our own people, even if we are victorious." It went against human nature, however—and the nature of General Staffs—to follow through the logic of his own prophecy.

Amorphous and without limits, the concept of a long war could not be scientifically planned for as could the orthodox, predictable, and simple solution of decisive battle and a short war. The younger Moltke was already Chief of Staff when he made his prophecy, but neither he nor his Staff, nor the Staff of any other country, ever made any effort to plan for a long war. Besides the two Moltkes, one dead and the other infirm of purpose, some military strategists in other countries glimpsed the possibility of prolonged war, but all preferred to believe, along with the bankers and industrialists, that because of the dislocation of economic life a general European war could not last longer than three or four months. One constant among the elements of 1914—as of any era—was the disposition of everyone on all sides not to prepare for the harder alternative, not to act upon what they suspected to be true.

Schlieffen, having embraced the strategy of "decisive battle," pinned Germany's fate to it. He expected France to violate Belgium as soon as Germany's deployment at the Belgian frontier revealed her strategy, and he therefore planned that Germany should do it first and faster. "Belgian neutrality must be broken by one side or the other," his thesis ran. "Whoever gets there first and occupies Brussels and imposes a war levy of some 1,000 million francs has the upper hand."

Indemnity, which enables a state to conduct war at the enemy's expense instead of its own, was a secondary object laid down by Clausewitz. His third was the winning of public opinion, which is accomplished by "gaining great victories and possession of the enemy's capital" and which helps to bring an end to resistance. He knew how material success could gain public opinion; he forgot how moral failure could lose it, which too can be a hazard of war.

It was a hazard the French never lost sight of, and it led them to the opposite conclusion from the one Schlieffen expected. Belgium was their pathway of attack too, through the Ardennes if not through Flanders, but their plan of campaign prohibited their armies from using it until after the Germans had violated Belgium first. To them the logic of the matter was clear: Belgium was an open path in either direction; whether Germany or France would use it depended on which of the two wanted war the more. As a French general said, 'The one that willed war more than the other could not help but will the violation of Belgian neutrality."

Schlieffen and his Staff did not think Belgium would fight and add its six divisions to the French forces. When Chancellor Bülow, discussing the problem with Schlieffen in 1904, reminded him of Bismarck's warning that it would be against "plain common sense" to add another enemy to the forces against Germany, Schlieffen twisted his monocle several times in his eye, as was his habit, and said: "Of course. We haven't grown stupider since then." But Belgium would not resist by force of arms; she would be satisfied to protest, he said.

German confidence on this score was due to placing rather too high a value on the well-known avarice of Leopold II, who was King of the Belgians in Schlieffen's time. Tall and imposing with his black spade beard and his aura of wickedness composed of mistresses, money, Congo cruelties, and other scandals, Leopold was, in the opinion of Emperor Franz Josef of Austria, "a thoroughly bad man." There were few men who could be so described, the Emperor said, but the King of the Belgians was one. Because Leopold was avaricious, among other vices, the Kaiser supposed that avarice would rule over common sense, and he conceived a clever plan to tempt Leopold into [an] alliance with an offer of French territory. Whenever the Kaiser was seized with a project he attempted instantly to execute it, usually to his astonishment and chagrin when it did not work. In 1904 he invited Leopold to visit him in Berlin, spoke to him in "the kindest way in the world" about his proud forefathers, the Dukes of Burgundy, and offered to re-create the old Duchy of Burgundy for him out of Artois, French Flanders, and the French Ardennes. Leopold gazed at him "openmouthed," then, attempting to pass it off with a laugh, reminded the Kaiser that much had changed since the fifteenth century. In any event, he said, his ministers and Parliament would never consider such a suggestion.

That was the wrong thing to say, for the Kaiser flew into one of his rages and scolded the King for putting respect for Parliament and ministers above respect for the finger of God (with which William sometimes confused himself). "I told him," William reported to Chancellor von Bülow, "I could not be played with. Whoever in the case of a European war was not with me was against me." He was a soldier, he proclaimed, in the school of Napoleon and Frederick the Great who began their wars by forestalling their enemies, and "so should I, in the event of Belgium's not being on my side, be actuated by strategical considerations only."

This declared intent, the first explicit threat to tear up the treaty, dumbfounded King Leopold. He drove off to the station with his helmet on back to front, looking to the aide who accompanied him "as if he had had a shock of some kind."

Although the Kaiser's scheme failed, Leopold was still expected to barter Belgium's neutrality for a purse of two million pounds sterling. When a French intelligence officer, who was told this figure by a German officer after the war, expressed surprise at its generosity, he was reminded that "the French would have had to pay for it." Even after Leopold was succeeded in 1909 by his nephew King Albert, a very different quantity, Belgium's resistance was still expected by Schlieffen's successors to be a formality. It might, for example, suggested a German diplomat in 1911, take the form of "lining up her army along the road taken by the German forces."

"Brush the Channel"

Schlieffen designated thirty-four divisions to take the roads through Belgium, disposing on their way of Belgium's six divisions if, as seemed to the Germans unlikely, they chose to resist. The Germans were intensely anxious that they should not, because resistance would mean destruction of railways and bridges and consequent dislocation of the schedule to which the German Staff was passionately attached. Belgian acquiescence, on the other hand, would avoid the necessity of tying up divisions in siege of the Belgian fortresses and would also tend to silence public disapproval of Germany's act. To persuade Belgium against futile resistance, Schlieffen arranged that she should be confronted, prior to invasion, by an ultimatum requiring her to yield "all fortresses, railways and troops" or face bombardment of her fortified cities. Heavy artillery was ready to transform the threat of bombardment into reality, if necessary. The heavy guns would in any case, Schlieffen wrote in 1912, be needed further on in the campaign. "The great industrial town of Lille, for example, offers an excellent target for bombardment."

Schlieffen wanted his right wing to reach as far west as Lille in order to make the envelopment of the French complete. "When you march into France," he said, "let the man on the right brush the Channel with his sleeve." Furthermore, counting on British belligerency, he wanted a wide sweep in order to rake in a British Expeditionary Force along with the French. He placed a higher value on the blockade potential of British sea power than on the British Army, and therefore was determined to achieve a quick victory over French and British land forces and an early decision of the war before the economic consequences of British hostility could make themselves felt. To that

end everything must go to swell the right wing. He had to make it powerful in numbers because the density of soldiers per mile determined the extent of territory that could be covered.

Employing the active army alone, he would not have enough divisions both to hold his eastern frontier against a Russian breakthrough and to achieve the superiority in numbers over France which he needed for a quick victory. His solution was simple if revolutionary. He decided to use reserve units in the front line. According to prevailing military doctrine, only the youngest men, fresh from the rigors and discipline of barracks and drill, were fit to fight; reserves who had finished their compulsory military service and returned to civilian life were considered soft and were not wanted in the battle line. Except for men under twenty-six who were merged with the active units, the reserves were formed into divisions of their own, intended for use as occupation troops and for other rear duty. Schlieffen changed all that. He added some twenty reserve divisions (the number varied according to the year of the plan) to the line of march of the fifty or more active divisions. With this increase in numbers his cherished envelopment became possible.

After retiring in 1906 he spent his last years still writing about Cannae, improving his plan, composing memoranda to guide his successors, and died at eighty in 1913, muttering at the end: "It must come to a fight. Only make the right wing strong."

Von Moltke

His successor, the melancholy General von Moltke, was something of a pessimist who lacked Schlieffen's readiness to concentrate all his strength in one maneuver. If Schlieffen's motto was "Be bold, be bold," Moltke's was, "But not too bold." He worried both about the weakness of his left wing against the French and about the weakness of the forces left to defend East Prussia against the Russians. He even debated with his Staff the advisability of fighting a defensive war against France, but rejected the idea because it precluded all possibility of "engaging the enemy on his own territory." The Staff agreed that the invasion of Belgium would be "entirely just and necessary" because the war would be one for the "defense and existence of Germany." Schlieffen's plan was maintained, and Moltke consoled himself with the thought, as he said in 1913, that "We must put aside all commonplaces as to the responsibility of the aggressor.... Success alone justifies war." But just to be safe everywhere, each year, cutting into Schlieffen's dying request, he borrowed strength from the right wing to add to the left.

Moltke planned for a German left wing of eight corps numbering about 320,000 men to hold the front in Alsace and Lorraine south of Metz. The German center of eleven corps numbering about 400,000 men would invade France through Luxembourg and the Ardennes. The German right wing of 16 corps numbering about 700,000 men would attack through Belgium, smash the famed gateway fortresses of Liège and Namur which held the Meuse, and fling itself across the river to reach the flat country and straight roads on the far side. Every day's schedule of march was fixed in advance. The Belgians were not expected to fight, but if they did the power of the German assault was expected to persuade them quickly to surrender. The schedule called for the roads through Liège to be open by the twelfth day of mobilization, Brussels to be taken by M-19, the French frontier crossed on M-22, a line Thionville-St. Quentin reached by M-31, Paris and decisive victory by M-39.

The plan of campaign was as rigid and complete as the blueprint for a battleship. Heeding Clausewitz's warning that military plans which leave no room for the unexpected can lead to disaster, the Germans with infinite care had attempted to provide for every contingency. Their staff officers, trained at maneuvers and at war-college desks to supply the correct solution for any given set of circumstances, were expected to cope with the unexpected. Against that elusive, that mocking and perilous quantity, every precaution had been taken except one—flexibility.

While the plan for maximum effort against France hardened, Moltke's fears of Russia gradually lessened as his General Staff evolved a credo, based on a careful count of Russian railway mileage, that Russia would not be "ready" for war until 1916. This was confirmed in German minds by their spies' reports of Russian remarks "that something was going to begin in 1916."

In 1914 two events sharpened Germany's readiness to a fine point. In April, England had begun naval talks with the Russians, and in June, Germany herself had completed the widening of the Kiel Canal, permitting her new dreadnoughts direct access from the North Sea to the Baltic. On learning of the Anglo-Russian talks, Moltke said in May during a visit to his Austrian opposite number, Franz Conrad von Hötzendorff, that from now on "any adjournment will have the effect of diminishing our chances of success." Two weeks later, on June 1, he said to Baron Eckhardstein, "We are ready, and the sooner the better for us."

The French View

General de Castelnau, Deputy Chief of the French General Staff, was visited at the War Office one day in 1913 by the Military Governor of Lille, General Lebas, who came to protest the General Staff's decision to abandon Lille as a fortified city. Situated ten miles from the Belgian border and forty miles inland from the Channel, Lille lay close to the path that an invading army would take if it came by way of Flanders. In answer to General Lebas' plea for its defense, General de Castelnau spread out a map and measured with a ruler the distance from the German border to Lille by way of Belgium. The normal density of troops required for a vigorous offensive, he reminded his caller, was five or six to a meter. If the Germans extended themselves as far west as Lille, de Castelnau pointed out, they would be stretched out two to a meter.

"We'll Cut Them in Half"

"We'll cut them in half!" he declared. The German active Army, he explained, could deploy some twenty-five corps, about a million men, on the Western Front. "Here, figure it out for yourself," he said, handling Lebas the ruler. "If they come as far as Lille," he repeated with sardonic satisfaction, "so much the better for us."

French strategy did not ignore the threat of envelopment by a German right wing. On the contrary, the French General Staff believed that the stronger the Germans made their right wing, the correspondingly weaker they would leave their center and left where the French Army planned to break through. French strategy turned its back to the Belgian frontier and its face to the Rhine. While the Germans were taking the long way around to fall upon the French flank, the French planned a two-pronged offensive that would smash through the German center and left on either side of the German fortified area at Metz and by victory there, sever the German right wing from its base, rendering it harmless. It was a bold plan born of an idea—an idea inherent in the recovery of France from the humiliation of Sedan.

The Shadow of Sedan

Under the peace terms dictated by Germany at Versailles in 1871, France had suffered amputation, indemnity, and occupation. Even a triumphal march by the German Army down the Champs Elysées was among the terms imposed. It took place along a silent, black-draped avenue empty of onlookers. At Bordeaux, when the French Assembly ratified the peace terms, the deputies of Alsace-Lorraine walked from the hall in tears, leaving behind their protest: "We proclaim forever the right of Alsatians and Lorrainers to remain members of the French nation. We swear for ourselves, our constituents, our children and our children's children to claim that right for all time, by every means, in the face of the usurper."

The annexation, though opposed by Bismarck, who said it would be the Achilles' heel of the new German Empire, was required by the elder Moltke and his Staff. They insisted, and convinced the Emperor, that the border provinces with Metz, Strasbourg, and the crest of the Vosges must be sliced off in order to put France geographically forever on the defensive. They added a crushing indemnity of five billion francs intended to hobble France for a generation, and lodged an army of occupation until it should be paid. With one enormous effort the French raised and paid off the sum within three years, and their recovery began.

The memory of Sedan remained, a stationary dark shadow on the French consciousness. "*N'en parlez jamais; pensez-y toujours*"(Never speak of it; think of it always) had counseled Gambetta. For more than forty years the thought of "Again" was the single most fundamental factor of French policy. In the early years after 1870, instinct and military weakness dictated a fortress strategy. France walled herself in behind a system of entrenched camps connected by forts. Two fortified lines, Belfort-Epinal and Toul-Verdun, guarded the eastern frontier, and one, Maubeuge-Valenciennes-Lille, guarded the western half of the Belgian frontier; the gaps between were intended to canalize the invasion forces.

Behind her wall, as Victor Hugo urged at his most vibrant: "France will have but one thought: to reconstitute her forces, gather her energy, nourish her sacred anger, raise her young generation to form an army of the whole people, to work without cease, to study the methods and skills of our enemies, to become again a great France, the France of 1792, the France of an idea with a sword. Then one day she will be irresistible. Then she will take back Alsace-Lorraine."

Through returning prosperity and growing empire, through the perennial civil quarrels—royalism, Boulangism, clericalism, strikes, and the culminating, devastating Dreyfus Affair—the sacred anger still glowed, especially in the army. The one thing that held together all elements of the army, whether old guard or republican, Jesuit or Freemason, was the *mystique*

d'Alsace. The eyes of all were fixed on the blue line of the Vosges. A captain of infantry confessed in 1912 that he used to lead the men of his company in secret patrols of two or three through the dark pines to the mountaintops where they could gaze down on Colmar. "On our return from those clandestine expeditions our columns reformed, choked and dumb with emotion."

Originally neither German nor French, Alsace had been snatched back and forth between the two until, under Louis XIV, it was confirmed to France by the Treaty of Westphalia in 1648. After Germany annexed Alsace and part of Lorraine in 1870 Bismarck advised giving the inhabitants as much autonomy as possible and encouraging their particularism, for, he said, the more Alsatian they felt, the less they would feel French. His successors did not see the necessity. They took no account of the wishes of their new subjects, made no effort to win them over, administered the provinces as *Reichsland*, or "Imperial territory," under German officials on virtually the same terms as their African colonies, and succeeded only in infuriating and alienating the population until in 1911 a constitution was granted them. By then it was too late. German rule exploded in the Zabern Affair in 1913 which began, after an exchange of insults between townspeople and garrison, when a German officer struck a crippled shoemaker with his saber. It ended in the complete and public exposure of German policy in the *Reichsland*, in a surge of anti-German feeling in world opinion, and in the simultaneous triumph of militarism in Berlin where the officer of Zabern became a hero, congratulated by the Crown Prince.

For Germany 1870 was not a final settlement. The German day in Europe which they thought had dawned when the German Empire was proclaimed in the Hall of Mirrors at Versailles was still postponed. France was not crushed; the French Empire was actually expanding in North Africa and Indo-China; the world of art and beauty and style still worshiped at the feet of Paris. Germans were still gnawed by envy of the country they had conquered. "As well off as God in France," was a German saying. At the same time they considered France decadent in culture and enfeebled by democracy. "It is impossible for a country that has had forty-two war ministers in forty-three years to fight effectively," announced Professor Hans Delbrück, Germany's leading historian. Believing themselves superior in soul, in strength, in energy, industry, and national virtue, Germans felt they deserved the dominion of Europe. The work of Sedan must be completed.

"Élan Vital"

Living in the shadow of that unfinished business, France, reviving in spirit and strength, grew weary of being eternally on guard, eternally exhorted by her leaders to defend herself. As the century turned, her spirit rebelled against thirty years of the defensive with its implied avowal of inferiority. France knew herself to be physically weaker than Germany. Her population was less, her birth rate lower. She needed some weapon that Germany lacked to give herself confidence in her survival. The "idea with a sword" fulfilled the need. Expressed by Bergson it was called *élan vital*, the all-conquering will. Belief in its power convinced France that the human spirit need not, after all, bow to the predestined forces of evolution which Schopenhauer and Hegel had declared to be irresistible. The spirit of France would be the equalizing factor. Her will to win, her *élan*, would enable France to defeat her enemy. Her genius was in her spirit, the spirit of *la gloire*, of 1792, of the incomparable "Marseillaise," the spirit of General Margueritte's heroic cavalry charge before Sedan when even Wilhelm I, watching the battle, could not forbear to cry, "*Oh, les braves gens!*"

Belief in the fervor of France, in the *furor Gallicae*, revived France's faith in herself in the generation after 1870. It was that fervor, unfurling her banners, sounding her bugles, arming her soldiers, that would lead France to victory if the day of "Again" should come.

Translated into military terms Bergson's *élan vital* became the doctrine of the offensive. In proportion as a defensive gave way to an offensive strategy, the attention paid to the Belgian frontier gradually gave way in favor of a progressive shift of gravity eastward toward the point where a French offensive could be launched to break through to the Rhine. For the Germans the roundabout road through Flanders led to Paris; for the French it led nowhere. They could only get to Berlin by the shortest way. The more the thinking of the French General Staff approached the offensive, the greater the forces it concentrated at the attacking point and the fewer it left to defend the Belgian frontier.

The doctrine of the offensive had its fount in the Ecole Supérieure de la Guerre, or War College, the ark of the army's intellectual elite, whose director, General Ferdinand Foch, was the molder of French military theory of his time. Foch's mind, like a heart, contained two valves: one pumped spirit into strategy; the other circulated common sense. On the one hand Foch preached a *mystique* of will expressed in his famous aphorisms, "The will to conquer is the first condition of victory," or more succinctly, "*Victoire c'est la volonté,*" and, "A battle won is a battle in which one will not confess oneself beaten."

In practice this was to become the famous order at the Marne to attack when the situation called for retreat. His officers of those days remember him bellowing "Attack! Attack!" with furious, sweeping gestures while he dashed about in short rushes as if charged by an electric battery. Why, he was later asked, did he advance at the Marne when he was technically beaten? "Why? I don't know. Because of my men, because I had a will. And then—God was there."

Though a profound student of Clausewitz, Foch did not, like Clausewitz's German successors, believe in a foolproof schedule of battle worked out in advance. Rather he taught the necessity of perpetual adaptability and improvisation to fit circumstances. "Regulations," he would say, "are all very well for drill but in the hour of danger they are no more use.... You have to learn to think." To think meant to give room for freedom of initiative, for the imponderable to win over the material, for will to demonstrate its power over circumstance.

But the idea that morale alone could conquer, Foch warned, was an "infantile notion." From his flights of metaphysics he would descend at once, in his lectures and his prewar books *Les Principes de la Guerre* and *La Conduite de la Guerre*, to the earth of tactics, the placing of advance guards, the necessity of *sureté*, or protection, the elements of firepower, the need for obedience and discipline. The realistic half of his teaching was summed up in another aphorism he made familiar during the war, "*De quoi s'agit-il?*" (What is the essence of the problem?)

Eloquent as he was on tactics, it was Foch's *mystique* of will that captured the minds of his followers. Once in 1908 when Clemenceau was considering Foch, then a professor, for the post of Director of the War College, a private agent whom he sent to listen to the lectures reported back in bewilderment, "This officer teaches metaphysics so abstruse as to make idiots of his pupils." Although Clemenceau appointed Foch in spite of it, there was, in one sense, truth in the report. Foch's principles, not because they were too abstruse but because they were too attractive, laid a trap for France. They were taken up with particular enthusiasm by Colonel Grandmaison, "an ardent and brilliant officer" who was Director of the Troisième Bureau, or Bureau of Military Operations, and who in 1911 delivered two lectures at the War College which had a crystallizing effect.

"Offensive à Outrance"

Colonel Grandmaison grasped only the head and not the feet of Foch's principles. Expounding their *élan* without their *sureté*, he expressed a military philosophy that electrified his audience. He waved before their dazzled eyes an "idea with a sword" which showed them how France could win. Its essence was the *offensive à outrance*, offensive to the limit. Only this could achieve Clausewitz's decisive battle which "exploited to the finish, is the essential act of war" and which "once engaged, must be pushed to the end, with no second thoughts, up to the extremes of human endurance." Seizure of initiative is the *sine qua non*. Preconceived arrangements based on a dogmatic judgment of what the enemy will do are premature. Liberty of action is achieved only by imposing one's will upon the enemy. "All command decisions must be inspired by the will to seize and retain the initiative." The defensive is forgotten, abandoned, discarded; its only possible justification is an occasional "economizing of forces at certain points with a view to adding them to the attack."

The effect on the General Staff was profound, and during the next two years was embodied in new Field Regulations for the conduct of war and in a new plan of campaign called Plan 17, which was adopted in May, 1913. Within a few months of Grandmaison's lectures, the President of the Republic, M. Fallières, announced: "The offensive alone is suited to the temperament of French soldiers.... We are determined to march straight against the enemy without hesitation."

The new Field Regulations, enacted by the government in October, 1913, as the fundamental document for the training and conduct of the French Army, opened with a flourish of trumpets: "The French Army, returning to its tradition, henceforth admits no law but the offensive." Eight commandments followed, ringing with the clash of "decisive battle," "offensive without hesitation," "fierceness and tenacity," "breaking the will of the adversary," "ruthless and tireless pursuit." With all the ardor of orthodoxy stamping out heresy, the Regulations stamped upon and discarded the defensive. "The offensive alone," it proclaimed, "leads to positive results." Its Seventh Commandment, italicized by the authors, stated: *Battles are beyond everything else struggles of morale. Defeat is inevitable as soon as the hope of conquering ceases to exist. Success comes not to him who has suffered the least but to him whose will is firmest and morale strongest.*

Nowhere in the eight commandments was there mention of matériel or firepower or what Foch called sureté. The teaching of the Regulations became epitomized in the favorite word of the French officer corps, le cran, nerve, or less politely, guts. Like the youth who set out for the mountaintop under the banner marked "Excelsior!" the French Army marched to war in 1914 under a banner marked "*Cran.*"

Over the years, while French military philosophy had changed, French geography had not. The geographical facts of her frontiers remained what Germany had made them in 1870. Germany's territorial demands, William I had explained to the protesting Empress Eugénie, "have no aim other than to push back the starting point from which French armies could in the future attack us." They also pushed forward the starting point from which Germany could attack France. While French history and development after the turn of the century fixed her mind upon the offensive, her geography still required a strategy of the defensive.

General Michel

In 1911, the same year as Colonel Grandmaison's lectures, a last effort to commit France to a strategy of the defensive was made in the Supreme War Council by no less a personage than the Commander in Chief designate, General Michel. As Vice President of the Council, a post which carried with it the position of Commander in Chief in the event of war, General Michel was then the ranking officer in the army. In a report that precisely reflected Schlieffen's thinking, he submitted his estimate of the probable German line of attack and his proposals for countering it. Because of the natural escarpments and French fortifications along the common border with Germany, he argued, the Germans could not hope to win a prompt decisive battle in Lorraine. Nor would the passage through Luxembourg and the near corner of Belgium east of the Meuse give them sufficient room for their favored strategy of envelopment. Only by taking advantage of "the whole of Belgium," he said, could the Germans achieve that "immediate, brutal and decisive" offensive which they must launch upon France before the forces of her Allies could come into play. He pointed out that the Germans had long yearned for Belgium's great port of Antwerp, and this gave them an additional reason for an attack through Flanders. He proposed to face the Germans along a line Verdun-Namur-Antwerp with a French army of a million men whose left wing—like Schlieffen's right—should brush the Channel with its sleeve.

Not only was General Michel's plan defensive in character, it also depended upon a proposal that was anathema to his fellow officers. To match the numbers he believed the Germans would send through Belgium, General Michel proposed to double French front-line effectives by attaching a regiment of reserves to every active regiment. Had he proposed to admit Mistinguette to the Immortals of the French Academy, he could hardly have raised more clamor and disgust.

"Les réserves, c'est zéro!" was the classic dogma of the French officer corps. Men who had finished their compulsory training under universal service and were between the ages of twenty-three and thirty-four were classed as reserves. Upon mobilization the youngest classes filled out the regular army units to war strength; the others were formed into reserve regiments, brigades, and divisions according to their local geographical districts. These were considered fit only for rear duty or for use as fortress troops, and incapable, because of their lack of trained officers and NCOs, of being attached to the fighting regiments. The regular army's contempt for the reserves, in which it was joined by the parties of the right, was augmented by dislike of the principle of the "nation in arms." To merge the reserves with the active divisions would be to put a drag on the army's fighting thrust. Only the active army, they believed, could be depended upon to defend the country.

The left parties, on the other hand, with memories of General Boulanger on horseback, associated the army with *coups d'état* and believed in the principle of a "nation in arms" as the only safeguard of the Republic. They maintained that a few months' training would fit any citizen for war, and violently opposed the increase of military service to three years. The army demanded this reform in 1913 not only to match an increase in the German Army but also because the more men who were in training at any one time, the less reliance needed to be placed on reserve units. After angry debate, with bitterly divisive effect on the country, the Three-Year Law was enacted in August, 1913.

Disdain of the reserves was augmented by the new doctrine of the offensive which, it was felt, could only be properly inculcated in active troops. To perform the irresistible onslaught of the *attaque brusquée*, symbolized by the bayonet charge, the essential quality was *élan*, and *élan* could not be expected of men settled in civilian life with family responsibilities. Reserves mixed with active troops would create "armies of decadence," incapable of the will to conquer.

Similar sentiments were known to be held across the Rhine. The Kaiser was widely credited with the edict "No fathers of families at the front." Among the French General Staff it was an article of faith that the Germans would not mix reserve units with active units, and this led to the belief that the Germans would not have enough men in the front line to do two things at once: send a strong right wing in a wide sweep through Belgium west of the Meuse and keep sufficient forces at their center and left to stop a French breakthrough to the Rhine.

When General Michel presented his plan, the minister of war, Messimy, treated it *"comme une insanité."* As chairman of the Supreme War Council he not only attempted to suppress it but at once consulted other members of the council on the advisability of removing Michel.

Messimy, an exuberant, energetic, almost violent man with a thick neck, round head, bright peasant's eyes behind spectacles, and a loud voice, was a former career officer. In 1899 as a thirty-year-old captain of Chasseurs, he had resigned from the army in protest against its refusal to reopen the Dreyfus case. In that heated time the officer corps insisted as a body that to admit the possibility of Dreyfus's innocence after his conviction would be to destroy the army's prestige and infallibility. Unable to put loyalty to the army above justice, Messimy determined upon a political career with the declared goal of "reconciling the army with the nation." He swept into the War Ministry with a passion for improvement. Finding a number of generals "incapable not only of leading their troops but even of following them," he adopted Theodore Roosevelt's expedient of ordering all generals to conduct maneuvers on horseback. When this provoked protests that old so-and-so would be forced to retire from the army Messimy replied that that was indeed his object. He had been named War Minister on June 30, 1911, after a succession of four ministers in four months and the next day was met by the attack of the German gunboat *Panther* on Agadir precipitating the second Moroccan crisis. Expecting mobilization at any moment, Messimy discovered the generalissimo-designate, General Michel, to be "hesitant, indecisive and crushed by the weight of the duty that might at any moment devolve upon him." In his present post Messimy believed he represented a "national danger." Michel's "insane" proposal provided the excuse to get rid of him.

Michel, however, refused to go without first having his plan presented to the Council whose members included the foremost generals of France: Gallieni, the great colonial; Pau, the one-armed veteran of 1870; Joffre, the silent engineer; Dubail, the pattern of gallantry, who wore his kepi cocked over one eye with the *"chic exquis"* of the Second Empire. All were to hold active commands in 1914 and two were to become Marshals of France. None gave Michel's plan his support. One officer from the War Ministry who was present at the meeting said: "There is no use discussing it. General Michel is off his head."

Whether or not this verdict represented the views of all present—Michel later claimed that General Dubail, for one, had originally agreed with him—Messimy, who made no secret of his hostility, carried the Council with him. A trick of fate arranged that Messimy should be a forceful character and Michel should not. To be right and overruled is not forgiven to persons in responsible positions, and Michel duly paid for his clairvoyance. Relieved of his command, he was appointed Military Governor of Paris where in a crucial hour in the coming test he was indeed to prove "hesitant and indecisive."

Messimy having fervently stamped out Michel's heresy of the defensive, did his best, as War Minister, to equip the army to fight a successful offensive but was in his turn frustrated in his most-cherished prospect—the need to reform the French uniform. The British had adopted khaki after the Boer War, and the Germans were about to make the change from Prussian blue to field-gray. But in 1912 French soldiers still wore the same blue coats, red kepi, and red trousers they had worn in 1830 when rifle fire carried only two hundred paces and when armies, fighting at these close quarters, had no need for concealment. Visiting the Balkan front in 1912, Messimy saw the advantages gained by the dull-colored Bulgarians and came home determined to make the French soldier less visible. His project to clothe him in gray-blue or gray-green raised a howl of protest. Army pride was as intransigent about giving up its red trousers as it was about adopting heavy guns. Army prestige was once again felt to be at stake. To clothe the French soldier in some muddy, inglorious color, declared the army's champions, would be to realize the fondest hopes of Dreyfusards and Freemasons. To banish "all that is colorful, all that gives the soldier his vivid aspect," wrote the *Echo de Paris*, "is to go contrary both to French taste and military function." Messimy pointed out that the two might no longer be synonymous, but his opponents proved immovable. At a parliamentary hearing a former War Minister, M. Etienne, spoke for France.

"Eliminate the red trousers?" he cried. "Never! *Le pantalon rouge c'est la France!*"

"That blind and imbecile attachment to the most visible of all colors," wrote Messimy afterward, "was to have cruel consequences."

In the meantime, still in the midst of the Agadir crisis, he had to name a new prospective generalissimo in place of Michel. He planned to give added authority to the post by combining with it that of Chief of the General Staff and by abolishing the post of Chief of Staff to the War Ministry, currently held by General Dubail. Michel's successor would have all the reins of power concentrated in his hands.

Messimy's first choice was the austere and brilliant general in *pince-nez*, Gallieni, who refused it because, he explained, having been instrumental in Michel's dismissal he felt scruples about replacing him. Furthermore he had only two years to go before retirement at sixty-four, and he believed the appointment of a "colonial" would be resented by the Metropolitan Army—"*une question de bouton*," he said, tapping his insignia. General Pau, who was next in line, made it a condition that he be allowed to name generals of his own choice to the higher commands which, as he was known for his reactionary opinions, threatened to wake the barely slumbering feud between rightist army and republican nation. Respecting him for his honesty, the government refused his condition. Messimy consulted Gallieni, who suggested his former subordinate in Madagascar, "a cool and methodical worker with a lucid and precise mind." Accordingly the post was offered to General Joseph-Jacques-Césaire Joffre, then aged fifty-nine, formerly chief of the Engineer Corps and presently Chief of the Services of the Rear.

Massive and paunchy in his baggy uniform, with a fleshy face adorned by a heavy, nearly white mustache and bushy eyebrows to match, with a clear youthful skin, calm blue eyes and a candid, tranquil gaze, Joffre looked like Santa Claus and gave an impression of benevolence and *naïveté*—two qualities not noticeably part of his character. He did not come of a gentleman's family, was not a graduate of St. Cyr (but of the less aristocratic if more scientific Ecole Polytechnique), had not passed through the higher training of the War College. As an officer of the Engineer Corps, which dealt with such unromantic matters as fortifications and railways, he belonged to a branch of the service not drawn upon for the higher commands. He was the eldest of the eleven children of a petit bourgeois manufacturer of wine barrels in the French Pyrénées. His military career had been marked by quiet accomplishment and efficiency in each post he filled: as company commander in Formosa and Indo-China, as a major in the Sudan and Timbuktu, as staff officer in the Railway Section of the War Ministry, as lecturer at the

Artillery School, as fortifications officer under Gallieni in Madagascar from 1900 to 1905, as general of a division in 1905, of a corps in 1908, and as Director of the Rear and member of the War Council since 1910.

General Joffre

He had no known clerical, monarchist, or other disturbing connections; he had been out of the country during the Dreyfus Affair; his reputation as a good republican was as smooth as his well-manicured hands; he was solid and utterly phlegmatic. His outstanding characteristic was a habitual silence that in other men would have seemed self-deprecatory but, worn like an aura over Joffre's great, calm bulk, inspired confidence. He had still five years to go before retirement.

Joffre was conscious of one lack: he had had no training in the rarefied realms of staff work. On a hot July day when doors in the War Ministry on the Rue St. Dominique were left open, officers glancing out of their rooms saw General Pau holding Joffre by a button of his uniform. "Take it, *cher ami*," he was saying. "We will give you Castelnau. He knows all about staff work—everything will go of itself."

Castelnau, who was a graduate both of St. Cyr and of the War College, came, like D'Artagnan, from Gascony, which is said to produce men of hot blood and cold brain. He suffered from the disadvantage of family connections with a marquis, of associating with Jesuits, and of a personal Catholicism which he practiced so vigorously as to earn him during the war the name of *le capucin botté*, the Monk in Boots. He had, however, long experience on the General Staff. Joffre would have preferred Foch but knew Messimy to have an unexplained prejudice against him. As was his habit, he listened without comment to Pau's advice, and promptly took it.

"Aye!" complained Messimy when Joffre asked for Castelnau as his Deputy Chief. "You will rouse a storm in the parties of the left and make yourself a lot of enemies." However, with the assent of the President and Premier who "made a face" at the condition but agreed, both appointments were put through together. A fellow general, pursuing some personal intrigue warned Joffre that Castelnau might displace him. "Get rid of me! Not Castelnau," Joffre replied, unruffled. "I need him for six months; then I'll give him a corps command." As it proved, he found Castelnau invaluable, and when war came gave him command of an army instead of a corps.

Joffre's supreme confidence in himself was expressed in the following year when his aide, Major Alexandre, asked him if he thought war was shortly to be expected.

"Certainly I think so," Joffre replied. "I have always thought so. It will come. I shall fight it and I shall win. I have always succeeded in whatever I do—as in the Sudan. It will be that way again."

"It will mean a Marshal's baton for you," his aide suggested with some awe at the vision.

"Yes." Joffre acknowledged the prospect with laconic equanimity.

Plan 17

Under the aegis of this unassailable figure the General Staff from 1911 on threw itself into the task of revising the Field Regulations, retraining the troops in their spirit, and making a new plan of campaign to replace the now obsolete Plan 16.

The staff's guiding mind, Foch, was gone from the War College, promoted and shifted to the field and ultimately to Nancy where, as he said, the frontier of 1870 "cuts like a scar across the breast of the country." There, guarding the frontier, he commanded the XXth Corps which he was soon to make famous. He had left behind, however, a "chapel," as cliques in the French Army were called, of his disciples who formed Joffre's entourage. He had also left behind a strategic plan which became the framework of Plan 17. Complete in April, 1913, it was adopted without discussion or consultation, together with the new Field Regulations by the Supreme War Council in May. The next eight months were spent reorganizing the army on the basis of the plan and preparing all the instructions and orders for mobilization, transport, services of supply, areas and schedules of deployment and concentration. By February, 1914, it was ready to be distributed in sections to each of the generals of the five armies into which the French forces were divided, only that part of it which concerned him individually going to each one.

Its motivating idea, as expressed by Foch, was, "We must get to Berlin by going through Mainz," that is, by crossing the Rhine at Mainz, 130 miles northeast of Nancy. That objective, however, was an idea only. Unlike the Schlieffen plan, Plan 17 contained no stated over-all objective and no explicit schedule of operations. It was not a plan of operations but a plan of deployment with directives for several possible lines of attack for each army, depending on circumstances, but without a given goal. Because it was in essence a plan of response, of riposte to a German attack, whose avenues the French could not be sure of in advance, it had of necessity to be, as Joffre said, "a posteriori and opportunist." Its intention was inflexible: Attack! Otherwise its arrangements were flexible.

A brief general directive of five sentences, classified as secret, was all that was shown in common to the generals who were to carry out the plan, and they were not permitted to discuss it. It offered very little for discussion. Like the Field Regulations it opened with a flourish: "Whatever the circumstance, it is the Commander in Chief's intention to advance with all forces united to the attack of the German armies." The rest of the general directive stated merely that French action would consist of two major offensives, one to the left and one to the right of the German fortified area of Metz-Thionville. The one to the right or south of Metz would attack directly eastward across the old border of Lorraine, while a secondary operation in Alsace was designed to anchor the French right on the Rhine. The offensive to the left or north of Metz would attack either to the north, or, in the event the enemy violated neutral

territory, to the northeast through Luxembourg and the Belgian Ardennes, but this movement would be carried out "only by order of the Commander in Chief." The general purpose, although this was nowhere stated, was to drive through to the Rhine, at the same time isolating and cutting off the invading German right wing from behind.

To this end Plan 17 deployed the five French armies along the frontier from Belfort in Alsace as far as Hirson, about a third of the way along the Franco-Belgian border. The remaining two-thirds of the Belgian frontier, from Hirson to the sea, was left undefended. It was along that stretch that General Michel had planned to defend France. Joffre found his plan in the office safe when he succeeded Michel. It concentrated the center of gravity of the French forces to this extreme left section of the line where Joffre left none. It was a plan of pure defense; it allowed for no seizing of initiative; it was, as Joffre decided after careful study, "foolishness."

EXHIBIT 1
Concentration of the Armies, August 4–14, 1914.

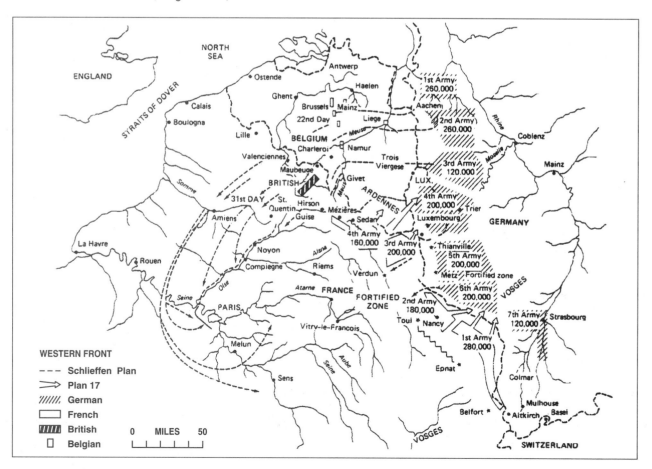

THE SWATCH[†]

By Arieh Ullmann

The Swiss Watch Industry in the Late 1970s

In 1978 when Dr. Ernst Thomke became managing director of ETA after a 20-year leave of absence from the watch industry, the position of this Swiss flagship industry had changed dramatically. Just like other industries suffering from the competitive onslaught from the Far East, the Swiss watch industry faced the biggest challenge in its four hundred years of existence. Once the undisputed leaders in technology and market share—which the Swiss had gained thanks to breakthroughs in mechanizing the watch manufacturing process during the 19th century—the Swiss had fallen on hard times.

[†]**Source:** This case was written by Arieh A. Ullmann, State University of New York, Binghamton. All information in this case is from published sources. Unless indicated otherwise, exhibit information is from SMH and Swiss Watchmanufacturers Federation annual reports. Distributed by the North American Case Research Association. ©1991. All rights reserved to the author and the North American Case Research Association.

In 1980, Switzerland's share of the world market, which in 1952 stood at 56%, had fallen to a mere 20% of the finished watch segment while world production had grown from 61 million to 320 million pieces and movements annually. Even more troubling was the fact that the market share loss was more pronounced in finished watches compared to non-assembled movements (exhibit 1). Measured in dollars the decline was not quite as evident, because the Swiss continued to dominate the luxury segment of the market while withdrawing from the budget price and middle segments.

The Swiss, once the industry's leaders in innovation, had fallen behind. Manufacturers in the United States, Japan and Hong Kong had started to gain share especially since the introduction of the electronic watch. Although in 1967 the Swiss were the first to introduce a model of an electronic wristwatch at the Concours de Chronometrie of the Neuchatel Observatory (Switzerland) smashing all accuracy records, they dismissed the new technology as a fad and continued to rely on their mechanical timepieces where most of their research efforts were concentrated. While the Swiss dominated the watch segments based on older technologies, their market shares were markedly lower for watches incorporating recently developed technologies (exhibit 2). Thus, when electronic watches gained widespread acceptance the Swiss watch

EXHIBIT 1
World Watch Production and Major Producing Countries, 1980

Country	Production (Million Pieces)			Market Share, %
	Electronic	Mechanic	Total	
Switzerland: watches	10.4	52.6	63.0	20
Incl. non-assembled movements	13.0	83.0	96.0	30
Japan: watches	50.4	17.1	67.5	21
Incl. non-assembled movements	53.8	34.1	87.9	28
United States: watches & movements	2.0	10.1*	12.1*	
Rest of Europe: watches & movements	4.5	57.2*	67.7*	42[†]
Rest of Asia: watches & movements	76.0	31.3*	113.0*	
Latin America: watches & movements		2.7*	2.7*	

*Includes unassembled movements.
[†]Without unassembled movements.

EXHIBIT 2
Switzerland's 1975 Share of
World Production by Type of
Technology

Technology	Year of Introduction	Stage of Product Life Cycle	Swiss Share, %
Simple mechanical	Pre-WWII	Declining	35
Automatic	1948	Mature	24
Electric	1953	Declining	18
Quartz (high frequency)	1970	Growing	10
Quartz (solid state)	1972	Growing	3

producers found themselves in a catch-up race against the Japanese who held the technological edge (exhibit 3).

The situation of the industry which exported more than 90% of its production was aggravated by adverse exchange rate movements relative to the U.S. dollar, making Swiss watches more expensive in the United States—then the most important export market. Until the early 1970s, the exchange rate stood at US$1 = SFr. 4.30; by the end of the decade it had dropped to about US$1 = SFr. 1.90.

Structural Change in the Industry

Throughout its history the Swiss watch industry was characterized by an extreme degree of fragmentation. Until the end of the 1970s frequently up to thirty independent companies were involved in the production of a single watch. Skilled craftsmen called suppliers manufactured the many different parts of the watch in hundreds of tiny shops, each of them specializing on a few parts. The movements were either

EXHIBIT 3
Share of Electronic Watches
of Annual Output

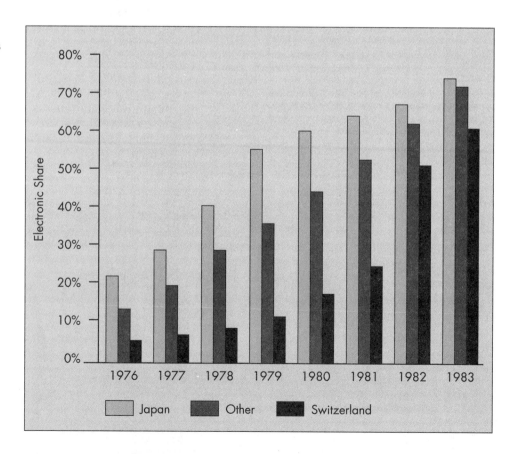

sold in loose parts (ebauche) or assembled to chablons by termineurs which in turn supplied the etablisseurs, where the entire watch was put together. In 1975 63,000 employees in 12,000 workshops and plants were involved in the manufacture of watches and parts. Each etablisseur designed its own models and assembled the various pieces purchased from the many suppliers. Only a few vertically integrated manufacturers existed which performed most of the production stages in-house (exhibit 4). The watches were either exported bearing the assembler's or manufacturer's brand name (factory label) via wholly-owned distributors and independent importers, or sold under the name of the customer (private label). By the late 1970s private label sales composed about 75% of Swiss exports of finished watches. In addition, the Swiss also exported movements and unassembled parts to foreign customers (exhibit 5).

This horizontally and vertically fragmented industry structure had developed over centuries around a locally concentrated infrastructure and depended entirely on highly skilled craftsmen. Watch making encompassed a large number of sophisticated techniques for producing the mechanical watches and this complexity was exacerbated by the extremely large number of watch models. The industry was specialized around highly qualified labor, requiring flexibility, quality, and first-class styling at low cost.

This structure was, however, poorly suited to absorb the new electronics technology. Not only did electronics render obsolete many of the watchmaker's skills that had been cultivated over centuries, it also required large production volumes to take advantage of the significant scale and potential experience effects. Whereas the traditional Swiss manufacturing methods provided few benefits from mass production, the extreme fragmentation from the suppliers to the distributors prevented even these. Furthermore, the critical stages in the value added chain of the watch shifted from parts and assembly—where the Swiss had their stronghold—to distribution where the Japanese concentrated their efforts. Encasement, marketing, wholesale and retail distribution, which the Japanese producers emphasized, represented over 80% of the value added.

Sales of mechanical watches in the budget and middle price segments dropped rapidly when electronic watches entered the market. Initially these were Instruments Inc., National Semiconductor Corp., Hughes Aircraft, Intel, and Time Computer. Due to rapidly rising production and sales volumes of electronic watches, prices dropped dramatically from $1,000 to $2,000 in 1970 to $40 in 1975 and less than $20 by the end of the 1970s. At this time most of the early American digital watch producers had started to withdraw from the watch business and it was the cheap digital watch from Hong Kong that flooded the market.

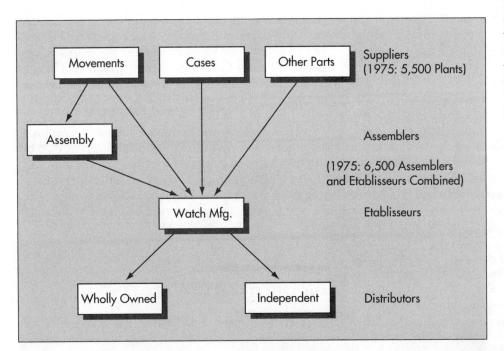

EXHIBIT 4
Traditional Structure of the Swiss Watch Industry

Source: Bernheim, R. A., *Koordination in Zersplitterten Märkten* ("Coordination in Fragmented Markets"), Paul Haupt Publ., Berne, 1981.

EXHIBIT 5
Swiss Exports of Watches, Movements, and Parts, 1960–1990

Year	Finished Watches		Assembled Movements		Unassembled Movements	
	Pieces*	Francs†	Pieces*	Francs†	Pieces*	Francs†
1960	16.7	767.2	8.2	192.7	n/a	n/a
1965	38.4	1334.4	14.8	282.7	n/a	n/a
1970	52.6	2033.8	18.8	329.5	n/a	n/a
1975	47.2	2391.2	18.6	329.1	5.4	44.0
1976	42.0	2262.4	20.0	343.0	8.0	54.2
1977	44.1	2474.5	21.9	381.3	15.8	94.8
1978	39.7	2520.0	20.6	380.3	18.7	103.5
1979	30.3	2355.6	18.6	371.1	20.2	121.0
1980	28.5	2505.8	22.5	411.8	32.7	189.2
1981	25.2	2880.2	19.9	382.5	27.5	160.5
1982	18.5	2754.6	12.7	256.4	14.5	81.0
1983	15.7	2676.6	14.6	247.1	12.7	76.8
1984	17.8	3063.9	14.5	235.0	14.6	98.5
1985	25.1	3444.1	13.4	220.4	18.8	138.9
1986	28.1	3391.0	13.3	213.4	19.4	133.3
1987	27.6	3568.0	11.1	179.4	20.9	122.8
1988	28.0	4128.8	12.2	202.8	31.9	162.1
1989	29.9	5080.0	12.6	217.7	28.4	136.3

*In millions
†In millions of current Swiss francs

As an indication of the eroded market power of the Swiss, the sale of assembled and unassembled movements had started to rise while exports of finished watches declined (exhibit 5)—a trend which negatively affected domestic employment.

The industry's misfortune caused large-scale layoffs, and bankruptcies started to increase steeply in the 1970s. Since the watch industry was concentrated around a few towns in the western part of Switzerland, the ensuing job losses led to regional unemployment rates unknown in Switzerland since the 1930s (exhibit 6).

ETA, where Dr. Thomke became managing director, was a subsidiary of Ebauches SA, which in turn was a subsidiary of ASUAG (General Corporation of Swiss Horological Industries Ltd.) ASUAG had been created in 1931 during the first consolidation period in the industry. It was Switzerland's largest watch corporation (total sales in 1979 were SFr. 1,212 million) and combined a multitude of companies under its holding structure including such famous brands as Certina, Eterna, Longines, and Rado. Ebauches, of which ETA

was part, was the major producer of watch movements for ASUAG and most of the other Swiss etablisseurs. The other large Swiss manufacturer was SSIH (Swiss Watch Industry Corporation Ltd.) which also was a creation of the same 1931 consolidation and whose flagships were Omega and Tissot. During the second half of the 1970s ASUAG suffered from declining 150 profitability and cash flow, poor liquidity, rising long-term debt, and dwindling financial reserves due to sluggish sales of outdated mechanical watches and movements which comprised about two thirds of ASUAG's watch sales. Diversified businesses outside the watch segment contributed less than 5% of total sales.

Turnaround at ETA

Ernst Thomke grew up in Bienne, the Swiss capital of watch making. After an apprenticeship in watch making

EXHIBIT 6
Swiss Watch Industry:
Companies and Employment

Year	Number of Companies	Employment
1960	2,167	65,127
1965	1,927	72,600
1970	1,618	76,045
1975	1,169	55,954
1976	1,083	49,991
1977	1,021	49,822
1978	979	48,305
1979	867	43,596
1980	861	44,173
1981	793	43,300
1982	727	36,808
1983	686	32,327
1984	634	30,978
1985	634	31,949
1986	592	32,688
1987	568	29,809
1988	562	30,122

with ETA he enrolled in the University of Berne where he first studied physics and chemistry and later medicine. After his studies he joined Beechams, a large British pharmaceuticals and consumer products company as a pharmaceutical salesman. In 1978, when his old boss at ETA asked him to return to his first love, he was managing director of Beecham's Swiss subsidiary and had just been promoted to Brussels. However, his family did not wish to move and so, after 18 years, he was back in watches.

When he took over, morale at ETA was at an all-time low due to the prolonged period of market share losses and continued dismissals of personnel. ETA's engineers and managers no longer believed in their capabilities of beating the competition from Japan and Hong Kong. Although ETA as the prime supplier of watch movements did not consider itself directly responsible for the series of failures, it was equally affected by the weakened position of the Swiss watch manufacturers. When Thomke assumed his role as managing director of ETA he clearly understood that, for a successful turnaround, his subordinates needed a success story to regain their self-confidence. But first a painful shrinking process had to be undertaken in order to bring costs under control. Production which used to be distributed over a dozen factories was concentrated in three centers and the number of movement models reduced from over 1,000 to about 250.

As a first step, a project called "Delirium" was formulated with the objective to create the world's thinnest analogue quartz movement—a record which at that time was held by Seiko. When Thomke revealed his idea to ETA's engineers they were quick to nickname it "Delirium Tremens" because they considered it crazy. But Thomke insisted on the project despite his staff's doubts. To save even the tiniest fraction of a millimeter some watch parts were for the first time bonded to the case instead of being layered on top of the watch back. Also, a new extra thin battery was invented. In 1979 the first watch was launched with Delirium movement and ETA had its first success in a long time. In that year, ASUAG sold more than 5,000 pieces at an average price of $4,700 with the top model retailing for $16,000.

The Delirium project not only helped to boost the morale of ETA's employees, it also led to a significant change in strategy and philosophy with ETA's parent, Ebauches SA. No longer was Ebauches content with its role as the supplier of movement parts. In order to fulfill its primary responsibility as the supplier of technologically advanced quality movements at competitive prices to Switzerland's etablisseurs, Ebauches argued, it was necessary to maintain a minimum sales volume that exceeded the reduced domestic demand. Therefore, in 1981 ETA expanded its movement sales beyond its then-current customers in Switzerland, France and Germany. This expansion meant sales to Japan, Hong Kong and Brazil. Ebauches thus entered into direct international competition with Japanese, French, German and Soviet manufacturers. In short, ETA claimed more control over its distribution channels and increased authority in formulating its strategy.

As a second step, the organizational culture and structure were revamped to foster creativity and to encourage employees to express their ideas. Management layers were scrapped and red tape reduced to a minimum. Communication across departments and hierarchical levels was stressed, continued learning and long-term thinking encouraged, playful trial-and-error and risk-taking reinforced. The intention was to boost morale and to create corporate heroes.

The third step consisted in defining a revolutionary product in the medium or low price category. By expanding even farther into the downstream activities, Thomke argued, ETA would control more than 50% instead of merely 10% of the total value added. Since 1970 the watch segments below SFr. 200 had experienced the highest growth rates (exhibit 7). These were the segments the Swiss had ceded to the competitors from Japan and Hong Kong. As a consequence, the average price of Swiss watch exports had steadily risen, whereas the competitors exported at declining prices. Given the overall objective to reverse the long-term trend of segment retreat, it was crucial to reenter one or both of the formerly abandoned segments. Thomke decided to focus on the low price segment. "We thought we'd leave the middle market for Seiko and Citizen. We would go for the top and the bottom to squeeze the Japanese in the sandwich."[1] The new concept was summarized in four objectives:

1. *Price:* Quartz-analogue watch, retailing for no more than SFr. 50.

2. *Sales target:* 10 million pieces during the first three years.

3. *Manufacturing costs:* Initially SFr. 15—less than those of any competitor. At a cumulative volume of 5 million pieces, learning and scale economies would reduce costs to SFr.10 or less. Continued expansion would yield long term estimated costs per watch of less than SFr. 7.

4. *Quality:* High quality, waterproof, shock resistant, no repair possible, battery only replaceable element, all parts standardized, free choice of material, model variations only in dial and hands.

The objectives were deliberately set so high that it was impossible to reach them by improving existing technologies; instead, they required novel approaches. When confronted with these parameters for a new watch, ETA's engineers responded with "That's impossible," "Absurd," "You're crazy." Many considered it typical of Thomke's occasionally autocratic management style which had brought him the nickname "Ayatollah." After all, the unassembled parts of the cheapest existing Swiss watch at that time cost more than twice as much! Also, the largest Swiss watch assembler—ETA's parent ASUAG—sold 750,000 watches annually scattered over several hundred models. In an interview with *The Sunday Times Magazine* Thomke told the story: "A couple of kids, under 30, said they'd go away and look at the Delirium work and see if they could come up with anything. And they did. They mounted the moving parts directly on to a moulded case. It was very low cost. And it was new, and that is vital in marketing."[2] The concept was the brainchild of two engineers. Elmar Mock, a qualified plastics engineer, had recommended earlier that ETA acquire an injection moulding machine to investigate the possibilities of producing watch parts made of plastic. Jacques Muller was a horological engineer and specialist in watch movements. Their new idea was systematically evaluated and improved by inter-disciplinary teams consisting of the inventors, product and manufacturing engineers, specialists from costing, marketing and accounting, as well as outside members not involved in the watch industry.

The fourth step required that ETA develop its own marketing. In the 1970s and early 1980s it did not have a marketing department. Thomke turned to some independent consultants and people outside the watch industry with extensive marketing experience in apparel, shoes and sporting goods to bring creative marketing to the project. Later, as Swatch sales expanded worldwide, a new marketing team was built up to cover the growing marketing, communications and distribution activities.

Product and Process Technology

A conventionally designed analogue watch consisted of a case in which the movement was mounted. The case was closed with a glass or crystal. The movement

[1]Moynahan, Brian, and Andreas Heumann, "The Man Who Made the Cuckoo Sing," *The Sunday Times Magazine,* August 18, 1985, p. 25.

[2]Moynahan/Heumann, op. cit.

EXHIBIT 7
World Watch Production by
Price Category, 1970 vs.
1980

Source: Thomke, E., Inder
Umsetzung von der Produktidee
Zur Marktreife liegt ein entschei-
dender Erfolgsfaktor ("In the
transation from product idea to
marketable product lies a key
success factor"), *Management-
Zeitschrift*, No. 2 (1985),
pp. 60–64.

Price Category	1970 Sales (Million Pieces)	1980 Sales (Million Pieces)	Growth, %
Less than 100 SFr.	110	290	264
100–200 SFr.	33	50	52
200–500 SFr.	20	20	0
More than 500 SFr.	7	10	43

included a frame onto which the wheels, the micromotor needed for analogue display, other mechanical parts as well as the electronic module were attached with screws. First the movement was assembled and then mechanically fixed in the case. Later the straps were attached to the case.

The Swatch differed both with regard to its construction as well as the manufacturing process.

Construction

First, the case was not only an outer shell, it also served as the mounting plate. The individual parts of the movement were mounted directly into the case—the Delirium technology was perfected. The case itself was produced by a new, very precise injection-molding process which was specifically developed for this purpose. The case was made of extremely durable plastic which created a super-light watch.

Second, the number of *components* was reduced significantly from 91 parts for a conventional analogue quartz watch to 51 (exhibit 8). Unlike in conventional watch assembly, the individual parts of the movement— the electronic module and the motor module—were first assembled in subgroups before mounting and then placed in the case like a system of building blocks.

Third, the *method of construction* differed in that the parts were no longer attached with screws. Components were riveted and welded together ultrasonically. This eliminated screws and threads and reduced the number of parts and made the product rugged and shock-resistant. As the crystal was also welded to the case, the watch was guaranteed water-resistant up to 100 feet.

Fourth, the tear-proof *strap* was integrated into the case with a new, patented hinge system which improved wearing comfort.

Fifth, the *battery*—the only part with a limited life expectancy of about three years—was inserted into the bottom of the case and closed with a cover.

Production

First, as a special advantage the Swatch could be assembled from one side only.

Second, because of this it was possible to fully automate the watch mounting process. Ordinary watches were assembled in two separate operations: the mounting of the movement and the finishing. The Swatch, however, was produced in one single operation (exhibit 9). According to representatives of the Swiss watch manufacturers, this technology incorporated advanced CAD/CAM technology as well as extensive use of robotics and was the most advanced of its kind in the world.

Third, due to the new design, the number of elements needed for the Swatch could be significantly reduced and the assembly process simplified. As a prerequisite for incorporating this new product technology, new materials had to be developed for the case, the glass and the micro motor. Also, a new assembly technology was designed and the pressure diecasting process perfected.

Fourth, quality requirements had to be tightened, because the watch could not be reopened and therefore, except for the battery, not be repaired. Given these constraints, each step in the manufacturing process had to be carefully controlled including the parts, the pre-assembled modules, the assembly process itself as well as the final product. This was especially important because in the past high reject rates of parts and casings indicated that many Swiss manufacturers had difficulties with quality control which damaged their reputation.

Overall, the new product design and production technology reduced the costs significantly and raised product quality above watches in the same price category produced by conventional technology.

Marketing

The new marketing team came up with an approach that was unheard of in this industry dominated by engineers.

Product Positioning. Contrary to conventional wisdom in the industry it was not the product, its styling and technical value that were emphasized, but its brand name. Quality attributes such as waterproofness, shock resistance, color, preciseness were less important than the association of the brand name with positive emotions such as "fun," "vacation," "joy of life." The watch was positioned as a high fashion accessory for fashion conscious people between 18 and 30. As it turned out many people outside this range

EXHIBIT 8
Swatch Components

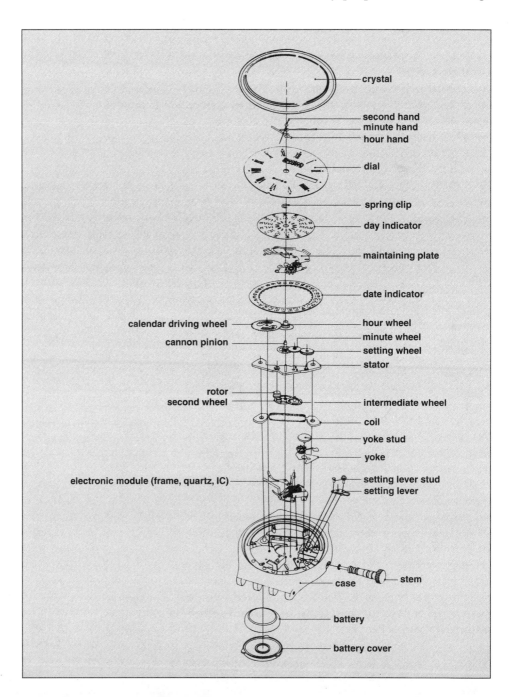

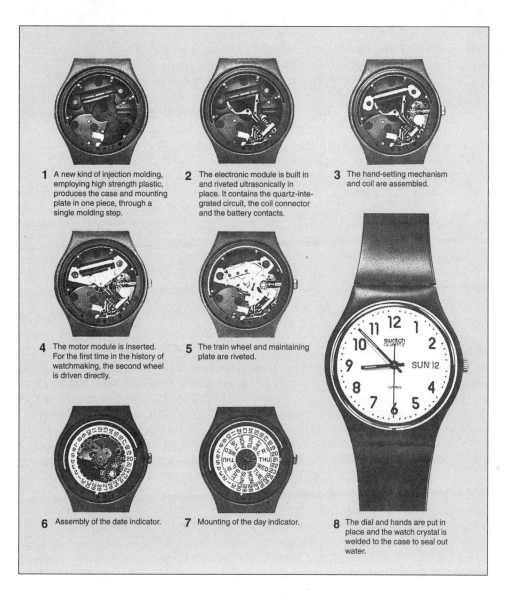

EXHIBIT 9
Swatch Assembly Process

1 A new kind of injection molding, employing high strength plastic, produces the case and mounting plate in one piece, through a single molding step.

2 The electronic module is built in and riveted ultrasonically in place. It contains the quartz-integrated circuit, the coil connector and the battery contacts.

3 The hand-setting mechanism and coil are assembled.

4 The motor module is inserted. For the first time in the history of watchmaking, the second wheel is driven directly.

5 The train wheel and maintaining plate are riveted.

6 Assembly of the date indicator.

7 Mounting of the day indicator.

8 The dial and hands are put in place and the watch crystal is welded to the case to seal out water.

started buying the Swatch. Jean Robert, a Zurich based designer, was responsible for Swatch's innovative designs.

Pricing. The price was set at a level that allowed for spontaneous purchases yet provided the high margins needed for massive advertising.

Distribution. As a high-fashion item competing in the same price range as some Timex and Casio models, the Swatch was not sold through drugstores and mass retailers. Instead, department stores, chic boutiques and jewelry shops were used as distribution channels. Attractive distributor margins and extensive

training of the retailers' sales personnel combined with innovative advertising ensured the unique positioning of the product.

Brand Name. In 1982 20,000 prototypes of 25 Swatch models were pretested in the United States, which was viewed as the toughest market, setting the trend for the rest of the world. The unisex models only differed in color of the cases and straps and the dial designs. It was during these pretests that Franz Sprecher, one of the outside consultants of the marketing team, came up with the name "Swatch" (Swiss + Watch = Swatch) during a brainstorming session with the New York based advertising agency concerning the product's positioning and name. Up until then Sprecher's notes repeat-edly mentioned the abbreviation S'Watch. During this meeting Sprecher took the abbreviation one step fur-ther and created the final name.

The Swatch Team

Besides Thomke, three individuals were crucial for the successful launching of the Swatch: Franz Sprecher, Max Imgrueth, and Jacques Irniger.

Franz Sprecher obtained a masters in economics and business from the University of Basle. Following one year as a research assistant and Ph.D. student he decided to abandon academia and enter the inter-national business world as a management trainee with Armour Foods in Chicago. After six months he returned to Switzerland and joined Nestle in international marketing. Two years later he became sales and marketing director of a small Swiss/Austrian food additives company. Later Sprecher moved to the positions of International Marketing Director of Rivella and then Account Group Manager at the Dr. Dieter Jaeggi Advertising Agency in Basle. Sprecher took a sabbatical at this point in his career and planned to return to the international business world as a consultant within a year. Towards the end of this period while thinking of accepting a position as a professor at the Hoehere Wirtschafts- und Verwaltungshochschule in Lucerne he received a phone call from Thomke concerning the new watch. Thomke told Sprecher: "You've got too much time and not enough money, so why don't you come and work for me." Sprecher then took over the marketing of the, as of yet unnamed, product as a freelance consultant. Today, he continues to consult for Swatch as well as for other brands such as Tissot and Omega.

Another important person involved in the creation of the Swatch was Max Imgrueth. Max Imgrueth was born in Lucerne, Switzerland. Following graduation from high school in St. Maurice, a small town in the Valais surrounded by high mountains, he went to Italy and studied art history in Florence and fashion and leather design in Milan. After a brief stint in linguistics he enrolled in business courses at the Regency Polytechnic in England and New York University. In 1969 he left the United States because he had difficulties in obtaining a work permit and started to work in a women's specialty store in Zurich, Switzerland. Two years later he switched to apparel manufacturing and

became manager for product development and marketing. In 1976 he was recruited by SSIH, owners of the Omega and Tissot brands. From 1976 to 1981 he was in charge of product development and design at Omega's headquarters in Bienne. Conflicts with the banks—which at that time de facto owned SSIH due to continued losses—over Omega's strategy led him to resign from his job and to start a consulting business. One of his first clients was ETA Industries which were just getting ready to test market the Swatch in San Antonio, Texas. He succeeded in convincing ETA that San Antonio was the wrong test market and that the Swatch as a new product required other than the traditional distributors. As a consequence New York and Dallas were chosen as primary test sites, and TV advertising and unconventional forms of public relations were tried. While working on debugging the introduction of the Swatch, he was offered the position of president of Swatch USA, a job which initially consisted of an office on Manhattan's Fifth Avenue and a secretary.

The third individual involved in the early phase of the Swatch was Jacques Irniger who joined ETA in 1983 as vice president of marketing and sales for both ETA and Swatch worldwide. In 1985 he was a board member of the Swatch SA, vice president of marketing and sales of ETA SA Fabriques d'Ebauches and president of Omega Watch Corp., New York. Irniger received his doctorate in economics from the University of Fribourg, a small city located in the French-speaking part of Switzerland. After training positions in marketing research and management at Unilever and Nestle he became marketing manager at Colgate Palmolive in Germany. After Colgate, he moved on to Beecham Germany as vice president of marketing. Before joining ETA he was vice president of marketing and sales for Bahksen International.

Market Introduction

The Swatch was officially introduced in Switzerland on March 1, 1983—the same year that ASUAG and SSIH merged after continued severe losses that necessitated a SFr. 1.2 billion bailout by the Swiss banks. During the first four months 25,000 Swatch pieces were sold—more than a third of the initial sales objective of 70,000 for the first 12 months. According to some distinguished jewelry stores located on Zurich's famous Bahnhofstrasse where Switzerland's most prestigious and expensive watches were purchased by an endless stream of tourists from all over the world, the Swatch did not compete with the traditional models. On the contrary, some jewelers reported that the Swatch stimulated sales of their more expensive models. The success of the Swatch encouraged other Swiss manufacturers to develop similar models which, however, incorporated conventional quartz technology.

Subsequent market introductions in other countries used high-powered promotion. In Germany, the launching of the Swatch was accompanied by a huge replica of a bright yellow Swatch that covered the entire facade of the black Commerzbank skyscraper in Frankfurt's business district. The same approach was used in Japan. On Christmas Eve 1985 the front of a tall building in Tokyo was decorated with a huge Swatch that was 11 yards long and weighed more than 14,000 pounds. Japan, however, turned out to be a difficult market for the Swatch. The 7,000 Yen Swatch competed with domestic plastic models half the price. Distribution was restricted to eleven department stores in Tokyo only and carried out without a Japanese partner. After six months it became obvious that the original sales target of SFr. 25 million for the first year could not be reached. The head of the Japanese Swatch operation, the American Harold Tune, resigned. His successor was a Japanese.

In the United States, initial sales profited from the fact that many American tourists coming home from their vacation in Switzerland helped in spreading the word about this fancy product which quickly became as popular a souvenir as Swiss army knives. U.S. sales of this $30 colorful watch grew from 100,000 pieces in 1983 to 3.5 million pieces in 1985—a sign that Swatch USA, ETA's American subsidiary, was successful in changing the way time pieces were sold and worn. No longer were watches precious pieces given as presents on special occasions such as confirmations, bar mitzvahs, and marriages, to be worn for a lifetime. "Swatch yourself," meant wearing two, three watches simultaneously like plastic bracelets. Swatch managers traveling back and forth between the United States and Switzerland wore two watches, one showing EST time, the other Swiss time.

The initial success prompted the company to introduce a ladies' line one year after the initial introduction, thus leading to 12 models. New Swatch varieties were created about twice a year. Also, special models were designed for the crucial Christmas season: In 1984 scented models were launched, a year later a limited edition watch called Limelight with diamonds sold at $100. The Swatch was a very advertising-intensive line of business. For 1985, the advertising budget of Swatch USA alone was $8 million, with U.S. sales estimated at $45 million (1984 sales: $18 million). In 1985, Swatch USA sponsored MTV's New Year's Eve show; the year before it had sponsored a breakdancing festival offering $25,000 in prizes, and the Fresh Festival '84 in Philadelphia.

Swatch managers were, however, careful not to flood the market. They claimed that in 1984 an additional 2 million watches could have been sold in the United States. In England, 600,000 watches were sold in the first year and the British distributor claimed he could have sold twice as many.

Continued Growth

The marketing strategy called for complementing the $30 time piece with a range of Swatch accessories. The idea behind this strategy was to associate the product with a lifestyle and thereby create brand identity and distinction from the range of look-alikes which had entered the market and were copying the Swatch models with a delay of about three months. In late 1985 Swatch USA introduced an active apparel line called Funwear. T-shirts, umbrellas, and sunglasses should follow in the hope of adding an extra $100 million in sales in 1986. Product introduction was accompanied by an expensive and elaborate publicity campaign including a four-month TV commercial series costing $2.5 million, an eight-page Swatch insert featuring a dozen Swatch accessories in *Glamour, GQ, Vogue,* and *Rolling Stone,* and a $2.25 million campaign on MTV. In January 1985 Swatch AG was spun off from ETA. The purpose of the new Swatch subsidiary was to design and distribute watches and related consumer goods such as shoes, leather and leather imitation accessories, clothes, jewelry and perfumes, toys, sports goods, glasses and accessories, pens, lighters and cigarettes. Swatch production, however, remained with ETA. Furthermore, licenses were being considered for the distribution of the products. All of these products as well as the watches were designed in the United States with subsequent adaptations for European markets.

This strategy of broadening the product line was, however, not without risks, because it could dilute the impact of the brand name. *Forbes* mentioned the examples of Nike which failed miserably when it tried to expand from runningwear to leisure wear, and so did Lewis when it attempted to attach its brand recognition to more formal apparel.[3] Yet Max Imgrueth was quick to point to other examples such as Terence Conran, a designer and furniture maker who succeeded in building a retail empire ranging from kitchen towels to desk lamps around his inexpensive, well-designed home furnishings aimed at the young.

Ensuring Success

At the end of 1985, 45,000 Swatch units were produced daily and annual sales were expected to reach 8 million pieces (1984: 3.7 million). The Swatch was so successful that by the end of 1984 Swatch profits above recovering all product related investments and expenditures contributed significantly towards ETA's overhead. The Swatch represented 75% of SMH's unit sales of finished watches and made it SMH's number one brand in terms of unit sales and the number two brand in terms of revenues, topping such prestige brands as Longines and Rado. SMH (Swiss Corporation for Microelectronics and Watchmaking Industries Ltd.) was the new name of the Swatch parent after the ASUAG-SSIH merger in 1983. Thanks to the Swatch SMH was able to increase its share of the world market (1985: 400 million units) from 1% to 3% within four years. The success also invigorated the Swiss industry at large (exhibit 5b). Despite this success the managers at Swatch continued to perfect and expand the Swatch line.

In 1986 the Maxi-Swatch was introduced which was ten times the size of the regular Swatch. Before the start of the ski season during the same year the Pop-Swatch was launched which could be combined with different color wristbands. As a high-technology extravaganza the Pop-Swatch could also be worn in combination with a "Recco-Reflector" which had been developed by another SMH subsidiary. The Recco reflected radar waves emitted from a system and thus helped to locate skiers covered by avalanches.

In 1987 Swatch wall models were introduced, and the Swatch Twinphone. The latter was not just colorful. It had a memory to facilitate dialing and, true to its origin, provided an unconventional service in that it had a built-in "party line," so that two people could use it simultaneously. 1988 saw the successful introduction of the Twinphone in the USA, Japan and the airport duty-free business as well as the expansion of the Pop-Swatch product line. The Swatch accessories line was discontinued due to unmet profit objectives and negative impact on the Swatch brand image.

In its 1989 annual report SMH reported cumulative sales of over 70 million Swatch pieces. Over 450 models of the original concept had been introduced during the first 7 years (exhibit l0). The Swatch had also become a collector's item. Limited edition models designed by well-known artists brought auction prices of SFr. 1,600, SFr. 3,900 and SFr. 9,400—about 25 to 160 times the original price!

In 1990 the "Swatch-Chrono" was launched to take advantage of the chronometer fashion. Except for the basic concept—plastic encasement and battery as the only replaceable part—it had little in common with the original model and represented a much more complex instrument. It had four micromotors instead of only one due to the added functions and was somewhat larger in diameter. Despite the added complexity it claimed to be as exact and robust as the original Swatch. As a special attraction the watch was available in six models and retailed for only SFr. 100. The company was also experimenting with a mechanical Swatch to be marketed in developing countries where battery replacement posed a problem. In this way the company hoped to boost sales in regions which represented only a minor export market for the Swiss.

The success of the Swatch at the market front was supported by a carefully structured organization. Just like the other major brands of SMH, the Swatch had its own organization in each major market responsible for marketing, sales and communication. These regional offices were supported by SMH country organizations which handled services common to all brands such as logistics, finance, controlling, administration, EDP and after-sales service.

The Swatch also meant a big boost for Thomke's career. He was appointed general manager of the entire watch business of the reorganized SMH and became one of the decision makers of the new management team that took over in January 1985. The "Swatch Story" was instrumental in the turnaround of SMH which only six years after the merger of two moribund companies showed a very healthy bottom line (exhibit 11).

The Future

Despite the smashing success of the Swatch and its contibution to the reinvigoration of the Swiss watch making industry, future success was by no means guaranteed.

---

[3]Heller, Matthew, "Swatch Switches," *Forbes*, January 1986, p. 87.

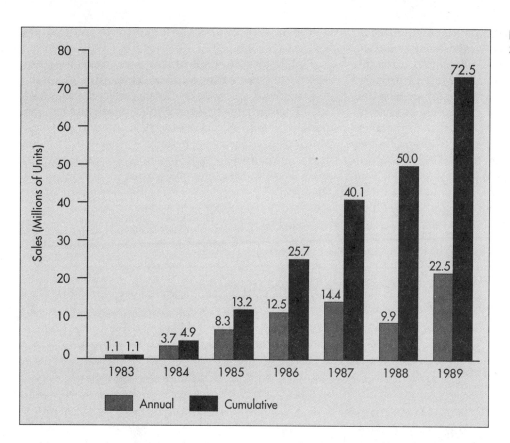

EXHIBIT 10
Swatch Sales

First, competition remained as fierce as ever. The 1980s were characterized by an oversupply of cheap watches because many manufacturers had built capacity ahead of demand. Prices dropped, especially for the cheapest digital watches, a segment that the Swiss avoided. However, several competitors switched to the more sophisticated analogue models and thus created competition for the Swatch. Many look-alikes with names such as Action Watch, A-Watch, etc., flooded the market.

Second, the Swiss had to guard their brand recognition—not just because of the diversification of the Swatch line. It was not clear whether the Swatch brand name was strong enough to create a sustainable position against the imitations. Also, the quality advantage of the Swatch was neither evident to the consumer nor a top priority for the purchasing decision.

A third issue was for how long the Swatch could maintain its technological advantage. By the late 1980s all imitations were welded together. In addition, many competitors, especially the Japanese, were larger than SMH and therefore able to support larger R&D budgets.

A fourth threat was market saturation. While countries with a GDP per capita of over $5,000 comprised only 17% of the world's population, they absorbed 87% of Swiss watch exports. The changes in watch technology and pricing during the last 10 years had increased watch consumption. In England, consumption grew from 275 watches per 1,000 inhabitants in 1974 to 370 watches 10 years later. In the United States the respective figures were 240 and 425 units of which 90% was made up of low price electronic models. While the average life of a watch was much shorter today and consumers had started to own several watches, market saturation could not be ruled out. Also, given the trendy nature of the Swatch it could fall out of fashion as quickly as it had conquered the market. For this situation SMH was not as well prepared as, say, Seiko or Casio, whose non-watch businesses were much stronger and contributed more in terms of overall sales and profits.

A fifth threat was the continued rapid development of technology especially in the field of communications. Increasingly, time measurement was evolving into one of several features of an integrated communication system. Watches were already integrated in a wide variety of products including household durables, computers, telephones. Several SMH subsidiaries involved in microelectronics, electronic components and telecommunications were busy developing products in this area and searching for applications in other markets as well. In the late 1980s SMH started to test prototypes of a combined watch/pager. In late 1990 Motorola introduced a combined watch/pager. It was not clear how SMH and its Swatch subsidiary would fare in this evolving era despite its high-technology sector which,

however, was smaller than that of its competitors (exhibit 12).

Finally, despite the success of the Swatch and of several mid-priced models under other brand names such as Tissot, the Swiss continued to experience higher than average unit prices for their watches. This was partially due to the success of their luxury mechanical watch pieces which were frequently encased in precious metal and adorned with precious stones. However, executives of Swiss companies expressed concern about this trend.

EXHIBIT 11
SMH: Financial Data
(in millions SFr.)

	1989	1988	1987	1986	1985	1984
Income Statement Data						
Sales revenues:						
Gross sales	2,146	1,847	1,787	1,895	1,896	1,665
Costs:						
Materials	793	681	670	759	812	714
Personnel	646	580	577	593	556	541
External services	346	331	335	356	360	286
Depreciation	80	71	73	68	61	60
Total operating costs	1,865	1,663	1,655	1,776	1,789	1,758
Operating profit (loss)	236	142	117	103	66	51
Income before taxes	209	126	90	82	72	38
Net income	175	105	77	70	60	26
Balance Sheet Data						
Assets:						
Current assets	1,194	1,065	1,103	1,080	1,070	1,049
Inventories	602	562	528	568	513	524
Fixed assets	529	510	533	507	456	451
Total assets	1,723	1,575	1,636	1,587	1,526	1,500
Liabilities and stockholders' equity:						
Short-term debt	367	384	442	503	524	501
Long-term debt	295	302	798	801	862	898
Total liabilities	662	686	1,240	1,304	1,386	1,399
Total shareholders' equity	892	760	697	648	490	420
Total liabilities & equity	1,723	1,575	1,636	1,587	1,526	1,500
Other Data						
Personnel: in Switzerland	8,822	8,385	8,526	9,323	9,173	8,982
Personnel: abroad	2,963	2,893	2,597	2,611	2,353	2,311
Personnel: total	11,785	11,278	11,123	11,934	11,526	11,293
Stock price high (SFr.)	560	395	490	700	410	—
Stock price low (SFr.)	378	178	150	375	127	—

EXHIBIT 12
SMH Subsidiaries, 1990

SMH Swiss Corporation for Microelectronics and Watchmaking Industries Ltd. Neuchâtel (Holding Company)

Company Name, Registered Offices	Field of Activity	Shareholding SMH Direct or Indirect, %
Omega SA, Bienne	Watches	100
Compagnie des montres Longines Francillon SA, Saint-Imier	Watches	100
SA Longines pour la vente en Suisse, Saint-Imier	Distribution	100
Columna SA, Lausanne	Distribution	100
Longines (Singapore) PTE Ltd, Singapore	Distribution	100
Longines (Malaysia) Sdn, Kuala Lumpur	Distribution	100
Montres Rado SA, Lengnau	Watches	100
Tissot SA, Le Locie	Watches	100
Certina, Kurth Freres SA, Grenchen	Watches	100
Mido G. Schaeren & Co SA, Bienne	Watches	100
Mido industria e Comercio de Relogios Ltda, Rio de Janeiro	Distribution	100
Swatch SA, Bienne	Watches	100
ETA SA Fabriques d'Ebauches, Grenchen	Watches, movements, electronic components and systems	100
ETA (Thailand) Co. Ltd, Bangkok	Watches and movements	100
Leader Watch Case Co. Ltd, Bangkok	Watch cases	100
Endura SA, Bienne	Watches	100
Lascor SpA, Sesto Calende (Italy)	Watch cases	100
Diantus Watch SA, Castel San Pietro	Watches and movements	100
Société Européenne de Fabrication d'Ebauches d'Annemasse (SEFEA) SA, Annemasse (France)	Watch components and electronic assembly	100
Ruedin Georges SA, Bassecourt	Watch cases	100
EM Microelectronic-Marin SA, Marin	Microelectronics	100
SMH Italia SpA Rozzano	Distribution (Omega, Rado, Tissot Swatch, Flik Flak)	100
SMH (UK) Ltd, Eastleigh	Distribution (Omega, Tissot)	100
SMH Australia Ltd, Prahran	Distribution (Omega, Tissot, Swatch, Flik Flak)	100
SMH Belgium SA, Bruxelles	Distribution (Omega, Tissot, Flik Flak)	100
SMH Ireland Ltd, Dublin	Distribution (Omega)	100
SMH Sweden AB, Stockholm	Distribution (Omega, Longines, Tissot, Certina, Swatch, Flik Flak)	100
SMH Uhren und Mikroelektronik GmbH, Bad Soden (Germany)	Distribution (Omega, Longines, Rado, Tissot, Certina, Swatch, Flik Flak)	100

Continued

EXHIBIT 12—*Continued*
SMH Subsidiaries, 1990

SMH SWISS CORPORATION FOR MICROELECTRONICS AND WATCHMAKING INDUSTRIES LTD. NEUCHÂTEL (HOLDING COMPANY)

Company Name, Registered Offices	Field of Activity	Shareholding SMH Direct or Indirect, %
SMH France SA, Paris	Distribution (Omega, Longines, Rado, Tissot, Certina, Swatch, Flik Flak)	100
SMH España SA, Madrid	Distribution (Omega, Tissot, Swatch, Flik Flak)	100
SMH Japan KK, Tokyo	Distribution (Longines, Tissot, Swatch)	100
SMH (HK) Ltd, Hong Kong	Distribution (ETA, Longines, Swatch, Flik Flak)	100
SMH (US) Inc., Dover Del.	Holding company	100
Hamilton Watch Co Inc., Lancaster Pa.	Distribution	100
Omega Watch Corp., New York	Distribution	100
Rado Watch Co Inc., New York	Distribution	100
Swatch Watch U.S.A. Inc., New York	Distribution (Swatch, Flik Flak)	100
ETA Industries Inc., New York	Distribution	
Unitime Industries Inc., Virgin Islands	Assembly	100
Movomatic USA Inc., Lancaster Pa.	Distribution (Movomatic, Farco)	100
Tissot (US) Inc., New York	Distribution	
Omega Electronics Equipment (US) Inc., Lancaster Pa.	Distribution	100
SMH (US) Services Inc., Lancaster Pa.	Service, watches	100
Technocorp Holding SA, Le Locie	Holding	100
Renata SA, Itingen	Miniature batteries	100
Oscilloquartz SA, Neuchâtel	High stability frequency sources	100
OSA-France Sarl, Boulogne-Billancourt	Distribution	100
Omega Electronics SA, Bienne	Sports timing equipment, score-board information systems	100
Omega Electronics Ltd, Eastleigh (UK)	Distribution	100
Lasag SA, Thun	Laser for industrial and medical application	100
Lasag USA, Inc., Arlington Heights Ill.	Distribution	100
Technica SA, Grenchen	Machine tools and tools	100
Meseitron SA, Corceiles	High precision length measurement (Cary) and automatic size control (Movomatic)	100
Farco SA, Le Locie	Bonding equipment	100
Comadur SA, la Chaux-de-Fonds	Products in hard materials	100
Nivarox-FAR SA, Le Locie	Watch components and thin wires	100
A. Michel SA, Grenchen	Industrial components and delay systems	100
Regis Mainier SA, Bonnetage (France)	Precision and watch components	97.5
Vuillemin Marc, Bonnetage (France)	Precision and watch components	70.1
Chronometrage Suisse SA (Swiss Timing), Bienne	Sports timing	100
Asulab SA, Bienne	Research and development	100
ICB Ingenieurs Conseils en Brevets SA, Bienne	Patents	100
SMH Marketing Services SA, Bienne	Services and licenses	100

STRATEGIC PLANNING AT OLDELFT†

By Ron Meyer

It was September 16, 1986, as Kees van Hoeven put the final touches on the presentation he would be giving to MBA students at the Rotterdam School of Management the next day. As Oldelft's corporate planner, he had been requested to give a lecture on the way strategic planning had been implemented in his company since it was initiated in 1979. Without hesitation, he had agreed to come to the school, as he had good reason to believe that this would be a stimulating exercise for the students, as well as for himself.

For the students, he realized, Oldelft was an interesting example of a relatively small high-tech firm operating in a turbulent global market. The company, with its head office situated near The Netherlands' largest technical university in Delft, specialized in products requiring advanced knowledge of optics, electronics, electronoptics ("optronics"), and precision mechanics. These products, with relatively short product life cycles, fell into three categories, namely, medical, defense, and industrial products. In all three cases, Oldelft's competition was global and fierce. Van Hoeven recognized that it would be of great interest to the students to observe to what extent textbook planning processes had been adapted to fit the needs and constraints of such a company.

His visit to Rotterdam, however, was very interesting personally as well. He had already played a prominent role in guiding the 1985 planning cycle at Oldelft, but he was now in charge of running "the circus," as the planning process was generally referred to. Since the

Oldelft strategic planning process was biannual, the first planning cycle under his supervision would lead to a final plan by the end of 1987. The first steps in this 1987 planning cycle would soon be taken, leaving him only a short period of time to review the manner in which the planning at Oldelft took place and to make changes where needed. Thus he welcomed the opportunity to exchange opinions on the strengths and weaknesses of the Oldelft planning process with a room full of MBA students. He was very curious to hear what kind of questions they would ask him and what kind of possible improvements they would propose.

The History of the Company

The Oldelft company was founded in 1939 by Oscar van Leer as the "Optical Industry The Old Delft." In its first years the company was quite small and specialized in handcrafted optical products, ranging from magnifying glasses and microscopes to cameras. At a very early stage, however, van Leer was able to lure an extremely capable man away from Philips to lead his company. This man was A. Bouwers, an engineer with a passion for research and development (R&D), who also proved to be a highly motivated entrepreneur.

Bouwers committed a large part of his time and a considerable portion of company funds to new product development, which in 1945 led to the first prototype of a photofluorographic camera with a concentric mirror system. This product, which was finally introduced in the market in 1950 as the Odelca, allows expensive full-sized X-rays to be substituted by far cheaper postcard-size ones. This product was a great success because it made nationwide tuberculosis examinations financially feasible.

Fuelled by his success, Bouwers maintained his policy of remaining at the forefront of technological innovation in the field of optics. In 1952, for instance, Oldelft introduced advanced aerial cameras for both low- and high-altitude reconnaissance. During this period, Bouwers also followed an aggressive

†**Source:** This case was prepared by Ron Meyer as a basis for class discussion rather than to illustrate either effective or ineffective handling of an administrative situation. Unless otherwise indicated, all information was obtained with the kind assistance of the Oldelft company. Some names in the text have been changed. This case was originally published as part of the strategic management course *Ondernemingsplanning II* (Corporate Planning) of the Dutch Open University. Copyright © 1991 Open Universiteit Heerlen.

acquisitions strategy, buying up large numbers of smaller optical companies. As one Oldelft manager put it, "No Dutch company with the word 'optical' in its name was safe."

By 1968, when Bouwers retired, Oldelft had expanded to a company with a turnover of about Dfl 35 million and more than a thousand employees. To the satisfaction of van Leer and the small number of other stockholders, Oldelft also proved to be very profitable, with a return on investment (ROI) ranging from 8 to 20 percent. To ensure that Oldelft would remain equally successful in future, Bouwers had also brought in an experienced R&D manager from outside the company to replace him. This was S. Duinker, head of the Philips laboratory in Hamburg, who has remained president of Oldelft since then.

The Years of Holding Course (1968–1975)

Duinker inherited a company operating in two very different markets, namely, the medical and defense markets. In the medical field Oldelft had developed radio therapy equipment, in addition to its Odelca X-ray cameras, and in the defense market Oldelft had established itself with reconnaissance cameras. Technology was the common theme linking these products and underlying Oldelft's R&D projects. In the late 1950s the company had supplemented its expertise in optics and precision mechanics with knowledge of the rapidly expanding field of electronics. The possibilities offered by these technologies by and large determined the thrust of Oldelft's product development strategy.

A second major factor determining Oldelft's product line was the breathing space left to it by larger companies. A former member of the executive board described the strategy Oldelft employed by using the analogy of a guerrilla fighter—Oldelft was small and flexible, and only moved in areas left open to it by its powerful competitors; yet it was ready to strike at these opponents should weak points in their flanks show up.

Oldelft's relations to its competitors were, however, not as antagonistic as this analogy might suggest. Actually, the contrary was often true, it being the case that many competitors were also suppliers of Oldelft, while others purchased important components from the company. Philips, for instance, was simultaneously competitor, supplier, and customer of Oldelft, depending on the product in question. This meant that Oldelft was very dependent on the cooperative relationships it was able to establish with other companies. Oldelft's contacts were especially essential in the medical sector, since OEM (original equipment manufacturer) sales accounted for a large portion of turnover.

Besides OEM sales, Oldelft's major medical customers were all professional users, mostly hospitals, spread throughout the world, though concentrated in Europe and North America. Although the medical customers of Oldelft were easily identifiable, the company's competitors were somewhat harder to classify. Due to the highly specialized nature of the medical products Oldelft sold, the company was in fact operating in a number of small segments of a substantially fragmented market. To a large degree, the competitors Oldelft encountered in each segment differed in name, number, and strength.

In the defense business the same held true. The company had a small number of clearly identifiable customers, namely, national governments of Western or developing nations, while the market niches in which the company operated were populated by a large number of nondominant competitors. This was where the similarities between the defense and medical markets ended, however. The defense industry, in which Oldelft participated, had characteristics all its own.

While the medical market could be said to be global due to the low level of protectionism practised by governments in this field, the defense market was quite the opposite. Governments are usually extremely hesitant to reward defense contracts to foreign companies, even though they might pay lip service to free trade. Moreover, in addition to discriminatory procurement policies, many governments are actively engaged in subsidizing and promoting nationally produced defense goods as well. This put Oldelft up against difficult competition in obtaining military contracts abroad. Yet being a Dutch company with a small home market, these foreign sales were essential for Oldelft. The company was severely export dependent, with 90 percent of its total turnover coming from abroad.

The defense market was also risky due to its sensitivity to shifting political winds. It is a Dutch law that all military products leaving the country require export permits, and these will not be granted if the country of destination is at war. This made Oldelft's exports vulnerable to political upheaval abroad. Especially since the lead time of a sale and the subsequent delivery can extend over a number of years, it could happen that a contract was signed with a country at peace and that war would break out before the products could be delivered.

The lead time of a sale in the defense industry could even be up to ten years in the case of new products, introducing a variety of additional problems for a company such as Oldelft. The length of this lead time was due not only to the extra time involved in producing and "debugging" new high-tech products but also to the government study groups in which defense contractors would need to invest years of their time before even being awarded the contract.

Despite these drawbacks, however, Oldelft made most of its profits in the defense market. Although winning a contract could prove extremely difficult, the margins on most contracts made all the trouble more than worthwhile. Company figures actually suggest that the medical products weren't profitable at all, although it can be difficult to do proper analysis in a small company. The medical products were retained, however, for a number of important reasons. The defense business tends to be rather cyclical and the medical products could be used to counterbalance this, for instance, when planning production-capacity usage. Furthermore, Oldelft learned that the technological spin-off from medical to defense was considerable and could assist in strengthening the company's competitive advantage.

Besides the potentially rich financial rewards, the defense industry had a second attractive point. Military customers were far more interested in the quality of the product than in its price and delivery period. This was to Oldelft's advantage, since low cost and speed were not company strong points, while product reliability was a well-acknowledged Oldelft characteristic. This was largely due to the company's perfectionist culture, which was especially prevalent in the R&D department. This culture ensured a product of high quality and technological sophistication, yet also caused relatively high costs, both in terms of time and money.

It should come as no surprise that the vice president in charge of commercial affairs at the time expressed mixed feelings about the Oldelft culture. While it did facilitate the development of high-quality products, it weakened Oldelft's competitive position in the price-sensitive medical market. The perfectionist culture, with its inherently long R&D lead times, also reduced Oldelft's ability to quickly enter new high-tech markets not yet dominated by larger companies.

His concern was strengthened by the fact that by 1974 most of Oldelft's products were in a late phase of their product life cycle, while there were few promising civil products in the pipeline. At the same time, profits had dipped, and the 1974 annual report showed the first loss in years.

The Advent of Strategic Thinking (1975–1976)

By 1975, this decline in the company's fortunes led the executive board to point to a cost reduction drive as a necessary step toward profit recovery. There was, however, no staff group available at the time that could do an overhead analysis. It was therefore decided to institute a policy advice council (Beleids Advies Raad, BAR). This BAR was a voluntary group, mostly made up of young aggressive managers with new ideas who wanted to update the rather conservative corporate culture.

The BAR quickly obtained status as it developed beyond a cost-cutting group to a more general corporate think-tank. Being attuned to the newest management techniques, the BAR soon requested authority from the executive board to look into the possibilities of setting up a long-term planning approach, as this was one of the latest management developments at the time.

The BAR's initiative was accepted, and the seven-man team embarked on the task of designing a large-scale planning approach for Oldelft. The corporate plan they envisaged would be centered on turnover projections for the next seven to eight years. Sales managers would be asked to estimate the turnover they expected in their areas of responsibility, making it possible to synchronize all else to fit these forecasts. One would be able to derive everything, from capital requirements to personnel planning, from these figures, so that an overall business blueprint could be made. This would nicely solve a large number of important Oldelft problems at once, such as the need to level out production-capacity usage.

President Duinker was rather surprised by the far-reaching BAR proposal, as he had a far more "visionary" company plan in mind. He had expected a type of general SWOT analysis, followed by a number of corporate objectives and policy guidelines. After a period of discussion, however, a compromise was struck, whereby both planning options would be worked out.

By April 1976 Duinker's idea of drawing up a document outlining the company's "objectives and policy principles" had taken shape. This hefty paper set out for the first time the company's long-term financial, social, commercial, and technological goals. It also laid down the fundamental policy guidelines that would be followed to achieve these goals. This was, in fact, the company's first attempt at explicitly formulating its mission and at putting to paper a number of its implicit strategic choices.

The foremost goal stated in this document was the primacy of continued independence over the goal of growth. This had never been a topic of discussion, as there had never been any reason to bring it up. It was realized, though, that the external environment was changing and that this would force the company to choose. The concentration ratio in many market segments was on the increase, and the funds needed to develop new products was also growing. This would put pressure on the company to merge or sell to a larger competitor in order to maintain growth. The executive board, however, clearly expressed that it would be its policy to remain independent, with company shares being widely spread.

While the intention was stated to periodically review the outlined objectives and policy principles, practice was that the document was neatly filed and rarely again exposed to daylight. The documents on strategy that the BAR in the meantime had been working on were going to be concrete plans, including serious operational targets. By September 1976 the first "strategic planning round" was started to obtain the turnover forecasts needed to work out the rest of the plans. There was but one problem in the BAR approach. No sales manager was willing to make a turnover prognosis eight years into the future. The extrapolation of current trends, it was realized, is dangerous in any case, but the unpredictability of the markets in which Oldelft operated made estimating impossible. The technological advances were seen as too fast and the number of competitors too unpredictable to even come close to an educated guess. No manager was willing to stick out his neck and try. The result was that the discussions dragged on and on, while very little was actually achieved.

The Impending Crisis (1976–1978)

In the meantime Oldelft's fortunes were slumping. In 1975 the company had been able to recover from the 1974 downturn, but by mid-1976 a sharp decline in sales had set in, and the short-term sales forecasts had taken a turn for the worse. By late 1977 it had become obvious that dramatic action would be necessary to prevent large-scale losses in the following years. An "action plan" was drawn up to reduce overhead costs quickly. This plan led to a severe cutback in production capacity and consequently to a reduction in the workforce from 1600 to 1300 employees.

It was realized, however, that these short-term savings would not be sufficient to ensure the continued viability of the company. There were a number of more fundamental problems that would have to be addressed as well. First, there was "serious doubt whether the present organizational structure, personnel and procedures would still fit the expected smaller scale of the company and whether they, in general, would be able to handle the commercial, technical and socio-economical problems." Second, it was recognized that it was "no longer self-evident that in the coming years Oldelft would be serving the same markets through the same distributing channels with the same products, developed and produced in the same way as before."[1] The executive board decided to thoroughly reexamine both the structure and strategy of the company. To assist in this difficult process of self-analysis, the consultancy firm of Arthur D. Little (ADL) was called in.

The Introduction of Strategic Decision Making (1978-1979)

ADL started the two-front study in May 1978, looking both at the organizational structure of Oldelft, and at the strategy and the strategy-formulating process of the company. This large team of mostly American consultants was lead by John Niemans. It was his main task to teach this technology-oriented company to think in market terms and to develop its ability to effectively engage in strategic decision making. This was quite a challenge, one Oldelft manager later recalled, as Niemans had little to build on. Strategic thinking was still in its embryonic phase at Oldelft, and most strategic decision-making concepts were new to the company's management.

By mid-1979 ADL had largely completed its task of reorganizing and reorienting Oldelft. This year-long process had led to a high number of important changes within the company. For instance, certain products were phased out, an important development program was cancelled, explicit make or buy decisions were made, and the company decided to substantially strengthen its

---

[1]Drawn from an internal company document announcing the hiring of ADL consultants.

position in electronics. Furthermore, strategic business units were implemented, in part to improve strategic decision-making ability.

Niemans had also given Oldelft the tools with which it would be able to carry out strategic planning on its own strength in future. He had given them a methodology and, in fact, had dragged the company through its very first strategic planning cycle. Not surprisingly, he also stressed the necessity for Oldelft to retain its ability to engage in strategic decision making. His advice, however, was not more concrete.

The First Attempts at Strategic Planning (1980–1981)

In 1980 the executive board decided to appoint the one-man market research department, presided over by the vice president for commercial affairs, as the coordinating body for the corporate strategic planning process. Mr. Verkade from this department was given the task of leading the first independent strategic planning cycle, generally along ADL lines. It was his opinion, however, that the ADL method was far too extensive to be implementable on a regular basis, so he introduced a simplified form. Before he could start with the actual process, though, Verkade left the company and was replaced by Mr. Jansen.

In the meantime, the last ADL people were finishing up their jobs of assisting in implementing the organizational changes, and Oldelft personnel were finally settling into the new situation. The years of upheaval, change, and uncertainty had left most employees with a desire just to get back to work. So when Jansen called on managers to participate in strategic planning meetings, very few had the time or the motivation to attend. The attractiveness that strategic planning had enjoyed due to its newness had also evaporated, making it even harder to get managers to come to planning sessions, especially since the sanctions for nonattendance were benign.

As gradually more and more managers dropped out of the strategic planning discussions, Jansen filled this vacuum by doing their strategic analyses for them. Within a short period of time, however, this task had become a full-time job, as the participation rate dropped ever lower. Jansen was pressed to write on and on. But as the company was actually far too large for one man to analyze, he got caught up in an endless writing process and never did catch up with the detailed facts. He was forced to generalize, and his analyses soon became too superficial for the line managers to consider seriously. This led these managers to dismiss strategic planning as a waste of time, justifying wholesale abandonment of meaningful cooperation. In this manner, in not more than a few months, Jansen had become isolated, and strategic planning had become nothing more than a one-man academic exercise.

The First Successful Independent Strategic Planning Cycle (1981)

During the same period, in 1981, the workers' council (Ondernemings Raad) proposed to have the head of the 1978 ADL team, John Niemans, appointed to the supervisory board. The executive board agreed, and thus invited a well-informed and outspoken person to join the company. Niemans, of course, was very interested to find out to what extent his recommendations had been carried out by the company. He was disappointed to see the strategic planning process being carried out so poorly.

The executive board agreed with this critique and took firm action to ensure that by the end of 1981 the first independent strategic planning cycle would be completed. The responsibility for accomplishing this was given to a man with more experience and weight than Jansen, namely, to the head of the commercial staff offices, Ab Baas. Compared with most other Oldelft managers, Baas had a strong background in company planning, as he was one of the driving forces behind the old BAR. He also had a reputation for getting things done and, unlike Jansen, had the wholehearted backing of the executive board to strengthen his position. To the line managers it was clear that participation in the new planning cycle was no longer voluntary, but compulsory.

Baas introduced a planning process almost totally along ADL lines. This combination of both bottom-up and top-down approaches has, to this day, remained the way in which Oldelft conducts its strategic planning. This process consists of four general steps, namely:

- the drawing up of situation analyses per business segment of the business units;
- the formulation of plans and options per business segment;
- the evaluation of all plans and options by the company's top management;

- the communication of the decisions taken to all relevant personnel.

The Situation Analyses

Baas introduced a hard-nosed approach to obtaining the relevant data on the business segments' external environments. He started by handing out almost-empty booklets to the five business segment managers. The only things printed in each booklet were the headings on each page denoting what the managers should put in the space below. It was the duty of these line managers to hand the booklets back in with all the pages filled. The amount of information Baas requested from each business segment was extensive, and it was the responsibility of each manager to gather all relevant data himself.

A completed situation analysis was made up of two key elements, namely, an analysis of the industry's maturity and a weighing of the business segment's competitive position, which together determined the company's strategic position. The industry's maturity was ascertained by analyzing current and expected trends, threats, opportunities, market segmentation, customers, technological change, market growth, and growth potential. This analysis would place the industry's maturity somewhere on a continuum from embryonic to aging (see figure 1).

The company's competitive position in each product market was determined by comparing Oldelft to its competitors on a large number of fronts. This assessment paid attention to differences between companies, as well as between products. Companies were checked for their strengths and weaknesses, for instance in the areas of R&D, finance, service and sales. Products were compared on the basis of price, quality and features. Together with the figures on the relative marketshares, this information placed each competitor somewhere on the continuum from weak to dominant.

In the ADL approach the industry maturity continuum and the competitive position continuum form the two axes of the strategic position matrix, displayed in figure 1. The strategic position resulting from this whole situation analysis is the most important factor determining which strategies should be developed for each business segment in future.

This whole process of establishing the business segments' strategic position was a complex, yet vitally important, first step in the planning cycle. To ensure the quality of the business segment managers' output, Baas held a number of meetings with each manager on his situation analysis. Baas invited all other Oldelft

FIGURE 1
Strategic Option Zones

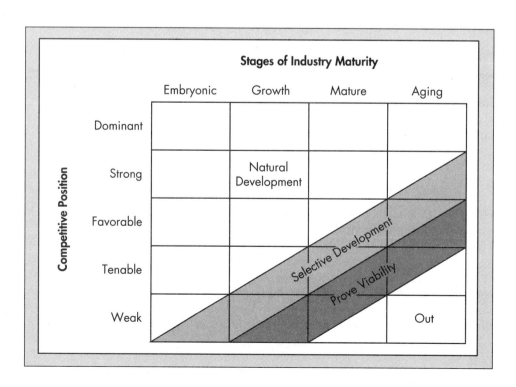

managers who had a stake in the business unit to attend these meetings as well, as broad input usually increases the accuracy of an assessment. Besides the business segment manager, Baas also requested the presence of product managers, sales managers (from home and abroad), plant managers, project managers, production coordinators, development unit managers, as well as relevant staff members and an occasional external consultant. On average, between ten and fifteen participants came to each meeting.

Plans and Options

Once the situation analyses had been completed, the business segment managers were asked to evaluate past plans and to supply new plans and options. These new plans, Baas made clear, were to be developed using the strategic position of the business segment as a reference framework. Just as with the situation analysis, a number of meetings with a broad, representative group were held to discuss and finalize the proposed plans.

After all the meetings with the business segments had been concluded, it was Baas's task to reorganize all information into a presentable form. To facilitate decision-making by the company's top management, it was also necessary for him to "translate" the business segments' options into comparable financial figures and to add a risk analysis to each of them. After considerable rewriting, this resulted in five business segment discussion papers, which were subsequently handed to top management.

The Corporate Scrums

These business segment analyses were the main input into the "corporate scrums," as the strategic decision-making discussions among the top managers are called in ADL-speak. The other two inputs provided by Baas were a financially and strategically consolidated view of the whole corporation and a socio-economic analysis of the outside world.

In total, three scrums were programmed to reach agreement on the strengths and weaknesses of the corporation, general goals, corporate strategies, business strategies, action plans, and resource allocation within the company. In each meeting there were ten to twelve participants, including the president of the company, the executive vice presidents, the so-called directors (heads of the most important departments and business units), the company controller, an ADL consultant, and Baas himself. Each scrum lasted two to three days and

was held outside the company offices to ensure that day-to-day business would not divert attention from the discussions at hand.

The first scrum evaluated past strategies and discussed strategic issues and financial performance. The second scrum drew conclusions about strategic issues and decided actions, strategies, and resource allocation to the business segments. Finally, the third scrum was dedicated to a discussion on socioeconomic analysis and the corporation's strengths, weaknesses, and general goals. This last scrum concluded with the selection of corporate strategies for the coming five year period.

While the planning horizon employed was five years, the emphasis of the plans was on the first two. Actions and resource allocations especially focused on the first two years. This was due to Baas having scheduled the following planning cycles to take place on a biannual basis (in 1983, 1985, 1987, and so on).

The Post-Scrum Booklets

After this decision-making process had been completed, Baas wrote up post-scrum booklets for each of the business segments. These documents each contained a finalized situation analysis, a list of the decisions taken on the business segments's proposed strategies and action plans, a forecast of the financial results for the next five years, and a specification of the amount of R&D resources allocated to each business segment. These booklets were subsequently sent to the ten to fifteen managers involved in the strategic planning process for each business segment. It was up to these managers to implement the plans along the general lines set out in each booklet. Besides these business segment booklets, Baas also drew up a consolidated booklet for the whole company, as well as a summary for staff personnel and the workers' council.

There was no formal review procedure built into the planning system. Managers were expected to act according to the plans, yet retained the flexibility to deviate from the plans if the circumstances arose.

During this whole process, which Baas was able to conclude by the end of 1981, occasional ADL support was called in, as no one had real expertise in "running such a show." Baas himself especially had few pretensions. It was typical of his style that he avoided the title of corporate planner, as he argued that he did not plan, but merely facilitated, the planning process. With a wink, he opted instead for the title of "circus director."

The Acceptance of Strategic Planning

While in 1981 the strategic planning process at times might have resembled a three-ring circus, by the third planning cycle, concluded in 1985, it had become well-rehearsed corporate practice. Gaining the acceptance of these production- and technology-oriented managers was a challenge for Baas. It was very difficult for him to motivate people to think and operate strategically, not only during the planning sessions but especially afterward. It was not only the corporate culture that frustrated Baas's attempts to gain acceptance for strategic planning but also the absence of both carrot and stick. There was no reward system geared to encourage participation in and compliance with the plans, nor was there any formal mechanism to control the managers' execution of them.

Despite these problems, by 1985 Baas had been able to embed the planning process in the company's way of running its business. By then, all fifty-odd participants had grown accustomed to the way Baas had implemented the ADL approach to strategic planning, and they had gotten used to the timetable Baas had drawn up for them to meet. This planning process timetable was spread out over a period of approximately one year. Baas started the process during November and used the period up until April to complete the pre-scrum booklets. The corporate scrums were subsequently planned for May and June. The period up until October was then used by the planning staff to draw up the post-scrum booklets for the business units (BUs), staff, and the worker's council.

Although Baas was the only person in the organization involved in guiding the planning process on a full-time basis, he was assisted during the busiest periods by three to four others. During the 1985 process, though, he did have a permanent assistant, namely, his young successor-to-be, Kees van Hoeven. Shortly after the completion of the third planning cycle, van Hoeven took over as corporate planner and Baas was promoted to head of the defense products business unit (see figure 2).

The Fourth Strategic Planning Cycle

With the fourth planning cycle slated for completion by October 1987 and with a lead time of about one year, van Hoeven's visit to the Rotterdam School of Management on September 17, 1986 was really going to be on the eve of the next planning period. He would be planning for a company that had changed somewhat since the days of the ADL studies. One important step had been the divestment of two noncore businesses, namely, Cine (film-cutting equipment) and Deltronics (medical equipment merchandizing). This left Oldelft with two remaining BUs. The medical products BU was made up of three business segments, namely X-ray (OEM), radio therapy, and ultrasound, while the other BU comprised the defense products.

All these products could be said to fit the "mission definition," formulated during the ADL consulting period, which was to "reveal the invisible." However, Oldelft did not feel restricted to a narrow interpretation of this mission, since it acted more as a good slogan that fit the range of products than as a guiding principle. In practice the company let itself be guided by the technologies involved in making certain products. Its lack of apprehension in interpreting its business-defining statement less strictly was demonstrated in 1984, when a new BU, industrial products, was created, and the Seampilot was introduced (see figure 3). This laser-based seam-tracking system for arc-welding automation employed the unique combination of optronics, electronics, and precision mechanics in which Oldelft specialized. This diversification into another civil market, it was hoped, would help offset the destabilizing influence of the irregular large-scale defense contracts.

The introduction of the ACAL gas detection system in the same year entailed a further widening of the mission definition interpretation. This system for nerve gas detection actually "reveals the unsmellable" and hence seems to fall outside Oldelft's traditional imaging business. The ACAL technology, however, is based on optronics' ability to identify discolorations caused by the gas and as such can be said to fall within a wider interpretation of "revealing the invisible."

Besides new products, another important change was that of the company's fortunes. Since the ADL studies Oldelft had recovered its former profitability, with its return on equity ranging from 5 percent to a high of 37 percent (see tables 1 and 2). These results had allowed the company to increase its R&D expenditures, and a number of promising new products had been introduced into the market.

Van Hoeven's position, too, was about to change. While he was still a member of the commercial staff office, as Baas had been, it had become obvious that an organizational reshuffling was in the making. The proposals within the executive board would have almost all commercial staff reporting under the

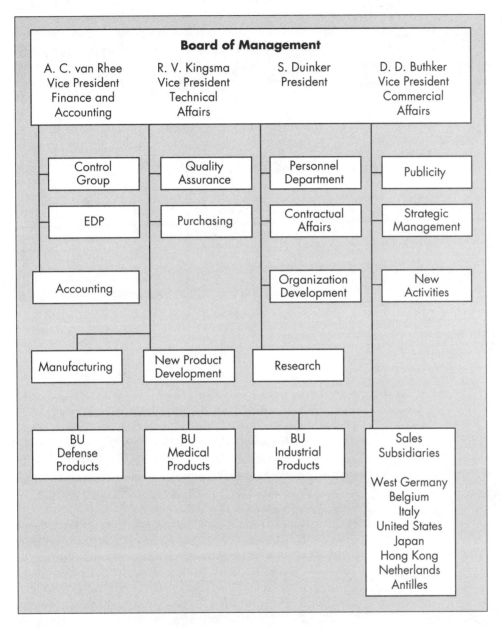

FIGURE 2
Proposed
Organisation Chart
(as of January 1, 1987)

individual business units instead of under the vice president for commercial affairs, Buthker, as now was the case. One of the few exceptions would be corporate planning, which would then no longer be reporting to the head of the commercial staff, but, rather, directly to the vice president for commercial affairs.

One of the things that was not altered much over the years was the company's approach to the planning process. Baas's attention during the first planning cycles had mainly been focused on getting strategic plans made. As mentioned before, he also exerted considerable effort at overcoming organizational resistance to planning and spent much time encouraging the highly product- and technology-oriented managers to think strategically. Only now that strategic planning had become more or less accepted was the time opportune for van Hoeven to review the planning methodology and implement improvements.

Hence, he welcomed the opportunity to exchange opinions on the strengths and weaknesses of the Oldelft planning process with the students and professors of the school. He was very curious to hear what kind of questions they would ask him and what kinds of possible improvements they would propose.

FIGURE 3
Present Product Age Guide

	Medical			Defense	Industrial
	X-ray	**Radio Therapy**	**Ultrasound**		
1956	Oldelca 100-camera				
1957					
1958					
1959					
1960					
1961					
1962					
1963					
1964	Oldelca 70-camera	Deccalix			
1965					
1966					
1967					
1968					
1969					
1970	Anodica 2-camera			Night vision equipment	
1971					
1972	Deltorax camera	Simulix			Indeca (NDT)
1973					
1974					
1975					
1976					
1977					
1978		Simtomix		F-16 HUD	
1979					
1980				Laser range finders	
1981	Anodica 6-camera				
1982					
1983			Transducers		
1984			Small parts scanner	ACAL (gas detection)	Seampilot
1985	Electrodelca		Linear arrays	Thermal observation	

TABLE 1
Financial Summary 1976–1985 in Dfl millions

	1976	1978	1980	1981	1982	1983	1984	1985
Results								
Sales	129.2	127.0	194.9	162.3	229.3	293.3	255.6	227.6
Salaries, wages and social security	(63.0)	(62.4)	(69.1)	(69.1)	(77.5)	(86.4)	(82.9)	(84.2)
Depreciation	(4.9)	(5.0)	(6.3)	(8.1)	(11.9)	(14.8)	(13.6)	(14.6)
Other operating cost	(48.9)	(60.0)	(103.9)	(68.9)	(99.9)	(146.3)	(122.7)	(111.9)
Operating result	12.4	(0.5)	15.7	16.2	40.0	45.8	36.4	16.9
Financial income and expenses	(8.4)	(9.5)	(11.7)	(11.4)	(11.8)	(6.3)	(3.5)	(4.1)
Taxation	(1.6)	(0.2)	–	(0.1)	(3.1)	(12.6)	(12.9)	(3.9)
Extraordinary income and expenses	0.6	0.6	(1.9)	–	(14.2)	(2.0)	(3.0)	(2.5)
Net income	3.0	(9.7)	2.1	4.7	10.9	25.0	17.1	6.4
Cashflow	7.9	(4.7)	9.7	13.2	38.0	43.0	41.2	14.0
Dividends	1.2	–	–	–	1.7	3.5	6.1	4.3
Assets								
Fixed assets	35.9	45.8	51.7	59.2	65.1	66.0	60.5	62.3
Inventories	71.9	72.7	75.4	79.1	74.5	74.7	96.0	67.4
Accounts receivable	40.0	72.3	80.8	56.9	67.2	86.0	116.6	93.2
Liquid resources	2.0	2.2	4.5	2.1	14.1	13.9	8.0	36.8
Total Assets	149.8	192.9	212.4	197.3	220.9	240.5	281.0	259.7
Liabilities								
Group equity	34.5	33.6	39.8	45.0	54.7	79.2	107.5	116.2
Long-term external liabilities	36.0	46.9	41.8	40.0	51.3	46.7	43.5	46.2
Short-term external liabilities	79.2	112.3	130.8	112.3	115.0	114.6	130.0	97.3
Total equity and liabilities	149.8	192.9	212.4	197.3	220.9	240.5	281.0	259.7

TABLE 2
Financial Ratios 1976–1985

	1976	1978	1980	1981	1982	1983	1984	1985
Sales and Results								
Sales increase over previous year in %	11.0	(14.2)	12.9	(16.7)	41.3	28.0	(3.0)	(11.0)
Net income as a % of sales	2.3	(7.6)	1.1	3.0	4.8	5.8	6.7	2.8
Net income as a % of average group equity	9.3	(28.8)	5.5	11.2	22.0	37.3	18.3	5.7
Dividend distribution as a % of net income	42	–	–	–	15	14	36	66
Equity								
Group equity as a % of total equity employed	22	17	19	23	25	33	38	45
Risk-bearing equity as a % of total equity employed	32	25	25	29	30	37	40	51
Working capital								
Inventory as a % of sales	56	57	39	39	32	25	38	30
Current assets/current liabilities	1.4	1.3	1.2	1.2	1.4	1.5	1.7	2.0
Working capital in Dfl. millions	34.7	34.8	29.9	26	41	60	90	100
Per share statistics								
Net income per share of Dfl. 10	4.82	(14.59)	n/a	7.12	16.43	36.11	21.05	7.55
Shareholders equity	53.37	50.46	n/a	67.53	82.18	114.53	132.56	136.58
Employees								
Number of employees at year end	1639	1448	1311	1319	1435	1412	1324	1321
Research and Development								
R&D costs as % of sales of own products	10.4	14.2	9.8	n/a	n/a	n/a	n/a	n/a
R&D costs as % of sales	n/a	n/a	n/a	6.5	6.8	8.9	8.4	11.0

■ KAO CORPORATION†

By Sumantra Ghoshal and Charlotte Butler

Dr. Yoshio Maruta introduced himself as a Buddhist scholar first, and as President of the Kao Corporation second. The order was significant, for it revealed the philosophy behind Kao and its success in Japan. Kao was a company that not only learned, but "learned how to learn." It was, in Dr. Maruta's word's, "an educational institution in which everyone is a potential teacher."

Under Dr. Maruta's direction, the scholar's dedication to learning had metamorphosed into a competitive weapon which, in 1990, had led to Kao being ranked ninth by Nikkei Business in its list of excellent companies in Japan, and third in terms of corporate originality (exhibit 1). As described by Fumio Kuroyanagi, Director of Kao's overseas planning department, the company's success was due not merely to its mastery of technologies nor its efficient marketing and information systems, but to its ability to integrate and enhance these capabilities through learning. As a result, Kao had come up with a stream of new products ahead of its Japanese and foreign competitors and, by 1990, had emerged as the largest branded and packaged goods company in Japan and the country's second largest cosmetics company.

Since the mid 1960s Kao had also successfully used its formidable array of technological, manufacturing and marketing assets to expand into the neighbouring markets of SE Asia. Pitting itself against long established multinationals like Procter & Gamble and Unilever, Kao had made inroads into the detergent, soap and shampoo markets in the region. However, success in these small markets would not make Kao a global player, and since

†**Source:** This case was written by Charlotte Butler, Research Assistant, under the supervision of Sumantra Ghoshal, Professor at INSEAD. It is intended to be used as a basis for class discussion rather than to illustrate either effective or ineffective handling of an administrative situation. Unless otherwise indicated, all exhibits are based on information provided by Kao Corporation. Reprinted with the permission of INSEAD. Copyright ©1992 INSEAD-EAC, Fontainebleau, France.

the mid-1980s, Kao had been giving its attention to the problem of how to break into the international markets beyond the region. There, Kao's innovations were being copied and sold by its competitors, not by Kao itself, a situation the company was keen to remedy. But would Kao be able to repeat its domestic success in the US and Europe? As Dr. Maruta knew, the company's ability to compete on a world-wide basis would be measured by its progress in these markets. This, then, was the new challenge to which Kao was dedicated: how to transfer its learning capability, so all-conquering in Japan, to the rest of the world.

The Learning Organization

Kao was founded in 1890 as Kao Soap Company with the prescient motto, "Cleanliness is the foundation of a prosperous society." Its objective then was to produce a high quality soap that was as good as any imported brand, but at a more affordable price for the Japanese consumer, and this principle had guided the development of all Kao's products ever since. In the 1940s Kao had launched the first Japanese laundry detergent, followed in the 1950s by the launch of dishwashing and household detergents. The 1960s had seen an expansion into industrial products to which Kao could apply its technologies in fat and oil science, surface and polymer science. The 70s and 80s, coinciding with the presidency of Dr. Maruta, had seen the company grow more rapidly than ever in terms of size, sales and profit, with the launching of innovative products and the start of new businesses. Between 1982 and 1985 it had successfully diversified into cosmetics, hygiene and floppy disks.

A vertically integrated company, Kao owned many of its raw material sources and had, since the 1960s, built its own sales organization of wholesalers who had exclusive distribution of its products throughout Japan. The 1980s had seen a consistent rise in profits, with sales increasing at roughly 10 percent a year throughout the decade, even in its mature markets (exhibit 2). In 1990, sales of Kao products had reached ¥620.4 billion

EXHIBIT 1

The Ranking of Japanese Excellent Companies 1990 (*Nikkei Business* April 9, 1990)

1.	Honda Motors	79.8
2.	IBM–Japan	79.4
3.	SONY	78.4
4.	Matsushita Electrics	74.5
5.	Toshiba	69.9
6.	NEC	69.8
7.	Nissan Motors	69.8
8.	Asahi Beer	67.4
9.	KAO	66.6
10.	Yamato Transportation	66.4
11.	Fuji-Xerox	66.3
12.	Seibu Department Store	66.2
13.	Suntory	65.8
14.	Nomura Security	65.4
15.	NTT (Nippon Telegraph & Telephone)	65.3
16.	Omron	65.1
17.	Ajinomoto	64.3
18.	Canon	64.3
19.	Toyota Motors	63.9
20.	Ohtsuka Medicines	63.8

Note: Points are calculated on the basis of the following criteria:

1. the assessment by Nikkei Business Committee's member corporate originality, corporate vision, flexibility, goodness;
2. the result of the researches among consumers.

($3,926.8 million), an 8.4 percent increase on 1989. This total consisted of laundry and cleansing products (40 percent), personal care products (34 percent), hygiene products (13 percent), specialty chemicals and floppy disks (9 percent) and fatty chemicals (4 percent) (exhibit 3). Net income had increased by 1.7 percent, from ¥17.5 billion ($110 million) in 1989 to ¥17.8 billion ($112.7 million) in 1990.

Kao dominated most of its markets in Japan. It was the market leader in detergents and shampoo, and was vying for first place in disposable diapers and cosmetics. It had decisively beaten off both foreign and domestic competitors, most famously in two particular instances: the 1983 launch of its disposable diaper brand Merries which, within twelve months, had overtaken the leading brand, Procter & Gamble's Pampers and the 1987 launch of its innovative condensed laundry detergent, the aptly named Attack; as a result of which the market share of Kao's rival, Lion, had declined from 30.9 percent (1986) to 22.8 percent (1988), while in the same period Kao's share had gone from 33.4 percent to 47.5 percent.

The remarkable success of these two products had been largely responsible for Kao's reputation as a creative company. However, while the ability to introduce a continuous stream of innovative, high quality products clearly rested on Kao's repertoire of core competences, the wellspring behind these was less obvious: Kao's integrated learning capability.

This leaning motif had been evident from the beginning. The Nagase family, founders of Kao, had modeled some of Kao's operations, management and production facilities on those of United States corporations and in the 1940s, following his inspection of United States and European soap and chemical plants, Tomiro Nagase II had reorganized Kao's production facilities, advertising and planning departments on the basis of what he had learned. As the company built up its capabilities, this process of imitation and adaptation had evolved into one of innovation until, under Dr. Maruta, a research chemist who joined Kao in the 1930s and became president in 1971, "Distinct creativity became a policy objective in all our areas of research, production and sales, supporting our determination to explore and develop our own fields of activity."

The Paperweight Organization

The organizational structure within which Kao managers and personnel worked embodied the philosophy of Dr. Maruta's mentor, the 7th century statesman Prince Shotoku, whose Constitution was designed to foster the spirit of harmony, based on the principle of absolute equality; "Human beings can live only by the Universal Truth, and in their dignity of living, all are absolutely equal." Article 1 of his Constitution stated that "If everyone discusses on an equal footing, there is nothing that cannot be resolved."

Accordingly, Kao was committed to the principles of equality, individual initiative and the rejection of authoritarianism. Work was viewed as "something fluid and flexible like the functions of the human body," therefore the organization was designed to "run as a flowing system" which would stimulate interaction and the spread of ideas in every direction and at every level (see exhibit 4 on page 656). To allow creativity and initiative full rein, and to demonstrate that hierarchy was merely an expedient that should not become a

constraint, organizational boundaries and titles were abolished.

Dr. Maruta likened this flat structure to an old fashioned brass paperweight, in contrast to the pyramid structure of Western organizations: "In the pyramid, only the person at the top has all the information. Only he can see the full picture, others cannot... The Kao organization is like the paperweight on my desk. It is flat. There is a small handle in the middle, just as we have a few senior people. But all information is shared horizontally, not filtered vertically. Only then can you have equality. And equality is the basis for trust and commitment."

This organization practised what Kao referred to as "biological self control." As the body reacted to pain by sending help from all quarters, "If anything goes wrong in one department, the other departments should know automatically and help without having to be asked." Small group activities were encouraged in order to link ideas or discuss issues of immediate concern. In 1987, for example, to resolve the problem of why Kao's Toyohashi factory could achieve only 50 percent of the projected production of Nivea cream, workers there voluntarily formed a small team consisting of the people in charge of production, quality, electricity, process and

EXHIBIT 2
The Trend of Kao's Performance

	Billions of Yen						Millions of US$
Years ended March 31	1985	1986	1987	1988	1989	1990	1990
Net Sales (Increase)	398.1	433.7 +8.9%	464.1 +7.0%	514.4 +10.9%	572.2 +11.2%	620.4 +8.4%	3,926.8
Operating Income (Increase)	16.5*	19.853*	31.7	36.5 +15.2%	41.4 +13.5%	43.5 +5.1%	275.5
Net Income (Increase)	9.4	10.5 +12.3%	12.9 +22.5%	13.4 +4.2%	17.5 +30.4%	17.8 +1.7	112.7
Total assets	328.3	374.4	381.0	450.4	532.3	572.8	3,625.5
Total shareholders' equity	114.4	150.9	180.2	210.7	233.8	256.6	1,624.1

*non-consolidated

Note: The U.S. dollar amounts are translated, for convenience only, at the rate of ¥156 = $1, the approximate exchange rate prevailing on March 30, 1990.

EXHIBIT 3
Review of Operations

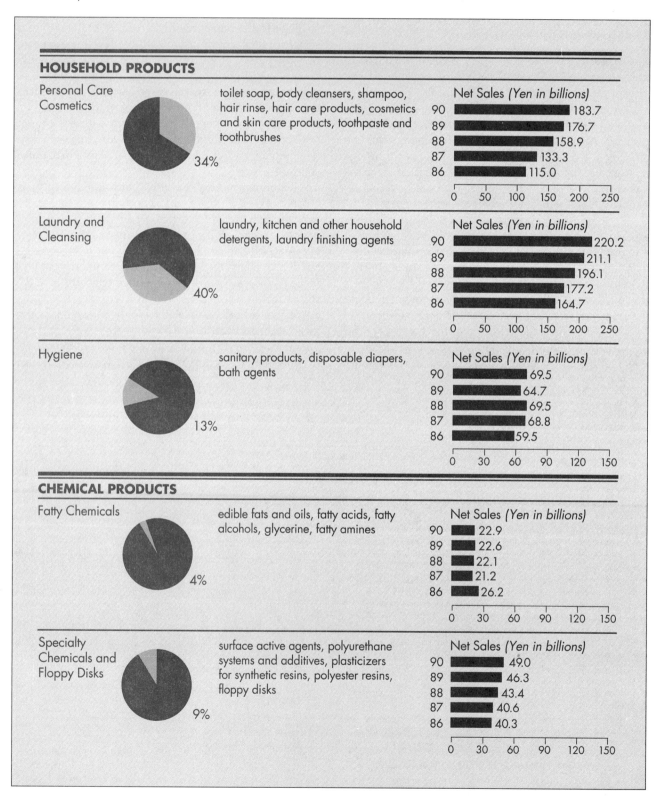

HOUSEHOLD PRODUCTS

Personal Care Cosmetics

toilet soap, body cleansers, shampoo, hair rinse, hair care products, cosmetics and skin care products, toothpaste and toothbrushes

34%

Net Sales (Yen in billions)

Year	
90	183.7
89	176.7
88	158.9
87	133.3
86	115.0

0 50 100 150 200 250

Laundry and Cleansing

laundry, kitchen and other household detergents, laundry finishing agents

40%

Net Sales (Yen in billions)

Year	
90	220.2
89	211.1
88	196.1
87	177.2
86	164.7

0 50 100 150 200 250

Hygiene

sanitary products, disposable diapers, bath agents

13%

Net Sales (Yen in billions)

Year	
90	69.5
89	64.7
88	69.5
87	68.8
86	59.5

0 30 60 90 120 150

CHEMICAL PRODUCTS

Fatty Chemicals

edible fats and oils, fatty acids, fatty alcohols, glycerine, fatty amines

4%

Net Sales (Yen in billions)

Year	
90	22.9
89	22.6
88	22.1
87	21.2
86	26.2

0 30 60 90 120 150

Specialty Chemicals and Floppy Disks

surface active agents, polyurethane systems and additives, plasticizers for synthetic resins, polyester resins, floppy disks

9%

Net Sales (Yen in billions)

Year	
90	49.0
89	46.3
88	43.4
87	40.6
86	40.3

0 30 60 90 120 150

machinery. By the following year, production had been raised to 95 percent of the target.

In pursuit of greater efficiency and creativity, Kao's organization has continued to evolve. A 1987 programme introduced a system of working from home for sales people, while another will eventually reduce everyone's working time to 1800 hours a year from the traditional level of 2100 hours. Other programmes have aimed at either introducing information technology or re-vitalising certain areas. 1971 saw the "CCR movement," aimed at reducing the workforce through computerisation. "Total Quality Control" came in 1974, followed in 1981 by Office Automation. The 1986 "Total Cost Reduction" programme to restructure management resources evolved into the "Total Creative Revolution" designed to encourage a more innovative approach. For example, five people who were made redundant following the installation of new equipment, formed, on their own initiative, a special task force team, and visited a US factory which had imported machinery from Japan. They stayed there for three months until local engineers felt confident enough to take charge. Over time, this group became a flying squad of specialists, available to help foreign production plants get over their teething troubles.

Managing Information

Just as Dr. Maruta's Buddha was the enlightened teacher, so Kao employees were the "priests" who learned and practised the truth. Learning was "a frame of mind, a daily matter," and truth was sought through discussions, by testing and investigating concrete business ideas until something was learned, often without the manager realizing it. This was "the quintessence of information... something we actually see with our own eyes and feel with our bodies." This internalised intuition, which coincides with the Zen Buddhist phrase *kangyo ichijo*, was the goal Dr. Maruta set for all Kao managers. In reaching it, every individual was expected to be a coach; both to himself and to everyone else, whether above or below him in the organization.

Their training material was information. Information was regarded not as something lifeless to be stored, but as knowledge to be shared and exploited to the utmost. Every manager repeated Dr. Maruta's fundamental assumption: "in today's business world, information is the only source of competitive advantage. The company that develops a monopoly on information, and has the ability to learn from it continuously, is the company that

will win, irrespective of its business." Every piece of information from the environment was treated as a potential key to a new positioning, a new product. What can we learn from it? How can we use it? These were the questions all managers were expected to ask themselves at all times.

Access to information was another facet of Kao's commitment to egalitarianism: as described by Kuroyanagi, "In Kao, the 'classified' stamp does not exist." Through the development of computer communication technologies, the same level of information was available to all: "In order to make it effective to discuss subjects freely, it is necessary to share all information. If someone has special and crucial information that the others don't have, that is against human equality, and will deprive us and the organization of real creativity."

Every director and most salesmen had a fax in their homes to receive results and news, and a bi-weekly Kao newspaper kept the entire company informed about competitors' moves, new product launches, overseas development or key meetings. Terminals installed throughout the company ensured that any employee could, if they wished, retrieve data on sales records of any product for any of Kao's numerous outlets, or product development at their own or other branches. The latest findings from each of Kao's research laboratories were available for all to see, as were the details of the previous day's production and inventory at every Kao plant. "They can even," said Dr. Maruta, "check up on the president's expense account." He believed that the increase in creativity resulting from this pooling of data outweighed the risk of leaks. In any case, the prevailing environment of *omnes flux* meant that things moved so quickly "leaked information instantly becomes obsolete."

The task of Kao managers, therefore, was to take information directly from the competitive environment, process it and, by adding value, transform it into knowledge or wisdom.

Digesting information from the market place in this way enabled the organization to maintain empathy with this fast moving environment. The emphasis was always on learning and on the future, not on following an advance plan based on previous experience. "Past wisdom must not be a constraint, but something to be challenged," Dr. Maruta constantly urged. Kao managers were discouraged from making any historical comparisons. "We cannot talk about history," said Mr. Takayama, Overseas Planning Director. "If we talk about the past, they (the top management) immediately

EXHIBIT 4
Organizational Structure

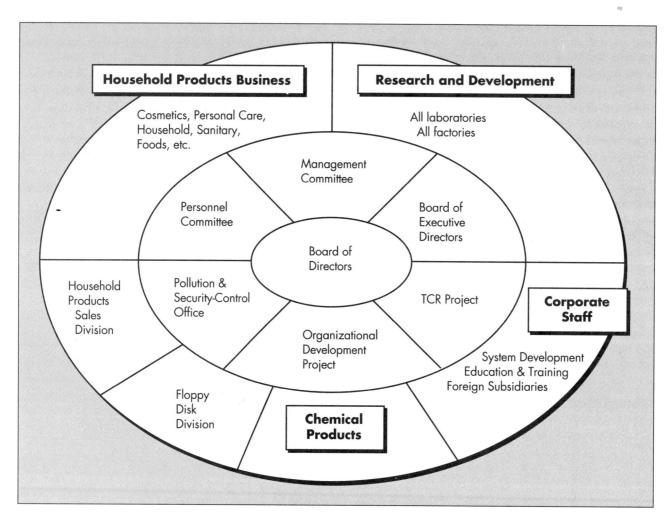

become unpleasant." The emphasis was rather, what had they learnt today that would be useful tomorrow? "Yesterday's success formula is often today's obsolete dogma. We must continuously challenge the past so that we can renew ourselves each day," said Dr. Maruta.

"Learning through cooperation" was the slogan of Kao's research and development (R&D); the emphasis was on information exchange, both within and outside the department, and sharing "to motivate and activate." Glycerine Ether, for example, an emulsifier important for the production of Sofina's screening cream, was the product of joint work among three Kao laboratories. Research results were communicated to everyone in the company through the IT system, in order to build a close networking organization. Top

management and researchers met at regular R&D conferences, where presentations were made by the researchers themselves, not their section managers. "Open Space" meetings were offered every week by the R&D division, and people from any part of the organization could participate in discussions on current research projects.

A number of formal and informal systems were created to promote communication among the research scientists working in different laboratories. For example, results from Paris were fed daily into the computer in Tokyo. The most important of these communication mechanisms, however, were the monthly R&D working conferences for junior researchers which took place at each laboratory in turn. When it was their own laboratory's turn to act as host, researchers could nominate anyone they wished to meet, from any laboratory in the company, to attend that meeting. In addition, any researcher could nominate him or herself to attend meetings if they felt that the discussions could help their own work, or if they wanted to talk separately with someone from the host laboratory. At the meetings, which Dr. Maruta often attended to argue and discuss issues in detail, researchers reported on studies in progress, and those present offered advice from commercial and academic perspectives.

The Decision Process

"In Kao, we try collectively to direct the accumulation of individual wisdom at serving the customer." This was how Dr. Maruta explained the company's approach to the decision process. At Kao, no one owned an idea. Ideas were to be shared in order to enhance their value and achieve enlightenment in order to make the right decision. The prevailing principle was *tataki-dai;* present your ideas to others at 80 percent completion so that they could criticise or contribute before the idea became a proposal. Takayama likened this approach to heating an iron and testing it on one's arm to see if it was hot enough. "By inviting all the relevant actors to join in with forging the task," he said, "we achieve *zoawase*; a common perspective or view." The individual was thus a strategic factor, to be linked with others in a union of individual wisdom and group strategy.

Fumio Kuroyanagi provided an illustration. Here is the process by which a problem involving a joint venture partner, in which he was the key person, was resolved: "I put up a preliminary note summarizing the key issues, but not making any proposals. I wanted to share the data and obtain other views before developing a proposal fully... This note was distributed to legal, international controllers to read... then in the meeting we talked about the facts and came up with some ideas on how to proceed. Then members of this meeting requested some top management time. All the key people attended this meeting, together with one member of the top management. No written document was circulated in advance. Instead, we described the situation, our analysis and action plans. He gave us his comments. We came to a revised plan. I then wrote up this revised plan and circulated it to all the people, and we had a second meeting at which everyone agreed with the plan. Then the two of us attended the actual meeting with the partner. After the meeting I debriefed other members, discussed and circulated a draft of the

letter to the partner which, after everyone else had seen it and given their comments, was signed by my boss."

The cross fertilization of ideas to aid the decision process was encouraged by the physical lay out of the Kao building. On the 10th floor, known as the top management floor, sat the chairman, the president, four executive vice presidents and a pool of secretaries (exhibit 5). A large part of the floor was open space, with one large conference table and two smaller ones, and chairs, blackboards and overhead projectors strewn around: this was known as the Decision Space, where all discussions with and among the top management took place. Anyone passing, including the president, could sit down and join in any discussion on any topic, however briefly. This layout was duplicated on the other floors, in the laboratories and in the workshop. Workplaces looked like large rooms; there were no partitions, but again tables and chairs for spontaneous or planned discussions at which everyone contributed as equals. Access was free to all, and any manager could thus find himself sitting round the table next to the president, who was often seen waiting in line in Kao's Tokyo cafeteria.

The management process, thus, was transparent and open, and leadership was practised in daily behaviour rather than by memos and formal meetings. According to Takayama, top management "emphasizes that 80 percent of its time must be spent on communication, and the remaining 20 percent on decision making." While top management regularly visited other floors to join in discussions, anyone attending a meeting on the 10th floor then had to pass on what had happened to the rest of his colleagues.

Information Technology

Information Technology (IT) was one of Kao's most effective competitive weapons, and an integral part of its organizational systems and management processes. In 1982, Kao made an agreement to use Japan Information Service Co's VAN (Value Added Networks) for communication between Kao's head office, its sales companies and its large wholesalers. Over time, Kao built its own VAN, through which it connected upstream and downstream via information linkages. In 1986 the company added DRESS, a new network linking Kao and the retail stores receiving its support.

The objective of this networking capability was to achieve the complete fusion and interaction of Kao's marketing, production and R&D departments. Fully integrated information systems controlled the flow of materials and products; from the production planning of raw materials to the distribution of the final products to local stores: no small task in a company dealing with over 1,500 types of raw materials from 500 different suppliers, and producing over 550 types of final products for up to 300,000 retail stores.

Kao's networks enabled it to maintain a symbiotic relationship with its distributors, the *hansha*. Developed since 1966, the Kao hansha (numbering 30 by 1990) were independent wholesalers who handled only Kao products. They dealt directly with 100,000 retail stores

EXHIBIT 5
Layout of Kao Offices

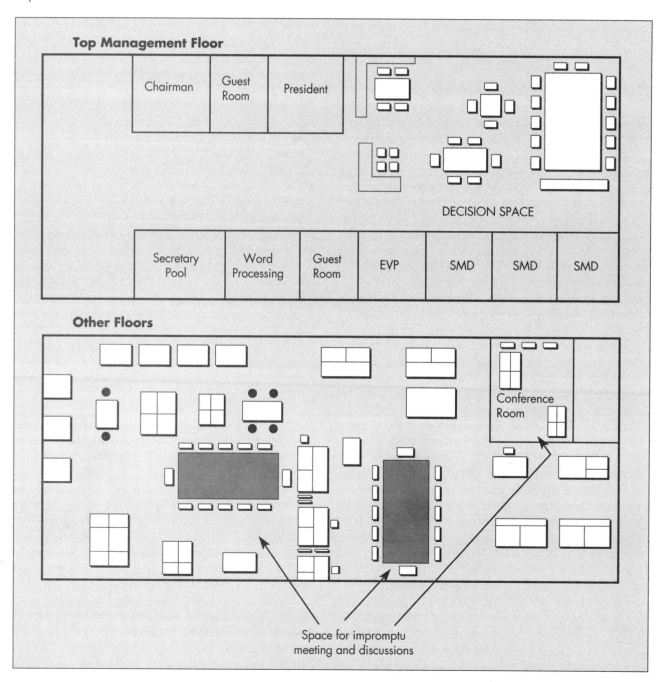

Space for impromptu meeting and discussions

out of 300,000, and about 60 percent of Kao's products passed through them. The data terminals installed in the hansha offices provided Kao with up-to-date product movement and market information, which was easily accessible for analysis.

Kao's Logistics Information System (LIS) consisted of a sales planning system, an inventory control system and an on-line supply system. It linked Kao headquarters, factories, the hansha and Logistics centres by networks, and dealt with ordering, inventory, production and sales data (exhibit 6). Using the LIS, each hansha sales person projected sales plans on the basis of a head office campaign plan, an advertising plan and past market trends. These were corrected and adjusted at corporate level, and a final sales plan was produced each month. From this plan, daily production schedules were then drawn up for each factory and product. The system would also calculate the optimal machine load, and the number of people required. An on-line supply system calculated the appropriate amount of factory stocks and checked the hansha inventory. The next day's supply was then computed and automatically ordered from the factory.

A computerized ordering system enabled stores to receive an deliver products within 24 hours of placing an order. Through a POS (point of sale) terminal, installed in the retail store as a cash register and connected to the Kao VAN, information on sales and orders was transmitted to the hansha's computer. Via this, orders from local stores, adjusted according to the amount of their inventory, were transmitted to Kao's Logistics centre, which then supplied the product.

Two other major support systems, KAP and RRS, respectively helped the wholesale houses in ordering, stocking and accounting, and worked with Kao's nine distribution information service companies: the Ryutsu Joho Service Companies (RJSs). Each RJS had about 500 customers, mainly small and medium sized supermarkets who were too small to access real-time information by themselves. The RJSs were essentially consulting outfits, whose mandate was to bring the benefits of information available in Kao VAN to those stores that could not access the information directly. They guided store owners by offering analysis of customer buying trends, shelf space planning and ways of improving the store's sales, profitability and customer service. The owner of one such store commented: "A Kao sales person comes to see us two or three times a week, and we chat about many topics. To me, he is both a good friend and a good consultant… I can see Kao's philosophy, the market trend and the progress of R&D

holistically through this person." According to Dr. Maruta, the RJSs embodied Kao's principle of the information advantage: their purpose was to provide this advantage to store owners, and the success of the RJSs in building up the volume and profitability of the stores was ample evidence of the correctness of the principle.

Kao's Marketing Intelligence System (MIS) tracked sales by product, region and market segment, and provided raw market research data. All this information was first sifted for clues to customer needs, then linked with R&D "seeds" to create new products. New approaches to marketing were sought by applying artificial intelligence to various topics, including advertising and media planning, sales promotion, new product development, market research and statistical analysis.

Additional information was provided by the Consumer Life Research Laboratory which operated ECHO, a sophisticated system for responding to telephone queries about Kao products. In order to understand and respond immediately to a customer's question, each phone operator could instantly access a video display of each of Kao's 500 plus products. Enquiries were also coded and entered into the computer system on-line, and the resulting data base provided one of the richest sources for product development or enhancement ideas. By providing Kao with "a direct window on the consumer's mind," ECHO enabled the company to "predict the performance of new products and fine tune formulations, labelling and packaging." Kao also used a panel of monitor households to track how products fitted into consumers' lives.

In 1989, Kao separated its information systems organization and established a distinct entity called Kao Software Development. The aim was to penetrate the information service industry which, according to Japan Information, was projected to reach a business volume of ¥12,000 billion ($80 billion) by the year 2000. In 1989, the market was ¥3,000 billion ($20 billion). One IBM sales engineer forecast, "by 2000, Kao will have become one of our major competitors, because they know how to develop information technology, and how to combine it with real organization systems."

In 1989 Kao's competitors, including Lion and Procter & Gamble, united to set up Planet Logistics, a system comparable to Kao's VAN. Through it, they aimed to achieve the same information richness as Kao. But Dr. Maruta was not worried by this development. Irrespective of whatever information they collected, he believed that the competitors would not be able to add the value and use it in the same way as Kao did: "As a company we do not spend our time chasing after what our rivals do. Rather, by mustering our knowledge, wisdom and ingenuity to study how to supply the consumer with superior products, we free ourselves of the need to care about the moves of our competitors. Imitation is the sincerest form of flattery, but unless they can add value to all that information, it will be of little use."

EXHIBIT 6
Kao's Information Network (*Nikkei Computer* Oct. 9, 1989)

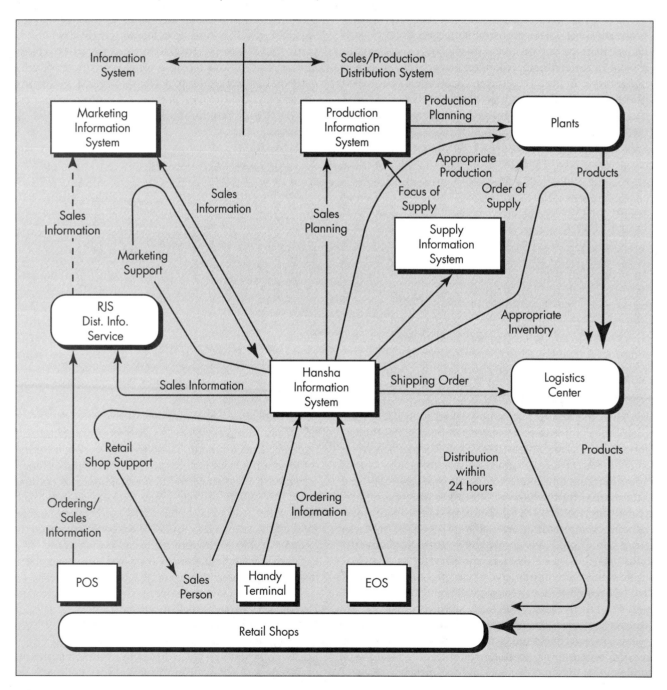

Sofina

The development of Sofina was a microcosm of Kao's *modus operandi*. It illustrated the learning organization in action since it sought to create a product that satisfied the five principles guiding the development of any new offering: "Each product must be useful to society. It must use innovative technology. It must offer consumers value. We must be confident we really understand the market and the consumers. And, finally, each new product must be compatible with the trade." Until a new product satisfied all these criteria, it would not be launched on the market. At every stage during Sofina's creation, ideas were developed, criticised, discussed and refined or altered in the light of new information and learning by everyone involved, from Dr. Maruta down.

The Sofina story began in 1965 with a "vision." The high quality, innovative product that finally emerged in 1982 allowed Kao to enter a new market and overtake well-established competitors. By 1990, Sofina had become the highest selling brand of cosmetics in Japan for most items except lipsticks.

The Vision

The vision, according to Mr. Daimaru (the first director of Sofina marketing), was simple: to help customers avoid the appearance of wrinkles on their skin for as long as possible. From this vision an equally simple question arose. "What makes wrinkles appear?" Finding the answer was the spring that set the Kao organization into motion.

Kao's competence until then had been in household and toiletry personal care products. However, Kao had long supplied raw materials for the leading cosmetics manufacturers in Japan, and had a technological competence in fats and soap that could, by cross pollination, be adapted to research on the human skin. Accordingly, the efforts of Kao's R&D laboratories were directed towards skin research, and the results used in the company's existing businesses such as Nivea or Azea, then sold in joint venture with Beiersdorf. From these successes came the idea for growth that steered the development of Sofina.

The Growth Idea

The idea was to produce a new, high quality cosmetic that gave real value at a reasonable price. Duringthe 1960s, there was a strong perception in the Japanese cosmetics industry that the more expensive the product, the better it was. This view was challenged by Dr. Maruta, whose travels had taught him that good skin care products sold in the United States or Europe were not as outrageously expensive. Yet in Japan, even with companies like Kao supplying high quality raw materials at a low price, the end product was still beyond the reach of ordinary women at ¥10-20,000.

As a supplier of raw materials, Dr. Maruta was aware of how well these products performed. He also knew that though cosmetics' prices were rising sharply, little was being spent on improving the products themselves, and that customers were paying for an expensive image. Was this fair, or good for the customer? Kao, he knew, had the capacity to supply high quality raw materials at low cost, and a basic research capability. Intensive research to develop new toiletry goods had led to the discovery of a technology for modifying the surface of powders, which could be applied to the development of cosmetics. Why not use these assets to develop a new, high quality, reasonably priced product, in keeping with Kao's principles?

To enter the new market would mean a heavy investment in research and marketing, with no guarantee that their product would be accepted. However, it was decided to go ahead; the product would be innovative and, against the emotional appeal of the existing competition in terms of packaging and image, its positioning would embody Kao's scientific approach.

This concept guided the learning process as Sofina was developed. It was found that the integration of Kao's unique liquid crystal emulsification technology and other newly developed materials proved effective in maintaining a "healthy and beautiful skin." This led Kao to emphasize skin care, as opposed to the industry's previous focus on make-up only. All the research results from Kao's skin diagnosis and dermatological testing were poured into the new product and, as Dr. Tsutsumi of the Tokyo Research Laboratory recalled, in pursuing problems connected with the product, new solutions emerged. For example, skin irritation caused by the new chemical was solved by developing MAP, a low irritant, and PSL, a moisturiser. By 1980, most of the basic research work had been done. Six cosmetics suitable for the six basic skin types had been developed, though all under the Sofina name.

During this stage, Kao's intelligence collectors were sent out to explore and map the new market environment. Information on products, pricing, positioning, the competition and above all, the customers, was analysed and digested by the Sofina marketing and R&D teams, and by Kao's top management. Again and again Dr. Maruta asked the same two questions: How would the new product be received? Was it what customers wanted?

The Growth Process

Test marketing began in September 1980, in the Shizuoka prefecture, and was scheduled to last for a year. Shizuoka was chosen because it represented 3.0 percent of the national market and an average social mix; either too rich or too poor, too rural or too urban. Its media isolation meant that television advertisements could be targeted to the local population, and no one outside would question why the product was not available elsewhere. The local paper also gave good coverage. In keeping with Kao's rule that "the concept of a new product is that of its advertising," the Sofina advertisements were reasoned and scientific, selling a function rather than an image.

Sofina was distributed directly to the retail stores through the Sofina Cosmetics Company, established to distinguish Sofina from Kao's conventional detergent business and avoid image blurring. No mention was made of Kao. Sofina's managers found, however, that retailers did not accept Sofina immediately, but put it on the waiting list for display along with other new cosmetics. The result was that by October 1980, Kao had only succeeded in finding 200 points of sale, against an object of 600. Then, as the real parentage of Sofina leaked out, the attitude among retailers changed, and the Sofina stand was given the best position in the store. This evidence of Kao's credibility, together with the company's growing confidence in the quality and price of the product, led to a change of strategy. The 30-strong sales force was instructed to put the Kao name first and, by November, 600 outlets had been found.

Sofina's subsequent development was guided by feedback from the market. Direct distribution enabled Kao to retain control of the business and catch customer responses to the product at first hand. To Mr. Masashi Kuga, Director of Kao's Marketing Research Department, such information "has clear added value, and helps in critical decision making." During the repeated test marketing of Sofina, Kao's own market research service, formed in 1973 to ensure a high quality response from the market with the least possible distortion, measured the efficacy of sampling and helped decide on the final marketing mix. This activity was usually supported by "concept testing, focus group

discussions, plus product acceptance research." Mr. Daimaru visited the test market twice or three times each month and talked to consumers directly. Dr. Marunta did the same.

Every piece of information and all results were shared by the Sofina team, R&D, Kao's top management, corporate marketing and sales managers. Discussions on Sofina's progress were attended by all of these managers, everyone contributing ideas about headline copy or other issues on an equal basis. Wives and friends were given samples and their reactions were fed back to the team.

From the reactions of customers and stores, Kao learned that carrying real information in the advertisements about the quality of the product had been well received, despite differing from the normal emphasis on fancy packaging. This they could never have known from their detergent business. Another finding was the importance of giving a full explanation of the product with samples, and of a skin analysis before recommending the most suitable product rather than trying to push the brand indiscriminately. They also learned the value of listening to the opinion of the store manager's wife who, they discovered, often had the real managing power, particularly for cosmetics products.

Decisions were implemented immediately. For example, the decision to improve the design for the sample package was taken at 3:30 P.M., and by 6:30 P.M. the same day the engineer in the factory had begun re-designing the shape of the bottle.

The results of this test marketing, available to the whole company, confirmed the decision to go ahead with Sofina. Kao was satisfied that the product would be accepted nationally, though it might take some time. A national launch was planned for the next year. Even at this stage, however, Mr. Maruta was still asking whether consumers and retail store owners really liked Sofina.

The Learning Extended

Sofina finally went on nationwide sale in October 1982. However, the flow of learning and intelligence gathering continued via the hansha and MIS. Kao, the hansha, the retailers and Sofina's customers formed a chain, along which that was a free, two-way flow of information. The learning was then extended to develop other products, resulting in production of the complete Sofina range of beauty care. In 1990, the range covered the whole market, from basic skin care to make-up cosmetics and perfumes.

In fact, the product did not achieve real success until after 1983. Dr. Tsutsumi dated it from the introduction of the foundation cream which, he recalled, also faced teething problems. The test result from the panel was not good; it was too different from existing products and was sticky on application. Kao, however, knowing it was a superior product that lasted longer, preserved and used their previous experience to convert the stickiness into a strength: the product was repositioned as "the longest lasting foundation that does not disappear with sweat."

In the early 1980s, while market growth was only 2-3 percent, sales of Sofina products increased at the rate of 30 percent every year. In 1990, sales amounted to ¥55 billion, and Kao held 15.6 percent of the cosmetic market behind Shiseido and Kanebo, though taken individually, Sofina brands topped every product category except lipsticks.

Within Japan, Sofina was sold through 12,700 outlets. According to Mr. Nakanishi, Director of the Cosmetics Division, the marketing emphasis was by that time being redirected from heavy advertising of the product to counselling at the point of sale. Kao was building up a force of beauty counsellors to educate the public on the benefits of Sofina products. A Sofina store in Tokyo was also helping to develop hair care and cosmetics products. A Sofina newspaper had been created which salesmen received by fax, along with the previous month's sales and inventory figures.

Knowledge gathered by the beauty advisers working in the Sofina shops was exploited for the development of the next set of products. Thus, Sofina "ultra-violet" care, which incorporated skin lotion, uv care and foundation in one, was positioned to appeal to busy women and advertised as "one step less". The Sofina cosmetics beauty care consultation system offered advice by phone, at retail shops or by other means to consumers who made enquiries. From their questions, clues were sought to guide new product development.

A staff of Field Companions visited the retail stores to get direct feedback on sales. Every outlet was visited once a month, when the monitors discussed Kao products with store staff, advised on design displays and even helped clean up. Dr. Maruta himself maintained an active interest. Mr. Kuroyanagi described how Dr. Maruta recently "came down to our floor" to report that while visiting a certain town, he had "found a store selling Sofina products, and a certain shade sample was missing from the stand." He asked that the store be checked and the missing samples supplied as soon as possible.

Despite Sofina's success, Kao was still not satisfied. "To be really successful, developing the right image is important. We've lagged behind on this, and we must improve."

As the Sofina example showed, in its domestic base Kao was an effective and confident company, renowned for its ability to produce high quality, technologically advanced products at relatively low cost. Not surprising then, that since the 1960s it had turned its thoughts to becoming an important player on the larger world stage. But could the learning organization operate effectively outside Japan? Could Kao transfer its learning capability into a very different environment such as the US or Europe, where it would lack the twin foundations of infrastructure and human resource? Or would internationalization demand major adjustments to its way of operating?

Kao International

When the first cake of soap was produced in 1890, the name "Kao" was stamped in both Chinese characters and Roman letters in preparation for the international market. A century later, the company was active in 50 countries but, except for the small neighbouring markets of South East Asia, had not achieved a real breakthrough. Despite all its investments, commitment and efforts over 25 years, Kao remained only "potentially" a significant global competitor. In 1988, only 10 percent of its total sales was derived from overseas business, and 70 percent of this international volume was earned in SE Asia. As a result, internationalization was viewed by the company as its next key strategic challenge. Dr. Maruta made his ambitions clear; "Procter and Gamble, Unilever and L'Oréal are our competitors. We cannot avoid fighting in the 1990s." The challenge was to make those words a reality.

The Strategic Infrastructure

Kao's globalization was based not on a company-wide strategy, but on the product division system. Each product division developed its own strategy for international expansion and remained responsible for its worldwide results. Consequently, the company's business portfolio and strategic infrastructure varied widely from market to market.

South East Asia   As exhibit 7 illustrates, Kao had been building a platform for production and marketing throughout South East Asia since 1964, when it created its first overseas subsidiary in Thailand. By 1990 this small initial base had been expanded, mainly through joint ventures, and the company had made steady progress in these markets. The joint ventures in Hong Kong and Singapore sold only Kao's consumer products, while the others both manufactured and marketed them.

One of Kao's biggest international battles was for control of the Asian detergent, soap and shampoo markets, against rivals like P&G and Unilever. In the Taiwanese detergent market, where Unilever was the long established leader with 50 percent market share, Kao's vanguard product was the biological detergent, *Attack.* Launched in 1988, Attack increased Kao's market share from 17 percent to 22 percent. Subsequently, Kao decided on local production, both to continue serving the local market and for export to Hong Kong and Singapore. Its domestic rival, Lion (stationary at 17 percent) shortly followed suit. In Hong Kong, Kao was the market leader with 30 percent share and in Singapore, where Colgate-Palmolive led with 30 percent, had increased its share from 5 percent to 10 percent. Unilever, P&G and Colgate-Palmolive had responded to Kao's moves by putting in more human resources, and consolidating their local bases.

In Indonesia, where Unilever's historic links again made it strong, Kao, Colgate-Palmolive and P&G competed for the second position. In the Philippines, Kao had started local production of shampoo and liquid soap in 1989, while in Thailand it had doubled its local facilities in order to meet increasing demand. To demonstrate its commitment to the Asian market where it was becoming a major player, Kao had established its Asian headquarters in Singapore. In that market, Kao's disposable diaper Merry had a a 20 percent share, while its Merit shampoo was the market leader.

North America

Step 1 – Joint venture   In 1976, Kao had embarked on two joint ventures with Colgate-Palmolive Company, first to market hair care products in the US, and later to develop new oral hygiene products for Japan. The potential for synergy seemed enormous; Colgate-Palmolive was to provide the marketing expertise and distribution infrastructure, Kao would contribute the technical expertise to produce a high quality product for the top end of the United States market.

1977 saw a considerable exchange of personnel and technology, and a new shampoo was specially developed by Kao for the United States consumer. Despite the fact that tests in three major United States cities, using Colgate-Palmolive's state-of-the-art market research methods, showed poor market share potential, the product launch went ahead. The forecasts turned out to be correct, and the product was dropped after 10 months due to Colgate-Palmolive's reluctance to continue. A Kao manager explained the failure thus; "First, the product was not targeted to the proper consumer group. High-price, high-end products were not appropriate for a novice and as yet unsophisticated producer like us. Second, the United States side believed in the result of the market research too seriously and did not attempt a second try… Third, it is essentially very difficult to penetrate a market like the shampoo market. Our partner expected too much short-term success. Fourth, the way the two firms decided on strategy was totally different. We constantly adjust our strategy flexibly. They never start without a concrete and fixed strategy. We could not wait for them."

The alliance was dissolved in 1985. However, Kao had learned some valuable lessons about United States marketing methods, Western lifestyles and, most of all, about the limitations of using joint ventures as a means of breaking into the United States market.

Step 2 – Acquisition   In 1988, Kao had made three acquisitions. In May, it bought the Andrew Jergens Company, a Cincinnati soap, body lotion and shampoo maker, for $350 million. To acquire Jergens' extensive marketing know-how and established distribution channels, Kao beat off 70 other bidders, including Beiersdorf and Colgate-Palmolive, and paid 40 percent more than the expected price. Since then, Kao has invested heavily in the company, building a new multi-million dollar research centre and doubling Jergen's research team to over 50. Cincinnati was the home town of P&G, who have since seen Jergens market Kao's bath preparations in the United States.

High Point Chemical Corporation of America, an industrial goods producer, was also acquired in 1988. As Kao's United States chemical manufacturing arm, it had since begun "an aggressive expansion of its manufacturing facilities and increased its market position." The third acquisition, Info Systems (Sentinel) produced application products in the field of information technology.

In Canada, Kao owned 87 percent of Kao-Didak, a floppy disk manufacturer it bought out in 1986. A new

EXHIBIT 7
The History of Kao's Internationalization

	Company	Year	Capital	Main Products
ASIA				
Taiwan	Taiwan Kao Co. Ltd	1964	90	detergent, soap
Thailand	Kao Industrila Co. Ltd	1964	70	hair care products
Singapore	Kao Private Ltd	1965	100	sales of soap, shampoo, detergents
Hong Kong	Kao Ltd	1970	100	sales of soap, shampoo, detergents
Malaysia	Kao Ptc. Ltd	1973	45	hair care products
Philippines	Pilippinas Kao Inc.	1977	70	fats and oils
Indonesia	P.T. PoleKao	1977	74	surfactants
Philippines	Kao Inc.	1979	70	hair care products
Indonesia	P.T. Dino Indonesia Industrial Ltd	1985	50	hair care products
Malaysia	Fatty Chemical Sdn. Bdn.	1988	70	alcohol
Singapore	Kao South-East Asia Headquarters	1988		
Philippines	Kao Co. Philippines Laboratory			
NORTH AMERICA				
Mexico	Qumi-Kao S.A. de C.V.	1975	20	fatty amines
	Bitumex	1979	49	asphal
Canada	Kao-Didak Ltd	1983	89	floppy disk
U.S.A.	Kao Corporation of Americal (KCOA)	1986	100	sales of household goods
	High Point Chemical	1987	100 (KCOA)	ingredients
	Kao Infosystems Company	1988	100 (KCOA)	duplication of software
	The Andrew Jergens	1988	100 (KCOA)	hair care products
U.S.A.	KCOA Los Angeles Laboratories			
EUROPE				
W. Germany	Kao Corporation GmbH	1986	100 (KCG)	sales of household goods
	Kao Perfekta GmbH	1986	80 (KCG)	toners for copier
	Guhl Ikebana GmbH	1986	50 (KCG)	hair care products
Spain	Kao Corporation S.A.	1987	100	surfactants
W. Germany	Goldwell AG	1989	100	cosmetics
France	Kao Co. S.A. Paris Laboratories			
Spain	Kao Co. S.A. Barcelona Laboratories			
W. Germany	Kao Co. GmbH Berlin Laboratories			

plant, built in 1987, started producing 3.5 inch and 5.25 inch diskettes, resulting in record sales of $10 million that same year. Kao viewed floppy disks as the spearhead of its thrust into the United States market. As Mr. Kyroyanagi explained: "This product penetrates the US market easily. Our superior technology makes it possible to meet strict requirements for both quantity and quality. Our experience in producing specific chemicals for the floppy disk gives us a great competitive edge." In what represented a dramatic move for a Japanese company, Kao relocated its worldwide head office for the floppy disk business to the United States, partly because of Kao's comparatively strong position there (second behind Sony) but also because it was by far the biggest market in the world. The United States headquarters was given complete strategic freedom to develop the business globally. Under the direction of this office a plant was built in Spain.

Europe   Within Europe, Kao had built a limited presence in Germany, Spain and France. In Germany, it had established a research laboratory, and through its 1979 joint venture with Beiersdorf to develop and market hair care products, gained a good knowledge of the German market. The strategic position of this business was strengthened in 1989 by the acquisition of a controlling interest in Goldwell AG, one of Germany's leading suppliers of hair and skin care products to beauty salons. From studying Goldwell's network of beauty salons across Europe, Kao expected to expand its knowledge in order to be able to develop and market new products in Europe.

Kao's French subsidiary, created in January 1990, marketed floppy disks, skin toner and the Sofina range of cosmetics. The research laboratory established in Paris that same year was given the leading role in developing perfumes to meet Kao's worldwide requirements.

Kao's vanguard product in Europe was Sofina, which was positioned as a high quality, medium priced product. Any Japanese connection had been removed to avoid giving the brand a cheap image. While Sofina was produced and packaged in Japan, extreme care was taken to ensure that it shared a uniform global positioning and image in all the national markets in Europe. It was only advertised in magazines like Vogue, and sales points were carefully selected; for example in France, Sofina was sold only in the prestigious Paris department store, Galeries Lafayette.

Organizational Capability

Organizationally, Kao's international operations were driven primarily along the product division axis. Each subsidiary had a staff in charge of each product who reported to the product's head office, either directly or through a regional product manager. For example, the manager in charge of Sofina in Spain reported to the French office where the regional manager responsible for Sofina was located, and he in turn reported to the Director of the Divisional HQ in Japan. Each subsidiary was managed by Japanese expatriate managers, since Kao's only foreign resource was provided by its acquired companies. Thus, the German companies remained under the management of its original directors. However, some progress was made towards localisation; in Kao Spain (250 employees) there were "only six to ten Japanese, not necessarily in management." Kao's nine overseas R&D laboratories were each strongly connected to both the product headquarters and laboratories in Japan through frequent meetings and information exchange.

Mr. Takayama saw several areas that needed to be strengthened before Kao could become an effective global competitor. Kao, he believed "was a medium sized company grown large." It lacked international experience, had fewer human resource assets, especially in top management and, compared with competitors like P&G and Unilever, had far less accumulated international knowledge and experience of Western markets and consumers. "These two companies know how to run a business in the West and have well established market research techniques, whereas the Westernization of the Japanese lifestyle has only occurred in the last 20 years," he explained. "There are wide differences between East and West in, for example, bathing habits, that the company has been slow to comprehend."

Kao attempted to redress these problems through stronger involvement by headquarters' managers in supporting the company's foreign operations. Mr. Kuroyanagi provided an insight into Kao's approach to managing its overseas units. He described how, after visiting a foreign subsidiary where he felt change was necessary, he asked a senior colleague in Japan to carry out a specific review. The two summarized their findings, and then met with other top management members for further consultation. As a result, his colleague was temporarily located in the foreign company to lead certain projects. A team was formed in Japan to harmonize with locals, and sent to work in the subsidiary. Similarly, when investigating the reason for the company's slow penetration of the shampoo market in Thailand, despite offering a technologically superior product, headquarters' managers found that the product positioning, pricing and packaging policies developed for the Japanese market were unsuitable for Thailand. Since the subsidiary could not adapt these policies to meet local requirements, a headquarters' marketing specialist was brought in, together with a representative from Dentsu — Kao's advertising agent in Japan — to identify the source of the problem and make the necessary changes in the marketing mix.

Part of Mr. Kuroyanagi's role was to act as a "liaison officer" between Kao and its subsidiaries. Kao appointed such managers at headquarters to liaise with all the newly acquired companies in Europe and Asia; their task was to interpret corporate strategies to other companies outside Japan and ensure that "We never make the same mistake twice." He described himself as "the eyes and ears of top management, looking round overseas moves, competitors' activities and behaviours and summarizing them." He was also there to "help the local management abroad understand correctly Kao as a corporation, and give hints about how to overcome the cultural gap and linguistic difficulties, how to become open, aggressive and innovative."

Kao's 1990 global strategy was to develop "local operations sensitive to each region's characteristics and needs." As Mr. Takayama explained, these would be able "to provide each country with goods tailored to its local climate and customs, products which perfectly meet the needs of its consumers." To this end, the goals of the company's research centres in Los Angeles, Berlin, Paris and Santiago de Compostela in Spain, had been redefined as: "to analyze local market needs and characteristics and integrate them into the product development process," and a small market research unit had been created in Thailand to support local marketing of Sofina. Over time, Kao hoped, headquarters' functions would be dispersed to SE Asia, the US and Europe, leaving to the Tokyo headquarters the role of supporting regionally based, locally managed operations by giving "strategic assistance." There were no plans to turn Jergens or other acquired companies into duplicate Kaos; as described by Dr. Maruta "We will work alongside them rather than tell them which way to go."

The lack of overseas experience among Kao's managers was tackled via a new ¥9 billion training facility built at Kasumigaura. The 16 hectare campus, offering golf, tennis and other entertainment opportunities was expected to enjoy a constant population of 200, with 10 days training becoming the norm for all managers. To help Kao managers develop a broader and more international outlook, training sessions devoted considerable attention to the cultural and historical heritages of different countries. A number of younger managers were sent to Europe and the United States, spending the first year learning languages and the second either at a business school, or at Kao's local company offices.

"If you look at our recent international activity," said Mr. Kuroyanagi, "we have prepared our stage. We have made our acquisitions… the basis for globalization in Europe, North America and South East Asia has been facilitated… We now need some play on that stage." Kao's top management was confident that the company's R&D power, "vitality and open, innovative and aggressive culture" would ultimately prevail. The key constraints, inevitably, were people. "We do not have enough talented people to direct these plays on the stage." Kao could not and did not wish to staff its overseas operations with Japanese nationals, but finding, training and keeping suitable local personnel was a major challenge.

Kao expected the industry to develop like many others until "there were only three or four companies operating on a global scale. We would like to be one of these." Getting there looked like taking some time, but Kao was in no rush. The perspective, Dr. Maruta continually stressed, was very long term, and the company would move at its own pace. "We should not," he said, "think about the quick and easy way, for that can lead to bad handling of our products. We must take the long term view… and spiral our activity towards the goal… We will not, and need not hurry our penetration of foreign markets. We need to avoid having unbalanced growth. The harmony among people, products and world wide operations is the most important philosophy to keep in mind… only in 15 years will it be clear how we have succeeded."

THE BODY SHOP INTERNATIONAL—THE MOST HONEST COSMETIC COMPANY IN THE WORLD†

By Andrew Campbell

Every year the cynics wait for The Body Shop to trip over its ideologically pure feet and every year they are disappointed. Although imitators have inevitably arisen, Body Shop benefits from being clearly identified as the leader of the pack in the growing market for toiletries and cosmetics aimed at the environmentally oriented, health conscious consumer.

The Body Shop "originates, produces and sells naturally based skin and hair products and related items through its own shops and through franchised outlets." The business has grown rapidly since it opened its first shop in Brighton in 1976, and in 1990 it had a turnover of £84.5m and 457 outlets in the UK and overseas. In the seven years since its flotation the company has increased both turnover and profits by a factor of nine, and has been described as "the share that defies gravity." This is despite the onset of a recession in retailing. Financial performance for the last five years is detailed in exhibit 1. Although it is not one of the largest retail operators, The Body Shop has been particularly influential because of its phenomenal success, its strong underlying philosophy and the press coverage it has received.

Much of the press coverage has centred around managing director Anita Roddick, a charismatic, outspoken and determined figure who has a simple formula to explain the secret of her legendary success: "I look at what the cosmetics trade is doing and walk in the opposite direction."

The extent of this success is such that she claims that The Body Shop is Britain's most international store. "We produce over 300 products sold in well over 300 shops from the Arctic Circle to Adelaide, covering 31 countries and 13 languages, without once diluting our image." Actually by February 1990 The Body Shop was operating with 457 shops, 139 in Britain and 318 in 37 other countries. A further 25 UK outlets and 180 overseas were due to open in the following 12 months, including a shop in Japan in October 1990. Preliminary research has been conducted into the feasibility of opening in Moscow.

Anita Roddick has won many accolades from the business community, including the Business Enterprise Award for company of the year, and Business Woman of the Year. In her acceptance speeches she savages corporate approaches to business and in particular traditional ways of doing business in the retail and cosmetics sectors: "Retailing itself has taught me nothing. I see tired executives in tired systems. These huge corporations are dying of boredom caused by the inertia of giantism. All these big retailing companies seem to be led by accountants and they seem to have become just versions of the post office or the department of motor vehicles.

"Retailing at the moment is a combination of war and sport in designer uniforms, with its obsession with corporate raiding, acquisitions of acres, strategies, niche markets, specialisation and empire building, where their only sense of adventure is in their profit and loss sheet. We have never once been seduced into believing we are anything more than simply traders."

Her belief is that the essential difference between The Body Shop and other retailers is explained in the words of Niemann Marcus: "Profit is not the objective of my business. It is providing a product and a service." So how does she do it? "It is so easy. First, know your differences and exploit them, then know your customers and educate them, then talk about the image of your company as well as the products, and finally be daring, be first and be different."

"One of the rules of any successful company is to find out what your original features are and shout them out from the rooftops. We have found that when you take care of your customers really well, and make them the focal point, never once forgetting that your first

†**Source:** Ashridge Strategic Management Centre, © 1991, revised February 1992. Reprinted by permission of the author.

EXHIBIT 1
The Body Shop's Financial Performance 1986–1990 (in £'000)

	1990†	1989†	1989††	1987*	1986*
Turnover UK & Eire	56,901	41,412	54,754	21,255	13,560
Turnover Overseas	27,579	13,997	18,253	7,221	3,834
Turnover —Total	84,480	55,409	73,007	28,476	17,394
Pre-tax profit	14,508	11,232	15,243	5,998	3,451
Earnings per share	10.0p	7.4p	10.2p	4.65p	2.58p
Number of outlets UK	139	112	112	89	77
Number of outlets overseas	318	255	255	186	155

	Group Turnover			Group Trading Profits		
	1990†	1989†	1989††	1990†	1989†	1989††
United Kingdom & Eire	56,901	41,412	54,754	13,486	9,745	13,015
Other EEC countries	6,962	4,136	5,445	1,566	904	1,254
Rest of Europe	3,910	2,717	3,966	996	932	1,270
USA	5,839	874	874	(1,941)	(1,632)	(1,820)
Rest of North America	5,860	3,194	4,244	1,481	887	1,082
Australasia	3,544	2,119	2,454	915	326	422
Asia	1,464	957	1,270	389	222	324
	84,480	55,409	73,007	16,892	11,384	15,547

* = Year ended September 30
† = Year ended February 28
†† = 17 months ended February 28

line of customers are your own staff, profitability flows from that."

The Body Shop has an extraordinary effect on people who come into contact with it. "It arouses enthusiasm, commitment and loyalty more often found in a political movement than a corporation," says journalist Bo Burlingham. "Customers light up when asked about it, and start pitching its products like missionaries selling Bibles." John Richards, director of retail research at County NatWest Securities, comments: "I've never seen anything like it. The nearest comparison would be something like flower power in the 1960s."

The Body Shop Story

Anita Roddick was one of four children of Italian immigrants and helped in the family cafe at the Sussex seaside resort of Littlehampton, which is still the base for her retailing empire. She has fond memories of the cafe, a popular meeting place for local children. "We had the first juke box in the town after the war, the first knickerbocker glories and the first Pepsi-Colas. I didn't know it then but I was receiving subliminal training for business life; I was at the centre of that magical area where buyer and seller come together."

At an early age she decided that she wanted to see the world and went to work for the International Labour Office of the United Nations in Paris. It was while travelling internationally for the UN that the seeds of her future calling were sown. Visiting such exotic spots as Polynesia, Mauritius and the New Hebrides, she observed the simple but effective way remote communities lived.

"I just lived as they did and watched how they groomed themselves without any cosmetic aids. Their skin was wonderful and their hair was beautifully clean." She watched the Polynesians scoop up untreated cocoa butter and apply it to their skin with remarkable results. She also observed Sri Lankans using pineapple juice as a skin cleanser, and later discovered that natural enzymes in it help remove dead cells.

Today, Anita spends about two months every year travelling the world picking up tips for natural ingredients to go into Body Shop products. "Women in other societies know that these well tried and tested ways work and do not need a scientist or advertising agency to sell them." When Anita gets back from a trip abroad she will regale managers with tales of her adventures. Walls in warehouses and factories are hung with words and images and displays of Third World art.

When she returned from her travels, Anita married and opened a restaurant with her husband Gordon. He too got the wanderlust and set off on a horse back ride from South America to New York that was to take him two years. She did not feel that she could cope with the restaurant on her own and decided to open a shop instead, selling skin and hair products made from the natural recipes gleaned on her travels.

"You cannot call this shop The Body Shop"

Starting with a bank loan of £4000, Anita Roddick opened the first Body Shop in Brighton in 1976 with a blaze of publicity. She was jammed between two funeral parlours who wrote her a letter saying, "You cannot call this shop the Body Shop," because the coffins would pass twice a day and they were expecting some cute photographer from *She* magazine to take that happy snap shot of the week. Her response was straightforward, as she recalls: "I have always been

petrified of headmasters and solicitors, but I think that the two most talented things that I have ever done in my life were to ignore those letters and then to use that to promote the company. So what I did was quite simple, and I think it should be standard practice for any young company setting up: the anonymous phone call! I rang up the local Evening Argus in Brighton and said to them, 'Do you know what is going on in Kensington Gardens? This poor woman on her own, with a new baby, whose husband is trekking across South America on a horse, is being intimidated by two Mafia undertakers. Her little shop is called THE BODY SHOP…'—I mean, I had written the story over the phone and we got our first free editorial. We have never ever paid for an advert since."

Many of the features which made The Body Shop different came about because of lack of funds in those early stages. The company could only afford 20 products to begin with, which was not enough to fill the shop. So making each product in 5 different sizes gave a wider range straight away. There are now over 300 products, but they can still be bought in 5 different sizes—customers like to be able to try the small sizes first. The Body Shop still uses the cheapest bottles, referred to in the early days by the Press as "urine sample bottles," and they can still be brought back for refills (a system originally introduced because they were in short supply, but now symbolic of the company's policy of recycling). Similarly symbolic are carrier bags which carry the question: "Why aren't telephone bills, gas bills, electricity bills, rate demands, income tax forms, public notices, circulars, newspapers, printed on recycled paper? This is a recycled paper bag. The Body Shop introduces changes for the better."

The success of The Body Shop grew out of Roddick's almost naive belief in herself and the value of sheer hard work. "We worked hard, therefore we survived," she says. "We didn't have any understanding of the commercial methods taught by business colleges. In fact I would suggest that anyone with an ounce of individuality should not go to a business school… because you are structured by academics who measure you in the science of business. They use a business language that is predictable, and where going out and doing is not part of the course."

The Body Shop expanded rapidly under the franchise system which developed a strong camaraderie through the help given to each franchise in setting up and through allowing everyone to do their own labelling. There are currently around 5000 applicants wanting to take up a Body Shop franchise, and it takes 3 years to succeed. "Unless you're absolutely obsessed you don't get a look in."

Applicants undergo strict vetting, including an offbeat questionnaire with unlikely questions such as: "How would you like to die? What is your favourite flower? Who is your heroine in history or poetry?" Roddick believes that basic business skills can be provided by the company but the right attitude and values cannot. "We have the back-up to teach almost anyone to run a Body Shop," she says. "What we can't control is the soul."

The Body Shop has managed to achieve a remarkable level of uniformity within their now global network of shops. "They are all the same—and they all work. I think it is interesting that we are not seen as an English company but as a cross-cultural one, with a product range with international ingredients."

Operations

In the early days bottles were filled, labelled and capped by hand and each order picked and filled individually. The process is now fully automated. There is a manufacturing department with a staff of 7 covering manufacturing, quality control, product development and customer complaints.

Twenty-five percent of manufacturing is done in-house, the rest by contract manufacturers. The range grows by 80-90% each year. In 1990 construction is due to be completed on new manufacturing and blow-moulding facilities as well as a research and development and office building in Littlehampton.

Each supplier to The Body Shop is required to sign a declaration guaranteeing none of the ingredients used has been tested on animals during the previous five years. To show its complete opposition to cruelty in the name of beauty, in 1989 The Body Shop resigned from the Cosmetic Toiletry and Perfume Association amid accusations that the trade body lacked the necessary passion and imagination to eliminate animal testing quickly enough.

Franchise System

At the start of the company, Anita and Gordon Roddick could not afford to open new shops themselves even though business was booming, so they developed the concept of "self-financing." If someone else would put up the money to open a new shop, the Roddicks would help with their expertise in running the operation, help re-fit the shop, and grant a licence to use the company name and sell the products. The company now has a franchise manager who provides a consultancy service and organises the relocation of older shops to prime sites.

The franchise system also operates overseas, with a head franchisee for a country or group of countries who is granted exclusive rights to use The Body Shop trademark and to distribute its products. Those who operate their own shops successfully are given the right to sub-franchise within their area, and have responsibility for training sub-franchisees.

As in the UK, shop designs and graphics are strictly enforced and franchisees have to stock 85% Body Shop products. Unlike the UK, however, no annual operating fees are charged to overseas franchisees and products are sold subject to an overseas distribution discount.

Scandinavia was the first overseas area in which The Body Shop became popular, followed by Canada which became the first overseas operation to manufacture products itself. Samples are still sent to the UK for quality control before each batch is bottled, and the "heart ingredients" are provided by Body Shop International and blended in the UK. Other ingredients are approved by the UK before manufacture in Canada.

The Body Shop Philosophy

In essence Anita Roddick promotes an ethical code of behaviour for the global citizen—and that includes multinational companies. She believes in the empowerment of people, through jobs, work, honest earning. "Our idea of success is the number of people we have employed, how we have educated them and raised their human consciousness, and whether we have enthused them with a breathless enthusiasm. Our solution to third world poverty is trade not aid."

The philosophy is explained to the customer as follows:

- The Body Shop continues to trade today on the same principles that have held firm since its beginning in 1976.

- We use vegetable rather than animal ingredients in our products.

- We do not test our ingredients or final products on animals.

- We respect our environment: we offer a refill service in our shops, all our products are biodegradable, we recycle waste and use recycled paper wherever possible, we use biodegradable carrier bags.

- We use naturally based, close-to-source ingredients as much as we can.

- We offer a range of sizes and keep packaging to a minimum: our customers pay for the product, not elaborate packaging or for more than they need (and this helps keep the prices down too).

The philosophy is put into practice on many levels, some more visible than the others:

- Our products reflect our philosophy.

- They are formulated with care and respect:
  –respect for other cultures;
  –respect for the past;
  –respect for the natural world;
  –respect for the customer.

- The Body Shop joined forces with Greenpeace over a two year period in a campaign to "Save the Whale" and in the UK we are involved with the Friends of the Earth during 1987-88, in a campaign to raise public awareness of the dangers of acid rain and other environmental hazards, and to encourage others to take positive action to protect their environment, such as recycling household and workplace waste.

Roddick and her employees have real enthusiasm for the company and its products. "I see business as a renaissance concept," she says, "where the human spirit comes into play. How do you ennoble the spirit when you are selling moisture cream? Let me tell you, the spirit soars when you are making products that are life serving, that make people feel better. I can even feel great about a moisture cream because of that."

There are some very visible manifestations of the company's philosophy in the way the company operates. For example, each employee at the Littlehampton head office has two wastepaper baskets, one for recyclable and one for non-recyclable waste. The company even runs training courses on recycling.

EXHIBIT 2
The Toiletries Industry

THE TOILETRIES INDUSTRY

The market for haircare products is complex and fragmented. In the UK in 1988 the total size of the skincare market alone was over £138 million. Although nearly 50% of the market for skincare creams and lotions is accounted for by the top 5 companies, a large number of small companies makes up the remaining 56%.

The shampoo market is also highly fragmented with the top 10-11 brands accounting for half the market and the other 80-90 competing for the rest. The conditioner market is becoming more and more competitive with many brands competing for a small market share. The top companies in the UK in terms of market share in both shampoos and conditioners are Elida Gibbs, Beecham, Alberto Culver, Johnson & Johnson and Revlon. The fastest growing brand is Timotei, which has a share of just under 10% and caters to two growing trends, that for "natural" products and that for a shampoo designed for frequent use without damaging the hair.

There is a wide spectrum of products, with new products or reformulations continually being introduced as companies seek to create or imitate new fashion fads. This means that advertising is used extensively, with the premium brands being advertised in upmarket women's glossy magazines. Television advertising is also used for both hair and skincare products, often aimed at educating the consumer about a new type of product. The proliferation of new products has also lead to a blurring of product categories, eg moisturising cleanser, conditioning shampoo.

The industry can be segmented by a number of different criteria, such as price range (premium, middle and budget); target market age group; function (health and hygiene, beauty products), and so on. Growth is mainly in upmarket product ranges and consumers are primarily women, although sectors which have shown high growth recently are products for men and own label products, with Boots now taking 6-7% of the market for cleansers,

Continued

Commitment by top management to such values is vital. "The people who make the policy decisions… must lead with integrity, commitment and passion, otherwise a cynicism pervades the whole place," says Roddick. "Corporate culture is the most important part of a growing company like The Body Shop—it is the values, the rituals, the goals, the hero's characteristic of a company's style."

The Responsibility of Profits

After The Body Shop was launched on the Unlisted Securities Market and the shops were all proving profitable, Roddick set up an environmental and communities department to translate her beliefs and concerns into practical projects. Each franchised outlet is required to take on a community project in its area, "which is there to give the young women in the organisation additional status and helps them realise that everyone has the ability to change the world for the better." All projects are taken on within working hours, and franchisees choose what they want to do. There is no coercion.

This determination to use private profit for public good is now reaching out to some of the remotest parts of the third world, where one of the latest projects is setting up a paper making plant in a Tibetan refugee camp. The paper is processed from pineapple and banana leaves and will be used for wrapping Body Shop products.

In Southern India, The Body Shop has set up a boys' town for destitute youngsters. The boys are taught rural craft and to make Christmas cards, and the money from the sales is put into trust funds. When the youngsters leave at the age of 16 they have the means to purchase a herd of sheep or a horse and cart, giving them a vital start. So far over 3,000 jobs have been created and the scheme has made about £100,000 profit, and supplies The Body Shop with soap bags and wooden foot massagers.

The whole process is seen to be self perpetuating with ingredients obtained from the Third World, providing work and sustenance for under-privileged

EXHIBIT 2–Continued
The Toiletries Industry

moisturisers and astringents. After Boots, the most important in the own label sector are Marks & Spencer, Sainsbury's, Yves Rocher and Superdrug. Safeway and Woolworths also have their own skincare ranges. In terms of distribution, supermarkets now account for about 30% of the total hair care market; there is a growing tendency to view such products as shampoo, hairspray and conditioners as "grocery" items, and they are increasingly sold in larger or "family size" packs. Another area where there has been growth recently is in anti-ageing products. Women (including younger women) are taking an increasing interest in the health of their skin and the adverse affects of wind, sun and polluted air.

Own label products are also a threat to established brands in the soap market, such as Imperial Leather, Lux and Shield. Sales of soap reached a peak in 1986 and the market is now thought to be declining, with products such as bath oil or foam overtaking soap for the first time in 1987. The two main trends in the soap market in recent years have been "fruity" soaps, first made popular by The Body Shop but imitated by others; pure, fragrance-free brands such as Simple and Pears; and liquid soap, which now accounts for around 5% of the total market.

The Body Shop dominates the UK market for natural make-up mainly because most manufacturers of "natural" cosmetics, such as Creightons, have not entered the colour cosmetics market. Health-oriented manufacturers of toiletries and makeup include Innoxa, whose slogan is "pure and beautiful" and which is the only makeup recognised by the British Medical Association.

As a result of the recent growth in environmental awareness throughout Europe, numerous small players have been active in the "green" cosmetics market. However, only Yves Rocher is a significant competitor for The Body Shop. Monsieur Rocher's passion is "plants and natural beauty" and this is explained in the Green Book of Beauty, a mail order catalogue for toiletries and makeup. Mail order constitutes the heart of this company's activities, and it has in addition more than 1,200 Beauty Centres worldwide.

societies, making products that are sold to the more fortunate, the profits of which are ploughed back into an educational programme which aims to make people more aware of the critical social issues of our time.

The plight of the inhabitants of the Amazon rain forest has been the subject of a worldwide campaign by the company, which has raised £250,000 for their defence. It has mobilised employees for petition drives and fund-raising campaigns, carried out through the shops and in company time. It has produced window displays, t-shirts, brochures and videotapes to educate people about the issues, and has even printed appeals on the side of its delivery trucks.

The Body Shop was the first company in Britain to use Jojoba oil in cosmetics. Jojoba is obtained from a desert plant and is a substitute for sperm whale oil. Apart from helping protect whales, there are other powerful reasons for using oil from the desert plant. Jojoba can be grown on some of the poorest land in the world, which is totally unsuitable for conventional crops, and in regions where people are living in abject poverty.

This approach isn't restricted to far away places. Chris Elphick of Community Learning Initiatives suggested that perhaps Roddick might care to go and practise some of her philosophies in Easterhouse, an area just to the east of Glasgow which has 56% male unemployment and frequent deaths from solvent abuse. Her response was predictable. Within 8 months she had won over all the local councillors, opened a soap factory called Soapworks and dedicated 25% of all profits to the local community. When asked about unions, she told them: "You only need unions when management are bastards. We will talk to you one to one if there is a problem." Employees are treated with respect and made to feel that their roles are important. Soapworks is involved in the community and has funded the building of a playground for local children. In the first full trading year Soapworks produced over four million bars of soap and expected to produce more than 15 million bars in 1990. A bath-salt filling line has been added, and the workforce now stands at 85.

The commitment to "profits with principles" is also evident in initiatives for employees, such as the £1 million invested in 1989 in building and equipping a workplace nursery for head office staff.

Journalist Bo Burlingham claims that the campaigning approach is part of a carefully researched and executed business strategy. Roddick wants causes that will generate excitement and enthusiasm in the shops, and says: "You educate people by their passions, especially young people. You find ways to grab their imagination. They're doing what I'm doing. They're learning. Three years ago I didn't know anything about the rain forest. Five years ago I didn't know anything about the ozone layer. It's a process of learning to be a global citizen. And it produces a sense of passion you won't find in a department store."

No Advertising

An important aspect of The Body Shop's product philosophy is that, in keeping with its claim to be the most honest cosmetics company, it does not call its products "beauty" products, nor does it use idealised images of women to sell them. Roddick explains: "The cosmetics industry is bizarre because it's run by men who create needs that don't exist, making women feel incredibly dissatisfied with their bodies. They have this extraordinary belief that all women want is hope and promise. They have this absolute obsession with not telling the truth, which is bizarre because some of the products they make are actually good. But to me it's dishonest to make claims that a cream that is basically oil and water is going to take grief and stress and 50 years of living in the sun off your face. It's bullshit to consistently endorse its main product line which is garbage, waste and packaging." Salespeople in The Body Shop are expected to be able to answer questions, but are trained not to be forceful.

The Body Shop does not advertise and its point of sale materials concentrate on giving information about the ingredients in the product, and educating the customer about its use. In fact, the information sheets about the products were first introduced because the products in the early days sometimes looked unappetising: "We thought we had to explain them because they looked so bizarre. I mean, there were little black things floating in some of them. We had to say these were not worms." Containers have clear, factual explanations of what is inside and what it is good for. On the shelves are notecards with stories about the products or their ingredients. There are stacks of pamphlets with such titles as *Animal Testing and Cosmetics* and *What is Natural?* There is a huge reference book called *The Product Information Manual* with background on everything Body Shop sells.

The level of information The Body Shop offers provides a powerful source of competitive advantage. It differentiates the company from its competitors, and it creates obstacles for would-be copycats. Customers feel they *know* its values and business practices, and the effect is to create a loyalty that goes beyond branding. "I've just taken what every good teacher knows," says Roddick. "You try to make your classroom an enthralling place…I'm doing the same thing. There is education in the shops. There are anecdotes right on the products, and anecdotes adhere."

Although the company does not advertise directly, good public relations is fundamental to their marketing strategy. Roddick quickly learned the same lesson as Marks & Spencer—that product advertising is unnecessary when a company has built up a strong and continuing public image. Says journalist Michel Syrett: "Roddick courts publicity. She makes herself deliberately available to the press and is a constant source of good copy. 'The press like us,' she commented at the CBI last year. 'I'm always available and I'm loudmouthed and quotable.' Her views on healthcare, environmental issues and the soullessness of big business are not manufactured and are entirely consistent with the aims and philosophy on which The Body Shop has been founded."

The money that would normally be spent on marketing is largely invested in the company's employees. "It takes more or less the same approach that it uses with customers, attacking cynicism with information," says Bo Burlingham. "It deluges employees with newsletters, videos, brochures, posters and training programmes, to convince them that while profits may be boring, business does not have to be."

There is a training centre in London which anyone in the company can attend free of charge. Courses are almost entirely devoted to instruction in the nature and uses of the products, and are so popular that the school cannot keep up with demand.

The company newsletter reads almost like an underground newsletter. Burlingham again: "More space is devoted to campaigns to save the rain forest and ban ozone-depleting chemicals than the opening of a new branch. Sprinkled throughout are quotes, bits of poetry, environmental facts and anthropological anecdotes."

The Move into Colour Cosmetics

It might appear to the casual observer that a move into colour cosmetics (makeup as opposed to skin and haircare products) would be inconsistent with this philosophy and approach. After all, the mainstream colour cosmetics industry is characterised by glossy advertising showing the customer an idealised image of the woman she could become if only she would use this or that eyeshadow or lipstick.

But Anita Roddick had the answer to any criticism there might be. She commissioned academic research on the psychology of makeup from Dr. Jean Ann Graham in the United States to prove that women derive psychological support from painting their faces. The range was launched in collaboration with Barbara Daly, a well-known makeup expert who had designed the Princess of Wales' makeup on her wedding day. The packaging was minimal and the design stylishly simple. Products were coded to guide customers as to which colours go together, and again information leaflets were available, as well as a video showing how to apply makeup using both a young and an older woman as models. The range has proved successful with customers and in 1989 represented around 10-15% of Body Shop's turnover, a steadily increasing proportion.

■ SPORTIS: CHALLENGE AND RESPONSE IN POST-COMMUNIST POLAND†

By Max Boisot

Sysky's Soliloquy: Part I

Michael Sysky, sales manager of Sportis, chuckled to himself as his car reached the outskirts of Marki, 20 kilometers outside Warsaw, where his firm's headquarters were located. The journey to work had given him the time to savour the irony of the current situation at Sportis.

Here they were, a small private concern employing little over 300 people, barely one year after the Polish "Big Bang" in which prices were freed up and the zloty devalued, facing the total collapse of their traditional domestic market. But what can Sportis do about it? Recognizing the need to develop its activities outside Poland in order to survive as a firm, in one bold leap Sportis enters the one major foreign market in which it knows it has a strong competitive advantage: not that of the United States, Japan, or Western Europe, of course—what chance would a small Polish firm like Sportis stand there?—but that of Poland's former political master, the Soviet Union. By western standards Sportis may be lacking in funds and in know how, mused Sysky, but as this move shows, it certainly is not short on entrepreneurship.

Of course, Sysky acknowledged, westerners may have found it difficult to work with the Soviets—differences in culture as well as in economic philosophy were likely to cause problems. But, he believed, the Poles may have the necessary flexibility to succeed where westerners may not.

†**Source:** ©1992 by Max Boisot. Reprinted by permission of Routledge, Chapman & Hall Ltd., from *East West Business Collaboration*, Max Boisot, Ed. This case was prepared by Max Boisot as the basis for class discussion rather than to illustrate either effective or ineffective handling of an administrative situation.

The "people" problem, however, was by no means the end of it. The joint venture agreement which Sysky had signed on March 2, 1991 on behalf of Sportis had, as Soviet partners, the fishing company of Murmanrybprom, and a garment repair firm called Silouhette. Both were located in the city of Murmansk, some 200 miles north of the Arctic circle. The last time Sysky was in town, the temperatures were 45°C below zero.

There are so many barriers to entry against western competition, reflected the sales manager as he passed through the company gates. After all, which US, German, Japanese or British company in their right mind would brave this frozen desolation, the anachronistic caprices of "old believers," and the now galloping entropy of the Soviet business system, in pursuit of a market which, if anything, was probably shrinking? Had not Gosplan just announced that domestic production had dropped by 11% last year and was it not common knowledge that in "Sovietspeak" 11% really means 16% or more, making due allowance for the duplicity and ignorance of central planners?

However, as any Pole worth his vodka will tell you, a shrinking market is not bereft of profitable opportunities. It may not offer much sustenance to a Siemens or an IBM, but it is a square meal to a Polish firm of 300 people; a firm that is "streetwise" in the Soviet Union and knows where to look. Like many Poles, Sysky felt he had got to know the Soviets—their way of thinking and their priorities—quite well. Geography had made the two countries neighbours and history had provided numerous opportunities to get acquainted—albeit not always happy ones.

Many Polish firms had come to realize that, in spite of the recent demise of Comecon and the Soviet's lack of hard currency, the Soviet market remained potentially a huge one for them (see exhibit 1 for a brief example of another such firm) and, paradoxically, for the very reasons that made the market unattractive to western investors. Supplies there are scarce and consumers are therefore not too choosy about quality. Western standards of quality are a luxury well beyond their foreign exchange allowance and, more generally, their financial reach. Polish, Czeck, and Hungarian goods which would not be given shelf space in sophisticated western markets, are well received and often much sought after in the Soviet Union. For East European firms that have the patience and the flexibility, such a market could be theirs for the taking.

Sportis certainly had the patience and the flexibility needed, thought Sysky, but he wondered, under current circumstances, whether it had the stamina. As he drew up in front of his office, he could not help recalling that Sportis's remuneration for its minority participation in

EXHIBIT 1
WZT: An Example of Another Polish Company Looking East

WZT

Sportis forms part of the small firm sector in Poland which today accounts for approximately 18% of economic activity. Some light may be thrown on the prospects of this sector by a brief description of the situation faced by a larger firm in the state-owned sector.

WZT is a medium-sized state-owned firm located about 15 kilometers from the centre of Warsaw and manufacturing televisions and professional recording equipment such as videocameras. The firm employs 5,000 people and is currently being prepared for privatization in the second half of 1991.

The firm's sales and output figures for 1988-90 are as follows:

Year	Sales ($)	Output volume	Black and White TV Sets (%)
1988	52 million	379,000 TVs	70
1989	70 million	402,000 TV	50
1990	96 million	370,000 TV	20

WZT accounts for 50% of TV sets manufactured in Poland and currently has 30% of the domestic market. Its nearest competitor in Gdansk accounts for 30% of domestic production and 25% of the domestic market. Foreign competition, however, is increasing as western firms set up local production. One US/South Korean joint venture, Curtis International, is already producing 100,000 sets a year locally at prices that WZT cannot hope to match. Its productivity per employee is too low—about one-third that of Philips. The firm is clear that if it is to survive after privatization it has to find a foreign partner.

Joint venture discussions are currently under way with several prospective partners—Sharp, Sony, Hitachi, from Japan, and Siemens, Philips, and Thomson from Europe, as well as a Taiwanese firm—on the manufacture of video equipment and a new TV chassis. These prospective partners are all seeking to build up strong positions in a rapidly growing domestic market and to use Poland as a platform from which to launch into the Soviet Union. None of them are in Poland to exploit low labour costs. WZT has maintained its links with its former Russian trading partners and is in the process of setting up a distribution network with private distributors in the western part of the Soviet Union. The firm, however, faces the same problems as western firms in the Soviet Union: how to get paid.

WZT perceives its main attraction to prospective joint venture partners to be its technically qualified staff and the domestic distribution network it is in the process of building up. Eighteen months ago, the firm thought of itself primarily as a manufacturer and owned just two retail outlets in Warsaw. It now owns eight retail outlets directly and has signed up distribution agreements with another 70 throughout the country.

Given its current product range and its technical base, the firm does not feel able to target western markets yet. If anything, the share of its output that is exported has been declining—12% of output in 1989, 7% in 1990. Discussions with prospective joint venture partners have also made it clear that the kind of technologies that would allow WZT to be more export-competitive are not on offer.

In preparation for its privatization, the firm's top management has been changed. The old Nomenklatura appointees have been replaced by younger managers—the new managing director, for example, is 33 years old and has no line management experience—although qualified people are not easy to find. This is hardly surprising when it is realized that an experienced research engineer is paid US$300 a month by WZT—less than half of what he can earn at Sharp's or in the blossoming private sector.

the Murmansk joint venture would be in fish—even dividend payments in the Soviet Union are made in the form of barter. "How many clothing manufacturers in western countries, can list fish on the balance sheet as part of their current assets and still stay in business?" he asked himself.

Origins and Growth

Life could be somewhat bleak for recently graduated young engineers in Poland in the late 1970s and early 1980s. Although they were required to work for a state-owned enterprise for a minimum of three years as a condition for studying at all, they knew, upon entering their respective firms, that unless they were prepared to sign up with the party and then bind themselves tightly to the nomenklatura, they were headed for nowhere as fast as their talents would carry them there. To preserve their sanity and that minimum level of motivation that imparts meaning to life, many resorted to moonlighting in those many eddies of the command economy that the state plan majestically sails by. Others, less concerned with job security, simply took time off.

So it was with Thomas Holc, a recent graduate in electrical engineering, who at the age of 20 was spending most of his time sailing and generally messing about in boats instead of crouching over a drawing board, as he should have been doing, designing lighting equipment for an obscure state engineering company. During his stolen leisure hours—and of these, at least, there was no shortage—Holc developed a great many contacts in the world of sailing and gained some insight into its functioning. He resolved that, when he was released from his current servitude, he would put this clandestine experience to some profitable and, hopefully, enjoyable use.

Although Poland at the beginning of the decade did not offer a particularly hospitable environment for such heretical entrepreneurial thoughts—martial law was only a few months away and the economy, weighed down with external debts, was taking one of its periodic nosedives—there were signs of a new attitude towards private business by the authorities, albeit one forced upon them by the dire circumstances that they then confronted. As far back as 1976 legislation had been passed encouraging the creation of private business in Poland by "foreigners" of Polish origin. Thomas Holc had a brother, Andrew Holc, living in London, who would be willing to "front" for him should he decide to

try something in this new climate. In 1980, therefore, Holc started collecting market data on a casual basis as well as investigating manufacturing processes. He did not have much money to invest at the time, but after seeing other budding entrepreneurs taking a chance and subsequently succeeding, he decided to have a try with an initial investment of one million zlotys and £1000 sterling. Sportis was created in 1983.

Shortly after the firm's creation, Holc came across an old ruin in the small village of Serock some 30 kilometers outside Warsaw, not far from a lake on which he used to sail. The local authority was willing to let him have the ruin for a nominal rent of two US dollars a month on condition that he restored it to its earlier condition. Once renovated, it was to be Sportis's first production facility.

Holc had originally intended to manufacture sails and life jackets there, primarily for exports, but he was thwarted in this strategy by small Far Eastern producers, located mainly in Hong Kong, who were able to sell a finished product on the world markets for a lower price than he would pay for his inputs in Poland—courtesy of the state pricing system. Yet, since the renovation of his new building was now nearing completion, and local staff had already been recruited and were being trained, Holc felt under pressure to get going with something, even if that something was not quite along the lines he had initially envisaged. Was not the ability to adapt, after all, the essence of entrepreneurship? Thus it was that for the first nine months of its existence Sportis found itself in the business of making trousers.

Gradually, however, the firm was able to shift to the manufacture of life jackets as originally planned, but for the domestic rather than the export market. Its product range consisted of fairly basic designs, mostly copied from catalogues, whose colours and shapes were slightly modified to suit the requirements of the Polish market. The Polish navy turned out to be an important customer for these life jackets, but the firm soon branched out into new product areas such as windproof clothing, tracksuits, and windcheaters.

Although Sportis was directly in touch with some end users such as the country's sea rescue services—70% of its sales at the time were in lifejackets—the bulk of its clients were state distributors such as Interster, Stoteczne Przedsiebiurstwo Handlv, Wewnetrzengo, and Handlomor, or state-owned or funded sports clubs acting as distributors. Having little or no direct contact with the market, the firm was unwilling to anticipate market demands and hence to invest in producing for stock. It would therefore only manufacture to order. Given the nature of the Polish economic environment, this turned out to be not such a bad strategy: the firm has been growing every year since outset.

This growth creates its own problems. In a political system committed to the public ownership of the means of production, whatever private sector exists—and in Poland at the time it did not exceed 5% of economic activity—does so because it is tolerated rather than encouraged. Consequently, not only did Sportis, during those years, receive no support whatever from state or local government—apart from the ruin it was offered in Serock—but its growth actually had to be covert if it was not to attract the disapproving gaze of the authorities. The Polish communist party continued to view the private sector—particularly that segment of it that could boast foreign connections—as a breeding ground for spies and a hotbed of capitalist corruption, and for that reason severely constrained its growth. The Warsaw city authorities were responsible for granting Sportis its production licence and would only do so if it was prepared to limit the size of its establishment to 60 employees and get its products approved. The firm, however, in line with current practice elsewhere, would be allowed to take on part-timers beyond its full-time staffing allocation, a concession which allowed it to share some staff with another firm, Christine, created almost at the same time as Sportis itself and owned by Thomas Holc's British wife. Christine was a manufacturer of women's clothes and it employed production processes not very different to those of Sportis and on a similar scale. There was clearly some scope for synergy between the two firms.

Continued growth and opportunities to diversify into survival suits and inflatable rescue boats led Sportis in 1989 to create a wholly owned subsidiary in the hamlet of Bojano, some 15 kilometers outside Gdansk and three hours by train from Warsaw. Production facilities are located in an extension of an old chicken hut and are reached by a dirt track. Ludwig Vogt, the director of the subsidiary and the inspiration behind it, had been a captain in the merchant navy and had spent time working in a testing station for sea rescue equipment. He had had dealings with Sportis for a number of years when acting as an adviser to the firm's clients and was recruited by Sportis largely on account of his detailed knowledge of customer requirements with respect to the products that the Bojano factory would be producing.

The choice of Gdansk as a location was strongly influenced by the fact that expansion could no longer be sensibly accommodated on the Serock site and that labour practices and attitudes in the Gdansk region seemed to be more flexible than around Warsaw. Another influencing factor was that Ludwig Vogt lived in Gdansk.

Current Performance

Sportis today finds itself in a radically different economic environment to that which confronted it nearly a decade ago. The opportunities discernible on the horizon for many Polish firms following the collapse of the communist order, are now counterbalanced by a number of looming threats. The fog of confusion that currently shrouds the country's real economic performance is undermining the fragile consensus so necessary for the difficult policy decisions that lie ahead. Indeed, even western counsels are divided on the matter of how well the country is doing and where it is headed. Inflation, at 5% a month, has improved greatly since 1990 but with the zloty now pegged to the dollar, it remains a major headache for firms which, having to turn outward towards exports, are caught in a vicious cost squeeze.

Official figures on the Polish economy may make grim reading—industrial production, it is claimed, fell by a third in 1990—but how reliable are they? Official statistics are designed to measure the state economy. Private industry is for the most part ignored. In a communist system in which the private sector was largely made up of Marx's "petty commodity traders" and never allowed to exceed more than 5% of national output, such neglect was understandable and probably not particularly harmful. Yet the Polish government's statistical office believes that the output of private industry (excluding farming) grew by over 50% in 1990 and now accounts for 18% of national income, up from 11% in 1989. And in the latter year, the government's statisticians estimate, the number of people employed in private enterprise grew by more than 500,000, bringing the total to 1.8-2 million people. These figures merely confirm what casual empiricism thrusts before the gaze of all foreign visitors to the country today: every Polish town now has its street markets where everything from imported toothpaste to once unavailable Polish ham can be bought; the area around Warsaw's palace of culture, for example, has been transformed into a vast oriental souk. Queues in post-communist Poland have virtually disappeared.

Yet if many of these mushrooming small private firms are doing well it is because they have positioned themselves at the consumer end of what was an archaic state distribution system and have been able to respond as nimble traders do everywhere to pent up consumer needs. Sportis as a production organization, by contrast, is placed upstream of the state distributors on which it has relied for a regular flow of orders as well as detailed feedback on what end users of its products required in terms of quality and performance.

The state distribution system on which Sportis was so dependent has now collapsed and it is of no consolation to the firm that its main state-owned competitor has collapsed along with it. Sportis is in the paradoxical position of being the sole domestic producer—indeed, with only modest imports in these products the firm has virtually a monopoly—in a market to which it currently has almost no access.

Sportis confronts this situation with no marketing organization to speak of. Michael Sysky, the Sales Manager, joined Sportis in 1985 but, until very recently, he was the only person in the organization involved in the selling function. As Sysky explains, marketing as such was never needed under the old system. The firm produced to order and luckily there were always orders in the distributor's pipeline. Exactly where the pipeline led to had never much bothered anyone.

To build up its marketing capacity, Sportis has now recruited a salesman who reports to Ludwig Vogt in Bojano and whose job it is to contact retailers directly. This is proving more difficult than expected: retailers are hard to identify and in the current economic climate as many are going out of business as are opening up. A further complication lies in trying to assess the current level of demand for Sportis products given the income levels that prevail in Poland at present (for one measure of Polish income see exhibit 2). Per capita income continues to decline, but no one seems to be able to say at exactly what rate. The traditional users of the firm's main products are all facing hard times—deep sea fishing firms in Poland are now selling off a large part of their fleets and many face bankruptcy—but with the reforms new market segments are also making their appearance, especially in the field of leisure.

Given the overall gloomy outlook, sales and profit levels at Sportis may offer some surprises. On paper, at least, it does not seem to be doing as badly as its domestic circumstances would suggest (see exhibit 3). There are two explanations for this.

The first is that in the last year Thomas Holc has reoriented Sportis towards external markets as originally intended (exhibit 3 shows the firm's foreign currency earnings). In addition to a growing Soviet business, the firm has started manufacturing under contract for Compass, a Swedish firm producing vest and life jackets for sailors. In 1990 Compass, facing rising labour costs at home, relocated its production in the Bojano plant and just held on to the design and marketing fuction. Bojano now produces between 120,000 and 150,000 pieces a year for its new Swedish client.

Sportis is also manufacturing under contract for Musto Ltd of Benfleet, in Essex (UK). Keith Musto, the owner, is an old friend of Thomas Holc from their sailing days. His firm, like Compass, specializes in protective clothing for sailors. He had originally intended to subcontract production operations to a Hong Kong firm but found the geographical distance too great for effective coordination. He then approached Sportis with a trial order, supplying it with both the designs and the raw materials. The firm now carries out six months worth of production for Musto each year and a joint venture between the two firms is currently under discussion. Both sides remain cautious on this matter, however, for they agree that Sportis is not yet sufficiently cost effective to be a viable joint venture partner.

A second possible reason why the sales and profit figures look so good is that the firm has no accounting system to accurately track and describe its present or past financial performance. Small private businesses in Poland were required to adopt the same socialist bookkeeping and accounting procedures as the larger state-owned enterprises. True to communist doctrine, the emphasis was on what was produced rather than on what was sold, and performance was judged on the value of outputs rather than the value of sales. In state-owned enterprises, of course, whether the firm made a profit or not was of no great account since any losses were usually made up by state subsidies. Furthermore, the financial data collected was placed at the service of the supervising authorities located externally rather than within the enterprises themselves, with the result that few firms knew how to convert a morass of bookkeeping data into usable accounting information that could help with managerial decision making.

Thomas Holc made a clear distinction between the figures that he used for external reporting—which usually showed either a loss or a small profit—and those that described the "real" business which he kept in his head. In the past, the supervisory authorities had required two quite distinct sets of books: one for the tax office and one for the state statistical office. Holc had little faith in the relevance of either set of data. Yet the figures that Holc kept in his head and which he used for the day-to-day running of the business, as he himself acknowledges, were often themselves only tenuously related to its performance. Like most Polish managers brought up under the old system, he was unfamiliar with the managerial use of balance sheets, income

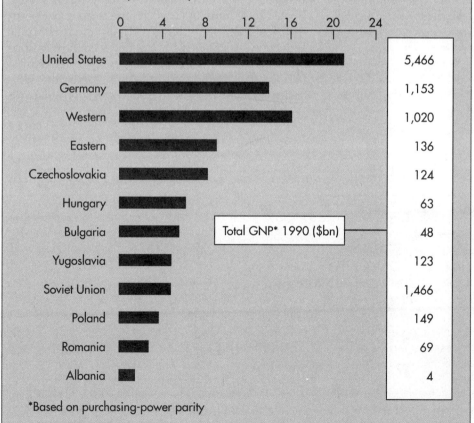

POST-COMMUNIST POVERTY

Economists have been quarreling for years about how poor the Soviet Union and Eastern Europe really are. The following chart shows new estimates by PlanEcon, a consultancy and authoritative communist-watcher based in Washington, DC.

To calculate incomes per head and GNP in dollar terms, an exchange rate has to be applied to local-currency figures (which are themselves pretty unreliable). Some estimates use the exchange rates available to businesses. This is unsatisfactory. The region's assorted economic policies mean that commercial exchange rates are volatile and distorted. Exchange rates based on purchasing-power parity are better; these compare incomes in terms of the goods that people buy with some allowance for quality. This is the measure used by PlanEcon.

The Soviet Union's GNP for 1990 comes out at roughly $1.5 trillion, giving a GNP per head of about $5,000. Soviet incomes vary widely by republic: from $6,740 in Latvia, $6,240 in Estonia, $5,960 in Belorussia, and $5,880 in Lithuania to $2,750 in Uzbekistan and $2,340 in Tadzhikistan (all these figures are for 1989). Poland, Eastern Europe's boldest reformer, is one of its poorest, with an income per head of just $3,910. In the region, only Romania and Albania are worse off.

GNP* Per Head, 1990 ($ thousands)

Total GNP* 1990 ($bn)

United States	5,466
Germany	1,153
Western	1,020
Eastern	136
Czechoslovakia	124
Hungary	63
Bulgaria	48
Yugoslavia	123
Soviet Union	1,466
Poland	149
Romania	69
Albania	4

*Based on purchasing-power parity

EXHIBIT 2
Post-communist Poverty
(*The Economist,* January 12, 1991)

statements, and flow of funds statements. These were documents that the firm produced—after a fashion— but it did so only for the tax office. They were never used internally. To keep track of his business Holc made use of productivity data in the raw form in which it was collected by Sportis's bookkeeper: measures of the productivity of different work teams; measures of time used by the staff; measures of direct and indirect costs; data on value added; summary data on monthly production; and so on.

Sportis's bookkeeper was trained in socialist bookkeeping methods. Holc would not describe her as an accountant in the western sense; he perceived her role primarily in terms of external reporting. She played a key role within the firm since only she was in a position to follow and interpret the myriad changes in financial regulations that affected it. She was happy to make bookkeeping data available to the Sportis managers but only on a request basis and usually only in the form in which it was collected. Indeed, who in the firm would know how to speak an alternative form? The result was that no one in Sportis was in a position to build up an overall picture of the firm's financial performance. Holc is well aware of the problems this could pose. A short while back, his wife's company, Christine, found itself in some difficulty when it turned out it had been running at a loss instead of making a profit as was believed.

He also knows that to get the firm's productivity up to competitive levels he must quickly establish a better control of costs. Until recently, this hardly seemed necessary. Inputs, including labour, were cheap, and were of an acceptable quality for the domestic market. Unrelenting inflation and the urgent need to find new markets abroad have changed all that. The point was driven home when Sportis was visited by the US firm Levi's, which was seeking out potential Polish subcontractors. In the course of discussions, it was discovered that, while it took Sportis 30 minutes to produce a pair of denims, the US firm could produce them in six-and-half minutes. "They thought that they would make us feel better by telling us not to be too despondent since, after all, it had taken Levi's a hundred years to reach such a level of productivity," commented Sysky ruefully.

The absence of an effective accounting system poses a more subtle challenge to Sportis than simply improving current productivity levels. With the company's growth and diversification—it is currently preparing to move into the production of oil booms based on the technology it is using for inflatable rescue boats—Holc increasingly feels the need to decentralize some management decisions. Some first steps have been taken. The sharing of staff with Christine—bookkeeper, sales manager, production manager, deliveries, purchasing, and administrative staff, and not least, Thomas Holc himself—was coming to an end. Sportis would maintain its head offices on Christine's production site at Marki but from now on the two firms would be run on an "arm's length" basis. (Exhibit 4 gives Sportis's staffing levels.) At the same time, Holc was preparing to delegate day-to-day responsibility for

EXHIBIT 3
Sales Figures, 1986–90

1986	1987	1988	1989	1990	
278.300.030	162.579.541	348.879.482	1.053.822.169	10.650.296.550	Total sales (zloty)
278.118.067	144.552.311	326.502.545	1.004.546.738	3.897.554.145	Domestic sales
181.963	18.027.230	22.376.937	49.275.431	6.752.742.405	Exports
	USD 21.784,83	GBP 8.321,70	GBP 6.867	GBP 4.168,70	
	NLG 14,476	DEM 480		USD 46.993,60	
	DKK 6.119,62	SEG 75.258	Skr. 113.200	Skr. 20.000	
				DKK 121.536	
				RBL 2.783.955	
	295.081.970	275.739.020	309.431.480		

*This is a direct transcription from the documents supplied by the Sportis bookkeeper and is a fair representation of Holc's information base.

operations in Bojano to Ludwig Vogt. Major investments and decisions on product policy would remain with Holc but the rest would soon be handed over to Vogt.

Yet since Sportis had no planning or budgeting system to speak of, and since most of the knowledge required to manage the firm remained locked in Holc's head, he wondered how the decentralization would work out in practice.

Strategic and Organization Issues

Given the new opportunities and challenges that it faces, how does Sportis see the future? Perhaps it would be more relevant to ask how Thomas Holc sees the future since he is the classic owner-manager and for the time being takes all the strategic decisions himself (Sportis is legally a "single-owner firm" and is not required by law to have a board of directors). Holc as chief executive nevertheless works closely with the sales manager (Sysky), the head of the Bojano operations (Vogt), and the bookkeeper, but he does so on a purely informal basis.

"Sportis is what westerners call a niche player," comments Holc, "producing differentiated products for a specialized market. I would like to see Sportis expand but not by switching to mass production techniques. This would bring about more changes than I could currently handle. A move towards automation and capital intensive production, greater investments in machinery and stocks, and, of course, bank loans. The current rate of interest on zloty loans is over 80%. Who needs it? I am not seeking the quiet life, but I don't want to die young either. Except for a small part of our production sold directly to retailers—about 10-15% of our total sales—we shall go on manufacturing to order." Holc recognizes that such an expansion strategy is not without its problems. The domestic market offers uncertain—although by no means negligible—prospects and while Sportis considers itself the most competitive (because it is the only) domestic producer, a number of the new distributors in its product markets are turning to imports rather than sourcing domestically.

The Soviet market which Sportis began to investigate a year ago is also full of pitfalls. "Many Polish firms were spoilt in their dealing with the Soviet Union," observes Sysky, "In the days of the centrally planned economy, selling to the Russians was a picnic. Everything was routed through a few large state trading organizations and all that a Polish manager had to do was to drop in and pick up his cheque. It was all routine. Today there are no more cheques. The main challenge is to find a customer who can pay you—in Vodka, Russian bears, or black market submarines, anything at all, in fact, but roubles. Unsurprisingly there is a lot of corruption about. Over there at present, it's everyone for himself."

"To do business with the Soviets," Sysky continued, "it is essential to build up mutual trust. Too many problems, both large and small, have to be overcome for people to trust a complete stranger. Take, for example, our new joint venture with Murmanrybprom: we drew up a legal agreement with them. Yet we know and they know many issues will arise that could not be anticipated by the agreement, and that once the joint

Location: Serock	
Production (direct)	39
Production (indirect)	9
Administration	8
Total number of employees	56
Location: Bojano	
Production (direct)	85
Production (indirect)	4
Administration	15
Total number of employees	104

Note: Some administrative staff work for both Sportis and Christine.

EXHIBIT 4
Staffing Levels

venture has been officially registered—any day now—our dealings with each other will be guided entirely by the quality of our personal relationship."

"In spite of such difficulties," Sysky then added, "the Soviet market remains a potentially attractive one for Sportis given the fragility of the domestic one. An added consideration is that western competitors are now showing their faces in the Polish market and this can only reduce the viability of small domestic producers working on their own."

"Given the Soviet Union's current problems, westerners are unlikely to show up there quite yet, thank God, and since Soviet customers are generally still quite undemanding—we are to them what the West has always been for us: an Eldorado that we can only dream about—our price/quality offering remains quite acceptable to them."

Did internationalization mean anything more for the firm than the Soviet Union or manufacturing subcontracts? Apparently not. Neither Holc nor Sysky felt that Sportis would be in any position to move into western markets for a long while yet. According to Holc:

> To enter western markets—many of them already saturated—with simple products like ours, would require greater marketing and organizational capacity than we currently dispose of. We would be dealing with new market segments sensitive to branding and fashion trends, and we currently lack the design capacity to respond.
>
> We might stand a better chance in the more industrial markets for protective wear and inflatables, where branding plays less of a role, but there we often meet protectionism disguised as mandatory technical standards. Sportis manufactures these products to established international standards, but many countries such as the US, Great Britain, and Germany, still insist on local retesting, greatly adding to our product costs and hurting our competitiveness.

Given its current lack of competitiveness in western markets, the subcontracting work that Sportis was currently undertaking for Compass and Musto was considered something of a sideline activity and not central to the firm's future business. Holc explained:

> Compass closed down its Swedish operations on account of labour problems such as recurring absenteeism and high social security costs. It transferred both its production and equipment to the Bojano site. But the firm really only sees us as a way of keeping down its labour costs. It does not appear willing to involve us in the higher value added parts of its operation. We remain a source of low cost inputs.

"In fact, not that low cost," Holc continued, "If our wage rates are low then so is our productivity. For this reason it is still unclear that the joint venture that we are currently discussing with Musto in the UK will prove profitable for either party."

Improving productivity remains the firm's major headache. It is caught in a major cost squeeze which it is finding hard to analyse and to deal with. Direct costs went up by 250% in the first 11 months of 1990 but productivity failed to increase at all. Worse, the local authority that leased Sportis the Serock site for a 10 year period now wants to increase the rent from US$2 a month to US$2,000 a month—and this 18 months before the rental agreement is due to expire. But with the zloty exchange rate now pegged to the dollar, none of these increases in operating costs can be passed on to the firm's foreign customers.

Sysky's Soliloquy: Part II

As he entered his car for the journey home at the end of the day, Michael Sysky sighed audibly. His thoughts returned once more to the Russian joint venture that he had negotiated.

From one perspective the firm was exploiting a competitive advantage by "working with the devil it knew." But for what benefit? Western and Japanese firms were not exactly queuing up to get into the Soviet Union and it was obvious why: earning an honest rouble, or preferably an honest dollar, there was proving to be more trouble than it was worth. Sysky had heard that these same firms also had their fingers burnt in China and for much the same reasons. Yet it seemed that South China was now overrun by small, nimble-footed entrepreneurs from Hong Kong, all discreetly making money in out of the way places, mostly beyond the reach of the Chinese bureaucracy. Could not the Murmansk operation be of the latter kind?

From another perspective, however, the move east for Sportis could be viewed as an escape from the new challenge from the west. The firm did not feel that it could be competitive in western markets—indeed, it was not even sure how much of its domestic market it would be able to hold on to if foreign competition hotted up there.

To become truly competitive in western markets, mused Sysky, Sportis would need to undergo a cultural transformation. People would have to pull together and cooperate with each other to an extent until now unknown in Polish firms. At present everyone just attends to his own job in the organization—perhaps a consequence of paying people on piece—and teamwork is virtually nonexistent. "We must be operating at least 40% below our existing productive potential because of poor work discipline and other work-related problems," he muttered to himself as he drove off. Things would be hard to change without making the management more professional. But how were they going to do that? Polish managers are all like Christine's recently departed production manager; if they are good enough to run your organization, then they are also good enough to run from it and to start their own, and that is exactly what they will do. No amount of bribery or blandishments will keep them loyal once they get an entrepreneurial twinkle in their eye.

Sysky wondered about the changes that Sportis would have to make to its organization in order to attract and retain the right people. Would Thomas Holc, the final arbiter of the firm's fate, be prepared to swallow them? Would Sysky himself be prepared to?

■ AMSTRAD PLC[†]

By John Hendry

Entrepreneurial Beginnings

Alan Sugar was a born entrepreneur. As a teenager in London's East End, his ventures ranged from boiling beetroots for a local greengrocer to cutting up rolls of 35mm film for resale. On leaving school he became a trainee statistician at the Ministry of Education but soon left to work for a small electrical firm. He continued to do work "on the side" as well, selling car radio aerials and other accessories from the back of a minivan in a street market. In 1968, at the age of 21, he set up his own company, AMS Trading Company (General Importers) Ltd, later shortened to Amstrad.

In 1970 Sugar saw an opportunity to go into manufacturing. One of the key selling points of hi-fi turntables was their plastic dust covers, most of which were made by an expensive vacuum-forming process. Sugar manufactured them by injection-moulding, which was a much cheaper process providing you could get sufficient volume, and he cornered the market. Soon after this he moved into hi-fi units themselves, as well as clock radios, cassette recorders and car radios and cassette players, assembling products from sub-units and components sourced in the Far East. By 1980 turnover had reached £8.8 million and profits £1.4 million, and in April 1980 the company was floated on the stock exchange. By 1983 turnover had soared to over £50 million and profits to £8 million. A small Hong Kong company had been formed to monitor and co-ordinate subcontracted manufacturing throughout the Far East.

---

†**Source:** ©1991 by John Hendry. This case was prepared by John Hendry as the basis for class discussion rather than to illustrate either effective or ineffective handling of an administrative situation. Excerpts from *The Sunday Times* are copyrighted. © Times Newspapers Limited 1985/89.

From hi-fis to personal computers

In the financial year 1982-83 Amstrad's sales were dominated by racked hi-fi systems, for which it had over 35% of the UK market. That year also saw the introduction of its colour televisions. In 1983-84 colour televisions accounted for over 90% of turnover, and Amstrad also introduced video cassette recorders. In June 1984 it also delivered its first home computer, and for the year 1984-85 computers composed nearly two-thirds of turnover, with televisions and video recorders making up most of the balance. The introduction of computers was also responsible for taking its exports up to 53% of total turnover, from just 13% the previous year. Thereafter, though both audio and video products continued to sell well, sales were dominated by computers. In August 1985 Amstrad introduced the CPC6128 personal computer with integral disk drive and monitor, and the PCW8256 word processor—computer, software, monitor, and printer all for £400. In April 1986 Amstrad bought the computer business of Clive Sinclair for just £5 million, giving it 75% of the UK home computer market. In September 1986 it introduced the PC1520, an IBM-compatible PC, the base model of which was also priced at just £400. In 1987 this was followed by the more powerful PC1640, and in 1988 by portable versions of both the 1520 and 1640. In the year 1987-88, professional computers (the IBM compatibles) accounted for about 55% of the 625 million turnover; home computers (rationalized into a small Sinclair range) about 20%; video recorders about 15% and audio and computer printers less than 5% each.

The Problems Begin

It was in about 1988 that things started to go wrong. Amstrad had run into trouble with its products before. An early launch into citizens' band radio and the initial launch of video cassette recorders were both failures,

EXHIBIT 1
Amstrad's 10-Year Record (Year end June 30)

	1980	1981	1982	1983	1984	1985	1986	1987	1988	1989
Key figures										
Turnover (excluding VAT) (£m)	8.8	14.1	28.1	51.8	84.9	136.1	304.1	511.8	625.4	626.3
Profit before taxation (£m)	1.4	2.4	4.8	8.0	9.1	20.2	75.3	135.7	160.4	76.6
Profit after taxation (£m)	1.1	1.2	2.6	5.3	5.7	14.0	52.0	93.4	105.1	51.1
Dividends pence/share (including tax credit)	0.06	0.11	0.14	0.16	0.19	0.27	0.49	0.97	1.87	1.87
Dividend cover (times)	5	3	6	10	8	14	27	24	14	6
Retained profit for the year (£m)	0.8	1.1	2.4	5.1	5.0	12.9	47.2	89.6	93.0	43.1
Earnings pence/share after tax	0.22	0.26	0.54	1.12	1.17	2.57	9.54	17.13	18.99	9.01
Share capital and reserves (£m)	3.7	4.8	7.2	12.3	29.2	42.2	88.1	179.5	256.2	310.8
Key ratios (%)										
Turnover growth over prior year	56.5	61.2	98.6	84.6	64.0	60.2	123.5	68.3	22.2	0.1
Profit before tax over prior year	49.9	74.6	100.8	68.6	13.3	121.1	273.5	80.3	18.2	–53.2
Profit before tax as a percentage of sales	15.5	16.8	17.0	15.5	10.7	14.8	24.8	26.5	25.6	12.2

but in both cases the company was able to cut its losses quickly and move on to other products. The hard disk version of the PC1520 encountered overheating problems, leading to delays while a revised model was launched incorporating a fan, but this proved to be only a minor hiccup in Amstrad's rampant growth. The problems of 1988, however, were more serious.

Up to this time, Amstrad products had been targeted firmly at the consumer. The PC1520 and PC1640 were described as business computers, but sold principally to individuals working or studying at home, the self-employed or very small businesses. In 1987, however, it announced the PC2000 range; a new range of up-market personal computers using fast 286 and 386 chips, which were supposed to take the company firmly into the corporate market. This range was originally due to be launched in late 1987, but design problems delayed the launch until September 1988. A chronic shortage of memory chips severely limited the early production, losing an estimated £50 million of sales, and a design error resulted in 7,000 machines being recalled in July 1989 at a cost of about £6 million. Demand was also much weaker than had been anticipated, and in September 1989 the range was relaunched at lower prices.

The chip shortage lasted for much of 1988 and 1989, and reflected the notorious cyclical nature of the silicon chip market. Despite press comment about a pending chip shortage as the electronic industry boomed in the late 1980s, Amstrad failed to act until it was too late. Then in October 1988 it rushed into paying £45 million for a small minority shareholding of a chip manufacturer, Micron Technology, in an effort to secure supplies. As Sugar commented some months later, "It was a lousy deal." The shares were worth, at most, £30 million.

In this same period, problems with a Taiwanese subcontractor led to a break in audio supplies in the crucial pre-Christmas selling period in 1988, and in the autumn of 1989 Amstrad pulled out of the audio market. An attempted move into the supply of satellite aerial dishes, seen as a major new market, suffered both from technical design problems and from delays in the launching of UK satellite TV. The launch of another major new product—a low-priced fax machine—was also delayed.

Finally, Amstrad ran into difficulties with its European subsidiaries. Throughout most of the 1980s it had only two overseas subsidiaries: a distribution company in France and the Hong Kong company. By the late 1980s the Hong Kong company employed 500 people: 100 managing the Far East subcontracting operations; the remainder working in a printer factory which acted as a testbed for production innovations, and provided a benchmark for assessing subcontractors' production. Faced with the prospect of European Community import controls, however, as well as with a need for shorter lead times and greater flexibility, it decided to move some of its production to Europe. In 1988, rather than simply subcontracting, it set up a joint manufacturing venture. However, it underestimated the problems of start-up, and the ensuing delays added to its existing supply shortages. Meanwhile, again in 1988, Amstrad also sought to increase control of its overseas distribution—previously contracted out—by setting up a series of distribution subsidiaries. Over an 18-month period 10 of these were set up, but the head office support needed was underestimated, and the firm quickly found itself carrying unwieldy inventories.

An End to Rapid Growth

The cumulative result of these and other problems was that Amstrad's turnover for the year 1988-89 was almost identical to that for 1987-88, bringing to an abrupt end its long history of rapid growth. At the same time profits collapsed by over 50% as operating margins fell from the company's traditional 25% to much nearer the industry average of 10%, while the share price dropped from over 200p in the summer of 1988 to under 50p in late 1989.

By the end of 1989 Amstrad was the dominant supplier of satellite dishes for the UK market, and the PC2000 range of computers was at last making a significant contribution to turnover. But inventories, though declining, were still high, and with personal computer product cycles shortening dramatically any out of date stocks were not going to be easy to shift. The

EXHIBIT 2
Amstrad's Consolidated Profit and Loss Account (£ thousand)

	1985	1986	1987	1988	1989
Turnover	136,061	304,150	511,798	625,426	626,323
Change in stocks and work in progress	1,686	4,298	52,222	(14,541)	173,766
Other operating income	512	348	858	1,838	1,524
Raw materials etc.	(103,539)	(207,130)	(399,998)	(382,046)	(599,791)
Other external charges	(7,316)	(18,924)	(20,470)	(47,175)	(67,922)
Staff costs	(3,594)	(4,672)	(7,261)	(15,781)	(24,338)
Depreciation	(1,047)	(1,168)	(1,645)	(2,759)	(4,824)
Other operating charges	(2,364)	(3,851)	(3,783)	(9,488)	(26,198)
Interest receivable	449	4,198	5,174	10,120	9,542
Interest payable	(691)	(1,965)	(1,183)	(5,188)	(11,475)
Profit before tax	20,157	75,284	135,712	160,406	76,607
Taxation	(6,147)	(23,279)	(42,313)	(55,258)	(25,517)
Profit after tax	14,010	52,005	93,399	105,148	51,090
Ordinary dividends	(1,027)	(1,893)	(3,816)	(7,903)	(7,957)
Extraordinary items	(42)	(2,954)	—	(4,287)	—
Retained profit	12,941	47,158	89,583	92,958	43,133

EXHIBIT 3
Amstrad's Consolidated Balance Sheet (£ thousand)

	1985	*1986*	*1987*	*1988*	*1989*
Fixed assets:					
Intangibles	160	379	284	69	382
Tangibles	6,883	7,219	11,620	22,949	44,428
Associated company			980	1,125	
Listed investments				42	44,574
	6,993	7,598	12,884	24,585	89,384
Current assets:					
Stocks	25,173	33,277	95,687	122,142	325,155
Trade debtors	23,660	38,325	54,809	130,629	100,432
Other debtors	1,418	3,523	9,343	12,115	22,740
Prepayments	614	333	601	931	1,299
Deferred taxation		3,755	1,934	1,336	6,422
Overseas taxation			1,833		1,409
Investments	257				
Cash	13,519	62,467	107,630	186,673	44,681
	64,641	141,680	271,837	453,826	502,138
Creditors (due within one year)	(28,614)	(61,175)	(105,202)	(222,232)	(276,792)
Net current assets	36,027	80,505	166,635	231,594	225,346
Total assets less current liabilities	43,020	88,103	179,519	256,179	314,730
Finance lease obligations					(3,920)
Provision for taxation	(850)				
Net assets	42,170	88,103	179,519	256,179	310,810
Capital	5,452	27,260	27,260	27,812	28,419
Share premium account	12,327			12,612	13,806
Revaluation reserve					9,848
Profit and loss account	23,785	60,235	151,055	214,551	257,533
Other reserves	606	608	1,204	1,204	1,204
Shareholders' funds	42,170	88,103	179,519	256,179	310,810

new fax machine, though imminent, was not yet in the shops; sales of home computers were declining; and the PC2000, on which the company's prospects largely depended was not making an impact on the main corporate market. It was selling well to small firms, but the primary reason for its development had been to take Amstrad out of this market, in which margins were being squeezed, and into the less price-sensitive mainstream business market. This move was still perceived as critical for Amstrad's future growth.

Facing the Future

Where had Sugar gone wrong? Comments in the press suggested that the problem was primarily one of management structure. Alan Sugar had built up the company with a minimal structure, keeping tight personal control over everything that went on and taking all the important decisions himself. The view was, however, that it had grown to a size where such an

EXHIBIT 4
Extract from the *Amstrad Annual Report 1985*

We are experts in design and engineering—one of our talents is to engineer products with all the specifications and facilities the market demands and delete those unusual facilities that are only employed by the minority. In short we produce what the mass market customer wants and not a 'Boffins ego trip.' We have identified trends and opportunities in the market and applied our philosophy of engineering, outstripping the competition on price and specification and, more importantly, on quality. The relationship with our Engineering Team…is quite unique. We have a team of people who can understand the commercial side as well as the technical side of product innovation.

Our other talents are in the procurement of component parts and in the understanding and reading of the semiconductor market…. We are also very flexible concerning the manufacturing territory for our products and in selecting the area most suitable for the item in question to be made. Our marketing skills and understanding the seasonable nature of our business is one of the main reasons for our success. Having the right inventory at the right time is important.

Alan Sugar

entrepreneurial approach was simply not feasible. Most of the problems of 1988-89 could, it was claimed, be traced back to overstretched management, and if Amstrad was to recover its stability and start moving forward again it would have to "join the adults" and become more professional. Sugar noted other reasons, including an undisciplined chase for profits to keep the stock market happy, but basically he seems to have agreed. In the autumn of 1989 he introduced a new and greatly extended corporate structure, reinforcing his top management team with several key new appointments and relinquishing some of his own executive power. He also strengthened considerably his new product development team, noting that Amstrad relied heavily on its stream of new products and could no longer risk expensive mistakes. His overall strategy, though, remained the same: to move into the corporate market; to continue to take control of overseas distribution; and to bring manufacturing increasingly into Europe and into the company, rather than relying on subcontractors.

Sunday Times, **January 27, 1985**

"The truck driver and his wife, the people I'm selling to, he associates a computer with those things he sees when he checks in at the airport on his way to Costa del wherever—it is, things with a keyboard and a screen."

"I think when this type of average man goes to a shop and sees—possibly what Sinclair and Acorn call a computer, to him—with respect—it looks like a pregnant calculator—he can't associate with it."

Sugar says the first generation of electrical, computer-type objects gave mum and dad a bit of a pain at home. "What was happening was that the kids were occupying the television, there were loads of wires all over the place—and then, the kids couldn't be bothered to set up the computer or game after a while, and a lot of the first generation of computers ended up with their cables wrapped around them and thrown under the staircase."

And with Amstrad's everything-with-chips, all-in-one box approach? "Mum and dad say 'that's the computer, it goes in Johnny's bedroom—and it stays there'."

Observer, **October 27, 1985**

Alan Sugar, founder and chairman of hugely successful Amstrad Consumer Electronics, is living proof that charm is not a necessary requisite to get along in business.

His manner is disconcertingly direct and the only obviously mild thing about the 38-year-old entrepreneur are the "extra mild" cigarettes he smokes with some ferocity. One of his favourite sayings is "cut the crap," which could be seen as the motto that has sped him, in under 20 years, from street-market trader to head of a public company worth around £150 million.

"Sure he's abrupt," says an employee, "but people are loyal to him because of his track record. He's fought his way up from nothing and he's not superior. If there's a box to be shifted while he's around, he'll do it himself."

Sugar doesn't like talking about himself and prefaces most personal statements with "I don't want to sound big-headed." But his Rolls Royce and shirt cuffs bear his initials and he's quick to identify the personal reasons for his success.

"I seriously believe that I have got an in-born talent. Some people are born with the talent to be a musician, others with a brain to be an engineer or programmer or doctor. I just have an aptitude towards business, trading and dealing. It's something you can't learn at university, it's just in you."

Employees say it is difficult to identify ranks within the organisation. But Sugar notes: "I'm very important to Amstrad. I think businesses in our sector need a spearhead. There are other businesses that have boards padded out with the right honourable lieutenants and flight marshals or whatever. But deep down, when you cut the crap, there is some spearhead there. In an industry like ours there is a prime motivator and that's me."

The simple philosophy that produced Amstrad's word processor and home computers is the same that brought success in audio equipment. Sugar put the amplifier, tuner, tape-deck and turntable into a neat glass-fronted cabinet, called it the Tower, priced it low and sold thousands.

"There's no innovation there. All we've done is taken a logical step. And there's a lot more of these steps that can be taken," he says.

Amstrad's products are made in the East, either bought-in or manufactured under contract. And in its past financial year, over 50 per cent of the company's revenue came from sales abroad with Amstrad risking little by selling direct to distributors who are responsible for marketing the product.

Financial Weekly, October 17, 1985

The design of the PCW8256 illustrates Amstrad's emphasis on the useful, and its impatience with the superfluous.

In the first place, it uses an 8-bit processor which is really yesterday's technology. The standard microprocessor these days is 16-bit, as with the IBM PC, and most manufacturers are now moving towards designs based on the 32-bit chip.

Sugar takes the view that, as far as the customer is concerned, the number of bits the processor can address is quite beside the point: "8-bit, 16-bit, 1-bit," he says, "who cares, so long as it works."

And it does work. Indeed, it works faster than some famous-name 16-bit machines, thanks to the dedicated word-processing software.

The Z-80 chip may be old hat, but it's proven and reliable, and is perfectly adequate to the task. Above all, it is dirt cheap, because of the huge volumes in which it is produced.

Sugar says the inherent limitations of 8-bit chip design have not held up development at all. He is, as usual, realistic about the PCW8256. If it has a two-year life, he'll be happy. But he expects it to last longer than that.

Amstrad's ability to create mass market products lies in its pricing strategy. The company has, until recently at any rate, left the trail blazing to others—to the Japanese in the audio and video markets and to the likes of Sinclair and Acorn in the computer market.

Sugar's trick is to extract from those pioneering products the key design and engineering elements, to apply his version of Occam's razor to the "illogical" bits and pieces, and then to re-package the device in ways that permit extremely aggressive pricing.

In his words, "We look at the competition, take it to bits, and see if we can engineer something similar or better—usually better, and cheaper. We identify the facilities that aren't useful and we ditch them to reduce costs."

It would be misleading to regard the result as a no-frills version of the original. "Techno-cosmetics" (as they are sometimes called) are as evident in Amstrad products as they are in those of the competition.

Amstrad was first to introduce the controversial double-cassette deck in its racked stereo products (a move that has infuriated the British Phonographic industry), and the company also pioneered remote control for audio systems.

In Sugar's book, there are frills, and frills. He is merciless with those that are merely the product of some boffin's ego trip, but he is swift to incorporate those that are "useful" in the sense that they appeal to his customers. Perhaps his greatest skill is his remarkable feel for such things. He, more than any other player in the customer electronics market, has a sense of what consumers want.

The "realism" that Sugar sets such store by is evident in Amstrad's remarkable agility when confronted by changes in the marketplace, and also in the company's uncanny sense of timing.

Growth over the past five years, which have seen annual sales multiply almost 16-fold, has not been accompanied by a corresponding increase in the size of the planning team. Sugar and half-a-dozen senior lieutenants, specialists in design, engineering, and finance, run the company from the ninth floor of Amstrad's headquarters in Brentwood. Sugar himself sits in the middle of an open-plan office, at a desk distinguished from all the others only by the presence of a large, leather, Chesterfield-type armchair.

From this modestly-appointed eyrie in north east London, Sugar and his assistants monitor and regulate a £136m a year company operating in markets stretching from Hong Kong to Chicago. It is a classic example of a small group decision-making system and it works just fine.

A new product or, more rarely, a new market idea, normally begins in Sugar's mind, the product of his feel for what his customers, people between 17 and 35 in the BC1C2D socio-economic groups, are yearning for.

The key criterion and normally the basis of Sugar's insight, is price.

He decides that if Amstrad can market a shelf-mounted audio system for £300, including speakers and incorporating a compact disc (CD) player, a twin cassette deck, a radio tuner, and a conventional record player, it will sell like hot cakes.

He convenes a meeting and asks his experts whether, by pruning any illogical and useless facilities, such a product can be produced at a cost sufficiently below £300 to show an adequate profit. The engineers go away and do their sums.

They re-convene and report their findings. If Sugar likes what he hears, the "go" button is pressed.

The marketing department (or at least that part of it outside Sugar's head) is not consulted. As Sugar puts it, "We go ahead with production as soon as we know we've got a winner."

Usually, they know they have such a winner when Sugar's gut feeling tells them so. He has a favourite metaphor to explain the point: "If we found a way of making £1notes for 50p, marketing wouldn't be the problem. The problem would be doing it."

The decision about where to make the new product is based on the physical size and shape and on the sourcing of components. If 90% of the components come from Japan, then the Far East is the logical place to manufacture. If, as in the case of the audio products, it is more of a belt and braces operation, perhaps involving substantial UK sub-contracting, then the product is as likely as not to be made at Amstrad's manufacturing and warehousing complex at Shoeburyness.

It is the product that defines the territory of manufacture, not marketing considerations or any idea of a proper balance between "in house" manufacture and sub-contracting.

Once launched, the sales performance of the new product is carefully monitored. The process begins with detailed sales forecasts and is backed up with a high-speed reporting system. New sales are immediately chalked up on blackboards in the office at the top of the Brentwood headquarters.

Sugar is realistic about sales reports: "We're not blinded by the odd extraordinary result or by a seasonal down-turn in sales. Some of our competitors were dazzled by their initial success. We're always a bit pessimistic."

The small decision-making group can react very swiftly to a genuinely surprising trend. Better than expected sales may lead to an increase in production, though this is not always possible. Worse than expected sales invariably lead to a reduction in production budgets or, when appropriate, to a complete withdrawal from the market.

The City appears not to have fully appreciated this agility. When it was concerned about the general level of computer sales earlier this year, it marked down Amstrad's shares. It should have known that the surest and earliest sign of disappointing sales at Amstrad is the company's prompt withdrawal from the market.

It's not as if there aren't any precedents. Amstrad pulled out of clock radios when the market collapsed; it withdrew from the CB radio market with a pocketful of profit when that business failed to match up to expectations; it ceased production of 22-inch colour TVs; and it stopped ordering video cassette recorders when quota agreements between Europe and Japan seriously undermined Sugar's pricing strategy.

The same pragmatism has characterised Amstrad's approach to export markets. Sugar pursues a zero-exposure export policy. Amstrad first finds an importer, and then he, the importer, puts up the finance. All sales to importers are irrevocable, and all are made on the basis of irrevocable letters of credit.

"If you have a good product," says Sugar, "people beat a path to your door. Most people seek us out. We just choose from the bunch."

Financial Times, **October 23, 1985**

Amstrad has two notable strengths. One is the way in which it puts together and markets very low cost products such as its recently launched word processor complete with printer for £459 including VAT. The other is the speed with which it gets itself out of problematical markets like colour television, video and of course CB radio.

Amstrad products are always aimed at the mass market, are usually very basic with no frills and are remarkably cheap. Sugar's favourite description of his typical customer is "the lorry driver and his wife."

"Amstrad's key strength is Alan Sugar's ability to identify a price-point at which a volume of product can be shifted. The company then aims for that price point in the whole design of the product, by working backwards and allocating the margins," says Robert Miller-Bakewell, analyst at stockbrokers Wood Mackenzie.

"We take our leaf out of the Japanese book. Only we do what they do quicker," says Sugar, founder, major shareholder and chief executive. "They are good at identifying volume markets, studying the available products and seeing how they can make them better and cheaper."

Like Amstrad home computers the attraction of the new word processor is not just that it is very cheap but that it is sold as a complete unit which only needs a plug.

When Amstrad first moved into the home market in summer 1984, rivals typically sold just the computer with some software and a heavy emphasis on technology and power. But in order to make them work you had to buy and assemble all the peripherals like screen, cables, and cassette or disc drive.

Amstrad entered the market with a computer that came complete with all those necessary peripherals. There was nothing stunning about the technology but it was an important repackaging of the product. Suddenly home computing was accessible to all those people who could not—or did not want to bother—with the trouble of assembling a "system."

Similarly, the new word processor is a personal computer with printer, the screen, a disc drive and a generally acclaimed word processing program. No other company offers a serious product at such a low price nor sells as a complete assembled package something which is attractive to the non-expert buyer—although extra blank discs must be purchased before it can be used. "We keep the product very simple," says Alan Sugar. "It comes in one box, with one power cord. You plug it in and it works."

The packaging of the product is not just a good marketing ploy, it is also an important key to Amstrad's

pricing and applies equally to the audio equipment, the home computers and the word processor. By linking all the constituent parts Amstrad can avoid duplicating many components from cardboard boxes to microchips.

Costs are cut further by keeping the product as basic as possible and not offering extra facilities, which Sugar believes very few people need or would use. On the computer side he is particularly contemptuous of reviewers who seem more interested in obscure functions than in the basics of the machine.

The third element which enables Amstrad to keep its costs low is its small company structure. Founded in 1968 by Sugar to sell tinted plastic covers for record players, the company is still very closely run by him and greatly depends on his instinctive entrepreneurial and managerial flair. There is very little middle management and most of the decisions seem to be made by Sugar—although he accepts this will have to change as the company grows.

The fourth reason for Amstrad's low costs is its willingness to subcontract work wherever possible. The most obvious and most important is manufacturing, which is largely done in the Far East. The home computers and the new word processor are both assembled by the subsidiary of a Japanese company in Korea.

Amstrad also subcontracts a number of other activities such as distribution. It does not want the overhead of a fleet of lorries during the quiet summer period.

The level of subcontracting has also helped Amstrad maintain its reputation for being fleet-footed. Indeed Sugar values this highly: "It is better to accept a lower margin, but have the flexibility to get out of something."

Amstrad has shown it can make mistakes but get out of trouble with little apparent difficulty. CB Radio was one business which Amstrad entered with enthusiasm. But the day CB Radio was legalised Sugar decided—correctly—that the widely-held projections for demand would not be met and sold his entire stocks. Amstrad was one of the few companies to make a profit out of CB.

Financial Weekly, **October 1, 1987**

Malcolm Miller, Amstrad's sales and marketing director, gave a hint of the speed culture. "We're doers" he said. "We get on with things. If you have a good idea, every day you waste talking about it is a day's lost profit."

And there are speed structures as well as a speed culture. Finance director Ken Ashcroft recalled what it was like when he joined the company: "It was a revelation to me to see the simplicity of decision-making."

Amstrad is built for speed from the bottom up. It has unbundled the traditional industrial package and turned manufacturing into a sub-contracted activity that can be used like a tap, to be turned up or down and on or off depending on market conditions and product development schedules.

Just as Amstrad lacks commitment to its products, so it lacks commitment to its manufacturing arrangements and component sourcing. The achievement Sugar takes most pride in over the past year is the change in the "bill of materials" for computer production from 95% Japanese to 50% Japanese since last January.

The wholesale flight from yen-priced components as the Japanese currency soared in foreign exchange markets required only a modest increase in the Amstrad purchasing department.

Managers of corporate treasury departments (Amstrad has one now) are used to shifting surplus cash in and out of currency at short notice but to change the whole currency mix of a manufacturing company's materials purchasing in so short a time is remarkable.

"It was natural to us," said Sugar, "because it was necessary for the survival of the margin."

Speed and agility are important secrets of Amstrad's success. The third essential ingredient is what might be called the company's vision system: its ability to identify market niches and—using its inner eye—to dream up the right products to fill them. Sugar himself makes a major contribution here.

Amstrad uses outside firms like MEJ Electronics (hardware) and Locomotive Software for product development (though the "in-house" R&D facility has been strengthened recently) but product ideas and associated marketing strategies come from Amstrad.

Sugar on customers: "I'm realistic and we are a marketing organisation so if it's the difference between people buying the machine or not, I'll stick a bloody fan in it. And if they say they want bright pink spots on it I'll do that too: What is the use of me banging my head against a brick wall and saying, 'You don't need the damn fan, Sunshine?' "

Financial Times, **August 1, 1988**

So while Amstrad notched up pre-tax profits of £90.12m on sales of £351.06m in the first half of this financial year,

its own workforce is small. In Hong Kong, Amstrad's Asian base, the company employs less than 500 people, around 400 of whom work in its small factory making printers.

Amstrad's cramped Hong Kong office hardly looks like a nerve centre for one of the most successful British companies of the decade. Shared with a textile concern and tucked away in Kowloon's jewellery quarter, about 70 engineers and administrators control the company's web of sub-contracting, purchasing and shipping arrangements in the Far East.

At the heart of these is Amstrad's network of major sub-contractors manufacturing the company's computer, audio and video products. Amstrad depends on them for its most fundamental requirement— products at the right price and quantity for the high streets of Europe. This explains the care with which a new sub-contractor is chosen.

In one recent case, says Stan Randall, Amstrad's head in Hong Kong, the company was impressed by the product coming out of a Taiwanese factory which it had not used before. Amstrad's Hong Kong engineers took the factory's products apart, studying the techniques used by their Taiwanese counterparts. They worked out a price and quality specification for a large quantity of a particular Amstrad product. "At that stage, the factory didn't even know we were interested in them," Randall says.

When Amstrad knew what it wanted and the price it was prepared to pay, its team visited the factory. They spent four days crawling over its procedures. Satisfied with what they found, they began negotiating an order for 200,000 of the products.

Amstrad keeps tight control over its sub-contractors. Randall, one of only two people from Britain employed by Amstrad in the Far East, insists on up to five of his Hong Kong engineers working full-time in a sub-contractor's factory when a new product is being introduced. Amstrad supervises and pays for the installation of new tooling for its products. Once a sub-contractor is bedded down, Amstrad maintains pressure on quality through a team of 20 inspectors, based in Hong Kong, who are constantly visiting the sub-contractors.

Randall, who was Amstrad's purchasing manager in the UK before setting up the company's subsidiary in Hong Kong in 1981, says Amstrad uses its printer factory there as a testing ground for innovative production ideas. Sandwiched into four floors in Kowloon, the plant will be churning out 50,000 printers a month by the end of the year. Printers were chosen as the sole product for Amstrad itself to make in the Far East because Amstrad's direct competitors own the other printer factories in the region.

Randall aims for a stable set of sub-contractors so that they learn to take Amstrad into their confidence about their future plans. Amstrad has been dealing with the Japanese company which makes its computers and word processors in a Korean plant for 14 years. "It's a long-term relationship. We have had some companies get very big on the back of Amstrad business," Randall says.

But he tries to remain highly flexible within his stable bedrock of sub-contractors and major suppliers. "You always have to keep your options open to move your production round the region," says Randall, a workaholic never far from his cellular phone.

Investors Chronicle, April 23, 1989

Last year Amstrad's operating margins were a huge 25 percent. That is more than double those of competitors such as Compaq, which like Amstrad is young and fast growing but unlike Amstrad sells premium-priced computers.

"The reason Amstrad earns so much is that the machines are underengineered and the company understaffed (last year Amstrad's 1,400 staff brought in sales of almost £1/2m a head). Margins could come all the way down to 10 percent," declares Keith Woolcock of CIBC Securities. At that level Amstrad would have made just £60m, profit last year, not £160m.

One way Amstrad is attempting to maintain its margins is by moving into the corporate computer market where buyers are less concerned with price than with hastle-free reliability.

The new range is the key to this strategy. Some Amstrad watchers believe it may have missed the boat. Others are more sanguine. The truth is no one really knows how successful the new range will be. No one doubts its importance. The existing machines still have plenty of mileage in them, particularly overseas. But like a shark Amstrad needs to keep moving. And with computers now accounting for around three-quarters of Amstrad's sales, it is hard to see how the consumer side could take up the slack if computers flag.

Sunday Times, April 23, 1989

Alan Sugar saw £52m clipped from his personal fortune in two days last week, after the second profits down-grade of the year for his troubled Amstrad consumer electronics group. The shares closed down 21p at 141p on Friday, as analysts forecast that profits would be £110m this year, compared with £164m in the year to June 1988.

But Sugar is not facing poverty; his stake in Amstrad is still worth £351m. However, he does need to recapture the City's confidence and to this end he is recruiting 10 financial and technical executives.

"Our problems are very simple," Sugar told the *Sunday Times*. "We have had such phenomenal growth over the past few years that we are still operating with a management team you would expect to be running a company a fraction of our size. From an engineering point of view we have too small a team to take on too big a task, and we are now paying the penalties in terms not only of our ability to design new products, but to maintain our existing ranges."

Sugar admitted failing to keep a tight hold on the financial reins. "There is nobody to blame but ourselves. It was entirely our own naivety in thinking we could take on products as advanced as the new business personal computers so quickly. They represent a much bigger dimension in technology," he said.

"We must strengthen ourselves in engineering and design," he said, "especially in our method of checking, testing and bringing products to the market so that they are rock solid as soon as they go into production. We've also got to get a team of heavy hitters on the financial side, to improve our product planning and take much more firm control of inventories, especially in our overseas subsidiaries."

Sugar said that a top priority must be "continuing to design a stream of products and bringing them swiftly to market. We can't take two years to design products; it must continue to be other companies copying us two years later. I don't mean that we should hire a vast force of design people, but we could do with more engineering foremen to manage the technical team."

Business, July 1989

His management style is not so much hands-on as hands-in. In 1984, when Fraser was settling in at Microsoft, Sugar rang him up. "He wanted to sell some piece of software on a volume deal with his new computer," Fraser says. "I quoted him our standard price, 60 pence a copy. He blew his top. 'I don't buy anything on that basis,' he roared. 'Don't you know the business I'm in? I sell yesterday's technology at tomorrow's prices. If people want Dolby [hi-fi noise reduction], I give them Dolby B, not Dolby C.' [Dolby B was introduced in 1968, Dolby C in 1980.] He said he wouldn't take the product. Boom. End of conversation. Over the years I had many thundering conversations down the phone with him about various things. It was always very abrupt, very blunt."

There is little escape from observation if a job is not done well. "In Amstrad you either last three weeks or you last forever," Sugar told his student audience. Stan Randall, after 18 years Amstrad's longest-serving employee says: "He walks constantly from department to department, from finance to marketing to sales to dispatch, spending five minutes here, ten minutes there, finding out what people are doing, helping out or pushing people along." The same applies when he visits the Hong Kong offices, where he knows many of the indigenous senior staff by first name.

At least once a week Sugar sees the heads of a foreign subsidiary. The R&D departments are used to having him stomp into their impromptu meetings and sit listening to the discussion before throwing in a question to stir them up. Keeping Amstrad alert in spirit and structure has been crucial to his success. "Every day you spend sitting around talking about an idea is a day of wasted sales," says Malcolm Miller, group sales and marketing director.

To push prices down the company plays suppliers off against one another. "It's attention to detail," Sugar explains. "Say the power cord on a unit costs £1.50. If we use 50,000 per month, in a year we spend on that one item alone, £900,000." Armed with that, the company looks to see if it can reduce its specification and at the same time searches for other suppliers.

"We may get the price reduced by 25 pence," Sugar continues, "and you may say—why waste your time? But 25 pence multiplied by 50,000 per month by 12 months is £150,000. As you can see, a good day's work for one bloke."

The early products contained some interesting touches from the Amstrad philosophy of providing the absolute minimum at the lowest price. One person who took the facia off an early Amstrad hi-fi found the button for "chrome/normal" cassette tapes was not connected. A hi-fi reviewer recalls an Amstrad speaker that appeared from the front to have two speaker cones, like high-priced rivals. When he took the front grille off, he found only one cone. The other had been painted on.

CANON: COMPETING ON CAPABILITIES†

By Sumantra Ghoshal and Mary Ackenhusen

In 1961, following the runaway success of the company's model 914 office copier, Joseph C. Wilson, President of Xerox Corporation, was reported to have said, "I keep asking myself, when am I going to wake up? Things just aren't this good in life." Indeed, the following decade turned out to be better than anything Wilson could have dreamed. Between 1960 and 1970, Xerox increased its sales 40 percent per year from $40 million to $1.7 billion and raised its after-tax profits from $2.6 million to $187.7 million. In 1970, with 93 percent market share world-wide and a brand name that was synonymous with copying, Xerox appeared as invincible in its industry as any company ever could.

When Canon, "the camera company from Japan," jumped into the business in the late 1960s, most observers were sceptical. Less than a tenth the size of Xerox, Canon had no direct sales or service organisation to reach the corporate market for copiers, nor did it have a process technology to by-pass the 500 patents that guarded Xerox's Plain Paper Copier (PPC) process. Reacting to the spate of recent entries in the business including Canon, Arthur D. Little predicted in 1969 that no company would be able to challenge Xerox's monopoly in PPC's in the 1970s because its patents presented an insurmountable barrier.

Yet, over the next two decades, Canon rewrote the rule book on how copiers were supposed to be produced and sold as it built up $5 billion in revenues in the business, emerging as the second largest global player in terms of sales and surpassing Xerox in the

number of units sold. According to the Canon Handbook, the company's formula for success as displayed initially in the copier business is "synergistic management of the total technological capabilities of the company, combining the full measure of Canon's know how in fine optics, precision mechanics, electronics and fine chemicals." Canon continues to grow and diversify using this strategy. Its vision, as described in 1991 by Ryuzaburo Kaku, President of the company, is "to become a premier global company of the size of IBM combined with Matsushita."

Industry Background

The photocopying machine has often been compared with the typewriter as one of the few triggers that have fundamentally changed the ways of office work. But, while a mechanical Memograph machine for copying had been introduced by the A.B. Dick company of Chicago as far back as 1887, it was only in the second half of this century that the copier market exploded with Xerox's commercialisation of the "electrophotography" process invented by Chester Carlson.

Xerox

Carlson's invention used an electrostatic process to transfer images from one sheet of paper to another. Licensed to Xerox in 1948, this invention led to two different photocopying technologies. The Coated Paper Copying (CPC) technology transferred the reflection of an image from the original directly to specialized zinc-oxide coated paper, while the Plain Paper Copying (PPC) technology transferred the image indirectly to ordinary paper through a rotating drum coated with charged particles. While dry or liquid toner could be used to develop the image, the dry toner was generally preferable in both technologies. A large number of companies entered the CPC market in the 1950s and 1960s based on technology licensed from Xerox or RCA (to whom Xerox had earlier licensed this technology).

†**Source:** This case was written by Mary Ackenhusen, Research Associate, under the supervision of Sumantra Ghoshal, Professor at INSEAD. It is intended to be used as a basis of class discussion rather than to illustrate either effective or ineffective handling of an administrative situation. Reprinted with the permission of INSEAD. Copyright ©1992 INSEAD, Fontainebleau, France.

693

However, PPC remained a Xerox monopoly since the company had refused to license any technology remotely connected to the PPC process and had protected the technology with over 500 patents.

Because of the need for specialized coated paper, the cost per copy was higher for CPC. Also, this process could produce only one copy at a time, and the copies tended to fade when exposed to heat or light. PPC, on the other hand, produced copies at a lower operating cost that were also indistinguishable from the original. The PPC machines were much more expensive, however, and were much larger in size. Therefore, they required a central location in the user's office. The smaller and less expensive CPC machines, in contrast, could be placed on individual desks. Over time, the cost and quality advantages of PPC, together with its ability to make multiple copies at high speed, made it the dominant technology and, with it, Xerox's model of centralized copying, the industry norm.

This business concept of centralized copying required a set of capabilities that Xerox developed and which, in turn, served as its major strengths and as key barriers to entry to the business. Given the advantages of volume and speed, all large companies found centralized copying highly attractive and they became the key customers for photocopying machines. In order to support this corporate customer base, Xerox's product designs and upgrades emphasized economies of higher volume copying. To market the product effectively to these customers, Xerox also built up an extensive direct sales and service organisation of over 12,000 sales representatives and 15,000 service people. Forty percent of the sales reps' time was spent "hand holding" to prevent even minor dissatisfaction. Service reps, dressed in suits and carrying their tools in briefcases, performed preventative maintenance and prided themselves on reducing the average time between breakdowns and repair to a few hours.

Further, with the high cost of each machine and the fast rate of model introductions, Xerox developed a strategy of leasing rather than selling machines to customers. Various options were available, but typically the customers paid a monthly charge on the number of copies made. The charge covered not only machine costs but also those of the paper and toner that Xerox supplied and the service visits. This lease strategy, together with the carefully cultivated service image, served as key safeguards from competition, as they tied the customers into Xerox and significantly raised their switching costs.

Unlike some other American corporations, Xerox had an international orientation right from the beginning. Even before it had a successful commercial copier, Xerox built up an international presence through joint ventures which allowed the company to minimize its capital investment abroad. In 1956, it ventured with the Rank Organisation Ltd. in the U.K. to form Rank Xerox . In 1962, Rank Xerox became a 50 percent partner with Fuji Photo to form Fuji Xerox which sold copiers in Japan. Through these joint ventures, Xerox built up sales and service capabilities in these key markets similar to those it had in the United States. There were some 5,000 sales people in Europe, 3,000 in Japan and over 7,000 and 3,000 service reps, respectively. Xerox also built limited design capabilities in both the joint ventures for local market customization, which developed into significant research establishments in their own rights in later years.

Simultaneously, Xerox maintained high levels of investment in both technology and manufacturing to support its growing market. It continued to spend over $100 million a year in R&D, exceeding the total revenues from the copier business that any of its competitors were earning in the early 70s, and also invested heavily in large-size plants not only in the U.S., but also in the U.K. and Japan.

Competition in the 1970s

Xerox's PPC patents began to expire in the 1970s, heralding a storm of new entrants. In 1970, IBM offered the first PPC copier not sold by Xerox, which resulted in Xerox suing IBM for patent infringement and violation of trade secrets. Canon marketed a PPC copier the same year through the development of an independent PPC technology which they licensed selectively to others. By 1973, competition had expanded to include players from the office equipment industry (IBM, SCM, Litton, Pitney Bowes), the electronics industry (Toshiba, Sharp), the reprographics industry (Ricoh, Mita, Copyer, 3M, AB Dick, Addressograph/Multigraph), the photographic equipment industry (Canon, Kodak, Minolta, Konishiroku) and the suppliers of copy paper (Nashua, Dennison, Saxon).

By the 1980s many of these new entrants, including IBM, had lost large amounts of money and exited the business. A few of the newcomers managed to achieve a high level of success, however, and copiers became a major business for them. Specifically, copiers were generating 40 percent of Canon's revenues by 1990.

Canon

Canon was founded in 1933 with the ambition to produce a sophisticated 35mm camera to rival that of Germany's world-class Leica model. In only two years' time, it had emerged as Japan's leading producer of high-class cameras. During the war, Canon utilized its optics expertise to produce an X-ray machine which was adopted by the Japanese military. After the war, Canon was able to successfully market its high-end camera, and by the mid-1950s it was the largest camera manufacturer in Japan. Building off its optics technology, Canon then expanded its product line to include a mid-range camera, an 8mm video camera, television lenses and micrographic equipment. It also began developing markets for its products outside of Japan, mainly in the U.S. and Canada.

Diversification was always very important to Canon in order to further its growth, and a new products R&D section was established in 1962 to explore the fields of copy machines, auto-focusing cameras, strobe-integrated cameras, home VCRs and electronic calculators. A separate, special operating unit was also established to introduce new non-camera products resulting from the diversification effort.

The first product to be targeted was the electronic calculator. This product was challenging because it required Canon engineers to develop new expertise in microelectronics in order to incorporate thousands of transistors and diodes in a compact, desk model machine. Tekeshi Mitarai, President of Canon at that time, was against developing the product because it was seen to be too difficult and risky. Nevertheless, a dedicated group of engineers believed in the challenge and developed the calculator in secrecy. Over a year later, top management gave their support to the project. In 1964, the result of the development effort was introduced as the Canola 130, the world's first 10-key numeric pad calculator. With this product line, Canon dominated the Japanese electronic calculator market in the 1960s.

Not every diversification effort was a success, however. In 1956, Canon began development of the synchroreader, a device for writing and reading with a sheet of paper coated with magnetic material. When introduced in 1959, the product received high praise for its technology. But, because the design was not patented, another firm introduced a similar product at half the price. There was no market for the high priced and incredibly heavy Canon product. Ultimately, the firm was forced to disassemble the finished inventories and sell off the usable parts in the "once-used" components market.

Move into Copiers

Canon began research into copier technology in 1959, and, in 1962, it formed a research group dedicated to developing a plain paper copier (PPC) technology. The only known PPC process was protected by hundreds of Xerox patents, but Canon felt that only this technology promised sufficient quality, speed, economy and ease of maintenance to successfully capture a large portion of the market. Therefore, corporate management challenged the researchers to develop a new PPC process which would not violate the Xerox patents.

In the meantime, the company entered the copier business by licensing the "inferior" CPC technology in 1965 from RCA. Canon decided not to put the name of the company on this product and marketed it under the brand name Confax 1000 in Japan only. Three years later, Canon licensed a liquid toner technology from an Australian company and combined this with the RCA technology to introduce the CanAll Series. To sell the copier in Japan, Canon formed a separate company, International Image Industry. The copier was sold as an OEM to Scott Paper in the U.S. who sold it under its own brand name.

Canon's research aiming at developing a PPC technical alternative to xerography paid off with the announcement of the "New Process" (NP) in 1968. This successful research effort not only produced an alternative process but also taught Canon the importance of patent law: how not to violate patents and how to protect new technology. The NP process was soon protected by close to 500 patents.

The first machine with the NP technology, the NP1100, was introduced in Japan in 1970. It was the first copier sold by Canon to carry the Canon brand name. It produced 10 copies per minute and utilized dry toner. As was the standard in the Japanese market, the copier line was sold outright to customers from the beginning. After two years of experience in the domestic market, Canon entered the overseas market, except North America, with this machine.

The second generation of the NP system was introduced in Japan in 1972 as the NPL7. It was a marked improvement because it eliminated a complex fusing technology, simplified developing and cleaning, and made toner supply easier through a new system developed to use liquid toner. Compared with the Xerox equivalent, it was more economical, more compact, more reliable and still had the same or better quality of copies.

With the NP system, Canon began a sideline which was to become quite profitable: licensing. The first generation NP system was licensed to AM, and Canon also provided it with machines on an OEM basis. The second generation was again licensed to AM as well as to Saxon, Ricoh, and Copyer. Canon accumulated an estimated $32 million in license fees between 1975 and 1982.

Canon continued its product introductions with a stream of state-of-the-art technological innovations throughout the seventies. In 1973 it added colour to the NP system; in 1975, it added laser beam printing technology. Its first entry into high volume copiers took place in 1978 with a model which was targeted at the Xerox 9200. The NP200 was introduced in 1979 and went on to win a gold medal at the Leipzig Fair for being the most economical and productive copier available. By 1982, copiers had surpassed cameras as the company's largest revenue generate (see exhibits 1 and 2 for Canon's financials and sales by product line).

The Personal Copier

In the late 1970s, top management began searching for a new market for the PPC copier. They had recently experienced a huge success with the introduction of the AE-1 camera in 1976 and wanted a similar success in copiers. The AE-1 was a very compact single-lens reflex camera, the first camera that used a microprocessor to control electronically functions of exposure, film rewind, and strobe. The product had been developed through a focused, cross-functional project team effort which had resulted in a substantial reduction in the number of components, as well as in automated assembly and the use of unitized parts. Because of these improvements, the AE-1 enjoyed a 20 percent cost advantage over competitive models in the same class.

After studying the distribution of offices in Japan by size (see exhibit 3), Canon decided to focus on a latent segment the Xerox had ignored. This was the segment comprised of small offices (segment E) who could benefit from the functionality offered by photocopiers but did not require the high speed machines available in the market. Canon management believed that a low volume "value for money" machine could generate a large demand in this segment. From this analysis emerged the business concept of a "personal side

desk" machine which could not only create a new market in small offices but potentially also induce decentralization of the copy function in large offices. Over time, the machine might even create demand for a personal copier for home use. This would be a copier that up to now no one had thought possible. Canon felt that, to be successful in this market, the product had to cost half the price of a conventional copier (target price $1,000), be maintenance free, and provide ten times more reliability.

Top management took their "dream" to the engineers, who, after careful consideration, took on the challenge. The machine would build off their previous expertise in microelectronics but would go much further in terms of material, functional component, design and production engineering technologies. The team's slogan was "Let's make the AE-1 of copiers!," expressing the necessity of know-how transfer between the camera and copier divisions as well as their desire for a similar type of success. The effort was led by the director of the Reprographic Production Development Center. His cross-functional team of 200 was the second largest ever assembled at Canon (the largest had been that of the AE-1 camera).

During the development effort, a major issue arose concerning the paper size that the new copier would accept. Canon Sales (the sales organisation for Japan) wanted the machine to use a larger-than-letter-size paper which accounted for 60 percent of the Japanese market. This size was not necessary for sales outside of Japan and would add 20-30 percent to the machine's cost as well as make the copier more difficult to service. After much debate world-wide, the decision was made to forego the ability to utilize the larger paper size in the interest of better serving the global market.

Three years later the concept was a reality. The new PC (personal copier) employed a new-cartridge based technology which allowed the user to replace the photoreceptive drum, charging device, toner assembly and cleaner with a cartridge every 2,000 copies, thus eliminating the need to maintain the copier regularly. This enabled Canon engineers to meet the cost and reliability targets. The revolutionary product was the smallest, lightest copier ever sold, and created a large market which had previously not existed. Large offices adjusted their copying strategies to include decentralized copying, and many small offices and even homes could now afford a personal copier. Again, Canon's patent knowledge was utilized to protect this research, and the cartridge technology was not licensed to other manufacturers. Canon has maintained its leadership in personal copiers into the 1990s.

EXHIBIT 1
Canon, Inc.: Ten-Year Financial Summary (in ¥ millions)

	1981	1982	1983	1984	1985	1986	1987	1988	1989	1990
Net sales:										
Domestic	144,898	168,178	198,577	240,656	272,966	274,174	290,382	348,462	413,854	508,747
Overseas	326,364	412,322	458,748	589,732	682,814	615,043	686,329	757,548	937,063	1,219,201
Total Sales	471,262	580,500	657,325	830,383	955,780	889,217	976,711	1,106,010	1,350,917	1,727,948
Percentage to previous year	112.5	123.2	113.2	126.3	115.1	93.0	109.8	113.2	122.1	127.9
Net income	16,216	22,358	28,420	35,029	37,056	10,728	13,244	37,100	38,293	61,408
Percentage to sales	3.4	3.9	4.3	4.2	3.9	1.2	1.4	3.4	2.8	3.6
Advertising expense	23,555	37,532	41,902	1,318	50,080	37,362	38,280	41,509	54,394	72,234
Research and development	14,491	23,554	28,526	38,256	49,461	55,330	57,085	65,522	75,566	86,008
Depreciation	22,732	27,865	30,744	39,995	47,440	55,391	57,153	57,627	64,861	78,351
Capital expenditure	54,532	46,208	53,411	75,94	91,7863	81,273	63,497	83,069	107,290	137,298
Long-term debt	39,301	53,210	60,636	99,490	134,366	166,722	222,784	206,083	277,556	262,886
Stockholders' equity	168,735	235,026	264,629	304,310	333,148	336,456	371,198	416,465	550,841	617,566
Total assets	505,169	606,101	731,642	916,651	1,001,044	1,009,504	1,133,881	1,299,843	1,636,380	1,827,945
Per share data:										
Net income:										
Common and common equivalent share	34.04	41.17	46.31	53.63	53.38	16.67	19.65	51.27	50.16	78.29
Assuming full dilution	33.35	38.89	45.02	53.37	53.25	16.67	19.64	51.26	49.31	78.12
Cash dividends declared	7.84	8.23	9.43	9.88	11.36	11.36	9.09	11.36	11.93	12.50
Stock price:										
High	1,248	934	1,294	1,336	1,364	1,109	1,282	1,536	2,040	1,940
Low	513	417	755	830	800	791	620	823	1,236	1,220
Average number of common and common equivalent shares in thousands	515,593	564,349	645,473	675,153	727,257	746,108	747,053	747,059	780,546	788,765
Number of employees	24,300	25,607	27,266	30,302	34,129	35,498	37,521	40,740	44,401	54,381
Average exchange rate ($1 =)	222	248	238	239	235	167	143	127	129	143

EXHIBIT 2
Sales by Product
(in ¥ millions)

Year	Cameras	Copiers	Other Business Machines	Optical & Other Products	Total
1981	201,635	175,389	52,798	40,222	470,044
1982	224,619	242,161	67,815	45,905	580,500
1983	219,443	291,805	97,412	48,665	657,325
1984	226,645	349,986	180,661	73,096	830,388
1985	197,284	410,840	271,190	76,466	955,780
1986	159,106	368,558	290,630	70,923	889,217
1987	177,729	393,581	342,895	62,506	976,711
1988	159,151	436,924	434,634	75,301	1,106,010
1989	177,597	533,115	547,170	93,035	1,350,917
1990	250,494	686,077	676,095	115,282	1,727,948

Building Capabilities

Canon is admired for its technical innovations, marketing expertise, and low-cost quality manufacturing. These are the result of a long-term strategy to becoming a premier company. Canon has frequently acquired outside expertise so that it could better focus internal investments on skills of strategic importance. This approach of extensive outsourcing and focused internal development has required consistent direction from top management and the patience to allow the company to become well grounded in one skill area before tasking the organisation with the next objective.

Technology

Canon's many innovative products, which enabled the company to grow quickly in the seventies and eighties are in large part the result of a carefully orchestrated use of technology and the capacity for managing rapid technological change. Attesting to its prolific output of original research is the fact that Canon has been among the leaders in number of patents issued world-wide throughout the eighties.

These successes have been achieved in an organisation that has firmly pursued a strategy of decentralized R&D. Most of Canon's R&D personnel are employed by the product divisions where 80-90 percent of the company's patentable inventions originate. Each product division has its own development center which is tasked with short- to medium-term product design and improvement of production systems. Most product development is performed by cross-functional teams. The work of the development groups is coordinated by an R&D headquarters group.

The Corporate Technical Planning and Operation centre is responsible for long-term strategic R&D planning. Canon also has a main research centre which supports state-of-the-art research in optics, electronics, new materials and information technology. There are three other corporate research centres which apply this state-of-the-art research to product development.

Canon acknowledges that it has neither the resources nor the time to develop all necessary technologies and has therefore often traded or bought specific technologies from a variety of external partners. Furthermore, it has used joint ventures and technology transfers as a strategic tool for mitigating foreign trade tensions in Europe and the United States. For example, Canon had two purposes in mind when it made an equity participation in CPF Deutsch, an office equipment marketing firm in Germany. Primarily, it believed that this move would help develop the German market for its copiers; but it did not go unnoticed among top management that CPF owned Tetras, a copier maker who at that time was pressing dumping charges against Japanese copier makers. Canon also used Burroughs as an OEM for office automation equipment in order to acquire Burroughs software and know-how and participate in joint development agreements with Eastman Kodak and Texas Instruments. Exhibit 4 provides a list of the company's major joint ventures.

Copier Market Segment	Number of Office Workers	Number of Offices	Working Population
A	300+	200,000	9,300,000
B	100–299	30,000	4,800,000
C	30–99	170,000	8,300,000
D	5–29	1,820,000	15,400,000
E	1–4	4,110,000	8,700,000

EXHIBIT 3
Office Size Distribution, Japan 1979

Source: Yamanouchi, Teruo, Breakthrough: The Development of the Canon Personal Copier, *Long Range Planning*, Vol. 22, October 1989, p. 4

Canon also recognizes that its continued market success depends on its ability to exploit new research into marketable products quickly. It has worked hard to reduce the new product introduction cycle through a cross-functional programme called TS 1/2 whose purpose is to cut development time by 50 percent on a continuous basis. The main thrust of this programme is the classification of development projects by total time required and the critical human resources needed so that these two parameters can be optimized for each product depending on its importance for Canon's corporate strategy. This allows product teams to be formed around several classifications of product development priorities of which "best sellers" will receive the most emphasis. These are the products aimed at new markets or segments with large potential demands. Other classifications include products necessary to catch up with competitive offerings, product refinements intended to enhance customer satisfaction, and long-run marathon products which will take considerable time to develop. In all development classifications, Canon emphasizes three factors to reduce time to market: the fostering of engineering ability, efficient technical support systems, and careful reviews of product development at all stages.

Canon is also working to divert its traditional product focus into more of a market focus. To this end, Canon R&D personnel participate in international product strategy meetings, carry out consumer research, join in marketing activities, and attend meetings in the field at both domestic and foreign sales subsidiaries.

Marketing

Canon's effective marketing is the result of step-by-step, calculated introduction strategies. Normally, the product is first introduced and perfected in the home market before being sold internationally. Canon has learned how to capture learning from the Japanese market quickly so that the time span between introduction in Japan and abroad is as short as a few months. Furthermore, the company will not simultaneously launch a new product through a new distribution channel—its strategy is to minimize risk by introducing a new product through known channels first. New channels will only be created, if necessary, after the product has proven to be successful.

The launch of the NP copier exemplifies this strategy. Canon initially sold these copiers in Japan by direct sales through its Business Machines Sales organisation, which had been set up in 1968 to sell the calculator product line. This sales organisation was merged with the camera sales organisation in 1971 to form Canon Sales. By 1972, after three years of experience in producing the NP product line, the company entered into a new distribution channel, that of dealers, to supplement direct selling.

The NP copier line was not marketed in the U.S. until 1974, after production and distribution were running smoothly in Japan. The U.S. distribution system was similar to that used in Japan, with seven sales subsidiaries for direct selling and a network of independent dealers.

By the late 1970s, Canon had built up a strong dealer network in the U.S. which supported both sales and service of the copiers. The dealer channel was responsible for rapid growth in copier sales, and, by the early 1980s, Canon copiers were sold almost exclusively through this channel. Canon enthusiastically supported the dealers with attractive sales incentive programmes, management training and social outings. Dealers were certified to sell copiers only after completing a course in service training. The company felt that a close relationship with its dealers was a vital asset that

EXHIBIT 4
Canon's Major International
Joint Ventures

Category	Partner	Description
Office Equipment	Eastman Kodak (U.S.)	Distributes Kodak medical equipment in Japan; exports copiers to Kodak
	CPF Germany	Equity participation in CPF which markets Canon copiers
	Olivetti (Italy) Lotte (Korea)	Joint venture for manufacture of copier
Computers	Hewlett-Packard (U.S.)	Receives OEM mini-computer from HP; supplies laser printer to HP
	Apple Computer (U.S.)	Distributes Apple computers in Japan; supplies laser printer to Apple
	Next, Inc. (U.S.)	Equity participation; Canon has marketing rights for Asia
Semiconductors	National Semiconductor (U.S.)	Joint development of MPU & software for Canon office equipment
	Intel (U.S.)	Joint development of LSI for Canon copier, manufactured by Intel
Telecommunications	Siemens (Germany)	Development of ISDN interface for Canon facsimile; Siemens supplies Canon with digital PBX
	DHL (U.S.)	Equity participation; Canon supplies terminals to DHL
Camera	Kinsei Seimitsu (Korea)	Canon licenses technology on 35mm Camera
Other	ECD (U.S.)	Equity participation because Canon values its research on amorphous materials

allowed it to understand and react to customers' needs and problems in a timely manner. At the same time, Canon also maintained a direct selling mechanism through wholly owned sales subsidiaries in Japan, the U.S. and Europe in order to target large customers and government accounts.

The introduction of its low-end personal copier in 1983 was similarly planned to minimize risk. Initially, Canon's NP dealers in Japan were not interested in the product due to its low maintenance needs and inability to utilize large paper sizes. Thus, PCs were distributed through the firm's office supply stores who were already selling its personal calculators. After seeing the success of the PC, the NP dealers began to carry the copier.

In the U.S., the PC was initially sold only through existing dealers and direct sales channels due to limited availability of the product. Later, it was sold through competitors' dealers and office supply stores, and, eventually, the distribution channels were extended to include mass merchandisers. Canon already had considerable experience in mass merchandising from its camera business.

Advertising has always been an integral part of Canon's marketing strategy. President Kaku believes that Canon must have a corporate brand name which is outstanding to succeed in its diversification effort. "Customers must prefer products because they bear the name Canon," he says. As described by the company's finance director, "If a brand name is unknown, and there is no advertising, you have to sell it cheap. It's not our policy to buy share with a low price. We establish our brand with advertising at a reasonably high price."

Therefore, when the NP-200 was introduced in 1980, 10 percent of the selling price was spent on advertising; for the launch of the personal copier, advertising expenditure was estimated to be 20 percent of the selling price. Canon has also sponsored various sporting events including World Cup football, the Williams motor racing team, and the ice dancers Torvill and Dean. The company expects its current expansion into the home automation market to be greatly enhanced by the brand image it has built in office equipment (see exhibit 1 for Canon's advertising expenditures through 1990.)

Manufacturing

Canon's goal in manufacturing is to produce the best quality at the lowest cost with the best delivery. To drive down costs, a key philosophy of the production system is to organize the manufacture of each product so that the minimum amount of time, energy and resources are required. Canon therefore places strong emphasis on tight inventory management through a stable production planning process, careful material planning, close supplier relationships, and adherence to the kanban system of inventory movement. Additionally, a formal waste elimination programme saved Canon 177 billion yen between 1976 and 1985. Overall, Canon accomplished a 30 percent increase in productivity per year from 1976 to 1982 and over 10 percent thereafter through automation and innovative process improvements.

The workforce is held in high regard at Canon. A philosophy of "stop and fix it" empowers any worker to stop the production line if he or she is not able to perform a task properly or observes a quality problem. Workers are responsible for their own machine maintenance governed by rules which stress prevention. Targets for quality and production and other critical data are presented to the workers with on-line feedback. Most workers also participate in voluntary "small group activity" for problems solving. The result of these systems is a workforce that feels individually responsible for the success of the products it manufactures.

Canon sponsors a highly regarded suggestion programme for its workers in order to directly involve those most familiar with the work processes in improving the business. The programme was originally initiated in 1952 with only limited success, but in the early 1980s participation soared with more than seventy suggestions per employee per year. All suggestions are reviewed by a hierarchy of committees with monetary prizes awarded monthly and yearly depending on the importance of the suggestion. The quality and effectiveness of the process are demonstrated by a 90 percent implementation rate of the suggestions offered and corporate savings of $202 million in 1985 (against a total expenditure of $2 million in running the programme, over 90 percent of it in prize money).

Canon chooses to backward integrate only on parts with unique technologies. For other components, the company prefers to develop long-term relationships with its suppliers and it retains two sources for most parts. In 1990, over 80 percent of Canon's copiers were assembled from purchased parts, with only the drums and toner being manufactured in-house. The company also maintains its own in-house capability for doing pilot production of all parts so as to understand better the technology and the vendors' costs.

Another key to Canon's high quality and low cost is the attention given to parts commonality between models. Between some adjacent copier models, the commonality is as high as 60 percent.

Copier manufacture was primarily located in Toride, Japan, in the early years but then spread to Germany, California and Virginia in the U.S., France, Italy and Korea. In order to mitigate trade and investment friction, Canon is working to increase the local content of parts as it expands globally. In Europe it exceeds the EC standard by 5 percent. It is also adding R&D capability to some of its overseas operations. Mr. Kaku emphasizes the importance of friendly trading partners:

> "Friction cannot be erased by merely transferring our manufacturing facilities overseas. The earnings after tax must be reinvested in the country; we must transfer our technology to the country. This is the only way our overseas expansion will be welcomed."

Leveraging Expertise

Canon places critical importance on continued growth through diversification into new product fields. Mr Kaku observed,

> "Whenever Canon introduced a new product, profits surged forward. Whenever innovation lagged, on the other hand, so did the earnings... In order to survive in the coming era of extreme competition, Canon must possess at least a dozen proprietary state-of-the-art technologies that will enable it to develop unique products."

While an avid supporter of diversification, Mr. Kaku was cautious.

"In order to ensure the enduring survival of Canon, we have to continue diversifying in order to adapt to environmental changes. However, we must be wise in choosing ways toward diversification. In other words, we must minimize the risks. Entering a new business which requires either a technology unrelated to Canon's current expertise or a different marketing channel than Canon currently uses incurs a 50 percent risk. If Canon attempts to enter a new business which requires both a new technology and a new marketing channel which are unfamiliar to Canon, the risk entailed in such ventures would be 100 percent. There are two prerequisites that have to be satisfied before launching such new ventures. First, our operation must be debt-free; second, we will have to secure the personnel capable of competently undertaking such ventures. I feel we shall have to wait until the twenty-first century before we are ready."

Combining Capabilities

Through its R&D strategy, Canon has worked to build up specialized expertise in several areas and then link them to offer innovative, state-of-the-art products. Through the fifties and sixties, Canon focused on products related to its main business and expertise, cameras. This prompted the introduction of the 8mm movie camera and the Canon range of mid-market cameras. There was minimal risk because the optics technology was the same and the marketing outlet, camera shops, remained the same.

Entrance into the calculator market pushed Canon into developing expertise in the field of microelectronics, which it later innovatively combined with its optics capability to introduce one of its most successful products, the personal copier. From copiers, Canon utilized the replaceable cartridge system to introduce a successful desktop laser printer.

In the early seventies, Canon entered the business of marketing micro-chip semiconductor production equipment. In 1980, the company entered into the development and manufacture of unique proprietary ICs in order to strengthen further its expertise in electronics technology. This development effort was expanded in the late eighties to focus on opto-electronic ICs. According to Mr. Kaku:

"We are now seriously committed to R&D in ICs because our vision for the future foresees the arrival of the opto-electronic era. When the time arrives for the opto-electronic IC to replace the current ultra-LSI, we intend to go into making large-scale computers. Presently we cannot compete with the IBMs and NECs using the ultra-LSIs. When the era of the opto-electronic IC arrives, the technology of designing the computer will be radically transformed; that will be our chance for making entry into the field of the large-scale computer."

Creative Destruction

In 1975 Canon produced the first laser printer. Over the next fifteen years, laser printers evolved as a highly successful product line under the Canon brand name. The company also provides the "engine" as an OEM to Hewlett Packard and other laser printer manufacturers which when added to its own branded sales supports a total of 84 percent of world-wide demand.

The biggest threat to the laser printer industry is substitution by the newly developed bubble jet printer. With a new technology which squirts out thin streams of ink under heat, a high-quality silent printer can be produced at half the price of the laser printer. The technology was invented accidentally in the Canon research labs. It keys on a print head which has up to 400 fine nozzles per inch, each with its own heater to warm the ink until it shoots out tiny ink droplets. This invention utilizes Canon's competencies in fine chemicals for producing the ink and its expertise in semiconductors, materials, and electronics for manufacturing the print heads. Canon is moving full steam forward to develop the bubble jet technology, even though it might destroy a business that the company dominates. The new product is even more closely tied to the company's core capabilities, and management believes that successful development of this business will help broaden further its expertise in semiconductors.

Challenge of the 1990s

Canon sees the office automation business as its key growth opportunity for the nineties. It already has a well-established brand name in home and office automation products through its offerings of copiers, facsimiles, electronic typewriters, laser printers, word processing equipment and personal computers. The next challenge for the company is to link these discrete products into a multifunctional system which will perform the tasks of a copier, facsimile, printer, and scanner and interface with a computer so that all the functions can be performed from one keyboard. In 1988, with this target, Canon introduced a personal computer which incorporated a PC, a fax, a telephone and a word processor. Canon has also introduced a colour laser copier which hooks up to a computer to serve as a colour printer. A series of additional integrated OA offerings are scheduled for introduction in 1992, and the company expects these products to serve as its growth engine in the first half of the 1990s.

Managing the Process

Undergirding this impressive history of continuously building new corporate capabilities and of exploiting those capabilities to create a fountain of innovative new products lies a rather unique management process. Canon has institutionalized corporate entrepreneurship through its highly autonomous and market focused business unit structure. A set of powerful functional committees provide the bridge between the entrepreneurial business units and the company's core capabilities in technology, manufacturing and marketing. Finally, an extraordinarily high level of corporate ambition drives this innovation engine, which is fuelled by the creativity of its people and by top management's continuous striving for ever higher levels of performance.

Driving Entrepreneurship: The Business Units

Mr. Kaku had promoted the concept of the entrepreneurial business unit from his earliest days with Canon, but it was not until the company had suffered significant losses in 1975 that his voice was heard. His plan was implemented shortly before he became president of the company.

Mr. Kaku believed that Canon's diversification strategy could only succeed if the business units were empowered to act on their own, free of central controls. Therefore, two independent operating units were formed in 1978, one for cameras and one for office equipment, to be managed as business units. Optical Instruments, the third business unit, had always been separate. Since that time, an additional three business units have been spun off. The original three business units were then given clear profitability targets, as well as highly ambitious growth objectives, and were allowed the freedom to devise their own ways to achieve these goals. One immediate result of this decentralization was the recognition that Canon's past practice of mixing production of different products in the same manufacturing facility would no longer work. Manufacturing was reorganized so that no plant produced more than one type of product.

Mr. Kaku describes the head of each unit as a surrogate of the CEO empowered to make quick decisions. This allows him, as president of Canon, to devote himself exclusively to his main task of creating and implementing the long-term corporate strategy. In explaining the benefits of the system, he said:

> "Previously, the president was in exclusive charge of all decision making; his subordinates had to form a queue to await their turn in presenting their problems to him. This kind of system hinders the development of the young managers' potential for decision-making."

> "Furthermore, take the case of the desktop calculator. Whereas, I can devote only about two hours each day on problems concerning the calculator, the CEO of Casio Calculator could devote 24 hours to the calculator... In the fiercely competitive market, we lost out because our then CEO was slow in coping with the problem."

In contrast to the Western philosophy of stand-alone SBUs encompassing all functions including engineering, sales, marketing and production, Canon has chosen to separate its product divisions from its sales and marketing arm. This separation allows for a clear focus on the challenges that Canon faces in selling products on a global scale. Through a five-year plan initiated in 1977, Seiichi Takigawa, the president of Canon Sales (the sales organisation for Japan), stressed the need to "make sales a science." After proving the profitability of this approach, Canon Sales took on the responsibility for world-wide marketing, sales and service. In 1981, Canon Sales was listed on the Tokyo stock exchange, reaffirming its independence.

Canon also allows its overseas subsidiaries free rein, though it holds the majority of stock. The philosophy is to create the maximum operational leeway for each subsidiary to act on its own initiative. Kaku describes the philosophy through an analogy:

> "Canon's system of managing subsidiaries is similar to the policy of the Tokugawa government, which established secure hegemony over the warlords, who were granted autonomy in their territory. I am "shogun" [head of the Tokugawa regime] and the subsidiaries' presidents are the "daimyo" [warlords]. The difference between Canon and the Tokugawa government is that the latter was a zero-sum society: its policy was repressive. On the other hand, Canon's objective is to enhance the prosperity of all subsidiaries through efficient mutual collaboration."

Canon has also promoted the growth of intrapreneurial ventures within the company by spinning these ventures off as wholly owned subsidiaries. The first venture to be spun off was Canon Components, which produced electronic components and devices, in 1984.

Building Integration: Functional Committees

As Canon continues to grow and diversify, it becomes increasingly difficult but also ever more important to link its product divisions in order to realize the benefits possible only in a large multiproduct corporation. The basis of Canon's integration is a three dimensional management approach in which the first dimension is the independent business unit, the second a network of functional committees, and the third the regional companies focused on geographic markets (see exhibit 5).

Kaku feels there are four basic requirements for the success of a diversified business: 1) a level of competence in research and development; 2) quality, low-cost manufacturing technology; 3) superior marketing strength; and 4) an outstanding corporate identity, culture and brand name. Therefore, he has established separate functional committees to address the first three requirements of development, production and marketing, while the fourth task has been kept as a direct responsibility of corporate management. The three functional committees, in turn, have been made responsible for company-wide administration of three key management systems:

- The Canon Development System (CDS) whose objectives are to foster the research and creation of new products and technologies by studying and continuously improving the development process;

- The Canon Production System (CPS) whose goal is to achieve optimum quality by minimizing waste in all areas of manufacturing;

- The Canon Marketing System (CMS), later renamed the Canon International Marketing System (CIMS), which is tasked to expand and strengthen Canon's independent domestic and overseas sales networks by building a high quality service and sales force.

Separate office have been created at headquarters for each of these critical committees, and over time their role has broadened to encompass general improvement of the processes used to support their functions. The chairpersons of the committees are members of Canon's management committee, which gives them the ability to ensure consistency and communicate process improvements throughout the multiproduct, multinational corporation.

Using information technology to integrate its worldwide operations, Canon began development of the Global Information System for Harmonious Growth Administration (GINGA) in 1987. The system will consist of a high-speed digital communications network to interconnect all parts of Canon into a global database and allow for the timely flow of information among managers in any location of the company's world-wide organisation. GINGA is planned to include separate but integrated systems for computer integrated manufacturing, global marketing and distribution, R&D and product design, financial reporting, and personnel database tracking, as well as some advances in intelligent office automation. As described by Mr. Kaku, the main objective of this system is to supplement Canon's efficient vertical communications structure with a lateral one that will facilitate direct information exchange among managers across businesses, countries, and functions on all operational matters concerning the company. The system is being developed at a total cost of 20 billion yen and it is targeted for completion in 1992.

Managing Renewal: Challenges and Change

Mr. Kaku was very forthright about some of the management weaknesses of Canon prior to 1975:

> "In short, our skill in management—the software of our enterprise—was weak. Management policy must be guided by a soundly created software on management; if the software is weak, the firm will lack clearly defined ideals and objectives. In the beginning we had a clearly defined objective, to overtake West Germany's Leica. Since then our management policy has been changing like the colours of a chameleon."

> "In the past our management would order employees to reach the peak of Mount Fuji, and then before the vanguard of climbers had barely started climbing, they would be ordered to climb Mount Tsukuba far to the north. Then the order would again be suddenly changed to climb Mount Yatsugatake to the west. After experiencing these kind of shifts in policy, the smarter employees would opt to take things easy by taking naps on the bank of the river Tamagawa. As a result, vitality would be sapped from our work force—a situation that should have been forestalled by all means."

Mr. Kaku's first action as President of Canon was to start the firm on the path to global leadership through establishing the first "premier company plan," a six-year plan designed to make Canon a top company in Japan. The plan outlined a policy for diversification and required consistently recurring profits exceeding 10 percent on sales.

EXHIBIT 5
Canon Organisation Chart

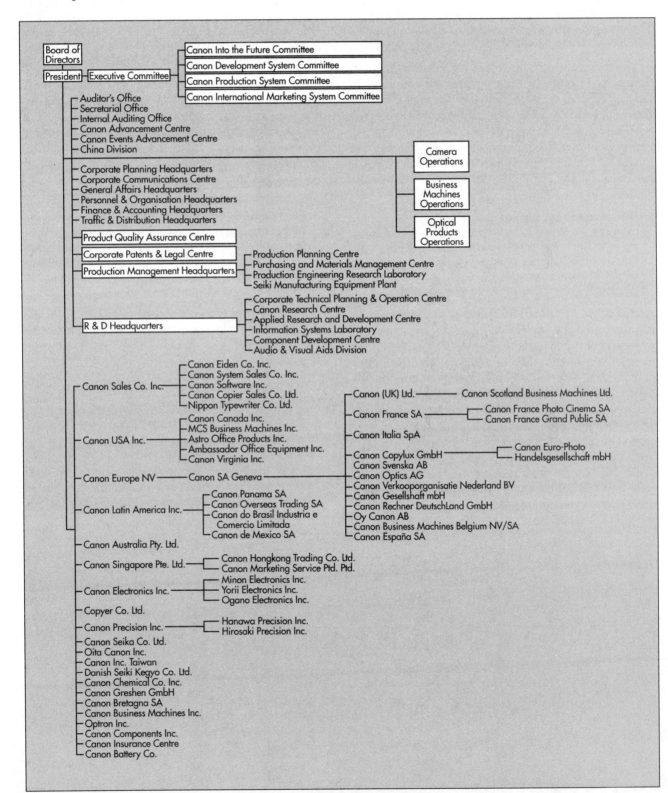

"The aim of any Japanese corporation is ensuring its perpetual survival. Unlike the venture businesses and U.S. corporations, our greatest objective is not to maximize short-term profits. Our vital objective is to continually earn profits on a stable basis for ensuring survival. To implement this goal, we must diversify."

By the time the original six-year plan expired in 1981, Canon had become a highly respected company in Japan. The plan was then renewed through 1986 and then again into the 1990s. The challenge was to become a premier global company, defined as having recurring profits exceeding 15 percent of sales. R&D spending was gradually increased from 6 percent of sales in 1980 to 9 percent in 1985 as a prerequisite for global excellence. As described by Mr. Kaku:

"By implementing our first plan for becoming a premier company we have succeeded in attaining the allegorical top of Mount Fuji. Our next objective is the Everest. With a firm determination, we could have climbed Fuji wearing sandals. However, sandals are highly inappropriate for climbing Everest; it may cause our death."

According to Mr. Kaku, such ambitions also require a company to build up the ability to absorb temporary reversals without panic; ambition without stability makes the corporate ship lose its way. To illustrate, he described the situation at Canon during the time the yen depreciated from 236 to the dollar in 1985 to 168 to the dollar in 1986. With 74 percent of Canon's Japanese production going to export markets, this sudden change caused earnings to fall to 4.6 billion yen, one tenth of the previous year. Some board members at Canon sought drastic action such as a major restructuring of the company and cutting the R&D budget. Mr. Kaku had successfully argued the opposite:

"What I did was calm them down. If a person gets lost in climbing a high mountain, he must avoid excessive use of his energy, otherwise his predicament will deepen... Our ongoing strategy for becoming the premier company remains the best, even under this crisis; there is no need to panic. Even if we have to forego dividends for two or three times, we shall surely overcome this crisis."

While celebrating the company's past successes, Mr. Kaku also constantly reminds his colleagues that no organisational form or process holds the eternal truth. The need to change with a changing world is inevitable. For example, despite being the creator of the product division-marketing company split, he was considering rejoining these two in the nineties:

"In the future, our major efforts in marketing must be concentrated on clearly defining and differentiating the markets of the respective products and creating appropriate marketing systems for them. In order to make this feasible, we may have to recombine our sales subsidiaries with the parent company and restructure their functions to fully meet the market's needs."

While constantly aware of the need to change, Kaku also recognizes the difficulties managers face in changing the very approaches and strategies that have led to past successes:

"In order for a company to survive forever, the company must have the courage to be able to deny at one point what it has been doing in the past; the biological concept of "ecdysis"—casting off the skin to emerge to new form. But it is difficult for human beings to deny and destruct what they have been building up. But if they cannot do that, it is certain that the firm can not survive forever. Speaking about myself, it is difficult to deny what I've done in the past. So when such time comes that I have to deny the past, I inevitably would have to step down."

SOCIÉTÉ GÉNÉRALE DE BELGIQUE†

By John Pringle and David Hover

In June 1988, the dust was finally settling after the largest cross-border takeover in European history. The Belgian industrial and financial giant, Société Générale de Belgique (SGB), had been acquired by the French holding company, Compagnie Financière de Suez. In its initial step at securing control over its latest acquisition, Suez had appointed Mr Hervé de Carmoy, previously the director of international operations at the British Midland Bank PLC and a Frenchman, as SGB's first Chief Executive Officer.

The mandate given de Carmoy was, however, still clear: define and implement a strategy to revitalise SGB and its many holdings and make the SGB empire a competitive and profitable force in Europe. It would not be an easy task. As the new Chief Executive Officer (CEO), de Carmoy assumed many of the managerial responsibilities of the former Governor of SGB, Mr René Lamy, who remained as Chairman of the SGB Board. By appointing a non-Suez executive to run SGB and initially keeping Lamy, a Belgian, as Chairman, Suez had sought to allay the suspicion harbored by many Belgians that Suez was intent on dominating and perhaps absorbing SGB. SGB was closely tied to Belgium, and the government, unions and public would be watching the changes made under de Carmoy with interest. Publicly, the Suez group professed interest in keeping SGB independent.

The company that de Carmoy found himself running in 1988 was a very large amalgamation of holdings in generally unrelated financial and industrial companies, concentrated in Belgium. Additionally, tradition was

†**Source:** This case was prepared by Research Associate David H. Hover, under the supervision of Professor John J. Pringle, as a basis for class discussion rather than to illustrate either effective or ineffective handling of a business situation. Copyright ©1991 by the International Institute for Management Development (IMD), Lausanne, Switzerland. IMD retains all rights. Not to be reproduced or used without written permission directly from IMD, Lausanne, Switzerland.

strong at SGB and the old order was deeply intrenched: many believed the nickname la vieille dame (the old lady) had been well earned. Founded in the early 1800s, the company had grown to become one of the pillars of the Belgian economy although it suffered from years of ineffective management and mediocre performance.

Historically, La Générale, as the company was more commonly known, had taken a passive approach to its subsidiaries, rarely interfering or showing much interest in their activities as long as dividends were paid. Complicating the problem, many of SGB's holdings were only minority stakes: SGB frequently relied on its ability to influence decision-making at the subsidiary level rather than taking formal control through majority ownership. However, changes in the commercial environment of Belgium, stemming from the increasing momentum behind the drive for a unified market in the European Community in 1992, were forcing all domestic businesses to adopt new ways of operating, and SGB was no exception.

Belgium and the European Community

Belgium is a small country of less than 10 million inhabitants sandwiched between France, Luxembourg, West Germany and The Netherlands. The population is divided into two primary cultural and linguistic groups: the French-speaking Walloons in the southern half of the country (Wallonia), and the Flemish-speaking (similar to Dutch) Flemings in the north (Flanders). The Flemish constituted approximately 56 percent of the country's population. In the 1980s, about 11 percent of the population lived in Brussels, the capital. Although French-speaking, the residents of Brussels were not considered Walloons.

Prior to World War II, economic growth had been concentrated in the south because of local deposits of coal and minerals (notably iron). After the war, however, the centre of economic activity shifted to Flanders as the coal and steel industries in Wallonia declined, exacerbating previously existing linguistic and cultural animosities between the two regions. Increased autonomy for Flanders and Wallonia had helped relieve some of the pressures, but a strong rivalry for political and economic gain remained.

Perhaps because of its history, cultural background and location, Belgium had been a founding member of the European Community and was an avid supporter of inter-European cooperation. One SGB executive described Belgium's relationship to Europe, "What is good for Europe is good for Belgium. Belgium will only survive within Europe. Belgians shouldn't be worried about who controls what."

La Vieille Dame

Société Générale de Belgique/Generale Maatschappij van België (the company's formal name in French and Flemish) was a part of Belgium. The company had been established in 1822 by the royal decree of the Dutch King, William I, as a development bank to promote industrial development in the southern part of the kingdom. The new bank was financed through contributions from the large banking families in Brussels and the King's own coffers. A history published in honour of the company's 150th anniversary identified the company's mission: "[SGB] would have as its object, participation in any undertaking of a useful character...able to take part in any limited company...and supply development funds for industry by way of loans or [shareholdings]."

After Belgium became independent in 1830, SGB continued its role as the region's development bank. During the early years of Belgium's independence, a large number of the company's shares which still belonged to the former King, William I, were repurchased by Belgian investors. Ironically, given the events in 1988, the nineteenth century repurchase was described in 1970 by a company historian as, "a necessary action if foreign takeover was to be avoided." Deepening the company's ties with Belgium, the Belgian royal family became closely associated with La Générale over the years although the nature of its influence remained obscure.

Through its banking and investment activities, SGB had accumulated substantial interest in companies throughout Belgium and its former colonies, particularly the Belgian Congo (Zaire). At the end of 1986, SGB had direct or indirect holdings in 1261 companies worldwide ranging from a railroad in Angola to a film production company in Los Angeles. In 1988, one Belgian

newspaper claimed SGB, through its subsidiaries and holdings, contributed a third of the total Belgian economic output.

SGB's long history as development bank and venture capital fund had created an unusual legacy. Some of the infant industries, including mining, railroads, and steel, in which SGB had acquired and maintained investments during the 1800s had become mature or declining industries in the late 1900s. While these industries had initially been very important to the economic development of Belgium and Europe, in 1988 they were considered by many to have little potential for future growth or profits.

Attempts at diversifying into new fields in the 1970s and 1980s had been generally unsuccessful. For example, one effort, ACEC, an electrotechnical equipment and computer manufacturer succeeded in accumulating extensive debts without making any significant in-roads into its targeted markets. Diversification remained an interest, however, and SGB maintained holdings in a number of companies in expectation of future growth opportunities.

An additional problem for SGB was that many of its ownership positions were relatively small. In general, SGB policy had been to hold equity investments at "a significant level, [but] seldom exceeding 50 percent." A "significant" level for SGB meant "sufficient to influence the activities of the company." The diverse and fragmented shareholder base of many of the companies partiality owned by SGB frequently allowed SGB to exert influence without having to purchase controlling interest. For example, because SGB was the largest stockholder in Generale Bank, it had been able to influence Bank policy, despite owning only about 20 percent of the stock. Although it permitted SGB to conserve capital, company management increasingly found minority ownership was insufficient to effectively guide strategy and implement the changes necessary to meet the challenges of the coming European internal market.

Europe 1992: Completing the Internal Market

A free internal market in which goods, services, people and capital would move unimpeded across national borders had been the objective when the Treaty of Rome was signed in 1957, creating the European Economic Community. Substantial progress in achieving a common market had been made since the EC was established, notably in the creation of a Community-wide customs union in 1968, but a truly integrated market remained elusive and significant barriers to free trade persisted. In the mid-1980s, however, the situation had begun to change.

When the EC established the customs union in 1968, it was anticipated that free flow of trade between the member countries would be substantially realised. Under the customs union, tariff levels were unified for trade within the EC. However, varying standards of taxation, safety, and product quality remained. Countries allowed only products meeting local standards to be imported. These non-tariff barriers continued to restrict the free movement of goods, services, people, and capital. Preoccupied with protecting domestic markets, member countries had resisted efforts to remove the remaining impediments to free trade. Few observers, especially during the late 1970s when poor economic conditions existed throughout Europe, thought the Community would ever achieve its goals.

During the early 1980s, however, EC member countries gradually began to realize that global competition was increasing and that Europe's divided markets were limiting the efficiency of European companies. The renewed interest led directly to the European Commission White Paper, *Completing the Internal Market*, published in 1985. In the Paper, the Commission set out a detailed agenda together with a timetable for establishing a single internal market among the member nations. The main objective of the programme outlined in the White Paper was to remove the remaining non-tariff barriers to trade within the Community and create an "area without frontiers" by the end of 1992.

Many of the Paper's key points, including its guiding principle to establish open frontiers, were embodied in the Single European Act, adopted in 1985 by the unanimous approval of the European Council of Ministers. In an important step toward speeding up the necessary legislative process to make the internal market a reality, the Act provided for majority (rather than unanimous) voting on many issues. By accepting majority voting, member states surrendered some of their sovereignty. Importantly, majority voting was not extended to fiscal policy regulations.

In total, the Commission had identified 286 regulatory issues that needed action before the internal market could be realized. By June 1988, approximately 60 of the necessary actions had been taken, and, although short of the final goal, the result had

meaningfully changed the way businesses operated in the Community. Many knowledgeable observers believed that "1992" was best viewed as a process and not a date; even if the 1992 deadline were missed, the major goals would be achieved.

Corporate Strategy at SGB in the 1980s

While Europe moved towards realization of the dream of the internal market, SGB had also worked on preparing itself for the new economic environment although progress had not been smooth. One of the major stumbling blocks for SGB was the stagnant and myopic senior management and Board of Directors. Before the restructuring which followed the takeover, the SGB Board had been comprised exclusively of SGB executives. Although an exaggeration, one executive was not far from the general perception when he described the qualifications for Board membership as "French-speaking and blue-blooded." Certainly, the vast majority of senior executives were French-speaking.

Board meetings had been sedate affairs; embarrassing questions were not asked by Directors, knowing similar questions about the results, strategy and difficulties at their own subsidiary would not be asked. Those SGB Directors also serving as the CEOs of subsidiaries, one observer later commented, saw their subsidiaries as personal fiefdoms; meddling in their internal affairs by the parent at "rue Royale" was not appreciated.[1] Reports to the Board were frequently based only on annual reports with almost no supporting documentation. Auditors, working on behalf of SGB, were known to have been denied access to subsidiaries—*pas de chiffres* (no numbers) was the effective response.

It was within this old traditional environment that René Lamy had become CEO in January 1981, determined to restore the glory and image of SGB. Beginning in 1979, the holding company had identified its role in coordinating and providing new ideas to the subsidiaries as an area needing further improvement. The effort to strengthen the centre of SGB and increase its control over the far-flung parts of the organisation took time to develop. As with many would-be Don

---

[1] SGB's headquarters were located at 30 rue Royale which formed one side of a square, the other sides of which were occupied by the Belgian parliament building and the royal palace.

EXHIBIT 1

SGB's Balance Sheet 1984–1987 (in BEF thousands)

	1987††	1987†	1986††	1986†	1985	1984
Assets						
Current assets						
Cash	15,297,000	834,256	12,751,000	60,330	119,155	30,430
Current investments	60,434,000	12,389,006	58,040,000	11,494,063	6,444,636	4,854,769
Accounts receivable	101,748,000	1,702,282	110,939,000	1,346,098	2,793,443	1,782,510
Inventory	103,071,000		110,573,000			
Notes receivable	7,747,000	443,337	5,382,000	45,662	85,148	540,148
Other	9,574,000	674,589	7,147,000	57,356	58,997	76,445
Fixed assets						
Financial Assets*						
Affiliated companies	89,315,000	54,309,979	78,030,000	47,973,624	41,804,979	36,872,576
Participating interests	35,958,000	13,749,798	22,722,000	8,784,703	8,525,384	6,974,449
Other financial assets	18,602,000	6,908,127	13,942,000	3,144,471	1,139,371	1,234,496
Formation expenses	3,944,000		1,982,000			
Intangible fixed assets	6,310,000		4,799,000			
Consolidation goodwill	9,056,000		2,087,000			
Tangible assets	101,315,000	697,576	94,636,000	729,290	760,911	795,971
Total	562,371,000	91,708,950	523,029,000	73,635,597	61,732,024	53,161,794
Liabilities						
Accounts payable						
Current notes payable	12,276,000	141,692	14,074,000	503,001	55,932	179,684
Financial debt	45,791,000	1,530,315	44,239,000	5,751,001	58,156	1,241,000
Trade debt	95,666,000	23,773	105,424,000	30,507	2682	12,736
Taxes & remuneration	18,333,000	131,358	18,730,000	169,625	102,110	103,570
Other	44,443,000	8,919,298	36,451,000	12,029,844	12,759,763	8,909,762
Notes payable	18,333,000		18,730,000			
Financial debt	86,409,000	8,898,037	67,969,000	1,072,075	1,596,378	1,684,503
Other	10,250,000	2,385,111	9,365,000	25,909	28,422	29,810
Other		1,105,206		207,733	269,168	91,199
Total	331,416,000	23,134,790	313,421,000	19,789,695	14,872,611	12,252,264
Provisions	27,367,000	1,017,911	22,217,000	1,035,650	1,330,450	1,067,954
Capital and reserves						
Capital	35,254,000	35,254,289	30,100,000	30,100,000	27,220,000	24,100,000
Reserves	38,240,000	14,911,807	37,133,000	14,848,773	13,392,872	13,380,872
Other	22,497,000	17,318,734	12,050,000	7,796,791	4,874,893	2,326,334
Exchange differences	(3,196,000)		(1,787,000)			
Third-party interests	110,793,000		109,896,000			
Accumulated profits		71,419		64,688	41,198	34,370
Total capital	203,588,000	67,556,249	187,392,000	52,810,252	45,528,963	39,841,576
TOTAL	562,371,000	91,708,950	523,029,000	73,635,597	61,732,024	53,161,794

*Primarily shares. †Unconsolidated. ††Consolidated (rounded to nearest million).

Note: Prior to 1986 the equity method was used for affiliates 20-50 percent held by SGB. All linked companies in which SGB had a direct holding were fully consolidated beginning in 1986. This was intended to provide a more accurate view of the group by representing SGB's effective control. As a result of the change, third-party interest in the 1986 group's equity went from 12 billion BEF (out of 90 billion BEF), to 110 billion BEF (out of 187 billion BEF) as stated above.

Quixotes, Lamy and the managers at "rue Royale" were up against a deeply entrenched opponent steadfast in its opposition to change.

In the company's 1981 annual report, the formation of a strategic management group was announced. Its ambitious goals included establishing future policy guidelines, monitoring the parts to ensure maximisation of growth and prevent over-diversification, and, finally, to oversee group strategy. The objective was the coherent synthesis of individual corporate programmes while improving the group's ability to find and exploit promising new areas of activity.

The tools to carry out the new policy were concentrated in the financial and organisational areas. Included would be a corporation-wide information system. Later, a human resources committee with representatives from the SGB Board and management, as well as the subsidiaries, was organized. The implementation, however, was slow. The 1984 annual report noted that only then were results (in the form of a report) being seen from the strategic planning initiative launched in 1981.

The growing competitiveness in world business was also noticed by SGB management, and statements about the need to ensure the efficiency of the company as a unit were made repeatedly. In the 1985 Annual Report a new organisational concept, which identified 10 Business Sectors, was planned:

> The grouping of available resources around [the 10 major subsidiaries] is designed to meet the basic criterion of efficiency. In effect the object is to put together a number of entities which are sufficiently integrated so as to enable a [united] policy of technical marketing and financial rationalization [creating new entities] better adapted to face up to international competition.

The company stressed, however, that strengthening SGB with respect to the subsidiaries did not imply that the decentralization concept was being abandoned.

Despite efforts to persuade the subsidiaries, resistance to the enhancement of SGB's power over the units was extensive and the implementation of Lamy's revitalisation plans was stymied. The poor rate of progress eventually attracted the attention of stockholders and, in turn, others interested in the potential returns available from reorganising or breaking up the company. In response to the many claims that SGB was directtionless during this period, Jean Duronsoy, a Gechem executive, stated later, "It isn't true that Lamy didn't have a strategy, and it also isn't true that Carlo De Benedetti did."

The Takeover

The battle of control for SGB, launched by Carlo De Benedetti in January and won by Suez in April 1988, ended with the largest cross-border takeover in Europe. Many of the biggest names in European finance had been involved in the struggle at one point in time or another. However, as Philippe Bodson, a member of the post-takeover SGB Board brought in as an ally to the Suez-led investor group, said afterwards, "The details of what happened during the takeover will perhaps always remain a mystery." Regardless, when Carlo De Benedetti, the CEO of Olivetti SpA, made his bid for control of SGB on January 18, 1988, he forever changed the course of the company's history.

The Belgians were seen by many as dedicated Europeanists. Prior to the Single European Act, cross-border takeovers, especially hostile ones, were unusual in Europe, although other foreign takeovers had been allowed in Belgium before. However, the SGB case was unique. It was the largest cross-border takeover ever conducted in Europe and, moreover, SGB was a significant economic and cultural force in Belgium. As one SGB executive noted, however, "SGB's former managers saw themselves as more important than the Belgian government did. Evidently, they didn't read the cards right.'[2]

SGB's attractiveness as a takeover target had been clear to the Board. In September 1987, an anti-takeover plan was prepared to operate in conjunction with the company's previously established contingent of loyal shareholders. The stockholders considered loyal to SGB management were mostly large French and Belgian corporations, many of which were also partly owned by each other and SGB. The group included: Groupe AG (20 percent held by SGB); Artois (a Belgian brewery); Assubel; Royale Belge (other large Belgian insurers); Compagnie Générale d'Electricité (a French telecommunications company); Cerus (an investment company); Suez; and others. Together these companies

---

[2]The immediate political situation in Belgium may also have been a factor in the SGB takeover. In December 1987, following a parliamentary dispute over economic reforms, the governing Belgian coalition failed, the government dissolved, and new elections were held. The election results gave fewer seats to the leading party in the previous coalition, forcing it to form a new coalition. While the new coalition was being organised, the country was run by a largely ineffectual interim government. By the time the new coalition government assumed power in May 1988, the battle for SGB was over.

EXHIBIT 2
SGB's Unconsolidated Income
Statement 1984–1987
(in BEF thousands)

	1987	1986	1985	1984
Charges				
A. Interest and debt charges	922,942	892,186	890,922	1,314,462
B. Other financial charges	1,169,556	533,123	94,689	221,342
C. Services and goods	194,652	149,686	106,691	107,377
D. Remuneration and pensions	354,279	356,828	335,057	289,618
E. Other	83,113	51,530	33,323	33,153
F. Depreciation	367,800	244,087	340,219	247,975
G. Amounts written off				
Financial assets	3,330,955	1,582,348	781,935	637,453
Current assets	285,266	20,208	4,974	49,294
H. Provisions	0	508,115	328,502	316,358
I. Loss on disposal*	17,731	156,422	71,596	9,812
J. Extraordinary charges	24,130	23,534	164,971	19,780
K. Income taxes	213	76,225	492	122
L. Profit	4,137,536	5,311,617	2,821,435	1,974,647
Total charges	10,888,173	9,905,909	5,974,806	5,221,393
Income				
A. Income from financial assets	4,314,080	3,974,250	3,571,159	3,176,566
B. Income from current assets	414,877	639,554	395,341	337,926
C. Other financial income	1,415,538	631,852	199,604	112,860
D. Income from services	79,137	78,164	73,977	70,923
E. Other current income	58,368	40,497	38,902	35,474
F. Write-backs	125,493	78,121	98,815	7,213
G. Write-backs of provisions	7,540	158,756	8,536	11,364
H. Gains on disposal*	4,169,840	4,278,451	1,557,906	1,427,777
I. Extraordinary income	289,699	23,574	10,021	34,620
J. Income tax adjustments	13,601	2,690	20,545	6,670
Total income	10,888,173	9,905,909	5,974,806	5,221,393

*Primarily from fixed financial assets.

owned approximately 25 percent of SGB's shares, enough, it was hoped, to thwart an attempted takeover.

The test came in January 1988. After bidding the price of SGB shares up to BEF 3250 (Belgian francs) from BEF 2230 ten days before, Carlo De Benedetti made his intention to control SGB public.[3] De Benedetti was well known as sophisticated investor interested in establishing a pan-European empire capable of fully exploiting the opportunities promised by the proposed internal market. He had also successfully purchased and revived Olivetti SpA, an Italian office automation company. De Benedetti held a seat on the Board of Directors at Suez and owned a majority of Cerus, among his many other interests.

Most observers were not surprised by De Benedetti's move, only by its size. By targeting one of Belgium's largest corporations, however, many wondered if he had attempted too much. Turning around Olivetti had been a major success but was on a much smaller scale than the reorganisation of a conglomerate like SGB. His action plan for SGB, if he won, was unknown. Many

[3]On March 7, the stock price hit a high of BEF 8530. The price in June 1988 ranged between BEF 4205 and BEF 5000.

	1987	1986
Operating income		
Turnover	336,804	341,012
Change in inventory	(75)	(1,543)
Other income	11,278	11,349
Operating charges		
Raw materials & consumables	174,016	170,692
Services, other goods	63,646	67,788
Remunerations, pensions	80,924	84,931
Other charges	23,456	21,969
Operating profit	5,965	5,438
Financial income (from:)		
Fixed financial assets	4,569	4,476
Current financial assets	5,716	6,170
Other financial income (non-interest)	6,534	6,277
Interest	(10,490)	(10,325)
Other charges	(7,736)	(6,577)
Extraordinary income	13,237	20,539
Extraordinary charges	(11,303)	(19,722)
Profit before taxes	6,492	6,276
Income taxes	(2,231)	(2,056)
Profit after taxes	4,261	4,221
Results of companies consolidated (using equity method)	6,509	5,262
Profit	10,770	9,482
Group share	3,611	6,334
Third-parties' share	7,159	3,148

EXHIBIT 3
SGB's Consolidated Income Statement 1986–1987 (in BEF millions)

assumed that De Benedetti would sell some of the poorer performing parts and use the proceeds to strengthen the remaining holdings. De Benedetti, perhaps in an attempt to deflect nationalistic criticism, denied that his intent was to break up SGB. Rather, he claimed to be interested in building a new management team capable of revitalising the company.

The alliance which wrestled control away from De Benedetti's grasp was formed by Maurice Lippens, the Chairman of Groupe AG, and consisted of a mix of Belgian and French shareholders, most of whom were members of SGB's original group of loyal shareholders. Suez, initially hesitant to enter the conflict, had been persuaded to act as the leading "white knight" and dominated the group. At the end of February, the group claimed more than 50 percent of the outstanding shares. Virtually all of SGB's shares were held by one of the two sides, and trading activity effectively ceased. Despite repeated attempts, the De Benedetti camp could only muster control of 47-48 percent of the shares. The Suez faction called for an extraordinary shareholders' meeting in April to decide the outcome.

At the extraordinary shareholders' meeting on April 14, 1988, it was clear that Suez had won, although De Benedetti was still in a position of power due to his large minority interest.

Compagnie Financière de Suez

The company that won control of SGB was itself a major conglomerate closely associated with its national colonial history. The company was founded in 1858 to build and operate the Suez canal. The canal, however, was nationalised in 1956 by President Nasser of Egypt, leaving the company floundering. Through a determined effort, the company changed its focus and gradually grew into the second largest *banque d'affaires,* a cross between a holding company and investment bank peculiar to France. The company was nationalised by the French government in 1982 and then re-privatised in mid-October 1987.

Suez could be described as a French counterpart to SGB: a large holding company with a multitude of minority positions in generally unrelated (French) businesses. At the centre of the Suez empire was Banque Indosuez, an investment bank owned 100 percent by Suez. When De Benedetti began his assault on SGB, Suez, partly held by De Benedetti's Cerus group and SGB, was a member of SGB's secure shareholders. Initially Suez stayed out of the contest but gradually came to oppose De Benedetti. Observers believed that Suez wanted to stop De Benedetti from acquiring SGB because, if he won, his next target would likely be Suez. The SGB purchase cost Suez almost $2 billion, financed primarily through new equity issues.

The Company, June 1988

SGB's many shareholdings had been organised into ten business sectors focused around the primary subsidiaries and related companies in the, 1985 reorganisation (see exhibit 4). Of the ten sectors, eight were considered "strategy holdings," while the other two sectors held companies which SGB considered important but not core operations. The strategic groups were Financial Services, Energy (including engineering, industrial contracting, electronics, telecommunications and media), Non-ferrous Metals, Cement, Transport, Diamonds, Chemicals, and International Trading. Exhibit 5 provides a breakdown of SGB's portfolio by relative value and dividends. Exhibit 6 provides information on ownership.

In the prospectus for a stock offering in October 1987, companies were considered affiliated enterprises or subsidiaries if SGB could control either the composition of the Board or management policy. In a number of cases where it could not exercise control, SGB, still a significant stockholder, was able to exert influence over important decisions. Companies in the latter group included Generale Bank, Groupe AG, and Arbed, among others. After 1986, if SGB were able to influence decisions, the results of the subsidiary would be fully consolidated in SGB's annual report, even if less than 50 percent were held. A final category existed in companies where SGB desired a "lasting relationship." Few holdings came under this heading, although SGB's interest in Royale Belge, Belgium's number two insurer, was listed.

Financial Services

The Financial Services sector was the largest of SGB's strategic groups in terms of both value and dividends. In 1987, the group accounted for 32.2 percent of the SGB's portfolio value and 41.8 percent of total dividend contributions. Growing out of the company's original mission as a development bank, the Financial Services group contained companies deeply rooted in SGB.

Tanks Consolidated Investments Tanks Consolidated Investments was a holding company centered around a large portion of SGB's "strategic reserves" and investments in international financial services. One of the company's major holdings was a 50 percent stake in the London-based subsidiary of Dillon, Read, the New York investment bank. Tanks also held 33.3 percent of Sodecom, an investment company fully owned by the SGB Group, in which part of SGB's shareholding in Groupe AG was located. Through Tanks, SGB held interests in a number of other companies, including Tanks Investments (Zimbabwe) and Benguela Railway in Angola.

Generale Bank Generale Bank was perhaps the most important of any single one of SGB's holdings. The bank was the largest in Belgium with 1,157 branches. Its overseas operations were significantly smaller, although international growth was a major objective. In anticipation of 1992, the bank had concluded an alliance with the Dutch bank Amro in early 1988. Under the agreement, the two banks exchanged shares equivalent to 10 percent of outstanding equity and had the option to increase cross-ownership to 25 percent in the future. Together the two banks would form one of the ten largest banking groups in Europe.

EXHIBIT 4
Group Organisation Chart
at December 31, 1987

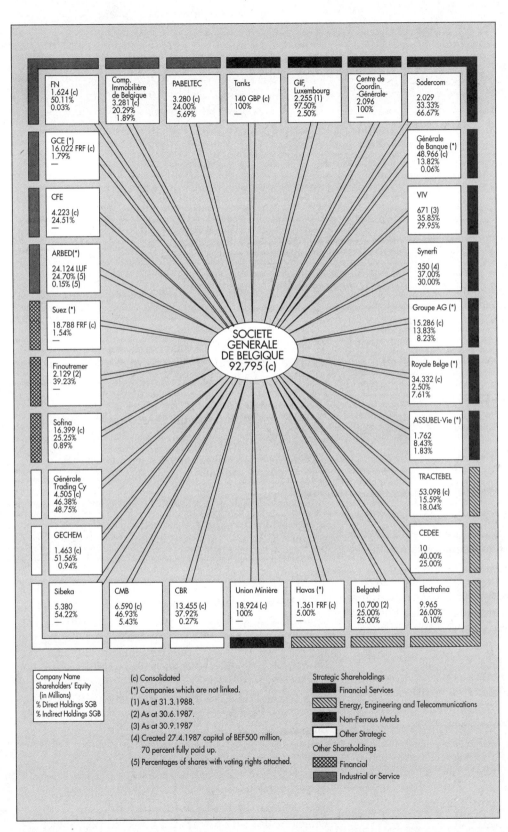

FN
1.624 (c)
50.11%
0.03%

Comp.
Immobilière
de Belgique
3.281 (c)
20.29%
1.89%

PABELTEC
3.280 (c)
24.00%
5.69%

Tanks
140 GBP (c)
100%
—

GIF,
Luxembourg
2.255 (1)
97.50%
2.50%

Centre de
Coordin.
-Générale-
2.096
100%
—

Sodercom
2.029
33.33%
66.67%

GCE (*)
16.022 FRF (c)
1.79%
—

Générale
de Banque (*)
48.966 (c)
13.82%
0.06%

CFE
4.223 (c)
24.51%

VIV
671 (3)
35.85%
29.95%

ARBED(*)
24.124 LUF
24.70% (5)
0.15% (5)

Synerfi
350 (4)
37.00%
30.00%

Suez (*)
18.788 FRF (c)
1.54%

Groupe AG (*)
15.286 (c)
13.83%
8.23%

Finoutremer
2.129 (2)
39.23%

Royale Belge (*)
34.332 (c)
2.50%
7.61%

Sofina
16.399 (c)
25.25%
0.89%

ASSUBEL-Vie (*)
1.762
8.43%
1.83%

SOCIETE
GENERALE
DE BELGIQUE
92,795 (c)

Générale
Trading Cy
4.505 (c)
46.38%
48.75%

TRACTEBEL
53.098 (c)
15.59%
18.04%

GECHEM
1.463 (c)
51.56%
0.94%

CEDEE
10
40.00%
25.00%

Sibeka
5.380
54.22%
—

CMB
6.590 (c)
46.93%
5.43%

CBR
13.455 (c)
37.92%
0.27%

Union Minière
18.924 (c)
100%
—

Havas (*)
1.361 FRF (c)
5.00%
—

Belgatel
10.700 (2)
25.00%
25.00%

Electrafina
9.965
26.00%
0.10%

Company Name
Shareholders' Equity
(in Millions)
% Direct Holdings SGB
% Indirect Holdings SGB

(c) Consolidated
(*) Companies which are not linked.
(1) As at 31.3.1988.
(2) As at 30.6.1987.
(3) As at 30.9.1987.
(4) Created 27.4.1987 capital of BEF500 million,
    70 percent fully paid up.
(5) Percentages of shares with voting rights attached.

Strategic Shareholdings

▰ Financial Services
▨ Energy, Engineering and Telecommunications
▰ Non-Ferrous Metals
☐ Other Strategic

Other Shareholdings

▨ Financial
▰ Industrial or Service

EXHIBIT 5
Shareholdings in Strategic Sectors (1987)

Sector	Book value* BEF Millions	Percentage	Estimated value BEF Millions	Percentage	Gross dividends (%) 1987	1986	1985
Financial services	22,482	30.7	29,102	32.2	41.8	34.8	35.6
Energy etc.	13,212	18.1	17,429	19.3	17.8	16.7	14.5
Non-ferrous metals	15,668	21.4	15,668	17.3	14.0	15.5	16.7
Cement	4,051	5.5	6,510	7.2	3.6	2.9	2.7
Transport	1,950	2.7	2,795	3.1	4.3	4.3	4.0
Diamond industry	1,517	2.1	2,782	3.1	6.6	7.1	7.5
Chemicals	1,650	2.3	1,789	2.0	0.0	4.4	3.7
International trading	613	0.8	949	1.1	2.5	2.6	2.6
Other financial	4,305	5.9	6,954	7.7	6.9	7.3	7.5
Other industrial	7,731	10.6	6,338	7.0	2.5	4.4	5.2
Total	73,179	100.0	90,316	100.0	100.0	100.0	100.0

*Unconsolidated.

Generale Bank
Abbreviated consolidated figures (BEF m)

	1987	1986
Total assets	2,175,143	2,080,365
Shareholders' equity (Group share)	48,986	47,252
Turnover (sales)	n/a	n/a
Profit (group share)	6,409	5,896

Groupe AG The Financial Services group, additionally, held SGB's interests in Groupe AG and Royale Belge, the number one and two insurance companies in Belgium respectively. Groupe AG had been instrumental in the takeover as Suez's main Belgian ally. Groupe AG was also an important holder of Generale Bank stock. Groupe AG had acquired substantial holdings in Assubel, a Belgian insurance company, during January 1988.

Groupe AG
Abbreviated consolidated figures (BEF m)

	1987	1986
Total assets	206,957	186,772
Shareholders' equity (Group share)	15,286	8,887
Turnover (sales)	n/a	n/a
Profit (group share)	4,126	2,728

Rounding out the Financial Services group were two venture capital companies, one each in Wallonia and Flanders, as well as specialised financial subsidiaries.

Energy, Engineering and Telecommunications

Energy; Engineering, Industrial Contracting and Technical Services; Electronics, Telecommunications and Media, was the formal designation for SGB's second largest sector by value. The sector accounted for 19.3 percent of the total portfolio value and 17.8 percent of gross dividends. As the name implied, this sector comprised a wide range of different activities, most of which were organised as subsidiaries of the primary company in the sector, Tractebel, making it a major conglomerate in its own right. Besides Tractebel, other holdings in the sector included Electrafina, Belgatel (a shareholder in Alcatel, a telecommunications joint venture between ITT and Compagnie Générale d'Electricité of France), and Havas (a French media and advertising company). When Havas was privatised by the French government in 1986, Société Générale de Belgique had purchased 5 percent on behalf of Tractebel. ACEC, an attempt at entering the electronic hardware business, was an unsuccessful subsidiary in this group and had accumulated extensive tax-deductible losses.

Tractebel SGB directly owned 15.6 percent of Tractebel and was its largest single shareholder. Six SGB Directors also sat on Tractebel's 30-man Board, including Lamy who served as chairman. Formed by the merger of two energy and related consulting companies at the bidding of SGB in 1986, Tractebel was one of the top five firms in market capitalisation on the Belgian stock exchange. The company had a complex holding structure, similar to SGB's, with interests ranging from nuclear power plants (66.3 percent of Belgium's power came from nuclear energy) to a specialty food company. The company's primary holdings were in three electric utilities, which together produced 92.6 percent of the power generated in Belgium. However, Tractebel's ownership of each was limited to about 25 percent. The other major shareholder was Groupe Bruxelles Lambert (GBL), another Belgian conglomerate.[4] The engineering and financial services units had grown directly out of the needs of the utilities and remained largely dependent on them for business.

Tractebel had made a number of diversification efforts over the years, including construction and robotics, inherited from FN Industrial Systems.

Tractabel
Abbreviated consolidated figures (BEF m)

	1987	1986
Total assets	120,224	91,141
Shareholders' equity (Group share)	53,098	48,324
Turnover (sales)	26,641	25,818
Profit (group share)	6,785	6,024

Non-ferrous Metals: Union Minière

The non-ferrous metals sector was operated through Union Minière, a wholly owned holding company, originally formed in 1906 to operate mines in the Belgian Congo. In 1987, the sector contributed 17.3 percent of the value of the portfolio and 14 percent of dividends. Its primary investments were in Metallurgie Hoboken-Overpelt (MHO), founded in 1919 to process the copper, gold, cobalt and other mineral ores coming from the Katanga mine in the Congo, and Vieille-Montagne, which began exploiting Belgian, zinc reserves before

---

[4]GBL was a major shareholder in the Belgian petrochemicals group Petrofina and was believed to be interested in controlling the company. SGB's 15.5 percent minority position in Petrofina (4.4 percent of which was held by Electrafin a joint subsidiary of SGB and GBL) acted as a counterweight to GBL's influence in the utilities.

1850. UM also mined and processed germanium, a promising semi-conductor, and recycled precious metals, especially platinum, from catalytic converters.

In 1987, UM made another loss despite rising prices in copper and stable prices in most other products. The operations of Vieille-Montagne suffered sharp losses as the Belgian franc appreciated against the US dollar, the reference currency for zinc. Vieille-Montagne operated two zinc: smelters, one with a 205,000 ton capacity (the largest in Europe) and the other with a capacity 180,000 tons. The operations at MHO, on the other hand, were profitable. MHO operated a 120,000 ton zinc smelter, although this operation was secondinary to the company's copper business. Total zinc smelter capacity in Europe, divided amongst fourteen companies, was approximately 1,730,000 tons per year (1988), 33 percent of world production.

The copper and zinc industries had faced an extended period of low growth, chronic excess capacity and intense competition from non-European suppliers during much of the 1980s. Forecasts for the industries expected more of the same, with only temporary price increases stemming from short-term supply constraints. One executive noted that, given the cyclical nature of the minerals processed by UM, it was advantageous to have a secure shareholder like SGB willing to take a long-term perspective. Under Lamy's SGB, however, the long-term perspective had been to gradually sell part of SGB's interest in UM once operating profits were generated, despite UM's dominant position in the industry and low-cost production facilities.

Union Minière
Abbreviated consolidated figures (BEF m)

	1987	1986
Total assets	80,388	80,648
Shareholders' equity (Group share)	18,924	20,106
Turnover (sales)	84,871	77,782
Profit (group share)	(831)	(734)

Cement: CBR

CBR was a manufacturer of ready-mix concrete and aggregates, 38 percent directly owned by SGB. In 1987, 7.2 percent of portfolio value and 3.6 percent of gross dividends were contributed by CBR. CBR's operations were concentrated in Europe and North America, and

EXHIBIT 6
Important Holdings by Sector (1987)

	Important subsidiary holdings (direct and indirect (%))	SGB ownership	
		Direct (%)	Indirect (%)
Financial			
Tanks		100.00	0.00
Dillon, Read Ltd.	50.00		
Benguela Railway Co.	90.00		
Sodecom		33.33	66.66
Groupe AG	7.83		
Generale Bank		13.82	0.06
Groupe AG		13.83	8.23
Generale Bulk	8.71		
Royale Belge		2.50	7.61
Assubel		8.43	1.83
Energy, engineering and other			
Tractebel		15.59	18.04
Petrofina	8.64	0.42	15.07
Belgatel	20.00	25.00	25.00
Havas		5.00	0.00
Electrafina		26.00	0.10
Tractebel	9.72		
Petrofina	4.39		
Non-ferrous metals			
Union Miniere		100.00	0.00
Metallurgie Hoboken-Overpelt	61.57		
Vieille-Montagne	50.15		
Cement: CBR		37.92	0.27
Transport: CMB		46.93	5.43
Diamond industry: Sibeka		54.22	0.00
Chemicals: Gechem		51.56	0.94
International trading: Generale Trading Cy		46.38	48.75
Other shareholdings:			
Sofina		25.25	0.89
Petrofina	1.59	0.42	15.07
Tractebel	8.16		
Belgatel	5.00		
Finoutremer		39.23	0.00
Petrofina	0.47		
CMB	1.99		
Belgamanche		50.00	0.00
Eurotunnel (s.a. and Plc.)	3.44		
Compagnie Financiere de Suez		1.54	0.00
Arbed (Voting shares only)		24.70	0.15
Compagnie Generale d'Electricite (CGE)		1.79	0.00
Fabrique Nationale Herstal (FN)		50.11	0.03
Browning (USA)	81.00		
Beretta	36.00		
FN Aeronautique	50.00		

were the fifth largest in the world. The cement industry was dependent on the general level of construction. CBR had made both revenue and productivity increases in recent years.

CBR
Abbreviated consolidated figures (BEF m)

	1987	1986
Total assets	32,787	35,350
Shareholders' equity (Group share)	13,455	11,665
Turnover (sales)	36,226	30,339
Profit (group share)	2,338	1,440

Transport: CMB

The CMB shipping line accounted for 3.1 percent of portfolio value and 4.3 percent of gross dividends. CMB had been able to maintain its profitability despite extensive excess supply in the maritime shipping industry. CMB's tramping operations (mostly iron ore and coal for the steel industry in Belgium and Luxembourg run through its Bocimar subsidiary) had increased market share as freight rates for bulk cargo improved. The important regular line operations had, however, suffered from the industry-wide 40 percent oversupply in container ships. CMB owned approximately 36 ships at the end of 1987, and chartered others as needed. The company also had smaller operations in road transportation and port facilities.

CMB
Abbreviated consolidated figures (BEF m)

	1987	1986
Total assets	38,907	42,509
Shareholders' equity (Group share)	6,590	6,585
Turnover (sales)	30,376	31,214
Profit (group share)	533	520

Diamonds: Sibeka

Sibeka was involved in the mining and processing of natural and synthetic diamonds, and the manufacturing of diamond tools. Sibeka contributed 3.1 percent of

SGB's portfolio value and 6.6 percent of gross dividends. SGB owned 54 percent of Sibeka directly. The company's 48 percent drop in profits between 1986 and 1987 was attributable to the persistence of poor market conditions in the diamond tools business. The important drill bit industry had been especially hard hit as the rate of oil exploration decreased. However, 1987 had been a good year for diamond jewellery. Sales of synthetic diamonds had also been strong over a number of years.

Sibeka
Abbreviated consolidated figures (BEF m)
(Consolidated figures were not available.)

	1987	1986
Total assets	5,978	5,608
Shareholders' equity	5,380	5,002
Turnover (sales)	n/a	n/a
Profit	218	420

Chemicals: Gechem

SGB owned 52 percent of Gechem, which accounted for 2 percent of the portfolio value. Plagued with flat results from its diverse range of activities, Gechem did not contribute dividends to SGB in 1987. Although ranked only seventh among SGB holdings in value, Gechem was important to the parent company and, thus, was the first target of de Carmoy's reorganisation plan. The company had not only lost BEF 2,236 million in 1987, but had, in fact, been a "problem child" for at least ten years.

Gechem was created by merging SGB's chemicals-related holdings in 1985. The fertiliser operations, which had been a loss, were sold off soon after the merger, and the remaining parts were reorganised as Recticel (polyurethane foams), Sadacem (metallic oxides and salts), PRB (munitions), and Omnichem (fine chemicals). Recticel was a world leader in the manufacturing of foams used for car seats, beds, acoustical applications, and packaging. Metallic oxides and salts were also a promising area for Gechem because of their substantial market presence. The munitions group suffered from poor market conditions and relatively dated products. Omnichem was a significant player in the severely fragmented fine chemicals industry. SGB was well aware that many parts of Gechem would be closed down if sold individually.

Gechem
Abbreviated consolidated figures (BEF m)

	1987	1986
Total assets	36,837	45,373
Shareholders' equity (Group share)	1,463	3,269
Turnover (sales)	39,125	54,976
Profit (group share)	(2,236)	(3,663)

International Trading: Generale Trading Cy

International Trading, which accounted for 1.1 percent of SGB's portfolio value and 2.5 percent of gross dividends, actively traded in non-ferrous metals for UM as well as other commodities for outside accounts. SGB and its subsidiaries (primarily UM) owned 95 percent of Generale Trading Cy.

Generale Trading Cy
Abbreviated consolidated figures (BEF m)

	1987	1986
Total assets	17,420	4,258
Shareholders' equity (Group share)	4,504	2,649
Turnover (sales)	42,258	7,792
Profit (group share)	(387)	357

Other Shareholdings:
Financial and Industrial or Services

The financial holdings sector accounted for 7.7 percent of SGB's portfolio value and 6.9 percent of dividends. The leading company in this group was the holding company, Sofina, and its important holdings in Tractebel and in Petrofina, a large petroleum refiner and a major player in the Belgian economy. Additionally, the sector contained SGB's 1.5 percent holding in Suez.

As with SGB's miscellaneous financial holdings, the industrial and services held in this sector were generally unrelated to the company's other holdings. Some of the holdings in this group were, however, important to SGB, especially Arbed and FN. Overall, the industrial and services holdings accounted for

7 percent of SGB's portfolio value and 2.5 percent of gross dividends.

Arbed In 1987, Arbed was one of the ten largest steel producers in Europe with an output of between 7 to 8 million tons per year. SGB held a minority position with 25 percent of Arbed's outstanding voting stock. The Luxembourg government owned 30 percent while the balance was held by others. Because of industry-wide difficulties, Arbed had posted a loss in 1987 after three years of good performance.

Arbed
Abbreviated consolidated figures (BEF m)
(Consolidated figures were unavailable.)

	1987	1986
Total assets	70,613	72,474
Shareholders' equity	24,124	26,627
Turnover (sales)	47,971	57,808
Profit	(2,217)	890

Fabrique Nationale Herstal – FN Located in Wallonia, Fabrique Nationale Herstal SA (FN) was famous for manufacturing light arms and munitions for military forces and for sports use throughout the world. Its Browning brand name in the USA was well known. Plagued by labour and management problems as well as poor market conditions, FN had been unprofitable since 1985. FN operated a small and slightly profitable aircraft engine group which did contract work for the larger engine makers such as Pratt & Whitney of the USA. The company received financial assistance from the Walloon regional government in 1987, underscoring its importance to the region.

Fabrique Nationale
Abbreviated consolidated figures (BEF m)

	1987	1986
Total assets	344,404	33,836
Shareholders' equity (Group share)	1,624	753
Turnover (sales)	23,762	28,092
Profit (group share)	(1,510)	(2,836)

The Future of SGB

De Carmoy was well aware of how much trouble and expense Suez had invested to secure control of SGB. His appointment had followed a much publicized battle for control, and the spotlight was now on him to perform. It was clear that Suez expected him to clean up the SGB house and improve its profitability quickly. Suez was intent on making SGB work and would ensure that the necessary means were available. Between the two companies (SGB and Suez) substantial financial resources were available; each company had the capacity to raise funds in many ways.

The central issue was how the company should be restructured. Georges Ugeux, the Finance Director appointed by de Carmoy, raised a key question, "How does the holding company add value?" It was clear that the other shareholders in the Suez camp would be unwilling to see SGB completely broken up even if buyers could be found and approval granted. Mr de Carmoy saw a great challenge ahead as he pondered the appropriate strategy for SGB. He was convinced that there were some excellent parts to SGB and, with the right management input, the company could become an important contributor to Suez.

CORPORATE STRATEGY AT GRAND METROPOLITAN†

By David Sadtler and Andrew Campbell

Allen Sheppard had become chief executive officer (CEO) of Grand Metropolitan (GrandMet) in 1986 and had added the chairmanship of the company in 1987. Since the company's founding in 1947, GrandMet had also been headed by two other chairmen—Maxwell Joseph and Stanley Grinstead—and each change in leadership had been accompanied by a significant shift in corporate strategy. Sheppard now faced a decision about whom should be given the opportunity to leave his mark on the company by succeeding him as the next CEO.

Two very capable senior GrandMet managers were the most obvious candidates for the job. Ian Martin, the chief operating officer (COO), had worked closely with Sheppard since he joined the company in the 1970s. He had successfully turned around and rejuvenated a number of GrandMet businesses, most notably Pillsbury, a U.S. acquisition. George Bull, CEO of GrandMet's food operations, had a strong marketing background and had successfully built up International Distillers and Vintners (IDV), GrandMet's most profitable division. Sheppard realized that whatever choice he made would have an important influence on the company's future corporate strategy. Therefore, he needed to think through the alternative candidates and the directions in which they would take the company. His decision would help to define a new era in GrandMet's history.

The corporation Sheppard would be turning over to his successor had grown dramatically since its inception and, as of 1993, was among the top fifteen United Kingdom public companies in market capitalization. Its past financial performance had been relatively strong (see exhibits 1, 2 and 3) and its spread of operations was quite broad (see exhibit 4). GrandMet's growth had been effected both through internal development and by way of an extremely active programme of acquisition (the major acquisitions in its corporate life are summarised in exhibit 6). It would be a challenge for any successor to improve on this impressive track record.

The Early Years

The business from which GrandMet emerged was founded by Max Joseph. Born in 1910, he became an estate agent and learned the property business prior to World War II. His business prospered. "Before he reached 30 he already owned a Rolls Royce and a house on Hampstead Heath."[1]

After war service, Max Joseph began purchasing hotels: the first was the Mandeville in 1947 and then the Washington in 1950. The next major purchase was the Mount Royal at Marble Arch, which was by far the biggest thus far. London hotels were followed by the acquisition of hotels in Monte Carlo, Paris, New York City, Madrid, and Amsterdam.

As the company grew, better financial control was required. Stanley Grinstead was hired in 1960 as chief accountant, followed by Ernest Sharp, to help strengthen financial and managerial control. This triumvirate ran GrandMet during the 1960s. Despite increasingly complex operations, the group remained unbureaucratic. Joseph was said to "panic" whenever there were more than six people at a meeting. He never himself had an office at GrandMet and ran the company and his other investments from an outside office nearby.

Joseph's basic theme was to purchase "trading property assets." The idea was that the cash flow of the properties acquired should be sufficient to cover the cost of the debt taken on to acquire them. Good management would increase the cash flow, and the value of the assets would rise because of inflation and the increasing demand for hotels. Joseph was buying assets that he believed would increase in value with debts he could service out of the cash flow. Joseph's skill in raising

†**Source:** This case was written by David Sadtler and Andrew Campbell, of Ashridge Management Centre, as the basis for class discussion, rather than to illustrate either effective or ineffective handling of an administrative situation. Used with permission.

[1]Peter Williamson and Bernard Rix, Grand Metropolitan PLC (A), 9-788-01, London Business School, 1988.

money and the strong asset base of the company enabled the process of acquiring good assets to continue apace. As one manager commented: "Joseph had a tremendous reputation in the city and a talent at closing deals." The company then went public in 1961, as Mount Royal, Ltd. In 1962 its name was changed to Grand Metropolitan Hotels.

In the mid- to late 1960s nonhotel acquisitions began. There were two criteria: (1) companies whose businesses were related to hotels (drinks, food, catering, pubs); and (2) asset-intensive businesses, in which the "trading property asset" concept could be continued and extended. The major acquisitions of this period began with Levy and Franks (1966), which included Chef & Brewer pub-restaurants, as well as off-license stores.

After several catering businesses, Express Dairy was purchased in 1969 for £32 million. Express provided one quarter of all milk products door-to-door in Britain, and also owned restaurants, hotels, and food stores. Joseph made an offer for the business within forty-eight hours of hearing it was available. Many of Express's depots were in valuable city-centre locations.

A move into a less-related business came in the early 1970s with the acquisition of Mecca, the bingo halls, dance halls, and casino group. It also contained food, drink, and leisure operations and was property intensive.

"With the exception of Express, all of the acquisitions to date had been on friendly terms. Max Joseph generally invited the former owners or top management

EXHIBIT 1
Grand Metropolitan Group: Adjusted Figures Balance Sheet 1983–1992 (in £ millions)

	1983	1984	1985	1986	1987	1988	1989	1990	1991	1992
Fixed assets										
Intangible assets – brands	0.0	0.0	70.2	119.3	608.0	588.3	2,652	2,317	2,464	2,492
Tangible assets	2,100.9	2,291.0	2,654.3	2,625.7	2,725.2	3,279.4	3,839	3,756	2,764	2,638
Investments	131.2	139.2	133.3	129.8	177.2	206.1	144	214	851	713
	2,242.1	2,430.2	2,857.8	2,874.8	3,510.4	4,073.8	6,635	6,287	6,079	5,843
Current assets										
Stocks	604.7	683.8	653.7	646.3	733.7	761.1	1,269	1,349	1,286	1,381
Debtors	618.5	693.4	731.0	731.4	827.5	873.5	1,451	1,541	1,561	1,830
Cash	51.3	106.9	143.4	88.0	113.4	137.8	215	243	261	309
Creditors										
Borrowings	(995.2)	(1,067.9)	(1,162.8)	(1,020.8)	(1,471.6)	(889.1)	(3,856)	(3,131)	(2,860)	(2,750)
Creditors	(869.2)	(986.9)	(1,063.3)	(1,084.4)	(1,269.6)	(1,463.9)	(2,547)	(2,534)	(2,304)	(2,265)
Provisions	(46.3)	(81.5)	(91.1)	(43.9)	(70.4)	(55.1)	(325)	(328)	(569)	(561)
	1,605.9	1,778.0	2,068.7	2,191.4	2,373.4	3,438.1	2,842	3,427	3,454	3,787
Summarised balance sheet										
Fixed assets	2,242.1	2,430.2	2,857.8	2,874.8	3,510.4	4,073.8	6,635	6,287	6,079	5,843
Other assets (excluding cash)	307.7	308.8	230.3	249.4	221.2	115.6	(152)	28	(26)	385
	2,549.8	2,739.0	3,088.1	3,124.2	3,731.6	4,189.4	6,483	6,315	6,053	6,228
Net borrowings	(943.9)	(961.0)	(1,019.4)	(932.8)	(1,358.2)	(751.3)	(3,641)	(2,888)	(2,599)	(2,441)
Net assets	1,605.9	1,778.0	2,068.7	2,191.4	2,373.4	3,438.1	2,842	3,427	3,454	3,787
Capital and reserves	1,566.4	1,744.1	2,035.2	2,164.8	2,345.1	3,406.7	2,810	3,401	3,422	3,759
Minorities	39.5	33.9	33.5	26.6	28.3	31.4	32	26	32	28
	1,605.9	1,778.0	2,068.7	2,191.4	2,373.4	3,438.1	2,842	3,427	3,454	3,787
Gearing	58.8%	54.0%	49.3%	42.6%	57.2%	21.9%	128.1%	84.3%	75.2%	64.5%

EXHIBIT 2
Grand Metropolitan Group: Adjusted Figures Profit and Loss Account 1983–1992 (in £ millions)

	1983	1984	1985	1986	1987	1988	1989	1990	1991	1992
Turnover	4,468.8	5,075.0	5,589.5	5,291.3	5,705.5	6,028.8	9,298	9,394	8,748	7,913
Operating profit	396.3	438.1	445.1	453.3	554.4	582.1	914	1,021	1,027	949
Associates profits	10.7	5.8	8.1	7.0	7.9	11.5	18	23	10	16
	407.0	443.9	453.2	460.3	562.3	593.6	932	1,044	1,037	965
Net exceptional items	(19.2)	(36.1)	(40.7)	0	0	0	0	0	0	0
Disposal of fixed assets	10.2	22.6	4.7	8.7	15.4	100.0	68	54	32	13
Sale or termination of businesses				(67.0)	(31.5)	305	502	112	(450)	41
Interest	(111.8)	(109.6)	(105.9)	(101.3)	(120.2)	(93.0)	(280)	(239)	(171)	(94)
Profit before taxation	286.2	320.89	311.3	300.7	426.0	905.6	1,222	971	448	925
Taxation	(83.3)	(85.6)	(64.4)	(61.1)	(90.0)	(250.8)	(337)	(305)	(223)	(295)
Profit after taxation	202.9	235.2	246.9	239.6	336.0	654.8	885	666	225	630
Minorities & pref. dividends	(5.0)	(4.0)	(4.7)	(2.8)	(2.8)	(8.3)	(8)	(6)	(7)	(6)
Profit attributable	197.9	231.2	242.2	236.8	333.2	646.5	877	660	218	624
Extraordinary items	1.6	(20.2)	29.9	0	0	0	0	0	0	0
Profit for year	199.5	211.0	272.1	236.8	333.2	646.5	877	660	218	624
Ordinary dividends	(58.0)	(67.1)	(79.2)	(87.5)	(103.1)	(129.1)	(167)	(198)	(218)	(246)
Transferred to reserves	141.5	143.9	192.9	149.3	230.1	517.4	710	462	(0)	378
Attributable profits/dividends	3.4	3.4	3.1	2.7	3.2	5.0	5.3	3.3	1.0	2.5

Note: Figures have been adjusted for FRS 3 going back to 1986. However, figures for 1983-1985 have not been adjusted.

to join the GrandMet board; examples included Frank Berni from Berni Inns and Eric Morley from Mecca. The result was a growth of the main board to 18. Many of the businesses continued to run much as they had prior to acquisition with little interference from the centre short of sorting out major problems as and when they arose. It is probably fair to say that neither Joseph nor Grinstead showed much inclination to become deeply involved in day to day operations."[2]

These acquisitions arose opportunistically and were executed very quickly, owing to the lack of bureaucracy. Complex analytical evaluation models were eschewed. Joseph only wanted to know that existing cash flow would "wash the face" of the cost of borrowing, and that the operations were something they could manage.

Then he would go ahead if he liked the "feel" of the business and the price looked attractive.

The same thinking was extended to the acquisition of the brewer, Truman, Hanbury, Buxton (THB). Also in the right sector and asset intensive, the acquisition of Truman turned out to be a difficult task; but after nine months, GrandMet's offer of £48 million was accepted. As with Express, Joseph noted that breweries were often on valuable city-centre sites.

The true significance of this acquisition became apparent when the possibility of the acquisition of Watney Mann, as a "follow-on" to THB, was presented to Joseph. This was a much larger brewery and constituted a very bold step for GrandMet: three separate offers were made and five different letters were sent to each of Watney's thirty thousand shareholders. When it was finally concluded at a cost of £435 million, it was the largest industrial acquisition in the United

---

[2]Williamson and Rix, op. cit.

EXHIBIT 3
Grand Metropolitan Group: Financial Performance by Segment (in £ millions)

	1983	1984	1985	1986	1987	1988	1989	1990	1991	1992
Turnover										
Food	737	778	778	750	825	1,253	2,872	3,506	3,026	2,647
Drinks	1,511	1,551	1,698	1,721	2,410	2,581	2,784	3,000	2,425	2,858
Retailing						1,671	2,040	2,531	2,051	1,540
UK Consumer Services	1,055	1,175	1,234.2	1,212	1,049					
US Consumer Products	864	1,235	1,502	1,270	635					
Hotels	301	336	378	338	333					
Discontinued					454	523	1,602	357	1,246	868
Total	4,468	5,075	5,590	5,291	5,706	6,028	9,298	9,394	8,748	7,913
Trading Profit										
Food	31	16	28	39	44	84	245	309	300	186
Drinks	177	206	228	244	323	316	389	473	454	505
Retailing						179	230	278	236	211
UK Consumer Services	74	67	75	83	79					
US Consumer Products	98	122	84	91	68					
Hotels	27	32	38	30	38					
Discontinued					20	75	103	22	81	47
Total	407	443	453	487	572	654	967	1,082	1,071	949

Discontinued:	**1987**	**1988**	**1989**	**1990**	**1991**	**1992**
	Liggett	Hotels	Hotels	Betting	Brewing	Express dairy
	Contract services	US soft drinks	Betting	Other	Tenanted pubs	B. King's distribution
	Diversified Products	Children's World	Other		Liquid milk &	
	Quality Care	Diversified Products			chilled products	
	Children's World	Quality Care			UK drinks wholesaling	
		Contract services			Off-licenses	
					Service restaurants	

Kingdom to date. It also included IDV, a wine and spirits operation, which GrandMet attempted to sell off after the acquisition. In the event, that divestiture failed and GrandMet was left with an uncomfortably high level of debt.

The Pressure of the 1970s

At about this time (1973), economic conditions in Britain deteriorated. This was the period of the three-day week, the secondary banking crisis, and a subsequent collapse in the property market. GrandMet had taken on large debts to acquire Watney Mann and, with the failure of

the disposal of IDV, was now coming under significant financial pressure. In 1974 the company announced the first fall in trading profit in its history.

The priority at this stage for GrandMet was therefore to generate sufficient trading profits to service its borrowings and to survive until the value of the property portfolio was again sufficient to underpin more investment. To this end, Max Joseph recruited Allen Sheppard from British Leyland to address the operating profitability of Watney Mann. At the same time, IDV was separated out from Watney Mann and set up as a separate business unit under Anthony Tennant, a former Truman director.

Sheppard and Tennant each set about building the strength of their respective operations and recruiting good managers to help them. Sheppard went about his task by dramatically cutting costs and head count at the breweries while at the same time revitalising regional brands. Profit and cash flow increased dramatically, and significant capital was released from the business. Similarly, at IDV, Tennant set about strengthening the position of the individual brands and promoting them effectively. Major rationalisation was not pursued.

Both business strategies worked, and by the end of the 1970s, GrandMet was once more in a strong financial position—its earnings had increased and its balance sheet was immeasurably stronger, owing in large measure to the revitalisation of the property market and its attendant effects on the assets in GrandMet's balance sheet.

During this period, GrandMet's financial affairs and the demands for control from the centre were becoming ever greater. Accordingly, in 1975 the first full-time financial director was appointed, and steps were taken to increase formal controls.

"GrandMet very nearly went under during the 1970s. It was touch and go on a number of occasions. Falling profits made it hard to service debt and falling asset values meant that the company was in danger of breaking its bank covenants. Then suddenly it all changed. Near the end of the 1970s, cash flow started to improve, asset values rose, and from having a perilous balance sheet GrandMet became one of the companies with strong asset backing," explained Peter Cawdron, Group Strategic Development Director.

U.S. Diversification

One of the legacies of the period of financial pressure and subsequent consolidation was a belief on the part of Joseph, Grinstead, and Sharp that they did not want in future to be so dependent on the U.K. economy, the collapse of which in the early 1970s had almost cost them the company. They were thus receptive to propositions to invest abroad.

The first such opportunity arose when it became apparent that IDV's United States distributor, The Paddington Corporation, could be acquired. This would involve acquisition of Paddington's parent, the Liggett Group, which was also one of the major cigarette manufacturers in the United States and possessed a number of other related businesses (soft drinks, bottling, fitness products, and Alpo dog food). While the logic of purchasing the U.S. distributor for the group's largest branded spirits product (J&B Scotch) was clear to all, Max Joseph was dubious about the deal, since it was not heavily property related and, being in the United States and in a number of unfamiliar businesses, represented a significant managerial stretch for GrandMet. Despite his opposition, however, Stanley Grinstead, who had now taken over as chairman, championed the acquisition and completed it in 1981 for $450 million.

Shortly thereafter the possibility of purchasing Intercontinental Hotels from financially pressed Pan Am arose. This was a more familiar business for GrandMet, and Joseph, Grinstead, and Sharp had little difficulty in making up their minds. The deal was done in one week for $500 million. Nonetheless, the Intercontinental Hotel acquisition represented a significant departure from GrandMet's previous approach to buying trading property assets, whether in hotels or elsewhere. Few of the hotels were owned; most were operated under management contracts. Thus there was little real asset backing to the large sum paid for Intercontinental.

Shortly thereafter, Joseph died. Grinstead set out to make his mark on GrandMet via a programmed search for acquisitions in "U.S. branded services." Grinstead believed that GrandMet needed a broader base of businesses. He predicted that service businesses would grow faster than manufacturing businesses and felt that the United States would provide a suitable balance to GrandMet's U.K. operations. These acquisitions included Children's World (a childcare operation), Quality Care (a home health-care company), and Pearle Optical (the largest U.S. optician chain). Pearle was acquired for $386 million, a nineteen times exit multiple. At this stage, financial analysts began to ask questions about the wisdom of the strategy and the extent of the financial gamble GrandMet was taking with such far-flung acquisitions.[3]

Operating Improvements

At the time of the U.S. diversification programme, major operational improvements were being effected in the existing portfolio. Allen Sheppard had assembled a team around him that included Clive Strowger (from British Leyland), Ian Martin (from ITT), and David Tagg, who subsequently became responsible for GrandMet's management development programmes. Together this

---

[3]"Glasnost at GrandMet," *Management Today*, October 1987.

team aggressively attacked the problems of the brewing business, separating it from the pub-retailing business. The brewery's workforce was cut by 50 percent (a reduction of 5,000), and £82 million of capital had been released by 1986. Significant changes were undertaken in the marketing of regional brands and in the management of the pub estates (which were segmented into different "brands" and market segments).

At the same time, the restaurant operations (especially Berni Inns) were further segmented and rationalised, and excess sites were disposed of. Similarly, Express Foods had been ailing and was assigned to Sheppard. He installed Clive Strowger in Express, and within two to three years, performance had increased dramatically. Again, rationalisation was the key, as peripheral businesses were disposed of, costs were cut, and marketing improved.

Thus the Sheppard team, which was now responsible for U.K. brewing and food operations, continued to apply its formula to all of the businesses in its portfolio: it rationalised costs, disposed of peripheral businesses, improved marketing, and took steps to build a system of delegation and empowerment of operating managers. The goal was to institutionalise the search for superior performance and continuous improvement.

The management philosophy created by Sheppard was attractive to a certain kind of highly energetic, often impatient manager who is prepared to become closely involved in operational details. One ex-GrandMet manager, now chief operating officer of another major company, and with wide experience of three other companies, stated, "I don't believe in going back. But Sheppard is the one manager I would willingly work for again." The philosophy was frequently referred to as "restless management" because of Sheppard's habit of jumping up and pacing around during meetings. It was also known as "the light grip on the throat" referring to Sheppard's insistence on performance improvement and belief in decentralization .

The building of IDV, which went through its sharpest internal growth phase in the early 1980s, produced what eventually became GrandMet's largest profit contributor. During this period, IDV introduced fifty-five new products and boasted 32 percent of the new products of the seven biggest drinks companies. "No new branded spirit in recent years has been more successful than Bailey's Irish Cream, introduced by GrandMet a decade ago and now the world's No. 1 liqueur."[4]

Anthony Tennant managed IDV with a style very different from Allen Sheppard's. His strategy was built on four planks: (1) own the distributors and get close to the customer; (2) commit to the development of new products; (3) maintain a heavy marketing spend; and (4) form alliances to aid geographic expansion.

"Tennant, first head of GrandMet's IDV and then as CEO of Guinness is the prime architect of the industry's new strategy. His strategic *coup de main* at GrandMet was persuading RJR Nabisco's boss Ross Johnson to sell him Heublein Inc. in 1987 for $1.2 billion, a stiff price at the time but a steal in retrospect. Heublein gave IDV 13% of the American spirits market and full ownership of the world's leading vodka brand, Smirnoff, enhancing a portfolio that already included top brands such as J&B Scotch and Gilbey's gin."[5]

Grinstead described the GrandMet approach in the 1986 annual report as follows: "The group has a varied portfolio of companies but at the same time ensures that each company is a substantial competitor in its own market place. It has developed through operational experience and market research, a remarkable knowledge of the hotel, leisure, food, property, retailing and alcoholic beverage markets in the United Kingdom and the United States in particular... The group has built brands in many markets which are of immense value and which are continuously maintained and strengthened by skilful marketing. In addition it has an enviable record of success in new brand introduction. The breadth of the Group's activities provides an exceptional opportunity for the training of management. The range and variety of its international markets allows the development of a cadre of senior management which compares very favourably with those of the other United Kingdom or Unites States corporations... These are some of the important ways in which Grand Metropolitan adds value to the planning and activity of its component companies."[6]

By 1986, however, despite significant improvement in U.K. operations and the sale of the cigarette operations of the Liggett Group, performance was proving disappointing. Although there were no financial pressures, the former high annual rate of growth in earnings per share had declined until growth disappeared in 1986. One observer noted that "Grinstead turned the company in a new direction without, however, putting in place all the controls necessary to ensure the strategy's success. Management

[4]"Profits Soar for Global Brands," *Fortune*, November 4, 1991.

[5]Ibid.
[6]*Grand Metropolitan Annual Report*, 1986.

EXHIBIT 4
GrandMet's Principal Group Companies

	Country of incorporation	Country of operation	Percentage of equity owned	Business description
Food				
ALPO Petfoods, Inc.	U.S.	U.S.	100%	Manufacture and marketing of dog food, cat food, and dog treats
Brossard Surgelés SA	France	France	100%	Manufacture and marketing of frozen bakery products
Conservas Chistu, SA	Spain	Spain	100%	Manufacture and marketing of fresh and shelf-stable vegetables
The Häagen-Dazs Company, Inc.[†]	U.S.	U.S., Japan Canada, Europe	100%	Manufacture and distribution of superpremium ice cream and frozen desserts
The Pillsbury Company[†]	U.S.	U.S.	100%	Manufacture, marketing, and distribution of bakery products, frozen and shelf-stable vegetables and frozen pizza
Pillsbury Canada Ltd.	Canada	Canada	100%	Manufacture, marketing, and distribution of vegetables, dough, and pizza snacks
Pillsbury GmbH[†]	Germany	Germany	100%	Manufacture and marketing of ready meals, canned soups, frozen gateaux, and savoury products
Pilstral SA[†]	France	Europe	100%	Manufacture of baked goods and coordination of the Green Giant vegetable business across Europe
Drinks				
AED SA	Spain	Spain	100%	Importation, distribution, and marketing of wines and spirits
R&A Bailey & Company	Ireland	Ireland—exporting worldwide	100%	Production, distribution, marketing, and exporting of cream liqueur
Carillon Importers Ltd.	U.S.	U.S.	100%	Importation, distribution, and marketing of wines, spirits, and other adult beverages
Cinzano SpA[†]	Italy	Worldwide	100%	Production, distribution, and marketing of vermouth; local distribution of wines and spirits
Croft & Ca Lda.	Portugal	Portugal—exporting worldwide	100%	Production, distribution, marketing, and exporting of port wine
Croft-Jerez SA	Spain	Spain—exporting worldwide	100%	Production, distribution, marketing, and exporting of sherry

Continued

was still highly decentralised; problems within subsidiaries were allowed to go too far before head office reacted. And despite the reorientation toward drinks and leisure, GrandMet still lacked sufficient focus."[7]

By 1986, the City had lost confidence in GrandMet and the shares were downrated accordingly. It was widely suggested that GrandMet (see exhibit 5) lacked coherence. Eventually bid rumours began to circulate, and one or two predators (e.g., Alan Bond in Australia) assembled share stakes. Shortly thereafter (1987) Stanley

Grinstead stepped down and Allen Sheppard took over as chairman. The heat was still on, however, and Sheppard was quoted as saying, "If I'm not careful, some nineteen-year-old will come along and break me up."

Portfolio Restructuring

Under Sheppard, two of GrandMet's three largest acquisitions were completed. First, Heublein, a project begun under Grinstead, was bought from Nabisco for

[7]"Tough team at GrandMet," *Financial Weekly*, January 21, 1988.

	Country of incorporation	Country of operation	Percentage of equity owned	Business description
Drinks (continued)				
Gilbey Canada Inc.[†]	Canada	Canada	100%	Production, distribution, marketing, and wholesaling of wines and spirits
Heublein Inc.[†]	U.S.	Worldwide	100%	Production, importing, and marketing of wines and spirits
International Distillers and Vintners Ltd.[†]	England	Worldwide	100%	Production, distribution, marketing, exporting, and importing of wines, spirits, and other adult beverages
Justerini & Brooks Ltd.	England	U.K.—exporting worldwide	100%	Distillation, marketing, and export of Scotch whiskey
S&E&A Metaxa SA[†]	Greece	Greece	100%	Production, distribution, and marketing of spirits
Sovedi France SA	France	France	100%	Importation, distribution, and marketing of wines and spirits
The Paddington Corp.	U.S.	U.S.	100%	Importation, distribution, and marketing of wines and spirits
Branded Retailing and Pubs				
Burger King Corporation[†]	U.S.	U.S., Canada Europe	100%	Fast-food retailing
Grand Metropolitan Estates Ltd.[†]	England	U.K.	100%	Management of the group's property activity
Inntrepreneur Estates Ltd.	England	U.K.	50%	Property investment company
The Chef & Brewer Group Ltd.	England	U.K.	100%	Management of pubs
Pearle Inc.[†]	U.S.	U.S., Netherlands	100%	Retailing of eye-care products and services
Corporate				
Grand Metropolitan Finance PLC	England	U.K.	100%	Financing company for the group

[†]Carries on the business described in the countries listed in conjunction with its subsidiaries and other group companies

£855 million, driven by the desire to control key brands like Smirnoff. Consistent with the style of the Joseph regime, this project was completed in four days and in the process doubled IDV's spirit sales.

The other major project was the acquisition in 1989 of Pillsbury for $5.7 billion. This was a bitter fight and one that involved protracted legal disputes and other classic American bid defense tactics. Pillsbury provided GrandMet with the keystone for a global food business, building on the smaller operations of Express, Alpo, and smaller regional businesses like Peter's Savoury Products. It also offered major rationalisation possibilities.

The GrandMet team moved quickly into Pillsbury's Minneapolis headquarters after the deal. Led by Ian Martin, head of U.S. operations for GrandMet, the team removed about one-third of the company's managers. Some 1,500 staff were fired before the year was out. An interview at the time described GrandMet's intentions to "revive Pillsbury's food business by trimming its excessive costs, rebuilding its famous but underexploited brands and developing new food products and markets." Ian Martin was quoted as saying, that "We've introduced more pace, momentum, and a hard edge to management." All major aspects of the operation were subject to intense scrutiny: "We're up to our armpits, studying issues such as production, distribution and quality. The real competitive edge is quality. If we get that right, the other things will follow."[8] Martin summarised the approach in another interview: "The three basics are cut costs, build brands and develop new products—in that order. That sounds like a cliche, like Onward Christian Soldiers, but it's true."[9]

The City initially was concerned about the size of the Pillsbury deal and the $750 million provision for restructuring costs. However, since interest cover for the group was high, there was little concern about debt pressure. Much of the concern was focused on GrandMet's ability to turn around Burger King, Pillsbury's fast food subsidiary, which was locked into a fierce war with McDonald's.

In parallel with these two major acquisition initiatives, the Sheppard team initiated what subsequently became referred to as "Operation De-clutter." All businesses that did not offer the promise of strong branding, dominant share position, and international scope (see section entitled "Vision 2000" below), were divested. Operation De-clutter and the focus on food, drinks, and retailing was built on the idea that global leadership in a few businesses is better than a less powerful presence in many. At the same time, Sheppard noted, "we considered and rejected the idea of becoming a single-cell business. This route would provide maximum focus; it would also expose us to a fair degree of risk—all our eggs would be in one basket."[10]

Sheppard's decisions in the betting shop business are illustrative of this strategy. Shortly after he became chairman, GrandMet bought William Hill to add to its Mecca operations and so became the largest and most profitable company in the U.K. industry. The strategy was to use the strength of the management in this sector to enter the U.S. market and so become an international leader. However, shortly after entering the U.S. market, Sheppard decided that the U.S. venture was too risky and would lower GrandMet's reputation in the U.S. market. He then sold the entire operation, showing a substantial profit.

In the chairman's statement in the 1987 report and accounts, Sheppard stated, that "The major business portfolio restructuring of the past 3 years has been completed and we are now in a position to develop rapidly in our chosen business areas." The disposal programme undertaken as part of Operation De-clutter had been a wide-ranging one, and that programme has continued to this day. The principal acquisitions and disposals of the past five years are summarized in exhibit 6.

Management Team

When Sheppard took over, he moved quickly to assemble his team of proven operating managers around him as a top team for the group. Strowger became finance director, while remaining responsible for food operations. Ian Martin took over GrandMet's American operations, and David Tagg became personnel director.

Anthony Tennant was recruited to become the chief executive of Guinness, following the scandal that ousted Ernest Saunders. Tennant was succeeded at IDV by George Bull, and the division continued with the same strategy and with a large degree of autonomy from the centre. "IDV is another world with a different style of management and jealous of its autonomy," commented one manager. "Recently GrandMet has begun to have more influence on IDV, putting pressure on us to improve operations, lower costs, and take some rationalisation decisions we have been avoiding."

Sheppard also resolved to build a strong and active board of directors. He recruited Richard Giordano of BOC, Frank Pizzitola of Lazards, John Harvey-Jones of ICI, Colin Marshall of British Airways, and David Simon of BP. The GrandMet board is an active and vigorous forum for debate and corporate governance. "Little time is spent on formalities. The agenda is divided into formal and action items and the formal part generally takes about 30 seconds," says Sheppard. "Then we discuss, not so much results to date as what actions we are taking to improve the results in the forecast period. Our discussions are very much to do with real live issues and action points rather than just reporting. We all feel quite passionately about the company and we've got ten people on the Board, all of whom regard themselves as chief executive."[11] Exhibit 7 summarises the backgrounds of GrandMet's current directors.

---

[8] "Squeezing the Doughboy," *Financial Times*, 3 July 1989.
[9] *Fortune*, op. cit.
[10] Allen Sheppard's speech of December 10, 1992, at the strategic planning conference in London.

[11] "Gripping Yarns," *Director*, August 1992.

United Kingdom	United States	International

Brewing
  Watneys
Consumer services
  Retailing (pubs and
    bookmakers)
  Gaming (casinos)
  Contract services
    (catering and private
    hospitals)
	Consumer products
	  Dog food
	  Soft drinks
	  Tobacco
	  Fitness products
	  Preschool nurseries
	  Food (cheese)
	  Home nursing
	  Opticians
		Hotels
		  Intercontinental hotels
		  Wine and spirits

EXHIBIT 5
GrandMet's Portfolio, 1985

Sheppard's new team made many other changes in management. Tagg changed nearly all the personnel directors, Strowger changed some of the finance directors, and in America Ian Martin changed whole layers of management. Sheppard was determined to stamp his restless management philosophy on the group as quickly as possible.

A key part of the central philosophy at GrandMet is the development and empowerment of operating managers. The personnel function, under David Tagg, carries wide-ranging responsibility in this regard. Williamson and Rix describe it thus: "GrandMet possesses a strong central personnel function which is designed to spot potential problems before they show up in reported financial results. It is there also to attract good management to train them, to understand their skills, so as to accumulate a critical mass of knowledge within the group, and a pool of proven managers who can be transferred into a subsidiary when problems arise or market developments necessitate unfamiliar shifts in strategy or organisation."[12]

Another key capability lies in the corporate acquisition team under Peter Cawdron, group strategy development manager and a former Warburgs banker: "Acquisitions are the result of a formal planning and review system underscored by the company's vision of the future. The corporate head office in London's Hanover Square initiates and assesses all major acquisitions and also undertakes studies on behalf of operating units in collaboration with them....GrandMet's acquisition strategy is an attacking one. It identifies what it wants, chooses its target, and goes for it. Consider the Pillsbury deal. Having decided to become a global food player and realised the need for rapid entry into the U.S.

market, GrandMet proceeded by screening every respectably sized food company in the United States, evaluating the respective businesses and their managements. All the major U.S. food companies were then assessed by charting them along two axes, desirability and do-ability, to determine which company appeared the best fit. Pillsbury stood out well above the others."[13]

Vision 2000

Early in the Sheppard regime, it became clear that a formalised statement of the business goals for the group was needed, both for internal and external consumption. Sheppard therefore assigned this job to Peter Cawdron, who undertook the task with the help of outside consultants and a wide-ranging programme of input from senior executives and board members; the project took twelve to fifteen months to complete. In the resulting document, entitled *Vision 2000*, Sheppard articulated a corporate statement of GrandMet's mission as follows:

"Grand Metropolitan is respected internationally for its management, enterprise and growth record. It is a dynamic and innovative company dedicated to success.

GrandMet specialises in highly branded consumer businesses where its marketing and operational skills ensure it is a leading contender in every market in which it operates. The nature of these businesses—in food, drinks and retailing—is complementary, which adds to the value of the group as a whole.

---

[12]Williams and Rix, op. cit.

[13]Roderick McNiel, "Acquisitions—The GrandMet Approach," *FT Mergers and Acquisitions International*, February 1991.

EXHIBIT 6
GrandMet's Strategic Acquisitions and Disposals Since 1987

ACQUISITIONS		
Food		**Price**
1988	Kaysens (frozen gateaux)	£21.5m
1988	Peter's Savoury Products (meat and pastry products)	£75m
1989	The Pillsbury Company (Green Giant, Pillsbury, Häagen-Dazs etc.)	£5,800m
1990	Belin Surgelés (French frozen cake company)	(not disclosed)
1990	Jus-rol (frozen pastry)	£46.5m
1991	Aunt Nellie's (glass jar-packed vegetables)	(not disclosed)
1991	Bistrial (French cake manufacturer)	(not disclosed)
1991	Jurgen Langbein (German soup company)	(not disclosed)
1992	McGlynn's Bakeries (U.S. frozen bakery products)	(not disclosed)
1992	Knack & Back (refrigerated dough)	(not disclosed)
Drinks		
1989	Sileno (Portuguese wine and spirit distribution)	(not disclosed)
1989	Metaxa (International brand; Greek/German distribution)	(not disclosed)
1989	Mont La Salle Vineyards (Californian wines and brandy)	(not disclosed)
1990	Anglo Española de Distribución SA (Spanish distributor)	(not disclosed)
1991	R & J Emmet pic (Irish liqueur)	£33m
1991	New Zealand Wines & Spirits	(not disclosed)
1992	Cinzano (vermouth and sparkling wines)	(not disclosed)
Retailing		
1988	Vision Express (U.S.) (eyecare)	£40m
1988	Eye + Tech (U.S.) (eyecare)	£32m
1989	EyeLab (U.S.) (eyecare)	(not disclosed)
1989	Burger King (see Pillsbury)	(see above)
1989	UB Restaurants (fast food restaurants)	£180m
1991	Inntrepreneur Estates formed (50/50 owned with Courage/Foster's Brewing Group)	(not disclosed)

Continued

Its style is about winning—never satisfied and always innovative. GrandMet strives to be a good employer and a good neighbour, and a contributor to the wealth and well-being of all the communities and environments in which it operates."

Sheppard underlined the importance he placed in the vision statement: "The investment of time and resource in the process of developing a Corporate Vision and long-term strategy for Grand Metropolitan has proved to be a major motivator and integrating force throughout the Group. It has channelled the energy of our managers to strive towards their highest aspirations. It has positioned us to exploit strategic opportunities much more quickly and efficiently in the future. Finally, but not least, it has caused us to build and enhance the strategic capability of the Corporate Centre. The whole process, together with our successful management philosophy, has given stimulus and credibility to Grand Metropolitan's ability to continue to add value to all its businesses in the years to come.'"[14]

A close look suggests that the centre of GrandMet has three influences:

- It creates a tough and challenging culture in which top management expects and demands superior operating

[14]Statement by Allen Sheppard, *The Development of a Long Term Strategy for Grand Metropolitan*, April 1989.

DISPOSALS

	Company	Reason	Price
1988	Soft Drink Bottling Plants	No brand control	£705m/£400m
1988	Inter-Continental Hotels	Level of investment required to obtain additional hotels to provide adequate long term returns to shareholders too high	£2bn/£1.2bn net
1989	London Clubs (casinos)	After hotels were sold did not fit strategy	£128m
1989	S&A Restaurants	To comply with U.S. licensing laws	£434m/£263m
1989	Van de Kamps (seafood)	No international branding potential	£140m/£89m
1989	Bumble Bee (seafood)	No international branding potential	£269m/£171m
1989	William Hill and Mecca retail betting interests	No international potential	£750m
1990	Wimpy table service restaurants	Not appropriate for conversion to Burger King	(not disclosed)
1990	158 Berni Restaurants	Upgrading business portfolio	£120m
1991	GrandMet Brewing	No international potential. Key brands not owned (£55m to be repaid after four years)	£316m
1991	Pizzaland/Pastificio/ Perfect Pizza	No international branding potential	(not disclosed)
1991	Wienerwald (German restaurant chain)	No international potential	(not disclosed)
1991	The Dominic Group (liquor retailers)	No international potential	£49.5m
1992	Express Dairy/Eden Vale	Commodity oriented, nonstrategic	£359m
1992	Express Ireland	Commodity oriented, nonstrategic	(not disclosed)
1992	BKDS (Burger King Distribution Services)	Noncore to Burger King strategy	(not disclosed)
1992	Eatfresh	No international potential	(not disclosed)
1992	Express foods	Commodity oriented, nonstrategic	£96m

performance and cost leadership. This often involves introducing radical culture change and shaking up management.

- It nurtures talent. GrandMet pays a great deal of attention to motivating people and moving them around so that they can make an impact on more than one business within the group. The careers of the top 150 executives in the company are periodically reviewed by the board. Sheppard himself is said to be expert not only at motivating individuals but at being sure they are in the right place to make the most of their particular abilities. He underlines his commitment both to management development and to business growth by encouraging risk taking. A failure is not a career-ender, and playing it safe is not acceptable.

- It strives simultaneously for operating improvements and enhanced branding. "Many companies are good at brand management and developing new products. Others are good at cost management and operating control. At GrandMet we are good at both in being able to release cash from operations and have the marketing skill to invest it wisely in brands," explained Allen Sheppard.[15]

In a 1990 interview in *The Times*, Sheppard expanded on his philosophy: "We have checks and balances in the corporate governing sense, but we don't believe in safety nets for our management. We don't have one-

---

[15]Speech to Strategic Management Society, October 1992.

and-a-half people doing each person's job. What one has to do is have absolutely excellent people and encourage them to take authority to do their own thing, like a small business. My job is to ride that anarchy, working within a strategic plan, rather like a herd of horses. I have to somehow capture all that movement; that is what management is all about."[16]

---

[16]"The Working Class Hero Who Turned His Back on the Party," *The Times*, December 22, 1990.

The Future

As Allen Sheppard reexamined GrandMet's choices for the future, he noted a number of important companies as his principal corporate strategy competitors:

- In spirits, GrandMet is the largest in case sales; two of the other three global operators, Allied Lyons and Guinness, are British; the fourth, Seagram, is Canadian; all are now emulating the generic strategy developed

EXHIBIT 7
GrandMet's
Board of Directors

Sir Allen Sheppard, *Chairman and Group Chief Executive*
Joined GrandMet as a director in 1975 after 18 years in the motor industry. He became group chief executive of GrandMet in 1986 and chairman in 1987. He is chairman of The Prince's Youth Business Trust and deputy chairman of Business in the Community. He is also chairman of London First and London Forum and a nonexecutive deputy chairman of Meyer International. Age 59.

Richard V. Giordano KBE (USA), *Deputy Chairman*
Chief executive of the BOC Group from 1979 to 1992 and chairman from 1985 to 1992. He is a nonexecutive director of the BOC Group, Reuters Holdings, The RTZ Corp, and Georgia Pacific Corp in the United States. Appointed nonexecutive director of GrandMet in 1984 and deputy chairman in 1991. Age 58.

Ian A. Martin, *Group Managing Director and Chief Operating Officer*
Became chairman and chief executive of Warney Mann & Truman Brewers in 1982 having joined the company in 1979. He was appointed to the board of GrandMet in 1985 and group managing director and chief operating officer in 1991. He is chairman of International Distillers & Vintners, GrandMet Inc, and the North American Advisory Committee. He is also a nonexecutive director of St. Paul Companies Inc and Granada Group. Age 57.

George J. Bull, *Chairman and Chief Executive, Food Sector*
Joined International Distillers & Vintners in 1962, prior to its acquisition by GrandMet and became chief executive in 1984. He was appointed to the board of GrandMet in 1985. He was appointed chairman and chief executive of the food sector and chairman of The Pillsbury Company in July 1992. He is also chairman of the Far East Business Development Advisory Committee. Age 56.

John B. McGrath, *Chief Executive, Drinks Sector*
Joined Warney Mann & Truman Brewers as group director in 1985 and appointed managing director in 1986. He was appointed managing director and chief operating officer of International Distillers & Vintners in 1991. He was appointed to the board of GrandMet in June 1992 and also became chief executive of the drinks sector. He was a prime mover in the creation of the Portman Group. Age 54.

David P. Nash, *Group Finance Director*
Joined the GrandMet board in December 1989, having previously held various positions in Imperial Chemical Industries and Cadbury Schweppes. He is chairman of GrandMet finance and other group finance and holding companies and is responsible for group information technology systems. He is chairman of the Eastern European Advisory Committee. Age 52.

Continued

by Tennant of reducing costs, building global brands, controlling distribution, and cranking out new products.

- In the food sector, GrandMet reckons it is eighth in the world "league table," the sector is dominated by three true giants, Philip Morris, the largest consumer products company in the world, Unilever, and Nestlé; all are financially strong and intensely acquisitive.

- The retailing sector is more fragmented; GrandMet faces rivals in each segment (e.g., McDonald's) and more

broadly spread rivals such as Pepsico (drinks, snacks, and fast food) and Whitbread (beer and restaurants).

Given this situation, Sheppard had to pick a successor who could set out the best strategic direction for the future. Therefore, he had to find an answer to two questions: in which direction should GrandMet's corporate strategy be developed, and who is the right person to accomplish this task?

EXHIBIT 7—Continued
GrandMet's Board of Directors

David E. Tagg, *Chief Executive, Property and UK Retailing and Group Services Director*
Joined Warney Mann & Truman Brewers as personnel director in 1980. He was appointed to the board at GrandMet in 1988. He is responsible for GrandMet Estates and is chairman of The Chef & Brewer Group and also responsible for the group personnel, legal, and company secretarial functions. He is chairman of the European Advisory Committee, GrandMet Community Services, and of the Group Pension Funds. He is a nonexecutive director of Storehouse. Age 52.

Sir John Harvey-Jones MBE
Was chairman of Imperial Chemical Industries from 1982 to 1987, having joined that company in 1956 from the Royal Navy. He is nonexecutive chairman of *The Economist* newspaper and nonexecutive deputy chairman of Guinness Peat Aviation Limited. Appointed a nonexecutive director of GrandMet in 1983 and deputy chairman from 1987 to 1991. Age 68.

Professor Dr. Gertrud Höhler (Germany), *Management Consultant, Höhler Consultants*
Founded Berlin-based Höhler Consultants in 1985. Her clients include the majority of the 50 largest companies in Germany. She serves on advisory councils for the German Federal Defence Ministry and the German Federal Ministry for Research & Technology. She has been professor of general literary studies and German studies at the University of Paderborn since 1972. Appointed a nonexecutive director of GrandMet in November 1992. Age 51.

Sir Colin Marshall, *Deputy Chairman and Chief Executive, British Airways*
Joined British Airways as chief executive in 1983 and became deputy chairman in 1989 having previously held positions in Sears, Avis, and Hertz. He is currently a nonexecutive director of The Midland Bank, IBM, U.K. Holdings, and HSBC Holdings. Appointed a nonexecutive director of GrandMet in 1988. Age 59.

David A. G. Simon CBE, *Group Chief Executive and Deputy Chairman, The British Petroleum Company*
Joined BP in 1961 and in 1982 became chief executive BP Oil International—BP's worldwide oil refining and marketing group. In 1986, he was appointed a managing director, BP Group, joining the group main board with responsibility for finance and Europe. He is currently chairman of BP Exploration, BP Oil, and BP Chemicals. Appointed a nonexecutive director of GrandMet in 1989. Age 53.

■ CHEMICAL LABOUR GROUPING, EEIG†

By Lluis Renart and Francesco Parés

It was early April 1990, and Joseba Garmendia[1] was looking forward to Easter to be able to at least take a few hours off to rest and reflect. In addition to being general manager, and co-owner of Química del Atlántico, S.A., Joseba Garmendia had taken upon himself the additional responsibility of being coordinator of Chemical Labour Grouping, European Economic Interest Grouping (CLG, EEIG). This grouping had been registered in the Bilbao Company Registry on March 13, 1990, and had been set up by four paint manufacturers from different European countries:

- Lacke und Farbe GmbH (LF), from Germany
- Marceau et Fils, S.A. (M), from France
- United Colours Ltd (UC), from the UK
- Química del Atlántico, S.A. (QA), from Spain.

The agreement had taken almost two years to negotiate.

Joseba Garmendia and the managers of the other three companies were very pleased about the way things had progressed up until the legalization of their groupings. Not only had new and exciting competitive prospects opened up for them on a European scale, but early during the agreement planning process they had started to put into practice certain cooperation mechanisms, specifically the joint purchase of certain raw materials which had already begun to produce very tangible results in their respective income statements.

However, Joseba Garmendia was also aware that the grouping was one of the first EEIG's formed in Europe and definitely the first that had been formally registered in Spain. None of its four partners had any experience in this type of alliance. The planning had been relatively smooth but they were now venturing into virgin territory, mapping the route as they walked.

Joseba Garmendia had written down a list of issues that had presented themselves during the process. Some of them seemed to suggest new opportunities of potential, while others could harbour dangers, or at least doubts. He was looking forward to the Easter holiday to be able to reflect on each of these issues.

Química del Atlántico, S.A. (QA)

Química del Atlántico, S.A. was founded in 1932. At about that time, it started to manufacture air-drying, nitrocellulose paints for automobile body repairs and was the first company to supply these products on the Spanish market.

In 1955, the company opened its plant in Baracaldo, a few kilometres from Bilbao; in 1990, this plant was still the corporate headquarters. Over the years, the company had steadily grown up and had opened two more factories: Portugalete and Santurce, both near the corporate headquarters. In 1990, QA's facilities occupied a surface area exceeding 60,000 square metres.

The company had consistently allocated significant effort and resources to research and development, as a result of which it had been able to launch products, systems and processes such as:

- polyester finishes for wood products
- baked enamels for refrigerators
- implementation of water soluble baths by immersion, used mainly in automobile factories
- paint application systems using electrodeposition
- powdered paints
- the Kolormatik system, able to select from among more than 5,000 hot or cold colours; basic or complementary colours; absolute or relative colours; monochromatic, polychromatic or achromatic colours; and obtain any range of tints or hues.

This desire to be always on the leading edge of technology had led the company to sign technology transfer agreements with companies such as Dai Nippon (Japan), Fuller O'Brian (USA), ICI (United

	1984	1985	1986	1987
Saudi Arabia	51.4	7.6	*	8.1
Egypt	18.4	13.2	*	16.2
Libya	13.6	7.6	2.3	*
Ecuador	3.9	*	*	*
France	*	19.5	*	*
Portugal	*	*	10.5	9.9
Andorra	*	*	5.0	*
Nicaragua	*	*	3.5	*
USA	*	*	*	13.5
Other countries	9.7	15.1	3.7	42.3
Total exports	97	63	25	90
Total QA sales	7,179	8,000	8,630	9,400

Note: The *Censo Oficial de Exportadores* only provides information on the four main countries that a particular company exports to in any one year. Therefore, the indication of an asterisk (*) means unknown.

EXHIBIT 1
Exports by Química del Atlántico, S.A.

Kingdom), Lacke und Farbe GmbH (Germany), and so on.

Química del Atlántico, S.A.'s sales turnover in 1985 amounted to about 8 billion pesetas.[2] Home decorating paints accounted for about 20 percent of this figure and automobile body repair paints (refinishing) accounted for 30 percent. Thus, these two types of paint represented 50 percent of QA's sales; that is, approximately half of the company's production consisted of standard paints manufactured for stock and subsequently sold through decorating shops and other retail outlets. The company estimated that its products were sold in 75 percent of the approximately 12,000 retail outlets existing in Spain in 1985.

The other 50 percent of QA's sales were paints manufactured to order for industrial customers. The most important industrial sector for QA were the automobile OEMs (Original Equipment Manufacturers), which accounted for about 30 percent of the company's total sales, with a volume of about 6,000 tonnes of paint. The remaining 20 percent was sold to other industrial sectors, such as domestic appliance manufacturers, automobile components and spare parts, toys,

metallographic industry (printing on tinplate or aluminium used in the manufacture of cans for food products or soft drinks), furniture, electrical material, railroad rolling stock, etc.

In 1986, QA's total workforce amounted to about 575 employees and this figure would remain virtually unchanged until 1990.

Química del Atlántico, S.A. had been the leader in the refinishing segment in Spain since the end of the Spanish Civil War with exactly three products: two black paints and one white paint. When SEAT started manufacturing cars in Spain towards the end of the 50s, QA was able to position itself well, sharing the client with Lory. Subsequently, other automobile OEMs and other paint manufacturers established manufacturing facilities in Spain. QA's management estimated that in 1985, the last year before Spain joined the EC, its company's market share in the specific segment of paint supply to Spanish automobile OEMs was about 15 percent. The classification of paint suppliers for that year in Spain would probably be the following:

Glasurit	(Basf)
Química del Atlántico	
Ivanow	(Akzo)
Herberts	(Hoescht, AG)
PPG	
Du Pont/Lory	(International Paints)

[2]The rate of exchange of the US dollar against the Spanish peseta reached an all-time high of 190 pesetas for one dollar in early 1985. From there, the US dollar stumbled to below 100 pesetas per dollar in 1990.

As yet, QA had had little export activity. As can be seen in exhibit 1, in recent years exports had accounted for less than 1.5 percent of the company's total sales.

January 1, 1986:
At Last We're in the EC!

After several years of contacts and hard negotiating, the treaty by which Spain became a member of the European Communities was signed in Madrid on June 12, 1985. This treaty specified that Spain, together with Portugal, would be fully-fledged members of the EC on January 1, 1986. The treaty provided for a seven-year transition period during which tariffs would be progressively reduced.

Joseba Garmendia remembered that in those early days in 1986 he had felt distinctly optimistic. QA had a strong competitive position in Spain, it had proprietary technology, and it hoped that during the transition period the cost of imported raw materials would steadily fall as a result of the tariff reductions. "Everything will go better," he had thought. And, to a large extent, he was right. Also, after several years of economic recession, the Spanish market was starting to pick up speed. QA closed 1986 with total sales amounting to 8.63 billion pesetas.[3] The budget for 1987 forecast a further substantial increase to 9.4 billion pesetas.

However, halfway through 1987, Joseba Garmendia started to become aware of certain changes that were taking place in the paint industry as a result of the 'import' from Japan of certain operating procedures that until then were little known in Spain:

— The 'kanban' or Just-in-Time, system, which demanded a greater degree of commitment and involvement from suppliers to their customers.

— The tendency to reduce the number of suppliers. It was mentioned that the Japanese automobile manufacturers had four times fewer suppliers than their Western counterparts.

— Stricter quality requirements, both in the products delivered and in the service provided: everything had to work properly the first time round, with no failures or delays or rejects.

— A tendency to extend these quality requirements to the supplier's own factory to increase its efficiency and thereby lower costs.

From 1988 onwards, Joseba Garmendia started to notice that the Spanish automobile OEMs were starting to put into practice these operating procedures:

— The number of suppliers was starting to be reduced, although this was offset by the fact that the "survivors" received larger orders. However, in exchange, the manufacturers demanded better sales prices.

— People were starting to talk about ODETTE, a telematic interface network that would link automobile production plants with their suppliers in real time, with the possibility of modifying almost instantly supplies, parts and component vendors' delivery schedules in response to changing needs.

— Total quality requirements were starting to be implemented.

— And, finally, the Spanish automobile OEMs, all of them belonging to large multinational groups, were asking QA a key question, "This paint you're supplying me in Spain, can you supply it to me just the same in the United Kingdom, or in Germany, or in France?"

At that time, approximately 30 percent of QA's sales were to automobile manufacturers. The storm clouds that were gathering over such a large part of its billing seemed to be becoming increasingly more threatening. In his gloomiest moments, Joseba Garmendia saw himself shut out from the OEM automobile market in the very near future. What could he do to prevent this from happening? In fact, although his sales turnover to the automobile OEM industry in Spain had remained constant in volume terms, his market share had probably fallen to about 10 percent.[4]

An Unexpected Telephone Call

It was Lothar Steinhübel, Lacke und Farbe GmbH's (LF) Managing Director and an old acquaintance of his. This German company had sold technology to Química del Atlántico, S.A. although the products manufactured using technology purchased from LF had never exceeded 1 percent of QA's total sales. Lothar

---

[3]"Fomento de la Producción," Special Issue, *Las 2.500 Mayores Empresas Españolas,* September 1987.

[4]Perhaps the most dramatic situation had happened in 1982 when General Motors opened its new factory in Figueruelas (Zaragoza): all the decisions were taken by GM-Opel in Germany so that QA was not even able to get itself homologated as a supplier.

Steinhübel asked him three questions regarding the OEM automobile industry.

1. Do you want to cooperate on more general business issues, beyond the field of technology transfer?

2. Are you prepared to operate at a pan-European level?

3. Are you prepared to include other partners in this cooperation system?

After answering 'Yes' to all three questions, Joseba Garmendia was invited to a meeting that would be held in Cologne (FRG) in September 1988. Also answering Steinhübel's invitation, in addition to Garmendia and Steinhübel, John Brown of United Colours Ltd was present at the meeting. The sole subject discussed at this meeting was the supply of paints to automobile manufacturers. The three men soon realized that their respective companies were all facing the same problem: "The automobile industry demands that we be able to supply them any product to any of their European plants at any time."

All three stated that they were prepared to face the challenge and to fight to keep their sales to the automobile industry. They felt that the solution lay in mutual cooperation and said that they were willing to get to work on the matter, although they were not yet sure what form this cooperation would take. One thing they were clear about was that they needed a fourth partner who, due to the European automobile manufacturers' production structure, should be French (see exhibit 2). One of them suggested the name of Marceau and the others agreed. They did not consider it necessary to include an Italian partner, at least not for the moment, as the only automobile manufacturer in Italy was the Fiat Group, which had its own domestic suppliers and in-house production of paints. Each of the partner companies ratified their desire to preserve their independence and freedom.

The 'territorial' aspect or functions of each partner within the alliance were established as follows: a complete paint supply transaction to an automobile manufacturer involves certain actions (mainly production) which are performed 'on-site' in the paint supplier's factory. However, such transactions also include a series of actions, mainly service, that must be performed 'off site' away from the paint factory, and sometimes even in the customer's factory. Consequently, it was agreed that each partner would obviously carry out all the production operations in its own factory. However, all the 'off-site' operations would be performed by the partner in each country, regardless of

who manufactured the paints being applied. This off-site operation included the operation of the 'mixing room' in each customer factory, logistics, implementation of Just-in-Time, etc.

In the course of the conversations, they also ascertained that each of the three manufacturers only supplied the automobile factories in their own country, with the sole exception of substantial quantities supplied by Steinhübel to a French plant operated by the Peugeot Group.

The Return Flight... and Some Reflections

At the end of the meeting, Joseba Garmendia caught the train back to Düsseldorf. When he arrived at the airport to catch his direct flight back to Bilbao, he found that all flights had considerable delays due to a strike. With the memories of the meeting still fresh in his mind, he went to one of the lounges and sat down to patiently wait for his flight to be called while he continued to think about what had been discussed in the meeting.

It was quite clear to him that all three paint manufacturers were facing more or less the same problems. However, in spite of having common interests, there were clear cultural differences, different ways of thinking. "I'll have to learn to put myself in their shoes," thought Garmendia.

While he sat waiting in the airport, another thought suddenly came to him: they had only been talking about the automobile industry, but it seemed very likely that other industries that were also customers of the same paint manufacturers would sooner or later make the same demands as the automobile industry. For example, the first could be the automobile component industry, followed shortly after by the domestic appliance manufacturers, which were concentrated in a few groups operating on a pan-European scale. Or the metal-lographic industry, which printed the metal sheets that were then turned into cans for use by a small number of soft drink brands.

Skipping from one idea to another, Joseba Garmendia realized that if Química del Atlántico, S.A. wanted to give on its own a commercially suitable response throughout Europe to the various industries currently supplied in Spain, it would come up against at least two problems:

EXHIBIT 2
Automobile OEMs in Europe at the End of 1988, and Location of Main Production Plants

	West Germany	United Kingdom	France	Spain	Other Countries
General Motors	X	X		X	
Ford	X	X		X	
Renault			X	X	Portugal
Peugeot-Citroën		X	X	X	
Volkswagen-Audi-Seat	X			X	
British Motors		X			
Nissan		X		X	
Mercedes	X			X	
BMW	X				
Volvo/Saab					Sweden
Fiat/Alfa Romeo/Lancia					Italy

1. A serious financial problem would be caused by the large investments required to adequately serve so many manufacturers in so many industries and in so many different countries. In fact, to sell paints to a large industrial customer, it is normally necessary to have at least two people per plant (point of supply) able to make 'in situ' the necessary corrections to the formulation and to supervise the paint application systems. It would also be necessary to have sufficient physical space to work, a buffer stock and office space to carry out invoicing and control tasks.

2. Furthermore, undoubtedly there would be control and communication problems caused by the need to operate in different cultures and using different languages.

Garmendia reached the conclusion that the only apparently viable option lay in cooperation.

But all these reflections raised one question which at that time he was unable to answer: "If at the Cologne meeting we only agree to cooperate in supplying the OEM automobile industry, what will Química del Atlántico, S.A. have to do to continue supplying customers in other industries? Will we have to form other alliances specialized in serving different industries?" In any case, Garmendia realized that although perhaps this alliance could coordinate their paint sales to other industries, that is, the entire range of paints manufactured 'to order,' under no circumstances would it extend to home decorating paint sales or sales to the car refinishing market segment.

A few days later, he received in Baracaldo the minutes of the Cologne meeting written by Steinhübel. In synthesis, it was the expression of "a summary of wills that pointed to something that could become a letter of intent."

Shortly before Christmas 1988, Garmendia and Steinhübel went to Paris to meet Pierre Marceau, managing director of Marceau et Fils, S.A. They did not carry with them any pre-prepared documents and their intention was just to ask him the same questions they had analysed in Cologne. Pierre Marceau had agreed to see them and after they had been talking with him for a short while, it soon became apparent to the visitors that he was concerned about the same problems. However, although courteous, the meeting was cold; Garmendia thought that it was because Marceau was aware that he was talking with competitors.

Garmendia had never been in Marceau et Fils, S.A. before. Later, he would remember that the offices seemed to have an air of Spartan austerity. He liked this and he felt that it went well with the idea of a company and management that seemed to have an 'industrial mentality' like Química del Atlántico, S.A.; i.e. a sober style with few people in the offices.

Marceau listened to them, seemed to understand their reasoning and asked them to provide him with some documentation on the project. It therefore seemed clear that he was interested in going forward together with them, although, at the end of the meeting, he explicitly told Steinhübel that this would mean finding some type of solution to the fact that they competed as suppliers to Peugeot in France.

Garmendia left the meeting very pleased, not only by the apparently positive results achieved but also by the favourable impression he had received of the French

EXHIBIT 3
Sales by Main Sectors

Source: Personal estimates by Joseba Garmendia.

	% sales to industrial customers	% sales to automobile OEMs	Volume sales to automobile OEMs in tonnes
Química del Atlántico, S.A.[1]	50%	30%	= 6,000 tonnes
Marceau et Fils, S.A.	50%	30%	= 5,600 tonnes
Lacke und Farbe GmbH	100%	60%	= 7,000 tonnes
United Colours Ltd[1]	90%	60%	= 6,000 tonnes

[1]The rest, both in the case of Química del Atlántico, S.A. and United Colours Ltd are sales of paint for home decorating and automobile refinishing.

manager's personality. In some way, he could relate better to him than to Brown or Steinhübel, not only because he found it easier to talk in French but also because they seemed to have similar ways of thinking. In short, there seemed to be a greater cultural affinity between Garmendia and Marceau than between Garmendia and Brown or Steinhübel. It seemed to Garmendia that this foursome relationship would be 'more balanced.' Garmendia also knew that while the percentage of sales to the automobile OEM industry varied for each one of the manufacturers, the volume of paint in tonnes sold by each of them to the automobile manufacturers was fairly similar (see exhibit 6).

1989: The Torch Changes Hands

The beginning of 1989 was marked by two events: on the one hand, Marceau and Steinhübel had to solve the problem of their competing for Peugeot, and Brown, on the other, seemed to be adopting a rather passive attitude.

For his part, taking as his basis the minutes of the Cologne meeting, Joseba Garmendia asked a Bilbao law firm to study the best way to give a legal framework to the project. It just so happened that Miguel Torres, one of the lawyers working in the firm, had prepared a study on Regulation 2137/85, which had been approved by the EEC Council of Ministers in 1985 and was to come into force on July 1, 1989. Consequently, the lawyer proceeded to write a new document on which to

base the cooperation between the four paint manufacturers, adapting it to the legal framework of the European Economic Interest Groupings (EEIG) (see exhibit 4).

It seemed to Joseba Garmendia that the legal form of the EEIGs was "just what the doctor ordered" for the type of cooperation they wanted to implement. He quickly summoned another plenary meeting, which took place in Paris in March 1989, that is, three months before the EEIG Regulation was to come into force.

When Garmendia presented in Paris the proposal to create the alliance by giving it the legal form of the EEIGs, the news of this new legal possibility came as a complete surprise to the other three manufacturers and it seemed to them to be exactly what they needed.

This caused a wave of enthusiasm in the meeting. However, John Brown, being more prudent and cautious, pointed out to his colleagues that they would have more than enough time to do things together and that they should not forget that it was very likely that their needs, interests and priorities were divergent. Therefore, Brown proposed that they start little by little and choose as their first area of joint action a subject: that seemed to be clearly to the best interests of all four: coordination of raw material purchasing policies and the consequent negotiation with suppliers. The aim was to show that cooperation could be undeniably *profitable* for all four. Joseba Garmendia, for his part, realized that if his purchasing volume was about five billion pesetas, among the four of them, they would have a purchasing power of about 20 billion pesetas! They all agreed to immediately start cooperating in this area.

EXHIBIT 4
Summary of the Main Requirements and Characteristics of a European Economic Interest Grouping

SUMMARY OF THE MAIN REQUIREMENTS AND CHARACTERISTICS
OF A EUROPEAN ECONOMIC INTEREST GROUPING (EEIG)

- It is governed by Regulation (EEC) No. 2137/85 of the European Council of July 25, 1985, applicable as from July 1, 1989.

- The EEIGs are a Community legal instrument whose purpose is to facilitate economic activity between its members, particularly at pan-European level.

- It is formed by means of the legalization of a 'grouping contract', which should then be registered in one of the EC Member States (the country in which the grouping's official address is situated).

- It shall be governed by the law of State in which the official address is situated.

- Its activity may only be ancillary to its members' economic activity.

- Companies or natural persons carrying out an economic activity may be members of an EEIG. Other legal bodies governed by private or public law may also be members. The members must have their official address and central administration in the Community. An EEIG may not have non-Community members.

- Its organs are the members acting collectively and the manager or managers. Other bodies may be provided for.

- Its purpose is not to make profits for the grouping itself. If profits or losses are obtained, these will be considered as belonging to the members and will be distributed among them (i.e., it is fiscally transparent).

- It may not invite investment by the public.

- The members are jointly and severally liable for the grouping's debts.

- New members will be admitted by unanimous decision.

- A member may be excluded if he causes or threatens to cause serious disruption or if he seriously fails in his obligations. Unless provided for otherwise, if one member withdraws, the grouping will continue for the other members.

- It may be wound up by unanimous decision of its members, unless the formation contract provides otherwise. It may also be wound up for other reasons, including by court order. If it is wound up, it must be liquidated.

- The EEIGs are subject to national laws governing solvency and cessation of payments.

- The grouping is not a holding company and the members continue to be economically, legally and financially independent. The grouping may not have shared capital.

- At present, the EEIG is the only supranational legal instrument available to carry out cooperation activities between partners from two or more European countries.

Upon returning to their respective factories, each of the four partners appointed one of their purchasing managers to sit on the Raw Material Joint Purchasing Committee. This committee started to act in a very flexible and informal manner. The suppliers' reaction was highly positive from the point of view of the newly grouped buyers. The committee found that by buying together in a coordinated fashion, they could obtain substantial discounts, averaging about 30 percent, on the prices each one had been able to buy at individually.

If we consider that the cost of raw materials accounted for about 70 percent of a paint's sale price, it was clear that the discounts that were being obtained would have a direct and immediate effect on each of the four manufacturers' profit and loss statement.

This excellent and very tangible result of their initial cooperation efforts encouraged them to continue and added more fuel to the cooperation process. As Joseba Garmendia said, "We were like Saint Thomas: seeing is believing. I think that that also marked the point

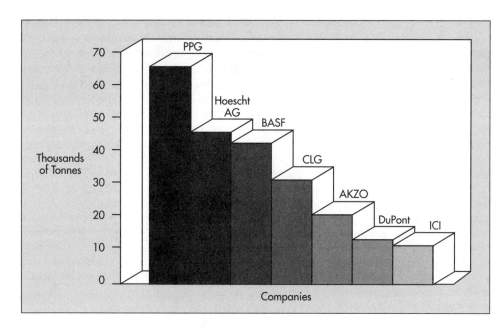

of no return. As soon as it was seen that joint purchasing gave tangible financial benefits, I don't think that any of us had any doubts any more as to the desirability of cooperating. It was clear that cooperating was useful and beneficial and that we should take it further."

More or less at the same time and without there being any specific declaration being made to such effect, Joseba Garmendia took on the responsibility for leading and coordinating the group.

As has already been said, the EC Regulation provided that EEIGs could be formed and formally registered after July 1, 1989 in the Member States that had passed suitable legislation. The corresponding Spanish legislation had been passed in the Congress but was stopped in its passage through the Senate by President Felipe Gonzalez's decision to dissolve Parliament and hold early elections. Consequently, the corresponding Spanish Act had not been enacted. However, on January 1, 1990, the Company Registry Regulation came into force, allowing EEIGs to be registered in Spain even in the absence of the above-stated legislation.

All four partners agreed that Joseba Garmendia should be responsible for forming the EEIG in Spain, no doubt because he and his lawyer had given legal form to the agreement and also because he was a 'neutral' partner between France and Germany, the English partner being the most passive and also the smallest of the four.

Thus, culminating the formation process, the grouping was formally and officially registered in the Bilbao Company Registry on March 13, 1990.

Reflections in Early April, 1990

Joseba Garmendia made an effort to put his ideas in order:

1. When he thought about everything that had been done until now and everything that was happening in the EEIG, the first thing that came to his mind was that, overall, the following changes had occurred:

    (a) Before 1986, Química del Atlántico, S.A. was one of the companies that 'called the shots' in the Spanish paint market: it was a company with a good brand image, three factories, a competent workforce and, above all, a high share of the Spanish paint market. In a Spanish ranking of paint manufacturers, QA held one of the top three places.

    (b) However, with Spain joining the EC, and even though the total sales forecast for 1990 would amount to about 12 billion pesetas, upon looking at Química del Atlántico, S.A.'s position within the entire EC, even though its image and strengths remained intact, its market share was virtually negligible. In an EC wide ranking, it would have come in at about 50th. As has already been indicated, its strategic position with respect to 'globalized' customer segments would probably have become increasingly untenable. In the medium term, difficult to determine exactly, it would perhaps be ruled out as a supplier to the major pan-European manufacturers of automobiles, domestic appliances, metallographic printing, etc.

(c) However, the formation of the EEIG repositioned the four manufacturers together as the fourth European supplier of paints sold to automobile manufacturers, only behind the big multinationals PPG, Hoescht and Basf and ahead of AKZO, Du Pont and ICI (see exhibit 5.) As PPG was a North American company, CLG, EEIG would be the third 'pure European' supplier. As Joseba Garmendia put it: "The alliance put us back among the EC big shots in automobile paints."

This not only seemed to be very important from a strategic viewpoint but it would also perhaps be vital within the framework of the Single Market that would come into force as from January 1, 1993.

Also, the mere announcement of the formation of the alliance to the main pan-European automobile OEMs had managed to get the four partners off the "list of small suppliers to be phased out." It seemed that they had managed to turn the tide in their favour. However, there was still a very important question to be settled: Would the four partners be able to successfully compete together against the big paint multinationals established in Europe? In other words, what could be their specific competitive advantages against suppliers as important as those that have been mentioned in the previous paragraphs?

2. The four partners had accepted that, in a particular country, all operations to be carried out in the car manufacturer's plants would be carried out by the partner located in the country concerned. In other words, none of the four were prepared to start up or supervise logistics operations (storage and unloading paint at destination), dilute 'concentrated' paint manufactured in the home country, make final adjustments, and so on, in any country that was not their own.[5] Only if one of the partners should refuse to supervise such operations for another partner could the said partner seek help from a third party.

Finally, the subject of what to do in the markets of other EC member countries seemed to remain open to future analysis and decision.

3. Thinking about the 'globalized customers' such as the automobile industry, Garmendia wondered what would happen in a case such as the following: An automobile brand decides to buy a certain type of paint for all or several of its European factories. A coordinated tender is sent by the EEIG and the manufacturer agrees to buy at a certain price. As all four companies are independent, it could happen that the sale price is attractive to some of the four but not other(s). Does the company that decides 'not to serve' have the right not to be involved in the operation? If this were to be so, it could harm those who have decided to serve, as the automobile manufacturer may demand or buy for all its plants or not buy for any.

4. Another subject open to discussion was that of technology transfer. For example, Marceau et Fils, S.A. had developed and sold paints for the French high-speed train (TGV). Spain had just decided in 1989 to build and run the high-speed train between Madrid and Seville. This would probably be followed by the Madrid Barcelona line, linking up with the French frontier. According to the agreements, Química del Atlántico, S.A. should supply the special paint for the Spanish high-speed train. How much should it pay Marceau et Fils, S.A. for the formula? Or, in other words, if the sale of high-speed paint to the Spanish railway company (RENFE) produced a certain gross profit, how should this gross profit be distributed between Química del Atlántico, S.A. and Marceau et Fils, S.A.?

5. Up to now, it had not been planned to designate any 'General manager' or 'Executive secretary' at the head of the EEIG. For the moment, Joseba Garmendia was carrying out these functions but could he or did he want to carry on performing them?

6. If a manager was recruited for the EEIG, what should be his/her personal profile? How should he/she be paid? What would be his/her duties? How should his/her performance be monitored?

7. As yet, it had not been decided whether any type of membership fee or economic contribution should be paid up, whether fixed or variable, one-off or regular, by the grouping's partners. So far, each company had paid for its own travel expenses, management time, etc. Should this system continue? Was it fair? Was it practical?

8. Who should be responsible for getting potential customers to approve the paints that the grouping's partners could supply?

---

[5] The final adjustments consisted of adding pine oils, silicones or other ingredients which favoured good application of the paint, in accordance with the temperature, humidity, air cleanness, etc., conditions in force at that time in the factory where cars or other objects were being painted.

EXHIBIT 6
Description of the BRITE/EURAM Programme

A COMMUNITY PROGRAMME FOR SAVING TRADITIONAL INDUSTRY

BRITE/EURAM is an association of programmes aimed at supporting cooperation in industrial research. This project, implemented by the EEC Commission, will be in force for four years after 1989 and will have a budget of almost 500 million ECUs (about 70 billion pesetas) to subsidize á fonds perdu R&D projects that meet the requirements detailed below.

The programme's main goals are to encourage technological research at industry level and to help achieve a greater competitiveness of manufacturing industries on the world markets. It also seeks to promote technology transfer between industrial sectors and particularly between sectors with a high proportion of SMEs who need to have access to new technologies to improve their performance.

The BRITE/EURAM programme seeks to provide, through investigation and technological development, (IDT), the technical resources required to improve products and processes.

The general areas in which BRITE/EURAM projects may be submitted are listed below. Participation in the programme is open to all industrial companies, research centres, and other interested institutions from EEC and EFTA countries.

The general conditions for inclusion are the following:
• The projects should be carried out cooperatively.
• At least two legally independent industrial companies should be involved and they must come from at least two Member States.
• The cooperating companies should be independent. Cooperation between a parent company and its subsidiary in another country will not be accepted.
• The projects should be innovative and not redundant with other R&D projects being performed in other EEC locations. If this is not the case, the proposers should prove that their project concerns an innovative application of a known technique for a product, in the development of a process or a new material.
• The project should last from two to four years.
• The project should have a clear industrial impact and be supported by a financial contribution from the participating companies.
• A research institution receiving in the form of direct payments an industrial financing amounting to 50% from named industrial sponsors involved in the conceptual management of the project, may qualify as an independent industrial company.
• The projects should be large-scale and cover a minimum of ten man-years and have a total cost ranging from one to five million ECUs.
• The consortium should accept joint responsibility for a substantial part of the costs: 50% of the costs will normally be financed by the community.

Proposal design and presentation
The proposals should be presented in three physically separate parts, as follows:

First part: Administrative and financial data. These will refer to the project proposed, cost breakdowns and an abstract or synopsis of the proposal or technical project.

Second part: Description of the proposal. This should include the applicants' purpose in presenting the proposal and their knowledge of the current situation worldwide in the field of research proposed. This part should provide evidence for the economic and technical benefits that the project's application will provide for the Community. and establish detailed technical and management plans to ensure success of the project.

Third part: Details on the association. The purpose of this part is to define the functions of the partners involved in the project and describe the industrial partners intentions as regards the utilization of the results. In this section, the merits of the institutions that will carry out the work and of the personnel that will supervise the research should be described. All the factors that may limit practical utilization of the results should also be pointed out.

After the proposals have been evaluated by a group of qualified experts appointed by the Commission, the Commission will publish a list giving the proposals selected and the names of the participants.

The CDTI (Centre for Technological and Industrial Research) is the (Spanish) body selected by the EEC to present the Spanish project to the Commission.

TECHNOLOGY IN ADVANCED MATERIALS
• Metal materials and metal matrix compounds
• Materials for magnetic, optical, electrical and super-conductivity applications
• Non-metallic materials for high temperatures
• Polymers and organic matrix compounds
• Materials for specialized applications

PRODUCT AND PROCESS DESIGN
AND QUALITY METHODOLOGY
• Quality, reliability and maintainability in industry
• Process and product assurance

APPLICATION OF MANUFACTURING TECHNOLOGIES
• Advanced manufacturing practices for specialized industries, many of which are SMEs
• Flexible material manufacturing processes, particularly manufacturing of clothing and footwear, but also other materials including those used in the preparation of composite materials and in the food and packaging industries

MANUFACTURING PROCESS TECHNOLOGIES
• Surface treatment techniques
• Moulding, assembly and joining
• Chemical processes
• Particle and powder processes

9. The EC had implemented a research aid programme called BRITE-EURAM (see exhibit 6). Only alliances of companies from several EC member countries could apply for these earmarked funds. CLG, EEIG had applied for one million ECUs in aid for a programme at the beginning of 1990. This programme would be implemented by the grouping members in cooperation with the Peugeot Group.

10. Joseba Garmendia was also reflecting on the following situation:

    In 1988, a Turkish trade mission visited Spain. A Turkish trade agent contacted QA and asked whether it would be prepared to supply powdered paint to Turkish companies to paint domestic appliances and automobile parts and components. The agent would provide the customers and would take care of the physical distribution. QA would invoice directly to the customers provided by the agent.

    An agreement was reached and supply was started in 1988. However, Garmendia was aware that by working in this fashion, 'in remote mode' as it were, without giving a good service to the customer 'in situ' adapted to each application's specific circumstances, neither was he providing the excellent level of service that QA usually provided to its customers in Spain nor was he obtaining full benefit of the possible additional market opportunities that could arise in Turkey.

    As QA was sure that it did not want to become a multinational company in the normal meaning of the word, that is, by establishing a local subsidiary in Turkey, the ideal solution would probably be to find a Turkish partner willing to manufacture and serve the Turkish customers.

    Garmendia wondered whether he did or did not have some kind of moral obligation to offer the other EEIG partners part of this business opportunity.

11. Not only had they started joint purchasing but at some moment of particular optimism they had talked of investing together in building a new resin factory which would be a captive supplier of this important raw material to the four grouped manufacturers. The investment would amount to about 400 million pesetas. Was it a good idea?

12. European legislation on the EEIGs stated very explicitly that the grouping's activities should confine themselves to areas that were ancillary to each of the member company's economic activities. However, could one expect that the grouping would become increasingly necessary for all four companies? And if this were so, would it lead to a merger between the companies?

While he reflected on all these issues, and perhaps on a few more that possibly had remained unmentioned or had not had time to come to the surface due to the short time the grouping had been operating, Joseba Garmendia wondered whether the EEIG that had been created could be considered as something solid or not. What difficulties or disagreements could arise between the partners? If disagreements should arise, how should they be settled?

At one point, the thought occurred to him that perhaps the four partners were going through a honeymoon period and that it would not be long before disagreements and disputes started to crop up. What could be done to avoid them and to achieve the consolidation of the EEIG which, in turn, would enable ambitious strategic goals to be achieved?

Perhaps one of the possible solutions would be to consider the EEIG as "a catalytically elastic solution." With this rather cryptic phrase, Garmendia meant that CLG, EEIG would be "like a forum for business opportunities, these being not only opportunities for new projects but also the opportunity to obtain profits by rationalizing production costs, technical homologations by customers, and that it be the companies themselves which, after stating their desire to share in a particular business opportunity, would establish bilaterally, trilaterally or multilaterally relationships with the partner that has presented the project, in accordance with each company's needs." However, if this were to be the case, should all the relationships and actions be optional? Or should there be certain actions that are, "obligatory by the mere fact of being members of CLG, EEIG?"

Whatever the case, Garmendia was convinced that if the grouping had been formed and started up, it had been "to win the war" and not to just win "battles," no matter how important these might be.

EXHIBIT 7
Design, Manufacture and Application of Industrial Paints in the Automobile Industry

DESIGN, MANUFACTURE AND APPLICATION OF INDUSTRIAL PAINTS IN THE AUTOMOBILE INDUSTRY

Although paint companies are usually included in the chemical sector of a country's economic activity, its manufacturing process is basically a physical process, consisting of mixing together a number of ingredients that do not chemically react with each other.

The total process of creating, manufacturing and applying a paint usually comprises four main phases or stages, which may coincide with the company's various technical-production departments.

1. Design or formulation

This department is set in motion by the task of solving a certain painting problem, which may be completely new for the company, or simply the need to improve a certain aspect or attribute of one of the formulae already existing in the company.

Its mission consists of developing a paint formula able to solve the particular problem or need and manufacturing a small sample of the formula in question. In other words, it carries out the product engineering.

Five possible types of ingredient can be used:

1.1 Resins

These give flexibility, adherence and protection (for example, against rusting.) They go from a liquid state to a polymerized state after application.

1.2 Pigments

These give colour.

1.3 Fillers

Such as barite or calcium carbonate. They give consistency.

1.4 Solvent

This is the vehicle that facilitates or enables application. After application, the solvent evaporates and disappears.

1.5 Additives

They give the paints certain properties. They are usually added in relatively small quantities.

2. Determination of the process

The following step, often carried out in another department, consists of determining the exact process to be carried out on an industrial scale to be able to manufacture the paint in question effectively and efficiently. Manufacture is by batches.

The basic task is to determine the machines (and their accessories) to be used, also stating how long each part of the process will last. In other words, it is not enough to carry out the product engineering but it is also necessary to carry out the process engineering.

3. The manufacturing process as such

The Manufacturing or Production Department implements the prescriptions given by the Design and Process Departments in order to obtain the paint in question in industrial quantities.

The manufacturing process as such usually consists of several stages or phases:

3.1 Dispersion/homogenization

This stage, also called sometimes 'First mixture' consists of mixing in a tank part of the ingredients in order to break up the lumps and disperse the pigment, which is the most expensive ingredient per kilogramme of component.

In this first mixture, it is customary to add 100% of the total pigment that the finished product will have, 100% of the fillers, about 60% of the resin and 20% of the solvent. The rest of these ingredients and the additives will be added towards the end of the process (stages further on).

3.2 Grinding or disintegration

The pigment's molecular dispersion is intensified in suitable machines, although *not* to the point of breaking its molecular structure.

3.3 Transformation/dilution tank

In this stage, the rest of the solvent and resin is added, in addition to the additives required to give the paint being manufactured required specific properties.

At this point, the actual characteristics of the paint manufactured are checked out in order to verify that it meets the prescribed specifications. It is at this point also that the colour can be controlled, in order to ensure that the specific batch has the exact hue prescribed.

3.4 Packaging

After verifying the characteristics of the batch that has been manufactured, it is then packaged.

In the case of industrial paints, including the paint supplied to the automobile manufacturers, the product is usually packaged in 200 litre barrels.

Continued

EXHIBIT 7—*Continued*
Design, Manufacture and Application of Industrial Paints in the Automobile Industry

4. The application process

If the paint has been manufactured for use in home decorating, it is packaged in smaller containers which will be sold through decorator shops and it will be applied by a professional painter or by the user himself.

However in the case of industrial paints and particularly in the case of the supply of paints to automobile manufacturers, the process is only completed when the paint is applied.

In other words, after the manufacturing process as such, carried out in the paint manufacturer's plant, there is another application process ('painting') which is carried out in the automobile manufacturer's plant.

Over the years, the paint manufacturers' responsibilities within the automobile production plant have steadily increased.

Specifically, at the beginning of 1990, the paint application process in an automobile production plant usually consisted of five stages:

4.1 Degreasing, phosphating, washing and drying of bodywork.

4.2 Application of the primer by means of a cataphoresis process consisting of immersing the bodywork in a large tank (up to 500 litre) to apply a very thin and fragile first coat of a neutral-coloured paint which gives it rust-resistant properties. The immersion is electrostatic, in other words, an electric charge is applied so that the paint adheres better to all parts of the bodywork.

4.3 Application of the sealant

This second coat of paint, also of a neutral colour (i.e., it is usually the same colour, regardless of the colour of the top coat that will be applied in the following stage (4.4)).

It gives body and elasticity to the paint, smoothing over rough spots and improving the adhesiveness of the top coat that will be applied next.

4.4 Application of the top coat

This is the coat that gives the colour that the buyer of the vehicle sees and appreciates. It may be an opaque or metallized coating.

4.5 Final bake, in which the polymerization takes place.

It should be stressed that the application process of the various coats of paint is a very important process for the automobile manufacturer, both as regards the maintenance of a certain production rate on the assembly line and as regards the quality of the final product.

Thus, if at one time the paint manufacturer could have thought that his mission ended when he delivered the 200 litre barrels of paint at the automobile manufacturer's goods inwards warehouse, over the years there has been a growing co-involvement process of the paint manufacturer in the final result obtained in the application of his products.

Therefore, the paint manufacturers usually have a technical representative, helped by one or two assistants, also employed by the paint manufacturer in each of the automobile production plants supplied by them. The mission of these people is to work closely with the automobile manufacturer's personnel in order to ensure that the application process takes place smoothly.

The technical representative usually has a physical space where he can 'correct the barrels' in at least two ways:

(a) Because the paint in the barrels supplied by the paint manufacturer usually has a higher viscosity or less liquid consistency than the viscosity for application. This means that solvents must be added to the barrels' contents to give them the optimal viscosity for application.

(b) Because the particular circumstances under which the paint is applied (relative humidity, air temperature, etc.) may vary from one day to the next as a result of which the paint must be adapted to the circumstances prevailing at any one time.

The managers of paint manufacturing companies admit that although they try to bring to bear all their scientific abilities, the application of paint continues to have something of alchemy, sometimes bordering on magic, about it.

It is therefore obvious that the paint manufacturer's technical representative in the automobile production plant plays a key role in two areas:

(a) In the technical area as such, due to his ability to solve or help to solve any problem that might crop up.

(b) In the human area, by maintaining an ongoing and close relationship with the automobile manufacturer's personnel in particular with the supervisors and managers responsible for the smooth operation of the painting line.

It is in this second area that the technical representative's people skills, the languages he may speak and a facility for cultural empathy may be decisive for the continued presence of a certain paint brand as supplier to an automobile manufacturer.

EXHIBIT 8
The Process of Selling Paints to Automobile Manufacturers

THE PROCESS OF SELLING PAINTS TO AUTOMOBILE MANUFACTURERS

The automobile manufacturers as a market segment of the paint manufacturers is characterized by:

- being composed of a few customers
- being present in a number of countries, i.e., being globalized
- able to buy paints in large volumes
- but very demanding, both from the financial viewpoint (mainly sales prices and conditions of payment) and from the technical viewpoint. Within the technical requirements, one should differentiate between those referring to the paint itself, those referring to the supply system (Just-in-Time, etc.) and those referring to paint application.

Using automobile manufacturer terminology, the paints are material production, that is, a supply provided by a supplier which is added to the final product.

As opposed to the 'non-production material', which are the ancilliary materials required to carry out the automobile manufacturing process but which are not included in the final product, that is, they are eliminated before the car is sold to the final consumer.

Stages in the buying process

1. Homologation of the paint manufacturer as possible supplier

The automobile manufacturer starts by carrying out an indepth analysis of the potential supplier as regards its technical capacity, economic capacity, organization level, quality assurance system, etc.

Nowadays, it is almost impossible to obtain new approvals in Europe. However, paint manufacturers, particularly the small and medium-sized manufacturers feel a growing threat of losing their approval, due to the strong tendency of automobile manufacturers to reduce the number of suppliers in general, including paint suppliers.

With the forthcoming single European market, which will come into force on 1/1/1993, this pressure has been stepped up considerably and the European manufacturers wish to only deal with suppliers able to serve them at a pan-European level.

By way of a final point, we will stress that the approval is of the supplier as a company, and not of a specific paint.

2. High level political decision

In a second phase, the automobile manufacturers take an initial decision as to rough percentages into which they wish to divide their paint purchases among the approved manufacturers.

One could perhaps make a distinction here between two major types of decisions or influences: those coming from the most senior levels of the company and those that come from the Purchasing Department. Consequently, in this second level, factors such as the relationships between the respective plants' parent companies (in Germany or in France...), the relationships established at local level, internal policies as regards the allocation of purchasing quota among the suppliers, and, of course, the prices and conditions the paint manufacturer is able to offer come into play.

3. Decision with respect to a specific product

Finally, the automobile manufacturer will allocate the purchase of a particular colour for a particular car model. Of course, the 'neutral' colour paints to be used in the cataphoresis (1st coat) or the sealant (2nd coat) or the waxes, etc. are also allocated.

At this level, the process is usually the following: At any time, which may be just before launching a new car model or before a restyling or at any time in which the automobile manufacturer wishes to launch on the market a new palette of colours for a particular model, the manufacturer will issue a set of specifications detailing the characteristics of the paint to be purchased.

In some cases, the paint manufacturer, working closely with the automobile manufacturer's design team, may manage to tip the balance in its favour by arranging that the specifications prescribed match better the characteristics of the paint that he is able to manufacture, although this may only occur when the supplier is able to offer some kind of innovation.

The usual procedure is that all the approved suppliers have access to the set of specifications issued. The suppliers send back an offer which obviously must fulfill the prescribed specifications.

From the technical and specifications viewpoint, what the customer usually asks for could be defined as "an unstable balance of characteristics," such as:

- gloss, colour and persistence over time
- ease of industrial-scale application
- hardness
- anti-rust or anti-acid protection
- no cratering

Continued

EXHIBIT 8—*Continued*
The Process of Selling Paints to Automobile Manufacturers

- no dripping of the paint (i.e., no tear or sheet formation)
- no bubbling due to gas being given off during the curing stage
- impact flexibility

Together with its offer, the supplier also has to send a sample which will be analysed by the customer's laboratory to verify that the paint ordered really has the characteristics and features asked for. This is normally checked out using standard and ad hoc testing procedures (STM standard, stability tests in special cubicles with saline mist or CO_2, Florida Test, etc.).

In fact, the continuous increase in the standards demanded by automobile manufacturers is one of the paint manufacturers' most powerful incentives to innovate. After achieving an innovation, the supplier may then apply it to other customer segments that are less demanding technologically. The next step is to perform a test run on the production line. The major automobile manufacturers (more than three million vehicles/year) usually have a special testing line.

If the paint passes the test, the Purchasing Department is authorized to send orders to the paint suppliers. This is usually done on the basis of allocating a certain paint hue for a certain model to a specific supplier. As the final consumers' preferences vary (for example, normally more white or red cars are sold than blue or green cars) the allocation of a particular colour implies the allocation of a certain purchasing volume. An average car's 'skin' usually requires purchasing and applying about 6.6 lbs. of primer (cataphoresis), about 8.8 lbs of filler-sealant and a further 8.8 lbs of top coat. These figures do not include the paint used for other components and miscellaneous vehicle parts.

Normally, the Purchasing Department sends an order for 3 months, of which the first month is 'firm' and the other 2 months are 'orientative.' The scheduling is reviewed monthly, except in the case of the cataphoresis primer, in which, due to the tank's large capacity, the contracts are medium and long-term, with annual price reviews.

As the Industrial Paints Sales Manager (including automobile) of Química del Atlántico, S.A. said:

This process is neither rigid nor excessively formalistic but is constantly evolving in a constant search for improvement. Thanks to a constant and close contact between supplier and customer, the former must strive to find out what concerns the latter, that is, what types of improvements in the characteristics of the paints used at any particular time may sufficiently interest the buyer to spark off a new buying process which, with luck, may culminate in the replacement of another supplier's paints by his paints.

Of course, all the suppliers are trying to do the same!

In addition to influencing purchasing volume through technical characteristics, the supplier may also influence it through aesthetic features, that is, through colour hues:

The subject of hues is very complex and also absolutely vital. Some pigment compositions may be difficult to obtain or imitate because the number of base pigments is limited for technical reasons (a new pigment requires lengthy and detailed tests to determine its durability, persistence of gloss, . . .). Therefore, the paint manufacturer usually takes the initiative to propose particular hues to the manufacturer's design department. If they are accepted, the paint manufacturer may have a certain advantage as he already knows the specific pigment composition that gives that exact hue.

Finally, the paint manufacturer can influence the volumes purchased by the automobile manufacturer through his technical representative who is in daily contact with the plant's painting team.

Situations may arise in either direction: the workers and supervisors on a line may work more or less openly against a supplier and find all sorts of minor defects and failures. Or, vice versa, even though Purchasing has established that the purchases of a certain paint be divided between two suppliers according to a certain percentage (e.g., 50%/50%), in the end, one of them sells 60% and the other 40% because the painting line personnel prefer to use the former's paints.

Of course, the variations in the quantities sold by each supplier may also be due to errors or mistakes by the paint manufacturer. Química del Atlántico, S.A.'s industrial director classified the possible errors or mistakes as follows:

Venial sin: when the automobile manufacturer's laboratory detects some variation or analytic difference in the paint that the supplier has been selling him month after month without this difference being detected in the painting line.

Mortal sin: when incidents occur in the painting line which require the painted products to be reworked or which cause complaints on the quality of the work done (for example, the appearance of craters or other failures).

Excommunication: when incidents occur that cause a decrease in the line speed or which even make it necessary to stop the line.

■ TAURUS HUNGARIAN RUBBER WORKS: IMPLEMENTING A STRATEGY FOR THE 1990s†

By Joseph Wolfe, Gyula Bosnyak, and Janos Vecsenyi

Many major decisions had been made by Taurus in the two years since its top management planning session. Yet the basic implementation of its diversification strategy had not been accomplished. Gyula Bosnyak, Director of Corporate Development Strategic Planning, recognized both the timing and the enormity of the events and issues involved. In 1988 the Hungarian government had passed its Corporation Law which put all state-owned firms on notice to privatize and recapitalize themselves. Not only did the firm have to deal with the mechanics of going public, it had to obtain the ideal mix of debt and equity capital to ensure solid growth for a company which was operating in a stagnant economy and a low growth industry. Top management was also concerned about the route it should follow to invigorate the company. It was

†**Source:** ©1991, 1992 by Joseph Wolfe, Gyula Bosnyak, and Janos Vecsenyi. This case was prepared by Joseph Wolfe, Gyula Bosnyak, and Janos Vecsenyi as the basis for class discussion rather than to illustrate either effective or ineffective handling of an administrative situation.

accepted that Taurus had to maintain or even improve its international competitiveness, and that it had to diversify away from its traditional dependence on the manufacturing of truck and farm tyres.

Rather than viewing this situation as a threat, Gyula had seen this as an opportunity for Taurus to deal with its working capital problem as well as to begin serious diversification efforts away from its basically non-competitive and highly threatened commercial tyre manufacturing operation. Now, in spring 1990, he was beginning to sort out his company's opinions before making his recommendations to Laszlo Geza, Vice President of Taurus's Technical Rubber Products Division, and Laszlo Palotas, the company's newly elected president.

Upon the nationalization of all rubber firms after the Second World War, the Hungarian government pursued a policy of extensive growth for a number of years. From 1950 to 1970 annual production increases of 12.5% a year were common while the rubber sector's employment and gross fixed asset value increased on average approximately 6.2% and 15.7% per year. Although growth was rapid, great inefficiencies were incurred. Utilization rates were low and productivity lagged by about 1.5-3.0 times that obtained by comparable socialist and advanced capitalist countries. Little attention was paid to rationalizing either production or the product line as sales to the Hungarian and CMEA countries appeared to support the sector's activities. At various times the nationalized firm

Mechanical goods	Hard rubber products
Latex foam products	Flooring
Shoe products	Cements
Athletic goods	Drug sundries
Toys	Pulley belts
Sponge rubber	Waterproof insulation
Insulated wire and cable	Conveyor belts
Footwear	Shock absorbers and
Waterproofed fabrics	vibration dampeners

EXHIBIT 1
Major Non-tyre Rubber Uses

produced condoms, bicycle and automobile tyres, rubber toys, boots, and raincoats (see exhibit 1).

During this period the government also restructured its rubber industry. In 1963 Budapest's five rubber manufacturers, PALMA, Heureka, Tauril, Emerge, and Cordatic, were merged into one company called the National Rubber Company. Purchasing, cash management, and investment were centralized, and a central trade and research and development apparatus was created. Contrary to the normal way of conducting its affairs, however, the company pioneered the use of strategic planning when the classic type of centralized planning was still the country's ruling mechanism.

In 1973 the company changed its name to the Taurus Hungarian Rubber Works, operating rubber processing plants in Budapest, Nyiregyhaza, Szeged, Vac, and Mugi as well as a machine and mould factory in Budapest.

As shown in exhibit 2 below and tables 5 and 6 at the end of this case, Taurus operated four separate divisions while engaging in a number of joint ventures. Sales increased annually to the 20.7 billion forint mark with an

EXHIBIT 2
Organizational Structure

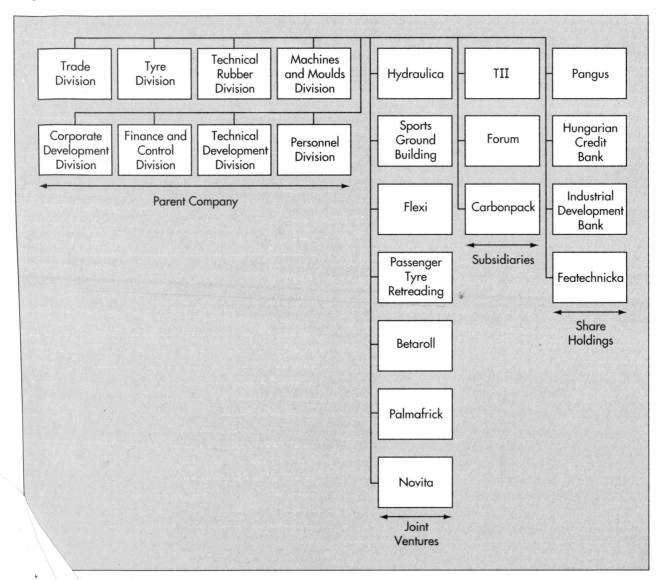

increasing emphasis on international business. (See tables 9 and 10 at the end of this case for Taurus's income statement and balance sheet.)

Tyre Division

The tyre division manufactured tyres for commercial vehicles after having phased out its production of automobile tyres in the mid-1970s. Truck tyres, as either cross-ply or all-steel radials, accounted for about 34% of the division's sales. Farm tyres were its other major product category as either textile radials or cross-ply tyres. Farm tyres were about 20% of the division's sales in 1988. A smaller product category included tyre retreading, inner tubes, and fork lift truck tyres. About 58% of the division's volume were export sales, of which the following countries constituted the greatest amount (in millions of forints):

United States	351.7
Algeria	298.2
Czechoslovakia	187.3
West Germany	183.5
Yugoslavia	172.0

The division had finished a capacity expansion financed by the World Bank in the all-steel radial truck tyre operation. Eleven new tyres within the "Taurus Top Tyre" brand were scheduled for the market of which two were completed in 1988 and another three in early 1990. The division was also developing a new super-single tyre under a licensing agreement with an American tyre manufacturer.

Technical Rubber Division

This division manufactured and marketed an assortment of rubber hoses, air-springs for trucks and buses, conveyor belts, waterproof sheeting, and the PALMA line of camping gear. The PALMA camping gear line had a 15% world market share while the company's rotary hose business was a world leader with 40% of all international sales. The demand for high-pressure and large-bore hoses was closely related to offshore drilling activity while the sale of air-springs for commercial vehicles was expected to increase as this technology gained increasing acceptance with vehicle manufacturers. The Soviet Union was this division's largest customer with 1988 sales of 380 million forints. In recent years, sales within the division had been distributed in the following fashion:

Large-bore high-pressure hoses	6.7%
Rotary hoses	27.1%
Hydraulic hoses	14.7%
Camping goods	18.0%
Waterproof sheeting	13.9%
Air springs	5.3%
Conveyor belts	14.3%

Machine and Moulds Division

This division manufactured products which were used in-house as part of Taurus' manufacturing process as well as products used by others. About 70% of its sales were for export and its overall sales were distributed as follows in 1988:

Technical rubber moulds	24.0%
Polyurethane moulds	17.0%
Machines and components	25.0%
Tyre curing moulds	34.0%

Trade Division

The Trade Division conducted CMEA purchases and sales for Taurus as well as performing autonomous distribution functions for other firms. Its activities served other Taurus divisions as well as those outside the company. It was expected that this division would continue to function as the Taurus purchasing agent while increasing its outside trading activities; its status regarding CMEA trafficking was in a state of flux.

Implementing the Taurus Strategy of Strategic Alliances

Gyula Bosnyak could see that the general rubber industry had fallen from a better than average industry growth performance in the 1960-70 period to one that was far inferior to the industrial average during the 1980-87 period (see table 7). He also saw that other industries, such as data processing, aircraft, medical equipment, and telecommunication equipment, had obtained sizeable growth rates from 1977-87. Moreover, he was extremely aware of the increasing concentration occurring in the tyre industry through the formation of joint ventures, mergers, co-operative arrangements, and acquisitions (see exhibit 3 and tables 3 and 4). It was obvious that at least the rubber industry's tyre segment had passed into its mature stage. In response to this, most major rubber companies had diversified away from the heavy competition within the industry itself, as well as attempting to find growth markets for their rubber production capacity. For the year 1987 alone Gyula listed the various strategic alliances shown in

EXHIBIT 3
Recent Activities of Various Tyre and Rubber Companies

RECENT ACTIVITIES OF VARIOUS TYRE AND RUBBER COMPANIES

Bridgestone Corporation: Bridgestone's acquisition of the Firestone Tire and Rubber Company in 1988 for $2.6 billion vaulted it into a virtual tie with Goodyear as the world's second largest tyre company, behind Michelin. The acquisition proved troublesome for Bridgestone, with Firestone losing about $100 million in 1989 causing the parent company's 1989 profits to fall to about $250 million on sales of $10.7 billion. Bridgestone had already invested $1.5 billion in upgrading Firestone's deteriorated plants and an additional $2.5 billion would be needed to bring all operations up to Bridgestone's quality standards. North American sales were $3.5 billion and the firm planned to quadruple the output of its La Vergen, Tennessee plant. Bridgestone was attempting to increase its share of the American tyre market, while slowly increasing its share of the European market as Japanese cars increased their sales there. In mid-1989 nine top executives were forced to resign or accept reassignment over disputes about the wisdom of the company's aggressive growth goals. Bridgestone was a major player in Asia, the Pacific, and South America where Japanese cars and trucks were heavily marketed.

Continental Gummi-Werke AG: Continental was West Germany's largest tyre manufacturer and was number two in European sales. It purchased General Tyre from Gencord in June 1987 for $625 million and was known as a premium quality tyre manufacturer. Continental entered a $200 million joint radial tyre venture in 1987 with the Toyo Tyre and Rubber Company and Yokohama Rubber Company for the manufacture of tires installed on Japanese cars being shipped to the American market. Another plan of the venture entailed manufacturing radial truck and bus tires in the United States.

Cooper Tire and Rubber Company: This relatively small American firm had been very successful by specializing in the replacement tyre market. This segment accounted for about 80% of its sales and nearly half its output was sold as private-labelled merchandise. Cooper had recently expanded its capacity by 12% with about 10% more capacity completed in 1990. About 60% of its sales were for passenger tyres while the remainder were for buses and heavy trucks. The company was attempting to acquire a medium truck tyre plant in Natchez, Mississippi to enable it to cover the tyre spectrum more completely.

Goodyear Tire and Rubber Co: Goodyear diversified into chemicals and plastics, and a California to Texas oil pipeline, as well as into the aerospace industry. Automotive products, which included tyres, accounted for 68% of sales and 76% of operating profits. Recent sales growth had come from African and Latin American tyre sales where the company had a dominant market share. Plant expansions were made in Canada and South Korea (12,000 tyres daily per plant) during 1991. Goodyear was attempting to sell off its All America pipeline for about $1.4 billion to reduce its $275 million per year interest charges on $3.5 billion worth of debt.

Michelin et Cie: Although it lost $1.5 billion between 1980 and 1984, Michelin had become profitable again. In late 1988 the company acquired Uniroyal/Goodrich for $690 million which made it the world's largest tyre company. Uniroyal had merged in August 1986 with the B F Goodrich Company, creating a company where 29% of its output was in private brands. Passenger and light truck tyres were sold in both the United States and overseas, and sales grew 44.5% although profits fell 11.1%. Michelin entered a joint venture with Okamoto of Japan to double that company's capacity to 24,000 tyres a day. While a large company, Michelin was much stronger in the truck tyre segment than it was in the passenger tyre segment.

Pirelli: After having been frustrated in its attempts to acquire Firestone, Pirelli purchased the Armstrong Tyre Company for $190 million in 1988 to gain a foothold in the North American market. Armstrong had been attempting to diversify out of the tyre and rubber industry by selling off its industrial tyre plant in March 1987. Pirelli, which was strong in the premium tyre market, obtained a company whose sales were equally divided between the original equipment and replacement markets and one which had over 500 retail dealers. In the acquisition process Pirelli obtained a headquarters building in Connecticut, three tyre plants, one tyre textile plant, and one truck tyre factory. Armstrong's 1988 sales were $500 million.

EXHIBIT 4
Strategic Alliances in 1987

Goodrich (USA) and Uniroyal (Great Britain) operate as a joint venture.

Pirelli (Italy) acquired Armstrong (USA).

Firestone (USA) acquired by Bridgestone (Japan) which has another type of alliance with Trells Nord (Sweden).

General Tire (USA) acquired by Continental Tyre (West Germany) which, in turn operates in co-operation with Yokohama Tyre (Japan). Continental also owns Uniroyal Englebert Tyre.

Toyo (Japan) operates in co-operation with Continental Tyre (West Germany) while also operating a joint venture in Nippon Tyre (Japan) with Goodyear (USA).

Michelin (France) operates in co-operation with Michelin Okamoto (Japan).

Sumitoma (Japan) operates in co-operation with Nokia (Finland), Trells Nord (Sweden), and BTR Dunlop (Great Britain).

exhibit 4, while exhibit 5 reviews the diversification activities of the company's major tyre competitors in 1989.

Within the domestic market, various other Hungarian rubber manufacturers had surpassed Taurus in their growth rates as they jettisoned low profit lines and adopted newer ones possessing greater growth rates. Taurus' market share of the Hungarian rubber goods industry had slowly eroded since 1970 and this erosion increased greatly in the decade of the 1980s due to the creation of a number of smaller start-up rubber companies, encouraged by Hungary's new private laws. While the company's market share stood at about 68% in 1986, Gyula estimated that it would only fall another 4% by 1992. Table 8 displays the figures and estimates he created for his analysis.

With the aid of a major consulting firm, Taurus had recently conducted an in-depth analysis of its business portfolio (see exhibit 6). It was concluded that the company operated in a number of highly attractive markets, but that its competitive position needed to be improved for most product lines. Accordingly, emphasis was to be placed on improving the competitiveness of the company's current product lines and businesses. With 1991 as the target year, Taurus was to implement two types of projects: software projects dealing with quality assurance programmes, management development and staff training efforts, and the implementation of a management information system; and hardware projects dealing with upgrading the agricultural tyre compounding process as well as upgrades in the infrastructures of various plants.

EXHIBIT 5
Major 1988 Rubber
Company Diversifications

Rubber company	Non-tyre sales (%)	Major diversification efforts
Goodyear	27.0	Packing materials, Chemicals
Firestone	30.0	Vehicle service
Cooper	20.0	Laser technology
Armstrong	N/A	Heat transmission equipment
General Tire	68.0	Electronics, Sporting goods
Carlisle	88.0	Computer technology, Roofing materials
Bridgestone	30.0	Chemicals, Sporting goods
Yokohama	26.0	Sporting goods, Aluminum products
Trelleborg	97.0	Mining, Ore processing
Artimos	N/A	Food processing
Nokia	98.0	Electronics, Inorganic chemicals

EXHIBIT 6
Taurus's Product Portfolio

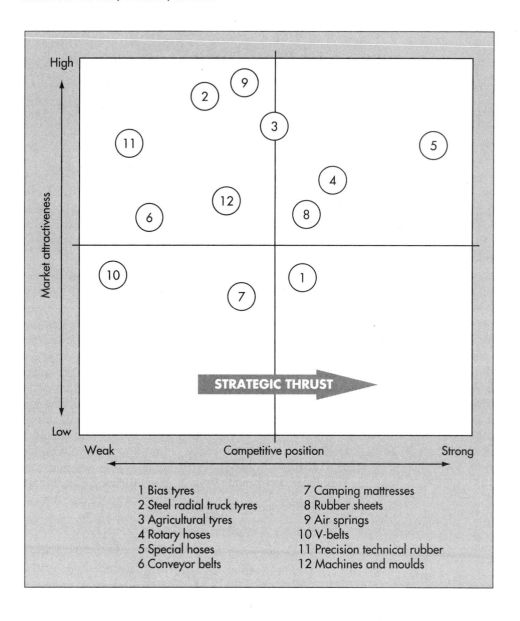

1 Bias tyres
2 Steel radial truck tyres
3 Agricultural tyres
4 Rotary hoses
5 Special hoses
6 Conveyor belts
7 Camping mattresses
8 Rubber sheets
9 Air springs
10 V-belts
11 Precision technical rubber
12 Machines and moulds

Fundamental to the desire within Taurus to be more growth oriented was its newly-enunciated strategy shown in exhibit 7. The company was seeking strategic alliances for certain business lines rather than growth through internal development which had been its previous growth strategy. While it was felt that internal development possessed lower risks, as it basically extended the company's current areas of expertise, benefited the various product lines already in existence, and better served its present customer base while simultaneously using the company's store of management knowledge and wisdom, internal development possessed a number of impediments to the current desires within Taurus for accelerated growth. Paramount was the belief that management was too preoccupied with current activities to pay attention to new areas outside the specific areas of expertise.

Now ranked at thirtieth in size in the rubber industry, Taurus found it was facing newly formed international combinations with enormous financial strength, strong market positions, and diverse managerial assets. Given the high degree of concentration in the rubber industry, and that even the largest firms had to accomplish international co-operative relationships, Taurus

EXHIBIT 7
Taurus's Strategy
for the 1990s

The decade of the 1990s is predicted to be a busy period for the rubber sector world-wide. There are strong factors of concentration in traditional manufacturing businesses and particularly in tyre operations. The role of substitute products is growing in several areas. On the other hand, the fast end-of-century growth of industrial sectors is expected to stimulate the development of sophisticated special rubber products. In the face of these challenges, Taurus bases its competitive strategy on the following:

— A continuous structural development programme has been started aimed at *increasing the company's competitive advantage* with scope to cover a range from manufacturing processes, through quality assurance, to the reinforcement of strengths and elimination of weaknesses.

— *Efficiency* is a prerequisite of any business activity. The company portfolio must be kept in good balance.

— Associated with profitability, the company keeps developing its sphere of operations, determining the direction of diversification according to the criteria of potential growth and returns.

— Our pursuit of competitive advantages and diversification must be supported by a powerfully expanding *system of strategic alliance and co-operation.*

determined that it too should seek co-operative, strategic alliances. In seeking these affiliations, the company would be open and responsive to any type of reasonable alternative or combination that might be offered, including participation with companies in the creation of new, jointly held companies, whether they were related or unrelated to the rubber industry. The only real criteria for accepting an alliance would be its profitability and growth potential.

In pursuing strategic alliances Gyula noted that the bargaining position differed greatly between the various business lines in the Taurus portfolio. As an aid to understanding its bargaining strategy with potential allies, the Taurus businesses were placed into one of three categories as shown in exhibit 6. Category I types were those where the Taurus bargaining position was relatively weak as it felt it had little to offer a potential suitor. Category II types were those where Taurus could contribute a sizeable "dowry" and had much to offer the potential ally, while Category III types were those businesses with mixed or balanced strengths and weaknesses.

The problem was how to restructure the company's current divisional activities to make them into rational and identifiable business units to outside investors, as well as serving Taurus's own needs for internal logic and market focus. Which product lines should be grouped together and what should be the basis for their grouping? Gyula saw several different ways to do this.

Products could be grouped based on a common production process or technology. They could be based on their capital requirements, grouped by markets served, or trade relations which have already been established by Taurus. Depending on how he defined the company's new SBUs, he knew he would be making some major decisions about the attractiveness of the company's assets as well as defining the number and the nature of Taurus's potential strategic alliances. As he explained:

"If I create an SBU which manufactures hoses, a good joint venture partner might be someone who manufactures couplings for hoses—this would be a match that would be good for both of us and it would be a relatively safe investment. If on the other hand I create a business which can use the same hoses in the offshore mining and drilling business, and this is a business that is really risky but one that could really develop in the future, what do I look for in partners? I need to find an engineering company that is undertaking large mining exploration projects. For every type of combination like this where I can create, I have to ask myself each time 'What are the driving questions?'"

In reviewing the company's portfolio he immediately saw three new SBUs that he could propose to Laszlo Geza. One SBU would serve the automobile industry through the manufacture of rubber profiles (rubber seals and grommets which provide watertight fits for car windows), V-belts for engines and engine components such as their air conditioning, power steering, and

EXHIBIT 8
Cooperation Potentials
by Product Line

Product Lines	Co-operation category		
	I	II	III
Truck Tyres	•		
Farm Tyres			•
Rotary hoses		•	
Speciality hoses			•
Hydraulic hoses	•		
Waterproofing sheets		•	
Belting	•		
Camping goods			•
Air-springs			•
Machines and moulds		•	
Precision goods			•

electrical units, and special engine seals. Another unit would serve the truck and bus industry by manufacturing the bellows for articulated buses and air springs for buses, heavy duty trucks, and long haul trailers. The last new SBU would target the firm's adhesives and rubber sheeting at the construction and building industry where the products could be used to waterproof flatroofs as well as serving as chemical-proof and watertight liners in irrigation projects and hazardous waste landfill sites. Although top management knew that "the house wasn't on fire" and that a careful and deliberate pace could be taken regarding the company's restructuring, Gyula wanted to make sure the proposals he was about to make to the Technical Rubber Products Division were sound and reasonable. Moreover, the success or failure of this restructuring would set the tone for future diversification efforts.

TABLE 1
Predicted World
Consumption of Rubber
(in millions of metric tons)

Type	1986	1987	1988	1989	1990	1991	1992
Synthetic	9.5	9.8	9.8	9.9	9.9	10.0	10.0
Natural	4.5	4.6	4.9	5.1	5.4	5.7	5.9
TOTAL	14.0	14.4	14.7	15.0	15.3	15.7	15.9

TABLE 2
Predicted Changes in Rubber
Demand by Geographic
Area (in thousands of metric
tons)

Geographic Area	1987	1992	Change (%)
North America	3,395	3,432	1.09
Latin America	788	944	19.80
Western Europe	2,460	2,953	20.04
Africa and Middle East	259	324	25.10
Asia and Oceania	3,060	3,541	15.72
Socialist Countries	4,057	4,706	16.00
TOTAL	14,019	15,900	13.42

Company	1984		1988	
	Sales (billion)	Profits (million)	Sales (billion)	Profits (million)
B. F. Goodrich (US)	3.40	60.6	n/a*	n/a
Bridgestone (Japan)	3.38	65.1	9.30	310.2
Cooper (US)	0.56	23.9	0.73	35.0
Firestone (US)	4.16	102.0	n/a**	n/a
GenCorp (US)	2.73	7.2	0.50	n/a***
Goodyear (US)	10.24	391.7	10.90	330.0
Michelin (France)	5.08	(256.5)	8.70	397.4
Pirelli (Italy)	3.50	72.0	7.01	172.1
Taurus (Hungary)	0.26	11.5	0.38	9.0
Uniroyal (US)	2.10	77.1	2.19	11.8

*Merged with Uniroyal in 1987.
**Acquired by Bridgestone in 1988.
***Acquired by Continental in 1987.

TABLE 3
Selected Company Sales and Profits (in US Dollars)

Top Market Shares in World Tyre Market		
Company	1985	1990
Goodyear	20.0%	17.2%
Michelin	13.0	21.3
Bridgestone	8.0	17.2

TABLE 4
Top Market Shares in World Tyre Market

Market	1980	1982	1984	1985	1986	1987	1988	1989
Export	2,560	2,588	3,704	4,055	4,517	5,349	6,843	7,950
Domestic	7,890	9,024	9,381	9,979	11,174	12,255	12,056	12,716
Total	10,450	11,612	13,085	14,034	15,691	17,604	18,899	20,666

TABLE 5
Total Company Sales (in millions of Forints)

	Tyres	Technical Rubber	Machines and Moulds	Trade
Revenues	8,547	7,183	242	4,694
Assets:				
Gross fixed assets	5,519	2,787	292	—
Net fixed assets	3,016	1,120	135	—
Inventones	1,126	545	104	—
Employees	4,021	3,851	552	198

Note: Machines and moulds sales includes output used in-house.

TABLE 6
Selected 1989 Division Performance Information (in millions of Forints)

TABLE 7
Comparative Average
Annual Growth Rates

Period	Rubber sector (%)	All industry (%)
1960-70	8.3	6.8
1970-80	4.0	4.1
1980-87	1.7	4.3
Average	5.0	5.1

TABLE 8
Percentage Share of Rubber
Goods Production between
Taurus and All Other
Hungarian Rubber
Manufacturers

	1970	1980	1986	1992
Taurus	95	80	68	65
All others	5	20	32	35

TABLE 9
Taurus's Income Statements,
1987-89 (in millions of
Forints)

Sources: 1987 and 1988 data
from 1988 company *Annual
Report;* 1989 data from internal
reports.

	1987	1988	1989
Basic activities	10,637.7	12,193.4	14,918.6
Non-basic activities	6,270.0	6,705.5	5,747.0
Total revenues	16,907.7	18,898.9	20,665.6
Direct costs	12,022.1	13,095.0	13,819.6
Indirect costs	4,235.6	4,963.3	5,714.8
Production and operating costs	16,257.7	18,058.3	19,534.4
Before tax profit	650.0	840.6	1,131.2
Taxes	290.0	386.0	491.4
After tax profit	360.0	454.6	639.8

Note: 1987 data adjusted to reflect the effects of tax changes initiated in 1988.

Assets	1987	1988	1989
Cash, bank deposits, and receivables	2,491.1	3,157.0	3,763.2
Inventories	2,749.6	2,803.8	2,888.3
Other current assets and capital investments	577.4	739.7	938.6
Current assets	5,818.1	6,700.5	7,590.1
Property	2,480.7	2,772.0	3,008.6
Machines and equipment	4,718.2	6,202.6	6,357.9
Fleet	46.3	46.4	48.6
Other	27.9	25.9	25.6
Fixed asset value	7,273.1	9,046.9	9,440.7
Accumulated depreciation	3,977.0	4,303.8	4,687.7
Unaccomplished projects	541.4	272.2	541.6
Total fixed assets	3,837.5	5,015.3	5,294.6
Total assets	9,655.6	11,715.8	12,884.6
Liabilities			
Short-term loans	1,531.7	1,684.3	1,444.0
Accounts payable	922.7	1,378.5	2,072.8
Accrued expenses	95.8	141.4	151.6
Provisions for taxes	(274.1)	195.0	34.7
1989 long-term debt service	267.0	129.9	314.3
Other liabilities due within 12 months	58.0	5.4	242.1
Total current liabilities	2,601.1	3,534.5	4,259.5
Provisions and non-current liabilities	61.4	335.1	0.4
Long-term loans	725.4	1,453.1	1,815.7
Equities and funds reserve	5,907.7	5,938.5	6,169.2
Current year after tax profit	360.0	454.6	639.9
Total equity and funds	6,267.7	6,393.1	6,809.0
Total liabilities	9,655.6	11,715.8	12,884.6

Note: 1987 data adjusted to reflect the effects of tax changes initiated in 1988.

TABLE 10
Taurus's Balance Sheet, 1987-89 (in millions of Forints)

ROYAL BOSKALIS WESTMINSTER: STRATEGIC POSITION, 1987†

By Ron Meyer

In early February 1987, the Dutch Federation of Dredging Contractors (Vereniging Centrale Bagger-bedrijf) released a report on the present state and the expected future of the Dutch dredging industry. The alarming findings of this report came as no surprise to those familiar with the industry, least of all to Hans Kraaijeveld van Hemert, chairman of the board of management of the world's largest dredging company, Royal Boskalis Westminster. He was already well aware of the fact that roughly 30 percent of the global commercial dredging fleet could be classified as structural overcapacity, mainly due to some companies' overambitious fleet expansion programs in a mature market. He also knew that the fierce competition resulting from the high number of idle dredging vessels was driving tendering beneath cost price, causing industrywide losses and threatening all dredging companies' long-term viability.

Van Hemert also largely agreed with the recommendations presented in the report. These entailed the creation of a scrap program to reduce the structural excess capacity of the entire industry's dredging fleet, later to be followed by a reduction in the number of competitors by way of mergers and acquisitions. For the successful implementation of this plan, however, it would be of the utmost importance that all dredging contractors cooperate. No company would be willing to reduce its own capacity unilaterally, to the benefit of all. Only the knowledge that all other dredging contractors would be making a comparable

sacrifice would be able to ensure everyone's participation in the scrapping plan. One major noncomplying dredging company could easily undermine the entire scheme, thereby prolonging the industry's slump.

Recent experiences did not encourage van Hemert to be overly optimistic about industrywide compliance with the plan. Earlier attempts to restore market discipline had failed, and there was still a considerable chance that some companies would prefer to run the risk of every man for himself. On the other hand, the industry's problems had never been so severe, which hopefully would convince companies that only a concerted effort by all would be able to fend off the impending decline of the industry's viability.

This left van Hemert and his board of management in the difficult position of plotting a course for Boskalis for the years to come. Faced with the dredging industry's problems and a number of years of financial losses, it would be a trying task to turn the company's fortunes around and secure its viability for the future.

The History of the Company

Boskalis Westminster's origins date back to the latter half of the nineteenth century, when the families Kraaijeveld and Van Noordenne first started to work together in the area of dredging. This cooperation was finally sealed in 1910 by the incorporation of the company Kraaijeveld en Van Noordenne in the village of Sliedrecht in The Netherlands, close to where the central office of the company is still situated. Due to the growing importance of the families Bos and Kalis within the company during these early years, the company name was changed to Bos en Kalis in 1931.

With a firm base successfully established in The Netherlands, international expansion quickly followed, initially in Europe and subsequently to all corners of the world. Actually, Boskalis was among the pioneer dredging contractors to operate in the Middle East, Africa, Canada, South America, Southeast Asia, and Australia.

†**Source:** This case was prepared by Ron J. H. Meyer as a basis for class discussion rather than to illustrate either effective or ineffective handling of an administrative situation. Unless otherwise indicated, all information was obtained with the kind assistance of the Royal Boskalis Westminster Company. This case was originally published as part of the strategic management course *Ondernemingsplanning II* (Corporate Planning) of the Dutch Open University. © Open Universiteit, 1991.

EXHIBIT 1
An Introduction to Dredging

An Introduction to Dredging

Dredging is the act of moving earth in a wet environment. Probably the most well-known type of dredging is the dredging performed in harbours, rivers, and canals. Sometimes it is necessary to deepen these facilities to allow ships with a heavier draught to make use of them, but more commonly dredging is required just to keep the harbours, rivers, and canals from silting up.

The applications of dredging are far more numerous than the two well-known ones above. Not only do dredgers deepen and maintain the existing "wet infrastructure," but they can also create harbours and canals from scratch. Dredgers can also create artificial islands and raise the level of existing land by using earth taken from the sea bottom. Furthermore, dredgers are involved in bottom and shore protection, including the building of dykes and breakwaters. Finally, they are also essential partners when building subsea pipelines.

Since dredgers operate in a wet environment, almost all dredging equipment is built into ships. Basically there are two types of dredging techniques, scooping and suction. Scooping is done by attaching buckets to a conveyor belt (similar to a large escalator) and letting these buckets scoop mud from the bottom and transport it up the conveyor belt to the water surface and into a waiting barge. While these bucket dredgers are still occasionally used they have largely been replaced by suction dredges, which (almost like giant vacuum cleaners) suck the earth up into their holds through a pipe. Since the earth that needs to be moved is not always loose mud, but often hard rock, two types of suction dredges have been developed. Cutter suction dredges are equipped with a suction pipe that first pulverizes the rock before sucking it up, while suction hopper dredges are solely intended for soft materials.

While these are the general categories of dredging ships, each category contains a number of general-purpose and specialized vessels. According to dredging contractor Jan Piet de Nul, the specialized ships are often the key to gaining a contract: "We were able to put our large suction ships to work in China because we had a ship with a very shallow draught that could go up front. These things happen very often. That's the secret of the determination of prices...: that little piece of work that is hard to do. Seventy percent of all contracts could be done by anyone; it's the thirty percent that's difficult that it's all about".[1]

In many countries permanent bases were established, thereby enabling the organization to operate as a local contractor, which was, and still is, very important due to the highly protectionist nature of the dredging business. A good example of the company's integration into a local business environment by means of a subsidiary was in the United Kingdom. Here a major dredging contract led to the formation in 1933 of a very successful British branch of the company, Westminster Dredging.

Not only did Boskalis spread its wings geographically, but it also diversified its services into nondredging businesses. During the 1970s especially the company expanded and diversified at an astonishing rate. By 1982 dredging accounted for only about 40 percent of the company's turnover of Dfl 2.5 billion. Its other activities were organized into four divisions: construction (20 percent), offshore pipelines and railroads (30 percent), engineering (2 percent), and agroindustrial (8 percent).

By 1984, however, Boskalis's 1982 profit of Dfl 26 million had turned into an operating loss of approximately Dfl 280 million, and the company was in serious difficulty. The company had encountered major problems in its construction division throughout 1982 and 1983, but had been able to tackle these by undertaking a large reorganization within the division. No sooner had these difficulties been dealt with, however, than a number of megaprojects in Algeria and Argentina, as well as a number of smaller projects in Nigeria, all mainly in the pipeline construction business,

---

[1] Henk Schol, "Baggeraars dreigen hun eigen doodgravers te worden" (Dredgers in danger of becoming their own gravediggers), *Elseviers Weekblad*, May 14, 1988.

almost simultaneously became problematic due to the local governments' inability or unwillingness to pay Boskalis for the services it had performed. Together with the disappointing results of most of the divisions of the company, this led to severe liquidity problems and deep-rooted doubts by the company's bankers whether Boskalis was viable enough to justify refinancing.

After extended negotiations between the Boskalis board of management and the company's bankers, and after an investigation by McKinsey consultants, the solution to the financial difficulties was found in the continuation of the dredging business and an orderly winding down of the rest of the group's activities. This was achieved by splitting Boskalis into two individual groups of companies. Royal Boskalis Westminster retained the dredging and dredging-related activities, while all other nondredging businesses—to be liquidated over a number of years—were grouped in a separate company, managed by a trust formed by the banks.

EXHIBIT 2
Financial Summary 1979–1986 (In Dfl Millions)

	1979	1980	1981	1982	1983	1984	1985	1986
Turnover								
Total Turnover (on work done)	1,570	2,392	2,681	2,529	2,150	990	530	470
Turnover Dredging	574	716	696	979	788	620	530	470
Total Turnover by region								
The Netherlands	408	462	381	386	425	116	160	116
Rest of Europe	553	788	556	774	549	317		
Africa	498	536	366	639	637	163		
Australia/Asia	41	11	13	19	44	17	370	354
The Americas	47	505	794	163	172	171		
Middle East	23	90	571	548	323	140		
Profit and Loss Account								
Gross operating income	271.3	261.5	252.4	264.7	173.9	(246.0)	55.3	47.7
Depreciation	(125.9)	(130.3)	(116.6)	(118.5)	(100.1)	(114.5)	(52.4)	(46.7)
Net operating income	145.4	131.2	135.8	146.2	73.8	(360.5)	2.9	1.0
Interest expenses	(47.6)	(68.7)	(75.8)	(79.0)	(56.1)	(85.0)	(11.1)	(6.3)
Earnings assoc. companies	(24.1)	7.6	(7.1)	(17.6)	(29.0)	3.7	0.3	0.8
Earnings before taxation	73.7	70.1	52.9	49.6	(11.3)	(441.8)	(7.9)	(4.5)
Taxation	(19.7)	(17.4)	(31.8)	(44.8)	(27.3)	(2.5)	0.5	(1.9)
Earnings after taxation	54.0	52.7	21.1	4.8	(38.6)	(444.3)	(7.4)	(6.4)
Extraordinary results	(38.2)	—	—	22.4	(6.9)	(7.1)	(2.4)	(3.1)
Minority interests	(2.1)	(1.2)	(0.7)	(1.4)	(1.9)	(2.2)	0.4	—
Net earnings	13.7	51.5	20.4	25.8	(47.4)	(453.6)	(9.4)	(9.5)
Dividends								
Cash	9.3	18.5	11.8	11.8	—	—	—	—
Shares	2.0	0.7	—	—	—	—	—	—
Cashflow	139.6	181.8	137.0	144.3	52.7	(339.1)	43.0	37.2

Note: The numbers between brackets are negative.

EXHIBIT 3
Financial Summary 1979–1986 (In Dfl Millions)

	1979	1980	1981	1982	1983	1984	1985	1986
Assets								
Fixed assets	610.9	667.8	840.0	1022.8	714.1	605.7	318.0	255.3
Inventories	35.9	39.6	50.2	44.1	48.0	43.4	40.6	26.6
Work in progress	56.2	104.7	38.6	71.6	110.1	1.4	8.7	(19.3)
Receivables and prepayments	569.5	756.5	858.4	747.9	896.5	450.0	217.4	226.5
Liquid assets	92.2	57.4	55.0	89.8	63.6	131.7	82.2	47.0
Total assets	1,364.7	1,626.0	1,842.2	1,976.2	1,832.3	1,232.2	666.9	537.1
Liabilities								
Shareholders' equity	403.8	434.3	489.8	509.8	459.3	14.9	169.3	155.0
Long-term liabilities	430.8	487.3	622.9	670.8	554.9	152.2	243.4	199.8
Short-term liabilities	530.1	704.4	729.5	795.6	818.0	1065.1	254.2	182.4
Total liabilities	1,364.7	1,626.0	1,842.2	1,976.2	1,832.3	1,232.2	666.9	537.1

Note: These figures have been corrected for differences in reporting practices in annual reports throughout the period 1979–1986.

This agreement, reached in December 1985 (but retroactive to January 1, 1985) and the reorganization that followed in its wake resulted in an additional loss of Dfl 170 million. This brought the net loss incurred by the company in 1984 to approximately Dfl 450 million, which almost wiped out the company's entire equity (see exhibits 2 and 3). It has also had an important impact on the ownership structure of Boskalis. Due to the reorganization, 85 percent of the shares are currently cumulative preferred shares, almost all of which are indirectly held by the company's bankers through the aforementioned trust.

The Business and Structure of the Company

The dredging and dredging-related activities, to which Boskalis has limited itself since the reorganization, include land reclamation, dry-earth moving, sand winning and supply, minor dredging-related pipe laying, coastal defence, bottom and shore protection, marine drilling and blasting, port and waterway engineering, surveys and site investigations, protection and stabilization of subsea pipelines and installations, as well as port and terminal operations.

These activities constitute a complete range of dredging services, enabling Boskalis to tackle almost all dredging projects unassisted. Unlike before 1985, however, Boskalis can no longer handle integrated engineering projects without outside help. For such large-scale projects requiring more than only the above-mentioned dredging expertise, Boskalis now frequently enters into joint ventures or operates as a subcontractor.

Contracts are almost always obtained via a tendering process, which can be very cost intensive. To be able to tender, site and soil investigations must be undertaken, which can take four people between four and eight weeks to complete. The associated costs generally hover between Dfl 500,000 and Dfl 1 million. At a "hitting rate" of approximately one contract for each ten tenders, this means Dfl 5–10 million must be built into the margin of each contract.

The company's range of operation is worldwide. In fact, between 70 and 80 percent of work done by Boskalis is outside The Netherlands. This global orientation is reflected in the company's organizational structure. While the head office, the support services, and a number of highly specialized subsidiaries are situated in The Netherlands, the bulk of the group's companies is spread geographically throughout the company's areas of operation (see exhibit 4).

EXHIBIT 4
Organizational Chart
(as of April 1, 1987)

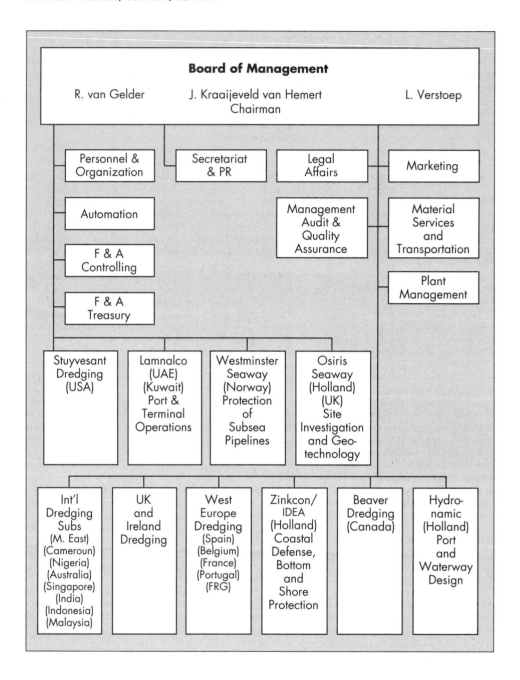

These regional units all have an individual responsibility as profit centers. They do not own any major pieces of capital equipment themselves, but rather lease these from the central office as required. An overview of the major dredging equipment at their disposal is given in exhibit 5. These ships are all relatively new (mostly not more than ten years old) and technically they are state of the art. The economic life span of an average ship is approximately twenty years.

The World Dredging Market

The world dredging market has always been noted for its highly protectionist nature. Only about a third of the total world market is accessible to nonlocal contractors. The other two-thirds is protected by various types of legislation and policies. The high degree of protectionism in the dredging industry can partially be explained by the fact that historically the large majority of the customers have been governments or government agencies, at both the local (e.g., port authorities) and national (e.g., ministries of public works) levels. Hence, governments have always had an important role in the well-being of their national dredging contractors.

In many countries dredging fleets are state owned and have therefore obtained near-monopoly power. Obviously this is the case in the Communist economies, but it also holds true in many Third-World nations. Similar to the nationalistic fervor they display in the airline industry, many of these countries also want to have their own dredging fleets. Naturally, the specialized shipyards in Western nations (for dredging material, mainly concentrated in The Netherlands) are anxious to encourage these sentiments. Generally, developmental aid agencies also look more favorably on financing the importation of ships than on the importation of dredging services, even though many Third-World dredging fleets are rusting away in their ports due to lack of expertise and maintenance funds.

Another highly protectionist country is the United States. The Jones Act only allows dredging to be done if

EXHIBIT 5
Boskalis Westminster's Fleet Size and Capacity

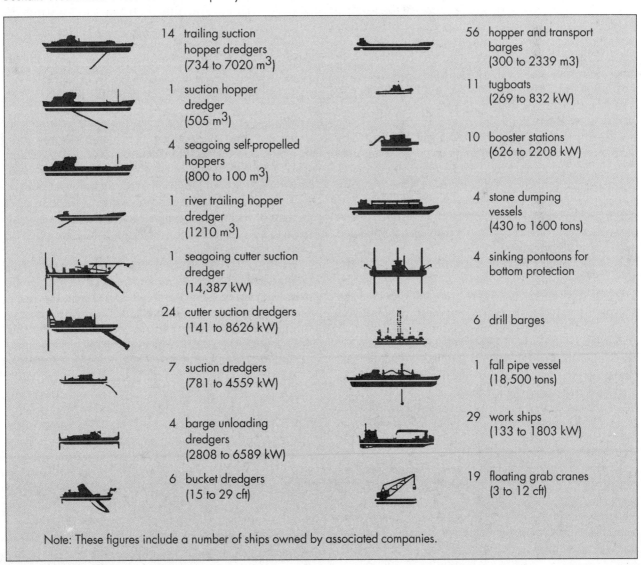

14 trailing suction hopper dredgers (734 to 7020 m³)	56 hopper and transport barges (300 to 2339 m3)
1 suction hopper dredger (505 m³)	11 tugboats (269 to 832 kW)
4 seagoing self-propelled hoppers (800 to 100 m³)	10 booster stations (626 to 2208 kW)
1 river trailing hopper dredger (1210 m³)	4 stone dumping vessels (430 to 1600 tons)
1 seagoing cutter suction dredger (14,387 kW)	4 sinking pontoons for bottom protection
24 cutter suction dredgers (141 to 8626 kW)	6 drill barges
7 suction dredgers (781 to 4559 kW)	1 fall pipe vessel (18,500 tons)
4 barge unloading dredgers (2808 to 6589 kW)	29 work ships (133 to 1803 kW)
6 bucket dredgers (15 to 29 cft)	19 floating grab cranes (3 to 12 cft)

Note: These figures include a number of ships owned by associated companies.

EXHIBIT 6

Size of the Nonprotected
International Dredging
Market

	1981	1983	1985	1986	1992
Volume (in billion m^3)	1.05	1.0	1.0	1.0	1.0–1.1
Value (in Dfl billions)	4.6	4.4	3.2	3.0	2.9–3.2

the ships are more than 75 percent American built, effectively ruling out competition from companies operating internationally. Some international dredgers have been willing to invest heavily in separate American ships, which cost two and a half times more to build than ships constructed in The Netherlands. However, these contractors run the exceptional risk that if work "dries up" in the States, these ships are too expensive to work anywhere else.

Protectionism manifests itself not only at the national level. In some countries, such as Great Britain, for instance, local port authorities demonstrate an outspoken preference for local dredging contractors. In other countries ports often have their own dredging ships and, due to their flexible bookkeeping, can convince themselves that they are much cheaper than outside contractors.

Governments and government agencies are still by far the most important dredging customers. Only to a smaller extent do private companies require the services of dredging contractors. Oil companies often make up the majority of these private sector customers. The importance of this market is declining, however, due to the reduction in offshore activities that has accompanied the drop in the price of oil.

Low oil prices have done more damage to the demand for dredging services than one might at first suspect. In the ten-year span from 1973 to 1983 the international dredging market expanded drastically as newly rich OPEC (Organization of Petroleum Exporting Countries) countries such as Nigeria, Libya, Algeria, and the Gulf states invested their "oil dollars" in large-scale infrastructure projects. Due to the drop in oil prices these countries have been forced to cut the number of new megaprojects, significantly reducing the number of large-scale contracts now available to international dredging companies.

In the industrialized nations there has been a similar trend away from new large-scale projects. Here, government budget cuts have been the most important factor limiting the number of new big contracts.

Yet, despite these indicators of possible market shrinkage, the actual size of the global dredging market has remained remarkably stable throughout the 1980s. Measured by volume of earth moved, the total market has remained constant at about 3 billion cubic meters a year, of which 1 billion is open for bidding by international contractors. What has changed is the composition of the demand. Large-scale projects have been replaced by small-scale projects and especially by maintenance work. Van Hemert estimates that in 1986 approximately half of all dredging work was maintenance.

While the market might not have altered much in volume during the 1980s, it has changed significantly in financial terms. In 1981 customers paid Dfl 4.6 billion for 1.05 billion cubic meters of dredging work. In 1986, however, they paid Dfl 3 billion for the same amount of work (see exhibit 6). This represents more than a 35 percent reduction in the revenues of the industry. The price index for a standard dredging package dipped 32 points between 1981 and 1986.

In Boskalis Westminster's home market, The Netherlands, the price drops have been less dramatic than in the international market as a whole. However, the Dutch dredging market has shrunk in volume throughout the 1980s, and predictions are that this downward trend will continue into the future (see exhibit 7).

As a consequence, the reasonable gross margin of 17 percent for the industry on a standard dredging package, which is generally considered to be necessary for this type of high-risk business, has been transformed into a margin of minus 20 percent. And there is little

EXHIBIT 7

Size of the Dutch
Dredging Market

	1981	1983	1985	1986	1992
Volume (in millions m^3)	185	175	165	165	150
Value (in Dfl millions)	620	600	560	510	470

reason to believe that in the near future prices will rebound to their former level.

There are two reasons for the fall in prices. One is the shift in the type of dredging done. While the international volume of work remained stable throughout the 1980s, the percentage of relatively expensive cutter work has shrunk in favor of the cheaper suction work. This revised makeup of the total demand has been responsible for a 10 percent drop in the aggregate value of all work done. The culprit responsible for the remaining 25 percent reduction in price is cutthroat competition.

The Competition

Boskalis is by no means the only Dutch company competing in the international dredging marketplace. Together with six other Dutch dredging companies, each with a turnover of more than Dfl 100 million, and a large number of smaller companies, they have a 50 percent share of the global nonprotected market. Their relative size expressed in millions of Dutch guilders turnover in dredging-related activities is shown in exhibit 8.

As exhibit 8 indicates, Boskalis's only main non-Dutch competitors are three Belgian companies (Dredging International, Jan de Nul, and Decloedt). The seven large Dutch dredgers together with these three Belgians control 90 percent of the international free market dredging fleet.

More figures on most of these companies, however, are difficult to obtain, since in most cases the dredging activities of each company only account for a part of the total turnover. Often the companies are involved in activities in which Boskalis also used to be active, including construction, offshore, engineering, and pipeline construction.

As might be suspected, the international market is very important to all of these companies, since the Dutch and Belgian markets are small relative to the high number of large local competitors. Dutch companies, for instance, on average acquire more than 75 percent of their work abroad. Boskalis is no exception, with 70 to 80 percent of its turnover resulting from work done outside The Netherlands (see exhibit 2).

This export dependency makes these companies very vulnerable to political and economic trends and crises throughout the world. So when after the peak year 1982 a large number of economic and political indicators (e.g., falling oil prices, growing dollar value, the Third-World debt crisis, increasing protectionism, government cutbacks) predicted a shrinkage of the international dredging market, dredging contractors scurried to take action to protect themselves.

They had all invested heavily in this capital-intensive industry in the late 1970s to have large ships at their disposal for the high number of megaprojects that were being planned. These substantial capital expenditures, however, necessitated a high turnover during the ten- to fifteen-year payback period of the ships. As the level of turnover was being threatened by a downturn in demand, most companies realized that extra efforts would be needed to maintain their level of activities. This, it was believed, could only be achieved by becoming more competitive. Only by undercutting the competitor's price would they be able to hold on to their acquired positions. Hence, steps were taken to bring down the dredging price per cubic meter.

		1985	1986
1.	Royal Boskalis Westminster (NL)	530	470
2.	Royal Volker Stevin Group (NL)	364	290
3.	Dredging International (B)	234	n/a
4.	Zanen Verstoep (NL)	203	117
5.	Hollandse Aannemingsmij (NL)	192	212
6.	Ballast-Nedam (NL)	173	115
7.	Van Oord Groep (NL)	161	161
8.	Jan de Nul (B)	156	n/a
9.	Decloedt (B)	151	n/a
10.	Broekhoven Zeist (NL, German parent)	126	93

EXHIBIT 8
Dredging Turnover of the Largest International Dredging Firms

EXHIBIT 9
Age Breakdown of the Global Dredging Fleet (vertical bars represent the total capacity of the ships built in each year)

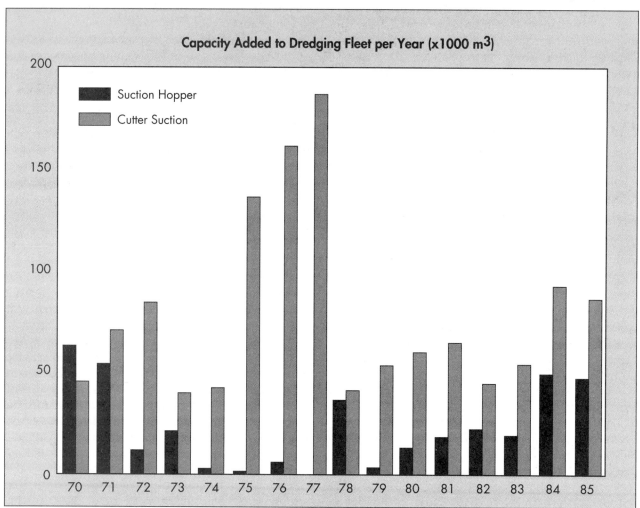

Capacity Added to Dredging Fleet per Year (x1000 m^3)

The solution found by some to attain this greater efficiency was the building of even bigger ships, with huge production capacities. Large sums were borrowed, especially in 1984 and 1985, to invest in ships with unparalleled capacities (see exhibit 9). The Dutch government encouraged this building wave by granting the dredging contractors investment premiums and by subsidizing the ailing shipbuilding industry. According to Leen Verstoep, member of the board of management of Boskalis, the government's contribution toward the cost of a new ship added up to between 30 and 40 percent of the total price.

Two developments proved this building spree to be an unfortunate solution. First, while demand remained constant in volume, it shifted toward smaller-scale projects for which these Goliaths were unsuitable. Their high mobilization and demobilization expenses made the deployment of small and middle-sized ships far more cost efficient. Second, since almost all of the major companies adhered to the same strategy of building big ships (Boskalis being a notable exception), no one's competitive strength increased sufficiently to gain a definitive edge. In effect, all that happened was that excess capacity was increased further and that dredgers were faced with even higher debts requiring servicing.

The pressure created by the oversupply of dredging services and the urgent need for turnover naturally expressed itself in pricing. On average, prices have dipped to 20 percent below the integral cost price, placing almost all dredging companies in the red. The

	1981	1983	1985	1986
Total turnover	2215	2064	1664	1450
Total earnings	161	137	−277	−307
Total cash flow	336	320	−75	−97

EXHIBIT 10

Aggregate Financial Results of Dutch Dredging Companies in 1986 (in Dfl Millions)

total losses of the Dutch dredgers in 1986 were estimated to be about Dfl 300 million, as exhibit 10 indicates. The smaller dredging firms, some of whom were unable to update their fleets and almost all of whom do not have the financial stamina to survive a succession of beatings, have been decimated. Between 1975 and 1986 forty-two Dutch dredging companies were purchased by larger competitors or simply went under. This amounts to a decrease in the number of smaller dredging contractors by more than 25 percent.

The heavy losses suffered by the dredging industry have forced most companies to implement major internal budget cuts, focused on short-term survival, often with a severe impact on the companies' long-term viability. The ranks of the companies' personnel, for instance, have been heavily trimmed in the drive to reduce costs. While in 1981 there were still 6,200 full-time employees in the Dutch dredging industry, in 1986 this had been reduced to 3,900, with more layoffs planned. Boskalis, too, has had to shed hundreds of jobs, leaving it in a difficult position. With a few exceptions almost all of Boskalis's fleet personnel have been with the company for more than fifteen years. The personnel shrinkages of the past have prohibited Boskalis from hiring new talented people to succeed the older generation. Hence, the seed of future personnel problems has already been sown. This in a company that, despite its capital intensity, recognizes that its highly skilled employees are a key success factor.

The industry's R&D budgets have also been hit hard by the companies' cost reduction drives. Most companies have cut back their individual R&D efforts to a fraction of their former size, and Boskalis, too, has been forced to considerably downscale its R&D programs. Collective fundamental research by the Dutch dredgers, which has been important in the past, is also being threatened. Furthermore, the leading Dutch builder of dredging ships, IHC, which—together with the technical departments of its more sophisticated clients—has been responsible for most of the important technological developments in dredging equipment since 1945, has been forced to virtually close its R&D

department due to the dismal outlook in the market for new dredging ships. Thus technological developments within the Dutch dredging industry seem destined to slow to a snail's pace.

The Dutch and Belgian dredgers currently still have an estimated fifteen-year technological lead over their other competitors. It is feared, however, that American, Italian, Greek, Japanese, and Korean dredging companies, most with the advantage of protected home markets, are closing in fast.

The CB Proposals

As the situation had become increasingly gloomy for the whole dredging industry by 1986, the Federation of Dutch Dredging Contractors, *Centrale Baggerbedrijf* (CB), commissioned a study into the present state and the future possibilities of the Dutch dredging industry. The report, published in February 1987, clearly spelled out the industry's problems. Although the data presented left considerable room for a debate on exactly how large the overcapacity of the international free-market dredging fleet actually was, it did confirm the widespread knowledge that it was unacceptably high. According to most definitions, the downtime of the Dutch fleet could be pegged at well over 50 percent.

This high idleness rate, the report continued, was driving dredging firms to cutthroat competition, since any income above variable cost could be used to service their debts or show some return on investment. The solution to the industry's predicament must therefore be sought in the restoration of viable prices by a sharp reduction of fleet capacity, to be followed by a decrease in the number of market parties.

Fleet-capacity reduction was the most pressing of these two necessary measures, the report argued, and therefore required immediate attention. However, cutbacks in the number of ships could only be attained if all fifty major Dutch dredging companies and the other major Western European contractors (mostly Belgians) were willing to cooperate in an industrywide scrapping plan. A large enough portion of the structural overcapacity would have to be taken out of the market permanently by scrapping ships to ensure price recovery.

In addition to scrapping ships, a ban would also be needed on the building of new ships in most categories. This measure would have to stay in effect until the dredging market could justify resumption of construction activities.

The report also contained the recommendation not to lay up ships temporarily and not to sell ships to third parties. The continuing existence of a large mothballed fleet, which could be quickly redeployed at any moment, would have a negative psychological impact on the price level, it was believed. Selling ships to third parties would obviously be out of the question, since this would not reduce global overcapacity, but rather would create additional competitors, thereby lessening the chance of reaching an industrywide agreement on cutting capacity. Only if the third party was a contractor working in a local protected market should the sale of a ship be allowed.

Implementation

The authors of the report predicted great difficulties in implementing these proposals, however, since it was of the utmost importance that none of the major dredging firms undermine the agreement. While all companies underwrote the report's conclusion that capacity should be reduced, few were happy with the prospect of having to scrap ships of their own. Only the knowledge that all other dredging contractors would be making an equal sacrifice, to the benefit of all, would be able to ensure everyone's participation in the scrapping plan. If, however, one major dredger abstained from cooperation, the other companies would perceive their capacity-cutting efforts to be unfairly profitable to this "defector." The discipline needed to adhere to the plan could thus be weakened by one company's unwillingness to conform, and wholesale desertion could easily follow.

This unpleasant scenario was by no means unrealistic given the high cost of conforming to the plan and the lucrative payoff that could be enjoyed if one were the only company to defect. Moreover, the absence of widespread consensus and market discipline had already become characteristics deeply embedded in the

industry's culture. Dredgers are "individualists and fighters," as the Belgian dredging contractor Jan Piet de Nul puts it.[2] According to the director of the CB, F. C. F. Sterrenburg, getting these people to sit around the same table and achieve a consensus is very difficult, especially "while in the marketplace they're at each other's throats."[3] Earlier plans to revitalize the Dutch dredging industry had also been thwarted at embryonic stage, so expectations were not running high.

Even if all companies grasped the seriousness of the situation and could be convinced that the "fight to the death" to which the industry was now headed was a "no-win" situation, the complexity of working out a cutback plan itself could lead to disunity and an abandonment of capacity reduction attempts. A number of dredging firms had recently undertaken scrapping programmes themselves, leading to a reduction of 60 ships and 150 barges over the last three years. Already these companies were stating that any new plans should take their previous efforts into account.

Other companies, too, had quickly presented extenuating circumstances to support their arguments that they should sacrifice less than their neighbours. Some were faced with the threat that a reduction in their fleet size would undermine their ability to provide a full range of services, thus lessening their competitiveness compared with bigger companies such as Boskalis. Others were being threatened by their bankers' uneasiness about losing collateral. These bankers might be more inclined to foreclose on some dredging contractors now and sell off their assets than to wait and possibly receive nothing at all. This would not only be a threat to the company involved, but would also affect others, since selling off cheap ships on the free market would probably attract a new market entrant with very low fixed costs. Because of this, the financially weak companies were in a position in which they could "blackmail" other companies into concessions.

Recognizing the high chance of failure by defection, the CB report does present a few proposals aimed at obtaining cooperation, although they are limited to the Dutch dredging companies. The most important is its request for Dfl 150 million in assistance from the Dutch government, spread over three years, which would be used to offset the price of cooperating with the plan.

---

[2]Henk Schol, "Baggeraars dreigen hun eigen doodgravers te worden" (Dredgers in danger of becoming their own gravediggers), *Elseviers Weekblad,* May 14, 1988.

[3]"FNV-bond wil sanering van de baggerindustrie" (FNV trade union wants restructuring of the dredging industry), *NRC Handelsblad,* April 8, 1988.

Furthermore, the report asks the government to punish defectors by excluding them from tendering on public works in The Netherlands for three years, as Dutch law allows. The Dutch government did not react negatively to these ideas, although it did make it clear that it would only participate if the dredging companies achieved a consensus.

Almost immediately after the presentation of the report to its members, the CB's general assembly unanimously endorsed the report's conclusions. A veteran in industrial restructuring, G. A. Wagner, was subsequently brought in to work out the restructuring recommendations and to research the possibility of further government assistance.

Haste was required, though, because most companies were enduring heavy losses and some were already taking steps undermining the scrapping plan even before it had been officially implemented. For instance, Zanen Verstoep, a company in one of the weakest positions, sold a large cutter suction ship to an Italian company at about the same time the CB's report was presented. Fears seemed justified that more of these sales would follow.

Boskalis Responds

The reaction of Boskalis to the storm gathering over the dredging industry has been one of taking a leading role in the capacity-cutting talks. A former member of the board of managing directors of Boskalis, J. Th. Meijers, is the chairman of the CB and is leading the discussions toward an industrywide agreement.

This role is not only in line with the company's position as largest dredging company, but also corresponds with its long-standing policy of limiting total fleet capacity. While in the last few years other dredging companies added ships with huge production capacities to their fleets, Boskalis sought to strengthen its position and renew its fleet by modernizing existing ships and by acquiring other companies. Even while the company was in the midst of its own restructuring problems, acquisition negotiations were commenced with a middle-sized Dutch dredging company, Breejenbout (net turnover in 1985 was Dfl 63 million) in May 1985. It finally purchased Breejenbout in November 1985 and in so doing solved its renewal problems for its trailer suction hopper fleet without adding to world market capacity. Moreover, Boskalis obtained a company with a sound reputation and was able to pay cash for Breejenbout, which was sold below its net equity value.

When in May 1987 the 1986 annual report was presented to the shareholders and again a negative result was announced, van Hemert was painfully aware that while the loss had been unexpectedly small and the ratios had been strengthened, the steps he and his board had taken until that moment had only been able to stem the losses. Although he was sure that they had set Boskalis on the right path toward recovery, his mind was still open to additional strategies that might enlarge the chance of a faster turnaround. But, he asked himself, what could these additional strategies be?

■ CINEPLEX ODEON CORPORATION†

By Joseph Wolfe

In mid-February 1989, Jack Valenti, head of the Motion Picture Association, reaffirmed the film industry's basic health by citing 1988 movie theater attendance figures surpassing 1 billion people for the seventh year in a row. While this magnitude translated into box office revenues of over $4.4 billion, there are indications the industry is in a state of both absolute and relative decline. It is also undergoing a restructuring that is fundamentally changing the nature of competitive practices for those in the film exhibition business. In the first instance, a lower proportion of America's aging population attends the movies each year, partially due to the use of VCRs for film viewing, the presence of television in both its broadcast and cable versions, and to other uses of the consumer's leisure time dollars. In the second instance, a great degree of owner concentration is occurring, due to separate actions by both the Hollywood producers of films and their exhibitors.

Despite the apparent decline of the motion picture theater as the major supplier of America's needs for mass entertainment, the Toronto-based firm of Cineplex Odeon has quickly become North America's second largest and most profitable theater chain through a series of shrewd and adventuresome acquisitions while creating a large number of up-scaled, multiscreened theaters in key cities and market areas. With 482 theaters and 1,809 screens in 20 states, the Washington, D.C., area, six Canadian provinces, and the United Kingdom, the firm posted record sales of $695.8 million and profits of $40.4 million in 1988 while standing on the verge of developing and operating more than 110 screens in the United Kingdom by 1991. Central to Cineplex Odeon's success is the firm's driven and often-abrasive chairman, president, and CEO, Garth Drabinsky. It is against the backdrop of the industry's fundamental changes and

basic decline that Drabinsky must chart his firm's future actions to insure its continued growth and prosperity.

The Motion Picture Theater Industry

The motion picture theater industry (SIC 783) has undergone a number of radical transformations since its turn of the century beginnings. The first movies were shown in cramped and hastily converted storefront locations called *nickelodeons*, so-named for their five-cent admission charges. Their numbers grew rapidly because the costs of entering this industry were relatively low and a plentiful supply of films was available in both their legal and pirated versions. By 1907, it was estimated the United States had about 3,000 movie theaters, mainly concentrated in the larger cities. Rural areas were serviced by traveling film shows, which made their presentations in the local town meeting hall.

The typical show lasted only 15 to 20 minutes, augmented by song slides or lectures. As the film medium's novelty declined, audiences began to clamor for more lavish and ambitious productions using recognizable actors and actresses. Feature-length movies replaced one-reel short subjects and comedies in the middle to late 1910s, and the theater industry's greatest building period began. Opulent, specially built structures soon became the focal point of every major city's downtown area. Often possessing more than 5,000 seats, they came complete with a pit orchestra and vocalists and chorus, baby-sitting facilities, elevators and grand staircases to a heaven-like balcony, numerous doormen, and a watchful and attentive fleet of uniformed ushers.

By the mid-1920s, over 19,000 theaters were in operation, and Hollywood's film producers began what was a continuing attempt to control via acquisitions the first-run exhibitors of their films. The battle was initially waged between Paramount and First National, but soon Loews (MGM), Fox, and Warner Brothers joined in, with First National being the major loser. By 1935, the twin realities of the Great Depression and the advent of sound films caused the number of theaters to plummet to about 15,000. Because of the nation's bleak economic outlook, many theaters had become too run-down or too costly to convert to the greater demands of sound films. Many Americans also substituted radio's free entertainment for their weekly lemming-like trek to the movies. Surviving theaters introduced the double feature to create more value for the entertainment dollar, while obtaining the major source of their profits from candy, soft drinks, and popcorn sales.

During World War II, motion picture attendance and Hollywood's profits reached their all-time highs, with about 82 million people a week going to the nation's 20,400 theaters. This pinnacle did not last long, however, as postwar incomes were spent on new cars, television sets, and homes built in the newly emerging suburbs. Motion picture attendance began its precipitous fall in 1947, with attendance reaching its all-time low of 16 million per week in 1971. The number of theaters followed the same downward trend, although a steady increase in the number of drive-in theaters temporarily took up some of the slack (see exhibit 1.)

The postwar period also saw the effects of the government's 1948 Consent Decree. By the early 1940s, Hollywood's five major studios had obtained control or interests in 17 percent of the nation's theaters. This amounted to 70 percent of the important large city first-run theaters. Although certain studios were stronger in different parts of the country—Paramount dominated New England and the South, Warner Brothers the mid-Atlantic region, Loews and RKO the New York-New Jersey area, and 20th Century-Fox the western states—each controlled all stages of the distribution chain from its studios (manufacturing), its film exchanges (wholesaling), and its movie theaters (retailing). Under the Consent Decree the studios could either divest their studios and film exchanges or get rid of their movie theaters. Hollywood chose to sell the cinemas, thereby opting to control the supply side of the film distribution system.

In an effort to arrest the decline in attendance and to counter the relatively inexpensive and convenient medium of black-and-white television in the 1950s, the film studios retaliated by offering movies that dealt with subject matter considered too dangerous for home viewing, shown in formats and hues beyond television's technical capabilities. Moviegoers heard the word "virgin" uttered for the first time, women "with child" actually looked pregnant, rather than merely full-skirted, and couples were shown in bed together without having to put one foot on the floor. From 1953 to 1968, about 28 percent of Hollywood's films were photographed and projected in a bewildering array of

Year	Theaters	Drive-ins	Total	Screens
1923	15.0		15.0	
1926	19.5		19.5	
1929	23.3		23.3	
1935	15.3		15.3	
1942	20.3	0.1	20.4	
1946	18.7	0.3	19.0	
1950	16.9	2.2	19.1	
1955	14.1	4.6	18.7	
1965	9.2	4.2	13.4	
1974	9.6	3.5	13.2	14.4
1980	9.7	3.6	13.3	17.6
1981	11.4	3.3	14.7	18.0
1984	14.6	2.8	17.4	20.2
1985	15.1	2.8	17.9	20.7
1986	16.8	2.8	19.6	22.8
1987*	17.9	2.8	20.7	23.6
1988*	18.1	2.7	20.8	24.3

*Estimated.

EXHIBIT 1
Number of U.S. Movie Theaters (in thousands)

widescreen processes, such as Cinerama, CinemaScope, RegalScope, SuperScope, Technirama, VistaVision, Panavision, Techniscope, and even three-dimensional color.

As movie attendance stabilized in the mid-1980s to a little more than 20 million patrons per week, two new trends have established themselves in the movie theater business. The first has been the creation of multiple screened theater sites, while the second trend has been Hollywood's reacquisition of theaters and theater chains as part of a general consolidation within the industry. Many theater chains have rediscovered the glitz and glamour of old Hollywood by either subdividing and rejuvenating old theaters or by constructing multiplexes from scratch in suburban malls and shopping districts. The economies of multiple screened operations are compelling at the local level. Rather than needing a separate manager and projectionist for each theater, a number of variously sized auditoriums can be combined and centrally serviced. Box office operations and concession stands can also be centrally managed and operated. The availability of a number of screens at one location also yields programming flexibility for the theater operator. A "small" film without mass appeal can often turn a profit in a room seating only 300 people, while it would be unprofitable and would be lost in a larger auditorium. Having a number of screens in operation also increases the likelihood the complex will be showing a hit film, thereby generating traffic for the other films being shown at the site. Having multiple screens also allows the operator to outfit various rooms with different sound systems (the THX System by Lucasfilm versus the standard four-track optical stereo system) and projection equipment (at least one 70mm six-track magnetic sound projector in addition to the usual 35mm projector), thereby offering the very finest possible viewing.

The second trend toward consolidation is occurring at all levels of the film distribution chain. A number of studios have recently purchased major theater chains after sensing a relaxation of the enforcement of the Consent Decree (in 1984, the Justice Department offered advance support to any studio financing a lawsuit to reenter the movie theater business) plus their promise to limit their ownership to less than 50 percent of any acquired chain. MCA, owner of Universal Studios, has purchased 49.7 percent of Cineplex Odeon, the Cannon Group has purchased the Commonwealth chain, and United Artists Communications purchased the Georgia Theatre Company, the Gulf States and Litchfield chains, and—in 1988 alone—the Blair, Sameric, Commonwealth

(from the Cannon Group) and Moss theater chains. Gulf & Western's Paramount Studios purchased Trans-Lux, Mann Theaters, and Festival Enterprises, while Columbia and Tri-Star (owned by Coca-Cola) bought the Walter Reade and Loews chains. On the retailing side, Cineplex Odeon has purchased the Plitt, RKO, Septum, Essaness, and Sterling chains, Carmike Cinemas has purchased Stewart & Everett, while AMC Entertainment purchased the Budco Theatres. Through these actions and others the top six chains now own nearly 40 percent of America's screens. This is a 67 percent increase in just three years.

Wholesaling operations have been drastically reduced over the years on a scale unnoticeable to the public but very significant to those in the business. When filmgoing was in its heyday, each studio operated as many as 20 or so film exchanges in key cities across the country. Hollywood's studios have since closed many exchanges, until they are now operating only five to eight branch offices each. Paramount recently merged its Charlotte and Jacksonville branches into its Atlanta office, while Chicago now handles the business once serviced by its Detroit, Kansas City, Des Moines, and Minneapolis branches. As observed by Michael Patrick, president of Carmike Cinemas, "as the geographical regions serviced by these offices increase, the ability of smaller exhibitors to negotiate bookings is diluted relative to the buying power of the larger circuits."[1]

Competitive Conditions

Despite the glamour associated with Hollywood, its start, its televised Academy Award Show, and such megahits as *Who Framed Roger Rabbit?*, *Rain Man*, and *Batman*, theater operators are basically in the business of running commercial enterprises dealing with a very perishable commodity. A movie is a merchandisable product made available by Hollywood and various independent producers to commercial storefront theaters at local retail locations. Given the large degree of concentration in the industry, corporate level actions entail the financing of both acquisitions and new construction, while local operations deal with the booking of films that match the moviegoing tastes of the communities being served.

[1]Michael W. Patrick, "Trends in Exhibition" in *The 1987 Encyclopedia of Exhibition*, ed. Wayne R. Green (N.Y.: National Association of Theatre Owners, 1988), p. 109.

To the degree a movie house merely retails someone else's product, the theater owner's success lies in the quality and not the quantity of products produced by Hollywood. Accordingly the 1987-88 Christmas season did not produce any blockbusters, while 1987's two big hits were *Beverly Hills Cop II* and *Fatal Attraction*, and 1986's hits were *Top Gun, Crocodile Dundee*, and *The Karate Kid, Part II.* Under these conditions of relatively few real moneymakers, the bargaining power shifts to the studios, leaving the exhibitors with more screens than they can fill with high-drawing films. Although the independent producers (the "indies")—such as the DeLaurentis Entertainment Group, New World, Atlantic, Concorde, and Cannon—are producing proportionally more films every year and the majors are producing fewer, their product is more variable in quality and less bankable. Additionally, theaters often pay a premium for the rights to exclusively show first-run movies in a given area or film zone, such as the May 1989 release of *Indiana Jones and the Last Crusade.* This condition hurts the smaller chains especially hard, because they do not have the resources to outbid the giant circuits.

Marketing research conducted by the industry has consistently found young adults are the prime consumers of motion picture theater entertainment. This group is rather concentrated but not organized. A study by the Opinion Research Corporation in July 1986 found those under the age of 40 accounted for 86 percent of all theater admissions. Frequent moviegoers constitute only 21 percent of the eligible film goers, but they account for 83 percent of all admissions. A general downward attendance trend has been occurring, as shown in exhibit 2, where 43 percent of the population never attended a film in 1986. The long-term demographics also appear to be unfavorable, because America's population is moving toward those age categories least likely to attend a movie. Those 40 and over make up only 14 percent of a typical theater's admissions, while they account for 44 percent of the nation's population. Those from 12-29 years of age make up 66 percent of

admissions, while accounting for only 36 percent of the population (see exhibit 3.)

It appears that certain barriers to entry into the motion picture theater industry exist. Economies of scale are present, with the advantage given to operations concentrated in metropolitan areas, where one omnibus newspaper advertisement covers all the chain's theaters. As shown in exhibit 4, the largest chains in the United States lost the least during the period of July 1984 to June 1985. Based on these results, scale economies appear to exist in the areas of operating costs, executive compensation, advertising, and rental expenses. Those choosing to enter the industry in recent years have done so through the use of massive conglomerate-backed capital. The possibility that an independent can open a profitable movie theater is very remote. "There's no way the small, independent operator can compete against the large screen owners these days," says John Duffy, cofounder of Cinema 'N' Drafthouse International, of Atlanta, Georgia[2] (see exhibit 5.) As a way of carving a niche for himself, Duffy's chain charges $2.00 for an "intermediate run" film but serves dinner and drinks during the movie, thereby garnering more than $5.00 in food revenue, compared to a theater's average $1.25 per admission.

Despite attempts by various theater owners to make the theater-going experience unique, customers tend to go to the most convenient theater that is showing the film they want to see at the time best for them. Accordingly, a particular theater chain enjoys proprietary product differentiation to the degree it occupies the best locations in any particular market area. Additionally, the cost of building new facilities in the most desirable areas has increased dramatically. Harold L. Vogel, of Merrill Lynch, Pierce, Fenner and Smith, has observed the average construction cost comes to over $1 million per screen in such areas as New York or Los Angeles.

---

[2]Quoted by Peter Waldman, "Silver Screens Lose Some of Their Luster," *The Wall Street Journal*, February 9, 1989, p. B1.

Attendance	1986	1985	1984
Frequently (At least once a month)	21.0%	22.0%	23.0%
Occasionally (Once in two to six months)	25.0	29.0	28.0
Infrequently (Less than once in six months)	11.0	9.0	8.0
Never	43.0	39.0	39.0
Not reported	0.0	1.0	2.0

EXHIBIT 2
Frequency of Attendance by Total Public, Ages 12 and Over

EXHIBIT 3
U.S. Population by Age Group for 1980, with Projections for 1990 and 2000

Age Range	Year	Number (in millions)	Percent of total	Percent Change
5–17	1980	47.22	20.7%	
	1990	45.14	18.1	–4.4%
	2000	49.76	18.6	10.2
18–24	1980	30.35	13.2	
	1990	25.79	10.3	–15.0
	2000	24.60	9.2	–4.6
25–44	1980	63.48	27.9	
	1990	81.38	32.6	28.2
	2000	80.16	29.9	–1.5
45–64	1980	44.49	19.5	
	1990	46.53	18.6	4.4
	2000	60.88	22.7	31.1
65 and over	1980	25.71	11.3	
	1990	31.70	12.8	23.3
	2000	34.92	13.0	10.2

Just as the motion picture was a substitute for vaudeville shows and minstrels at the turn of the century, radio and now television have been the major somewhat interchangeable substitutes for mass entertainment in America. Most recently cable television, pay-per-view TV, and videocassettes have eaten into the precious leisure time dollar. It has been estimated that 49.2 million homes now subscribe to cable television, 19.0 million homes have pay-per-view capability, and 56.0 million homes have a VCR, with 20.0 percent of those homes having more than one unit. The greatest damage to theater attendance has been accomplished by videocassettes, which deliver over 5,000 titles to viewers, at a relatively low cost, in the comfort of their own living rooms. As Sumner Redstone, owner of the very profitable National Amusements theater chain, says, "Anyone who doesn't believe videocassettes are devastating competition to theaters is a fool."[3]

Although the motion picture medium has been characterized as one that provides visual mass entertainment, those going to movies must ultimately choose between alternative forms of recreation. In that regard skiing, boating, baseball and football games, books, newspapers, and even silent contemplation vie for the consumer's precious time. Exhibit 6 shows the movie theater industry has declined in its ability to capture both America's total recreation dollars or its thirst for passive spectator entertainment. During the period from 1984 to 1987, the greatest increases in consumer recreation expenditures were for bicycles, sports equipment, boats, pleasure aircraft, and television and radio equipment and their repair.

Different marketing strategies are being employed in an attempt to remain viable in this very competitive industry. Some chains, such as Cinemark Theaters and Carmike Cinemas, specialize in $1 or low-price second-run multiplexed theaters in smaller towns and selected markets. In a sense they are applying Wal-Mart's original market strategy of dominating smaller, less-competitive rural towns. Others, such as General Cinema, United Artists Communications, and AMC Entertainment, favor multiplexed first-run theaters in major markets. Within this group, AMC Entertainment has been a pioneer as a multiscreen operator. It opened its first twin theater in 1963 and its first quadplex in 1969. As of mid-1988, AMC was operating 269 complexes with 1,531 screens, with most of its expansion in the Sunbelt. General Cinema has been diversifying out of the movie theater business through its nearly 60.0 percent interest in the Neiman Marcus Group (Neiman-Marcus, Contempo Casuals, and Bergdorf Goodman) and 18.4 percent interest in Cadbury Schweppes. Most recently, General Cinema sold off its soft drink bottling business to PepsiCo for $1.5 billion to obtain cash for investments in additional nontheater operations.

---

[3]Quoted by Stratford P. Sherman, "Movie Theaters Head Back to the Future," *Fortune*, January 20, 1986, p. 91.

EXHIBIT 4
Average Operating Results for Selected Motion Picture Theater Corporations, By Asset Size, July 1984–June 1985

Results	Smaller-sized		Middle-sized		Larger-sized	
Revenues	$224,171	100.0%	$4,476,042	100.0%	$151,545,455	100.0%
Cost of operations	93,917	41.9	1,780,066	39.8	54,707,909	36.1
Operating income	130,254	58.1	2,695,976	60.2	96,837,546	63.9
Expenses:						
Compensation of officers	6,788	3.0	150,647	3.4	2,121,636	1.4
Repairs	5,497	2.5	74,134	1.7	2,438,504	1.6
Bad debts	170	0.1	4,196	0.1	82,661	0.1
Rent	32,195	14.4	315,841	7.1	11,489,901	7.6
Taxes (excluding federal tax)	12,904	5.8	179,881	4.0	5,689,843	3.8
Interest	8,045	3.6	117,216	2.6	8,031,999	5.3
Depreciation	8,866	4.0	269,122	6.0	8,954,959	5.9
Advertising	16,004	7.1	152,745	3.4	5,689,843	3.8
Pensions and other benefit plans	—	—	42,662	1.0	771,504	.5
Other expenses	70,971	31.7	1,682,992	37.6	55,245,207	36.5
Net profit before taxes	(31,186)	(13.9)	(293,460)	(6.6)	(3,678,421)	(2.4)
Current ratio	1.0		1.3		0.7	
Quick ratio	0.6		1.0		0.5	
Debt ratio	140.6		52.9		74.2	
Asset turnover	3.0		1.3		1.0	

A great amount of building has occurred in the theater industry in the past few years. Since 1981, the number of screens has increased about 35 percent, but the population proportion attending movies has actually fallen. Additionally, the relatively inexpensive days of "twinning" or quadplexing existing theaters appears to be over, and the construction of totally new multiplexes is much more expensive. Exhibit 7 shows that operating profit margins peaked in 1983 at 11.7 percent, and they have fallen dramatically since then as the industry has taken on large amounts of debt to finance the construction of more and more screens, now generating 24.6 percent fewer admissions per screen. Many operations are losing money, although certain economies of scale exist and labor-saving devices have allowed industry employment to fall slightly, while the number of screens has increased substantially. The Plitt theaters were money losers before being acquired by Cineplex Odeon, and AMC Entertainment lost $6.0 million in 1987 and $13.8 million in 1988 on theater operations. Carmike was barely profitable in 1986, and General Cinema's earnings from its theater operations

Circuit	Headquarters	Screens
United Artists Communications	Denver, Colo.	2,677
Cineplex Odeon	Toronto, Canada	1,825
American Multi-Cinema	Kansas City, Mo.	1,531
General Cinema	Chestnut Hill, Mass.	1,359
Carmike Cinemas	Columbus, Ga.	742

EXHIBIT 5
North America's Largest Theater Circuits in 1988

EXHIBIT 6
Motion Picture Exhibitors'
Share of Entertainment
Expenditures

Year	Consumer Expenditures	Recreation Expenditures	Spectator Expenditures
1929	0.94%	16.6%	78.9%
1937	1.01	20.0	82.6
1943	1.29	25.7	87.6
1951	0.64	11.3	76.3
1959	0.31	5.6	61.0
1965	0.21	3.5	51.2
1971	0.18	2.7	47.7
1977	0.56	5.8	34.8
1983	0.16	2.4	41.9
1986	0.14	1.9	37.3
1987	0.14	1.8	36.9
1988	0.13	1.8	36.5
1989*	0.13	1.7	36.1

*Estimated by the casewriter

have fallen for the past three years, although the operation's assets and sales have been increasing. Generally speaking, about half the nation's motion picture theaters and chains have been unprofitable in the 1980s, while numerous chains have engaged in the illegal practice of "splitting," wherein theater owners in certain markets decide which one will negotiate or bid for which films offered by the various distributors available to them.

The Cineplex Odeon Corporation

Today's exhibition giant began in 1978 with an 18-screen complex in the underground garage of a Toronto shopping center. Garth Drabinsky, a successful entertainment lawyer and real estate investor (see exhibit 8), joined with the Canadian theater veteran Nathan Aaron (Nat) Taylor in this enterprise. After three years and dozens of new theaters, Cineplex entered the American theater market by opening a 14-screen multiplex in the very competitive and highly visibleLos Angeles Beverly Center. Despite the chain's growth, it was only marginally profitable. When the fledgling chain went public on the Toronto Stock Exchange in 1982, it lost $12.0 million on sales of $14.4 million.

Cineplex nearly went bankrupt but not through poor management by Drabinsky or Taylor. Canada's two major theater circuits, Famous Players (Paramount Studios) and the independent Odeon chain, had pressured Hollywood's major distributors into keeping their first-run films from Cineplex. But in 1983, Drabinsky, who as a lawyer had written a standard reference on Canadian motion picture law, convinced Canada's version of the U.S. Justice Department's antitrust division that Famous Players and Odeon were operating in restraint of trade. Armed with data gathered by Drabinsky, the Combines Investigative Branch forced the distributors to sign a consent decree, thus opening all films to competitive bidding. Ironically, without the protection provided by its collusive actions, the 297 screen Odeon circuit soon began to lose money, whereupon Cineplex purchased its former adversary for $22 million. The company subsequently changed its name to Cineplex Odeon.

In its development as an exhibition giant, the chain has always been able to attract a number of smart, deep-pocketed backers. Early investors were the since-departed Odyssey Partners, and, with a 30.2 percent stake, the Montreal-based Claridge Investments & Company, which is the main holding company of Montreal financier Charles Bronfman. The next major investor was the entertainment conglomerate MCA Incorporated, of Universal City, California. MCA purchased 49.7 percent of Cineplex's stock (but is limited to a 33.0 percent voting stake because of Canadian foreign-ownership rules) in January 1986 for $106.7 million. This capital infusion gave Cineplex the funds to further pursue its aggressive expansion plans.

Item	1979	1981	1983	1985	1987
Tickets sold (000,000)	1,121	1,067	1,197	1,056	1,086
Average admission per screen	65,575	58,422	63,387	49,936	47,797
Capital expenditures (000,000)	$19.0	$57.4	$77.6	$164.0	$515.7
Profit margin	9.3%	9.1%	11.7%	11.6%	8.8%

EXHIBIT 7
Per Screen Admissions,
Capital Expenditures, and
Operating Profit Margins

As Drabinsky said at the time, "There's only so much you can do within the Canadian marketplace. It was only a question of when, not where, we were going to expand."[4] In short order the company became a major American exhibitor by acquiring six additional chains. Some rival and fearful exhibitors, because of Drabinsky's quest for growth via the acquisition route, have been tempted to call him Darth Grabinsky. (See exhibit 8.)

Despite these rumblings, Cineplex Odeon has reshaped the moviegoing experience for numerous North Americans. Many previous theater owners had either let their urban theaters fall into decay and disrepair or they had sliced their larger theaters into unattractive and sterile multiplexes. Others had built new but spartan and utilitarian facilities in suburban malls and shopping centers. When building their own theaters from either the ground up or when refurbishing an acquired theater, Cineplex pays great attention to making the patron's visit to the theater a pleasurable one. When the Olympia I and II Cinemas in New York City were acquired, a typical major renovation was undertaken. Originally built in 1913, the theater seated 1,320 and was billed as having "the world's largest screen." New owners subsequently remodeled it in 1939 in an art deco style, and in 1980 it was renovated as a triplex, with a fourth screen added in 1981. As part of Cineplex's renovation, the four smaller auditoriums were collapsed into two larger 850-seat state-of-the-art wide-screened theaters featuring Dolby stereo sound systems and 70mm projection equipment. Its art deco design was augmented by postmodern features, such as marble floors, pastel colors, and neon accents.

Whether through new construction or the renovation of acquired theaters, many Cineplex cinemas feature entranceways made of terrazzo tile, marble, or glass. The newly built Cinema Egyptien in Montreal has three auditoriums and a total seating capacity of 900. It is replete with mirrored ceilings and handpainted murals rendered in the traditional Egyptian colors of Nile green, turquoise, gold, lapis lazuli blue, and amber red. Historically accurate murals measuring 300 feet in length depict the daily life and typical activities of the ancient Egyptians. Toronto's Canada Square office complex features a spacious, circular art deco lobby, with a polished granite floor and recessed lighting highlighted by a thin band of neon encircling the high domed ceiling. On the lobby's left side, moviegoers can snack in a small cafe outfitted with marble tables, bright red chairs, and thick carpeting. In New York City the chain restored the splendor and elegance of Carnegie Hall's Recital Hall as it was originally conceived in 1981. The plaster ceilings and the original seats were completely rebuilt and refinished in the gold and red velvet colors of the great and historic Carnegie Hall.

Just to make the evening complete, and to capture the high profits realized from concession operations, patrons of a Cineplex theater can typically sip *cappuccino* or taste any of the 14 different blends of tea served in Rosenthal china. Those wanting heavier fare can nibble on croissant sandwiches, fudge brownies, carrot cake, or a *latte macchiato*, while freshly popped popcorn is always served with real butter. In-theater boutiques selling movie memorabilia to add to the dollar volume obtained from the moviegoer were created but discontinued, due to unnecessarily high operating costs.

This glamor does not come cheaply, because the chain usually charges the highest prices in town. For those in a financial bind, the American Express credit card is now honored at many of the chain's box offices. Cineplex broke New York City's $6 ticket barrier by raising its prices to $7, thus incurring the wrath of Mayor Ed Koch, who marched in picket lines with other angry New Yorkers. Cineplex's action also caused the New York state legislature to pass a measure requiring all exhibitors to print admission prices in their newspaper advertisements. When justifying the

[4]Quoted by David Aston in "A New Hollywood Legend Called—Garth Drabinsky?" *Business Week*, September 23, 1985, p. 61.

EXHIBIT 8
Cineplex Odeon
Theater Acquisitions

Odeon	Septum
Plitt Theatres	Essaness
RKO Century Warner Theaters	Sterling Recreation Organization
Walter Reade Organization	Maybox Movie Centre, Ltd.
Circle Theatres	

increased ticket price, Drabinsky said the alternative was "to continue to expose New Yorkers to filthy, rat-infested environments. We don't intend to do that."[5] Instead of keeping prices low, $30 million was spent refurbishing Cineplex Odeon's 30 Manhattan theaters to attract better-paying customers. Another unpopular and somewhat incongruous action, given the upscale image engendered by each theater's trappings is the running of advertisements for Club Med and California raisins before its films. Regardless of the anger and unpopularity created among potential patrons, Cineplex is not interested in catering to the "average" theater patron. Rather than trying to attract the mass market, the theater chain aims its massive and luxurious theaters at the aging Baby Boomers, who are becoming a greater portion of America's population.

Over the years, Cineplex Odeon and Garth Drabinsky have received high marks for their creative show business flair. As observed by theater industry analyst Paul Kagan, "Garth Drabinsky is both a showman and a visionary. There were theater magnates before him, but none who radiated his charisma or generated such controversy."[6] These sentiments are reiterated by Roy L. Furman, president of Furman Selz Mager Dietz & Birney, Inc., one of Drabinsky's intermediaries in the Plitt acquisition. "Too many people see the [theater] business as just bricks and mortar. Garth has a real love for the business, a knowledge of what will work and what won't."[7] When a new Cineplex Odeon theater opens, it begins with a splashy by-invitation-only party, usually with a few movie stars on hand. Besides his ability to attract smart investors, Drabinsky believes moviegoers want to be entertained by the theater's ambience as well as by the movie it shows. Accordingly, about $2.8 million (about $450,000 per screen) is spent when building one of the chain's larger theaters, as opposed to the usual $1.8 million for a simple no-frills sixplex. "People don't just like coming to our theaters," says Drabinsky, "They linger afterward. They have another cup of *cappuccino* in the cafe or sit and read the paper. We've created a more complete experience, and it makes them return to that location."[8] He later expanded on this observation, saying, "This company has attempted to change the basic thinking. We've introduced the majesty back to picture-going."[9]

Drabinsky dates his fascination with the silver screen to his childhood bout with polio, which left him bedridden much of the time from the ages of 3 to 12. His illness also imbued him with a strong sense of determination, and this resolution has helped to drive Cineplex Odeon forward. No one speaks for the company except Drabinsky, and he logs half a million miles a year visiting his theaters and otherwise encouraging his employees. The energetic CEO likes to drop by his theaters unannounced to talk with ushers and cashiers, and he telephones or sees 20 to 25 theater managers a week. His standards are meticulously enforced, often in a very personal and confrontational manner. He has been known to exemplify his penchant for detail by stooping in front of one of his ushers to pick up a single piece of spilled popcorn.

The combative nature that helped Drabinsky break the Famous Players and Odeon cartel in the early 1980s still resides with him. When Columbia pictures temporarily pulled its production of *The Last Emperor* out of distribution, he retaliated by cancelling 140 play dates of the studio's monumental bomb, *Leonard Part 6* starring Bill Cosby. "Some people are burned by his brashness," says Al Waxman (formerly of the television series "Cagney & Lacey"). "There is no self-denial. He stands up and says, 'Here's what I'm doing.' Then he

[5]Quoted by Richard Corliss, "Master of the Movies' Taj Mahals," *Time*, January 25, 1988, pp. 60-61.
[6]Ibid., p. 60.
[7]Aston, "A New Hollywood Legend," p. 62.

[8]Quoted by Alex Ben Block, "Garth Drabinsky's Pleasure Domes," *Forbes*, June 2, 1986, p. 93.
[9]Mary A. Fischer, "They're Putting Glitz Back into Movie Houses," *U.S. News & World Report*, January 25, 1988, p. 58.
[10]Block, "Garth Drabinsky's Pleasure Domes," p. 92.

does it."[10] As his long-time mentor Nat Taylor has observed, "He's very forceful, and sometimes he's abrasive. I think he's so far ahead of the others that he loses patience if they can't keep up with him."[11] This nature may have long-term negative consequences for Cineplex, however, because Drabinsky has recently had heated arguments with Sidney Jay Sheinberg, president of MCA Incorporated, the head of the circuit's largest shareholder group.

In addition to its motion picture theater operations, Cineplex Odeon has been engaged in other entertainment-related ventures, such as television and film production, film distribution, and live theater. In the latter area, the company is restoring the Pantages Theatre in downtown Toronto into a legitimate theater for the housing of its $5.5 million production of Andrew Lloyd Webber's *The Phantom of the Opera*, scheduled for Fall 1989.

Cineplex also began a 414-acre motion picture entertainment and studio complex in Orlando, Florida, as a joint venture with MCA Incorporated, but sold its stake to an American unit of the Rank Organization PLC for about $150 million in April 1989 after having invested some $92 million in the project. Various industry observers felt Cineplex withdrew from the potentially profitable venture to help reduce its bank debt, which had grown to $640 million.

The firm also created New Visions Pictures as a joint venture with a unit of Lieberman Enterprises, Inc., in August 1988, to deliver 10 films over a two-year period. Cineplex Odeon also owns Toronto International Studios, Canada's largest film center. This operation licenses its facilities to moviemakers and others for film and television production. In a related motion picture production move, Cineplex acquired The Film House Group, Inc., in 1986, to process 16mm and 35mm release prints for Cineplex Odeon Films, another one of the company's divisions, and for other distributors. After doubling and upgrading its capacity in 1987, it sold 49 percent of its interest to the Rank Organization in December 1988 for $73.5 million. Rank exercised its one-year option to buy the remaining portion of The Film House Group shortly thereafter.

The company has also engaged in various motion picture distribution deals and television productions, none of which have been commercially successful. Cineplex has distributed such films as Prince's *Sign o' the Times*, Paul Newman's *The Glass Menagerie*, The

Changeling with George C. Scott, and *Madame Sousatzka* starring Shirley Maclaine, while its television unit contracted 41 new episodes of the revived "Alfred Hitchcock Presents" series for the 1988-89 television season. The series, however, was cancelled. For future release, Cineplex is financing five low-budget ($4 million to $5 million each) films joint-ventured with Robert Redford's Wildwood Enterprises through Northfork Productions, Inc. The five movies will be distributed through Cineplex Odeon Films.

Garth Drabinsky's financial dealings and his ability to attract capital to his firm has always been very important to its success. Serious questions have been raised, however, into the propriety of some of Cineplex's financial reporting methods. Charles Paul, a vice president of MCA Incorporated and a Cineplex board member, says various members are very concerned about the company's financial reporting practices and procedures. In a highly critical report distributed by Kellogg Associates, a Los Angeles accounting and consulting firm, a number of questionable practices were noted. Most frequently cited is Cineplex's treatment of the gains and losses associated with asset sales, with the overall effect being an overstatement of operating revenues. As an example, Cineplex treated its gain of $40.4 million from the sale of The Film House Group as revenue, rather than as extraordinary income. The report also criticized (1) Cineplex's $18.7 million write-off on the value of its film library, thereby "postponing" losses on the sale of American theaters, and (2) its inclusion of the proceeds from the sale of theaters as nonoperating income in its cash flow statement but calling it operating revenue in its profit and loss statement. In 1988 alone, Cineplex reported a profit of $49.3 million from the sale of certain theater properties.

Also of concern is the role that asset sales play in the company's revenue and cash flow picture. Jeffrey Logsdon, a Crowell Weedon analyst, believes Cineplex has been selling its assets just to keep operating, citing as evidence the sale of both The Film House Group and its 50 percent stake in MCA's Universal Studios tour project to the Rank Organization. Exhibit 9 demonstrates how Cineplex's revenue sources have changed since 1985, with box office receipts constantly falling and property sales constantly rising. Over the period shown, the sale of theater assets has increased 98 percent as a source of corporate revenues. Additionally, the return on those sales, based on selling price over acquisition costs, has fallen every year from a high of 139.1 percent in 1985 to the low of 13.3 percent in 1988.

---

[11] Aston, "A New Hollywood Legend," p. 63.

EXHIBIT 9
Cineplex Odeon's Revenue
Sources

Revenue Source	1988	1987	1986	1985
Admissions	51.1%	62.5%	64.5%	68.0%
Concessions	16.5	18.2	20.0	20.0
Distribution and other	22.5	11.1	8.6	7.0
Property sales	9.9	8.0	6.8	5.0

There is also a question about whether Cineplex can continue its current growth rate via acquisitions and debt financing. The cost of acquisitive growth may become more expensive, because many of the bargains have already been obtained by Cineplex or other chains. The early purchase of the Plitt Theater chain in November 1985 cost about $125,000 per screen, although the bargain price for Plitt may have been a one-time opportunity, because it had just lost $5 million on revenues of $ 111 million during the nine months ending June 30, 1985. To get into the New York City RKO Century Warner Theaters chain in 1986, Cineplex had to pay $1.9 million per screen, while it paid almost $3.0 million a screen in 1987 for the New York City-based Walter Reade Organization. Overall, Cineplex Odeon paid about $276,000 each for the screens it acquired in 1986, and some are questioning the prices being paid for old screens, as well as the wisdom of expanding operations in what many see is a declining and saturated industry. A past rule of thumb has been that a screen should cost 11 times its cash flow; but some experts feel a more reasonable rule should be 6 to 7 times its cash flow, given the glut of screens on the market. The changing effects of Cineplex's acquisition and debt structure since 1984 have been summarized in exhibit 10.

Given the nature of the North American market and Cineplex Odeon's penchant for growth, it is currently implementing a planned expansion into Europe. Cineplex is scheduled to build 100 screens in 20 movie houses throughout the United Kingdom by 1990, and it has further plans in Europe and Israel for the early 1990s. Exhibit 11 lists the comparative per capita motion picture attendance rates found in various European countries. Other exhibitors are also interested in bringing multiscreened theaters to Europe. In addition to Cineplex's plans, Warner Brothers, American Multi-Cinema, Odeon, and National Amusements have announced their intentions of opening a total of more than 450 screens in the United Kingdom, with further theaters scheduled for later dates.

While few deny the attractiveness of the theaters owned and operated by Cineplex, the firm may have overextended itself both financially and operationally (see exhibits 12 and 13.) Is Cineplex Odeon on the crest of a new wave of creative growth in North America and Europe, or does it stand at the edge of an abyss? Is consolidation or a thorough review of past actions in order? What next moves should Garth Drabinsky and Cineplex make to continue the firm's phenomenal success story?

EXHIBIT 10
Selected Summary Financial
Data (in $ millions)

	1989*	1988	1987	1986	1985	1984
Revenue	710.0	695.8	520.2	357.0	124.3	67.1
Net profit	43.0	40.4	34.6	22.5	9.1	3.5
Net profit (%)	6.1	5.8	6.6	6.3	7.3	5.3
Long-term debt	720.0	600.0	464.3	333.5	40.7	36.1
Interest	52.6	40.2*	33.8	16.4	3.9	2.1
ROE (%)	10.2	10.3	11.0	18.1	40.7	30.5

*Estimated

Country	Visits Per Year
United States	4.4
Great Britain	1.4
Canada	2.8
France	1.9
West Germany	1.9
Italy	1.6

EXHIBIT 11
1988 Per Capita
Attendance Rates

EXHIBIT 12
Cineplex Odeon Corporation—Consolidated Statement of Income (in $ thousands)

	1988	1987	1986	1985
Revenue:				
Admissions	$355,645	$322,385	$230,200	$ 84,977
Concessions	114,601	101,568	71,433	24,949
Distribution, post production and other	156,372	61,216	30,846	7,825
Sale of theatre properties	69,197	34,984	24,400	6,549
	695,815	520,153	356,989	124,300
Expenses:				
Theatre operations and other expenses	464,324	371,909	258,313	89,467
Cost of concessions	21,537	18,799	13,742	5,980
Cost of theatre properties sold	61,793	21,618	11,690	2,736
General and admin. expenses	26,617	17,965	15,335	5,701
Depreciation and amortization	38,087	23,998	14,266	3,678
	612,358	454,289	313,346	107,562
Income before the undernoted	85,457	65,864	43,643	16,738
Other income	3,599	—	—	(330)
Interest on long-term debt and bank in-debtedness	42,932	27,026	16,195	3,961
Income before taxes, equity earnings, preacquisition losses and extraordinary item	44,124	38,838	27,148	13,107
Income taxes	3,728	4,280	6,210	3,032
Income before equity, earnings, preacquisition losses and extraordinary item	40,396	34,558	21,138	8,075
Add back: Pre-acquisition losses attributable to 50% interest Plitt not owned by the corporation	—	—	1,381	—
Equity in earnings of 50% owned companies	—	—	—	1,021
Income before extraordinary item	40,396	34,558	22,519	10,374
Extraordinary item	—	—	—	9,096
Net income	$ 40,396	$ 34,558	$ 22,519	$ 10,374

EXHIBIT 13
Cineplex Odeon Corporation—Consolidated Balance Sheet (in $ thousands)

	1988	*1987*	*1986*
Assets:			
Current assets:			
Accounts receivable	$ 151,510	$ 42,342	$ 20,130
Advances to distributors and producers	26,224	10,704	4,671
Distribution costs	10,720	10,593	4,318
Inventories	7,450	8,562	6,978
Prepaid expenses and deposits	5,505	4,683	4,027
Properties held for disposition	25,557	22,704	16,620
Total current assets	226,966	99,588	56,744
Property, equipment, and leaseholds	824,836	711,523	513,411
Other assets:			
Long-term investment and receivables	130,303	49,954	14,292
Goodwill (less amortization of $2,758; 1987—$1,878)	53,966	52,596	40,838
Deferred charges (less amortization of $7,724; 1987—$1,771)	27,100	12,015	6,591
	211,369	114,565	61,721
Total assets	$1,263,171	$925,676	$631,876
Liabilities and Shareholders' Equity			
Current liabilities:			
Bank indebtedness	$ 21,715	$ 20,672	$ 30
Accounts payable and accruals	107,532	74,929	47,752
Deferred income	21,967	755	—
Income taxes payable	5,651	4,607	1,926
Current portion of long-term debt and other obligations	10,764	5,965	6,337
Total current liabilities	167,629	106,173	55,945
Long-term debt	663,844	449,707	317,550
Capitalized lease obligations	14,849	14,565	15,928
Deferred income taxes	10,436	13,318	11,142
Pension obligations	6,326	4,026	3,668
Minority interest	25,144	—	—
Stockholders' equity:			
Capital stock	283,739	289,181	212,121
Translation adjustment	13,348	1,915	(3,591)
Retained earnings	77,856	46,791	19,113
	374,943	337,887	227,643
Total liabilities and shareholders' equity	$1,263,171	$925,676	$631,876

■ SCANDINAVIAN AIRLINES SYSTEM IN 1988†

*By Sumantra Ghoshal with
Ronald Berger Lefèbure, Johnny
Jorgensen and David Staniforth*

When the Scandinavian Airlines System (SAS) group financial results for the fiscal year 1986-87 were released, it marked the trinational transport group's sixth straight profitable year, and their best year ever with a net operating income of Skr. 1.6 billion on revenues of Skr. 23.9 billion. This was a huge improvement over the situation in 1981 when losses were mounting and the airline was rapidly losing market share. A summary of the company's recent financial results, along with relevant exchange rates, are shown in exhibit 1.

Much of the credit for the company's dramatic turnaround was ascribed to Jan Carlzon who succeeded Carl-Olov Munkberg as president and CEO in 1981. Carlzon quickly initiated a number of major changes in the airline and its associated companies. He reoriented SAS towards the business travel market and gave top priority to customer service. This involved a complete reorganization of the company and a major decentralization of responsibility. As a result, SAS had become the leading carrier of full-fare traffic in Europe. Carlzon had joined SAS as executive vice-president in 1980, after serving as president of Linjeflyg, the Swedish domestic airline. Previously, he had been managing director of the SAS tour subsidiary Vingresor.

Despite these successes, dramatic as they were, the company still faced considerable threats and many analysts questioned if it could survive as a viable competitor in the increasingly global and competitive airline industry. Its population base of only 17 million

spread out over a large area was too small by itself to support a comprehensive international traffic system. In addition, its geographic location at the periphery of Europe was a disadvantage when compared to Western Europe's densely populated areas.

The most pressing problem was the airline's operating costs, which were among the highest in the industry (see exhibit 2.) It was estimated that labour charges accounted for 35 percent of SAS's total costs, compared with only 25 percent for the major US carriers since deregulation, and 18 percent for the large Asian airlines. The evolution of the US "mega-carriers" was a major concern as they eyed Europe as an area for continued expansion.

Senior managers of the company were fully aware of these challenges. In discussing future developments in the airline industry, and SAS's role in particular, Helge Lindberg, group executive vice president, noted:

> "I doubt very much that SAS can survive alone as a major intercontinental airline. We need to expand our traffic system in order to compete with major European carriers having much larger population bases, as well as with the major American and Asian carriers who maintain considerably lower operating costs. We need to develop with other partners a global traffic system with daily connections to the important overseas destinations. The nature of our industry is such that if you are not present in the market the day the customers wish to travel, the business is lost. Another priority is to reduce our costs. Our social structure in Scandinavia leaves us with one of the highest personnel costs in the industry, coupled with the fact that increased emphasis on service caused us to lose our traditional budget consciousness over the past few years. A third major issue is to develop a competitive distribution system, a problem we are about to solve in partnership with Air France, Iberia and Lufthansa, with the so-called Amadeus system."

The Turnaround

Sweden, Denmark, and Norway had always shared a common interest in creating an ambitious air service, both to link their scattered communities, and to ensure a

†**Source:** © 1988 by INSEAD-CEDEP, Fontainebleau, France
This case was prepared by Ronald Berger Lefèbure, Johnny Jorgensen and David Staniforth, Research Assistants, under the supervision of Sumantra Ghoshal, Associate Professor at INSEAD. It is intended to be used as the basis for class discussion rather than to illustrate either effective or ineffective handling of an administrative situation. Unless stated otherwise, exhibit data have been obtained from SAS.

EXHIBIT 1
SAS Group Financial and Operating Results, 1977/78–1986/87

Financial Summary—Group	1977/ 1978	1978/ 1979	1979/ 1980	1980/ 1981	1981/ 1982	1982/ 1983	1983/ 1984	1984/ 1985	1985/ 1986	1986/ 1987
Operating revenue	7,050	8,066	9,220	10,172	12,807	15,972	18,005	19,790	21,585	23,870
Operating expenses	(6,437)	(7,551)	(8,920)	(9,664)	(11,895)	(14,696)	(16,415)	(18,256)	(19,369)	(21,514)
Depreciation	(347)	(360)	(391)	(430)	(474)	(483)	(545)	(574)	(863)	(1,126)
Financial & extra items	(140)	(7)	28	(129)	10	(192)	(77)	57	162	443
Net operating income	126	148	(63)	(51)	448	601	968	1,017	1,515	1,663
Exchange Rate Skr./$US	4.60	4.15	4.17	5.61	6.28	7.83	8.70	7.40	6.91	6.40
Revenue by business area										
SAS Airline Consortium						12,600	14,151	15,434	16,495	17,510
						79%	79%	78%	76%	73%
SAS International Hotels						732	843	948	1,083	1,230
						5%	5%	5%	5%	5%
SAS Service Partner						1,681	2,049	2,393	2,712	3,223
						11%	11%	12%	13%	14%
SAS Leisure (Vingresor)						1,311	1,474	1,537	1,897	2,379
						8%	8%	8%	9%	10%
Other						456	460	390	415	730
						3%	3%	2%	2%	3%)
Group eliminations						(808)	(972)	(912)	(1,017)	(1,202)
						−5%	−5%	−5%	−5%	−5%
Total						15,972	18,005	19,790	21,585	23,870
Income by business area										
SAS Airline Consortium						461	729	811	1,207	1,453
						77%	75%	80%	80%	87%
SAS International Hotels						14	21	67	72	73
						2%	2%	7%	5%	4%
SAS Service Partner						75	15	81	123	180
						12%	2%	8%	8%	11%
SAS Leisure (Vingresor)						41	43	81	133	141
						7%	4%	8%	9%	8%
Other						17	5	(15)	(31)	(99)
						7%	4%	−1%	−2%	−6%
Group Eliminations						(25)	(21)	(7)	(22)	(85)
						4%	−2%	−1%	−1%	−5%
Extraordinary items						18	176	−1	34	0
						3%	18%	0%	2%	0%
Total						601	968	1,017	1,516	1,663

Operating statistics SAS Airline	1977/ 1978	1978/ 1979	1979/ 1980	1980/ 1981	1981/ 1982	1982/ 1983	1983/ 1984	1984/ 1985	1985/ 1986	1986/ 1987
Cities served	98	102	103	105	99	93	91	88	89	85
Kilometers flown (millions)	123	124	20	113	113	120	124	125	136	n/a
Passengers (thousands)	7,886	8,669	8,393	8,413	8,861	9,222	10,066	10,735	11,708	n/a
Cabin load factor (%)	56.4%	59.9%	59.4%	60.9%	63.6%	65.5%	67.2%	67.2%	66.2%	68.9%
Employees	16,010	16,755	17,069	16,425	16,376	17,101	17,710	18,845	19,773	n/a

Airline	1982	1983	1984	1985	1986
Singapore Airlines	36	36	33	32	30
British Caledonian	37	37	29	35	38
United Airlines	39	39	38	44	40
KLM	35	29	26	35	44
Pan American	34	36	38	36	n/a
British Airways	40	38	31	37	44
Delta	42	43	43	45	44
Lufthansa	51	44	40	53	57
Swissair	54	47	41	53	58
Sabena	53	43	44	56	63
SAS	53	53	50	65	76

EXHIBIT 2
Comparison of Airline
Operating Costs
(US cents per available
tonne–kilometer)

role for Scandinavia among the world's international airlines. They first considered a joint airline in the 1930s when all three countries wanted to establish a route to America. No firm agreement was reached until 1940 however, when they decided to operate a joint service between New York and Bergen, on Norway's west coast. This plan was unfortunately scuttled by the German invasion three days later.

The Bermuda conference on international air travel in 1946 put an end to any hopes of true freedom of the air, and served to underline the importance of developing a common airline in order to establish a stronger world presence. The three countries agreed upon an ownership structure, and in the summer of 1946 a DC-4 lifted off from Stockholm bound for Oslo and New York bearing the Scandinavian Airlines System name. Sweden controlled three-sevenths of the new airline and Norway and Denmark two-sevenths each, with ownership split 50: 50 between the respective governments and private interests.

SAS gained a strong foothold in the European market—at the expense of the Germans who were forbidden from establishing their own airline—and quickly developed a worldwide route network. The airline established numerous firsts in the early years of worldwide air travel, beginning with the Swedish parent company ABA in 1945, who were the first to re-establish transatlantic service after the war. SAS pioneered the Arctic route in 1954 with a flight from Copenhagen to Los Angeles via Greenland, and in 1957 inaugurated transpolar service to Tokyo, cutting travel time by half. The Scandinavians were the first to operate the French Caravelle, introducing twin-engine jet travel within Europe, and worked with

Douglas Aircraft to develop the ultra-long range DC-8-62, capable of flying non-stop to the US west coast and Southeast Asia. A list of the airline's major milestones is shown in exhibit 3. SAS had often looked for overseas partners, and purchased 30 percent of Thai Airways International in 1959. This stake was bought back by the Thai government in 1977, but the two airlines had since entered into a co-operative service agreement.

The 1960s and early 1970s were the golden years for the airline. Apart from 1972 when profits shrank to $8 million due to currency fluctuations, average annual net profits from 1969-75 were between $15 million and $20 million. In the late 1970s, the second oil stock had a severe effect on profits, and the airline sustained considerable losses in 1979-80 and 1980-81.

SAS had developed close relationships with Swissair and KLM. An agreement between the three airlines (the KSSU agreement) was signed in 1969 with the objective of strengthening technical co-operation and of jointly assessing any new aircraft entering the market. For example, it was agreed that SAS would be responsible for overhauling the Boeing 747 engines of all three airlines, while the other partners performed other joint maintenance activities.

Although the trinational airline had generally functioned smoothly, there had been some problems among the constituent groups, particularly when Denmark joined the EEC in 1973. This underlying rivalry was reflected in Norway by the statement, "SAS is an airline run by the Swedes for the benefit of the Danes," in reference to the airline's head office in Stockholm and its main traffic hub at Kastrup airport in Copenhagen. Nonetheless, the larger traffic base and

EXHIBIT 3
SAS Milestones

Source: *The SAS Saga:* Anders Buraas, Oslo 1979

1946—July 31—August 1
DDL, DNL, and SILA found SAS for the operation of intercontinental services to North and South America.

1946—September 17
Route to New York opened.

1946—November 30
Route to South America opened.

1948—April 18
ABA, DDL, and DNL form ESAS to co-ordinate European operations.

1948—July 1
SILA and ABA amalgamated.

1949—October 26
Route to Bangkok opened.

1950—October 1
ABA, DDL, and DNL transfer all operations to SAS in accordance with a new Consortium Agreement dated February 8, 1951, with retroactive effect.

1951—April 18
The Bangkok route is extended to Tokyo.

1951—April 19
Route to Nairobi is inaugurated.

1952—November 19
First transarctic flight by commercial airliner.

1953—January 8
The Nairobi route extended to Johannesburg.

1954—November 15
Polar route to Los Angeles inaugurated.

1956—May 9
Pre-war route to Moscow reopened.

1957—February 24
Inauguration of North Pole short cut to Tokyo.

1957—April 2
SAS participates in formation of Linjeflyg.

1957—April 4
Route opened to Warsaw.

1957—April 16
First flight to Prague.

1958—October 6
Agreement of cooperation signed by SAS and Swissair.

1959—August 24
SAS and Thai Airways Co. establish THAI International.

1960—July 2
Monrovia added to South Atlantic network.

1961—October 1
SAS Catering established as subsidiary.

1962—May 15
Inauguration of all-cargo service to New York.

1963—May 4
Route opened across top of North Norway to Kirkenes.

1963—November 2
First service to Montreal.

1964—April 2
Route to Chicago inaugurated.

1965—April 5
Non-stop service New York—Bergen begun.

1966—September 2
Inauguration of service to Seattle via Polar route.

1967—November 4
Opening of Trans-Asian Express via Tashkent to Bangkok and Singapore.

1968—March 31
Dar-Es-Salaam added to East African network.

1969—November 1
Route opened to Barbados and Port-of-Spain in West Indies.

1970—February 18
KSSU agreement ratified.

1971—April 3
Trans-Siberian Express to Tokyo inaugurated.

1971—November 1
SAS participates in formation of Danair.

1972—April 5
Route to East Berlin opened.

1972—May 24
New York-Stavanger route opened.

1973—November 4
All-cargo express route opened to Bangkok and Singapore.

1973—November 6
Dehli added to Trans-Orient route.

1975—September 2
Inauguration of Svalbard route, world's northernmost scheduled service.

1976—April 21
Route opened to Lagos.

1977—April 7
Kuwait added to Trans-Orient route.

1977—November 2
Opening of Gothenburg-New York route.

increased bargaining power afforded by the union had helped to make SAS a major world airline.

Problems Facing SAS in 1981

When Jan Carlzon assumed the presidency of SAS in August 1981, he realized that major changes would have to be made to restore the airline and associated companies to profitability, and to meet the growing challenges of an increasingly competitive industry. After 17 profitable years, the SAS group had posted operating losses of Skr.63.1 million and Skr.51.3 million in fiscal years 1979-80 and 1980-81 respectively. This dramatic decline had given rise to rumours that the three constituent countries were considering disbanding SAS and running their own separate airlines.

In addition to the problems that beset the industry—the international recession, higher interest rates and fuel costs, overcapacity and less-regulated competition—specific problems had plagued SAS in recent years. The airline had been losing market share, even in its home territory; its fleet mix and route network did not meet market needs, and its reputation for service and punctuality had deteriorated. For example, on-time performance (defined as percentage of arrivals within 15 minutes of schedule) had slipped from over 90 percent to 85 percent—a major drop by airline standards.

In addition, many regular travellers from Norway and Sweden were increasingly avoiding Copenhagen's troublesome Kastrup airport—SAS's major hub—in favour of more attractive and efficient terminals at Amsterdam, Frankfurt or Zurich. Under the umbrella of regulation, bad habits had developed within the company's management ranks. Carlzon felt that SAS, like most airlines, had allowed itself to become too enamoured with technology—new aircrafts, new engines—often at the cost of meeting the customer's needs. They had become a product-driven airline instead of being a service-driven one. A typical example was the acquisition of the state-of-the-art Airbus A300 aircraft in the late 1970s. These larger planes required high load factors to be profitable and this necessitated lower flight frequency—not in the best interests of customers who needed frequent and flexible flight schedules. In the past, when air travel was still somewhat of a novelty, customers had been willing to plan their trips according to a particular airline's schedule, and had even been willing to sacrifice some time to do so. The market had since changed, and experienced travellers now chose flights to suit their travel plans, not vice-versa. "In the past, we were operating as booking agents and aircraft brokers," said Carlzon. "Now we know, if we want the business we must fight for it like the 'street fighters' of the rough-and-tumble American domestic market."

New Strategy—"The Businessman's Airline"

Faced with the situation of a stagnant market, general overcapacity in the industry, and continuing loss of market share to competitors, Carlzon recognized that a new strategy was necessary to turn SAS around. In a similar situation when he was the president of Linjeflyg, Carlzon had decided to increase flight frequency and cut fares dramatically in order to improve aircraft utilization and boost load factors. These actions had proven to be very successful and profitability had

improved substantially. However, the market SAS operated in was quite different from that of Linjeflyg, and it was not clear that a similar strategy could be applied successfully. Another possible option was to initiate a major cost reduction program aimed at obtaining a better margin from a declining revenue base. This strategy would have required significant staff cuts, fleet reduction, and an overall lower level of flight frequency and service.

In the airline industry, the most stable market segment was the full-fare paying business traveller who provided the vast majority of revenues. First class travel within Europe was declining, mainly because businesses could not justify the extra expense, especially during a recession. All the major, scheduled airlines were after the business traveller, and some had created a separate "business" class priced at a 10-20 percent premium over economy, which offered many of the amenities of first class.

SAS chose the strategy of focusing on the business traveller. As described by Helge Lindberg, then executive vice president-commercial, "although other options were considered, we quickly decided there was no alternative but to go after the business traveller segment with a new product which offered significant advantages over the competition." In the words of Jan Carlzon: "We decided to go after a bigger share of the full-fare paying pie." There were a number of risks involved in this strategy. Increasing investment to provide an improved level of service at a time of mounting losses could bankrupt the airline if revenues did not improve sufficiently. On the other hand, if investment was the way to go, perhaps it could be better spent on more efficient aircraft so as to reduce costs. Another concern was that differentiating the product could alienate the tourist class passengers, especially among Scandinavian customers, who might resent any increase in passenger "segregation." In spite of these considerable risks, management increased expenditures and staked the future of the airline on their ability to woo the European business traveller away from the competition.

As a result, first class was dropped and "EuroClass" was introduced, offering more amenities than competing airlines' business classes, but at the old economy fare. (A similar service, First Business Class, was introduced on intercontinental routes, where first class was retained.) Thus any passenger paying the full fare would be entitled to this new service, which included separate check-in, roomier seating, advance seat selection, free drinks, and a better in-flight meal.

EXHIBIT 4
Example of EuroClass
Advertisement, 1981

Source: *Advertising Age* 1981

SAS Advertisement:

"Of the eight major airlines competing in Sweden for European traffic, five do not
give you separate check-in and seating, separate cabin or free drinks. Of the three
remaining airlines, two do not give you extra room and larger seats. Only one airline
in Europe has EuroClass which gives you more service and comfort for the economy
fare."

Lufthansa Advertisement:

"You can still fly first class in Europe!"

The other European airlines reacted strongly. Air France saw EuroClass as a serious threat to its own "Classe Affaires", which cost 20 percent more than economy, and at one point refused to book any EuroClass fares on its reservation system. Other airlines protested to their local government authorities, but to no avail, and the new fare structures were allowed to remain. SAS backed up the new service with the largest media advertising campaign ever launched by the airline (see exhibit 4.)

In conjunction with the new EuroClass services, a drive was launched to improve flight schedules and punctuality. The aircraft fleet mix was modified in order to meet the demands of increased flight frequency. The recently acquired, high-capacity Airbus aircraft were withdrawn from service and leased to SAS's Scanair charter subsidiary since they were not suitable for the frequent, non-stop flights which the new schedule demanded. For the same reason some Boeing 747s were replaced by McDonnell-Douglas DC-10s, and the older DC-9s were refurbished instead of being replaced since they were of the right size for the new service levels.

On certain short-distance routes such as Copenhagen-Hamburg, a new "EuroLink" concept was introduced. This involved substituting 40-passenger Fokker F-27s for 110-passenger DC-9s and doubling flight frequencies to provide a more attractive schedule. In short, the previous high fixed-cost, high capacity fleet was changing into a lower fixed-cost, high frequency one. This evolution of the SAS fleet is shown in exhibit 5.

Every effort was made to differentiate the business traveller product as much as possible from the lower priced fares. In this respect, "Scanorama" lounges were introduced at many of the airports served by SAS in an effort to further improve service. These lounges were for the exclusive use of the full-fare paying passenger and offered telephones and telex machines and a more relaxing environment to the business traveller. A joint agreement with the Danish Civil Aviation Authority was reached to invest in refurbishing Kastrup airport to bring it up to competitive standards. The objective was for Kastrup to be Europe's best airport by the end of the decade.

The introduction of these new products and related services represented a change in the overall philosophy of SAS. All tasks and functions within the organization

EXHIBIT 5
Evolution of SAS's Fleet

Aircraft type*		Seat Capacity	1977/ 1978	1978/ 1979	1979/ 1980	1980/ 1981	1981/ 1982	1982/ 1983	1983/ 1984	1984/ 1985	1985/ 1986	1986/ 1987
Boeing	747	405	3	4	4	5	5	3	5	5	2	0
Airbus	A300	242	0	0	2	4	1	1	0	0	0	0
McDonnell-Douglas	DC-10-30	230	5	5	5	5	5	5	6	8	9	11
	DC-8-62	n/a	5	5	2	3	3	3	3	3	3	0
	DC-8-63	170	5	3	4	2	2	2	2	2	2	0
	DC-9-21	75	9	9	9	9	9	9	9	9	9	9
	DC-9-33	(freight)	2	2	2	2	2	2	2	2	2	2
	DC-9-41	100/122	45	49	49	49	49	49	49	49	49	49
	DC-9-81	133	0	0	0	0	0	0	0	0	6	8
	DC-9-82	156	0	0	0	0	0	0	0	0	6	8
	DC-9-83	133	0	0	0	0	0	0	0	0	0	4
Fokker	F-27	40	0	0	0	0	0	0	4	6	9	9
Total			74	77	77	79	76	74	80	84	97	100

*Aircraft owned or leased by SAS that were leased to other operators are not included in this table.

were examined. If the business traveller benefited from a particular service or function, it was maintained or enhanced, otherwise it was cut back, or dropped altogether. Managers were urged to look upon expenses as resources; to cut those that did not contribute to revenue, but not to hesitate in raising those that did. Administrative costs were slashed 25 percent, but at the same time an extra Skr. 120 million was invested on new services, facilities, aircraft interiors, and other projects that affected the passengers directly. As a result, annual operating costs were increased by Skr.55 million at a time of deep deficits and continuing losses. Furthermore, these additional investments for improved service delayed the acquisition of new, more efficient aircraft to replace the ageing DC-9 fleet.

The results of this new strategy were dramatic. Full-fare paying passenger traffic rose over 8 percent in the first year, and profits rose to Skr.448 million for the 1981-82 fiscal year. In punctuality, SAS improved on-time performance to 93 percent, a record in Europe. The share of full-fare paying passengers rose consistently, and by 1986 it had risen to 60 percent, giving SAS the highest proportion of any airline in Europe. Accompanying this change in passenger mix were impressive profit gains. In 1986 SAS turned in the third best profit performance

among the world's major airlines with a net operating profit of Skr. 1.5 billion (a comparison of financial and operating results of major world airlines is shown in exhibit 6).

Corporate Cultural Revolution

Due in part to the protected, stable growth environment, the SAS organization was not ready to meet new competitive challenges without a major restructuring. Previously, the reference point had been fixed assets and technology, with emphasis on return on investment, centralized control, and orders from top management. Across the board cost-cutting was the usual approach to improve profits and to adapt to changing market conditions. The customer interface had been neglected. As described by a senior manager of the company:

"In those days, many employees felt that passengers were a disturbing element they had to contend with, rather than the ones who were in fact paying their salary. Taking control of a situation, and bypassing the regulations in order to please a customer were not the things to do in SAS."

EXHIBIT 6
Comparison of Major World
Airlines' Statistics, 1986

Source: *Air Transport World,*
June 1987

	Passengers	(thousands)		RPKs	(millions)
1.	Aeroflot	115,727	1.	Aeroflot	188,056
2.	United	50,690	2.	United	95,569
3.	American	45,983	3.	American	78,499
4.	Eastern	42,546	4.	Eastern	56,164
5.	Delta	41,062	5.	Delta	50,480
6.	TWA	24,636	6.	TWA	48,100
7.	All Nippon	24,503	7.	Northwest	46,346
8.	Piedmont	22,800	8.	British Airways	41,405
9.	USAir	21,725	9.	Japan Air Lines	38,903
10.	Continental	20,409	10.	Pan American	34,844
22.	SAS	11,700	30.[†]	SAS	12,471

	Fleet size	(No. aircraft)		Employees	
1.	Aeroflot	2,682	1.	Aeroflot	500,000
2.	United	368	2.	American	51,661
3.	American	338	3.	United	49,800
4.	Northwest	311	4.	Eastern	43,685
5.	Eastern	289	5.	Federal Express*	43,300
6.	Delta	253	6.	Delta	38,901
7.	Continental	246	7.	British Airways	37,810
8.	CAAC (China)	241	8.	Air France	35,269
9.	TWA	167	9.	Lufthansa	34,905
10.	Republic	165	10.	Northwest	33,250
18.	SAS	106	22.	SAS	19,773

	Operating revenue	(US $ million)		Operating profit	(US $ million)
1.	United	6,688	1.	American	392
2.	American	5,857	2.	Federal Express*	365
3.	Air France	4,747	3.	SAS	260
4.	Japan Air Lines	4,578	4.	Delta	225
5.	Eastern	4,522	5.	Cathay Pacific	206
6.	Delta	4,496	6.	Swissair	200
7.	Northwest	3,598	7.	Northwest	167
8.	TWA	3,181	8.	USAir	164
9.	Federal Express*	2,940	9.	Continental	143
10.	Pan American	2,580	10.	KLM	131
11.	SAS	2,387			

*Freight only.   [†]Estimated

Thus personal initiative was discouraged, and adherence to the company policy manuals was the norm. A large corporate staff was needed to run this bureaucracy, with layers of middle management to follow up directive from the top. Throughout the organization the morale of employees was low, and the level of co-operation among them, such as between ground staff and air crews, was not always the best. "There was a feeling of helplessness, and a fear for the future of the company," remarked an SAS pilot when asked to comment on the situation prevailing prior to 1981.

A transformation "from bureaucrats to businessmen" was essential, and an emphasis on the customer was needed. A major reorientation had been contemplated by Carlzon's predecessor, Carl-Olov Munkberg, but it was felt that implementation of a new organization would be more effective under a new CEO. "New brooms sweep clear," remarked Carlzon in relating his decision to replace or relocate 13 of the 14 executives in the management team of SAS. Helge Lindberg, the sole survivor in the top management team, was put in charge of the day-to-day running of the airline. Lindberg's extensive knowledge and experience was valued by Carlzon, who saw him as a "bridge between old and new," and a valuable asset now that the time for change had arrived.

In the past, SAS had focused on instructions, thereby limiting potential contributions from the employees. A key element of the cultural revolution under Carlzon was a new emphasis on information instead of instructions. The practical implications of this were that any employee in the "front line" (i.e. in the SAS-customer interface) should have the decision-making power necessary to do, within reasonable limits, whatever that person felt appropriate to please the customer. Each "moment of truth," when the customer encountered the service staff, would be used to its full potential so as to encourage repeat business. "Throw out the manuals and use your heads instead!" was the message from Lindberg. The underlying assumptions, made explicit throughout the organization, were that an individual with information could not avoid assuming responsibility and that hidden resources were released when an individual was free to assume responsibility instead of being restricted by instructions.

Some of the tools used by Carlzon in the reorganization were personal letters and several red booklets ("Carlzon's little red books") distributed to all employees. In these booklets the company's situation

and its goals were presented in very simple language, using cartoon-like drawings to emphasize their importance (see example in exhibit 7). Some employees found this form of communication too simple, but overall, the response was very positive. In his first year Carlzon spent approximately half of his time travelling, meeting with SAS employees all over the world. This made it very clear to everyone that management was deeply committed to turning things around, and helped to implement the changes quickly.

Education was considered necessary to reap the full benefits of the new organization, and both managers and front-line staff were sent to seminars. The courses for the front-line personnel were referred to by many as the "learn-to-smile seminars," but the real benefits probably resulted more from the participants' perception that the company cared about its employees, than from the actual content of the courses.

Certain problems were encountered in the process of change. Confusion and frustration were typical reactions of many middle managers when they suddenly found themselves bypassed by the "front line," on the one hand, and by the top management, on the other. "You can't please everyone, and some people will have to be sacrificed," said an SAS manager when asked to comment on this problem. Cross-training of employees to perform several tasks was attempted, but met with resistance from the unions. An example was the "turnaround" check—a visual check of the aircraft performed between each flight. This could very well be done by the pilots, but the mechanics' union insisted upon this task being done by their people, resulting in higher operating costs.

Another problem was that the first reorientation had short-term goals, and when these were achieved, the early momentum diminished. By 1984 SAS had received the "Airline of the Year" award from the Air Transport World magazine, and its financial situation had improved dramatically. These factors led to a feeling of contentment, and people started to fall back into old habits. Demands for salary increases were again raised. Some people thought that SAS was now out of danger, and wanted to harvest the fruits of hard work. Small "pyramids" started to crop up in the organization, and it became evident that the problems in the middle management were not solved. "The new culture was taking roots, but we had problems keeping up the motivation," noted Lindberg.

Consequently, a "second wave" of change was launched, and new goals with a much longer time

EXHIBIT 7
Examples from "Carlzon's
Little Red Books"

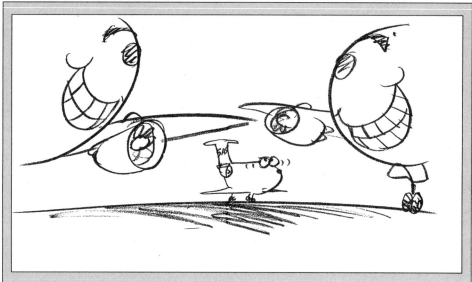

Hopeless Odds

When we looked around a year ago, our hopes of "getting our nose up" were sinking.
Demand had stopped increasing. We could no longer regard ourselves rich, i.e. there was
less hope for continued growth and thus automatically increased revenues. The competition
got harder. How could we survive?

Continued

horizon were outlined. Management wanted to prepare the company for the coming liberalization in the airline industry, and ensure a level of profitability sufficient to meet upcoming fleet replacement needs. The ultimate goal was for SAS to be the most efficient airline in Europe by 1990.

The Second Wave

SAS wanted to integrate the various elements of the travel package offered to the business traveller: to develop a full service product for the full-fare paying passenger. In the words of Lindberg: "We wanted to be a full service, door-to-door travel service company. We aimed to offer a unique product which we could control from A to Z." To meet this objective, the SAS service chain concept was established by creating a distribution system and network of services that met the needs of the business travellers, from the time they ordered their tickets to the time they got back home. This meant that the development of a hotel network, reservation system, and credit card operation were decisive for the company's future.

SAS International Hotels (SIH)

In 1983 SIH became a separate division within the SAS Group. A new concept, the SAS Destination Service—"ticket, transport and hotel package"—was introduced in September 1985. SAS market research indicated that ground transportation and hotel reservations ranked high among the needs of business travellers. Indeed, surveys also indicated that more than 50 percent of Scandinavian business travellers had no prior knowledge of the hotels where they had been booked, and thus would appreciate the standards and facilities guaranteed by the SAS Destination Service. The hotels where guaranteed reservations could be made under this scheme totalled 80, and the chain, already one of the biggest in the world, was marketed as SAS Business Hotels. With this new service, passengers were able to order airline tickets, ground transportation, and confirmed hotel reservations with one telephone call.

At each SAS destination where public transport from the airport to the city centre was time consuming or

EXHIBIT 7—*Continued*
Examples from "Carlzon's
Little Red Books"

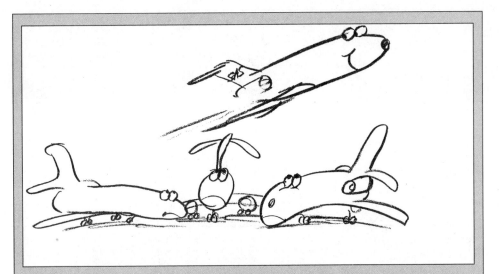

Certain Competitors "Throw in the Towel"

At the time when SAS achieves its best result ever, the majority in the airline industry are doing poorly. The IATA companies are this year losing around US$2 billion! But they should be Making a profit of US$3 billion (7.5 percent of turnover) to have a chance of meeting their future aircraft investments. From this we can draw two conclusions:

• SAS is not like the other IATA companies. Our result is nothing less than a world sensation.

• The IATA companies will probably fight for their lives in the future—just as we started to do a year and a half ago. They will probably use all their force to beat us in the coming rounds.

Note: Translation from Swedish by casewriters

complicated, a door-to-door limousine service was made available at reasonable prices to full-fare paying passengers. A helicopter shuttle service was introduced for travellers transferring between New York's Kennedy and LaGuardia airports. Many of the hotels featured SAS Airline Check-in. This meant that passengers could check their luggage and obtain boarding-passes before leaving the hotel in the morning, and then go directly to the gate at the airport for afternoon or evening departures. With the creation of the SAS Destination Service, a complete door-to-door transport service was offered, and it reflected SAS's conviction that, to a large extent, the battle for full-fare paying passengers would be won on the ground. The total product had to be seen as an integrated chain of services for the business travel market, including reservations, airport limousines, EuroClass, hotels, car rentals, airline check-in at the hotel, hotel check-in at the airport, airport lounges, and the SAS 24-hour telephone hotline.

SAS Reservation System

SAS was facing a rising number of reservation transactions: one million in 1980, and two million in 1983. This demand created the need for an integrated information system, and a network able to accept higher access without increasing the response time. To respond to this need, the company introduced a new reservation system in 1984. Developed at a cost of over Skr.250 million, the new system had more than 13,000 terminals around the world which were connected with SAS's centralized computing centre. The company believed that innovative and aggressive applications of computerized information and communication technology would decide which airlines would survive. The strategy was to ensure that SAS products found the shortest and least expensive access to the market, either directly or via travel agencies. Management believed that the company had to retain independence from credit card companies and the huge distribution systems of the major US airlines. By creating its own information

EXHIBIT 8
Selected Operating Data for
US CRS Systems

	Sabre (American)	Apollo (United)	System One (Texas Air)	Pars (TWA/ NWA)	Datas II (Delta)
Terminals: USA	54,800	40,688	21,450	17,907	9,600
Abroad	316	330	100	352	300
Subscriber locations	13,018	8,944	6,350	4,816	3,100
Agency sales processed (% of total) Jan–June 1986*	43	30.1	8.5	8.5	4.1
RPMs of airlines (% US) Jan–May 1987	14.136	17.125	19.212	17.766	12.317
Revenues† ($m)	336	318	n/a	n/a	n/a
Profits 1986	412	n/a	n/a	n/a	n/a
Airline booking fees:					
Basic ($)	1.75	1.85	1.75	1.75	1.50
Direct access ($)	2.00	1.85	1.75	1.75	1.50
Direct access airlines as of July 1987	13	30	20	13	5
Current strengths	Size Depth of data Most	Size Depth of data	Aggressiveness	Pricing Corporate Base Flexibility	

*USA only, Sabre estimate

†American is the only airline reporting publicly; Apollo estimate as published previously by the author and not disputed by the company

and communication system to assure continued direct access to markets, SAS would have control of the complete purchase process.

Controversy over ticket distribution had increased in Europe and European carriers manoeuvered to protect their national markets. The threat of competition from the US systems and the danger of losing control of the distribution process forced Europe's major airlines to improve and update their computer reservation systems. (A summary of the major American systems can be found in exhibit 8.) In 1987 SAS joined a computer reservation system (CRS) study group formed by Air France, Lufthansa, and Iberia. Later that year, the group announced its intention to develop one of the world's largest and most complete reservation and distribution systems. Known as AMADEUS, the system was expected to provide travel agencies with product and service information, reservation facilities for a worldwide array of airlines, hotels, car rentals, trains, ferries, and ticketing and fare quoting systems. Representing a total investment of US$270 million, the

system was scheduled to be operational in mid-1989, and was expected to handle 150 million annual booking transactions. Finnair (Finland), Braathens SAFE (Norway), Air Inter and UTA (France) had joined the AMADEUS group by the end of 1987. A competing system, known as GALILEO, was also announced in 1987 grouping, among others, British Airways, KLM, Swissair, Alitalia, and Austrian Airlines.

Credit Cards

In 1986, through the acquisition of Diners Club Nordic, SAS took over franchise rights in the Nordic countries for the Diners Club card, which had 150,000 card holders in Scandinavia, Finland, and Iceland. The annual sale of hotels and transport services was a multibillion kronor business in Scandinavia. SAS alone sold Skr.11 billion worth of airline tickets in Scandinavia during its 1984/1985 fiscal year. Credit card purchases accounted for 13 percent of these sales, and the share was steadily rising. The credit card acquisition was seen

EXHIBIT 9
SAS Group Structure

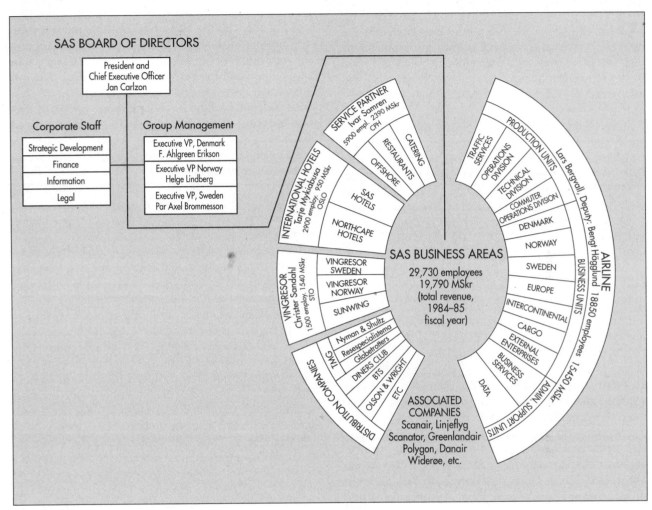

as an important element in SAS's distribution strategy, being a practical tool for the business traveller.

SAS Service Partner (SSP)

SSP, an SAS subsidiary in the catering business, was expanded from 12 international airline flight kitchens to an enterprise with more than 7,000 employees in over 100 locations. The subsidiary operated in 13 countries from the US to Japan, delivering 18 million airline meals a year. SSP was made up of a group of independent companies in airline catering and the international restaurant business. In 1984 SSP catered for more than 100 airlines, operated flight kitchens for several others,

and ran airport restaurants in all three Scandinavian countries as well as in England and Ireland. It had a separate unit for its Saudi Arabian business, which was expected to have possibilities for growth in the Middle and Far East. In the early 1980s, Chicago had been chosen as the entry point in a planned expansion among US airports. Despite the cyclical nature of the airline business, the subsidiary had remained consistently profitable. SAS believed that more and more airlines would concentrate on operating aircrafts, and leave service industry tasks like catering to specialist companies. British Airways was an example, having handed over its short and medium haul catering at London's Heathrow airport to SSP.

Other Related Activities

SAS had also begun to offer a dedicated service to US magazine publishers wishing to distribute their products in Europe. The airline offered a fast freight and delivery service at a reasonable price through a single distribution system, and management believed this to be a growing market. This new activity allowed otherwise unused cargo capacity to be put to productive use.

The role of Vingresor, an SAS subsidiary since 1971 and Sweden's largest tour-operator, was also expanded considerably. All-inclusive tours on charter flights from Sweden and Norway remained the basic service offered. Additional service products such as Vingresor's resorts with hotels in Europe and Africa had been developed, as well as a travel program including the Vingresor family concept.

New Group Structure

In March 1986 SAS was reorganized into five independent business units: the airline, SAS Service Partner, SAS International Hotels, SAS Leisure (Vingresor), and SAS Distribution (see exhibit 9.) The rationale was that each of these businesses faced very different strategic demands and, therefore, each was required to have its own management team to allow for more aggressive business development in an increasingly competitive climate. The same philosophy was pushed further down the line: for example, the new organization restructured the airline's route sectors into separate business units functioning as independent profit centres. The SAS group management, consisting of the chief executive officer, three executive officers and three executive vice-presidents representing Denmark, Norway, and Sweden, was expected to focus primarily on overall development of the SAS group's business areas.

It had been planned to introduce the new organization as early as 1984, but Carlzon had felt that the time was not ripe because the airline was involved in a public debate on air safety and there were problems with various trade union groups. "Now, I fear we might have waited too long. It has become clear that the two jobs cannot be combined. The burdens of the day-to-day operation of the airline and work on the future development of it and other business units are simply too heavy," he commented in 1986.

1988: Facing the Future

Looking ahead to the turn of the century, management of SAS was concerned about the future of the company. The globalization trend in the airline industry was gaining momentum, exemplified by the actions of giants like British Airways and American Airlines. BA had made it clear that it did not intend to stop growing after its acquisition of British Caledonian and the so-called "marketing merger" with United Airlines, in which the two carriers agreed to coordinate flight schedules and marketing programs, offer joint fares, and share terminals in four US cities. American Airlines was moving into Europe, having recently closed a leasing deal covering 40 new wide-body aircraft. "Globalization is inevitable," commented Carlzon. "Nobody will fly European unless we have a shake-out and become more efficient." This underlined the threat of being relegated to a regional carrier, and SAS's need to unite with other airlines to create a "Pan-European" system.

Aircraft replacement was another threat to SAS. The average age of its 60-strong DC-9 fleet (exclusive of the newer MD-80s) was 25 years, and an upcoming EEC directive on noise levels could, if put into effect in 1992, ground 30 aircraft. The required investment in new aircraft was estimated at Skr.40 billion over the next decade, which translated into one new plane per month from 1988 until the year 2000. This process of replacement had started, with the purchase of nine Boeing 767s for transatlantic traffic. To be able to finance these projects, the airline had to attain a gross profit level of 13 percent (before depreciation), compared to 11 percent in 1986. This increase was difficult to achieve in an increasingly competitive environment and one in which SAS had a cost disadvantage with respect to other airlines.

Partnerships or mergers with other airlines was clearly an attractive option, but the company had been frustrated in its attempts to develop such relationships. In the spring of 1987 SAS entered into negotiations with Sabena of Belgium with the goal of merging the operations of the two companies. Sabena was 52 percent state-owned and the Belgian government had expressed an interest in selling part of its holding to the private sector. With US$3.3 billion in sales, the merged carrier would have been Europe's fourth largest. Sabena chairman Carlos Van Rafelghem had stated that any accord with SAS would involve combining medium-

and long-distance networks in a system based on hubs in Copenhagen and Brussels. The negotiations failed, however, mainly on the issue of the degree of integration. SAS wanted to include all of Sabena's operations, including hotels and catering, while the Belgian carrier was only interested in merging the airline systems.

In the fall of that same year, SAS launched a bid to acquire a major shareholding in British Caledonian Airways. SAS was eager to expand its traffic base and gain access to BCal's American, African, and Middle East destinations, and to the carrier's Gatwick Airport hub outside London. A battle for control with British Airways ensued, with BA emerging the winner,

having paid £250 million, more than double the original bid. A major issue during the takeover battle was the implication of SAS gaining control of a British airline. The question of national control was important because of bilateral agreements. If BCal were deemed to be non-British, the foreign partner in an agreement might revoke the airline's licences on routes to that country.

By the middle of 1988, it was clear to the corporate management of SAS that, while past actions had led to a sound base for the future, they were not sufficient by themselves to ensure long-term viability of the company. Within the rapidly changing environment, a new thrust was necessary, and had to be found without much delay.

■ CARTIER: A LEGEND OF LUXURY†

By Sumantra Ghoshal, François-Xavier Huard and Charlotte Butler

The Birth and Growth of a Legend

In 1817, a man named Pierre Cartier returned from the Napoleonic Wars and opened a shop in the Marais, Paris's artisan quarter, where he sculpted powder horns and decorative motifs for firearms. His son, Louis-François (1819-1904) adapted to the more peaceful and prosperous times of the Restoration by becoming first the apprentice and later, in 1847, the successor of Monsieur Picard, a "maker of fine jewellery, novelty fashion and costume jewellery.' In 1859, Louis-François opened a shop on the Boulevard des Italiens, flanked by the favourite cafés of the smart set. He soon attracted the attention and patronage of the Princess Eugénie, cousin of Napoléon III and soon to become Empress of France.

Alfred Cartier took over from his father, Louis-François, in 1874. In the turbulent decade following the collapse of the Second Empire and the revolt of the Communards, the company survived by selling the jewels of La Barucci, a famous courtesan of the time, in London. Like his ancestors, Alfred adapted to changing times and the whims of a new set of customers, the wealthy bourgeois, adding objets d'art, clocks, snuff boxes and fob watches to his range of wares. His son, Louis, became his associate in 1898.

†**Source:** This case was written by François-Xavier Huard and Charlotte Butler, Research Associates, under the supervision of Sumantra Ghoshal, Associate Professor at INSEAD. It is intended to be used as a basis for class discussion rather than to illustrate either effective or ineffective handling of an administrative situation. Reprinted with the permission of INSEAD. Copyright ©1990 INSEAD-CEDEP, Fontainebleau, France. Revised 1992.

Louis Cartier

"Cartier… the subtle magician who breaks the moon into pieces and captures it in threads of gold."
—Jean Cocteau

Louis brought to the firm his "creativity, his commercial genius and an extraordinary dynamism." Full of curiosity, passionately interested in artistic and technical innovation, Louis introduced platinum into jewellery settings, making them lighter and easier to wear, and showed a distinctive flair for design. His was the inspiration for new items such as the watch with a geometric hull, designed for his friend, the Brazilian pilot Santos Dumont. Jewellery designer Jeanne Toussaint (1887-1978) added her creativity to that of Louis. The result was the famous animal collection, including the beast that was to become Cartier's best-known international trade-mark, the fabulous jewelled panther.

Cartier moved to the Place Vendôme, home of the greatest names in jewellery, but Louis had no intention of allowing Cartier to become just another jewellery firm. The clockmaker, Jaeger and Lalique, the goldsmith and luxury glass manufacturer, both worked for him. At the 1925 World Fair, it was clear that rather than cling to the company of traditional jewellers, Louis preferred to mix with people from other creative fields, such as the couturiers Lanvin and Louis' father-in-law, Worth.

With his brothers, Louis opened shops in London (1902) and New York (1908), while at the Court of St. Petersburg he established Cartier as a rival to Fabergé. Cartier ruled over the crowned heads of Europe, "the jeweller of kings and the King of jewellers." Royal warrants came from Edward VII of England (Louis created 27 diadems for his coronation), Alphonse XII of Spain and Charles of Portugal.

In the early decades of the 20th century, Cartier reached its apogee. There was not a monarch, business tycoon or film star who was not a client. Louis even conquered the literary world, designing the swords carried by authors such as Mauriac, Duhamel, Maurois and Jules Romains for their enrollment as members of the Académie Française. And it was Jean Cocteau who, in 1922, inspired Louis to create his famous ring composed of three interlocking circles, a magical symbol in Indian legend.

But Louis' descendants were to live through less glorious times. The Second World War engulfed many of the clients who had been the mainstay of the great jewellery houses and, after four generations of entrepreneurial, successful Cartiers, the firm seemed to lose its sense of direction. The New York store was sold, amid some dispute and discord within the family.

In 1964, a man came knocking at the door of the legendary jewellers. He was a manufacturer of mass-produced cigarette lighters, an inventive spirit who had applied all the latest technical refinements to the development of a new product. To mark the event, he wanted to decorate this new product with silver and christen it with one of the great names of the jewellery establishment. Rejected by other jewellers, he made his way to Cartier.

Robert Hocq

Robert Hocq was the head of Silver Match. A self-educated man, his dreams were forged among the machines in his workshop. Trailing behind the great names of Dupont and Dunhill, Silver Match had adopted the "copied from America" style of the new consumer society, furnishing disposable lighters to the mass market. Positioned in the middle range, the Silver Match lighters were sold through tobacco shops.

Robert Hocq had defined the market he was aiming for—the gap between his current products and the "super luxury" of Dunhill and Dupont. All that his lighters needed was "a little something" that would elevate them to the realm of "authentic" luxury goods. And in a world of plastic and cheap imitations, he needed the guarantee that only a name associated with true luxury could provide. Whether prompted by the need for money or the memory of past innovations, in 1968 Cartier agreed to grant Hocq a temporary licence.

The lighter's original design, a simple column in the Greek architectural style encircled by a ring, was slowly elaborated. Two radical innovations were incorporated. First, its oval shape was a direct descendant of Louis Cartier's favourite form, then quite unknown in the world of lighters. Second, Robert Hocq introduced the use of butane gas. The sale of gas cartridges would be a lucrative sideline even though, for the moment, clients were more accustomed to using liquid fuel.

To commercialise the new products, Le Briquet Cartier S.A. was established. The lighters were to be sold through the same outlets as Silver Match, a network of retailers. By 1968, the deal had been finalised and Robert Hocq turned to the task of finding the right person to sell his Cartier lighter.

Alain Perrin

The candidate who entered Robert Hocq's office, did so in response to an advertisement he had seen in the paper. The meeting began at six o'clock in the evening, and ended at midnight over an empty bottle of whisky. Alain Perrin often exhausted those around him whether at home, at the twelve schools he attended or during the long nights of his student days. He had arm-wrestled with Johnny Halliday, dined with the Beatles and, in short, led the Parisian life of insouciance of the 60s generation. Born into a family of scientists, he dreamt only of a business carrier. While at the Ecole des Cadres he imported Shetland sweaters for his friends. Cutting school to race all over trading sweaters for farmers' old furniture, he earned the nickname "King Pullover."

After the death of his father in 1965, Alain Perrin directed his ebullient energy towards more serious objectives. He returned to school to finish his studies and then began work in a paper recycling company. Bored by this, he started his own company dealing in antiques. One shop led to another, and finally to three.

In May 1969, he was still only 26.

On the road, a suitcase of the new Cartier lighters in his hand, Perrin visited those existing Silver Match clients who seemed best suited to the new product's image; wholesalers and fine tobacco stores or civettes. The lighter was an immediate success. The civettes gave it star billing; to be able to handle a Cartier product was tantamount to selling real jewellery. In competing with traditional jewellers, this gave them a long-sought legitimacy.

All profits were reinvested by Hocq in order to acquire the permanent and exclusive right to the Cartier name. His relations with Cartier grew ever closer.

Hocq's activities were not confined to lighters. Two days after Cartier acquired a 70-carat diamond in a New York sale, Richard Burton bought it for 14.5 million francs as a gift for Liz Taylor. Cartier's profit on the deal was minimal but the publicity surrounding the sale was invaluable. Orchestrated by Hocq, the event was a media coup for Cartier.

In 1971, backed by a group of financiers, Robert Hocq bought the jewellery business and the Paris and London shops from the Cartier family. In 1976, he bought back the New York store. Alain Dominique Perrin became General Manager of the lighter division.

Must Lighters

In 1972, the trademark "Les Must de Cartier" was born.

When the lighters were first launched in December 1969, Robert Hocq was discussing the project with a colleague. Tapping a magazine advertisement, Hocq asked him "Cartier... what exactly does Cartier mean to you." In English, the man answered: "Cartier is a must, Sir." At the time, the reply baffled Hocq, but several years later, he remembered the incident.

> "Modern man has a need to let the world know that he has succeeded. To do this, he needs to be able to buy symbols of social prestige. True luxury objects produced by the great jewellers cannot give him the recognition he yearns for, since they are exclusively one-of-a-kind."
> "Must lighters are the materialization of social status."

In 1974, following the example of Dupont, Cartier pens joined the lighters in shop windows. Whereas the lighter was, by its very nature, connected with tobacco shops, pens opened up new distribution channels. In 1975, the addition of leather goods opened up yet another.

With the Cartier pen-lighter duo, stores were no longer selling an object but a prestige concept. At the same time, Cartier was anxious to expand distribution of its jewellery. However, although lighters and pens could hold their own amidst displays of necklaces and rings in neighborhood jewellery stores, Cartier jewels were simply not meant to be surrounded by the ordinary and anonymous.

Exclusive Cartier boutiques were created. In them, under the slogan "Les Must de Cartier" and set against the rich bordeaux red chosen for the line, Cartier jewels were displayed to advantage. Later on, leathers, lighters and pens too were shown against this same distinctive setting. Strict guidelines defined the product mix, decoration and service which each distributor had to provide. Cartier then began sending inspectors round to monitor discreetly that these conditions were being respected.

The Must line was not to everyone's taste. The very select Comité Colbert excluded Cartier from its membership and shortly afterwards Cartier withdrew from the Syndicat de Haute Joaillerie, the organisation of fine jewellers which represented the most prestigious houses of the Place Vendôme. For a time, relations between "that cowboy Perrin" and the other jewellers were strained.

In 1973, Cartier founded a new company under the emblem "Les Must de Cartier," to be kept entirely separate from its jewellery interests. Alain Perrin became its President. Concerned that too much of the jewellery business was concentrated in the Paris area (65% of sales), he convinced Robert Hocq that the concept and products should be exported.

> "I needed to move from the state of an elegantly sleepy retailer to that of a young, contemporary, international concern, capable of creating products for a world-wide market, and not just Paris, London or New York."

Once a year, Alain Perrin travelled round the world. In ten to twelve stops from the Middle East to Australia, from Hong Kong to the United States, he picked up orders and sold the universality of the Must concept.

Must Watches

Buying back the New York store in 1976 led to a new activity.

As a jeweller, Cartier made a solid gold watch: the Tank. Its reputation (which went back to Louis Cartier) had inspired innumerable imitations. The American market in particular was infested by a plague of watches in plated brass, copies of the Tank. For 500 or 1,000 francs, an imitation of the real thing (costing 10,000 to 15,000 francs) could be bought. Even the New York store, long out of the control of the Cartier family, was selling this type of imitation.

To end these shoddy practices, Alain Dominique Perrin fought fire with fire. He brought out a vermeil watch, based on an original model. This meant that for only 2,000 francs more than the price of a cheap imitation, people could buy themselves a real Cartier watch, a true descendant of the masterpieces created by Louis Cartier in solid gold and brilliants.

The extension of the luxury Must line into watches allowed Cartier to surpass Dupont. From then on, Cartier's line of lighters, pens, leathers and watches were always displayed quite separately. Retailers had to reserve "a space within a space" for them in their stores and the style of presenting the goods had to be in keeping with (and directly inspired by) the Must boutiques.

Perfume

The idea of launching a perfume, planned for 1981, presented a dilemma.

On the one hand, the very nature of the product contradicted Cartier's expressed wish to limit itself to "lasting products which clients covet and to which they become attached." Cartier had originally resolved only to produce objects that were "never thrown out."

On the other hand, perfume was inevitable. Historically, it had been the first diversification channel for every luxury brand, and constituted the most obvious path in the public mind.

A further problem was how to launch the perfume—and hence follow in the footsteps of most other luxury brands—without breaking another of Cartier's golden rules: "Avoid what is already being done."

Cartier's product managers came up with the idea of a "case/refill." The case was conceived as an object in the Cartier tradition, lasting forever and never going out of fashion—an expensive product priced well above the competition—while the refill, in utilitarian plastic, would be priced well below the competition for the same quantity of perfume. The bevelled shape of the refill would ensure that it could not stand upright or be used without the case. Sale of the perfume to a client without a case would be forbidden.

The idea seemed simple yet seductive. Opposition came from market specialists, who did not believe that it would work. Previous similar attempts, albeit limited, had failed.

But Cartier's marketing team felt that the Cartier cachet would overcome any reservations in the perfume market, and that the very novelty of the case, "a totally new gift idea," would open up a whole new area of marketing. Perrin decided to go ahead with the launch. It was an immediate success.

At a later date, having legitimized its entry into the perfume market, Cartier brought out its perfume in a classic bottle—with a leather pouch. It was presented as a "travel" version.

> "In the luxury market, it's the survival of the fittest. You have to have the largest market share and be the most creative. Then you can do as you like with the market."

Transition

In 1979, Robert Hocq was run over and killed by a car while crossing the Place Vendôme. His daughter Nathalie became head of the group until 1981, when she moved to the United States. At that time, the Must collection represented a turnover of 250 million francs. The same year, Must and Cartier Joaillier merged, regrouping under the name Cartier International. Alain Dominique Perrin became President of the Board of Directors.

In 1983, Cartier was acquired by the Richemont group, a 3.3 billion Swiss francs tobacco and luxury goods conglomerate of South African origin.

The Forces of Creativity

On becoming President of the company following the Richemont takeover in 1983, Alain Perrin announced to Business Week, "By 1990 we'll show a turnover of 300 million dollars." The actual turnover in 1990 reached US$950 million, representing an average annual growth rate of 27% per year over 10 years (exhibit 1). Consolidated sales, including other brands acquired or under licence, amounted to US$1.350 billion. A 1990 McKinsey study evaluated the world luxury market at US$50 billion in retail sales, thus giving the Cartier brand 4% of sales—the largest for any single brand—in a highly fragmented market.

In jewellery, representing 25% of its turnover, Cartier is one of the world leaders after the US firm Winston. It is number one in the sale of luxury watches (40% of the market and 550,000 annual sales), and deluxe leather goods (10% of turnover) with 1.6 million articles sold in 1989 (exhibit 2).

According to Alain Perrin, creativity is the engine that has powered Cartier to this spectacular success. For him, it is the soul, the very essence of the group. Under Perrin, the lifeblood of the company is derived from the friction between a series of dualities. Thus, creation at Cartier is yesterday's memory, juxtaposed with today's insights into the environment. Perrin loves to cultivate such disequilibrium because "It forces us to move forwards."

> "One of the best sources of profit is creativity. Creativity is what? It is doing something your competitors do not do. Or doing it first. Or doing it stronger or better. Everything that is creative contains a plus on something… and creativity is the backbone of Cartier."

EXHIBIT 1
Cartier: Rate of Growth,
1985-90

Source: *Le Figaro,*
December 10, 1990

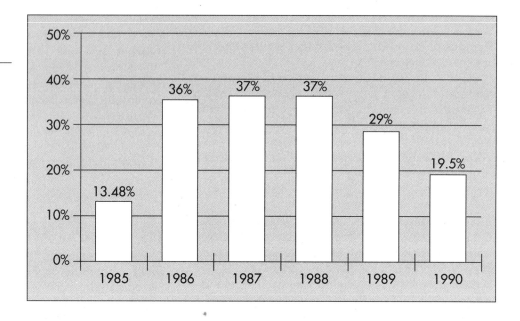

Product Development

The design for every new Cartier product is discussed and prepared according to a very precise process involving all the 200 people working at Cartier International. The launch of a product takes two to three years. A "product plan" three years ahead of the launch describes the evolution of the line: one major launch per year and spin-offs from each major project.

Nothing is launched until Perrin is convinced Cartier can "do it right." "I'd rather lose one year than introduce a half-baked concept."

Once the designs have been selected, the Drafting department elaborates models and prototypes "while stressing quality and keeping in constant contact with

EXHIBIT 2
Cartier: Sales by Product

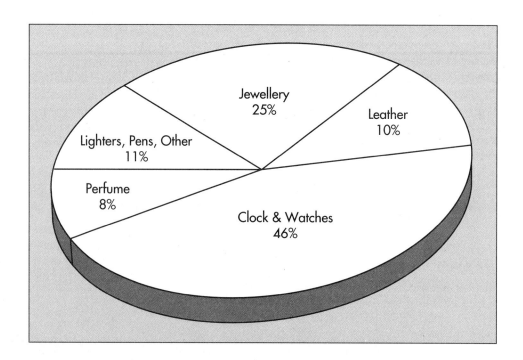

the creator." In order to reproduce the audacity of the designs, technical creativity is added to artistic imagination.

> "The oval pen was a real brain teaser, one which the best specialists in the business refused to touch when we consulted them. It took us two years to bring out the product, since we had to design and produce our own cartridge. We patent designs every year."

Such creativity rests on this paradox: "Each product is an exceptional creation, but we invent nothing."

The Old . . .

Cartier's past is where the search for present creativity begins. Each new product launched has its ancestor among the collections of chalk and pastel drawings made by Louis Cartier and represents "the spirit of creation and the style of Cartier, adapted to our time and to the trends we are setting for the future."

At the turn of the century, a piece of Cartier jewellery destined for the mistress of a client was accidently delivered to his wife. To avoid a repetition of this error, Cartier began to keep exhaustive records on clients, the models they chose and the gems used. These records became Cartier's archives.

> "The first lesson a product manager has to learn is how to navigate his or her way through our archives. In this treasure trove, we search for ideas which will fall onto fertile ground, germinate, ripen and one day, when the time is right, be launched onto a market which is not quite ready for it."

While looking at an archive photograph of the governor of Marrakesh and at the massive watch that Louis Cartier had made for him, Alain Perrin predicted that "One day we'll have to launch a watch like that." Today, "the Pasha watch is one of our star products, and has brought large watches back into fashion."

Perrin had already delved into the archive's rich seam of ideas for the Must line. When he became President, its use became systematic. Consequently, the company began to develop lines whose names—Santos, Panthère, Pasha, Cougar—owed nothing to the American culture of the sixties and seventies that dominated elsewhere.

. . . And The New

Cartier's business is to be a trend-setter not a follower; "to influence people in their behaviour, in their choice, in their taste... Other companies follow customers; but customers follow Cartier." To do this, "We spend a lot of time and money on surveying the market and the competition... on getting the information that will lead us to understand and make decent forecasts on trends."

Perrin has files on each of his major competitors going back twenty years. "I know more about them than they do about themselves." He even has "people making window checks on competitors' products all over the world, all the year round."

> "Starting from concrete information on competition, on distribution, on consumption, on people's choices, on political trends, on fashion, all these ingredients at the end give us the quality of information that we need to be able to create a product which we know will be fashionable, and have an influence on the culture of the year 2000."

Image

For Perrin, brand image is the basis of an effective marketing strategy. "Luxury, for the client and the manufacturer alike, means communicating around a brand in the same way that jewellery communicates around a gem." But promotion should be based on the name and image of the company rather than the product.

> "Our brand name was built very slowly, and it's set in concrete. We survive economic, political and regional conflicts without disturbance. Crises seem to stimulate the market for high value added products. In recent years we have even witnessed a growing demand for relatively old Cartier jewels. This is unhoped-for support for our image."

Perrin is proud of Cartier's pioneering marketing methods. "We were the first to use heavy marketing, the first to communicate in the way we do, the first to use heavy public relations to create events around culture, promote artists, and probably the first to succeed in controlling our distribution as we did." He enjoys manipulating the opposite marketing poles of secrecy and publicity.

Secrecy . . .

Through secrecy about past events affecting the company, Cartier is able to protect its legend.

> "One of our strengths is our ability to maintain a certain mystery about the economic entity which is the company. We bring magic and dreams to consumers who don't want

to see their favourite brands discussed in the media, and lacking any sense of the romantic."

According to Perrin, breaching this secrecy could bring the luxury industry crashing down. Thus, he regards going public as a sure way to perdition. "Waging public battles on the floor of the stock exchange is a serious error for the luxury goods sector. It kills the magic. My craft is to make money with magic." Luxury businesses who go public "risk losing their soul. A luxury business has nothing to gain from seeing its name indiscriminately positioned in alphabetical order in the daily quotations listing."

... And Publicity

But then again, "Cartier is a name which lives in the news." The luxury goods sector is an important consumer of publicity. Cartier's public relations department has a team of 20 people, and each new product launch is accompanied by astounding creative pageantry, courtesy of a company called Delirium.

Undoubtedly, Perrin himself is Cartier's best communication tool. A high profile figure, he is photographed everywhere; beside Elton John on his French tour, at the launch of the "restos du coeur" (soup kitchens set up by the French comedian, the late Coluche), on the slopes of a fashionable ski resort, at a Red Cross benefit or attending a conference at HEC (a leading French business school).

Another powerful weapon is Cartier's universal implantation.

> "I remember," notes a competitor, "finding myself in a tiny airport deep in the heart of Venezuela. The very first thing I saw as I got off the plane and entered the makeshift building was a Cartier watch."

Cartier files all the magazine photos or articles which mention its name, or that of one of its products. Its picture gallery includes the tennis player Jimmy Connors, Dynasty star Linda Evans, French film star Jean-Paul Belmondo, Pakistan's ex-Prime Minister Benazir Bhutto, and also "rogues" such as Libya's President Ghadafi, the ex-gangster Mesrine, giving his companion a Cartier necklace just hours before being shot down by the police. The sale of the Duchess of Windsor's jewels "among which ours were prominent" also served Cartier well.

Another famous picture shows Perrin perched on the top of a steam-roller, the day in 1981 when he destroyed 4,000 counterfeit Cartier watches. The defence of the Cartier name against counterfeiters costs the company nearly US$3.5 million a year.

Cartier has created its own highly effective communication and marketing weapon: the use of sponsorship and culture.

> "By marrying Cartier with contemporary art we seduced the anti-luxury and anti-uniform population. We also seduced the media which, since 1981, had been cool towards the luxury goods industry. By positioning the firm in the future rather than in the past, we at last managed to reach a younger clientèle."

Most famous is the "Cartier Foundation for Contemporary Art," a cultural centre established just outside Paris in response to a 1983 market survey which found that young people were interested in contemporary art, and that 70% of those attending exhibitions were less than 25 years old. A meeting place, as well as an exhibition and seminar centre, the Foundation hosts young artists from across the world and offers them financial support. Exhibitions have included a retrospective dedicated to the "Solex," the little moped symbolising a whole generation of young Frenchmen and women, and another on the cars of Enzo Ferrari.

> "Sponsorship is an impressive form of communication. It unites Cartier's employees around an adventure which attracts both the media and the public across the world. Patronage costs Cartier 30 to 40 million francs a year. But it earns us media coverage worth 200 to 250 million francs."

Marketing

Perhaps Perrin's trickiest balancing act has been to maintain Cartier's image as an elite purveyor of expensive luxuries while thriving in the mass markets of watches, wallets and pens.

Exclusivity ...

At the fusion of Cartier Joaillers and Les Must in 1981, demarcation lines were established to keep the Must line clearly separate. In the company's London office in Bond Street, "Must people worked upstairs, Cartier people downstairs." To compensate for the Must "wide distribution" image and to keep the Cartier name close to its roots, the "high jewellery" business was relaunched. By developing a line of "signed" jewels with extremely limited editions, Cartier strengthened its

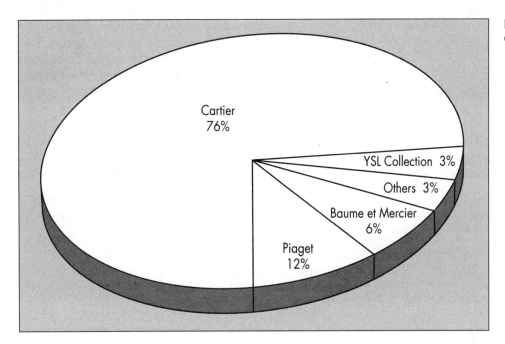

EXHIBIT 3
Cartier: Sales by Brands

Cartier
76%

YSL Collection 3%

Others 3%

Baume et Mercier
6%

Piaget
12%

presence in the US$50,000-$100,000 market segment (the top of the jewellery market goes above US$100,000).

One of Cartier's principles is never to test any of its products commercially. "Our products, whether we are talking about a piece of fine jewellery or a Must pen, must be exclusive. There has to be a "certain something' that makes them stand out, something that goes against the norms. We do "anti-marketing'."

. . . And Volume Sales

"With the Must line I was perfectly conscious that by producing thousands of watches or pens instead of one-of-a-kind objects, I was running the risk of affecting the image of our company. If it is true that men and women wish to call attention to themselves by having a Cartier lighter or pen or sunglasses, it is also true that they wish to be recognised as part of an exclusive milieu and not as just anyone."

Quality must never be sacrificed. "The same care must be exercised over each of the 300 operations necessary to the making of a lighter as in the 1,400 hours it took to make the Odin necklace (US$600,000). Industrial quality has to stand comparison with the traditional, painstaking care of the individual craftsman. Cartier's workshop has 67 craftsmen, setters, polishers and jewellers, "three times more than most leading jewellers."

Cartier's success in watchmaking illustrates the manipulation of these contradictions. Cartier's adversary was Rolex, whose massive sporty wrist-watches in steel and gold had set the trend. Alain Perrin felt that a watch of equal quality, but with more creative lines and more style could become an effective rival to the Swiss brand. Through his efforts, a large clientèle was now familiar with luxury products. Their appetites whetted, they were demanding more...

However, he also believed that the Must line would not be strong enough to compete against Rolex. The Must concept, used and reused since 1972, risked becoming stale through repetition.

Perrin decided that henceforth, Cartier would develop its exclusive collections under a generic name taken from Cartier's history. "I was going to put products inspired by the exclusive designs of Louis Cartier within the reach of thousands of people."

On October 20th, 1978 twenty Mystère jets brought Cartier's guests to Paris's Le Bourget airport from the four corners of the world. Among them were Jacky Ickx, Ursula Address and Santos Dumont's grandson. They were to be present at the launch of the "Santos Dumont," a wrist-watch with a shape inspired by the famous aviator's watch. The first watch to have screws on its body, it was "immediately copied by the competition." In 1981, it was followed by another success, the first moonphase Pasha watch.

In 1990, Cartier overtook Rolex as the world leader in luxury time-pieces.

Distribution

"We had to get Cartier out of the temple... We had to shake Cartier out of its retailer's lethargy in order to make it a profitable luxury goods company, distributing internationally."

"Leaving The Temple"

Cartier's journey into the light had begun when Perrin set off round the tobacconists with his suitcase full of lighters. The move signalled Cartier's move away from the discreet salons of the jewellers and its entry into the wider world of the gift shop.

By December 1989, 33% of Cartier's revenues (15% of volume) came from its network of 135 stores. The rest came from concessions. Cartier used its profits gradually to purchase all the distributors controlling its 7,500 name-brand points of sale. This takeover was complete by 1990.

In Japan, Cartier entered the market early in 1971 by renting the usual corner spaces in hotels and department stores. By 1989, Cartier had bought an entire building, cancelled the contract with its importer and in its place established a joint venture (Cartier controlling 51% of the shares) to manage the 16 Japanese points of sale.

"It's the only way to consolidate our margins and control our brand name. The retail margin accumulated with the gross margin is what makes us profitable. But more importantly, it's the assurance that the name will be represented as it ought to be, whether it's in Melbourne, Madrid or Paris."

Logistics

In the mid 1980s, Cartier was confronted by an almost total blockage of its logistics system. "We were no longer able to guarantee supplies, but at the same time we were troubled by an increase in intermediary inventory. Our network took some hard knocks." Cartier responded by reinforcing the coordination between sales and production and introducing a sophisticated computer system. This system was designed around 13 months

sales projections and was piloted from Freiburg in Switzerland by Cartier's General Agent (Switzerland is a duty-free zone where products can be circulated quickly with the minimum of customs formalities). Freiburg, Cartier's central supplier, manages all plant deliveries and covers sub-contractors supplying all 22 sales affiliates. It then centralises the statistics needed to update sales and manufacturing plans.

Freiburg also controls the customer service file. "We have to be able to repair all our models, including those we no longer produce. After-sales service is assured indefinitely. It's a valuable contact with clients and it makes them return to our stores." Product maintenance costs Cartier 7 million dollars each year, and represents 240,000 repairs.

Strategy

Focus...

Cartier is one of the very rare luxury houses that will not allow any licensing of its name (with the exception of the development of a brand of cigarettes, a decision imposed by the holding company which also owns Rothmans). Perrin will never develop a new line simply because there is a market for it. Except for scarves, he has not ventured into the fashion businesses. "There is no Cartier make-up, clothes, shoes or ties, and as long as I am here there never will be."

"Cartier could do what the other luxury houses do: a little bit of everything. We haven't wanted that, since every name has strict limits. Our business is gems, jewellery, watch making, lighters, pens."

... And Diversification

On the other hand, "We have developed all of our traditional products. Now, Cartier is condemned to external growth." Acquisitions will prevent the Cartier name becoming over-exposed and besides, "If there is something that can add to the group, it is better to buy it than to leave it to your competitors."

Every acquisition is designed "to consolidate our leadership in the luxury industry." Thus, in 1988, Cartier bought the two Swiss watch-makers, Baume & Mercier (70,000 watches per year in a market segment close to that of the Must line) and Piaget (17,000 watches in an exclusive market "more than Rolls Royce, maybe Lagonda"). They were, says Perrin, "sleeping beauties." He has separated the two "for their own good. I don't want them to talk to each other any more." Cartier also acquired the distinguished jewellers Aldebert (80 million FF in annual sales), which has 7 stores in Paris, Cannes and Monte Carlo.

Since 1989, Cartier has held a 6% share in Yves Saint Laurent, the high fashion firm for which it had produced a line of jewellery. A contract with Ferrari allows Cartier to go beyond the defined limits of luxury goods, as it did years ago with cigarette lighters (exhibit 3).

> "We wanted to introduce our expertise, our distribution, our know-how into the male and female accessory businesses. The deals also set a kind of barrier at the bottom of the pyramid... With Ferrari and Yves St. Laurent we have got the market share we could not have got with the Cartier name."

> "We will go no further in diversification, which has remained relatively restrained."

Management

> "If you decentralise creativity too much it is no longer creativity, it's a mess... the information must come from the satellites, from the subsidiary or from the markets, but the final decision must come from one man."

Absolutism...

Under Perrin, absolutism lives on in France: "In a company with a strong name, a strong personality, the President must be in charge."

Perrin is the ultimate arbiter of what is produced by the firm. It is he who decides which products will be launched, he who examines, refuses or approves each of the 1,200 designs submitted to him by the marketing department, he who pulls apart each product before its launch. "I am," he says, "that kind of man. I want to participate very much in the creativity, in the production, in the quality. I am an active executive."

But all these choices are, he maintains, "the choices of any good manager... anybody could be Alain Perrin at the head of Cartier."

> "At Cartier, we are a management team. I can disappear tomorrow morning... My management people are very able to go on... The team is built around Cartier, not around me... It took twenty years, but there is no recipe... It is by finding the people to match... It is the quality of these people which guarantees our growth."

Observers note a sense of shared excitement among a workforce embarked on "the adventure of Cartier." "Everyone sees him, and he enters anyone's office at any time. Ask anyone here and you'll get the impression that they know him personally. They'll tell you, 'his greatest assets are his attentiveness to others and his great generosity'."

Such a direct relationship can cause difficulties. It is an area where Perrin's balancing act has occasionally failed. When Perrin took over the management of Cartier, he was assisted by an executive committee composed of the fifteen managers responsible for different areas of the company. However, Cartier's expansion rendered this system increasingly difficult, whereupon Perrin appointed a General Manager. Unsurprisingly, Perrin's direct, impulsive and omnipresent management style had trouble accommodating this new structure and so he modified it, transforming the General Manager into a Vice President. Three General Managers were then appointed to run the operational functions of Marketing, Finance and Operations (coordinating the sales affiliates from Freiburg).

Perrin also has a group of close advisers, "people who have been with me for a long while, between about six and twelve years." They help him with his top management tasks of creation, communication and production and have been selected because "I found in them all the qualities that I don't think I could find in myself. So let's say I am looking for complementary colleagues." He also uses them as "a task force to check and control what is being completed and achieved on the operational side."

Any occasional conflicts between the normal line organisation and his advisory group, Perrin sees as another source of creative energy.

> "A company without conflict is a company without life... If you take it the positive way, a conflict must end up with something creative. So I believe in conflicts." His role is to "be the referee" of this "calculated chaos," so that it does not result in paralysis.
>
> "If you know how to manage conflict, it ends up being very constructive."

...And Autonomy

At the same time, Perrin insists that "a company is not only a money machine" but "a mosaic of men and women... a place where people live together... And the relationships that you have to create inside a company are human relationships, they give everyone the opportunity to express themselves." One of Cartier's great successes has been "in motivating people... And you cannot motivate the 4,600 people working for Cartier if you don't give them the absolute conviction that a soul exists..."

At Cartier, this soul is composed of "the partners plus the management," and before taking any final decision, the top man "must take the time and go round the world if necessary, and listen to the partners."

At Cartier, it is "natural for many, many people around me in this company to come up with a new concept... They can always try, they know they can try... The art of management is to put the ideas of others together. Creativity is something you manage exactly like an industry."

Perrin believes that "everybody has within himself a fantastic power of creation and of interpretation." The modern executive is "one who knows how to use what is inside the brain of the people, not only what he knows, not only his techniques, but his power of creation."

"The secret of Cartier" says Perrin, "is that we try to extract something from everybody, and give everybody the chance to participate in the creation." And by this, he means not just the product, but "the way you decorate a new office, the way you organise a new factory, a new distribution network... I like to have creative meetings, and this is the way we work."

"You must allow people the freedom to express themselves. I very often say in meetings, and we all do the same, express yourself. If you say something stupid, don't worry, we will let you know. But I prefer people to say ten stupid things, because the eleventh one will be the idea."

A New Temple

In 1990, Cartier International was installed in its new offices on the rue François ler in Paris. Housed in one of the city's grandest former private residences, Cartier is within striking distance of the large foreign luxury shops on the avenue Montaigne, and demonstrably a long way from the old-style jewellers of the Place Vendôme. All its stores will eventually be transformed along the same lines as this new corporate headquarters.

A considerable investment programme will see the renovation of the boutiques. There will be room for leisurely browsing, as well as intimate alcoves in which to personalise private sales. Luminous window displays in green, ivory and mushroom tones will be reduced in size and show only a few items. The centrepiece will be a column decorated in gold leaf, against which some of Cartier's most exclusive jewels will be thrown into sharp relief.

The next generation of acolytes in the Cartier temple is also being assured. Recruitment is based on student placements. Every year, a hundred students work in the company, vying to fill twenty positions. In 1990, Cartier created a sales school, Sup de Luxe, which will train salespeople from the stores as well as distributors of Cartier products.

Perrin prefers managers who have "experienced the terrain." "The manager who is only a technocrat and who has never gone out into the field, talked to a client or gone to a factory and talked to the workers, worked with them, understood how to transform a piece of steel into a watch... understood what the process of production is really like, as well as distribution... is somebody who is less complete."

"When you hire four guys D-day, and after two years look at them, one has been everywhere and knows everybody, and this is the one you are going to promote right away... One day, the fact that he has learnt so much from all kinds of horizons will help him have a broader view and have this famous intuition, the power to make a decision... The others are already stuck in one direction, doing what they do best."

Global Strategy

The expansion of Cartier outside France began in the 1970s, with the export of the Must concept. By 1991, Cartier was present in 123 countries with 145 boutiques and a network of 10,000 concessions.

Cartier spread early to Hong Kong (1969) and Japan (1971). At the time, few believed there could be a market for Cartier's products in the Far East.

To fight off the competition in Hong Kong, Cartier played its cultural card and launched the "Cartier Master Series" in 1988. The first year was "an unbelievable success." By 1990, Hong Kong had five boutiques and 114 retailers and was one of Cartier's three regular international launching pads, along with Paris and New York.

And yet, Perrin is clear that Cartier will never stray too far from its heartland. "We must be strong at home.

America represents 20%, of which the greater part is the United States, and Asia 25%." Since 1983, Cartier has gradually pulled back from the Middle East market (only 3% in 1990, which left the company less exposed to the effects of the Gulf War) (exhibit 4).

> "Our European penetration is a voluntary strategy. Europe is the origin of luxury. It is a product of our culture. I believe that the market most loyal to the artistic professions is the one that has conceived them. I will always ensure that Europe never represents less than 50%. Most of the major names have chosen the opposite strategy and Asia claims between 60% and 80% of their revenues. But who can guarantee that there won't be a reversal in the Asian market?"

In the early 1990s, Cartier looks to expand into Eastern Europe. Openings are planned in Budapest, Warsaw, Prague and Moscow. The Cartier name is already known in Hungary. At the turn of the century, Louis Cartier directed the company from a palace in Budapest, where he lived for six months of the year while pursuing an affair with the beautiful Hungarian woman who became his second wife.

Meanwhile, Cartier is strengthening its position in the American market. A consumer research firm was commissioned for study to identify areas with the most highly paid populations. Shops will be opening in San Diego, San Jose, Phoenix... "We're going to places where money flows like ice in the sun..."

Integrated Manufacturing

Perrin sees the integration of its industrial facilities as Cartier's next major strategic challenge. The process will be led from Saint Imier in Switzerland, the headquarters of Cartier's industrial arm, CTL (Luxury Technology Company).

With the exception of a few smaller outfits and its jewellery workshop, Cartier has hitherto lacked the means to manufacture its other products. Some of them, such as glasses frames (introduced in 1983 and manufactured by Essilor) and perfumes, are subcontracted to major industrial companies. For the rest, Cartier depends on networks of small local craftsmen who have traditionally supplied the fashion and luxury goods industry. Paris is rich in such craftsmen, who are closely tied to the greatest names in jewels. Cartier's leather goods are produced in France, Italy and Spain. Nothing comes from the Far East.

In 1988, Cartier completely integrated its cigarette lighter and pen production by opening a plant in Freiburg (100 employees) and another in Franconville (200 employees).

Next, "We decided that the artisan watch manufacturing in Switzerland should be integrated, as this activity accounts for more than 40% of sales." Relations with the watch-makers, to whom Cartier

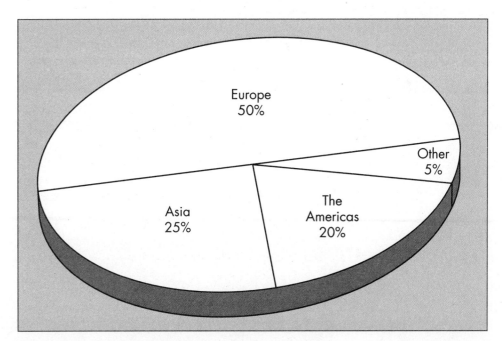

EXHIBIT 4
Cartier: Sales by Region

subcontracted 80% of its watch-making business, had been strained. "Respect for deadlines among some of our sub-contractors had deteriorated drastically. The big companies are fighting to dominate a network of manufacturers who are themselves struggling to keep up with the expansion of the business."

In 1989, Cartier invested in a 50% shareholding in Cristallor, the watch-case manufacturing affiliate of Ebel (a very exclusive Swiss manufacturer and a long-time Cartier sub-contractor). With Piaget and Baume & Mercier, Cartier also acquired two manufacturing companies, Prodor and Complications. Further additions have resulted in an industrial armoury which Perrin hopes will make Cartier invincible first in watches, and then in jewellery. Since October 1991, the majority of watches made by the company have been assembled at the plant in Saint Imier. As a result, Cartier has reversed the proportion of watches it sub-contracts.

In the future, Cartier will be able to manufacture 75% of its production, the remaining 25% will give the company flexibility. "This push towards integration allows us to consolidate our margins and our quality, and affirms our leadership."

By a twist of fate, Piaget and Rolex face each other on opposite sides of the street in Geneva. Alain Perrin likes to feel the vibrations from his closest rival so nearby. "In 1991," he predicted, "the battle will really start."

The future of the luxury industry, considers Perrin, will be "in the hands of two or three or four groups, no more." The names that will dominate? "Cartier, of course, as number one. Chanel. Vuitton. Dior. Yves St. Laurent. Dunhill. Hermes..."

Cartier is planning a three-pronged strategy: to reinforce its presence where it is already strong, to expand in Eastern Europe and, in anticipation of 1993 and the end of duty-free shopping, to open shops in every European airport. These will become "centres of luxury products, at the expense of alcohol, tobacco and perfume."

But even as he describes the changes to prepare for the future, Perrin is equally emphatic about the inherent continuity and timelessness of the company.

"There is no significant change in the spirit of Cartier between 1847 and 1990, and there will be none by 2000 or 3000... Cartier has been the companion of all the success stories of the world for 150 years. As long as the world is the world, that success story will never cease."

SAATCHI & SAATCHI WORLDWIDE: GLOBALIZATION AND DIVERSIFICATION†

By Ron Meyer

Robert Louis-Dreyfus, chief executive of Saatchi & Saatchi Worldwide (Saatchi), was faced with what business journalists would euphemistically call a challenge. His company had run up considerable losses in 1989 and 1990, largely due to preferred dividends and extraordinary items, but had been able to remain marginally profitable on regular (pretax) operations. In the first six months of 1991, however, even this turned into a £4 million loss, and the outlook for the near future was dim. According to the *Wall Street Journal* there appeared to be no signs of recovery in the key advertising markets for the rest of 1991, or even through 1992.[1] Furthermore, while Louis-Dreyfus had done much to improve the company's equity position, mostly by selling off peripheral businesses, Saatchi was still burdened by a heavy debt load. It was clear that Louis-Dreyfus had to act quickly to ensure the short-term survival of his financially troubled company. However, he also had to set out a clear strategy to improve the firm's long-term prospects.

Louis-Dreyfus had been hired as chief executive officer (CEO) in January of 1990 at the moment that Saatchi had been balancing on the brink of financial insolvency, due to its empire-building acquisition spree. He undertook a full financial and strategic review that concluded that the board's decision to concentrate on the communications business (advertising, direct marketing, public relations, media services, and so on) and to turn away from the concept of a full-range services company was correct. The case for selling a broad package of services to multinationals, from advertising to computer expertise and management consulting, could make sense, but the bottom-line results indicated that the company had overpaid when buying these businesses. By mid-1991, Louis-Dreyfus had disposed of ten out of twelve of the consulting businesses (for a total net extraordinary costs in 1989 and 1990 of £99 million) and had pushed through a recapitalization plan, which provided some short-term breathing space.

Long-term survival, however, would have to come from turning around the company's core advertising business. In the past many philosophical and heated debates about "globalization" had occurred in the office of Maurice Saatchi, one of the two founding brothers. Now Louis-Dreyfus had to decide whether the company's vision to offer "global" advertising services was to remain the company's central strategy for the future or whether there were other alternatives open.

The Triumphant Early Years (1970–1986)

The Saatchi brothers founded their company in the Soho district, London's ad agency heartland, in 1970. Charles Saatchi, described as one of the most eccentric and reclusive businessmen since Howard Hughes, was barely twenty-seven years old at the time, and brother Maurice was twenty-four.

The agency soon built up a reputation for simple, provocative ads. The 1971 print ad promoting contraception, for example, showed a pregnant man and asked, "Would you be more careful if it was you who got pregnant?" The agency came to prominence in 1979 with the advertising campaign that helped the Conservatives oust the Labour Party in Britain and put Margaret Thatcher in office. "Labour Isn't Working," said one poster depicting a long line of unemployed people.

†**Source:** This case was written by Ron J. H. Meyer, with the assistance of Nancy Peterson and Kathleen Pinnette, as a basis for class discussion rather than to illustrate effective or ineffective handling of an administrative situation. This case was compiled from publicly available sources and supplemented by information kindly provided by Saatchi & Saatchi. Copyright © 1994 by Ron Meyer, Rotterdam School of Management, Erasmus University.

[1] *Wall Street Journal*, "Saatchi Posts First Half Loss, Sees No Pickup," September 6, 1991.

EXHIBIT 1
Eighteen Years of
Uninterrupted Growth

Date	Pretax profits (£ millions)	Noteworthy events
1970		Saatchi & Saatchi formed.
1975	0.4	Merger with Compton Partners to construct publicly quoted company.
1979	2.4	Saatchi & Saatchi becomes largest U.K. agency.
1981	3.6	Second agency network started by acquisition of Dorland Advg. Saatchi becomes largest European agency group.
1982	5.5	Saatchi becomes a worldwide agency network by the acquisition of Compton Communications in the United States.
1983	11.2	U.S. stock exchange listing obtained.
1984	20.0	Enters consulting market with acquisition of Hay Group.
1985	40.4	Forms marketing services by acquisition of Rowland (PR), Siegal & Gale (design), and Howard Marlboro (sales promotion).
1986	70.1	Major expansion in advertising with acquisition of Dancer Fitzgerald Sample, Backer & Spielvogel, and Ted Bates Worldwide. Saatchi becomes world's largest agency group.
1987	124.1	Paris listing obtained. Acquisition of Litigation Sciences and Peterson & Company. Merged nineteen units into two global networks: Saatchi & Saatchi Advertising Worldwide, ranking No. 2, and Backer Spielvogel Bates Worldwide, ranking No. 3.
1988	138.0	Formation of Zenith centralized media buying. Acquisition of Gartner information systems consultancy. Becomes world's tenth largest consulting firm. Tokyo listing obtained.

They were an unlikely pair to conquer Madison Avenue, but in the 1980s, the Iraqi brothers focused their attention on just that. Maurice and Charles were ignored or laughed at when they announced that they someday would rule over the world's largest advertising agency. By 1988, after a long spree of acquisitions, their concern employed 16,600 people in 58 countries, and had client billings of $13.5 billion, giving it control of 5 percent of the worldwide advertising market, according to *Advertising Age*. The company's biggest international accounts included British Airways, Proctor & Gamble, Sara Lee, Johnson & Johnson, and Toyota. Saatchi's competitors were no longer laughing.

The brothers had set themselves on their spectacular growth course by acquiring other advertising companies. The largest coup was the $400 million buyout in 1986 of Ted Bates agency, based in New York. This triumph allowed Saatchi to take the title of the world's biggest ad business. In the meantime the Saatchi's had also set their sights on the consulting business, announcing that Saatchi would become the largest consultancy too. The purchase of twelve consultancy firms, including big companies like Hay Management, proved they were serious.

The Saatchi's were eminently successful, or so it would seem when looking at the numbers. *Money Observer* reported (January 1989) only thirty-seven U.K. companies had succeeded in raising their dividends by more than 10 percent a year over the previous decade. Saatchi was the leader of the pack, achieving a compound average of over 20 percent, due to record-breaking new business gains of 4 percent of the U.K. advertising market. Exhibit 1 outlines Saatchi's growth and major acquisitions between 1970 and 1988.

The Seeds of Destruction (1986–1988)

While the financial highlights up to 1988 looked quite impressive (see also exhibits 2 and 3), Saatchi's appetite for acquisitions was accompanied by some symptoms of

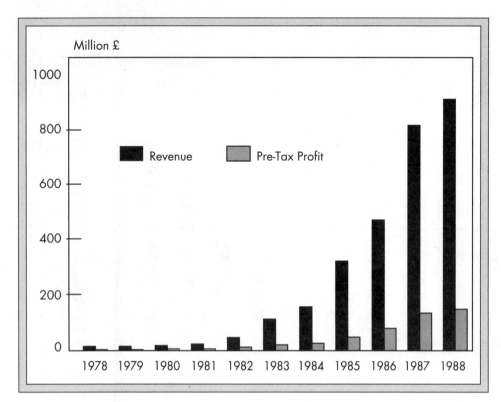

EXHIBIT 2
Saatchi's Revenue and Pretax
Profits, 1978–1988

indigestion. Following the purchase of Bates in 1986, a string of client account losses and staff departures plagued the company. Especially in the United States, Saatchi lost several accounts due to the fact that client companies did not want to deal with the same ad agency as their competitors had. Large consumer product companies, such as Proctor & Gamble and Colgate-Palmolive, were concerned about confidentiality and conflicts of interest because their merged ad agency now also carried a competitor's account, so they withdrew hundreds of millions of dollars worth of business.

One of the important staff departures was that of Marten Sorrell, Saatchi's top financial executive[2]. His expertise was sorely missed, when, soon after his departure, Saatchi bought out Ted Bates for what many view as an exorbitant price. Besides his financial expertise Sorrell had also played cheerleader to investors at Saatchi. After his departure, no one replaced him as an intermediary between management and the

shareholders. This reinforced the perception that the brothers were interested in other things besides Saatchi and shareholder value.

Another problem was that some of Saatchi's acquisitions, like Hay, had completed their earn-out periods. Some executives feared that those companies no longer had the incentive to keep the profit increases going as strongly. Poorly handled earn-out deals encouraged the selling shareholders to milk the business, because that's the way they get the maximum earn-out.

Then in 1987 the brothers undauntedly attempted to bid for two British banks, Midland and Hill Samuel. This backfired on them miserably and signalled shareholders to their apparent lack of focus. For the first time shareholders of the publicly owned company and others openly began to question the brothers' strategy for the business. Had the company's vast growth, by means of aggressive acquisitions, truly added value to the companies purchased? Or was Saatchi, as some critics claimed, an example of "dyssynergy"?

As problems started to mount, Saatchi's share price showed a significant drop (see exhibit 4), which presented the company with further difficulties. The key

---

[2]Mr. Sorrell, a brilliant empire builder, went on to make the WPP Group the biggest global ad company (see exhibit 7) by buying J. Walter Thompson and Ogilvy & Mather, thus overtaking Saatchi's lead position.

EXHIBIT 3
Saatchi's Earnings and
Dividends per Share,
1978–1988

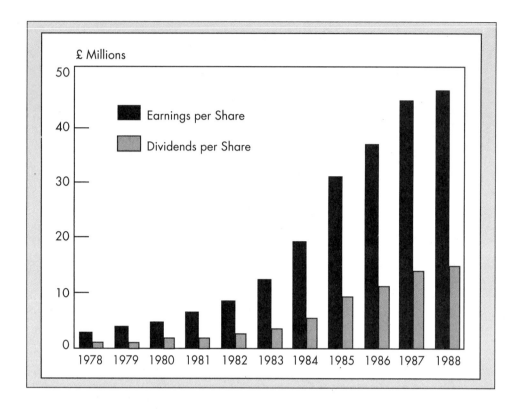

to Saatchi's growth in the 1980's was its high stock price, a weak dollar, and a policy of buying companies on an instalment plan. Saatchi's strong price-earnings ratio, which topped twenty-seven times, allowed it to raise capital in London for a downpayment on acquisitions followed by performance-based payments typically over three to five years. The declining dollar helped to make the American acquisitions relatively cheap. However, when the share price fell, the company could no longer raise money.

The Unravelling Giant (1989–1991)

By early 1989 it had become clear to Saatchi's directors that the company's financial results would take a turn for the worse. After eighteen years of nonstop growth, Saatchi's operating profit in the first half of 1989 was set to decline by approximately 40 percent compared with the first half of 1988. Publicly Saatchi bravely stated that "we see this as a pause for breath in our growth," and claimed that there was no deep or secret reason for the weak financial results. It was merely a case of advertising suffering because some U.S. clients were

worried about the "new" Bush administration and the budget deficit. Ad spending postponed from the first half to the second half that year had caused the damage. However, by mid-June of 1989 Saatchi had seen itself forced to put its consultancy division up for sale.

Saatchi had collected a mishmash of twelve consulting companies offering advice ranging from employee compensation and jury selection to real estate strategies and computer systems. Victor E. Millar, head of Saatchi Consulting, was given the assignment to dispose of all of these companies as quickly as possible.

The pressure to sell was high, as the company was strapped for cash. All the profits for the year would be used for dividends; therefore a sale would provide breathing space. Selling proved more difficult though as buyers were interested in bits and pieces, due to the wide variety of services Saatchi owned. Also, the urgency of the sale, from Saatchi's perspective, encouraged lower bids. The company was at first weary to sell these businesses at such a tremendous loss. Hesitation only worked against Saatchi, and when it finally completed its divestments, it sold the businesses for about £100 million after initially expecting between £250 and £350 million.

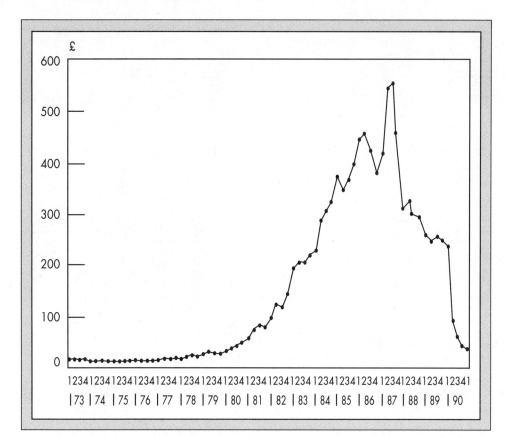

EXHIBIT 4
Saatchi's Long-Term Share
Price, 1973–1990

The company that had been unable to pay preferred dividends in October 1990 confirmed that it would be unable to pay dividends on its ordinary shares in early 1991. Huge fiscal year net losses were triggered by massive writedowns on its disposal of the consulting businesses for 1990. The company said the write-downs, amounting to £76.9 million, reflected a hard-nosed decision by Saatchi to take its lumps in 1990 (see exhibit 5).

In January 1991 Saatchi unveiled a major recapitalization plan to save itself from insolvency. At the time analysts believed it was unlikely the troubled company would be able to redeem the original shares in 1993. The plan was revised in February to allow the troubled advertising company to survive intact but proposed handing over control to its preferred shareholders.

The plan, which was approved in March 1991, gave Saatchi's Europreference holders 65 percent of the company, and handed the two largest holders, ESL and London-based St. James's Place Capital, a seat apiece on

the board. Both also provided additional capital to the company by underwriting a sizable chunk of a new £55 million rights offering. With the consultancy businesses divested and the balance sheet strengthened, Saatchi was now prepared to move forward in its strategy of focusing on its communications businesses.

Saatchi's "Total Communication Services" Strategy

The Saatchi brothers relinquished responsibility as joint chief executives on January 1, 1990, handing the position over to the French-born advertising executive, Robert Louis-Dreyfus. Maurice and Charles remained on the board, and Maurice also stayed on as chairman. The new chairman's role was to focus on client relationships and broader strategy, while that of the chief executive was to concentrate on operational management and to

EXHIBIT 5
Consolidated Profit and Loss
Account (in £ millions)

	1990	1989	1988
Turnover	4,353.6	4,364.1	3796.1
Revenue (gross profit)	808.1	973.5	862.2
Profit ordinary activities before exceptional items and tax	35.8	61.3	116.4
Exceptional items	(0.2)	(39.5)	21.6
Profit ordinary activities before tax	35.6	21.8	138.0
Taxation on profit on ordinary activities	(23.1)	(37.2)	(50.4)
Profit (Loss) on ordinary activities	12.5	(15.4)	87.6
Minority interests	(5.3)	(2.9)	(3.7)
Preference dividends	(28.5)	(18.2)	(8.8)
Extraordinary items	(76.9)	(22.0)	
Profit attributable to ordinary shareholders	(98.2)	(58.5)	75.1
Ordinary dividends	(14.2)	(25.1)	
Retained profit (loss)	(98.2)	(72.7)	50.0
Profit (Loss) per ordinary share (in pence)	(15.3)	(23.1)	48.1

assume profit responsibility toward the board. The choice of Louis-Dreyfus fell in line with Saatchi's announced plan to sell consulting and concentrate on communication services (see exhibit 6).

Louis-Dreyfus announced his strategy to expand Saatchi's share of the advertising pie, primarily through internal growth as opposed to Saatchi's traditional method of acquisitions. When he took over at Saatchi, the major international agencies controlled about 18 percent of total ad revenue worldwide, with Saatchi's share about 25 percent of that (see exhibits 7 and 8). In the next ten years, Louis-Dreyfus predicted, the major agencies' share of total ad revenue would double, and "I would like to increase our share of the

EXHIBIT 6
Saatchi's Directors in 1990

Saatchi, Maurice, BSc Econ, 44, chairman. Worked on new business development at Haymarket Publishing from 1968 to 1970, when he formed Saatchi & Saatchi. Chairman of Saatchi since 1985. Trustee of the Victoria and Albert Museum and governor of the London School of Economics.

Louis-Dreyfus, Robert, MBA, 44, chief executive. In 1982 appointed COO of IMS, the leading pharmaceutical market research company; in 1984 CEO. Negotiated sale of IMS to Dun & Bradstreet in 1988. Joined Saatchi as chief executive in January 1990.

Levitt, Theodore, PhD, 66, Non-executive director. Currently emeritus professor of business administration at Harvard. Appointed in March 1991.

Mellor, Simon, BSc, 36, director. Joined Saatchi in 1976. Director of corporate communications since November 1990.

Russell, Thomas, PhD, 59, Non-executive director. Elected director of IMS in 1984 and chairman in 1987.

Saatchi, Charles, 47, director. Co-founder.

Scott, Charles, FCA, finance director. CFO of IMS from 1986 until he joined Saatchi in January of 1990.

Sinclair, Jeremy, 44, deputy chairman. Founding member of Saatchi.

Rank	Organization	Gross Income ($ millions)	% Growth (over 1989–90)
1.	WPP Group	2,712.0	12.9
2.	Saatchi & Saatchi	1,729.3	9.7
3.	Interpublic Group	1,649.8	10.4
4.	Omnicom Group	1,335.5	13.4
5.	Dentsu	1,254.8	(0.6)
6.	Young & Rubicam	1,073.6	16.0
7.	Eurocom Group	748.5	58.5
8.	Hakuhodo	586.3	0.1
9.	Grey Advertising	583.3	19.1
10.	Foote, Cone & Belding Communications	563.2	5.9

EXHIBIT 7
Top Ten Advertising
Organizations in 1990

sector to a third from 25%."[3] Louis-Dreyfus intended to achieve such spectacular internal growth by implementing a two-pronged strategy, namely, by offering "one stop shopping" and "global communications services."

Saatchi had learned from its past experience in consulting that cross-reference of clients between service companies has its limits, but believed that this was not a problem for the closely related communications activities. Saatchi's managers believed that a client buying Saatchi's advertising services would also be willing to let the Saatchi Group take care of its other

communication needs such as direct marketing, public relations, and market research. Having the total range of communications services, it was felt, would maximize the opportunities for cross-reference and might attract new clients preferring "one-stop shopping." Louis-Dreyfus therefore agreed that Saatchi should keep all its communication service companies (see exhibit 9) and should hold regular meetings at the national level to determine cross-referral opportunities.

While there were opportunities for synergy, there was also the threat of conflicting client accounts among the company's ad agencies. Saatchi therefore decided to create two distinct and separate advertising agency networks, which were seen to be in direct competition with one another, thus ensuring client confidentiality.

[3]*Business Week,* "Saatchi's New Chief Sees Slow Turnaround, with a Return to Earnings Stride in 1994," March 22, 1990.

Rank	Agency	Gross Income ($ millions)	% Growth (over 1989–90)
1.	Young & Rubicam	1,001.4	15.7
2.	Saatchi & Saatchi Advertising Worldwide	825.7	11.5
3.	Ogilvy & Mather Worldwide	775.3	10.8
4.	McCann-Erikson Worldwide	744.7	11.3
5.	BBDO Worldwide	723.8	10.2
6.	Backer Spielvogel Bates Worldwide	715.6	8.0
7.	J. Walter Thompson	690.7	10.3
8.	Lintas Worldwide	676.5	10.4
9.	DDB Needam Worldwide	625.2	16.2
10.	Grey Advertising	583.3	19.1

EXHIBIT 8
Top Ten U.S.-Based
Consolidated Agencies in
1990

EXHIBIT 9
Saatchi's Communication
Activities

Activity	Company	Clients
Advertising	**Saatchi & Saatchi Advertising Worldwide** No. 2 International Advertising Agency 135 offices in 32 countries	General Mills, Sara Lee, Proctor & Gamble, J&J, Hewlett Packard, Toyota
	Backer Spielvogel Bates Worldwide No. 6 International Advertising Agency 159 offices in 46 countries	Philip Morris, Hyundai, King Fisher, Rover, BAT Industries, Mars
	Independent Agencies Campbell, Mithun, Esty No. 16 Advertising Agency in U.S. 7 offices in U.S. and Canada	Chrysler, Kroger, ConAgra, Texaco, 3M
	KHBB: No. 17 Advertising Agency in U.K. **AC&R:** No. 38 Advertising Agency in U.S. **Hall Harrison Cowley:** U.K. regional network	
Direct Marketing	**Kobs & Draft Worldwide** No. 6 International Direct Marketing Agency 21 offices in 18 countries	Chase Manhattan, IBM, Mars, Rover
Public Relations	**Roland Worldwide** No. 6 International Public Relations Company 29 offices in 19 countries	Du Pont, J&J, Mars, P&G, Sandoz
Media Services	**Zenith Media Worldwide** Established 1988, offices in London, Paris, Madrid, Barcelona, and Milan	Allied Lyons, Amstrad, Philip Morris
Other	**Howard Marlboro Group**—In-store marketing **HP:ICM**—Face-to-face communications **Siegal & Gale**—Corporate identity and design **National Research Group**—Market research **Yankelovich Clancy Shulman**—Market research	

Saatchi's Global Marketing Approach

The second, long-standing aspect of Saatchi's strategy, besides being a total communications services company, was to build up the company's capability for launching "global" advertising campaigns. Maurice and Charles had been early converts to the idea of global marketing, championed by Theodore Levitt of Harvard Business School. The idea basically holds that cultures are becoming so similar that products can be marketed the same way everywhere. Louis-Dreyfus supported the global advertising notion, but with more caution

than the Saatchi brothers. He agreed that Saatchi was right to expand into different markets to serve multinational clients, but added, "Creativity isn't the same everywhere. You can't apply the same principles in England, France and America."[4]

While warning against excessive "globalization," Louis-Dreyfus by no means abandoned his belief in the basic premises. He and Maurice recruited Theodore Levitt to the company board in March of 1990 and reiterated that global marketing is an evolutionary process. Thus, Saatchi will be at the forefront of

---

[4]Graham Thomas, vice chairman of Saatchi, in a memorandum to the authors dated April 8, 1992.

EXHIBIT 10
An Example of Transnational
Advertising

PAN-EUROPEAN ADVERTISING FOR PROCTOR & GAMBLE

Proctor & Gamble (P&G) is Saatchi's number one client, with operations in 130 countries. About 70 percent of P&G's business is done in world brands, of which Pampers is one of the most famous. It was introduced to the U.S. market in 1968 as the first disposable diaper in the world. Expansion followed in the mid-1970s, first in Europe and followed by the Middle East and Asia. Today it is brand leader in fourteen European markets and has recently been launched in Poland and Yugoslavia, with Hungary to follow soon. But today's success was not always the case.

In the early eighties Pampers had not kept up with technical developments, and by the mid-eighties had found itself squeezed by low-cost competitors moving up-market, leading to lower prices and sagging profitability. In 1985 the company relaunched with an upgraded product in all European markets. Millions of dollars were invested in new production lines. All countries shared the same objectives: rebuild share and maintain profitability in the face of higher product costs.

However, while the objectives were the same, the marketing executions differed in each country. Since there was no agreed learning on "what really worked," each country did what it judged best for its market. Advertising, media, promotional activity were done on an individual market basis. There were ten different TV campaigns produced across Europe. The results of the launches were disappointing across Europe, as the exceptional product performance did not match the higher prices and unexpected product issues surfaced. The problem became worse when each country tried to fix it their own way. R&D, agencies, and the plant had several requests from each country to address.

As Pampers reached its lowest point at the end of 1985, the company realized it needed to fundamentally reorganize in order to survive. The right balance needed to be found between global, European, and local marketing. The most significant issues identified were lowering manufacturing costs by striving for economies of scale, searching for innovative product initiatives with pan-European application, and sharing worldwide and European ideas in areas such as product, packaging, advertising, and direct marketing. In 1986 the European diaper business was reorganized into a pan-European operation to reap transnational synergies. Two new senior positions were created at P&G, namely, a divisional manager with volume and profit responsibility for the total diaper business across Europe, and a European marketing manager.

Saatchi decided to reorganize its team to mirror the P&G structure. Together the companies worked on "keeping it simple and back to basics." The basis for the advertising development came out of the previous experience gleaned from ten different pieces of advertising. The pan-European approach meant that Saatchi has given P&G much less advertising (through standardization), but of much higher quality (by transferring learning effects across borders). Since 1987 the formula has been an undeniable success, as the following Euro volume growth figures show:

Index vs. previous year	
1986	100
1987	110
1988	132
1989	127
1990	127

EXHIBIT 11
Primary West European
Clients

Country	MNC Clients	Local Clients	Total 1990 ($ m)
Austria	15	20	65
Belgium	24	11	15
France	53	30	275
Germany	42	35	238
Ireland	17	15	23
Italy	26	20	286
Netherlands	37	20	73
Spain	25	31	131
United Kingdom	60	41	745

implementing this strategy for clients who compete transnationally, but will also rededicate itself to those clients currently operating only in local environments. A listing of Saatchi's Western European clients, multinational versus local, is set forth in exhibit 11. Multinational clients are those operating in more than one country, but needn't necessarily be pursuing transnational standardization, although they could potentially in the future.

To be able to offer multinational clients global advertising campaigns, Saatchi has arranged its advertising business within a regional and worldwide matrix (see exhibit 12). On the one hand the company is organized geographically, with agencies in each country of operation and coordination between neighbouring countries achieved by means of regional management boards. On the other hand Saatchi is also organized by client, whereby worldwide account directors (WADs) and regional account directors (RADs) are responsible for representing multinational client needs across all agencies. WADs and RADs are currently running the twelve biggest international accounts.

Saatchi's Future

In May 1990 Saatchi's shares rose slightly following the news that Louis-Dreyfus had dismissed Roy Warman and Terry Bannister, two senior managers at Saatchi.

EXHIBIT 12
Organizational Diagram of
Saatchi's Advertising
Business

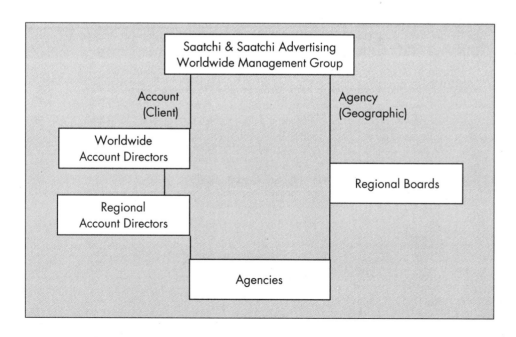

EXHIBIT 13
Estimated World Advertising
Expenditure (annual %
change)

	1991 vs. 1990		1992 vs. 1991		1993 vs. 1992		1994 vs. 1993	
	Current Prices	Constant Prices	Current Prices	Constant Prices	Current Prices	Constant Prices	Current Prices	Constant Prices
Major Media*								
North America	−1.8	−5.9	1.4	−2.2	3.2	−0.8	3.3	−0.7
Europe	3.4	−2.0	8.0	2.4	8.3	2.2	8.8	2.1
Asia/Pacific	6.0	1.7	8.1	3.9	8.3	3.6	8.5	3.8
Latin America	11.8	n/a	14.6	n/a	18.0	n/a	18.6	n/a
ROW	9.6	n/a	9.9	n/a	11.4	n/a	12.3	n/a
Subtotal**	2.0	−2.9	5.5	0.7	6.6	1.3	7.0	1.4
Direct Mail								
North America	4.7	0.6	5.1	1.2	5.1	1.0	5.0	0.9
Europe	4.0	−1.4	5.0	−0.6	7.0	0.8	8.0	1.4
Other Media***								
U.S.	5.0	0.7	5.0	1.3	5.0	1.0	5.0	1.0
Japan	4.3	1.1	5.6	2.7	5.7	2.2	5.7	2.2
Total	2.7	−2.0	5.4	0.9	6.3	1.3	6.7	1.4

*TV, print, radio, cinema and outdoor
**Constant prices exclude Latin America and the rest of the world
***Includes point-of-sale, sales promotion expenditure

The dismissals were interpreted by the markets as a sign that Louis-Dreyfus had won strategic control of the company from the Saatchi brothers, and that he now had the authority to get to grips with its financial problems.

A year later, as the share price continued to drop, Louis-Dreyfus had implemented the recapitalization plan that strengthened the Saatchi balance sheet and divested its consulting business for a loss. The company had its strategy of total communications service and global advertising on track. However, the operating margins were still under great pressure and would continue to fall during 1991. Furthermore, world advertising expenditure was expected to decline in 1991 (see exhibit 13).

Meanwhile, Maurice Saatchi, chairman, rededicated the company to the principles of creativity that had built it in the first place and offered a new definition of great advertising. "It means creative work that is so simple and direct that it strikes a chord in humans everywhere," he said. But the question on Louis-Dreyfus's mind was whether this was enough to get Saatchi out of the red.

■ NOKIA DATA[†]

By Kamran Kashani with Robert Howard

Early in 1989, the top management of Nokia Data was mapping the key elements of the firm's strategy for growth and international expansion through the mid-1990s. In the previous year, the Finnish computer company had acquired the Data Systems Division of Sweden's LM Ericsson as a first step towards becoming a major player in the European market for information technology. However, despite the acquisition, less than a quarter of Nokia Data's $1.2 billion sales were generated outside the Nordic market1, where it now held the leading position. Management intended to improve the company's spotty international presence by aggressively expanding onto the large but also highly competitive markets in the rest of Europe.

A cornerstone of Nokia Data's European growth strategy was what management referred to as a "multi-domestic" approach. Management believed that in the fast maturing European market for computers, the key to competitive advantage lay in customer orientation achieved through a strong local identity and domestically tailored marketing programs in each European country. Thus, local hardware and software customization, local branding, local marketing, and local sales and support services constituted the main elements of Nokia Data's "multi-domestic" approach.

Top executives were keenly aware that their planned approach went counter to industry practices, which were increasingly emphasizing pan-European integration and marketing. In fact, some Nokia managers had expressed doubts regarding the wisdom of the "multi-domestic" approach. According to Kalle Isokallio, President of Nokia Data:

> "We have a different view of the industry than what one reads in the papers. Our industry is no longer high growth or high tech. Both sales and technology are maturing. In this competitive market, we can't compete with majors like IBM or Siemens in volume or new technology. We don't have the resources. Where we can outperform them is by being closer to the computer buyer who prefers to buy from a domestic supplier. In every country where we compete, therefore, we want to be considered as one of the top domestic vendors. Pan-European identity and integration doesn't make sense for us. We are too small for that."

The Nokia Group

Nokia was founded in 1865 in the village of Nokia, Finland, as a timber and paper company. In the subsequent 100 years, Nokia grew and diversified into tires, power transmission, radio, telecommunications, electronics and computer technology. In 1988, the Nokia Group of companies had sales of $5,500 million, earned a net profit of $215 million, and spent 5 percent of net sales on research and development. With its 44,000 employees, Nokia conducted operations in 32 countries, 17 of which had manufacturing facilities. By 1988, the Nokia Group of companies was Finland's largest publicly traded industrial enterprise. In addition to Helsinki, Nokia shares were listed on the stock exchanges in Stockholm, London, Paris and Frankfurt. (See exhibit 1 for information on the Nokia Group of companies.)

Nokia Information Systems (NIS)

Nokia's experience with computers dated from 1962, the year when Nokia Electronics was formed to capitalize on the company's recent purchase of its first mainframe. At this time, Nokia implemented a timesharing system with outside companies to handle

1The Nordic market consisted of the three Scandinavian countries (Sweden, Norway, and Denmark), plus Finland.

Industry Segment	1988	1987	1986
Electronics			
Information Systems	1170*	459	336
Telecommunications	359	364	197
Mobile Telephones	271	214	178
Consumer Electronics	1432	678	441
Cables and Machinery			
Cables	557	529	438
Machinery	255	188	163
Electrical Wholesaling	245	180	75
Paper, Power and Chemicals			
Paper	628	589	447
Chemicals	130	110	81
Rubber and Floorings			
Rubber Products	342	337	271
Floorings	75	64	51
Group Total	5237	3500	2519

*less inter-division sales and sales between industry segments

EXHIBIT 1
The Nokia Group of Companies Sales (in $ Millions)

bookkeeping and other data processing activities. In the late 1960s, Nokia began serving as a sales agent for Honeywell, marketing its complete product line of mainframes, terminals and printers to the Finnish market. During this period, Nokia management combined their increasing knowledge of hardware with their data processing know-how from timesharing. In the early 1970s, Nokia developed, manufactured and sold its own minicomputer.

Throughout the 1970s, the Honeywell product line represented a main source of revenue at Nokia Electronics. However, in 1977, prompted by the growth of its customer base in the banking and retailing sectors, Nokia formed a separate department for its own products. In 1981, Nokia expanded its product offering further with its first personal computer, the Mikro Mikko 1. In 1985, Nokia Electronics was split into four divisions: Information Systems, Telecommunications, Mobile Telephones, and Consumer Electronics.

As of 1987, the Honeywell line accounted for 40 percent of Nokia Information System's revenues in Finland. Honeywell's role was limited to manufacturing, performed in the US, Italy or Scotland, and to providing operating system software. Aside from adding its own terminals to Honeywell's computers, Nokia was responsible for all applications of software,

and post-sales services. In 1987, Nokia Information Systems enjoyed the leading market share in Finland, where it generated 75 percent of its total sales.

Nokia Data

With limited growth opportunities in the small Finnish market, Nokia management began searching for an acquisition candidate within the Nordic countries. In 1988, Nokia Information Systems purchased the Data Systems unit of the Ericsson Group in Stockholm and merged the two operations to form Nokia Data. Data Systems produced and marketed a range of minicomputers, personal computers, telephone exchanges and printers throughout Europe in addition to Hong Kong and Australia. Aside from keeping sales offices in North America and other overseas markets, the Ericsson Group retained a 20 percent share ownership in Nokia Data. Nokia, on the other hand, was able to strengthen its share of the Nordic countries market and gained the opportunity to expand into Germany, France, Britain and a number of other European markets. Management believed that increased geographic coverage translated into greater credibility among Nokia's customers and helped ensure the company's survival in the Nordic countries at a time of industry consolidation. By the end of 1988, with sales of $1.2 billion, Nokia Data was the largest computer company in the Nordic countries. The firm employed 8,500 employees, had subsidiaries in 10 European countries, and a European installed base of over 700,000 terminals and personal computers. (See exhibit 2 for the Nokia Data reporting structure.)

The Information Technology Industry

In its broadest sense, information technology (IT) was defined as the industry which combined the data processing and storage power of computers with the distance-transmission capabilities of telecommunications. The industry included all types of computers, word processors, printers, plotters, disk drives, telephones, telephone networks, public databases and relative software. Virtually all organizations used these products. In Western Europe, the manufacturing, finance, retail and public sectors accounted for the largest expenditures. In 1987, the worldwide market for IT was valued at $407 billion with volume distributed heavily among three geographic markets: North America, 38 percent; Europe, 26 percent; and Japan, 30 percent. For 1989, total industry sales were forecast to reach $505 billion.

Nokia's Data Business

In the vast information technology field, Nokia Data management defined its core business as the sector of the computer industry that focussed on terminals, personal computers and related networks. While the total European computer industry in 1987 was valued at $86 billion, management estimated its industry sector accounted for $20-22 billion.

Nokia Data's product offering included terminals, personal computers, minicomputers, local area networks (hardware connected to share and exchange information among a group of users), and the related communication links for connecting different brands and classes of computers. In addition to hardware, Nokia Data provided application software and services tailored to meet the needs of its five primary customer segments — in retailing, banking and insurance, manufacturing, government, and general business. Typical examples of general business applications included materials administration, purchasing, order handling, invoicing, database management, word processing, graphics and spreadsheets. Across Europe, the five segments in which Nokia Data competed were forecast to grow between 7 percent and 10 percent per year through the early 1990s.

Markets and Competition

In Europe, Nokia Data competed directly and indirectly with a large number of firms. (Exhibit 3 shows the top 25 manufacturers in the European data processing market, ranked by their total volume of business in the region.) Nokia Data's management believed that such rankings were misleading because not all firms competed in the market sector defined as terminals, personal computers, networks, and related products and services. Instead, to delineate the competition, management used the diagram shown in exhibit 4, which clustered industry participants around four product/system zones: terminals, personal computers, local area networks and systems. The four zones differed in their volume potential and product/systems configuration. (See exhibit 5 for a summary of Nokia Data's key competitors and their product offerings along the four zones.)

Terminals   The European terminal market, consisting of keyboards and screens, represented approximately 6 percent of the European sector in which Nokia Data competed and was valued at $2.2 billion. Terminals had no data processing power of their own and, hence, had to be connected to a host computer. Sales were divided between add-on terminals (90-95 percent), where customers expanded an existing system by adding new terminals, and upgrades (5-10 percent), where customers substituted new terminals for old. The terminal market was contested for by mainframe and minicomputer suppliers, such as IBM and DEC, which were able to sell their own terminals on the strength of their computers, and by a large number of component suppliers. Among these were Memorex Telex of US origin and SEL of Germany, which made terminals compatible with existing computers as well as disk drives, cassettes and other computer accessories. Across Europe, Nokia Data management considered IBM, Memorex Telex and Olivetti as their primary competitors in the terminal market.

Typical customers for terminals included large organizations, such as banks and insurance agencies, that processed data with a large central computer and a score of dispersed terminals. Customers purchasing

EXHIBIT 2
Partial Organization Chart

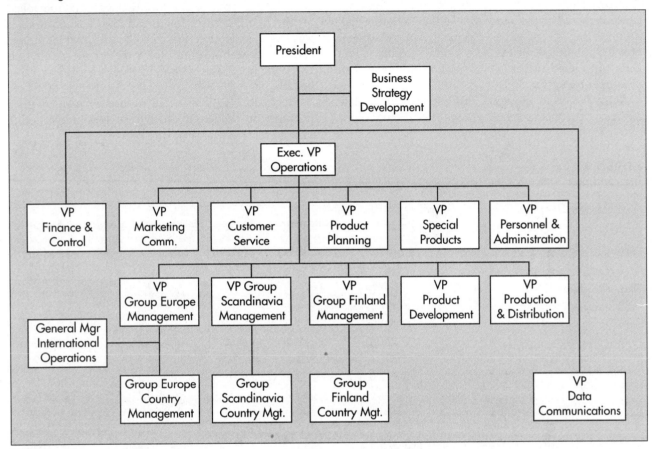

terminals from component suppliers, instead of the large computer companies, cited price as an important factor. More recently, ergonomics had become a criterion as it was believed to contribute to improved employee comfort and productivity. Since the terminal market was primarily an add-on market, functions performed for the customer were installations and, when necessary, after-sales repair.

According to Nokia Data management, keys to success in the terminal market were compatibility with hardware from the major computer companies, competitive pricing, and credibility as a terminal supplier. Credibility, a sales manager clarified, meant a supplier was known for dependable products and was large enough to survive any industry shakeout.

In unit sales, the terminal market was projected to remain stagnant through the early 1990s and decline thereafter. In 1989 the market was becoming increasingly competitive. The average terminal prices in Europe had declined by about 8 percent in recent months.

Personal Computers   In 1988, the European personal computer market was valued at $11 billion and expected to reach $18 billion by 1993. Competitors in this zone were well-known personal computer manufacturers such as IBM, Olivetti, Siemens, Amstrad, Apple and Compaq. These firms were further classified by Nokia Data management according to their origin and historic customer base. More specifically, IBM, Siemens and Olivetti, for example, had begun with and enjoyed established reputations in the business community, and were described by Nokia Data management as having an "institutional" market background. On the other hand, Amstrad, Apple and Compaq, a few among a large number of companies, were originally associated with the mass market and said by management to have a "consumer" background.

From 1984 to 1987, the share of all personal computers sold by the institutional group in Europe had declined from 45 percent to 35 percent, with the balance of sales accounted for by the consumer group. Nokia Data considered that it had a more institutional than consumer background.

Regardless of their original customer base, by the late 1980s, competitors from both groups offered stand-alone personal computers direct to large accounts and via retail outlets to the medium-sized and small business and consumer markets. Typically, larger accounts relied on the manufacturer for installation and after-sales services. Smaller accounts as well as individual buyers relied on the manufacturer's dealer or repair network for help, a process which was considered less reliable.

According to Goran Hermannson, a marketing manager in Sweden, in order to succeed in marketing

EXHIBIT 3

The 25 Largest Computer Companies Competing in Europe in 1987

Rank	Company	Origin	Total Revenue ($ million)	European Revenue ($ million)	Europe as % of Total	Estimated Revenues from Nokia Data's Industry Sector*	Major European Markets
1	IBM	USA	50,485.7	18,332.5	36	3520	F, D, I, UK
2	Siemens	Germany	5,703.0	4,961.6	87	357	D
3	Olivetti	Italy	4,637.2	3,802.5	82	1041	I, D, F
4	Digital (DEC)	USA	10,391.3	3,533.0	34	73	F, D, I, UK
5	Nixdorf	Germany	2,821.5	2,652.2	94	266	D, F, UK
6	Groupe Bull	France	3,007.5	2,345.8	78	30	F, E, UK
7	Unisys	USA	8,742.0	2,272.9	26	28	F, CH
8	Philips	Netherlands	2,601.6	2,055.2	79	271	NL, D, B, L
9	Hewlett-Packard	USA	5,000.0	1,800.0	36	0	F, D, I, UK
10	STC	UK	2,123.9	1,720.4	81	40	UK
11	NCR Corp.	USA	5,075.7	1,583.6	31	144	D, F, UK, NL
12	IM Ericsson**	Sweden	1,511.6	1,284.9	85	—	S, D, DK
13	Alcatel NV	France	2,052.1	1,272.3	62	229	F
14	Inspectorate	Switzerland	1,225.0	1,033.0	84	0	CH
15	Societe Générale	France	970.1	970.1	100	0	F
16	Atlantic Computers	UK	959.7	892.7	93	0	UK
17	Honeywell Bull	USA	2,059.0	885.4	43	21	F, E, I, UK
18	Memorex Intl	Netherlands	1,041.1	832.9	80	54	D, NL
19	Wang Laboratories	USA	3,045.7	822.3	27	49	F, D, I, UK
20	Mannesmann AG	Germany	686.0	617.0	90	90	D
21	Apple Computer	USA	3,041.2	547.4	18	204	F, S
22	Cap Gemini Sogeti	France	682.3	545.8	80	0	F
23	Econocon Intl	Netherlands	674.3	525.9	78	0	NL
24	Amstrad plc	UK	533.0	501.0	94	250	UK, F, E
25	Amdahl Corp.	USA	1,505.2	493.1	33	0	F, D, I, UK

* Nokia Data's industry sector is defined as terminals, personal computers, LANs and vertical systems installed in the company's five end-user segments

** Figures are for year-end 1987, prior to Nokia Information System's acquisition of the Ericsson Data Systems Division. Following the acquisition by Nokia Data in 1988, parts of the company were sold off.

EXHIBIT 4
Nokia Data's Industry Sector: Product/Service Zones

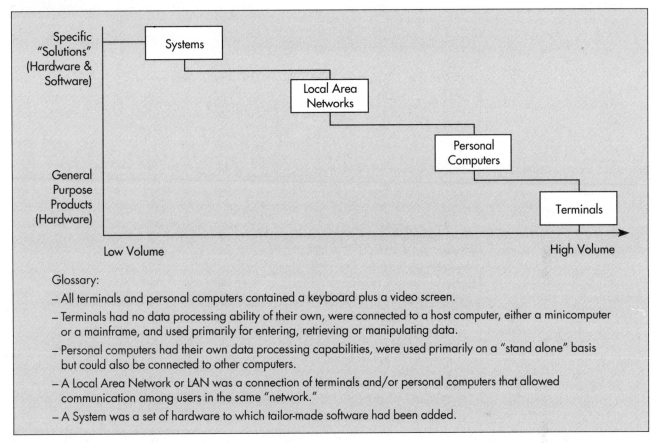

Glossary:

– All terminals and personal computers contained a keyboard plus a video screen.

– Terminals had no data processing ability of their own, were connected to a host computer, either a minicomputer or a mainframe, and used primarily for entering, retrieving or manipulating data.

– Personal computers had their own data processing capabilities, were used primarily on a "stand alone" basis but could also be connected to other computers.

– A Local Area Network or LAN was a connection of terminals and/or personal computers that allowed communication among users in the same "network."

– A System was a set of hardware to which tailor-made software had been added.

personal computers to large accounts, a hardware supplier had to be known for reliable products and perceived by the customer as large enough to survive the computer industry's eventual consolidation. Companies from the institutional group had an advantage because they already enjoyed a reputation as suppliers of mainframes and minicomputers. More recently, compatibility with hardware from multiple vendors had become an important factor for supplying personal computers to large accounts. Major institutional companies such as IBM, which had traditionally employed its own proprietary systems, were now facing increasing pressure to abandon these in favor of industry standards and multiple vendor compatibility.

Nokia Data management believed that to succeed in the mass market, on the other hand, a supplier needed low manufacturing costs, extensive retail distribution and a favorable price/performance image in the eyes of

the customer. Examples of such companies included Amstrad, Commodore and Compaq.

Local Area Networks (LANs)   LANs were a collection of computers, printers, cables and other communications links which allowed a network of users to process data and communicate with one another.

In addition to hardware, LANs were equipped with operating systems software, applications software, and sophisticated LAN management software that allocated data processing among the computers in a network. As a concept in computing, LANs were relatively new to the industry, represented $670 million of the $20-22 billion segment in which Nokia Data competed, and were expected to grow 20-30 percent per annum through the middle 1990s. Although LANs could include mainframes and minicomputers, they were built primarily using personal computers. One advantage of LANs was its attractive cost-performance ratio. An

EXHIBIT 5
Nokia Data's Main
Competitors

Company/Product	Systems*	LANs	PCs	Terminals
IBM	All	X	X	X
Siemens	M, G, GB, I	X	·X	X
Olivetti	B, R, GB	X	X	X
Digital (DEC)		X		X
Nixdorf	All	X		X
Bull	GB, M	X	X	X
Unisys	GB, M	X	X	X
Philips	B, I, M, GB	X	X	X
STC	GB, M	X		X
NCR	B, R	X	X	X
Alcatel				X
Memorex				X
Wang	GB	X	X	X
Mannesmann	All	X	X	
Apple	GB	X	X	
Amstrad				
Compaq		X	X	
Commodore			X	

*Nokia Data management defined systems competitors as those offering "solutions" in the company's five end-user segments. Yet, because the management viewed the competition in terms of industry standards, proprietary systems, and horizontal product offering, a number of the companies listed in exhibit 3 were not seen as direct competitors.

Note: B = Banking   R = Retail   G = Government
       I = Insurance   M = Manufacturing   GB = General Business

independent estimate showed that it cost less than $10,000 per employee to set up a network of personal computers, versus $12,000 for a seat at a minicomputer and $14,000 at a mainframe. In addition to lower hardware costs, networks eliminated the inefficiencies of multiple training staffs, multiple software packages and data transmission costs.

Typical customers in the LAN segment, according to Goran Hermansson, were companies or departments with fewer than 100 personal computer users. He explained that it was technically easier to implement LAN solutions in smaller companies than in ones with hundreds of personal computers. In addition, he believed that the LAN technology was less popular with central data processing management in larger companies because it allowed individual departments to decide on their own systems independently.

Due to the complexity associated with the design, installation and maintenance of a LAN, service accounted for a large portion of the purchase price. In addition, customers were keenly aware of the importance of vendor support in the early phases of a LAN's installation. In the words of one Nokia Data customer, it was important to have "someone to shoot" if something went wrong.

According to Nokia Data management, to be successful as a LAN supplier, a company had to enjoy the same qualifications as a personal computer vendor, namely, reliable products, hardware compatibility in a multi-vendor environment, and customer perceived longevity. In addition, it had to have the technical know-how to act as a systems integrator, connecting products from one or many vendors. Most important, a LAN supplier had to be willing to service a network that contained products from vendors other than itself and guarantee against a network failure.

Because LANs were built primarily with personal computers, competitors came from both the institutional and the consumer groups. In the institutional group, Nokia Data's largest competitor in Europe was IBM, although companies such as Olivetti and Philips were strong in their local markets. The largest competitor in the consumer group was Compaq.

Systems   At Nokia Data, a system was defined as a set of hardware and software products tailored to meet a specific need within an industry or industry segment. A system could consist of terminals sold with tailor-made software utilizing a client's existing mainframe or minicomputer. Alternatively, a system could be based on LAN products, complemented by customized software. In 1988, the European systems business was estimated to be $7 billion and projected to grow 10-15 percent annually through the early 1990s.

As with the personal computer market, systems competitors were categorized by Nokia Data management into institutional and consumer groups. The distinguishing feature between these groups, according to a Nokia Data sales executive, was knowledge about their customers' industries. He explained that companies like IBM and Siemens had accumulated a vast base of experience in industries such as insurance, banking, and manufacturing where centralized data processing, using mainframes and terminals, had been practiced for over two decades. On the other hand, newcomers such as Compaq and Amstrad, with a consumer background, relied more on the industry knowledge of third parties, including value added resellers (VARs) to compete in the systems market.

Systems customers were typically large organizations which sought to decentralize their data processing activities to a department or work group level. Decentralized data processing was attractive as it eliminated the users' dependence on a single computer, particularly important in organizations such as banks where a computer breakdown might force shutdown of operations.

Leif Lindfors, a Sales Manager for Sweden, believed that, as in the LAN market, success in systems required reliable hardware and software. However, he explained, the most important requirement for success in systems was to have a salesforce with industry-specific knowledge, assisted by a technical support staff capable of developing customized software. Nokia Data management identified its primary systems competitor as IBM followed by other institutional companies such as Unisys, Siemens, Olivetti, Nixdorf and Philips.

Industry Trends

Industry observers, as well as Nokia Data executives, believed several trends were influencing the level and nature of competition in the European data processing market. Among these trends were slowing growth, improved price-performance ratio of hardware, growth of decentralized computing, emergence of industry standards, proliferation of VARs, and the anticipated European integration towards a single market after 1992.

Slowing Growth   In the late 1980s, the overall growth in the European computer industry was slowing down to single digits. As of 1988, annual growth had declined for the first time below 10 percent, and some analysts were predicting only 6 percent yearly growth through 1992. Mainframes and minicomputers had experienced the biggest decline in growth rates as customers shifted to lower-cost computing alternatives such as personal computers and LANs. In fact, analysts expected mainframe and minicomputer sales to grow at only 8 percent and 3 percent, respectively, into the early 1990s. Demand for personal computers, however, was expected to remain strong, with 10 percent growth forecast through 1992.

Price-Performance Ratio   Advances in computer chip technology had substantially reduced the cost of computing power during the 1980s, a trend that was expected to continue into the 1990s. For example, in 1981, a mainframe capable of processing one million instructions per second cost over $400,000; by the early 1990s, the hardware with similar performance was expected to be priced round $50,000. More importantly, the computing power associated with some earlier mainframes was, by 1988, available in a desktop computer at a fraction of the cost, a trend referred to in the industry as "downsizing." Furthermore, as more and more processing power was provided to end-users, analysts believed that powerful personal computers would replace terminals connected to mainframes and minicomputers.

Decentralized Computing   In the early days of computing, companies needed a mainframe and a multitude of dumb terminals to perform all data processing centrally. The first step toward decentralization occurred with minicomputers, allowing users to process up to 95 percent of their data within their own departments. The next step in decentralization came with the personal computer, placing data processing capability directly on the end-user's desk. Personal computers were, however, limited in their computing capacity and, as stand-alone hardware, did not allow communication among users.

The recent arrival of LAN technology provided an alternative means to decentralize computing by distributing data processing among a work group's or a department's interconnected computers. The use of personal computers in a network gave LANs a computing capacity similar to minicomputers at a fraction of the cost. In the opinion of many analysts, downsizing and distributed processing together were subtantially changing the way companies competed in the computer industry. One analyst believed that decentralization was providing end-users with more say in computer purchase decisions, leading to an increasing number of specialized narrow segments. The net result, according to another observer, was that the more expensive minicomputer and mainframes would lose sales to the less costly personal computer-based LANs.

Industry Standards   Throughout the 1980s, minicomputer and mainframe manufacturers such as IBM, DEC and Siemens, sold their hardware with proprietary software, thus locking customers into a specific data handling method. Having made a substantial investment in hardware and software, few customers were willing to purchase new systems from other manufacturers, a decision which could entail difficult and expensive tasks of rewriting old programs.

In contrast to proprietary systems, US-based AT&T developed and licensed UNIX, a non-proprietary operating system that allowed different brands of computers to communicate with each other. Preferred by an increasing number of computer buyers, the use of UNIX-based hardware and software was on the rise worldwide. Industry observers believed that interconnectivity would become an important buying criteria in the 1990s.

Proliferation of VARs

During the 1980s, the focus of competition in the computer industry had shifted away from hardware towards software and services. Staffan Simberg, Vice President Group Europe, attributed this trend to the "commoditization" of computers, where substantive technological differences in hardware were narrowing among different manufacturers. Another factor was what many in Nokia Data managment referred to as the

"declining technical sophistication of the average buyer." Increasingly, computer decisions in small to medium-sized companies were being made by non-computer people who were more concerned with the quality of "solutions" than the technicalities of the "black box."

The two trends combined had given rise to value added resellers (VARs), independent companies who filled a gap between manufacturers and small to medium-sized clients. VARs bought hardware from a variety of producers, adding customized software and services for narrow vertical user segments such as the legal and medical professions, specialized retailers, plumbing and farming. VARs competed among themselves and with computer manufacturers in the LANs and systems markets. From modest levels in the 1970s, the number of VARs in Europe had grown in recent years to several hundred. Together, they accounted for an estimated $3 billion in industry sales.

To use a VAR for competitive advantage, explained one Nokia Data sales executive, a company had to provide hardware with an attractive price and encourage the resellers to develop applications in their special end-user segments. In an average installation, 65 percent of the price paid by a customer was accounted for by the cost of hardware to the reseller; the rest went to cover expenses, including costs associated with application development, and margins.

European Integration   The European Economic Community (EEC) had chosen 1992 as the date to integrate its internal market by liberalizing trade and removing barriers among its twelve member states. Increased competition among manufacturers in an open market implied that government procurement could no longer favor a local vendor over another vendor from the EEC. Hence, 1992 posed a serious challenge to national computer companies where 50 percent of sales was to the local government. Increased competition was also expected to lead to concentration in the industry, as companies strove to achieve critical mass and economies of scale. Recent examples of such activities included Alcatel, formed though the merger of ITT's European business and the French CGE group; and Memorex Telex, formed by the merger of Memorex International and the US Telex organization.

Also, in anticipation of 1992, companies such as Apple, IBM, Siemens and Olivetti were integrating regional operations towards a "European" posture and identity. In the case of Apple, its management had recently created a European research and development center in Paris. "We want to form a strong European identity so that we are able to be part of the European economy."[2] By adopting a regional profile, both European and non-European companies wanted to be better positioned to compete for local government bids after 1992, when procurement policies were no longer biased toward domestic suppliers. In this respect, Olivetti's Executive Vice President, Elserino Piol, maintained, "The European companies that remain 'national champions' are going to suffer after 1992." The same article concluded, "Europe's computer makers have all opted for the same survival strategy. Each is scrambling to go pan-European as fast as possible."[3]

Nokia Data's European Strategy

At the end of 1988, Nokia Data manufactured its products in Sweden and Finland, and operated wholly-owned sales and service branches in all four Nordic countries (Sweden, Norway, Denmark, Finland) in addition to Germany, the Netherlands, Spain, the UK, France and Switzerland. In Germany, Nokia Data's largest non-Nordic countries operation, the company employed a total of 450 in sales and service. Nokia Data also used sales agents, who had previously sold Nokia Information Systems or Ericsson Data System products, in Finland, Sweden, Belgium, Austria, Italy, Portugal, Hong Kong and Australia.

The company assembled most of its products in its own facilities; a minor share of total production was subcontracted to third parties in Nordic countries as well as the Far East. Management saw definite advantages to sourcing internationally and using its own facilities for assembly. Currently, components purchased as far away as the US and the Far East accounted for 70 percent of the total cost of production; the rest of the cost was divided equally between labor and plant overhead. Efficient sourcing and materials management were considered critical to overall cost performance. A recent estimate indicated that well-run procurement and manufacturing operations, including rationalized purchasing and investment in modern assembly, could potentially save the company as much as 40 percent on the production costs of terminals and PCs. One-half of the projected savings would have come from reduced materials cost. Some Nokia Data

[2] *Business Marketing*, September 1988
[3] *Business International*, September 12, 1988

executives believed that while potential for savings existed, it probably was less than the estimated 40 percent.

Nokia Data marketed what management called its "horizontal products"— terminals, personal computers and LAN-based hardware — in all markets. With minor exceptions, these products were based on non-proprietary technologies. "Vertical systems," as management called them, were sales of hardware and software to target segments in banking/insurance, retailing, manufacturing, government and general business. Nokia Data did not use VARs in a market until management believed the company had a strong local presence. Hence, as of 1988, VARs were only used in Finland and Sweden. Less than 3 percent of the company's sales were generated through sales agents or VARs.

In Finland, Nokia Data used the Mikko brand for its entire line. In all other markets, Nokia Data used the Alfaskop brand name acquired from Ericsson Data Systems.

Although its products were sold as far away as Hong Kong and Australia, 95 percent of Nokia Data's sales were concentrated in Europe with Finland, Sweden, and Germany representing 40 percent, 25 percent and 11 percent of total sales respectively. (See exhibits 6, 7 and 8 for a summary of Nokia Data's sales by country, segment and product.)

Senior managers thought of their company as a sales-driven organization. Although major strategic decisions were made by product groups at headquarters, the regions and country management in larger markets wielded significant influence on short-term policies and sales action. For example, although product design was a headquarters decision, a local sales operation could ask for the development of a special terminal and keyboard for a large order. Local managers in new and "strategic" markets such as Germany, France and Spain were measured and rewarded based on sales performance. In the more established markets such as Finland and Sweden, both sales and profitability were considered in performance evaluation.

Competitive Standing

Top management at Nokia Data believed that they enjoyed a number of competitive advantages in their sector of the computer industry. In particular, they believed that the large institutional competitors had been slow to respond to the growing customer demand for multi-vendor connectivity and were, consequently,

EXHIBIT 6
1988 Sales Summary By Segment (in $ millions)

Country	SF	S	DK	N	D	NL	E	UK	Others	Total	% Total
Retail	34.4	12.1	21.1	2.7	3.0	0	8.3	0	0	81.6	7
Banking/Insurance	199.8	144.3	4.5	14.5	23.5	2.7	19.4	0.7	6.0	415.4	35
Manufacturing	75.4	92.3	9.7	11.0	25.0	15.9	13.6	24.5	9.4	276.8	24
Government	88.1	50.4	23.7	6.8	74.5	17.2	7.7	0.6	1.5	270.5	23
General Business	106.0	3.3	4.3	4.1	5.3	1.2	1.5	0	0	125.7	11
Total	503.7	302.4	63.3	39.1	131.3	37.0	50.5	25.8	16.9	1170.0	100
% Total	43	26	5	3	11	3	4	2	2	100	

Notes: SF = Finland   NL = Netherlands
         S = Sweden   E = Spain
         DK = Denmark   CH = Switzerland
         N = Norway
         D = Germany   Others = Belgium, Italy, Austria, Portugal, Hong Kong, Australia

up to one year behind Nokia Data in developing the necessary LAN expertise. Companies from the consumer group, on the other hand, were believed to be even further behind in developing networking expertise and, in addition, lacked the industry knowledge of the institutional companies, including Nokia Data. One executive commented that the company's two decades of experience in the banking and retail sectors, combined with its ability to design solutions around hardware from other vendors, were important factors in achieving the 35 percent and 25 percent market shares in the Nordic countries banking and retail segments, respectively.

Nokia Data's other competive strengths were believed to include the financial backing of a large parent, the Nokia Corporation, the company's small size and its industry reputation as an ergonomic trendsetter. Because of its smaller size, the company was thought to be more able to keep pace with the evolving industry trends than its larger competitors such as IBM. Furthermore, ergonomics, translated into improved user comfort and productivity, was proving to be a distinct advantage against the smaller manufacturers as well as larger competitors from the institutional group. As an example, Goran Hermansson, pointed to the fact that Ericsson, although not a technological forerunner, pioneered the separate keyboard and the tilt-and-swivel

screen on personal computers. A more recent innovation was Nokia Data's positive display screen with sharp black characters on a paper white background designed to reduce eye strain.

Despite these advantages, Yrjänä Ahto, Vice President Marketing Communication, believed Nokia Data was not sufficiently known outside the Nordic countries, a fact which some customers interpreted as "a risky company" to do business with. Furthermore, although top management considered Nokia Data's size to be an asset, some European country managers believed the company was too small, lacking the critical mass and resources necessary to compete with big players like IBM.[4]

Future Strategy

Nokia Data's top management aimed to make their company a leading supplier of terminals, personal computers, LANs and systems for the European business community. The management wanted to achieve this goal within the next five years and without

[4]IBM Europe's operations included 15 plants in six countries in addition to nine R&D facilities, seven scientific centers, and sales and service units in all markets. The company claimed a high degree of European content (92 percent) in its products and integrated manufacturing across the continent.

EXHIBIT 7
1988 Sales Summary By Product And Service Category (in $ millions)

Country	SF	S	DK	N	D	NL	E	UK	F	CH	Others	Total	% Total
Terminals	56.3	103.6	34.8	10.2	67.0	13.9	24.1	8.6	5.2	10.4	15.5	349.6	29.9
Personal Computers	117.2	137.3	14.2	18.8	54.5	18.0	12.1	6.7	9.0	5.3	7.9	401.0	34.3
Peripherals	8.4	10.2	0.2	1.1	0	0.6	4.0	0	0	0	0	24.5	2.1
Minicomputers	56.0	30.2	8.6	7.5	2.1	2.2	5.8	8.6	2.2	0.3	2.9	126.4	10.8
LANs	10.7	13.7	2.9	0.6	3.5	0.9	1.2	0.9	0.2	0	0	34.6	2.9
Service & Misc	226.2	1.5	1.2	0.3	1.2	0.9	2.4	0.2	0	0	0	233.9	20.0
Total	474.8	296.5	61.9	38.5	128.3	36.5	49.6	25.0	16.6	16.0	26.3	1170.0	100
% Total	40.6	25.4	5.3	3.3	11.0	3.1	4.2	2.1	1.4	1.4	2.2	100	

Note: The Service & Misc figure for Finland includes sales of a large number of turn-key systems projects estimated at around $200 million in total. Peripherals included specialized banking printers, plotters and Personal Identification Number (PIN) Keyboards.

Country Codes: SF = Finland   E = Spain
                 S = Sweden   UK = United Kingdom
                 DK = Denmark   F = France
                 N = Norway   CH = Switzerland
                 D = Germany   Others = Belgium, Italy, Austria, Portugal, Hong Kong, Australia
                 NL = Netherlands

acquisitions. The targeted turnover for 1993 was set at $2.5 billion, equally distributed between the Nordic countries and the rest of Europe. The targeted revenues represented an annual growth rate of 6 percent in Nordic countries and 35 percent outside.

For the next three years, the company planned to concentrate on non-Nordic markets where it operated wholly-owned subsidiaries. With the exception of minicomputers, Nokia Data planned to sell its full line in each market. Management believed that its own minicomputer, based on a proprietary operating system, was not competitive in a market that increasingly demanded multi-vendor connectivity.

Outside the Nordic countries, management also aimed to increase Nokia Data's presence in its five target segments by following the product pathway shown in exhibit 4, starting with the sale of terminals. Company executives believed that purchases from Nokia Data had to build on a client's existing systems, because customers had already made substantial investments with other companies in hardware, software and training. Also, because Nokia Data was not well known outside the Nordic countries, management believed that

the first step had to be perceived by the customer as having little, if any, risk. "Consequently," explained Yrjänä Ahto, "terminals were the logical entry point with new clients as they were far less complex than a LAN or a system and considered less risky. Thereafter, as the company becomes better known and as customers upgrade terminals to personal computers and LANs, Nokia Data can move up the product line, growing in size and perceived ability to deliver at the upper end."

Within its five end-user segments, management planned to target the larger organizations with over 500 terminals tied to minicomputers or mainframes but with few personal computers. According to management, sales to large customers were the fastest way to generate volume and to build Nokia Data's image as a reliable supplier of computer products and services, especially when the client was a public organization, like a local PTT, for example.

Since 1988, the company had undertaken an extensive European advertising campaign in both local and international media to improve its awareness level and consolidate its corporate image. In 1988, $14 million

EXHIBIT 8
Nokia Data Sales by
Products Category (1988)

	$ Million	Units	$ Average Price
Terminals	349.6	161106	2170
Personal Computers	401.0	125312	3200
Peripherals	24.5	21993	1114
Minicomputers	126.4	1973	64065
LANs	34.6	245	141224*

*Includes related terminals, central processing equipment and connections.

worth of press advertisements promoted the company's products as "built by Europeans for Europeans." Headlined "For the European Generation," the standardized series of color advertisements promoted the company's Alfaskop brand. They appeared in the international edition of such magazines as *The Economist, Time, Newsweek* and *Fortune*. (See exhibit 10 at the end of this case for sample advertisements.)

Multi-domestic Implementation

Nokia Data's senior management believed that a strong local identity and presence in each major European country was crucial to achieving the company's ambitious strategic goals. More specifically, top management aimed to decentralize decision-making by adopting what they referred to as a "multi-domestic" approach. This approach contrasted with pan-European integration and implied a strong country management voice in local activities.

According to senior managers, a multi-domestic implementation of the company's expansion strategy would affect many aspects of its operations. For example, activities such as product development, production and marketing were to be delegated to the local organizations that had reached a minimum size. Local branding, in particular, was believed essential for a favorable local identity. Management believed that companies which used the same brand in every market did so to their detriment. "A local image," commented Ahto, "is simply not possible without a local brand — even for companies like IBM which manufacture in almost every European country." Similarly, local manufacturing allowed a company to differentiate itself from the competition by reflecting local tastes more closely. As one top executive commented, "Ultimately, I only care about what the customer wants, even if it's

only a red terminal or a blue keyboard." (The main elements of multi-domestic approach are summarized in exhibit 9.)

Nokia Data's multi-domestic approach went counter to strategies adopted by others in the industry. In 1988, for example, Apple Computer began to integrate its European operations under the control of a stronger Paris headquarters. According to the company, Apple's national subsidiaries would continue to take care of their own local markets while Paris looked for pan-European customers and ways to transfer effective strategies region-wide. In the words of an Apple executive, "When one Apple company comes up with an excellent marketing scheme, Paris headquarters will be responsible for trying to introduce it into other EC countries."[5]

Siemens also had recently restructured its operations to improve competitiveness outside its home market, Germany. Aiming to become a "truly global player," one member of top management was quoted as saying, "In five years, Siemens will be a completely different company. Among Europeans, we will be one of the most aggressive."[6] In recent advertisements (shown in exhibit 11 at the end of this case), the company had billed itself as "the top European computer company in the world market." On another front, IBM was recently capitalizing on the 1992 European integration issue by promoting the concept of integrated operations for a single European market. In a company-sponsored publication called "1992 Now," IBM Europe's President was quoted as saying "...in IBM, we manage our European manufacturing activities as if it were 1992."

Nokia Data's outspoken president, Kalle Isokallio, believed that a pan-European approach was "nonsense"

[5]*Business Marketing,* September 1988
[6]*Business Week International,* February 20, 1989

as it assumed homogeneous European markets. He thought that the 1992-related harmonization might bring uniform technical standards, but buyer behavior would still be nationally oriented. To illustrate, Isokallio described a typical German customer as someone "who never buys a prototype and signs nothing but a lengthy and detailed contract." In sharp contrast, he pointed to a typical French customer, "who is willing to try new innovative products and sign a contract on the back of a Gauloise cigarette pack." Kalle Isokallio explained that in a non-homogenous EEC, characterized by trends toward decentralized computing and narrow market segments, manufacturers had to get close to their customers. Therefore, he emphasized, "local identity" was the key, with a minimum level of local production, some local development and strong local brands.

As of early 1989, the company's local presence varied among markets. In Finland and Sweden, for example, management believed they were rightfully a "domestic" company because of local production, local development and, most importantly, local brands. "Yet," explained Ahto, "before we can claim to be domestic in non-Nordic countries, we must reach a minimum size. After that, we can start local production and introduce a local brand. But, before we reach that critical mass, we will try to be 'European'."

Management Discussions

Although Nokia Data management at all levels agreed with the strategic goal of long-term viability through rapid growth, there was less consensus on the specifics of how that might be achieved. For example, concern was expressed at both the headquarters and country organizations about whether the company would be able in the near future to take advantage of the growth in LANs and vertical systems. For one thing, some argued, the company did not enjoy the needed name recognition in most European markets to be considered a credible supplier of highly technical LANs or sophisticated vertical systems. Furthermore, others argued that even where the company had an established reputation, as in most of the Nordic countries, it was for terminals and personal computers rather than the more advanced LANs and systems. "We have too much of an ordinary hardware supplier image," complained Nils Wilborg, head of the Information Department in the Swedish country organization. On a related point, Ingvar Persson, Vice President of Product Planning, explained that while competition centered around hardware in the 1970s and around software in the 1980s, the distinguishing feature in the future would be in services. "Yet," he emphasized, "the market views us as a hardward vendor, not a service provider."

Doubts were also expressed regarding the practicality of and the rationale behind the multi-domestic approach. Jürgen Olschewski, the German Managing Director, believed the Nokia Data's small size in his country was a big obstacle to becoming a full-fledged manufacturing, marketing, and service operation. Nevertheless, he agreed with top management that a strong German identity would be an asset in competing against firms such as IBM or Compaq with no local image. A few others wondered, on the other hand, if a multi-domestic approach might not fragment the company too much to compete effectively against the larger and more integrated competitors.

Conclusion

Nokia Data's top management knew that some of their colleagues were concerned about the company's future direction. Yet, they believed that Nokia Data's fortunes in a maturing industry depended on innovative thinking and quick action close to customers—elements which they thought were inherent in their overall strategy for growth and multi-domestic approach. Explained Ahto, "Our plans for the future are in line with the corporate culture which we want to establish within Nokia Data — a culture which emphasizes profit performance, business orientation, speedy decision-making and fast action. Doing business under tough conditions has always been fun at Nokia. We want to continue having fun in the future."

EXHIBIT 9
Elements of Nokia Data's
Multidomestic Approach

Research and Development

As Nokia Data implemented its multidomestic approach across Europe, management planned to consolidate basic product development such as video display and keyboards in Sweden. Market-specific development, such as language translation and application software, however, would all be performed locally.

Production

The management believed local manufacturing was one of the conditions needed for a local identity. Hence, Nokia Data planned to set up production facilities in each market, once an economically viable minimum sales volume, estimated at around 50,000 personal computers or terminals annually, was achieved. Sourcing of components was to be centralized in Sweden.

Segmentation

As of 1989, Nokia Data's penetration in each of its five primary segments varied considerably across different national markets. As part of local, say in local strategies, country management would decide which of the five segments to concentrate on. Local management could also decide to develop a share of its business in segments not considered primary by Stockholm.

Branding

Management believed that the Mikko name in Finland and the Alfaskop name in Norway, Sweden and Denmark were viewed by those markets as local brands with local image. Outside Scandinavia, management planned to introduce local brands but not until Nokia Data's local brands were perceived to offer Nokia Data a decided advantage especially over non-local international brands.

Communication

At the end of 1988, Nokia Data's subsidiaries used the same pictures, advertisements and brochures, localized only through text translation. In the future, however, each subsidiary would work from a general framework defined in Stockholm, taking responsibility for local execution. Aside from local campaigns designed to promote local brands, Nokia Data headquarters would continue a European-wide English language corporate advertising campaign in international publications.

Distribution

Currently, decisions regarding the use of VARs or sales agents and the extent of their contribution to local marketing were headquarters decisions. In the future, as sales through such channels increased, local organizations would play a primary role in such decisions.

Pricing

As in the past, future pricing decisions at Nokia Data would be the responsibility of country managers. Aside from pricing in accordance with market conditions, local organizations were to pay Stockholm a transfer price set at their market price, less the local margin of 30-40 percent. However, no central control on local pricing was foreseen.

Customer Service

In the past, Nokia had maintained more service points than sales offices in a local market, a factor which managment believed helped to reassure customers of speedy availability of help when needed. In the future, that policy would not change. But, under local management, the customer services concept was to be broadened to incorporate "Careware," a comprehensive package designed to meet the total needs of most clients.

Continued

EXHIBIT 9–Continued
Elements of Nokia Data's
Multidomestic Approach

The Careware Concept, formulated in Stockholm for implementation in local organizations, went beyond normal after-sales service and included presales consulting, planning and testing, installation, technical and educational services. Careware was divided into six groups of "Customer Service Products." The following list represents the content of Careware Services.

Nokia Data's Customer Careware

Operational Services
Educational and Training
Systems Evaluation
Network Services
On-site Service Representative
Total Customer Service Responsibility
System Security Services
Stand-by Customer Service
Safety Tests and Check-ups
Terminal Cleaning

Installation Services
Project Management and Administration
Cabling
Product Installation
Customizing

Nokia On-Site/Remote Services

Customer Carry-In Services

Nokia Software Services

Nokia Time and Material Service

		Central	Local
R&D:	Basic Product Design	X	
	Applications Software		X
PRODUCTION:	Procurement		
	Coordination	X	
	Purchasing		X
	Manufacturing		X
MARKETING:	Advertising:		
	General Framework	X	
	Execution		X
	Branding		X
	Segmentation		X
	Sales Force		X
	Distribution		X
	Pricing (end user price)		X
	Servicing		X

*This chart refers to future division of responsibilities under a multidomestic approach.

EXHIBIT 10
Nokia Data Sample
Advertisement

EXHIBIT 10
Nokia Data Sample
Advertisement

EXHIBIT 10
Nokia Data Sample
Advertisement

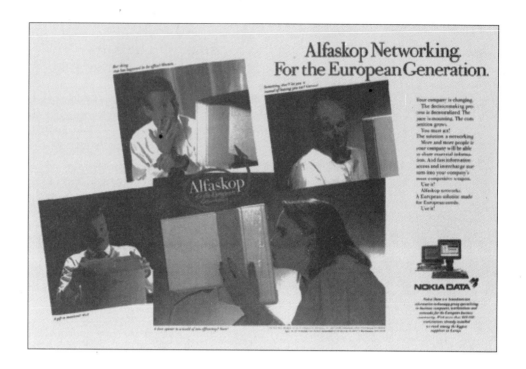

EXHIBIT 11
Siemens Sample
Advertisement

■ PHARMA SWEDE: GASTIRUP†

By Kamran Kashani with Robert Howard

Early in 1990, Bjorn Larsson, advisor to the president and the head of Product Pricing and Government Relations for Pharma Swede, in Stockholm, Sweden, was reviewing the expected consequences of "1992" on Gastirup in Italy. Gastirup was a drug for the treatment of ulcers. Since its introduction in Italy in 1984, this innovative product had achieved considerable success in its category of gastrointestinal drugs. However, the success had come as a result of pricing the drug at a significant discount below the prevailing prices for the same product in the rest of Europe. Higher prices would have disqualified Gastirup from the government reimbursement scheme, the system by which the state health insurance agency reimbursed patients for pharmaceutical expenditures. The government-negotiated prices for Gastirup in Italy were 46 percent below the average European price.

Bjorn Larsson was concerned that, with the anticipated removal of all trade barriers in Europe, Gastirup would fall victim to massive parallel trading from Italy to the higher-priced countries in the region. Furthermore, with the increased coordination among government health insurance agencies, also foreseen in the years following 1992, price differences among EEC countries were expected to narrow. This likely development highlighted the need for a consistent pricing policy throughout Europe.

As head of Product Pricing and Government Relations, it was Bjorn Larsson's responsibility to recommend the actions that top corporate and local Italian management should take to avert potential annual losses for Gastirup, projected in the $20-$30 million range. Among alternatives being considered, the most extreme was to forego the large and growing Italian market altogether and concentrate the product's sales elsewhere in Europe. The Italian market for Gastirup had grown to $27 million in recent years and accounted for 22 percent of European sales. Another option was to remove Gastirup from the Italian government reimbursement scheme by raising the prices to levels close to those prevailing in the higher-priced countries. This action would most likely reduce the drug's sales in Italy by as much as 80 percent. Still another alternative was to take legal action in the European Court of Justice against the Italian government's reimbursement scheme and the related price negotiations as barriers to free trade. Finally, the company could take a "wait and see" attitude, postponing any definitive action to a time when the impact of "1992" was better known.

Company Background

Pharma Swede was formed in 1948 in Stockholm, Sweden; it concentrated solely in pharmaceuticals. In 1989, the company employed over 2,000 people and earned $50 million on sales of $750 million, distributed among its three product lines: Hormones (20 percent), Gastrointestinal (50 percent), and Vitamins (30 percent). Gastirup belonged to the gastrointestinal product category and, as of 1989, accounted for roughly $120 million of Pharma Swede's sales. (See exhibit 1 for a breakdown of Pharma Swede's sales.)

International Activities and Organization

As of December 1989, Pharma Swede had wholly-owned subsidiaries in 11 countries in Western Europe, where it generated 90 percent of its sales. The balance of sales came from small operations in the United States, Australia and Japan.

†**Source:** This case was prepared by Professor Kamran Kashani, with the assistance of Research Associate Robert C. Howard, as a basis for class discussion rather than to illustrate either effective or ineffective handling of a business situation. This case was developed with the cooperation of a company that wishes to remain anonymous. As a result, certain names, figures and facts have been modified.

Product Line	1987	1988	1989
Hormones	90	130	150
Vitamines	175	205	225
Gastrointestinal	200	290	375
Total	**465**	**625**	**750**

EXHIBIT 1
Sales (in $ millions)

Due to high research and development costs as well as stringent quality controls, Pharma Swede centralized all R&D and production of active substances in Stockholm. Partly as a result of these headquarters functions, 60 percent of the company's expenditures were in Sweden, a country that represented only 15 percent of sales. However, the politics of national health care often required the company to have some local production. Consequently, a number of Pharma Swede's subsidiaries blended active substances produced in Sweden with additional compounds and packaged the finished product.

Pharma Swede had a product management organization for drugs on the market (see exhibit 2.) For newly developed drugs, product management did not begin until the second phase of clinical trials, when decisions were made as to where the new products would be introduced and how. (See exhibit 3 for the different phases of a new product's development.) Besides country selection, product management at headquarters examined different positioning and price scenarios, and determined drug dosages and forms. It had the final say on branding and pricing decisions, as well as basic drug information, including the package leaflet that described a drug's usage and possible side effects. As one product manager explained, the marketing department in Stockholm developed a drug's initial profile and estimated its potential market share worldwide. However, it was up to local management to adapt that profile to their own market.

As an example, in 1982 headquarters management positioned Gastirup against the leading anti-ulcer remedy, Tomidil, by emphasizing a better quality of life and 24-hour protection from a single tablet. To adapt the product to their market, the Italian management, with the approval of Stockholm, changed the name to Gastiros and developed a local campaign stressing the drug's advantages over Tomidil, the oral tablet which had to be taken 2 or 3 times a day.

EXHIBIT 2
Partial Organization Chart

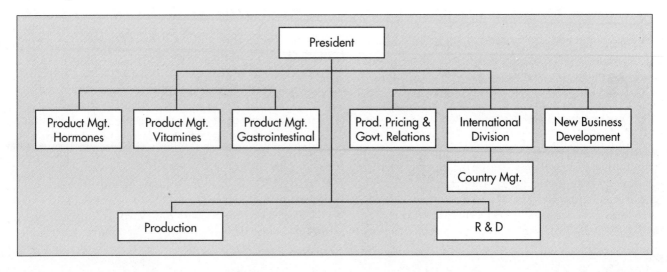

EXHIBIT 3
The Development of a New Drug

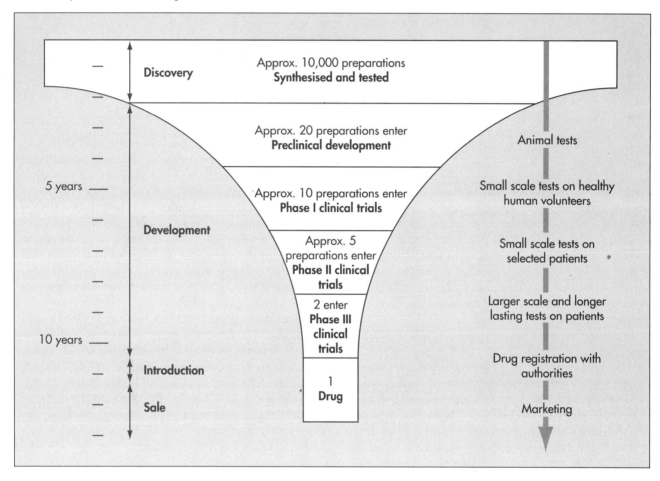

As a rule, headquarters limited its involvement in local markets. It saw its role as one of providing technical or managerial assistance to country management who were responsible for profit and loss.

Product Pricing and Government Relations

The Product Pricing and Government Relations department, located at the headquarters, was a recently established function within the company. It prepared guidelines for subsidiary management to use in negotiating drug pricing and patient reimbursement policies with local government agencies. The department was divided into Government Relations and Product Pricing. Those in Government Relations followed ongoing political events and prepared

negotiating positions on such issues as employment creation through local production.

The role of Product Pricing, headed by Bjorn Larsson, was to determine the "optimum" price for new products. An optimum price, Bjorn explained, was not necessarily a high price, but a function of price-volume relationships in each market. An optimum price also reflected the cost of alternatives, including competitive products and alternative treatments like surgery, and the direct and indirect costs of non-treatment to society and the government. Each of these criteria helped to quantify a product's cost-effectiveness or, as government authorities saw it, its treatment value for money.

Using cost effectiveness data in price negotiations was a recent development in the pharmaceutical industry and corresponded to the increasing cost consciousness among public health authorities. Economic exercises which were initially performed in Stockholm to measure a drug's treatment and socioeconomic benefits were repeated with local authorities during negotiations. In Bjorn Larsson's opinion, the latest measure of "non-treatment cost" was becoming an important factor. He explained that a thorough understanding of the direct and indirect costs of an illness had come to play a key role in whether or not a government was willing to pay for a product by granting it reimbursement status, as well as the magnitude of that reimbursement. According to industry observers, the task of marketing to governmental agencies had become crucial in recent years as public agencies were scrutinizing drug prices more carefully. (See exhibit 4 for an overview and further description of Product Pricing and Government Relations.)

The Pharmaceutical Industry

As of 1989, approximately 10,000 companies worldwide competed in the $180 billion pharmaceutical industry. Industry sales were concentrated in North America, Western Europe and Japan, with the 100 largest companies in these areas accounting for nearly 80 percent of all revenues. Western Europe alone accounted for an estimated 25 percent of total volume.

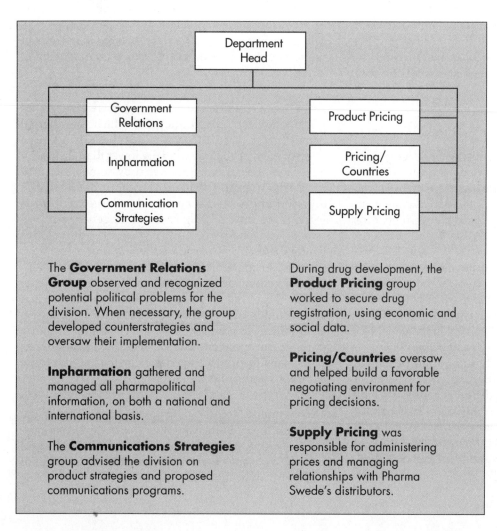

EXHIBIT 4
Product Pricing and Government Relations

The **Government Relations Group** observed and recognized potential political problems for the division. When necessary, the group developed counterstrategies and oversaw their implementation.

Inpharmation gathered and managed all pharmapolitical information, on both a national and international basis.

The **Communications Strategies** group advised the division on product strategies and proposed communications programs.

During drug development, the **Product Pricing** group worked to secure drug registration, using economic and social data.

Pricing/Countries oversaw and helped build a favorable negotiating environment for pricing decisions.

Supply Pricing was responsible for administering prices and managing relationships with Pharma Swede's distributors.

The industry classified pharmaceutical products according to how they were sold and their therapeutic status. In the first instance, pharmaceutical sales were classified into two categories, ethical and over-the-counter (OTC). Ethical drugs, with four-fifths of all pharmaceutical sales worldwide and a 10 percent annual growth rate, could only be purchased with a doctor's prescription. These drugs were branded or were sold as a generic when original patents had expired. OTC drugs were purchased without a prescription; they included both branded and generic medicines such as aspirin, cough syrups and antacids. At Pharma Swede, ethical drugs accounted for more than 90 percent of total sales.

Ethical drugs were also classified into therapeutic categories, of which gastrointestinal was the second largest, representing 15 percent of industry sales. Within the gastrointestinal category there were a number of smaller segments, such as anti-ulcer drugs, used to control and treat digestive tract ulcers, anti-diarrhoeas and laxatives. In 1989, the ethical anti-ulcer drug segment was valued at $7 billion worldwide and growing at 18 percent a year, faster than the total prescription market.

Trends in Europe

In parallel with worldwide trends, several factors were expected to play a role in shaping the future of the European pharmaceutical industry. Among these were an aging population, rising R&D and marketing costs, greater competition from generics, and government cost controls.

Aging Population Europe's stagnating population was gradually aging. The segment of the population over 55 years old was forecast to grow and account for between 33 percent and 40 percent of the total by the year 2025—up from below 25 percent in the mid-1980s. During the same period, the segment below 30 years of age was forecast to drop from about 40 percent to 30 percent. The "graying of Europe" was expected to have two lasting effects on drug consumption. First, low growth was projected in the sales of drugs normally used by children or young adults. Second, drug companies marketing products for age-related diseases, such as cancer, hypertension and heart ailments, could expect growing demand.

Rising R&D and Marketing Costs Research and development expenses included the cost of identifying a new molecule and all the tests required for bringing that molecule to the market. Generally, for every 10,000 molecules synthesized and tested, only one made it through the clinical trials to appear in the market. Product development costs were estimated to average $120 million per drug, from preclinical research to market introduction. Industry estimates for research and development expenses averaged around 15 percent of sales in the late 1980s, with some companies spending as much as 20 percent of sales on new drugs. Research in more complex diseases like cancer, as well as lengthy clinical trials and government registration processes, had raised these costs recently.

Marketing costs has also increased due to a general rise in the level of competition in the industry. In the early-1980s, pharmaceutical firms spent, on average, 31 percent of sales on marketing and administrative costs. By 1987, the ratio had increased to 35 percent and was still rising. Some companies were reported to have spent unprecedented sums of $50-60 million on marketing to introduce a new drug.

Growth of Generics Generic drugs were exact copies of existing branded products for which the original patent had expired. "Generics," as these drugs were known, were priced substantially lower than their originals, and were usually marketed by some other firm than the inventor. Price differences between the branded and generics could be as large as 10-to-1. Depending on the drug categories, generics represented between 5 percent and 25 percent of the value of the total prescription drug market in Europe, and their share was expected to grow. For example, in the UK, sales of generic drugs had grown to represent an estimated 15 percent of the total National Health Budget and were forecast to reach 25 percent by 1995. In line with efforts to contain costs, governments in many parts of Europe were putting increased pressure on physicians to prescribe generics instead of the more expensive branded drugs.

Government Role Governments were one of the strongest forces influencing the pharmaceutical industry in Europe where, in conjunction with public and private insurance agencies, they paid an average of two-thirds of health care costs. In Italy, for example, 64 percent of all ethical pharmaceutical expenditures were covered by the public health care system. In Germany, France and the UK, the respective shares were 57 percent, 65 percent, and 75 percent. These ratios had risen considerably throughout the 1960s and 1970s.

European governments were facing two opposing pressures: to maintain high levels of medical care while trying to reduce the heavy burden placed on the budget for such expenditures. Influence on pharmaceutical pricing, according to industry experts, had become an increasingly political as well as economic issue.

Not surprisingly, government agencies seeking to reduce health insurance costs increasingly encouraged the use of generics. In fact, before the advent of generics and official interventions, well-known branded drugs which had lost their patents in the 1970s, such as Librium or Valium, often maintained up to 80 percent of their sales for several years. In contrast, by the late 1980s, it was more likely that a drug would lose nearly 50 percent of its sales within two years after its patent expired.

Gastirup

Under circumstances not completely understood, gastric juices—consisting of acid, pepsin and various forms of mucous—could irritate the membrane lining the stomach and small intestine, often producing acute ulcers. In serious cases, known as peptic ulcers, damage extended into the wall of the organ causing chronic inflammation and bleeding. Middle-aged men leading stressful lives were considered a high-risk group for ulcers.

Ulcers were treated by four types of remedies: antacids, H-2 inhibitors, anticholinergics, and surgery. Antacids, containing sodium bicarbonate or magnesium hydroxide, neutralized gastric acids and their associated discomfort. Some of the more common OTC antacid products were Rennie and Andursil. In contrast, H-2 inhibitors such as ranitidine reduced acid levels by blocking the action of the stomach's acid-secreting cells. Anticholinergics, on the other hand, functioned by delaying the stomach's emptying, thereby diminishing acid secretion and reducing the frequency and severity of ulcer pain. Finally, surgery was used only in the most severe cases, where ulceration had produced holes in the stomach and where ulcers were unresponsive to drug treatment.

In 1989, the world market for non-surgical ulcer remedies was estimated at $8 billion, with most sales distributed in North America (30 percent), Europe (23 percent), and Japan (5 percent). Worldwide, H-2 inhibitors and OTC antacids held 61 percent and 12 percent of the market, respectively.

The Oral Osmotic Therapeutic System

Gastirup, introduced in 1982 as Pharma Swede's first product in the category of ulcer remedies, used ranitidine as its active ingredient. As of 1982, ranitidine was available as a generic compound, after having lost its patent protection in that year. The US-based Almont Corporation was the original producer of ranitidine and its former patent holder.

What distinguished Gastirup from other H-2 inhibitors, including ranitidine tablets produced by Almont and others, was not its active ingredient, but the method of administration called the oral osmotic therapeutic system (OROS). In contrast to tablets or liquids taken several times a day, the Oral Osmotic Therapeutic System was taken once a day. Its tablet-like membrane was specially designed to release a constant level of medicine over time via a fine laser-made opening. By varying the surface, thickness and pore size of the membrane, the rate of drug release could be modified and adapted to different treatment needs. Furthermore, the release of the drug could be programmed to take place at a certain point in time after swallowing the tablet. Consequently, drug release could be timed to coincide with when the tablet was in the ulcerated region of the upper or lower stomach. (See exhibit 5 for a diagram and brief description of the OROS.)

Drugs supplied via OROS had certain advantages over the others. First, because of a steady release of the medicine, they prevented the "high" and "low" effects often observed with the usual tablets or liquids. Furthermore, the time-release feature also prevented over-functioning of the liver and kidneys. In addition, because drugs contained in an OROS had to be in the purest form, they were more stable and had a prolonged shelf life. Pharma Swede management believed that drugs administered by OROS could lead to fewer doctor calls, less hospitalization, and reduced health care costs for insurance agencies and governments.

Because OROS was not a drug per se but an alternative method of drug administration, it was sold

EXHIBIT 5
The Oral Osmotic
Delivery System

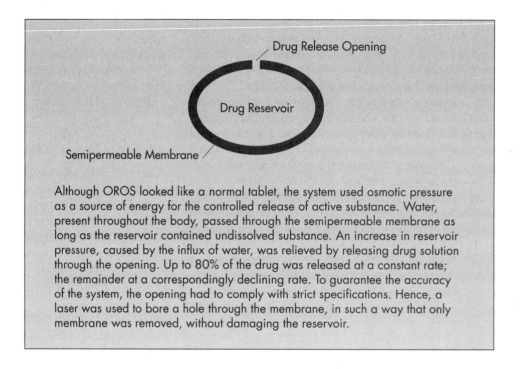

Although OROS looked like a normal tablet, the system used osmotic pressure as a source of energy for the controlled release of active substance. Water, present throughout the body, passed through the semipermeable membrane as long as the reservoir contained undissolved substance. An increase in reservoir pressure, caused by the influx of water, was relieved by releasing drug solution through the opening. Up to 80% of the drug was released at a constant rate; the remainder at a correspondingly declining rate. To guarantee the accuracy of the system, the opening had to comply with strict specifications. Hence, a laser was used to bore a hole through the membrane, in such a way that only membrane was removed, without damaging the reservoir.

in conjunction with a particular pharmaceutical substance. By the end of 1989, Pharma Swede was marketing three drugs using OROS. Gastirup was the company's only OROS product in the gastrointestinal category; the other two were in the hormones category. The management of Pharma Swede characterized the use of OROS as an attempt to introduce product improvements which did not necessarily rely on new molecules but on new "software," leading to improved ease of use and patient comfort.

Ranitidine, the active ingredient in Gastirup, was not made by Pharma Swede, because of its complex manufacturing process and the fact that since 1982 it was available from a number of suppliers both inside and outside Sweden. Gastirup OROS tablets were manufactured by the company in Sweden; final packaging, including insertion of the drug information sheet, was done in a number of European countries including Italy.

Patent Protection

OROS was developed and patented by the Anza Corporation, a US company that specialized in drug delivery systems. In Europe, Anza had applied for patents on a country-by-country basis. Patent protection

was twofold: OROS as a drug delivery system, and its use with specific drugs. The more general patent on OROS was due to expire in all EEC countries by 1991. The second, and more important patent for Gastirup, covered Oral Osmotic Therapeutic Systems containing ranitidine. This latter patent, exclusively licensed to Pharma Swede for Europe, would expire everywhere on the Continent by the year 2000.

Although Pharma Swede sold more than one OROS product, it had an exclusive license from Anza for only the ranitidine-OROS combination. Over the years, a number of companies had tried to develop similar systems without much success. To design a system that did not violate Anza's patents required an expert knowledge of membrane technology which only a few companies had.

Competition

Broadly speaking, all ulcer remedies competed with one another. But, Gastirup's primary competition came from the H-2 inhibitors in general, and from ranitidine in particular. Since 1982, when ranitidine joined the ranks of generics, it was produced by a number of companies in Europe and the US. Despite increased competition, ranitidine's original producer, the US-based Almont

Corporation, still held a significant market share worldwide.

Almont had first introduced its Tomidil brand in 1970 in the US. After only two years, the product was being sold in 90 countries capturing shares ranging between 42 percent and 90 percent in every market. Tomidil's fast market acceptance, considered by many as the most successful for a new drug, was due to its high efficacy as an ulcer treatment and its few side effects. The drug had cut the need for surgery in an estimated two-thirds of cases. Pharma Swede attributed Tomidil's success also to centralized marketing planning and coordination worldwide, high marketing budgets and focused promotion on opinion leaders in each country. Although Almont was not previously known for its products in the ulcer market, and the company had little experience internationally, Tomidil's success helped the firm to grow into a major international firm in the field.

In the opinion of Pharma Swede management, Tomidil's pricing followed a "skimming" strategy. It was initially set on a daily treatment cost basis of five times the average prices of antacids on the market. Over time, however, prices were reduced to a level three times those of antacids. After 1982, the prices were cut further to about two times those of antacids. In 1990, competing tablets containing ranitidine were priced, on average, 20 percent below Tomidil for an equivalent dosage. In that year, Tomidil's European share of drugs containing ranitidine was 43 percent.

Pharma Swede management did not consider antacids and anticholinergics as direct competitors because the former category gave only temporary relief, and the latter had serious potential side effects.

Results

Gastirup's sales in Europe had reached $120 million by the end of 1989, or 7 percent of the ethical anti-ulcer market. (See exhibit 6 for a breakdown of sales and shares in major European markets.)

Pricing

Gastirup was premium priced. Its pricing followed the product's positioning as a preferred alternative to Tomidil and other ranitidine-containing tablets by improving the patient's quality of life and providing 24-hour protection in a single dosage. While competitive tablets had to be taken two or three times daily, the patient needed only one Gastirup tablet a day. The risk of forgetting to take the medicine was thus reduced as was the inconvenience of having to carry the drug around all the time. Because of these unique advantages, substantiated in a number of international clinical trials, management believed that using Gastirup ultimately resulted in faster treatment, and reduced the need for surgery. Gastirup was priced to carry a significant premium over Tomidil prices in Europe. The margin over the generics was even higher. (See exhibit 7 for current retail prices of Gastirup and Tomidil across Europe.)

Pharmaceutical Pricing in the EEC

Drug pricing was a negotiated process in most of the EEC. Each of the 12 member states had its own agency to regulate pharmaceutical prices for public insurance reimbursement schemes. From a government perspective, pharmaceuticals were to be priced in accordance with the benefits they provided. Although the pricing criteria most frequently cited were efficacy, product quality, safety and patient comfort, European governments were putting increasing emphasis on "cost-effectiveness," or the relationship between price and therapeutic advantages. Among diverse criteria used by authorities, local production of a product was an important factor. As a result of individual country-specific pricing arrangements, there were inevitably widespread discrepancies in prices for the same product across Europe.

For new products, price negotiations with state agencies began after the drug was registered with the national health authorities. Negotiations could last for several years, eventually resulting in one of three outcomes: no price agreement, a partially-reimbursed price, or a fully-reimbursed price. In the event of no agreement, in most EEC countries the company was free to introduce the drug and set the price, but the patient's cost for the product would not be covered by health insurance. In many EEC countries, a drug that did not receive any reimbursement coverage was at a severe disadvantage. Partial or full reimbursement allowed the doctor to prescribe the drug without imposing the full cost on the patient. Any price adjustment for a product already on the market was subject to the same negotiation process.

Once agreement was reached on full or partial reimbursement, the product was put on a reimbursement scheme, also called a "positive list"—a list from

854

EXHIBIT 6

Sales (in $ millions) and
Market Shares in Major
European Markets in 1989

Countries	Total Market*	Gastirup	Tomidil	Others**
	(100%)	(% Share)	(% Share)	(% Share)
Belgium	41	2 (5%)	16 (39%)	23 (56%)
France	198	15 (8%)	61 (31%)	122 (61%)
Germany	318	30 (9%)	51 (16%)	237 (75%)
Italy	394	27 (7%)	110 (28%)	257 (65%)
Netherlands	81	8 (10%)	25 (31%)	48 (59%)
Spain	124	5 (4%)	11 (9%)	108 (87%)
Sweden	34	10 (29%)	5 (15%)	19 (56%)
United Kingdom	335	18 (5%)	97 (29%)	220 (66%)
All Europe	**1,673**	**120 (7%)**	**486 (29%)**	**1,054 (63%)**

* All ethical anti-ulcer remedies
** Includes branded and generic drugs

which doctors could prescribe. Germany and the Netherlands were the two exceptions within the EEC employing a "negative list," a register containing only those drugs which the government would not reimburse. Drugs on the reimbursement list were often viewed by the medical profession as possibly better than non-reimbursed products. (See exhibit 8 for a summary of price setting and reimbursement practices within the EEC.)

Pricing Gastirup in Italy

Pharmaceutical pricing was particularly difficult in Italy. Health care costs represented 8 percent of the country's gross domestic product and one-third of the state budget for social expenditures. Government efforts to

contain health care costs resulted in strict price controls and a tightly managed reimbursement scheme. Italy was considered by Pharma Swede management as a "cost-plus environment" where pricing was closely tied to the production cost of a drug rather than its therapeutic value.

In May 1982, Pharma Swede Italy submitted its first application for reimbursement of Gastirup. The submitted retail price was $33 per pack of ten 400-milligram tablets. On a daily treatment cost basis, Gastirup's proposed price of $3.30 compared with Tomidil's $1.35. Although priced 25 percent lower than the average EEC price for Gastirup, Italian authorities denied the product admission to the positive list. They argued that Gastirup's therapeutic benefits, including its one-a-day feature, did not justify the large premium

Countries	Gastirup	Tomidil	Gastirup / Tomidil
Belgium	$3.86	$2.47	+56%
Denmark	5.96	3.94	+51%
France	3.69	2.12	+74%
Germany	5.31	3.54	+50%
Greece	3.43	2.36	+45%
Italy	2.40	1.35	+78%
Netherlands	5.66	3.11	+82%
Portugal	3.13	2.24	+40%
Spain	4.03	2.82	+43%
Sweden	5.91	4.22	+40%
United Kingdom	5.40	3.10	+74%

EXHIBIT 7
Retail Prices in Europe (Daily Treatment Cost in 1989)

over the local price of Tomidil, which was already on the reimbursement scheme. Tomidil and another generic ranitidine-containing brand were produced locally, while Gastirup was to be manufactured in Sweden and only packed in Italy.

Despite the rejection by authorities, Pharma Swede chose to launch Gastirup in Italy without the reimbursement coverage. Management hoped to established an early foothold in one of Europe's largest markets. Hence, early in 1983, Gastirup was introduced in Italy at a retail price of $37 for a pack of 10 units, and under the brand name Gastiros. This price translated into a daily treatment cost of $3.70, or 16 percent below the EEC average retail price of Gastirup and nearly three times that of Tomidil in Italy.

The response of the Italian market to Gastiros was better than management had expected. Following an intensive promotional campaign aimed at the general practitioners, sales reached $500,000 a month, or 2 percent of the market. Meanwhile, the number of requests for reimbursement received by the Italian health care authorities from patients and doctors was growing daily. Management believed that these requests were putting increased pressure on the authorities to admit the product to the positive list.

In a second round of negotiations, undertaken at the initiative of management nine months after the launch, Pharma Swede Italy reapplied for reimbursement status

based on a price of $31 per pack of 10 units. This price represented a daily treatment cost of $3.10 and was 30 percent below the EEC average. Once again the price was judged too high and the request was rejected. In November 1984, management initiated a third round of negotiations, and in April 1985 Gastiros was granted full reimbursement status at $24 per pack, a price which had not changed since.

Gastirup's Italian sales and market share among H-2 inhibitors grew substantially following its inclusion in the reimbursement scheme. By 1989, factory sales had reached $27 million, representing a dollar share of 7 percent of the market. Gastirup was Pharma Swede Italy's single most important product, accounting for nearly a quarter of its sales.

In Italy, as in other countries, Pharma Swede distributed its products through drug wholesalers to pharmacies. Typical trade margin on resale price for pharmacies was 30 percent. Gastiros' factory price to wholesalers of $15 per pack of 10 tablets had a contribution margin of $3 for the Italian company, which paid its parent $1 for every 400-milligram tablet imported from Sweden. The transfer price was the same across Europe. In turn, the parent earned $0.70 in contribution for every tablet exported to its local operations. The variable cost of producing the tablets included raw materials and the licensing fees paid to Anza.

EXHIBIT 8
Price Setting and
Reimbursement in the EEC

Country	Price Setting	Reimbursement
Ireland	No price control for new introductions.	Positive list (prescription recommended) Inclusion criteria: • efficacy/safety profile • cost-effectiveness profile
	Prices of prescription drugs are controlled through PPRS (Pharmaceutical Price Regulation Scheme). Control is exercised through regulation of profit levels.	Positive list for NHS prescriptions (National Health Service) Inclusion criteria: • therapeutic value • medical need
Belgium	Price control by the Ministry of Health on the basis of cost structure.	Positive list (Ministry of Health) Inclusion criteria: • therapeutic and social interest • duration of treatment • daily treatment costs • substitution possibilities • price comparison with similar drugs • Co-payment: 4 categories (100 percent, 75 percent, 50 percent, 40 percent)
Greece	Price control by the Ministry of Health based on cost structure (support of local industry appears to be of importance).	Positive list (IKA, Social Security Ministry)
Portugal	Price and reimbursement negotiations with the Ministry of Health and Commerce based on: • local prices • lowest European prices • therapeutic value • cost-effectiveness	Positive list Inclusion criteria: • therapeutic value • international price comparison • cost-effectiveness
Spain	Price control based on cost structure.	Positive list (Social Security System) Inclusion criteria: • efficacy/safety profile • cost-effectiveness

Continued

EXHIBIT 8—Continued
Price Setting and
Reimbursement in the EEC

Country	Price Setting	Reimbursement
France	Price control for non-reimbursable products. Price negotiations with the Ministry of Health for reimbursed products.	Positive list (Transparence Commission and Directorate of Pharmacy and Pharmaceuticals, within the Ministry of Health) Inclusion criteria: • price • therapeutic value • potential market in France • (local R&D) Co-payment: 4 categories (non-reimbursable, 40 percent of retail price, 70 percent of retail price, 100 percent of retail price)
Luxembourg	Price control by the Ministry of Health. Prices must not be higher than in the country of origin.	Positive list Inclusion criteria: • therapeutic value • cost-effectiveness
Italy	Price control for reimbursed drugs by CIP (Interministerial Price Committee), following guidelines of CIPE (Interministerial Committee for Economic Planning) based on cost structure.	Positive list (Prontuario Terapeutico Nazionale National Health Council). Reimbursement criteria: • therapeutic efficacy and cost-effectiveness • innovation, risk-benefit ratio and local research also considered.
FR Germany	No direct price control by authorities.	Negative list. Reference price system since January 1989. Principles: • Drugs will only be reimbursed up to a reference price. • Patient pays the difference between the reference and retail prices. Co-payment: DM 3 per prescribed product (1992: 15 percent of drug bill).
Netherlands	No price control by authorities.	Negative list. Reference price system since January 1988.
Denmark	Price control based on: • cost structure • "reasonable" profits	Positive list. Inclusion criteria: • efficacy/safety profile • cost-effectiveness profile

Lifting the Trade Barriers

As "1992" drew closer, Pharma Swede management believed that two important issues affecting the European pharmaceutical industry would be manufacturing location and drug pricing. In the past, many of the cost-constraint measures taken by authorities had, by design or coincidence, an element of protectionism and represented national trade barriers. For example, local authorities might refuse a certain price or reimbursement level unless the sponsoring company agreed to manufacture locally. Under current EEC regulations, such actions were considered barriers to trade and illegal.

As a countermeasure to such barriers, companies could take legal action against local agencies at the European Court of Justice. With the support of the European Federation of Pharmaceutical Industries Associations (EFPIA), drug firms could sue the agencies for violating the EEC regulations. Although the EFPIA had won 12 cases over the preceding decade, litigation processes lasted sometimes up to seven years, and the results were often partial and temporary in value. Nonetheless, industry participants were relieved that, after 1992, the element of local production linked to price negotiation would disappear.

Since December 1988, under a new EEC regulation called the Transparency Directive, government pricing decisions were open to review by the pharmaceutical companies. The directive served to eliminate any interference with the free flow of pharmaceutical products within the community caused by price controls or reimbursement schemes. It required state agencies to explain how they set drug prices in general as well as in each case. If not satisfied, companies that believed they had been discriminated against could appeal a ruling on price, first to local courts, thereafter to the EC Commission and, ultimately, to the European Court of Justice.

In addition, the new law required that agencies act quickly when a new drug was approved for sale or when a company asked for a price adjustment. On average, it had taken Pharma Swede one year to reach agreement on a price for a new product. Price adjustments for old products, on the other hand, had taken as long as two years because of delays by local authorities.

Another development related to the creation of a single European market was the expected harmonization in pharmaceutical prices and registration systems among member states. Bjorn Larsson and others in the industry believed that, across Europe, pharmaceutical price differences would narrow in a two-stage process: initially as a result of the transparency directive, and thereafter as part of a more comprehensive market harmonization. Bjorn thought that harmonization was a gradual process and that the completion of a single European market would occur at the earliest between 1995 and 2000.

Aside from narrowing of the differences in drug prices, possible outcomes for the post-1992 environment included a pan-European registration system and harmonized health insurance. Some observers predicted that a harmonized drug registration system would be put in place sometime between 1992 and 1995, although the exact form it might take remained open. Pharma Swede management believed it was unlikely that such a system would discriminate against non-EEC firms. Harmonization of national health insurance systems, a longer-term consequence of 1992, was not expected before 1995. Industry analysts believed that, in the interim, the states would continue to press for cost containment on a national basis. Private pan-European insurance offerings, on the other hand, were expected to increase with deregulation and the completion of the internal market .

The Problem

Prior to 1992, Europe's parallel trade in pharmaceutical products had been limited to less than 5 percent of industry sales. Each country had local language packaging and registration requirements that tended to restrict or prohibit a product's acceptance and distribution in neighboring markets. Furthermore, according to some Pharma Swede managers, products produced in certain countries, such as Italy or France, suffered a poor quality image in other markets, such as Germany and England. National sentiments aside, distributors seeking to capitalize on parallel imports had to have approval from local authorities which often implied repackaging to meet local requirements.

Where parallel imports had been a minor problem in the past, they posed a serious challenge to drug firms, including Pharma Swede, in the post-1992 environment when such trade would be protected by law. Hans Sahlberg, the company's product manager for gastrointestinal drugs, explained that government insurance agencies were already examining price and

EXHIBIT 9
Relative Retail Prices of Gastirup (EC = 100)

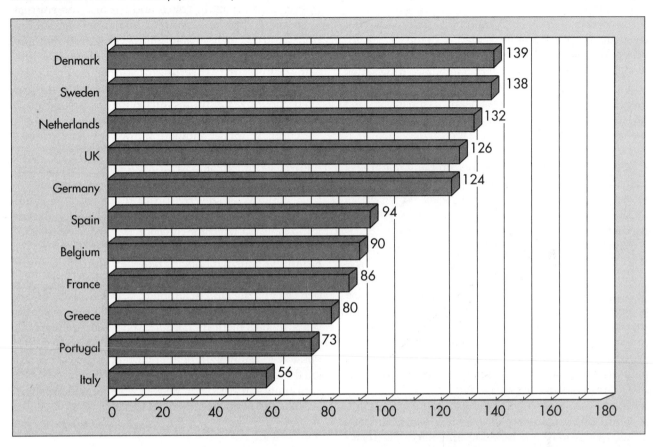

reimbursement issues on a European-wide basis. For drugs already on the market, it was only a matter of time before authorities reimbursed on the basis of the lowest priced parallel import. As an example, this implied that Gastirup, priced at $2.40 per tablet in Italy and $5.40 in Germany, would be reimbursed in Germany at the lower price of imports from Italy. If this proved true, German revenue losses from Gastirup alone could amount to $17 million on current sales. Furthermore, if a system should emerge after 1992 mandating a single EEC price, Pharma Swede would have to revamp its entire price setting policy.

Management Options

With the upcoming changes in Europe, Gastirup's pricing discrepancies had become a source of major management concern. If not carefully managed, Bjorn and his colleagues believed that the company could lose money, reputation or both. (See exhibit 9 for relative prices of Gastirup in Europe.)

In looking for options to recommend to top management at headquarters and at the Italian operation, Bjorn and his staff developed four alternatives. The first, and the most extreme option, was to completely remove Gastirup from the Italian market and concentrate sales elsewhere in Europe. This action would be in defence of prices in the more profitable markets. This alternative was not Bjorn's first choice as it implied sales revenue losses of $27 million. It also went counter to Pharma Swede's policy of marketing all its products in every European country. Bjorn feared that such a move would lead to heated discussions between headquarters and local management in Italy. It could even seriously damage the company's public reputation. "How," asked Bjorn, "could Pharma Swede, an ethical drug company, deal with public opinion aroused by the apparently unethical practice of denying Gastirup to the Italian market?"

As another alternative, Bjorn could suggest removing Gastirup from the reimbursement scheme by raising prices to levels closer to the EEC average. Such action would place Gastirup in the non-reimbursed drug status and lead to an estimated 80 percent loss in sales. Since the magnitude of this loss was nearly as great as in first option, headquarters did not believe the Italian management would be any more receptive. Moreover, if Gastirup were removed from the reimbursement scheme, both the product and the company might lose credibility with the medical profession in Italy. According to Bjorn, many doctors perceived the drugs on the reimbursement list as "economical" and "really needed."

Nonetheless, shifting the drug to non-reimbursement status would shift the financing burden from the government to the patient, thus coinciding with the Italian government's view that patients should assume a greater financial role in managing their health. With an increased emphasis on cost containment, such a proposal was liable to appeal to Italian authorities, Bjorn expected full support for this proposal from managers in high-priced markets whose revenues were jeopardized by low-priced countries such as Italy.

There was, however, a possibility that changing the reimbursement status might backfire. Hans Sahlberg recalled a case in Denmark where, after removing a class of cough and cold drugs from reimbursement, Danish authorities came under pressure from a group of consumer advocates and were forced to reverse their decision. If Pharma Swede requested that Gastirup be removed from the Italian reimbursement scheme and the government were forced to reverse that position, the company's public image and its standing with local authorities might be damaged.

Still, a third option was to appeal to the European Commission and, if necessary, start legal action before the European Court of Justice. As Bjorn explained, the artificially-regulated low drug prices in Italy placed higher priced imported drugs at a disadvantage and, hence, acted as a barrier to the free movement of pharmaceutical products. Since the EFPIA has sued and won a similar case against Belgium, Bjorn believed that Pharma Swede might have a good case against the Italian government. But as much as Bjorn might want to pursue legal action, he recognized the risks inherent in using a legal mechanism with which Pharma Swede had no prior experience.

Headquarters management, on the other hand, looked favorably at this option as it provided the opportunity to settle "once and for all" the conflict with the Italian government over pharmaceutical pricing. Local management, however, feared that any legal action would create resentment and sour the atmosphere of future negotiations. At any rate, legal action could take several years and might even jeopardize Gastiros' status in Italy as a reimbursed drug.

A fourth option entailed taking a "wait and see" attitude until the full effects of "1992" became better known. Bjorn explained that for the next two to three years, governments would continue to concentrate on price controls. After 1992, pressure for harmonization would reduce differences in drug prices, thought it was impossible to project the direction the prices might take. As an estimate, the Product Pricing and Government Relations staff had calculated that uniform pricing translated to an EEC-wide general decrease of 10 percent in drug prices, although prices in Italy would probably rise by about 15 percent. Thus, for the next few years, management at Pharma Swede could monitor the changes within the EEC and prepare as carefully as possible to minimize any long-term price erosion. Bjorn felt this option argued for vigilance and "having all your ammunition ready." But, he was not sure what specific preparatory actions were called for.

Conclusion

With the integration of Europe in sight, top management was deeply concerned about the impact that the changing regulatory environment might have on Pharma Swede's operations. Gastirup was the first product to feel the effects of harmonization, but it would not be the last. A decision on Gastirup could set the pace for the other products. In evaluating the alternative courses of action for Gastirup, Bjorn had to consider their likely impact on several stakeholders, including the country management in Italy, the management in high-priced countries and at headquarters, the Italian and EEC authorities, and the medical profession at large. Bjorn was not sure if any course of action could possibly satisfy all the parties concerned. He wondered what criteria should guide his proposal to the company president, who was expecting his recommendations soon.

CAP GEMINI SOGETI: BUILDING A TRANSNATIONAL ORGANIZATION†

By Tom Elfring

As the hundreds of group managers of Cap Gemini Sogeti (CGS) poured into the conference building in Prague on this nice summer day, June 25, 1992, the company's executive chairman, Serge Kampf, wondered what their ideas would be regarding the transformation of the organization. After all, he had not only called these managers together to present his own vision of what the future organizational form might look like, but also to get their input and to arrive at decisions that would be widely supported throughout the company. Kampf realized that restructuring the organization would be a difficult task, but he also knew that to continue the company's success it was imperative that CGS and the large number of recently acquired firms be moulded into a coherent transnational company.

Although reorganizations are always difficult, CGS had quite a few factors making the task more easy. CGS was a growing firm in a growing industry—worldwide CGS held the fourth place in the "big league" of information technology service companies, while in Europe CGS was by far number one. Internally, Kampf could also count on widespread support for his efforts to build CGS into a global company. During the four day Marrakesh Rencontre in June 1990, the 550 attending group managers had opted overwhelmingly for a strategy of globalization, with the intent of belonging to the top three information technology services corporations worldwide. This bottom-up decision had created a shared vision of the company's future and willingness throughout the organization to change.

†**Source:** © 1994 by Tom Elfring. This case was prepared by Tom Elfring, Rotterdam School of Management, Erasmus University, with the assistance of Saskia van Rijn. This case is intended for classroom discussion, not to illustrate the effective or ineffective handling of a managerial situation. Unless mentioned otherwise, all information was obtained with the kind assistance of Cap Gemini Sogeti. The author would like to thank Ron Meyer for his useful comments. Used with permission of the author.

However, Kampf and CGS were also faced with some daunting challenges. First, competition within the information technology services industry had grown increasingly intense since 1990 and the firm's net income had suffered as a consequence. Second, after the Marrakesh Rencontre, CGS had acquired a large number of companies that needed to be merged into the CGS organization. Finally, building an effective transnational organization would probably mean that the company's well-known strict decentralization policy would need to be adapted, either marginally or radically. Any further move away form the high level of local autonomy, however, would probably meet with some anxiety, it not resistance.

To Serge Kampf it was clear that the group managers' bold Marrakesh decision for a global push was a vote "for a dream or a nightmare." Since June 1990 he had brought together many of the building blocks for the envisioned global company, but now at this Prague Rencontre it was up to group managers to help realize the dream. The building blocks needed to be brought together to form an effective transnational company. Of course, the question was, how? What type of organizational setup and systems would suit the demands of a knowledge-intensive service firm operating on an international scale? To this pressing question the group managers—and Serge Kampf—needed to find an answer.

The Company's History

The growth of Cap Gemini Sogeti had been built on its ability to "make computer systems work" and meet the requirements of the client. The Cap Gemini Sogeti Group's official birthdate was January 1, 1975. In that year Gemini Computer System merged with the Cap/Sogeti Group. The latter group was the result of a merger between Cap, a computer services firm, and Sogeti, a business management and information-processing company. At that time Cap had 780 employees, Gemini employed about 320 people, and Sogeti was the smallest, with 250 workers on the payroll.

Cap Gemini Sogeti started out with European subsidiaries in Great Britain, The Netherlands, Switzerland, and Germany, but most of its business was conducted in France. This new Cap Gemini Sogeti Group had a good start in life through powerful (French) government patronage and the national management tradition of contracting out services instead of performing these tasks themselves.

Cap Gemini Sogeti (CGS) grew from small autonomous groups of programmers-for-hire scattered around France, with a common policy of tight financial control and a thoroughly professional reputation. During the 1980s, CGS acquired a large number of mostly smaller firms in Europe and some in the United States. They improved their position in the market for professional information technology services, such as information technology (IT) consulting, customized software, and education and training. Their expansion in the 1980s was centered on these services, and CGS achieved an average annual growth rate of about 30 percent, of which roughly two-thirds was due to internal growth. The remaining one-third had been the result of friendly acquisitions and alliances. This seemed to be the only way to provide global coverage some of the clients required.

An important acquisition was that of Sesa (Société d'Études des Systèmes d'Automation) in 1987. It could be seen as a turning point, because Sesa was a distinguished French software house with a broader corporate culture than the narrowly based CGS, with its origins in "body shopping," hiring out computer specialists on a daily basis to work on customers' contracts. In the late eighties, CGS concentrated on the integration of the Sesa team and on consolidating and streamlining its organization, thereby improving its profitability.

___

CGS's Current Position

Cap Gemini Sogeti is now Europe's number one computer services and consulting company and one of the industry's leaders worldwide. Located in fifteen European countries and the United States, the group specializes in software services, its goal being to assist its clients in drawing the greatest possible benefit from information technologies. Ever since its creation in 1975, the group has upheld a strong development policy, multiplying its revenues, profits, and size. In 1992, however, CGS incurred the first losses in its history. The

net group loss of $14.9 million is partly due to $60 million worth of restructuring (see exhibits 1 and 2.)

Cap Gemini has always had a certain gloss and sparkle (even by French standards). It is proud, elitist, almost arrogant and has a single-minded devotion to developing methods and tools for writing better, more accurate software. In France, especially in government circles, software skills are equated directly with pure intellectual effort and are much prized, which has resulted in substantial government backing and patronage. Much of Cap Gemini's success was said to be due to its simple management strategy; it concentrated on what it does best (professional software engineering) and wasted little time arguing about whether it should be selling computer hardware, applications packages, or administrative services, all of which have diluted the effort of many other software houses. It articulated this philosophy to its employees continuously.

Michel Berty, general secretary of Cap Gemini Sogeti, described his satisfaction with people with well-developed minds. Two-thirds of Sogeti's employees have an advanced engineering degree. "They are good," he says. "They have learned to work and to reason. Human qualities are also essential but are not always so well developed."

One of Cap Gemini's formulas for success has been an inviolate decentralization policy that stipulates that when any of its branches—250 in 1989—reaches 150 staff, it splits in two, and a new manager is appointed to head the new branch. Eric Lutaud, a member of the corporate development team at Cap Gemini Sogeti, explains: "We are so decentralized that at any point in time we have several people doing things that are not kosher."

This highly decentralized style of organization, however, was subject to very strong financial controls. Cap Gemini believed local operations had to be in the hands of locally hired managers to be successful. "To keep in touch with fast-moving IT markets, we work in terms of bottom-up, not top-down." Unlike most European firms, Cap Gemini tied compensation to performance.

Besides the responsibility for innovations at the local level, CGS also had a more traditional and centralized unit to look to for innovations. In 1984 Cap Gemini Sogeti created Cap Gemini Innovation, specializing in applied research. Its principal missions included staying on the leading edge of new technologies, experimenting with and validating technical advances in the profession, and transferring skills among the teams taking part in group projects. This research and

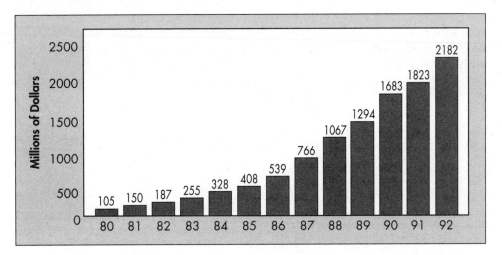

EXHIBIT 1
CGS Revenue, 1980–1992

development policy was carried out jointly at four research centers in France, Belgium, and The Netherlands, bringing together researchers and technicians from more than ten countries. The sums invested in this activity have grown steadily since 1985, at which time they represented $20 million; at the end of 1991, the figure had climbed to $109 million.

Traditionally Cap Gemini Sogeti's business was the provision of general technical backup for customers' data-processing departments. But the most profitable and fastest-growing part of the business results from companies wanting Cap Gemini Sogeti to design and set up a specific project. For this you need staff with in-depth knowledge of the customer's sector (see exhibits 3 and 4.)

From One to Four Related Businesses

The number of different types of services related to IT has grown tremendously in the past decades. The move from a very focused firm to one with a more complete service offering was rather gradual in the 1980s but has accelerated in the 1990s. The driving forces for the swift move to a full-service offering were a combination of market, product, and knowledge considerations. First, some of the existing clients from the original professional services group (IT consulting, customized software, and education and training) asked for related products/services such as management consultancy, facilities management, and systems integration. In

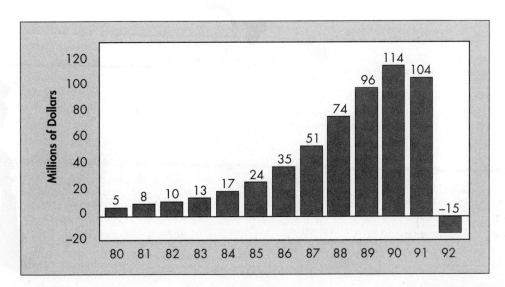

EXHIBIT 2
CGS Net Income,
1980–1992

EXHIBIT 3
A Comprehensive
Range of Services

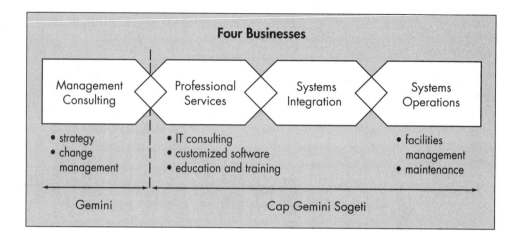

addition, some of those new areas showed much higher growth rates than the original core service. And the clients in those new service categories were also potential clients for the professional services group. Second, the expansion by acquisitions and alliances had also been partly knowledge driven. The degree to which targeted firms were able to fill in the gaps in the CGS skills portfolio was a serious consideration. The takeover of Hoskyns was valuable in terms of its competencies in facilities management. Hoskyns's specialty is outsourcing, or running a customer's entire data-processing department, a business that was growing at 25 percent a year, nearly twice as fast as other computer services. Its other main lines of business were IT consultancy and systems integration. The development of the market for facilities management was more advanced in the U.K. than in continental Europe. CGS used the Hoskyns competencies to expand its firm's operations in continental Europe.

Facilities Management

Contemporary corporations expect their information systems to keep pace with competitiveness. That is the function of their IT departments, which must be able to accommodate growing technological complexity, be easily adaptable, make practical use of their experts' time and stay fully in control of quality and costs. In its response to each of these criteria, facilities management (FM) has proven its effectiveness as a powerful resource for helping companies implement their strategies and achieve their objectives, while allowing them to

EXHIBIT 4
Information Technology
Services by CGS

Facilities Management:	taking over all or part of a client's IT resources (hardware, software, and staff) and running this operation for a given time period and with commitment to results.
Systems Integration:	providing a client with a complete IT solution integrating hardware and software, with a commitment to respect established costs and delivery times.
IT Consultancy:	involves analyzing an IT problem and developing solutions; designing, planning, and organizing information systems: implementing solutions either by developing customized software, or by adapting already-existing applications.
Management Consulting:	helping and assisting firms to transform their business by integrating disciplines such as strategy, operations, and information technology.

concentrate on their own business. The acquisition of Hoskyns marked the commitment of Cap Gemini to move into that market in a serious way.

Hoskyns brought to the Cap Gemini Sogeti group its expertise and market-leader position in the U.K., and 3500 employees. The twenty-five years of experience in FM accumulated by the managers and staff of Hoskyns enabled Cap Gemini Sogeti to make a grand entrance into facilities management. It also led to a second strategic breakthrough: achieving a leading position in Great Britain. However, one of the U.K. managers, who was working in continental Europe, remarked that the approach to facilities management in the U.K. differed quite substantially from practice on the continent. In particular, the content of the contracts between clients and service-provider varied because they were based on disparate approaches. For example, the U.K. manager generally wanted to stay in control of the operations, while in the Scandinavian countries joint ventures with equal shares are often established to regulate facilities management contracts, and in The Netherlands quite a number of partnerships with minority shares are to be found.

CGS strengthened its position in the facilities management market and in the Scandinavian market simultaneously by an $88.3 million friendly bid for Programator, its Scandinavian competitor, in February 1992. In joining forces with Programator, Cap Gemini Sogeti confirmed its stated goal of becoming the number one computer services company and market leader in northern Europe. In acquiring Programator, which generated 40 percent of its turnover from facilities management, CGS mainly targeted the FM market in Scandinavia and thus pursued its FM development strategy. As a result of this operation, Cap Programator was the uncontested professional services leader in this region, unequalled in terms of number of locations, and able to handle all types of IT projects at both local and international levels. The acquisition of Programator should have enabled CGS to generate a turnover of more than $500 million in northern Europe in 1992.

Consultancy

When more and more of CGS's customers asked for collaboration on problems of major technology projects linked to their specific activity, Sogeti created a consulting group that was structurally and professionally independent of Cap Gemini Sogeti. Gemini Consulting was created by bringing together

three leading consultancy firms: the MAC Group, United Research, and Gamma International. "United Research, MAC Group and Sogeti are betting that the increased speed of corporate decision making will mean that a linked network of consultants will succeed where individual firms cannot. In the past," says Scott Parker, co-managing director of MAC, "companies hired one consulting firm to plan their strategy, then engaged another to help implement it. Today, the markets are moving too fast for that. If your product life cycle is two years, you can't use up one year studying the issue. So MAC, which specializes in strategy; United Research, which helps organizations manage change; and Sogeti, whose units design IT systems, will pool their specialties to take a project from strategic planning through implementation."

A business analyst was, however, a bit sceptical about the related diversification of CGS into other services. "In particular, inclusion of consultancy in their integrated service offering looks nice in theory but might be difficult to implement. I hope they've learned from the problems encountered by Saatchi and Saatchi and also by Arthur Andersen in offering consultancy services as part of the package."

In 1992 Gemini Consulting took a controlling interest in Gruber, Titze and Partner (GTP), Germany's third largest management consultancy firm. The skills of Gemini and GTP were complementary, and the combined operation (340 consultants in Germany) would boost Gemini's presence in Germany and become its largest subsidiary in Europe.

Gemini Consulting was legally, organizationally, and culturally separate from Cap Gemini Sogeti. The major reason was that the culture, the organization, and the internal management procedure at Gemini Consulting are integral to and inseparable from the firm's ability to deliver the results its partner-clients expect. And these were quite different from the Cap Gemini Sogeti way of doing business.

Systems Integration

Systems integration involves submitting all-in-one bids to deliver working packages of hardware and software that, for instance, will automate a factory or computerize a billing process. The customers' primary focus is no longer on choosing what equipment to buy but on maximizing the contribution of IT to the enterprise's success and well-being. Systems Integration submits all-in-one bids to deliver working packages of hardware and software.

In the SI process, the integrator often selects technology, builds interfaces, and provides integration, installation, operation, training, and technology refreshment. Systems Integrators develop, implement, and manage for their customers all the technologies used to provide information as a strategic corporate asset. While they work in close partnership with their customers to address business needs, the customers ultimately control their business and the direction it is going in. The value of systems integrators and systems managers is their technical resources and in-depth understanding of their customers' markets. Cap Gemini Sogeti argued that they could be trusted more, as they were free from the pressure to peddle their own merchandise (see exhibit 5.)

The four related businesses CGS did serve represented about 38 percent of the total market of IT services. However, there was still a huge part of the total IT services market in which CGS wasn't involved, like tax audit consulting, packaged software (systems products, applications products), turnkey systems and hardware sales, and processing and network services.

Increasingly, customers of IT-service firms, such as CGS, require that the service suppliers have prior knowledge about the industry from which the customer stems. An understanding of the particular industrial context is beneficial for the customer because no time is wasted by the supplier in investigating the industrial setting and introducing IT applications. As a result the service suppliers can judge relatively quickly and accurately what it takes to satisfy customers' demands. By showing in-depth knowledge of the clients' industrial context, service suppliers can more convincingly argue that they can indeed offer state-of-the-art IT solutions. In a number of cases the competitive context and demanding clients in a particular country forced the local Cap Gemini unit to find innovative solutions. These innovative solutions, being developed in one country, can be applied by other CGS units working in other countries.

One aspect of organizational capabilities concerns the creation of optimum conditions for pooling application expertise generated from completed projects. It becomes important as a skill for full-service suppliers, and CGS had developed some capabilities for the upgrading of organizational memory. The solutions implemented were aided by IT-based tools such as electronic bulletin boards and extensive electronic mail facilities (including voice mail). In addition, it appeared that these formal aspects of routines were complemented by the reliance on informal networks of professionals who cooperated in previous project-teams.

EXHIBIT 5
Market for IT Services

The "Big League" in IT Services		1990 European Revenues, $ Millions		
	$ Millions		**Country**	**Revenue**
1. EDS (excluding GM revenue)	2,788	1. Cap Gemini Sogeti	France	1,464
2. IBM (about 3.3% of the total revenue)	2,280	2. Finsiel	Italy	875
3. Computer Sciences Corp (3/31/91)	1,738	3. EDS + SD Scicon	U.S.A.	300†
4. Cap Gemini Sogeti	1,683	4. IBM	U.S.A.	700
5. Anderson Consulting (about 75% of total)	1,420	5. Sema Group	France	559
		6. O.I.S. (Olivetti)	Italy	667
		7. Sligos	France	532
Next ones are far below:		8. GSI	France	375
Finsiel (Italy)	875	9. Volmac	Holland	347
Sema Group (France)	667	10. CGI	France	325
CSK (Japan)	618	11. Axime	France	325
Olivetti (Italy)	559	12. Programator	Sweden	298
Sligos (France)	532	13. Logica	U.K.	253
SD-Scicon (U.K.)	412	14. CISI	France	250
		†=estimated revenue in Europe		

Information could also be acquired at competence centres, which provided line managers with skills related to a given technique or application. Development of project routines helped to structure project management. Organizing for cross-market opportunities was based on knowledge of the industry represented in reference databases developed by CGS that offered descriptions and information on activities.

Reconfiguration of the Competitive Context

Cap Gemini Sogeti's strategies were partly a response to the changes in the European competitive context. The acquisitions and alliances were necessary to gain market share and remain one of the top players in a fast-concentrating market. An industry analyst concluded that the industry had entered a Darwinian phase: those who failed to get stronger would be absorbed. One element of growth strategies is to increase geographical coverage. The need to be present in more countries was closely related to the internationalization of the business community and in particular to the fact that a rising number of clients throughout Europe wanted IT-system developers to create systems that worked across national boundaries.

The setup of the international support division was motivated by the need to offer solutions to multinational clients. This unit combines the commercial and technical support functions required by the operational groups. These ranged from providing assistance in technical developments, such as quality assurance and research and development (R&D) programs, to marketing developments. The latter focused on initiating and coordinating international projects and, if necessary, dealing with the top management of client companies.

The move from one to four related businesses can be seen as a result of the changes in the way business was done. Spotting business opportunities for each other became increasingly important. CGS was beaten in its home market by competitor Arthur Andersen when they were given a systems-integration contract for the Paris Stock Exchange after Andersen consulted for the French treasury ministry. Cooperation with the newly formed Gemini Consultants, however, had been similarly beneficial. A United Research (one of the partners in Gemini Consulting) contract with Mobil Oil Corporation in the United States led to a contract for CGS to work on Mobil's European distribution network.

CGS's new service offering matched the cross-marketing capabilities of competitors such as the large accountancy/consultancy firms.

A different but related aspect in these cross-marketing efforts was CGS's ability to achieve boardroom access. Cooperation with Gemini Consulting provided a direct link to the top management of client companies. That is important because, as a result of growing complexity and uncertainty, IT management had become an essential corporate function affecting large parts of the organization. Decisions concerning investments in information technology were very often made at the middle-management level, in particular by managers of the IT departments. Increasingly, however, because of the growing corporate importance and complexity of IT investments, it had become a concern of top management.

Besides the growing competition from the large accountancy conglomerates, the IT services market was also attractive for the large computer manufacturers. They were expanding their service activities to compensate for declining profit margins on hardware. CGS had a strong selling point in its objectivity and independence from the computer equipment vendors. The strategies of IBM could have a substantial influence on CGS performance, since about 60 percent of its clients were IBM users. Its relationship with the struggling U.S. giant was a mixture of competition and collaboration.

Probably the most serious competitive threat came from Electronic Data Systems (EDS), the IT services firm owned by General Motors. EDS was boosting its European sales and trying to expand its non-GM business. Just as with CGS, EDS had been trying to grow in Europe as fast as possible. For example, SD-Scicon, one of the main European IT services firms in the 1980s, sold its German subsidiary (Scientific Control Systems, SCS) to CGS. To counter that move and the takeover of Hoskyns, EDS reacted in 1991 by buying, after a serious takeover fight, the U.K. part of SD-Scicon (see exhibit 6.)

The Marrakesh Rencontre

At the Marrakesh meeting in June 1990, it was decided that the hallmarks of the group were to be a comprehensive service and a well-run organization staffed by highly motivated men and women.

These managers were presented with a choice between three different strategies: staying local but adding some new related services; expanding

Company (country, main business)	Year	Type
Sesa (France, software house)	1987	Takeover
SCS (Germany, computer services)	1990	Takeover
Hoskyns (United Kingdom, facilities management)	1990	Takeover
Daimler-Benz (Germany, industrial group)	1991	Alliance
Debis Systemhaus (Germany, software services)	1991	Merger
Programator (Sweden, facilities management)	1991	Take-over
MAC Group (U.S., management consultancy)	1991	Alliance
United Research (U.S., management consultancy)	1991	Alliance
Volmac (Netherlands, software house)	1992	Alliance
GTP (Germany, management consultancy)	1992	Takeover

geographical coverage with the existing focus of service provision; or expanding the service offering in combination with achieving global presence. Each of these strategies was discussed intensively with regard to content and implications. When the results of the poll were announced, it became clear that the managers had opted overwhelmingly for the third strategy, global presence.

The Current Organizational Structure

The director of the newly formed Cap Volmac in the Benelux remarked that internal coordination and cooperation in the worldwide operations of Cap Gemini Sogeti should improve quickly, because only then can CGS really profit from the trend of increasing client demand for IT services—showing that they can indeed offer the promised solutions.

CGS's alliance with Daimler-Benz in 1991 was a direct result of the decisions taken in the Marrakesh meeting and represented a response to the changes in competitive context as sketched above. CGS obtained financing of $585 million through this alliance, concluded after a year of negotiations in July 1991. It gave Germany's largest industrial group 34 percent of Sogeti, the holding company that owns 58 percent of Cap Gemini Sogeti (see exhibit 7.) Daimler-Benz also has the option of taking full control of Sogeti and Cap Gemini in February 1995. However, Serge Kampf, who controls Sogeti through another holding company, SKIP, has the option of buying back the 34 percent Daimler-Benz stake starting in 1994, before the German group can exercise its option.

In addition, CGS set up a joint venture with Debis Systemhaus, Daimler's software arm. In the joint venture, Sogeti's German activities and Daimler's informatics operations were brought together. Debis was a newcomer to the computer industry, it being established in 1990 as a 100 percent subsidiary of Daimler-Benz providing services internally as well as working with outside companies. The Systemhaus had a staff of 3,600 people with revenue of over $400 million. The largest percentage of its business was in IT services, and it covered a wide range of services, from software packages to full-system implementation, and from consultancy and training to computer centre, network, and telecommunications management.

One of the challenges for Cap Gemini Sogeti was to integrate the acquisitions and alliances of local companies and the local CGS units. The establishment of a new Cap Gemini Benelux, to be named Cap Volmac, an alliance of existing CGS units and Volmac was representative for challenges encountered by CGS in increasing geographical coverage. In February 1992, the alliance and shares exchange between CGS and Volmac, the leading Dutch IT services firm in which CGS already had a small stake, was made public. This move was in line with the attempts of CGS to increase its European market coverage and met the demand from multinational clients to handle IT services contracts spanning several countries. For CGS the strong market position of Volmac in facilities management, one of the new lines of business with above-average growth rates, was particularly attractive. CGS and Volmac would pool their activities in the new firm in the Benelux region. Sixty percent of Cap Volmac would be owned by a new holding group. The other

EXHIBIT 7
Capital Structure after
Alliance with Daimler-Benz

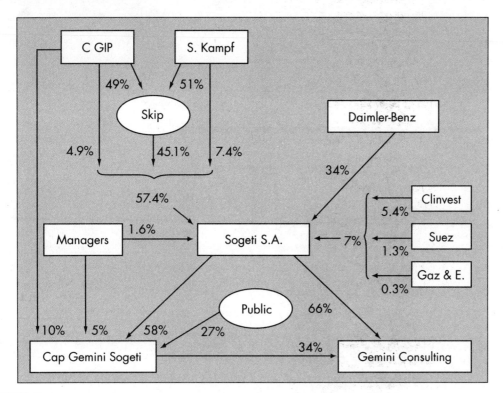

40 percent would be divided between Volmac's existing public shareholders, institutional investors and the World Software Group, which was Volmac's holding company. The new holding group would in turn be roughly two-thirds owned by CGS and one-third by the World Software Group. The new Cap Volmac had around 4,000 staff and annual sales of slightly under $500 million.

The Prague Rencontre

The main issues to be discussed by the participants of the Prague Rencontre on June 25, 1993, were the following:

> How can the existing organizations (such as Hoskyns, Programator, Volmac, and Debis) be integrated and "welded" more cohesively into the group, as changes in demand increase?
>
> What should the organizational structure look like?
>
> How can expertise of acquired companies be retained when experts can leave so easily?
>
> How can a common company culture be created?
>
> How can cross-selling be made a success?
>
> What role can Gemini play in the restructuring?

With respect to these issues and the necessary changes, Serge Kampf remarked that important CGS values such as cooperation, teamwork, and manager mobility should be respected, and he emphasized that "even though we want to rebuild a new house together, we cannot destroy the foundations of the old one." What such a house should look like was the question he hoped the Prague Rencontre delegates would be able to resolve.

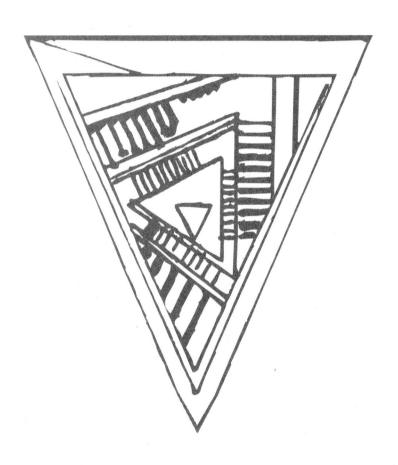

Name Index

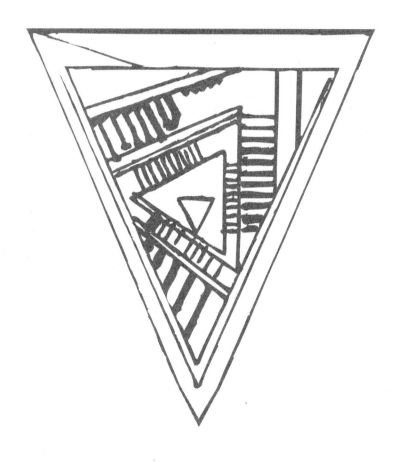

Subject Index

B
Breakpoints, 366, 390-404
Budgeting, 50, 93-94
Buyers
    innovation driven by, 530
    power of, 165-166
    relations with, *see* cooperation

C
Capabilities
    based competition, 231-239
    evaluation of, 180, 191
    international, 521-522
    organisational, 216-217, 232-239, 239-243, 252-260
    predator, 237-239
    school of thought, 214-217
    strategic, 320, 332, 343
Chaos
    and self-organisation, 469-470
    school of thought, 414, 416
    theory, 467-471
Chief executive officer, *see* leadership
Collaboration, *see* cooperation
Competence,
    core, 236-237, 245, 248-251, 264, 290-301
    distinctive, 40, 70, 73
Competition
    analysis of, 156-168
    capabilities-based, 231-239
    sources of, 162
    time-based, 225-231, 233
Competitive
    advantage, 10, 11, 25, 40, 168-175, 189-191, 218-260, 266, 274-287, 290, 332, 518
    advantage of nations, 481, 529-539
    cycles, 403
    dynamics, 409-410
    position, 10-11, 156-168, 218-225, 381-390
    scope, 219-221
    shifts, 393-394

Context
    European, *see* European context
    industry, *see* industry context
    international, *see* international context
    organisational, *see* organisational context
    strategy, *see* strategy context
Contingency
    approach, 415
    planning, 128
Control
    chaos perspective of, 472
    corporate systems of, 263-265, 301-315
    perspective, 414
    systems, 66, 92-93, 146, 198-199, 202-209, 431
Cooperation
    arrangements, 323-331
    competitive, 336-343
    conditions for success, 577-580
    intra-organisational, 450-454
    objectives of, 324-330, 337-339
    relationships, 318-331, 333, 346
    within Europe, 561-562, 571-574
    see also networks
Corporate
    centre, 264-266, 301-315
    management styles, 265, 301-315
    restructuring, 231
    supervisory board, 266, 103-104

D
Design school of thought, 38, 69-79
Diversification, 55, 238, 263-315, 343, 536

E
Entrepreneurial
    school of thought, 69, 77
Environmental
    analysis, 145, 147, 156-168, 253-254, 276, 529-531
    change, 67, 80, 395-398

cycles, 398-404
    determinism, 19, 365, 408
    selection, 368, 369-373
    scanning, 46, 125, 396
    school of thought, 69, 364-366
    variables, 47
Ethics, 43, 148, 181
European
    business strategies, 565-569
    competition, 563-565
    context, 543-596
    convergence, 592
    distribution, 557-558
    industrial restructuring, 544, 561-562, 571-580
    integration, 543-570
    management, 544-545, 570, 580-590
    managers, 588-589, 591-596
    myopia, 545
Evaluation
    overrationalised, 104
    strategic options, 45-50, 146-147, 186-192

F
Fit, 10-11, 49, 188-189, 214-216, 244, 349-350
Forecasting
    of industry evolution, 375-380
    techniques, 147
Formulation, *see* strategy formulation

G
Global
    cash flow, 515-517
    integration of activities, 505-511
    standardisation, *see* international standardisation
    strategic coordination, 505-511
    thinking, 494-495
Globalisation
    definition of, 478-479, 482, 490
    evolution of, 484, 511-514
    of competition, 480, 485, 514-520